Tolley's Taxwise I
2009/10

Income Tax
National Insurance
Corporation Tax
Capital Gains Tax and Stamp Duty

Authors:
Rebecca Benneyworth FCA BSc
Lynnette Bober ACA CTA MA (Cantab)
David Heaton FCA CTA of Baker Tilly
Julie Ward CTA
Contributors from Grant Thornton UK LLP
Contributors from Winter Rule LLP
General Editor:
Rebecca Benneyworth FCA BSc

Members of the LexisNexis Group worldwide

United Kingdom	LexisNexis, a Division of Reed Elsevier (UK) Ltd, Halsbury House, 35 Chancery Lane, London, WC2A 1EL, and London House, 20–22 East London Street, Edinburgh EH7 4BQ
Argentina	LexisNexis Argentina, Buenos Aires
Australia	LexisNexis Butterworths, Chatswood, New South Wales
Austria	LexisNexis Verlag ARD Orac GmbH & Co KG, Vienna
Benelux	LexisNexis Benelux, Amsterdam
Canada	LexisNexis Canada, Markham, Ontario
China	LexisNexis China, Beijing and Shanghai
France	LexisNexis SA, Paris
Germany	LexisNexis Deutschland GmbH, Munster
Hong Kong	LexisNexis Hong Kong, Hong Kong
India	LexisNexis India, New Delhi
Italy	Giuffrè Editore, Milan
Japan	LexisNexis Japan, Tokyo
Malaysia	Malayan Law Journal Sdn Bhd, Kuala Lumpur
New Zealand	LexisNexis NZ Ltd, Wellington
Poland	Wydawnictwo Prawnicze LexisNexis Sp, Warsaw
Singapore	LexisNexis Singapore, Singapore
South Africa	LexisNexis Butterworths, Durban
USA	LexisNexis, Dayton, Ohio

© Reed Elsevier (UK) Ltd 2009

Published by LexisNexis

A CIP Catalogue record for this book is available from the British Library.

ISBN: 9 780754 537229

Typeset by Letterpart Ltd, Reigate, Surrey

Printed and bound by Polestar Wheaton's Ltd

Visit LexisNexis Butterworths at www.lexisnexis.co.uk

ABOUT THIS BOOK

For over 30 years Tolley's Taxwise I has provided practitioners with a practical means of keeping up to date with changing legislation by way of worked examples. The publication is updated annually to show the changes introduced by the Finance Acts.

The publication is useful as a manual for staff and practitioners giving guidance as to the layout of computations and notes explaining both the law and practice relating to taxation issues. In addition, the worked examples provide a comprehensive study aid to students of taxation, allowing the testing of theoretical knowledge on practical examples of a style that could well form the basis of an examination question for professional qualifications.

Coverage

A selection of taxation examples based on the legislation current for 2009/10, complete with annotated solutions.

The examples are preceded by a summary commencing on page (xxi) of the main provisions of the Finance Act 2009, which received Royal Assent on 21 July 2009.

The book is not an exhaustive work of reference but it shows the treatment of all the points that are most likely to be encountered.

The contents list starting on page (v) shows the broad coverage of each example. In addition, there is a general index at the back of the book to assist in the location of specific points.

Reference to ITTOIA 2005 are to the Income Tax (Trading and Other Income) Act 2005.

The authors

Rebecca Benneyworth FCA BSc; **Lynnette Bober** ACA CTA MA (Cantab); **David Heaton** FCA CTA of Baker Tilly; **Julie Ward** CTA; contributors from **Grant Thornton UK LLP** (see below); and contributors from **Winter Rule LLP** (see below) – continuing the original work of Arnold Homer FCA CTA TEP, and Rita Burrows MBA ACIS CTA.

Additional technical consultants: **Peter Gravestock** FCA CTA (Fellow) ATT, Past President of the Association of Taxation Technicians, tax lecturer and author; **Amanda Sullivan** CTA (Fellow) TEP BA (Hons).

Grant Thornton UK LLP is a leading business and financial adviser, and are a member firm within Grant Thornton International. Our tax teams have the know-how to advise on overall tax exposure and work with clients in dealing with the complexities of both the UK and international tax systems. Our advisers can assist with all taxes including income and corporation tax, stamp duty land tax, tax investigations, employment tax, financial planning, VAT and capital taxes. Our panel of expert contributors to the Tolley's Taxwise I 2009–10 edition are as follows:

Rachel Ellis, Associate Director, Recovery and Reorganisation Tax

Joanne Gracie, Manager, Private Client

Nick Harrop, Senior Tax Manager, Corporate Tax

David Hill, Director, International Tax

Stephen Hill, Associate Director, Recovery and Reorganisation

Francesca Lagerberg, Head of Tax

Gillian McGill, Tax Manager, Corporate Tax

Paul Smith, Director, International Tax

Lindsey Wicks, Senior Tax Manager, National Tax Office

The contributors from **Winter Rule LLP** are:

John Endacott FCA CTA (Fellow) BSc (Econ) – John has considerable experience of advising on capital gains tax. He has been a tax partner at Winter Rule for over ten years and prior to that worked for KPMG and Coopers & Lybrand.

John is a well-known author and lecturer on tax matters. He was shortlisted for Tax Writer of the Year in the LexisNexis Awards in 2009. He is a contributor to *Simon's Taxes* and author of various works including *Tolley's Tax Planning*, *TAXLine Tax Planning*, *Tolley's Capital Gains Tax Planning*, *Finance Act Handbook*, and various articles for specialist tax publications. He has also been a member of the Technical Committee of the ICAEW Tax Faculty and a tax examiner for both the ICAEW and the CIOT.

Anthony Meehan CTA ATT MA BA (Hons) – Anthony started his career with KPMG before joining Winter Rule. He won the Spofforth Medal for the best paper on Taxation of Individuals, Trusts and Estates in his CTA exams and specialises in advising high net worth individuals on capital gains tax planning.

Steve York CTA ATT BSc – Steve joined Winter Rule, where he trained, in 1996. He has specialised in advising high net worth individuals on capital gains tax planning. He is a co-author of the chapter on capital gains tax planning in *Tolley's Tax Planning*.

Peter Penneycard FCA BA – Peter has practised tax for over 30 years, in industry and in public practice both large and small. He currently advises SMEs and their owners on most taxes – income, corporation and capital gains taxes, VAT, insurance premium tax and SDLT. He is often quoted in the general and technical press.

The Winter Rule Tax Team have also written *Tolley's Capital Gains Tax Planning under the New Regime*.

Companion publication

Tolley's Taxwise II 2009–10 (covering Inheritance Tax and Taxation of Trusts and Estates).

Contents

Contents

Index

Abbreviations

AMV	=	actual market value
art	=	Article
ATCA	=	Advance Thin Capitalisation Agreement
CAA	=	Capital Allowances Act
Cf.	=	compare
CFC	=	Controlled foreign company
CGT	=	Capital gains tax
CGTA 1979	=	Capital Gains Tax Act 1979
CIR	=	Commissioners of Inland Revenue ('the Board')
CIS	=	Construction Industry Scheme
CRCA	=	Commissioners for Revenue and Customs Act
CT	=	Corporation tax
CTSA	=	Corporation tax self-assessment
CTT	=	Capital transfer tax
CTTA 1984	=	Capital Transfer Act 1984
CUP	=	Comparable uncontrolled price
EC	=	European Communities
ECJ	=	European Court of Justice
EEC	=	European Economic Community
EFRBS	=	Employer-financed Retirement Benefits Scheme
EU	=	European Union
Ex D	=	Exchequer Division
FA	=	Finance Act
FII	=	Franked investment income
FOIA 2000	=	Freedom of Information Act 2000
FY	=	Financial year
HC(I)	=	High Court (Ireland)
HL	=	House of Lords
HMRC	=	Her Majesty's Revenue and Customs
ICTA	=	Income and Corporation Taxes Act 1988
IHT	=	Inheritance tax
IHTA 1984	=	Inheritance Tax Act 1984
IR	=	Inland Revenue
ISAs	=	individual savings accounts
ITA	=	Income Tax Act 2007
ITEPA 2003	=	Income Tax (Earnings and Pensions) Act 2003
ITTOIA 2005	=	Income Tax (Trading and Other Income) Act 2005
IUMV	=	initial unrestricted market value
LIVR	=	Limited information value report
MSCs	=	managed service companies
MSCP	=	managed service company provider
NIC	=	National insurance contribution
NMW	=	National minimum wage
pa	=	per annum
PEPs	=	personal equity plans
PIDs	=	property income distributions
pm	=	per month
POA	=	Payments on account
POCA 2002	=	Proceeds of Crime Act 2002
QCBs	=	qualifying corporate bonds
RBPA	=	Renovation of Business Premises in disadvantaged Area
s	=	Section
SA	=	Self-assessment
Sch	=	Schedule

List of Abbreviations

SE	=	Societas Europaea
SED	=	Seafarers' earnings deduction
SI	=	Statutory instrument
SIPPs	=	self-invested personal pensions
SSCBA 1992	=	Social Security Contributions and Benefits Act 1992
SP	=	Revenue Statement of Practice
Sp C	=	Special Commissioners
TCGA 1992	=	Taxation of Chargeable Gains Act 1992
TOISAs	=	TESSA only Individual Savings Accounts
TMA 1970	=	Taxes Management Act 1970
UAP	=	Upper accruals point
UEL	=	Upper earnings limit
VAT	=	Value added tax
VATA 1994	=	Value Added Tax Act 1994

PERSONAL TAX RATES

1. Income tax is chargeable on taxable income, ie that part of income which remains after all allowable deductions, including personal allowances, have been made.

   Prior to 6 April 2008, capital gains were taxed according to income tax rates and bands. From 6 April 2008 a single CGT rate of 18% (subject to entrepreneurs' relief) applies instead.

   With effect from 6 April 2008, the starting rate was abolished although a savings starting rate remains. Savings are treated as the highest slice of income after dividend income.

   The rates of tax for 2008/09 and 2009/10 are:

   | | *2009/10* | | | *2008/09* | | |
	Rate	*On*	*Tax on full band*	*Rate*	*On*	*Tax on full band*
		£	£		£	£
Savings income:						
Starting savings rate *	10%	2,440		10%	2,320	
Non-savings income:						
Basic rate	20%	37,400	7,480.00	20%	34,800	6,960.00
Higher rate on excess over basic rate limit	40%			40%		

   *The starting rate for savings is 10% for both 2009/10 and 2008/09, but as savings income ranks above non-savings income, it applies only to the extent that net income from non-savings sources does not exceed the band of £2,440 (2008/09 £2,320).

   If the starting rate for savings is applicable, it forms part of the basic rate band, not an addition to it.

   Dividends are taxed as shown below in both years.

Tax-credit inclusive dividends	10% (dividend ordinary rate) up to basic rate limit, † 32.5% (dividend upper rate) thereafter. †

   † Non-UK source dividends

   From 6 April 2008, dividends from non-UK companies of which the recipient owns less that 10% attract a tax credit of 1/9th of the grossed up amount. From 22 April 2009 this tax credit is extended to all dividends from foreign companies which are based in a territory with which the UK has a double taxation agreement which includes a non-discrimination clause.

   Finance Act 2009 includes legislation to introduce a further higher rate of tax from 6 April 2010. The rate will be 50% and it will apply to taxable income in excess of £150,000. Dividends within this band will be taxed at 42.5% rather than 32.5%.

2. Discretionary and accumulation and maintenance trusts are charged on non-dividend income at a single rate, called 'the rate applicable to trusts', which is currently 40%. This rate will increase on 6 April 2010 to 50%. A standard rate band of £1,000 applies to the first slice of income chargeable at the rate applicable to trusts. Trustees of other trusts are liable at the basic rate of 20%.

   The rate of tax for discretionary and accumulation and maintenance trusts on dividend income, called 'the dividend trust rate', is 32.5% for 2008/09 and 2009/10. This rate will then correspondingly increase to 42.5% from 6 April 2010. Trustees of other trusts pay tax on dividend income at 10%.

   Trusts for vulnerable people can elect to be taxable as if the income of the trust were the income of the beneficiary.

3. Personal allowances for 2008/09 and 2009/10 are:

	2009/10 £	*2008/09* £
Personal allowance:		
Under 65	6,475	6,035
65 to 74	9,490	9,030
75 and over	9,640	9,180
Excess allowance over basic amount of	6,475	6,035
reduced by £1 for every £2 by which income exceeds	22,900	21,800
Age-related married couple's allowance (tax saving thereon 10%) †		
Elder born before 6 April 1935 and under 75	N/A	6,535
Elder 75 or over	6,965	6,625
Excess allowance over basic amount of	2,670	2,540
reduced by £1 for every £2 by which income exceeds	22,900	21,800

† Reduced in tax year of marriage by 1/12th for each complete month (running from 6th day of one month to 5th day of next) in that year prior to the date of marriage

	2009/10 £	*2008/09* £
Blind person's relief (available to each blind person, whether single or married)	1,890	1,800

Life assurance relief as a deduction of 12.5% from premiums payable where the life assurance contract was entered into before 14 March 1984.

Maximum allowable premiums either:

(a)   one-sixth of total income, or

(b)   £1,500

whichever is greater.

4.   Tax credits for 2008/09 and 2009/10 are:

Credit element	Annual amount	
	2009/10 £	2008/09 £
Family element of CTC	545	545
Baby element of CTC	545	545
Child element of CTC	2,235	2,085
Disability element of CTC[1].	2,670	2,540
Severe disability element of CTC[1].	1,075	1,020
Basic element of WTC	1,890	1,800
Couple's or lone parent element of WTC[2].	1,860	1,770
30 hour element of WTC	775	735
Disability element of WTC[4].	2,530	2,405
Severe disability element of WTC[4].	1,075	1,020
50-plus return to work element of WTC[2,3,4].	1,300	1,235
50-plus return to work element of WTC, 30 hour rate[3,4].	1,935	1,840
For both working credit and child tax credit		
– first income threshold	6,420	6,420
– first withdrawal rate	39%	39%
– second income threshold	50,000	50,000
– second withdrawal rate	1 in 15	1 in 15
– first threshold (those entitled to child tax credit only)	16,040	15,575
Childcare element		

Credit element	Annual amount 2009/10 £	2008/09 £
Percentage of eligible costs	80%	80%
Maximum eligible costs (weekly)	£	£
– one child	175	175
– two or more children	300	300

Footnotes

1. The disability element of CTC is paid for each child for whom a Disability Living Allowance (DLA) is due or if the child is registered blind. If the higher care component of DLA is due then the severe disability element is paid.

2. The 16–29 hours 50-plus element is not payable in addition to the couple's element unless the claimant is responsible for a child or qualifies for the disability element of WTC.

3. The two 50-plus elements are mutually exclusive ie a claimant working 18 hours gets the £1,235; a claimant working 30 hours gets £1,840, both being paid in addition to the other elements.

4. If both claimants in a joint claim are disabled or entitled to the 50-plus element then the award will include two elements per couple.

TAXATION OF DIRECTORS AND OTHERS IN RESPECT OF CARS

INCOME TAX CAR BENEFITS CHARGES

Car benefits charge is based on CO_2 emissions and ranges from 10% to 35% of list price (for details see Example 10). The taxable benefit for cars registered after 31 December 1997 with no CO_2 emissions figures is 15%, 25% or 35% of list price depending on engine size (the 15% and 25% rates being increased by 3% for diesel cars). The taxable benefit for pre 1 January 1998 cars is 15%, 22% or 32% of list price depending on engine size. The taxable benefit for cars with no cylinder capacity is 35% of list price (32% for pre-1 January 1998 cars), except for electric cars, for which the charge is 9%. Special provisions apply to electric, very low emission diesel cars and environmentally friendly cars, such as those running wholly or partly on road fuel gas or E85 fuel.

The list price is restricted to a maximum of £80,000, and is reduced by up to £5,000 in respect of a capital contribution from the employee.

For cars 15 years old or more at end of tax year with a market value of £15,000 or more, market value (up to £80,000) is substituted for list price if higher.

The benefit is reduced proportionately if the car is not available for part of the year.

CAR FUEL BENEFIT SCALES

Car fuel benefit is calculated using the same CO_2-based percentage rates as are used for calculating car benefits, ranging from 20% to 35% of a set figure.

The percentage rates are applied to the following figures:

	2003/04 to 2007/2008	2008/09 & 2009/10
Basis figure	£14,400	£16,900

VAN BENEFITS

Benefits for vans weighing up to 3,500 kg are as follows:

	2008/2009 and 2009/10
Van and fuel benefit with restricted private use	£3,000
Additional fuel scale charge for unrestricted private use	£500

The basis for accounting for VAT fuel for private mileage changed for VAT accounting periods beginning on or after 1 May 2008.

VAT scale charges are based on carbon emissions, according to the following table which is effective for VAT accounting periods starting on or after 1 May 2009. The VAT element must be calculated by using the VAT inclusive fraction. The VAT element has not been published this year due to the change in rate of the standard rate from 15% to 17.5% on 1 January 2010.

CO_2 band	3 monthly Scale Charge	1 monthly
120 or less	126	42
125	189	63
130	189	63
135	189	63
140	201	67
145	214	71
150	226	75
155	239	79
160	251	83
165	264	88
170	276	92
175	289	96
180	302	100
185	314	104
190	327	109
195	339	113
200	352	117
205	365	121
210	378	126
215	390	130
220	403	134
225	416	138
230	428	142
235 or above	441	147

TAX FREE HMRC APPROVED MILEAGE RATES FOR BUSINESS USE OF OWN TRANSPORT FOR 2003/04 TO 2009/10

	First 10,000 business miles	*Additional business miles*
Cars and vans	40p	25p
Motor cycles	24p	24p

	First 10,000 business miles	*Additional business miles*
Bicycles	20p	20p
Passenger payments, car or van only, per passenger	5p	5p

NATIONAL INSURANCE CONTRIBUTIONS

National insurance contribution rates from 6 April 2009 are as follows:

Class 1 contributions

Lower earnings limit:	£95	a week	(previously £90)
Earnings threshold (employers and employees):	£110	a week	(previously £105)
Upper earnings limit (employees only):	£844	a week	(previously £770)

Employees

11% of weekly earnings between	£110 and £844	(previously £105 and £770)
Reduced rate for married women and widows with valid certificate of election	4.85% on weekly earnings as above	

For both categories of employees an additional 1% is chargeable for 2009/10 on the balance of earnings over £844 (£770 for 2008/09) per week.

Employers   12.8% on all earnings over £110 per week (previously 12.8% and £105)

CONTRACTED OUT EMPLOYEE

Reduction in 'not contracted out' contributions, applicable to weekly earnings from £110 to £770:

	Salary related schemes	*Money purchase schemes*
Employees	1.6%*	1.6%*
Employers	3.7%*	1.4%*

* Employees and employers also receive these rebates on earnings between £95 and £110 a week, on which they do not pay contributions. If an employee's rebate exceeds his contributions, the excess rebate goes to the employer.

Employers' Class 1A and Class 1B contributions			12.8%
Class 2 contributions			
Self-employed flat rate	£2.40	a week	(previously £2.30)
Small earnings exception	£5,075	a year	(previously £4,825)
Class 3 contributions			
Voluntary contributions	£12.05	a week	(previously £8.10)
Class 4 contributions			
8% of profits between	£5,715 and £43,875		(previously 8% on profits between £5,435 and £40,040)

and 1% of all profits above £43,875 (2008/09 £40,040).

CAPITAL GAINS TAX

Major changes to the calculation of gains for capital gains tax for individuals and trusts were introduced with effect from 6 April 2008. From this date gains are calculated without applying indexation or taper relief, and all gains are based on 1982 rebased values. The resulting gain, after the annual exemption, is taxed at a flat rate of 18%. This does not apply to chargeable gains for corporation tax.

Total net gains of individuals for 2009/10 not exceeding £10,100 (2008/09 £9,600) are exempt. The remaining gains are taxed at the capital gains tax rate of 18%. Personal representatives are entitled to the annual exemption, currently £10,100, for the year of death and the next two years. Gains not covered by the exemption are taxed at 18%

Gains of trusts in which the settlor retains an interest are taxed as the settlor's gains. For other trusts, the trustees are entitled to an annual exemption of £5,050 (2008/09 £4,800), divided equally between trusts created by the same settlor, subject to a minimum exemption of £1,010 for each trust (2008/09 £960). Gains in excess of the exemption are charged at 18% for both discretionary trusts (including accumulation and maintenance trusts) and for other trusts.

CAPITAL GAINS TAX ACTUARIAL TABLE FOR LEASES (TCGA 1992 SCH 8)

Years	Percentage	Years	Percentage
50 (or more)	100.000	24	79.622
49	99.657	23	78.055
48	99.289	22	76.399
47	98.902	21	74.635
46	98.490	20	72.770
45	98.059	19	70.791
44	97.595	18	68.697
43	97.107	17	66.470
42	96.593	16	64.116
41	96.041	15	61.617
40	95.457	14	58.971
39	94.842	13	56.167
38	94.189	12	53.191
37	93.497	11	50.038
36	92.761	10	46.695
35	91.981	9	43.154
34	91.156	8	39.399
33	90.280	7	35.414
32	89.354	6	31.195
31	88.371	5	26.722
30	87.330	4	21.983
29	86.226	3	16.959
28	85.053	2	11.629
27	83.816	1	5.983
26	82.496	0	0
25	81.100		

If the duration of the lease is not an exact number of years, find the percentage for the number of whole years and add to it for each extra month one-twelfth of the difference between that percentage and the next higher percentage (counting an odd 14 days or more as one month).

CAPITAL GAINS TAX TAPER RELIEF FOR INDIVIDUALS, PERSONAL REPRESENTATIVES AND TRUSTEES UP TO 5 APRIL 2008

Gains on disposals of business assets on or after 6 April 2002* up to 5 April 2008			Gains on disposals of non-business assets on or after 6 April 1998 up to 5 April 2008		
Whole yrs in qualifying period	% reduction available	% of gain chargeable	Whole yrs in qualifying period	% reduction available	% of gain chargeable
1	50	50	1	–	–
2 or more	75	25	2	–	–
			3	5	95
			4	10	90
			5	15	85
			6	20	80
			7	25	75
			8	30	70
			9	35	65
			10 or more	40	60

For non-business assets, an extra year was included in the qualifying period if the asset was owned before 17 March 1998 (except where anti-avoidance provisions apply).

* For business assets owned before 17 March 1998, the taper relief rates were 7.5% for disposals in 1998/99, 15% for disposals in 1999/2000, 25% for disposals in 2000/01 and 50% for disposals in 2001/02.

Taper relief was abolished from 6 April 2008.

CORPORATION TAX RATES

Financial years (ie beginning 1 April)	2004	2005	2006	2007	2008 & 2009
Corporation tax full rate (%)	30	30	30	30	28
Small companies' rate (%)	19	19	19	20	21
Marginal relief limits (£000's)					
lower	300	300	300	300	300
higher	1,500	1,500	1,500	1,500	1,500
Marginal relief calculation					
$(M - P) \times I/P \times$ fraction	11/400	11/400	11/400	11/40	7/400
Effective marginal rate	32.75%	32.75%	32.75%	32.50%	29.75%
Starting rate (%)	0	0			
Marginal relief limits (£000's)					
lower	10	10			
higher	50	50			
Marginal relief calculation					
$(R2 - P) \times I/P \times$ fraction	19/400	19/400			
Non-Corporate Distribution Rate	19%	19%			
Effective marginal rate	23.75%	23.75%			

The full rate for corporation tax for the financial year commencing 1 April 2010 will be 28%.

Foreword

It was announced in the 2007 budget that the small companies' rate would rise to 22% from 1 April 2009, but this was deferred until 2010.

The small companies rate for ring fence profits remains at 19%.

INDEXATION ALLOWANCE

Indexation allowance is based on the retail prices index, and is calculated to three decimal places (which means to one decimal place when expressed as a percentage), except for calculations in respect of the post 31 March 1982 holding of quoted securities, which are not rounded. After April 1998 indexation allowance is relevant only for companies.

The retail prices index was re-based to 100 in January 1987. To avoid complications where two different bases are used, the examples in this book are based on the following table (see overleaf), in which the figures for months before January 1987 have been re-calculated to the new base. This does, however, give some differences from the precise figures because of rounding. The precise figures are published monthly by HMRC and in various other publications.

As a result of changes to capital gains tax from 6 April 2008, the retail price index is not used in computing gains for individuals and trusts from that date. The index is still required for computation of chargeable gains for corporation tax purposes.

	1982	1983	1984	1985	1986	1987	1988	1989
January		82.61	86.84	91.2	96.25	100.0	103.3	111.0
February		82.97	87.2	91.94	96.6	100.4	103.7	111.8
March	79.44	83.12	87.48	92.8	96.73	100.6	104.1	112.3
April	81.04	84.28	88.64	94.78	97.67	101.8	105.8	114.3
May	81.62	84.64	88.97	95.21	97.85	101.9	106.2	115.0
June	81.85	84.84	89.2	95.41	97.79	101.9	106.6	115.4
July	81.88	85.3	89.1	95.23	97.52	101.8	106.7	115.5
August	81.9	85.68	89.94	95.49	97.82	102.1	107.9	115.8
September	81.85	86.06	90.11	95.44	98.3	102.4	108.4	116.6
October	82.26	86.36	90.67	95.59	98.45	102.9	109.5	117.5
November	82.66	86.67	90.95	95.92	99.29	103.4	110.0	118.5
December	82.51	86.89	90.87	96.05	99.62	103.3	110.3	118.8

	1990	1991	1992	1993	1994	1995	1996	1997
January	119.5	130.2	135.6	137.9	141.3	146.0	150.2	154.4
February	120.2	130.9	136.3	138.8	142.1	146.9	150.9	155.0
March	121.4	131.4	136.7	139.3	142.5	147.5	151.5	155.4
April	125.1	133.1	138.8	140.6	144.2	149.0	152.6	156.3
May	126.2	133.5	139.3	141.1	144.7	149.6	152.9	156.9
June	126.7	134.1	139.3	141.0	144.7	149.8	153.0	157.5
July	126.8	133.8	138.8	140.7	144.0	149.1	152.4	157.5
August	128.1	134.1	138.9	141.3	144.7	149.9	153.1	158.5
September	129.3	134.6	139.4	141.9	145.0	150.6	153.8	159.3
October	130.3	135.1	139.9	141.8	145.2	149.8	153.8	159.5
November	130.0	135.6	139.7	141.6	145.3	149.8	153.9	159.6
December	129.9	135.7	139.2	141.9	146.0	150.7	154.4	160.0

	1998	1999	2000	2001	2002	2003	2004	2005
January	159.5	163.4	166.6	171.1	173.3	178.4	183.1	188.9
February	160.3	163.7	167.5	172.0	173.8	179.3	183.8	188.9
March	160.8	164.1	168.4	172.2	174.5	179.9	184.8	190.5
April	162.6	165.2	170.1	173.1	175.7	181.2	185.7	191.6
May	163.5	165.6	170.7	174.2	176.2	181.5	186.5	192.0
June	163.4	165.6	171.1	174.4	176.2	181.3	186.8	192.0
July	163.0	165.1	170.5	173.3	175.9	181.3	186.8	192.2
August	163.7	165.5	170.5	174.0	176.4	181.6	187.4	192.6
September	164.4	166.2	171.7	174.6	177.6	182.5	188.1	193.1
October	164.5	166.5	171.6	174.3	177.9	182.6	188.6	193.3
November	164.4	166.7	172.1	173.6	178.2	182.7	189.0	193.6
December	164.4	167.3	172.2	173.4	178.5	183.5	189.9	194.1

	2006	2007	2008	2009
January	193.4	201.6	209.8	210.1
February	194.2	203.1	211.4	211.4
March	195.0	204.4	212.1	211.3
April	196.5	205.4	214.0	211.5
May	197.7	206.2	215.1	212.8
June	198.5	207.3	216.8	213.4
July	198.5	206.1	216.5	
August	199.2	207.3	217.2	
September	200.1	208.0	218.4	
October	200.4	208.9	217.7	
November	201.1	209.7	216.0	
December	202.7	210.9	212.9	

SUMMARY OF MAIN INCOME TAX, CORPORATION TAX, CAPITAL GAINS TAX AND STAMP TAX PROVISIONS OF FINANCE ACT 2009

Finance Act 2009 reference		*Example*
s 1–3	*Income tax – rates for 2009/10*	*1*

The basic and higher rates for 2009/10 are 20% and 40% respectively. The basic rate limit is £37,400 and the personal allowance for those under 65 is £6,475. The personal allowances for those aged over 65 are as set out on page xii.

s 4   *Personal allowances for those with income exceeding £100,000*

With effect from 6 April 2010, for those individuals with an income exceeding £100,000 the personal allowance is reduced in accordance with the same formula that is used for the restriction of age allowances where the income exceeds the relevant threshold. The definition of income is 'adjusted net income' and so is after pension contributions and gift aid payments.

s 5 and Sch 1   *Abolition of personal allowances for Commonwealth citizens*

With effect from 6 April 2010, personal allowances are no longer available to individuals solely on the ground of them being Commonwealth citizens. However, most non-residents will continue to qualify for personal allowances on other grounds either under the UK domestic legislation or double tax treaties.

s 6 and Sch 2   *Increase in income tax rates from 6 April 2010*

This section inserts the new 50% income tax rate for individuals and trustees and the new higher dividend rate of 42.5%. The amendment is prospective and so will not be inserted into the legislation until the 2010/11 tax year.

s 7   *Corporation tax – rates for the financial year 2010*   *49*

The main rate of corporation tax for the year 2010 will remain at 28%. The rate of tax on ring fenced profits remains at 30%.

s 8   *Small companies rate for fraction for the financial year 2009*   *50*

The small companies' rate for the financial year 2009 is maintained at 21% with marginal relief and a fraction of 7/400. The rate of tax on ring fenced profits remains at 19% with appropriate marginal rate relief.

s 10   *SDLT – Thresholds for residential property*   *84*

The threshold at which SDLT becomes payable on residential property will be £175,000 until 31 December 2009 when it will revert to £125,000.

s 23 and Sch 6   *Temporary extension of loss carry back provisions*

A temporary loss relief is introduced which for income tax applies to losses in the years 2008/09 and 2009/10 and for corporation tax applies for accounting periods ending after 23 November 2008 and before 24 November 2010. The provision is an extended loss carry back arrangement subject to various restrictions including a £50,000 limit.

Finance Act 2009 reference		*Example*
s 24	*First-year capital allowances for expenditure in 2009/10*	

As a temporary measure, first-year allowances are reintroduced at a rate of 40% for expenditure in 2009/10 for income tax and for the year to 31 March 2010 for corporation tax purposes.

s 25   *Agreements to forego tax reliefs*

This section enables HM Treasury to override certain provisions of the Corporation Taxes Acts that provide for businesses to automatically benefit from certain tax reliefs. It is being introduced in connection with the Asset Protection Scheme which was introduced to support the UK banks.

s 26 and Sch 7   *Contaminated and derelict land*

Part 14 of CTA 2009 is amended to extend relief not just for contaminated land but also for derelict land.

s 27 and Sch 8   *Venture capital schemes*   93

A number of technical amendments are made to EIS, VCT and CVS arrangements. For individuals, the previous restrictions in respect of the amount of EIS relief that can be carried back are removed. This change applies to 2009/10.

s 28 and Sch 9   *Group relief – equity status of preference shares*

ICTA 1988, Sch 18 is amended to exclude certain further types of preference shares from qualifying as equity holders for the purposes of establishing ownership.

s 29 and Sch 10   *Sale of lessor companies – technical changes*

Technical amendments are made to FA 2006, Sch 10 which deals with the sale of lessor companies.

s 30 and Sch 11   *Expenditure on cars and motor cycles*   9

New rules for tax relief on expenditure on cars and motor cycles apply from 6 April 2009 for income tax and 1 April 2009 for corporation tax. These rules were originally published in a technical note in December 2008. The rate of capital allowances on cars will now be determined by the CO_2 emissions. Those exceeding 160 g/km will be separately pooled with a WDA at 10% (assuming no private use) whereas cars with CO_2 emissions of less than 160 g/km will be added to the main pool and so attract relief at 20%. Motor cycles are excluded from the definition of cars.

s 31 and Sch 12   *Reallocation of chargeable gains or loss within a group*   83

This changes the way in which the election in TCGA 1992 s 171A operates. As a result it extends the relief to deemed gains.

Finance Act 2009 reference		*Example*
s 32 and Sch 13	*Stock lending – insolvency of borrower*	79

This makes technical amendments to the way in which the capital gains tax provisions apply on stock lending where a borrower becomes insolvent. This arises from problems that were encountered in the financial difficulties of late 2008.

s 33	*Financial Services Compensation Scheme (FSCS) payments*	

Where a payment is received under the FSCS then where it is deemed to represent interest it is to be treated for all tax purposes as a payment of interest. Accordingly, a higher rate tax liability can arise or a refund of income tax where appropriate.

s 34–37 and Sch 14–17	*Taxation of Foreign profits, etc*	55

These measures change the taxation of foreign profits for corporation tax purposes. The change to the rules follows a long period of consultation and includes changes to HM Treasury consent rules and to controlled foreign company (CFC) rules. The CFC holding company exemption and the Acceptable Distribution Policy are both amended with effect from 1 July 2009. The dividend exemption rules are contained in a new CTA 2009 Part 9A and are effective from 1 July 2009. The restriction of financing costs contained in s 35 and Sch 15 is effective for accounting periods beginning on or after 1 January 2010.

s 38 and Sch 18	*Foreign currency accounting*	73

This provision is introduced to ensure that there is a consistent approach to the translation of foreign currency amounts into sterling to avoid losses arising due to exchange rate differences of measurement.

s 39	*Certain distributions of offshore funds taxed as interest*	

As certain distributions from offshore funds are equivalent to interest, the tax treatment has changed with effect from 22 April 2009 and a new section is introduced to achieve this (ITTOIA 2005 s 378A).

s 40 and Sch 19	*Foreign distributions – individuals*	

For corporation tax, most foreign distributions are now exempt but for individuals, it is necessary to continue to consider the double tax relief position. This extends to the provision introduced by FA 2008 s 34 and Sch 12 whereby non-UK source dividends are treated in an equivalent way to UK source dividends.

s 41 and Sch 20	*Loan relationships*	49, 51–52, 55–56, 63

For accounting periods beginning on or after 1 April 2009, the loan relationship rules in respect of connected parties are amended such that for companies, a restriction will only apply where the creditor company is located in a 'non-qualifying territory'.

Finance Act 2009 reference		*Example*
s 42	*Release of trade debts, etc*	
	This section amends CTA 2009 to extend the loan relationship rules to debts released that have been incurred in the course of a trade or property business.	
s 43 and Sch 21	*Foreign exchange matching – anti-avoidance*	
	With effect from 22 April 2009, CTA 2009 Part 5 Chapter 3 is amended to include further anti-avoidance provisions.	
s 44 and Sch 22	*Offshore funds*	
	A new definition of offshore fund is introduced.	
s 45	*Investment trust dividends – taxation as interest*	
	This section provides for HM Treasury to make regulations to enable certain dividends of investment trusts to be taxed as interest receipts.	
s 46 and Sch 23	*Insurance companies*	63, 73
	This provision replaces the existing guidance on the tax treatment of long-term insurance funds and make various other amendments to the provisions relevant to the insurance companies.	
s 47	*Lloyd's – equalisation reserves*	
	This section introduces a provision to enable HM Treasury to make regulations in respect of Lloyd's equalisation reserves.	
s 48 and Sch 24	*Disguised interest*	
	CTA 2009 Part 6 is amended to make provision for returns from certain financial arrangements that are economically equivalent to interest to be taxed as loan relationships.	
s 49 and Sch 25	*Transfer of income streams*	
	The statutory rules dealing with tax planning involving the transfer of income streams are expanded to ensure that receipts derived from a right to receive income are treated as income for the purposes of corporation tax and income tax. For income tax purposes, new rules are inserted into ITA 2007 Part 13 Chapter 5A.	
s 50 and Sch 26	*SAYE schemes*	85
	These provisions introduce certain practical and administrative amendments to the operation of SAYE savings schemes.	

Finance Act 2009 reference		*Example*
s 51–52 and Sch 27	*Remittance basis*	98

Minor amendments are made to the remittance basis rules that were introduced by FA 2008. Please note: Example 98 within this book incorporates some of the changes made by FA 2009.

s 53–54 and Sch 28	*Car benefits*	9, 10, 58

Changes are made to the rules for benefits in kind arising on the private use of cars with effect from 6 April 2011. Specifically, the car price cap of £80,000 is abolished, the lower threshold is reduced to 125g/km and for electrically propelled cars, the appropriate percentage is reduced to 9%. For 2009/10 onwards, a disabled driver who holds a blue badge is entitled to use the list or notional price of an equivalent manual car instead of that of an automatic car when computing the relevant benefit.

s 55 *Exemption from benefit for health screening*

This provision introduces an exemption from income tax on a benefit in kind where health screening or medical check ups are provided each year. It also exempts the provision of a non-cash voucher or credit token to achieve the same end result. The provision is included in a new section ITEPA 2003 s 320B.

s 56 *MEPs Pay*

Following changes to the remuneration arrangements of MEPs, it is necessary to make changes to the double taxation relief arrangements. This is because the tax is deducted by the European Community and so would not otherwise qualify for double tax relief.

s 57	*Double tax relief on underlying dividends*	35, 55, 71–72

The mixer cap in ICTA 1988 s 799 is retrospectively amended from 1 April 2008. This is to correct a discrepancy that arose following the reduction in the main rate of corporation tax to 28%.

s 58 and Sch 29	*Manufactured overseas dividends*	55, 71

Anti-avoidance provisions are introduced to counter the avoidance of corporation tax using manufactured overseas dividends.

s 59 *Double taxation – payments made by reference to foreign tax*

This section restricts the available double taxation relief where a payment is made to either the claimant or a connected person. The double tax relief is then restricted to the net amount suffered.

s 60 *Double taxation – anti-fragmentation*

This provision clarifies the basis on which profits must be calculated for double tax relief purposes and applies only to banks.

Stop Press

Finance Act 2009 reference		*Example*
s 61 and Sch 30	*Financial arrangements – avoidance*	20, 39, 51

Various anti-avoidance provisions are introduced to prevent tax planning involving certain financial arrangements.

s 62 *Transfers of trade to obtain terminal loss relief*

This provision has been introduced to prevent the exploitation of terminal loss relief in ICTA 1988 s 393A by means of an artificial transfer of trade to another company.

s 63 and Sch 31 *Sale of lessor companies – anti-avoidance*

FA 2006 Sch 10 is amended to ensure that it applies as the Government intended to the sale of an intermediate lessor company.

s 64–65 and Schs 32–33 *Leases of plant or machinery and films – anti-avoidance*

These provisions are introduced to counter avoidance involving the leasing of plant or machinery or in respect of long funding leases of films.

s 66 and Sch 34 *Real Estate Investment Trusts (REITs)*   97

This provision makes minor amendments to the rules on REITS contained in FA 2006 Part 4.

s 67 *Deductions for employee liabilities*

In order to counter avoidance ITEPA 2003 s 346 is amended, and s 555 is effectively amended, to prevent a deduction of an employment related liability by an employee where the main purpose, or one of the main purposes, is the avoidance of tax.

s 68 *Employment loss relief*

This provision amends ITA 2007 s 128 and prevents a deduction of an employment loss where it is derived from arrangements a main purpose, or one of the main purposes of which, is the avoidance of tax.

s 69 *Loss relief – losses from contracts for life assurance*

In order to counter certain anti avoidance schemes, legislation is introduced to put beyond any doubt that income tax loss relief does not arise from offshore life insurance policies. This provision has effect for 2009/10 and transitional provisions could apply to 2008/09.

s 70 *Intangible fixed assets and goodwill*

Amendments are made to CTA 2009 Part 8 in respect of internally generated goodwill.

ss 71 *Taxable benefit – living accommodation*

This provision is introduced to counter avoidance of benefits-in-kind on the provision of living accommodation to employees where a payment is made by means of a lease premium rather than by rent.

Finance Act 2009 reference		*Example*

s 72 and Sch 35   *Pensions – special annual allowance charge*   37

This provision introduces a restriction for higher rate tax relief on pension contributions for those individuals with relevant income of £150,000 or more. This applies in respect of pension payments on or after 22 April 2009. These rules are to apply for 2009/10 and 2010/11. New provisions are due to be introduced with effect from 6 April 2011 which will operate differently. Relevant income is the individual's total income for a year. An individual will be caught by these new provisions if their income was £150,000 or more in either of the two previous tax years concerned. Individuals are permitted to continue to have higher rate tax relief on regular pension contributions or in respect of £20,000 (if higher). Given that the self-employed tend to make low regular contributions with annual single premium contributions, a late amendment was made to the Finance Bill which introduced a further measure that allows a higher special annual allowance which is the lower of £30,000 or the average of their irregular pension contributions for 2006/07, 2007/08 and 2008/09. These provisions are known as anti-forestalling provisions.

s 75   *Power to make retrospective non-charging provision*

This provision provides that any or all of the regulations made under FA 2004 Part 4 can apply retrospectively as long as they do not increase any person's tax liability (FA 2004 s 282 is amended).

s 80   *SDLT – leasehold enfranchisement*   84

This provision extends FA 2003 s 74 to deal with the position where tenants of flats exercise their collective rights under various housing acts.

ss 81–82   *Registered social landlords and shared ownership arrangements*   84

These provisions extend certain more favourable SDLT treatments involving registered providers of social housing and shared ownership arrangements.

s 83 and Sch 37   *Stock lending – insolvency*   84

As with the change introduced by s 32, this provision make similar changes for stamp taxes in respect of stock lending arrangements where one of the parties becomes insolvent.

s 84 and Sch 38   *Oil industry – capital allowances*

These provisions amend the rules providing for tax relief for decommissioning costs in the oil industry.

s 86 and Sch 40   *Oil – chargeable gains*

These provisions introduce a no gain/no loss transfer for companies swapping licences for fields within the UK continental shelf.

Finance Act 2009 reference		*Example*
s 87 and Sch 41	*Oil production assets put to alternative uses*	
	Amendments are introduced for corporation tax purposes where assets are reused to move them out of ring fenced trades.	
s 90 and Sch 44	*Supplementary charge – reduction for certain new oil fields*	
	These provisions introduce a new allowance (Field Allowance) which can be used to reduce the company's adjusted ring fenced profits from oil and gas production in the UK and UK continental shelf.	
s 92	*HMRC charter*	
	It is now necessary for HMRC to prepare and maintain a charter which will set out the standard of behaviour and values to which HMRC will aspire in dealing with taxpayers and others.	
s 93 and Sch 46	*Duties of senior accounting officers of large companies*	
	This provision enables HMRC to take action against the officers of large companies if the company fails to establish and maintain appropriate tax accounting arrangements.	
s 94	*Publishing details of deliberate tax defaulters*	
	This provision enables HMRC to publish the names of the persons who are penalised for deliberate tax defaults where the tax lost exceeds £25,000.	
s 95–96 and Sch 47–48	*Information and inspection powers*	
	These provisions make amendments to FA 2008 Sch 36 which contain the new information and inspection powers of HMRC.	
s 98–99 and Sch 50–51	*Record keeping and time limits*	
	These provisions make amendments to the various requirements of different taxes in terms of record keeping and time limits in order to bring in consistency as part of the merger of HMRC and the move to a new investigation and management regime.	
s 100 and Sch 52	*Recovery of overpaid tax*	
	The 'error or mistake relief' provisions are replaced by new rules for the recovery by the taxpayer of tax overpaid. The new rules apply to claims made on or after 1 April 2010.	
s 101–105 and Sch 53–54	*Interest*	
	These provisions introduce various changes to ensure that the rules for interest are consistent across the various taxes managed and operated by HMRC.	

Finance Act 2009 reference		*Example*
s 106–109 and Sch 55–57	Penalties	41, 44, 46

These provisions introduce a new penalty regime for failure to make returns on time or to pay tax on time. The regime is consistent across the various taxes managed and operated by HMRC. Reasonable excuse provisions are included.

s 110 and Sch 58 — *Recovery of debts under PAYE*

This is a practical provision giving more flexibility for HMRC to collect small tax liabilities over a longer period through PAYE.

ss 111 — *Managed payment plans*

This section introduces time to pay arrangements which have been introduced in order to support businesses through the recession.

s 123 and Sch 61 — *Alternative finance investment bonds*

These provisions facilitate the acquisition and disposal of real property in connection with such bonds and provide that they do not incur liability to SDLT or tax in respect of chargeable gains and that entitlement to capital allowances is maintained.

s 124 — *Mutual societies – tax consequences of transfer of business*

It has been identified that there are barriers to the transfer of businesses between mutual societies and this section enables regulations to be made by HM Treasury to better facilitate such transfers.

s 126–127 — *Interpretations and title*
These give abbreviations, interpretations and the name of the Act.

PROVISIONS NOT COVERED IN THIS SUMMARY

Finance Act 2009 reference

s 9 and Sch 3	VAT – extension of reduced standard rate and anti-avoidance provisions
ss 11–22	Excise and environment taxes and duties
ss 73–74	Financial Assistance Scheme and FSCS
ss 76–79 and Sch 36	Various VAT provisions
s 85 and Sch 39	Blended oils for PRT purposes
s 88 and Sch 42	Former licences and former oil fields – PRT
s 89 and Sch 43	Abolition of provisional expenditure allowance – PRT
s 91 and Sch 45	Oil – miscellaneous amendments for PRT purposes
s 97 and Sch 49	HMRC powers to obtain contact details for tax debtors
s 112	Customs & Excise enforcement powers
s 113–116	Gaming duties
s 117–121	Environmental taxes and duties
s 122	Inheritance tax on agricultural property and woodlands in the EEA
s 125	National savings

Question

Christopher Thackery, aged 50, is married to Helen, aged 39, and they have a son, Mark, aged 14. Their respective incomes are as follows:

Christopher Thackery:

		£
(i)	Salary as a sales representative for year ending 5.4.2010 (tax deducted under PAYE £6,657)	35,165
(ii)	Bonus based on the company profits for the accounting year to:	
	31 March 2009 (paid 1 June 2009)	4,600
	31 March 2010 (paid 1 June 2010)	4,750

		Year ended 5 April 2010 £
(iii)	Investment income	
	Dividends received from UK companies (exclusive of dividend tax credits)	1,701
	Net interest received from Midwest Bank	976
	National Savings Bank interest (Easy Access Savings)	1,600
	Interest on National Savings Certificates	815
	Interest arising on overseas bank accounts	180
	Rental income	4,930

Helen Thackery:

(i)	Profits from hairdressing business operated since 1993	
	Year to 31.7.2009	6,080
	Year to 31.7.2010	7,500
(ii)	Building society interest – net amount received in year ended 5.4.2010	732

Mark Thackery:

Mark has a building society account, the source of capital being gifts from his father. The interest for the year ended 5.4.2010 was £24. The account has been registered for interest to be paid gross. He also has dividends of £360 on shares given to him by his grandfather.

Outgoings year ended 5 April 2009

Christopher paid mortgage interest of £4,320 on a home loan of £84,000. He also paid £3,000 interest on a loan to buy the rented property, which had been let throughout the year at a full rent. The couple do not incur any childcare costs and Helen is nominated as the main carer of Mark.

(i) Compute the income tax due (or repayable) for each family member for the year 2009/10 and show what tax credits are due, based on Helen and Christopher's 2009/10 income.

(ii) State the tax treatment and reduction in liability arising if Christopher Thackery paid £800 net in 2009/10 into a personal pension plan, and compare that treatment with a similar contribution by Helen Thackery.

Ignore foreign taxation.

Answer

(i) **Income Tax Computations 2009/10**

   Christopher Thackery

	£	£
Non-savings income:		
Salary	35,165	
Bonus (paid 1 June 2009)	4,600	39,765
Rental income (4,930 less interest paid 3,000)		1,930
		41,695
Non-dividend savings income		
National Savings Bank	1,600	
Midwest Bank interest (976 + tax deducted 244)	1,220	
Foreign bank interest	180	3,000
Dividend income		
UK dividends received (1,701 + dividend tax credit 189)		1,890
		46,585
Personal allowance		6,475
Taxable income		40,110

Tax thereon: On non-savings income

					£
	Basic rate	35,220	@	20%	7,044
On savings income other than dividends					
	Lower rate	2,180	@	20%	436
	Higher rate	820	@	40%	328
On dividend income					
	Upper rate	1,890	@	32½%	614
		40,110			

			£
Tax liability			8,422
Less: Tax deducted	– under PAYE	6,657	
	– by Midwest Bank	244	
Tax credits on UK dividends		189	7,090
Tax due			1,332

   Helen Thackery

	£	£
Business profits (yr ended 31 July 2009)		6,080
Building society interest (732 + tax deducted 183)		915
		6,995
Personal allowance		6,475
Taxable income		520

	£	£
Tax thereon: @ savings starting rate 10%		52
Less: Tax deducted		183
Tax repayable		131

Tax Credits

Helen, as carer, will receive child tax credit in respect of Mark. The relevant income for tax credits being:

	£
Christopher (as above)	46,585
Helen (as above)	6,995
	53,580
Less: Investment income disregard	300
	53,280

As this is more than £50,000 the amount due is the family element of £545 less taper of £219, giving a net award of £326. This is paid four weekly to Helen (with Child Benefit) during the year, assuming Helen and Christopher renewed their award by 31 July 2009 and their income for 2008/09 was at a similar level. For more detail on tax credits see Example 7.

Mark Thackery

Mark's building society interest of £24 is covered by his personal allowance, so he has no income tax liability, hence his entitlement to receive gross interest. His dividend income is similarly covered by his personal allowance. Tax credits on dividends are not, however, repayable, so he will effectively suffer the notional tax credit of (1/9 × 360 =) £40 shown on the dividend voucher. Although the source of the bank interest was funds gifted by his father, this is not taxable on Christopher as it is less than £100.

(ii)   **Payment of a personal pension premium**

Christopher Thackery's personal pension premium of £800 is net of basic rate tax. The gross premium is therefore £1,000. Providing the payment is within the limits allowed, no tax relief is withdrawn from such a payment even if the payer has no tax liability. Relief is available on the amount up to the individual's earnings for the year (subject to an overall maximum of £245,000 for 2009/10). For someone like Christopher who is liable to higher rate tax, the extra relief over and above the basic rate tax retained at source is given by extending the basic rate limit by the amount of the premium, so that in Christopher's case the revised limit is £38,400. The position would therefore be as follows:

		£			£
Taxable income as in (i)					40,110
Tax thereon:	On non-savings income				
	Basic rate	35,220	@	20%	7,044
	On non-dividend savings income				
	Lower rate	3,000	@	20%	600
	On dividend income				
	Ordinary rate	180	@	10%	18
	Upper rate	1,710	@	32½%	556
		40,110			8,218

	£	£
Less: Tax deducted and dividend tax credits as before		7,090
Tax due		1,128

Thus the effect of paying a pension premium of £1,000 gross, £800 net, is to give relief of:

Reduction of tax due (1,332 – 1,128)	204
Tax relief given by deduction from premium	200
	£404

The relief is more than 40% because the effect of increasing the basic rate band by £1,000 in this case is to move £820 of non-dividend savings income out of the higher rate band into the lower rate band, saving 20% = £164, plus £180 of dividend income into the ordinary rate band, saving 22½% = £40 giving a total reduction of tax of (164 + 40 =) £204, plus the tax of £200 deducted from the payment. The effective rate of tax saving on the premium is 40.4%.

Helen Thackery would also pay the premium of £1,000 net of basic rate tax. Since she is not a higher rate taxpayer the premium would not affect her tax liability and she would retain the £200 deducted at source, even though only £52 tax was charged on her income. If the premium had instead been paid into a retirement annuity contract, gross, rather than net her position would have been:

	£	£
Business profits	6,080	
Less: Retirement annuity premium	1,000	5,080
Non-dividend savings income		915
		5,995
Personal allowance		6,475
Taxable income		Nil
Tax deducted from savings income		183
Tax repayable		183

Thus the tax saving from paying a retirement annuity premium of £1,000 would be (£131 previously repayable compared with £183 now repayable =) £52, ie her total tax liability without paying the premium.

The payment of £1,000 (gross) to a pension plan by either Helen or Christopher would slightly increase their tax credits entitlement as the taper on the family element would reduce to £152, bringing the net award to £393, an increase of £67.

Explanatory Notes

Scope of income tax charge

1.   Income tax is charged broadly on the world income of UK residents, subject to certain deductions for earnings abroad and for individuals who are not ordinarily resident or not domiciled in the UK (see Examples 5 and 12). Non-residents are liable to income tax only on income that arises in the UK. The UK excludes the Channel Islands and the Isle of Man. The introduction of a Scottish Parliament has brought with it the right for that Parliament to increase or decrease the basic rate of income tax by up to 3%. It is intended that any Scottish variable rate would apply only in place of the *basic* rate

of tax and would not affect the starting, lower, higher or dividend rates of tax for income tax purposes. There would also be some circumstances where income would be charged at the normal basic rate instead of the Scottish rate. As capital gains are charged at a flat rate of 18% the Scottish rate would not affect the tax liability on such gains.

Certain aspects of UK tax are affected by the provisions of the European Union, EU law taking precedence over UK law. The EU treaty limits the right of member states to impose taxes, and requires that the laws of member states do not discriminate against members of other states. Furthermore the UK tax legislation must be compatible with the European Convention on Human Rights and, from October 2000, the Human Rights Act 1998.

From 1 January 1999 businesses may pay their taxes in euros, although liabilities will still be calculated in sterling and under- or overpayments may arise because of exchange rate fluctuations before payments are actually credited by the tax authorities. SI 1998/3177 prevents unintended tax consequences arising in the UK as a result of the adoption of the euro by other EU states.

Taxable income

2. An individual's income for tax purposes is called his total income (ITA 2007 s 23). It is the sum of all income of that person computed in accordance with the provisions of the Income Tax Acts. In addition to provisions within the Income Tax Act 2007 trading and other income (eg property) is computed under the Income Tax (Trading and Other Income) Act 2005 (ITTOIA 2005). Each source of income is known as a 'component' of total income. Under the legislation expenses can often be deducted from income in arriving at the taxable amount. In the case of dividends the taxable amount is the amount received plus the related tax credit (equal to 1/9 of the dividend received). Earnings and pensions are taxed in accordance with the Income Tax (Earnings and Pensions) Act 2003 (ITEPA 2003).

After totalling all components of income, certain payments are deducted to arrive at total income, namely allowable interest (see note 14). Where relevant, trading losses are also deducted. Part (ii) of the example illustrates that retirement annuity premiums reduce earnings, and thus total income, whereas personal pension contributions do not. Gift aid donations to charity or to registered community amateur sports clubs do not reduce total income, relief being given in the same way as for personal pension contributions, but see Example 3 explanatory note 1 for the special personal pension contributions and gift aid rules in relation to age allowance and Example 39 part (c) for the different treatment of personal pension contributions and gift aid donations for top slicing relief on life insurance policies. See also Example 2.

Income exempt from tax

3. Certain income is exempt from tax, the principal items being as follows:

    (i) Interest and bonuses on National Savings Certificates.

    (ii) Income from TESSA Only Special Savings Accounts (TOSSAs) and Individual Savings Accounts (ISAs).

    (iii) Terminal bonuses on Save As You Earn (SAYE) contracts.

    (iv) Prizes (including Premium Bond prizes) and bettings winnings.

    (v) The stipulated capital element of a purchased life annuity.

    (vi) Statutory redundancy payments (and certain other payments on termination of employment).

    (vii) Educational grants and scholarships.

    (viii) Maintenance payments.

(ix) Qualifying sickness and unemployment insurance payments (such as benefits paid from permanent health insurance policies, income protection insurance, mortgage payment protection insurance, and insurance to meet loan repayments or domestic bills).

(x) Damages and compensation for personal injury (whether received as a lump sum or by periodic payments).

(xi) Some state benefits, including wounds and disability pensions, war widows' pensions, disability living allowance, child benefit, attendance allowance, severe disablement allowance, income support (except to the unemployed and to strikers), jobfinder's grant, payments and training vouchers under the Jobmatch programme, tax credits, housing benefit, pensioners' Christmas bonus, pensioners' winter allowance and pension credits (see Example 9 explanatory note 1 for details of taxable state benefits).

Tax is not normally payable on cashbacks and rebated commissions received by someone as an ordinary retail customer (see HMRC Statement of Practice 4/97).

Charging income to tax

4.   The tax year runs from 6 April to 5 April. Income is taxed on a 'current year basis', which means that the taxable income is always that of the tax year (except for business income, for which the taxable income is normally the profits of the accounting year ending in the tax year).

Employment earnings are charged to tax when they are received (or when remitted to the UK for certain non-domiciled or not ordinarily resident individuals, see Example 12), regardless of the year in which they were earned. Christopher's bonus received in June 2009 is thus charged in 2009/10, even though it was earned in the previous tax year.

5.   In working out how much tax is payable, certain payments, eg pension premiums (see explanatory note 12), donations to charity (see explanatory note 13), and allowable interest payments under headings (i) to (vi) in explanatory note 14, qualify for tax relief at the taxpayer's highest tax rate, although in the case of personal pension premiums the minimum tax saving is the tax of 20% deducted from the premium, as illustrated in part (ii) of the example in relation to Helen Thackery. Patent royalties are also paid net of basic rate tax (except where paid by one company to another – see Example 5 part (a)), but in this case the relief may not be retained by a non-taxpayer (see explanatory note 13). Certain qualifying investments, such as under the Enterprise Investment Scheme or Venture Capital Trust Scheme (see Example 93), give relief at 20% and 30% respectively of the investment. Qualifying investments in Community Development Finance Institutions give relief at 5% of the investment for up to five years (see Example 93).

6.   As well as being able to save tax on certain payments, taxpayers may claim various tax allowances. Married couple's allowance is available only to a couple one of whom was born before 6 April 1935.

The age-related personal allowance and the increased married couple's allowance for the over 75s first apply in the tax year in which the taxpayer (or for married couple's allowance, the elder of the two) reaches the relevant age (or would have reached that age if he/she had not died earlier in the tax year). For detailed notes see Example 3. The personal allowance and blind person's relief, where relevant, reduce statutory income and save tax at the payer's highest tax rate. Married couple's allowance and maintenance relief for the over 65s save tax at 10% for 2009/10. The tax saving is given by reducing the tax payable by the appropriate amount. See Example 8 for the way this is done through the PAYE system. Although still called the married couple's allowance, the allowance is also available to members of a registered civil partnership provided that at least one of the partners was born before 6 April 1935.

In addition, a family unit or a single person may be able to claim tax credits. These are payable if the claimant(s) have low income or a child. For details see Example 7.

7.   Life assurance relief is given at 12½% of premiums on qualifying policies taken out up to 13 March 1984. It is not given on policies taken out after that date. The relief is obtained by paying the

premium net. The maximum amount of premiums qualifying for relief on pre 13 March 1984 policies is £1,500 or one sixth of total income whichever is the *greater*. It is therefore possible for a non-taxpayer to obtain relief on premiums up to £1,500. For detailed notes on life assurance see Example 39.

Rates of tax

8.   On income other than savings income, tax is payable for the tax year 2009/10 at the basic rate of 20% on the first £37,400 and the higher rate of 40% on income above that.

Different rates apply to savings income, the main items of which are dividend income, interest from banks and building societies, interest on company debentures and government stocks, the income element of a purchased life annuity (see Example 4 explanatory note 3) and accrued income charges on the sale/purchase of interest-bearing securities (see Example 6) (ITA 2007 ss 8 and 9). Savings income is taxed as the top slice of income (except for termination payments – see Example 11 explanatory note 9. Savings income is subdivided into dividends and other savings income, with dividends being treated as the top slice of the savings income. Tax is payable on savings income other than dividends at the savings starting rate of 10% until the £2,440 limit is used (the savings starting rate limit) then at the basic rate of 20% on income up to the basic rate limit of £37,400 and at 40% thereafter. The savings starting rate only applies to the extent that taxable non-savings income does not exceed the £2,440 limit. Dividend income is taxed at the dividend ordinary rate of 10% on income up to the basic rate limit and the dividend upper rate of 32½% thereafter. The rates on dividends and other savings income apply not only to UK income but also to foreign savings income (except for income charged to tax on a remittances basis, to which the normal non-savings income rates apply – see Example 5). Relief is available for foreign tax deducted. The savings income rates do not apply to other investment income, such as rents or to annuities (other than purchased life annuities), or to other taxable income even if the underlying source is savings income (see Example 2 part (b)).

Tax at 20% is deducted from UK building society and bank interest received (except National Savings Bank interest) unless a non-taxpayer (or in this example, his parent on his behalf) has registered to receive interest in full. For details see Example 5.

Shareholders receive a tax credit of 1/9th (representing 10% of the tax credit inclusive amount) on UK dividends and also on dividends from foreign companies in which they own less than 10% of the shares. The maximum credit that can be set against the tax payable is, however, restricted to 10% of taxable income (ITTOIA 2005 s 397). See Example 4 explanatory note 9 for the effect of this restriction on a higher rate taxpayer whose income consists wholly of dividends. Non-taxpayers cannot recover the tax credits on dividends. Tax deducted from other savings income is repayable.

The self-employed pay Class 4 national insurance contributions based on their profits, Class 4 contributions being collected along with income tax (see page (xv)).

9.   Shareholders owning in excess of 10% of the shares in a foreign company also benefit from a non-repayable tax credit, provided the company is located in a country where tax equivalent to corporation tax is levied on the profits.

Taxation of the family

10.   Income and capital gains of a married couple are taxed on each of them separately. Each is entitled to a personal allowance and annual exemption. The age-related married couple's allowance goes to the husband, unless an election is made to transfer all or half of it to the wife. In any event, any unused tax saving may be transferred to the other spouse if income is too low to use it. For the detailed provisions see Example 3.

Although still called the married couple's allowance, the allowance is also available to members of a registered civil partnership provided that at least one of the partners was born before 6 April 1935.

For couples married on or after 5 December and for all civil partners, the higher of the two incomes will be used to determine the allowance (as opposed to that of the husband for couples married before that time).

By contrast entitlement to tax credits is dependent upon the total income of the couple computed in accordance with the rules for tax credits. For the detailed provisions see Example 7.

11.   The income of unmarried children under 18 is treated as the parent's, if it derives from funds transferred to the child or settled on the child by the parent. There are certain exceptions, including income of up to £100 a year, which covers Mark's building society interest in this example. For further details see Example 2.

Personal pension premiums and retirement annuity premiums

12.   UK residents under 75 may pay contributions to buy themselves a pension. The detailed provisions are in Examples 37 and 38. Generally, people paying under pre 1 July 1988 contracts (retirement annuity contracts) may pay the premiums gross and obtain tax relief at their marginal rate by deducting the premiums from their taxable earnings. However, they may now be paid net of basic rate tax like other pension premiums, including stakeholder pension premiums, and higher rate relief where relevant is given in the payer's self-assessment or coding notice. The extra higher rate relief is given by extending the basic rate band by the amount of the payment, as shown in part (ii) of the example for Christopher Thackery.

(For further details, see Example 37.)

Those with relevant income (as defined) of more than £150,000 may suffer a tax charge if they increase their pension contributions in 2009/10 or 2010/11 against the normal regular contributions paid previously. From 2011/12 contributions paid by those with income in excess of £150,000 will not attract tax relief at the taxpayer's marginal rate. (See Example 38 for further details).

National insurance contributions are not deducted in calculating earnings for pension contribution purposes (FA 2004 s 189(2)), and pension scheme payments (either under personal, stakeholder, retirement annuity or occupational schemes) are not deducted in calculating earnings or profits on which national insurance contributions are calculated (SSCBA 1992 Sch 2 para 3).

Position of non-taxpayers in relation to tax relief deducted from payments

13.   The tax deducted from personal pension premiums may be retained by both taxpayers and non-taxpayers.

The taxation of royalties has been changed by ITA 2007. It is now mandatory to deduct income tax from such payments. The tax deducted is then collected as part of the taxpayer's self-assessment. Non-taxpayers or those who can only partly cover the charge will therefore need to file a self-assessment and account for the tax due.

Where tax has been deducted at source from gift aid donations to charity then the taxpayer needs to have paid sufficient tax to cover the amount deducted. The tax paid for this purpose includes income tax, non-repayable tax credits on dividends and capital gains tax (see Example 90).

Allowable interest

14.   Before 6 April 2000 relief was available to someone aged 65 or over who had taken out a loan to buy a life annuity, the loan being secured on the only or main residence of the borrower/annuitant. The relief was at the then basic rate of 23% on the first £30,000 of a qualifying loan. Relief for such loans remains available (under the Mortgage Interest Relief At Source (MIRAS) scheme where appropriate) for loans taken out before 9 March 1999 (or for which a written offer had been made before that date), providing the property was the borrower's main residence immediately before that date. Despite the reduction in the basic rate to 20%, relief for home annuity loans continues at 23% (ICTA s 353(1AA)). If the taxpayer leaves the property, eg to move into a nursing home, or remortgages the

property, or moves to a different property, the relief will continue so long as the loan or replacement is still outstanding (ICTA 1988 s 365). Relief is no longer available from 6 April 2000 on any other home loans.

Relief at the payer's marginal rate is available for interest on loans under the following headings.

(i) Loans to buy plant or machinery, for example an office machine, for use in a partnership or in one's employment (ITA 2007 s 390). Relief in this case is restricted to interest payable not later than three years after the end of the tax year in which the loan was made. Where there is part private use, relief is restricted to the business proportion of the interest. Employees cannot claim relief for plant and machinery unless it is *necessarily* provided for use in their employment (ITA 2007 s 390 & CAA 2001 s 36).

(ii) Loans to buy shares in or lend money to a close company that is a trading or property investment company, providing the borrower either owns more than 5% of the ordinary share capital, or owns some share capital and has worked for the greater part of his time in the management or conduct of the company in the period since obtaining the loan to the time the interest is paid (ITA 2007 s 392). The loan interest does not qualify for relief if either income tax relief or capital gains deferral relief has been given in respect of the shares under the enterprise investment scheme (see Example 93).

(iii) Loans to a partner to buy an interest in a partnership or to lend money to it, providing the borrower is still a partner when the interest is paid and providing he is not a limited partner or a partner in an investment limited liability partnership (see Example 26) (ITA 2007 s 398).

(iv) Loans to personal representatives to pay inheritance tax on a deceased person's personal property (ie property other than freehold land and buildings), in respect of interest paid within one year from the making of the loan (ITA 2007 s 403).

(v) Loans for the purchase of shares in unquoted employee-controlled trading companies by their full-time employees or spouses (ITA 2007 s 396).

(vi) Loans to acquire a share or shares in a co-operative (ITA 2007 s 401).

In no circumstances can bank overdraft interest be deducted from *total* income, no matter for what purpose the overdraft is used. Relief is only available for bank overdraft interest where it is paid in connection with a business and is thus deductible as a business expense under the trading rules where it relates to let property (see Example 97).

Where the claim for allowable interest relates to trading purposes then if the interest cannot be offset within the tax year it may be added to trading losses carried forward (see Example 29) or included in a terminal loss claim (see Example 32) (ITA 2007 s 88).

Self-assessment

15. Around one third of taxpayers are technically required to 'self-assess' the amount of income tax and capital gains tax payable, although HMRC will still work out the tax if the taxpayer wants them to, providing returns are sent in early enough or filed via the Internet. Most taxpayers, however, account for their tax under PAYE and by deduction at source. HMRC issue assessments themselves in some circumstances, in particular where they discover that tax has been underpaid because the taxpayer has failed to disclose relevant information.

If Christopher Thackery receives a self-assessment tax return, then he is required to compute his 'tax due for 2009/10 before payments on account'. This will be the tax liability less tax deducted at source (ie PAYE tax, tax deducted by banks and building societies etc and dividend tax credits).

Note that the reduction of the tax liability in respect of dividend tax credits is restricted to 10% of the income actually charged to tax (see Example 4 explanatory note 9).

In Christopher Thackery's case, the tax due arises because National Savings Bank Easy Access Savings Account interest, rental income and foreign bank interest have been received without deduction of tax, and higher rate tax is due on £2,710 of investment income. The actual liability will always be slightly different from the exact figure because of the rounding of allowances and rates under the PAYE system, and the possible offset of untaxed interest against allowances under PAYE (see Example 8 explanatory note 1).

Because of the nature of Christopher's income no payments on account will have been made. Provided Christopher files his tax return by 31 October 2010, or electronically by 30 December 2010 HMRC will collect the amount due by way of an adjustment to his PAYE code number in 2011/12 (see Example 8 explanatory note 13). If the return is filed too late for a coding adjustment, the tax due must be paid by 31 January 2011. For detailed notes on self-assessment see Example 41.

Question

(a)   Mr Victor, a married man aged 55, has the following income for 2009/10:

	£
Non-savings income (gross)	29,950
Savings income (dividends of £10,800 + dividend tax credits £1,200)	12,000

His two children, Arthur aged 23 and Brian aged 15, are beneficiaries under an accumulation and maintenance trust set up by Mr Victor in 1992, under which the children are entitled to the income at age 18. The trust's investments comprise interest-bearing securities. In 2009/10 the income of the trust was £4,000, the trustees paying £2,000 gross in respect of each of the children and deducting tax therefrom at the appropriate rate. Brian has no other income. Arthur is a post graduate student at university and in addition to the trust income he has vacation earnings of £800 (from which no tax has been deducted) and a research grant.

Mrs Victor does not work, her only income being savings income of £11,810 (gross).

Show the tax position of Mr Victor and his children for 2009/10, assuming that the family income for tax credits for 2008/09 amounted to £60,000, and a claim for tax credits was made in 2008/09, showing Mrs Victor as the main carer of Brian.

(b)   Outline:

(i)   the broad principles of the income tax treatment of trusts;

(ii)   tax-effective transfers by parents to their infant children;

(iii)   tax planning possibilities for husband and wife.

(c)   Set out the tax treatment relating to:

(i)   financial support to adopters;

(ii)   receipts from foster care.

Answer

(a)   **Mr Victor and his children – Income tax computations 2009/10**

Arthur's income from the trust is his in his own right and tax will have been deducted by the trustees at the basic rate of 20%. Brian's income will be treated as his father's income, taxable not as savings income but as miscellaneous income (ITTOIA s 629). The trustees will have deducted tax at 40% (see part (b)(i) note 4 of the example). The tax position is therefore as follows:

Mr Victor

				£
Non-savings income, including Brian's income from the trust				31,950
Savings income (dividends)				12,000
				43,950
Personal allowance				6,475
Taxable income				37,475
Tax thereon:				
On non-savings income	25,475	@	20%	5,095
On dividend income (part)	11,925	@	10%	1,192
On dividend income (balance)	75	@	32½%	24
	37,475			
Tax liability				6,311
Less: Tax deducted – by trustees	800			
Tax credits on dividends	1,200			2,000
Tax payable				4,311

Brian

Brian has no taxable income, his only income being treated as his father's under the parental settlement rules, since he is under 18 and unmarried.

Arthur

Arthur's trust income is not treated as his father's because he is over 18.

His research grant is exempt from tax. His trust income of £2,000 plus his vacation earnings of £800 are below his personal allowance of £6,475 so he can recover from HMRC the tax of £400 deducted from the trust income.

Tax Credits

Mrs Victor, as carer, will be entitled to tax credits for the couple, the amount being computed on their joint income for 2008/09 adjusted to actual for 2009/10 provided the claim was renewed by 31 July 2009. In this case a claim was made and the initial award notice would show nil.

When final details of income were filed that claim would be amended to:

	£
Income	
Mr Victor (as above)	43,950
Mrs Victor	11,810
	55,760
Less: Disregard	300
	55,460
Family element award	545
Less: Excess income (55,460 – 50,000 =) 5,460 × 6.67%	364
Tax credits payable	181

(b)   (i)   Tax treatment of trusts

The tax treatment of trusts is dealt with in detail in the companion to this book, Tolley's Taxwise II 2009/10. The broad principles are as follows:

1.   The settlor remains liable for income tax on the trust income if he or his spouse/civil partner has retained an interest in the settlement or where the settlement transfers income but not capital. Spouse/civil partner does not include a future, former or separated spouse/civil partner or the settlor's widow(er) or surviving civil partner (ITTOIA 2005 s 624).

These provisions do not apply to annual payments made for commercial reasons in connection with an individual's business. There are also exceptions for outright gifts between spouses/civil partners, and for various arrangements made on separation or divorce. There is no charge on the settlor to the extent that the trust income is given to charity (see Example 90 explanatory note 5).

All income treated as the settlor's income under ITTOIA 2005 s 624 is charged to tax in accordance with whichever provisions of the Income Tax Acts as would have applied had the income arisen directly to the settlor. So savings income of the trust is taxed as savings income of the settlor.

2.   Even if a settlement is of capital in which the settlor does not retain an interest, if income of the settlement is paid to or for the benefit of an unmarried child of the settlor who is under 18, it is treated as the settlor's income, subject to the exceptions in part (b)(ii) of the example (ITTOIA 2005 ss 626–627). The tax deducted by the trustees from the payment counts as tax paid by the settlor (ITA 2007 s 494(3)). If the settlor has to pay any further tax he is entitled to recover it from the trustees, or from the person who received the income (ITTOIA 2005 s 646), (but see part (b)(ii) of the example). The income charged as the settlor's income under ITTOIA 2005 s 629 is treated as miscellaneous income and it does not count as savings income. This applies even if the income is derived from dividends, because such income comes from the general pool of income in the trust.

3.   Where someone has an interest in possession in a trust, ie the right to income (usually a life interest), the trustees are liable to tax at the dividend ordinary rate of 10% on tax credit inclusive dividend income, the lower rate of 20% on other savings income and at the basic rate on other trust income (without any deduction for their expenses) and they deduct tax at the appropriate rate from income payments to the life tenant. Non-taxpaying beneficiaries can claim repayment of the tax deducted, except that the tax credits on dividend income are not repayable. Arthur in part (a) of the example would not therefore have been able to reclaim tax if the trust's income had been dividend income.

4.   Where the trust is a discretionary trust (including accumulation and maintenance trusts), the trustees are liable to tax at the trust dividend rate of 32½% on tax credit inclusive dividend income (of which the tax credit covers 10%) and at 40% on other income, after deducting

trust expenses (ITTOIA 2005 s 568). The first £1,000 of discretionary trust income is instead liable at the rates set out at 3 above, that is dividends 10%, other savings income 20%, non-savings income 20% (FA 2005 s 14). Even though tax on dividends is paid at only 32½%, the trustees deduct tax at 40% on payments to beneficiaries (and non-taxpaying beneficiaries may claim repayment of the tax deducted), but the trustees cannot treat the tax credits on the trust's dividend income as covering part of the tax at 40% to be accounted for by them on the payments to the beneficiaries (ITA 2007 s 498).

5.   Special rules apply from 2004/05, by election, where it is a trust with a vulnerable beneficiary. In order to qualify the beneficiary must be entitled to all of the income and the property must be held for the vulnerable beneficiary absolutely. If the beneficiary qualifies as a minor he/she must be absolutely entitled to the property at 18. A vulnerable person is either a disabled person who is incapable of administering their affairs by reason of a mental disorder, or a person in receipt of attendance allowance, or disability living allowance (higher or middle rate), or a minor (under 18) where one or both parents have died. The election enables the tax liability of the trust to be computed using the tax rates and allowances applicable to the vulnerable beneficiary. The treatment extends to capital gains tax. For full details see Tolley's Taxwise II 2009/10.

(ii)   Tax-effective transfers by parents to infant children

Children are taxpayers in their own right, no matter how young they are, and they are entitled to the personal allowance against their income. This does not apply to certain income from their parents, as indicated in (i) above. The following items are not caught by the parental settlement rules:

1.   Income deriving from funds provided by the parent if it is less than £100 a year. The £100 income limit applies separately to each parent.

2.   National Savings Children's Bonus Bonds for children under 16. The maximum holding per child is £3,000 in the current issue plus earlier issues of the Bonds. All interest and bonuses are tax-free, but no further returns are earned after the child's 21st birthday.

3.   Premiums of up to £270 a year on a qualifying friendly society life assurance policy for a child under 18. The returns under the policy are exempt from tax, but friendly societies are not able to reclaim dividend tax credits.

4.   Contributions of up to £3,600 a year to a personal pension policy on behalf of a child, such contributions being paid net of basic rate tax, which is retained whether or not the child is a taxpayer. The contributions would probably be exempt from inheritance tax under the rules for regular gifts out of income (inheritance tax is dealt with in detail in the companion to this book, Tolley's Taxwise II 2009/10). The child cannot draw pension benefits from the fund until he/she reaches age 55.

Parents can also establish accumulation and maintenance settlements for their children, the income from which is not treated as theirs unless and to the extent that it is used for the maintenance or education of children who are under 18 and unmarried, as illustrated in part (a) of the example.

The effect of Brian's trust income of £2,000 being treated as Mr Victor's income in part (a) of the example is to make part of Mr Victor's income liable to higher rate tax liability and to reduce the family's claim for child tax credit. As stated in (i) note 2, the settlor has the right to recover from the trustees any additional tax payable by him. ITTOIA 2005 s 619A states that the settlement income is regarded as the top slice of the settlor's income. This is, however, overridden by ITA 2007 s 16 requiring savings income to be treated as the top slice of income. Although the settlement income is in fact savings income, it is not treated as such in Mr Victor's hands. The effect for Mr Victor is that the settlement income falls within the basic rate tax band.

In fact, the inclusion of the trust income increases his overall tax liability by £417, because the trust income is charged to tax at 20%, costing £400, and it moves £75 of his dividend income that would have been charged at 10% into the 32½% rate band, costing £17. Mr Victor is entitled to treat the tax at 40% deducted by the trustees from the trust income (£800) as paid by him (see (i) note 2). The loss of tax credits, £2,000 @ 6.67% = £133, is not recoverable from the trustees.

Income arising on bare trusts created by parents in favour of their children under 18 on or after 9 March 1999, and income from funds added to existing trusts on or after that date is taxed as income of the parent, unless covered by the £100 limit dealt with above.

Bare trusts created under a parent's will are still effective, and also bare trusts created by other relatives, although it is not possible to make a reciprocal arrangement for someone to create a trust for his relative's children and for the relative to do the same for his children. A disadvantage of bare trusts is that the child cannot be prevented from having the property put into his own legal ownership at age 18.

Bare trusts created by parents are still effective for capital gains purposes, so that it is possible to use such trusts to acquire investments for children that produce capital growth rather than income.

It is possible for a child aged 16 or 17 to hold a cash ISA. It should be noted that if the funds used for that ISA are provided by the parents then the interest arising within the ISA will be taxable on the parent (subject to the £100 limit referred to at (ii) note 1 above).

(iii)   Tax planning for married couples and civil partners

As far as capital gains tax is concerned, each member of a couple is entitled to the annual capital gains tax exemption. Losses of one may, however, not be set against gains of the other. Transfers of assets between them in tax years when they are living together for all or part of the year are made on a no loss/no gain basis. See Example 76.

It may be sensible for a couple to rearrange their affairs in order to obtain the maximum benefit from being taxed separately, for example if one party has insufficient income to use his/her personal allowance. Care should be taken with dividends as the tax credits are not repayable. However it may be possible to transfer part or all of the age-related married couple's allowance to increase the tax payable by one partner in order to use up dividend tax credits that would otherwise be lost.

It is not possible for one party to give the other the right to part of his/her income without transferring the capital, but outright transfers of capital, with no right for the transferring party to control the capital or derive a benefit from it, are tax effective (ITTOIA 2005 s 624). (The fact that the individual who gave the asset away later gets it back on the other's death, or as a gift, does not make the transfer ineffective providing the initial gift was not made with any express or implied stipulation as to what the receiving individual could do with it.) An attempt by two directors owning all the shares in a company to increase their wives' income by issuing them with preference shares (for which the wives paid a nominal amount) carrying rights to 30% of the profits but no voting rights nor rights to participate in surplus assets was treated as an income settlement, and thus ineffective in *Young v Pearce, Young v Scrutton* (1996).

In Tax Bulletin 64 (April 2003) HMRC issued further guidance on the settlements legislation and how they felt it could apply to individuals and businesses in non-trust situations. They listed factors they would consider in deciding whether the settlements legislation should be applied:

–   A main earner draws a low salary leading to enhanced dividends paid to shareholders who are family members.

–   Disproportionately large returns on capital investments.

–   Different classes of shares enabling payment of dividends only to shareholders paying lower rates of tax.

–   Waiver of dividends to enable higher dividends to be paid to those liable at lower rates of tax.

–   Income being transferred from a person making most of the business profits to a friend or family member who pays a lower rate of tax.

Common situations which HMRC felt could invoke the settlement rules were:

– Shares are issued that carry only restricted rights.

– Shares are gifted that carry only restricted rights.

– Income of a company is derived mainly from a single employee but shares are held by others.

– A share in a partnership is gifted or transferred at below market value.

– Dividend waivers occur.

– Dividends are only paid on certain classes of shares.

– Dividends are paid to a settlor's minor children.

HMRC confirms that ITTOIA 2005 s 624 will not apply if there is no 'bounty' or if the gift is to a spouse/civil partner and is an outright gift which is not wholly, or substantially, a right to income, eg a gift of shares in a quoted company.

The Tax Bulletin article gives various examples of where HMRC considers that the settlements legislation will apply. Their view was originally upheld in the case of *Jones v Garnett* (2005) where shares were held by husband and wife and the main earner (Mr Jones) drew a salary below the going rate for the work he had done. As a result the dividend paid to Mrs Jones was deemed to arise from the 'bounty' created by the failure to draw a salary at the going rate. Therefore, under s 660A ICTA 1988 (now ITTOIA 2005 s 624), that dividend income was taxable on Mr Jones. The Court of Appeal disagreed with the HMRC view and held that there was no bounty provided when Mrs Jones acquired her share in the company. The House of Lords unanimously dismissed HMRC's appeal in July 2007. They held that while the arrangements constituted a settlement, the exemption for outright gifts between spouses/civil partners applied (ITTOIA 2005 s 626). Consequently, Mrs Jones was assessable on the dividends she received even though most of the profit was as a result of Mr Jones's efforts. Following the Lords decision, HMRC announced that they intend to legislate to 'reverse' the decision. Although a consultation document setting out proposed new legislation addressing this problem was issued in December 2007, this was widely criticised, and concern was expressed as to how the proposed legislation would apply in practice. The draft legislation was reconsidered during 2008 and both pre-Budget report 2008 and Budget 2009 announced that the legislation was not to be implemented at present. It is possible that this could be re-introduced in the future. Where capital transfers are made, and the property consists of mortgaged property, one point that needs watching is that if the liability to pay the mortgage is taken over by the transferee, stamp duty land tax is payable (unless the transfer is certified as not liable to duty because the consideration is £125,000 or less for residential property, £150,000 or less for non-residential).

Spouses and civil partners normally own joint property as 'joint tenants', which means each has equal rights over the property and when one dies it goes automatically to the other. The joint tenancy can, however, be severed and replaced by a 'tenancy in common' in which the share of each is separate, and may be unequal, and may be disposed of in lifetime or on death as the individal wishes. Where property is in joint names, it is deemed to be owned equally for income tax purposes unless it is actually owned in some different proportions and a joint declaration is made to that effect (ITA 2007 s 836). Declarations apply to income arising on or after the date of the declaration. For a declaration to be valid, notice must be given to HMRC (on Form 17) within the period of sixty days beginning with the date of the declaration. The form only covers the assets listed on it. Any new assets must be covered by a separate form. Tax Bulletin 63 (February 2003) makes it clear that normally bank and building society joint accounts are held in such a way that each owner is equally entitled to the whole account. Form 17 can only be used for these accounts if the parties have formally changed the legal basis on which the account is held.

The provisions of ITA 2007 s 836 deeming joint ownership do not apply if the property is shares in a close company. Instead the income from the shares must be divided between husband and wife in accordance with their actual ownership rights in the shares.

The deemed equal ownership is not relevant for capital gains purposes. The actual underlying beneficial ownership determines the capital gains treatment (see Example 76 part (a)).

(c)   (i)   **Financial support to adopters**

Where a family receives financial support from a local authority or adoption agency the amount received is free of income tax under ITTOIA 2005 s 744.

(ii)   **Foster carers (ITTOIA 2005 part 7 chapter 2)**

A standard tax exemption applies to foster carers which, together with an optional simplified method of computing taxable profits for those foster carers whose income exceeds the exempt amount provides a simple basis for calculating taxable income.

The exempt limit is the sum of

–   £10,000, per residence, per full tax year (s 808), plus

–   £200 per week for a child aged under 11, and £250 per week for a child aged 11 or older (s 811).

Where a foster carer's gross receipts exceed the above limits, then, instead of computing their business profits using the normal rules, they can elect to deem their profit as being the excess of gross receipts from foster care over the exempt limits. The election must be made by the first anniversary of the 31 January after the year of assessment, or such longer period as HMRC may allow (s 818). (There is statutory provision for the deadline to be extended if there is a late adjustment to the profits from the provision of foster care (s 819).) A carer who is exempt or using the simplified method of computing profits is not entitled to capital allowances (s 826). No balancing charge or balancing allowance arises when they become exempt or elect to go into the simplified scheme. If the foster carer goes back to using the normal method of computing profits he or she can claim capital allowances on assets still held at the start of that period, including assets purchased during the periods when he or she was exempt or using the simplified scheme (ss 824–827).

If a taxpayer ceases to trade as a foster carer whilst within the exempt limit, then any overlap relief due on cessation is given as a loss (s 828).

Question

(a)   Richard White is a single man aged 68 with pension income of £23,000, building society income of £2,600 (gross) and dividend income of £180 plus dividend tax credits of £20. He paid a gift aid payment of £800 (net) to his local church during the year.

Calculate the income tax payable for 2009/10.

(b)   John Brown, aged 75, married Ann Old, aged 72, on 10 May 2009. Their incomes for 2009/10 are as follows:

John Brown:	Pension	14,600	
	Building society interest	11,000	£25,600
Ann Old:	Pension	17,900	
	Dividends (inc tax credits)	12,000	£29,900

Calculate the income tax payable by each of them for 2009/10.

(c)   John and Jane Stone were divorced in 1987. Since that time John (who has remarried) has paid maintenance of £3,000 pa to Jane (who has not remarried). They are both aged 75. Their income in 2009/10 is as follows:

	John £	Jane £
Pension	35,040	8,810
Building society interest (amounts received)	2,480	240
Dividends (amounts received)	5,850	855

Compute the net tax payable by or repayable to John and Jane for 2009/10.

(d)   D Partid died on 10 June 2009 aged 74. He would have been 75 in September 2009. His income for the period from 6 April 2009 to the date of his death was as follows:

State pension	£3,500
Dividends (cash amount received)	£1,800
Building society interest credited	£800

He left a widow aged 45 and a child aged ten. Mrs Partid, who does not work, had income for 2009/10, of building society interest (net of 20% tax) of £1,600 and taxable state benefits following her husband's death, amounting to £9,080 (gross) in total.

Show the tax and tax credits position of Mr and Mrs Partid for 2009/10 assuming they made a joint claim to child tax credit before Mr Partid died, and Mrs Partid made a single claim by 11 September 2009. Assume that both Mr Partid's, and Mrs Partid's, income for 2008/09 was greater than the income for 2009/10 and show only the final award tax credits figure.

(e)   Julia Jones, a single lady, will be 60 on 28 December 2009. She is entitled to a state pension of £100 per week. She will continue to work for at least one year at a salary of £62,000 pa. She has savings income of £1,400 pa gross but no other pension provision.

Set out the tax liability (using 2009/10 allowances and rates throughout) arising on the state pension on the assumption that Julia:

(i)   Takes the pension of £100.00 per week from her 60th birthday.

(ii)   Defers her pension until she ceases employment on her 61st birthday where she will receive a pension of £110 per week.

(iii)   As in (ii) but Julia takes a lump sum of £5,500 with an ongoing pension of £100 per week.

(iv)   Continues to work until her 65th birthday then taking a lump sum of £32,825 plus a pension of £100 per week.

(v)   Indicate what would happen if Julia died before she took her deferred pension.

Answer

(a) **Income tax payable by Richard White for 2009/10**

	£	£	£
Pension			23,000
Building society interest (2,080 + 520)			2,600
Dividends (180 + 20)			200
			25,800
Personal allowance (age 68)		9,490	
Reduced by:			
Income	25,800		
Less: Gift aid donation (gross)	1,000		
	24,800		
Age allowance income limit	22,900		
One half of excess of	1,900	950	8,540
Taxable income			17,260
Tax thereon:			
On non-savings income	14,460 @ 20%		2,892
On non-dividend savings income	2,600 @ 20%		520
On dividend income	200 @ 10%		20
	17,260		
Tax payable			3,432

Notes

(i) As tax payable of £3,432 exceeds the tax on the gift aid payment of £200 no adjustment is required for that tax.

(ii) Where gift aid payments are made by taxpayers entitled to age allowance, total income for age allowance purposes is reduced by the gross gift (ITA 2007 ss 36 and 58). Richard paid a net gift of £800 on which tax of £200 (£800 × 20/80) is deemed deducted, giving a gross gift of £1,000. Thus the restriction of allowances by one-half of excess income over £22,900 is based on the reduced income of £24,800 not the actual income of £25,800.

(iii) If Richard makes annual payments under gift aid of £800 (£1,000 gross), he could consider electing to carry back part of his 2010/11 gift aid payment to 2009/10. Provided that payment is made and the election is made before the tax return for 2009/10 is filed and before 31 January 2011 in any event, a carry back of £1,000 would further reduce income for age allowance to £23,900, thus reducing the restriction by a further £500 and saving tax of £500 @ 20% = £100. See Example 90 at explanatory note 8 for the effect on any payments on account.

(b)   **Tax position of John Brown and Ann Old for 2009/10**

John Brown

	£	£
Pension	14,600	
Building society interest	11,000	25,600
Personal allowance (age 75)	9,640	
Reduced by ½ × (25,600 − 22,900)	1,350	(8,290)
Taxable income		17,310

Tax thereon:					
On non-savings income	6,310	@	20%	1,262	
On non-dividend savings income	11,000	@	20%	2,200	
Tax payable					3,462

Ann Old

	£	£
Pension	17,900	
Dividends	12,000	29,900
Personal allowance (Additional age-related allowance of £3,015 forgone due to income level)		(6,475)
Taxable income		23,425

Tax thereon:					
On non-savings income	11,425	@	20%	2,285	
On dividends	12,000	@	10%	1,200	3,485
Less: Married couple's allowance (elder aged 75)				6,965	
Reduced by ½ × (29,900 − 22,900)			3,500		
Less: reduction in personal allowance			3,015	485	
				6,480	
Less: 1/12th of £6,480				540	
				5,940	
Tax saving at 10%					594
Tax payable					2,891

Notes

(i)   Only claimant's income affects married couple's allowance, even if it is given by reason of other spouse's/civil partner's age.

(ii)   The married couple's allowance is reduced by half the excess of the claimant's income over £22,900, less the restriction already made to the personal allowance, before being reduced by 1/12th for each tax month before the date of marriage.

(iii)   Tax would be saved if income-producing assets were transferred from the claimant to the other spouse/civil partner to avoid the claimant's allowances being affected by the income limit. However, this should be done carefully as the other spouse/civil partner might end up with more income in the year and so would be the individual entitled to the allowance. This is less of an issue for couples who *married* before 5 December 2005 (see note (iv) below). See also explanatory note 4.

(iv)   If the marriage had taken place in May 2005 instead of May 2009 then married couple's age allowance would be given to the husband. Thus, John would receive the tax saving which would have been calculated as follows:

Married couples allowance (elder aged 75)		6,965
Reduced by ½ × (25,600 – 22,900)	1,350	
Less: reduction in personal allowance	1,350	Nil
		6,965
Tax saving @ 10%		697

This is a difference of £103 in married couple's allowance.

The difference can be explained by John having an additional entitlement to age allowances of £485 (at 10%) plus the fact that a full-year's married couple allowance is available rather than merely 11/12ths (worth an additional £540 at 10%).

(c)   **Net tax payable by or repayable to John and Jane Stone for 2009/10**

John Stone

	£			£
Pension				35,040
Building society interest (2,480 + tax deducted 620)				3,100
Dividends (5,850 + tax credits 650)				6,500
				44,640
Personal allowance (age 75, but see note (i))				6,475
Taxable income				38,165
Tax payable thereon:				
On non-savings income	28,565	@	20%	5,713
On non-dividend savings income	3,100	@	20%	620
On dividends (part)	5,735	@	10%	574
On dividends (balance)	765	@	32½%	249
	38,165			7,156
Less: Married couple's age allowance (basic amount – see note (i))	2,670			
Relief for maintenance to former wife (see note (ii))	2,670			
	5,340	@	10%	534
Tax payable				6,622

Jane Stone

	Income £	Tax deducted £
Pension	8,810	
Building society interest (240 + tax deducted 60)	300	60

	Income £	Tax deducted £
Dividends (855 + non-repayable dividend tax credits 95)	950	
	10,060	
Personal allowance (age 75)	9,640	
Taxable income	420	
Tax payable thereon:		
On dividends 420 @ 10%	42	
Less: Dividend tax credits, restricted to 10% of taxable income of £420 (see note (iii))	42	–
Tax repayable		60

Notes

(i)   John is aged 75, but his income is too high for him to benefit from the increased personal allowance of £9,640. He is, however, entitled to the basic married couple's allowance of £2,670 regardless of his income (see explanatory notes 1 and 2).

(ii)   Maintenance received is not taxable. Maintenance relief is only available for payers who satisfy the relevant conditions (see explanatory notes 5 and 6) and one of the parties to the marriage was born before 6 April 1935. The relief is 10% of maintenance paid to a maximum of 10% of £2,670.

(iii)   Dividend credits can be used to reduce tax payable (up to a maximum of 10% of taxable income – see Example 1 explanatory note 8), but are not repayable.

(d)   **Tax position of Mr and Mrs Partid for 2009/10**

Mr Partid

	Income £	Tax deducted £
State pension	3,500	
Building society interest (800 + 200)	1,000	200
Dividends (1,800 + 200 non-repayable tax credit)	2,000	–
	6,500	200
Personal allowance (would be aged 75 during tax year)	(9,640)	–
Tax repayable		200

Personal representatives will notify HMRC that married couple's allowance of £6,965 is to be transferred to the widow.

Mrs Partid

	£	£
Total income, including savings income of (1,600 + 400) = 2,000		11,080
Personal allowance		6,475
Taxable income		4,605
Tax thereon: Non-savings income		
2,605 @ 20%	521	

		£	£
Non-dividend savings income			921
2,000 @ 20%		400	
Less: Married couple's age allowance (transferred from husband)	6,965 @ 10%		697
Tax due			224
Tax deducted at source			400
Tax repayable			176

Tax Credits – Mr and Mrs Partid (joint claim)

Award period 6 April 2009 to 10 June 2009 = 66 days

Eligibility   WTC – No
                     Childcare – No
                     CTC – Yes
                     Family element – Yes

Income – 2009/10	Mr Partid £	Mrs Partid £	Total £
State taxable benefits	–	9,080	9,080
Other income (including state pension)	6,500 +	2,000 – 300 =	8,200
Income for Tax Credits – Mr & Mrs Partid			17,280
Income for award period 66/365 × 17,280			3,125

Maximum claim
    CTC   6.13
    Family element   1.50

	66 days		
Relevant period	×	7.63 =	504

Restricted by

		£	
Income		3,125	
Income threshold	66/365 × 16,040	2,900	
39% ×		225	88
Tax Credits payable			416

Tax Credits – Mrs Partid (single claim)

Award period 11 June 2009 to 5 April 2010 = 299 days

Eligibility – CTC and Family element

Income – 2009/10

		£	
Employment (state taxable benefits)		9,080	
Other income	(2,000 – 300)	1,700	
		10,780	
Income for award period	299/365 × 10,780		8,831

Maximum claim
    CTC   6.13

Family element		1.50	
	299 days		
Tax Credits payable	×	7.63	2,281

Amount is not restricted as income £8,831 is below the threshold income level of 299/365 × 16,040 = £13,140

(e)   **Deferral of state pension**

(i)   **Tax liability on state pension – commencing 2009/10**

Julia has income of (£62,000 + £1,400) £63,400 before drawing her state pension and is therefore a 40% taxpayer. Her tax liability on state pension is

State pension –
14 weeks @ £100 = £1,400 @ 40% =   £560

2010/11
Julia will have other income of at least (£46,500 + £1,400) in 2010/11 and is
still a higher rate taxpayer
Liability on state pension
52 weeks @ £100 = £5,200 @ 40% =   £2,080

2011/12
Assuming Julia ceased paid employment in December 2010 her liability
in 2011/12 (aged 61) is

		£
State pension		5,200
Savings income		1,400
		6,600
Personal allowance		(6,475)
Liable at 10% (savings income)		125 = £13

When Julia reaches age 65 in December 2014 her age allowance will exceed her income and she will have no liability from 2014/15 onwards.

(ii)   **Deferral for one year**

If Julia defers her state pension then her liability on pension becomes

2010/11
State pension (income as in (i) above)   £
14 weeks @ £110 = £1,540 @ 40% =   616

2011/12, 2012/13 and 2013/14

		£
State pension		5,720
Savings income		1,400
		7,120
Personal allowance		(6,475)
Liable at 10%		645 = £65

From 2014/15 onwards Julia's age allowance will exceed her income and she will have no liability to tax.

(iii) Drawing a lump sum

If Julia opts to take the lump sum of £5,500 that amount is taxable when received at the rate applicable to her total income

2010/11   £

Earnings	46,500
Other income	1,400
	47,900

Rate applicable (£47,900 is greater than the personal allowance plus the basic rate limit of £37,400) is 40%

Tax on lump sum £5,500 @ 40%	2,200
Tax on state pension 14 weeks @ £100 = £1,400 @ 40%	560
Tax liability on state benefits	2,760

However, Julia may elect to receive the lump sum on 6 April 2011 instead of 28 December 2010. (She could also delay receiving her state pension to 6 April 2011 which would increase the lump sum payable.)

In 2010/11 the resultant tax liabilities would be

On state pension (as above) £1,400 @ 40% = £560

In 2011/12 the tax liabilities would be

	£
State pension	5,200
Other income	1,400
Total income before lump sum	6,600

Rate applicable (£6,600 is less than the basic rate limit) is 20%.

Tax on lump sum £5,500 @ 20%	1,100
Tax on total income (as in (i) above) £125 @ 10% =	13
	1,113

(iv) Drawing pension at age 65

Similar rules would apply at age 65, ie tax at 40% would be due on the lump sum unless Julia deferred receiving the amount until 6 April 2015 when 20% would apply.

(v) Death

If Julia dies after deferring her state pension, but before opting to take the lump sum or increased pension, no amount would be payable to her estate as she is single. (See note (c) below.)

Notes

(a) The Pensions Act 2004 amended Schedule 5 to the Social Security Contributions and Benefits Act 1992 (SSCBA 1992) with effect from 5 April 2005 to increase the subsequent pension payable following deferment and also to enable the deferred pension to be taken as a lump sum with no increase in state pension. State pension includes Basic Pension, SERPS, S2P and Graduated Pensions (SSCBA 1991 Sch 5 para A1).

Deferral must be for a minimum period of five weeks and gives an uprating of pension of 1% for each five weeks of deferral (10.4% pa uplift) (SSCBA 1992 Sch 5 para 2A).

To take a lump sum the minimum deferral period is one year. The lump sum is the pension foregone increased by Bank Base Rate plus 2% compounded. At a bank rate of 0.50% that gives an increase of 2.50% pa (SSCBA 1992 Sch 5 para 3B).

(b)   The lump sum is not treated as income but is taxed at a flat rate based upon taxable income (excluding the lump sum) for the year (F(No2)A 2005 s 7).

If total income (excluding lump sum) for 2009/10 is:

Nil	the rate is	0%
£1 to £37,400	the rate is	20%
£37,401 upward	the rate is	40%

The limit being the basic rate limit for the relevant years.

Because it is likely that the pensioner will have other income in the year of retirement, provision is made for the deferral of the lump sum to the first day of the following fiscal year (F(No 2)A 2005 s 8(5)). This would reduce the tax rate for Julia from 40% to 20%. In practice it will often be more advantageous also to defer taking the state pension until the first day of the new tax year. The lump sum would then be further increased by the additional pension deferred which otherwise for Julia would have been taxed at 40%.

(c)   If a state pension is deferred and the taxpayer dies before opting to take a lump sum or enhanced pension then the benefits are lost unless there is a surviving spouse or civil partner. If the deceased taxpayer had a spouse or civil partner then, provided the period of deferment is at least twelve months, the surviving spouse (partner) may elect to receive a lump sum based upon basic state pension plus one-half of the additional pension deferred (SSCBA 1992 Sch 5 para 3C). Alternatively, the surviving spouse (partner) may take an enhanced pension of an amount equal to the increase the deceased would have been entitled to had deferment ceased on the date of death. This applies after five weeks of deferment.

(d)   Deferral will reduce a claimant's income for the purpose of drawing benefits or council tax benefit. However, when the increased pension is drawn entitlement to such benefits may be reduced. To mitigate the effects of taking a lump sum the amount received (net of tax) is disregarded in calculating such benefits.

(e)   A lump sum is taxable in the applicable year of assessment, that is the tax year in which the first pension payment date falls, or if the pensioner dies before the beginning of that year, the tax year in which the pensioner dies (F(No 2)A 2005 s 8(2)). The actual date of payment of the lump sum is not relevant (s 8(8)).

If a surviving spouse elects for a lump sum the applicable year of assessment is the tax year in which their spouse dies (s 8(4)).

If the lump sum is not payable until the following tax year then it is taxed in the following year unless the pensioner dies before the start of the following tax year in which case it is taxed in the year of death (s 8(6)).

Explanatory Notes

Age-related allowances

1.   Each of a married couple (or members of a registered civil partnership) is entitled to a personal allowance based on their own age. Higher allowances apply to someone aged 65 or over in the tax year, the allowances for 2009/10 being £9,490 for someone aged 65 to 74 and £9,640 for someone

aged 75 or over. The higher age-related allowances are reduced by half of the excess of the net total income over a certain limit (£22,900 for 2009/10) and this limit applies to each spouse/civil partner separately.

The allowances are not, however, reduced below the basic personal allowance (£6,475 for 2009/10). The net total income for the purpose of age allowances is after deducting annual payments (and where relevant, trading losses). Retirement annuity premiums paid under the pre 1 July 1988 rules are deducted from relevant earnings and therefore also reduce total income. This no longer applies in respect of personal pension contributions. Relief for such contributions is given by deducting and retaining basic rate tax at source, higher rate relief where relevant being given by extension of the basic rate limit (see Example 1 part (ii)) and total income is not affected. However, by virtue of ITA 2007 s 58, total income for age allowances is reduced by the gross amount of the pension premium as for gift aid payments (as to which see part (a) note (ii) of the example).

2.   The married couple's allowance is no longer available unless at least one spouse or civil partner was born before 6 April 1935. Where available, the allowance is given as a reduction of tax payable, rather than as a deduction from taxable income, and saves tax at 10%. For 2009/10 the allowance is £6,965. The allowance is reduced if the claimant's total income is over £22,900, the reduction being equal to half of the excess over £22,900, but not so as to reduce the allowance below a basic allowance of £2,670 (ITA 2007 ss 36 and 37). See note 1 for the definition of total income.

For marriages before 5 December 2005, the allowance was always given in the first instance to the husband. A married woman is, however, entitled as of right to half the basic allowance, ie £1,335, if she makes a claim (on Form 18) to that effect. Alternatively the couple may jointly claim for the *whole* of the basic allowance of £2,670 to be given to the wife. In either case, the claim must be made *before* the beginning of the relevant tax year, ie before 6 April 2010 for 2010/11 (except in the year of marriage, when the claim may be made within that tax year). The allowance will then be allocated in the chosen way until the claim is withdrawn, or where a joint claim has been made for the whole of the basic allowance to go to the wife, until the husband makes a fresh claim for half of that amount. The withdrawal or husband's claim must also be made before the beginning of the tax year for which the revised allocation is to take effect (ITA 2007 s 47).

The husband is entitled to any extra allowance over the basic £2,670, and it is his income level that determines how much of the extra allowance is available.

Following the introduction of the Civil Partnership Act 2004, civil partners are also allowed the allowance with effect from 2005/06 provided that at least one partner was born before 6 April 1935. For such couples, the allowance is initially allocated to the partner with the higher total income in the year. This allocation also applies to married couples whose marriage is on or after 5 December 2005 (ITA 2007 s 46).

A husband and wife who got married before 5 December 2005 can elect for the new rules to apply. The election must be made jointly, before the start of the first year to which it is to apply and it cannot be withdrawn.

If the tax payable by either spouse/civil partner is too low to use the tax saving to which he/she is entitled on the married couple's allowance, that spouse/civil partner may notify HMRC (on the tax return or on Form 575) that the excess is to be transferred to the other spouse/civil partner (s 47). The time limit for making the claim is four years from the end of the tax year.

Where there are other deductions from tax payable, the married couple's allowance is treated as the last deduction (except for double taxation relief on foreign income) (ITA 2007 s 27), thus maximising the amount that is available to be transferred to the other spouse/civil partner.

Allowing a wife to claim half of the basic married couple's allowance by right gives greater equity, although more than four fifths of the allowance still goes to the husband unless he agrees for the wife to claim a further £1,335. There would be a cash flow benefit from transferring the allowance if the wife is an employee paying tax weekly or monthly on her earnings and the husband is self-employed paying tax on his business profits as part of his half-yearly payments on account and balancing payments under self-assessment.

In addition, although where a husband claims the allowance, any unused tax relief may be transferred to the wife, relief for the basic allowance would be given earlier by making the advance claim to transfer it if it was known that the husband would not be paying enough tax to use it.

It should be noted that a claim to transfer half or all of married couple's allowance to the spouse/civil partner prior to the start of the tax year may save tax if the transferor is likely to have unused non-repayable tax credits on dividends. The increase in the transferor's taxable income because of the transfer of allowances may enable the dividend credits to be used, with the transferee using the transferred allowance against his/her own liability.

3. The effect of the restriction of the age-related personal allowance when income exceeds the limit is to increase the taxable income by 1½ times the extra income. The marginal rate of tax on the extra income depends on the mix of dividend income, other savings income and non-savings income. If there is no savings income the marginal rate is 30% (ie 1½ × 20%). If there is non-dividend savings income the marginal rate will be somewhere between 15% (ie 1½ × 10%) and 30% depending on the respective amounts of non-dividend savings income and non-savings income. Where the income includes dividend income, the marginal rate will also be between 15% (ie 1½ × 10%) and 30%, depending on the income mix.

If the income is high enough to cause a restriction in married couple's age allowance, as in part (b) of the example, the marginal tax rate on that part of the excess income is only 5% higher than the normal rate, since the reduction affects the married couple's allowance that saves tax at only 10%.

Married couple's allowance – year of marriage/entering into a civil partnership

4. The married couple's allowance is available to those born before 6 April 1935 irrespective of the date of marriage or civil partnership.

In the year of marriage or registration, the allowance is reduced by 1/12th for each complete tax month (ending on the 5th) before the wedding/registration date (ITA 2007 s 54).

Where a party's income is sufficiently above the income limit for the married couple's allowance to be affected (his personal allowance first having been reduced to the normal £6,475 level), the income restriction is applied first, and the resulting allowance is then reduced according to the date of marriage/registration, as shown in part (b) of the example.

The effect of the income limit for age allowances on marginal tax rates is stated in note 3 above. Ann Old's marginal rate in part (b) of the example is 20% on non-savings income, 10% on dividend income and 20% on non-dividend savings income (unless taxable income exceeds the basic rate limit of £37,400).

Suppose Ann Old had received some shares from her husband resulting in an increase of dividend income (including the tax credits) of £1,000 (and a corresponding decrease in her husband's income). This would have reduced the value of the married couple's allowance by (£500 × 11/12 at 10% =) £46.

John Brown, however, would have regained an additional £500 of his age-related personal allowance. With income being taxed at 20%, this would have saved him an additional £100.

Year of separation – married couple's allowance and maintenance payments

5. For a couple one or both of whom was born before 6 April 1935, the married couple's allowance is given in full in the tax year of separation, but it is not available in later tax years except where someone born before 6 April 1935 remarries or enters into a civil partnership (or a younger person marries or enters into a civil partnership with a person who *was* born before 6 April 1935).

6.   All maintenance payments are exempt from tax in the hands of the recipient and they are received in full without tax being deducted (ITTOIA 2005 s 727). Where either of a separated or divorced couple was born before 6 April 1935 the payer may claim a deduction from his/her tax liability at 10% on up to £2,670 (index linked) of maintenance paid to the spouse/civil partner (either for the recipient's own maintenance or for the benefit of a child under 21) (ITA 2007 s 453). Relief is not available if payments are expressed to be payable direct to a child, even though actually paid to the wife (*Billingham v John* 1997). The maintenance relief is not increased where there is more than one ex-spouse/civil partner receiving maintenance.

The full maintenance relief is given in the year of separation, as well as the married couple's allowance. Payments due after the recipient remarries do not qualify for relief. If the payer remarries or enters into a civil partnership he/she will still be entitled to maintenance relief as well as any married couple's allowance.

The above provisions also apply to maintenance paid under court orders and written agreements the proper law of which is that of a part of a European Community member state, or a member state of the European Free Trade area forming part of the European Economic Area. For a list of the relevant countries see HMRC Manual, Relief Instructions Re 1190 (ITA 2007 s 453 (previously ICTA 1988 s 347B)).

No relief is available for payments which are voluntary and not made under a legal obligation.

Child Support Agency

7.   Maintenance assessed by the Child Support Agency qualifies for tax relief in the same way as maintenance under a court order (ITA 2007 s 453), and maintenance collected by the Agency for a divorced or separated spouse qualifies for relief as if it had been paid direct to the spouse. Maintenance paid to the Department for Work and Pensions for a spouse/civil partner who receives income support also qualifies for relief as if it had been paid to the spouse/civil partner.

Life assurance relief

8.   Husband and wife continue to get relief for life assurance premiums on each other's lives even after they are divorced (ICTA 1988 Sch 14 para 1) provided that the policies were issued before 14 March 1984. The relief of 12.5% of the premiums is given by deduction at source and does not affect the tax payable.

Age-related allowances in year of death

9.   The higher allowances for someone aged 65 or over (or 75 or over) are available in the tax year in which the relevant birthday falls, even if the person dies earlier in the tax year.

Married couple's allowance, where available, is given to the husband unless a claim has been made for all or half of the basic allowance to go to the wife. The full allowance is available in the year of death of either husband or wife.

The surviving spouse may have transferred to him/her any part of the allowance claimed by the other spouse that the other's income is too low to use, providing the personal representatives notify HMRC accordingly (ITA 2007 s 51).

All the allowances available to a wife in the year of her husband's death are available against *any* of her income for the full tax year.

(See note 2 above for civil partners and marriages after 4 December 2005.)

Dealing with the deceased's estate

10.   When someone dies, the tax position of the deceased for the year of death must be dealt with by the personal representatives, who also have a tax liability in respect of transactions carried out by them in completing the administration of the estate. Under self-assessment, the normal time limit for

enquiring into a tax return is twelve months from the date the return is filed (see Example 41 note 13). To minimise delays in winding up estates and trusts, and in distributing estate or trust property, HMRC have announced that they will, on request, issue tax returns before the end of the tax year of death, or of winding up an estate or trust, and will give early confirmation if they do not intend to enquire into the return. For more on the taxation of the deceased's estate, see Tolleys Taxwise II 2009/10.

The personal representatives will not usually be able to settle the deceased's tax liabilities until probate is obtained. The deceased's tax district should be asked to arrange for the HMRC Accounts Office not to issue any further Statements of Account in the meantime. By HMRC Concession A17, interest on tax falling due after death will not start to run until thirty days after the grant of probate.

11.   For further provisions on taxation of spouses and civil partners see Example 2.

Tax Credits

12.   The claim for tax credits for the period to date of death will be based upon the joint income of the claimants. It would appear that the calculation is based upon their income for the whole tax year (SI 2002/2006 reg 3(1)) apportioned to the award period of 66 days (SI 2002/2008 reg 8(3) Step 3).

For the period after date of death Mrs Partid is a sole claimant. Again, it is her income for the whole of the tax year that is relevant. This time the £300 disregard applies wholly to her income. The result is then apportioned to the award period of 299 days.

Because Mr and Mrs Partid do not work the income threshold for CTC is used, £16,040 per year.

State retirement pension counts as 'pension income' for tax credit purposes and benefits from the £300 disregard. Other taxable state benefits are counted in full along with employment income, student income and miscellaneous income (see Step 2, SI 2002/2006 reg 3(1)).

If Mr and Mrs Partid had been entitled to any payment of non-taxable pension credit then the income threshold does not apply and full CTC is payable.

For further details about tax credits see Example 7.

National insurance contributions

13.   Julia Jones will not be required to pay Class 1 primary (employee) national insurance contributions on any earnings after she reaches pensionable age (age 60 on 28 December 2009). However, her employer will continue to be liable to pay secondary (employer) contributions on her earnings.

Question

(a)   Doreen, a widow since 1995, is aged 74. Her income in the year ended 5 April 2010 consisted of:

	£
Retirement pension	6,460
Building society interest – cash amount received*	2,347
3½% War Loan interest (£2,000 of the stock was sold March 2010)	105
National Savings Bank interest	85
Purchased life annuity (gross amount, including agreed capital element £632)	790
Dividends received from UK companies	630

*   Doreen has not registered to receive interest gross.

Doreen's grandchildren, James aged 17 (still at school) and Bertha aged 13, have lived with her and been maintained by her since their parents were killed in an aeroplane crash in 1997. They have an interest in a discretionary trust set up by the wills of their parents and during 2009/10 the trustees paid the sum of £990 to help with an educational trip abroad for Bertha. Bertha does not have any other sources of income.

Calculate the amount of Doreen's and Bertha's income tax repayments for 2009/10 together with tax credits payable to Doreen, assuming that Doreen's income for tax credits in 2008/09 amounted to £7,685, and Doreen renewed a claim to tax credits by 31 July 2009.

(b)   In 2009/10 John, a single man aged 60, has pension income of £3,850 (no tax deducted under PAYE). He also has building society interest of £4,800 (cash amount received). He made a gift aid payment to the local church amounting to £400.

Calculate John's income tax repayment for 2009/10.

(c)   Nigel, a widower aged 50, makes a single gift aid donation to a registered community amateur sports club of £800 in 2009/10. Show the tax saving arising from the payment if Nigel's income is:

	(i) £	(ii) £	(iii) £
Salary	44,000	25,000	25,000
Building society interest (gross amount)	3,000	20,000	11,000
Dividends (including dividend tax credits)	1,000	3,000	12,000
	48,000	48,000	48,000

Answer

(a)   **Doreen – Income tax repayment 2009/10**

	£	Income £	Income tax paid £
Non-savings income			
Retirement pension		6,460	
Savings income other than dividends			
Building society interest (2,347 + 587)	2,934		587
3½% War Loan interest (see explanatory note 1)	105		
National Savings Bank interest	85		
Income element of annuity (see explanatory note 3)	158	3,282	32
Savings income – dividends			
630 + dividend tax credit 70		700	
Net total income		10,442	619
Personal allowance (65 to 74)		9,490	
Taxable income		952	
Income tax thereon (see explanatory note 5):			
On non-dividend savings income	252 @ 10%	25	
On dividends	700 @ 10%	70	
		95	
Less: Tax credits on dividends		70	
Tax payable			25
Repayment due			594

Bertha – Income tax repayment 2009/10

	Income £	Income tax paid £
Non-savings income		
Income from discretionary trust (see explanatory note 4)		
(990 + (40/60) 660)	1,650	660
Personal allowance		
(£6,475, but restricted to income)	1,650	
	–	
Tax repayable		660

Tax Credits – Doreen

Initial award 2009/10
Eligibility   WTC – No
                Childcare – No
                CTC – Yes
                Family element – Yes

Income – 2008/09	
(below threshold)	£7,685

	£
Maximum claim applies	
CTC – 2 children, £5.72 × 2 × 365	4,176
Family element, £1.50 × 365	548
Tax credits payable	4,724

Income for 2009/10		
As for income tax	10,442	
Less: Disregard	300	£10,142

Less than £25,000 increase – no adjustment

However, the tax credit rates have increased for 2009/10. Therefore, Doreen is entitled to the following elements:

	£
CTC – 2 children, £6.13 × 2 =	12.26
Family element, £1.50 =	1.50
	13.76

As income below threshold of £16,040 a daily amount of £13.76 will be payable until James leaves school.

(b)   John – income tax repayment 2009/10

		Income £	Income tax paid £
Non-savings income			
Pension		3,850	–
Savings income other than dividends			
Building society interest (4,800 + 1,200)		6,000	1,200
		9,850	1,200
Personal allowance		6,475	
Taxable income		3,375	
Income tax thereon:	2,440 @ 10%	244	
	935 @ 20%	187	431
	3,375		
Repayment due			769

Note:

As tax chargeable of £431 exceeds the tax of £100 retained on the charitable gift (400 net + 100 tax @ 20% = £500 gross), the repayment is not restricted.

(c)   Nigel – tax relief on gift aid donation 2009/10

Nigel is a higher rate taxpayer, so his basic rate threshold is increased from £37,400 to £38,400 as a result of the gift aid payment of £800 net, £1,000 gross. Where a higher rate taxpayer has income from a number of sources, the effect of extending the basic rate band is to give relief at 20% plus the marginal rate otherwise chargeable on the slice of income that moves below the basic rate threshold as a result of the extension.

The position in Nigel's case is therefore as follows:

	(i) £	(ii) £	(iii) £
Salary	44,000	25,000	25,000
Building society interest	3,000	20,000	11,000
Dividends	1,000	3,000	12,000
	48,000	48,000	48,000
Personal allowance	6,475	6,475	6,475
Taxable income	41,525	41,525	41,525

Tax due without gift
Non-savings income:

					(i)	(ii)	(iii)
37,400 /	18,525 /	18,525 @	20%		7,480	3,705	3,705
125 /	– /	– @	40%		50	–	–

Non-dividend savings income:

					(i)	(ii)	(iii)
– /	18,875 /	11,000 @	20%		–	3,775	2,200
3,000 /	1,125 /	– @	40%		1,200	450	–

Dividends:

					(i)	(ii)	(iii)
– /	– /	7,875 @	10%		–	–	788
1,000 /	3,000 /	4,125 @	32½%		325	975	1,341
38,965	38,965	38,965			9,055	8,905	8,034

Tax due with gift
Non-savings income:

					(i)	(ii)	(iii)
37,525 /	18,525 /	18,525 @	20%		7,505	3,075	3,075

Non-dividend savings income:

					(i)	(ii)	(iii)
875 /	19,875 /	11,000 @	20%		175	3,975	2,200
2,125 /	125 /	– @	40%		850	50	–

Dividends:

					(i)	(ii)	(iii)
– /	– /	8,875 @	10%		–	–	888
1,000 /	3,000 /	3,125 @	32½%		325	975	1,016
38,965	38,965	38,965			8,855	8,705	7,809

	(i)	(ii)	(iii)
Saving of higher rate/upper rate tax	200	200	225
Basic rate tax retained out of gift aid payment	200	200	200
Tax saving	400	400	425

This represents a tax saving of (i) 40%, (ii) 40% and (iii) 42.5%.

This is because the £1,000 income that has moved below the basic rate threshold is:

(i) Salary, giving tax saving of 20% + 20% = 40%

(ii) Building society interest, giving tax saving of 20% + 20% = 40%

(iii) Dividends, giving tax saving of 20% + 22.5% = 42.5%

Explanatory Notes

Interest on Government Stocks and National Savings Bank accounts

1. Interest on 3½% War Loan is always paid gross (half yearly in June and December). By selling some of her stock in March 2010, Doreen effectively received three months' interest (ie from December

2009) as part of her capital proceeds. There are 'accrued income scheme' provisions to treat such amounts that accrue on any marketable securities other than shares as income. The provisions do not, however, apply where the nominal value of all securities held does not exceed £5,000. This exception applies in Doreen's case, since £105 represents interest on £3,000 stock (£2,000 of which has now been sold), so the provisions would not apply to her March 2010 sale. For details of the scheme see Example 6.

2.   Interest on National Savings Bank accounts is received in full without tax being deducted. For details see Example 5.

Purchased life annuities

3.   When a life annuity is purchased for a lump sum, part of the annual payment is deemed to be a return of the capital and is not taxable. The rate of tax deducted at source on the income element is the lower rate of 20%. The capital element is determined by HMRC, with the usual rights of appeal (ITTOIA 2005 s 717 Part 6 Chapter 7). Doreen will receive a cash sum of £758, being £158 income less £32 tax = £126 plus £632 capital.

Income from a discretionary trust

4.   The payment towards Bertha's educational trip counts as her income and since it is paid from a discretionary trust its value is after tax of 40% not 20% (ITA 2007 s 493 – see Example 2 part (b)(i) note 4). An income tax repayment claim can be made on behalf of Bertha to recover the £660 tax deducted since her income is covered by her personal allowance. See note 12 below as to why vulnerable trust treatment does not apply.

Order of deductions

5.   A taxpayer may offset allowances and reliefs against income of different descriptions in the most advantageous order unless the legislation provides otherwise (ITA 2007 s 23). As far as tax rates are concerned, the legislation provides that savings income is to be treated as the highest part of income, and that dividend income is to be treated as the highest part of the savings income (ITA 2007 s 12). As the savings starting rate applies only to non-dividend savings income, the most advantageous way of offsetting the personal allowance will normally be first against non-savings income, then non-dividend savings income, then dividend income. Married couple's allowance, where available, is given as a reduction of tax payable rather than being offset against income. Any surplus married couple's allowance may be transferred to a spouse/civil partner. The legislation provides for the allowance to be treated as the last deduction, except for double taxation relief on foreign income, thus maximising the unused amount available to be transferred (ITA 2007 s 47 – see Example 3 explanatory note 2).

Dividends carry a non-repayable dividend tax credit at 1/9th of the amount received, ie 10% of the tax credit inclusive amount. The dividend tax credits are set against the tax chargeable (rather than being deducted in arriving at it) (ITTOIA 2005 s 397). They are therefore taken into account after reliefs and allowances that reduce the tax chargeable.

Age-related allowances – income restriction

6.   The personal allowance is increased where a person is sixty-five years of age or over at any time in the year of assessment, and is further increased in the tax year in which the person reaches seventy-five years of age. The allowance is reduced by one half of the excess of net total income over £22,900, but cannot be reduced below the normal personal allowance of £6,475 (ITA 2007 ss 36 and 37). Age-related married couple's allowance is similarly reduced by half the excess income over £22,900 less any reduction made in the personal allowance, but the allowance is not reduced below £2,670.

7.   Note that net total income for the purpose of the age allowance income limit means income after deducting gross gifts to charities and personal pension contributions (ITA 2007 ss 36 and 58) (see

Example 3 explanatory note 1). See Example 90 for the detailed provisions on charitable gifts and gifts to amateur sports clubs and Examples 37 and 38 for the treatment of pension contributions.

Repayment claims

8.   Repayments arise where tax is deducted at source from some income and other income is too low to utilise available allowances. Someone whose income is expected to be covered by available allowances can register to receive bank and building society interest in full (see Example 5). This would have benefited Doreen in part (a) of the example, although she would still have had to claim repayment of the tax deducted from the life annuity. A claim however is not available to Doreen because a claim to receive interest in full cannot be made where income is expected to exceed allowances, even where a repayment is due. HMRC will, however, refund overpaid tax of £50 or more before the end of the relevant tax year (see HMRC leaflet IR 110). Repayment claims may be made outside the self-assessment system. HMRC do not require the claims to be supported by tax vouchers, although they may call for extra information if they cannot calculate the repayment from the information shown on the claim form.

Where someone is taxed under PAYE, an overpayment of £10 or less is not repaid unless a specific claim is made. It will usually be dealt with by a coding adjustment in the following year (SP 6/95). (For detailed notes on PAYE see Example 8.)

9.   John in (b) and Nigel in (c) could not have registered to receive building society interest gross as both have income chargeable to tax.

Nigel should submit a self-assessment return as a higher rate taxpayer. If his income had been wholly subject to PAYE, the income tax deducted would amount to £9,130 and he would be entitled to a repayment of (40% − 20%, ie) £200 because of the gift aid payment. Accordingly all higher rate taxpayers making qualifying gift aid donations to charity will need to request a self-assessment return to obtain the higher rate relief if one is not sent automatically each year.

Note that if Nigel's income of £48,000 had been wholly dividend income, his tax position taking into account the gift aid payment of £1,000 gross would be:

			£
Dividend income (including non-repayable dividend tax credits of £4,800)			48,000
Personal allowance			6,475
Taxable income			41,525
Tax thereon:	38,400	@ 10%	3,840
	3,125	@ 32½%	1,016
Tax due			4,856
Less: Dividend credits (restricted*)			4,153
Tax remaining payable			703

*   The maximum tax credits that may be set against taxable income are 10% of the dividends brought into charge to tax, ie the taxable income of £41,525. The tax remaining payable is thus 22½% of £3,125.

10.   If Nigel in part (c) of the example had income in 2008/09 liable to higher rate tax, and the marginal income was dividend income whereas in 2009/10 it is salary, then it would be advantageous to make a carry back claim for the Gift Aid donation. The gift to the community amateur sports club would have to have been made before 31 January 2010 and before submission of the 2008/09 tax return. The relief against dividend income in 2008/09 would give a tax saving at 42.5%, whereas against salary in 2009/10 the saving would only be at 40%. There would also be a cash-flow advantage in the carry back.

11.   Where a taxpayer is entitled to a tax repayment then it is possible to specify on the self-assessment return (but not on a repayment claim) a charity to receive part or all of that repayment. It is necessary to enter the charity code at box 5 on the separate SA100 Charity form. The code is obtained from the website (www.hmrc.gov.uk/charities/charities-search.htm) or by ringing 0845 9000 444. Furthermore, by ticking box 6, the repayment will be increased by the basic rate tax deemed deducted. If John at (b) above had received a self-assessment tax return and had nominated his church to receive the repayment, the amount paid to the church would be

$$£769 \times \frac{100}{80} = £961$$

This would also be a deemed gift aid donation made by John at the date the amount is paid to the church, say December 2010, and higher rate tax relief could be claimed in 2010/11 of £961 × 20% = £192 (assuming John was a higher rate taxpayer in 2010/11).

No claim is possible to relate the amount back to the previous year as by the very process the gift cannot be made until the 2009/10 tax return is filed and processed. It is a requirement of the gift aid carryback claim that the claim is made prior to the filing of the relevant tax return, therefore the relevant date has passed at the time the gift is made to the charity.

12.   Although special tax treatment is available for trusts with vulnerable beneficiaries these rules cannot apply to Bertha or James in part (a).

In order to claim special treatment the beneficiary must be a disabled person or a relevant minor. A disabled person is a taxpayer who is incapable of administering his/her own property by reason of a mental disorder or a person in receipt of attendance allowance or disability living allowance (higher or middle rate). A relevant minor is a person under 18 where one or both of the parents have died. Bertha and James are therefore relevant minors. In addition the trust must also qualify. To do so the property must be held for the benefit of the vulnerable person absolutely. The beneficiary must be entitled to all of the income, and where the beneficiary is a minor they must be entitled to the property at 18. In the case of Bertha and James the trust is a discretionary trust and therefore does not qualify. In the same way if the trust had been an accumulation and maintenance trust for the children where they become entitled at age 25, again Bertha and James would not have been able to claim vulnerable trust treatment.

Where special treatment is claimed, available by election, the tax liability of the trust is computed in the normal way. The trustees then make a claim to reduce that liability to the amount due treating the trust income and capital gains as being the income or gains of the vulnerable beneficiary computed by adding those amounts to the actual income and gains of the beneficiary. The increase in the liability of the individual is the trusts tax liability. See Tolley's Taxwise II 2009/10 for a computation of such a claim.

Question

(a)   Outline the sources of income chargeable to tax as savings and other income, indicate how income tax is collected and when income tax is deducted at source from such income.

(b)   In relation to the information given for each person shown below state the basis of assessment under which the income will be chargeable to UK income tax.

Ignore double taxation relief.

   (i)   B Nice, who was born in England (as were his parents and grandparents) emigrated to Canada in 1991 when he was twenty-five years of age. On 1 May 2003 he returned to England for an extended holiday to visit relatives and expects to stay for at least five years. In December 2003 he instructed his Canadian bankers to remit his debenture interest from Jackboots (Montreal) Ltd to his temporary London bank account and continue this until further notice. The debentures have been held since 1993.

   (ii)   M Layber, a Spaniard, has been staying with friends in England for the last five years and has transferred his share of the profits from a Spanish partnership to provide his living expenses.

   (iii)   Fred Senior now permanently resides in England and is entitled to a pension from his previous employers in Germany. He has not remitted any of his pension during the past five years, during which it was paid into a current account overseas.

   (iv)   Romeo, who is domiciled, resident and ordinarily resident in the UK, receives interest from a foreign government which is payable through a London paying agent. He also receives dividends from various foreign companies. Both sources of income have been held for many years.

Answer

(a)   **Income assessable**

Under ITTOIA 2005 part 4 interest and investment income is chargeable to income tax as savings income on the income paid in the fiscal year. This includes:

Chapter 2	Interest
Chapter 3	Dividends – UK companies
Chapter 4	Dividends – non-UK companies
Chapter 5	Stock dividends
Chapter 6	Release of a loan to a participator in a close company
Chapter 7	Purchased life annuities
Chapter 8	Profits from deeply discounted securities
Chapter 9	Gains from contracts for life assurance
Chapter 10	Distributions from unauthorised unit-trusts
Chapter 11	Transactions in deposits
Chapter 12	Futures and options
Chapter 13	Sales of foreign dividend coupons

In addition tax is charged as non-savings income by part 5 of ITTOIA 2005 on:

Chapter 2	Receipts from intellectual property
Chapter 3	Films and sound recordings
Chapter 4	Telecommunication rights
Chapter 5	Settlements
Chapter 6	Income from estates
Chapter 7	Annual payments
Chapter 8	Income not otherwise charged to tax

Employment income, employment related annuities (retirement annuities) and pensions are chargeable under the Income Tax (Earnings and Pensions) Act 2003 (ITEPA 2003) as non-savings income (see Examples 8–13).

Trading income is charged as non-savings income under ITTOIA 2005 part 2, and property income under ITTOIA 2005 part 3.

The other parts of ITTOIA 2005 deal with:

Part 6	Exempt income
Part 7	Rent-a-room and foster carers
Part 8	Special rules for foreign income
Part 9	Partnerships

Tax is chargeable on the sum of income from all sources liable to UK tax subject to allowable deductions and reliefs.

Self-assessment

A taxpayer is required to self assess their personal liability to tax (see Examples 40 and 41). Having computed their liability under self-assessment, subject to certain de minimis limits, provisional payments on account of the income tax on all sources of income are payable half-yearly on 31 January in the tax year and 31 July following, based on the net income tax liability of the previous tax year (after deducting PAYE tax and tax at source). The payments on account and the amounts of tax deducted at source and under PAYE are compared with the final income tax and capital gains tax liability for the tax year, and a balancing payment is made or repayment claimed on or before the following 31 January (see Example 41).

For 2009/10 the rate of tax on income up to the basic rate limit (£37,400) is 20% on non-savings income, 20% on savings income other than dividends and 10% on dividends, the rates applicable to income above that limit being 40% and 32½% on dividend income. However, where non-savings income is less than £2,440, a starting rate of 10% applies to savings income within that band (treating it, as usual, as the top slice of income). These rates apply to both UK and foreign savings income, except for any foreign income that is taxed on a remittances basis, to which the non-savings tax rates apply.

Deduction of tax at source

Tax is deducted at source from many sources of savings and other income, the rate of tax deducted from interest, royalties and annual payments being the basic rate of 20%. Tax is not deducted at source from most National Savings interest (see explanatory note 4). Nor is tax deducted from interest, patent royalties and annuities paid by a company to another company that the paying company reasonably believes to be liable to corporation tax on the amount received or is an EU company, and payments by and to local authorities. The range of people to whom companies and local authorities may pay such amounts gross includes bodies exempt from tax, such as charities, pension funds, and those managing ISAs, TESSAs and PEPs (ITA 2007 s 930 onwards). See explanatory note 9 re special provisions for royalty payments by companies to certain recipients entitled to double tax relief. Tax is not deducted at source from copyright royalties unless they are paid to non-residents (see explanatory note 7). Retirement annuities and other employment-related annuities have been brought within the PAYE scheme from 6 April 2007. (FA 2004 Sch 36 para 43 and FA 2005 Sch 10 paras 60, 61(a), 64(2).) Prior to this, such annuities were paid net of basic rate tax (or gross where the annuitant was a non-taxpayer and completed a Form R89).

Interest on all gilt edged securities (other than bearer gilts) acquired on or after 6 April 1998 is paid gross, unless the holder applies to receive it net (ITA 2007 s 892). (Interest on 3½% War Loan is always paid gross.) Those already holding stocks on 6 April 1998 are treated as having applied for net payment, but may apply at any time for gross payment. The provisions for paying interest gross also apply to bearer gilts (ITA 2007 s 893 and s 1024).

Company debenture interest is paid net of tax except when paid to another company etc as indicated above or where the debenture stock is a listed security (see later in this note). The same applies to interest paid by banks other than the National Savings Bank, or by licensed deposit takers (specified by Treasury order) or building societies, unless it is paid to an individual who can register to receive the interest in full (see below) or the interest comes within a specified exception, the main exceptions being as follows (ITA 2007 part 15 chapter 2 s 850 onwards, SIs 1990/2231, 1990/2232):

(i)   Certificates of deposit (including certificates issued in 'paperless' form) and sterling or foreign currency time deposits, providing the loan is not less than £50,000 and is repayable within five years.

(ii) General client deposit accounts with building societies or banks operated by solicitors and estate agents.

(iii) Accounts held at overseas branches of UK and foreign banks and building societies. (See explanatory note 12.)

(iv) Bank and building society accounts and accounts with other deposit holders, where the account holder is not ordinarily resident in the UK and has provided a declaration to that effect (see Example 36).

(v)   Bank and building society accounts in the names of charities.

(vi) Bank and building society accounts in the names of companies, clubs and societies.

(vii) Accounts held by Individual Savings Account and Personal Equity Plan managers (see Example 92).

(viii) Interest on cash received by a building society in respect of an agreement for the sale and repurchase of securities.

There is a general requirement in ITA 2007 s 874 to deduct tax at source from interest paid to a non-resident, subject to any express provisions to the contrary. There are such express provisions for certain bank and building society interest (see (iv) above), and exemption from tax is sometimes provided under a double tax agreement. See Example 36 for further details.

Interest on all quoted eurobonds is paid gross to both individuals and companies (ITA 2007 s 882). A quoted eurobond is any interest-bearing security issued by a company that is listed on a recognised stock exchange. 'Company' for this purpose includes a building society, so that building society permanent interest-bearing shares (see Example 63 explanatory note 1) are within the definition of eurobond.

Where a taxpayer is not ordinarily resident in the UK (see below) tax is not deducted on UK government stocks. Nor is tax deducted where the recipient is exempt from tax, such as interest paid to UK charities (exempt under ITA 2007 s 532). ITA 2007 s 597 gives HMRC power to make specific regulations relating to the deduction of tax on Government stocks that are not within the gross payment provisions.

Under FA 2005 s 51 returns from alternative finance arrangements are to be treated as interest for the purposes of ITTOIA 2005. This will include returns from arrangements that do not involve the receipt or payment of interest in adherence with Shari'a law. Such agreements and returns are economically equivalent to conventional banking product interest. However, they were not previously taxed as interest. Under this legislation the profit is taxed as savings income.

Registering to receive interest in full

An individual may register to receive bank and building society interest and interest on deposits with local authorities in full if he expects his total taxable income to be below his available allowances (ITA 2007 s 852, SIs 1990/2231, 1990/2232). The relevant forms (R85) may be obtained from banks, building societies and local authorities or from tax offices. A separate form is needed for each account. A parent can register the account of a child under 16 if the child's total income will be less than the personal allowance (£6,475 for 2009/10), providing not more than £100 income arises from parental gifts (a separate £100 limit applying to income from gifts from each parent).

The account holder must tell the bank or building society straight away if his circumstances change so that he is no longer eligible to receive interest in full, and he should contact his tax office about any tax he may have to pay. Where tax has been underpaid it is collected either by adjustment to a PAYE coding or in the taxpayer's self-assessment. A penalty of up to £3,000 may be imposed if someone fraudulently or negligently certifies that he is entitled to register to receive interest in full, or if he fails to notify that he is no longer entitled to receive interest in full (TMA 1970 s 99A). HMRC is notified by banks and building societies of amounts of interest credited.

It is not possible to register to receive gross interest on some accounts and not on others, and those who expect to have some taxable income cannot register, even though they will be entitled to a refund. It is, however, possible to claim a refund before the end of the tax year if it amounts to £50 or more. Smaller refunds will only be made after the end of the year.

Interest on late paid debts

Under the Late Payment of Commercial Debts (Interest) Act 1998 statutory interest is payable where payment is delayed on certain contracts for the supply of goods or services. Such interest is not annual interest and is brought into tax as a trading receipt under ITTOIA 2005. The interest is paid gross and will normally be an allowable deduction for trading concerns. Similar tax treatment applies to interest payable under the terms of a trading contract. In the case of a company interest is included in the loan relationships regime. If interest for late payment is received by an individual other than in the course of business then it will be taxable at the savings rate (either 10% or 20%, depending on the amount of non-savings income).

Remittance basis

Where a taxpayer is not domiciled in the UK, or not ordinarily resident in the UK, then they may claim under ITA 2007 s 809B to be liable to tax on a remittance basis in respect of income and gains arising abroad. If the remittance basis is successfully claimed then tax will be due on the full amount received in the UK within the tax year without deductions.

However, the availability of the remittance basis was significantly curtailed from 2008/09. The automatic right to be taxed on the remittance basis applies only where the unremitted income and gains do not exceed £2,000 in the tax year. Otherwise the remittance basis must be claimed by those entitled to it. A claim will result in the loss of UK personal allowances and CGT annual exemption, and for those resident in the UK for seven out of the previous nine years can only be made on a payment of £30,000, representing a UK tax charge on unremitted income. For more details of the remittance basis from 2008/09 onwards see Example 98.

(b)   (i)   **B Nice**

Since it was B Nice's intention to remain in England for at least five years on his return in May 2003, he would have been regarded as resident and ordinarily resident from the date of his return and treated as a new permanent resident. He has a UK domicile of origin which will have been retained unless he acquired a domicile of choice in Canada, but such a change requires a high standard of proof. This will depend partly upon whether B Nice has settled permanently in one particular Canadian province.

His debenture interest from Jackboots (Montreal) Ltd will be assessable in the UK.

If he has retained his UK domicile the basis of assessment will be the full amount of interest arising in the current tax year (whether remitted to the UK or not).

If he had acquired a Canadian domicile, however, he would be charged only on a remittance basis and the source would be treated as acquired when income was first remitted, the assessable income in each tax year being the amount remitted in that year.

The 10% savings starting rate on non-dividend savings income up to the savings starting rate limit of £2,440 applies to savings income from abroad, unless the income is charged on a remittance basis, in which case the tax rates for non-savings income apply.

(ii)   **M Layber**

M Layber is not domiciled in the UK, but he is resident here. He is accordingly chargeable to tax on that part of his Spanish profits that is remitted to the UK, according to the remittances basis rules outlined in (i) above. However, M Layber will only be automatically entitled to the remittance basis if his unremitted income and gains are less than £2,000 each tax year. If the unremitted amount from all overseas sources exceeds this amount, M Layber will have to make a claim to the remittance basis, and this will result in the loss of his UK personal allowance and CGT annual exemption. So if his unremitted income and gains exceed the de minimis, M Layber will need to consider how much the loss of allowances will impact on his UK tax liability, and whether claiming the remittance basis would be beneficial. M Layber should also be aware that the position will change if he remains in the UK for a further two years, as after that he would become liable to the remittance basis charge of £30,000 per annum in order to benefit from the remittance basis. He should seek advice about his UK tax position on foreign income and gains, taking into account the double tax relief available in order to be aware of his likely future UK tax liabilities.

(iii) Fred Senior

Fred Senior is resident and ordinarily resident in the UK. If he is also domiciled here he will be charged to tax on his German pension under ITEPA 2003 s 573 whether he remits it to the UK or not, but subject to a deduction of 10% (the basis of assessment being the same as indicated in (i) above). If he is not domiciled in the UK he will not be charged to tax on the pension at all unless it is remitted, provided his total unremitted income and gains do not exceed £2,000 per annum. If it is remitted, he will be charged on the full amount of the remittance with no percentage deduction according to the rules outlined in (a) above.

(iv) Romeo

Since Romeo is resident, ordinarily resident and domiciled in the UK, the interest will be taxed at 20% and the dividends at 10%, to the extent that his income does not exceed the basic rate limit. If his non-savings income does not exceed £2,440, the 10% savings starting rate will be available on the interest income up to that limit.

Explanatory Notes

Interest received by companies

1. For companies, all interest payable and receivable, including interest from abroad, is brought into account under loan relationship rules calculating the company's income, together with profits and losses on disposals. The detailed provisions are in Example 63. Tax is not deducted from interest paid by a company to a company within the charge to corporation tax or to certain other recipients, or from interest on listed company securities, as indicated in part (a) of the example.

Basis of assessment

2. Income tax is charged on all amounts computed under ITEPA 2003, ITTOIA 2005 and ITA 2007. On interest the amount is the full amount of interest arising in the tax year (ITTOIA 2005 s 370).

3. Interest 'arises' on the date it is received. In the case of a bank account the interest arises when it is credited to the account. For non-corporate taxpayers there are no adjustments to take account of interest that is merely accruing. Different rules apply to companies (see Example 63).

National Savings investments, ISAs and TESSAs

4. National Savings and Investments offer a wide range of investments. Income bonds (including guaranteed income bonds) carry interest which is paid without deduction of tax monthly. Capital bonds carry guaranteed interest that is credited gross each year. The interest is accumulated until the bond is cashed in, but tax is charged on the interest when credited. Fixed rate savings bonds pay interest net of tax annually at rates fixed a year at a time, and the bonds can be cashed at any anniversary date without interest penalty. Higher rate taxpayers will have extra tax to pay and those liable at less than the lower rate may claim a refund. National Savings Certificates, which may be fixed-interest or index-linked, carry interest which is accumulated until they are repaid, and the interest is free of all taxation. Premium bonds earn no interest at all, and any prizes are free of all taxation. For children under 16, National Savings Children's Bonus Bonds are available, under which all interest and bonuses are tax-free. For details see Example 2 part (b)(ii) note 2.

5. Interest on the cash component of Individual Savings Accounts (ISAs) and on Tax Exempt Special Savings Accounts (TESSAs) is exempt from tax providing the rules of the schemes are satisfied. For details see Example 92.

Accrued income scheme

6.   For sales of interest bearing securities (but not shares), the accrued income provisions of ITA 2007 s 619 onwards apply. These are illustrated in Example 6.

The accrued income provisions prevent income tax being avoided by selling securities just before an interest payment date, thus receiving the interest as part of the capital proceeds. The rules do not apply if the nominal value of all the securities held by an individual in the tax year in which the next interest payment on the securities falls due or in the previous tax year does not exceed £5,000.

Deduction of tax at source from copyright and patent royalties

7.   Where copyright royalties are paid, basic rate tax is not deducted at source unless:

(a)   the owner's usual place of abode is outside the UK (ITA 2007 s 906) (and even then, tax is not deducted if the royalties are paid to a non-resident professional author)

or

(b)   the copyright is held as an investment and the royalties are deemed to be annual payments subject to deduction of tax under ITA 2007 s 902.

Copyright royalties that are paid in full are a normal trading expense. If they are paid net by individuals they are deducted from total income.

8.   The treatment of patent royalties is different from that of copyright royalties. The Income Tax Act 2007 has changed the tax treatment of charges on income (annual payments and patent royalties). The approach is intended to remove many of the complexities in the original legislation. It is now mandatory to deduct income tax at the basic rate (unless covered by ITA 2007 s 902(3)). The tax so deducted is then collected as part of the payer's self-assessment. Relief is now given for annual payments and patent royalties as a deduction in calculating net income.

Treatment of royalties in computing income

9.   For companies patents and copyrights are dealt with under the rules for intangible assets, and are brought into account either as trading income or non-trading income. For details see Example 66.

A company paying royalties to a non-resident may pay gross, or deduct tax at a reduced rate according to the provisions of the relevant double tax treaty, if it believes the recipient to be entitled to double tax relief (ITA 2007 s 911). If the company's belief turns out to be incorrect, however, the company will have to account for the tax that should have been deducted, plus interest and possibly penalties.

10.   Where copyright royalties are received by individual authors, composers etc, the income is income of their profession. Royalty receipts from purchased copyrights will be intellectual property charged under ITTOIA 2005 s 579.

11.   The position of patent royalties received by individuals is similar. Where they are received by the inventor, the receipts are taxed as earned income (FA 2004 s 189 new (2A)).

The Tax Law Rewrite project changed the definition of relevant UK earnings. As before and stated above, patent income arising to an individual who devised an invention counts as relevant UK earnings, but the exceptions previously in TA 1988 s 833(5C) and (5E) have been removed. These prevented earned income treatment for patents that had been purchased (ie, held as an investment). A wider range of patent income now potentially qualifies as 'relevant UK earnings'.

Foreign Income

12.   Income from abroad is taxed in the UK as illustrated in part (b) of the example. These rules may, however, be affected by double tax agreements, which in many cases provide for the normal statutory rules to be varied.

Non-residents are not liable to tax on foreign income. UK residents who are not domiciled in the UK and citizens who are resident but not ordinarily resident in the UK can make a claim to be charged to tax only when foreign income is brought into the UK, known as the remittance basis. The remittance basis is automatically available to a small number of individuals, but otherwise must be claimed which will result in the loss of UK personal allowances and CGT exemption. Long-term residents can only make a claim to be taxed on the remittance basis by paying a remittance basis charge of £30,000 per annum. See Example 98 for an extensive example of the remittance basis.

Other UK residents are charged on the income arising abroad, whether it is remitted or not. If the income is a foreign pension, the taxable amount is only 90% of the amount arising (TA 1988 s 65(2) as applied by ITEPA 2003 s 575(2)). (This also applies to a foreign public service pension taxed under the pension income rules – ITEPA 2003 s 617.) Pensions payable by the governments of Germany and Austria to victims of Nazi persecution are, however, totally exempt from tax (ITEPA 2003 s 642).

Where income that is charged on the 'arising' basis has not been brought into the UK, it is converted into sterling at the exchange rate on the date it arises. Where there are frequent credits, an average exchange rate for the year may be used, using rates published by HMRC, providing the amounts are not materially affected and the averaging basis is adopted consistently.

For detailed notes on the meaning of residence and ordinary residence see Example 12. Someone's country of domicile is broadly the country in which he has his permanent home. Under UK law a child acquires his father's domicile as his domicile of origin at birth, unless he is illegitimate (or his father died while the child was a minor), in which case he acquires his mother's domicile. The domicile of origin may be changed to a domicile of choice, but a very high standard of proof is required to show a change of domicile. An ongoing HMRC review is taking place on possible changes to the law of domicile, but meanwhile, significant changes were made to the remittance basis of taxation for UK resident non UK domiciled or not ordinarily resident individuals from April 2008, as detailed above in part (a).

13.   Relief for foreign trading losses is given only against the foreign trading profits (ITA 2007 s 95).

Foreign rental income of individuals is taxed in broadly the same way as UK rental income, and the same rules apply in general to companies (see Example 97). The 'furnished holiday letting' provisions do not apply to overseas property. Losses on foreign lettings are deducted from total letting income from overseas property, any unrelieved amount being carried forward to set against later overseas letting income, but relief may now be available on furnished holiday accommodation in the EEA as for the UK until the end of 2009/10 when the special tax advantages of furnished holiday lettings are abolished.

Relief is available for foreign tax suffered on overseas income taxed in the UK. For details see Example 36.

Foreign partnerships

14.   The partnership business in part (b) (ii) is apparently controlled and carried on abroad. Even so, the profit shares of partners who are resident, ordinarily resident and domiciled in the UK are charged in the UK. For a UK resident partner who, like M Layber, is not domiciled and/or not ordinarily resident in the UK, however, it is only profits earned in the UK that are charged. Profits earned abroad are taxed on the remittances basis, as indicated in part (b) (ii) of the example.

Foreign business profits are not liable to Class 4 national insurance contributions (SSCBA 1992 s 16).

Tax Credits

15.   For tax credits foreign income is computed on an arising basis whether or not remitted or excluded from UK liability by a double taxation agreement. There is an exception for unremittable income (SI 2002/2006 reg 3(3)). The 10% relief for foreign pensions is given (SI 2002/2006 reg 12(3)(b), as amended by SI 2003/732), as are the equivalent exemptions for victims of Nazi persecution, foreign

social security payments, and the exemptions in various Extra Statutory Concessions (see Reg 12(3)(c) for further details). It appears that relief for foreign trading losses could be set against total tax credit income of the claimants under Step 4 of Reg 3 (see Example 7(b)) but no relief is available for a loss arising on a property let overseas.

Special withholding tax

16.   Where a UK taxpayer has savings in Austria, Belgium or Luxembourg a special withholding tax may be applied (but not before 1 January 2005). This can be avoided by authorising any paying agent to report information about the income to HMRC authorities or by obtaining a certificate from HMRC. Such a certificate will be valid for up to three years.

If 'special withholding tax' is suffered then full credit will be given against the individual's income tax or capital gains tax liability with any excess being repayable (unless relief has also been obtained in another jurisdiction). Relief will be given for foreign tax before special withholding tax so as to maximise the benefit of double taxation relief.

UK income tax liability of non residents

17.   The UK tax liability for non-UK resident individuals and trustees on certain sources of income is broadly limited to the amount of tax deducted at source from that income. The UK tax liability is calculated by excluding certain sources of income from the computation of total income, and adding the tax deducted from that income, to the liability but without reference to personal allowances (ITA 2007 s 811).

The sources of income disregarded for this purpose is given in ITA 2007 s 813. For example, a non-resident individual who receives a net dividend of £1million from a UK company would have no higher rate liability to UK tax, provided personal allowances are not claimed. This is because dividend income is 'disregarded savings and investment income' by ITA 2007 s 825(1)(a) and s 811 provides that the UK tax liability is limited to the tax credit on that dividend. If personal allowances were claimed instead (assuming they are available under a double tax agreement or otherwise) the UK tax liability would be as follows:

				£	£
Dividend income (gross)					1,111,111
Personal allowance					(6,475)
Taxable income					1,104,636
Tax thereon:	37,400	@	10%	3,740	
	1,067,236	@	32½	346,852	350,592
Less: tax credit on taxable dividend					(110,464)
Liability if personal allowances claimed					240,128

Other sources of income disregarded for this purpose include most UK savings and investment income, defined in ITA 2007 s 825, annual payments (s 826), most pension income, including UK state pensions (s 813(3)), social security income and disregarded transaction income (s 814).

Under s 811, the limit of the UK liability is calculated without reference to personal allowances, age-related allowances, blind person's allowance, married couples' allowance, or any tax reliefs that would otherwise be due under ITA 2007 ss 457–459.

Question

A.

Briefly set out the basic principles of the Accrued Income Scheme giving details of:

(a)   securities affected by the scheme;

(b)   persons affected by the scheme;

(c)   how the accrued income scheme works.

B.

Interest on 8½% Treasury Stock is paid half yearly on 25 January and 25 July, the stock going ex-dividend on 18 January and 18 July.

Mr Pinter bought £100,000 nominal stock ex-dividend for settlement on 21 January 2010. He sold the stock cum-dividend for settlement 11 June 2010.

Show the accrued income adjustments arising from these transactions.

Answer

A.

The accrued income scheme was originally introduced as an anti-avoidance measure to prevent the process known as 'bond-washing'. 'Bond-washing' was a practice whereby holders of securities (such as government stocks or corporate bonds) would dispose of their stocks immediately prior to the date on which interest became payable. The price obtained for the security included the 'accrued interest' on the stock, but the profit on the security was taxed under the capital gains rules rather than being treated as income (as it would have been had the interest actually been received).

This practice was particularly prevalent at a time when CGT rates were lower than those applying to income tax. It also allowed taxpayers to use capital gains tax exemptions and reliefs against profits which would otherwise have been treated as income.

The accrued income scheme provisions are in Income Tax Act 2007 (ITA 2007) part 12. They set out how to compute accrued interest on a sale or purchase of stocks and bonds.

(a)   Securities affected by the scheme (ITA 2007 s 619)

The accrued income scheme applies to interest-bearing marketable stocks and bonds including:

- British Government securities ('gilts');

- building society permanent interest bearing shares (PIBS);

- local authority bonds; and

- company debentures and loan stock.

The scheme does not apply to ordinary or preference shares in a company, units in a unit trust, bank deposits or National Savings Certificates.

(b)   Persons affected by the scheme

The accrued income scheme does not apply to companies (ITA 2007 s 5). Any profits made by companies on the sale and acquisition of securities are dealt with under the 'loan relationships' rules (see Example 63).

The scheme applies to individuals, trusts and estates. However the vesting of securities in personal representatives on a person's death is not subject to the accrued income scheme provisions (ITA 2007 s 620(2)(a)), nor is a transfer to a legatee by the personal representatives in the interest period in which death occurs (ITA 2007 s 636).

Individuals are not caught by the accrued income scheme if the nominal value of their total holdings does not exceed £5,000 at any time in both:

- the tax year in which the next interest date falls; and

- the previous tax year

(ITA 2007 s 639).

Individuals are not caught by the scheme if they are not resident and not ordinarily resident in the UK (ITA 2007 s 643).

For individuals who are resident in the UK but are not UK domiciled, the scheme only applies to UK securities (ITA 2007 s 644).

The scheme does not apply to traders in securities, for whom these transactions represent trading profits (ITA 2007 s 642).

(c)   How the accrued income scheme works

To make the required tax adjustments under the accrued income scheme it is necessary to determine whether a sale or purchase was 'cum-dividend' or 'ex-dividend'. The term 'cum' means 'with' and 'ex' means 'without', therefore a transaction with the right to the next dividend is 'cum-dividend' and a deal without the right to the next dividend is 'ex-dividend'.

It is common practice to use the terms 'ex-div' and 'cum-div' even though the return on the investment is in fact interest and perhaps the terms 'ex interest' and 'cum interest' would be more appropriate. The HMRC guidance on this area uses the terms 'ex-div' and 'cum-div'.

All stocks will have an ex-div date. Most stocks pay interest every six months (although some pay annually and some pay quarterly). If an investor holds stock at the ex-div date, the investor will be entitled to receive the next interest payment, even if the investor disposes of the stock before the actual date on which the interest is paid. There may be a few weeks between the ex-div date and the date on which the interest is physically paid.

Once the ex-div date has passed, the market price for the stock will go down. This is because a purchaser will not thereafter have a right to the net interest payment and will therefore offer a lower amount to purchase the stock.

The price of the stock will vary for many reasons, one of which is that the purchase price will or will not include the right to the next interest payment. A transaction cum-div will be priced to include the right to receive the next interest payment in full even though the stock will have been owned for less than the full interest period.

All securities have a 'nominal value'. This is the value on which interest payments are calculated. The nominal value is also the value at which the stocks will be redeemed. However, the 'nominal value' is unlikely to be the same as the market value of the stock. All accrued income will be calculated on nominal values. Market values are irrelevant for income tax.

The accrued income scheme calculates the 'accrued interest' every time stock is bought and sold and allocates this interest between buyer and seller. The accrued income is effectively the increase or reduction in the price of the stock depending on whether the stock has been purchased or sold 'cum-div' or 'ex-div'.

In practice, most taxpayers who buy and sell stock will receive a contract note and details of any accrued income will be shown on that contract note.

The way in which the accrued interest scheme works depends on whether:

- the taxpayer is the buyer or seller; and

- if the stock is being transferred 'cum-div' or 'ex-div'.

There are therefore four possible scenarios:

1.   A person selling stock cum-div.

   Selling 'cum-div' means that the buyer will be entitled to the next interest payment. Therefore the price of the stock will be increased by accrued interest. This accrued interest, known as the 'accrued income profit', is taxable on the seller at the time of the next interest payment.

   The accrued interest is calculated on a daily basis from the date of the previous interest payment through until the date of settlement based upon the gross interest payable.

   It is taxed as 'miscellaneous income' and is entered on an individual's self-assessment tax return at boxes 1 and 3 on page Ai 1 of the Additional Information pages (SA101).

   The income is taxed in the tax year in which the next interest date falls. For instance, if the next interest date following settlement is 30 April 2010, the accrued income charge is taxed in 2010/11.

2.   A person selling stock ex-div.

Selling 'ex-div' means that the seller will be entitled to the next interest payment, therefore the price of the stock will be decreased by accrued interest. That amount is known as the 'accrued income loss' and is a deduction from the next interest payment on that security before entering onto the self-assessment tax return.

3.   A person buying stock cum-div.

A purchaser of securities 'cum-div' will be entitled to the full amount of interest payable on the next interest date, therefore the price paid will be increased by the accrued interest. That amount is the 'accrued interest loss' because it represents the return of the investor's own funds when the interest is paid. It is deducted from the amount paid before inclusion in the self-assessment tax return.

4.   A person buying stock ex-div.

When buying 'ex-div' there is no entitlement to the next interest payment therefore the price paid is reduced by the 'accrued interest profit'. That amount is taxed at the date of the next interest payment by inclusion in the self-assessment tax return (boxes 1 and 3 on page Ai 1 of the Additional Information pages (SA101)).

B.   **Mr Pinter – purchase and sale of 8½% Treasury Stock**

Treatment of the purchase for settlement on 21 January 2010

This is a purchase ex-div, therefore the seller will receive the full half-year interest to 25 January 2010 of £4,250. The purchase price will have been reduced to take into account the interest due from 22 January 2010 (the day after the settlement date) and 25 January 2010. This amounts to:

$$\text{Days from 22 January to 25 January 2010 } \frac{4}{365} \times £8,500 = £93.15$$

The seller is entitled to an accrued income loss of £93.15 to reduce his taxable income for 2009/10 (in which the next interest payment date, 25 January, falls) and Mr Pinter will have an accrued income profit on the same amount for that year.

Treatment of the sale for settlement on 11 June 2010

This is a sale cum-div therefore the buyer will receive the full half-year interest to 25 July 2010. The purchase price will have been increased to take into account the interest due between 26 January 2010 and 11 June 2010. This amounts to:

$$\text{Days from 26 January to 11 June 2010 } \frac{137}{365} \times £8,500 = £3,190.41$$

Mr Pinter will have an accrued income profit of £3,190.41 in 2010/11 (in which 25 July 2010 falls) and the buyer is entitled to an accrued income loss of the same amount for that year.

The accrued income loss reduces the taxpayer's savings income, and thus saves a basic rate taxpayer 20%. Accrued income profits are taxed at the savings rate if available (ITA 2007 s 18(3)(d)).

If Mr Pinter is a basic rate taxpayer he will obtain tax relief in 2009/10 at 20% on £93.15 and pay tax in 2010/11 at 20% on £3,190.41. If the other parties are basic rate taxpayers, they will get relief at 20% in each case. If anyone is a higher rate taxpayer then the applicable rate will be 40%.

Explanatory Notes

Capital gains tax

1.   Capital gains tax (CGT) essentially charges tax on the profit made by an investor on the sale of an asset. The disposal of a security could therefore give rise to a CGT charge as well as an accrued income adjustment.

The contract note for the sale and purchase of securities will normally detail the amount of any accrued income. For CGT, exclude any accrued income loss from acquisition cost and add any accrued income profit to acquisition cost as otherwise there will be an element of double counting or double taxation. On sale, deduct any accrued income profit and add any accrued income loss to sale proceeds.

Most securities liable to the accrued income scheme, such as British Government stock, qualifying corporate bonds and building society PIBS, are exempt from CGT, however some securities, such as non-sterling loan stocks, are chargeable to CGT.

Tax credits and tax treatment of accrued income

2.   Accrued income profits and losses are taken into account in computing income for tax credits (SI 2002/2006 reg 14(2)(ix)). The profit increases income of the tax year in which the next income payment, after the settlement date, falls. Accrued income loss reduce the interest received on the next interest date. Profits and losses are not netted off unless they relate to the same stock with the same interest payment date.

Discounted securities

3.   Taxpayers other than companies are subject to special rules dealing with discounted securities (ITTOIA 2005 ss 427–460). The accrued income scheme does not apply to such securities. The discounted security rules apply where the issue price is lower than the redemption price by more than ½% per year between issue and redemption, or, if that period exceeds 30 years, by more than 15%. Investors are charged to income tax in the tax year of disposal, at savings rate (if available), on the profit. If a loss arises on securities acquired before 27 March 2003 then that loss may be offset against the total income of the year, (for trustees against income from discounted securities only) otherwise loss relief is not available (ITTOIA 2005 s 454).

On death there is a deemed disposal at market value with tax charged accordingly. Transfers from the personal representatives to legatees are also deemed disposals with income tax being charged on the estate on the difference between value at death and value at transfer.

Variable rate securities

4.   The rules set out above apply to all securities that have interest that is:

●   fixed;

●   fixed by reference to a published base rate; or

●   at a rate fixed by reference to a published index of prices (eg RPI, CPI etc).

If interest is otherwise variable then ITA 2007 s 627 and s 635 apply. These provisions require the transferor to calculate taxable interest in a just and reasonable manner, but no adjustment (in practice, relief) applies for the transferee.

Question

A.

(a)   Outline the basic principles of tax credits, setting out the criteria to be satisfied for eligibility for

    (i)   Working tax credit (WTC)

    (ii)   Childcare element of WTC

    (iii) Child tax credit (CTC).

(b)   How is 'income' computed for tax credits?

(c)   What changes in circumstances must be reported to HMRC, and by what date?

(d)   What is an 'award period', and why are separate calculations required for each 'relevant period' within the award period?

(e)   What information must be provided at the end of each fiscal year and how will underpayment/ overpayment of tax credits be dealt with?

B.

(a)   Brian and Angela Smith are married. Brian is self-employed preparing accounts to 31 December each year. Angela is employed. Both usually work more than 30 hours per week. They have one child, Joanna, date of birth 30 June 2006. She attends an approved nursery costing £165 per week. Because Angela is pregnant she has increased the time Joanna spends at the nursery and from 5 January 2010 the cost increases to £200 per week. On 1 March 2010 Colin was born. No nursery costs were incurred for Colin in 2009/10. Angela was still on statutory maternity leave at 5 April 2010.

Their income for 2008/09 per their tax returns was:

	Brian	Angela
Self-employment	18,810	
Per P60		22,700
Per P11D – Car		2,160
– Medical		640
Investment income (gross)	180	520

Brian pays £133.33 per month (net) to a personal pension policy and Angela pays £40 (net) per month under gift aid to the local church.

Their income for 2009/10 per their tax returns was:

	Brian	Angela
Self-employment		
(Accounts y/e 31/12/09) – Loss	(2,800)	
Per P60		16,100
Per P11D – Car		2,160
– Medical		700
Investment Income (gross)	20	140

Included in Angela's P60 for 2009/10 is Statutory Maternity Pay of £2,326 for 10 weeks and Statutory Sick Pay of £193. Brian will make a claim under ITA 2007 s 64 to carry his loss back to 2008/09.

A renewal claim for tax credits for 2008/09 was filed by Brian and Angela on 30 July 2008 and renewal information provided on 6 July 2009. Notification of increase in nursery costs and the birth of Colin were given on 5 May 2010.

Compute the tax credits payable to Angela or Brian during 2009/10 (the provisional award), and the under/overpayment arising for 2009/10 after calculation of the final award.

(b)   Re-compute the position on the assumption that instead of a loss the accounts of Brian for the year ended 31 December 2009 showed a profit of £35,000.

Answer

A.   (a)   Basic principles

Tax credits were introduced as a form of 'negative income tax' with effect from 6 April 2003. The primary legislation is the Tax Credits Act (TCA) 2002 which is supplemented by numerous statutory instruments. The aim of the legislation is to provide help to those on low income who are working and those with children. The method of award is based upon the family unit. The claim is based on joint income of the couple where:

–   this is a married couple living together and not permanently separated; or

–   a man and a woman living together as husband and wife; or

–   a same-sex couple (from 5 December 2005).

If the claimant is a lone parent or someone who is aged 25 or over and working at least 30 hours per week, then the claim is based on the income of that person. Special rules apply to those with a disability which puts them at a disadvantage in getting a job.

An award is made per day. The elements of tax credits are computed by dividing the yearly amount by the number of days in the tax year (SI 2002/2008 regs 6–9) and rounding up to the nearest penny. All days with the same entitlement within the award period are aggregated and are known as a 'relevant period'.

Income is based upon broadly the taxable income of the fiscal year. That is again divided by the number of days in the tax year and applied to the relevant periods.

The first award of tax credits is provisional and is based on the income of the preceding year, ie for 2009/10 the claim is initially based upon the income of 2008/09. The income disregard is £25,000 (SI 2006/963 reg 4) making the relevant income, for most claimants, the lower of the income of the preceding year, or, the income of the current year. For example for a 2009/10 claim (assuming income has not increased by more than £25,000 when comparing 2008/09 income with 2009/10 income) the award is based on the lower of the income for 2008/09 or 2009/10.

Because claims have to be made within three months of the commencement of the year, to prevent loss of credits, protective claims are necessary for any claimants who think that their income for the current year could be low enough to make them qualify. Claims should be made by 6 July in the tax year. This could apply to claimants with:

(i)   children,

(ii)   self-employed income, or

(iii)   employment where income may significantly reduce within the fiscal year.

For some awards the amount of credits will be constant, providing income falls between certain bands (this will apply to many entitled to the 'family element' of CTC only). For this type of award a claimant will receive on automatic renewal pack at the year-end and the claim will continue. Any changes of circumstances, or income falling outside the levels set out in the pack, must be notified to HMRC by 31 July.

The claim must be made at the time that eligibility arises; an award can only be backdated up to three months prior to the date of submitting a completed claim. Thus to claim tax credits for 2009/10 in full a claim must be made by 6 July 2009. If, for example, a claim was submitted on 2 August 2009 then the award period would commence on 2 May 2009 and only 340 days of credits would be payable for 2009/10.

An award in payment at 5 April 2009 will continue to be paid until the renewal pack is returned, or 31 July if earlier. Any alteration to existing claims will be backdated to 6 April provided the information is provided by 31 January.

If the forms are not returned by 31 July then tax credit payments will cease.

If the forms are not returned by 31 January then increased claims based on the renewal information will only be backdated three months. Furthermore HMRC will institute proceedings to recover tax credit payments made between 6 April and 31 July.

All other claimants will file details of income at the year-end. This will be used to correct the claim to 'actual' and also form the basis of claim for the following year. A return will be required by 31 July 2009 for 2008/09. If income is not known at that time an estimate should be used with the return being corrected by the following 31 January ie in the above example by 31 January 2010.

Any underpaid credit will be paid to the claimant and any overpaid amount is recovered by HMRC. In computing overpayments, the first £25,000 increase in income between the preceding year and the current year is ignored.

Eligibility for tax credits are set out below.

(i)   Working Tax Credit (WTC)

A person is entitled to Working Tax Credit if they are working at the date of claim, or will commence work within seven days and are:

–   aged at least 16, and working for not less than 16 hours per week and have a child for whom he or his partner is responsible, or

–   aged at least 16, working for not less than 16 hours per week, and have a disability that puts him at a disadvantage in getting a job and satisfy either the 'qualifying benefit test' or the special 'fast-track' rules to qualify for a disability element, or

–   aged at least 25, and working not less than 30 hours per week, or

–   aged at least 50, returning to work after qualifying for certain out-of-work benefits for at least the previous six months and working not less than 16 hours per week.

Work must be expected to continue for at least four weeks, and must be for payment.

In arriving at hours normally worked customary or paid holiday and unpaid time allowed for meals, etc is disregarded.

A person is treated as engaged in qualifying remunerative work for any period during which they are on statutory maternity, paternity or adoption leave providing that they were in qualifying work before they went on leave. This also applies to the self-employed providing that they would have qualified for statutory maternity, paternity or adoption leave if they had been an employee. Any additional non-statutory leave does not count as a period in work eg unpaid additional maternity leave.

In the same way, a person is treated as being in qualifying remunerative work for the first 28 weeks if they are receiving Statutory Sick Pay or various other benefits because of illness. This provision is also applied to the self-employed as appropriate.

The disability element of WTC is paid if the claimant has a physical or mental disability which puts them at a disadvantage in getting a job, eg seeing, hearing, communicating with people, mobility, mental disability, or exhaustion and pain, and satisfies the 'qualifying benefit' test or the special 'fast-track' rules.

There are three 'qualifying benefit' tests. Either the claimant is receiving one of the following:

–   Disability Living Allowance

–   Attendance Allowance

–   Industrial Injuries Disablement Benefit with Constant Attendance Allowance (CAA)

–   War Disablement Pension with CAA or Mobility Supplement

–   A vehicle provided under the Invalid Vehicle Scheme

or they must have received one of the following in the previous six months:

–   Incapacity Benefit at the short-term higher rate or the long-term rate

–   Income based Jobseeker's Allowance*

–   Income Support*

–   Severe Disablement Allowance

–   Council Tax Benefit*

–   Housing Benefit*

　　* This must include a Disability Premium or a Higher Pensioner Premium.

or they have been training for work in the last eight weeks following a period of receiving certain disability benefits.

There is also a set of fast-track rules for those who are finding it hard to stay in work because of a disability. They allow a claimant to qualify for the disability element earlier than under the 'qualifying benefit' tests above.

The Severe Disability element is payable if the claimant is entitled to a Disability Living Allowance (Highest Care Component) or Attendance Allowance (Higher Rate).

For more detail on all these disability elements see *WTC2 Child Tax Credit and Working Tax Credit A Guide* or SI 2002/2005 regs 9 and 17 (as amended).

All WTC payments are made by HMRC directly to the claimant.

The annual income threshold is £6,420 (£5,220 for 2007/08) with credits being reduced by 39p (37p 2007/08) for every £ of income over the threshold. The credits available for 2009/10 are shown in the rates and allowances on page (xii).

(ii)   Childcare element of WTC

A claimant is entitled to claim for childcare if they are eligible for WTC even if, because of the 39% tapering, the amount payable is nil. The claimant(s) must have one or more children and pay for registered or approved childcare. The childcare element is 80% (2005/06 70%) of the amount payable with a maximum cost of £175 per week for one child or £300 per week for two or more children. If the claim is by a couple both partners must work at least 16 hours unless one partner is incapacitated or is an in-patient at a hospital or is in prison.

Payment of this element of WTC is made to the main carer with the Child Tax Credit (CTC).

Approved care is care provided for a child by a registered childminder or an accredited organisation. Childcare can be claimed until the Saturday following the 1 September following a child's 15th birthday, or a further year if the child is disabled.

To compute the average weekly childcare costs one of the following methods is used depending on the method of payment:

–   If the charges are for a fixed weekly amount take the weekly amount for the last four weeks and divide by 4;

–   If the charges are for a fixed monthly amount multiply that amount by 12 and divide by 52;

- If the charges vary take the amount paid in the last 52 weeks (or the last 12 months) and divide by 52;

- If childcare costs have not yet commenced, or have started in the last 52 weeks then an estimate of the costs for the next 52 weeks (divided by 52) is used;

- If payment of childcare is expected to last for less than 52 weeks then the estimated total is divided by the expected weeks of provision;

- If costs decrease for at least four weeks in a row by £10 per week or more, or childcare ceases, then notification of this change in circumstance is required within one month. The method of calculation of the new average weekly cost is determined by the original method used. If that was the same amount paid weekly then the new average weekly cost is the amount to be paid in the next four weeks divided by 4. In all other cases the new average weekly cost is the estimated amount payable over the next 52 weeks divided by 52 (use the expected number of weeks of payment in both places in the above calculation if provision is for less than 52 weeks);

- If one of the claimants is on statutory maternity, paternity or adoption leave they are still treated as being in work for the purposes of having qualifying childcare costs, but only in respect of any existing children of the family for whom they incur childcare costs. They cannot claim childcare for the new child.

Approved child care means care provided by:

- registered childminders, nurseries and play schemes

- out-of-hours clubs on school premises run by a school or a local authority

- childcare schemes run by school governing bodies under the 'extended schools' scheme

- childcare schemes run by approved providers

- in England and Scotland certain approved childcare provided in the claimants' home.

A claim cannot be made for childcare provided in the claimants' home by a relative, or for the child's education.

Where childcare is provided in the home of a relative then that relative must also provide care to children who are not related. Thus a relative (eg aunt or grandparent) will not normally be able to qualify for looking after the relative's child in their own home even if they are an approved childcare provider. In order to make a claim the relative would also need to look after a non-related child. (SI 2005/93).

(iii)   Child Tax Credit (CTC)

CTC is paid directly to the main carer, usually the mother. In order to claim CTC it is necessary to be responsible for a child or qualifying young person.

A child is a person who has not attained the age of 16 and they remain a child for tax credit purposes until immediately before the 1 September following their 16th birthday.

A qualifying young person is a person aged under 20 who is either in full-time non-advanced education or, has ceased full-time education, and has registered for work or training with the Careers Service, Connexions Service or the Department of Employment and Learning in which case, CTC continues for a further 20 weeks after he ceases full-time education.

If a child or young person dies the entitlement ceases eight weeks following death (but not beyond the date when the qualifying young person would have reached age 20).

If the child or qualifying young person has a child of their own, only one claim for CTC can be made in respect of that newborn child. If the intermediate parent is under 16 then the grandparents would claim for both 'children' as no claim by the intermediate parent would be possible. If the intermediate parent was 16 or over then the claim could be made by the parent and the grandparent would not then be able to claim for their 'young person'. This would require the intermediate parent to be supporting the child however. If that was not the case then the grandparent could continue to claim for both providing that the intermediate parent still qualified as a young person.

Being responsible for a child (or qualifying young person) means that the child must normally live with the claimant. If the child lives with more than one potential claimant(s), the claim is to be made by the person or couple having 'main responsibility' for the child. Parties can jointly elect which of them satisfies the main responsibility test. In the absence of such an agreement HMRC make the decision and in order to do so they will ask questions to discover:

–   which address does the child give as a contact address, or for mail

–   where the child spends most nights, goes to after school

–   who keeps clothes/toys/belongings

–   who buys their clothes, food, underwear, provides pocket money

–   which is the registered address for healthcare, social worker, health visitor

–   whether there are any court orders determining responsibility.

The various elements of CTC, available for 2009/10, are shown in the rates and allowances on page (xii). Most of the credits are tapered in the same way as they are for WTC, ie a reduction of 39p for every £ of income over the threshold. If the claimant is also entitled to WTC the threshold remains at £6,420 (£5,220 for 2007/08). Taper will reduce WTC (excluding childcare) before CTC. It then reduces childcare and finally CTC. If the claimant is only entitled to CTC, eg the claimant is not working, or is a student or student nurse, the threshold is £16,040 (£15,575 for 2008/09).

The family element of CTC is tapered last and at a different rate. The full £545 pa (or £1,090 for the 12 months after birth) is payable until income exceeds the higher of income at which the 39% taper ceases (see table at note 7 below), or the second threshold of £50,000 pa. At which point family element is tapered away at the rate of £1 for every £15 of further income, a withdrawal rate of 6.67%. This gives a cut off point of around £58,000 or £66,000 in year of birth. (These thresholds can alter if there are more than two children and maximum childcare costs and/or disability elements in the claim.)

Child Tax Credit is paid in addition to Child Benefit of £20.00 per week for the first child and £13.20 per week for every other child. Claimants in receipt of income support or income based jobseeker's allowance are automatically entitled to the maximum amount of WTC and CTC (TCA 2002 s 7 and SI 2002/2008 reg 4).

Claimants in receipt of pension credit who are also responsible for a child will be entitled to the full amount without the taper provisions applying (SI 2003/2170).

(b)   Income for tax credits

Income for tax credits is computed for the claimant, or joint claimants, for the fiscal year. The amounts to include or exclude are set out in SI 2002/2006 as amended. The legislation requires the income to be computed in the following manner.

Step 1

Add together

–   Pension income

–   Investment income, including chargeable event gains (before top-slicing relief)

–   Property income

–   Foreign income

- Notional income

If the result is £300 or less, treat as nil. If the result is more than £300 only the excess is included. The £300 applies on a per claim basis ie the income of a couple is added together and the £300 deducted from the sum.

Step 2

Add together

- Employment income

- Social Security income

- Student income (ie certain student dependant grants)

- Miscellaneous income.

Step 3

- Add together Steps 1 and 2.

Step 4

Add trading income to Step 3 or deduct a trading loss of the year from Step 3. This could be the trading loss of a partner.

From the above is deducted

- Gift Aid payments (gross)

- Pension payments (gross).

Where a Gift Aid contribution is carried back by election, then it is deductible for tax credits in the fiscal year of payment.

Employment Income

Employment income means:

- Any earnings received in the tax year, including any money's worth (see below)

- Any expense payment chargeable to income tax

- Any non-cash voucher, credit token or cash voucher, chargeable to income tax (excluding childcare vouchers)

- Any termination payment chargeable to income tax

- Any SSP

- Any SMP, SPP or SAP to the extent that it exceeds £100 per week per person (note the rate of SMP for 2009/10 is £123.06 per week)

- Benefit in kind on cars and car fuel and the taxable part of any mileage allowances

- Any amount subject to tax by ITEPA 2003 s 225 (restrictive undertakings)

- Any strike pay.

The definition appears to exclude all other taxable benefits in kind but those earning £8,500 or more are taxed on the full cost of any assets transferred to them rather than on the second-hand value so that the figures returned on the P11D are used.

Employment income does not include:

- Pension income

- Qualifying removal expenses (under £8,000)
- Payments covered by most ITEPA 2003 expenses claims (travelling costs, professional fees etc)
- Items covered by specific concessions eg staff suggestion schemes
- Deemed earnings under IR 35
- Employer provided childcare vouchers.

From employment income may be deducted:

- Travel expenses
- Fees and subscriptions to professional bodies
- Employee liability insurance
- Entertainers expenses
- Fixed sum deductions
- Personal security assets and services
- Give As You Earn donations
- Allowable expense claims
- Allowable claims for mileage allowance relief (ie where the employer has paid less than the mileage allowance rates).

Pension Income

This includes pensions paid by

- The Crown
- Annuities under a Retirement Benefit Scheme, Superannuation Scheme, etc, Unapproved Pension Payments.
- Lump sums payable where state pension has been deferred.
- Taxable lump sums arising from commutation of trivial pension policies.

Trading Income

This is the profit or loss for the year disregarding averaging.

Student Income

This means any grant under the Education (Student Support) Regulations 2002 other than

- A grant for a dependent child,
- A grant for books, travel or equipment.

Investment Income

This is investment income as calculated for income tax but without top-slicing relief for chargeable events.

Property Income

This is as for income tax (ie excluding non-taxable rent a room income). It is the amount chargeable to tax ie after deduction of losses brought forward (box 38 on SA tax return property pages).

Foreign Income

This means income arising outside the UK which is **not**

–   Employment income

–   Trading income

–   Investment income.

Foreign income is computed on an income arising basis whether or not remitted. The 10% relief for certain foreign pensions is given.

Foreign income includes any income arising or income that has been excluded from UK liability by a double taxation agreement.

Notional Income

Notional income means income, which a claimant is treated as having, but which he does not in fact receive.

This includes amounts treated as income under ITTOIA 2005, including:

–	s 277	Premium on rent
–	s 409	Stock dividends
–	s 415	Release of a loan to a participator by a close company
–	s 624	Income rising under a settlement where the settlor retains an interest
–	s 629	Payments to unmarried minor children of the settlor
–	s 633	Sums paid to settlor otherwise than as income
–	s 652	Income from the residue on an estate
ITA 2007 s 628		Accrued income scheme
FA 2004 s 84 & Sch 15		Benefit charge on pre-owned assets

If a claimant has deprived himself of income for the purpose of securing entitlement to, or increasing the amount of, a tax credit he is treated as having that income. This could include dividends not received because of a dividend waiver.

If income would become available to a claimant upon making an application for that income he is treated as having that income.

If a claimant provides a service for less than full value to another person who could afford to pay, then trading income or employment income is deemed to include the full value. This does not apply where the claimant is a volunteer, or is engaged to provide the service by a charitable or voluntary organisation and the Board are satisfied that it is reasonable for the claimant to provide the service free of charge.

Miscellaneous Income

This includes any other income chargeable not already included above, such as an amount taxable on change of accounting basis (including UITF 40).

(c)   Changes in circumstances

The tax credits rules require a claimant to notify within one month any changes in

(i)   the claiming unit (eg starting to live with a partner or separating from a partner), including being part of a same-sex unit,

(ii)   childcare payments where certain reductions in payments occur, or

(iii)   ceasing to be 'in the UK' (see explanatory note 4).

(iv)   changes in hours worked where the level decreases below 30, or 16 hours per week,

(v)   changes in the number of children eligible for the tax credits within the claiming unit.

Failure to notify can result in a penalty not exceeding £300.

Other changes in circumstances, which would result in an increase in credits, should be notified within three months because the entitlement to the new element of the claim can only be backdated for three months.

Changes which have to be notified, and which carry the potential £300 penalty, are:

–   Date of marriage (if claiming as a single person)

–   Date of commencement to live as a couple

–   Date ceased to live as a couple (including death)

–   Decrease in childcare payments to nil or by £10 a week or more

–   Claimant leaves the UK for 8 weeks or more at the beginning of a temporary absence of 52 weeks or less (the period is extended to 12 weeks in circumstances of illness or bereavement)

–   Claimant leaves the UK for a period which will be more than 52 weeks

–   Partner of claimant returns to the UK after period of absence during which they were treated as not being 'in the UK' (see explanatory note 4 for more detail on these 'residence rules').

–   Birth or Death of a child

–   Change in the 'main responsibility' for a child

–   Child ceases full-time education after 1 September following their 16th birthday

–   Changes to the number of working hours.

Other changes in circumstances which should be notified at some time are:

–   Increase in childcare of £10 a week or more lasting four weeks in a row

–   Changes to entitlement to disability elements

It is also obviously useful to tell HMRC about changes of employer, address, bank account or childcare provider.

Changes in income can be notified in year, or at the year-end. If there is an increase in excess of £25,000 pa over the income of the previous year the tax credit award will be recalculated and an overpayment of tax credits may have to be returned to HMRC.

If income decreases then it is advisable to notify the reduction to HMRC. This will increase the tax credits award. The recalculated daily rate is paid from the date of notification, but the increase from the previous 6 April to date of notification is not normally paid until the final award notice is issued after notification of actual income for the year. This is to try and avoid substantial overpayments arising where income bounces back up later in the tax year. For example, Sam is made redundant in July. When he notifies (instantly), his tax credits are recalculated for the whole tax year based on the new lower estimate of income but the increase is only paid in respect of the period from July. The potential overpayment from April to July is withheld to prevent an overpayment if Sam's income increases for any reason. This is common; for example, he finds new employment, then, the tax credit system struggles with substantial increase in income (back to the previous year level) occurring close to the end of the tax year as there would not be sufficient time to collect the overpayment.

Tax Credits interact with Housing Benefit and Council Tax benefits, so it is necessary to notify the Local Authority of any change in the level of award.

(d)   Four-week run on

Any award of WTC may run on for four weeks (from April 2007) following the claimant's hours dropping below the 16/30 hours per week. The measure is designed to reduce overpayments and to ease the transition from tax credits to benefits. This applies when claimants cease to work or start working fewer hours per week.

Claimants, where entitled, will be eligible to claim income support or Job Seeker's Allowance and other income-related benefits whilst in receipt of the WTC four-week run on. Under social security legislation, WTC will be treated as income for benefit purposes.

(e)   Award periods and relevant periods

An award period is normally a fiscal year, however if eligibility first arises in the year, eg on birth of first child, it is the period from the date of eligibility (or three months before date of claim if later) to the end of the fiscal year. If eligibility ceases before the end of the year then the award period ceases on that day.

Within the award period each day is considered separately, however all days with the same entitlement are aggregated and that period is known as a 'relevant period'.

In all instances the average income of the year of claim is used. This is normally the lower of the income for the fiscal year, or, for the preceding fiscal year, as computed for Tax Credits, divided by the number of days in the year and multiplied by the number of days in the relevant period to give the income for the relevant period.

The same principle is used to calculate the maximum award for a relevant period although the childcare credit rules are slightly different to allow for the fact that there are weekly, rather than daily, maxima.

(f)   Year-end procedures

A claimant is required to provide such information as will enable HMRC to confirm the claim made and to continue payments for the following year. In many instances this will only require notification if the income of the family unit was not within certain limits.

Where a recomputation applies the renewal information will require a declaration of actual income by 31 July. If actual income is not known estimates must be provided and the form marked to show an estimate has been used. The actual figures must be filed by 31 January following.

If income has reduced and additional tax credits are due the amount will be paid directly to the claimants.

If income has increased by £25,000 or less no adjustment will be made to the income part of the claim for the year under review. The increased income will be used in recomputing the provisional award for the following year, ie the award now being paid.

If income has increased by more than £25,000 the excess over £25,000 is taken into account resulting in an overpayment of credits at the rate of 39% of the excess (or, if a claim for family element only, 6.67%). The excess payments will be recovered from future tax credit awards wherever possible (see explanatory note 6). Otherwise direct payment will be required. The amount is recovered as tax and is due within 30 days of the notice. On application overpayments may be repaid by 12 monthly instalments without interest. TCA 2002 s 37 provides for interest to be charged on overpayments of tax credits but only where the overpayment is attributable to the fraud or neglect of any person. In cases of hardship application may be made to arrange for repayment of the overpayment over a period in excess of 12 months.

TCA 2002 s 29(5) also provides for overpayments to be recovered through the PAYE system but currently HMRC are unable to use this provision.

In the case of a joint claim, both members of the family unit are required to sign claim forms and both have to repay any excess, ie there is a joint and several liability (TCA 2002 s 28(4)).

B.   (a)   **Brian and Angela Smith – Tax Credits Claim 2009/10**

Initial award based on 2008/09 income

Award period

Date of renewal claim	– 30 July 2008
Date of eligibility (made prior to 31 July)	– 6 April 2008
Renewal pack returned	– 6 July 2009
Award period 6 April 2009 to 5 April 2010	(365 days)
Relevant period – initially the whole year	(365 days)

Initial eligibility

WTC	–	Yes both work full time
Childcare	–	Yes
CTC	–	Yes for one child (not under one)
Family element	–	Yes

Income

		£	£
Investment income			
Brian		180	
Angela		520	
		700	
Less:		300	400
Self-employment			
Brian		18,810	
Less: Personal pension	$\left(£1,600 \times \dfrac{100}{80}\right)$	2,000	16,810
Employment			
Angela – P60		22,700	
Car		2,160	
		24,860	
Less: Gift Aid	$\left(£480 \times \dfrac{100}{80}\right)$	600	24,260
Base income on PY basis for 2009/10			41,470

Maximum claim (per day)

		£
WTC	– Basic	5.18
	Second adult	5.10
	30 hours	2.13
CTC	– One child	6.13
	– Family element	1.50

			£
Relevant period = 365 days ×		20.04 =	7,315
Childcare, £165 × 80% × 52			6,864
			14,179
Restricted by			
Income	41,470		
Income threshold	6,420		
39% ×	35,050	=	13,670
			509
But not below Family element 365 × 1.50		=	£547.50

Payable at the rate of £10.52 pw (£42.11 per 4 week) to Angela (the first or last payment is adjusted to include rounding).

Award revised to actual, calculation of final award

Award period 6 April 2009 to 5 April 2010 (365 days)

Relevant periods

| Changes | – | Childcare from 5 January 2010, but not notified until 5 May 2010, therefore increase claim from 5 February 2010 |
| | – | Birth of Colin – 1 March 2010 (notified 5 May 2010 ie within 3 months) |

6 April 2009 to 4 February 2010	305 days
5 February 2010 to 28 February 2010	24 days
1 March 2010 to 5 April 2010	36 days

Income

	£	£	£
Investment income			
Brian	20		
Angela	140		
	160		
Less: £300 restricted to	160		–
Employment			
Angela – P60	16,100		
Less: SMP 10 weeks @ £100	1,000		
	15,100		
Car	2,160		17,260
Less: Trading loss		2,800	
Personal pension		2,000	
Gift Aid		600	(5,400)
Income for tax credits 2009/10			11,860

Maximum claim (per day)

		6/4/09 – 4/2/10 £	5/2/10 – 28/2/10 £	1/3/10 – 5/4/10 £
WTC	– Basic	5.18	5.18	5.18
	Second adult	5.10	5.10	5.10
	30 hours	2.13	2.13	2.13
CTC	– Child	6.13	6.13	12.25
	– Family element	1.50	1.50	2.99
		20.04	20.04	27.65

× days in relevant period:

6/4/09 – 4/2/10 = 305

5/2/10 – 28/2/10 = 24

1/3/10 – 5/4/10 = 36

		£	£	£
		6,112	481	995
Childcare (per relevant period):				
£165 × 52 × 305/365 × 80%		5,736		
£175/7 = £25 × 24 × 80%			480	
£175/7 = £25 × 36 × 80%				720
Maximum credits due	£14,524	11,848	961	1,715
Restricted by		£	£	£
Income £11,860		9,910	780	1,170
Threshold £6,420		5,365	422	633
		4,545	358	537
× 39%	£2,122	1,773	140	209

Payment of claim (calculation of under payment)

	£
– As WTC to worker	
Maximum	
(5.18 + 5.10 + 2.13) × 365	4,530
Less: restriction	2,122
To Brian or Angela per claim	2,408
– As WTC and CTC to carer	
Balance of TC (14,524 – 4,530)	9,994
Paid in year	545
Payable to Angela	9,449

Angela and Brian's initial award for 2010/11 will be based on 2009/10 income and their circumstances at the time of renewal. It will be necessary to know whether Angela is going back to work after her period of statutory maternity leave because this will determine whether the couple can continue to claim the childcare element. If she does return to work, and incurs childcare costs for both children, a different maximum of £300 per week will apply. The higher family element of £1,090, £2.99 per day, will be payable up to 28 February 2011. If Brian believes that he will make a profit in the year to 31 December 2010 of a similar level, to year ending 31 December 2008 then it would be advisable to notify HMRC of the increased earnings levels so that an overpayment does not arise from 6 April 2011.

(b) Revised Income 2009/10

	£	£
Investment income – as above		–
Employment – as above	17,260	
Less: Gift Aid	600	16,660
Self-employment	35,000	
Less: Personal pension	2,000	33,000
		49,660
Original income		41,470
As increase is less than £25,000 – ignore		8,190

Claim is recomputed using the actual circumstances of the year but still using the income figure of £41,470.

Maximum claim

	6/4/09 – 4/2/10	5/2/10 – 29/2/10	1/3/10 – 5/4/10
	£	£	£
As above: Maximum credits due £14,524	11,848	961	1,715
Income: £41,470	34,653	2,727	4,090
Threshold: £6,420	5,365	422	633
	29,288	2,305	3,457
× 39%	11,422	899	1,348
Credits due: Family element only £1.50/ £2.99 per day	£458 (× 305)	£36 (× 24)	£108 (× 36)
Actual credits	426	62	367
Entitlement is higher of family element or actual	458	62	£367

Total credits due £887 (458 + 62 + 367), less paid in year £545 = £342 payable to Angela (representing increased family element and some child element payable because of the increased childcare costs).

Explanatory Notes

Eligibility

1. The above sets out the main criteria for eligibility. Reference should be made to 'WTC2 – Child Tax Credit and Working Tax Credit' a HMRC booklet which sets out the rules for eligibility in detail with more information on childcare, disability, severe disability and fast track claims. Help can also be obtained from the Helpline on 0845 300 3900 or 0845 603 2000 (Northern Ireland).

Claims

2.   Agents must file a Form 64–8 signed by each of the claimants in order to receive information about tax credits from HMRC. Copies of claim forms can be obtained from 01772 235 623. If an agency or community organisation actually assists customers in completing the tax credits claim form, then they can receive multiple copies of the claim form via the orderline on 0845 366 7820.

Trading Losses

3.   If a taxpayer suffers a trading loss then *three* separate loss claims will be required ie:

   (a)   Income Tax – Claim under:

   (i)   trade loss relief against general income (ITA 2007 s 64); or

   (ii)   early trade loss relief (ITA 2007 s 72); or

   (iii) carry forward trade loss relief (ITA 2007 s 83); or

   (iv)   carry forward where trade transferred to a company (ITA 2007 s 86); or

   (v)   terminal trade loss relief (ITA 2007 s 90); or

   (vi)   trade losses treated as CGT loss (ITA 2007 s 71).

   (See Examples 29–32.)

   (b)   Class 4 national insurance contributions – Claim against income liable to Class 4 only (SSCBA 1992 Sch 2.3(4)) (see Example 48).

   (c)   Tax Credits – Claim against income of the *couple* or single claimant for year of loss only (SI 2002/2006 reg 3(1)). Any amount not used in this way may be deductible from trading income from the same source of the claimant in subsequent years. Uncommercial losses are not relievable.

Separate schedules will be needed to compute the carried forward amount for each claim.

Where the taxpayer with the loss has had more than one relevant period within the year, it is thought that the loss is restricted by the relevant days of the claims made. Where a loss claim (or gift aid or pension claim) is made a Form TC 825 is completed and filed with HMRC. In circumstances where a couple have parted HMRC will notify the loss to be used in future years, eg Alan lived with Beth until 30 July 2009. They parted, and on 6 February 2010 he moved in with Carol. In 2009/10 Alan had a loss of £14,000. Beth's income (for tax credits) is £17,000 and Carol £10,000.

The income calculation is always for the full fiscal year.

	Alan & Beth £	*Alan* £	*Alan & Carol* £	
Alan	Nil	Nil	Nil	
Partner	17,000		10,000	
Less: Loss	14,000	–	10,000	
	3,000		Nil	
Days in relevant period	116	190	59	
Loss used				
(116/365 × 14,000)	4,449	Nil		
(59/365 × 10,000)			1,616	
Loss for year				14,000
Used re Alan and Beth			4,449	
re Alan			Nil	
re Alan and Carol			1,616	6,065
Loss to carry forward				7,935

Loss claims should be made after claims for Gift Aid or pension payments as any excess loss can be carried forward.

Being 'in the UK' and Temporary Absences

4.   When computing *income* for tax credits the income tax definitions of Resident, Ordinarily Resident and Domicile are used although this is not of much practical relevance since virtually all worldwide income counts for tax credit purposes.

When considering entitlement (ie whether someone can claim tax credits) different rules are relevant. TCA 2002 s 3(3) requires the claimant(s) to be 'in the UK'. This requires physical presence in the UK on the days of entitlement.

The Tax Credits Residence Regulations (SI 2003/654) state that a person shall not be treated as being 'in the UK' if they are not ordinarily resident here, although this does not apply to a Crown servant posted overseas or his partner. Certain EC workers are treated as being ordinarily resident, as are certain persons in the UK as a result of compulsion by law. CTC is a family benefit under EC law and some claimants will qualify regardless of the requirements of these regulations.

Persons who are ordinarily resident for tax credit purposes (see HMRC Manual at TCTM 02003 as to what ordinary residence means for tax credit purposes) can also be treated as being 'in the UK' for certain periods of temporary absence. This is an absence which is not expected to be for more than 52 weeks in total. In this situation the first 8 weeks of absence are ignored. This is extended to 12 weeks if the absence or continued absence is due to the illness of the claimant or the illness/death of his partner, or his or his partner's child or qualifying young person, or a close relative of his or his partner.

It follows that if a claimant, who is part of a couple, works abroad for a temporary period, then for the first 8 weeks they will still be treated as a couple and a joint tax credit claim will be available. After 8 weeks the partner in the UK must notify the absence of the other (within one month) and the partner remaining in the UK will become a single claimant. This *may* increase the claim as only the UK partner's income will be counted. (If there are no children the claimant remaining in the UK would lose the couple's element of WTC assuming that they were working themselves and therefore entitled to WTC.)

Unfortunately the provision that deems a person as being resident for up to 8 or 12 weeks of absence does not also deem them to be working in the UK. This means that a parent remaining in the UK with children will lose their entitlement to claim childcare credits during that period. This is because the tax credits claim is by a couple, but one member (the parent overseas) is not working in the UK.

On the return of the overseas worker a further notification will be required (within one month) and the claim must revert to a joint claim. If the claimant was not part of a couple the only notification which has to be made is their own lengthy or permanent departure from the UK. When the individual returns to the UK they will have a choice as to whether they make a new claim to tax credits. They will obviously have to do so within three months of qualifying in order to get the maximum entitlement.

Penalties

5.   There is a penalty for fraudulently or negligently making incorrect statements etc in connection with tax credit claims, or notifications of changes in circumstances, limited to a maximum of £3,000 per offence.

There is a maximum penalty of £300 initially and £60 per day thereafter for failure to provide information when required.

There is a separate penalty for failure to notify certain changes in circumstances within one month (three months before April 2007):

- Changes in the claiming unit (eg starting to live with a partner or separation), or ceasing to be 'in the UK'.

- Falls in childcare costs to nil or by £10 per week or more for four or more weeks.

- Ceasing to be 'in the UK'.

- Changes in hours worked (decrease below 30 or 16).

- Changes in eligible children.

Any changes in income arising from an enquiry for income tax may have a corresponding effect upon a claim for tax credits. In the same way any agreed alteration of income for tax credits may affect income tax and possibly national insurance.

Overpayments

6.   Where HMRC become aware of an overpayment in a year, eg notification of change in circumstances or increase in income, they will automatically recover the amount from the tax credits due to be paid for the remainder of the year. If this causes hardship then the claimant may apply for a top-up payment, however, such amounts will be recovered by becoming an overpayment at the year-end.

To determine 'hardship', HMRC will use the same maximum deduction rates as for year-end recoveries.

For year-end overpayments and in-year overpayments (from April 2006) the maximum deduction from future awards of tax credits will be:

If claiming maximum WTC/CTC	–	10% of current tax credit award
If claiming family element of CTC only	–	100% of current tax credit award
In all other cases	–	25% of current tax credit award.

In the first instance the restriction applies to a tax credits award of the same type. Therefore if the overpayment is WTC the maximum recoverable will be 10% (or 25%) of the WTC payable only. If no WTC is payable for the year then the restriction applies to CTC payable in the year.

In exceptional circumstances HMRC will not recover an overpayment. This will be where the overpayment was due to an HMRC mistake and the claimant believed that the award was correct. See Code of Practice 26 for further details.

For joint claims both parties remain liable for overpayments even if they no longer live together. However, HMRC will take into account the circumstances of the individual case in deciding how to take proceedings to recover the overpayment. This can include asking for one former partner to pay all or most of the amount due, or by taking different forms of action against each partner.

Employer provided childcare vouchers

7.   An employer can provide his employees with childcare vouchers to the value of up to £55 per week (from 6 April 2006). Such vouchers do not count as income for tax credits and are not liable to income tax or national insurance. (See Example 9 explanatory note 24 for the conditions attached to the vouchers in order to obtain tax free status.)

Care must be taken when claiming tax credit childcare to ensure that the amount of childcare claimed is net of the cost covered by such vouchers.

Although this would appear a generous tax-free perk, in fact in most cases where 39% taper applies no benefit will arise as most employers will restrict salary by an amount equal to the tax-free voucher provided. The adverse effect on net income being per week

			£	£	£
Before voucher					
Childcare				55	
Covered by tax credits – 80%				44	
Net cost (from net pay)					11.00
With Voucher					
Childcare £55 – £55 voucher				Nil	
Loss of salary				(55.00)	
Net of Tax	@ 20%		11.00		
NI	@ 11%		6.05	17.05	
				(37.95)	
Less increase in tax credits					
£55 (reduction in income)	@	39%		21.45	(16.50)
Difference in net income – Loss					(5.50)

However, in the first year of change there is a further complication of the £25,000 income disregard. If the employee had the choice between a £55 per week rise and a £55 per week tax-free childcare voucher and tax rates were as above then it would cost the employee £1,401 to take the voucher. This is because the taper would not apply to the increase in pay assuming that the family unit had no other alteration in income.

			£	£	£
Increase in salary				2,860	
Less: Tax	@	20%	572		
NI	@	11%	315	887	
				1,973	1,973
Increase in income less than £25,000 – no clawback					
Childcare costs				2,860	
Covered by tax credits – 80%				2,288	572
Net increase in pay					1,401
Compared with					
Childcare voucher				2,860	
Childcare costs				2,860	Nil

At maximum childcare costs, 39% (2007/08 37%) taper applies until a couple's income is as below:

No of Children	1	2	3	4	5
2009/10	42,420	61,484	67,215	72,946	78,676
2008/09	41,471	60,151	65,497	70,843	76,189
2007/08	41,058	60,098	65,085	70,071	75,058
2006/07	40,436	59,260	64,030	68,800	73,570

Marginal rate

8. The National Minimum Wage increased in October 2009 to £5.80 per hour. Therefore, someone in full-time employment should earn at least £8,000 per annum. The marginal tax rate for 2009/10 for a family on tax credits earning in excess of £6,420 is 70%. This is made up of income tax at 20%, NIC at 11% and tax credit withdrawal at 39%.

Pension contributions

9. As shown in question B, Brian's losses and the £25,000 income disregard interact very favourably for claimants. The same is true for one-off pension contributions.

Matthew and Georgina have three children (aged 9 years old, 6 years old and 5 months). Matthew works full-time earning £35,200 per annum while Georgina cares for the children.

Matthew pays £1,000 (net) into his personal pension. The gross contribution received by his fund amounts to £1,250. The pension contribution reduces the family's income for tax credit purposes for the current and following tax year increasing their tax credits by £488 per year (1,250 × 39%). This amounts to tax relief of 98% as follows:

Increase in pension fund	1,250
Less: tax relief at source	(250)
Increase in tax credits current year	(488)
Increase in tax credits for following year	(487)
Cost to Matthew	25
Rate of relief	98%

*   Anti-maximisation rules exist to prevent the abuse of the £25,000 income disregard which state 'if a claimant has deprived himself of income for the purpose of securing entitlement to, or increasing the amount of, a tax credit, he is treated as having that income.'

Enquiries

10.   For interaction of tax credits and self-assessment see Example 46.

Other examples showing tax credits

11.   For further examples of tax credits see Example 40.

Example 2	–	Restriction of family element
Example 3(d)	–	Year of death
Example 4(a)	–	Use of previous year income
Example 9	–	Benefits
Example 12 explanatory note 14	–	Absence from UK
Example 29	–	Trading losses
Example 30	–	Opening years – choice of accounting period
Example 33	–	Averaging claims
Example 39	–	Chargeable event gains
Example 90	–	Charitable giving

Question

A.

Your firm has recently been instructed to act as advisers to a newly incorporated manufacturing company, Byrd Ltd.

Mr Tallis, the managing director of Byrd Ltd, has requested you to write to him summarising the major points in the operation of a Pay As You Earn (PAYE) scheme in order that he can ensure his new part-time accounts assistant is operating the scheme correctly and maintaining the necessary records.

You have established that the staff complement comprises two full-time working directors, one employee earning £8,400 per annum (plus substantial reimbursed expenses), the accounts assistant, who is a graduate, earning £16,000 per annum and several part-time employees each earning approximately £80 per week.

Write to Mr Tallis setting out the information requested and ensuring that your letter covers the following specific points:

(a)   requirements on employees joining and leaving,

(b)   records required for operation of PAYE, NI and other employer obligations,

(c)   calculation of pay and payment of monies to HMRC, and

(d)   end of year returns and forms.

Note: Ignore the requirements of the statutory sick pay, statutory maternity pay, statutory adoption pay and statutory paternity pay schemes.

B.

In connection with the HMRC Form P11D explain:

(a)   the purpose of this form,

(b)   when, by whom, and in respect of whom, it is necessary to complete and submit the form,

(c)   the major contents of the form.

Outline the purpose and contents of Form P9D.

Answer

A.   Operating PAYE

Smith & Co,
Old Street, Newtown.
1 October 2009

Mr Tallis
Managing Director, Byrd Ltd.

Dear Mr Tallis,

As requested I summarise below the major points in the operation of a Pay As You Earn (PAYE) scheme and other payroll responsibilities.

(1)   Basic documentation – A New Employer's Starter Pack is available from the HMRC helpline on 0845 60 70 143. This includes tax and national insurance tables and employers' help books, together with an order form for obtaining relevant forms and employers' guides explaining the scheme. The Employer's CD-Rom is an invaluable resource, and contains most employer forms, guidance and tables and includes calculators, forms to fill in on-screen and step-by-step help for people new to running basic payroll. There is also free payroll software on the CD-Rom suitable for smaller businesses, or you may wish to invest in a software product which will complete all of the calculations automatically. There is a wide range of software products on the market with a correspondingly wide range of prices. The accounts assistant should familiarise himself with the workings of the scheme and refer to the employers' guides on points of difficulty. The guidance available on the internet is always the most up to date, so it is better to use that as a source of information rather than paper versions, which can become out of date quite quickly. The employers area is signposted from the main HMRC homepage (www.hmrc.gov.uk), and includes a huge range of information for employers, including a diary to remind your staff when routine payroll tasks need to be completed. Local HMRC business support teams also run various courses on operating a payroll scheme that your new assistant could attend and the details of when these occur is marked in the Employers' diary. You will need to book a place to attend, but there is no charge. Help for existing employers is available from the helpline on 0845 71 43 143. It is also possible to obtain PAYE forms from the Employer's Forms and Online Order Service at www.hmrc.gov.uk/menus/formmenu.htm, or you can print most forms from the CD-Rom, where they are stored in PDF format. There is also an internet service for PAYE at www.hmrc.gov.uk. More details of this are at (11) below.

(2)   All new employees should be asked for parts 2 and 3 of Form P45 given to them by previous employers or by Jobcentre Plus if they have been drawing jobseeker's allowance. The best help available for those taking on a new employee is on the HMRC employers' website. The item 'Take on a new employee' is listed under the first menu list which starts "I want to ..." This sets out how to check that the employee can legally work for you, and what to do with the P45 they present to you. The guidance leads you through each step, including preparing a deductions working sheet to record their pay and tax. In summary, for employees who produce Form P45, a deductions working sheet should be made out according to the instructions in the employer's day-to-day payroll help book E13, and part 3 of the P45 sent to HMRC – by online submission if the employer is geared up to do so – from 2011 online submission will be mandatory for all businesses. Part 2 is retained. These procedures must be followed whether or not the employee's pay with you will exceed the tax and national insurance thresholds, so it is particularly important in relation to the part-time employees. Care must be taken to check whether the employee is subject to a student loan repayment deduction. This is shown in Box 5 on Form P45 by the inclusion of the letter Y (see (10) below).

(3)   If a new employee does not produce Form P45, the online guidance on taking on a new employee specifies the action to be taken. In the case of the part-time employees earning below the Lower Earnings Limit (£95 for 2009/10), if they certify on Form P46 that the employment with you is their only or main employment and that they do not receive a pension, HMRC do not have to be notified but the Form P46 must be retained, and records must be kept of the employee's name, address and pay. If the employee, either at the start or subsequently, earns more than the Lower Earnings Limit, Form P46 must be submitted to HMRC. Online submission of P46 will also be mandatory from 2011.

(4)   When an employee for whom a deductions working sheet is in use leaves, Form P45 must be completed, the top copy sent to HMRC and the bottom three copies (including part 1A which is the employee's copy) handed to the employee. Once again, mandatory electronic submission will apply to this form from 2011.

(5)   Records should be kept of the name, address, national insurance number and date of birth of each employee for whom a deductions working sheet has been prepared, and it would be advisable to have this information available for all employees even if a deductions working sheet is not in use. It is also necessary to record the employee's gender. HMRC cautions in the guidance that asking for date of birth should be delayed until after an employee is engaged, lest you breach the Age Discrimination legislation.

(6)   On each pay day the details of pay and the tax and employer's and employee's national insurance thereon, together with any student loan deduction (calculated in each case from the tables, or using appropriate computer software) must be recorded on the P11 deductions working sheets or computer equivalent. The accounts assistant will need a summary sheet of the total pay and the total tax and national insurance due. Within fourteen days after the end of each tax month, ie by the 19th (22nd if paid electronically), a cheque for the total amount due for the month must be received by HMRC Accounts Office with an accompanying payslip (supplied by HMRC). Electronic payments do not need to be accompanied by a payslip. If your average monthly total payments of PAYE, NIC and student loan deductions for the current year are less than £1,500 you may choose to pay HMRC quarterly rather than monthly. This is easily arranged by completing a Form P31. If for any month you have no deductions to remit (eg, because of recovering statutory maternity pay), you should submit a 'nil' payslip so that HMRC knows that no payment should be received.

(7)   Details of what counts as pay are given in the employers' guides. Broadly it covers all cash payments and also benefits in kind if they can be readily converted into cash. There are more stringent rules relating to directors and to employees earning at a rate of £8,500 per annum or more (this limit includes the value of the expenses and benefits). Reimbursed expenses are included under these stricter provisions unless HMRC grants a dispensation allowing the expenses to be ignored, in which case they do not have to be recorded on Form P11D (see 8 below). Details of the nature of any expenses reimbursed should be supplied to the tax office and a dispensation requested. In any event, reimbursed expenses do not count as pay for deduction purposes, but must be recorded on Form P11D if a dispensation is not granted. An employee will not be included in a dispensation if it would have the effect of reducing his taxable earnings (not just pay) below £8,500, so a dispensation will not be available for the employee who earns £8,400.

Certain amounts will be included in gross pay for national insurance, but not for income tax. These amounts are liable to Class 1 national insurance contributions when paid but are treated as benefits for PAYE and included on Form P11D. See Chapter 5 of CWG2 'Employer's Further Guide to PAYE and NICs' for the detail on these payments.

(8)   At the end of the tax year you will be required to send year-end documents to HMRC. This process is best done by using the online facility, whether using commercial software, or the HMRC submission facility. Form P14, which in paper version are in three parts, must be completed for each employee in respect of whom entries were required on the deductions

working sheet (Form P11). A Form P14 must be completed if an employee has earned £95 or more in any pay week even though no deductions are shown. Two parts of Form P14 are for HMRC and the third part constitutes the Form P60 (details of pay and tax deducted) for the employee. If you complete these forms online, you will need to print the employee version, Form P60, and also one copy for your backup records. Form P35 must be completed listing the total tax and total national insurance for each employee, and the aggregate totals should reconcile with the wages records and records of payments to HMRC through the year. The completed Form P35 and two copies of each P14 should be sent to HMRC by 19 May. Form P60 must be issued on paper to employees by 31 May. The electronic process allows employers to complete the forms online and submit, receiving a confirmation of receipt almost immediately.

A Form P11D must be completed for each director and employee earning at a rate of £8,500 or more, showing details of all benefits provided other than anything already included as pay on the deduction working sheets, or covered by a dispensation, or in respect of which you have entered into a PAYE settlement agreement with HMRC to settle the tax liability for all relevant employees. The boxes on the form that are relevant for Class 1A national insurance contributions (see (9) below) are colour coded. If expenses payments in excess of £25 to non-P11D employees have not been treated as pay (other than reimbursed business expenses and expenses paid in accordance with a scale agreed with the tax office), or certain benefits have been provided to non-P11D employees, Form P9D must also be completed. Forms P11D and P9D should be sent to HMRC by 6 July and copies must be provided by that date to anyone employed at 5 April. If an employee has left after 5 April, the copy may be sent to his last known address. You are not *required* to give copies to employees who leave *during* the year unless they make a written request, but it would be sensible and helpful to the employee to do so. This could be done either at the time the employee leaves or when issuing copies to other employees at the year-end. There is not currently any plan to require electronic submission of Forms P11D.

(9)   Class 1A employers' national insurance contributions, currently at 12.8% of the cash equivalent of benefits, are payable annually in arrears on the provision of all taxable benefits. The amount due is calculated annually from the P11D entries and is payable to the Accounts Office using the special payslip by 19 July 2010 for 2009/10 (22 July 2010 if payment is made electronically). The payment is shown on Form P11D(b) which must be filed with the PAYE tax office by 6 July. Interest is charged from the day after the July due date on any late payment.

When company cars and fuel are first provided to employees, and when cars cease to be available, HMRC must be notified on Form P46 (Car) within 28 days after each quarter to 5 July, 5 October, 5 January and 5 April.

(10) Where a student took a student loan as a new borrower after August 1998 then repayment of those loans will be collected by way of a deduction from salary. You are not required to take any action unless you receive a start notice (SL1) or a P45 with the student loan indicator set. The first deduction date will be on the next pay date. For new employees 'Y' in the SL box on Form P45 triggers the deduction. The repayment is 9% of the excess of earnings over £288.46 per week (£1,250 per month). Deductions must continue until a stop notice (SL2) is received. Earnings will be the amount computed for national insurance purposes.

(11) HMRC encourages the use of the internet by smaller employers to submit Forms P14, P35, P11D, P11D(b), P9D, P45 and P46. Employers may also receive Forms such as P6 (coding details) and P9 (code amendments) via the internet.

An employer with 50 or more employees must use electronic communications with HMRC for year-end returns for PAYE/NI. It is anticipated that all employers will be required to use year-end electronic communications from 2009/10.

Large and medium-sized employers (those with 50 or more employees) are required to file in-year PAYE forms online. Small employers (with fewer than 50 employees) will be required to file in-year forms online from April 2011. Employers will need to remain aware and read news items to ensure that they are up to date with the current situation.

Large employers (250+ employees) are obliged to pay PAYE/NI and associated amounts electronically. If any employer pays PAYE/NI electronically, or through the bank, the cleared payment must arrive by the 22nd of the month (or the previous bank working day if the 22nd is a bank holiday or falls on a weekend). A large employer will be charged a surcharge if they pay late more than twice or do not pay electronically.

(12)   Interest is charged on PAYE, NIC, student loan and CIS deductions that remain outstanding 14 days after the end of the tax year, ie, from 19 April 2010 for 2009/10 (22 April for e-payers), except for Class 1A contributions, where interest runs from the due date of payment, ie 19 July 2010 for 2009/10 (again, 22 July for e-payers). There are also penalties if you are late sending in Forms P14, P35, P11D, P11D(b) or P9D, or if you deliberately or carelessly (previously fraudulently or negligently) provide incorrect information in a P11D, P11D(b) or P9D or in relation to a PAYE return. For student loan deductions there are penalties for fraudulently or negligently making incorrect deductions, or making or receiving incorrect payments. Such interest and penalties are not deductible in computing the tax liabilities of the employer. The penalties for incorrect returns are based on the behaviour giving rise to the inaccuracy, and where errors have been made after taking reasonable care, no penalty is charged. Where an employer fails to take reasonable care the penalty can be up to 30% of the potential lost revenue, but the system allows substantial discounts for disclosing the errors to HMRC in full. Penalties for dishonesty are considerably higher.

(13)   If your company failed to pay national insurance contributions because you had been fraudulent or negligent, you, as a director of the company, could be held personally liable for the failure. It is essential that you make sure that the payroll is properly administered and that all liabilities are paid by the due date.

(14)   As you have more than four people on your payroll, you will be obliged to designate a 'stakeholder pension provider' within three months of starting business, after discussion with your employees. If employees so wish, you are required to make the pension deductions from their pay. You must stop deductions when asked to do so, but you need not accept instructions from any employee to change contributions more than once in any six-month period. The employee contributions, which are net of basic rate tax, are deducted from net pay. They do not affect the amount of PAYE or national insurance contributions payable. Employers are not obliged to contribute to the scheme, but if they do so the payments do not have to be included in the payroll for tax and NI purposes. The amounts deducted from employee wages must be paid to the stakeholder provider not later than the 19th of the following month. If you fail to do so, a report will be sent to the regulatory authority. Persistent offences will result in fines being imposed upon the company.

This is only an outline of the main points of the PAYE scheme, and if there are any points of difficulty I will be happy to discuss them with you.

Yours sincerely,

A N Other

B.   Form P11D

(a)   The purpose of Form P11D is to give HMRC details of expenses payments and benefits provided in the tax year to directors or to employees earning at the rate of £8,500 per annum or more. The form also enables the employer to compute his liability to Class 1A national insurance on benefits. A copy must be provided to employees and directors to enable them to complete their self-assessment tax returns and, if they wish, to work out their own tax. The form must show not only payments and benefits provided by the employer himself but also by anyone else where the employer has arranged for that other person to provide the payments or benefits. Insignificant private use of assets and services mainly used for work purposes is exempt from tax (and national insurance contributions) and is not included on Forms P11D (ITEPA 2003 s 316). The exemption does not apply to potentially high value items, such as motor vehicles, boats, aircraft, and alterations to living accommodation. The Treasury has the power to issue regulations exempting minor benefits (ITEPA 2003 s 210).

(b)   Form P11D is required to be completed by employers and sent to HMRC, with a copy to the employee/director, by 6 July after the end of the tax year. There are penalties if the forms are submitted late, or if the employer fraudulently or negligently provides incorrect information in the form.

A form has to be completed for each director and for each employee earning at the rate of £8,500 per annum or more, except those for whom no expenses payments or benefits have been provided, when employers are simply required to confirm to HMRC on Form P11D(b) that all the necessary Forms P11D have been completed and returned. (Form P11D(b) is also used to notify the amount of Class 1A contributions due, as indicated in part A of the example at note (9)). The due date for Form P11D(b) is the same as for Form P11D, ie 6 July following the tax year.

The definition of 'director' includes every director except one who

(i)   earns less than £8,500 per annum, and

(ii)   owns not more than 5% of the ordinary share capital of the company, and

(iii) either works full-time or works for a charitable or non-profit making body.

In determining whether or not the £8,500 earnings limit is reached all expenses payments and the cash equivalent of all benefits must be included (computed according to the special rules for directors and employees earning £8,500 or more). Where a car is provided all payments reimbursed by the employer in respect of the car as well as the benefits charge for the car and (if private fuel is provided) for car fuel must also be included (although the reimbursements do not form part of the taxable pay since they are covered by the charges for car and car fuel provision). Only certain deductions can be made from this total figure (eg, payroll giving, contributions to an employer's pension scheme, whether normal contributions or AVCs). For the full list see ITEPA 2003 s 218(4).

A third party who has provided expenses payments or benefits to an employee or director other than by arrangement with the employer must provide details of the cash equivalents to the employee/director by 6 July following the end of the tax year. This does not apply to corporate hospitality unless the provision was in return for services rendered by the employee/director or the provision was directly or indirectly procured by the employer, or by someone connected with him. Nor does it apply to gifts costing not more than £250 in total from the same donor (ITEPA 2003 s 324). Taxable third party benefits not arranged by the employer are subject to a Class 1A national insurance liability that is payable by the provider. Tips and items included in a Taxed Award Scheme are also excluded, although they are taxable. (Under the Taxed Award Scheme the third party is already required to provide information to the employee – see explanatory note 8.) The third party does not have to provide information to HMRC unless required to complete a return under TMA 1970 s 15 or the Class 1A charge arises on third party benefits.

(c)   The major contents of Form P11D are details of the provision of cars and car fuel for private use, beneficial loans, relocation expenses, excess mileage allowances for use of the employee's own car (see Example 9 explanatory note 20), vans made available for private use, private medical etc treatment and insurance, general expenses allowances for business travel, travelling and subsistence, entertainment, home telephone benefits, subscriptions, services supplied, vouchers and credit cards, assets given or transferred to the director/employee, or placed at his disposal, taxable nursery provision and educational assistance, provision of living accommodation, and income tax paid for a director and not deducted from his wages. Except where HMRC have given a dispensation (see part A(7)) or the tax liability has been settled by the employer under a Taxed Award Scheme or by a PAYE Settlement Agreement (see explanatory note 9), all other expenses payments and benefits must also be shown, including payments made on the employee's behalf and not repaid.

Payments include those made by credit card or any other means. HMRC's view is that the figures quoted must include value added tax where appropriate. Dispensations would most commonly be given for travelling and subsistence expenses, professional subscriptions and entertainment.

Employers must calculate and show on the form the cash equivalent of all the benefits. The amounts reported by the employer do not take into account any reduction for allowable expenses, for which the employee must make his own claims (see below). Employers may obtain from HMRC optional working sheets for living accommodation, cars and fuel, vans, beneficial loans and relocation expenses. These are also included on the employers' CD-Rom.

Except where special valuation rules apply, the cash equivalent of benefits is normally the marginal cost to the employer of providing them, less any amount made good by the employee. Where the employer gives the employee a voucher (other than a childcare voucher for less than £55 per week), the taxable value for the P11D is the price paid by the employer to buy the voucher, which may be at a discount to face value if vouchers are bought in bulk.

If, unusually, an asset given to an employee is worth more second-hand than it cost the employer to buy it, the market value is taxed instead of the cost. If the asset has already been used in the business and has depreciated (eg, a car), the second-hand value is taken as the cash equivalent.

The cash equivalent for cars is based upon the list price of the car and its carbon dioxide emissions figure and the fuel benefit is calculated by applying the percentage based upon the emissions figure to £16,900 pa. A fixed charge may apply for private use of a van, with an extra fixed amount if fuel is provided for any private mileage that is other than insignificant. (See Example 9 at explanatory note 18.)

The provision of living accommodation attracts a charge equivalent to its annual value less any rent paid, plus an additional charge if the cost of the accommodation exceeds £75,000, plus a further charge in respect of running costs if applicable, although this element is limited to 10% of pay.

Where other assets are provided for the employee's use the cash equivalent is 20% of the market value at the time the asset is first provided, proportionately reduced if the asset is also used for business purposes. For computer equipment first made available before 6 April 2006, the first £2,500 of market value is ignored. A single mobile phone can also be provided for the employee tax-free.

The cash equivalent of beneficial loans is the difference between the interest paid by the director/employee, if any, and interest calculated at a rate prescribed by statutory instrument. Loans to buy the main residence are within the beneficial loans rules (see Example 58 explanatory note 5).

If any of the expenses included on the form are incurred 'wholly, exclusively and necessarily in the performance of the duties of the employment' the director/employee may submit a claim under ITEPA 2003 s 336 for an appropriate deduction.

Taxable benefits are liable to Class 1A national insurance and must be shown separately from expenses. For example, if an employer provides private medical insurance for an employee or his family, that is a benefit on which tax and Class 1A national insurance contributions are due. However, if the insurance is to cover medical risks whilst working overseas for the employer, that is an expense not giving rise to a tax or NI liability. If the contract for the purchase of a benefit is made by the employee but paid by the employer, that is a payment made on behalf of the employee liable to Class 1 national insurance contributions (employer's and employee's contributions). It must also be shown on Form P11D and is liable to income tax, but not under PAYE. See explanatory note 8 re benefits provided under the Taxed Award Scheme.

Payments made to employees in respect of reasonable additional costs incurred as a result of working from home can be exempt from tax and are not reported on Form P11D. Where the amount paid does not exceed £3 per week, no justification is necessary for the payment, provided the employee works from home under arrangements reached with the employer to their mutual convenience. Where the amount paid exceeds this amount, the payment is tax-exempt to the extent that it represents a reimbursement of additional expenses incurred as a result of working from home. This can include additional costs of broadband connection if appropriate. Employers may wish to seek a dispensation in respect of higher payments. Guidance is available in the Employment Income Manual which is the internal guidance available to HMRC staff. The manuals are available on the internet at www.hmrc.gov.uk/thelibrary by selecting 'staff manuals'. Paragraph EIM 01472 and the following pages provide plenty of information to support employers on this topic.

Form P9D

The purpose of Form P9D is to give HMRC details at the end of the tax year of taxable benefits and expenses payments for employees earning at a rate less than £8,500 and to provide those details to the employees so that they may enter the amounts in their self-assessment tax returns if they receive them. The time limits for sending in the forms and the penalties for late submission and incorrect information are the same as for Forms P11D. No Class 1A national insurance liability arises on benefits shown on Form P9D.

The main contents of the form are expenses payments totalling more than £25 for the tax year (other than those wholly for business purposes, or for which relief is available, such as the first £8,000 of relocation expenses), payments made on the employee's behalf, gifts (at second-hand value), non-cash vouchers (including the excess of luncheon vouchers over 15p a day but excluding childcare vouchers up to £55 per week), and living accommodation.

Explanatory Notes

PAYE codings

1. The foregoing covers the main features of the PAYE scheme and the requirements for completing Forms P11D and P9D. The PAYE regulations are in SI 2003/2682. The tax calculation is made using code numbers notified by HMRC on Form P6. The code represents the tax allowances and deductions the employee is entitled to, reduced by amounts needed to cover other adjustments, such as benefits charges for cars and fuel, or to avoid too much income being charged at the basic rate where someone has more than one employment. Another adjustment in the past was the Allowance Restriction to restrict the tax saving to 10% on age-related married couple's allowance, but this ceased for the under 75s from 6 April 2009. An adjustment is still possible for those aged over 75. Where the employee has untaxed income from other sources it is frequently deducted from the employee's allowances to avoid tax having to be accounted for separately on that other income. Inevitably, coding adjustments will often be based on estimates and will not result in the exact amount of tax due being collected, so that year-end adjustments or adjustments to the next year's coding may have to be made. In *Blackburn v Keeling* the Court of Appeal held that a loss likely to

arise in 2003/04 could not be included in a 2002/03 code. The taxpayer was a name in various Lloyd's syndicates and claimed carry-back relief for losses to be declared in May 2003.

2.   The code number is the amount of the allowances less the last digit, so that the code for a single person entitled to the personal allowance of £6,475 is 647L. Most codes are three numbers followed by a suffix. For example, suffix L denotes single personal allowance, P age-related allowance for someone aged 65 to 74 and Y age-related allowance for someone aged 75 or older. The suffixes enable HMRC to implement changes in these allowances by telling employers to adjust the codes by a specified amount. Some codes have a prefix instead of a suffix, eg prefix D which is used to collect higher rate tax, and prefix K which is used to collect tax on an excess of an employee's taxable benefits or a pensioner's state pension over available allowances. The maximum tax deducted from any payment of earnings under K codes is, however, restricted to 50%. Other codes are BR, which means basic rate tax applies, 0T, which means no allowances are available, NT, which means no tax is to be deducted and T, which means the code is only to be changed if a specific notification is received from the tax office.

3.   The tax tables work on a cumulative basis, so that the allowances are spread evenly over the tax year, unless for some reason it would be inappropriate for the cumulative basis to apply in a particular case (for example, where a coding is reduced to take account of an increase in a separate source of untaxed income), and to apply the tax tables on a cumulative basis would result in a very large decrease in take-home pay for one particular week/month. In such cases, the deductions for the remainder of the tax year are made on a non-cumulative or week 1/month 1 basis which means that one week's or month's proportion of the allowances due for the tax year is given against each week's/month's pay. When this basis is used it is shown in the code, eg '647L Wk 1'.

Employees joining and leaving

4.   The P45/P46 procedure enables the cumulative basis to be continued from one employment to another where appropriate. Form P45 has a separate part 1A for the employee and the form shows a separate figure for the pay and tax in that employment if it differs from the cumulative figures (ie, if pay from a previous employer is included in the totals). Where a new employee does not produce Form P45, then the employer must fill in a Form P46 and ask the employee to certify

(a)   that this is his first job since 6 April and he has not drawn taxable jobseeker's allowance or taxable incapacity benefit or a state or occupational pension, or

(b)   that the employment is now his only job but he has had another job since 6 April or has received taxable JSA or incapacity benefit, but does not receive a pension of any kind, or

(c)   that he has another employment or receives a pension.

The treatment of completed Forms P46 depends on the circumstances. For employees who state that they receive a pension, the forms must be sent to HMRC and tax must be deducted at the basic rate (PAYE code BR is used). Otherwise, the forms are not sent to HMRC if the employee's earnings do not exceed the NI lower earnings limit (£95 a week for 2009/10). A deductions working sheet must be prepared in order to record the amount paid, and to account for tax and national insurance contributions as and when pay exceeds the earnings threshold. The Forms P46 must be retained, together with details of the employee's name, address, date of birth and gender and amount of pay. For employees earning more than the lower earnings limit, Forms P46 are sent to HMRC. Where employees earn in excess of the tax threshold (£125 per week for 2009/10), tax is deducted on the normal cumulative basis for type (a) cases and on a week 1 or month 1 basis for type (b) cases, using code 647L W1/M1 until a code number is received. Employees paid between the NIC threshold and the tax threshold will be liable to national insurance contributions, but no tax until the tax threshold is reached.

If the employee does not complete any of the statements on Form P46, then the form as completed by the employer is sent to HMRC and tax deducted at basic rate until further instructions are received. National insurance contributions are only operated once the NIC threshold (£110 per week for 2009/10) is reached.

Where an employee is retiring on a pension paid by the employer, the employer completes Form P46(Pen) instead of Form P45, sending it to HMRC (normally by electronic transmission) and giving the employee a copy. Tax on the pension is then deducted using the existing code but on a week 1/month 1 basis until further instructions are received.

Accounting for PAYE

5. Employers do not have to use the deductions working sheets and year end Forms P14 supplied by HMRC, and may use their own approved substitutes for either or both. The substitutes can be in the form of computerised records, and employers may transmit information online (see part A note (11) of the example).

6. Employers who expect their average total monthly payment for PAYE, national insurance and student loan deductions (and taking into account sub-contractors' deductions for those in the construction industry where appropriate), to be less than £1,500 may pay quarterly, 14 days after 5 July, 5 October, 5 January and 5 April, instead of monthly. New employers must notify HMRC accordingly but existing employers need not do so unless they receive a demand from the Accounts Office (SI 2003/2682).

Car and car fuel provision

7. The calculation and treatment of benefits in kind for directors and employees earning £8,500 or more is dealt with in detail in Example 9. Where employees are provided with cars and/or fuel, or car/fuel provision is withdrawn, employers have to provide details to HMRC on Form P46(Car) within 28 days after each quarter to 5 July, 5 October, 5 January and 5 April. For company cars and fuel details see Example 10.

Taxed Award Schemes

8. Where employers or third parties have entered into a 'Taxed Award Scheme' with HMRC, under which the scheme providers agree to pay the tax on non-cash incentive awards at either basic rate or basic and higher rate, certificates showing the entries to be made in tax returns are given to employees by scheme providers separately from Forms P11D, and relevant information is also provided separately to HMRC. Class 1 national insurance contributions are payable on the tax paid by scheme providers, but not on the prizes themselves. Where the benefits are provided by a third party, Class 1A rather than Class 1 contributions are payable. Where the employer has not arranged for the awards to be provided, the third party *must* pay both the Class 1A contributions and the associated tax.

PAYE Settlement Agreements (PSAs)

9. Some employers enter into PAYE settlement agreements (PSAs) with HMRC under which they pay a lump sum to cover the tax liability of their employees on expenses and benefits that are minor or irregular, or where it would be impracticable to apply PAYE (for example where benefits are shared) (ITEPA 2003 ss 703–707). Items covered by the PSA need not be shown on Forms P35, P14, P11D and P9D, nor are they shown on employees' tax returns. Once a PSA has been negotiated with HMRC, it may be renewed annually for later years, subject to adjustment for changed circumstances. The employer's payment under the PSA is due by 19 October (22 October for e-payment) following the end of the tax year. Class 1B national insurance contributions are payable for 2009/10 at 12.8% on the benefits etc taxed under the PSA, to the extent that there would have been a national insurance liability under Class 1 or Class 1A. In addition a Class 1B liability of 12.8% is due on the

tax payable under a PSA (SSCBA 1992 s 10A and SI 2001/1004 regs 41, 42). The Class 1B contributions are payable by employers at the same time as they pay the tax on the PSAs.

Items included in a PSA are not part of the income reportable on the employee's self-assessment tax return and the national insurance contributions are not credited to the employee's account.

Interest is charged on overdue tax and Class 1B contributions from the 19 October (22 October for e-payers) due date.

Penalties for late and incorrect employer returns

10.   Employers need to be fully aware of the requirements of the PAYE scheme, because there are penalties for late filing of year-end forms, and interest is charged where the tax and national insurance due for a tax year has not been received by HMRC by 19 April or 22 April if paid electronically (SI 2003/2682 reg 82). Interest on Class 1A contributions runs from the day after the 19 July (or 22 July for e-payers) due date (see part A note (9) of the example). See note 9 above re interest on late-paid income tax and Class 1B contributions under PSAs.

The statutory penalty for late Forms P14 and P35 is £100 for every 50 employees (or part of 50) for each month or part-month the return is late. In practice the penalty is limited to the *higher* of £100 and the total of the tax and national insurance contributions for the year that should be shown on the return. The initial penalty for each late Form P11D or Form P9D is up to £300, and there is a further penalty of up to £60 a day if the failure continues. The penalties for inaccuracies on returns which lead to a loss of tax (or potential loss of revenue) are geared to the behaviour giving rise to the penalty. There is no penalty for mistakes having taken reasonable care, but in other circumstances the penalty will be:

–   for inaccuracies arising from carelessness – 30%;

–   for inaccuracies arising from dishonesty which is not concealed – 70%;

–   for inaccuracies arising from dishonesty with concealment – 100%.

These penalties are subject to reductions when the inaccuracy is disclosed to HMRC. In general, penalties for disclosure when the taxpayer is not under threat of discovery are less than those where the disclosure is made after an enquiry commences. The minimum penalties when disclosure has occurred are:

Type of behaviour	Minimum penalty – unprompted disclosure	Minimum penalty – prompted disclosure
Careless	0%	15%
Deliberate understatement	20%	35%
Deliberate with concealment	30%	50%

The monthly penalties stated above for late Forms P14 and P35 also apply to late P11D(b) Class 1A returns, but based only on the number of P11Ds in respect of which Class 1A liability arises, rather than all P11Ds (due date 6 July as indicated in note (9) of part A of the example). The automatic penalty is not charged if Forms P35 and P14 are received by HMRC within seven days of 19 May, and for P11D and P11D(b) when received by 19 July (filing date 6 July).

HMRC also have power to visit employers' premises to undertake PAYE audits, and as well as the PAYE audit teams they have compliance officers who concentrate particularly on expenses payments and benefits for P11D employees and any international expenses and payments. PAYE audits and the penalty and interest provisions are dealt with in Example 45. HMRC new compliance checks are dealt with in Example 41 explanatory note 13.

Date when earnings regarded as paid

11.   ITEPA 2003 s 686 lays down rules to determine when a payment of, or on account of, employment income is to be regarded as being made for the purpose of applying PAYE, so that the definitions of payment for PAYE purposes and receipt for assessment purposes match.

The general rule is that PAYE must be applied at the date income is paid.

Payment is deemed to occur on the earliest of:

(a)   the date on which the payment is made;

(b)   the date on which an employee becomes entitled without restriction to remuneration;

(c)   the date on which sums on account of director's remuneration are credited in the company's records;

(d)   the end of a period during which a director's remuneration is determined;

(e)   the time when a director's remuneration is determined, if that is after the end of the period to which the remuneration relates.

Any restriction on the right to draw money is ignored.

Normally directors' remuneration is determined by the company in a general meeting. HMRC will therefore treat the date of the annual general meeting at which the accounts are approved as the date of legal entitlement.

Pay in the form of readily convertible assets and tax avoidance arrangements

12.   Under provisions in ITEPA 2003 ss 696 and 702 relating to income tax and SI 2001/1004 Schedule 3 relating to national insurance contributions, PAYE tax and Class 1 national insurance contributions must be accounted for when an employee is provided with marketable assets such as stocks and shares, gold bullion, futures and commodities, assets subject to a fiscal warehousing regime, assets that give rise to cash without any action being taken by the employee, assets in the form of debts owed to the employer that have been assigned to the employee, and assets for which trading arrangements exist or are likely to come into existence. The convertible assets provisions apply equally where vouchers and credit tokens are used to provide the assets, and the legislation has been strengthened to ensure that the vouchers provisions operate as intended. It has also been made explicit that the convertible assets provisions apply to agency workers and to those working for someone in the UK but employed and paid by someone overseas.

Benefits chargeable under the convertible assets provisions are treated as notional pay for PAYE, and the tax and national insurance due is deducted from actual cash payments made either when the notional payment is made or later in the same income tax month. If there is insufficient pay, the employer must still pay over the amount due with his remittance for that month, the payment then being treated as tax paid by the employee (ITEPA 2003 s 710). If the employee does not then make good that amount to the employer within 90 days of the provision of the asset, he is treated for tax purposes as having received further pay of that amount (ITEPA 2003 s 222), such pay being shown on year-end Forms P11D and P9D.

PAYE/NI applies where pay is provided in the form of the enhancement of the value of an asset owned by the employee (such as paying premiums to increase the value of an employee-owned life policy).

PAYE/NI also applies where an employee is taxable on the exercise, assignment or release of a share option, or when a risk of forfeiture is lifted, or when shares are converted into shares of a different class, if the shares can be readily realised for cash. Options exercised under an HMRC-approved scheme are generally not subject to PAYE/NI. The tax provisions are mirrored in the national insurance legislation. See Example 85 for further details. Employers and employees can jointly elect for the liability for employer's Class 1 national insurance contributions to be transferred from the employer to the employee, with the amount payable being a deduction from the taxable amount arising on an unapproved share option (see Example 48 explanatory note 14).

PAYE must also be applied to notional payments from certain tax avoidance schemes. This applies PAYE from the later of 19 July 2006 and the deemed date of payment to tax avoidance schemes effected from 2 December 2004 onwards (FA 2006 s 92 and s 94).

Self-assessment

13.   Under self-assessment, those who pay all their tax through PAYE are not required to self-assess, although if they wish to do so they may require HMRC to send them a return. The time limit for making this demand is five years from 31 October following the end of the tax year, eg by 31 October 2015 for 2009/10 (ITEPA 2003 s 711). If an employee's return shows an underpayment of less than £2,000, then providing the return is submitted by 30 October (or if filed electronically by 30 December) following the tax year, eg by 30 October 2010 for 2009/10, the underpayment will be dealt with by a PAYE coding adjustment unless the employee wishes to pay it directly. Where there is an overpayment of PAYE tax, those who do not self-assess will still be able to make a repayment claim outside the self-assessment system. See Example 43 for the position regarding coding claims under self-assessment and HMRC's power to enquire into such claims.

14.   Even if employees do not have to fill in tax returns under self-assessment, they must still keep records relating to their tax liabilities. Records must be retained for 22 months from the end of the tax year, unless the employee is also self-employed or receives rents from property letting, in which case the retention period is five years ten months. If HMRC enquires into the employee's tax affairs, records must be retained until the end of the enquiry if later than the normal period (TMA 1970 s 12B). Relevant records include Forms P60, P11D or P9D, P45 or P160 and P46(Pen) for pensioners, information to support expenses claims and coding notices. Such records should also be retained for tax credit claims.

Charitable donations under payroll deduction scheme

15.   Participating employers may arrange for their employees to have deductions made from their pay for donation to charities of the employee's choice through an agent or agency charity (ITEPA 2003 s 713). The earnings are taken into account net of the deduction for PAYE purposes, so that the figure of pay on the year-end Form P60 is after making the deduction (but the deduction does not reduce earnings for national insurance purposes). The deduction must be made under a scheme authorised by HMRC and subject to regulations made by statutory instrument (SI 1986/2211).

The employer may deduct as an expense against profits any expenses incurred in operating a payroll giving scheme, including payments to an approved agency to meet the agency's expenses in running a scheme (ICTA 1988 s 86A and ITTOIA 2005 s 72).

For detailed notes on charitable donations see Example 90.

Miscellaneous points

16.   Where someone receives employment & support allowance (ESA) based on contributions rather than a means test, the benefit is taxable. For those liable to tax under PAYE (eg on an occupational pension), tax on the ESA is collected by a coding adjustment. Those not subject to PAYE on other income have tax deducted directly from the benefit by the Department for Work and Pensions under a simplified form of PAYE.

17.   For the detailed provisions on employers' and employees' national insurance contributions, see Example 48.

18.   When fixing employees' pay, employers are required to comply with the requirements of the National Minimum Wage Act 1998 and the National Minimum Wage Regulations 1999 (SI 1999/584). There are also various burdens imposed on employers in order to implement aspects of Government policy. As indicated in the example, employers are required to collect repayments of student loans through PAYE. They will also be required to give paid time off for studying or training to employees satisfying stipulated criteria. Employers who do not either have an occupational pension scheme that all employees are eligible to join within one year of starting work or provide employees with access to a personal pension scheme satisfying various conditions (in particular that the employer contributes an amount equal to at least 3% of the employee's earnings), must offer access to a registered stakeholder

pension scheme if they have five or more employees, of whom at least one meets the conditions to be provided with such access (see Example 38 for details of personal pension schemes).

If a Scottish variable tax rate is introduced, it will affect employers in England if one of their workers is classed as a Scottish resident. In that event, an 'S' indicator will be shown on coding notices and HMRC will notify employers when to start and stop applying the Scottish variable rate.

Help for new and small businesses is provided by HMRC Advice Teams, who will give general advice on tax and national insurance and run workshops to help employers to comply with PAYE obligations. Electronic communication is in the process of being implemented on a mandatory basis as indicated in Part A note (2) of the example.

19.   Employers may make special PAYE arrangements for foreign national employees (known as tax equalisation) under which the employers meet all or part of the employees' tax and provide a professional adviser to deal with employees' UK tax affairs. A guide to tax equalisation is provided in Revenue Help Sheet 212 – see HMRC's Tax Bulletins of October 1997, June 1998, June 2002 and February 2006.

20.   Special arrangements can also be made with HMRC where an employee working outside the UK is subject to double taxation, both under PAYE and by withholding in the foreign country – see HMRC Procedures Manual Appendix 5 and Tax Bulletin of February 2003.

21.   Where an employee working abroad does not pay income tax on his earnings, but must pay national insurance contributions, special payment arrangements can be made – see HMRC Procedures Manual Appendix 7B and Tax Bulletin 81 of February 2006.

22.   Shares purchased as partnership shares by an employee under an approved Share Incentive Plan are bought out of salary before the deduction of PAYE or NI, the maximum amount being the lower of £1,500 pa or 10% of salary. For full details see Example 85.

23.   For details of the employer's responsibility to deduct PAYE on tips and gratuities together with the national insurance liability on such payments, see Example 48 at part (d).

Question

Honiton is employed by International Megabytes plc, and has a gross salary for 2009/10 of £46,000 before deducting pension contributions of 5%. In June 2008 the company required him to transfer to the Newcastle office so that he could supervise the installation of a new reporting system in that area. It is anticipated that this assignment will last for two years and at the conclusion of that period he will return to work in the head office in Swindon.

During his stay in Newcastle he is living with his wife and youngest child in a company house, which cost £80,000 in 1994 and has an annual value of £700. His older children are remaining at the family home in Swindon. The company paid certain of the household bills for the Newcastle house, which for the year ended 5 April 2010 were as follows:

	£
Electricity	530
Gas	710
Gardener	240
Redecoration	680

In addition the company furnished the house at a cost of £10,400. Honiton pays the company £70 per month by way of contribution towards the cost of his accommodation.

The company provides him with a car (CO_2 figure 190 grams per kilometre) which had a list price of £18,600 when purchased new in August 2008. He pays for all petrol but is reimbursed by the company for the full amount, including private petrol amounting to £1,765. For the duration of his stay in Newcastle his wife has been provided with a car (CO_2 figure 143 grams per kilometre) bought new in February 2004, list price £9,200. Honiton contributes £35 per month towards the provision of this car. His wife pays for all her petrol.

Honiton spends time working away from the office, and has a fully equipped office at home in Newcastle, including a laptop computer costing £1,500 which he uses extensively for work, a Blackberry costing £200 used when out on business, and a desk and other furniture in his home office. The company pays for broadband subscription costs on a package which allows unlimited use; the contract is in the company's name and costs £30 per month. Data charges for the Blackberry cost £25 per month; the contract is in the company's name.

Other benefits provided are:

(i) Medical insurance costing £1,480 under a company scheme. This included £300 for additional medical cover for Mr Honiton for periods spent outside the UK on company business. (Mr Honiton received hospital treatment during the year, for which the insurance company paid £750.)

(ii) Meals in the company's staff dining room. The dining room, which is open to all staff at the Newcastle office, provides subsidised lunches at £1.50 against an estimated cost of £4. On the basis of 240 working days the subsidy is worth £600 in a full year.

(iii) The Newcastle office runs a creche for the children of staff. Honiton's daughter, age 3, attends the creche twice a week. The cost, which is borne by the company, is £250.

(iv) During the year the company paid Mr Honiton's travelling expenses amounting to £6,750 and reimbursed entertaining incurred by him of £1,560. These amounts relate wholly to company activities.

In July 2009 Honiton and his family went on holiday to Minorca as a prize in the company's productivity increase scheme. The cost of the holiday was £2,200.

The company operates a staff loan scheme at 2% per annum interest. In December 2008 Honiton borrowed £6,000 for personal expenditure. The loan is for a period of five years with no repayment for the first two years. The official rate of interest is 4.75% from 1 March 2009 and was 6.75% before. Assume the rate remains unchanged for the remainder of 2009/10.

Honiton received an award of £250 for passing the examinations of the Computer Institute.

(a)   Compute the amount assessable as employment income for 2009/10, setting out the amounts on which Class 1 and Class 1A national insurance contributions are payable.

(b)   Comment on any differences between Mr Honiton's remuneration for income tax: for Class 1 national insurance purposes and for tax credits.

Answer

(a)   **Honiton – amount assessable as employment income for 2009/10**

	£	£	£
Salary		46,000	
Less: Pension contributions 5%		2,300	43,700
Taxable benefits:			
Provision of living accommodation –			
Annual value	700		
Running expenses (530 + 710 + 240 + 680)	2,160		
Use of furniture 20% × 10,400	2,080		
Additional charge on accommodation costing more than £75,000			
(80,000 – 75,000) = £5,000 @ 4.75%	237		
	5,177		
Less: Contribution	840	4,337	
Provision of car –			
Car charge 18,600 × 26%		4,836	
Fuel scale charge 16,900 × 26%		4,394	
Provision of mobile phone		–	
Provision of car for wife –			
9,200 × 16%	1,472		
Less: Contribution (providing this is paid as a condition of the car being available for private use)	420	1,052	
Medical insurance	1,480		
Less: re Overseas business trips	300	1,180	
Travel and subsistence	8,310		
Less: Incurred wholly for company activities	8,310	–	
Prize – holiday in Minorca		2,200	
Interest on beneficial loan of £6,000 @ 4.75%	285		
Less: Amount paid (2%)	120	165	
Award for passing Computer Institute exams		250	18,414
			62,114

Class 1 and Class 1A national insurance contributions

Class 1 contributions

	£	£
Salary	46,000	
Cash award	250	
	46,250	
Primary (employee's) contributions		
11% × (43,875 – 5,715)	4,198	
Plus		
1% × (46,250 – 43,875)	23	4,221

Secondary (employer's) contributions
12.8% × (46,250 − 5,715)   5,188

Class 1A (employer's) contributions on taxable benefits

	£	£
Benefits as above	18,414	
Less: Cash award	250	
	18,164	

Contributions due 19 July 2010
12.8% × 18,164   2,325

(b)   **Differences between pay for tax, for national insurance and for tax credits**

Pay for national insurance purposes is broadly the same as pay for income tax, but the main difference is that it is taken before deducting the employee's occupational pension contributions and charitable payments under the payroll giving scheme. Employee contributions to personal or stakeholder pension plans are deducted from pay after both PAYE and NIC have been deducted. Payments in kind are excluded from pay for Class 1 national insurance unless they are specifically chargeable under the provisions of SI 2001/1004 reg 25 and Sch 3. These charging provisions also cover vouchers which may be exchanged for any of the relevant items. The payments in kind that are specifically treated as pay are gilt-edged stock, company loan stock, futures, options, certificates of deposit, units in authorised unit trusts, company shares, marketable assets such as gold or commodities, gemstones and certain alcoholic liquor, relocation expenses in excess of £8,000, and *any* asset (including a voucher) for which trading arrangements exist to enable it to be exchanged for an equivalent amount (see Example 8 explanatory note 12).

HMRC takes the view that payments in kind are to be regarded as pay for Class 1 national insurance purposes if they can be turned into cash by mere surrender, rather than needing to be sold, so premium bonds would count as pay for Class 1 but the gift of a television set would not. Cash vouchers, vouchers exchangeable partly for cash, and nearly all other vouchers count as pay for Class 1, the main exceptions being qualifying childcare vouchers and luncheon vouchers up to 15p per day.

Although payments in kind escape a Class 1 national insurance charge except as indicated above, employers have to pay a separate charge – Class 1A contributions – on virtually all benefits provided to P11D employees that are not charged to PAYE tax and Class 1 contributions (see explanatory note 24 about the provision of childcare). The amounts chargeable to Class 1A contributions are the amounts of the taxable general earnings that are outside Class 1 and Class 1B liability and are taken from the entries on Forms P11D. The charge does not apply if the benefit is *wholly* offset by a matching deduction for tax purposes. Where, however, there is both business and private use, Class 1A contributions are payable on the full amount, even though employees are entitled to a deduction for the business proportion for tax purposes. Class 1A contributions are payable annually in arrears, the payment for 2009/10 being due by 19 July 2010 (22 July for e-payment).

The Class 1A chargeable amount includes the amounts of the car and car fuel benefits that are charged to income tax for employees' private use. Class 1A contributions are similarly payable on the flat-rate taxable amounts for private use of employer-provided vans and fuel in such vans.

If an employer provides private fuel for an employee's own car or van, Class 1A rather than Class 1 contributions are payable if the employer provides the fuel directly, or pays for it by way of credit card, agency card, etc, providing the fact that the fuel was being bought on behalf of the employer was explained in advance so that the contract for the purchase is made between the employer (with the employee acting as his agent) and the supplier. There is no reduction in the chargeable amount for business use. If the employee buys the fuel personally and reclaims the cost, Class 1 employer's and employee's contributions are payable on the full amount, except to the extent that records are available to identify the business mileage. Instead of paying for private and business fuel for employees' own vans, it is usually more tax-efficient for a business mileage allowance to be paid using HMRC authorised mileage rates (see explanatory note 20).

Pay for tax credits includes earnings received in the year together with taxable amounts relating to cars and car fuel, readily convertible assets, non-cash vouchers, credit tokens, cash vouchers and any amounts paid to settle a pecuniary liability of an employee. The amount is reduced by allowable contributions to pension schemes and give as you earn charitable donations.

Honiton would therefore include the following employment income in any claim for tax credits.

	£	£
Salary (net of pension)		43,700
Car – self	4,836	
– wife	1,052	
Fuel	4,394	
Award re exams	250	10,532
		54,232

Assuming that Mr and Mrs Honiton have no other income in 2009/10 and that the base year (2008/09) income was more than £54,232 their entitlement to a family element of CTC would be:

	£	£
Family element		545
Restricted by		
Income	54,232	
Income threshold	50,000	
6.67% ×	4,232	282
		263

providing that they completed their annual review by 31 July 2009.

(See Example 7 for further details of income for Tax Credits.)

Explanatory Notes

Assessable income

1.   The tax charge under ITEPA 2003 covers earnings from employment and also pensions, both from employers and from the State, and some other social security benefits.

Taxable social security benefits include:

- Bereavement allowance
- Carer's allowance
- Incapacity benefit and contributory employment & support allowance
- Income support
- Jobseeker's allowance
- Statutory adoption pay   }
- Statutory maternity pay   }   Taxable whether paid through payroll by the employer or paid by the DWP

- Statutory paternity pay   }
- Statutory sick pay   }

Non-taxable social security benefits include:

- Long-term incapacity benefit which began before 13 April 1995

- Increases in taxable benefits in respect of a child

- Attendance allowance

- Child benefits

- Tax credits

- Council tax benefit

- Disability living allowance

- Housing benefit

- Industrial injuries benefit

- Pensioner's Christmas bonus and winter fuel allowance

- Pension credits

- State maternity allowance

- Bereavement payments (lump sum)

2. Employees are taxed on their earnings, which includes any salary, wage or fee, any gratuity or other profit or benefit of any kind (ITEPA 2003 s 62). To be earnings from the employment, the remuneration must be in return for the employee 'acting as or being an employee' (*Hochstrasser v Mayes*, HL 1959). It broadly means something that is a reward for services rendered in the employment, but the case of *Hamblett v Godfrey* (1986) showed that the test is wider, and covered payments made to employees at GCHQ Cheltenham to compensate them for giving up their right to be in a trade union, because the rights were connected with the employer/employee relationship. The related Special Commissioners cases of *Boothe v Bye* and *Wilson v Bye* in 1995 held that payments to retain two directors as employees to the date the company was sold were from their employments. In *White v IRC SpC 357* in January 2003, housing allowance paid outside the employee's contractual terms was held to be from the employment. (A payment to compensate an employee for loss of rights under a share option scheme on his ceasing to be eligible following a management buy-out was, however, held to be not taxable in *Wilcock v Eve* 1994, although this decision has been overtaken by a change in the law – see ITEPA 2003 Part 7 Chapter 5.)

A payment by the employer for a debt for which the employee is legally responsible (referred to as meeting a pecuniary liability of the employee) counts as pay both for tax and national insurance. Class 1 national insurance contributions are payable at the time of payment, but tax is not deducted under PAYE (which only applies on payments made directly to the employee) and the payments are reported on Forms P11D and P9D at the year-end (see Example 8 part B). This rule applies to payments for home telephone bills if the *employee* is the subscriber, unless the employer does no more than meet the cost of business calls excluding rental. It does not apply if the *employer* is the subscriber. In either case there would be a charge on P11D employees (see explanatory notes 11 and 12), subject to a claim for a deduction for the cost of the business calls. Where there is no Class 1 charge (ie, the employer is the subscriber) there will be a Class 1A charge on the full amount of the bill, unless the telephone is only available for business use.

3. Where employees receive commissions and discounts from their employers, the commissions count as pay even if paid to or passed on to the customer or invested for the customer's benefit. HMRC have, however, stated that where the transaction is at arm's length and is a normal part of the employer's business, the employee will usually be able to claim a deduction under the 'wholly, exclusively and necessarily' expenses rule (see explanatory note 5). Commissions on employees' own transactions also count as pay, unless the same commissions are available to the general public. Discounted prices for an employee's own transactions as distinct from commission sacrifices do not normally result in a

tax charge, but if the cost to the employer exceeds the price paid, P11D employees are charged to tax on the excess. 'Cashbacks' as inducements to employees to enter into transactions are not taxable if they are available on the same terms to the general public. For further details see SP 4/97 (updated in 2005).

4.   The charge is on taxable earnings *received* in the tax year (ITEPA 2003 s 15). Earnings are treated as received on the earliest of the following (s 18):

(a)   when actual payment is made of, or on account of, the earnings

(b)   when a person becomes entitled to payment of, or on account of, the earnings

and in the case of directors

(c)   when sums on account of the earnings are credited in the company's accounts or records (whether or not there are any restrictions on the director's right to draw the earnings)

(d)   the end of a period, where the earnings for the period are determined before it ends

(e)   the time when the earnings for a period are determined, if that is after the end of the period.

Normally directors' remuneration is determined by the company in general meeting unless the shareholders agree on some other occasion to remunerate the directors with certain sums. HMRC therefore usually treat the date of the annual general meeting at which the accounts are approved as the date of legal entitlement.

There are parallel rules to determine when income is deemed to be paid for PAYE (ITEPA 2003 s 686) (see Example 8 explanatory note 11).

Allowable expenses

5.   Certain expenses may be deducted from the earnings to arrive at the taxable pay. The general expenses rule is in ITEPA 2003 s 336, which provides that if an employee is 'obliged to incur and pay out of earnings … qualifying travelling expenses, or any amount (other than qualifying travelling expenses) incurred wholly, exclusively and necessarily in the performance of the duties of the employment' he may claim a deduction for those expenses. For detailed notes on travelling expenses see Example 13 explanatory note 6.

For expenses not reimbursed by the employer, it is notoriously difficult to meet the wholly, exclusively and necessarily test and the quite separate requirement that the expenditure must be incurred in the performance of the duties. HMRC's EIM manual acknowledges the problem at paragraph 31637 'because the general rule for employee expenses is extremely restrictive it is tempting to conclude that no expense could ever be deductible'. It later states 'however the rule is intended to permit some deductions' but does not give any indication what they might be.

Numerous cases have failed to obtain a deduction under this section including *Fitzpatrick v CIR* and *Smith v Abbott* (1994) which involved journalists buying competitors' newspapers and more recently the case of *Hinsley v HMRC* (SpC 569) in which an airline pilot was obliged to reimburse his training costs when he left the company's employment.

After the Special Commissioner's decision in favour of HMRC in *Consultant Psychiatrist v Revenue and Customs Commissioners* (SpC 557) 2006, HMRC have updated their Employment Income Manual. The case involved a psychiatrist employed by an NHS trust who claimed a deduction under ITEPA 2003 s 336 for training in an area that was desirable for her professional development and necessary for her continuing professional development. Paragraph EIM 32530 has been extended to include 'no deduction is due for the costs of continuing professional education. That is so even if participation in such activities is compulsory, and failure to do so may lead to the employee losing his or her professional qualifications, and/or their job. Continuing professional education is not a duty of the employment for the purpose of section 336.' This analysis does not accord with the Special Commissioner's decision, which was that the claim failed because the employee was not performing any duties under her contract when undergoing the training, a point that turned on the contractual situation of the individual concerned. An exemption would also have been due if the work-related training had been funded by the employer (ITEPA 2003 s 250).

An employee can claim a deduction for living costs at a temporary workplace (attended for 24 months or less, which is not the whole period of the employment contract), but this does not extend to the costs of spouse/partner or children (ITEPA 2003 ss 336 and 337).

Some expenses that are not covered by the general rule in s 336 are specifically allowed by statute, such as contributions to registered pension schemes, most professional subscriptions that are relevant to the employment (ITEPA 2003 ss 343 and 344), and charitable donations under the payroll giving scheme (ITEPA 2003 ss 713–715).

To avoid unnecessary work, payments by employers in respect of expenses for which the employee could obtain a deduction are not normally treated as pay under the PAYE scheme, so that the employee does not have to make an expenses claim, but there are special rules for those earning £8,500 per annum or more and for directors (see below at explanatory note 11 onwards).

Provision of living accommodation

6.   The annual value of accommodation provided for an employee is specifically chargeable to tax (less any rent paid), no matter how little he earns, except where it is provided in the performance of his duties (ITEPA 2003 s 99). This exception does not apply to a director unless he owns not more than 5% of the ordinary share capital and either works full-time or works for a charitable or non-profit making company. If the employer pays the employee's council tax and water charges, the payments count as taxable benefits unless the accommodation is within the s 99 rules for job-related accommodation, in which case the payments escape tax (ITEPA s 314) and also national insurance contributions (SI 2001/1004 Sch 3 Part VIII para 10).

Where the cost of the accommodation provided exceeds £75,000 an additional charge is made, even if the employee escapes the annual value charge by paying rent to cover it. The additional charge is calculated as follows:

Cost plus improvements less £75,000 @ beneficial loan interest rate at *beginning* of tax year (6 April 2009 – 4.75% as used in the example).

If the employee is paying rent in excess of the annual value of the property, the excess reduces the additional charge. Employees exempt from the charge on annual value because the accommodation is job-related are also exempt from the additional charge. (S 99 disapplies the whole of Chapter 5 of Part 3 of ITEPA 2003 which includes the additional charge.)

Both the charge on annual value and the additional charge are scaled down pro rata if the accommodation is provided for only part of the year, and are also reduced to the extent that part of the property is used exclusively for business.

Annual values for UK properties are based on rateable values, even though domestic rates have been abolished. However, this is only HMRC practice as the legislation strictly assesses the market rent for the first £75,000 of value. Where no annual value is available, or where there is a material change of circumstances, employers should estimate what the annual value would have been under the rating system. Special rules apply in Scotland.

For properties outside the UK the annual value will be the rent that could be obtained for the property let on an annual basis, unfurnished, on the assumption that the landlord meets costs of repairs and insurance and the tenant meets all other costs customarily borne by the tenant (HMRC Manual EIM 11441).

If the employee earns at the rate of £8,500 per annum or more, or is a director, the cost of the provision of services in relation to the accommodation (ie heating, lighting, cleaning, repairs, maintenance, decoration and the provision of furniture) is chargeable as a benefit in addition to the provision of the accommodation itself. This applies even if the employee is provided with the accommodation in the performance of his duties, although in that case the charge for the provision of services cannot exceed 10% of the employee's emoluments excluding the value of those services (ITEPA 2003 s 315) (see Example 58 part (c) for an illustration).

There is specific legislation in ITEPA 2003 ss 64 and 109 which prevents salary sacrifice schemes being used to reduce the tax charge for the provision of living accommodation.

Relocation expenses

7.   When an employee is relocated and his existing home is not within reasonable travelling distance of his new workplace, qualifying removal expenses and benefits are exempt up to a maximum of £8,000 per move so long as they are paid or provided in the period from the date of the job change to the end of the next following tax year (or the end of a later tax year if HMRC grant an extension). Allowable expenses include expenses of disposing of the old property and buying another, removal expenses, providing replacement domestic goods, travelling and subsistence (including temporary accommodation), and bridging loan expenses (ITEPA 2003 Part 4 Chapter 7). A payment to an employee to compensate him for a fall in value when he sells his home does not qualify and is fully taxable. The company house in Newcastle is Honiton's permanent location for the duration of his assignment, rather than temporary accommodation while he seeks a permanent home, and it does not therefore qualify under the relocation expenses provisions. If Honiton had incurred expenses in moving to the Newcastle house they would have qualified up to the £8,000 limit.

Where an employee sells his home to the employer or to a relocation company on terms that give him the right to share in any later surplus, there would be a taxable benefit if the value of that right plus the amount initially paid to the employee exceed the open market value of the property.

Employers do not have to operate PAYE on qualifying relocation payments, but qualifying expenses payments and benefits in excess of £8,000, and all non-qualifying expenses and benefits, must be reported on year-end P11D returns. The taxable benefit is liable to Class 1A national insurance contributions for P11D employees where the employer provides the benefit (such as a bridging loan) and Class 1 where the employer reimburses a cost incurred by the employee. Both PAYE and Class 1 national insurance contributions are payable on non-qualifying expenses payments.

For the capital gains treatment where an employee sells his home to a relocation company see Example 81 explanatory note 14.

Employee liability insurance etc

8.   The cost of employee liability insurance, professional indemnity insurance and work-related uninsured liabilities is not a taxable benefit if paid by the employer and is an allowable expense if paid by the employee (ITEPA 2003 s 346). National insurance contributions are not payable on such benefits. Relief can continue for six years after the year in which the employment ceased (ITEPA 2003 ss 555–564).

Vouchers

9.   Cash vouchers are treated as pay and are chargeable to tax (and Class 1 national insurance contributions) at the time of receipt (ITEPA 2003 s 81). Non-cash vouchers (other than certain childcare vouchers – see explanatory note 24 below) are also treated as pay, but are dealt with by year-end notification on Forms P11D/P9D (except where they are used in connection with the provision of assets that can be readily converted into cash, in which case they are also charged to tax and Class 1 national insurance contributions under PAYE – see Example 8 explanatory note 12).

The benefit is the cost of the voucher plus the cost of the goods and services for which it may be exchanged (ITEPA 2003 s 87). Vouchers are sometimes used in connection with incentive award schemes (see SP 6/85 for the costs to be taken into account and see Example 8 explanatory note 8 for notes on such schemes). There is a specific exemption for vouchers used to obtain a car parking space (ITEPA 2003 s 266(1)(a)). Class 1 national insurance contributions are charged on most non-cash vouchers, subject to certain exceptions that mainly mirror income tax provisions but also including qualifying childcare vouchers (SI 2001/1004 Sch 3 Part V). For detailed notes on the national insurance position on vouchers see Example 48 part (b).

Non-P11D employees – salary sacrifice arrangements etc

10. For employees and directors who are not within the special rules outlined in note 11 below, the charging rules of ITEPA 2003 do not apply to benefits in kind except where:

    (a)   A specific amount of salary has been sacrificed for the benefit, in which case under the principle established in *Heaton v Bell* 1969 the amount forgone is taxable (subject to what is said in note 6 re living accommodation), or

    (b)   The benefit can be converted into cash, in which case the taxable amount is the second-hand value.

P11D employees/directors

11. Special rules apply to the computation of benefits of lower paid employees, that is, those earning at a rate less than £8,500 per annum (ITEPA 2003 Part 3 Chapter 11). All employees earning at a rate of £8,500 or more are subject to the normal rules. Directors who do not own more than 5% of the ordinary share capital and either work full-time or work for a charitable or non-profit making company are subject to the special rules if they earn less than £8,500 per annum. All other directors are included in the normal rules whatever they earn (ITEPA 2003 s 216).

    Earnings for the purpose of the £8,500 rule are calculated inclusive of expenses payments and benefits and *before* deducting any allowable expenses other than employees' contributions to the employer's pension scheme and some other reliefs (ITEPA 2003 s 218).

    The expenses payments made by an employer for his employee are notified annually to HMRC on Form P11D (see Example 8). Employers may ask HMRC to grant a dispensation (notice of nil liability) under ITEPA 2003 s 65 in relation to expenses that would be allowable under the ITEPA 2003 s 336 'wholly, exclusively and necessarily' rule or other rules allowing deductions from employment income. If the dispensation is granted the expenses do not have to be shown on the Form P11D, so that they are not treated as pay. Dispensations are most frequently given for travelling and subsistence expenses, professional subscriptions and entertainment. They do not apply to a particular employee if the effect would be to reduce the employee's earnings below the £8,500 limit. Dispensations are also effective for national insurance contributions. Forms P11D do not need to show items covered by a PAYE settlement agreement (see Example 8 explanatory note 9), nor details of non-cash incentives under 'Taxed Award Schemes', to which special provisions apply (see Example 8 explanatory note 8). No entries are required for mileage allowance payments that do not exceed the statutory limits (see explanatory note 20).

    See Example 8 explanatory note 14 for the record-keeping responsibilities of employees under self-assessment.

12. Virtually all benefits received are chargeable to tax as earnings, but the employee/director may then make a claim for expenses incurred 'wholly, exclusively and necessarily' in the performance of his duties. The benefits provisions apply not only to benefits provided to the employee himself, but also benefits to his 'family or household', defined as his spouse/civil partner, children and their spouses/civil partners, parents, and his servants, dependants and guests (ITEPA 2003 s 721(4) & (5)).

    Benefits consisting of the private use of assets and services used for performing the duties of the employment are, however, exempt, if the private use is insignificant, except for motor vehicles, boats, aircraft and alterations to living accommodation (ITEPA 2003 s 316 – see Example 8 part B(a)). Under ITEPA 2003 s 210 HMRC have the power to exempt minor benefits. They have used this power to exempt any private use of hearing aids and other equipment, services or facilities provided to disabled people under the Access to Work Programme or Disability Discrimination Act 1995 to enable them to do their work (but this still does not include the 'excluded benefits' as given in ITEPA 2003 s 316(5) and listed above).

The effect of the benefits provisions is to treat all amounts arising from the employee's or director's employment as taxable (unless they are specifically exempt) and to place the onus of an expenses claim on him. This is mitigated by the provisions for dispensations and PAYE settlement agreements. This example illustrates many of the provisions. Other points are covered in Example 58.

The employee/director is charged on the 'cash equivalent' of the benefit. This normally means the cost to the employer (including VAT where appropriate in the view of HMRC, whether recovered or not) less any amounts made good by the employee. In the case of *Pepper v Hart*, HL 1992, concerning a schoolmaster who paid reduced fees for his son, it was confirmed that cost for in-house benefits means the additional cost of providing the benefit, ie, its marginal cost, and not a proportion of total costs.

Special rules apply where an asset has been used by an employee before it is given to him (see explanatory note 21) and to the calculation of the benefit of cheap loans and private use of cars and vans (see explanatory notes 26, 13 and 18 respectively).

Virtually the only benefits that escape tax for employees earning at a rate of £8,500 or more and directors are:

(a)   a single mobile telephone when the contract is in the name of the company (ITEPA 2003 s 319 – see explanatory note 19);

(b)   free canteen meals (see explanatory note 23);

(c)   certain computer equipment available to employees generally and first made available before 6 April 2006 (ITEPA 2003 s 320 – see explanatory note 27);

(d)   employers' contributions to provide for a retirement or death benefit, except where insuring against insolvency under an unfunded retirement benefits scheme (ITEPA 2003 s 307) or employers' contributions to a registered pension scheme (ITEPA 2003 s 308);

(e)   the provision of a parking space for a car, van, motor cycle or bicycle (or voucher to obtain one) at or near the place of work or reimbursement of an employee's expense in obtaining such a parking space near his work (ITEPA 2003 s 237);

(f)   works bus services (ITEPA 2003 s 242) and subsidised public transport (ITEPA 2003 s 243) (see explanatory note 28);

(g)   provision of cycles and safety equipment for use mainly for travel to work or for business journeys (ITEPA 2003 s 244 – see explanatory note 29);

(h)   the provision of services or assets to protect the employee from a special security threat, such as from terrorists (ITEPA 2003 s 377);

(i)   the provision of creche facilities to any value or, from 6 April 2005, approved child care or child care vouchers of up to £55 per week (£50 before 6 April 2006) (ITEPA 2003 ss 270A and 318–318D – see explanatory note 24);

(j)   certain entertainment and gifts (ITEPA 2003 ss 264 and 265 – see explanatory note 31);

(k)   stress counselling and outplacement counselling for redundant employees (ITEPA 2003 s 310);

(l)   welfare counselling services available to employees generally (SI 2000/2080);

(m)   in-house sports facilities (ITEPA 2003 s 261);

(n)   the payment or reimbursement by the employer of personal expenses such as newspapers and phone calls up to a VAT-inclusive amount of £5 a night (£10 if outside the UK) where an employee is away from home overnight on business (ITEPA 2003 s 240);

HMRC have confirmed that no benefit charge arises where an employee uses recreational facilities or canteen facilities on the premises of another employer where the employees of that employer work at the same site and use the same facilities. See also explanatory notes 8 and 35.

Private use of employer-provided cars

13. The private use of a car provided by the employer attracts a benefits charge, unless the car qualifies as a 'pool car' under ITEPA 2003 s 167 or as an 'emergency vehicle' under ITEPA 2003 s 248A, or is otherwise not commonly used as a private vehicle and unsuited to private use (such as a Formula 1 racing car, or a hearse). A pool car is one that is used by more than one employee, is not normally garaged at an employee's home, and where the private use, if any, is merely incidental to the business use (see SP 2/96 for HMRC's interpretation of incidental private use). An emergency vehicle is a car made available to a member of the fire, police or ambulance service to enable them to respond quickly to emergencies by taking the vehicle home. Special rules apply to cars used by employees in the motor industry – such as those of salesmen and engineers – see HMRC employment income manual.

    The charge for private use of taxable cars is based on the list price (currently up to a maximum of £80,000) (ITEPA 2003 Part 3 Chapter 6). The value includes accessories supplied with the car (other than mobile phones) and any accessory costing £100 or more that is added later, but not including accessories for disabled employees. Replacement accessories only increase the taxable value of the car to the extent, if any, that they are superior to the old ones, ie they cost more than accessories that are equivalent to the old ones.

    The list price is the manufacturer's, importer's or distributor's list price of an individual car at the time of first registration (including delivery and VAT, but excluding road tax), not the price actually paid. Cars valued at more than £15,000 and at least 15 years old at the end of the tax year are taxed according to their open market value if more than the list price. An employee contribution of up to £5,000 towards the initial cost of a car reduces the cost on which the tax charge is based (ITEPA 2003 s 132).

    The charge is a percentage of price graduated according to the level of the car's carbon dioxide emissions (see Example 10 part (a) for the relevant percentages).

    The taxable benefit covers all benefits connected with the provision of the car including the London Congestion Charge except private fuel (see below) and the provision of a chauffeur (ITEPA 2003 s 239(5)).

    Where the employee makes a payment to the employer as a condition of the car being available for private use, this sum reduces the taxable benefit (ITEPA 2003 s 144).

Provision of private fuel

14. There is a separate additional charge for the provision of private fuel in an employer-provided car, based on the percentage used for the car benefit (see Example 10), whether the cost of the fuel is reimbursed or paid directly (ITEPA 2003 ss 149–153).

    The fuel charge is not varied according to the level of business mileage. It is not reduced by any contribution made by the employee unless the employee makes good to the employer the whole cost of the fuel for his private use, in which case there is no assessable benefit.

    The fuel charge is calculated by applying the percentage applicable to the car benefit to £16,900. Where free fuel ceases to be provided during the tax year, the benefit is reduced pro rata (unless fuel is again provided later in the same tax year, in which case a full year's charge will apply).

    HMRC have issued advisory fuel rates for company cars that can be used to charge employees for fuel provided by the employer (eg, by allowing the use of a fuel card) for private miles travelled in the company car, or to reimburse employees for fuel they buy that is used for business miles travelled in the company car. If the employer prefers he may provide evidence of actual costs and substitute them for the advisory rates. Without such evidence any excess payment will be liable to PAYE and Class 1 national insurance contributions (but the fuel scale will not apply). Failure to charge for fuel provided for all private miles in an employer's car will result in the scale charge being applied. The scale charge cannot apply where the employee drives his own car: any fuel provided for business purposes will be taxable on its cost.

Company cars – advisory fuel rates for company cars from 1 July 2009

These rates apply to all journeys on or after 1 July 2009 until further notice. As rates are updated, they appear here: http://www.hmrc.gov.uk/cars/advisory_fuel_current.htm

Engine Size	Petrol *From 1.7.09*	Diesel *From 1.7.09*	LPG *From 1.7.09*
1400cc or less	10p	10p	7p
1401cc to 2000cc	12p	10p	8p
Over 2000cc	18p	13p	12p

The rates are acceptable to HMRC for VAT purposes (see explanatory note 20). For more on the decision whether to accept free fuel or not, see Example 10(c).

Change of car and periods of unavailability

15.   Where the car is not available for part of the year, the car charge and fuel charge are reduced proportionately. It is treated as not available for any day if it was not made available until after that day, or ceased to be available before that day, or if it was incapable of being used at all for not less than 30 consecutive days. Where a car is unavailable for less than 30 days, a temporary replacement of similar quality is ignored and the same car is regarded as provided throughout.

Employers have to give HMRC details of the first provision and the cessation of provision of cars and car fuel to employees on Form P46 (Car). The form must be submitted within 28 days after each quarter to 5 July, 5 October, 5 January and 5 April. These returns are no longer required in practice where an employee's company car is changed during the year. Details of all car and fuel provision are also required on year-end Forms P11D.

VAT and national insurance on cars and fuel

16.   In addition to the income tax charges, the employer has to pay VAT on the provision of fuel for private use. VAT is not payable on the provision of the car itself, even if the employee makes a payment for private use, unless the employer recovered all of the input tax on the acquisition of the car, or leases it from a lessor who reclaimed all the input tax on it, in which case a payment by the employee would attract VAT. Employer's Class 1A national insurance contributions are payable both on the provision of fuel in a car provided by the employer and the provision of the car itself (see part (b) of the example and also Example 48). The national insurance charges are based on the income tax figures, taking into account any reduction for any employee contributions for the use of the car.

Unlike the income tax and national insurance charges, the VAT scale charges apply to all employees who are provided with fuel no matter what they earn, and no matter whether the car is owned by the employer or the employee, except where an employee has paid for the fuel in full, including VAT, in which case the output VAT has to be accounted for. The VAT fuel scale charges are shown at the front of the book.

From 1 May 2007 the VAT scale charges are based on the CO_2 emissions, now using a table starting at 120 g/km to set the emissions bands. The rates were updated in May 2009.

See note explanatory 19 re VAT on mobile phones.

Cars or cash

17.   Because of the increased levels of scale charges for income tax, and the added burden of VAT and national insurance, it is often more cost effective for an employer not to provide fuel for private use.

It may also be more effective not to provide a car but to pay the employee for use of his own car using the approved mileage allowance rates (see explanatory note 20), although these have not been increased for some time. Because the employee will not have the option of claiming for actual costs this method will be most useful in the case of older cars which have high list prices or any cars with high business mileage. In most other cases the facility to claim actual costs against the employer's profits will outweigh any increase in the taxable benefit in kind for the employee.

Some employers may offer employees extra salary in place of private use of the company car and/or fuel. Non-P11D employees could be taxed on the salary forgone if they are allowed to switch at any time between cash pay or company car. P11D employees are charged to tax and national insurance on what they actually get, either car or cash (ITEPA 2003 s 119).

Private use of vans

18.   A fixed tax charge applies for private use of vans with a laden weight of 3.5 tonnes or less (ITEPA 2003 ss 154–166). The taxable amount is reduced by any payment by the employee for private use.

There is no benefit in kind charge where a van is primarily provided to an employee for business purposes but the employee is permitted to take the vehicle home (ordinary commuting). All other private use of the vehicle must be disallowed. However, the legislation does permit other private use if it is insignificant.

Examples of insignificant use published by HMRC include an employee who:

●   takes an old mattress or other rubbish to the tip once or twice a year;

●   regularly makes a slight detour to stop at a newsagent on the way to work;

●   calls at the dentist on his way home.

Examples of use which is NOT insignificant include an employee who:

●   uses the van to do the supermarket shopping each week;

●   takes the van away on a week's holiday;

●   uses the van outside of work for social activities.

Where the above exemption does not apply the taxable amount is a fixed charge of £3,000 per annum where an employee has exclusive private use of a van. In addition where fuel is provided for private mileage the charge will be increased by a further £500 to £3,500. The taxable benefit is reduced proportionately if the van is not provided for the whole year, or is unavailable for thirty consecutive days or more, or for periods when the van is a shared van.

Where vans are shared between several employees, the fixed charges of £3,000 and £500 are apportioned among the users. It is up to the employer to carry out the apportionment. The calculation for unavailability is done first, then that for shared use, then the reduction for payments for private use.

If a van is accepted as a van for VAT purposes then it will normally be treated in the same way by HMRC for income tax. A twin cab pickup with a load capacity of more than one tonne will be treated as a van. The addition of a weatherproof top over the loading area is treated as reducing the official payload by 45kg, and the load capacity must not be reduced to below 1 tonne if the vehicle is to be treated as a van rather than a car. Car-derived vans will be treated as cars unless they meet the technical criteria specified by HMRC. A description of such car-derived vans is available on www.hmrc.gov.uk/vat/sectors/motors/what-is-car.htm

A van charge is reduced proportionately if the vehicle is not available for a period of not less than 30 consecutive days. If a van is provided part way through a year, or available only for part of the year, then again a pro-rata charge applies.

Where the van is made available concurrently to more than one employee for private use by the same employer then the cash equivalent is worked out as if the van was not shared and then that charge is reduced on a just and reasonable basis to apportion the charge between the users.

Where it is a condition of the van being made available for private use that the employee is required to pay for, and does pay for, that use, the cash equivalent is reduced correspondingly.

Vans qualifying as 'pooled' do not result in a benefit on the employees that use them. A van qualifies as pooled using the same tests as for cars if:

- it was not normally kept overnight at or near any of the employees' homes;

- employees' private use was incidental to business use;

- it was in a pool for use by employees or one or more employers and it was used by employees and not used by one them to the exclusion of others.

The fuel benefit applies if any fuel is provided for more than insignificant private use. It will not apply if fuel is made available for business travel only, or the employee is required to make good the cost of private travel and in fact does so.

As for cars, no benefit charge applies for emergency vehicles (fire, police or ambulance vehicles normally fitted with a flashing blue light) where private use is prohibited except on an emergency call out.

Mobile phones

19.   The provision of a single mobile phone is not taxable on the employee. The contract must be in the name of the company. However, no charge will be imposed in respect of any mobile phones provided for the employee's use (or the use of members of his family or household) before 6 April 2006 (ITEPA 2003 s 319).

When the employee has more than one mobile phone on which private calls can be made, he may choose which phone is to be the taxable phone for the year. The benefit in kind is calculated by taking into account the cost of the handset (which is frequently very low or even zero) and the monthly charges from the service provider. The benefit is reduced by deducting any amounts incurred wholly, exclusively and necessarily in the performance of the duties – that is the element relating to business use. However, no deduction is ever possible for the fixed rate airtime charges, which normally provide 'inclusive minutes'. A deduction for business use is only available in respect of minutes billed over and above the standard monthly charge.

Despite the income tax exemption, private use by employees affects the input VAT that employers may recover. HMRC have, however, announced that input VAT may be recovered on the cost of the phones and on standing charges and also on call charges if private use is not permitted. If the employer charges employees for private use, input VAT on calls may be recovered in full but output VAT must be accounted for in the charges to employees. If no charge is made input VAT must be apportioned appropriately.

Business use of own vehicle, motor cycle or bicycle

20.   Where an employee uses his own transport for business purposes, he is entitled to relief for the business use and may calculate the deduction by using fixed rates (ITEPA 2003 ss 229–236).

The fixed rates are as follows:

Cars and vans: First 10,000 miles in tax year	40p per mile
Each additional mile	25p per mile
Motor cycles	24p per mile
Bicycles	20p per mile

Payments by the employer up to the fixed rates for business mileage using an employee's own transport are not liable to tax or Class 1 national insurance. Any excess is liable to Class 1 national insurance (see below) and for tax purposes the excess will be shown on Forms P11D and on Forms P9D if it exceeds £25.

If the employer does not pay mileage allowances, or pays less than the fixed rates, the employee may claim an appropriate expenses deduction (mileage allowance relief) in his tax return. Employees may not claim based on actual costs, and the fixed rate cannot be increased by relief for loan interest paid or capital allowances.

Class 1 national insurance contributions are charged on business mileage allowances for cars and vans only to the extent, if any, that they exceed the authorised rates applicable to the first 10,000 miles, ie, 40p per mile. If, instead of paying a mileage allowance, the employer reimburses the employee's fuel costs, the reimbursement counts as pay for Class 1 contributions, excluding the business proportion providing this is supported by mileage records. Class 1A rather than Class 1 contributions would be payable if an employer's credit card or agency card was used to buy fuel as agent of the employer, as indicated in part (b) of the example.

In addition to the mileage allowance payment, an employer may also pay up to 5p per passenger per mile free of tax and national insurance for fellow employees carried in the employer's or employee's car or van where the journey constitutes business travel for both driver and passengers. The employee cannot claim any relief if the employer does not pay the passenger rate.

Journeys for which the employer can reimburse the employee must meet the definition of business travel. Extensive guidance on this subject is given by Booklet 490. In broad terms, a journey to a place where the duties of the employment are to be performed is an allowable journey unless that journey is normal commuting, described as a journey between a permanent workplace and a place which is not a workplace. See Example 13 explanatory note 6 for more details of allowable travel.

Employers have to pay the VAT scale charges on private fuel provided for employees' own cars. They currently can reclaim the input tax if they reimburse the cost to the employees, and can claim input tax on the fuel element of a mileage allowance, but not on the part of the allowance that is for repairs etc. The advisory rates in note 14 should be used for this purpose. Following a March 2005 decision by the European courts that ruled that recovery of VAT paid by an employee was illegal, HMRC issued Value Added Tax (Input Tax) (Road Fuel Purchased by Employees) (Order) 2005. This confirms that fuel purchased by employees on behalf of their employer is VAT recoverable, provided it is used in the business in making taxable supplies and is supported by a VAT receipt. This leaves the financial position for employers unchanged, but adds the administrative requirement for a VAT receipt to be retained, although there is no requirement for any particular VAT receipt to be related to any particular business journey or claim.

Use of employer-provided assets other than cars, vans or living accommodation

21. Where an employee has the use of an asset other than a car, van, living accommodation or land, the cash equivalent of the benefit is 20% of the market value of the asset at the time of its first provision plus the full amount of any expense incurred in providing the asset (hence the charge on Honiton for the use of the furniture in the company house). The cash equivalent is reduced proportionately where there is partial business use of the asset, and is also reduced pro rata if the asset is only provided for part of the year. If the ownership of the asset is subsequently transferred to an employee then he is charged to tax at that time on the *higher* of:

(a) The market value of the asset at the time of the transfer of ownership.

(b) The market value at the time of the original provision less the total amounts charged on any employee as benefits under the benefits code of ITEPA 2003 for the use of the asset.

This calculation does not apply to the transfer of a previously-loaned computer if the computer was first made available to the employee before 6 April 2006 or of a bicycle previously used for qualifying journeys to an employee at market value (ITEPA 2003 s 206(6)).

Medical insurance

22. The cost of medical insurance provided by the employer is assessable on directors and employees earning at the rate of £8,500 or more under the general charging provisions of the benefits code (ITEPA 2003 Part 3 Chapter 10). The cost of any medical treatment paid by the insurance scheme is irrelevant. The measurement of the benefit is *what it cost to buy* that insurance. There is an exception for both tax and national insurance for the cost of medical insurance and/or medical treatment while an employee is working abroad (ITEPA 2003 s 325 and SI 2001/1004 Sch 3 Part VIII).

Meals and luncheon vouchers

23. Employees are not taxed on the benefit of free or subsidised meals if the meals are provided for the staff generally on the employer's own premises or in a canteen located elsewhere (but if a public restaurant was used, there would have to be an area separate from that open to the general public), or where using the canteen situated at the place of employment run by another employer where the facilities are not taxable on that employer's staff. (ITEPA 2003 s 317). Where companies do not have such separate facilities, the provision of luncheon vouchers is covered by the voucher provisions of ITEPA 2003 s 89 (see explanatory note 9), but luncheon vouchers of 15p per day are not chargeable. If their value exceeds 15p per day, the excess is chargeable on all employees and is reported at the year-end on Forms P11D/P9D. The same value is treated as pay for Class 1 national insurance contributions. The full cost of the vouchers is allowable as an expense to the employer.

Child care

24. The provision of child care facilities for children aged under 18 is fully exempted from the employee benefits charging provisions (ITEPA 2003 s 318). The exemption does not cover supervised activity provided primarily for educational purposes.

    The facilities may be provided jointly with other employers, voluntary bodies or local authorities, but each employer must be partly responsible for finance and management. The premises must be registered where required by law, and they cannot be domestic premises. In addition the exemption covers another employer's staff, who work at the providing employer's premises, when using the childcare facilities.

    The exemption does *not* cover cash allowances or paying the employee's childcare bills. Such provision for child care expenses is liable to Class 1 national insurance as for tax. A limited exemption applies to the provision of vouchers or the provision by the employer of child care in facilities other than the employer's and in circumstances that meet certain conditions.

    An employer may provide vouchers for qualifying child care to a value not exceeding £55 per week to employees. Such vouchers are free of tax and national insurance (employers and employees). The employer may also pay the voucher provision costs in addition to the £55. The vouchers must be accessible to all employees or to all persons working at the location where the scheme operates. The child only qualifies up to 1 September after their 15th birthday (plus an extra year if they are disabled). A similar relief is available on employer-contracted child care. Both father and mother can receive vouchers to the value of £55 per week under this provision for the same child, even if they both work for the same employer. See also booklets IR115 and E18 (2008) (ITEPA 2003 ss 318–318D). It is possible to combine the provision of child care with equivalent salary sacrifice.

    For details of tax credits claimable in respect of qualifying child care costs and details of when it is disadvantageous to receive tax-free child care vouchers see Example 7.

Examination prizes

25. The definition of earnings under the benefits code will catch a cash prize paid at the employer's discretion to an employee. This is also counted as earnings for tax credits. If the payment is in kind then it will be liable to Class 1A national insurance instead of Class 1 and excluded for tax credits.

Beneficial loans

26. P11D employees who have interest-free or favourable interest rate loans from their employers are taxed on the shortfall of the interest charged compared with the official rate (ITEPA 2003 Part 3 Chapter 7). The official rate is normally fixed for the whole tax year, although there is provision for the rate to be changed if interest rates move significantly during the year. The rate from 6 April 2009 is 4.75%. There is no tax charge on loans made to employees on commercial terms by employers who lend to the general public or if the loan is a qualifying loan for interest relief (see Example 1 explanatory note 14). Nor is there any charge if the total of all beneficial loans does not exceed £5,000 at any time in the tax year. See Example 58 for further notes and a detailed illustration of the beneficial loans rules.

Equipment and facilities provided for the performance of the duties

27. Where provision of a computer falls within ITEPA 2003 s 316, no benefit arises. To be exempt under this section private use must not be significant and it must have been provided solely to enable the employee to perform their employment duties. If there is a mixed motive no exemption is available. Section 316 is widely drafted and would also cover an iPod or broadband use, provided the business needs merit the provision. This exemption will therefore cover the provision and related costs of the home office equipment, laptop computer and Blackberry, which is regarded as a computer rather than a mobile phone. In establishing whether private use is significant, a qualitative approach is taken, to avoid the need for employers to record the business and private use on a time basis. If the provision is required to enable the employee to perform his duties, then the private use is regarded as insignificant.

Where an employee is taxable on the private use of a computer, the benefit is calculated as in 21 above, ie, based on 20% of the cost of the computer (including VAT) plus related expenditure, eg, insurance and maintenance. Output VAT on the provision of the computer for private use should also be charged, based on the VAT fraction of the private proportion of the estimated depreciation for the year. Where computer equipment was first made available to employees generally before 6 April 2006 (including members of their family or household), the benefit is chargeable to income tax and Class 1A national insurance only to the extent that the cash equivalent (*before* reduction for business use etc) exceeds £500.

The transfer of ownership of the computer will not give rise to the charge set out in 21 above provided the employee pays full market value and provided it was first made available before 6 April 2006.

Where the employer also provides broadband internet facilities under a contract in his name, and no breakdown between business and private use is possible, then HMRC accepts that no benefit in kind is chargeable, provided the facility is made available solely for the employee to perform his duties. This obviates the need to monitor business and private use.

Subsidised transport

28. There is no benefit in kind charge on the provision by an employer of a free or low cost works bus service, free or subsidised travel on local public stopping bus services used by employees to travel to or from work, or employer financial or other support for other bus services used for such journeys providing in this latter case that the employees do not obtain the service on more favourable terms than other passengers (ITEPA 2003 s 242). A works bus must have 9 or more passenger seats, be used for qualifying journeys, and must be available to the employees generally. It may be used for limited purposes during a working day without the employees incurring a benefit, eg, to take them shopping in the lunch break.

Bicycles

29. Workplace parking for bicycles and motor cycles is free of tax and national insurance (ITEPA 2003 s 237). Furthermore an employer may provide a cycle (and safety equipment) for commuting and

business journeys (ITEPA 2003 s 244). The offer of cycles and equipment must be available to the employees generally and used mainly for qualifying journeys. Transfer of ownership at market value will not give rise to a tax charge (as set out in 21 above). Alternatively an employee may provide his own cycle for business journeys, claiming an allowance of 20p per business mile as indicated in note 20 above. If the employer pays less than 20p per business mile the employee may make a tax claim for the shortfall.

To encourage employees to travel to work by cycle, employers may provide 'cyclist breakfasts' without a tax charge on the employee. This is available even if only part of the employee's journey to work is by bicycle.

Car sharing arrangements

30. Where employees car share and the arrangements break down in exceptional circumstances (eg, the driver is required to return home during working hours because of illness of spouse/children) then the employer may provide transport to take the employees home without a charge to tax.

Entertaining expenses (including staff entertaining) and gifts

31. If an employee receives amounts specifically for entertaining, or is specifically reimbursed for entertaining expenses he has incurred (such as the £1,560 received by Honiton in this example), those expenses are deductible in calculating taxable income provided the expenses are disallowable in the employer's computation of taxable income (ITEPA 2003 s 357). They are disallowed in the employer's computation of taxable profit and employers who are trading organisations must tick a box on Form P11D to indicate that this has been done. Employees of charities that are exempt from income and corporation taxes need not meet the disallowance test, although UK-based employees of foreign businesses with no taxable UK presence can often be affected.

If an employee pays entertaining expenses out of his salary or out of a round-sum allowance not specifically earmarked for entertaining, he is assessed on the full salary or allowance and may not claim any deduction, but the employer is allowed to deduct the full salary or allowance paid to the employee in his profit computation.

The benefit arising from entertaining provided to employees by third parties is not charged to tax, unless it has been procured by the employer or it relates to services performed or to be performed in the employment (ITEPA 2003 s 265). Gifts to employees from third parties of up to £250 in a tax year are exempt (ITEPA 2003 s 324), unless they are procured by the employer or relate to services that are part of the employee's normal duties. Section 264 provides that employees are not charged on the benefit of one or more annual parties etc that are open to staff generally, providing the cost to the employer for each person attending (including employees' guests) does not exceed £150 a year (VAT-inclusive). If the total cost per person for all annual functions exceeds £150 the exemption can be claimed on one or more of the functions for which the total cost does not exceed £150. For the treatment of entertaining expenses for the employer see Example 15 explanatory note 7.

Scholarships and training courses

32. Although income in the form of scholarships and educational grants is exempt from tax for the recipient under ITTOIA 2005 s 776, scholarships awarded to children of employees are assessable on the parent (ITEPA 2003 ss 211–215) unless they are fortuitous awards paid from a trust fund or scheme under which not more than 25% of the total payments relate to employees (whether P11D employees or not).

33. An employee is not taxed on the payment or reimbursement by his employer of the cost of a training course providing it satisfies stipulated criteria (ITEPA 2003 Part 4 Chapter 4). The provisions cover not only directly job-related training but also training in health and safety and to develop leadership skills. As well as the direct costs, the exemption covers learning materials, examination fees and registration of qualifications. Travelling and subsistence expenses are allowed to the same extent as they would be for employment duties.

Where employees are retrained in new work skills when they are about to leave or have left their present jobs, they are not taxed on the benefit of the expenses of retraining which are paid for or reimbursed by the employer, and the employer is able to deduct the cost in calculating taxable profits (ITEPA 2003 s 311).

Employees on full-time and sandwich courses at universities and colleges lasting 1 year or more may receive pay of up to £15,480 a year tax- and NIC-free while they are on the course (Revenue Statement of Practice 4/86 updated 1 September 2007 and SI 2001/1004 Sch 3 Part VII para 12).

Long service awards

34. An employer may make a non-taxable award in kind to an employee to mark not less than 20 years of service. The award must have a value not exceeding £50 per year of service and tax-free awards cannot be made at intervals of less than 10 years (ITEPA 2003 s 323). Vouchers exchangeable only for goods may be NIC-free if the long service award qualifies as tax-free (SI 2001/1004 Sch 3 Part V para 6) but not if they are vouchers to obtain readily convertible assets or exchangeable for cash.

Homeworkers' expenses

35. Payments by the employer for reasonable additional household expenses incurred in carrying out duties of the employment at home under home-working arrangements are exempt from income tax under ITEPA 2003 s 316A. To minimise the need for record keeping employers can pay up to £3 per week (£156 per year) without supporting evidence of the costs the employee has incurred (EIM01476). Payments over and above this amount must be reimbursement of reasonable additional household expenses incurred, which can extend to the payment of broadband contract in the name of the employee, provided this is an additional cost that the employee incurred as a result of working from home.

National insurance

36. For detailed notes on national insurance contributions see Example 48. For the special rules relating to marketable assets such as gold and commodities see Example 8 explanatory note 12.

Pre-owned assets

37. From 6 April 2005 a free-standing income tax charge arises where a taxpayer has the use or enjoyment of land, chattels or intangible assets previously owned by them or financed by gifts made by the taxpayer in the previous seven years. For detailed notes see Example 91.

Tips and gratuities

38. See Example 48 part (d) for the tax and national insurance treatment of gratuities.

Pension provision

39. HMRC have confirmed that tax-efficient pension contributions will be relievable by employers as deductible business expenses if the overall remuneration level is reasonable for the work done (BIM46035).

Late-night taxis home

40. A member of staff who works late and for whom a taxi home is provided is not taxable on the cost of the taxi provided that the late night working conditions are met and the journey is one of no more than 60 in the tax year. The late-night working conditions must all be met for the taxi to be tax free:

● the employee is required to work later than usual, and at least until 9pm;

● this occurs irregularly;

- by the time the employee leaves work public transport has ceased, or it would not be reasonable to expect the employee to use it; and

- the transport is by taxi by road or similar.

For more information about the administration of late-night taxi payments, and the records that HMRC expects employers to keep, see the Employment Income Manual at EIM 21831.

Question

(a) Explain the method of calculation of the cash equivalent of the benefit applicable to a motor car used privately.

(b) Set out the method to be used if the vehicle does not have a CO_2 emissions figure.

(c) John Hodges is employed by Cecil Ltd. He travels 7,000 business miles and 8,000 private miles per annum in his company car, which he will change in January 2010. His employer has offered John a choice of car from the following list:

Car	CO_2 emissions figure	Fuel type	Expected list price plus accessories £
VW Passat 2.3 V5	223	Petrol	19,905
VW Passat 1.9 TDI Sport	154	Diesel	20,900
BMW 740 (1997 model)	–	Petrol*	39,875**
Ford Galaxy 2.3	242	Petrol	19,460
Toyota Prius T Spirit 1.8 VVT-i	92	Petrol hybrid	21,210

* 4,398 cc

** Second-hand price in 2010 £10,000

Advise John of the amounts on which income tax would be charged in 2010/11 in respect of each car assuming the car was available from 6 April 2010.

(d) Comment on the advisability of Cecil Ltd providing fuel for John to use privately in the company car.

Answer

(a) **Computation of cash equivalent of car benefit**

  Carbon dioxide emissions figure

Where a car is provided by an employer to an employee or member of his family or household the cash equivalent of the benefit is based on the published carbon dioxide (CO_2) emissions figure (in grams per kilometre) for a given car. That figure is determined by the manufacturer using an EU standard test.

Many aspects affect the emissions figure, including the size and efficiency (state of tune) of the engine, fuel used, transmission (manual, automatic, two- or four-wheel drive) and accessories (eg, air conditioning). Each model variant will have a separate emissions figure. For cars registered from 1 March 2001 the official emissions rating appears on Form V5, the registration document, to which reference should be made or on the internet at www.vca.gov.uk. For cars registered between 1 January 1998 and 1 March 2001 the official emissions figure can be obtained from a booklet published by the Vehicle Certification Agency, 1 The Eastgate Office Centre, Eastgate Road, Bristol, BS5 6XX or on the Internet, at www.vcacarfueldata.org.uk or www.smmt.co.uk/co2/co2intro.cfm

The emissions figure is rounded down to the nearest whole 5 grams below, eg, CO_2 emissions figure 187 g/km becomes 185 g/km, and is then converted to a percentage using the HMRC table shown below. Cars are expected to become more environmentally friendly and the scale figures are being progressively reduced. Emission figures are not rounded down for the purposes of determining whether a car is a qualifying low emissions car (QUALEC).

The maximum percentage to be applied to the list price of the car is 35%. In calculating the benefit, the list price is capped at £80,000 (see Example 9 explanatory note 13 for detailed notes on the meaning of list price) until 5 April 2011, when this cap will be removed.

CO$_2$ Emissions Figure – Cars registered from 1/1/98 – CO$_2$ emissions in grams per km

2008–2009 to 2009–2010	2010–2011	2011–2012 onwards	Percentage of car's price taxed
120*	120*	120*	10
135	130	125	15
140	135	130	16
145	140	135	17
150	145	140	18
155	150	145	19
160	155	150	20
165	160	155	21
170	165	160	22
175	170	165	23
180	175	170	24
185	180	175	25
190	185	180	26
195	190	185	27
200	195	190	28
205	200	195	29
210	205	200	30
215	210	205	31
220	215	210	32
225	220	215	33
230	225	220	34
235	230	225	35

* From 2008/09 qualifying low emissions cars have a percentage of 10%. No alternative fuel discounts apply to these cars.

Special provisions for particular circumstances

Diesel cars have a lower CO$_2$ figure than the equivalent petrol models. To maintain an equitable balance of taxable benefits with petrol vehicles (because diesel drivers would otherwise have much lower taxable benefits than petrol drivers who have very similar company cars), the percentage is increased by 3% (but only up to the maximum 35%). The 3% surcharge does not apply to diesel cars first registered before 1 January 2006 that meet the Euro 4 emissions standard.

Disabled drivers who are required to use an automatic car because of their disability may use the CO$_2$ figure of the equivalent manual car and, from 6 April 2009, where the automatic version is more expensive than the manual, disabled drivers may use the list price of the equivalent manual car (ITEPA 2003 s 124A).

If a normally fuelled car is converted to use gas, the cost of conversion is excluded from list price. However, a car designed to use gas or bi-fuels at manufacture receives no reduction from list price in cases where the car benefit is taxed by reference to the CO$_2$ emissions figure. Such cars currently benefit from a lower % rate – see below – but the discounts are to be withdrawn from 6 April 2011 so that the focus is solely on the actual CO$_2$ emissions rating rather than the fuel type.

Electric cars are taxed on 9% of list price and this will continue after the 2011 changes to the other discounts for alternative fuels have been withdrawn. Gas cars have a CO$_2$ figure. Bi-fuel cars have two CO$_2$ figures, the lower (invariably the gas figure) being used to calculate the relevant percentage. Other provisions applying to alternative fuel cars are:

– The cost of conversion is disregarded in deciding the list price for bi-fuel gas and petrol cars where conversion is after type approval.

– 2% discount for bi-fuel gas and petrol cars where manufacture of or converted before type approval (to be abolished in 2011).

–   3% discount for hybrid electric and petrol cars (to be abolished in 2011).

–   6% discount for electric only cars (the 9% resulting rate will be unchanged in 2011).

–   2% discount for cars capable of running on E85 fuel (from April 2008 until April 2011).

Periods of unavailability, older cars, payments by employee etc

A reduction for periods of unavailability of at least 30 consecutive days is available. The list price is reduced by capital contributions made by an employee not exceeding £5,000. There are no discounts for business use or for the age of the vehicle. Where the car provided is more than 15 years old at the end of the tax year (classic cars) and has a market value exceeding £15,000 then market value is substituted for list price, currently up to the maximum figure of £80,000, although this cap is to be abolished from April 2011. Where a payment is made by the employee as a condition of the car being made available for private use, this amount is deducted from the computed benefit in kind.

Second cars are charged at the same rate as first cars, even if there is no business use.

(b)   Computation of cash equivalent where CO_2 figure is unavailable

Cars registered before 1 January 1998 do not have a CO_2 emissions figure computed to the relevant standard. The percentage of list price is based on engine size, but with no discounts for age, as follows:

Engine size (cc)	Percentage of car's price taxed
0–1400	15%
1401–2000	22%
2001 and over	32%
Cars without a cylinder capacity (eg, rotary-engined cars)	32%

A limited number of cars produced on or after that date will also not have a CO_2 figure, eg, kit cars, imports of specialised cars from outside the EU, home-built cars. The percentage to be used is then:

Engine size (cc)	Percentage of car's price taxed
0–1400	15%*†
1401–2000	25%*
2001 and over	35%
Cars without a cylinder capacity (eg rotary engined petrol cars)	35%

* Plus 3% supplement for diesel cars.

† Electrically propelled cars also attract this rate. The figure for such cars will fall to 9% from April 2011.

(c)   John Hodges – cash equivalent of benefits

	List price £	%	2010/11 £
VW Passat 2.3 V5	19,905		
CO_2 figure 223 = 220		33	6,568
VW Passat 1.9 TDI Sport	20,900		
CO_2 figure 154 = 150			
(19% + 3% diesel supp)		22	4,598
BMW 740 (used 1997 model)	39,875		
Over 2000 cc		32	12,760
Ford Galaxy 2.3	19,460		
CO_2 figure 235		35	6,811
Toyota Prius T Spirit 1.8	21,210		

	List price £	%	2010/11 £
CO_2 figure 92 = QUALEC		10	2,121

Thus the most expensive traditional car in the schedule (the VW Passat 1.9 TDI, the cost of the second-hand BMW to the employer being £10,000) gives the second lowest tax charge (£4,598) and the cheapest car (the BMW) gives the highest tax charge (£12,760). The lowest taxable benefit comes from the Toyota Prius, an electric hybrid with ultra-low emissions. It is the most expensive to buy, but it is also the only car in the list on which the employer could claim a 100% first-year capital allowance.

Because 'perk cars' have the same charge as business cars, it may be very tax-efficient to provide a perk car, especially where the emissions percentage is low (say 21% or lower). The provision of a car where the percentage is high (say 29% or higher) is unlikely to be cost-effective. The provision of a business car may continue to be tax-effective if the emissions figure is low (and very low emissions should mean high capital allowances) or private miles are high. The provision of an employee's own car and payment of mileage allowances at the HMRC approved rate is likely to be more tax-efficient in the case of older, larger cars such as the BMW above where the taxable benefit is over 127% of the second-hand cost of the car.

(d) Provision of fuel for private use

In most circumstances, the provision of fuel for private use in a company car is not cost-effective because the benefit is an 'all or nothing' charge that will be assessable in full, even if the employee only uses £1 of private fuel which he does not reimburse. *Impact Foiling Ltd and others v Revenue and Customs Commissioners* (SpC 562) 2006 demonstrates the cost of failing to record and check business and private mileage accurately. The two directors in this case were found to have kept inaccurate mileage logs that underestimated private mileage for 2002 to 2004. In January 2005 the company invoiced the directors for the full cost of fuel for the periods, but the Commissioners upheld the fuel benefits as the directors had not made good the cost of private fuel in the relevant year.

An increase in salary to compensate for the employees buying their own fuel can be at a lower figure than the cost of the fuel purchased. The price of fuel and the advisory fuel scale will alter over the life of the car, but the principle can be illustrated using current figures and rates. In the case of John Hodges he would have a tax charge on a benefit for 2009/10 as follows (annual amounts, pro-rata to actual dates car provided):

VW Passat 2.3 V5	16,900 × 33%	£5,577
VW Passat 1.9 TDI Sport	16,900 × 22%	£3,718
BMW 740	16,900 × 32%	£5,408
Ford Galaxy 2.3	16,900 × 35%	£5,915
Toyota Prius	16,900 × 10%	£1,690

Cecil Ltd could use the advisory fuel rates for company cars (see Example 9 explanatory note 14) or actual costs.

Assuming fuel consumption as shown below, and assuming the price of fuel to be petrol 100p per litre = £4.55 per gallon, diesel 110p per litre = £5.00 per gallon, the position would be:

		Actual cost per mile	Advisory scale rate from 1/7/09
VW Passat 2.3 V5	31.4 mpg	14½p	18p
VW Passat 1.9 TDI Sport	55.1 mpg	9p	10p
BMW 740	24.2 mpg	19p	18p
Ford Galaxy 2.3	27.7 mpg	16p	18p
Toyota Prius T Spirit 1.8	72 mpg	8p	12p

Assuming that John Hodges is a basic rate taxpayer, the salary increase required and overall savings to Cecil Ltd (disregarding VAT) might be:

If Cecil Ltd provides private fuel for VW Passat 1.9 TDI Sport

	£	£
Fuel cost to Cecil Ltd for 15,000 miles		
272 gallons @ £5.00	1,360	
Class 1A national insurance on fuel charge £3,718 × 12.8%	476	1,836
Cost to John		
Tax on £3,718 @ 20%	744	

If John buys fuel and charges Cecil Ltd for 7,000 business miles, using advisory fuel scale rates

	£	£
Fuel cost (as above)	1,360	
Less: business use 7,000 miles @ 10p	700	
Net cost to John	660	
Tax saved as above	744	
Saving to John	84	
Cost of business fuel to Cecil Ltd 7,000 miles @ 9p		630
Saving to Cecil Ltd		1,206

If Cecil Ltd provides private fuel for the BMW

	£	£
Fuel cost to Cecil Ltd for 15,000 miles		
620 gallons @ £5.00	3,100	
Class 1A national insurance on scale charge £5,408 × 12.8%	692	3,792
Cost to John		
Tax on £5,408 @ 20%	1,082	

If John buys fuel and charges Cecil Ltd for 7,000 business miles, using actual costs

	£	£
Fuel cost (as above)	3,100	
Less: business use 7,000 miles @ 18p	1,260	
Net cost to John	1,840	
Tax saved as above	1,082	
Extra cost to John	758	

		£	£
Extra salary required to compensate:		1,099	
Less: Tax @ 20%	220		
NI @ 11%	121	341	
		758	
Cost of business fuel to Cecil Ltd 7,000 miles @ 18p		1,260	
Salary increase to John		1,099	
Employer's NI on additional salary @ 12.8%		141	2,500
Saving to Cecil Ltd			1,292

The calculations are assumed to be VAT neutral. Similar, smaller savings would apply to the other cars considered, even including the Toyota where the taxable benefit is relatively small.

Question

(a)   Explain the tax treatment of lump sum payments made when an employee takes up employment (sometimes called 'golden hellos').

(b)   On 31 December 2009 Gordon Jones retired from his employment with Widgets International plc after 30 years' service, the first 12 of which were at the company's overseas branch. He received a lump sum ex gratia payment of £100,000.

Show how much of the £100,000 is taxable.

(c)   Mrs Baines retired from her employment on 31 October 2009 because of a permanent disability. She was awarded an ex gratia lump sum payment of £40,000 on that day.

Show how much of the £40,000 is taxable.

(d)   Mrs Juliette Brassington, managing director of T & S Textiles Ltd, was made redundant on 5 September 2009. She received £25,000 as compensation for loss of office and was also given her company car at its agreed value of £5,000.

Show the amount on which she is taxable in respect of the redundancy package.

(e)   Gerry Scattergood was made redundant from Shillingford in 2009/10 after many years service.

Upon leaving he was paid a lump sum of £40,000 which has been accepted by HMRC as compensation for loss of office. He also received £2,000 statutory redundancy pay.

Gerry's taxable income for 2009/10, before considering the £40,000, amounted to £27,300, none of which was savings income.

Calculate the tax ultimately payable on the £40,000 termination payment.

(f)   Supposing the statutory income of £25,300 of Gerry Scattergood for 2009/10 in part (e) had included jobseeker's allowance totalling £600, state how this will have been dealt with for tax purposes.

Answer

(a)   Where a lump sum payment is made to a prospective employee, it is necessary to decide whether the payment is taxable under the general earnings rules as remuneration for future services, or whether it represents compensation for some right or asset given up on taking up the employment, in which case it escapes a general earnings charge. These are essentially questions of fact to be decided by the tribunal, with the usual rights of appeal.

In *Jarrold v Boustead* 1964 a signing-on fee to a rugby football player to compensate him for giving up his amateur status was held not to be taxable. The same applied to an allotment of shares to an accountant to compensate him for giving up his position as senior partner in his own firm and taking on employment as managing director with a former client company (*Pritchard v Arundale* 1971). But in the case of *Glantre Engineering Ltd v Goodhand* 1983, a payment to the company's accountant when he took on the role of financial director with the small, dynamic but relatively new company was held to be an inducement to take up the employment rather than compensation for leaving his previous employment with a nationally known firm of accountants. Similarly, a payment by Nottingham Forest Football Club to Peter Shilton when he was transferred to Southampton was held to be an inducement to join Southampton rather than an ex gratia payment on leaving Nottingham Forest (*Shilton v Wilmshurst*, HL 1991). It is clear therefore that great care needs to be taken when considering the tax treatment of such payments.

Sometimes a lump sum is paid in return for the individual agreeing to restrict his conduct or activities in some way, for example agreeing not to leave to take up employment with a competitor within a certain period of time (often called a 'golden handcuff'). All payments in respect of such restrictive covenants are taxed as pay in the normal way, and the employer is allowed to deduct them as an expense (ITEPA 2003 s 225). If an employee makes such an agreement in return for a non-cash benefit, the value of the benefit still counts as pay for tax and national insurance contributions (ITEPA 2003 s 226). HMRC do not regard s 225 as applying where the only restrictive undertaking additional to those in the contract of employment given by the employee is that he will not pursue an action against the employer concerning the termination of his employment (Statement of Practice SP 3/96).

(b)   **Gordon Jones**

HMRC may take the view that Gordon has simply retired, which would mean that the ex gratia payment represents an arrangement to provide a benefit from an employer-financed retirement benefits scheme (EFRBS) and is therefore taxable in full under ITEPA 2003 Part 6 Chapter 2, in which case none of the provisions granting full or partial exemption relating to overseas service (ITEPA 2003 ss 413 and 414) or the £30,000 exemption (ITEPA 2003 s 403(1)) will be available. Normally a tax-free lump sum on retirement can only be paid from an approved pension scheme. However, some terminations of employment of older workers, while really dismissals for redundancy or waning competence, are described as early retirement to save embarrassment for all concerned. HMRC accepts (see EIM15022) that it is necessary to establish the true reason for the termination: if Gordon's departure is in fact a dismissal rather than a retirement, it could still be possible to treat the payment as falling within s 401, benefiting from both foreign service relief and the £30,000 exemption.

If the payment is not regarded as caught under ITEPA 2003 s 394 (non-approved pension payments), the position will be as follows:

	£
Ex gratia sum on retirement – 31 December 2009	100,000
Less: Exemption under ITEPA 2003 s 403	30,000
	70,000
Less: Exemption for overseas service (see note 6(c) (ii)) 12/30ths	28,000
Taxable part of £100,000	42,000

No national insurance is due on compensation payments. If the payment is made to Gordon on the day he leaves the employment and before his P45 has been issued, it is taxable under PAYE at the normal rates. If the payment is made after the termination and after the issue of the P45, the company is obliged to deduct only basic rate tax under PAYE, but Gordon will have to pay any higher rate tax due under self-assessment.

(c) **Mrs Baines**

Mrs Baines's ex gratia lump sum should be wholly exempt from tax under the 'golden handshake' provisions because it arises through her disability (ITEPA 2003 s 406). Unless the disability was the result of an accident, however, the payment will possibly be regarded as being received under an employer-financed retirement benefits scheme, in which case it will be chargeable to tax in full under ITEPA 2003 Part 6 Chapter 2.

(d) **Mrs Juliette Brassington**

The golden handshake provisions apply both to cash payments and benefits in kind, but only if they are not otherwise chargeable to tax. If an ex gratia payment or benefit represents a reward for past services, it will be charged to tax under the general earnings provisions, in which case national insurance will also be due, Class 1 on the cash and Class 1A on the benefit. If it is not, it may be regarded as a benefit from an EFRBS (see (b) above). HMRC have, however, stated that this will not normally apply to a straightforward redundancy package. Unless the car is regarded as a reward for past services or an EFRBS non-cash benefit, therefore, its value will be exempt from tax under ITEPA 2003 s 403(1), along with the compensation payment of £25,000. In view of the amounts involved it would have been more straightforward if Mrs Brassington had been given a redundancy payment of £30,000, then allowed to buy the car from the company at the market value of £5,000.

(e) **Gerry Scattergood – Tax payable on lump sum termination payment**

	£		£
Termination payment			40,000
Exempt under ITEPA 2003 s 403(1)	30,000		
Less: Required to cover statutory redundancy	2,000		28,000
Taxable portion remaining			12,000
Less unused part of basic rate band (37,400 – 27,300)			10,100
Taxable at the higher rate			1,900
Tax payable:	10,100	@ 20%	2,020
	1,900	@ 40%	760
	12,000		£2,780

(f) The jobseeker's allowance of £600 received by Gerry Scattergood, although taxable, will have been paid to him in full, and if he was still unemployed at the end of the tax year the benefit office will have worked out his tax position by reference to his coding and sent him any refund due. If he has underpaid tax the underpayment will normally be collected by a coding adjustment for a later year. If he had started work again before the end of the tax year, the benefit office would have refunded any tax overpaid to that point and given him a Form P45 to produce to his new employer. Compensation payments do not prevent an unemployed person getting unemployment credits for national insurance purposes for the period covered by the compensation.

Explanatory Notes

Golden handcuffs

1. The rules in relation to lump sum payments on commencement of employment are explained in part (a) of the example.

Termination payments and benefits

2. A payment or benefit received in connection with the termination of the holding of an office or employment or any change in its functions or earnings, whether made in pursuance of any legal obligation or not is, if not otherwise chargeable to tax, chargeable to tax under ITEPA 2003 Part 6 Chapter 3. Special rules do, however, apply to the calculation of the taxable amount.

    Section 403 can apply to a termination payment received in the UK by a taxpayer who is neither resident nor ordinarily resident in the UK in the tax year and who did not perform any UK duties in that year. The exemption and reliefs in note 6(c) will apply where appropriate.

3. Tax is charged in the tax year or years in which payments and benefits arise, after applying the reliefs and exemptions in note 6 below. The £30,000 exemption is allocated to the earliest payments and benefits received. If both payments and benefits are received in the same tax year, the exemption is used first against cash payments then against benefits. Benefits are valued using the benefits code, or if an asset has appreciated since the employer acquired it, the market value at the relevant time using the 'money's worth' principle (ITEPA 2003 s 415(2)(a)). Where the benefit is a beneficial loan, the taxable amount is treated as interest paid (ITEPA 2003 s 416), so that relief is available if the loan is a qualifying loan (see Example 1 explanatory note 14).

4. The proviso 'This chapter does not apply to any payment chargeable to income tax apart from this Chapter' in ITEPA 2003 s 401(3) is a reminder that a lump sum payment is not automatically exempt from the normal rules of taxing remuneration. The test is broadly whether the lump sum payment arises from *cessation of the employment or duties*, rather than a payment for services already performed or to be performed in the future.

    If it can be seen to relate to services already performed (eg, the contract of service provides for a twelve months' employment at £300 per month and a lump sum of £6,400 at the cessation of the twelve months' employment) or to services to be performed (eg, the employee is currently paid £20,000 per annum, and he agrees to accept £15,000 per annum for the next five years in consideration of a lump sum of £20,000 now), the payment will be caught as general earnings and liable to Class 1 national insurance contributions in the normal way.

    HMRC have sought to treat enhanced redundancy payments as liable to tax and national insurance contributions in the normal way where the arrangements had become part of the terms of the contract of employment. This was held not to be correct in the case of *Mairs v Haughey* 1993, the House of Lords deciding that the relevant factor was whether the payments were for services rendered by the employees or because their jobs had ceased to exist. It can be argued that the same reasoning should apply to all compensation for loss of office, whether it is contractual or not. It is important, however, that any payment must not be specifically provided for in the employment contract (even if the payment is discretionary), or be part of an established practice on the part of the employer. Such payments could be regarded as made under the terms and conditions of the employment and would be liable to both tax and national insurance. HMRC won the case of *EMI Group Electronics Ltd v Coldicott* in the High Court in 1997 (confirmed by the Court of Appeal in 1999) on the grounds that pay in lieu of notice in that case was a contractual substitution for earnings, whereas in the *Mairs v Haughey* case the payment was a contractual substitution for a redundancy payment. HMRC also won the case of *Richardson v Delaney* in 2001, which related to compensation based on a compromise agreement varying a taxable provision within the contract of employment.

If a contract of employment provides for a payment to be made, or that the employer has the right to make a payment to determine the contract lawfully, if the notice in the contract is not given to the employee, HMRC argues that it will always be earnings liable to tax and national insurance. Where the contract does not so provide, or the employer demonstrably chooses not to exercise the right to make a payment in lieu (see *Cerberus Software Ltd v Rowley* [2001] EWCA Civ 497) and the employer requires the employee to leave immediately, he will be in breach of the contract of employment and the payment will represent compensation for that breach. Care should, however, be taken with the consequential employment law implications of the employer failing to honour the terms of the employment contract. See Tax Bulletin 63 February 2003 for HMRC's view on the tax treatment of payments in lieu of notice.

Benefits under employer-financed retirement benefits schemes

5.   Certain payments and benefits received on termination of employment are treated as benefits under an employer-financed retirement benefits scheme rather than being taxed under the provisions of ITEPA 2003 Part 6 Chapter 3. This applies where there are 'arrangements' to provide relevant benefits, so that tax is chargeable under ITEPA 2003 s 394. Before 6 April 2006 schemes were known as unapproved retirement benefits schemes. Now unregistered schemes are known as employer-financed retirement benefits schemes. Generally, the taxation post-6 April 2006 differs in some important ways from the old regime but transitional rules apply for some former unapproved retirement benefits schemes in respect of certain payments on or after that date. The general rule is that relevant benefits received from the scheme will be charged to tax as employment income under ITEPA 2003 s 394.

The key difference is that the meaning of relevant benefits differs for unapproved schemes.

Generally, a relevant benefit is any pension, lump sum, gratuity or other like benefit given:

(a)   on retirement or on death, or

(b)   in anticipation of retirement, or

(c)   after retirement or death in connection with past service, or

(d)   on or in anticipation of or in connection with any change in the nature of the employee's service, or

(e)   by virtue of a pension sharing order or provision.

For unapproved schemes, only cash benefits counted as 'relevant benefits'. For employer-financed schemes, both cash and non-cash benefits count as 'relevant benefits'.

However, it does not include benefits provided solely by reason of an employee's disablement or death by accident occurring whilst he or she is in the employer's service, nor benefits provided on ill-health.

In addition, relevant benefits (for employer-financed schemes) do not include

(i)   pension income within Part 9 ITEPA 2003, or

(ii)   benefits chargeable under Schedule 34 FA 2004 (relevant non-UK schemes).

There must be a 'scheme' for a charge to arise under the non-approved or employer-financed retirement benefits scheme legislation.

The definition for both schemes is essentially the same and states that it 'includes a deed, agreement, series of agreements or other arrangements' providing for relevant benefits. SP13/91 explained that a scheme may be quite informal. It includes, for example:

– A decision at an employer's meeting

– A decision by an employee with delegated authority or in accordance with a policy

– The making of a payment under a plan, pattern, policy, practice or decision-making process or custom.

Although SP13/91 has been withdrawn with effect from 6 April 2006 because of the introduction of the simplified pensions regime, that does not affect HMRC's interpretation of 'scheme'.

Under SI 2006/210 and ITEPA 2003 s 393B, there is no tax charge on the payment of a lump sum by an employer-financed retirements benefit scheme under the rules that were in place before 6 April 2006.

Where the benefits include a beneficial loan, the amount taxable under ITEPA 2003 s 394 in respect of the loan is treated as interest paid (ITEPA 2003 s 399), so that relief is available if the loan is a qualifying loan (see Example 1 explanatory note 14).

Reliefs and exemptions

6. If it can be established that a payment is not otherwise chargeable to tax and therefore falls to be treated under the special rules for lump sum payments, ITEPA 2003 s 403 et seq gives certain exemptions and reliefs as follows:

(a) Certain amounts received are wholly exempt, viz:

– Payments and benefits for entering into a restrictive covenant (since caught specifically under ITEPA 2003 s 225, as shown in part (a) of the example).

– Payments made in connection with the employee's death, injury or disability.

– Benefits under registered pension schemes.

(b) In addition, the first £30,000 of other sums received does not attract tax (any statutory redundancy payments being included in this figure (ITEPA 2003 s 403)).

(c) If part of the service in the employment is performed overseas, then the following rules apply:

(i) *No tax at all is charged* where the foreign service comprises:

In any case, three-quarters of the whole period of service; or

the whole of the last ten years, if the service exceeded ten years; or

if the service exceeded twenty years, half of the period of service including any ten out of the last twenty years (ITEPA 2003 s 413).

(ii) *If the foreign service is not covered under the above provisions* the taxable amount is reduced by the proportion of foreign service to total service (ITEPA 2003 s 414).

(iii) Any lump sum benefits from an overseas pension scheme are exempt from tax in the same way as other amounts received if (i) above applies, and are proportionately chargeable as in (ii) if (i) does not apply (Revenue concession A10).

(iv) Foreign service means that the employee was not resident and not ordinarily resident in the UK or he was entitled to the 100% deduction for non-UK work.

Legal costs

7.   If an employee incurs costs in obtaining a termination payment they do not reduce the taxable amount. Where, however, an employer pays an employee's legal costs in obtaining the payment, HMRC will not treat the payment of costs as a taxable benefit if the payment is made by the former employer direct to the employee's solicitor under a specific terms of a compromise agreement following an out of court settlement, or if it is made to the employee under a Court Order (HMRC Concession A81).

Way in which tax is collected and reporting requirements

8.   To the extent that a termination payment exceeds £30,000 it is treated as pay for PAYE purposes if it is paid before the employee leaves, and is entered on the tax deduction working sheet and Form P45, with PAYE being applied in the normal way. If the payment is not made until after the employee has left and been issued with Form P45, the payment is still taxed under PAYE, but the employer is required to deduct tax at the basic rate. Class 1 national insurance is not payable on the termination payment.

The employee will pay the whole of the tax on benefits, and any higher rate tax due on cash payments, in his self-assessment, or claim a refund if appropriate. The due date of payment is 31 January after the end of the tax year, eg 31 January 2011 for 2009/10, and interest on underpaid tax, if relevant, would run from that date. Although making the payment after the employee has left defers the payment of tax for a higher rate taxpayer, it may result in increased payments on account for the following year (perhaps necessitating a claim to reduce them because they result from a one-off event), since the balance of tax payable forms part of the tax paid directly rather than through PAYE.

As far as the employer is concerned, unless the termination settlement is wholly cash, or the total value of the settlement including benefits is estimated not to exceed £30,000, the employer must provide details to HMRC not later than 6 July following the end of the tax year in which the termination settlement was awarded (copies being provided to employees to enable them to complete their tax returns). The details should cover the total value of the settlement, the amounts of cash and the nature of the benefits to be provided and their cash equivalents, indicating which, if any, amounts and benefits are to be provided in later years. No further report needs to be submitted unless, exceptionally, there is a subsequent variation increasing the value of the termination settlement by more than £10,000, in which case a report must be sent to HMRC by 6 July following the tax year of variation. If a report is not submitted because the value is originally estimated not to exceed £30,000, but it subsequently exceeds that amount, a report and employee copy must be provided by 6 July following the tax year in which the value is increased. The employer is liable to a penalty of up to £300 if he fails to submit a report, plus up to £60 a day from the time the £300 penalty is imposed until the report is submitted. If an incorrect report is submitted the penalty is geared to the lost revenue, according to the behaviour giving rise to the inaccuracy. A mistake having taken reasonable care is not subject to a penalty. See Example 8 note 10 for more details about the penalties for inaccuracies in returns from April 2009.

Top-slicing rules

9.   Where the income of the year in which a termination payment is received includes dividend or savings income, then although the dividend / savings income is treated as the top slice of income for all other purposes (except in relation to tax charges on life assurance policies), it is taken into account before termination payments (ITA 2007 s 1012).

In part (e) of the example, therefore, if Gerry Scattergood's other income of £27,300 had included dividend income of £5,000, the rates of tax payable by him would have been:

On non-savings income

On dividend income	22,300	@ 20%
	5,000	@ 10%
	27,300	
On compensation (as before)	10,100	@ 20%
	1,900	@ 40%
	12,000	

Without the special rule the increase in tax payable would have been:

Increase of	£5,000 @ (20–10)% =	500
Less saving of	£5,000 @ (40–32 ½)% =	375
		125

Where practicable, the termination of employment should be timed so as to reduce the employee's liability at the higher rate. If the employee's income will fall after he leaves, for example, it would be better to defer some or all of the termination payment to the beginning of a new tax year so that little or none of his employment earnings are included in his income.

Jobseeker's allowance

10. Jobseeker's allowance is means-tested after the first six months and is not payable in any event to those over pensionable age.

   The receipt of a termination payment does not affect entitlement to non-means-tested jobseeker's allowance (based on national insurance contributions paid) except to the extent that it represents pay in lieu of notice. However, it does affect entitlement to the means-tested allowance if the taxpayer then has more than £6,000 capital, and if capital exceeds £16,000 the means-tested allowance is not available.

   Jobseeker's allowance is chargeable to tax as social security income under Part 10 of ITEPA 2003, as indicated in part (f) of the example. In most cases an overpayment rather than an underpayment will arise, because the amount received is usually less than the available personal allowance. The taxpayer does not get a refund, however, until he starts work again, or until the end of the tax year if he remains unemployed.

   If employees are on strike, they may be able to claim income support. Employers cannot make tax refunds to employees while they are on strike. (Refunds would normally be due because no wages would be paid to utilise the tax-free pay the employee is entitled to each week.) Even if the strike continues beyond the end of the tax year the employee will not receive any refund from the employer. The employer will give him a statement at the tax year-end showing any refund due for that tax year and the refund will be made by the tax office when his position for the year is finalised.

Tax Credits

11. Because entitlement to WTC and CTC is based upon actual income for the whole fiscal year redundancy can have the effect of reducing average earnings and increasing entitlement. However, a claim can be backdated by only three months. It may be considered appropriate to put in a protective claim by 6 July in any tax year if redundancy is a possibility, or as soon as loss of employment may occur, to maximise credits. Any amount taxable under Chapter 3 of Part 6 of ITEPA 2003 will be income for tax credits (ie amounts in excess of £30,000 etc) as will any payment for entering a restrictive covenant to which ITEPA 2003 s 225 applies. Strike pay counts as income for tax credit purposes. However, benefits under Chapter 2 of Part 6 of ITEPA 2003 are not included as income.

Question

A.

(i) Explain in the context of income tax what is meant by the term 'resident and ordinarily resident in the UK', indicating the factors to be taken into account in deciding whether an individual is so resident and ordinarily resident.

(ii) When would an individual's employment income be taxed on the 'remittance' basis?

B.

Your client Dance is a British subject who until now has been resident, ordinarily resident and domiciled in the UK. He proposes to take a contract of employment with a UK company where most of his duties will be performed outside the UK. The contract will initially be for a period of two years but if he enjoys working abroad Dance anticipates that on its expiry he will either extend the contract or obtain other employment outside the UK.

He is uncertain if income from employment in these circumstances will be charged to UK income tax and he has asked you to write to him explaining the rules which will determine the position. He has also asked you specifically to answer the following questions:

(1) Will interest on the savings which he makes from employment abroad be taxable in the UK?

(2) If his wife goes with him, and takes up employment in the foreign country where he is based, will her income be taxable in the UK?

(3) If he lets his house whilst he is abroad will the income from that be liable to UK taxation?

Write to Dance explaining the assessability to UK income tax of his income in the circumstances he outlines and answering the specific questions that he has raised.

C.

To what extent is the following income taxable in the UK?

(a) Salary of C Sawyer, who is resident and ordinarily resident in the UK and is employed by a UK company. Some of the duties are performed abroad in each tax year. He is not a seafarer.

(b) Salary of F Aristo, who is not ordinarily resident in the UK and has a permanent job with a UK company, the duties being performed mainly abroad.

(c) Salary of Y D Dandy, who is domiciled in the USA. He has lived and worked in the UK for ten years, his employer throughout having been an American company. During 2009/10 he was given three months' unpaid leave to undertake a special employment contract with a German company. He has left his earnings from the employment in a German bank account to use on holiday trips.

D.

On 1 June 2009 Soames, who works full time for Glasnost plc, was sent by the company to set up their Moscow operation. During his tour of duty in Russia he has returned to the UK on leave from time to time. The inclusive dates of his visits to the UK are as follows:

10 August 2009 to 22 August 2009

11 December 2009 to 10 January 2010

29 August 2010 to 12 September 2010

On the basis of the above information write a memorandum indicating the earliest date on which he could return permanently to the UK in order to qualify as a non-resident for the period of absence.

Answer

A.   (i)   **Residence and ordinary residence**

The question of whether someone is resident and/or ordinarily resident in the UK is always considered in relation to the tax year. The two concepts are quite separate, and someone can be resident without being ordinarily resident and vice versa. By Revenue Concession A11, the year of arrival in the UK and the year of departure may be split into 'resident' and 'non-resident' periods (for further details see Example 35). Time spent in the UK is normally defined, for the purpose of testing residence status in UK tax law, by the number of days of presence in the UK. This is based on being physically present in the UK at midnight at the end of the day, except when that presence is merely as a transit passenger who carries out no other functions while in the UK. For years before 6 April 2008, only whole days of presence were counted for this purpose.

In order to be regarded as resident in a particular tax year, the individual must normally be present in the UK for at least part of that year. Under ITA 2007 s 829, a UK citizen who goes abroad for some temporary purpose is, however, treated as remaining resident in the UK. In the case of *Reed v Clark* 1985, it was not ruled out that such a person could in principle be regarded as resident even though he was absent from the UK throughout the year, although on the facts of the case Mr Clark was found to have been non-resident when he did not set foot in the UK at all during the year. Conversely, a visitor who is in the UK for a one-off *temporary* purpose and not with the intention of establishing his residence here is not treated as resident in a tax year unless his visits amount in the aggregate to 183 days. Having UK accommodation available for use is ignored in deciding whether someone is in the UK for such a temporary purpose (ITA 2007 s 831).

Someone who comes to the UK with the intention of remaining for at least three years, or to work for at least two years, is regarded as resident from arrival, the tax year being split as indicated above (concession A11). (This would be reviewed if the circumstances changed.) If that did not apply, the person would be regarded as a short-term visitor.

A visitor will also be regarded as resident (and ordinarily resident) if he makes regular, substantial visits to the UK. HMRC normally regard an average of 91 days a year over four tax years as constituting such visits. If it is clear from the outset that the individual will be visiting to this extent, he will be resident from 6 April in the first year he visits. If the intention to visit for at least 91 days each year is not known at the outset, residence will begin from 6 April of the year in which the intention to visit regularly to this substantial extent becomes clear, and in any event the individual is regarded as resident (and ordinarily resident) from the fifth tax year onwards.

Any days spent in the UK because of circumstances beyond the individual's control are disregarded for the purpose of the 'regular, substantial visits' provisions, but not for the 183 days rule (SP2/91).

The location of an individual's ordinary residence can be regarded as the country where he is habitually resident. The position regarding regular visitors is indicated above. Those who come to the UK with the intention of staying for at least three years are regarded as ordinarily resident from arrival (although HMRC will review this status if the facts reflect a shorter stay). Otherwise, they are regarded as ordinarily resident from the beginning of the tax year after the third anniversary of their arrival (SP 17/91). If, however, they remain in the UK and buy property in the UK, or lease property for three years or more, or form a firm intention to stay for at least three years, ordinary residence commences from the tax year in which that event occurs, or from the day of arrival if it occurs in the tax year of arrival. An individual who buys UK property, but does not intend to remain in the UK for three years, can have his status changed to not ordinarily resident if this is advantageous, provided he leaves the UK within three years, disposes of the property and makes the appropriate claim.

Former UK residents who have gone to live abroad are subject to these UK visits rules in the same way as foreigners, but it would be sensible for someone who has gone to live abroad to remain away for a whole tax year to demonstrate a clear break with the UK.

Someone who is employed or self-employed and goes abroad to work full-time for a period spanning at least a complete tax year is normally regarded as non-resident from the day after the date of departure and as a new permanent resident from the date of returning to the UK, providing interim UK visits are less than 183 days in any tax year and less than 91 days a year on average (taken over a period of up to four years). The same applies to those who accompany or later join their spouse/civil partner, whether or not they are working full-time abroad.

Someone who goes to live abroad permanently, or for at least three years, without taking up full-time work will still be regarded as non-resident from the date of leaving providing the absence covers a complete tax year and UK visits average fewer than 91 days a tax year.

See also the Revenue's Tax Bulletin of April 2001 for HMRC's views on the interpretation of the residence rules in relation to mobile workers.

Under self-assessment, individuals certify their own residence/ordinary residence status in their tax returns, and HMRC will no longer give prior rulings, although they may make enquiries about residence status as part of an enquiry into a return, in which case supporting evidence will probably be called for. Evidence of leaving the UK permanently could be selling the UK home and buying one abroad. If someone who was not working full-time abroad continued to own UK property, he would need to be able to show that this was consistent with his stated intention of living abroad for three years or more.

(ii)   Remittance basis

The remittance basis can be claimed by UK resident non-domiciled, or not ordinarily resident individuals. ITA 2007 Part 14 Chapter A1 deals with the remittance basis rules.

The remittance basis is only available as follows:

Where the unremitted foreign income and gains for the year do not exceed the de minimis of £2,000. In this case, the remittance basis is automatically available to the taxpayer. The unremitted foreign income and gains is the amount of income that would be chargeable to tax (on the arising basis) less the amount remitted in that year. No claim is necessary, and there is no tax payable in respect of the foreign unremitted income. (ITA 2007 s 809C). The employment income would be brought into charge under ss 22 or 26 of ITEPA 2003. (ITA 2007 s 809E.)

Because these rules, first introduced in April 2008, were found to be unduly harsh in relation especially to low income foreign migrant workers who work in the UK on a seasonal basis and also work in their home countries or elsewhere overseas, Finance Act 2009 introduced a limited higher threshold in ITA 2007 ss 828B and 828C. Where a non-domiciled employee with UK duties is UK-resident in a tax year but does not make a claim to use the remittance basis, which means he is taxable in the UK on his worldwide income and gains, the UK tax otherwise attributable to his foreign income and gains is waived where the following conditions are met:

- he has no more than £10,000 of foreign employment income or gains, all of which is taxed overseas;

- he has no more than £100 of foreign interest, all of which is taxed overseas;

- he has no other foreign income or gains for the year;

- if the foreign income and gains were included for UK tax purposes he would still be a basic (or even savings) rate taxpayer; and

- he is not issued with a notice to file a return by HMRC.

Other than when these low-earner rules apply, where the unremitted foreign income and gains exceed £2,000 the remittance basis is only available on a claim by the taxpayer (although even where the unremitted foreign income and gains are below £2,000 the taxpayer may, if he chooses, elect not to take advantage of the £2,000 exemption). The effect of a claim for remittance basis is to deny the personal allowance, blind person's allowance and the effect of any married couple's or civil partner's allowances. Any tax relief on life assurance premiums, and capital gains tax annual exemption would also be denied (ITA 2007 s 809F). For long-term resident individuals – those aged over 18 and resident for at least seven of the preceding nine tax years (whether or not they were then aged over 18) – the remittance basis claim involves paying a flat-rate tax charge of £30,000 (the remittance basis charge, or RBC) as an alternative to declaring and paying full UK taxes on the unremitted income and gains for that year. Those non-domiciled individuals who have not been UK-resident for seven of the last nine years can claim to use the remittance basis without paying the RBC, albeit with the other consequences such as loss of personal allowances. Individuals can opt into and out of the remittance basis from year to year. (ITA 2007 s 809G.)

B.   Non-residence and income arising abroad

15 October 2009

Dear Mr Dance,

With reference to your proposed contract of employment under which most of your duties will be performed abroad during a two-year period, which will possibly be extended, I give below an outline of the income tax position that will arise.

If you are employed full-time abroad for a period which includes a full tax year, you will be treated as not resident and not ordinarily resident from the day following your departure, unless your UK visits during your term abroad amount to 183 days or more in any one tax year, or 91 days or more per annum on average over a period of up to four tax years (disregarding in the 91-day count any days on which you were here for exceptional circumstances such as medical treatment or family weddings, etc). If on leaving the UK you take a holiday before starting the overseas employment, your non-resident period will start later, when you leave the UK to take up the employment. Any day on which you are physically present in the UK at midnight is regarded as a day in the UK, unless you are merely transiting the UK. If you eventually returned to the UK, you would be treated as a new permanent resident from the date of your return (but not for the earlier part of that tax year). If your wife accompanied you (or later joined you) she would be treated in the same way, whether or not she was employed abroad.

As long as you and your wife are treated as non-resident, you will not be liable to UK tax on any of your income abroad, either from employment or interest on foreign savings accounts. You would, however, remain liable on any earnings from employment duties in the UK (unless regarded as merely incidental to your earnings abroad), on the rent from your UK house and (subject to certain exceptions) on any investment income arising in the UK – the splitting of the year into resident and non-resident periods is relevant in your case only to overseas employment income and overseas investment income, so it would be more tax-efficient to deposit any savings into a non-UK bank while you are non-resident. If the rent from the UK house is paid to you outside the UK the payer will be required to deduct basic rate tax and account for it to HMRC unless you agree with HMRC to include any tax due in your self-assessment. As a non-resident British subject you would be entitled to claim personal allowances against the income liable to UK tax, and any rents would be taxable after offsetting any mortgage interest, agent's costs, etc.

If the nature of your UK duties is such that your contract cannot be regarded as full-time employment abroad, your two-year absence would probably be insufficient for you to be regarded as non-resident. In that event both your UK and foreign income would remain liable to UK tax. Your wife would still be regarded as non-resident if she was employed full-time abroad for a period spanning a full tax year.

I should mention also that the national insurance rules are separate and different. Your liability will depend on where you go and for how long. If your employer is sending you to a European Economic Area state or Switzerland, you will probably be liable to continue to contribute to the UK national insurance scheme, and be excluded from the host state scheme, even though you may be away for several years, as there are special rules for so-called 'migrant workers' to protect their social security pension entitlements in their home state. Your employer will need to apply for an E101 certificate from HMRC in Newcastle. Similar arrangements exist with certain other non-EEA states (eg, USA, Canada, Japan). If you are sent by your UK employers to work for them in a non-EEA state with which the UK has no social security treaty, you will continue to pay UK NIC for the first 52 weeks of overseas work, but then liability will cease until you come back to the UK to work. If you plan to stay overseas permanently when you leave, the 52-week liability will not apply and you ought to consider protecting your state pension entitlement by making voluntary NI contributions, although that is a decision that can be deferred for a few years.

This area of tax and NI law is complex and can also be affected by the double tax treaty and social security treaty between the UK and the other country. It would be helpful for us to go into the details fully before you finalise your arrangements. If you will telephone my office I will be happy to arrange a meeting.

Yours sincerely,

A.N. Adviser

C.   **Taxable Earnings**

(a)   Since C Sawyer is resident and ordinarily resident in the UK and not a seafarer, he is taxable on all his earnings, for both UK and foreign duties, with a UK employer.

(b)   F Aristo is taxable in respect of earnings for his UK duties (unless the employment is one which is in substance performed abroad and the UK duties are regarded as merely incidental to the foreign duties). If he is resident, even though not ordinarily resident, in the UK then he will also be liable in respect of any earnings from abroad which he *remits* to the UK. He will further be liable on unremitted earnings from abroad unless his total unremitted foreign income and gains (from all sources) does not exceed £2,000 in the relevant tax year. If he wishes to claim the benefit of the remittance basis, he will lose the benefit of his UK tax allowances. He is currently not ordinarily resident, but if in the future he becomes resident *and* ordinarily resident, once he has been UK resident for seven out of the last nine years will be liable to a remittance basis charge of £30,000 on his unremitted foreign income and gains if he chooses to claim the remittance basis.

(c)   Since Y D Dandy has lived in the UK for ten years he is undoubtedly regarded as resident and ordinarily resident. His UK earnings are therefore taxable.

As a non-UK domiciled person who is a long-term resident and has a foreign employer, he will only be able to benefit from the remittance basis if his foreign income from all sources does not exceed £2,000. In the event that this limit is exceeded, Y D Dandy would be liable to a remittance basis charge of £30,000 per annum on his unremitted earnings if he chose to claim the remittance basis. This is very unlikely to be cost-effective, since as an American citizen he will probably be taxable on the income in the US anyway, and the US may not give relief for the remittance basis charge. Dandy may therefore be better off paying UK tax on the unremitted earnings, and claiming double taxation relief. The earnings for the German work may be taxable in Germany anyway, unless exempted under Article 11(3) of the UK-Germany double tax agreement. The treaty exempts income from short-term (ie, less than 183 days) employment visits provided the costs of Dandy's UK employment for the period are not recharged to a fixed base or permanent establishment of the UK employer in Germany. If Dandy is working for a branch of his UK employer and cannot claim exemption from German tax under Article 11, he will pay German tax on his German income and, under the UK-Germany double tax agreement, the UK will give relief by reducing the UK tax liability on the German income by the German tax payable on that income, up to the amount of the UK tax due on that income. In this event, subsequent remittance to the UK will not affect his tax position. The interaction of the UK, German and US tax systems will be complex.

D.   Memorandum re overseas tour of duty by Soames for Glasnost plc

1.   In order to qualify as a non-resident, Soames must be employed full-time abroad for a period covering at least one complete tax year. Visits to the UK are permitted provided they are less than 183 days in a tax year and less than 91 days a year on average. UK departure days and certain exceptional days can be ignored by HMRC practice. By Revenue Concession A11 the tax years of departure and return may be split into resident and non-resident periods.

2.   Soames's visits to the UK are clearly less than the allowable 91 days on average and he is employed full-time in Russia. However, he will not complete one full tax year of absence until 6 April 2011. Provided he does not return permanently to the UK before that date he will be treated as non-resident from 1 June 2009 and his salary whilst in Russia will not be liable to UK tax. Otherwise he will remain UK-resident and fully liable to UK tax on his overseas earnings.

3.   Soames is likely to be liable to both UK tax and Russian tax on the same income if he remains UK-resident, but double tax relief should be available under the UK-Russia double tax agreement. Reference should therefore be made to the double tax treaty between the countries, which overrides the normal legislation.

Explanatory Notes

Income Tax (Earnings and Pensions) Act 2003

1.   The detailed rules relating to employment income chargeable to tax are contained in Part 2 with overseas provisions in Chapter 5 (ss 20 to 41).

2.   ITEPA 2003 s 15 applies to the earnings for any tax year in which the person holding the employment is resident, ordinarily resident and domiciled in the UK. (See Example 5 explanatory note 12 for the meaning of domicile.) The charge covers the full amount of the earnings received in the tax year, whether they are earned in the UK or abroad. Earnings of seafarers during a 'long absence' abroad qualify for a 100% deduction (see explanatory note 8).

3.   ITEPA 2003 s 27 applies to UK earnings for any tax year in which the person holding the employment is not resident in the UK. The section provides that the amount chargeable to tax is the earnings in respect of duties performed in the UK.

4.   The charge on *remittances to the UK* consists of:

   (i)   Earnings from an employment wholly abroad with a foreign employer by an employee who is resident, ordinarily resident but not domiciled in the UK (ITEPA 2003 s 22).

   (ii)   Earnings for the non-UK duties of someone resident but not ordinarily resident in the UK (ITEPA 2003 s 26).

   However, the availability of the remittance basis is now severely restricted, as described above in part A(ii).

5.   Where earnings are for a tax year before an employment starts, they are treated as being for the first tax year of the employment, and earnings for a tax year after an employment ends are treated as earnings for the last tax year of the employment (ITEPA 2003 s 17). Although these earnings before and after the employment is held are deemed to be 'for' the specified tax year, they are nevertheless taxed in the year of receipt. The deeming rules simply ensure that there is a taxable source for the receipt when none exists in reality at that time.

6.   Taxable earnings are therefore based on the amount *received in* the tax year (ITEPA 2003 ss 18 and 19, and ss 31 and 32). This applies even if the employment is no longer held in the tax year in which the emoluments are received (ITEPA 2003 ss 17 and 30). Where earnings are received after someone

dies, however, they are treated as income of the deceased before his death. Tax is charged on the personal representatives and is a debt payable out of the deceased's estate (ITEPA 2003 s 13). Note that the Class 1 national insurance contributions rules differ: if entitlement arises to a payment of employment earnings before death, but payment is delayed until after death, NICs are still chargeable. However, if entitlement to a payment of earnings arises after death (eg, where a bonus becomes payable based on accounts drawn up after death) there can be no Class 1 liability as there is no employed earner at the time of payment.

Earnings during absences abroad

7.   The circumstances in which someone is regarded as becoming non-UK resident are outlined in part A(i) of the example. Where an absence does not establish non-residence, there is no longer any deduction in respect of earnings abroad except for those who qualify as 'seafarers', as indicated in note 8.

8.   (a)   A 100% seafarers' earnings deduction (SED) is available to seafarers in respect of earnings during a 'long absence' abroad in periods when they remain ordinarily resident in the UK. The definition of seafarers explicitly excludes those employed on offshore installations for oil/gas exploration or extractions (ITEPA 2003 ss 378–385 as amended by FA 2004, with 'offshore installation' now defined in ITA 2007 s 1001). Following the decision in *Torr and Others v CIR* [2008] a jack-up drilling rig, FPSO, MODU, flotels and various other ships and ship-like structures used in the offshore oil and gas industry may now be treated as an offshore installation, depending on whether they are put to a 'relevant use' while 'standing or stationed' (see EIM33104). Those working on these vessels, despite being at sea on a ship, will therefore not qualify for seafarers' earnings deduction: the SED is meant for merchant seamen rather than rig workers.

       (b)   To qualify for the 100% deduction, the duties of an employment or successive employments must be performed wholly or partly abroad during an *eligible period* of at least 365 days. The earnings for a period of leave spent overseas immediately following a qualifying period also qualify for the 100% deduction, provided the earnings are for the tax year in which the eligible period ends rather than the next following year.

              An *eligible period* must either consist entirely of days of absence or consist partly of such days and partly of days included by reason of the following:

              Where a period consisting entirely of days of absence ends, it may be linked to an earlier eligible period to make a single qualifying period providing that there are no more than 183 intervening days and that the total days spent in the UK do not exceed one half of the total number of days *in the whole period*. Note that the one half rule must not be overstepped when looking at the position at the end of *each* absence abroad. Days on which the individual is not resident in the UK cannot be used as part of an eligible period.

       (c)   A person is not regarded as absent from the UK on any day unless he is absent at the end of it (ITEPA 2003 s 378(4)).

       (d)   Earnings qualifying for the 100% relief are calculated *after* pension contributions, capital allowances and allowable expenses (ITEPA 2003 s 381). Charitable donations under the payroll deduction scheme are not, however, on the list of items to be deducted.

       (e)   Where an employment is partly in the UK and partly abroad, the earnings must be apportioned to arrive at the amount qualifying for the 100% deduction on the basis of 'the proportion ... that is reasonable having regard to the nature of and time devoted to the duties performed outside and in the United Kingdom, and all other relevant circumstances' (ITEPA 2003 s 380(2)).

9.   Where the duties of an employment are substantially performed abroad, then any UK duties which are merely incidental to the performance of the foreign duties are regarded as performed abroad

(ITEPA 2003 s 39). This rule was rigidly interpreted in the case of *Robson v Dixon* 1972, where a British airline pilot employed by KLM Dutch Airlines and based at Amsterdam (commuting thereto from London), who performed less than 5% of his total take-offs and landings at Heathrow, was held not to be within this provision because it was the *quality* and not the *quantity* of the UK duties that had to be taken into account.

However, one should note the cases of *Shepherd v HMRC* (2006) and *Grace v CRC* [2008] EWHC 2708 (Ch). In *Shepherd v HMRC*, an individual claimed to have left the UK for Cyprus and kept his visits to the UK below the 91-day and 183-day thresholds. However, the Court held that he had not sufficiently left the UK in the first place (his work as a pilot was based in London and he retained a UK lifestyle) and therefore he was held to have remained UK-resident and ordinarily resident. In *Grace v CRC*, a British Airways long haul pilot who is a British Overseas Citizen with homes in Cape Town and Sussex was found by a Special Commissioner to have lost his UK residence and ordinary residence after he had spent more than seven consecutive days in the UK on only three occasions in six years, whereas he had done this over 60 times in Cape Town, where he spent most of his off-duty time, in the same period. However, the High Court overruled the decision, finding that, because he maintained a house in the UK which he visited regularly, a fact that remained the same both before and after he bought his South African home, he did not cease to be UK-resident: he merely became resident in both the UK and South Africa. There had been no distinct break in the quality of his UK residence.

10. Another case which has produced a large amount of publicity is *Gaines-Cooper v HMRC* (2006) SpC 568. Briefly, Robert Gaines-Cooper was born in the UK but claimed to be resident and domiciled in the Seychelles, where he had maintained a home since the 1970s. He argued that under IR20 his visits to the UK did not create residence. He maintained a UK private residence where his wife and child lived, because the child was at school in England; he had a number of worldwide businesses and assets but only spent a matter of weeks in the Seychelles during the years under appeal. The Commissioners stated that they should apply the law rather than IR20 and on the basis that he spent more time in the UK than in the other country, he was therefore UK-resident. They also concluded that his purpose in the UK was not a temporary one and therefore TA 1988 s 336 (now ITA 2007 s 831) was not available to him.

The case generated an outcry that HMRC was failing to follow its guidance (IR20). In response, it published an HMRC Brief in January 2007. This sets out its view that the 91-day test (in IR20) only applies to individuals who have left the UK and Mr Gaines-Cooper failed to meet this condition. The brief states that there has been no change in practice in relation to residence following this case and HMRC will continue to:

- treat an individual who has not left the UK as remaining resident here;

- consider all the relevant evidence, including the pattern of presence in the UK and elsewhere, in deciding whether or not an individual has left the UK;

- apply the 91-day test (where HMRC is satisfied that an individual has actually left the UK) as outlined in IR20, normally disregarding the days of arrival and departure in calculating days under this test. However, this practice has been overtaken by changes introduced in Finance Act 2008 s 22, which defines a day spent in the UK as a day on which the individual is present at the end of the day, unless he is a transit passenger.

The case highlights the practical difficulties of the residence rules.

Travelling and board and lodging expenses

11. Certain expenses which might not normally satisfy the ITEPA 2003 s 336 expenses rule (see Examples 9 and 13) are allowable in the case of employments abroad. These are:

    (i) *Travelling expenses* (ITEPA 2003 ss 341 and 342)

Where the employee is resident and ordinarily resident in the UK, and the duties of the employment are performed wholly outside the UK, and if the employer is a foreign employer the employee is domiciled in the UK, a deduction is allowed for the expenses of:

(a)   Travelling from the UK to take up the employment and returning to the UK at the end of the employment. Where the travel expenses are only partly attributable to the taking up or termination of the employment the deduction is restricted accordingly (ITEPA 2003 s 341).

(b)   Travelling between the UK and foreign places of employment, where the employee has two or more employments and performs the duties of one or more abroad (the deduction being restricted as in (a) if the travel is only partly for the purposes of the employment) (ITEPA 2003 s 342).

(ii)   *Travel expenses in other circumstances*

Where the employee is resident and ordinarily resident in the UK a deduction is allowed against the benefits charge where certain travel costs are met, or reimbursed, by the employer. The rules allow for any number of visits to and from the UK. This only applies where the employee is absent from the UK wholly and exclusively for the purpose of performing the duties of one or more employments *or* the duties are performed partly outside the UK and the journey is made wholly and exclusively for the purpose of performing them or returning after performing them (ITEPA 2003 s 370).

Relief would be available both for travelling and subsistence expenses under the general expenses rule in ITEPA 2003 s 336 for an employee who performed part of his duties abroad, whether the expenses were borne by the employer or the employee (see Example 13).

(iii)   *Board and lodging expenses* (ITEPA 2003 s 376)

Where the employee is resident and ordinarily resident in the UK, and the duties of the employment are performed wholly outside the UK, and where the employer is a foreign employer the employee is domiciled in the UK, a deduction is allowed against the benefits charge when foreign accommodation and subsistence costs are met, or reimbursed by, the employer. If the accommodation or subsistence is only partly for the purpose of enabling the employee to perform the duties of the employment, the deduction is restricted accordingly.

(iv)   *Family visits* (ITEPA 2003 s 371)

The travelling expenses of not more than two round trips in any one tax year by the employee's spouse/civil partner and children (under 18 at the beginning of the outward journey) to visit the employee are allowed as a deduction, providing the employee is absent for a continuous period of at least sixty days (either in a single tax year or straddling two tax years), and providing the payments are met or reimbursed by the employer (the deduction thus offsetting the benefits charge). As in (iii) this relief is given where the employee is resident and ordinarily resident in the UK.

There is also a special exemption for the payment or reimbursement by the employer of personal incidental expenses of up to £10 a night (ITEPA 2003 s 241(3)(b)), but this cannot be used to duplicate one of the deductions above. The £10 is applied to incidental overnight expenses averaged out over the number of days in each separate period of absence, ie, if an employee is overseas for 30 consecutive nights, he can claim up to £300 for non-business expenses (newspapers, laundry, match tickets, etc) for that particular trip. If the personal expenses exceed the £10 limit, they all become taxable.

(v)   *Travelling expenses of employees not domiciled in the UK* (ITEPA 2003 ss 373–375)

Reliefs similar to those given to UK resident and ordinarily resident employees are available to expatriate employees working in the UK. The costs of travelling between home and a permanent workplace are normally taxable earnings if paid by the employer, but non-UK domiciled employees may claim a deduction from their UK earnings for expenses paid or reimbursed by the employer in respect of unlimited journeys to and from the UK by the employee, and up to two return journeys per tax year for spouse/civil partner and children (subject to the same sixty day rule as in (iv) above). The reliefs are, however, only available where the employee was either not resident in the UK in either of the two tax years before the tax year of arrival in the UK, or was not in the UK at any time during the two years immediately preceding his arrival, and they are limited to a period of five years from the qualifying date of arrival in the UK. Relief is restricted where only part of the journey is for the specified purpose.

Self-assessment and non-residence

12. Self-assessment has posed problems for employees who start an absence abroad during the tax year. They will not be able to claim to be non-resident in their tax return due on the following 31 January since they will not qualify at that time, so they will have to indicate in the return that they are claiming split-year treatment under Concession A11. They would usually have arranged, by submitting a Form P85, not to pay tax under PAYE from the start of the absence, and indeed may claim a PAYE refund because they have unused allowances and basic rate band at the date of departure. An underpayment, with interest, will arise if their overseas period of absence is unexpectedly curtailed such that they never achieve non-resident status.

Rent payable to non-resident

13. Non-residents are broadly liable to UK tax on income arising in the UK. Where rent is paid direct to someone outside the UK, it must be paid net of basic rate tax unless the non-resident has agreed with HMRC to settle his tax liability directly (ITA 2007 s 971 – see Example 97 explanatory note 11). Non-resident British, Manx, Channel Island, EEA nationals, Commonwealth citizens and certain others may be entitled to claim UK personal allowances, and many others may be able to do so under the non-discrimination clauses in the UK's double tax treaties. Commonwealth citizens remain eligible only until 5 April 2010 (FA 2009 s 5 and Sch 1) but they will then also rely on treaty reliefs. For further details see Example 35.

Tax Credits

14. In order to claim tax credits it is normally necessary to be 'ordinarily resident' and 'in the UK'. Ordinary residence for this purpose has a different meaning from the one for income tax. For definitions and detailed rules see Example 7 at explanatory note 4.

    If a claimant leaves the UK permanently then notification is required within one month of departure. If the claimant leaves the UK temporarily but the absence exceeds eight weeks then notification is required within one month of the end of the eight weeks of absence. A penalty of up to £300 may be levied for failure to notify. (The eight-week rule may be extended to twelve weeks in certain circumstances.)

    If the claimant who has left the UK was claiming tax credits as part of a couple, notification will be required within three months of return.

    In the situation where one member of a couple goes abroad to work for periods in excess of 8/12 weeks, a family will have to make both joint and single claims to tax credits during the fiscal year. For the joint claims the income will be that of the couple. For the single claim the income will be that of the individual remaining in the UK.

    For example, John and Joan have one child aged 12. John works overseas on a three months on, one month off basis. He is not a Crown servant. He earns £36,600 p a. Joan does not work and they have no other taxable income. During 2009/10 he was in the UK from:

    6 April 2009 to 30 April 2009

    2 August 2009 to 7 September 2009

24 December 2009 to 24 January 2010.

John and Joan claim tax credits on 10 February 2009. Joan notifies John's departures and returns on time, and establishes her entitlement to make single claims at the same time.

John and Joan – Award periods:

6 April 2009 to 25 June 2009 (8 weeks after 30 April)	81 days
2 August 2009 to 2 November 2009 (8 weeks after 7 September)	93 days
24 December 2009 to 20 March 2010 (8 weeks after 24 January)	87 days

Claim is for family element only of £1.50 per day (John's income for these periods is too high to entitle John and Joan to any fast taper credits).

261 days @ £1.50 =   £392

Joan – Award periods:

26 June 2009 to 1 August 2009		37 days
3 November 2009 to 23 December 2009		51 days
21 March 2010 to 5 April 2010		16 days
Claim is	£	
CTC	6.13	
Family element	1.50	
	7.63	per day

104 days @ £7.63 =   £794

Note: Joan has no income and therefore the claim cannot be restricted. In order to claim the child must normally live with Joan in the UK. There is no entitlement to WTC as Joan does not work. See Example 7 explanatory note 4 for the unexpected restriction to WTC childcare claims during periods of temporary absence.

The example assumes John's work is outside the European Economic Area. The situation for those with rights under EC legislation can be more complicated.

Question

(a) Mark, who runs a garage business providing vehicle repairs, has written to you asking for advice about the mechanics who work in his garage. They wish to be treated as self-employed, and Mark has asked for your views on whether or not this is possible, the tax implications for him of their being so treated, and the potential risk to him if he treats them as self-employed and subsequently HMRC deem them to be employees.

Prepare brief notes for a meeting with Mark to discuss the matter.

(b) Wanda, a single woman, has recently returned to the UK after working overseas for a number of years. She is undecided whether to accept an offer of full-time employment from a company located near her home, or to set up her own consultancy business using her home as the base for her business.

You have advised her that the rules governing the deductibility of expenses for employees differ from the rules for self-employed persons. Wanda has now asked for a report summarising the position.

Prepare the report for Wanda, covering the basic rules for allowable expenditure, and their application in particular to travelling expenses (both within and outside the UK), subscriptions, and clothing.

(c) Ken Brown is employed as a clerk in the local factory, but has for many years been interested in antiques and he has pursued this as his hobby in most of his spare time.

In order to finance a holiday in the Bahamas, however, Ken had recently started buying and selling antiques for which he charged less than the normal retail price but nevertheless made a reasonable profit. When discussing this with a friend, he was told that he would have to pay income tax on this income as he was in fact carrying on a trade.

Consider whether or not Ken is carrying on a trade, giving your reasons fully and referring to leading cases in this area.

(d) In January, Lily cleared out her loft to make way for a loft extension and decided to sell the large quantity of old clothes, toys, books etc she had accumulated on eBay. This was so successful that in March she set up her own eBay shop. In July, Lily was approached by a friend to sell their old items for a percentage of funds realised, and in August she started to attend markets and car boot sales with a view to buying items for resale.

Review Lily's activity at each of the months mentioned above, and consider whether it constituted trading.

Answer

(a)   **Notes for meeting with Mark on employed or self-employed status of mechanics**

1.   The main distinction between trading income from self-employment taxable by ITTOIA 2005 part 2 and employment income taxable under ITEPA 2003 is that the former income is generated under contracts for services and the latter from a contract of service or contract of employment (ITEPA 2003 s 4(1)(a)). HMRC have issued factsheets ES/FS1 and ES/FS2 giving guidelines to help in the decision. (A separate publication CIS 349 is available for those in the construction industry.) There is also an online tool at www.hmrc.gov.uk/calcs/esi.htm to assist in determining employment status in most general cases.

2.   Factors pointing to employment are that the individual works wholly or mainly for one business, that he needs to carry out the work in person, to take orders as to when and how to do it, to work at the premises of those providing the work, or at a place determined by them, and to work directed hours at an hourly, weekly or monthly rate, and that he is paid for overtime, sickness and holidays. An entitlement to a pension through the contributions of those for whom he works is also one of the indicators.

3.   Factors pointing to self-employment are that the individual risks his own capital and bears any losses arising, that he controls whether, how, when and where he does the work, provides his own equipment, is free to employ or subcontract others to do the work he has undertaken, and is required to bear the cost of correcting faulty work.

4.   None of the factors is in itself conclusive in one direction or the other, and all the circumstances need to be taken into account. Nevertheless, two factors pointing towards self-employment are usually highly persuasive (if not determinative of the issue). First and most importantly, the unrestricted right for the person to select a substitute to do the work: a worker who does not have to provide personal service cannot be working under a contract of service. Alternatively, but carrying less weight, there is the lack of mutual obligation between the worker and the person requesting the work that is beyond the scope of the currently agreed project. Every contract involves mutual obligations, but if the nature of those obligations is that the worker is free to work elsewhere at any time, and to take on his own helpers at his own expense so that he can do two tasks at once, and to work how and when he pleases provided the service is delivered to the agreed timescale, the mutual obligations needed for a contract of service will be absent. However, where a contract provides for the use of substitutes and the freedom to arrange delivery of the service as the worker sees fit, these contractual terms have to be genuine and not merely included in a contract in order to satisfy the tax authorities. Written evidence, such as contracts, invoices, VAT registration, will have a considerable bearing on the decision, but HMRC may also interview the workers and customers to establish whether the real contracts differ from the paper evidence.

5.   If the mechanics were treated as self-employed, Mark would pay for their services in full and they would be liable for tax and Class 2 and Class 4 self-employed national insurance contributions. If their turnover was high enough they would have to register for VAT. Alternatively, they might choose to voluntarily register for VAT.

6.   Applying the general principles of what constitutes self-employment, however, it seems likely that HMRC would regard the mechanics as employees. If Mark treats them as self-employed without seeking a ruling in advance, and they are later deemed to be employees, he will be liable for tax and national insurance contributions. That amount might not be recoverable, or recoverable in full, from the employee, especially if the individual is no longer working for Mark. A deduction will normally be allowed for any settlement of the liability by the employer. There would also be penalties based on the tax and NI underpaid if the failure is considered to have occurred through lack of care or deliberate failure. Interest would also be

charged at the statutory rate from 19 April after the end of the tax year (for years before 2009/10) or from the normal monthly payment date (from 2009/10 onwards) until the date the liability was settled. There is no deduction available against Mark's profits for the penalties or interest. HMRC would not initiate collection of the tax from the mechanics unless they were held to have known that Mark had wilfully failed to deduct tax.

A case heard by the Special Commissioners (*Demibourne Ltd v HMRC* (2005)) highlights the difficulties of getting a worker's status wrong. In that case, a worker was treated as self-employed. He was therefore paid gross and he declared his earnings on his self-assessment return (and paid the tax accordingly – no NI was due as he was over state pension age). Subsequently, HMRC queried the worker's status on a PAYE enquiry. They considered that the worker was in fact an employee and raised a determination on the company under SI 2003/2682 reg 80 for the PAYE due but unpaid. By this time it was too late for the worker to reclaim his incorrectly self-assessed tax from HMRC and the employer had no right of recovery from the employee.

The Special Commissioner agreed that the worker was an employee and therefore that the reg 80 determination should be upheld. However, he realised that this would have meant HMRC receiving the tax twice (once from the worker and once from the employer) at the expense of the employer. He suggested that HMRC gave a credit for the tax already accounted for although such a request could not be binding on HMRC. Following the case of Demibourne, HMRC abandoned its long-standing arrangement of allowing an equitable offset of tax paid by individuals while they were treated as self-employed in arriving at the PAYE settlement due. In many cases they requested 100% of any unpaid tax and NI from the employer. The employer had then, to the extent possible, to recover amounts from its employees and the employees had then, to the extent possible, to amend their self-assessments. HMRC was concerned that, once an employer had concluded a contract settlement after a status investigation, it could no longer be liable for the tax that had been offset. However, a worker could legitimately require a refund of the self-assessed tax, as it had never been due. This never happened in practice, but the concern about fairness and protecting revenue led to the issue of new regulations.

After extensive consultation, HMRC issued amending Regulations in 2008 (SI 2008/782) which introduce a new power for HMRC to make a direction transferring the liability for the PAYE not deducted to the employee in cases where self-assessment tax has been paid on the earnings. (New Reg 72E to 72G inserted in SI 2003/2682) This removes the anomaly created by the *Demibourne* decision.

7. HMRC have one person in each of its area offices nominated to deal with questions on an individual's status. Mark should contact his local tax office to ask for a ruling. It would also be acceptable to use the online ESI tool to arrive at a view on status provided the results were properly documented, by printing and retaining the responses at the conclusion of the test.

8. Tax and NI contributions are charged on deemed salary when personal services equivalent to a disguised employment are provided through an intermediary such as a partnership or limited company. The charge is on the intermediary, therefore the client cannot be liable for the tax and national insurance of the worker where an intermediary is used. Mark could safeguard his position by insisting that his workers can only provide services to him other than as an employee if a partnership or limited company is used as an intermediary.

(b)

To: Wanda
From: A N Adviser   17 October 2009

Rules governing the deductibility of expenses for employees compared with the rules for self-employed persons

1. The main difference in the expenses treatment for employees compared with the self-employed is that employees are allowed to deduct expenses that are wholly, exclusively and necessarily incurred in the performance of the duties of their employment, whereas the self-employed are allowed to deduct expenses that are incurred wholly and exclusively for the purpose of their trade, profession or vocation, without any requirement that the expenses should be necessary.

2. Dealing first with employees, the general expenses rule is found in ITEPA 2003 s 336, which provides that an employee is allowed to deduct expenses wholly, exclusively and necessarily incurred in performance of his duties. Sections 337 to 342 of ITEPA 2003 give relief for certain travelling expenses, with additional provisions for overseas travel in ss 370 to 375.

3. (i) Travel expenses are allowed where they are either in the performance of the duties of the employment or for 'necessary attendance' at a temporary workplace (ITEPA 2003 ss 337–340).

    The full cost of travelling on business direct from home and associated subsistence expenses is allowed, unless the journey is ordinary commuting to/from your permanent workplace. Fixed mileage allowance payment rates may be used if the travel is in your own vehicle.

    If you are temporarily sent from your normal workplace to a different workplace for up to 24 months, returning to your normal place of work thereafter, you are allowed relief for the related travelling, accommodation and subsistence expenses. This will not apply if the temporary posting is expected to exceed 24 months. If it does in fact exceed or looks as if it will exceed 24 months the expenses are allowable up to the time that fact became known.

    (ii) If *part* of the duties of an employment are performed abroad, it is specifically provided by ITEPA 2003 s 370 that travel expenses *paid or reimbursed by the employer* for any journey from any place in the UK to the overseas destination and back again are allowed, providing the duties can only be performed abroad and that the 'wholly and exclusively' rule is satisfied (see s 370(4) and (5)). The provisions of ITEPA 2003 s 338 outlined in (i) above would, however, give relief for the expenses of travelling abroad wholly for business whether the cost was borne by the employer or the employee, and would in addition give relief for subsistence expenses. ITEPA 2003 s 371 also provides relief for up to two journeys a tax year by a spouse and children to visit an employee working abroad for 60 days or more, but this is not relevant in your case. Similarly if *all* the duties of your employment are performed abroad, you are entitled to a deduction for the expenses of travelling abroad to take up the appointment and returning to the UK thereafter if your earnings include an amount in respect of such travel (ITEPA 2003 s 370(1)–(3)) ie, they are again paid or reimbursed by your employer. You are also allowed relief for board and lodging expenses in similar circumstances (ITEPA 2003 s 376).

    (iii) If *all* the duties of one or more employments are performed abroad and providing you are resident and ordinarily resident in the UK (and domiciled here if your employer is a foreign employer), you are entitled to a deduction for the expenses of travelling abroad to take up the appointment, travelling between the appointments, and returning to the UK thereafter. For this relief there is no requirement for the payments first to have been met by your employer (ITEPA 2003 ss 341, 342). You are entitled to deduct an appropriate part of the expenses if the travelling is only partly for the purposes of the employment (ITEPA 2003 ss 341(5) and 342(8)).

    (iv) Where someone makes a dual purpose visit (eg a business trip combined with a holiday), either in the UK or abroad, this will not deny relief for the expenses providing the journey had to be made in the performance of the duties of the employment. If, however, a deduction is being claimed under ITEPA 2003 s 370 to balance an expenses payment by an employer (as in (ii) above), it will be denied if the journey has both a business and a private purpose. The cost of any journey that was specifically private would obviously be disallowed (for example, if your employer required you to go to Paris, but you went to the South of France on holiday first).

4. Subscriptions that are payable in order to be able to carry on particular employments, for example, that of an architect, health professional or teacher (ITEPA 2003 s 343), are specifically allowable by statute. This also applies to other professional subscriptions to bodies of persons approved by HMRC, providing the activities of the body are relevant to the employment (ITEPA 2003 s 344).

    Subscriptions other than approved professional subscriptions must satisfy the general rule that they be 'wholly, exclusively and necessarily incurred' and very few subscriptions would qualify. A list of subscriptions may be obtained at www.hmrc.gov.uk/list3

5. The expense of clothing is not allowed unless it is protective clothing or a uniform. This is so even if the clothing is worn only at work.

6. If you are required by an employer to work from home, you will probably incur extra costs of heating, lighting and telephone charges. Most home expenses would have been incurred anyway (eg, council tax, insurance, telephone rental) so they do not meet the test of being wholly, exclusively and necessarily incurred in the performance of the duties. However, as an administrative concession, HMRC will allow an employer to pay an allowance of £3 per week (in addition to the cost of business telephone calls) tax- and NI-free towards the extra costs of home workers. Any expenses incurred solely for business use, such as the employer having a new broadband connection installed at the home, should still be deductible, but HMRC will sometimes require evidence of business use.

7. Turning now to the position of the self-employed, the general rule is found in ITTOIA 2005 Chapter 4, which provides that a self-employed person cannot deduct expenses unless they are 'wholly and exclusively laid out or expended for the purposes of the trade, profession or vocation' (s 34), and that the expenditure must be of an income and not a capital nature (s 33).

8. As far as travelling expenses are concerned, the cost of travel from home to work base is not allowed, and journeys that are partly for business and partly for private purposes are disallowed. There is no distinction between travelling expenses in the UK and abroad, unless the trade, profession or vocation is carried on wholly abroad, in which case the cost of travelling abroad and back again, and between two separate foreign businesses, is allowed, providing the absence is wholly and exclusively for the purpose of performing the functions of one or more of the businesses (ITTOIA 2005 ss 92–94).

    Where a self-employed person's work base is his home, all business travelling from the home base is allowed, even if there is only one person for whom work is done. But merely doing some of your work at home does not enable you to claim the cost of travelling from home to the main work base.

9. Subscriptions to trade associations, although not usually satisfying the general expenses rule, are allowed providing the association has entered into an agreement with HMRC to pay tax on the excess of their receipts over their allowable expenses. Other subscriptions would need to satisfy the general rule.

10. As far as clothing is concerned, the self-employed are in no better position than employees, and unless clothing is special or protective clothing the cost is not 'wholly and exclusively' for the purposes of the business.

    The position is different for value added tax, because there is no 'wholly and exclusively' requirement. Input tax can be recovered if the clothing is for business purposes, with an apportionment if there is part private use.

11. As far as home working expenses are concerned, most home expenses for self-employed workers also have a dual purpose, which should mean that they are not deductible, but it is accepted that some proportion of costs can be attributable to the part of the home used as an office. In practice, a deduction may be claimed for the element of mortgage interest or rent, insurance and utilities costs that corresponds to the business use area where that part is wholly and exclusively for business use. This may in practice be a matter of negotiation with HMRC. The cost of a separate business telephone line should be fully deductible. Any part of the home set aside exclusively for business use may attract business rates and may affect the principal private residence exemption for CGT.

12 To summarise, although the requirements for expenditure to be allowable in an employment are more stringent than for the self-employed, there are a large number of areas, in particular those dealt with in this report, where the treatment is broadly the same.

(c)

In order to decide whether activities constitute trading, the starting point is the basic definition of a trade in ITA 2007 s 989, which states that the word trade 'includes any venture in the nature of trade'.

On its own the definition is not very helpful, but it has been given legal interpretation in many cases that have come before the courts.

In 1955 the Royal Commission on the Taxation of Profits and Income established six 'badges of trade', which represent the major considerations to be taken into account in deciding whether or not a trade is being carried on. These were:

(1)   The subject matter of the realisation

(2)   The length of the period of ownership

(3)   The frequency or number of similar transactions by the same person

(4)   Supplementary work on or in connection with the property realised

(5)   The circumstances that were responsible for the realisation

(6)   Motive.

Some or all of these would usually be present in trading activities, although the absence of any one or more would not necessarily indicate that a trade was not being carried on.

In relation to subject matter, it was considered in *CIR v Fraser* (1942) that there were only three reasons for purchasing an article: for own use or consumption, as an investment possibly to yield income, or for resale at a profit, ie, for the purpose of trading. The very nature of some assets will point towards trading rather than investment or own use. In *CIR v Rutledge* (1929), for example, there was an isolated purchase of 1 million rolls of toilet paper. And in *Wisdom v Chamberlain* (1969), concerning the short-term purchase and resale of silver bullion as a hedge against devaluation, it was clear that the asset itself gave the owner no aesthetic pleasure or pride of ownership. In both cases the profits were held to be assessable as trading profits.

A long period of ownership may indicate investment rather than trading. Obviously many assets appreciate in value with the passage of time, and holding assets to realise capital gains rather than buying and selling short-term to realise income has been widespread practice among those liable to income tax at higher rates. A quick sale, on the other hand, may not necessarily indicate trading, for example, when an asset is received as an inheritance and is disposed of shortly afterwards.

An isolated profitable transaction has been held to be trading, as in the case of *CIR v Rutledge* (above). Frequent repetition of transactions obviously constitutes even stronger evidence of trading, and it may be particularly important where the nature of the asset is not such as to be usually regarded as trading stock, eg *Leach v Pogson* (1962), where the taxpayer was held to be trading in establishing and selling driving schools. But there is a prima facie presumption against trading for speculative dealings in securities, and making 200 such transactions in about three years was held not to be trading in *Salt v Chamberlain* (1979).

Where an asset is resold after being processed or worked on in some way, this may indicate trading, eg, buying in bulk and breaking down into smaller saleable units. A leading case in this area is *Cape Brandy Syndicate v CIR* (1921), where a syndicate imported brandy, blended it, re-casked it and resold it.

A need for ready money to meet a sudden emergency would be clear evidence of the absence of a trading motive on the sale of an asset.

The lack of a profit motive is not conclusive evidence against trading (re Duty on Estate of Incorporated Council of Law Reporting for England and Wales, 1888). But clearly the existence of a profit motive is a very strong indicator that a trade exists.

In January 2007 HMRC issued a new Internet-based guide (www.hmrc.gov.uk/guidance/selling/index.htm) for people who trade online, through classified adverts and car boot sales. This sets out six examples of individuals selling and examines whether they are trading. It also lists their nine badges or indicators of trading as follows:

Indicators of trading	Points to consider
1. Profit seeking motive	An intention to make a profit supports trading.
2. The number of transactions involved	Systematic and repeated transactions support trade.
3. The nature of the goods sold	Are the goods only capable of being turned to advantage by being sold? Or do they yield income, or give enjoyment though pride of ownership?
4. Existence of similar trading transactions	Was this a one-off transaction or part of a pattern that suggests trading?
5. Changes to the goods	Were the goods repaired, modified or improved to sell them more easily?
6. The way the sale was carried out	Were the goods sold in a way that indicates trading, or to raise cash in an emergency?
7. The source of finance	Was money borrowed to buy the goods? Were any profits to be used to repay the loan?
8. Interval of time between purchase and sale	Goods being traded are usually bought then sold quickly.
9. Method of acquisition of the goods	Goods acquired by an inheritance, or as a gift, are less likely to be the subject of trade.

Applying these general considerations to the circumstances of Ken Brown's activities, it is clear that he will almost certainly be held to be carrying on a trade.

His original activity of purchasing antiques as a hobby, and presumably owning them for lengthy periods and reselling some of them from time to time, would be regarded as investment rather than trading. Antiques would give him pride and pleasure in their ownership, and their appreciation in value over time would give the opportunity to realise a profit on his investment. But the nature of his activities has changed with the commencement of short-term buying and selling. It was stated in the case of *Hawes v Gardiner* (1957), that what started as a hobby may develop into a trade, and that is almost certainly the case here. Ken's intention of holding for personal enjoyment and investment has changed to frequent buying and selling short-term to make an immediate profit.

As a result of the change of Ken's hobby to a trade, there is also a liability to Class 2 national insurance. Ken must notify the change as soon as his intention is altered, by submitting form CWF1 to HMRC's National Insurance Contributions Office at Newcastle upon Tyne, by calling the helpline on 08459 15 45 15 or registering online. Failure to notify before 31 January following the end of the tax year of commencement will result in a penalty geared to the lost contributions and the behaviour leading to the failure (SI 2001/1004 reg 87A) in line with the direct tax changes made by Finance Act 2008 Sch 41. Failures in respect of businesses that started before 6 April 2009 were and remain subject instead to a £100 penalty if notification was not made within three months of commencement. The penalty will not be charged if throughout the period of failure to notify Ken would have been able to claim exception from Class 2 national insurance because his expected earnings were below the small earnings exception limit (£5,075 for 2009/10).

(d)

January

Selling unwanted items that have been lying around in the attic is probably not sufficient to constitute a trade. The original purchases were presumably made for personal use. If items are being sold for more than their original cost, it is necessary to consider capital gains tax, but assuming they were individually worth less than £6,000 per item they would be exempt as chattels.

March

As stated under (c) above, the way a sale is carried out is a badge or indicator of trading. Setting up an online shop makes her activities appear more 'commercial'. However, no one factor can outweigh the others and provided the 'stock' being sold is still the same as before, Lily has not commenced trading. HMRC are known to monitor online retailers looking for unregistered businesses. It would therefore be prudent to retain proof, where reasonably practical, that the items being sold relate to her personal items.

July and August

Selling items on behalf of another person/buying stock for resale constitutes trading and Lily should register her business as soon as possible. Lily will also have to maintain records that allow her to separate the resale of her own personal items and 'business' transactions.

E-trading has grown phenomenally in recent years. EBay trading in particular often starts as a personal project to resell unwanted items and then develops into a business. This can generate problems for individuals who fail to register and fail to separate personal transactions from business ones. EBay has improved its guidance to users on their obligations to register with HMRC. It also makes various reports to HMRC. HMRC in turn use various tools to monitor for online unregistered traders.

Explanatory Notes

Employment or self-employment

1.   The distinction between employment and self-employment is often hard to draw. It is not set out in the legislation. Instead it is a question of fact based upon a series of tests developed from case law. A number of different elements have to be considered and a picture needs to be drawn from all the relevant factors. The question was well summarised by Mummery J in *Hall v Lorimer*, the summary being approved by Nolan LJ when the case went to the Court of Appeal (1993): 'In order to decide whether a person carries on business on his own account it is necessary to consider many different aspects of that person's work activity. This is not a mechanical exercise of running through a check list to see whether they are present in, or absent from, a given situation. The object of the exercise is to paint a picture from the accumulation of detail. The overall effect can only be appreciated by standing back from the detailed picture which has been painted, by viewing it from a distance and by making an informed, considered, qualitative appreciation of the whole.'

The difficulty is determining what weight to give to any individual item and what conclusion to draw from the whole. Very few tests or facts give a conclusive answer. The strongest single indicator of self-employment is the exercised ability to provide a substitute. A contract of service (employment) cannot exist unless it contains an obligation on the part of the employee to provide his/her services personally. In the case of *Express & Echo Publications Ltd v Tanton* (1999), it was made clear that if a worker did not have to perform the duties personally then he could not be an employee. However, the reverse, ie the requirement to undertake the duties personally, does not automatically make the worker an employee (*McManus v Griffiths* (1997)), but will be a strong pointer, and it has proven to be very helpful to HMRC in IR35 cases where it has been argued that, eg, an IT worker is in disguised employment.

The courts use the test of 'mutual obligations' extensively. If no obligations exist there can be neither a contract of service nor a contract for services. Thus where a person may, but need not, be asked to perform a service and, if asked, is free to decline to provide the service asked for, there exists no mutuality of obligation and thus no contract of service. Between engagements, the person would certainly not be an employee. Note, however, mutual obligations may be created by custom and habit, which in turn may give rise to an enforceable contract of service. Once the contract is made, however, the key to determining whether it is one 'of service' or 'for services' is the nature of the mutual obligations in that contract, which involves considering a number of factors.

The major factor to take into account is the 'economic reality'. How much freedom does he have and what risks does he run, since these are very different when comparing employed and self-employed workers. Is the worker really in business on his own account? Does he have the ability to subcontract work to others? Is he responsible for his own actions? In summary, can he gain or lose by his own actions?

In any given case all of the factors will not be relevant. Each case must be determined on its own facts. The factors include:

– Mutual obligations – long-term, personal commitment, or something more loose for the delivery of a project to a timetable

– Substitution, the ability to subcontract work

– Financial risk

– Is there a written (or unwritten) contract of service

– Business management, own office, notepaper etc

– Number of providers of work

– Provision of business and public liability or professional indemnity insurance

– A proper accounting system

– Contract for fixed term or job

– Basis of remuneration

– Capital invested in business

– Equipment – who provides major items

– Control or, more importantly, the right of the work-giver to control the method and manner of performance of the duties

– Place of duties

– Provision of benefits, sick pay, holiday pay or pension scheme

– Organisation (integration with client's business).

2.   Over the years HMRC have taken a different view in relation to various activities, and has succeeded in some cases taken before the courts, eg *Sidey v Phillips* (1987), where a non-practising barrister who lectured part-time on legal subjects and had two other separate sources of earnings was held to be an employee, and *Walls v Sinnett* (1987), where a part-time lecturing appointment held by a professional singer was also held to be an employment. They had succeeded in the much earlier (1973) case of *Fall v Hitchen*, where a dancer on a six-month Equity contract was held to be an employee. They have, however, now decided that self-employment will usually be more appropriate for most people in the performing arts (although they will often be deemed to be employed for NI purposes unless they are paid a fee per performance rather an hourly rate). Employment treatment will be restricted for income tax purposes to cases where someone receives a regular salary to perform in a series of productions, with a period of notice required to end the contract, such as permanent members of orchestras, and of opera, ballet and theatre companies. Where entertainers are taxed as employees they may claim a deduction for agent's fees up to a maximum of 17½% of their earnings in the relevant tax year (ITEPA 2003 s 352).

HMRC have lost some other cases, including the case of *McMenamin v Diggles* (1991), in which a barrister's senior clerk had changed his contractual arrangements to bring himself into the self-employed category, and *Hall v Lorimer* mentioned in 1 above (CA 1993), concerning a vision mixer who undertook short-term engagements for various production companies. The Revenue won the case of *Barnett v Brabyn* (1996), where they successfully argued that the taxpayer was self-employed despite only working for one client, but lost the case of *Andrews v King* (1991), where they argued that a gangmaster should be treated as self-employed. The court disagreed, holding that Andrews was selecting workers and hiring on behalf of his employers.

In *Parade Park Hotel & Paul May v HMRC* (2007) SpC, M, a builder and decorator worked for several years as the odd-job man at a small hotel. He was an alcoholic and his attendance was patchy. He had little other work and provided his own tools. M could refuse work and choose his own hours. The proprietor of the hotel would list work needing to be done in a book and M would do it as it suited him. The case involved a review of mutuality of obligation with the defence arguing the hotel was never obliged to provide work and M was never obliged to carry it out. The commissioners found there was no mutuality and insufficient control to constitute a contract of service.

The case highlights the current approach of the courts where there is no determinative written contract of an irreducible minimum requirement for three components to be present for a contract of service of:

- mutuality of obligation (ie, a commitment on both sides to offer and accept work on a regular basis);

- control (ie, a commitment by the employer to give direction and control and by the worker to accept the directions); and

- personal service (ie, a commitment by the worker to do the work himself, with no right to employ another to do it).

Where one or more of these components is missing, the contract cannot be one for service regardless of other factors indicating otherwise. This court approach is not always followed by HMRC's status inspectors.

3.   The same treatment should apply both to tax and national insurance, but someone (in any business) who has been retrospectively reclassified as self-employed has the option of not claiming a refund of Class 1 contributions, so that the contributions will remain on his record for the purpose of earnings-related pension. Employers will be able to reclaim their share of the Class 1 contributions wrongly paid for such self-employed workers, subject to SSA 1998 s 54, which provides for a time limit of one year after the end of the year in which the Class 1 contribution is wrongly paid. Earlier contributions are deemed to have been correctly paid irrespective of the employment status. This also applies to Class 1A and 1B contributions. Where contributions have been wrongly paid in the belief that someone was an employee, then after the end of the next following tax year (eg after 5 April

2010 for contributions paid in respect of 2008/09) the contributions will be treated as having been correctly paid for the relevant period, which means there will be no need for the HMRC National Insurance Contributions Office (NICO) to amend the contribution record of the worker concerned or to make repayments. The rules on NIC for entertainers are different – see Tax Bulletin 65 June 2003.

4. Contractors in the construction industry are required to certify on their monthly CIS returns that none of their subcontractors is an employee. Penalties are charged if this statement is false. Construction workers whose services as self-employed subcontractors are supplied by employment agencies are taxed as employees (see Example 89 for full details).

5. From 6 April 2000, under the 'IR35' rules, the provision of personal services that amounts to disguised employment through a partnership or limited company is 'looked through' and the individual is treated as an employee of the partnership or limited company supplying his services and a deemed employment payment, subject to PAYE and NIC, is imputed to him on 5 April at the end of the year (see Example 86 for full details).

    The application of these rules was temporarily thrown into some doubt following the employment case of *Cable and Wireless v Muscat CA* (2006). In that case an individual was held to have been an employee even though engaged through a personal service company. However, the facts were unusual, in that Mr Muscat was required by the employer to transfer into the personal service company, and the court found that he had never in fact ceased to be an employee of his original employer. HMRC wisely refused to take precedent from this employment law case and a subsequent employment law case has attempted to rein back in the principle (see Taxation magazine dated 2.7.07 'Back to source').

6. The main points of difference between employment and self-employment are dealt with in part (a) of the example, and part (b) illustrates some of the consequences in terms of allowable expenditure.

Travelling and subsistence expenses

The treatment of employees' travelling expenses is dealt with in ITEPA 2003 ss 337–342. Relief is given for travelling expenses, that is, amounts necessarily expended on travelling in the performance of the duties of the employment, or other travelling expenses which are attributable to the necessary attendance of the employee at any place in the performance of his duties and are not expenses of ordinary commuting or private travel.

Ordinary commuting broadly means travel from home to the permanent workplace. Private travel means travel between home and a place that is not a workplace, or between two places neither of which is a workplace. A permanent workplace is a workplace that is not a temporary workplace, and a temporary workplace is a workplace the employee attends to perform a task of limited duration or for some other temporary purpose. A workplace is not a temporary workplace if the employee works there continuously for a period of more than 24 months or if the employment itself is only expected to last for all, or almost all, of the period at that workplace. Where home is a permanent workplace, it is nevertheless still home, so travel between such a home and another permanent workplace (eg, by those who work part-time from home and part-time from an office) is still ordinary commuting, as shown by the decision in *Lewis v Revenue and Customs Commissioners* [2008] STC (SCD) 895.

Work at a particular place is regarded as continuous if the duties of the employment fall to be performed to a significant extent at that place (significant being regarded by HMRC as 40% or more). Site-based employees with no permanent workplace are allowed the cost of travelling to and from home and subsistence while away providing the job at the site is expected to and does last for not more than 24 months. As and when it becomes clear that the job will last for more than 24 months, travel and subsistence expenses are taxable from that time. Site-based employees are not allowed relief for subsistence expenses if they have no permanent home, because subsistence expenses must be attributable to the business travel.

Employees are entitled to relief for the full amount of qualifying travelling expenses. The full cost of meals and accommodation while travelling or staying away on business is allowable as part of the cost of travel. Business travel includes travelling on business from home where the journey is to (or from) a temporary workplace, or where the nature of the employment requires the employee to carry out his duties at home (but doing work at home for convenience rather than because of the nature of the job does not turn the home into a workplace). Where a journey has both a business and a private purpose, the expense will be allowed if the journey is substantially for business purposes.

As far as national insurance contributions are concerned, the rules are the same as for income tax, except that mileage payments may be made at 40p for every mile without NIC becoming due whereas for income tax there is a 10,000 mile limit before the lower rate of 25p applies. Contributions will normally be payable only if the employer makes a payment to the employee that exceeds the cost of a business journey.

Relevant cases concerning travelling expenses for the self-employed are *Horton v Young* (1971), where the expenses of travelling from home to the sites of the main contractor by a bricklaying subcontractor were allowed, and *Newsom v Robertson* (1953), where a barrister's expenses of travelling between his home, where he did some of his work, and his London chambers were disallowed. In the High Court case of *Powell v Jackman* (2004) the Court found that a milkman's business base was not his home, where he kept his business records, nor his depot where he kept his milk float, but that he had a defined area of business being his milk round, so the cost of travel from home to that base area was not deductible.

Clothing

As far as clothing is concerned, it has been held in various cases concerning employees (*Woodcock v IRC* (1977), *Hillyer v Leeke* (1976)) that clothing is 'partly for cover and comfort' and thus does not come within the 'wholly and exclusively' rule. The same rules were applied in the case of *Mallalieu v Drummond* (1983), relating to a self-employed barrister. However, protective clothing and uniforms that are not suitable for private use (eg, bearing printed or sewn-in business logos) will still qualify for both employees and self-employed workers.

Nature of a trade

7.   Parts (c) and (d) of the example indicate the main considerations in determining whether or not a trade exists. Where there are one or more isolated transactions it has to be decided whether they are 'in the nature of trade' or merely the conversion of capital in one form into capital in another. A purchase and sale is either a trading transaction or a capital transaction. There is no other interpretation, and a charge could not, for example, be raised under the 'miscellaneous profits or gains' provisions.

8.   The badges of trade mentioned in part (c) of the example were reviewed in the case of *Marson v Morton* 1986, in which it was held that the sale of land originally bought as an investment to be held for a year or two but in fact sold only a few months later was not 'an adventure in the nature of trade'. The following points were made, which re-state and in some respects add to the indicators listed by the Royal Commission:

   (i)   Although not conclusive, lack of repetition is a pointer that may indicate something other than a trade.

   (ii) Is the transaction related to the taxpayer's existing trade or trades?

   (iii) Was the subject matter a typical trading commodity which can only be turned to advantage by realisation?

   (iv) Was the transaction carried out in a typical trading way for that type of commodity?

   (v)   If the item was bought with borrowed money, that points to an intention to short-term re-sale (the judge, strangely, did not make a distinction between long-term and short-term borrowings, which itself can often be a useful indicator).

   (vi) Was the item re-sold in one lot or broken down into smaller lots?

(vii)   What was the intention of the purchaser at the time of purchase?

(viii) Did the item yield either enjoyment or pride of ownership, or produce income, any of which would point to investment rather than trading?

The judge stated that 'in 1986 it is not any longer self-evident that unless land is producing income it cannot be an investment'.

Mutual trading

9.   Where there is mutual trading, so that the people carrying on the trade and the customers are the same persons, as with members' clubs, any resulting surplus is not taxable as a trading profit, because it represents an excess of the members' contributions over the association's expenditure. This does not extend to trading with those who are not members, since the principle of mutuality does not then apply. Care must be taken to put into place a system to clearly identify the turnover attributable to members, so as to eliminate the non-taxable proportion. Many 'club licences' no longer restrict bar sales only to members. The club would also be taxable on any other profits, such as investment income and capital gains, and as an unincorporated association other than a partnership it would be liable to corporation tax rather than income tax and/or capital gains tax (see Example 49 explanatory note 1). Banks and building societies are able to pay interest to clubs without deducting tax, so the clubs will be due to account for corporation tax on the full amount of the interest at the appropriate rate. HMRC may be prepared to treat a club as dormant if it is mainly for recreational and other non-commercial purposes, even though there is strictly a small tax liability. Unless HMRC have given written notification of dormant status, however, clubs must complete returns and account for tax under the self-assessment system. Where dormant status has been granted, clubs must notify HMRC within twelve months after the end of the relevant accounting period if their circumstances change, or if chargeable assets are likely to be disposed of (see HMRC's Guide to corporation tax self-assessment CTSA/BK2). See also www.hmrc.gov.uk/guidance/clubs-societies.htm.

HMRC have stated they will not seek returns or tax from clubs or unincorporated associations, where the annual corporation tax liability is expected to be below £100. See also Example 90 part B and explanatory notes 10 to 12 for the tax exemptions for registered amateur sports clubs.

Illegal trading

10.   It is established case law that profits of illegal trading are nonetheless taxable. The unlawful nature of the contracts cannot be used as a defence to avoid paying tax on the proceeds. Hence the profits from illegal gambling machines were assessable in *Mann v Nash* (1932), from illegal street betting in *Southern v AB* (1933) and from prostitution in *CIR v Aken* (1988). As to betting, it was held in *Partridge v Mallandaine* (1886) that a racecourse bookmaker's profits were assessable as the profits of a vocation even though he could not at law enforce the wagering contracts. In contrast someone whose means of livelihood was betting on horses from his private address at starting prices was held not to be carrying on a trade (*Graham v Green*, 1925). If any contract is for an illegal purpose, it cannot be a contract of service as it is void, either by statute or in common law. The worker under that contract will therefore be a self-employed earner for tax and NI purposes.

Trading or investment

11.   The general conclusion to be drawn from the legislation and case law is that in cases where an activity is not clearly established as a trade at the outset, there may nonetheless come a point where its character is such that it may be challenged as a trading activity. An example is buying and selling Krugerrands. Occasional purchases and sales of Krugerrands with fairly lengthy intervening periods of ownership would be treated as capital transactions subject to capital gains tax. If, however, the scale and frequency of the transactions became such as to indicate a trading motive they would be challenged by HMRC as assessable as trading income.

12.   Individuals pay tax on gains at 18% rather than income tax rates, and companies pay tax at the same rates on both income and gains. There are, however, significant differences between the treatment of income and gains that need to be borne in mind, particularly the following.

Capital profits of companies are reduced by an indexation allowance. For individuals the indexation allowance (up to April 1998) and taper relief were available for periods up to April 2008 but the charge is now at the flat rate of 18%, subject in certain cases where entrepreneurs' relief is available to a reduction to 10%. Capital profits may also be eligible for some relief or even exemption, including, for individuals, an annual exemption of (currently) £10,100. Income profits, on the other hand, may be reduced or eliminated by paying pension premiums, or acquiring tax-efficient investments. Trading losses may be set against total income and capital gains, whereas capital losses may only be set against capital gains (except for losses on shares subscribed for in an unquoted trading company).

Question

Define capital expenditure and revenue expenditure and receipts and explain how they are treated differently for tax purposes.

Answer

Capital and revenue expenditure

The terms capital and revenue expenditure are not defined in the legislation. However, profits must be calculated in accordance with generally accepted accounting practice (GAAP) (ITTOIA 2005 s 25 for income tax and CTA 2009 s 46 for corporation tax). GAAP means UK GAAP or, where appropriate, International Financial Reporting Standards (IFRS). There are provisions to prevent groups of companies gaining a tax advantage by one company using IFRS and another UK GAAP. The normal accounting distinction between capital and revenue expenditure is that expenditure that is going to affect only the current accounting period is revenue expenditure, whereas expenditure that is going to give benefit to the business over more than one accounting period is capital expenditure.

For individuals and trustees, interest is a revenue item whatever the nature of the loan (ITTOIA 2005 s 29). Capital expenditure (s 33) and capital receipts (s 96) are excluded from profits unless specifically included by legislation. For example, the deduction of part of a short lease premium is spread over the term of the lease and revenue profits are reduced by capital allowances on certain capital assets. Capital expenditure that does not qualify for capital allowances forms part of the allowable cost for capital gains purposes, but on certain assets, such as leases, the expenditure is deemed to waste away over the tax life of the asset, so that no tax relief at all is given for the expenditure that is so treated. The same applies to any revenue expenditure that is specifically disallowed, such as entertaining expenses.

The tax treatment of capital and revenue expenditure has been varied for companies, with certain items being taken out of capital gains and brought into the computation of revenue profits. The main areas are the treatment of loan relationships (see Example 63) and the treatment of goodwill and intangible assets (see Example 66). In other instances, companies are entitled to deduct a greater amount from profits than the expenditure incurred, in particular in relation to research and development expenditure (see Example 52). These differences need to be borne in mind when considering what follows.

In determining the treatment of expenditure as revenue or capital, guidance can be obtained from the cases that have come before the courts. These cases often give conflicting opinions however. Lord Wilberforce, in the 1979 case of *Tucker v Granada Motorway Services Ltd* said that 'reported cases are the best tools that we have, even if they may sometimes be blunt instruments'. It is important to remember that the cases are only a guide, and each new situation must be considered on its own facts. In the case of *Vodafone Cellular Ltd v Shaw* (CA 1997 – see below) the judge in the High Court said that the decision involved 'a measure of gut reaction' in an area with 'an over-abundance of case law and the danger of over-citation'.

A case that considered the distinction between capital and revenue was *CIR v John Lewis Properties plc* (2003). In that case the Court of Appeal set out certain tests to determine whether an item is capital or revenue:

1. If the item is long lasting it is more likely to be a capital item. On the other hand, if it is appropriate to classify the item as part of the fixed, rather than the circulating capital of the business, then it will be a capital item even though it has a brief life. The context is therefore important.

2. The value of the asset is important, the higher the relative value the more likely the item is capital.

3. The fact that a payment causes a diminution in value of the asset is important but this diminution need not be permanent. It should be judged at the time of the disposal, and the size of the reduction is material.

4. A single lump sum payment is more likely to be capital and a series of recurring payments revenue.

5. Where a disposal of an asset is accompanied by the transfer of risk this indicates a capital transaction.

In some of the older cases, two different tests emerged. The first was the distinction between fixed and circulating capital (essentially the difference between the fixed and current assets of a business) and the second was the 'enduring benefit' test stated in *Atherton v British Insulated and Helsby Cables Ltd* (1926): 'When an expenditure is made not only once and for all, but with a view to bringing into existence an asset or an advantage for the enduring benefit of a trade, I think that there is very good reason (in the absence of special circumstances leading to an opposite conclusion) for treating such an expenditure as properly attributable, not to revenue, but to capital'. This case was cited by HMRC in the Vodafone case mentioned above, HMRC contending that a cancellation payment by Vodafone to escape from a requirement to pay 10% of their profits by way of annual fees to an American company holding 15% of Vodafone's shares yielded an enduring benefit to Vodafone and was therefore a capital payment. This was rejected by the court, but the Commissioners and the High Court found against Vodafone on the grounds that the payment, although accepted as revenue expenditure, benefited not only the parent company but its subsidiaries as well, so that it failed the 'wholly and exclusively' test in what is now CTA 2009 s 54(1)(a). This decision was reversed by the Court of Appeal, which held that the *purpose* of the payment was to remove a liability from Vodafone and it did exclusively benefit that company, even though the *effect* was to benefit the other companies in the group as well.

In the Tucker case mentioned above, the House of Lords considered that the first step was to decide on what asset the expenditure had been incurred. (So if it was a current asset, such as a motor vehicle for resale by a car dealer, sums spent on putting it into saleable condition would be revenue expenditure.) If the asset was a capital asset, it was then necessary to consider the nature of the expenditure, so that expenditure linked to its acquisition or disposal (such as legal expenses on buying or selling a property) would be capital expenditure, whereas expenditure on maintaining and repairing it would be revenue. This general principle has been extended to the treatment of liabilities, particularly in the field of exchange losses, where it was held by the House of Lords in *Beauchamp v Woolworth* (1989) that capital borrowing was something that is to be borrowed once and for all and income borrowing is going to recur every year. The company's exchange losses on repaying substantial sums that it had borrowed for a five-year period were therefore capital losses and could not be deducted in calculating income profits. (Special rules now apply to the treatment of exchange gains and losses relating to companies – see Example 63 explanatory note 2.)

Repairs or improvements

One of the key areas where the distinction is important is that of repairs. There are two aspects, first the treatment of repairs to newly acquired assets, and second the question of whether an item is a repair and thus allowable or an improvement or renewal and thus not allowable.

Where a newly acquired asset is repaired, the expenditure will not be allowed for tax purposes if the repairs must be done in order to bring the asset into use in the business (*Law Shipping v CIR* (1924)). If the asset is usable and commercially viable in its existing state, the subsequent repair expenditure will be allowable (*Odeon Associated Theatres Ltd v Jones* (1972)).

As far as improvements are concerned, the essential question is whether you are left with what you had originally or whether you have something extra. Money spent by a railway company in increasing the number of sleepers under each rail was capital expenditure, but expenditure on replacing worn rails and sleepers was revenue expenditure (*Rhodesia Railways Ltd v Income Tax Collector of Bechuanaland Protectorate* (1933). This case also raises the question of renewals. What needs to be decided is what is the entirety. If you incur expenditure on renewing a subsidiary part of an asset, you have repaired the asset. If you replace the entire asset, you have incurred capital expenditure. Thus the cost of demolishing and rebuilding a colliery chimney was held to be capital expenditure, since the chimney was the entirety (*O'Grady v Bullcroft Main Collieries Ltd* (1932)), whereas the cost of removing and replacing a factory chimney was a repair to part of the factory building and was allowable (*Samuel Jones & Co (Devondale) Ltd v CIR* (1951)).

These long standing provisions have been modified by FA 2008 s 73, which inserted s 33B into CAA 2001, which introduced a statutory test of capital vs revenue in relation to a new class of assets known as integral features. Expenditure on replacement features is classified as capital expenditure (attracting the relevant capital allowances) if more than 50% of the current replacement cost of the asset is spent in any 12-month period (which may span two accounting periods).

Provisions

The 1998 case of *Jenners Princes Street Edinburgh Ltd v CIR* raised the question of when a sum is expended for repairs. The departmental store had carried out a survey relating to external repairs and at the year-end was in the process of granting contracts to carry out the repair work. The actual work was done in the following two years. The Special Commissioners agreed with the company that a specific provision had been made, that it accorded with sound commercial accounting principles and therefore the amount had been 'expended' in the accounting sense even though not paid out.

In the 1999 case of *Herbert Smith v Honour* the High Court held that the expected future loss on a lease of vacated premises was an allowable deduction in the year of vacating the property, the provision being required under Financial Reporting Standard 12 (FRS 12) issued September 1998, which states that 'if an entity has a contract that is onerous, the present obligation under the contract should be recognised and measured as a provision'.

Under FRS 12, provisions must be made, and can only be made, when at the balance sheet date 'a business has a present obligation (legal or constructive) as a result of a past event, it is probable that expenditure will be required to settle the obligation, and a reliable estimate can be made of the obligation'.

In addition, post balance sheet events must be considered in arriving at the quantification of the provision. For example, a stock obsolescence provision cannot value stock at an amount below that subsequently achieved on an actual sale, ie its net realisable value. In the same way a provision cannot be made against a debt which has subsequently, but before the finalisation of the accounts, been paid in full. If settled at a reduced amount then the provision is restricted to the actual loss (FRS 21).

HMRC set out their views in Tax Bulletin 44 issued December 1999 and Working Together Issue 13, published June 2003. A provision will be deductible provided it is a revenue amount, the provision is required by GAAP, does not conflict with statute and can be accurately quantified.

Income recognition

Where the business supplies services under a contract, the income for the period must include all services performed up to the balance sheet date, irrespective of any arrangements which prevent those services being billed for until later. The value of partially completed services is not treated as work in progress, but is recognised as income and the related profit included in the reporting period. This is in accordance with FRS 5 Application Note G and applies particularly to professional businesses.

Goodwill and intangible assets

Another Accounting Standard that has a particular bearing on tax computations is FRS 10 – Goodwill and intangible assets. FRS 10 broadly requires *purchased* goodwill and intangible assets (but not internally created goodwill and intangibles) to be written off over the expected economic life of the asset. In some cases the tax law prescribes a different treatment, for example, expenditure incurred by individuals on goodwill is wholly capital expenditure and a deduction against profits cannot be made. FRS 10 does, however, affect the tax treatment of some payments for intangible assets, a particular example being transfer fees for football (and other sports) players. As indicated above, the treatment of goodwill and intangible assets for companies changed from 1 April 2002, the treatment now being largely as prescribed by accounting standards.

Capital profit or trading income

Similar principles to those outlined above are used to distinguish receipts which are part of the trading income from capital profits. Receipts of the trade form part of income, whereas capital receipts are dealt with under the capital gains rules.

The disposal of trading stock clearly gives rise to trading income, whereas the amount received for disposal of a fixed asset is a capital receipt. Particular difficulty arises in relation to compensation payments. Lump sums are not necessarily capital receipts. It depends on whether the compensation is to make good damage to, or for the physical destruction of, a capital asset of the business.

Compensation relating to the cancellation of trading contracts, including agency contracts, is usually treated as a trading receipt, unless the contract is so dominant that its loss accounts for substantially the whole of the company's trade (*Barr Crombie and Co Ltd v CIR* (1945)), or the contract regulates the whole structure or framework of the trade (*Van den Berghs Ltd v Clark*, (HL 1935)). The Van den Berghs decision was followed in the case of *Sabine v Lookers Ltd* (1958), where the Court of Appeal held that compensation for a material variation of a 'continuity clause' that had previously given a car distributor an ongoing option to renew its main distributorship was a capital receipt because the agreement 'governed Lookers' whole trade and was not merely one of several contracts or engagements'.

Explanatory notes

1. In the absence of a specific statutory provision, the trading rules would not permit a deduction for expenses incurred prior to the commencement of trade. Such expenses are, however, specifically dealt with in ITTOIA 2005 s 57, which provides that pre-trading expenditure incurred by an individual within seven years prior to the commencement of a trade, which would have been allowable expenditure if it had been incurred after the commencement, is treated as incurred on the first day of trading and is thus allowable as an expense of the first accounting period. The same applies to companies, except for pre-trading interest, for which different rules apply (see Example 49 explanatory note 6).

2. Legal charges on acquiring an asset such as a lease are part of the capital cost and are not allowed in computing taxable profits. HMRC will by concession allow the cost of *renewing* a short lease (ie one with 50 years or less to run) but not the cost of the original acquisition.

3. For full details of the tax treatment of intangible assets for companies see Example 66.

Question

D E Flour is a wholesale merchant who has been in business for many years, making up his accounts to 31 March each year. The following is a summary of his Profit and Loss Account for the year to 31 March 2010:

			£
Sales			897,251
Less: Cost of sales			782,359
Gross profit after warehouse wages etc			114,892
Rent from temporary letting of surplus warehouse space			10,000
Bank interest			90
Profit on sale of equipment			78
Dividend on holding of shares in Export and Import plc			314
			125,374
Less: Salary – Mrs Flour		10,000	
Other salaries		39,846	
Rates and insurances		3,200	
Light and heat		2,000	
Telephone		1,520	
Repairs		6,250	
Motor car expenses:			
Flour's own car	3,000		
Warehouse manager's car	1,600	4,600	
Bank interest		90	
Loan interest		2,250	
Bad and doubtful debts		138	
Legal and professional expenses		1,206	
General expenses		2,810	
Depreciation		800	
Business use of home		456	
Management salary – D E Flour		12,000	87,166
Net profit			38,208

The following further information is available:

1.   Mrs Flour assists with the book-keeping and other clerical duties. Her salary was paid monthly at the rate of £720, a further £1,360 bonus being paid at the end of April 2010 and included in creditors.

2.   Mrs Doe (Mrs Flour's widowed mother) lives on the premises and it is calculated that one-quarter of the insurance, light and heat relate to the living accommodation. She does not act as caretaker.

3.   Rates and insurance comprise:

	£
Business rates	2,100
Council tax (Mrs Doe)	620
Insurances	480
	3,200

4.   The telephone is used mainly for business, but there is an extension in the living accommodation and it is calculated that one-tenth of the expenditure relates to private use.

5.   Repairs comprise:

	£
Work on staff toilets	400
Redecoration of showroom	850
Division of large room into three private offices	5,000
	6,250

The toilets although usable were in a very bad state of repair when the premises were purchased in March 2009.

Had the large room not been converted into three private offices, the ceiling would have required repairing at a cost of £1,000.

6.   The expenses for Flour's car are the total running expenses for the year. Flour's mileage in the year to 31 March 2010 was as follows:

Home to business	4,000
Purely private journeys	4,000
Purely business journeys	10,000
Trip to south of England (Flour spent the week there, two days at the annual conference of Wholesalers' Trade Association and the remaining five days on holiday travelling round the region)	2,000
	20,000 miles

The warehouse manager's car had been purchased new in the year for £10,000. He uses the car 50% for private purposes. No private petrol is provided.

7.   The premises from which trade was carried on were purchased at the beginning of the year, having previously been rented. The loan interest relates to the purchase thereof. The premises are larger than Flour currently needs, so he has let a small part on a monthly basis until his business expands.

8.   The bad debts account was:

	£			£
Trade debts written off	390	Specific debt reserve }	B/F	230
		2% of debtors reserve }		800
Loan to customer written off	54			
		Debts recovered (previously charged and allowed in computing trading profits)		
Specific debt reserve } C/F	250			
2% of debtors reserve }	1,000			526
		Profit and loss account		138
	1,694			1,694

9.   Legal and professional expenses were:

	£
Legal costs – debt collection	250
negotiation of loan re premises	316
Accountancy	640
	1,206

10. (a) General expenses comprise:

	£
Printing and stationery	500
Annual payment through gift aid to local hospital (gross)	40
Subscription – trade association	70
Gift to local charity	30
Entertaining expenses and gifts (see below)	2,120
Donation to the Hospital Saturday Fund to which all the employees belong	50
	2,810

(b) Entertaining expenses and gifts were made up as follows:

	£
Entertaining customers	550
Christmas gifts to staff	366
Gift to employee on marriage	50
Gifts to customers	
One pocket diary to each customer at Christmas – cost £3.40 each	850
Expenses of staff dinner at Christmas	304
	2,120

11. Flour maintains an office at his home. He has been charged business rates on the office amounting to £306, and the lighting and heating costs are estimated at £150.

12. (a) Mr Flour has taken various goods for his own use or consumption, the selling price being £864 and the cost price £558. He has paid for these goods at cost price, £558 being included in his sales for the year.

(b) His mother owns a small grocery shop. Flour has in June 2009 professionally valued her stock for which he would normally charge a fee of £500 since this is one of the activities of his trade. He did not, however, make any charge.

13. All amounts are adjusted appropriately for VAT.

Using the format of the full self-employment pages, SA103F, compute the trading profit for tax purposes (before deducting capital allowances).

Answer

Computation of Net Business Profit for tax purposes for the year ended 31 March 2010

	£	£	Explanatory Note
Turnover		897,251	
		_____	
Other business income		10,404	2

	£	Disallowable £	
Less:			
Cost of goods bought for resale	782,359		
Construction industry – payments to subcontractors	–		
Wages, salaries and other staff costs	49,846		
Car, van and travel expenses	4,600	1,500	14
Rent, rates, power and insurance costs (£3,200 + £2,000 + £456)	5,656	1,240	3(a), 15
Repairs & renewals of property and equipment	6,250	5,000	3(b), 5
Telephone, fax, stationery and other office costs (£1,520 + (£2,810–£2,120)	2,210	192	3(a), (d), 6, 8
Advertising and business entertainment costs	2,120	550	7
Interest on bank and other loans	2,250	562	9
Bank, credit card and other financial charges	90		
Irrecoverable debts written off	138	254	3(c)
Accountancy, legal and other professional fees	1,206	79	10
Depreciation and loss/(profit) on sale	722	722	3(e)
Other expenses	12,000	12,000	4
Total expenses/disallowable expenses	869,447	22,099	
	_____	_____	
Net profit		38,208	
Goods etc taken for own use	306		13
Total additions to net profit or deductions from net loss		22,405	
Income, receipts and other profits included in business income or expenses but not taxable as business profits	404		2
Total deductions from net profit or additions to net loss		404	
		_____	
Net business profit for tax purposes		60,209	
		_____	

Explanatory Notes

All references in these notes are to ITTOIA 2005 unless otherwise stated.

Self-assessment – self-employment pages

1. For tax purposes, the profit shown in a trader's accounts has to be adjusted in accordance with the tax rules to arrive at the taxable profit (or allowable loss) for the accounting period. Section 25 requires profits for a trade to be calculated in accordance with generally accepted accounting practice, subject to any adjustment required or authorised by law. For information on the effect of Accounting Standards on tax computations relating to capital and revenue expenditure – see Example 14.

   Under self-assessment, the accounts figures are shown in tax returns in a standardised format on the self-employment pages, except for certain very large partnerships – see Example 42 explanatory note 5. The headings under which information must be given are those shown in the example. Taxpayers whose accounts include a balance sheet are also required to show the balance sheet details on the return. Those whose turnover is less than the VAT registration threshold (£68,000 for 2009/10) may instead complete the short self-employment pages, SA103S, which provides for a simpler summary of allowable expenses only, and no balance sheet. As an alternative, from 2009/10 they may simply enter their expenses as a single figure in box 9 of SA103S (or box 30 of SA103F) and need provide no additional analysis.

   The net business profit arrived at after the various tax adjustments is reduced by capital allowances to arrive at the taxable profit (see Example 18).

Non-trading income

2. The 'other income' comprises rent of £10,000, bank interest of £90 and the dividend of £314. The profit on sale of equipment of £78 is not included because it is netted off against the depreciation figure (see explanatory note 3(e)). The interest and dividends are excluded from the taxable income because they are taxable under other provisions. The same should strictly apply to the rent from letting, but where a small part of business premises is let because it is temporarily surplus to requirements and is likely to be used by the business within three years, the rent may be treated as part of the trading income.

Expenditure 'wholly and exclusively' for the trade

3. Unless it is covered by a specific statutory provision, expenditure is not allowable in computing profits unless it is wholly and exclusively for the purposes of the trade (s 34). A payment that satisfies the general rule is even so not allowable if it is a criminal payment, such as a bribe or protection money to terrorists, or a payment made in response to threats, menaces, blackmail and other forms of extortion. This restriction includes any payment made overseas which, if it were made in the UK, would constitute a criminal offence (s 55).

   A distinction is drawn between expenditure incurred in the capacity of trader, and in the capacity of taxpayer, the latter being an appropriation of profit and not allowable. So the expenses of an appeal against business rates would be allowable, since they relate to the trade, whereas the expenses of an appeal against a tax assessment would not, because they are incurred in the capacity of taxpayer. In the case of accountancy expenses, some of the expense is clearly related to the agreement of the tax liability on the profits, but by HMRC practice the full amount is allowable. This does not extend to the expense of preparing self-assessment returns and calculating capital gains, but HMRC accepts that the additional costs are likely to be minimal for someone whose personal tax affairs are straightforward. The relief for accountancy expenses does not apply to additional accounting charges relating to an in-depth investigation of the trader's affairs by HMRC. Such expenses are only allowed if no adjustment to profit results from the investigation, or where there is an adjustment to the current year only and the additional profits do not arise out of negligent or fraudulent conduct (Statement of Practice SP 16/91). Under self-assessment, HMRC is able to undertake random audits under the 'enquiry' procedure, in addition to their powers to investigate cases of fraudulent or negligent conduct or inadequate disclosure (see Example 41 explanatory notes 13 and 15).

The wholly and exclusively provision in s 34 is interpreted in practice in the following way:

(a) Living expenses and private payments are not allowable as they are not for the purpose of the trade. Therefore the expenses of the living accommodation occupied by Flour's mother-in-law are not allowable. The accommodation expenses would be allowable if she were acting as caretaker and therefore occupying the accommodation as an employee.

The council tax relating to Mrs Doe is also a private payment. If she had been an employee, then unless the accommodation was necessary for her to do her job the payment would have been treated as part of her wages for both tax and national insurance contributions, and would be reported on Form P11D for employees earning £8,500 per annum or more and for directors, or on Form P9D for other employees (for details of the PAYE provisions see Example 9). In these circumstances it would be an allowable deduction from Mr Flour's profits.

The disallowed premises costs of £1,240 comprise ¼ of the insurance and light and heat (£120 and £500 respectively) and the council tax of £620. 1/10th of the telephone costs, ie £152, is part of the disallowance of £192 on general administrative expenses (the other £40 relating to the charitable gift aid – see explanatory note 3(d)).

(b) Nothing can be allowed for repairs which might have been but have not been carried out. The £1,000 which would have been spent on the large room ceiling repair is therefore not allowable and the whole cost of dividing the room into offices is capital expenditure (see explanatory note 5).

(c) Debts cannot be written off except for bad debts that were incurred wholly and exclusively for the purpose of the trade, doubtful debts to the extent that they are respectively estimated to be bad and debts released by the creditor in a voluntary arrangement under the 1986 Insolvency Act. (The debtor in a voluntary arrangement will not have to bring into his trading profit debts that have been released in this way, but debts released other than under such arrangements must be treated as a trading receipt – ITTOIA 2005 s 97.) A general bad debts provision is therefore disallowed when it is made. If it is subsequently increased the increase is disallowed, and if it is decreased, the decrease is excluded from the profit. For detailed notes on deductibility of provisions see Example 14.

Writing off a loan to a customer is not allowable (unless lending money is part of the taxpayer's trade), since it was not for trading purposes. The disallowance of £254 comprises the increase of £200 in the general reserve and the loan of £54 written off. Writing off a loan to an employee where the loan was made by reason of the employment would (in the absence of special circumstances) be an allowable expense to the employer – but the employee would usually be liable to tax on the amount so released. The employer would need to show that the loss was connected with or arose out of the trade. For the detailed provisions on employee loans see Example 58.

(d) Payments such as pension contributions for the sole trader or under the 'gift aid' scheme (personal donations – see Example 90 for details) are not allowed as trading expenses. ITA 2007 has removed ITTOIA 2005 s 51 which previously prevented patent royalties from being deducted in calculating trade profits. Patent royalties can therefore be deducted if they are wholly and exclusively for the purpose of the trade. Patent royalties that do not meet the wholly and exclusively test above would be deducted under ITA 2007 s 448 in calculating an individual's net income.

(e) Any capital items and expenses connected with the acquisition or disposal of capital items are not allowable (the depreciation of equipment of £800 is thus not allowable and the profit on sale of equipment of £78 is not included in the taxable profit, giving a net disallowance of £722). By concession, the legal costs of *renewing* a short lease (ie for 50 years or less) are allowable. See Example 14 for the tests that apply to determine capital expenditure.

Family wages and drawings

4.　Mrs Flour's salary and bonus are allowable provided they can be shown to be commercially justifiable (ie wholly and exclusively for the trade). Earnings that are paid after the end of the account to which they relate may only be taken into account in that period if paid within nine months after it ends and as long as a valid provision exists at the balance sheet date, in accordance with GAAP. Otherwise they are deducted in the period in which they are paid (s 36). These provisions do not affect Mrs Flour's bonus since it is paid within one month. The bonus will form part of Mrs Flour's income for 2010/11 (in which it is received).

The payment described as a management salary to Mr Flour actually represents drawings of profit and is not allowed. The same applies to profit shares allocated to partners that are described as salaries, interest, etc.

Repairs

5.　The repair work on the staff toilets and indeed the decorating of the showroom is allowable since there was no question of these not being usable at the time of acquisition (*Odeon Associated Theatres Ltd v Jones* (1972)). If repairs are necessary before an asset can be used in a business, they are part of the capital cost. Expenditure on extensions, improvements and additions is capital expenditure and is not allowable, as in the case of the division of a room into three offices in the example.

Entertaining, gifts, donations and subscriptions

6.　The donation to the Hospital Saturday Fund is allowable since it is for the benefit of employees.

7.　Expenditure on entertaining and gifts is covered by s 45 which disallows expenditure on entertaining and gifts except for the following:

(a)　Gifts carrying a conspicuous advertisement, not consisting of food, drink or tobacco and not exceeding £50 per person per annum (s 47(3)). This covers Flour's expenditure on diaries.

(b)　Gifts for employees (s 47(4)). The wedding gift will come under this heading. It may escape tax in the hands of the employee if it can be regarded as having been made on personal grounds (even though there is a link between the payment and the employment), but not if it is regarded as paid as a reward for or in return for acting as or being an employee.

Expenditure on staff entertaining (s 46(3)), although allowable to the employer as being for the benefit of staff, will result in a benefits charge on a director or P11D employee, unless covered by the £150 exemption (see Example 9 explanatory note 31). The VAT position on staff entertaining costs is that input tax can be recovered on the proportion relating to employees only and not that relating to other guests (since entertaining expenses other than those relating to staff are disallowed – see explanatory note 16).

(c)　Gifts to charities (s 47(5)) (other than gift aid payments – see 3(d)), providing they are *wholly* and *exclusively* for the purposes of the trade. It will usually be difficult to show a trading motive for a gift to a charity. The trader may be able to show that being known as a subscriber to the charity benefits his trade. A modest gift to a charity with which the trader has a direct connection could usually be justified on 'wholly and exclusively' grounds. It has been assumed that this applies to Flour's gift to the local charity. HMRC have stated that subscriptions to hospitals, churches, chapels etc are not normally regarded as admissible except in a small community where the trader is the dominant employer and the employees are the predominant users of the facilities. There are separate provisions to allow relief for gifts of trading stock to charities and educational establishments (s 108). For details see Example 49 explanatory note 4(vi) and Example 90.

Where a business makes sponsorship payments of a revenue nature, they are allowed providing they satisfy the 'wholly and exclusively' rule, ie the purpose must be to provide the payer with a commensurate benefit, usually in the form of advertising.

8. Subscriptions to trade associations are normally allowable, the association bearing tax on any excess of its subscription income over its allowable expenses. Any other subscriptions need to be considered under the 'wholly and exclusively' rule.

Finance costs

9. Whilst disallowing capital expenditure in computing profits, s 29 and s 34 permit the deduction of interest paid wholly and exclusively for the trade. The loan interest has therefore been allowed, except for the proportion relating to the mother-in-law's living accommodation (assumed to be one-quarter).

10. The incidental costs of raising loan finance (excluding stamp duty) are allowed providing that the interest on the loan qualifies as a deduction from profits (so the private proportion of ¼, ie £79, is disallowed) (s 58). HMRC have stated that if a life policy is taken out as a condition of obtaining loan finance, the premiums would not be 'incidental costs' of obtaining the finance, although any incidental costs of taking out the policy would be.

11. Interest paid (or received) on delayed payment on contracts for the supply of goods or services will be a revenue expense (or trading receipt). The interest is not subject to deduction of tax at source (see Example 5 part (a)).

Security expenditure

12. Expenditure to meet a special threat to the personal security of a sole trader or partner, such as from terrorists, is allowable subject to various restrictions (s 81). Revenue expenditure, such as on bodyguards, is allowed as a business expense. Capital expenditure, such as on alarm systems and bullet resistant windows, qualifies for capital allowances (see Example 18 part (a)). Where expenditure is incurred in relation to employees, there are parallel provisions to exempt the employee from any benefit in kind charge on the security assets and security services provided.

Goods and services for own use

13. Own goods are generally thought to be accounted for at selling price (*Sharkey v Wernher* (1956)), which was given statutory effect by FA 2008 Sch 15 which inserted Chapter 11A. There is no rule requiring services to be accounted for at any greater figure than the charge made (*Mason v Innes* (1967)). It has been suggested by a number of leading commentators that the decision in *Sharkey v Wernher* is no longer appropriate, which may explain its introduction into statute. VAT is due on the price paid by the business.

Motor expenses

14. Motor expenses are capable of division into a part which is wholly and exclusively for the purposes of the trade and a part which is not, the former part being allowable on an apportionment basis (s 34(2)). Private motoring includes home to business travelling even though there are some duties undertaken at the private residence for which an allowance is made in computing profits (*Newsom v Robertson* (1953)). Half of the expenses on Flour's car have been disallowed on the basis of 10,000 private miles. Expenses that are *partly* for business are not allowed. The essential point is whether the trader had only a business purpose in mind when incurring the expenditure. If so the expenditure would be allowable, even if some incidental private benefit was obtained. But if there was more than one purpose, even if the trading purpose was the main one, the whole of the expenditure is strictly

disallowed. For this reason the trip to the south of England, having both a private and a business purpose, is disallowed. HMRC may be prepared to accept a claim for a proportion of travelling expenses for a mixed purpose journey on the basis of the time spent on business. This could not be done on a mileage basis for Flour's trip, because he has clearly covered extra miles during his holiday. Under self-assessment, a trader's assessment of such a business element would only be questioned if HMRC enquired into his return or later made a discovery that it contained an inaccuracy which was careless or deliberate, or that insufficient disclosure of the area of doubt had been made. In addition to claiming the appropriate proportion of running expenses, Flour will be able to claim the same proportion of capital allowances (see Example 20 explanatory note 12). For those whose turnover does not exceed the VAT threshold (£68,000 from 1 May 2009), HMRC have stated that they will accept traders using the HMRC Authorised Mileage Allowance Rates (see page (viii)) to compute allowable motoring expenses, capital allowances then not being claimable in addition. The trader can only change the basis of claim to actual costs on a change of motor vehicle.

Private use by *employees* does not cause any restriction either in allowable running expenses or in capital allowances. If the employee earns £8,500 or more or is a director, the private use will be the subject of a benefit in kind charge (see Example 9).

If a trader leases a motor car on or after 6 April 2009, and its official emissions rating exceeded 160 g/km CO_2 , then the allowable hire charge is restricted to 85% (ITTOIA 2005 s 48 as amended by FA 2009 Sch 11) (see Example 20 explanatory note 18).

Business use of home

15.   Where a room at home is used for business purposes, a deduction may be claimed for the additional costs of the business use, such as light and heat. Where part of a property is used for business purposes, business rates are payable if the business use prevents the continued domestic use of that part of the property. This means strictly that there must always be mixed use to avoid a business rates charge, and where a room is exclusively set aside as an office business rates should be payable. Where business rates are not paid, the appropriate part of the council tax may be deducted as a business expense. The inclusion of £456 in the premises costs covers the home expenditure on rates, light and heat.

In January 2007, HMRC issued new guidance on the use of home by the self-employed. This has been incorporated into HMRC's Business Income Manual at BIM47800. The guidance states that expenses can be apportioned using area, usage or time. The guidance includes examples and the higher the claim, the more likely the claim will be calculated by reference to more than one of these points eg, calculated on area and then time-apportioned. The guidance confirms that, in the right circumstances, it is possible to claim a portion of:

- Insurance – a portion of general household or where separate business insurance, that policy only in full.

- Council tax.

- Mortgage interest.

- Rent.

- Repairs and maintenance – examples include the full cost of decorating an area used solely for business purposes and the relevant portion of general redecoration of the exterior/roof.

- Cleaning.

- Heat, light and power.

- Telephone – including portion of line rental and all aspects of use including incoming calls where appropriate.

- Broadband – a flexible approach is suggested for all inclusive packages.

- Metered water – although the guidance incorporates the idea of apportioning some expenses that would be incurred regardless (eg, mortgage interest/council tax) there still seems to be a historic reluctance to accept claims for fixed water rates hence the title heading 'metered' water. That said, guidance to childminders (which predates this guidance) allows them to claim 10% of their water regardless of whether metered or fixed.

The guidance also states that where a claim is small and there is only minor business use of the home, for example the taxpayer writes up their business records at home, HMRC should accept a claim based on any reasonable basis. Their examples include a round sum figure of £3 per week for such use.

Value added tax

16. As a VAT registered trader Flour will account for VAT on his sales (including the sale of equipment), less a deduction for allowable input VAT he has suffered. He cannot claim a deduction for the VAT on business entertaining. It was, however, decided in the case of *Thorn EMI plc v C & E* (1994) that input tax should be apportioned where expenditure is partly for business entertaining and partly for other business purposes. He will have to pay a VAT scale charge for his private car fuel and this is similarly not deductible. If he had provided private fuel to employees, he would have to pay VAT scale charges for each employee, but the amounts charged would have been included as part of his deductible car expenses. As far as the car bought for the warehouse manager is concerned (and any other cars bought, but not commercial vehicles) Flour will not be able to reclaim the input VAT, but he can claim capital allowances on the VAT-inclusive amount. The VAT-inclusive cost is presumably £10,000, since the example states that amounts have been adjusted appropriately for VAT and no adjustment is appropriate in this instance.

As far as cars that are leased rather than purchased are concerned, leasing companies are entitled to reclaim input VAT in full on cars acquired for leasing. (The same applies to other businesses that use cars wholly for business purposes, such as self-drive hire firms and driving schools.) Where the leasing company has recovered the input VAT, the lessee may recover only 50% of the input VAT on the leasing charges if there is any use of the car for private purposes. The disallowed input VAT forms part of the deductible leasing charges in computing profit (subject to any restriction for private use by a sole trader or partner).

Where a VAT registered trader makes a gift of business goods costing more than £50, VAT output tax will be due based upon input tax claimed on the goods. However, if the gift is to a charity for resale in a charity shop the supply will be zero-rated.

A non-VAT registered trader includes VAT as part of his allowable expenses or capital costs, subject to the disallowance of VAT on business entertaining and on any private use proportion. A partly exempt trader may recover any non-deductible input VAT in a similar way. Some approximation may be necessary in allocating the VAT to the various items of expenditure and this will be accepted by HMRC providing it is reasonable.

For the treatment of VAT where small business flat rate scheme is used see Tax Bulletin 64. Expenses should then be shown as VAT inclusive and the amount payable to HMRC can either be deducted from the VAT inclusive turnover or shown as an expense in 'other expenses' on the tax return. The maximum turnover for the flat rate scheme is £150,000 so it is not available to Flour.

National insurance

17. As an employer, Flour will have to pay employers' Class 1, Class 1A (and if appropriate Class 1B) national insurance contributions, which are deductible in arriving at his taxable profit (see Example 48 for details). He will also have to pay self-employed Class 2 and Class 4 contributions, but these are not tax deductible (see Example 48).

Interest surcharges and penalties on income tax and VAT paid late

18. These are not deductible in arriving at the taxable figure of business profits, this includes interest on late paid CIS deductions, NI and student loan repayments (s 54).

Miscellaneous

19. This example deals with the treatment of most common items of expenditure. For the treatment of expenditure incurred prior to the start of a trade, see Example 14 explanatory note 1. For the treatment of premiums paid on short leases, see Example 99 part (h). Other points are dealt with in Example 49.

Question

Please note: This will apply to unincorporated businesses and limited liability partnerships (LLPs) carrying on a trade.

In (a) and (b) below, all calculations are to be taken to the nearest month.

(a)   Show the assessments arising in the following four examples, assuming that the traders all started in business on 1 January 2009 and made profits (net of capital allowances) as shown:

(i)	Year to 31 December 2009	£12,000
	Year to 31 December 2010	£18,000
(ii)	Six months to 30 June 2009	£3,000
	Year to 30 June 2010	£17,000
(iii)	15 months to 31 March 2010	£3,750
	Year to 31 March 2011	£16,000
(iv)	16 months to 30 April 2010	£4,400
	Year to 30 April 2011	£18,000

(b)   Show the assessments for the final tax year for the businesses in (a) if they had all continued to make up accounts annually to the dates shown and had ceased on 31 August 2013, the profits for each of them in the final two years being at the rate of £5,000 a month and the final accounting periods being:

(i)   8 months from 1.1.2013 to 31.8.2013

(ii)   14 months from 1.7.2012 to 31.8.2013

(iii)   5 months from 1.4.2013 to 31.8.2013

(iv)   16 months from 1.5.2012 to 31.8.2013

(c)   (i)   State how trading stock is valued on discontinuance of a business.

        (ii)   State how post cessation receipts and expenditure are treated.

(d)   Explain the provisions regarding the taxation of the income of barristers in years six to eight of their practice.

Answer

References in this example are to the Income Tax (Trading and Other Income) Act 2005 (ITTOIA 2005) unless otherwise stated.

(a) Although s 203(3) states that apportionments should be made in days, all calculations in the example have been taken to the nearest month in accordance with s 203(4) which permits apportionments either in days, or months, or months and fractions of months, providing the chosen method is used consistently. The 2008/09 profit in part (i) of the example works out at £3,000 when apportioned in months, with the overlap profit being the same amount. It would be 95/365 of £12,000, ie £3,123 if apportioned in days, and the overlap profit would then be £3,123.

Where a business makes up accounts to 31 March, HMRC is prepared to treat an apportionment of profit for a period of 5 days or less as nil in accordance with s 209. On this basis, a business that started on 1 April 2009 and made up accounts to 31 March 2010 would have no assessable profit in 2008/09 and would pay tax in each succeeding year on the profit of the year to 31 March; overlap profits would not arise unless the accounting date was changed. HMRC is similarly prepared to treat a change of accounting date to 31 March as being equivalent to a change to 5 April (per s 220(5)), all existing overlap relief being deducted at the time of the change (see Example 28 part (c) for an illustration).

					£
(i)	2008/09	1.1.09 – 5.4.09	3/12 ×	12,000	3,000
	2009/10	Yr to 31.12.09			12,000
	2010/11	Yr to 31.12.10			18,000

Overlap profit 1.1.09 – 5.4.09 (3 months)   £3,000

(ii)	2008/09	1.1.09 – 5.4.09	3/6 ×	3,000	1,500
	2009/10	1.1.09 – 31.12.09			
		1st 6 mths		3,000	
		6/12 × 17,000		8,500	11,500
	2010/11	Yr to 30.6.10			17,000

Overlap profit: 1.1.09 – 5.4.09 3/6 × 3,000   1,500
                 1.7.09 – 31.12.09 6/12 × 17,000   8,500

Total overlap profit (9 months)   £10,000

(iii)	2008/09	1.1.09 – 5.4.09	3/15 ×	3,750	750
	2009/10	1.4.09 – 31.3.10	12/15 ×	3,750	3,000
	2010/11	Yr to 31.3.11			16,000

Overlap profit 5 days from 1.4.09 – 5.4.09   –

(iv)	2008/09	1.1.09 – 5.4.09	3/16 ×	4,400	825
	2009/10	6.4.09 – 5.4.10	12/16 ×	4,400	3,300
	2010/11	1.5.09 – 30.4.10	12/16 ×	4,400	3,300
	2011/12	1.5.10 – 30.4.11			18,000

Overlap profit 1.5.09 – 5.4.10 (11 months)   £3,025

Relief for the overlap profits is given either when the business ceases or on an earlier change of accounting date if more than twelve months' profits is being taxed in one year.

(b)   If the businesses in (a) closed down on 31 August 2013, the tax year of cessation would be 2013/14. The profits of the final accounting period would be:

In (a)(i)	8 months to 31.8.13	£40,000
In (a)(ii)	14 months to 31.8.13	£70,000
In (a)(iii)	5 months to 31.8.13	£25,000
In (a)(iv)	16 months to 31.8.13	£80,000

The final assessments would be as follows:

(i)	Profits 1.1.13 to 31.8.13	40,000	
	Less overlap relief	3,000	£37,000
(ii)	Profits 1.7.12 to 31.8.13	70,000	
	Less overlap relief	10,000	£60,000
(iii)	Profits 1.4.13 to 31.8.13		
	(No overlap relief)		£25,000
(iv)	Profits 1.5.12 to 31.8.13	80,000	
	Less overlap relief	3,025	£76,975

(c)   (i)   *Valuation of trading stock*

The valuation of stock and work in progress is dealt with in Chapter 12 of ITTOIA 2005.

Any unsold trading stock at the date of discontinuance of a business is treated as follows:

1.   Any stock sold to an unconnected UK trader who can deduct the cost of it in his computation of assessable trading profits is brought into the final accounts or computations at the amount for which it is sold (s 173). Where stock is transferred with other assets, the consideration is apportioned on a just and reasonable basis.

2.   Any stock sold to a UK trader who is connected with the vendor (eg through a family link, or as companies in the same group), is treated as sold for an arm's length price (s 177). If, however, that amount is greater than both the actual sale price and the cost of the stock, the two parties may make a claim to use the higher of cost and sale price instead of arm's length value. The claim must be made within two years after the end of the chargeable period (ie tax year or company accounting period) in which the trade ceased (s 178).

3.   Any other stock (eg stock given away or retained for private purposes) is adjusted in the final income tax computation to reflect the amount it would have realised if it had been sold in the open market at the discontinuation of the trade (s 175(4)).

4.   The provisions of notes 1 to 3 do not apply where a business ceases because of the death of the sole proprietor (s 173(4)), and the closing stock is valued at the lower of cost and market value. Its acquisition value for executors or beneficiaries is, however, its market value at the date of death, both for capital gains purposes and for income tax purposes if they carry on the business. Work in progress is valued at consideration received, or at market value if no consideration (s 184). In the case of a profession the taxpayer may elect for work in progress to be valued at cost. An excess amount subsequently received being treated as a post-cessation receipt (s 185). The election must be made within one year from 31 January following the tax year of cessation.

(ii)   *Post-cessation receipts*

Where income is received after a business has ceased, and it has not been included in the final accounts, it is charged to tax under Chapter 18, at s 242. The taxable amount may be reduced by any expenses, capital allowances or losses that could have been set against it if it had been received before the business ceased (s 254). The taxable amount is treated as earned income of the tax year in which it is received. If, however, the income is received in a tax year beginning not later than six years after the cessation date, an election may be made to have it taxed as if it had been received on the date of cessation (s 257). The election must be made within one year from 31 January following the tax year in which the amount is received. Although the tax adjustment from backdating is calculated by reference to the earlier year, the claim is treated as relating to the tax year in which the amount is received and is given effect by increasing the tax payable for that later tax year. The additional tax is not, however, treated as part of the tax *assessed* for the later year and does not therefore affect payments on account for the next following year (see Example 43).

The treatment of post cessation receipts is particularly relevant to barristers within the first seven years of practice, because they normally prepare their accounts on the basis of cash received rather than on an earnings basis.

Post-cessation expenditure

Where qualifying payments are made within seven years after cessation (or debts for which provision was not made in the final accounts become irrecoverable), then unless there are post-cessation receipts against which the amounts may be set, a claim may be made to set them against the total income and capital gains of the tax year in which the payment is made (or the debt proves to be irrecoverable) (ITA 2007 s 96). The claim must be made within twelve months after 31 January following the end of the relevant tax year.

Qualifying payments are those made wholly and exclusively for professional indemnity insurance, or to remedy defective work, goods or services, or paid by way of damages in respect of such defects, including related legal and other professional expenses, or in respect of debt recovery costs.

The relief for post cessation expenses does not apply for corporation tax purposes, nor is any relief given when computing income for tax credit purposes.

(d)   Barristers are permitted to compute their income on a cash basis or on an invoiced basis for the first seven years of their practice. (ITTOIA 2005 s 160). However, they must apply the basis selected consistently. If during that period the barrister elects to prepare his accounts under generally accepted accounting practice (GAAP), then he may no longer use the concessionary basis provided by s 160, and must subsequently use GAAP for all subsequent periods of account.

When the concessionary basis comes to an end, either by the barrister reaching the end of seven years after commencement, or by electing to move to a GAAP basis before that time, the resulting uplift in income (adjustment income) arising from the change in accounting basis may be spread forwards over ten years as follows (ITTOIA 2005 s 238):

(i)   in each of the first nine years an amount of the lower of:

–10% of the adjustment income, or

–10% of the profits of the profession for that year before capital allowances,

(ii)   in the tenth year, the remaining adjustment income is chargeable to tax.

The adjustment income is the prior year adjustment required on a change in basis and thus is the opening amount chargeable as income under normal rules less any debtors already accounted for if the invoiced basis has been used. The income adjustment will be calculated under GAAP, and may require recognition of profit on uninvoiced work as required by UITF 40. For a full description of the impact of UITF 40 see Example 24 note 5. The separate adjustment relating to the adoption of UITF 40 will not apply to barristers, as they benefit from a ten-year spread under s 238 in any event.

If the barrister ceases trading at any time during the ten-year period over which the adjustment income is spread, the remaining amount is spread over the balance of the ten years, but without applying the 10 per cent of current profits rule at (i) above.

In any year, the barrister may elect to be taxed on a larger amount than that provided for by s 238, simply entering a different amount in box 69 on the Self Employment Full pages SEF4 (s 239). The additional amount brought into tax affects the initial amount of adjustment income calculated so that all subsequent periods are affected. The amount deducted from the adjustment income is

$A \times 10/T$,

where A is the additional amount brought into tax and T is the time remaining after the tax year in which the adjustment is made.

Explanatory Notes

Current year basis of assessment

1. Trading profits are charged to tax on the 'current year basis', which broadly means the profits of the accounting year ending in the current tax year. The detailed rules are given below. Businesses commencing on or after 6 April 1994 have used the current year basis from the outset. For businesses already in existence at that date the current year basis took effect from 1997/98, with 1996/97 being a transitional year.

Current year basis rules and overlap relief

2. The current year basis rules are contained in Chapter 15 of Part 2 of ITTOIA 2005. The essence of the rules is that businesses will be taxed over their lifetime on the taxable profits made. Although overlaps occur on commencement and possibly on changes of accounting date, they are dealt with by calculating the amount of profit that has been double charged (overlap profit) and allowing that amount as a deduction either when the business ceases or on an earlier change of accounting date if and to the extent that more than twelve months' profit is being taxed in one year. It is possible, however, that tax will be charged overall on more than the profits earned, for example where there are insufficient profits and/or other income against which to set overlap profits (see explanatory note 5).

A record needs to be kept not only of the amount of any overlap profits but also the length of the overlapping period. If an overlap period shows a loss, it must be recorded as an overlap of nil for the appropriate period. This is important because overlap relief is given at the time of a change of accounting date if and to the extent that more than twelve months' profit would otherwise be chargeable in one year (see Example 28 part (c)). Self-assessment returns provide for entries to be made for overlap profits brought forward and carried forward.

Opening years

3. The rules for the opening tax years are as follows (ITTOIA 2005 ss 199 to 201):

    Year 1   Profit from date of commencement to the end of the tax year

Year 2   (a)   If there is an account of at least twelve months ending in year 2, profits of twelve months to the end of that account (as in (a)(i) and (iii) in the example)

(b)   Where the first account ends in year 2 but is for less than twelve months, profits of twelve months from commencement (as in (a)(ii) in the example)

(c)   Where no account ends in year 2, profits of the tax year itself (as in (a)(iv) in the example)

Year 3   Normally profits of accounting year ending in the tax year, but with special rules for *onwards*   changes of accounting date, under which the basis period will never be less than twelve months but may be longer. (Changes of accounting date are dealt with in Example 28.) If, however, the tax year is the first year in which there is an accounting date not less than twelve months after commencement (as in the third year 2009/10 in part (a)(iv) of the example), the profits of twelve months to the accounting date are taken, even though the accounting period itself is longer.

Where there are losses, a loss that would otherwise be taken into account in two successive years is not included in the computation for the second year (see Example 30 for an illustration).

4.   When a taxpayer acquires a new source of income, details must be shown in his return for the tax year in which income first arises. If the taxpayer does not receive a tax return for that tax year, he must notify HMRC within 6 months after the end of the year that he is chargeable to tax, otherwise interest and penalties may arise (TMA 1970 s 7 – see Example 41 note 5). This is particularly important for new businesses. However, for Class 2 national insurance a new business must be notified within three calendar months after the calendar month of commencement. In this example the businesses commenced in January 2009 and notification would be required by 30 April 2009. Failure to notify gives rise to a penalty of £100 (SI 2001/1004 reg 87) – see Example 13 part (c). The penalty for failure to notify will be amended for obligations arising on or after 1 April 2010, and will in future be behaviour based, broadly similar to the structure for penalties for inaccuracies described in Example 8 note 10. All the businesses in part (a) of the example have taxable profits for 2008/09, even though their first accounts would not have been available until 2009/10 or later. Even though accounts may not be available in time, the tax finally found to be due for any year attracts interest from the original due date. It is important, therefore, to make estimated payments in order to avoid the interest charge (see Example 17). The legislation does not stipulate the length of the first account (or of subsequent accounts) but clearly the interest provisions discourage taxpayers from preparing a very long account to delay their tax liabilities.

Cessation of business

5.   The basis period for the tax year in which a business ceases is from the end of the basis period for the previous tax year to the date of cessation, unless the business ceases in the second tax year, in which case the basis period for that tax year is from 6 April to the date of cessation (s 202). This means that there will often be two accounts that together form the final basis period, for example if in part (b) of the example the trader in part (a)(iv), instead of making up a 16 month account, had made up an account for the year to 30 April 2013 and a final 4 month account to 31 August 2013.

Any overlap profit for which relief has not already been given is deducted in full from the assessable profit of the last *tax year* (as distinct from the profit of the final period of account), and if that results in a loss, the normal loss reliefs will be available. See Example 32, in particular explanatory note 5.

6.   Part (b) of the example shows how overlap relief is dealt with on cessation. It should be noted that choosing an accounting year-end of 30 April still has the cash flow benefit of delaying the assessment of profits while the business continues, as shown in parts (a)(iii) and (iv) of the example, in which profits are broadly being earned at the same rate in both cases but are being taxed a year later in part (iv). However, on cessation this results in a final basis period that includes 11 months of the previous tax year.

This is illustrated in part (b)(iv) of the example, where the basis period is 16 months, even though the business ceases only 5 months into the tax year. Although the available overlap relief covers 11 months' profits, the overlap profits were at a much lower rate than those being earned on cessation, hence the difference between the final assessment on the business with the 31 March year end (£25,000) and that on the business with the 30 April year end (£76,975). If there had been a loss in the first accounting period there may be no overlap relief at all.

Capital allowances

7.   Capital allowances are treated as a trading expense of the accounting period. If the accounting period is shorter or longer than twelve months, the annual writing down allowances are reduced or increased proportionately (see Example 18 part (b)).

Transitional overlap relief

8.   Under the previous year basis of assessment, profits were charged more than once when a business started, and sometimes on a change of accounting date, balanced by profits escaping tax for an equivalent length of *time* when the business ceased. Under the current year basis, profits may also be charged more than once at the start and on changes of accounting date, but the balancing adjustment when the business ceases is equal to the *amount* of profits that were double charged (see explanatory note 2).

On the replacement of the previous year basis by the current year basis, all profits up to 5 April 1997 were treated as having been taxed under the previous year basis rules, but the profit for the period from the end of the basis period for 1996/97 to 5 April 1997 was also included in the taxable profits for 1997/98 under the current year basis. This profit therefore represents a transitional overlap profit, for which relief will be given as in explanatory note 2, ie when the business ceases, or possibly earlier if the accounting date is changed. Unlike normal overlap profits, transitional overlap profits were calculated *before* capital allowances. Where, as a result of a change of accounting date, further overlap profits arise, these will be merged with transitional overlap profits to form a single figure.

Change of accounting basis, cash basis for barristers and advocates

9.   For periods of account beginning after 6 April 1999, business profits must be computed in accordance with generally accepted accounting practice, subject to any statutory taxation adjustments required (ITTOIA 2005 s 25). The main effect of the introduction of this section was that income should be accounted for on an earnings basis, and not on a cash or invoiced basis, as had applied previously.

However, an exception was included for new barristers and advocates, who may account for income either on a cash basis or an invoiced (fee note) basis for periods of account ending not more than seven years after commencement (ITTOIA 2005 s 160). Thereafter they must account for income under GAAP, which will require the computation of income on a time spent basis where services are supplied under a contract, as required by UITF 40.

The adoption of a full earnings basis constitutes a change of accounting policy, for which accounting standards require that the previous year's figures are adjusted onto the new basis, commonly known as a prior year adjustment. However, these earlier years have already been subject to tax, and rather than reopen the self-assessments for the previous years, the cumulative effect of the adjustment to previous years is taxed in the year of change, and known as adjustment income.

The adjustment income thus generated by this change in accounting basis can be spread over the ten years following the date of the change, as described in part (d) of the example. The amount brought into tax is limited to 1/10th of the profit before capital allowances in the first nine years, with the balance taxable in the tenth year.

If the barrister ceases practice, the charge continues for the remainder of the ten-year period without restriction by reference to profits.

An election may be made to pay all or part of the charge earlier, for example to utilise the basic rate band, or if there are allowable losses which can be set off.

The amount of adjustment income charged to tax in any year counts as relevant earnings for the purposes of calculating registered pension scheme contributions. It does not, however, attract Class 4 national insurance contributions.

If, exceptionally, the change resulted in a reduction of profits, that amount can be deducted in the year in which it arises, if appropriate generating a trading loss.

For details of the spreading provisions applying generally to businesses on the adoption of UITF 40 see Example 24 note 5.

Question

Please note: This will apply to unincorporated businesses and limited liability partnerships (LLPs) carrying on a trade.

On 31 January 2008 David, a supervisor with a building supplies company, was made redundant. During the next twelve months he applied for many jobs, and attended a number of interviews but without success. On 1 February 2009, he set up his own business as a self-employed plumber providing services to local houseowners. He is a single man and has income from other sources of around £6,000 per annum.

His turnover for the first three months was £2,000 per month which David expects to rise by £200 per month in each quarter to a turnover of £2,800 per month in the quarter to April 2010. He estimates his turnover in future years to increase above the April 2010 level of £8,400 per quarter by approximately 10% per annum.

David estimates that his profits, adjusted for tax purposes, will be approximately 80% of his turnover.

He is considering preparing his first accounts either for the year to 31 January 2010 and annually thereafter, or for the 15 months to 30 April 2010 and annually thereafter.

(a)   What are the tax consequences of David's accounts being prepared annually to 30 April, rather than 31 January?

(b)   State whether David is *required* to register his business for VAT purposes and irrespective of whether David is required to register or not, whether he is *able* to register if he so wishes, and the advantages or disadvantages of registration.

Answer

(a) David's anticipated turnover and resulting estimated profits for the alternative accounting dates are:

		Turnover £	Profits (80%) £
Year to 31 January 2010			
1st quarter 3 × 2,000	6,000		
2nd quarter 3 × 2,200	6,600		
3rd quarter 3 × 2,400	7,200		
4th quarter 3 × 2,600	7,800	27,600	22,080
Year to 31 January 2011			
Turnover: To 30.4.08 3 × 2,800	8,400		
For next 3 quarters @			
(8,400 × 110% =) 9,240	27,720		
	£36,120	Say 36,000	28,800
15 months to 30 April 2010			
1st 12 months	27,600		
5th quarter 3 × 2,800	8,400	36,000	28,800
Year to 30 April 2011			
Turnover (8,400 × 4) × 110%	£36,960	Say 37,000	29,600

The taxable profits arising are:

Accounts to 31 January annually			£
2008/09	1.2.09 – 5.4.09 2/12 × 22,080		3,680
2009/10	1.2.09 – 31.1.09		22,080
2010/11	1.2.10 – 31.1.11		28,800
			54,560

Overlap profits 1.2.09 – 5.4.09 £3,680

Accounts to 30 April annually			£
2008/09	1.2.09 – 5.4.09 2/15 × 28,800		3,840
2009/10	6.4.09 – 5.4.10 12/15 × 28,800		23,040
2010/11	1.5.09 – 30.4.10 12/15 × 28,800		23,040
			49,920

Overlap profits 1.5.09 – 5.4.10
11/15 × 28,800 £21,120

In each case the overlap profits represent the difference between the profits earned and the profits charged to tax, ie (54,560 – 3,680 =) £50,880 with a 31 January year-end and (49,920 – 21,120 =) £28,800 with a 30 April year-end.

If David makes up accounts to 30 April, therefore, there is a reduction in the taxable profits of the first three years of (54,560 – 49,920) = £4,640. If profits continue to rise, there will be an ongoing benefit of paying tax each year on earlier, lower profits. With a year-end of 31 January the taxable profits are very little different from the profits of the tax year itself, whereas with a year-end of 30 April nearly all the taxable profit relates to the previous year.

Unless there are losses for which relief is unavailable, however, the profits eventually charged to tax under the current year basis are the same as the profits earned. Paying tax each year on lower profits than have actually been earned is therefore effectively building up an amount of deferred profits on which tax must be paid when the business ceases. Furthermore, there is no inflation proofing of the overlap relief.

Say David ceased business on 31 January 2012, not having changed his accounting date in the meantime. The position in the final year would be:

Accounts to 30 April annually
2011/12   Profits of 21 months from 1.5.10 to 31.1.12 less overlap relief of £21,120
Accounts to 31 January annually
2011/12   Profits of 12 months from 1.2.11 to 31.1.12 less overlap relief of £3,680

Clearly if the rate of profits in 2011/12 is much higher than when the business started, the final assessment with the 30 April year-end will be very much higher than with the 31 January year-end.

As well as giving lower taxable profits when profits are rising, so long as the business continues, a 30 April year-end gives more time for preparation of accounts and tax computations. Under self-assessment, tax returns are due by 31 January following the tax year, eg by 31 January 2010 for 2008/09 if filed online, but 31 October after the end of the tax year if filed on paper, eg by 31 October 2009 for 2008/09. This normally allows 21 months' preparation time with a 30 April year-end, compared with twelve months with a 31 January year-end. The 30 April year-end, however, makes the calculation of tax bills more difficult at the start of the business.

In addition, a 30 April year-end could be beneficial for a tax credits claimant. Knowledge of the profits to the 30 April in the tax year will alert a claimant to the possibility of a claim for credits and this can then be more easily made by the 31 July deadline. A 30 April year-end could also mean that actual figures are available by 31 July following a year-end to complete any tax credits renewal form.

A year end early in the tax year, such as 30 April, can allow scope for pre-tax year end planning. For example, personal pension contributions can be made before the end of the tax year to maximise higher rate tax relief as profits are likely to be known before the end of the tax year. A year end close to the end of the tax year, such as 31 March, does not allow for any degree of accuracy in such planning.

In addition, the introduction of the 50% tax rate for income in excess of £150,000 which takes effect from 6 April 2010 means that some businesses could benefit from a change of year end to accelerate profits into 2009/10 from 2010/11 (for example changing from 30 April to 31 March). However, each case should be looked at on its own merit.

No matter which year-end is chosen, David has taxable profits for 2008/09, the tax on which is due for payment on 31 January 2010. Since the accounts will not be finalised by that date with either year-end, he will have to estimate the amount due, and will be charged interest from that date if his estimate falls short of the actual figure. (If he overestimates, he will receive a much lower rate of interest on the repayment than is charged on an underpayment.) He will know the exact amount of his profits sooner if he makes up accounts to 31 January. Furthermore, any tax due for 2008/09 will affect payments on account for 2009/10, unless it is covered by the de minimis limits, interest being payable from the half-yearly due dates of 31 January 2010 and 31 July 2010 based on the final figure of tax due for 2008/09. Estimated payments on account may therefore also be required, although in David's case the 2008/09 tax may be below the de minimis limits of £1,000 or 20% of the tax due.

Where taxable profits are lower as a result of the choice of year-end there will also be a saving in Class 4 contributions if the profits fall within the slice on which contributions are charged at the full rate. This would be the case for David in 2009/10, and probably in 2010/11 as well.

(b)   As far as VAT registration is concerned, David is required to register at any time if his turnover in the next *thirty days* is expected to exceed the VAT threshold (currently £68,000). He is also required to register at the end of any *month* if his turnover in the year ended on the last day of that month exceeded the threshold, unless HMRC is satisfied that his turnover in the coming year will not exceed (from 1 May 2009) £66,000.

Clearly David's turnover is expected to be below these limits for at least the first few years. He may register voluntarily if he wishes. This will not be to his advantage, because he would have to charge VAT to the houseowners for whom he works, and they would not be able to recover it, and he would also have to comply with the administrative requirements for keeping records and accounting to HMRC for the VAT charged to his customers (less a set-off for VAT he has suffered) although this could be simplified by using the Flat Rate Scheme.

If he remains non-registered, the VAT that he incurs forms part of the cost of the item concerned. If the item is an allowable deduction against his profit, such as his purchases of materials, he will save tax on the VAT suffered. If it is not, it may qualify for capital allowances, in which case the VAT forms part of the cost on which allowances are given. Where the asset is a chargeable asset for capital gains tax, any VAT not recovered forms part of the allowable expenditure taken into account when the asset is disposed of. Some VAT is not recoverable at all, such as on business entertaining.

Explanatory Notes

Choice of accounting date

1.   For the detailed provisions on opening and closing years' assessments, see Example 16. Self-assessment is dealt with in Example 41.

2.   Under the current year basis, the profits earned are normally taxed over the life of the business, any overlaps at the outset and on changes of accounting date being reflected in overlap relief when the business ceases. The effect of high inflation, however, could mean that overlap relief is of limited value in real terms. A year-end of 30 April has an ongoing cash flow benefit where profits are rising and also a benefit in the time for preparing accounts and computations, as indicated in the example.

If a year-end of 31 March is chosen, no overlap relief arises, since HMRC is prepared to treat the accounting year as equivalent to the tax year (see Example 16 part (a)), so there is no adverse effect from inflation. If a business with a different year-end faces falling profits, switching to a 31 March year-end would trigger any available overlap relief and would reduce the ongoing assessments (see Example 28 part (c)).

Notifying liability and sending in returns

3.   Not all taxpayers regularly receive tax returns for completion. By TMA 1970 s 7, a taxpayer is required to notify HMRC if he is liable to tax for any tax year, the notification being required to be made not later than six months from the end of that tax year (TMA 1970 s 7 – see Example 40 explanatory note 5). In David's case, if he does not get a return, he needs to notify HMRC that he has taxable income for 2008/09 not later than 5 October 2009. As stated below, David will be required to register his new business with HMRC within three months. Normally this registration will result in HMRC issuing a tax return for the relevant year with no notification being required under s 7.

4.   Penalties arise both for failure to send in a return on time (TMA 1970 s 93) and for failure to notify liability to tax (TMA 1970 s 7), although Finance Act 2008 amends the penalty for failure to notify to a tax geared penalty based on behaviour, which will take effect in respect of obligations arising on or after 6 April 2010. For the interest provisions see Example 44 and the penalty provisions Example 46.

Class 2 and 4 national insurance contributions

5.   A self-employed person is liable to pay Class 2 and Class 4 national insurance contributions. Class 2 contributions are due if earnings are expected to exceed the exemption limit (£5,075 for 2009/10). It is necessary to notify liability within three calendar months after the calendar month of commencement of self-employment (see Example 13 part (c)). Notification for Class 2 also acts as notification for income tax, although a separate penalty of £100 applies for failure to notify for Class 2 in addition to the income tax penalty mentioned at 4 above. This will be abolished in 2010 and replaced with a new behaviour based tax geared penalty.

Class 4 national insurance contributions are calculated on profits net of capital allowances. Under self-assessment, they are calculated by HMRC if the taxpayer does not wish to calculate his own tax and submits his return either online or by 31 October following the end of the tax year, and otherwise by the taxpayer. The Class 4 contributions are payable at the same time as income tax, so they are included in half-yearly payments on account. See Example 48 for detailed notes on national insurance contributions.

Question

(a) Lindley, LJ in *Yarmouth v France* (1887) said 'Plant ... includes whatever apparatus is used by a businessman for carrying on his business – not his stock in trade which he buys or makes for sale, but all goods and chattels, fixed or moveable, live or dead, which he keeps for permanent employment in his business'.

Discuss in the light of later cases and legislation how far this statement can be said to be true today.

(b) Where assets qualify for plant and machinery allowances, explain what expenditure may be taken into account, and state the date on which the expenditure is treated as incurred.

(c) Briefly explain when plant and machinery allowances may be available in respect of leased assets.

(d) Explain the various rates of capital allowances available, and give details of common allowances on expenditure other than plant and machinery.

(e) Explain the way in which capital allowances are given to traders and investors.

(f) Explain the meaning of the expression 'connected person' in relation to capital allowances, and outline the treatment of transactions between connected persons.

Answer

References in this example are to the Capital Allowances Act 2001 (CAA 2001) unless otherwise indicated.

(a) **Meaning of 'plant'**

The meaning of the words 'plant' and 'machinery' has been considered by the courts on many occasions. 'Machinery' is given its ordinary meaning, but no definition of 'plant' that can be regarded as all embracing has been arrived at. Many of the cases described below have treated parts of buildings and structures as plant. CAA 2001 ss 21 to 23 attempt to clarify the boundary between plant and buildings, and to limit any further additions to the 'plant' category, while not disturbing the effect of existing case law. The legislation specifically states that an asset cannot be plant if its principal purpose is to insulate or enclose the interior of the building or provide an interior wall, floor or ceiling intended to remain permanently in place.

For many years, books in a professional library were held not to be plant following *Daphne v Shaw* (1926), but this was overruled in *Munby v Furlong* (1977), since when the professional libraries of solicitors etc have been accepted as plant.

The case of *Yarmouth v France* was heard in 1887 and it concerned not taxation but employer's liability. An employee who had been injured by his employer's horse claimed under the workers' compensation provisions that he had been injured by his employer's 'plant', and the courts found in his favour.

The statement made by the judge in that case still forms the basis of the accepted definition of plant, and it was expanded in the war damage compensation case of *J Lyons & Co Ltd v AG* (1944) to emphasise that the basic distinction is between apparatus *with* which the trade is carried on and the setting *in* which it is carried on. This was echoed in the case of *Jarrold v John Good & Sons Ltd* (1962), where expenditure by a firm of shipping agents on moveable office partitioning which was used in order to give them maximum continuing flexibility in relation to the subdivision of their floor space was held to be on plant. Similarly, expenditure by a ship repairing company on the concrete work used in the construction of a dry dock and on excavating the land for the dock was held to be expenditure on plant (*IRC v Barclay, Curle & Co Ltd* (1969)), as was expenditure on a swimming pool at a caravan site (*Cooke v Beach Station Caravans Ltd* (1974)).

On the other hand, the 'setting' argument was used to disallow pre-fabricated moveable buildings used as a laboratory and gymnasium in a school (*St John's School v Ward* (1975)), the canopy over a petrol station (*Dixon v Fitch's Garages Ltd* (1975)), a false ceiling in a restaurant (*Hampton v Fortes Autogrill Ltd* (1980)), a floating ship used as a restaurant (*Benson v Yard Arm Club Ltd* (1979)), a fan-inflated polythene tennis court cover in a tennis coaching business (*Thomas v Reynolds* (1987)), car wash halls and sites (*Attwood v Anduff Car Wash Ltd CA* (1997)) and the structure of an electrical substation (only the equipment within it qualifying as plant – *Bradley v London Electricity plc* (1996)).

Two cases heard during 2004 show how subtle the distinction can be between plant and setting. In *Shove v Lingfield Park*, the Court of Appeal, overturning the finding of the Special Commissioner, held that an artificial surface on a racetrack allowing racing throughout the year was part of the setting. On the other hand, the Scottish Court of Session held that the construction of a five-a-side pitch could qualify for allowances (*CIR v Anchor International Ltd*).

Several cases have gone partly for and partly against the taxpayer. In *Cole Bros v Phillips* (1980), the electrical switchboard and most of the electrical equipment in a department store were held to be plant, but not certain light fittings whose only function was to provide light in areas with few windows. The court held in that case that items had to be considered individually and not as a single installation. In the case of *Carr v Sayer* (1992), it was held that permanent quarantine kennels were not plant but temporary, moveable, quarantine kennels *were* plant. In two 1992 cases, heard together, concerning single storey warehouses (*Hunt v Henry Quick Ltd* and *King v Bridisco Ltd*), it was held that platforms erected to increase the floor space in the warehouses were plant, but lighting beneath the platforms was not. A glasshouse constructed as a 'planteria' to protect plants and create an appropriate growing environment, but without any mechanical controls, was not plant (*Gray v Seymours Garden Centre* (CA 1995)). HMRC accepts, however, that glasshouses that incorporate a sophisticated, probably computerised, system to control and monitor temperature, humidity etc will usually qualify as plant, and they confirmed in their Tax Bulletin of June 1998 that such glasshouses will not normally be 'long life assets' (as to which see Example 20 explanatory note 21).

Although the question of what is and what is not plant is broadly a functional test, some of the cases involving buildings used by the public have held that various items forming part of the setting created atmosphere and thus performed the function of making the premises more attractive to customers. This has been applied to decor, murals, light fittings etc in hotels (*IRC v Scottish and Newcastle Breweries Ltd* (1981)) and to decorative screens in the shop front windows of building societies (*Leeds Permanent Building Society v Proctor* (1982)). But in *Wimpy International Ltd v Warland* (1988), only expenditure on light fittings was held to be plant on this criterion. Expenditure on shopfronts, floor and wall tiles, suspended ceilings, and mezzanine and raised floors was all disallowed, with the exception of one ceiling made of metal strips with gaps for visual interest. The Court of Appeal emphasised in that case that the starting point was the decision of the Appeal Commissioners. They considered there were two tests, the premises test and the business use test, and the business use test was only considered if the premises test was satisfied. Under the premises test, something which becomes part of the premises, instead of merely embellishing them, is not plant, except in the rare cases where the premises are themselves plant, like the dry dock in Barclay Curle, and the computerised glasshouses mentioned above. Under the business use test, if the item is not part of the premises and is not stock in trade, it is plant if it is used in carrying on the trade. (Although initial expenditure on a shopfront is disallowed, HMRC allows the cost of a subsequent replacement as a trading expense, except to the extent that the replacement does more than merely replace the original, ie any improvement element is disallowed.)

These principles were reconsidered by the Special Commissioners in *J D Wetherspoon plc v HMRC* (2007) in the context of wood panelling in a pub. It was held by the Special Commissioners that the panelling had become so standardised in the chain of pubs that it no longer represented a feature in its own right and had become subsumed as part of the building.

The distinction between plant and premises has been further confused by statute. FA 2008 introduced s 33A which provides that expenditure on integral features (as defined) are to qualify as if on plant or machinery provided that the purpose of the feature is not to insulate the interior of a building or to provide an interior wall, floor or ceiling which is intended to remain permanently in place. The meaning of integral feature includes some assets that were previously treated as plant but also some that were previously excluded from the definition of plant. Integral features are defined as the following:

- an electrical system (including a lighting system);

- a cold water system;

- a space or water heating system, a powered system of ventilation, air cooling or air purification and any floor ceiling comprised in such a system;

- a lift, escalator or moving walkway;

- external solar shading.

It can be seen, therefore, that although the statement in *Yarmouth v France*, as expanded in *J Lyons & Co Ltd v AG*, still forms the essence of the currently accepted definition of plant, the extent of its application is frequently contested before the courts and often some very narrow distinctions are drawn.

(b)   **Qualifying expenditure**

On assets that qualify for capital allowances, the expenditure that may be taken into account is qualifying capital expenditure incurred in the *chargeable period* (s 6 – see (e) below). If expenditure is funded by borrowing, it is still treated as having been incurred, although interest on the borrowing is allowed as a business expense and not as part of the capital cost (*Ben-Odeco Ltd v Powlson* (1978)).

It is specifically provided by s 25 that expenditure on alterations to an existing building incidental to the installation of plant or machinery is treated as expenditure on plant or machinery. *In J D Wetherspoon plc v HMRC* (2007) it was held that this was limited to preparatory expenditure (for example excavation works required for the installation of the plant or machinery) and certain consequential expenditure so far as it was objectively necessary for the proper functioning of the plant or machinery. In the latter category fell partitions around toilets in a pub but the test excluded easy-wipe tiles in the pub's kitchen.

Where plant and machinery is moved from one site to another, the cost of removal and re-erection, if not allowed as an expense, may be treated as expenditure on plant and machinery for capital allowances. Where plant and machinery is demolished and replaced, the net cost of demolition is treated as expenditure on the replacement plant and machinery. If the plant and machinery is not replaced, the demolition cost is treated as qualifying expenditure for the period in which it is incurred (s 26).

Where someone brings into a trade plant and machinery that has been given to him, the plant and machinery is treated as having been bought at that time for its open market value (s 14). The same applies where plant and machinery that has previously been used other than for trading purposes is brought into a trade, except that if the cost is less than market value, the cost figure is substituted (or, for connected persons transactions, the cost to the connected person if less) (s 13).

Where a building is constructed and plant and machinery is installed therein, it will be necessary to apportion ancillary expenses such as professional fees of architects, surveyors and engineers and overhead costs between the building and the plant. Since such expenses often form a significant part of the cost, it is important to ensure that the allocation is appropriate and supported by the facts.

Certain expenditure that would not otherwise qualify as expenditure on plant is specifically treated as such, namely:

–   Expenditure on adding thermal insulation to a building (s 28)

–   Expenditure on safety at sports grounds (ss 30 to 32)

–   Expenditure on security assets, such as alarm systems and bullet-proof windows, to improve the personal security of those under *special* threat, eg from terrorists (s 33).

In all these cases, the disposal value in respect of such expenditure is treated as nil (s 63).

Expenditure on integral features (as defined) qualifies as expenditure on plant and machinery (see above) (s 33A).

Conversely, expenditure on plant or machinery is not qualifying expenditure if incurred for leasing under a long-funding lease (s 34A).

If a trader other than a finance lessor acquires plant and machinery on hire purchase, the full capital cost is treated as incurred as soon as the asset is brought into use (s 67). The hire purchase charges are a revenue expense allowed over the term of the contract. Where plant and machinery is acquired under a lease, except for long-funding leases it is the lessor and not the lessee who is entitled to the allowances, whether the lease is an operating lease or a finance lease. Special anti-avoidance provisions apply to finance leases (see Example 20 part A (a)).

Where a third party (for example, the Government, or a local authority) makes a contribution or subsidy towards cost, that amount is excluded from the qualifying expenditure (subject to certain exceptions) (s 532). Where such contributions are paid by traders or investors, the payer can claim allowances even though he does not strictly have an interest in the asset (ss 537 to 541).

Date expenditure treated as incurred

Section 5 provides that expenditure is deemed to be incurred on the date on which the obligation to pay becomes unconditional, but if any part of the payment is not due until more than four months after that date, that part of the expenditure is regarded as incurred on the due date of payment. The due date of payment is also substituted where the unconditional obligation to pay is earlier than normal commercial usage and the sole or main benefit is that expenditure would be treated as incurred in an earlier chargeable period. The date when the obligation to pay becomes unconditional depends on the terms of the contract. It will usually be either the invoice date or the delivery date. Where ownership is transferred in one chargeable period but the obligation becomes unconditional in the first month of the next, the obligation is regarded as having arisen in the earlier period. (This sometimes happens on a large construction contract, where the ownership of the asset is transferred, but the obligation to pay does not become unconditional until, for example, an architect's certificate is presented.)

Where expenditure on plant and machinery is incurred prior to the commencement of a trade, it is deemed to be incurred on the first day of the trade (s 12).

(c)   **Leased assets**

Allowances on leased assets

Capital allowances on plant and machinery are not normally available unless the plant and machinery belongs to the taxpayer at some time in the relevant period (s 11). Allowances are, however, available for expenditure incurred by a tenant on lifts, heating and ventilating equipment, etc, even though in law such items become landlord's fixtures. Where such fixtures are not bought outright but are acquired on lease, either by a landlord or a tenant, there are provisions to enable the allowances to be given to the equipment lessor, instead of to the landlord or the tenant as the case may be. These provisions are dealt with in more detail in Example 20.

Long funding leases

Since 1 April 2006 expenditure on assets acquired for the purpose of long-funding leasing have ceased to qualify for plant and machinery allowances (s 34A). Instead, the lessee is entitled to be treated as the owner of the expenditure (s 70A).

A long-funding lease is, broadly, a lease longer than seven years. Leases of between five and seven years are long-funding leases if:

(a)   they are treated as finance leases under GAAP;

(b)   the residual value of the plant or machinery is 5% or less of the market value at the commencement;

(c)   the total rentals due in the first year (if less than those due in the second year) are between 90% and 100% of the second year's rentals; and

(d)   the total rentals due in any year after the second (if greater than those due in the second year) are between 100% and 110% of the second year's rentals.

Certain leases of plant or machinery for a building or leased with land are excluded (ss 70G, 70R and 70U).

(d)   **Rates of allowance on plant and machinery and other important capital allowances**

Rates of capital allowances on plant and machinery

For 2009/10 the rates of capital allowances on plant and machinery are as follows:

- An annual investment allowance (AIA) of up to £50,000, available on all plant and machinery including integral features, but with the exception of cars. The annual amount is available only once to a group of companies and other related parties (see Example 21).

- A first-year allowance of 40% on expenditure incurred between 1 April 2009 (6 April for income tax) and 31 March 2010 (5 April for income tax). This is given on additions to the main pool only, and is not available on cars or assets used for leasing. This is available on additions in excess of the annual investment allowance.

- A writing down allowance of 20% on assets in the main pool. This can be given in addition to the annual investment allowance on additions which do not qualify for first-year allowances.

- A writing down allowance of 10% on assets in the special rate pool. This is also available on additions in excess of the annual investment allowance.

Industrial buildings allowances (Pt 3) and agricultural buildings allowances (Pt 4)

After plant and machinery allowances, the next two most valuable allowances were industrial buildings allowances and agricultural buildings allowances. They are currently being phased out and will be fully withdrawn with effect from 1 April 2011 (or, for income tax purposes, from 6 April 2011). Those allowances are considered in more detail in Example 22.

Prior to their withdrawal, the basic scheme of those allowances was to provide relief for capital expenditure over a 25-year period, with 4% of the expenditure being relieved in each year.

Businesses premises renovation allowances (Pt 3A)

Businesses which incur expenditure on converting or renovating a building (or structure) in a disadvantaged area may qualify for an allowance. The building has to have been unused throughout the year before the commencement of the conversion or renovation work (s 360C).

The business is entitled to a 100% 'initial' allowance in the chargeable period in which the expenditure was incurred (s 360G). To the extent that any expenditure is unrelieved, relief of up to 25% of the expenditure may be relieved as a writing-down allowance in subsequent chargeable periods (s 360J).

The allowance is available in respect of expenditure incurred on or after 11 April 2007.

Flat conversion allowances (Pt 4A)

Property businesses which incur expenditure on converting or renovating business premises so as to create a 'low-value' flat may qualify for an allowance. The flat must be suitable for use as a dwelling and be held for short-term letting (leases of five years or shorter) (s 393D). Section 393D also specifies that the flat must have no more than four rooms (as defined) and must be accessible to the street without passing through the business premises.

A low-value flat is one whose market rent matches or falls below the limits specified in a table in section 393E. That table specifies thresholds depending on the number of rooms in the flat and whether or not the flat is in Greater London.

The property business is entitled to a 100% 'initial' allowance in the chargeable period in which the expenditure was incurred (s 393H). To the extent that any expenditure is unrelieved, relief of up to 25% of the expenditure may be relieved as a writing-down allowance in subsequent chargeable periods (s 393K).

(e)   **Capital allowances given to traders and investors**

Some capital allowances are given by way of a deduction when calculating the profits of a trade, profession, employment or property business following a claim in a tax return; others are given by a claim made other than in a return (s 3).

Capital allowances given in taxing a trade etc or property business

Capital allowances given in taxing a trade, profession, employment or property business are treated as an expense of the relevant *chargeable period*, both for individuals and companies. The meaning of chargeable period is as follows (s 6):

Chargeable period – companies:

For a company the chargeable period is the company's accounting period. An accounting period for corporation tax cannot exceed twelve months (ICTA 1988 s 12(3)), so a period of account that exceeds twelve months is split into a twelve-month chargeable accounting period or periods and the remainder.

Chargeable period – individuals:

For sole traders and partners, the chargeable period is the period of account. A period of account is a period for which accounts are made up. The legislation prescribes rules for overlaps and gaps in periods of account, but in practice these will virtually never arise, because it would be very unusual for a business to produce more than one set of accounts for the same period, or to have a period for which accounts were not made up at all.

If a period of account is longer or shorter than 12 months, annual writing down allowances are proportionately increased or reduced. But if a period of account exceeds 18 months it is regarded for the purpose of computing allowances as being split into successive 12 month periods plus the balance (s 6(6)). The aggregate allowances for the separate periods are then treated as a business expense of the whole period. This prevents undue advantage being gained as a result of the long account, as follows:

For a company – account made up for 26 months to 31.7.2010

If s 6(6) had not been enacted:

	£
Plant and machinery expenditure brought forward	100,000
Additions November 2008 (in excess of annual investment allowance)	20,000
	120,000
Writing down allowance 20% × 26/12	52,000
Written down value carried forward	68,000

Applying s 6(6):

	£
Plant and machinery expenditure brought forward	100,000
Additions November 2008 (in excess of annual investment allowance)	20,000
	120,000
Writing down allowance 20% for first 12 months	24,000
	96,000
Writing down allowance 20% for next 12 months	19,200
	76,800
Writing down allowance 20% × 2/12	2,560
Written down value carried forward	74,240

The s 6(6) rule restricts the allowances for the period to £45,760 instead of £52,000.

Where qualifying expenditure is incurred by an employee, or by an individual investor (including landlords of let property), the chargeable period for allowances is the tax year itself. The chargeable period for company investors is the accounting period, as for trading companies. As indicated on page 18.3, capital allowances in connection with let property (including capital allowances on leased plant and machinery where the lettings are in the course of carrying on a property business) are treated as an expense of the property business (s 248).

Capital allowances given by a claim made other than in a return

Allowances are given by a separate claim where plant and machinery is leased other than in the course of a 'qualifying activity', for example, a trade or property letting (see Example 20 explanatory note 1). Such leasing is referred to in the legislation as 'special leasing' (s 19). Leasing in such circumstances will be extremely rare. For income tax, relief for any such item of let plant and machinery is given against income from similar special leasing activities, unless the *lessee* does not use it for a trade etc throughout the relevant accounting period, in which case the set-off in that period is restricted to the time proportion of the accounting period that the plant and machinery has been leased (s 258). Excess allowances are carried forward to set against similar leasing income in later years. Similar rules apply for corporation tax, except that a claim may be made for excess allowances to be surrendered in a group relief claim (ICTA 1988 s 403ZB), or carried back against previous accounting periods for an equivalent period of time to that in which the excess occurred, unless the plant and machinery had not been used by the *lessee* for a trade etc for the whole of the relevant accounting period, in which case the treatment of the allowance is the same as for income tax (ss 259, 260).

Capital allowances claims

Claims for capital allowances by both traders and investors (other than claims relating to 'special leasing', as indicated above) are made in tax returns. For details see Example 43.

Treatment of excess allowances

Excess allowances relating to a trade form part of a trading loss for which the usual loss reliefs are available.

Where an individual makes a claim for capital allowances on assets used in his employment, then in the unlikely event that the allowances exceed his employment income, the excess is available for a loss claim against other income under ITA 2007 s 64 (s 262 and annex to Explanatory Notes to the Act).

The treatment of excess allowances for which relief is available by a special claim is indicated above.

For individuals carrying on a 'property business', excess allowances form part of a UK property business loss. A claim may be made, for the tax year of loss or the following tax year, to set an amount equal to the capital allowances included in the loss against total income (ITA 2007 s 118). The time limit for the claim is one year from 31 January following the end of the tax year. Any loss not relieved in this way is carried forward against future rent income.

A corporate investor's capital allowances are similarly incorporated within the company's UK property business loss but no separate claim relating to excess allowances may be made. Relief for a company's UK property loss is given against the total profits of the same accounting period. A claim may be made (within two years after the end of the accounting period) for any remaining loss to be surrendered to another company in the same group under the group relief provisions (see Example 64). Otherwise it is carried forward to set against the *total* profits of later accounting periods.

From 1 April 2008, companies (but not unincorporated traders) have been entitled to tax credits in respect of trading losses that arise, to the extent that they relate to the obtaining of first-year allowances in respect of expenditure on energy-saving plant or machinery (s 45A) or environmentally-beneficial plant or machinery (s 45H). The rules apply only until 31 March 2013.

The tax credits equal 19% of the surrenderable loss subject to a cap, being the higher of the company's PAYE and NICs payments for the chargeable period and £250,000 (CAA 2001 Sch A1).

(f)   **Connected persons – definition**

The basic definition of connected persons in ITA 2007 s 993 (for income tax) and ICTA 1998 s 839 (corporation tax) covers close family, trustees, partners, and companies one of which controls the other or under common control. Close family means spouse, relatives, and relatives' spouses and civil partners (relative being brother, sister, ancestor or lineal descendant). As far as business partners are concerned, however, s 993(4) (or s 839) provides that partners are *not* connected with fellow partners and their spouses/civil partners and relatives in relation to acquisitions or disposals of partnership assets pursuant to genuine commercial arrangements. An expanded definition of connected persons is used in relation to *plant and machinery* in s 266, however, which brings partnership transfers within its scope.

Effect on plant and machinery allowances

First-year allowances and the annual investment allowance (see Example 20 explanatory note 2) are not available on assets acquired from a connected person (s 217).

When plant and machinery is disposed of, the disposal value to be brought into account is normally the net sale proceeds, except that it cannot exceed the original cost (or, where plant has been transferred between connected persons, the highest price paid by any of the connected persons – ss 61 and 62). Where, however, the plant and machinery is sold for less than its open market value, open market value is substituted unless the buyer's expenditure will be taken into account for capital allowances or there will be a benefit taxable on an employee under the benefits code (ss 61, 63(1)). Normal intra-group transfers can therefore be made at the price paid on the transfer if the companies so wish, but there is no provision to use written down value. Intra-group transfers relating to £12,000+ cars must, however, be treated as made at open market value (or the expenditure incurred or treated as incurred if less) (s 79).

Where a *trade* is transferred between connected persons (as defined in s 266 and ITA 2007 s 993 and ICTA 1988 s 839), the disposal value for plant and machinery is the open market value, but first-year allowances are not available (s 265(4)). An election may, however, be made within two years of the transfer for a deemed disposal value such as gives no balancing allowance or balancing charge. The transferor then gets no allowances in the period of transfer, and the transferee stands in the transferor's shoes as regards allowances and balancing charges (ss 266, 267). The main instances when this applies are on incorporation of a business, or on a transfer of trade between companies in the same group (but see below under *Reconstructions* where there is 75% common ownership). Partnership changes are not treated as a cessation of the business, so the capital allowances computation is not affected.

Effect on other allowances

Where property other than plant and machinery is transferred between connected persons, or between bodies one of whom controls the other or controlled by the same persons, the property is treated as having been sold at open market value (ss 567, 568). An election may however, be made not later than two years after the transfer, for the transfer of industrial and enterprise zone buildings, hotels and research and development assets to be treated as made at written down value, so that balancing adjustments do not have to be made (s 569). This is relevant, for example, where a business is incorporated, or where assets are transferred from one group company to another.

Reconstructions

The above provisions relating to plant and machinery and other property transferred between connected persons are not relevant where a trade is transferred from one company to another, and at some time within one year before and two years after the transfer, the same persons own three quarters or more of the trade. This is treated by ICTA 1988 s 343 as a reconstruction of a company without a change of ownership. As far as the capital allowances computation for the period of transfer is concerned, first-year allowances on plant and machinery are claimed by whoever incurred the expenditure and balancing adjustments are made on the company carrying on the trade at the time of the disposal. Writing down allowances are split on a time basis. ICTA 1988 s 343 also provides for trading losses to be carried forward into the successor company, subject to anti-avoidance provisions in ICTA 1988 s 344 if the successor company does not take over the predecessor's unpaid liabilities.

Tax avoidance schemes

Where a business enters into artificial transactions which depress the market value of an asset prior to its sale to a connected person then the balancing allowance on disposal is blocked. However, the acquirer can claim allowances only on the reduced price. This provision applies in relation to any balancing event occurring on or after 27 November 2002 and applies only where there is a tax avoidance scheme.

Explanatory Notes

Chargeable periods

1. For detailed notes on chargeable periods for capital allowances see part (b) of this example and for the allowances for plant and machinery in detail, including the annual investment allowance, see Examples 19, 20 and 21. For provisions on disclaiming capital allowances see Examples 19 and 20.

2. Capital allowances for individuals relate to the period of account, and writing down allowances are proportionately reduced or increased if the period of account is less than or more than 12 months, subject to special rules for periods exceeding 18 months (see part (b)) and for finance lessors (see Example 20 part (a)).

Qualifying expenditure

3. The rules permitting expenditure thermal insulation to qualify for plant and machinery allowances were relaxed with effect from 6 April 2008 (income tax) and 1 April 2008 (corporation tax). Previously they applied only to traders and insulation in industrial buildings. They now apply to any qualifying activity other than ordinary or overseas property businesses (for which a straightforward deduction is available (ITTOIA 2005 s 312, ICTA 1988 s 31ZA)). The rules are also disapplied in respect of dwelling houses (CAA 2001 s 35).

4. Fire safety expenditure required by a fire authority following an application for a fire certificate under the Fire Precautions Act 1971 previously qualified as plant and machinery expenditure (former CAA 2001 s 29). This provision did not cover all fire safety expenditure and, rather than extend the relief to all such expenditure, the Government withdrew it altogether with effect from 1 April 2008 (corporation tax) and 6 April 2008 (income tax) (FA 2008 s 72).

Question

All figures in the following examples are as adjusted for VAT purposes.

(a)   AB, whose business qualifies as small, is a long established trader making up accounts annually to 30 September. Using the following information relating to the years to 30 September 2008 and 2009, show the capital allowances claimable on the plant and machinery main pool for 2008/09 and 2009/10. All additions post-April 2009 qualify for first-year allowance.

	£
Pool written down value brought forward at 30.9.07	150,000

Disposal proceeds totalled £15,000 in the year to 30 September 2008 and £9,500 in the year to 30 September 2009.

	Additions £
Year to 30 September 2008 –	
General plant (November 2007)	35,000
Computer (June 2008)	17,000
Year to 30 September 2009 –	
General plant (October 2008)	33,000
Van (May 2009)	28,000

(b)   Margaret was made redundant by Hi Fi plc on 31 March 2007. On 1 May 2007 she registered for VAT and commenced a trade as a producer and distributor of musical records and tapes. Her first accounts covered the seventeen months to 30 September 2008 and accounts were made up annually to 30 September thereafter.

Capital expenditure on and disposals of business assets up to 30 September 2009 were as follows:

9 April 2007	Jaguar 3600cc car costing £17,400. Business use has been provisionally agreed at 70%.
1 May 2007	Office fixtures and fittings costing £6,000.
2 November 2008	Installation of computerised musical and recording equipment costing £20,000.
23 March 2009	Video equipment costing £10,000.
1 April 2009	Computer used as a music design system costing £23,300.
4 June 2009	New mixing deck costing £8,000. This amount was after deducting a part-exchange allowance of £2,000 for a mixing deck bought in December 2007 for £2,800.
18 August 2009	Computer costing £7,000.

Prepare capital allowances computations for the first two accounting periods, assuming Margaret wishes to claim allowances as early as possible, and indicate how relief will be given. State any elections required and the time limit by which they should be made.

(c)   Calculate the optimum capital allowances claims for the relevant income tax year or chargeable accounting period, in respect of the following businesses.

If any options or elections are available these should be indicated and explained.

(i)   Falstaff is a single man entitled to a personal allowance of £6,475 in 2009/10. For the year ended 30 November 2009 his adjusted business profits before capital allowances were £9,350.

The written down value brought forward of assets on which capital allowances are claimed was £10,500.

On 7 March 2009 he purchased new plant costing £8,000.

He has no income other than from the business.

(ii)   B Wise Ltd, a manufacturing company, has adjusted profits (before capital allowances) of £80,000 for its accounts year ended 31 December 2009.

The written down value of the capital allowances pool as at 1 January 2009 was £42,500.

In the year ended 31 December 2009:

1 January 2009   Purchased new plant costing £142,500
1 March 2009   Sold plant for £6,000 (it had cost £7,500)

B Wise Ltd has a single subsidiary company and this company has incurred a trading loss in the corresponding accounting period which results in group relief being available of £42,800. The subsidiary is not able to carry back the loss and is not expected to trade profitably for some years to come. No AIA claim has been, or will be made, by the subsidiary company.

(d)   C and D had been in business for many years, making up accounts annually to 5 April and sharing profits 3:1. The following information relates to their plant and machinery in the year ended 5 April 2010:

Written down values brought forward at 6.4.09:

	£
Main pool	47,000
Car used by C (original cost £12,956)	5,600
Car used by D	21,000
Disposal proceeds during period:	
Van (original cost £7,500)	3,500
Car used by works manager (original cost in 2007 £9,000)	4,000
C's car	6,500
Additions during period:	
October 2009 Car to replace that used by works manager; CO_2 emissions 145 g/km	14,500
December 2009 Replacement van	13,000
January 2010 New fixtures (qualifying for main pool)	55,800
March 2010 Replacement car for C; CO_2 emissions 187 g/km	23,000

The partners' cars were used privately to the extent of one third. The works manager's car was used one quarter privately.

An amount of £1,200 relating to an electric sign bought in May 2009 had been disallowed in computing trading profit.

(i)   Compute the maximum capital allowances available for 2009/10.

(ii)   Without making computations, state what the position would be if the motor cars were owned personally by C and D.

Comment on the treatment of capital allowances for partnerships.

(e)   (i)   B Green (London) Ltd, a trading company, has adjusted profits (before capital allowances) of £15,000 for its accounting year ended 31 March 2010. The company does not have any associated companies. The written down value of the capital allowances plant pool at 1 April 2009 was £6,400. On 1 May 2009 the company purchased a new car costing £14,000 with a carbon dioxide emissions figure of 109 grams.

Show the optimum claim for capital allowances for the year to 31 March 2010.

(ii)   Show the revised optimum claim for capital allowances in (i) above if B Green (London) Ltd had losses of £11,000 brought forward from the accounting year ended 31 March 2009.

Answer

(a)

AB – Capital Allowances Computation 2008/09 and 2009/10

		Main pool £	Total allowances £
2008/09 (1.10.07 to 30.9.08)			
Written down value brought forward		150,000	
Additions – Computer	17,000		
AIA	(17,000)		17,000
Disposals		(15,000)	
		135,000	
WDA at hybrid rate 22.5%		(30,375)	30,375
Additions (general plant)	35,000		
FYA 50%	(17,500)	17,500	17,500
		122,125	64,875
2009/10 (1.10.08 to 30.9.09)			
Additions – (general plant and van)	50,000		
AIA	(50,000)		50,000
Disposals		(9,500)	
		112,625	
WDA 20%		(22,525)	22,525
Additions (van – balance of cost)	11,000		
FYA 40%	(4,400)	6,600	4,400
Written down value carried forward		96,700	76,925

(b) **Margaret – capital allowances computations**

		Main pool £	Computer (short life asset) £	Jaguar (30% private) £	Total allow-ances £
Period to 30 September 2008					
Purchases 9.4.07, 1.5.07		6,000		17,400	
FYA 50%		(3,000)			3,000
WDA 3,000 × 17/12				(4,250) (× 70% = 2,975)	2,975
WDV		3,000		13,150	5,975
Year to 30 September 2009					
Qualifying for AIA	53,300				
AIA	(50,000)				50,000
		3,300			
Disposal 4.6.09		(2,000)			

		Main pool £	Computer (short life asset) £	Jaguar (30% private) £		Total allow-ances £
		4,300				
					(× 70% =	1,841
WDA 20%		(860)		(2,630)	1,841	860
Additions (post-6/4/09) –						
– pool	10,000					
– short life			7,000			
FYA 40%	(4,000)	6,000	(2,800)			6,800
		9,440	4,200	10,520		59,501

The capital allowances will be deducted as trading expenses in arriving at the trading profit or loss of each accounting period. Assuming Margaret makes profits, the profits will be charged to tax as follows:

2007/08	Profit from 1.5.07 to 5.4.08	$= 11/17 \times$ 1st profit
2008/09	Profit from 1.10.07 to 30.9.08	$= 12/17 \times$ 1st profit
	Overlap profits 1.10.07 to 5.4.08 (6 months)	
2009/10	Profit for year to 30.9.09	

The effect of the overlapping income tax basis periods for 2007/08 and 2008/09 is that over the two years relief will be given for 23/17 of the capital allowances of £5,975 = £8,084. The extra relief of £2,109 is, however, reflected in a similar reduction in the overlap relief available in respect of the six months to 5 April 2008.

An election to treat the computer bought on 18 August 2009 as a short life asset must be made within the self-assessment time limit of one year from 31 January following the tax year in which the relevant accounting period ends, ie period to 30 September 2009 ends in 2009/10 giving a date of 31 January 2012.

(c) (i) **Falstaff – 2009/10**

	£
Falstaff's assessable profits are	9,350
and he has a personal allowance of	(6,475)
which leaves him with income unabsorbed of	2,875

He should therefore claim capital allowances for 2009/10 of £2,875 only, in order to reduce his income to the point where it is fully absorbed by his personal allowance (see explanatory note 5).

Capital allowances computation for year to 30 November 2009

	Pool £	Total Allowances £
WDV brought forward at 1 December 2008	10,500	
Additions 7 March 2009 (AIA not claimed)	8,000	
	18,500	
Writing down allowance (20% × £18,500 = £3,700) restricted to	(2,875)	2,875
WDV carried forward to account commencing 1 December 2009	15,625	

Alternatively Falstaff could consider leaving some profits within the tax charge at 20% (plus 8% Class 4 national insurance). This would give a tax saving (at the cost of a cash-flow disadvantage) if he is likely to be paying tax in the near future at 40% plus Class 4 contributions of 1%. This example ignores the impact of tax credits.

A variation would be to claim AIA of 100% restricted to £2,875 with no WDA. The tax savings would be the same.

(ii) **B Wise Ltd – Chargeable accounting period to 31 December 2009**

	£
B Wise Ltd has profits before capital allowances of	80,000
against which group relief is available of	42,800
which would leave unabsorbed profits of	37,200

The capital allowances claim should therefore be restricted to this figure (see explanatory notes 5 and 6). The computation will be as follows:

		Pool £	Total Allowances £
WDV brought forward at 1 January 2009		42,500	
Additions	142,500		
AIA	37,200		37,200
		105,300	
		147,800	
Sale proceeds		(6,000)	
		141,800	
Writing down allowance not claimed			
WDV carried forward at 31 December 2009		141,800	

(d)   C and D

(i)   Capital Allowances Computation 2009/10

	Main pool	C's first car	C's second car (private use)	D's car (£12,000+)	Total allow-ances
	£	£	£	£	£
B/f from 2008/09 (period ended 5.4.09)	47,000	5,600		21,000	
2009/10 (period ended 5.4.10) Disposal		(6,500)			
Balancing charge		900	(2/3= 600)		BC £600
Additions qualifying for AIA Sign £1,200 May 2009 Fixtures £55,800 Jan 2009 Total AIA £50,000					50,000
Surplus additions	7,000				
Additions – cars not qualifying for AIA	14,500		23,000		
Disposals Van	(3,500)				
Cars	(4,000)				
	61,000	(Max)	23,000	21,000	
WDA 20%	(12,200)			(3,000) (2/3=	12,200
WDA 10%			(2,300) 1,533)	2,000)	3,533
	58,800				
Additions Van £13,000 Dec 2009 FYA 40% (£5,200)	7,800				5,200
Cf to 2010/11	66,600		20,700	18,000	70,933

The capital allowances as computed will be deducted from the assessable profits, the balancing charge will be added to the profits, and the resulting amount will be divided three quarters to C and one quarter to D.

(ii)   If instead of the motor cars being partnership assets they had been owned personally by C and D, then the allowances on them would have been computed separately but still claimed by the partnership. They would not have been taken into account in computing the partnership profit divisible between the partners in the profit sharing ratio but would instead have been deducted separately from each partner's profit share. The total capital allowances, including those on the partners' cars, would be shown on the partnership self-assessment tax return and the share of profits after capital allowances (both partnership and individual) on the partnership statement. The net figure is then transferred to the tax returns of C and D respectively. For example, in 2009/10 the adjusted profit of the year to 5 April 2010 would be reduced by AIA and the writing down allowances on the main pool totalling £64,700, the balance being split three quarters to C and one quarter to D. D's share would then be reduced by his capital allowances of £2,000 and C's share would be reduced by net allowances of (1,533 – 600) = £933.

(iii)   Partnership capital allowances are treated as a trading expense of a period of account and are deducted in arriving at taxable profits. Partners are taxed separately on their shares of the profit as if it had arisen from a separate individual trade. Allowances on assets that are partnership assets reduce the overall profit and allowances relating to a partner's own property reduce his share of the profit as indicated in (ii) above, but in both cases the allowances must be claimed in the partnership return and cannot be claimed separately by an individual partner.

(e)   (i)   **B Green (London) Ltd – Chargeable accounting period to 31 March 2010**

Capital allowances computation	Main pool	Car	Total Allowances
WDV brought forward at 1 April 2009	6,400		
Additions		14,000	
First-year allowances (100%) – restricted		(13,720)	13,720
Writing down allowances (20%)	(1,280)		1,280
WDV carried forward at 31 March 2010	5,120	280	15,000

Alternatively, the company could have claimed all the first-year allowance and made a partial claim for the writing down allowances. However, that would subsequently increase the potential balancing charge on the disposal of the car.

On the other hand, it might be more likely that a balancing charge would first arise on the disposal of plant and machinery in the main pool. In this case, it might be more appropriate to take a full first-year allowance in respect of the car.

The company could also have claimed up to 100% FYA on the low emissions car and a corresponding partial writing down allowance in the main pool.

(ii)

	£
B Green (London) Ltd has profits before capital allowances of	15,000
The amount of profits covered by the loss brought forward is	11,000
Leaving profits to be covered by capital allowances of	4,000

Capital allowances computation	Main pool £	Total allowances £
WDV brought forward at 1 April 2009	6,400	
Additions 1 May 2009 (100% FYA not claimed)	14,000	

Capital allowances computation	Main pool £	Total allowances £
	20,400	
Writing down allowance (20% × 20,400 = 4,080) restricted to	4,000	4,000
WDV carried forward at 31 March 2010	16,400	

Explanatory Notes

Basis period for capital allowances

1. Capital expenditure on plant and machinery is taken into account according to the chargeable period in which it is incurred (CAA 2001 ss 2 and 6). Capital expenditure incurred before a trade starts is treated as incurred on the first day of trading, as with Margaret's expenditure in April 2007 prior to commencing trading in May 2007 in part (b) of the example (CAA 2001 s 12).

    See Example 18 part (b) for detailed notes on the chargeable period rules. Where a period of account exceeds 12 months but does not exceed 18 months, writing down allowances are proportionately increased, as shown in part (b) of the example.

2. For a further detailed illustration of the application of the plant and machinery provisions and detailed notes on other aspects, including the provisions for allocating assets to pools, the treatment of short life and long life assets and the availability of 100% first-year allowance for low emission cars see Example 20.

Rates of writing-down allowances

3. Until 2007/08 writing-down allowances were at an annual rate of 25%. This was reduced to 20% for most assets (see Examples 20 and 21). For chargeable periods spanning the introduction of the new rules (1 April 2008 for corporation tax, 6 April 2008 for income tax), the rate available is the average applying for the chargeable period. Strictly, any apportionment should be by days but the following example uses months.

    For example, suppose a company prepares accounts to 31 December each year. The effective rate of writing-down allowances for the year to 31 December 2008 is:

    ¼ × 25% + ¾ × 20% = 21¼%

    Statute requires percentages to be rounded up to the nearest two decimal places. (FA 2008 s 80.)

Small pools

4. For accounting periods beginning on or after 1 April 2008 (6 April for income tax) s 56A permits pool balances of £1,000 or less to be written off immediately rather than reduced proportionately until the cessation of a business. This applies only in respect of the main (20%) pool and the special rate (10%) pool.

    The £1,000 limit is proportionately increased or reduced in cases of longer or shorter chargeable periods or where the qualifying activity has not been carried on for the whole of the chargeable period.

Capital allowances claims and disclaimer

5. Both individuals and companies must make a specific claim for capital allowances, claims being made in tax returns (CAA 2001 s 3). Where the individual or company does not wish to claim all the plant

and machinery allowances they are entitled to, the claim may be restricted to the amount required (CAA 2001 ss 52(4) and 56(5)). Allowances may be left unclaimed to avoid wasting personal allowances or other reliefs, as shown in part (c) of the example. The availability of first-year allowances on certain expenditure provides another reason for partial claims, as shown in part (d) of the example. If there would otherwise be a balancing charge, all or the appropriate part of expenditure on which a first-year allowance is available may instead be included in the pool to cover a balancing charge (CAA 2001 s 58(5)).

6. Following CAA 2001, all writing down allowances may now be claimed wholly or only in part.

7. Under income tax self-assessment capital allowances are subject to the same time limits as other entries in a return, ie any amendment must normally be made within 12 months after the 31 January filing date for the return.

Companies are able to make, vary and withdraw capital allowances claims up to two years after the end of their accounting period. If the profits are not finally settled by that time, later time limits apply.

For detailed notes on claims procedures see Example 43.

8. If B Wise Ltd in part (c)(ii) of the example had claimed the full available allowances of £75,800 (AIA of £50,000 plus WDA of £25,800) its profits would have been reduced to (£80,000 – £75,800 =) £4,200 and group relief restricted to that amount. The subsidiary company would then have been left with an unrelieved loss of £38,600 to carry forward, with no prospect of early relief in view of its anticipated unprofitable trend.

Private use

9. Note in part (d) of the example that the private use restriction for the use of cars applies only to the cars used by the partners. Private use of assets by *employees* does not require any restriction of the capital allowances. The employees are charged on the benefit under the benefit code provisions of ITEPA 2003.

Business use of partner's own assets

10. Where partners own assets personally and use them in the business, the same capital allowances are available as if the partnership owned them (CAA 2001 s 264), but the allowances are deducted in arriving at each partner's assessable profit, as indicated in part (d)(ii) of the example.

Cars

11. For cars purchased prior to 1 April 2009 (6 April 2009 for income tax), cars costing in excess of £12,000 are put into single asset pools. The purpose of this pool was to limit the writing-down allowance each year to £3,000.

Although the main rate of writing-down allowance has been reduced to 20%, the restriction of £3,000 is unchanged.

One unexpected advantage of single asset pooling for cars is that balancing allowances might be available on the disposal of a vehicle. This is not available for assets in the main pool until a cessation of the qualifying activity.

12. The £12,000 cost limit does not apply to qualifying hire cars or cars which are entitled to 100% first-year allowances (s 74(2)).

13. Cars purchased on or after 1 April 2009 (6 April 2009 for income tax) are subject to the new capital allowance regime, under which allowances are determined by CO_2 emissions.

– New cars with emissions of no more than 110g/km are subject to 100% first-year allowance, the net WDV of nil being treated as added to the main pool unless the car has private use in an income tax business.

- Cars with emissions of no more than 160g/km (including second hand low emission cars) are added to the main pool where they will attract 20% WDA.

- Cars with emissions of more than 160g/km are added to the special rate pool where they will attract 10% WDA.

- Cars with private use in income tax businesses will remain subject to the single asset pooling rules and will attract WDA based on their emissions.

The main consequence of this new regime is that balancing allowances are no longer available on cars added to the pools. The self employed and partners with private use adjustments will find that they benefit from accelerated allowances under the new regime, but companies will suffer significant delays in obtaining the benefit of expenditure on cars.

First-year allowances

14. A first-year allowance of 40% on expenditure incurred between 1 April 2009 (6 April for income tax) and 31 March 2010 (5 April for income tax). This is given on additions to the main pool only, and is not available on cars or assets used for leasing. This is available on additions in excess of the AIA.

First-year allowances were also available to small and medium-sized enterprises at a rate of 40% until April 2008. However, small enterprises were occasionally allowed to claim 50% first-year allowances. This was the case for expenditure incurred in 2004/05 (or the financial year 2004 for companies) and again for expenditure incurred in 2006/07 and 2007/08 (or the financial years 2006 and 2007 for companies).

Annual investment allowance

15. Businesses incurring capital expenditure on plant or machinery after 31 March 2008 (or after 5 April 2008 in the case of unincorporated businesses) are now given an annual investment allowance. Subject to some exceptions (eg expenditure on cars), the first £50,000 of expenditure on plant and machinery in any year is immediately relievable. Groups of companies have only a single AIA allocated to the group as a whole which may be claimed as desired. The allowance is discussed further in Example 21.

Value added tax

16. Value added tax is not taken into account as part of the expenditure for capital allowances if it is recoverable through the VAT system (see Example 15 note 16). Similarly, output VAT on disposals is excluded from disposal proceeds. VAT on cars is not normally recoverable, and in that event it forms part of the cost for capital allowances, as shown in this example. On the sale of a car VAT is not normally due but there are special rules for second-hand car dealers and in some other circumstances.

Special rules also apply for items of plant costing £2,000 or more (VAT inclusive) where the trader has elected to use the small business flat rate scheme. In those cases VAT input tax is recoverable and capital allowances are only due on the net cost. On the sale of these items output tax at 17.5% is payable but only the net sale proceeds are included in the capital allowances pool. For capital assets costing less than £2,000, under the flat rate scheme both output and input VAT-inclusive figures are used in the capital allowances computation. The only exception to this rule is where the asset was purchased before the trader joined the scheme in which case the VAT-exclusive price is deducted from the pool on sale. (Where the VAT-exclusive price is shown in the capital allowances pool, the sale is not included in the turnover for the purposes of the flat rate scheme and the output tax at 17.5% must be accounted for separately.)

Question

A.

Alley plc, a company that qualifies as medium-sized, carries on a trade of multiple retailing. The company has traded for many years making up accounts to 31 December annually.

The company acquired some lorries under a finance lease for a two year period, 1 September 2009 to 31 August 2011. The lease rental payments are £485,000 per annum and the lorries have been capitalised in the accounts at £750,000, that amount being the cost of the lorries to the lessor company on 1 September 2009. Alley plc has charged depreciation on the lorries and the interest element of the rental payments in its accounts. The lessor company makes up accounts to 30 November annually.

The company made the following purchases and sales of plant and machinery in the two years ended 31 December 2010:

- 4 January 2009 purchased computer equipment costing £180,000.

- 12 January 2009 purchased three vans for £60,000.

- 21 March 2009 purchased a desk and office furniture for £6,600.

- 7 June 2009 purchased a motor car for use by the chairman for £16,000; the CO_2 emissions were 210 g/km.

- 19 June 2009 sold two motor cars for £3,000 each, which had previously cost £9,500 each in 2004.

- 31 March 2010 purchased shop fittings for £45,000.

- 14 May 2010 disposed of the car purchased for use by the chairman for £7,000. It was replaced by the acquisition on lease of a new Jaguar with a retail value of £28,000 and CO_2 emissions of 174 g/km, on which lease payments of £6,500 were made in 2010. These were charged in arriving at the operating profit.

In October 2010 the company spent £100,000 on repairs to its electrical systems. It would have cost £180,000 to replace the systems.

The written down value at 1 January 2009 for the main pool was £104,100.

(a)   Show the treatment of the leased lorries and the leased Jaguar car for Alley plc and also indicate the capital allowances treatment of the lorries for the lessor company.

(b)   Compute the capital allowances on plant and machinery for the two years ended 31 December 2010, assuming that the maximum reliefs are claimed as early as possible.

B.

A Part and D Lot, two unconnected, long established traders whose businesses qualify as small enterprises and who make up accounts to 31 December, each have sufficient profits in the year to 31 December 2009 to take advantage of the maximum capital allowances claimable. The following information relates to their VAT adjusted purchases and disposals of plant and machinery in the main pool in that year:

20.2 PLANT AND MACHINERY: LEASED ASSETS, LONG-LIFE ASSETS AND INTEGRAL FEATURES

	A Part £	D Lot £
Written down value b/f	200,000	650,000
Purchases qualifying for first-year allowance/AIA:		
February 2009	100,000	100,000
May 2009	850,000	850,000
Disposal proceeds (no plant sold for more than cost)	600,000	600,000

Show the capital allowances each should claim.

Answer

A. Alley plc

(a) **Tax treatment of leased items**

Lorries under finance lease

The lorries acquired by Alley plc under the finance lease, although capitalised in the company's accounts, are not treated as purchased for tax purposes. Instead the rental payments of £485,000 per annum are treated as a trading expense. The payments must be allocated to periods of account under the accruals concept. Where the Accounting Standard SSAP 21 has been applied, Revenue Statement of Practice (SP3/91) permits the charge to comprise a mixture of the finance charge element and the accounting depreciation charge.

Assets acquired on long-funding leases are treated differently (CAA 2001 ss 70A–70YJ). Finance leases are also subject to detailed anti-avoidance provisions (see explanatory note 23). As far as the lessor company is concerned, the expenditure of £750,000 on the lorries qualifies for a restricted writing down allowance covering the three-month period from 1 September to 30 November 2009. The legislation puts this into effect by restricting the allowable expenditure in the first period, but the whole of the remaining expenditure goes into the pool at the end of that period, so it is more straightforward to apply the restriction to the writing down allowance. The position is therefore as follows:

Lessor company's year to 30 November 2009 – relevant entries in plant and machinery pool

	£
Cost of lorries 1 September 2009	750,000
WDA 20% × 3/12ths	37,500
Written down value carried forward	712,500

Jaguar car leased for use by chairman

Alley plc is entitled to a deduction from its profits in respect of the Jaguar car lease payment in the year to 31 December 2010. Since the car emits more than 160g/km, Alley plc cannot deduct the full amount paid of £6,500. The restriction is 15% of the lease payments, so 85% is allowed for tax.

So £975 will be disallowed and £5,525 allowed.

(b) **Alley plc – Capital allowances on plant and machinery for two years ended 31 December 2010**

	Main pool	Short life asset computer	Special rate (10%) pool	Total Allowances
Yr ended 31.12.2009	£	£	£	£
WDV bf 1.1.09	104,100	–	–	–
Additions not qualifying for FYA or AIA:				
Car (7.6.09)			16,000	
Sales proceeds (19.6.09)	(6,000)			
	98,100			

	Main pool	Short life asset computer	Special rate (10%) pool	Total Allow-ances
Additions qualifying for AIA but not FYA:				
Computer equipment (4.1.09)		180,000		
Vans (12.1.09)	60,000			
Furniture (21.3.09)	6,600			
	66,600			
AIA	(50,000)	16,600		50,000
		114,700	180,000	
WDA 20%		(22,940)	(36,000)	58,940
WDA 10%			(1,600)	
		91,760	144,000	14,400
Yr ended 31.12.2010				
Sale proceeds (14.5.10)			(7,000)	
			7,400	
Additions on which FYA not available:				108,940
Electrical system repairs (October 2010)	100,000			
Annual investment allowance	(50,000)			50,000
Balance to 10% pool			50,000	
WDA 20%		(18,352)	(28,800)	47,152
WDA 10%			(5,740)	5,740
		73,408		
Additions qualifying for FYA				
Shop fittings (31.3.10)	45,000			
FYA 40%	(18,000)	27,000		18,000
WDV cf 31.12.10		100,408	115,200	51,660	120,892

B. **A Part and D Lot – Capital allowances claims for year ended 31 December 2009**

		A Part Main pool £		D Lot Main pool £
WDV bf at 1 January 2009			200,000	650,000
Purchases on which FYA not claimed				
February 2009 (none available)	100,000		100,000	
May 2009	350,000			
AIA	(50,000)		(50,000)	
			400,000	50,000
Disposal proceeds			(600,000)	(600,000)

	A Part Main pool £	D Lot Main pool £
		100,000
WDA 20%		(20,000)
Purchases qualifying for FYA		850,000
less taken into account above (850,000	500,000	
less 350,000)		
FYA 40% × 500,000/850,000	(200,000)	(340,000)
WDV cf	300,000	590,000

If A Part had claimed the full first-year allowance of 40% on £850,000, it would have amounted to £340,000, but there would have been a balancing charge of (£600,000 − (£200,000 + £50,000) = £350,000), giving him a net allowance of (£340,000 + £50,000 − £350,000) = £40,000 compared with £250,000 as shown. D Lot has a sufficient balance of qualifying expenditure to cover his disposal proceeds, so he should claim the available FYA in full.

Explanatory Notes

All references in these notes are to CAA 2001 unless otherwise stated.

Qualifying expenditure and qualifying activities

1. For a company, the entitlement to capital allowances depends on qualifying expenditure incurred in the chargeable accounting period. Expenditure on a building preparatory to the installation of plant and machinery counts as expenditure on plant and machinery (s 25). For detailed notes on the expenditure qualifying for relief and the timing of reliefs, including the chargeable period provisions relating to allowances for income tax purposes, see Example 18.

    Plant and machinery allowances are available to those carrying on 'qualifying activities'. The main examples of qualifying activities are trades, professions, vocations and employments, property letting businesses, including furnished holiday lettings businesses until 5 April 2010, and special leasing businesses (as to which see Example 18 part (b) under *Capital allowances given by a claim made other than in a return*) (s 15). Allowances must be calculated separately for each qualifying activity (s 11).

    FA 2006 brought some changes to the availability of capital allowances in respect of leased assets. They apply to leases longer than seven years (in some cases to leases longer than five years). See note explanatory 24 below.

Allowances available

2. The allowances available are first-year allowances, writing down allowances and balancing allowances. In some instances a balancing charge is made to take away allowances previously given. Writing down allowances and balancing allowances and charges are dealt with under a 'pooling' system, as outlined later in these notes. This note and notes 3 to 5 deal with first-year allowances (FYAs). Where claimed, FYAs are given instead of the first year's writing down allowance.

Although expenditure incurred before a trade starts is normally treated as incurred on the first day of trading (s 12), the actual date of the expenditure is the relevant date for FYAs. Where available, FYAs are given in full regardless of the length of the chargeable period (unless they are not or only partly claimed – see explanatory note 10).

From 1 April (6 April, income tax) 2009 the definition of a car has been changed to exclude motor cycles and include hire cars (cars used as taxis, daily hire cars and cars leased to the disabled).

FYAs are not available on transactions between connected persons (see Example 18 part (f)), or where obtaining allowances was the sole or main benefit of the sale (ss 213 to 217). Under the provisions of s 46, FYAs are not available on expenditure incurred in the period in which the trade ceases, nor on cars or taxis (other than low emission vehicles as indicated in note 8), motor cycles (for periods up to 1 April 2009), ships, railway assets, most long life assets (see note 21), and machinery and plant for leasing or letting on hire, whether in the course of a trade or otherwise. FYAs are also not available if there was a change in the nature or conduct of a trade carried on by someone other than the person who incurred the expenditure and obtaining an FYA was one of the main benefits that could be expected to arise from the change (s 46).

Pre-April 2008

3. Under ss 44 and 52, small and medium-sized businesses as defined may claim FYA of 40% for the chargeable period in which qualifying expenditure is incurred. For the year commencing 1 April 2007 (6 April 2007 for an unincorporated business) a small enterprise can claim FYA of 50%.

A small/medium-sized business is defined by reference to the Companies Act definition, adapted to apply to unincorporated businesses as well (ss 47 to 49). To qualify for financial years ending on or after 30 January 2004, the business must satisfy two of the following conditions in the current or previous year (and for companies in a group, the group must be small/medium-sized when the expenditure is incurred):

– Turnover must not be more than £22.8 million (previously £11.2 million)

– Assets must not total more than £11.4 million (previously £5.6 million)

– There must not be more than 250 employees

To qualify as 'small' a business must satisfy at least two of the following criteria in the current or previous year (and if a company is a member of a group, the group must also be 'small'):

– Turnover not more than £5.6 million (previously £2.8 million)

– Assets not more than £2.8 million (previously £1.4 million)

– Not more than 50 employees.

UK company members of a foreign group will not qualify unless the foreign group is small/medium-sized.

First-year allowances are available at 100% for expenditure on energy saving and environmentally beneficial plant and machinery and plant and machinery for gas refuelling stations (see explanatory note 7), and electric and low emission cars (see explanatory note 8).

From April 2008

4. From April 2008 the special rules giving first-year allowances to small and medium-sized businesses were removed. The 100% allowances for environmentally-friendly assets continue.

Instead, expenditure on plant and machinery qualifies for the proposed annual investment allowance (£50,000). The first £50,000 of qualifying expenditure will be written off in the year of expenditure. For businesses incurring larger amounts, the excess will be allocated to the main (20%) or special expenditure (10%) pool.

From April 2009

5.   For expenditure incurred on or after 1 April 2009 (6 April for income tax businesses) there is a first-year allowance of 40% available to all businesses, irrespective of size. The allowance is given only on expenditure allocated to the main pool, and is not available on cars or assets used for leasing. The FYA lasts for twelve months and will not apply to expenditure incurred after 31 March 2010 (5 April for income tax). It is given in addition to the AIA.

Computers

6.   Computer software is an intangible asset, but it is specifically provided that capital expenditure on licensed software (except where acquired with a view to sub-licensing) and electronically transmitted software qualifies for plant and machinery allowances (s 71). Software is usually either developed 'in house' or acquired on lifetime licence for a particular user or users rather than being purchased outright. If licensed software is acquired on rental, the rentals are charged against profit over the life of the software. Where a lump sum is paid, HMRC normally takes the view that the cost of software with an expected life of less than two years may be treated as a revenue expense and deducted from profit. Otherwise it will usually be treated as capital expenditure for which plant and machinery allowances may be claimed (under the short life asset rules if appropriate). The treatment of in-house software is broadly similar, being either treated as capital or revenue depending on the expected period of use. HMRC have stated that expenditure on modifications in connection with EMU and the introduction of the Euro will normally be revenue expenditure.

   From 1 April 2002 separate rules apply for companies in relation to intangible assets. Computer software treated as part of the cost of the related hardware is not affected by these rules. Software that is not so treated will be dealt with under the intangible assets provisions unless the company makes an election for capital allowances to apply. The election must be made within two years after the end of the accounting period in which the expenditure was incurred. Once made the election is irrevocable. For the detailed provisions on intangible assets see Example 66.

Energy saving and environmentally beneficial plant and machinery

7.   From 6 April 2001 (1 April 2001 for companies) 100% FYAs are available on new plant and machinery that is energy-efficient (ss 45A–45C). From 1 April 2003 this is extended to include environmentally beneficial plant and machinery. The FYA is available for qualifying expenditure on combined heat and power plant, boilers, motors, variable speed drives, lighting systems, refrigeration equipment, pipe insulation, heat pumps, radiant and warm air heaters, compressed air equipment, solar thermal systems, environmentally beneficial machinery and thermal screens. Qualifying products are listed on the UK Energy Technology List, which is available on the Internet at www.eca.gov.uk. Businesses purchasing relevant products may establish whether the 100% FYA is available by obtaining a certificate from the manufacturers, or alternatively via the website.

   The rules for fixtures in ss 172 to 204 (see explanatory note 30) have been adapted to enable energy service companies to claim the 100% first-year allowances on qualifying energy saving plant and machinery as outlined above where the plant and machinery is provided and becomes a fixture on a client business's premises, and the plant and machinery is operated by the energy service company under an energy services agreement.

   Under s 45E, 100% first-year allowances may be claimed for expenditure incurred between 17 April 2002 and 31 March 2013 inclusive on new plant and machinery for gas refuelling stations.

   From 17 April 2002 the general exclusion from FYAs of plant for leasing (see explanatory note 2) does not apply to plant and machinery for leasing that is energy-saving plant and machinery (s 45A), low emission cars (s 45D – see explanatory note 8), gas refuelling equipment (s 45E) or from 1 April 2003 environmentally beneficial plant (s 45H).

Low emission cars

8.   Expenditure on certain new cars purchased between 17 April 2002 and 31 March 2013 inclusive is eligible for 100% FYAs (s 45D). The eligible cars are those with a carbon dioxide emissions figure of 110 grams or less, bi-fuel cars where the lower emissions figure is 110 grams or less, and electric cars. 'Car' for this purpose includes a taxi but does not include a motor cycle. Before 1 April 2008, the emission threshold was 120 grams.

Such cars are also excluded from the restrictions relating to cars costing more than £12,000 (see explanatory note 17).

Annual investment allowance

9.   The annual investment allowance (AIA) replaces the first-year allowance regime for small and medium sized enterprises. It is available to all businesses (whatever their size) but will proportionately be of more value to smaller enterprises.

Up to £50,000 of annual expenditure may be deductible immediately for tax purposes. This can be expenditure that would otherwise be allocated to either the main pool or to the special rate pool. But the allowance is not available in respect of expenditure on cars.

Given the fact that expenditure is generally written off more slowly in the special rate pool, it would be generally favourable for such the annual investment allowance to be allocated to such expenditure in preference to expenditure qualifying for the main (20%) pool.

See also Example 21, in particular where claims are to be made by related businesses.

Partial claims for allowances

10.   Individuals and companies *need not claim* the full allowances available on plant and may instead claim the amount which gives the most favourable tax position taking all other circumstances into account (ss 52(4) and 56(5)). The main reason for making partial claims for allowances is to enable the taxpayer to claim other reliefs or allowances that cannot be claimed in a later period. As far as first-year allowance is concerned, allowances may sometimes be higher if it is only partly claimed. For an illustration see (b) above.

Pooling

11.   Expenditure on plant and machinery is pooled for the purposes of writing down allowances, balancing allowances and balancing charges (s 53). There are three kinds of pool, single asset pools, class pools and the main pool. Where someone carries on more than one qualifying activity, separate pools are required in relation to each activity.

Single asset pools (which contain only one asset) are required for:

(i)   A car costing more than £12,000 (other than a low emission car) purchased before 1 April 2009 (6 April for income tax) (s 74) (see explanatory note 17).

(ii)   A short life asset (s 86) (see explanatory note 20).

(iii)   An asset used privately by the proprietor (s 206) (see explanatory note 16).

Class pools (which may contain more than one asset) are required for:

(i)   Long life assets and integral features (see explanatory note 21).

(ii)   Expenditure on assets leased outside the UK (s 109) (see explanatory note 29).

All other qualifying expenditure goes into the main pool.

Writing down allowances and balancing adjustments

12.   The calculation of the capital allowances position on the pool depends on whether the disposal proceeds are more than or less than the available qualifying expenditure (s 55), ie the disallowed expenditure brought forward, plus additional qualifying expenditure in the current period (other than expenditure on which FYA is claimed), less any disposal proceeds. (Businesses are not in fact *required* to bring expenditure into the pool in the earliest available period, so that if for example some of the expenditure was omitted in error it could be brought in when the error was discovered.) If the proceeds *exceed* the disallowed expenditure, a balancing charge is made to withdraw the excess allowances (but see explanatory note 14 re the limit on the disposal proceeds). This may occur either while the business is continuing or on cessation.

Where the proceeds are less than the available expenditure, the available allowance is either a writing down allowance of 20% per annum on the reducing balance method (see explanatory note 13 re accounting periods of more or less than 12 months), or a balancing allowance if the period is the 'final chargeable period'. Before 1 April 2008 (or, 6 April 2008 for income tax), the rate of the writing down allowance was 25%.

For a single asset pool, the final chargeable period is the period in which the asset is disposed of. For the main pool and class pools the final chargeable period is that in which the qualifying activity is permanently discontinued (s 65), although this is varied slightly for assets leased abroad (see explanatory note 29). A balancing allowance does not arise other than in the final chargeable period even if, say, the whole plant in the main pool were destroyed by fire and the compensation fell short of the balance on the pool. In those circumstances, the pool balance after deducting the compensation would continue to attract writing down allowances.

Where a claim for first-year allowance is made, the balance of expenditure (including a nil balance) is strictly not allocated to a pool until (at earliest) the commencement of the following period, unless the asset is also disposed of in the period in which it is acquired. In practice it is sensible to bring the balance of the expenditure into the relevant pool at the end of the period of expenditure, so that it forms part of the opening figure for the next period.

The practical working order in respect of a pool for periods other than the final chargeable period is as follows (although some steps are clearly not relevant for single asset pools):

	£	£
Written down value (WDV) brought forward	?	
Add: Expenditure qualifying for AIA	?	
AIA	(?)	X
Balance of expenditure allocated to pool	?	
Add: Expenditure not qualifying for AIA or FYA or on which AIA/FYA not claimed	?	
Less: Disposal proceeds	(?)	
	X	
WDA on X (or balancing charge if X is a negative figure)	(?)	X
Expenditure qualifying for FYA	?	
FYA	(?)	X
Balance of expenditure allocated to pool	?	
WDV carried forward	X	
Total allowances		X

In the final chargeable period, if the qualifying activity is discontinued in that period, first-year allowance is not available (see explanatory note 2) and there would be a balancing allowance rather than a writing down allowance if X was positive. On a single asset pool, if an asset was disposed of in the period in which it was acquired for less than its cost, there would be a balancing allowance on the shortfall. If it was disposed of in that period for more than cost, it would not be brought into account for capital allowances at all and the capital profit would be dealt with under the capital gains legislation (see Example 95).

Accounting periods of more than or less than 12 months (s 56)

13. If a company's chargeable accounting period is less than 12 months the writing down allowance is proportionately reduced.

   Under the income tax rules, capital allowances are treated as a trading expense of a period of account, which may be more or less than 12 months. Writing down allowances are proportionately decreased where the accounting period is less than 12 months and increased where the accounting period exceeds 12 months (but there are special rules for accounting periods exceeding 18 months – see Example 18 part (e)).

   For both companies and individuals, the writing down allowance is proportionately reduced if a qualifying activity has been carried on for only part of the accounting period (s 56).

Limit on disposal proceeds

14. If plant is disposed of for more than its cost, the disposal proceeds brought into the computation are limited to the original value placed into the pool, except when the plant was acquired from a connected person, in which case the limit of disposal proceeds is the highest price paid by one of the connected persons (s 62). For the connected persons rules see Example 18 part (f).

   A capital profit is dealt with under the capital gains legislation (see Example 95).

Hire purchase

15. Hire purchase does not prevent allowances being given as though there were an outright purchase at the time of the first use of the relevant asset, except for finance lessors (see explanatory note 23) (s 67). The cash price is therefore brought in at that time and the subsequent instalments of capital ignored, the interest element being charged in arriving at taxable profit.

Private use

16. Where directors or employees are allowed to use company assets, such as cars, for private purposes, this does not affect the employer's allowances. The employee is charged on the benefit under the benefits code of ITEPA 2003, if he is a director or an employee earning £8,500 pa or more. The reason for keeping the car used by the chairman separate from the car pool in this example is that it cost more than £12,000, so that allowances have to be restricted, as indicated in explanatory note 17. If it had cost £12,000 or less it would have been included in the pool in the usual way.

   It is only where business assets are used partly for private purposes by the *proprietor* of the business (ie by a sole trader or by partners) that the capital allowances are restricted. In these circumstances the asset is kept separate in a single asset pool (s 206). The asset is written down by allowances calculated on the full cost, but only the business fraction is allowed in calculating taxable profits. When the asset is sold there is a final adjustment by way of balancing charge or balancing allowance (again restricted to the business fraction). If more than one asset is used privately then a separate single asset pool is set up for each asset (s 54). For an illustration see Example 19 part (a).

£12,000+ cars purchased before 1 April / 6 April 2009

17. Where a car, other than a low emission car, costs more than £12,000 a single asset pool is set up for it (s 74). 'Car' for this purpose is defined as a mechanically propelled road vehicle (including a motor cycle) other than one primarily suited for carrying goods or a vehicle not commonly used as a private

vehicle and unsuitable to be so used. Qualifying hire cars (ie cars normally hired to the same person for less than 30 consecutive days and less than 90 days in any twelve months and cars let to someone receiving the mobility component of disability living allowance or a mobility supplement) are not subject to the £12,000 restriction and they go into the main pool.

The writing down allowance is restricted to £3,000 per annum and where there is private use (see explanatory note 16), to the business fraction of £3,000 (ss 75, 77). Once the written down value falls to £15,000 or less WDAs are calculated at 20% per annum in the usual way, but the car remains in the single asset pool until it is disposed of. There is no limit on a balancing allowance. Cars will remain in a single asset pool for five years after the new rules commence (see below) at which point the car will be moved to the appropriate pool.

Cars purchased on or after 1 April / 6 April 2009

18.   Cars are allocated to a pool according to their official CO_2 emissions, as follows:

   –   new cars with emissions of no more than 110g/km are subject to 100% first-year allowance, the net WDV of nil being treated as added to the main pool unless the car has private use in an income tax business;

   –   cars with emissions of no more than 160g/km (including second hand low emission cars) are added to the main pool where they will attract 20% WDA;

   –   cars with emissions of more than 160g/km are added to the special rate pool where they will attract 10% WDA;

   –   cars with private use in income tax businesses will remain subject to the single asset pooling rules and will attract WDA based on their emissions.

No balancing allowances are therefore available on cars in future unless the car is subject to a private use adjustment. This is illustrated in the example by the treatment of the chairman's car sold on 14 May 2010.

Leased cars

19.   For leases entered into on or after 1 April 2009 (6 April for income tax) the lease restriction is simply 15% of the rentals where the emissions of the car exceed 160 g/km. There is no restriction on lease rentals for cars with emissions of up to 160 g/km. The allowable deduction may be further reduced where there is private use as set out in explanatory note 16.

Although a hire purchase agreement is an agreement for hire, with an option to purchase, it is expressly provided by ITTOIA 2005 s 49(2) that the hire charge restriction does not apply to a hire purchase agreement under which the option to purchase is exercisable on payment of an amount not exceeding 1% of the retail price of the car when new.

For leases before 1 April 2009 where a car was hired, and its retail price when new exceeded £12,000 and it was not a low emission car, the allowable hire charge that could be deducted in computing profits was restricted by applying the fraction

$$\frac{12,000 + P}{2P}$$

where P was the retail price when new (ITTOIA 2005 s 48). If there was a subsequent rebate of rentals, the amount brought in as a taxable receipt was reduced in the same proportion (s 48(4)). The retail price of a car when new was either the actual price paid by the lessor for the car when new, if known, or the manufacturer's list price less any generally available discount (Tax Bulletin April 2000).

Short life assets

20. Where a trader purchases machinery or plant for use wholly and exclusively for the purposes of the trade, an election may be made to treat the machinery or plant as a short life asset (s 85). The asset is then kept in a single asset pool. The scheme is intended to apply when a trader expects to dispose of an item of machinery or plant at less than its written down value within four years from the year of its acquisition, and it is particularly relevant for assets with a high rate of obsolescence, such as computers. (The normal 20% WDA system takes ten years to write off approximately 90% of any expenditure.)

The election for short life asset treatment is to be made by companies within two years after the end of the chargeable period in which the capital expenditure was incurred (or, where the capital expenditure was incurred on different dates, as is the case with the building expenditure preparatory to the installation of the computerised control system in this example, within two years after the end of the period in which the first expenditure was incurred). For individuals the time limit is one year from 31 January following the tax year in which the relevant accounting period ends. When a short life asset is sold within four years after the end of the period in which the capital expenditure was incurred (or the first capital expenditure if it was incurred on different dates), there is a final adjustment by way of a balancing charge or balancing allowance.

However, if the short life asset is not sold within that time its written down value is transferred to the main pool and thereafter dealt with as if it had never been in a single asset pool.

Example

EF makes up accounts annually to 31 December. In April 2007 he acquired plant costing £10,000. On the basis that a short life asset election was made, show the capital allowances available in the following cases (ignoring the possibility of first-year allowances):

(1)   The plant is sold in the year ended 31 December 2009 for (i) £3,000 and (ii) £6,000; and

(2)   The plant is not sold by 31 December 2011.

EF – Short life asset election

(1)   *Plant sold in yr ended 31 December 2009*

			(i) For £3,000 £	(ii) For £6,000 £
2007/08	Year ended 31.12.07	Cost	10,000	10,000
		WDA 25%	2,500	2,500
			7,500	7,500
2008/09	Year ended 31.12.08	WDA 21.25%	1,594	1,594
			5,906	5,906
2009/10	Year ended 31.12.09	Sale proceeds	3,000	6,000
	Balancing allowance (charge)		2,906	(94)

(2)   *Plant not sold by 31 December 2011*

			£
WDV after allowance for 2008/09 as above			5,906
2009/10	Year ended 31.12.09	WDA 20%	1,182
			4,724
2010/11	Year ended 31.12.10	WDA 20%	945

				£
				3,779
2011/12	Year ended 31.12.11	WDA 20%		756
WDV transferred to main pool				3,023

For further illustrations of the short life assets provisions see Example 19 part (b).

Short life asset treatment does not apply to machinery or plant otherwise dealt with outside the main pool, as detailed in explanatory notes 11, 16 and 17 above.

Long life assets

21. Special rules apply to long life assets (ss 90 to 104). These rules apply to expenditure on or after 26 November 1996. Expenditure on a second-hand asset is included if the special rules applied to the vendor in respect of that asset.

Long life assets are those with an expected economic life of 25 years or more. The provisions do not apply to machinery or plant in dwelling houses, retail shops, showrooms, hotels or offices, nor to cars (nor to certain ships and railway assets bought before the end of 2011). There is also a de minimis limit of £100,000 a year (reduced pro rata for companies with associated companies). There are various provisions to prevent the de minimis limit being exploited.

Assets within the provisions are pooled in a separate class pool known as the special rate pool and writing down allowances were initially given at 6% per annum on the reducing balance method. This was revised to 10% with effect from 1 April 2008 (6 April for income tax). A balancing adjustment does not arise on disposal unless the trade has also ceased. In many cases the expenditure would alternatively qualify for industrial buildings allowances, and businesses may choose which allowances to claim, although with the withdrawal of IBA's from 2011 this choice is a theoretical rather than practical option.

From April 2008 the long-life asset main pool has been extended to include integral features. The rate of allowances also increased from 6% to 10% per annum. Expenditure on cars with CO_2 emissions of more than 160 g/km is also allocated to this 'special rate' pool with effect from 1 April 2009.

Transitional rules for special rate expenditure

22. For chargeable periods straddling the introduction of the special rate pool (1 April 2008 or 6 April 2008 for corporation tax and income tax respectively), the rate of writing down allowance is averaged.

Thus in the case of GH Ltd below, the rate of writing down allowances applying to the year ended 30 September 2008 will be:

$(184/366 \times 6\%) + (182/366 \times 10\%) = 7.99\%$ (statutorily rounded up to 2 decimal places).

However, for all capital expenditure incurred after the introduction of the new rules, the new rate of 10% will be available. This differs from the transitional rules for the main pool where all expenditure in the transitional chargeable period attracts writing down allowances at the average 'hybrid' rate.

Example

GH Ltd incurred the following expenditure on long life assets in its accounting years to 30 September 2007 and 2008. It had not previously acquired any long life assets.

1 January 2007	£350,000
1 October 2007	£150,000
30 August 2008	£250,000

Show the capital allowances claim in respect of these assets.

GH Ltd – capital allowances on long life assets – years to 30 September 2007 and 2008

	Long life assets pool
	£
Year to 30 September 2007	
Purchases (not qualifying for FYA)	350,000
WDA 6%	(21,000)
	329,000
Year to 30 September 2008	
Additions prior to 1 April 2008	150,000
	479,000
WDA hybrid rate 7.99%	(38,273)
Additions on or after 1 April 2008	250,000
WDA 10%	(25,000)
	225,000
WDV carried forward	665,727

HMRC have given guidance on the long life assets rules in their Tax Bulletin of August 1997. See also the HMRC manuals at CA 23781.

Finance leases

23. For accounting purposes assets acquired under operating leases are treated as owned by the lessor, whereas assets acquired under finance leases are treated as owned by the lessee. Complex anti-avoidance provisions relating mainly to finance leases are included in ss 213 to 233. These rules have been augmented by Finance Act 2004 with additional restrictions on certain sale/lease and leaseback schemes to prevent double benefits accruing. In addition, FA 2006 introduced rules that ensure that assets acquired on long funding leases qualify for capital allowances in the hands of the lessee rather than the lessor (CAA 2001 ss 70A–70YJ). See below.

The main targets of the legislation are finance leases involving lower rentals with compensating capital payments (the capital sums being taxed at lower rates or possibly not at all, either through indexation allowance or by using a separate leasing company in which the shares are sold rather than the asset), and finance leases with back loaded payments, ie with rents concentrated towards the end of the lease. The provisions align the tax treatment more closely with the recognised accounting treatment. The receipt of a 'major lump sum' is treated as a disposal for capital allowances purposes and the rental income for tax purposes is normally the higher of the actual rent and the earnings recognised in the lessor's commercial accounts.

The first writing down allowance for finance lessors is restricted on a time basis according to the period from the date the expenditure is incurred to the end of the accounting period, as illustrated in part (a) of the example (s 220). Where a finance lessor obtains an asset on hire purchase, he will be entitled to capital allowances only as and when the capital expenditure is incurred, rather than being entitled to allowances on the full capital cost at the outset as indicated in explanatory note 15 (s 229). There are rules to prevent unused past allowances being transferred to finance lessors through sale and leaseback arrangements (ss 221 to 228). Provisions also limit the amount of lease rentals that may be deducted by the lessee where there has been a sale or lease followed by a finance leaseback (ss 228A to 228G). The term 'finance lease' is defined in s 219 as meaning arrangements which are, according to generally accepted accounting practice, treated as a finance lease or a loan in the books of one or more of the parties.

First-year allowances are not available on plant and machinery for leasing, as indicated in explanatory note 2.

FA 2006 introduced some anti-avoidance measures – particularly looking at the sale of lessor companies and the use of losses by leasing partnerships. CAA 2001 s 228K removed the restriction on the disposal value where the lessor is required to bring in a disposal value but remains entitled to some or all of the rentals payable after that time. Even where the limit would not have applied, the disposal value is the actual consideration plus the net present value of these amounts to which the lessor remains entitled.

FA 2008 has further eroded avoidance opportunities by introducing ICTA 1988 s 785A, which is designed to tax certain capital receipts (such as premiums) in connection with plant and machinery leases. FA 2008 led to the consequential repeal of certain aspects of CAA.

For HMRC's interpretation of various aspects of the rules on finance leases, see their Tax Bulletin of April 1997 and their manuals at CA28600.

Long funding leases

24. CAA 2001 ss 70A–70YJ provide an exception to the general tax rule that restricts capital allowances to the legal owner of an asset. The purpose of the rules is to bring closer alignment between the economic effect of a transaction and the tax consequences.

    Where the rules apply in respect of an operating lease, the deemed capital expenditure is the market value of the plant or machinery at the beginning of the lease (or, if later, when the asset is first used) (CAA 2001 s 70B).

    Where the rules apply in respect of a finance lease, the deemed capital expenditure is the present value of the minimum lease payments plus any unrelievable pre-commencement rentals (CAA 2001 s 70C).

25. A long funding lease (CAA 2001 s 70G) is a lease which is:

    •   not a short lease (see below);

    •   not an excluded lease because of background plant or machinery (ie equipment that one would ordinarily expect to be installed in a building to add functionality to the building (CAA 2001, s 70R)); and

    •   not excluded because the plant is attached to land but:

        –   is not background plant or machinery, and

        –   either:

            –   is worth no more than 10% of the value of any background plant or machinery, or

            –   is worth no more than 5% of the land and buildings (s 70U).

26. A short lease is:

    •   one of five years or less in duration, or

    •   a finance lease:

        –   with a lease term of between five and seven years;

        –   where the expected implied residual value at the end of the lease is 5% or less than the commencement value;

        –   the first-year rentals in the first year are at least 90% of those in the second year; and

–   the rentals in any year after the second year are no more than 10% more than those in the second year (s 70I).

Leasing plant and machinery together with land and buildings

27.   Where plant and machinery is leased out as part of a letting of land and buildings, the property lettings are treated as a qualifying activity for plant and machinery allowances both for income tax and corporation tax (ss 15, 16). The effect is that a landlord's expenditure on plant and machinery is pooled, and relief is given when expenditure is incurred rather than when the particular letting commences (except for expenditure before the first property is let, which is treated as incurred when the first letting starts – s 12). Except as indicated in explanatory note 28, allowances are not available on furniture and furnishings in dwelling houses, for which a wear and tear allowance is usually given instead (see Example 97 explanatory note 6). For the way in which relief is given for excess allowances see Example 18 part (b). See also explanatory note 26 for the restriction on loss claims by an individual with excess allowances on leased plant and machinery and explanatory note 28 for the special rules relating to fixtures.

28.   There are special provisions in s 19 relating to machinery and plant let other than in the course of a qualifying activity, but these circumstances will rarely arise (see Example 18 part (e)).

Where equipment leasing is a trade, the capital allowances are treated as a trading expense, and can therefore create or increase a trading loss. There is no restriction on the relief available for such a loss incurred by a company. If such a loss is incurred by an individual, however, the relief available is restricted to set-off against later rental income, rather than being set against other income under ITA 2007 ss 64 and 72 (see Examples 29 and 30), unless the trade is carried on by the individual for a continuous period of at least six months in, or beginning or ending in, the tax year of loss, and the individual devotes substantially the whole of his time to that trade (ITA 2007 s 75). See also explanatory note 23 re finance leases and explanatory note 30 re fixtures. There are some anti-avoidance provisions relating to leasing in ITA 2007 ss 76–78 concerning partnerships with one or more company members.

29.   Plant and machinery leased to non-residents for use overseas usually attracts writing down allowances of only 10% on the reducing balance basis, with all such expenditure being kept in a separate class pool (s 109). The final chargeable period for the pool is the period at the end of which there can be no more disposal receipts in any later period (s 65).

Fixtures

30.   Sections 172 to 204 contain special rules relating to fixtures, ie plant and machinery that in law is treated as part of the building in which it is installed or otherwise fixed. The main intention of the provisions is to enable allowances to be claimed by whoever incurs capital expenditure on fixtures, whether or not that person has an interest in the land or buildings. The provisions are lengthy and complex, and what follows is only a brief summary.

As indicated in explanatory note 28, landlords may claim relief for expenditure on fixtures (other than in dwelling houses). Allowances on fixtures may also be claimed by a tenant if he incurs the expenditure (s 176). Where fixtures are provided by equipment lessors, a joint election may be made by the equipment lessor and the equipment lessee (who may be the owner or tenant of the property) for the equipment lessor to claim the allowances (s 177). Equipment lessors cannot claim allowances on fixtures in dwelling houses, nor can they claim allowances on fixtures leased to non-taxpayers, such as charities. An exception is made for expenditure by equipment lessors incurred between 28 July 2000 and 31 December 2007 on boilers, radiators, heat exchangers and heating controls installed in low income homes under the Government's affordable warmth programme (s 180).

Allowances are not available on any amount in excess of the original cost of the fixtures when new plus any costs of installation (s 185). Vendors and purchasers may make a joint election (within two years of the date of the contract) fixing how much of the purchase price of a building relates to fixtures, the agreed amount being limited, however, to the vendor's original cost (s 198). Strictly elections should be made in respect of each fixture, but HMRC will accept a single election covering all the fixtures in a single property. Where a claim in a tax return becomes incorrect, for example, because of such an election, the claimant must notify an amendment to the return within three months after becoming aware of that fact (s 203). In the absence of an election under s 198, s 562 requires a 'just apportionment' of the purchase price between building and fixtures. See Example 18 part (a) for comments on apportionment.

There are anti-avoidance provisions to prevent double allowances and to prevent allowances on fixtures being artificially accelerated.

See explanatory note 7 re the special provisions to enable energy service providers to claim 100% allowances on energy saving plant and machinery that becomes a fixture.

Integral features

31.   From April 2008 expenditure on integral features ceased to qualify for the main pool and expenditure on such assets will be allocated to the new 10% pool. Section 33A provides that expenditure on integral features (as defined) are to qualify as if on plant or machinery provided that the purpose of the feature is not to insulate the interior of a building or to provide an interior wall, floor or ceiling which is intended to remain permanently in place. The meaning of integral feature includes some assets that were previously treated as plant but also some that were previously excluded from the definition of plant. Integral features are defined as the following:

   •   an electrical system (including a lighting system);

   •   a cold water system;

   •   a space or water heating system, a powered system of ventilation, air cooling or air purification and any floor or ceiling comprised in such a system;

   •   a lift, escalator or moving walkway;

   •   external solar shading.

Expenditure on repairs to integral features will be treated as capital expenditure, and disallowed in computing profits if more than 50% of the current replacement cost of the asset is spent during any twelve-month period. Capital allowances can be claimed on the expenditure as s 33A classifies it as expenditure on replacement features.

VAT capital goods scheme

32.   For value added tax, a capital goods scheme applies to items of computer equipment with a tax-exclusive value of £50,000 or more per item, and land and buildings with a tax-exclusive value of £250,000 or more. Under the scheme, adjustments may be made over a period of five years for computers and buildings on a ten-year or shorter lease and over ten years for other land and buildings where the VAT exempt/taxable use of the asset varies during the adjustment period, VAT being payable or repayable accordingly.

Any VAT adjustments are reflected in capital allowances computations, extra expenditure being treated as incurred when any additional VAT is paid and VAT refunds being taken into account when received. Where an additional VAT liability relates to expenditure that qualifies for first-year allowance, the FYA is also available on the additional VAT amount.

The date the VAT is treated as paid or repaid for the purpose of deciding in which capital allowances period the adjustment has to be made will normally be six months after the end of the taxpayer's VAT year. The adjustment to the plant and machinery pool therefore occurs in the period in which that date falls. If the adjustment relates to a building qualifying for capital allowances, the VAT adjustment is added to or deducted from the residue of expenditure at that date and writing down allowances are recomputed over the remainder of the building's life. Very few buildings that qualify for capital allowances are affected by VAT capital goods scheme adjustments. The main instance is enterprise zone buildings.

Renewals basis

33.   As an alternative to claiming capital allowances on plant and machinery, the renewals basis may be used. The original cost of an item does not qualify for any relief, but as and when it is replaced, the full cost of the replacement is charged against profit, excluding any amount representing additions or improvements. A trader may change from the renewals basis to capital allowances for all items in a particular class of plant and machinery by bringing their commercial written down value into the pool (Revenue Concession B1).

Question

A.

Describe the operation of the annual investment allowance.

B.

Explain how the annual investment allowance is allocated to different businesses in common or overlapping ownership.

C.

Explain briefly how expenditure in a plant and machinery pool may be immediately relieved without the qualifying activity being brought to an end.

D.

Explain how and when the following might write off the balance of expenditure in their main pools. Assume that each wants the maximum allowance as early as possible.

(a)   Darren prepares his business accounts to 5 April each year. As at 6 April 2009, his main pool contains a balance of £1,100. Darren incurs no capital expenditure during the years to 5 April 2011.

(b)   Shelley prepares accounts to 31 March each year. As at 1 April 2008, the balance in her main pool is £800.

(c)   Danny prepares his business accounts to 31 December each year. As at 31 December 2008, his main pool contains a balance of £1,200. Danny incurs no capital expenditure during the two years to 31 December 2010.

(d)   Debbie purchases a computer on 4 July 2007 which she uses wholly for the purposes of her trade. The computer and related equipment cost her £3,000. Debbie's only other unrelieved capital expenditure is £850 in respect of a car (also wholly used for business purposes) which she bought in 2005. Debbie prepares accounts to 30 June each year.

Answer

Except where stated otherwise, all statutory references are to CAA 2001.

A. Annual investment allowance

Finance Act 2008 contained measures that were intended to simplify the tax procedures for smaller businesses by giving them, in many cases, an immediate write-off for capital expenditure. The regime allowing certain environment-friendly expenditure to qualify for 100% first-year allowances remains.

Although the measures are intended to benefit the smaller business, the rules apply to all. However, the financial cap on the allowance means that the measures will be more of a nuisance than a benefit to larger enterprises.

The measures provide for an annual allowance (the annual investment allowance) of £50,000. Businesses are entitled to an immediate write-off of up to £50,000 of their qualifying expenditure in any year. Any balance of expenditure will be allocated to the pools and would qualify for writing-down allowances in the ordinary way.

The AIA is available in respect of qualifying expenditure incurred on or after:

- 1 April 2008 for corporation tax purposes;

- 6 April 2008 for income tax purposes (s 38A(4)).

Who qualifies for the annual investment allowance?

The AIA is available to individuals and companies. It is also available to partnerships if all the members are individuals (s 38A).

Therefore, trustees and partnerships with corporate partners will not be eligible for the annual investment allowance.

When AIA is not available

The AIA is not available in the following cases (s 38B).

1. In the chargeable period in which the qualifying activity is permanently discontinued.

2. In respect of capital expenditure on a car.

3. In respect of expenditure incurred wholly for the purposes of a ring-fence trade.

4. Where there is a change in the nature or conduct of the qualifying activity and obtaining the AIA might objectively be seen as a main benefit of making the change.

5. Where the plant or machinery was acquired for other purposes, for long-funding leasing or where it was acquired as a gift.

Claiming the AIA

The AIA is equal to £50,000 (or the amount of AIA qualifying expenditure if lower) (s 51A(5)).

If the taxpayer's chargeable period is longer or shorter than a year, the value of the AIA is proportionately adjusted (s 51A(4)).

If the AIA is allocated to expenditure on plant or machinery that will not be used wholly for the purposes of the qualifying activity, then the AIA is subject to a just and reasonable reduction (s 205).

Unused AIA may not be carried forward. Conversely, the AIA is not compulsory. Consequently taxpayers who would rather defer the allowances until a later year are not required to claim the AIA in full or at all. However, even in such circumstances any unused element may not be carried forward.

B.   AIA and businesses under common control

Individuals and partnerships

For individuals and partnerships, an AIA is generally available in respect of each qualifying activity carried on. Therefore, supposing an individual owned a confectioner's, ran a tuition service and was also a partner (with another individual) in a farming business, that individual would be entitled to two AIAs in addition to the AIA available to the partnership.

However, there are restrictions if there are two or more qualifying activities which are:

- carried on by a partnership or an individual;

- controlled by the same person; and

- related to each other.

Where this applies, there will be a single AIA available to the person(s) carrying on the qualifying activities.

Qualifying activities are related if either:

- they are carried on from the same premises; or

- they are within the same 'NACE classification' under European Law (s 51J).

Companies

Companies are subject to four restrictions.

1.   First, companies are entitled to only one AIA, irrespective of how many qualifying activities they carry on (s 51B).

2.   Secondly, groups of companies are entitled to only one AIA (s 51C).

3.   Groups of companies under common control are entitled to only one AIA if they are related to each other (s 51D).

4.   Other companies under common control are entitled to only one AIA if they are related to each other (s 51E).

As with unincorporated taxpayers, companies are related if at the end of the chargeable period, they carry on qualifying activities from the same premises.

However, the other definition of related differs slightly from that applying with respect to unincorporated businesses. Companies are also related if more than 50% of each company's turnover is derived from qualifying activities within the same NACE classification (s 51G).

Note that there is no restriction that seeks to limit allowances when an individual carries on a trade and also controls a company.

When restrictions apply

When the AIA is restricted, the taxpayers can choose how to allocate the allowance between the chargeable activities or companies.

C.   Small pools

Given that the introduction of the AIA was intended to relieve smaller businesses of the need to compute plant and machinery allowances in respect of most assets, representations were made to the Government to allow small balances following existing expenditure to be similarly relieved.

The Government responded to this request with the introduction of s 56A. It permits balances of £1,000 to be written off immediately. However, it operates only in respect of the main pool and the special rate pool.

Therefore, it will not be available in respect of single asset pools (eg short-life asset pools, car pools or pools for expenditure not used wholly for business purposes).

The £1,000 limit is considered immediately before a writing-down allowance might be given. Therefore, it cannot be applied if the acquisitions in a chargeable period (plus any brought forward available qualifying expenditure) exceed the threshold unless disposal receipts taken into account bring the pool balance below the £1,000 level.

The £1,000 level is adjusted proportionately in chargeable periods which are longer or shorter than a year.

Section 56A applies in respect of chargeable periods commencing on or after 1 April 2008 (corporation tax) or 6 April 2008 (income tax).

D.

(a) Darren

Darren is entitled to claim a 20% writing down allowance (£220) in respect of the expenditure in the main pool for the year to 5 April 2010. This will reduce the available qualifying expenditure to £880.

In the year to 5 April 2011, Darren may claim an immediate write off of the balance of the expenditure giving him an allowance of £880 in that year (s 56A).

(b) Shelley

Shelley might expect to be able to claim an immediate write off of her available qualifying expenditure in respect of the 2008/09 tax year (corresponding with her trading accounting period ending 31 March 2009). However, for income tax purposes, section 56A applies only with respect to chargeable periods beginning on or after 6 April 2008. Consequently, Shelley's first eligible chargeable period is that beginning on 1 April 2009.

Therefore, Shelley must claim (supposing she wants the maximum allowances) writing down allowances of 20.06% (she is entitled to five days' worth of allowance at 25%) in 2008/09 (amounting to £161).

The balance of expenditure (£639) may be claimed as an expense in 2009/10 under s 56A (assuming no further capital expenditure).

(c) Danny

Danny would ordinarily claim writing down allowances of 20% × £1,200 = £240 in the year to 31 December 2009. This would permit Danny to write off the balance of the expenditure (£960) in the year to 31 December 2010 (2010/11 tax year).

However, Danny may extend the accounting period by three months. This means that the £1,000 small pool limit in section 56A(3) is increased to £1,250 allowing an immediate write off in the 2009/10 tax year of the full balance of £1,200.

(d) Debbie

First-year allowances of 40% are available on the computer equipment in the year ended 20 June 2008, leaving a balance of £1,800. The balance of expenditure of £3,850 looks to be too high for section 56A to be of any relevance. However, if the expenditure on the computer were allocated to a short-life asset pool, the remainder of the pool balance would be within the limit by 30 June 2009.

Explanatory Notes

1. The AIA is not available in respect of expenditure on a car. The meaning of car has been changed from 1 (6) April 2009 to exclude motorcycles and include hire cars (cars used as taxis, daily hire cars and cars leased to the disabled). Vans, are excluded from the definition. HMRC have confirmed that some double-cab pickups also fall outside the definition of car (see HMRC Manuals EIM23045), so these also qualify for AIA.

2. The AIA applies in respect of chargeable periods in which capital expenditure is incurred. See s 12 for the meaning of this.

3. For chargeable periods straddling the commencement date (1 or 6 April 2008) the AIA is proportionately reduced to reflect only periods from the commencement date. Thus, for a company's accounting period from 1 October 2007 to 30 September 2008, the AIA will be approximately £25,000. That will be available only in respect of expenditure after the commencement date.

4. It will generally be advisable for the AIA to be allocated to expenditure qualifying for the special rate (10%) pool before expenditure which may be allocated to the 20% pool. This is because the former would otherwise be written off more slowly than the latter.

    Care should be taken before allocating the AIA to expenditure destined for a single asset pool. In the case of assets used only partly for the purposes of a qualifying activity, the AIA will be similarly restricted. In respect of other assets, the AIA might lead to a balancing charge when the asset is disposed of.

    However, different considerations may apply if a taxpayer's marginal rates are likely to differ in future years.

Question

A.

Outline the allowances available in respect of the conversion of redundant space over business premises into flats.

B.

When may tax relief be claimed for the renovation of business premises in disadvantaged areas?

C.

IJ, a sole trader, prepares accounts to 30 June annually. On 31 July 2007 he acquired patents having ten years to run at a cost of £5,000. The patents were sold outright for £6,000 on 30 April 2010.

Show the tax position for all the years.

D.

KL, a sole trader, has been in business for many years and makes up accounts to 30 September annually. In December 2009 he incurred capital expenditure of £100,000 on research and development. He also gave £20,000 to the South Riding University in June 2009 to be used for scientific research connected with his trade.

Show how these payments will be treated for tax purposes.

E.

MN makes up accounts annually to 30 April. In May 2007 he paid £8,400 for know-how for use in his trade. On 31 August 2009 he ceased trading. The business was not transferred to anyone else but he sold the know-how for £9,000.

Show the capital allowances available to him.

Answer

A. **Conversion of redundant space over business premises into flats**

Provisions in CAA 2001 ss 393A to 393W give relief for expenditure incurred on or after 11 May 2001 on converting parts of business premises into flats. The conversion must take place within the existing boundaries of the building, except as is required to provide access to the new flats.

Allowances available

An initial allowance of 100%, which may be claimed wholly or in part, is available to owners and occupiers of qualifying properties for expenditure on the renovation or conversion of redundant space above shops or offices into qualifying flats for residential letting (s 393H). On any amount not claimed as an initial allowance, a writing-down allowance of 25% per annum of the original qualifying expenditure may be claimed, which again can be reduced to a specified amount (CAA 2001 ss 393J and 393K). The initial allowance will be withdrawn if the flat fails to qualify, or is sold before being let (s 393I).

Qualifying properties are defined as those meeting the following requirements (s 393C):

* the property must have been built before 1980;

* there must be not more than four floors above the ground floor (excluding attics unless used as dwellings or part dwellings);

* the upper floors must have been constructed primarily for use as dwellings and must either be unoccupied or used only for storage within the year before conversion;

* the ground floor must be authorised for business use within rating classes A1, A2, A3, B1 or D1(a), which broadly means retail shops, financial and professional services, food and drink, other offices, research and development and light industrial use, and medical etc services, such as doctors' and dentists' surgeries.

Qualifying flats (s 393D) are defined as follows:

* each flat must be self-contained with external access separate from the ground floor premises;

* each flat must have no more than four rooms, excluding kitchen, bathroom, cloakroom and hallways;

* the flat must be held for short-term letting (ie not more than five years), and must not be let to a person connected with the person who incurred the conversion expenditure;

* the flat must not be a high value flat as defined by s 393E (ie with expected rental values in excess of specified limits, higher limits applying to flats in Greater London).

Balancing adjustments

A balancing adjustment will be made if the flat is sold, a long lease (exceeding 50 years) is granted, the person who incurred the expenditure dies, the flat is demolished or destroyed, or the flat ceases to be a qualifying flat. Since the available initial allowance is 100%, the adjustment will normally be a balancing charge, which cannot exceed the allowances given. There will be no balancing adjustment if the balancing event occurs more than seven years after the time when the flat was first available for letting. Allowances are not transferable to a purchaser.

Way in which allowances are given

Allowances are treated as expenses of a property business. For the treatment of excess allowances see Example 18 part (e).

B. **Renovation of business premises in disadvantaged areas**

Finance Act 2005 Sch 6 introduced a new business premises renovation allowance (BPRA) from 11 April 2007 for a period of five years. This gives tax relief on 100% of the cost of renovating or converting business property where the building has been unused for one year and is situated in either Northern Ireland or an area specified as a development area by the Assisted Areas Order 2007 (SI 2007/107).

BPRA is available as a capital allowance to an individual or company being an initial allowance of up to 100% of the qualifying expenditure (CAA 2001 s 360G). If any part of the initial allowance is disclaimed a writing down allowance of up to 25% of the qualifying expenditure is available in subsequent years until costs are fully claimed (CAA 2001 s 360J). No balancing charge or allowance will occur providing there is no disposal event within seven years of the premises being brought back into use (s 360M). No allowance is available to the purchaser of the renovated building.

Qualifying expenditure means any capital expenditure, including fixtures, used on the repair, conversion or renovation of the building into a qualifying business premise (s 360B).

The building must have been last used for the purpose of a trade or profession, or as an office. It must have been unused for at least one year before the expenditure is incurred and situated in either Northern Ireland or an area specified as a development area by the Assisted Areas Order 2007 (SI 2007/107). It must not have been used wholly or partly as a dwelling (s 360C).

The renovated building must be a qualifying business premises, that is, premises used or available for use for the purpose of a trade, profession or vocation or as an office. It must not be used wholly or in part as a dwelling (s 360D).

The initial allowance is available in the chargeable period in which the qualifying expenditure is incurred (s 360G) but will be withdrawn if the building is sold before first letting or use (s 360H).

A balancing allowance or charge occurs if the building is disposed of within seven years of being available for use. Normally sale price (or market value) is compared with the unclaimed residue to arrive at the adjustment, any balancing charge to be restricted by restricting proceeds to cost. In the case of death proceeds are to equal the residue of unclaimed expenditure (s 360O).

C. **IJ – Patents Allowances**

			£
2008/09	Year ended 30 June 2008	Cost	5,000
		WDA 25%	1,250
			3,750
2009/10	Year ended 30 June 2009	WDA 25%	938
			2,812
2010/11	Year ended 30 June 2010		
	Sale proceeds 30 April 2010 (limited to original cost)		5,000
	Balancing charge		2,188

The capital profit of £1,000 is taxed (ITTOIA 2005 ss 587–599) over six years commencing with the year in which it is received, ie 2010/11(unless IJ elects under s 590(3) to have all the tax charged in one sum in2010/11).

D. **KL – Research and development**

December 2009 capital expenditure qualifies for capital allowances of £100,000 in 2010/11(chargeable period year to 30 September 2010).

June 2009 gift of £20,000 to South Riding University is treated as a trading expense of the accounting year to 30 September 2009, reducing the assessable profit in 2009/10.

E.   MN – Know-how

			£
2008/09	Year ended 30 April 2008	Cost	8,400
		WDA 25%	2,100
			6,300
2009/10	Year ended 30 April 2009	WDA 25%	1,575
			4,725
2010/11	1 May 2009 to 31 August 2010		
	Sale proceeds		9,000
	Balancing charge (not restricted to allowances given)		£4,275

Explanatory Notes

Patents

1.   Where a trader incurs expenditure on devising and patenting an invention etc or in connection with a rejected patent application, the expenditure is allowable in computing trading profits (ITTOIA 2005 s 89). Where a trader purchases patent rights, he is entitled to capital allowances of 25% per annum on a reducing balance basis for expenditure. This rate has not changed despite the changes to the rates available for plant and machinery allowances.

Balancing adjustments are made on sale. If the sales proceeds exceed original cost, the capital profit is *not* charged to capital gains tax. It is charged over six years commencing with the tax year of receipt, unless the trader elects to have the whole amount charged in the year of receipt (ITTOIA 2005 ss 587–599).

For companies, the treatment of patents changed from 1 April 2002. Capital allowances will not normally apply in respect of patent rights acquired on or after that date and the acquisition and disposal of the rights, and royalty payments on them, will be dealt with under the intangible assets rules. For details see Example 66. Capital allowances continue to be available in respect of patents already owned by companies on 1 April 2002.

Research and development

2.   Following FA 2000 s 68 and Sch 19, the term 'scientific research' has been largely replaced in the legislation by 'research and development', which is defined as covering activities that are treated as such in accordance with generally accepted accounting practice, subject to HMRC having power to issue regulations to include/exclude specified activities.

Where a trader incurs capital expenditure on research and development related to his trade he is entitled to a capital allowance equal to the full amount of that expenditure (CAA 2001 ss 437–451). The normal rules for chargeable periods apply. Expenditure on land is, however, excluded. Expenditure on dwellings is also excluded, except that where a building is used partly as a dwelling and partly for scientific research and not more than one quarter of the expenditure on the building relates to the dwelling, the whole of the expenditure is allowable.

Balancing adjustments are made upon the asset ceasing to belong to the trader. For this purpose, disposal value is taken into account rather than sale proceeds. Disposal value is defined as:

(a)   the proceeds of sale, if the asset is sold at open market value or higher;

(b)   the deemed proceeds of sale if the asset is deemed to be sold because of its destruction; it is treated as sold immediately before its destruction for any insurance proceeds, compensation, demolition proceeds etc (any demolition costs being added to the expenditure);

(c)   open market value, in any other event (CAA 2001 ss 443–445.).

See Example 52 for the treatment of revenue expenditure on research and development, including enhanced deductions and tax credit payments available to companies in certain circumstances.

Know-how

3.   Know-how allowances are dealt with in CAA 2001 ss 452 to 463. Know-how means industrial information and techniques of assistance in manufacturing or processing goods or materials, working (or searching for) mineral deposits or carrying out agricultural, forestry or fishing operations. HMRC considers that the term does not include commercial know-how, such as information about marketing, packaging or distributing a product.

If know-how is sold as part of a business that is being disposed of, the payment is treated both as regards the seller and the buyer as a payment for *goodwill*, unless they jointly elect (within two years of the disposal) for it to be treated as a payment for know-how (ITTOIA 2005 s 194). If the election is made, or if know-how is disposed of other than as part of a business, capital allowances are available by way of annual writing down allowances of 25% on a reducing balance basis. Any additional expenditure is added to the written down value and any sale proceeds deducted before the writing down allowance is calculated. A balancing charge is made if know-how is sold for more than the written down value, and either a balancing charge or allowance is made when the trade ceases. Unlike balancing charges on other types of assets, a balancing charge is not restricted to the allowances that have been given in respect of the know-how, so if it is sold for more than cost, the excess is charged to tax within the balancing charge (CAA 2001 s 462).

For acquisitions by companies on or after 1 April 2002, know-how is dealt with under the rules for intangible assets. See Example 66 for details.

It appears (whether by design or oversight) that the 25% rate of writing-down allowance has not been reduced despite the rate being changed for plant and machinery allowances with effect April 2008.

Conversion of redundant space over shops and offices into flats

4.   The 100% allowances for the conversion of redundant space over shops and offices into flats for short-term letting dealt with in parts (B) and (C) of the example were introduced as part of the Government's measures to regenerate Britain's towns and cities. The provisions are very detailed, and care needs to be taken to make sure the rules are complied with.

Question

A.

(a)   Set out when an industrial buildings allowance is available; and

(b)   briefly explain what comprises 'qualifying trade' and 'qualifying expenditure' for industrial buildings allowances.

B.

Calculate the capital allowances and/or balancing charges arising in the following cases (assuming, except in (d), that the annual accounting date is not changed):

(a)   Arthur, a manufacturer of storage tanks, has been in business for several years, preparing accounts to 31 October annually. In the year ended 31 October 2008 he purchased land costing £100,000 and spent £300,000 on construction costs of a building for use in his trade. The building was not, however, used in that year, being first brought into use in November 2008.

(b)   Arthur, instead of purchasing the land and constructing the building himself, purchased the land and building from a builder for £500,000 on 1 March 2009; £100,000 being applicable to the land. The building was brought into use immediately. The cost of construction to the builder was £350,000.

(c)   Arthur, rather than building himself or purchasing from a builder, takes advantage of a trade depression to acquire an unused factory unit from Unfortunate Ltd, who had incurred construction costs of £200,000 in 2008 on land costing £100,000, intending to use the factory itself, but then had to dispose of the factory because of financial difficulties, selling to Arthur in December 2008 for £350,000 (including land £120,000). Arthur brought the building into use immediately.

(d)   Roy took a ninety-nine year lease of an industrial building from the Barchester District Council, paying a premium of £110,000 on 1 January 2008 in his first accounting period of fifteen months to 31 March 2009. The building was immediately brought into use in his trade of manufacturing ships tackle. The construction costs to the local authority were £120,000 excluding the land in the six months to June 2007 and Roy is to pay an annual rent of £3,000. Roy and the local authority each signed within the appropriate period the election under CAA 2001 s 290.

(e)   Spares Ltd, a UK company that manufactures components for the motor industry and makes up accounts annually to 31 October, incurred capital expenditure as shown below on a new freehold factory in the year to 31 October 2008, the factory being immediately brought into use for manufacturing.

	£	£
Land		36,000
Levelling land and digging foundations		24,000
Building – Factory	208,000	
Drawing office	28,000	
Factory canteen	32,000	
Sales office	52,000	320,000
Sports pavilion		20,000
		400,000

(f)   Benedict is a manufacturer making up his accounts to 31 December in each year. In February 2009 an industrial building, which originally cost Benedict £100,000 excluding land and on which allowances had been given resulting in a residue of expenditure at 31 December 2008 of £70,000, was destroyed by fire. Receipts from sales of scrap amounted to £2,500; the cost of demolition was £4,000 and insurance proceeds were £125,000.

(g) Honey, who makes up accounts to 31 March annually, built a factory for use in his manufacture of leather goods, the construction being completed in October 1993 and the factory brought into use on 1 March 1994. The construction cost was £320,000. He sold the factory on 1 March 2009 for £500,000 excluding land.

(h) Suppose Ivor was the purchaser from Honey in the above example. Calculate the allowances due to him. Explain how this would differ if the purchase price were instead: (i) £40,000 and (ii) £240,000 respectively excluding land.

(i) Pennicot, who prepares accounts to 31 December, sold four buildings on 31 December 2008 to Herbert, an unconnected manufacturer who also makes up accounts to 31 December. Herbert uses all four buildings for industrial purposes.

Details of the buildings are as follows:

1st Building

Building completed September 1962 at cost of £30,000 excluding land and brought into use 31 December 1962. Rate of initial allowance 5% and rate of writing down allowance 2%. Consistently used for industrial purposes except for a period of temporary disuse throughout 1971. Insulation against loss of heat added December 1989 at cost of £12,500. Sales proceeds (excluding land) £100,000 plus £10,000 for heat insulation.

2nd Building

Building completed 1974 at cost of £75,000 excluding land and brought into use 31 December 1974. Rate of initial allowance 40%. Used for industrial purposes until September 2000. Used as offices from that date until the date of sale. Sale proceeds (excluding land) £240,000.

3rd Building

Built 1985 at cost of £300,000 excluding land. Rate of initial allowance 25%. Date of first use 31 December 1985. Used for industrial purposes apart from a period of non-industrial use from 1 October 1992 to 31 March 1995. Sale proceeds (excluding land) £272,000.

4th Building

Built 1995 at cost of £1,000,000 excluding land. Date of first use 1 October 1995. Used as industrial building until 30 June 2000. Used for non-industrial purposes from 1 July 2000 to date of sale. Sale proceeds (excluding land) £500,000.

Show the allowances or charges that will arise to Pennicot for all relevant years and the allowances available to Herbert for 2009/10.

(j) Archer commenced farming on 1 July 2004, making up accounts annually to 30 June. He incurred qualifying capital expenditure of £100,000 on agricultural buildings in March 2005. On 30 September 2008 he transferred the farm to Oakes, a farmer who makes up accounts annually to 31 March. Show the allowances available to each of Archer and Oakes assuming no further changes are made and neither of them changes his accounting date.

(k) (i) Nicholas, a farmer who has made up his accounts to 30 April for many years, incurred £50,000 of expenditure on the construction of a barn on 1 January 2008 which was brought into use immediately. Calculate the allowances due in respect of the expenditure.

(ii)   Show the position if the barn in (i) above were sold for £45,000 on 1 October 2009 to Reginald, an established farmer who makes up accounts to 31 January.

Assume that neither Nicholas nor Reginald changes his accounting date during the writing down period.

Explain the differences had the sale been agreed before 21 March 2007 (but effected on 1 October 2009).

(l)   Somerset acquired the freehold of a farm on 1 April 2002 paying £350,000 for the land and buildings. No agricultural buildings allowances remain available on the buildings purchased. The farm is let to Essex for £6,000 per annum payable half yearly in advance on 1 April and 1 October. Essex makes up his farm accounts to 31 March in each year. Somerset incurred the following further capital expenditure on the farm:

		£
10 June 2002	Grain store	22,000
31 March 2003	Fencing	3,000

Essex incurred capital expenditure on the farm as follows:

25 July 2002	Drainage system	15,000
10 January 2003	Extension to farmhouse	33,000

On 1 October 2008 Kent took over the tenancy of the farm from Essex, paying £40,000 to Essex in respect of his capital expenditure. Kent makes up accounts to 30 June annually.

On 1 August 2009 Somerset sold his freehold interest in the farm to Cornwall for £500,000, Kent continuing as tenant.

(i)   What agricultural buildings allowances are due to each person concerned (none of whom is connected in any way with any of the others)?

(ii)   Calculate the chargeable gain on the sale of the freehold by Somerset.

Assume that the 2008 and 2009 disposals were not agreed before 21 March 2007.

(m)   Rufus, a single man who owns the freehold of a farm property, incurred capital expenditure of £300,000 on new farm buildings (not including a farmhouse) in October 2007. He leased the buildings to a farming tenant from 1 May 2008, the tenant paying rent of £15,000 a year quarterly in advance. Rufus has no other agricultural income, but his income from other sources in 2008/09 is £30,000 (none of it being rents). Show his taxable income for that year and for 2009/10 (assuming that Rufus's income continues at the same level).

Answer

A. Industrial buildings allowances – qualifying expenditure

(a) Industrial building allowances

Industrial buildings allowances are available if expenditure has been incurred on the construction of a building or structure for use:

– for a qualifying trade,

– as a qualifying hotel,

– as a qualifying sports pavilion, or

– as a commercial building or structure in an enterprise zone.

All such buildings are defined as industrial buildings (CAA 2001 s 271).

(b) Qualifying trade and qualifying expenditure

A qualifying trade is defined in CAA 2001 s 274, the most common qualifying trades being manufacturing or processing goods or materials, but including a variety of other undertakings such as those concerned with transport, sewerage, water, electricity, hydraulic power, tunnels, bridges, mines, highways, agricultural operations on land occupied by someone else and fishing. Buildings used to store goods and materials before and immediately after manufacture or processing are included, as are buildings to store goods and materials on arrival in the UK by any means of transportation. It was held in the case of *Girobank v Clarke* (CA 1997) that the cheques and other documents processed at a data processing centre were not goods and materials, so the centre did not qualify. Nor did a cash and carry wholesale warehouse, although some minor processing activities were carried on (*Bestway (Holdings) Ltd v Luff* (1998)). By HMRC practice, buildings used for warehousing and storage by traders and wholesalers where the goods are to be used for an industrial process are included provided the storage forms a significant, separate and identifiable part of the trade and is conducted as a trade in its own right. No allowance will be due if the activity is a necessary and transitory incident of the conduct of the wholesale business (Revenue's Tax Bulletin December 1999).

In *Maco Door & Window Hardware (UK) Ltd v HMRC* (2006), the Court of Appeal overturned the High Court decision and held that a warehouse qualified for IBAs since the storage goods were a distinct component of the taxpayer's wholesale trading operation.

Buildings are not used for the purposes of a qualifying trade if they are used as retail shops, showrooms, hotels, offices, or for purposes ancillary to those purposes (CAA 2001 s 277). In the case of *Sarsfield v Dixons Group plc*, a distribution warehouse operated as a separate undertaking by an associated company of a major retailer was held to be ancillary to the retail trade and did not qualify as a transport undertaking (CA 1998). Works offices are treated as in use for a qualifying trade as a result of the decision in *CIR v Lambhill Ironworks Ltd* (1950) and buildings used for the maintenance or repair of goods and materials are included (unless they are, or are part of, a retail business, or are used by a non-industrial business to maintain or repair goods or materials employed in that business). HMRC treats a motor dealer's vehicle repair workshop as an industrial building if it is completely separate from the vehicle sales area, does not have a reception, and public access is discouraged. Allowances would be restricted to the extent that vehicles for resale were repaired in the workshop.

There is a specific provision to include buildings provided for the welfare of workers in a qualifying trade, such as canteens (CAA 2001 s 275). A sports pavilion qualifies if it is provided for the welfare of workers in *any* trade (CAA 2001 s 280).

Where part of a building is outside the definition of industrial building, the whole building qualifies for relief providing the expenditure on the non-industrial part does not exceed 25% of the total cost. This only applies where the non-industrial part is housed within the same building, not where it is a separate building (CAA 2001 s 283).

Where a building qualifies as an industrial building, the expenditure that qualifies for relief is the capital expenditure on the construction of the building, excluding the cost of the land (CAA 2001 s 272), but including the cost of preparing the site for building, such as cutting, tunnelling and levelling (CAA 2001 s 273). Any subsequent capital expenditure on extensions and improvements to the building qualifies for relief as if it were a separate building. Revenue expenditure does not qualify, but it is expressly provided that where repair expenditure on an industrial building has not been allowed as a trading expense, the expenditure is treated as having been incurred on the construction of an addition to the building (CAA 2001 s 272(2)(3)). The relief is available to the person who incurs the construction expenditure, and there may be several people claiming relief on the same building, for example, the original owner in respect of the original expenditure, and a subsequent lessee or sub-lessee who incurs further capital expenditure on the building.

B. **Capital allowances and/or balancing charges**

(a) **Arthur – Construction**

	£
Cost of land – not available for relief	–
Construction costs – year ended 31 October 2008	300,000
Writing down allowance not available in 2008/09 since building not in use at end of basis period for that year (ie at 31 October 2008)	–
If the law was not changed Writing down allowances 2009/10 to 2033/34 inclusive @ 4% (before abolition) = £12,000 per annum for 25 years	300,000

However, because of the abolition of the allowance, actual entitlement will be as follows:

- in 2009/10 (chargeable period, the year to 31 October 2009), £300,000 @ (156 × 3% + 209 × 2%)/365 = £7,282

- in 2010/11 (chargeable period, the year to 31 October 2010), £300,000 @ (156 × 2% + 209 × 1%)/365 = £4,282

- in 2011/12 (chargeable period, the year to 31 October 2011), £300,000 @ (156 × 1% + 209 × 0%)/365 = £1,282

- thereafter, Nil.

(b) **Arthur – Purchase from builder**

The cost to the builder is irrelevant, but the value of the land must still be eliminated. Allowances are therefore due on £400,000. The building is not in use at the end of the basis period for 2008/09 (year ended 31 October 2008), and writing down allowances will be given at 4% (as reduced during the phasing out period) as follows:

- in 2009/10 (chargeable period, the year to 31 October 2009), £400,000 @ (156 × 3% + 209 × 2%)/365 = £9,710

- in 2010/11 (chargeable period, the year to 31 October 2010), £400,000 @ (156 × 2% + 209 × 1%)/365 = £5,710

- in 2011/12 (chargeable period, the year to 31 October 2011), £400,000 @ (156 × 1% + 209 × 0%)/365 = £1,710

- thereafter, Nil.

(c) Arthur – Purchase of unused building

Value of land must be eliminated.

Lower of cost of construction £200,000 or price paid for building £230,000 available for relief; therefore relief based on £200,000 @ 4% as follows.

- in 2009/10 (chargeable period, the year to 31 October 2009), £200,000 @ (156 × 3% + 209 × 2%)/365 = £4,855

- in 2010/11 (chargeable period, the year to 31 October 2010), £200,000 @ (156 × 2% + 209 × 1%)/365 = £2,855

- in 2011/12 (chargeable period, the year to 31 October 2011), £200,000 @ (156 × 1% + 209 × 0%)/365 = £855

- thereafter, Nil.

(d) Roy – Purchase of long lease

Premium paid on grant (less than construction costs) January 2007	£110,000

Roy would get writing down allowances at 4% per annum, ie £4,400 in the chargeable period in which the interest in the building is acquired, ie the period to 31 March 2009. The writing down allowance is proportionately reduced *or increased* if the chargeable period is less than or more than one year. Roy's allowance (before phasing out provisions are applied) for the 15-month period to 31 March 2009 is therefore 15/12 × £4,400 = £5,500, which is restricted as follows:

1.1.08 – 5.4.08 95 days @ 4% + 6.4.08 – 31.3.09 360 days @ 3% = £4,400

In subsequent years, he will get allowances reduced as follows:

- in 2009/10 (chargeable period, the year to 31 March 2010), £110,000 @ (5 × 3% + 360 × 2%)/365 = £2,215

- in 2010/11 (chargeable period, the year to 31 March 2011), £110,000 @ (5 × 2% + 360 × 1%)/365 = £1,115

- in 2011/12 (chargeable period, the year to 31 March 2012), £110,000 @ (5 × 1% + 361 × 0%)/366 = £15

- thereafter, Nil.

The rates of allowances are also subject to variation in cases of changes of accounting dates. (See explanatory note 2.)

(e) Spares Ltd – Qualifying expenditure

	£
Levelling land and digging foundations	24,000
Building (sales office included since not more than 25% of (£320,000 + £24,000))	320,000
Sports pavilion	20,000
Expenditure qualifying for allowances	364,000

Since the building is brought into use in the year to 31 October 2008, writing down allowances will commence in that year. They will be given at the rate of 4% per annum, ie £14,560, subject to the phasing out the allowance from April 2008 as follows:

- year ending 31 October 2008, £364,000 @ (152 × 4% + 214 × 3%)/366 = £12,432

- year ending 31 October 2009, £364,000 @ (151 × 3% + 214 × 2%)/365 = £8,786

- year ending 31 October 2010, £364,000 @ (151 × 2% + 214 × 1%)/365 = £5,145

- year ending 31 October 2011, £364,000 @ (151 × 1% + 214 × 0%)/365 = £1,505

- thereafter, Nil.

Unlike the provisions for individuals outlined in (d) above, corporation tax chargeable accounting periods never exceed 12 months (see Example 52 explanatory note 2).

(f)   Benedict – Demolition costs – surplus on sale

Because the fire occurred after 20 March 2007, no balancing adjustment arises. However, the disposal will be subject to capital gains tax in respect of the excess of the proceeds over the original cost.

(g)   Honey – Sale of industrial building

		£
1993/94 Construction cost year ended 31 March 1994		320,000
WDA 4%	12,800	
	12,800	
1994/95 to 2007/08 WDAs 4% for 14 years	179,200	192,000
Residue of qualifying expenditure at 31 March 2008		128,000
Sold during year ended 31 March 2009 (2008/09)		500,000
Surplus on sale		372,000
No balancing charge – as sale after 20 March 2007.		£192,000

(h)   Ivor – Purchase of second-hand industrial building

	(g) £
Residue of qualifying expenditure at sale	128,000
Divided by 9 years of life remaining out of 25 (ie from March 2009 to March 2018) Writing down allowance per annum (subject to phasing out of allowances)	£35,556

Thus Ivor's capital allowances are based upon the residue at the time of the sale and not the purchase price. This applies when the purchase price exceeds the original qualifying expenditure as is the case here (FA 2007 s 36(3)).

It would also apply if: (i) the purchase price were less than the residue; or (ii) the purchase price exceeded the residue but was less than the original qualifying expenditure.

The precise allowance available to Ivor will depend on Ivor's accounting date.

As the sale has taken place after 11 March 2007, there could be a further adjustment to the writing-down allowance in the chargeable period of the sale if the sale were tax-motivated and Ivor and Honey were connected parties (CAA 2001 s 313A).

(i)   Pennicot – Temporary disuse and non-industrial use

1st Building

			£
Cost 1962			30,000
1963/64	Initial allowance 5%	1,500	
	WDA 2%	600	2,100
			27,900
1964/65 to 2007/08	WDAs 2% for 44 years (temporary disuse in 1971 ignored – note 13)		26,400
Residue of qualifying expenditure before sale			1,500

Sale proceeds – 31.12.08   £100,000

No balancing charge 2008/09 as sale after 20 March 2007.

December 1989 expenditure of £12,500 on heat insulation qualified for allowances as plant and not as part of the industrial building expenditure. The proceeds of sale relating to the heat insulation expenditure are ignored (see explanatory note 7).

2nd Building

			£
Cost 1974			75,000
1975/76	Initial allowance 40%	30,000	
	WDA 4%	3,000	
1976/77 to 1988/89	WDAs 4% for 13 years	39,000	
1989/90	WDA (balance)	3,000	75,000

Since the building is 25 years old at December 1999, the period of non-industrial use after that date is irrelevant, there will be no balancing charge on Pennicot when he sells the building and no allowances are available to Herbert.

3rd Building

			£
Cost 1985			300,000
1986/87	Initial allowance 25%	75,000	
	WDA 4%	12,000	87,000
			213,000
1986/87 to 1993/94	WDAs 8 years at 4%		96,000
			117,000
1994/95 to 1996/97	Notional WDAs 3 years at 4%		36,000
			81,000
1997/98 to 2002/03	WDAs 6 years at 4%		72,000
2003/04	WDA (balance)		9,000
Residue of qualifying expenditure before sale			–

Adjusted net cost of building

	£
Cost	300,000
Sale proceeds – 31.12.08	272,000
	28,000

No balancing adjustment as sale after 20 March 2007.

4th Building

		£
Cost 1995		1,000,000
1996/97 to 1999/00	WDAs 4 years at 4%	160,000
		840,000
2000/01 to 2008/09	Notional WDAs 8 years at 4% (no restriction applied in arriving at residue before sale)	320,000
Residue of qualifying expenditure before sale		520,000

No balancing adjustment because sale on or after 21 March 2007.

Herbert

	1st building £	3rd building £	4th building £
Residue of expenditure at sale	1,500	Nil	520,000
Divided by unexpired life at date of sale	4 yrs*	2 yrs**	11.75 yrs***
WDAs to Herbert (subject to phased withdrawal)	£375	Nil	£44,255

* 31.12.08 – 31.12.12 = 4 years

** 31.12.08 – 31.12.10 = 2 years

*** 31.12.08 – 30.9.20 = 11.75 years

In view of the phased withdrawal of IBAs, Herbert's actual allowances in respect of the first and fourth buildings will be as follows:

	1st building £	4th building £
Residue of expenditure at sale	1,500	520,000
Divided by unexpired life at date of sale	4 yrs	11¾ yrs
WDAs to Herbert (subject to phased withdrawal)	£375	£44,255
2009/10 (year to 31 December 2009) (95 × 75% + 270 × 50%)/365	£212	£25,007
2010/11 (year to 31 December 2010) (95 × 50% + 270 × 25%)/365	£118	£13,944
2011/12 (year to 31 December 2011) (95 × 25% + 270 × 0%)/365	£24	£2,880
Thereafter	Nil	Nil

(j)   **Archer and Oakes**

The writing down period is the 25 years from the beginning of Archer's period of account in which the expenditure is incurred, ie from 1 July 2004 to 30 June 2029. Allowances will be given as follows:

Archer

	£
Qualifying expenditure (March 2005)	100,000
WDAs 4 yrs to 30.6.08 @ £4,000 per annum	(16,000)
WDA to 30.9.08 (yr to 30.6.09) 3/12 × 4,000	(1,000)
WDV transferred to Oakes	83,000

Note that although the allowances are restricted from 6 April 2008, the written down value is still reduced by the full allowance that would have been given were it not for the phasing out provisions.

Oakes

	£
WDV transferred from Archer	83,000
WDA yr to 31.3.09 (from 1.10.08) 6/12 × 4,000	(2,000)

As part of the phased withdrawal of agricultural buildings allowances, Oakes will obtain the following allowances in later years:

- in 2009/10 (chargeable period, the year to 31 March 2010), £100,000 @ (5 × 3% + 360 × 2%)/365 = £2,014

- in 2010/11 (chargeable period, the year to 31 March 2011), £100,000 @ (5 × 2% + 360 × 1%)/365 = £1,014

- in 2011/12 (chargeable period, the year to 31 March 2012), £100,000 @ (5 × 1% + 361 × 0%)/366 = £14

- thereafter, Nil.

(k)   **Nicholas**

(i)   Expenditure of £50,000 on barn in January 2008 is in the period of account to 30 April 2008. The writing down period is therefore the 25 years from 1 May 2007 to 30 April 2032.

The expenditure would be written off by writing down allowances of £2,000 per annum over the 25-year period but for the phased withdrawal of the relief, the first allowance, being due in 2008/09. The allowance is therefore restricted from the outset and is calculated as follows:

- in 2008/09 (chargeable period, the year to 30 April 2008), £50,000 @ (341 × 4% + 25 × 3%)/366 = £1,966

- in 2009/10 (chargeable period, the year to 30 April 2009), £50,000 @ (340 × 3% + 25 × 2%)/365 = £1,466

- in 2010/11 (chargeable period, the year to 30 April 2010), £50,000 @ (340 × 2% + 25 × 1%)/365 = £966

- in 2011/12 (chargeable period, the year to 30 April 2011), £50,000 @ (340 × 1% + 25 × 0%)/365 = £466

- thereafter, Nil.

(ii)   But for the phased withdrawal of the allowances, writing down allowances would have continued at £2,000 per annum until the expenditure was fully relieved.

The allowances to Nicholas would therefore have ceased in the tax year 2011/12 (the sale taking place in the chargeable period for that year, ie in the year to 30 April 2011).

But for the changes, Nicholas would have been entitled to a final writing down allowance proportionate to the length of the chargeable period to the date of sale, ie 1.5.10 – 1.10.10 = 5/12 × £2,000 = £833. The total writing down of the qualifying expenditure attributable to Nicholas would therefore be 2008/09 to 2010/11 = 3 years @ £2,000 + £833 in 2011/12 = £6,833, leaving unrelieved expenditure of £43,167.

(The actual allowances available to Nicholas are of course reduced by FA 2008 s 85 but this does not affect the actual writing-down of the expenditure.)

Reginald is entitled to allowances on the balance of £43,167, commencing in 2010/11, based on his accounting year to 31 January 2011. This would end (but for the withdrawal of the allowance) in the period of account in which the last day of the writing down period (30 April 2032) falls, ie in the year to 31 January 2033, affecting the tax year 2032/33.

The first allowance is based on an amount proportionate to the part of the period of account falling after the date of sale, ie from 1.10.10 – 31.1.11 = 4/12 × £2,000 = £667. However, this will be reduced further by FA 2008 s 85 to:

£667 × (64 × 50% + 301 × 25%)/365 = £196

In the successive years, Reginald's allowances would be:

- in 2011/12 (chargeable period, the year to 31 January 2012), £50,000 @ 4% × (64 × 25% + 301 × 0%)/365 = £88

- thereafter, Nil.

If the sale had been agreed before 21 March 2007 and Nicholas and Reginald could have elected for a balancing adjustment. In such case, the position would have been as follows:

Nicholas

	£
Cost 1 January 2008	50,000
2008/09 to 2010/11 WDAs 4% per annum	6,000

	£
Residue of qualifying expenditure before sale	44,000
Year to 30.4.11 (tax year 2011/12)	
Sale proceeds October 2010	45,000
Balancing charge (trading receipt of accounting year to 30.4.11)	1,000

Reginald

Year to 31.1.11 (tax year 2010/11)	
Residue of qualifying expenditure before sale	44,000
Add balancing charge on vendor	1,000
	45,000

Divided by balance of writing down period at date of sale, ie 21 yrs 7 mths (the chargeable period starting on 1.5.07 – see (i)) from 1.10.10 to 30.4.32, = WDA of £2,085 per annum. But for the phased withdrawal of the allowances, Reginald would have been entitled to a writing down allowance for the 4 months from 1.10.10 to 31.1.11 = 4/12 of £2,085, ie £695, then allowances at £2,085 per annum for 21 years from the year ended 31 January 2012 to the year ended 31 January 2032, with a final allowance of £520 in the year to 31 January 2033 (in which the writing down period ends). Actual allowances, however, are:

- in 2010/11: £695 × (64 × 50% + 301 × 25%)/365 = £204

- in 2011/12 (chargeable period, the year to 31 January 2012), £2,085 × (64 × 25% + 301 × 0%)/365 = £91

- thereafter, Nil.

(l) **Somerset**

(i) Writing down period for the expenditure in June 2002 and March 2003 is 25 years from 6.4.2002 to 5.4.27 (basis period for an investor is the tax year itself).

		£	Allowances available £
2002/03	Grain store	22,000	
	Fencing	3,000	
		25,000	
	WDA 4%	1,000	1,000
		24,000	
2003/04 to 2008/09	WDAs 4% per annum for 6 years	6,000	6,000
		18,000	
2009/10	WDA 4% to 1.8.09 = 4 mths (subject to adjustment below)	333	333
	WDV transferred to Cornwall	17,667	

Somerset's actual allowance for 2009/10 will be reduced by 50% to £167.

Cornwall

2009/10	WDV transferred from Somerset	17,667	
	WDA 4% from 1.8.09 to 5.4.10 = 8 mths	667	667

| | | | WDV carried forward | 17,000 |

Actual allowances are as follows:

2009/10: 50% × £1,000 = £500

2010/11: 25% × £1,000 = £250

2011/12 and subsequently: Nil.

Essex

Writing down period is 25 years from 1.4.2002 to 31.3.2027.

		£	Allowances available £
2002/03	(yr to 31.3.03)		
	Drainage system	15,000	
	One third farmhouse extension (£33,000)	11,000	
		26,000	
	WDA 4%	1,040	1,040
		24,960	
2003/04 to 2007/08	WDAs 4% per annum	5,200	5,200
		19,760	
2008/09	WDA 4% from 1.4.07 to 30.9.08 = 6/12	520	520
	WDV transferred to Kent	19,240	

Essex's actual allowance for 2008/09 will be reduced by 25% to £390

Kent

		£	Allowances available £
2009/10	(yr to 30.6.09)		
	WDV transferred from Essex	19,240	
	WDA 4% from 1.10.08 to 30.6.09 = 9/12 (subject to adjustment below)	780	780
	WDV carried forward	18,460	

Actual allowance in 2009/10 is reduced to:

£26,000 × 4% × ¾ × (187 × 75% + 178 × 50%)/365 = £490

If Kent continues as tenant to the end of the writing down period (and does not change his accounting date), his allowances would have been (but for the withdrawal of the relief):

2010/11 to 2026/27 17 years @ £1,040 per annum	18,720
2026/27 (based on year to 30 June 2026, in which the writing down period ends) WDA (balance of allowances)	780
Total allowances given	26,000

Actual WDAs however are:

- in 2010/11 (chargeable period, the year to 31 October 2010): £1,040 × (187 × 50% + 178 × 25%)/365 = £393

- in 2011/12 (chargeable period, the year to 31 October 2011): £1,040 × (187 × 25% + 178 × 0%)/365 = £133

- thereafter, Nil.

(m)   **Chargeable gain on sale of farm by Somerset in 2009/10**

	£	£
Sale proceeds August 2009		500,000
Cost of land and buildings April 2002	350,000	
Expenditure June 2002	22,000	
Expenditure March 2003	3,000	
	375,000	
		125,000

The farm will not qualify for entrepreneur's relief.

(n)   **Rufus – tax position 2008/09 and 2009/10**

If Rufus claims the maximum agricultural buildings allowances, and elects to set the allowances against his total income in 2008/09 and 2009/10 (see note 19), the position will be:

Agricultural buildings allowances

	£
2008/09	
Expenditure	300,000
WDA 4%	12,000
	288,000
2009/10	
WDA 4% (subject to reduction below)	12,000
WDV carried forward	276,000

Actual WDA for 2008/09 will be 75% × £12,000 = £9,000, and for 2009/10 will be 50% x £12,000 = £6,000.

Tax position 2008/09

	£
Non-agricultural income	30,000
Property business loss (agricultural buildings allowance – see note 20)	9,000
	21,000
Personal allowance	(6,035)
Taxable income	14,965

Tax position 2009/10

			£
Profits of property business (see note 20):			
Farm rent 1.5.09 to 5.4.10:			
3 qrs @ £3,750	11,250		
1.2.10 to 5.4.10 65/90 × 3,750	2,708	13,958	
Less: agricultural buildings allowance		6,000	7,958
Other income			30,000
			37,958
Personal allowance			(6,475)
Taxable income			31,483

If any property business loss in the form of unused allowances had remained after setting against total income in 2008/09 (and if necessary 2009/10), it could have been set against only income from the property business in later years (see note 20).

Explanatory Notes

Industrial buildings

Definition of industrial building

1. Following CAA 2001, the term 'industrial buildings' covers not only buildings in use for qualifying trades but also qualifying hotels, qualifying sports pavilions, and commercial buildings or structures in an enterprise zone (CAA 2001 s 271). Note that for the 'qualifying trades' part of the definition, the building must be *in use* for a qualifying trade, the most common of which are indicated in part A of the example. Note also that part of an industrial building may be outside the definition, provided that the expenditure on that part does not exceed 25% of the total cost of the building (10% for expenditure before 16 March 1983). Where a building was in an enterprise zone, there is no restriction on the use to which it may be put, except that a private dwelling does not qualify.

   See Example 18 part (a) re apportioning expenditure between the building and any plant and machinery within it.

Allowances available

2. Industrial buildings allowances are given as follows:

   (a) Initial allowance (when available) in respect of expenditure in a chargeable period.

(b) Writing down allowance where the building is an industrial building at the end of the relevant period (CAA 2001 s 309).

The writing down allowance is scaled down proportionately if a corporation tax accounting period is less than 12 months. For income tax, allowances are given for periods of account, and are proportionately increased or reduced if the account is for more or less than 12 months (CAA 2001 s 310) (see part D(d) of the example and Example 18 part (e)).

3. The initial allowance is not currently available (except for buildings in enterprise zones), but it has been available at various rates over the years, the most recent rates being as follows:

Date expenditure incurred	*Initial allowance*
13 November 1974 to 10 March 1981	50%
11 March 1981 to 13 March 1984	75%
14 March 1984 to 31 March 1985	50%
1 April 1985 to 31 March 1986	25%
1 November 1992 to 31 October 1993	20%

Where a building has qualified for initial allowance and there is an additional VAT liability under the capital goods scheme which is treated as additional expenditure on the building, the initial allowance is available on the additional expenditure.

4. Writing down allowances where expenditure was incurred after 5 November 1962 are initially calculated on a flat 4% of cost (2% for expenditure on or before that date) to the original claimant, except for enterprise zone buildings (CAA 2001 s 310 & Sch 3.66). However, as part of the phased withdrawal of allowances, allowances in respect of the financial year 1 April 2009 to 31 March 2010 (or, for income tax, the 2009/10 tax year) are cut by a quarter.

Thus, in the typical case, allowances will be worth only 2% of the expenditure (or 1% for pre-5 November 1962 expenditure). There will be a further reduction for financial year 2010 (or 2010/11 for income tax) of another quarter (taking the effective rate of allowance to 1% (or ½%). After 31 March 2011 (or 5 April 2011 for income tax) the allowances will cease to be available.

For chargeable periods that span two financial years (or tax years), the reduction in the allowance is proportionately adjusted. For example, suppose a company prepares accounts for the year to 31 December 2010. But for any withdrawal of the industrial buildings allowance, the company would have a writing-down allowance of £28,000. Its actual allowance will be:

£28,000 × [90 × 50% + 275 × 25%]/365 = £8,726 (FA 2008 s 85).

A second-hand purchaser does not get the same rate of relief as the original claimant. He gets allowances on the residue of qualifying expenditure after the sale (which usually means the amount he pays or the original building cost, whichever is lower) divided by the part of the tax life remaining at the date of purchase. The tax life of a building runs from the date the building was first used for 50 years for expenditure incurred on or before 5 November 1962, and for 25 years for expenditure after that date (CAA 2001 s 311 and Sch 3.67). If a building that has previously been used other than as an industrial building is acquired by an industrial user, the industrial user can claim writing down allowances over the remainder of the building's 25 (or 50) year life. Notional allowances are taken into account for the years when the building was not in industrial use (see explanatory note 13). When the sale takes place during the phased withdrawal of allowances, the full writing down allowance without reduction is deducted from the written down value of the building in arriving at the residue before sale.

The change to the current year basis for income tax does not affect the calculation of the writing down allowance for a second-hand purchaser, since it is based on the balance at the purchase date of the 25 (or 50) year period from the date the building was first used.

Partial claims for allowances

5.   The initial allowance may be only partially claimed by both individuals and companies (CAA 2001 s 306). As stated above, the allowance is presently available only for enterprise zone buildings.

It is also possible to disclaim a writing down allowance wholly or in part (CAA 2001 s 309). This could be done to avoid wasting other reliefs and allowances, as shown in Example 19 parts (c) to (e). The effect of disclaiming industrial buildings writing down allowance would be that the writing down period would be extended until the expenditure was fully written off, unless the building was sold in the meantime. Balancing adjustments cannot be made after the end of the 25 (or 50) year writing down period (see explanatory note 9), but this does not prevent writing down allowances continuing after the end of that period for someone whose ownership started before the writing down period expired.

Cost of construction

6.   Allowances are given in respect of the cost of *construction* of the building. The cost of construction includes the costs of preparing the site. Where the site preparation includes demolishing existing buildings, then unless the buildings had been used for industrial purposes so that the demolition costs are taken into account in the balancing adjustment (see explanatory note 9), the demolition costs form part of the construction costs. Where a newly erected building is bought unused, the purchaser gets allowances on the cost of construction or the price he pays, whichever is the lower (unless he buys from the builder, in which case he gets allowances on the full purchase price – CAA 2001 ss 294 to 297). Since the allowances are given on the construction of the building no relief is available for the land (CAA 2001 s 272). Where capital expenditure is incurred on extensions and additions it is treated as expenditure on a separate building with its own writing down life and allowances are given to whoever incurred the expenditure, so that allowances may go to a lessee, or sub-lessee, as indicated in part A of the example.

Where plant and machinery is purchased with a building, the purchase price needs to be apportioned and plant and machinery allowances can then be claimed on the appropriate part of the purchase price (see Examples 18 part (a) and 20 explanatory note 27).

Thermal insulation

7.   If expenditure is incurred, either by the occupier or by a landlord, *in adding* any insulation against loss of heat in an industrial building in use for a qualifying trade, this qualifies as expenditure on plant and machinery and attracts allowances as such. When the building is sold, the disposal value of the thermal insulation expenditure is treated as nil, so that any sale proceeds are ignored. A purchaser does not get any relief on a payment to the vendor in respect of the insulation, since the legislation refers to expenditure in *adding any insulation*, whereas the insulation is already part of the building when a purchaser acquires it (CAA 2001 ss 27 and 28).

Lease premiums

8.   A trader who pays a premium on a *short* lease (not exceeding fifty years) can deduct, in computing his profits over the period of the lease, the amount assessable on the landlord as additional rent (see Example 99 explanatory note 11). No such relief is available for the payment of a premium on a *long* lease, which is regarded wholly as a capital matter. If the lessor and lessee so elect, however, the grant of the long lease can be treated as the sale of the building, with any capital sum paid being treated as the sale proceeds. The election must be made in writing within two years from the date on which the lease takes effect. This provision is aimed mainly at giving relief where a public body builds new factories to encourage local industries, but it applies to any long lease of an industrial building (CAA 2001 s 290). It is not, however, available for transactions between connected persons (CAA 2001 s 291). For the meaning of 'connected persons' see Example 18 part (f).

Balancing adjustments on disposal

9.　　When a building that is, or has been, an industrial building is sold during its 25-year (or 50-year) life, a balancing adjustment used to be made (CAA 2001 s 314). The demolition cost of a building is added to the residue of qualifying expenditure before the sale, for the purposes of calculating the balancing allowance or charge (CAA 2001 s 340). See explanatory note 6 re demolition costs incurred on a non-industrial building.

There was no balancing adjustment on the seller, and no allowances are available to the purchaser, in cases of buildings sold after their writing down life, as shown in part E(j) of the example in relation to the second building. Even though the benefit of the capital allowances is retained by the seller, they are not deducted from the cost/31 March 1982 value in the capital gains computation when computing a gain.

Finance Act 2007 provides that balancing adjustments cease to be made on balancing events on or after 21 March 2007. However, this rule does not apply in respect of buildings in enterprise zones or in respect of disposals under pre-21 March 2007 contracts (which have not been significantly varied after 20 March 2007) which are completed before 1 April 2011.

10.　　Any balancing adjustment on the seller was calculated as follows (CAA 2001 ss 318 to 320):

(a)　If the building had been in industrial use (or used for research and development) throughout the period of ownership, the balancing charge or allowance was the difference between the sale proceeds and the written down value (residue of qualifying expenditure) before the sale, except that a balancing charge could not exceed the allowances given, any capital profit being dealt with under the capital gains rules (CAA 2001 ss 318 and 320).

In arriving at the residue of qualifying expenditure, initial allowances were treated as written off at the time of the expenditure (s 333) and writing down allowances at the end of the chargeable period (s 334).

(b)　If the building had not been in industrial use (or used for research and development) throughout the period of ownership s 319 applied:

(i)　Where the sale, insurance, salvage or compensation moneys are *not less than* the capital expenditure, the balancing charge made was equal to the allowances given.

(ii)　Where the proceeds are *less than* the capital expenditure or are nil:

A.　If the adjusted net cost of the building exceeds the allowances given, a balancing allowance was made equal to the excess

B.　If the adjusted net cost of the building is less than the allowances given, a balancing charge was made equal to the shortfall.

'Adjusted net cost' means the capital expenditure on the building less the disposal proceeds, reduced by the proportion of the period of ownership which the non-qualifying use bears to the whole, as illustrated in part E(j) of the example.

11.　　As indicated in explanatory note 4, a purchaser of a second-hand industrial building gets relief on the residue of qualifying expenditure after the sale. This is defined as (CAA 2001 s 313):

The residue of qualifying expenditure before the sale

Less any amount by which the sale proceeds fall short of that residue (s 337(2)), or

Plus (for sales agreed before 21 March 2007) the balancing charge made on the seller, but not so as to give a residue of expenditure after the sale any greater than the sale proceeds (s 337(3) and (4)).

In arriving at the residue of qualifying expenditure before the sale, notional allowances for a period of use for non-industrial purposes must be taken into account – s 336.

Put simply, where there has been no non-industrial use the purchaser gets allowances on the original building cost or the amount he pays, whichever is less. Where there has been a period of non-industrial use the purchaser gets allowances on the seller's residue of qualifying expenditure before the sale plus (where applicable) any balancing charge, or the amount he pays, whichever is less, as illustrated in part E(j) of the example.

Any writing-down allowances available to the purchaser are reduced as per explanatory note 4 above.

12.   For any transaction on or after 12 March 2008, FA 2008 has inserted section 313A to CAA 2001. It is an anti-avoidance measure designed to prevent tax advantages from being obtained during the transitional period. Where there is a tax-motivated sale of the relevant interest to a connected person or to a person under common control and the buyer and seller have different chargeable periods, the buyer's writing down allowances in the chargeable period which includes the sale is limited by the following fraction:

$$DI/CP$$

where

DI is the number of days in the chargeable period for which the buyer has the relevant interest and

CP is the number of days in the chargeable period.

Temporary disuse

13.   Temporary disuse as an industrial building does not prevent the continuity of allowances (CAA 2001 s 285). But if the building is put to other non-industrial use when not being used as an industrial building then no writing down allowances are given during that time and notional allowances have to be taken into account.

The notional allowances affect the residue of qualifying expenditure that is taken into account in the calculation of a second-hand purchaser's writing down allowance (see explanatory note 11). They are not, however, brought into the calculation of the balancing adjustment on the seller, because the period of non-industrial use is taken into account by reducing the total amount for which allowances are available to the seller in proportion to the period of non-industrial use (see explanatory note 10).

Capital Allowances – Hotels

14.   (a)   Relief is available for expenditure incurred after 11 April 1978 on the construction of a qualifying hotel, using broadly the same rules as those that apply to industrial buildings in use for qualifying trades.

      (b)   *Qualifying Hotel (CAA 2001 s 279)*

            Buildings of a permanent nature open at least four months in the seven months from April to October inclusive. The building must have at least ten letting bedrooms which are available to the public generally and not normally in the same occupation for more than one month. Services should normally include breakfast, evening meals, cleaning rooms and making beds.

      (c)   The hotel must be used for purposes of trade (i) throughout the twelve months ending with the last day of the relevant accounting period; or (ii) if the hotel was first used on a date after the beginning of those 12 months, by reference to 12 months beginning with the date of first use.

            A hotel that does not qualify under (i) because it has less than ten letting bedrooms can qualify under (ii) from the date of having at least ten letting bedrooms, as if that date were the date of first use.

      (d)   Qualifying expenditure includes that on any building provided for the welfare of hotel workers (CAA 2001 s 275).

(e)   Expenditure incurred by an individual trader or a partnership does not qualify for relief if it relates to accommodation which during the time the hotel is open in the season (April–October) is normally used as a dwelling by that trader or a partner or by their family or household. As with other industrial buildings, however, this does not apply if the dwelling part of the building does not exceed 25% (previously 10%) (CAA 2001 s 283).

(f)   Allowances available (except for hotels in enterprise zones) are:

Initial allowance 20% for expenditure incurred before 1 April 1986 or contracted for in the year to 31 October 1993 – in the chargeable period or basis period when the expenditure is incurred.

Writing down allowance – 4% to first user. Residue of qualifying expenditure after the sale (as with other industrial buildings) to a purchaser who did not himself incur the expenditure, spread over remainder of 25-year tax life.

Balancing allowances and charges apply. There may be a restriction on a balancing adjustment if during the tax life of the hotel it qualified for part but not all of the time.

(g)   Where the building ceases to qualify as a hotel because of a change of use but a sale is not made, there is a deemed sale at market value two years after the time when it ceased to qualify and a balancing allowance or charge will arise (CAA 2001 s 317).

Temporary disuse does not, however, mean that the building ceases to qualify or that the deemed sale at market value is to apply; but the temporary disuse cannot extend beyond two years after the end of the chargeable period in which the disuse commences.

Way in which allowances are given on let property

15.   The various buildings allowances are available to the owner of a building in respect of expenditure he has incurred on a building which is to be let under a lease or tenancy. (If the lessee or tenant himself incurs capital expenditure on extensions, additions etc, he will be entitled to allowances on that expenditure.) Occupation by a licensee of the owner or tenant is treated as occupation by the owner/tenant.

Any available initial allowance (which presently applies only to enterprise zone expenditure) is given when the expenditure is incurred (CAA 2001 ss 5 and 305), and writing down allowances commence when the building is brought into qualifying use (CAA 2001 s 309). The chargeable period for a lessor is the tax year itself (or company chargeable accounting period) (CAA 2001 s 6).

For both individuals and companies, the allowances are treated as an expense of a property business (CAA 2001 s 353 – see Example 18 part (e), which also deals with the treatment of excess allowances). An individual may claim to set a property business loss created by capital allowances against any other income of the year to which the loss relates, or of the following year, as indicated in part E(l) of the example (Maurice Rest Homes), with any balance remaining being carried forward against later rent income (ICTA 1988 s 379A). The time limit for the claim against general income is one year from 31 January following the tax year to which the claim relates.

Sale after cessation of trade

16.   Where an industrial building is sold after a trade ceases and a balancing charge arises, the charge is treated in the same way as a post-cessation receipt under ICTA 1988 s 103 or 104(1) for the purpose of enabling unrelieved losses, expenses and capital allowances to be set against it (CAA 2001 s 354). For notes on post-cessation receipts and expenses see Example 16 part (c)(ii).

VAT capital goods scheme

17. Where a qualifying building costing £250,000 or more is used by a VAT partly exempt business (such as an office in an enterprise zone used by a bank), VAT adjustments may be required under the capital goods scheme, and those adjustments are reflected in the capital allowances computation. For details see Example 20 explanatory note 32.

Agricultural buildings

Expenditure qualifying for allowances

18. Agricultural buildings allowances are available where the owner or tenant of agricultural land incurs capital expenditure on farmhouses, farm buildings, cottages, fences or other works. The expenditure must be for the purposes of 'husbandry' (CAA 2001 s 361). The meaning of husbandry given in s 362 does not actually define the term, but it effectively means farming. Husbandry is explicitly stated in s 362 to include intensive rearing of livestock or fish for human consumption and the cultivation of short rotation coppice. HMRC allow relief for a farm shop, except to the extent that stock is bought in rather than produced on the farm. Where the expenditure is on a farmhouse, not more than one third qualifies for relief. The allowance of up to one third of the expenditure is provided for by CAA 2001 s 369. The same fraction cannot be used for the part of the establishment charges of the farmhouse that are deducted from the farming profit. The claim in respect of these charges must be based on the extent of business use of the farmhouse.

Allowances are not available in respect of buildings and works on forestry land.

Allowances available and writing down period

19. For expenditure after 31 March 1986, the allowances available are annual writing down allowances at 4% over 25 years (CAA 2001 s 373), except for expenditure under a contract entered into between 1 November 1992 and 31 October 1993, for which a 20% initial allowance was also available providing the buildings or works were brought into use before 1 January 1995. Allowances may be disclaimed wholly or in part. Any balancing allowance will, however, take into account all allowances that have been or *could have been* claimed. Furthermore no claim is available after the end of the 25-year period. It is therefore highly unlikely to be advantageous to disclaim a writing down allowance.

However, as part of the phased withdrawal of allowances, allowances in respect of the financial year 1 April 2009 to 31 March 2010 (or, for income tax, the 2009/10 tax year) are cut by a quarter.

Thus, in the typical case, allowances will be worth only 2% of the expenditure (or 1% for pre-5 November 1962 expenditure). There will be a further reduction for financial year 2010 (or 2010/11 for income tax) of another quarter (taking the effective rate of allowance to 1% (or ½%). After 31 March 2011 (or 5 April 2011 for income tax) the allowances will cease to be available.

For chargeable periods that span two financial years (or tax years), the reduction in the allowance is proportionately adjusted. For example, suppose a company prepares accounts for the year to 31 December 2010. But for any withdrawal of the agricultural buildings allowamce, the company would have a writing-down allowance of £28,000. Its actual allowance will be:

£28,000 × [90 × 50% + 275 × 25%]/365 = £8,726 (FA 2008 s 85).

The initial allowance was given for the chargeable period related to the incurring of the expenditure. The first writing down allowance was not given in the same period as the initial allowance unless the buildings or works were brought into use by the end of that period. Unless there is a sale on which a balancing adjustment is made (see below), the 25-year writing down period will be shortened according to how much of the initial allowance was claimed.

Where there is no initial allowance, the first writing down allowance is given in the chargeable period relating to the incurring of the expenditure, the 25-year writing down period running from the first day of that period. The chargeable period for traders is the period of account for income tax and the chargeable accounting period for corporation tax (CAA 2001 s 6) (see explanatory note 20 for the chargeable period for investors).

Chargeable period for investors

20. For investors the chargeable period for the allowances is the tax year for income tax and the chargeable accounting period for corporation tax. For individuals, any available agricultural buildings allowances are treated as an expense of the individual's property business (as to which see Example 97). If no such business exists (ie if no letting has commenced), the individual is nonetheless treated as if he were carrying on such a business (CAA 2001 s 392). To the extent that an individual's capital allowances exceed property income from all sources in any tax year, a claim may be made for the excess to be set against the total income of that tax year or the following tax year or, if the loss is large enough, both tax years (ITA 2007 ss 118 and 120). The time limit for the claim is one year from 31 January following the tax year. For further points on the way allowances are given to investors, including the provisions relating to companies, see Example 18 part (e).

Disposal of agricultural buildings

21. Where agricultural buildings are disposed of, the former and new owners (if the disposal was agreed before 21 March 2007) may jointly elect for a balancing adjustment (CAA 2001 ss 381 and 382), and in the event of demolition or destruction the election is by the former owner. The election must be notified to the inspector by individuals within one year from 31 January following the end of the tax year. The time limit for companies is two years from the end of the chargeable accounting period (CAA 2001 s 382(6)(b)).

The balancing adjustment is calculated by taking the residue of qualifying expenditure before the sale and comparing it with the sale, insurance, salvage etc moneys. A balancing charge cannot exceed the allowances given. The new owner gets writing down allowances based on the residue of qualifying expenditure before the sale plus any balancing charge or less any balancing allowance.

That amount is divided by the unexpired part of the writing down period, to arrive at the annual writing down allowance. It is therefore necessary to calculate how much of the 25-year period from the first day of the chargeable period related to the incurring of the expenditure remains at the date of sale. This then determines the annual rate of writing down allowance, which will be proportionately increased or reduced for accounting periods of more or less than 12 months. Thus in part (b) of the example, following an election for a balancing adjustment, Reginald gets his first allowance for the four months from 1.10.10 (the date of sale) to 31.1.11 (the end of his accounting period).

22. Where an election is not made as outlined in explanatory note 21 above, the former owner gets a final writing down allowance for the chargeable period in which the sale occurs, the allowance being proportionate to the period from the start of that period to the date of sale. The new owner is entitled to relief for the balance of the expenditure, and he similarly gets his first allowance reduced according to the period from the date of sale to the end of *his* chargeable period (CAA 2001 s 375). The tax year in which the event is taken into account may be different for seller and purchaser where the accounting dates differ. For example, the last allowance to Nicholas in part (b) is given in 2011/12, whereas the first allowance to Reginald is in 2010/11.

23. The whole of the claimant's interest in the land has to be transferred for the allowances to be given to the purchaser. Thus an owner cannot transfer the allowances to a tenant by granting him a leasehold interest, as distinct from selling the freehold. Likewise a tenant must transfer his tenancy (like Essex did to Kent in the example) and not grant a sub-lease in order to pass the allowances on to the new tenant. Where an interest in land is a tenancy and the tenant transfers his interest, it is deemed to have been transferred:

(a) to the incoming tenant if he makes any payment to the outgoing tenant in respect of assets representing the expenditure in question,

(b)   in any other case, to the landlord (CAA 2001 s 368).

The allowances also revert to the landlord if the tenant surrenders his lease without taking a new lease.

Thus if in this example Kent had made no payment to Essex upon taking over the tenancy, the remaining allowances would have accrued to the then owner Somerset. On the transfer of his interest to Cornwall, Somerset would in turn have passed on the agricultural buildings allowances remaining to be given.

Capital gains tax

24.   Capital allowances are not taken into account in computing a gain for capital gains tax (TCGA 1992 s 41). The main reason is that the allowances are normally withdrawn by balancing adjustments, but the section makes no special provision for situations where that does not apply, for example, where no election is made for a balancing adjustment on the sale of agricultural buildings (and also where industrial buildings are disposed of after their writing down life has expired).

In the calculation of the gain to Somerset in part (c)(ii) of the example, there is accordingly no restriction of the allowable expenditure by reference to the allowances he has received, even though no income tax balancing adjustment was made.

Question

(a) The partnership of A, B and C commenced on 1 September 2008, accounts being made up annually to 31 August. They shared profits A one half, B one third, C one sixth after a salary of £6,000 to C. The profits for the first two years, net of capital allowances on partnership assets, were as follows:

	£
Year to 31 August 2009	42,000
Year to 31 August 2010	48,000

In addition each partner uses his own car for the business, capital allowances being due as follows:

	Yr to 31.8.09 £	Yr to 31.8.10 £
A	2,500	2,500
B	1,800	1,350
C	2,000	1,833

Show the tax position of each partner arising out of the above, and state what the situation would be if C left the partnership on 31 October 2011, A and B sharing profits in the same ratio as before.

(b) Partners D and E have been in business for fifteen years, sharing profits equally and making up accounts annually to 30 April. F joined as an equal partner on 1 January 2010.

Profits net of capital allowances around the time F joined were as follows:

Year to 30 April 2010	£36,000
Year to 30 April 2011	£45,000

Show the assessable income arising to each partner in respect of these profits and indicate their position regarding overlap relief.

(c) G, H and J have been in partnership for many years, making up accounts annually to 30 June and sharing profits and losses equally. The partners were entitled to transitional overlap relief of £25,500 each. G retired on 30 September 2009. H and J continued as equal partners. Recent profits were as follows:

		£
Year to 30 June 2009		84,000
Year to 30 June 2010:		
1 July 2009 to 30 September 2009	25,650	
1 October 2009 to 30 June 2010	51,300	76,950

Show the assessable income arising to each partner in respect of these profits and the treatment of overlap relief.

(d)   K and L have traded in partnership since 2001 as consultants, making up accounts to 5 April. They work on the basis of hourly billing, but have experienced delays in invoicing and billing. Due to loss of contracts, profits are expected to decrease over the coming years, as follows:

Year to	Profit before capital allowances £	Capital Allowances £
05/04/2006	50,000	6,000
05/04/2007	40,000	7,000
05/04/2008	30,000	4,000
05/04/2009	20,000	5,000
05/04/2010	20,000	3,000

As at 5 April 2005 the reasonably estimated billable time in unfinished work amounted to £20,000 over and above work in progress valued at cost. As a result of adoption of UITF 40, the profit element was recognised for the first time in the accounts to 5 April 2006.

Calculate

●   profits assessable to tax for all years, and

●   state what the position would be had the business ceased on 5 April 2007.

(e)   Outline the treatment of partnership non-trading income.

Answer

(a) **Partnership of A, B and C**

Division of profits:

	Total £	A £	B £	C £
Year to 31.8.09				
Salary	6,000			6,000
Balance 3:2:1	36,000	18,000	12,000	6,000
	42,000	18,000	12,000	12,000
Less: capital allowances on partners' cars	6,300	2,500	1,800	2,000
	35,700	15,500	10,200	10,000
Year to 31.8.10				
Salary	6,000			6,000
Balance 3:2:1	42,000	21,000	14,000	7,000
	48,000	21,000	14,000	13,000
Less: capital allowances on partners' cars	5,683	2,500	1,350	1,833
	42,317	18,500	12,650	11,167

Assessments on individual partners:

	A £	B £	C £
2008/09			
1.9.08 – 5.4.09			
7/12 × profit share for yr to 31.8.09	9,042	5,950	5,833
(which constitute overlap profits eligible for subsequent relief)			
2009/10			
1.9.08 – 31.8.09	15,500	10,200	10,000
2010/11			
1.9.09 – 31.8.10	18,500	12,650	11,167

If C left the partnership on 31 October 2011, the profit of the year to 31 August 2012 would be split as to the first 2 months between A, B and C according to their profit sharing arrangements and the remaining 10 months between A and B according to their profit sharing arrangements.

C's 2011/12 income from the partnership would comprise his share of the profit of the year to 31 August 2011 and his 2 months' share of the profit of the year to 31 August 2012, reduced by overlap relief of £5,833. A and B would continue to be taxed each year on their shares of the profits, and would get their overlap relief when they left the business or on an earlier change of accounting date if and to the extent that more than 12 months' profit was charged to tax in one year.

(b)   **Partnership of D, E and F**

Individual profit shares:

	Total £	D £	E £	F £
Year to 30.4.2010				
1.5.09 – 31.12.09 (8 mths)	24,000	12,000	12,000	
1.1.10 – 30.4.10 (4 mths)	12,000	4,000	4,000	4,000
	36,000	16,000	16,000	4,000
Year to 30.4.11	45,000	15,000	15,000	15,000

D and E will be taxed on their shares in 2010/11 and 2011/12. They are entitled to transitional overlap relief on their shares of the profits (*before* capital allowances) for the 11 months from 1 May 1996 to 5 April 1997 (the full 12 months to 30.4.97 being assessed in 1997/98).

F will be taxed as follows:

				£
2009/10	1.1.10 – 5.4.10			
	3/4 × 4,000			3,000
2010/11	1.1.10 – 31.12.10			
	1.1.10 – 30.4.10	4,000		
	1.5.10 – 31.12.10			
	8/12 × 15,000	10,000		14,000
2011/12	Yr to 30.4.11			15,000

F will be entitled to overlap relief on the following profits (which are *after* capital allowances):

1.1.10 – 5.4.10	3,000	
1.5.10 – 31.12.10	10,000	£13,000

(c)   **Partnership of G, H and J**

Taxable profits and overlap relief

Ignoring differences between taxable profits and actual profits, the profits of the two years to 30 June 2010 will be divided between the partners as follows:

	Total £	G £	H £	J £
Yr to 30.6.09	84,000	28,000	28,000	28,000
Yr to 30.6.10:				
To 30.9.09	25,650	8,550	8,550	8,550
To 30.6.10	51,300		25,650	25,650
	76,950	8,550	34,200	34,200

Assessments

	Total	G	H	J
2009/10 (yr to 30.6.09)	84,000	28,000	28,000	28,000
On retirement of G,				
period to 30.9.09		8,550		
Less overlap relief		(25,500)		

		11,050	28,000	28,000
2010/11 (yr to 30.6.10)	76,950			
Less allocated to G	(8,550)			
	68,400		34,200	34,200
Overlap relief cf			25,500	25,500

(d) **Partnership of K and L, and UITF 40 spreading**

As the uplift arose from adoption of UITF 40 in a year ending on or after 22 June 2005, it may be spread over a maximum of six years, as follows:

Adjustment profit (UITF 40 amount)   £20,000

Tax the lesser of:

Year to	Profit before capital allowances	*(a)* 1/3 of adjustment profits	*(b)* 1/6 of profits before capital allowances	*(c)* Balance Remaining	Add the lesser
05/04/2006	50,000	6,667	8,333	–	6,667
05/04/2007	40,000	6,667	6,667	13,333	6,667
05/04/2008	30,000	6,667	5,000	6,666	5,000
05/04/2009	20,000		3,333	1,666	1,666
05/04/2010	20,000		3,333	0	0

Taxable Profits

	Profit before capital allowances	Capital allowances	Profits after capital allowances	Adjustment income	Assessable
2005/06	50,000	6,000	44,000	6,667	50,667
2006/07	40,000	7,000	33,000	6,667	39,667
2007/08	30,000	4,000	26,000	5,000	31,000
2008/09	20,000	5,000	15,000	1,666	16,666
2009/10	20,000	3,000	17,000	–	17,000

If the business had ceased on 5 April 2007, spreading would still be available, but the criterion of one-sixth of profit disappears, so the result would be as follows:

Adjustment profit   £20,000

Tax the lesser of:

Year to	Profit before capital allowances	*(a)* 1/3 of Adjustment profit	*(b)* 1/6 of Profit before capital allowances	*(c)* Balance Remaining	Add the lesser
05/04/2006	50,000	6,667	8,333	–	6,667
05/04/2007	40,000	6,667	6,667	13,333	6,667
05/04/2008	–	6,667	–	6,666	6,666

Taxable Profits

	Profit before capital allowances	Capital allowances	Profit after capital allowances	Adjustment income	Assessable
2005/06	50,000	6,000	44,000	6,667	50,667
2006/07	40,000	7,000	33,000	6,667	39,667
2007/08	–	–	–	6,667	6,667

See explanatory note 5 for details of changes in accounting basis.

Class 4 national insurance does not apply to the adjustment income.

(e) **Partnership non-trading income**

Non-trading partnership income, such as rents and interest, is taxed separately on each partner (ITTOIA 2005 s 851). The way in which each partner's taxable income is arrived at depends on whether the income has been taxed at source.

If the income is taxed at source (or, in the case of dividends, is accompanied by a tax credit), then although it is divided according to the sharing arrangements of the partnership accounting period, each partner must show the income relating to each tax year in his own self-assessment. Shares of taxed income, together with the tax thereon, are therefore shown in partnership tax returns for the tax year rather than for the accounting period (see Example 42).

As far as untaxed income is concerned, it is treated as if it arose in a separate notional trade that started when the partner joined the firm (not when he started business on his own if he was a sole trader before becoming a partner) and ceased when he left (even if he continues as a sole trader, and even if the source of income actually ceased much earlier). A partner will therefore be entitled to overlap relief in respect of untaxed non-trading income in the same way as for trading profits when he joins the firm. The overlap relief will be given by reducing his share of the non-trading income when he leaves the firm (unless it has been given on an earlier change of accounting date), even if he then carries on business alone (s 854). This is different from overlap relief relating to the trade (see explanatory note 3). If the partner's share of non-trading income in the relevant tax year is less than the overlap relief to be deducted, the balance is relieved against other income of that tax year (s 856). Relief for any transitional overlap profits arising on the change to the current year basis of assessment is given in the same way as for normal overlap profits.

Explanatory Notes

All statutory references are to ITTOIA 2005 unless otherwise stated.

Basis of assessment

1. Businesses starting on or after 6 April 1994 are taxed under the current year basis rules, which are dealt with in Example 16.

Taxation of trading profits

2. The trading profits of the accounting period are shared between the partners according to their sharing arrangements, and each partner's share is regarded as his profit from a separate business (s 853). A new partner is therefore treated as commencing a new business when he joins (as illustrated in part (b) of the example), unless he had previously carried on the business as a sole trader, and a partner is treated as ceasing business when he ceases to be a partner (as illustrated in parts (a) and (c) of the example), unless he continues the business as a sole trader. Unless given on an

earlier change of accounting date, overlap relief is given when the partner leaves the partnership, or if he continues the business as a sole trader, when the sole trade ceases (s 856). The partnership itself is not treated as discontinued on a change of partners except where none of the old partners continue.

Although partners are taxed separately on their profit shares, there will still have to be overall agreement by the partners as to the amount of partnership profit and the division of the profits.

If there are large prior share salaries, etc in the partnership's profit sharing agreement, it is entirely possible that even if the firm as a whole has a taxable profit (or loss), the allocation will result in some of the partners showing a large profit with others showing losses (or vice versa). For tax purposes, the allocation of a partnership's profits between the partners must result in a straight apportionment of the actual profits made by the partnership. If the allocation of the profits using the firm's profit sharing arrangements for all the partners produces both profits and losses, then the actual profit will need to be reallocated between the profit making (or loss making) partners alone in proportion to the profits initially allocated to them. The same applies for losses.

In summary, if the partnership as a whole makes a profit, then no individual partner can claim a loss (or vice versa) – s 850(2)–(6).

Non-trading income

3.   Non-trading partnership income is divided according to the sharing arrangements in the accounting period (ss 850 and 851). If it is *untaxed* income, it is taxed as if it arose from a separate deemed trade, which is treated as having started when the partner joined the firm and ceased when a partner leaves the firm (*not* when the source of income ceases) (ss 849 and 851). The rules for overlap relief apply equally to untaxed non-trading income.

In a tax year in which overlap relief on non-trading income is to be deducted (ie usually in the year when the partner leaves the firm, but possibly earlier if the accounting date is changed), then if it exceeds the partner's non-trading income it may be set against any other income of that year (s 856(3)). There is, however, no provision for carrying any excess back to an earlier year.

There are no overlap problems with income that is taxed at source and dividends carrying tax credits. Such income is allocated to the appropriate tax year as indicated in part (e) of the example.

Calculation of overlap relief

4.   The detailed rules on the calculation of overlap relief are in Example 16. Even though partners may share profits and losses equally, their overlap relief may have been calculated at different times, so that the amounts of profits on which each has paid tax more than once are different. On a cessation of business, therefore, the profits assessable on each equal partner will reflect the differences in the overlap relief available. In part (c) of the example G, H and J became equal partners at the same time and each is entitled to the same amount of overlap relief. In part (b), although D, E and F are equal partners, the overlap relief available to D and E is based on their profit shares for the 11 months to 5 April 1997, whereas that for F is based on his profit shares for the 3 months to 5 April 2010 and the 8 months to 31 December 2010.

UITF 40 and changes in accounting basis

5.   UITF 40 was issued by the Accounting Standards Board on 10 March 2005 to clarify existing UK accounting standards, particularly FRS 5 and Application note G. It is concerned with recognising at the year-end an element of profit that has not yet been realised, but where a right to remuneration has accrued. Work under a letter of engagement providing for remuneration at hourly rates would normally give rise to such an element of profit, as the right to remuneration builds up by the hour. UITF 40 is effective for all accounting periods beginning on or after 22 June 2005, and is applicable to all contracts for services, not just financial services.

Adoption of FRS 5 resulted in businesses including a credit for work in progress in their accounts in earlier years. However, this had normally been valued at the lesser of cost and net realisable value.

The accounts therefore already contained a credit for costs on partially completed work, such as staff time and overheads. It usually excluded any element of profit, or the remuneration of partners or sole practitioners that is a component of profit. UITF 40 requires that the profit earned by the year-end, but not realised until after the year end, should be accrued as revenue in the accounts.

This resulted in accelerated recognition of profit in some businesses providing services, generating a one-off uplift in the year that the new accounting policy was adopted.

The measures for spreading the uplift apply when the new policy is adopted in accounting periods ending on or after 22 June 2005, and beginning before that date. FA 2006 Sch 15 provided measures to identify the profits to be spread, and to specify to which year they should be spread. The profit that may be spread is limited to that arising from the adoption of UITF 40 (or IFRS equivalent), and not from any other change of accounting policy.

The legislation does not provide guidance of how to calculate the profit uplift, which remains entirely the province of accounting standards. The profit element is reduced by foreseeable future under-recoveries, over-runs or additional costs, but if any profit remains, the proportion earned by the year end must be included in the accounts as accrued income. Quantification of the amount derives from accounting standards and judgement.

The uplift was incorporated into the accounts as a prior year adjustment, in the period in which UITF 40 was adopted. The adjustment included in the 5 April 2006 accounts was the value of work at 5 April 2005. The adjustment spread forward is the value of work done at the accounting date under UITF 40, less the value of WIP originally in the 5 April 2005 accounts, which was eliminated as a result of the change in accounting policy.

The adjustment, and elements taxed in subsequent years under the spreading provisions is not taxed as trading profit, but as 'adjustment income'. It is not liable to Class 4 national insurance contributions, but counts as income for purposes of tax credits and as relevant earnings for registered pension schemes.

The self-assessment Help Sheet IR238, which is available from the HMRC website, explains HMRC's view of the procedure.

The uplift may be deferred for tax by spreading over up to six years according to the following rules:

Year	The amount to be charged is
1	Lesser of: 1/3 of original amount or 1/6 of profit
2	Lesser of: 1/3 of original amount or 1/6 of profit
3	Lesser of: 1/3 of original amount or 1/6 of profit
4	Lesser of: 1/3 of original amount or 1/6 of profit or remainder
5	Lesser of: 1/3 of original amount or 1/6 of profit or remainder
6	The whole remaining amount

Unless the UITF uplift is more than 50% of normal profits, or unless profits decline, the spread will be over three years rather than six. As additional taxable income increases payments on account, the payment of tax will be spread over an even shorter period. The profit for the purposes of this calculation must exclude capital allowances, and any spreading adjustments available under other legislation.

An election may be made to accelerate the spreading in any year. Any amount accelerated reduces the 'original amount' in the calculation above. The election must be made by all partners jointly, except in the case of cessation when they may elect individually. This may be useful for utilising allowances or flattening fluctuations in income. The election must be made within one year of the normal tax return filing date.

If the business ceases completely, the spreading may continue on the basis of one-third of the original amount.

The taxable amount is entered into box 3.82 on the partnership return and box 11A of the partnership statement. The partners' share of the taxable amount is entered in box 11A on the partnership statement for each partner. The partners' share is then transferred to box 9 on the partnership pages of the SA return – page FP1 (full partnership) or SP1 (short partnership).

Effect of ITTOIA 2005 s 25 on changes in the basis of accounting adopted by a business

The provisions of ITTOIA 2005 part 2 Chapter 17 deal with a change of accounting basis, and apply where there is a change from a previously acceptable basis to a new acceptable basis. They also apply where there is a change, either in law or practice, in the way accounts are adjusted for tax purposes. The provisions apply for changes occurring in a period of account ending on or after 1 August 2001. All changes in the basis of accounting or computation are adjusted for. The aggregate adjustment is brought into account as adjustment income or adjustment expense, arising on the last day of the first period of account to which the new basis applies. However, if the adjustment results in expenses which have been allowed for tax purposes being disallowed, but subsequently allowed in a later period, the tax relief obtained so far is retained, and the relevant expenses in subsequent periods disallowed until the reversal has worked its way through. Thus a business will not suffer a large disallowance in one period, only to gain the tax relief in subsequent periods, such as may happen on the adoption of FRS 12, accounting for provisions.

For details of the spreading provisions applying to barristers at the end of the adoption of the cash or invoiced basis of accounting see Example 16 part (d).

Partnership self-assessment

6. For the self-assessment provisions as they relate to partnerships see Example 42.

Limited liability partnerships

7. A further type of commercial structure known as a 'limited liability partnership' (LLP) is available. An LLP has limited liability as though it were a limited company but its members are taxed as though it were a partnership as long as it is carrying on a trade. For details see Example 26.

Question

The partnership of Pipe and Ross has traded since 1991 in the business of chartered architects and decided to merge with another similarly long-standing partnership of architects, Simpson, Taylor and Venables, to form the new firm of Pipe Simpson with effect from 6 October 2009. Pipe and Ross have made up their accounts to 5 July each year and Simpson, Taylor and Venables have made up accounts to 5 May each year. The recent tax adjusted profits and sharing arrangements have been as follows:

		Pipe & Ross £			*Simpson, Taylor & Venables* £
Year to 5 July 2009		58,400	Year to 5 May 2009		85,600
Period to 5 October 2009		23,750	Period to 5 Oct 2009		33,250

	Profit share %	*Overlap relief bf* £		*Profit share* %	*Overlap relief bf* £
Pipe	60	21,870	Simpson	40	28,600
Ross	40	14,580	Taylor	30	21,450
			Venables	30	21,450

No formal notices of change of accounting date have been or are being given in respect of the accounts to 5 October 2009.

The partnership merger accounts are to be made up to 5 July and profits are to be shared as detailed below:

To 5 July 2010

First slice of £10,000 per annum to each partner.

Balance split:

Pipe	22%
Ross	16%
Simpson	22%
Taylor	20%
Venables	20%

From 6 July 2010

Profits shared equally.

The profit for the period 6 October 2009 to 5 July 2010 amounted to £121,000 and for the year to 5 July 2011 £200,000.

(a) Compute the taxable profits for the years 2009/10 to 2011/12, the division between the partners and the overlap relief to be carried forward at 5 April 2012.

Answer

(a) **Assessable profits – ITTOIA 2005, Part 2**

Individual assessments

Partners are individually assessable on their shares of the profits for the accounting period ended in the tax year as follows:

	Pipe £	Ross £	Simpson £	Taylor £	Venables £	Total £
2009/10						
(yr to 5.7.09)	35,040	23,360				58,400
(yr to 5.5.09)			34,240	25,680	25,680	85,600
2010/11 (period to 5.7.10 – merger on 6.10.09)						
6.7.09 to 5.10.09	14,250	9,500				23,750
6.5.09 to 5.10.09			13,300	9,975	9,975	33,250
6.10.09 to 5.7.10:						
First slice (9/12)	7,500	7,500	7,500	7,500	7,500	37,500
Balance	18,370	13,360	18,370	16,700	16,700	83,500
						121,000
Less: 2 months' overlap relief (Simpson, Taylor & Venables only) 2/11 (see explanatory note 2)			(5,200)	(3,900)	(3,900)	
	40,120	30,360	33,970	30,275	30,275	
2011/12 (yr to 5.7.11)	40,000	40,000	40,000	40,000	40,000	200,000
Overlap relief cf	21,870	14,580	23,400	17,550	17,550	

Note:

Strictly there is a later accounting date in 2009/10 for each of the old partnerships (5 October 2009). The temporary use of a new date need not, however, trigger the change of accounting date rules unless the taxpayers choose to notify the change under ITTOIA 2005 s 217. If no notification is made, the old date continues to apply (see Example 28).

Explanatory Notes

New firm or continuing firm

1. This example is somewhat different from the normal one involving admission of a new partner or retirement of a partner, in that it involves the merger of two businesses to form one new business. This does not cause the cessation of a trade or commencement of a new one for any partner who is a member of both the old and new businesses unless the new business is different in nature from either of the two previous businesses. In that event it would be advisable to seek the view of HMRC as to whether the merger can be regarded as the continuation of an existing business or whether it has resulted in a new business emerging, in which case all partners in the previous firms would be regarded as having ceased trading (with the full amount of any available overlap relief being given) and having recommenced in a new venture.

Overlap relief

2.   Since the partnerships are old-established businesses who have made up accounts regularly to the same accounting date each year, transitional overlap relief will have arisen on the change to the current year basis of assessment (see Example 16 explanatory note 8). The transitional overlap period for Pipe and Ross was the period from 6 July 1996 to 5 April 1997, ie nine months, and for Simpson, Taylor and Venables the period from 6 May 1996 to 5 April 1997, ie eleven months. Since the 2010/11 basis period for Simpson, Taylor and Venables runs for the 14 months from 6 May 2009 to 5 July 2010, each partner is entitled to deduct a two months' proportion of his available overlap relief, ie 2/11ths as shown in part (a) of the example.

Self-assessment returns

3.   The basic rules for dealing with self-assessment for partners are in Example 42. This example deals with a merger, and accordingly no individual ceases to trade. Therefore the cessation provisions do not apply even though the old partnerships cease.

As indicated in the example, the old firms need not notify HMRC of a change of accounting date to 5 October, but accounts have even so been made up to 5 October 2009, which ends in 2009/10. In view, however, of 5 October not having been formally adopted as a new accounting date, the partners' shares of the profits of that period do not form part of their individual assessments for 2009/10. Those profits to 5 October 2009 instead form part of their 2010/11 income.

Simpson, Taylor and Venables have changed their accounting date from 5 May to 5 July consequent upon the merger, but the accounts to 5 July 2010 are made up by the new merged firm.

It is necessary for a partnership return to be completed by the new merged firm for 2009/10. The position regarding returns is as follows:

2009/10

Pipe and Ross:

A partnership return will be required to the date of cessation on 5 October 2009. The return will include accounting details for the year to 5 July 2009 and a second set of trading income pages for the period 6 July 2009 to 5 October 2009 (with a comment in the additional information box that the profit of this period will form part of the taxable profits to 5 July 2010).

There will be two partnership statements, one covering the year to 5 July 2009 and the other covering the period 6 July 2009 to 5 October 2009. The statements will also include taxed interest etc for the period 6 April 2009 to 5 October 2009.

Simpson, Taylor and Venables:

Again, a return with two sets of trading statements and partnership statements will be required, covering the year ended 5 May 2009 and the period 6 May 2009 to 5 October 2009.

Pipe Simpson

This partnership will have a separate unique tax reference number and the return will not include accounts, as no accounts ended in the year to 5 April 2010. The return will show a start date of 6 October 2009 and the partnership statement will include details of taxed interest etc for the period 6 October 2009 to 5 April 2010.

2009/10

No returns will be required from the former partnerships.

Pipe Simpson:

A partnership return will be required, including the accounting details for the period 6 October 2009 to 5 July 2010. The partnership statement will cover the same period for trading and untaxed non-trading income. The taxed income will be for the year ended 5 April 2011.

Note: In the personal returns for 2010/11, the individual partners will complete separate partnership supplementary pages for each business, eg Pipe will complete a partnership page for the income from Pipe and Ross for the period 6 July 2009 to 5 October 2009 and a further partnership page for the income from Pipe Simpson for the period 6 October 2009 to 5 July 2010. However, no entry will be required for a commencement or a cessation, as each individual has continued to trade throughout the year. Presumably the overlap profits will be brought forward on the pages for Pipe and Ross and carried forward on the pages for Pipe Simpson.

Question

(a) The Ben Williams Partnership carries on a retail trade and is UK resident. For the past 20 years its partners to 30 June 2009, all of whom are UK resident, have been Ben Williams Ltd, Henderson Traders Ltd and John Wilson. The first £100,000 profit is allocated to John Wilson and the remaining profits are shared:

Ben Williams Ltd	56%
Henderson Traders Ltd	42%
John Wilson	2%

The partnership prepares its accounts to 31 December, as do the two corporate partners. John Wilson has transitional overlap relief brought forward of £46,700.

On 1 July 2009 Daniel Grant joined the partnership. He is entitled to a prior charge share of profits of £30,000 plus 1% of profits, Henderson Traders Ltd's share of profits reducing to 41% from that date.

Assume that profits and capital allowances, both for income tax and corporation tax purposes, are as follows:

Year to	Profits (before capital allowances) £	Capital allowances £
31.12.2008	5,200,000	70,000
31.12.2009	5,000,000	65,000
31.12.2010	5,500,000	76,000

Show the amounts assessable on each partner in respect of the three years concerned, and state when tax will be payable.

Ignore Class 4 national insurance contributions.

(b) Sharon Smith and Daniel Brown propose to commence trading on 1 January 2010 as S and D LLP, a limited liability partnership of chartered surveyors. Write brief notes for them setting out the legal and taxation aspects of an LLP.

Answer

(a) Where partnerships have both individual and corporate partners, separate computations have to be made for income tax and corporation tax, the computations being made *before* deducting shares of capital allowances according to the partnership agreement (see explanatory note 2). The total partnership profits for corporation tax purposes may therefore differ from those for income tax purposes. The example assumes, however, that profits are the same in each case. The division of the capital allowances, and the profit shares taking the capital allowances into account, are therefore as follows:

	Total	Ben Wil- liams Ltd	Henderson Traders Ltd	John Wilson	Daniel Grant
Division of capital allowances	£	£	£	£	£
Year to 31.12.2008	70,000	39,200	29,400	1,400	
Year to 31.12.2009					
To 30.6.09	32,500	18,200	13,650	650	
To 31.12.09	32,500	18,200	13,325	650	325
	65,000	36,400	26,975	1,300	325
Year to 31.12.2010	76,000	42,560	31,160	1,520	760
Division of profits					
Year to 31 December 2008					
First allocation	100,000			100,000	
Share of balance					
(56:42:2)	5,100,000	2,856,000	2,142,000	102,000	
	5,200,000	2,856,000	2,142,000	202,000	
Less: Capital allowances	70,000	39,200	29,400	1,400	
	5,130,000	2,816,800	2,112,600	200,600	
Year to 31 December 2009					
1.1.09 to 30.6.09					
First allocation	50,000			50,000	
Share of balance					
(56:42:2)	2,450,000	1,372,000	1,029,000	49,000	
	2,500,000	1,372,000	1,029,000	99,000	
1.7.09 to 31.12.09					
First allocation	65,000			50,000	15,000
Share of balance					
(56:41:2:1)	2,435,000	1,363,600	998,350	48,700	24,350
	5,000,000	2,735,600	2,027,350	197,700	39,350

Less: Capital allowances	65,000	36,400	26,975	1,300	325
	4,935,000	2,699,200	2,000,375	196,400	39,025
Year to 31 December 2010 First allocation	130,000			100,000	30,000
Share of balance (56:41:2:1)	5,370,000	3,007,200	2,201,700	107,400	53,700
	5,500,000	3,007,200	2,201,700	207,400	83,700
Less: Capital allowances	76,000	42,560	31,160	1,520	760
	5,424,000	2,964,640	2,170,540	205,880	82,940

Amounts assessable on partners

The corporate partners are assessable on their shares as shown above.

The assessable profits of the individual partners are as follows:

John Wilson

John Wilson will be assessable on his shares as shown above in 2008/09, 2009/10 and 2010/11 the assessments being based on the accounting period ending in the tax year.

Daniel Grant

2009/10	1.7.09 – 31.12.09		39,025	
	1.1.10 – 5.4.10	3/12 × 82,940	20,735	£59,760
2010/11	Yr to 31.12.10			£82,940

Overlap relief:
3 mths from 1.1.10 – 5.4.10 as above   £20,735

Due date of payment of tax liabilities

Self-assessment applies both for income tax and corporation tax (see explanatory note 8). Ben Williams Ltd and Henderson Traders Ltd will be required to make quarterly payments on account of corporation tax if their profits are £1.5 million or above.

John Wilson and Daniel Grant will include their profits in their self-assessment returns. Payments on account will be made on 31 January and 31 July each year, based on the partner's *total* net income tax liability for the previous year, with a balancing payment (or claim for a refund) on the next 31 January.

The self-assessment returns will show overlap relief carried forward of £46,700 for John Wilson and £20,735 for Daniel Grant.

(b) **Limited liability partnerships**

Under the Limited Liability Partnerships Act 2000 it is possible to carry on a business with a view to profit through the medium of a limited liability partnership (LLP). This is achieved by two or more persons registering an incorporation document with the Registrar of Companies. The subscribers are known as members although the term 'partner' is normally used. Thereafter new members can be added by agreement of existing members, and members may leave as long as at least two remain. There is no upper limit. Broadly a member will have limited liability as if operating through a limited company.

The members have the functions of both shareholders and directors of limited companies. The internal organisation of the LLP is similar to a partnership and is governed by agreement (formal or otherwise) of the members. There is no minimum capital requirement. Members can be obliged to contribute to the assets of the LLP on winding up. Normally each member will be required to provide capital and it may be appropriate for the agreement to provide that any undrawn profits will be added to capital. Accounts will be required as for a limited company, as will an audit (except for certain small LLPs), and filing requirements are as for limited companies.

Normally a member's liability will be restricted to capital provided plus undrawn profits. If this is below a specified amount, a member may be required to contribute on winding up. As for a limited company, an individual can, however, still remain personally liable under the law of tort where a duty of care to another exists. This particularly applies to professional firms. Furthermore, members can be sued for wrongful or fraudulent trading and can be disqualified from being a member of an LLP.

Taxation aspects of LLPs

Members of an LLP carrying on a trade are essentially taxed as if they were members of a partnership (ITTOIA 2005 s 863 and TCGA 1992 s 59A). All activities of the LLP are treated as carried on by the members and property is held by the members. All references to a partnership in the tax legislation include an LLP. On liquidation, however, the transparency of the LLP is lost and instead the LLP is treated for income and capital gains purposes as a company.

The transfer of a partnership to an LLP will be tax neutral, eg no balancing adjustments for capital allowances, the existing overlap relief of a partner continues, no capital gains charges or SDLT. National insurance Class 2 and 4 contributions are payable as before. A single partnership tax return can be made for the tax year of change. It is not possible to re-register a limited company as an LLP or to convert an LLP to a limited company.

Anti-avoidance legislation applies to LLPs that are property investment or investment LLPs (defined in ICTA 1988 s 842B and ITA 2007 s 399(6) and s 1004(1)) to prevent abuse. No interest relief is available on loans used to buy an interest in, or lend money to, such partnerships (ITA 2007 s 399). Other provisions affect pension funds, insurance companies and friendly societies.

An LLP is treated as an entity for VAT, registration being by Form VAT1. The LLP can become part of a VAT group.

Tax treatment of trading and professional losses

Where professional partnerships, such as S and D LLP chartered surveyors, operate through an LLP, loss relief will be due as for an unlimited partnership, except that relief for losses will be restricted to a member's subscribed capital. Undrawn profits will normally be regarded as a debt of the LLP rather than part of a member's capital unless the members' agreement provides otherwise. Where the restriction causes losses to be unrelieved, the unrelieved amount will be carried forward and treated as a loss available for relief against other income under ITA 2007 s 64 and s 72 in later years, subject to the 'subscribed capital' restriction in those years (ITA 2007 ss 107 to 114).

Winding-up

When a liquidator is appointed (or, if earlier, when a winding-up order is made), the tax treatment changes. Any income will thereafter belong to the LLP and will be taxed as that of a corporate body. Any chargeable gains will be computed by reference to the date the asset was acquired by the LLP and taxed on the LLP. Members will then be taxed (or obtain relief) on the gain/loss arising on their capital interest, the base cost being determined by the historical capital contribution made by the member to the LLP as if it had been a limited company. This treatment does not apply on an informal winding-up without the appointment of a liquidator.

Where, in respect of the acquisition of a share in an LLP asset, a member had claimed business assets rollover relief under TCGA 1992 ss 152, 153, or gains on depreciating assets had been held over under TCGA 1992 s 154, or the acquisition cost had been reduced by gifts holdover relief under TCGA 1992 s 165 or s 260, then on appointment of a liquidator the postponed gain will become chargeable (TCGA 1992 s 156A and s 169A).

Explanatory Notes

Treatment of partnerships with company members

1.   Where a partnership has company members, the normal income tax rules of ITTOIA 2005 part 9 apply to partners who are individuals (see Example 24), but special rules CTA 2009 Part 17 apply to corporate partners.

Computation of profits

2.   Two computations are made, one for income tax using income tax principles and one for corporation tax using corporation tax principles. The reason for having two separate computations is that there are various points of difference in the computations, in particular:

   (a)   Interest paid by a company is dealt with under the loan relationships rules, whether or not tax is deducted at source, and if it relates to the trade it is taken into account (usually on an accruals basis) in arriving at the trading profit. (See Example 63 for full details of loan relationships rules.)

   (b)   Different rules apply in relation to transactions in financial instruments (see Example 63) and the treatment of intangible assets (see Example 66).

   (c)   The rules for calculating rental income of individuals and companies are broadly the same, but there are some differences that affect the computation.

Deduction of tax from payments of interest and patent royalties

3.   Companies no longer deduct tax from interest or patent royalties in most circumstances (see Example 5 part (a)). Where tax is deducted, it is deducted at 20% from interest. Companies should strictly account for any tax deducted on the normal quarterly basis, but their shares may not be known at the appropriate time. Unless HMRC agrees to special arrangements, the company would have to account for tax on an estimated basis and adjust it later. Individuals would retain the tax deducted at source and any higher rate relief due would be given in calculating the tax due under self-assessment.

Treatment of company's share of profits

4.   The share allocated to each company partner is reduced by the capital allowances and charges allocated to that company. The company's share of interest paid will be taken into account on an accruals basis either as a trading expense or in arriving at a loan relationship credit surplus or deficit (see Example 49 explanatory note 5). The company's share of patent royalties paid will also be taken into account on an accruals basis under the intangible assets rules (see Example 66). The profit is charged to corporation tax as if it arose from a separate trade carried on by the company. Each corporate partner must include its share of the profits in its own corporation tax return. If the accounting periods of the company and partnership are different, the partnership share is time apportioned to the accounting periods of the company. If a loss arises the normal loss reliefs are available, subject to some anti-avoidance provisions.

Treatment of individual partners' profit shares

5.   The share of the capital allowances relating to the individual partners is treated as a trading expense and deducted from the profit, each individual partner's share then being dealt with according to the normal rules. Each individual will include his share of the profits in the partnership pages of his own self-assessment return (see explanatory note 8).

6. Daniel Grant is entitled to overlap relief as shown in respect of the profits taxable both in 2009/10, when he joined the partnership, and 2010/11. John Wilson's transitional overlap relief brought forward relates to the changeover to the current year basis of assessment in 1997/98, and was based on the profits from the end of the 1996/97 basis period to 5 April 1997, ie from 1 January 1997 to 5 April 1997. Overlap relief is given on a change of accounting date if more than twelve months' profits would otherwise be chargeable, or when the partner ceases in business.

Changes of partner

7. As far as changes of partner are concerned, the firm is not treated as ceasing when an individual partner joins or leaves. Similarly, changes in the corporate partners do not have any effect on the continuance of the partnership business, unless a change occurs in which none of the company partners continues but one or more new company partners joins the partnership. In that event the trade is treated as having been transferred to a different company.

Self-assessment

8. Self-assessment was introduced for income tax purposes from 1996/97 and for corporation tax for accounting periods ending after 30 June 1999. Under the self-assessment provisions, partnerships are required to send in partnership returns (TMA 1970 s 12AA). This applies even if there are no individual partners in the partnership. Where all the partners are companies, accounts and computations must be submitted with the partnership return (see Example 42 explanatory note 5).

   If all the partners are individuals, the due date for sending in the partnership return is 31 January following the end of the tax year. If all partners are companies, the return is due 12 months after the end of the accounting period. In both cases where notice to submit a return is received late, the due date becomes 3 months from the date the notice is received.

   For partnerships with both company and individual members, the due date for the partnership return is the later of the company date and the date for individuals.

   The due date of filing for income tax returns is 31 October for paper returns, and 31 January for electronic returns.

   For the year to 31 December 2009, the due filing date is therefore the later of 31 December 2010 and 31 January 2011 for electronic returns (ie 31 January 2011), or the later of 31 December 2010 and 31 October 2010 for paper returns (ie 31 December 2010).

   The individuals and companies also have to file their separate returns, the due dates for those separate returns being the same as stated above for partnerships of all individuals or all companies.

Limited partnerships

9. Under the provisions of the Limited Partnership Act 1907, it is possible for one or more partners to restrict liability for partnership debts to the amount of the limited partner's agreed capital contribution, providing there is at least one general partner with unlimited liability. The limited partner cannot take part in the management of the partnership, and his share of partnership profits would normally rank as unearned income.

   A company could act as either a limited partner or a general partner in such a partnership, and if a limited company is the general partner this effectively limits the liability of that general partner.

10. Certain reliefs available to a limited partner cannot exceed the amount of the partner's agreed capital contribution plus undrawn profits (ITA 2007 ss 104 and 105). The main items concerned are reliefs for trading losses (including capital allowances) against the partner's income (or company profits) other than trading income, group relief for companies and interest paid in connection with the trade by an individual. Income Taxes Act 2007 s 103C limits trade loss relief against other income or capital gains ('sideways' relief) to £25,000 per fiscal year per limited partner or 'non-active' partner. Relief is denied under this anti-avoidance legislation where the main purpose of making a

contribution to a partnership is to obtain tax relief. A limited partner is also not entitled to relief for interest on a loan to buy an interest in a partnership, or lend money to it (see Example 1 explanatory note 14 (iii)).

11. The national insurance treatment of limited partners who are individuals depends on the circumstances. Class 2 national insurance contributions are payable by someone who is 'gainfully employed' otherwise than as an employee (SSCBA 1992 s 2(1)(b)). Class 4 contributions are payable where profits are 'immediately derived' from carrying on a trade, profession or vocation (SSCBA 1992 s 15(1)). Although a limited partner cannot take part in managing the business, he may participate in a lesser capacity, and if he does, contributions will be payable.

Limited liability partnerships

12. As indicated in part (b) of the example, the Limited Liability Partnerships Act 2000 enables partnerships to adopt a structure that limits the liability of members, without the restriction on taking part in the business that applies to limited partners under the provisions outlined in explanatory note 9 above. Similar restrictions apply in LLPs for limited and non-active partners as in explanatory note 10 above in relation to reliefs, including the cap of £25,000 per year for offset of trading losses against other income or gains. The restriction on relief for interest on loans to buy an interest in, or lend money to, the partnership applies, however, only to partners in investment and property investment LLPs. The loss relief provisions are also different, in that undrawn profits cannot be included in the amount up to which loss relief may be claimed unless the members' agreement provides otherwise, but unrelieved losses may be carried forward and treated for the purposes of ITA 2007 s 64 and s 72 as if they had been incurred in the next period. For an illustration see Example 34 part (d).

13. Also as indicated in part (b) of the example, certain rolled over or heldover gains are deemed to be made by members of an LLP when a liquidator is appointed.

14. For information on how an LLP is formed see Example 27 at explanatory note 5.

15. Mixed structures involving LLPs and private limited companies are becoming relatively commonplace as a way of having the benefit of limited liability, retaining profits at the small companies' rate and drawing earned income subject to Class 4 national insurance rather than employees and employers contributions under Class 1.

Question

Computer Aids
Lower Place
North Westock
Devon
25 July 2009

Mr T Jones
Brown Jones & Co
Taxation Practitioners
2 High Street
London

Dear Mr Jones,

As you know I have traded personally for some years selling electronic parts. I have recently experienced a substantial increase in turnover and, hopefully, profits.

I do not wish to transfer my business to a limited company as I understand this will require a number of legal formalities and extra costs. However, I would be grateful for any tax planning advice you may be able to offer me. I would be happy to pay my wife a very substantial salary or to have her as a partner in the business if this was advisable. Her participation has, in fact, increased significantly as a result of the growth of the business.

Yours sincerely,

I N Putt

Your files show that the tax adjusted profits for the last few years were:

Year ended 31 March 2007	£30,000
Year ended 31 March 2008	£38,000
Year ended 31 March 2009	£45,000

The profits for the year to 31 March 2010 are expected to be £70,000 and to increase to £100,000 for the following year, with further increases as the business expands.

Mrs Putt is employed by her husband. Her salary has been limited to £4,700 per annum paid monthly while the business was being established and she and her husband have no other sources of income.

Mr and Mrs Putt were both born in 1973. Neither has made any pension provision. They do not have children.

Write to Mr Putt comparing the tax position if his wife remains as his employee at an appropriately increased salary with the position if she joins him in partnership, setting out the steps you advise him to follow and briefly mentioning any other tax planning points you consider appropriate.

Answer

Brown Jones & Co
Taxation Practitioners
2 High Street
London
15 August 2009

Mr I N Putt
Computer Aids
Lower Place
North Westock
Devon

Dear Mr Putt,

Thank you for your letter of 25 July asking me to advise you in connection with your micro electronics business.

It is clear that your anticipated current profits will give you a significant tax liability at the higher rate and unless action is taken to adopt a more tax effective structure this will get worse as profits increase. A saving in higher rate tax could be made if your wife's income was increased and your own reduced since your wife has the same level of tax allowances and starting/basic rate bands as you do.

You could pay your wife an increased salary for the year to 31 March 2009 so long as it was paid before 31 December 2009 and included as a creditor in your accounts. However, this is only possible if the obligation existed at 31 March 2009. If the salary was increased substantially, however, the increased amount would need to be justifiable as being 'wholly and exclusively for the purposes of the trade' and a salary of say half your expected profit would clearly be open to challenge. Under self-assessment HMRC will accept the figures shown in your return unless they open an enquiry into the return, but if such an enquiry was raised and it was eventually decided that the salary was not justifiable, your profits could be retrospectively amended and you would be liable to tax, interest, and possibly penalties on the additional profits if you were considered to have failed to take reasonable care over your tax affairs.

Even if such a large increase could be supported in view of your wife's increased participation in the business activities, the extra salary would result in a substantial amount of extra national insurance contributions for both yourself as employer and your wife. The increased salary would be taxed as your wife's income under PAYE at the time of payment and employer's and employee's national insurance contributions would also be payable. The reduction in your profits as a result of the increased salary would affect your tax payable for 2008/09. Your part of the national insurance cost as employer would also reduce your taxable profits, while the total contributions may enhance the potential social security benefits to which Mrs Putt is entitled, especially State Second Pension (S2P).

It is possible to increase your wife's salary to the earnings threshold (currently £110 per week, £476 per month) without attracting employer's or employee's national insurance. As you pay monthly you could increase Mrs Putt's pay from August to £476, without a national insurance cost. In a full year this would use almost all of her personal allowance but not her basic rate band. The £476 limit applies to each month individually.

You should be aware that if you pay your wife more than £95 per week (£411 per month) then you are obliged to open a PAYE scheme and complete year end returns even though no amount is deductible from your wife's salary or payable by you as employer. This is beneficial as the earnings will ensure qualification for both the basic state pension and also an enhanced level for S2P purposes.

If instead you formed a partnership with your wife, the following points should be noted:

(1)   Providing her profit share was not out of all proportion to her contribution to the business in terms of time, skill, financial investment or acceptance of risk, it should not be vulnerable to attack by HMRC as an arrangement for the avoidance of tax.

(2)   Although as a partner your wife would have to pay both Class 2 national insurance contributions at a fixed weekly rate, and Class 4 contributions on her profit share, these would amount to far less than the combined employer/employee contributions on an equivalent salary. However, these contributions do not qualify for S2P purposes.

(3)   If a partnership is formed say from 1 September 2009, then an equal split of profits may be realistic from a tax point of view for the period to 31 March 2010, although allocating a slightly higher share to your wife would eliminate your higher rate tax for the year. It would be important to be able to show that her share of income was fair and reasonable and commercial, so that HMRC could not argue that there was any element of bounty. The extent to which your wife invests in the business, and takes on risks of liabilities as a partner, are important here. You and your wife may be able to vary the profit sharing agreement in subsequent years to make sure that optimum use was made of personal allowances and basic rate band, again providing the arrangement was commercially justified and could not be shown to be pure bounty.

A partnership with your wife will be more tax effective in your circumstances than increasing her salary, but there are some disadvantages to the formation of a partnership as follows:

(1)   As a partner your wife will join you in bearing full legal liability for the debts and liabilities of the business. In the extreme this means that you could both be made bankrupt if the firm's debts could not be met. In the present healthy state of your business this does not present a problem. If this matter causes you concern please let me know and I will provide full details of a limited liability partnership which may then be more suitable, but it has substantially the same administrative and legal burdens as a limited company.

(2)   Self-employed national insurance contributions do not give entitlement to jobseeker's allowance and the self-employed do not get earnings-related S2P pension when they retire.

If you decide to form a partnership, it will be advisable to have a properly drawn partnership agreement, and I will be happy to assist you in arranging for this to be done. Your wife should be named on the letterheading and a partnership bank account should be opened. The change needs to be notified to your VAT office within 30 days, but a change of VAT number will not usually be necessary. Your wife needs to contact the national insurance contributions office within three months of the change to make arrangements to pay flat rate Class 2 contributions. These can be paid either by monthly direct debit or on a quarterly basis on receipt of a bill from the national insurance contributions office. The Class 4 contributions are calculated by reference to her profit share, and are payable to HMRC along with income tax.

The partnership will have to file a partnership return with HMRC, the profit allocation for the year ending 31 March 2010 assessable in 2009/10 being reflected in each of your personal self-assessment returns.

It is not necessary to consider tax credits. As you do not have children, you would only be eligible for working tax credits (WTCs) and your household income is well in excess of the relevant threshold. In any case, the allocation of income between the two of you will not change your overall household income.

As I have previously suggested to you, it would be sensible for you and your wife to make provision for pensions by paying contributions to a registered pension plan.

The amount you can contribute will effectively only be limited by your taxable earnings in any year. The individual yearly contributions limit for 2009/10 of £245,000 and the lifetime fund limit of £1,750,000 are unlikely to cause a restriction for the next few years. Under the new rules the relevant income is that of the actual fiscal year and there are no provisions to carry premiums backwards or forwards. The premiums continue to be paid net of basic rate tax and higher rate relief given by self-assessment.

When you have had a chance to consider my proposals, I shall be happy to meet you to discuss them in further detail and to deal with the necessary documentation.

Yours sincerely,

T Jones

Explanatory Notes

Forming a partnership

1.   HMRC will not accept that a partnership exists merely because the parties say so. There must be an agreement, which should preferably although not necessarily be in writing, and there must be evidence that the agreement has been acted on. See Example 26 re limited liability partnerships.

Although partners are free to divide profits in whatever way they wish according to the provisions of the partnership agreement, the division being accepted as valid for tax purposes, the settlements provisions of ITTOIA 2005 part 5 Chapter 5 are wide enough to catch artificial partnership arrangements between husband and wife where a spouse joining a partnership takes a profit share out of all proportion to the contribution made. However, the success of Mr and Mrs Jones in *Jones v Garnett* (2007), otherwise known as Arctic Systems, means that such a challenge by HMRC is currently unlikely.

It is therefore possible for many husband/wife partnerships to decide on profit shares for tax saving reasons providing the arrangements are not a sham. (The important factor to consider is that a deserted spouse may be left to meet the firm's liabilities.) A salary, on the other hand, must be wholly and exclusively for the purposes of the trade, and there is also a significant difference in terms of national insurance contributions, there being no upper ceiling for employer's contributions (at 12.8%) (see note 2).

National insurance contributions

2.   National insurance contributions are a very significant consideration when comparing the tax position of an employee and a partner. The contributions of a self-employed person earning £43,875 for 2009/10 are £3,053, compared with £9,082 combined employer/employee contributions on the same level of earnings. Above £43,875 the self-employed pay 1% whereas the combined employer and employee rate is 13.8%. The comparison is affected by the employer's contributions in respect of his employees being tax deductible, whereas the contributions of a self-employed person are not tax deductible, but the difference remains high. This point is also relevant when considering at what profits level it would be advantageous to incorporate a business, because directors pay national insurance contributions as employees. See Example 48 for further details. See also Example 88 regarding choice of business medium.

Registered pension premiums

3.   A registered pension premium within the permitted limits is paid net of basic rate tax, and the tax relief may be retained whether or not the payer is a taxpayer (FA 2004 ss 188 to 195). Mrs Putt could therefore pay a premium on or before 5 April 2010 of up to £4,700, deducting tax therefrom (or £5,720 if the salary is increased). Alternatively Mr Putt, as employer, could make a payment for her of up to any amount, subject to being able to show that the total remuneration package is commercial. (See Example 37). This would be paid gross, but would attract tax relief at the rate

applicable to the business profits, which might be higher rate. The contract would still be in the name of Mrs Putt, and the resultant pension taxed on her.

In the same way Mr Putt could pay up to 100% of his share of profits for 2009/10 into a registered pension fund, obtaining basic rate tax relief by deduction and higher rate relief via his tax return. Premiums paid in year do reduce the payments on account for the following year.

Although pension funds are exempt from tax, they cannot recover the tax credits on dividends, so that the value of an individual's personal pension fund is reduced accordingly. For the detailed provisions on registered pension plans see Example 37.

Potential tax position of Mr & Mrs Putt for 2009/10

4. If no action is taken, Mr Putt's estimated 2009/10 income of £70,000 would be reduced by his personal allowance of £6,475 to £63,525, so that £26,125 would be taxable at 40% (the higher rate threshold being £37,400).

    If Mr Putt took his wife into partnership on 1 September 2009, his wife being entitled to half of the profits from that date, then assuming the profits for the year to 31 March 2010 were £72,742 (being the estimated profits of £70,000 plus the wife's salary for seven months saved by taking her into partnership), the position would be:

	Husband £	Wife £
Salary to 31.8.09 5/12 × 4,700		1,958
Profit share:		
1.4.09 – 31.8.09 5/12 × 72,742	30,309	
1.9.09 – 31.3.10 7/12 × 72,742 = 42,433, split equally	21,216	21,217
	51,525	23,175
Personal allowance	6,475	6,475
Taxable income	45,050	16,700

Mr Putt's income in the higher rate band would be reduced from £26,125 to £7,650 (which may be further reduced if he paid a registered pension contribution), while Mrs Putt would pay tax at basic rate. Mr Putt would pay self-employed national insurance contributions of around £3,129, while Mrs Putt would pay seven months' Class 2 contributions = £73 plus Class 4 contributions at 8% on (21,217 – 5,715 =) £15,502 = £1,240, giving a total of £1,313.

By comparison, if Mr Putt continued as a sole trader his national insurance liability would have been:

			£
Class 2	52 × £2.40		125
Class 4	43,875– 5,715 = 38,160	@ 8%	3,053
	70,000 – 40,040 = 29,960	@ 1%	261
			3,439

National insurance has therefore increased by (3,129 + 1,313 – 3,439) = 1,003

Whereas income tax has decreased by

		£	£
Mr Putt	26,125 –7,650 = 18,475 × 40%	7,390	
Less: Mrs Putt increase			
	16,700 × 20%	3,340	4,050

£ £

Overall saving 3,047

(Previously Mrs Putt was unable to use £1,775 (6,475 – 4,700) of her personal allowance.)

Limited Liability Partnership

5. A Limited Liability Partnership (LLP) is formed by completing the necessary documentation available from Companies House, website www.companieshouse.gov.uk, and filing it with the appropriate signatures and fee. Most are formed through formation agents as for private limited companies. Its name must end with 'LLP' or 'Limited Liability Partnership', and names are subject to the same restrictions as company names. LLPs may not choose a name closely similar to an existing company's name, and vice versa.

The LLP has similarities to a company in that it is a separate legal entity contracting in its own right, it provides limitation on individuals' liability, and has accounting and administrative burdens similar to those of companies. It has similarities with traditional partnerships in that the partners (known as 'members') are taxed on a very similar basis to that for traditional partnerships. Unless salaried, the members are taxed under the same income tax rules as partners, the basis periods are as for partnerships, and benefits in kind rules do not apply to assets such as cars. On liquidation, however, the LLP becomes subject to corporation tax.

LLP administration

The disclosure requirements for LLPs are similar to those for companies, although the LLP does not have a Memorandum of Association. The Members' Agreement is a private document.

The LLP must have at least two members, and members' names must be notified to Companies House in the prescribed form, as for officers in the case of limited companies. A minimum of two members must be designated as 'designated members', who are in particular responsible for the filing and compliance obligations. The LLP must complete an annual return, and notify changes of members details, of accounting periods, and place details of mortgages or charges on record.

The LLP has very similar arrangements for setting an Accounting Reference Date, appointing auditors, for filing accounts, and similar penalties for non-compliance, as a limited company. Abbreviated accounts are available to small and medium-sized LLPs as for private limited companies.

Limited liability

In comparison to a traditional partnership, the LLP carries an increased administrative burden, so its attraction is likely to lie in the limitation of liability.

As the LLP is a separate legal entity which contracts and holds property in its own right, in the case of a prudently run LLP, its liabilities should be limited to its assets. The individual partners are therefore not jointly and severally liable for all business debts as in a traditional partnership. As for companies, in the case of an individual acting negligently or in contravention of professional guidelines, a legal challenge may seek to look through the corporate veil and hold an individual personally responsible. A liquidator may seek to recover any funds (eg loans, profit, expenses) or property withdrawn from the LLP within two years of commencement of winding-up if the member knew or had reasonable grounds for believing that the firm would be made insolvent by the withdrawal.

The members should therefore consider the solvency of the LLP before withdrawing funds. The LLP offers significant limitation of liability in comparison with traditional partnerships.

Tax should not be the major consideration in deciding between a traditional partnership and an LLP, as the tax treatment of both formats is intended by legislation to be as nearly identical as possible. The profits of both are taxed to income tax in a very similar manner, and potential benefits (for example, cars) are taxed under the income tax rules for disallowance for private use, not under the PAYE benefits in kind rules.

Question

State the rules for arriving at assessable profits following a change of accounting date, and show the computation of the assessable profits for all relevant years for the following traders, assuming they made up accounts to the dates shown (having not previously changed their accounting dates), and earned profits net of capital allowances as stated:

(a)   *Franky Flew*

(business started in 1986)

	£	
Year ended 31 August 2008	12,000	
8 months ended 30 April 2009	28,800	
Transitional overlap profit	19,025	(217 days)

(b)   *Harlech*

(business started 1 January 1998)

	£	
Year ended 31 December 2007	21,600	
16 months ended 30 April 2009	32,000	
Overlap profit	4,200	(3 months)

(c)   *Baines*

(business started in 1975)

	£	
Year ended 30 April 2009	70,000	
11 months ended 31 March 2010	45,540	
Transitional overlap profit	63,343	(340 days)

(d)   *Duffryn*

(business started in 1990)

	£	
Year ended 31 July 2007	45,600	
20 months ended 31 March 2009	70,000	
Year ended 31 March 2010	39,600	
Transitional overlap profit	36,011	(248 days)

Indicate what the position would have been if, instead of making up the 20-month account, Duffryn had made up accounts for:

(i)   12 months to 31 July 2008, making a profit of £42,000 and 8 months to 31 March 2009, making a profit of £28,000, or

(ii)   18 months to 31 January 2009, making a profit of £63,000, or

(iii) 21 months to 30 April 2009, making a profit of £73,500.

Answer

Change of accounting date

Under ITTOIA 2005 s 214, an accounting change, ie a change from one accounting date to another, is treated as made in the first tax year in which accounts are not made up to the old date, or are made up to the new date, or both. In order for the change to become effective at the time it is made, then unless the change takes place before the end of the third tax year, the following rules must be satisfied (s 217):

1. The first account to the new date does not exceed 18 months.

2. Notice of the change is given to HMRC by 31 January next following the tax year of change.

3. Either:

    (a) No earlier change has been made in any of the 5 previous tax years

    or

    (b) The notice sets out the reasons for the change and HMRC either accept that the change is for bona fide commercial reasons or do not notify their dissatisfaction within 60 days of receiving the notice. (Obtaining a tax advantage is not a bona fide commercial reason.) If HMRC object to the change, the taxpayer has a right of appeal.

The fact that (apart from in the second and third tax year) HMRC does not recognise a change of accounting date unless the change is notified to them means that accounts may be made up to an intermediate date for commercial reasons, for example when a partner leaves, without the annual accounting date being altered (see explanatory note 2).

The provision that the new accounts period must not exceed 18 months does not prevent a longer account being made up. It merely prevents the account being recognised until the change of accounting date conditions can be satisfied, as illustrated in part (d) of the example. Thus, if the rules are not satisfied for the first relevant year, the change to the new date is treated as made in the next following year and so on until the rules are satisfied (s 219). (See Example 16 explanatory note 4 re the effect of making up a long first account in a new business, such an account not, of course, being covered by the change of accounting date rules.)

Where the change of date occurs in the second or third tax year, or the provisions of s 217 apply, the basis period for the tax year in which the change occurs depends on the 'relevant period', ie the period from the end of the basis period for the previous tax year to the new accounting date in the current tax year. (Note that depending on the periods for which accounts are made up, there may not be an account made up to the new date in the current year – see (b) below.) If the relevant period is less than 12 months the basis period for the tax year of change is 12 months to the new date. If the relevant period is more than 12 months, the basis period is that longer period. What this means is that if the new date is *earlier* in the tax year than the old date, the basis period will be 12 months and profits will be double charged, for which overlap relief will be available in due course. If the new date is *later* in the tax year than the old date, more than 12 months' profit will be charged in the tax year of change, but the assessable profit will be reduced by the appropriate proportion of any available overlap profits according to the excess of the basis period over 12 months compared with the length of the period in which the overlap profits arose (see (c) and (d) below).

Taxpayers need to maintain a running computation of overlap relief and the period to which it relates. The overlap period may be calculated in days, months, or months and fractions of months. For businesses in existence at 5 April 1994, transitional overlap relief on the changeover to the current year basis of assessment was maximised by calculating the overlap period in days. If that was done, it would then be necessary to work out overlap relief in days during the life of the business. Where a change of accounting date creates further overlap relief, the relevant period and amount are added to existing overlap relief to give a new single period and amount. Where a change of accounting date uses up some overlap relief, this reduces the period and amount of overlap relief carried forward. Where there is a loss in an overlap period it must be counted as a profit of nil for the appropriate period (see Example 31 for illustrations).

Assuming that transitional overlap relief had been calculated in days in parts (a), (c) and (d) and new business overlap relief in months in part (b) of the example, and also assuming that the rules in 2 and 3 above are satisfied, the position is as follows:

(a)   Franky Flew

The change of accounting date takes place in 2009/10. The 'relevant period' is 1.9.08 to 30.4.09, which is less than 12 months, so the basis period for 2009/10 is the *year* to 30.4.09, giving assessable profits of:

1.5.08 – 31.8.08 123/365 × 12,000	4,044
8 mths to 30.4.09	28,800
	£32,844

The profits of £4,044 have also been taxed in 2008/09, so they are added to the transitional overlap profit, the combined amount of (19,025 + 4,044 =) £23,069 then relating to a period of (217 + 123 =) 340 days. The overlap profit will qualify for relief on a later change of accounting date to the extent that more than 12 months' profits is being charged, or otherwise on cessation.

The change of accounting date does not affect any other tax year.

(b)   Harlech

The change of accounting date takes place in 2008/09, since accounts are not made up to the old date in that year (or in fact to the new date, since no account ends in 2008/09). Assessments before 2008/09 are not affected, the 2007/08 assessment being as follows:

2007/08 (1.1.07 – 31.12.07)	£21,600
Overlap relief 1.1.97 – 5.4.97 (3 months)	£4,200

The 'relevant period' is 1.1.08 to 30.4.08 (ie the date of the new year-end in 2008/09). Since that period is less than 12 months, the assessable profit is based on 12 months to the new date. This gives the following results for 2008/09 and 2009/10:

2008/09	Yr to 30.4.08			
	1.5.07 – 31.12.07	8/12 × 21,600	14,400	
	1.1.08 – 30.4.08	4/16 × 32,000	8,000	£22,400
2009/10	Yr to 30.4.09	12/16 × 32,000		£24,000

The profits of £14,400 for 8 months have also been taxed in 2007/08, so they will be added to the initial overlap profit of £4,200, with the total amount of £18,600 covering an overlap period of 11 months qualifying for relief in a later year.

(c)   Baines

The change of accounting date takes place in 2009/10, since accounts are made up to the new accounting date in that year, and the 'relevant period' is 1.5.08 to 31.3.10. As that period exceeds 12 months, it is the basis period for 2009/10.

On the change of accounting date to 31 March, the transitional overlap relief is given in full against the 2009/10 assessment, since 31 March may be regarded as equivalent to the tax year (see Example 16 part (a)).

The assessment is therefore as follows:

		£	£
2009/10	Yr to 30.4.09	70,000	
	11 months to 31.3.10	45,540	
		115,540	
	Less Transitional overlap relief	63,343	52,197

The change of accounting date does not affect any other tax year.

(d) Duffryn

The first year affected by Duffryn's change of accounting date is 2008/09. Since the change involves an account of more than 18 months, however, it cannot satisfy the conditions of s 217, so assessments continue to be based on the old accounting date until the conditions are satisfied. The assessment for 2008/09 is therefore based on the year to 31.7.08, ie 366/610 × £70,000 = £42,000.

The s 217 conditions can be satisfied for 2009/10, since they are considered in relation to the account of 12 months to 31 March 2010. The 'relevant period' is the 20 months from 1.8.08 to 31.3.10, so the 2009/10 assessment is as follows:

244/610 × £70,000	28,000
Yr to 31.3.10	39,600
	£67,600

Where an accounting date is changed to 31 March, all overlap relief is given at that time as indicated in (c) above, so that the transitional overlap relief of £36,011 will be given against the 2009/10 assessable profit, reducing it to £31,589.

If Duffryn had made up accounts for 12 months to 31.7.08 and 8 months to 31.3.09

The change would take place in 2008/09 and two accounts would be made up to dates within that tax year. The s 217 conditions would be satisfied and the relevant period would be 1.8.07 to 31.3.09, covering 20 months. The position and comparison with the single 20-month account would therefore be as follows:

		Two accounts £	20-month account £
2008/09	Yr to 31.7.08	42,000	
	1.8.08 to 31.3.09	28,000	
		70,000	
	Less: Transitional overlap relief	36,011	
		33,989	42,000
2009/10	Yr to 31.3.10	39,600	31,589

If Duffryn had made up accounts for 18 months to 31.1.09

The s 217 conditions would not be breached and the relevant period would be the 18 months from 1.8.07 to 31.1.09. Since that period exceeds 12 months, it would be the basis period for 2008/09. Duffryn has transitional overlap relief of £36,011 for 248 days. Since the basis period for 2008/09 would exceed 12 months by 184 days, 184/248 of the overlap relief of £36,011, ie £26,718, would be given against the 2008/09 assessable profit, leaving 64 days of overlap relief amounting to £9,293 to be given in the future. The position would therefore be as follows:

2008/09 18 mths to 31.1.09		63,000
Less: Transitional overlap relief		26,718
		£36,282

If Duffryn had made up accounts for 21 months to 30.4.09

The conditions of s 217 would again be broken, and it would take a further year before they could be satisfied, because in 2009/10 the account that ends in that year is the 21-month account, so the accounting change would be ignored and the basis period would be the year to 31.7.09. The change would be effective in 2010/11, since the 12-month account to 30 April 2010 can satisfy the s 217 conditions. The relevant period would then be 1.8.09 to 30.4.10, and since this is less than 12 months, the basis period for 2010/11 would be 12 months to 30.4.10 The position would therefore be as follows:

2008/09	Yr to 31.7.08 366/640 × £73,500	£42,033
2009/10	Yr to 31.7.09	
	274/640 × £73,500 + 92/365 × profits of year to 30.4.10	
2010/11	Profits of yr to 30.4.10	

The profits of the 92 days from 1.5.09 to 31.7.09 would be overlap profits which would be added to the transitional overlap profits, the combined amount qualifying for later relief then relating to a period of (248 + 92 =) 340 days.

Explanatory Notes

Changes of accounting date

1. As indicated in the example, where accounts are made up to an earlier date in the tax year, this results in profits being charged more than once. The amount double charged represents an overlap profit, for which relief is available either on a further change of accounting date if more than 12 months' profit would otherwise be taxed in one year or on cessation. Where on a change of date the new date is later in the tax year, more than twelve months' profit will be charged, as indicated in parts (c) and (d) of the example, and an appropriate proportion of earlier overlap profits will be deducted.

    Part (d) of the example illustrates that if profits of a business with overlap relief start to fall, the ongoing assessments may be reduced by switching to a 31 March year-end. The extended basis period that results from changing to the 31 March accounting date is offset by the fact that the profits are reduced by the whole of the overlap relief.

Notification of changes

2. As indicated in the example, changes of accounting date are not recognised unless they are notified to HMRC, except where they occur in the second or third tax year (ITTOIA 2005 ss 200 and 215).

    Where a business ceases and accounts to the date of cessation are to a date other than the annual accounting date, the cessation provisions of s 202 override the change of accounting date provisions for the final tax year. Depending on the dates to which accounts are made up, the change of accounting date rules may apply for the penultimate year, but this may be overcome by not notifying HMRC of the change as indicated above.

    Where, however, a business is of very short duration, and a long account is made up to the date of cessation, a change of accounting date might technically occur in the second or third tax year for which no notification is required. HMRC have, however, stated that they will not object if computations are submitted on the basis that the old date continues to apply. For example:

Business starts 1 July 2007 and makes up accounts to 30 November 2008. The business ceases on 31 May 2010 and accounts are made up for the 18 months to that date. The basis periods are:

2007/08	1.7.07 – 5.4.08 (9/17 × 1st accounts)
2008/09	1.12.07 – 30.11.08
2009/10	Technically the change of accounting date rules should apply to give a basis period of the 12 months to 31.5.09, but HMRC will allow basis period to be left at: 1.12.08 – 30.11.09 (12/18 × 2nd accounts)
2010/11	1.12.09 – 31.5.10 (6/18 × 2nd accounts)

Overlap relief would be computed on profits of 4 months from 1.12.07 – 5.4.08 and relieved in 2010/11.

Question

(a)   William Smith, a married man aged 50, whose wife is aged 45, has been trading for some years preparing accounts to 31 December each year. He made a trading profit of £10,000 for the year to 31 December 2008 and a trading loss of £16,000 for the year to 31 December 2009. He has reorganised the business and expects to show a profit of around £11,000 in 2010, increasing in later years. Capital allowances have been taken into account in these figures. The business is undertaken on a commercial basis and he works more than ten hours a week. William does not want to take advantage of the extended three-year loss carry back provisions for 2009/10 losses as his 2006/07 and 2007/08 income was low and only just covered his personal allowance.

His unearned income for 2008/09 and 2009/10 was as follows:

	2008/09 £	2009/10 £
Rental income	3,840	6,500
Bank interest (gross amounts)	880	655

Smith's wife's income is £10,000 per annum from full-time employment.

In 2008/09 Smith had sold some shares he had inherited many years ago and made a chargeable gain of £11,000. He had no capital losses brought forward and he had no capital transactions in 2009/10.

Indicate what claims are available to Smith in respect of the 2009 loss and state the time limits involved.

Show the availability of a claim for tax credits and the effect of a claim made on:

  (i)   1 July 2009; or

  (ii)   1 July 2010.

The couple do not have any children.

(b)   James, a sole trader has been trading successfully for many years as a graphic designer. He produces advertising material for well-known high street banks / insurance companies. A number of mergers by his major clients resulted in substantial extra work and high profits when the client's products needed rebranding. This leads to James taking on new premises and staff. Towards the end of 2008 his work quickly dried up and he was forced to make a number of staff redundant. He was unable to quickly change his rental lease agreement. Business is now improving and he hopes to move back into profits by 2011. He has no other income. His taxable profits / losses for recent years are:

	£
Year ended 31 March 2006 profit	60,000
Year ended 31 March 2007 profit	120,000
Year ended 31 March 2008 profit	125,000
Year ended 31 March 2009 loss	(185,000)
Year ended 31 March 2010 loss	(60,000)

(1)   Show how the 2008/09 and 2009/10 losses can be carried back and relieved under the extended loss relief given under FA 2009 Sch 6.

(2)   Show how the position would change if the profits for 2006/07 only amounted to £30,000.

Class 4 national insurance contributions are payable between:

| 2008/09 | £5,435 and £40,040 | @ | 8% plus 1% on the excess over £40,040 |
| 2009/10 | £5,715 and £43,875 | @ | 8% plus 1% on the excess over £43,875 |

Answer

(a)   Loss claims available to William Smith in respect of 2009 loss

The loss of £16,000 in the year to 31 December 2009 is treated as the loss of the tax year 2009/10 (see explanatory note 1(b)). The loss claims available to Mr Smith are as follows:

(i)   He may carry forward the loss to set against his first available later profits from the same trade (carry forward trading loss relief ITA 2007 s 83).

(ii)   He may claim to set the loss against his total income of 2009/10 or 2008/09, or, if he wishes, of both years (trade loss relief against general income ITA 2007 s 64).

(iii)   He may claim to set the balance of the loss after a general income (s 64) claim (and after any other claims, such as under s 64 for the previous year) against his capital gains for the tax year(s) of the s 64 claim (ITA 2007 s 71).

The time limit for the carry forward of trading loss relief claim is five years from 31 January following the tax year (TMA 1970 s 43). However, this time limit will reduce to four years from the end of the tax year from April 2010. Once the loss claim has been established, relief is given automatically against the first available later trading profits.

The time limit for claims under s 64 and against capital gains is one year from 31 January after the tax year of loss (ITA 2007 s 64(5)), ie by 31 January 2012 for a 2009/10 loss.

The effect of the different claims would be as follows:

(i)   Carry forward trading loss relief ITA 2007 s 83

The loss would be set against the trading profit of the year to 31 December 2010. If this is £11,000 as expected, there would still be an unrelieved loss of £5,000 to carry forward to a later year. Smith's other income currently covers his personal allowance, although this might not be the case in 2010/11. The claim would reduce or eliminate the tax and Class 4 national insurance contributions for 2010/11, which is payable by way of payments on account on 31 January 2011 and 31 July 2011, with a balancing payment (or repayment) on 31 January 2012. Tax would remain payable for 2008/09 and 2009/10.

(ii) and (iii) Claim against general income of 2009/10 and/or 2008/09, and possibly against 2008/09 capital gains

Smith's income tax position for the relevant years before loss claims is as follows:

2009/10

	£
Trading income (loss in yr to 31.12.09)	–
UK property income	6,500
Savings income	655
	7,155
Personal allowance	(6,475)
Taxable income	680
Tax thereon at 10% (savings starting rate)	68

2008/09

				£
Trading income				10,000
UK property income				3,840
Savings income				880
				14,720
Personal allowance				(6,035)
Taxable income				8,685
Tax thereon:				
	8,685	@	20%	1,737
Class 4 national insurance contributions				
(10,000 – 5,435 =)	4,565	@	8%	365
				2,102

His capital gains tax liability in 2008/09 is (11,000 – annual exemption 9,600) =
£1,400   @   18% =   £252

Clearly a claim in 2009/10 would not be appropriate, since his personal allowance would be wasted and very little tax would be saved.

His income of 2008/09 does not fully cover the loss, so if he makes a claim for that year he cannot avoid wasting his personal allowance. The claim would save tax and Class 4 national insurance of £2,102 and leave an unrelieved loss of (16,000 – 14,720 =) £1,280, which could be carried forward under trading loss relief provisions against future profits of the same trade. Relief would be obtained at the basic rate in 2010/11 if his anticipated profit is realised. The loss carried forward for Class 4 national insurance purposes would be £6,000 being loss of £16,000 relieved against trading income only of £10,000 (see explanatory note 4).

Alternatively, Smith could set the balance of the loss of £1,280 against his 2008/09 capital gains of £11,000. The loss of £1,280 would reduce the gains to £9,720 less annual exemption £9,600 = £120. Tax thereon would be at 18%, amounting to £22, so that the extra tax saved through the claim would be (252 – 22 =) £230.

Optimum loss claim(s)

Claiming the maximum relief under general income (s 64), including relief against capital gains, means that the 2008/09 personal allowance is wasted and the remainder of the loss saves tax at 20%.

Furthermore, under self-assessment, carried back losses do not affect the calculation of payments on account either for the loss year or the next following year (see explanatory note 5), and interest on tax and Class 4 national insurance contributions refunded as a result of the loss claim is payable only from 31 January following the loss year. Assuming Smith made a s 64 claim for 2008/09 (possibly extended to capital gains), his tax position would be as follows:

2008/09	Income tax, Class 4 national insurance and capital gains tax totalling £2,102 refunded; a further capital gains tax refund of £230 made if loss set against gains. No interest on refund unless made after 31 January 2011 (balancing payment date for 2009/10).
2009/10	Payments on account would be based on tax/national insurance of (2,102 – 176 on savings income =) £1,926 payable directly for 2008/09. He would be entitled to a refund of (1,926 – 68 =) £1,858, unless he had claimed to reduce payments on account. Repayment supplement would be payable on the overpaid payments on account from the payment dates.

| *2010/11* | Payments on account would not be required, because the 2009/10 tax of £68 is below the de minimis level of £1,000 (£500 before 2009/10). |

If the loss is carried forward under s 83, tax might be saved at the basic rate, depending on the level of his 2010/11 income, and there could be further relief in a later year if his 2010/11 trading profits do not fully cover the loss.

Smith may be able to delay the decision on what loss claim(s) to make until he is reasonably certain of the level of his 2010/11 income. On the other hand, he may need to make the general income (s 64) claim in order to obtain immediate cash repayments.

Tax credits and trading loss

William Smith and his wife have tax credits income for 2008/09 of £24,420 ([14,720 − 300] + 10,000).

They are eligible for WTC as both work full-time and are over 25. However, the award would be 'nil' based on this level of income; they are not entitled to child tax credit or the childcare element of WTC.

In 2009/10 William incurs a trading loss of £16,000.

For tax credits this is offset against the family income giving income for tax credits for 2009/10 of:

Investment income		
William	7,155	
Less:	300	6,855
Employment		
Mrs Smith		10,000
		16,855
Less: Trading loss		(16,000)
Income for tax credits		855
WTC claim (per day)		
Basic	5.18	
Second adult	5.10	
30 hours	2.13	
365 days ×	12.41	£4,530

Providing a claim is made by 6 July 2009 (ie six months before the end of the accounting period in which the loss occurs) the full tax credit will be payable, otherwise the claim is backdated three months from the actual date of claim.

Mr and Mrs Smith will therefore receive:

(a)	Claim on 1 July 2009	£4,530
(b)	Claim on 1 July 2010 backdated to 1 April 2009 ie 5 days × £12.41 =	£62

A provisional award would also be made for 2010/11 at the rate of £12.41 per day. However, when the actual income is known for 2010/11 it is possible that no award may be due and much of the £12.41 per day paid for 2010/11 is potentially repayable. However, increases of income up to £25,000 are disregarded so some tax credit would be due provided income does not exceed £43,035 (4,530 × 100/39 + 6,420 + 25,000).

Where the trading loss exceeded the family's income for 2009/10 this would give rise to an unrelieved 'tax credit' loss. This unrelieved 'tax credit' loss could be carried forward and relieved against the first available profits of William Smith from the same business. For example, assume an unrelieved tax credit loss of £945, income for 2010/11 for tax credits might then become:

	£	£
Investment income (say)	5,045	
Less:	300	4,745
Employment income – Mrs Smith		10,000
Trading income (say)	11,000	
Less trading loss b/f	945	10,055
		24,800

This would result in a 'nil' award for 2011/12 but would not affect the provisional payments made for 2010/11.

	£
Income 2010/11	24,800
Income disregard threshold 2009/10	25,000
Income for tax credits 2010/11 (as 2009/10)	Nil

(b)   James

(1)   Extended loss relief for 2008/09 and 2009/10 losses

The extended loss carry back relief was introduced as a temporary measure to help businesses suffering losses in 2008/09 and 2009/10. Under the enhanced provisions losses arising in these two tax years can be carried back for three years.

	2005/06 £	2006/07 £	2007/08 £	2008/09 £	2009/10 £
Profit / loss	60,000	120,000	125,000	(185,000)	(60,000)
2008/09 loss c/back		(50,000)	(125,000)	175,000	
2009/10 loss c/back		(50,000)			50,000
Revised profit / loss c/fwd	60,000	20,000	-	(10,000)	(10,000)

The current one-year carry back (s 64) of trading losses against all income remains unchanged. Hence the 2008/09 loss carried back to 2007/08 is unlimited in amount.

However a cap of £50,000 exists to limit the amount of losses that can be carried back two / three years. The cap applies for each year of loss as shown above where £50,000 of the 2008/09 and £50,000 of the 2009/10 losses have been carried back to 2006/07.

The losses unrelieved for 2008/09 of £10,000 and 2009/10 of £10,000 are carried forward under s 83.

(2)   2006/07 profits revised to £30,000

	2005/06 £	2006/07 £	2007/08 £	2008/09 £	2009/10 £
Profit / loss	60,000	30,000	125,000	(185,000)	(60,000)
2008/09 loss c/back	(20,000)	(30,000)	(125,000)	175,000	
2009/10 loss c/back					
Revised profit / loss c/fwd	40,000	-	-	(10,000)	(60,000)

The £50,000 cap applies to the total losses which can be carried back two / three years. Therefore the 2008/09 loss carried back to 2006/07 amounts to £30,000 allowing losses of £20,000 (£30K + £20K = £50K total) to be carried back to 2005/06.

The losses must be offset against profits of the most recent tax year before those from an earlier year. As can be seen above, this results in the 2009/10 loss not being able to be relieved under these rules as no profits remain in the previous three years(having been reduced to zero by the 2008/09 loss). The loss is therefore carried forward under s 83.

A 2008/09 loss can only be offset against 2005/06 profits if it is off sufficient size and the 2006/07 profits are less than £50,000.

In addition, if a business makes a loss in 2008/09 and 2009/10, the extended loss relief will only be of benefit for the 2009/10 loss if:

- the 2008/09 loss was insufficient to wipe out all the 2006/07 profits; or

- the 2006/07 profits were higher than £50,000 so profits remain in charge after offsetting the max 2008/09 losses.

See explanatory note 8 for further details.

Explanatory Notes

Loss reliefs available – income tax

1. The reliefs available for a trading loss are as follows:

    (a) The loss may be carried forward to set against the first available later profits from the *same trade* (ITA 2007 s 83). Where part of a loss remains unrelieved after other loss claims, the balance is carried forward under this section. The amount will include any allowable interest, relieved outside the accounts, incurred for trading purposes and not utilised in the year (ITA 2007 s 88).

    (b) The loss of a tax year may be set against the net total income of that tax year, or of the previous tax year, or, if the loss is large enough and the claimant so wishes, of both tax years (ITA 2007 s 64). Unrestricted relief for trading losses against general income is not available unless:

        (i) the trade is commercial (s 66); and

        (ii) the individual spends an average of more than ten hours a week personally engaged in activities of the trade (s 74A).

        The first condition is met if the trade is carried on throughout the period on a commercial basis and with a view to the realisation of profits.

        FA 2008 restricted sideways loss relief for 'non-active' individuals. An individual carries on a trade in a non-active capacity where they spend an average of less than ten hours a week personally engaged in activities of the trade. In such circumstances, no sideways loss relief is available where tax avoidance arrangements exist. Otherwise, there is an annual limit of £25,000 on the total amount of sideways loss relief that an individual can claim from all trades carried on in a non-active capacity.

        Where claims are to be made for both available years, relief may be given in the order specified by the claimant. The trade does not have to have been carried on in the previous year. If relief is claimed in a tax year both for a loss of that year and a loss carried back from the following year, the current year's loss is relieved first (s 65).

        Losses are calculated using the *same basis periods* as are used for calculating profits, for claims under general income (s 64) and early trade-loss relief (s 72) (s 61 and s 62). Where a loss would otherwise enter into the calculations for two tax years, for example in the first year of business or on a change of accounting date, it is taken into account only in the first year. For an illustration see Example 31, which also deals with the calculation and treatment of overlap relief where losses are involved.

(c) FA 2009 Sch 6 introduced a temporary three year carry back for losses arising in the tax years 2008/09 and 2009/10. See explanatory note 8.

(d) For new businesses, relief may be claimed under early trade-loss relief (s 72) where losses are incurred in the first four tax years. For details see Example 30.

(e) A general income (s 64) claim may be extended to include set-off against capital gains, in either or both of the tax year of loss and the previous year (ITA 2007 s 71). The claim against income of the claim year must be made first (personal allowances therefore being wasted) and the loss available to set against capital gains is also reduced by any other loss relief claimed, for example under general income claim (s 64) in the previous year or by carry back under early trade-loss relief (s 72) in a new business. The amount of capital gains *available* to relieve the trading loss is the amount of the capital gains of the relevant year after deducting current and brought forward capital losses, ignoring any later claim that affects the chargeable gains for the year (TGCA 1992 s 261B). Having identified the amount *available* for relief in this way, that amount is then treated as an allowable capital loss of the relevant year and is therefore relieved *in priority* to brought forward capital losses. Where there are no losses brought forward, the claim may mean wasting all or part of the annual capital gains exemption. Where there are capital losses brought forward this will sometimes avoid wasting annual exemption, but in some cases there would be no immediate tax saving and it would be a question of whether the taxpayer wanted to have unrelieved trading losses carried forward or unrelieved capital losses carried forward.

In most instances it would probably be preferable to have unrelieved trading losses carried forward rather than capital losses, but if the business had closed down, the reverse would apply. If a later claim, such as a claim to business assets rollover relief, reduces the amount of the gains against which s 71 relief has been claimed, the s 71 losses which thereby become unrelieved are carried forward for relief against later gains, but they cannot be relieved in any tax year after the tax year in which the trade ceases (TGCA 1992 s 261B). Such losses must therefore be separately identified in the amount of unrelieved capital losses carried forward (see Example 95 explanatory note 11).

(f) For 2008/09 onwards, capital gains in excess of the annual exemption are taxed at a flat rate of 18%.

(g) Where a business has ceased, terminal trade-loss relief may be claimed under ITA 2007 s 90 in respect of the loss of the last twelve months (see Example 32).

Time limits for claims etc

2. A valid loss claim must state the source of the loss, the year of loss, and either the year of claim or the statutory reference under which the relief is claimed. The time limit for loss claims under general income (s 64) and early trade (s 72) is one year from 31 January following the tax year of loss. The time limit for claims under carry-forward (s 83) and terminal relief s 90 is 5 years from 31 January following the tax year of loss/cessation. Late claims cannot be accepted, but in very limited circumstances HMRC may grant relief as if a claim had been made within the time limit (see Tax Bulletin December 1994). Finance Act 2008 reduces the period allowed for claims to four years from the end of the tax year; this reduction will take effect from April 2010.

HMRC have stated that where claims are made under general income (s 64) both against the current year's and the previous year's income, the loss will be dealt with according to the order in which the claims are made, so that if the claim relating to the previous year were made first, the loss would be set against the previous year's income first. If both claims were made together the loss would be set off according to the order specified by the claimant. Where, however, relief is claimed in one tax year in respect of a loss both of the current year and of the following year, the current year's loss is relieved first (ITA 2007 s 65).

Capital allowances

3.   Capital allowances are currently automatically included in loss claims, since they are deducted as trading expenses in arriving at the trading result. There is some flexibility, in that some capital allowances may be wholly or partly disclaimed. See Examples 18 and 19 for further details on capital allowances.

Class 4 national insurance contributions and trading losses

4.   Class 4 national insurance contributions are payable on profits above the lower threshold, as indicated in the example, and they are included in the calculation of payments of account and balancing payments (or repayments) under self-assessment. Although a trading loss may be set against non-trading income following a claim under general income s 64, it reduces only trading profits for the purpose of calculating Class 4 national insurance contributions. Mr Smith's future profits for Class 4 will therefore be reduced by any part of the loss set against non-trading income under the s 64 claims. The self-assessment return provides a working sheet to calculate the appropriate adjustment to be made in the return. For detailed notes on national insurance contributions see Example 48.

Effect of carryback claims on payments on account and repayment supplement

5.   Carrying back a loss for relief in an earlier year has an unwelcome effect on payments on account. The tax saving from the carryback claim is *calculated* by reference to the tax rates of the earlier year, but relief is given *in relation to* the later year. Since the tax of the earlier year is not altered, the claim does not affect payments on account for the loss year (although the refund flowing from the loss claim may enable those payments to be discharged or repaid). Nor does it affect the payments on account for the next following year, which are based on the tax *assessed* for the loss year.

Similarly, repayment supplement on any repayment arising out of a carryback claim does not relate to the payment dates for the carryback year. Supplement is not payable unless the claim is given effect after 31 January following the loss year, and in that event it runs from that 31 January (see Example 44 for an illustration).

Losses and registered pension scheme contributions

6.   See Example 37 explanatory note 15 for the effect of loss claims on earnings for registered pension scheme contributions.

Losses and tax credits

7.   This example illustrates the need for all self-employed persons, working full-time and over 25, to make a protective claim for tax credits each year. When William Smith made a claim in July 2009 it is probable that he expected to make a profit for 2009 and therefore was not entitled to tax credits. In the event the business incurred a loss and an award of £4,530 is payable. If he had waited until the loss was quantified then the award is only paid from three months prior to claim ie for a claim on 1 July 2010 payment from 1 April 2010 to 5 April 2010. Thus William Smith has lost £4,468 by not making a protective claim.

The initial claim for trading loss relief under tax credits is always against the joint income of the claimants (Mr & Mrs Smith) in the year of loss. There are no provisions for carry back.

Any remaining trading loss for tax credits is carried forward and relieved against the first available later profits for tax credits from the same trade (SI 2003/2815). This will not normally be the same amount carried forward as for ITA 2007 s 83 (see note 1 above). This would apply regardless of the claim made for loss relief for income tax or capital gains. Thus if William Smith had decided to make a s 83 claim only the carry forward to 2010/11 would be £16,000 relieved as to £11,000 in that year with a further carry forward of (say) £5,000, for income tax but the tax credit claim would be as above.

The loss claims for income tax, Class 4 national insurance and tax credits are all stand-alone claims. In this example William Smith may obtain relief for his trading loss as to:

	£
Income tax (say without CGT) 2008/09	2,102
2010/11 £1,280 @ 20% – Income tax	256
£6,000 @ 8% – Class 4 national insurance contributions	480
Tax Credits (claim made 1 July 2009)	4,530
Tax Credits 2010/11	4,530
	11,898

An effective rate on a loss of £16,000 of 74%.

Extended loss relief FA 2009 s 23

8.   The three-year carry back under FA 2009 Sch 6 para 1 only applies to losses for the tax years 2008/09 and 2009/10. Losses for these two years can be relieved under the normal s 64 one-year carry back and then up to £50,000 carried back to the two previous tax years. (Note that the £50,000 applies to each of the tax years in which a loss is incurred.) The carry back to years two and three is only against profits from the same trade, as opposed to the normal one-year carry back against total income. The condition for claim is that at least one claim under s 64 has been made, or there is no income in either the year of the loss or the preceding year against which a claim might be made. Therefore in the year preceding the loss, the taxpayer has the option of claiming against total income under s 64 or against trading profits only under FA 2009 Sch 6. In this case a claim under s 64 in the year of the loss would be mandatory.

Losses must be offset against profits of the most recent tax year before those from earlier years.

For accounting periods of less than a year the £50,000 limit is time apportioned.

Any loss remaining after the extended loss relief claim is carried forward against future profits from the same trade under the normal s 83 rules.

The provisions for losses incurred during the first four tax years, or during the final year in which a trade, profession or vocation is carried on remain unchanged.

Question

You have been consulted by R Bridges, aged 30, who commenced business as an engineering consultant on 1 August 2008. He had previously been employed, his taxable salary being:

2005/06	£45,000
2006/07	£35,000
2007/08	£35,000

He was unemployed from 6 April 2008 to 1 August 2008, receiving taxable benefits of £2,785.

He has a part-time bookkeeper who has prepared a draft profit and loss account to 31 March 2010 covering the first twenty months' trading which showed:

	£	£
Fees receivable		27,384
Less: Office rent, rates and insurance	9,344	
Office salaries	7,527	
Travelling expenses	1,210	
Motor expenses	4,740	
Stationery, postages and telephone	2,079	
Professional indemnity insurance	2,400	
General expenses	385	27,685
Loss for the period		(301)

You ascertain:

(i) On 1 August 2008 Bridges bought a motor car for £15,400 which he used both for business and private purposes as to three-quarters and one-quarter respectively. The car's emissions are 155g/km.

(ii) At the same time he bought a computer and printer for £2,600 and subsequently purchased a scanner in August 2009 for £600. The scanner has been included in Stationery in the accounts.

(iii) Although expenses accrued evenly over the entire period, of the total fees receivable only £5,617 related to the first eight months. Fees receivable and expenses are estimated to be the same for April 2010, but profits are now increasing strongly and are expected to reach £35,000 in the year to 31 March 2011 and to continue to rise thereafter.

(iv) Bridges is a single man. His savings income has been:

	Building society interest (gross amounts) £	Dividends (including dividend tax credits) £
2005/06	2,100	1,300
2006/07	1,400	600
2007/08	1,000	920
2008/09	2,500	1,100
2009/10	1,400	300

Assume the savings income remains the same for 2010/11 to 2012/13 ie Interest £1,400 gross Dividends and tax credits £300.

(v) Bridges is registered for VAT and all amounts are shown net of recoverable input tax.

(vi) Bridges informed the tax and national insurance offices of his self-employment in October 2008. He has paid Class 2 contributions from commencement. He received a 2008/09 tax return in April 2009, but has not yet completed it.

(vii) You have agreed with Bridges to advise on the optimum tax claims, and will prepare accounts either to 31 March 2009 (and 2010) or for twenty months to 31 March 2010.

Tax data:

	2005/06 £	2006/07 £	2007/08 £	2008/09	2009/10
Personal allowance	4,895	5,035	5,225	6,035	6,475
Tax rates:					
10% on	2,090	2,150	2,230	2,320*	2,440*
Basic rate	22%	22%	22%	20%	20%
Basic rate limit	32,400	33,300	34,600	34,800	37,400
Savings rate on income up to basic rate limit	20%	20%	20%	n/a	n/a
Dividend rate on income up to basic rate limit	10%	10%	10%	10%	10%

40% higher rate tax thereafter, or dividend upper rate of 32.5%.

* Starting rate applies only to savings income for 2008/09 onwards. If taxable non-savings income is above this limit, the starting rate is not applicable.

Advise Bridges on how to finalise his draft accounts for submission to HMRC, and on his optimum loss claim(s), and compute the tax payable or repayable for 2008/09 and 2009/10.

Comment on the availability of claims for tax credits for 2008/09 and 2009/10.

Answer

The alternatives suggested are to complete accounts for two separate periods of eight and twelve months, or to complete accounts for twenty months to 31 March 2010.

The profits or losses and tax payable under each alternative are:

(1)   Two Accounts

	£	8 months to 31.3.09 £	12 months to 31.3.10 £
Fee income		5,617	21,767
Expenses	27,685		
Less: Scanner	(600)		
One-quarter car expenses	(1,185)		
Divisible 8: 12	25,900	(10,360)	(15,540)
Capital allowances (see below)		(4,100)	(2,610)
	Loss	(8,843)	Profit 3,617

Capital allowances

	Car £		Pool £	Total allowances £
Period 1.8.08 to 31.3.09:				
Purchases	15,400		2,600	
Qualifying AIA			(2,600)	2,600
WDA (8/12 × 3,000 max)	(2,000)	× 75%		1,500
	13,400		0	4,100
Period 1.4.09 to 31.3.10:				
WDA @ 20%	(2,680)	× 75%		2,010
Addition Aug 2009			600	
Qualifying AIA			(600)	600
WDV c/fwd	10,720		0	2,610

Assessable profits

		£
2008/09 (1.8.08 to 31.3.09)		–
Loss in basis period	8,843	
S 72 loss claim 2005/06	(8,843)	
2009/10 (yr to 31.3.10)		3,617

Tax repayable

Taxable income:

	2005/06 £	2008/09 £	2009/10 £
Employment income	45,000	2,785	–
Trading income			3,617
Building society interest	2,100	2,500	1,400
Dividends (including tax credits)	1,300	1,100	300
	48,400	6,385	5,317
Less: Loss relief under s 72	(8,843)		
	39,557		
Less: Personal allowance	(4,895)	(6,035)	(6,475)
	34,662	350	NIL

Tax repayable following loss claim:

			2005/06		2008/09	2009/10
			Tax without Loss Claim £	Tax with Loss Claim £		
Taxable Income (34,662 + 8,843)			43,505	34,662		

Without Loss	With Loss		Tax Rate		
2,090	2,090	@	10%	209	209
–	1,138	@	20%		228
30,310	29,172	@	22%	6,668	6,418
1,300	1,300	@	32½%	422	422
9,805	962	@	40%	3,922	385
43,505	34,662				
				11,221	7,662

	2005/06		2008/09	2009/10
Tax repayable following loss claim		(3,559)		
Tax @ 10%			35	0
Less: Non-repayable tax credits			(35)	(0)
Tax due			–	–
Tax deducted at source on building society interest @ 20%			(500)	(280)
Tax repayable			(500)	(280)
Total repayable: (3,559 + 500 + 280)				4,339

Notes:

Although Bridges has earnings below the Class 2 national insurance contributions exemption limits (2008/09 £4,825), repayment for 2008/09 had to be claimed by 31 December 2009. It is possible that Bridges would prefer to maintain a full national insurance record for maximum benefits.

No Class 4 contributions are due, but as the loss has been fully relieved against non-trading income, an equivalent loss can be carried forward for Class 4 purposes from 2008/09 to 2009/10. After deducting £3,617 in that year (on which no contributions would in fact have been payable), £5,226 of the loss remains to be carried forward to 2010/11.

(2) **One Set of Accounts**

	20 months to 31.3.10 £
Loss per draft accounts	(301)
Scanner	600
One-quarter car expenses	1,185
	1,484
Capital allowances (see below)	(6,690)
Revised loss	(5,206)

Capital allowances

	Car £		Pool £	Total allowances £
Period 1.8.08 to 31.7.09:				
Purchases	15,400		2,600	
Qualifying for AIA			(2,600)	2,600
WDA max as less than 20%	(3,000)	× 75%		2,250
	12,400		0	
Period 1.8.09 to 31.3.10:				
WDA (8/12 × 20%)	(1,653)	× 75%		1,240
Addition			600	
AIA			(600)	600
WDV c/fwd	10,747		0	6,690

Assessable profits

	£	£
2008/09 (1.8.08 to 5.4.09)		–
Loss in basis period 8/20 × £5,206	2,082	
S 72 loss claim 2005/06	(2,082)	
2009/10 (yr to 31.3.10)		–
Loss in basis period 12/20 × £5,206	3,124	
S 72 loss claim 2006/07	(3,124)	

Tax repayable

	2005/06 £	2006/07 £	2008/09 £	2009/10 £
Employment income	45,000	35,000	2,785	–
Trading income			–	–
Building society interest	2,100	1,400	2,500	1,400
Dividends (including tax credits)	1,300	600	1,100	300
	48,400	37,000	6,385	1,700
Less: Loss relief under s 72	(2,082)	(3,124)		
	46,318	33,876		
Less: Personal allowance	(4,895)	(5,035)	(6,035)	(6,475)
	41,423	28,841	350	–
Tax repayable:				
2,082 @ 40%	(833)			
3,124 @ 22%		(687)		
Tax payable @ 10%			35	
Less: Non-repayable tax credits			(35)	
			–	

Tax repayable

		2008/09 £	2009/10 £
Tax deducted at source repayable to Bridges			
Building society interest @	20%	(500)	(280)
Total repayable: (833 + 687 + 500 + 280)			£2,300

Note:

Similar comments apply re Class 2 national insurance contributions as for separate accounts. For Class 4, again the loss has not been relieved against trading income, the loss carried forward being £5,206.

Tax Credits

2008/09

		£	£
Income for base year (2007/08)			
Employment income			35,000
Investment income	– Building Society	1,000	
	– Dividends	920	
		1,920	
Less:		300	1,620
			36,620

Eligibility

R Bridges worked full-time throughout and is aged over 25. He is eligible but the award based on 2007/08 income will be nil, as his income is too high.

When he commenced self-employment on 1 August 2008 he should have claimed working tax credits (WTC) within three months ie by 2 November 2008. If he had done so he would have been entitled to WTC for the period 1 August 2008 to 5 April 2009 at the rate of:

WTC claim (per day)			
Basic	4.94		
30 hours	2.02		
249 days ×	6.96	=	£1,733

Although income for 2007/08 is too high, the revised income based upon actual income for 2008/09, gives a full award.

Income – 2008/09 (two sets of accounts)		
Taxable benefits		2,785
Building society interest	2,500	
Dividends (including tax credits)	1,100	
	3,600	
Less:	300	3,300
		6,085
Less: Loss (two accounts)		(8,843)
Loss to relieve in 2009/10		(2,758)
Income for tax credits		nil

Or	
One set of accounts	
Income as above	6,085
Less: Loss	(2,082)
	4,003
Income threshold	6,420
no restriction of WTC	nil

If the claim is made after 7 July 2009, and therefore no WTC is payable for 2008/09, the loss is still deemed to have been used in 2008/09 as set out above.

If he had made a provisional claim for tax credits for 2009/10 by 7 July 2009, then his claim for 2009/10 would be:

(i)   Two Accounts – 2009/10

		£	£
Self-employment			3,617
Investment income	– Building Society	1,400	
	– Dividends	300	
		1,700	
Less:		300	1,400
			5,017
Less: loss brought forward			(2,758)
			2,259

WTC claim (per day)

Basic	5.18	
30 hours	2.13	
365 days ×	7.31	£2,668

(ii)   One Account – 2009/10

	£	£
Self-employment		nil
Investment income (as above)		1,400
		1,400
Less: Loss for year	3,124	
Loss carried forward	(1,724)	(1,400)
WTC – as above		£2,668

For 2010/11 the tax credits income will be provisionally based upon 2009/10 and a full award will be made.

However, when the income for that year is known the award will be withdrawn in part depending upon the profits for that year as follows:

				Two Accounts £	One Account £
Profit for y/e 31.3.11				35,000	35,000
Investment income	– Building Society	1,400			
	– Dividends	300			
		1,700			
Less:		300		1,400	1,400
				36,400	36,400
Less: Loss brought forward					(1,724)
				36,400	34,676
Income disregard				25,000	25,000
				11,400	9,676
Threshold				6,420	6,420
				4,980	3,256
× 39%				£1,942	£1,270
As the maximum WTC (using 2009/10 rates) is:					
365 × £7.31				2,668	2,668
Revised award				726	1,398

The difference in tax credit award between one set of accounts or two is therefore £667.

Overall conclusion on accounts submission

As the income tax repayment is 4,339 – 2,300 = £2,039 lower with one account compared with two accounts, it is advisable to submit separate accounts to HMRC even though the tax credits award may be £667 lower on that basis.

Explanatory Notes

Notifying new sources of income and sending in tax returns

1. The rules for opening years' assessments do not prevent a taxpayer deciding the period covered by the first accounts. If a tax return is not received, however, HMRC must be notified not later than 5 October following the tax year that a new source of income has been acquired, ie by 5 October 2009 in the case of Bridges. For further details see Example 16 explanatory note 4. For Class 2 national insurance, a business is required to notify HMRC immediately. Failure to notify before 31 January following the end of the tax year of commencement results in a penalty geared to the tax lost and the behaviour leading to the failure: careless, deliberate but not concealed and deliberate and concealed (FA 2008 Sch 41). Businesses that started before 31 January 2009 were subject to a penalty of £100 if notification was not made within three months unless profits are below the small earnings exemption limit (SI 2001/1004 reg 87 – see Example 48 part (a) for details).

    Although Bridges notified HMRC in good time, he should have sent in his 2008/09 tax return by 31 January 2010. Failure to send in the return currently attracts a fixed penalty of £100, rising after six months (see Example 41 explanatory note 12), but the fixed penalty cannot exceed the tax payable for the year, which in this case is nil (and in fact Bridges is entitled to a refund of the tax deducted from his savings income). Penalties for late returns will change as a result of FA 2009, although the precise commencement date of the new penalties has not yet been announced. The change will remove the capping of the penalty at the tax outstanding, so Bridges would be liable to a £100 fixed penalty in the future, followed by daily penalties once the return is three months late. (See Example 41 explanatory note 12.)

Effect of basis periods: overlap relief, tax credits, cessation

2. For the basis periods in the opening years see Example 16 explanatory note 3.

    Where accounts are made up to 31 March annually, the problem of overlap profits does not arise. If accounts are made up other than to 31 March (or 5 April), and the accounts for the opening period show a loss, then it is probable that the overlap relief available will be nil. For example, if Bridges had made up accounts for the 21 months to 30 April 2010 showing a loss of £5,206, his assessments would be:

2008/09 (1.8.08 to 5.4.09)		Nil
S 72 loss available 8/21 (carryback to 2005/06) =	£1,983	
2009/10(6.4.09 to 5.4.10)		Nil
S 72 loss available 12/21 (carryback to 2006/07) =	£2,975	
2010/11 (yr to 30.4.10)		Nil
S 72 loss available 1/21 (carryback to 2007/2008) =	£248	

    (Overlap period 1.5.09 to 5.4.10 = 11 mths shows loss, therefore overlap relief nil. There is no doubling up of losses and the loss for the period 1.5.09 to 5.4.10 is allowed in 2009/10 only.)

    As a consequence of the above, Bridges would waste most of his personal allowance in 2010/11, and he would not be able to set off his dividend tax credits. He would, however, have no tax liability in that year and his claim for tax credits would be significantly increased.

    With a 30 April year-end full tax credits (as calculated for 2009/10 above) would be claimable (subject to claim by 6 July within the tax year) for:

2009/10	£2,668
2010/11 (using 2009/10 rates)	£2,668

    If, for example, Bridges had ceased business on 31 March 2013, having made profits as follows, assuming the same profits for years/periods to 31 March or 30 April for simplicity:

Year to 31 March or 30 April 2011		£30,000
Year to 31 March or 30 April 2012		£46,000
Year or 11 months to 31 March 2013		£27,500

With 31 March year-end, he would have been taxed on those profits in 2010/11, 2011/12 and 2012/13, amounting to £103,500, with possibly a small higher rate tax liability in 2011/12.

With 30 April year-end, he would have assessable profits as follows:

			£
			£
2010/11			–
2011/12			30,000
2012/13	Yr to 30.4.2012	46,000	
	11 mths to 31.3.2013	27,500	
		73,500	
	Less: overlap relief	–	73,500
			103,500

Although the total assessable profits are the same with either year-end, it is clear that a significant amount of higher rate tax would be payable for 2012/13 with the 30 April year-end. This would need to be set against the benefit of paying no tax in 2010/11, paying less tax in 2011/12 and the increased tax credits in 2010/11 as above. The effect on Class 4 national insurance contributions also needs to be considered (see note 7 below).

Early trade losses relief s 72

3. Where a loss is incurred in any of the first four tax years of a new business, relief may be claimed under ITA 2007 s 72 against the *total income* of the previous three tax years, *earliest* first (ITA 2007 s 73). ITA 2007 ss 61 and 62 provide that losses made in a tax year means losses made in the basis period for the tax year. This is subject to section 63, which prohibits double counting.

4. As with a general income claim (s 64), relief cannot be claimed under s 72 unless the trade is conducted on a commercial basis and under s 74 it is also necessary to show that a profit could reasonably have been expected in the loss period or within a reasonable time thereafter.

Capital allowances

5. Capital allowances are treated as trading expenses of the accounting period and writing down allowances are proportionately reduced or increased if the period is less than or more than 12 months. If, however, the period exceeds 18 months, it is split into a 12-month period plus the remainder, as illustrated in the example in relation to the 20-month account (see Example 18 part (e)).

See Example 19 for notes on the changes to the capital allowances system.

Repayment supplement

6. For losses, repayment supplement on repayments arising from carryback claims is payable from 31 January following the loss year (TMA 1970 Sch 1B). It runs to the date the repayment order is issued (see Example 44).

National insurance

7. The amounts payable (using 2009/10 rates for later years) with a 31 March year-end would be:

31 March y/e		2008/09 £	2009/10 £	2010/11 £	2011/12 £	2012/13 £
Class 2		120*	125*	125	125	125
Class 4		–	–			
(30,000 – 5,206 – 5,715)	@ 8%			1,526		
(43,875 – 5,715)	@ 8%				3,053	
(46,000 – 43,875)	@ 1%				21	
(27,500 – 5,715)	@ 8%					1,743
Total		£6,963	120	125	1,651	3,199	1,868

*   Subject to a claim for repayment for small earnings exemption if made. Whereas with a 30 April year-end the liability would be:

30 April y/e		2008/09 £	2009/10 £	2010/11 £	2011/12 £	2012/13 £
Class 2		120*	125*	125*	125	125
Class 4						
(30,000 – 5,206 – 5,715)	@ 8%				1,526	
(43,875 – 5,715)	@ 8%					3,053
(73,500 – 43,875)	@ 1%					296
Total		£5,495	120	125	125	1,651	3,474

*   Subject to a claim for repayment for small earnings exemption if made.

Giving a saving of £1,468 (6,963 – 5,495).

Effect of accounting date on loss claims

8.   There are points for and against making up accounts to a date early in the tax year (see notes 2 and 7 above and Example 17). Where losses are concerned, making up accounts to 30 April restricts the losses that may be taken into account in s 72 claims where successive losses are made in the early years of a new business. For example, if such a business started on 1 May 2007, the first accounts being either for the 11 months to 31 March 2008 or for the 12 months to 30 April 2008, the position regarding s 72 claims would be:

	Accounts to 31 March	Accounts to 30 April
2007/08	Loss of 11 months to 31.3.08	11/12 × loss to 30.4.08
2008/09	Loss of yr to 31.3.09	1/12 × loss to 30.4.08
2009/10	Loss of yr to 31.3.10	Loss of yr to 30.4.09
2010/11	Loss of yr to 31.3.11	Loss of yr to 30.4.10

The s 72 loss claims would cover 47 months with the 31 March year-end and only 36 months with the 30 April year-end.

Overall, if there is a loss in the opening period which will cause personal allowances and lower rate bands to be wasted, and it is expected that significant amounts of higher rate tax will be payable in the near future, it is advisable to use a 31 March (or 5 April) year-end. The position on tax credits (see explanatory note 2) and national insurance (see explanatory note 7) should also be considered.

Anti-avoidance provisions

9.   ITA 2007 s 74 contains anti-avoidance provisions to prevent husband and wife transferring a trade from one to the other after the first four years of assessment and effectively starting again.

ITA 2007 s 110 onwards restrict the relief for trading losses in the first four years of assessment to capital contributions made by the partner where the claimant is a partner who does not spend a significant amount of time personally engaged in the trade. See Example 34 part (e).

ITA 2007 s 74A (inserted by FA 2008) contains anti-avoidance provisions to prevent the offset of losses against other income by sole traders. The restrictions apply where the sole trade is not carried on by the individual spending a significant amount of time personally engaged in the trade, which is carried on on a commercial basis with a view to the realisation of profits as a result of the trading activities. This parallels the similar provision for partners. The limit on relief is £25,000 in total in any tax year, but there is no relief at all if the loss arises in connection with tax avoidance (ITA 2007 s 74B).

Miscellaneous

10. Bridges needs to show his accounting results in his tax returns in standard format. For an illustration see Example 15. For capital allowances on plant see Example 20, for the disclaimer rules see Example 19 and for the rules on VAT registration see Example 17 part (b). For rules on tax credits see Example 7.

Question

(a) Hamilton commenced trading on 1 January 2008, making up accounts annually to 31 December. He made a loss of £18,000 in the year to 31 December 2008. Show how the loss will be taken into account for tax purposes.

What would be the overlap relief position if Hamilton made up an account of 18 months from 1 January 2010 to 30 June 2011, having made a profit of £36,000 in the previous twelve months. Assume the change of accounting date complies with the requirements of the legislation.

(b) Riddell started a new business on 1 December 2008 and had the following results:

6 months from 1 December 2008 to 31 May 2009	Profit	£9,000
Year to 31 May 2010	Loss	£20,400
Year to 31 May 2011	Profit	£16,200

Show the alternative ways in which Riddell could obtain relief for his loss, assuming that he has enough other income to obtain full relief for any loss claimed under ITA s 64 or s 72.

(c) Raleigh, a single man, commenced business on 1 July 2008, making up accounts annually to 30 June. He had been employed at a salary of £10,000 per annum up to that date, but his business became his only source of income. His profits for the year to 30 June 2009 were £36,000. His early profitability was not sustained, and subsequent results were as follows, Raleigh having decided to change his accounting date to 31 December in 2011:

Year to 30 June 2010	Profits	£28,000
18 months to 31 December 2011	Profits	£13,000

Show Raleigh's taxable business profits for all relevant years and indicate what claims are available to him.

(d) Drake, a single man who had been in business for many years, making up accounts to 30 April, had the following results (after capital allowances) in recent years:

Year to 30 April 2007	Profit	£30,000
Year to 30 April 2008	Profit	£24,000
Year to 30 April 2009	Loss	£18,000

His transitional overlap profit was £34,000, the overlap period being 340 days. He has no other sources of income.

(i) Show his tax position for the relevant years;

(ii) Show what the position would have been if he had changed his accounting date to 31 March, and had made a loss of £16,500 in the 11 months to 31 March 2009.

For tax rates and allowances see Example 30.

Class 4 national insurance contributions are payable on the following profits:

2007/08	£5,225 to £34,840	@	8% and 1% thereafter
2008/09	£5,435 to £40,040	@	8% and 1% thereafter
2009/10	£5,715 to £43,875	@	8% and 1% thereafter

Answer

(a)   **Hamilton – losses and overlap relief**

Loss of £18,000 in first year to 31 December 2008 will be taken into account as follows:

2007/08 1.1.08 – 5.4.08	Loss, therefore assessment nil. 3/12 × £18,000 = £4,500 loss available for relief under s 64 and/or s 72.
2008/09 1.1.08 – 31.12.08	Loss, therefore assessment nil. Balance of loss, ie £13,500, available for relief under s 64 and/or s 72.

Any part of the loss of £18,000 not relieved under s 64 or s 72 would be carried forward under s 83.

For overlap relief purposes, even though there is a loss in the first twelve months, there is an overlap from 1.1.08 to 5.4.08, ie 3 months to the nearest month, with an overlap profit of nil. This must be aggregated with any subsequent overlap to establish the amount of overlap profit and the period to which it relates.

The 18 month account to 30 June 2011 would result in the following basis periods (see Example 28):

2009/10	Year to 31 December 2009
2010/11	Year to 30 June 2010
2011/12	Year to 30 June 2011

There is therefore a 6 months' overlap from 1.7.09 to 31.12.09 with overlap profits of £18,000. This is aggregated with the previous overlap to give a total overlap period of 9 months with a total overlap profit of (nil + £18,000 =) £18,000. If at a later date Hamilton changed his accounting date back to 31 December (again complying with the requirements of the legislation), he would be taxed on 18 months' profits at that time, reduced by *6/9ths* of the overlap profits of £18,000, ie £12,000, leaving overlap profits of £6,000 for 3 months to carry forward.

(b)   **Riddell – losses and overlap relief**

2008/09	1.12.08 – 5.4.09		
	4/6ths × £9,000 profit		£6,000
2009/10	Since no 12 month account ends in the second year, the basis period is 1.12.08 to 30.11.09:		
	Profit to 31.5.09	9,000	
	Loss 1.6.09 – 30.11.09 (6/12 × £20,400)	(10,200)	
	Loss available for relief	£(1,200)	
	Profit		nil

Profit of £9,000 is offset by an equivalent amount of loss in arriving at nil assessment. £6,000 of the profit of £9,000, ie for the 4 months from 1.12.08 to 5.4.09, is an overlap profit for which overlap relief will be available (see explanatory note 1).

2010/11	Basis period is 1.6.09 to 31.5.10 but cannot include loss to 30.11.09 since already taken into account in 2009/10. Since there is still a loss in the remainder of the period, the assessment is nil and the loss available for relief is 6/12 × £20,400 = £10,200.
	There is a further overlap period of 6 months from 1.6.09 to 30.11.09 with an overlap profit of nil (since there is a loss in the period). This is aggregated with the previous 4 month overlap period to give a total overlap period of 10 months with an overlap profit of (6,000 + nil =) £6,000.

2011/12   Assessable profit £16,200.

£9,000 of the loss was offset against profit in arriving at the nil assessment for 2009/10. If relief for the 2009/10 loss of £1,200 and the 2010/11 loss of £10,200 has been claimed against other income, the loss will therefore have been fully relieved. If no claims have been made against other income, there will be losses of £11,400 brought forward to set against the 2011/12 assessment.

(c)   **Raleigh's tax position**

Assessable business profits are as follows:

				£
2008/09	1.7.08 – 5.4.09	9/12 × 36,000		27,000
2009/10	Yr to 30.6.09			36,000
(overlap profits 1.7.08 to 5.4.09 £27,000)				
2010/11	Yr to 30.6.10			28,000
2011/12	1.7.10 – 31.12.11		13,000	
	Less: overlap profits			
	6/9 × 27,000		18,000*	
	Loss		5,000	
	Therefore assessable profit			nil

     * 3 months' overlap relief amounting to £9,000 carried forward.

Raleigh has a loss of £5,000 for 2011/12, for which s 64 relief may be claimed against his total income of 2011/12 or 2010/11. Since the 2011/12 income is nil, the claim will be made for 2010/11. Before loss relief his tax position for 2010/11 is:

			£
Business profits			28,000
Personal allowance			6,475
Taxable income			21,525
Tax thereon (using 2009/10 rates):	21,525 @ 20%		4,305

The loss of £5,000 will therefore save tax of £5,000 @ 20% = £1,000.

There will also be a saving in Class 4 national insurance contributions because the profits of £28,000 are below the upper earnings limit of £43,875 (2009/10 rates), so that the reduction to £25,000 gives a saving of £5,000 @ 8% = £400.

Although *calculated* by reference to Raleigh's 2010/11 tax position, the loss relief will be given in relation to the tax year of loss, ie 2011/12. If he has made any 2011/12 payments on account, they will be refunded, as will the tax saving of £1,400 from the loss claim (see explanatory note 3).

(d)   **Drake's tax position – loss with change of accounting date**

     (i)   *Tax position for relevant years*

		£
2007/08 (yr to 30.4.07)		30,000
2008/09 (yr to 30.4.08)		24,000
2009/10 (yr to 30.4.09)		nil
Loss available for relief	£18,000	

Relief for the loss could be claimed in 2009/10 or in 2008/09. Assuming no other income, the carryback to 2008/09 would be preferable unless Drake is likely to be a higher rate taxpayer in

2010/11 (yr to 30.4.10). Although there is a loss in 2009/10, there is no need to carry it back further under the relief introduced by FA 2009 Sch 6, as the loss will be fully relieved against 2008/09 income, and to carry back further would require that 2008/09 income has been extinguished. See Example 29 explanatory note 8 for details of FA 2009 three-year loss carry back.

Tax position	2007/08	2008/09 before loss	2008/09 after loss	2009/10
	£	£	£	£
Trading income	30,000	24,000	24,000	nil
Less: s 64 loss claim			(18,000)	
			6,000	
Less: Personal allowance	(5,225)	(6,035)	(6,035)	
	24,775	17,965	nil	
Tax: 2,230 @ 10%	223			
22,545/17,965 @ 22%/20%	4,960	3,593	–	
	5,183	3,593		
Class 4 NIC:				
8% × (30,000 – 5,225)	1,982			
8% × (24,000/6,000 – 5,435)		1,486	45	
	7,165	5,079	45	nil
Tax and NIC repayable			£5,034	

(ii) *With change of accounting date to 31 March 2009*

Assessments		£	£
2007/08 – as above			30,000
2008/09 (1.5.07 to 31.3.09)			
yr to 30.4.08 Profit		24,000	
period ended 31.3.09 Loss		(16,500)	
		7,500	
Less: overlap relief		(34,000)	nil
Loss available for relief		(26,500)	

The loss may be relieved in 2008/09 or 2007/08. Assuming no other income, the carryback to 2007/08 would be preferable unless Drake is likely to be a higher rate taxpayer in 2009/10 (ie accounts year ended 31 March 2010).

Tax position	2007/08 before loss		2007/08 after loss	2008/09
	£		£	£
Trading income	30,000		30,000	nil
Less: s 64 loss claim			(26,500)	
			3,500	
Less: Personal allowance		(5,225)	(3,500)	
		24,775	nil	
Tax and NIC (as above)	7,165		nil	nil
Tax and NIC repayable			£7,165 (and no liability in 2008/09)	

By changing his accounting date to a date nearer to 5 April, Drake has increased his available loss by means of overlap relief. In this example he has fully used the available overlap relief, as the change is to 31 March, and as a result has wasted part of his personal allowances. A change to 28 February would give an estimated repayment of:

		£
2008/09 (1.5.07 to 28.2.09)		
yr to 30.4.08		24,000
period ended 28.2.09 (say)		(14,000)
		10,000
Less: overlap relief 309/340 × 34,000		(30,900)
Loss available for relief		(20,900)

	2007/08 *after loss* £
Trading income	30,000
Less: s 64 loss claim	(20,900)
	9,100
Less: Personal allowance	(5,225)
	3,875

Tax:	2,230	@	10%	223
	1,645	@	22%	362
				585
Class 4 NIC (9,100 − 5,225)		@	8%	310
				895

With a February year-end the loss of £1,500 in March (and £1,500 in April) would reduce the assessable profits of 2009/10 (yr ended 28.2.10) and overlap relief of £34,000 − £30,900 = £3,100 would be carried forward at the cost of £895 payable for 2007/08. This is not as favourable as the position with the 31 March year-end.

Explanatory Notes

Overlap profits and overlap period

1. Under the current year basis, care needs to be taken in the calculation of overlap profits and the overlap period.

   ITTOIA 2005 s 204 defines an overlap profit as profits which arise in a period which falls within two basis periods (HMRC have stated that overlap periods may be calculated in days, months, or months and fractions of months providing the chosen method is used consistently). HMRC's booklet SAT 1 paragraph 4.6 states that any overlap period must be identified as such, even if it shows a loss, and the period must be aggregated with any subsequent overlap period, as illustrated in parts (a) and (b) of the example. This affects the amount of overlap relief that may be claimed where more than twelve months' profit is being taxed in one year because of a change of accounting date.

2. Transitional overlap profits qualifying for relief on the change to the current year basis (see Example 16 explanatory note 8) are treated as overlap profits (ITTOIA 2005 Sch 2.52).

3. As indicated in Example 29 explanatory note 1(b), s 64 losses under the current year basis are calculated for the same periods as profits (ITA 2007 ss 61 and 62). Where, therefore, there is an account of more than twelve months showing a loss, the loss is the loss of the tax year in which that account ends. The loss in such an extended basis period is increased by the appropriate amount of overlap relief.

In part (c) of this example, the long account does not in itself show a loss, but the profit is turned into a loss by the overlap relief deduction. In part (d) of the example the change of accounting date to a date nearer to 5 April enhances the available loss relief, and also has the effect of turning a profit into a loss.

See Example 43 for the way in which relief arising from carry-back loss claims is given and the position regarding repayment supplement.

National insurance contributions

4.   National insurance contributions are dealt with in Example 48.

Tax Credits

5.   Examples 7, 29 and 30 set out the rules for tax credits and the interaction with trading losses. It should be noted that any loss relieved under income tax provisions by way of carryback does not apply for tax credits. The unreduced profits and income of the earlier year are included in the computation of income for tax credits. The loss as computed for a fiscal year is initially offset against the joint income for tax credits of the claimants, any remaining trading loss for tax credits is then carried forward and relieved against the first available profits of the same trade for tax credits only.

Question

(a)   Sewell has been trading as a sole trader for many years, making up accounts to 30 September each year. As a result of serious decline in trade he decided to cease trading at 31 January 2010.

His results after capital allowances for the last few periods of trading have been:

Profit (loss)	£
Year ended 30 September 2006	21,000
Year ended 30 September 2007	15,000
Year ended 30 September 2008	6,000
Year ended 30 September 2009	5,000
4 months to 31 January 2010	(20,000)

Overlap relief available was £11,579.

   (i)   Compute the amount of losses arising and show how these losses may be relieved.

   (ii)   State what alternative form of relief is available to Sewell if the trade were to be transferred to a limited company solely in exchange for shares in the company.

(b)   From the following details of the income of Waterloo, a sole trader who has been carrying on the business of light engineering since 1970, show details of all taxable profits covered by the figures given and how relief for the loss on cessation may be obtained.

Tax adjusted profits or losses (after capital allowances):

	Profit £	Loss £
Year to 30 June 2006	94,100	
Year to 30 June 2007	60,500	
Year to 30 June 2008	13,200	
Year to 30 June 2009	8,000	
9 months to 31 March (when business ceased)		100,600

Overlap relief available was £9,900.

Waterloo is a single man and he has no income other than from the business.

(c)   Trafalgar, a single man, ceased business on 30 June 2009. His results in the period leading up to the cessation were as follows:

	Profit £	Loss £
Year to 31 December 2006	8,000	
Year to 31 December 2007	13,000	
Year to 31 December 2008	4,000	
6 months to 30 June 2009		19,200
Overlap relief available was		5,800

Trafalgar had previously had no other sources of income, but he took up employment after ceasing trading and earned £15,000 in 2009/10.

Show the alternative loss claims available to Trafalgar and calculate his tax position for the relevant years. For tax allowances and rates for years before 2009/10 see Example 30, for Class 4 national insurance rates see Example 31, and for earlier years.

2006/07	£5,035 to £33,540	@	8% and 1% thereafter
2007/08	£5,225 to £38,840	@	8% and 1% thereafter

Answer

(a) (i) **Sewell – terminal loss relief**

The position before loss relief is as follows:

				£
2006/07	(yr to 30.9.06)			21,000
2007/08	(yr to 30.9.07)			15,000
2008/09	(yr to 30.9.08)			6,000
2009/10	(1.10.08 to 31.1.10)			
	To 30.9.09	5,000		
	To 31.1.10	(20,000)		
	Loss	(15,000)		

The whole of any available overlap relief is included in the terminal loss of the final tax year (see explanatory note 5).

The losses available for relief are calculated as follows (see explanatory notes 1 to 5):

General income ITA 2007 s 64

Loss of 2009/10 comprises the loss of £15,000 in the 16 months to 31 January 2010, augmented by the overlap relief of £11,579, giving a loss of £26,579.

Terminal trade loss relief ITA 2007 s 90

Terminal loss relief is claimed in preference to FA 2009 s 23 three-year carry back as it is more beneficial.

£5,000 of the loss has already been relieved against the profit of the year to 30 September 2009 in arriving at the 2009/10 nil assessment and cannot be included in the terminal loss. The terminal loss is therefore as follows:

Loss	1.2.09 – 5.4.09:	
	Profit therefore	–
Loss	6.4.09 – 31.1.10:	
	To 30.9.09 6/12 × 5,000 profit	(2,500)
	To 31.1.10 (20,000 – 2,500 loss already	
	relieved against balance of profit)	17,500
	Overlap relief	11,579
		£26,579

The same amount is thus available for relief both under s 64 and s 90.

If Sewell has no other income the terminal loss would be relieved against trading profits as follows:

2009/10		–
2008/09		6,000
2007/08		15,000
2006/07	(reducing assessable profit to £15,421)	5,579
		£26,579

Had any loss remained unrelieved after setting against the 2006/07 profit, no further relief would be available.

Personal allowances of 2007/08 to 2008/09 would be wasted.

If Sewell has other income, the s 64 claim would be against the *total* income of 2009/10 and/or 2008/09. Unless the other income is very substantial, however, the terminal loss claim would still be preferable, because it would leave the other income to cover personal allowances.

(ii) Alternative relief available to Sewell

If the trade were transferred to a limited company solely in exchange for shares, then so long as the shares continued to be held, the loss could be carried forward and relieved against income received by Sewell from the company, both earned income (eg director's fees) and unearned income (eg dividends).

(b) Waterloo – Assessable profits and relief for losses

The tax position before relief for the loss on cessation is as follows:

		£
2006/07	Yr to 30.6.06	94,100
2007/08	(yr to 30.6.07)	60,500
2008/09	(yr to 30.6.08)	13,200
2009/10	21 months to 31.3.10	Nil

Claims under ITA 2007 s 64 are not relevant, since Waterloo has no income other than from the business. However, Waterloo has the choice of relief under FA 2009 Sch 6, which provides a three-year carry back against trading profits, and terminal loss relief under ITA 2007 s 90. Although the relief is very similar, with a loss the size of Waterloo's in the final period, the capping of relief available in the earlier years at £50,000 means that terminal loss relief will be preferable. The position is therefore as follows:

Terminal trade loss relief under s 90

			£
Loss 1.4.09 – 5.4.09:	Profit 5/365 × 8,000		Nil
Loss 6.4.09 – 31.3.10			
6.4.09 – 30.6.09	Profit 86/365 × 8,000	(1,885)	
1.7.09 – 31.3.10	Loss	100,600	
		98,715	
	Overlap relief	9,900	108,615
Terminal loss available for relief			108,615
Set against:			
2008/09 profits			(13,200)
2007/08 profits			(60,500)
2006/07 profits (balance)			(34,915)
			–

Leaving profits assessable in 2006/07 of (94,100 – 34,915) = £59,185

(c) Trafalgar – loss relief available on cessation of business

Before loss relief claims Trafalgar's taxable profits are as follows:

		£
2006/07 (yr to 31.12.06)	Profit	8,000

		£
2007/08 (yr to 31.12.07)	Profit	13,000
2008/09 (yr to 31.12.08)	Profit	4,000
2009/10 (6 mths to 30.6.09)	Loss	–

If terminal trade loss relief is claimed under ITA 2007 s 90, followed by s 64 claim

Terminal trade loss relief

		£
Loss 1.7.08 – 5.4.09:		
Profit 1.7.08 – 31.12.08 6/12 × 4,000	(2,000)	
Loss 1.1.09 – 5.4.09 3/6 × 19,200	9,600	7,600
Loss 6.4.09 – 30.6.09 3/6 × 19,200	9,600	
Add overlap relief (see explanatory note 5)	5,800	15,400
Terminal trade loss available for relief		23,000

Since there are no trading profits in 2009/10, the terminal loss will be relieved as follows:

	£
2008/09	4,000
2007/08	13,000
2006/07	6,000
	23,000

Leaving assessable profits in 2006/07 of (8,000 – 6,000 =) £2,000.

Relief against general income s 64

	£
Loss of 200/10 (19,200 + overlap relief 5,800)	25,000
Less: already relieved	23,000
Loss available for relief	2,000

Trafalgar's 2009/10 income of £15,000 will be reduced to £13,000.

If loss relief is claimed under ITA 2007 s 64, followed by s 90 claim

Relief under s 64

	£
Loss of 2009/10 (19,200 + overlap relief 5,800)	25,000
Set against 2009/10 employment income	15,000
Loss remaining unrelieved	10,000

There would be no point in making a s 64 claim for 2008/09 since there is no non-trading income and the terminal loss claim is available against the trading profits.

Terminal trade loss relief

The part of the terminal loss relieved under s 64 is regarded as being (15,000 – 2,000) = £13,000, since £2,000 of the s 64 loss is not included in the terminal loss (see explanatory notes 2 and 4(b)). The terminal loss is therefore as follows:

		£
Loss 1.7.08 – 5.4.09:		
Profit 1.7.08 – 31.12.08	(2,000)	
Loss 1.1.09 – 5.4.09 3/6 × 19,200	9,600	
	7,600	
Less: already relieved under s 64	(7,600)	–
Loss 6.4.09 – 30.6.09 as above	15,400	
Less: already relieved under s 64 (13,000 – 7,600)	(5,400)	10,000
Terminal loss available for relief		10,000

This will be set against the 2008/09 profits of £4,000 and £6,000 of the 2007/08 profits of £13,000, leaving £7,000 assessable for that year.

Tax position with alternative loss claims

Taxable income after loss claims

	Terminal loss relief first £	S 64 claim first £
2006/07	2,000	8,000
2007/08	–	7,000
2008/09	–	–
2009/10	13,000	–
	15,000	15,000

Tax and Class 4 national insurance contributions payable

2006/07	(2,000 – 5,035)				–	
	(8,000 – 5,035)	= 2,965	@	10%/22% + 8%		631
2007/08	(7,000 – 5,225)	= 1,775	@	10%+ 8%	–	320
2009/10	(13,000 – 6,475/5,715)	= 6,525	@	20% + 7285 @ 8%	1,888	–
					1,888	951

There is therefore a reduction of £937 in the tax and Class 4 national insurance contributions payable if the s 64 claim is made first. Under self-assessment there is no longer any repayment supplement advantage from carry-back claims, and there is a disadvantage in terms of payments on account (see Example 29 explanatory note 5).

Explanatory Notes

Calculation of losses available for relief

1. Under the current year basis rules, losses under ss 64 and 72 are calculated not only in the same way as profits but also for the *same periods* (subject to excluding any loss already included in a previous tax year where basis periods overlap) (ITA 2007 ss 61 and 62). The terminal loss rules have not, however, been properly adapted to fit in with the accounting period treatment, and terminal losses still have to be calculated separately for the parts of the last twelve months falling up to and after the end of the tax year. This may restrict the terminal loss available for relief where there is a profit in part of the last twelve months (see note 4(a)), eg in part (c) of the example £2,000 of the loss of

£19,200 in the last six months does not form part of the terminal loss, although Trafalgar does in fact get relief for it under s 64 because he has other income in 2009/10 (see note 2).

2. Where more than one loss claim is available in respect of a loss, the strict position is that losses that reduce trading profits (such as terminal losses) take priority over losses that reduce total income (such as s 64 losses). If, however, relief under s 64 has become final before relief is given under s 90, the s 64 relief will not be altered. The HMRC Manuals state that in practice a taxpayer may choose which claim he wishes to become final first.

The effect of making alternative claims is shown in part (c) of the example. The calculation of the terminal loss where the s 64 claim is made first is not clear. The view has been taken that the amount of relief given under s 64 may be regarded as covering first that part of the loss that is excluded from the terminal loss because of the way in which the terminal loss is calculated. This enables relief to be given overall for the full amount of the loss in that example. It is considered that this approach would be acceptable to HMRC.

Calculation of terminal trade loss and relief available

3. The terminal loss is calculated under ITA 2007 s 90 as follows:

   (a) the loss (if any) made in the trade in the period beginning with the start of the final tax year and ending with the cessation; and

   (b) the loss (if any) made in the trade in the period consisting of so much of the previous tax year as falls in the 12 months prior to the cessation.

4. The following points should be noted:

   (a) If 3 (a) or (b) is a profit it is treated as nil in the computation – it is *not* deducted from the terminal loss, as shown in part (a) of the example. If, however, there is a profit for *part* of the period concerned, it is taken into account in *arriving at* the loss for (a) or (b), as shown in parts (a) and (b) of the example.

   (b) The terminal loss cannot include any loss for which relief has already been obtained (eg under s 64 or s 83). See note 2 regarding the interpretation of this provision.

If a terminal loss claim is made, the loss is set first against the trading profits of the final tax year and then against the trading profits of the three previous tax years, latest first. ITA 2007 s 92 provides relief for the terminal loss against interest and dividends from the trade where trade profits are insufficient to fully utilise the loss.

Overlap relief

5. ITTOIA 2005 s 205 provides for overlap relief to be taken into account in computing the result of the *tax year of cessation*. This means that it does not need to be apportioned over the last 12 months in the terminal loss calculation. This is confirmed by paragraph 4.30 of HMRC's self-assessment guide SAT 1. For the calculation of transitional overlap relief see Example 16 explanatory note 8.

Transfer of a business to a company

6. Where a business is transferred to a company by a sole trader or partners in exchange solely or mainly for shares in the company, then it is provided by ITA 2007 s 86 that any income from the company, such as director's fees and dividends, can be regarded as trading income for the purposes of a carry-forward trade loss (s 83) claim, providing that the business has been carried on and the shares held throughout the tax year for which the claim is made (or in the tax year in which the transfer takes place, for the whole of the remainder of that year). In practice HMRC give the relief providing at least 80% of the shares are retained.

Temporary extension of loss carry back for 2008/09 and 2009/10 losses FA 2009 s 23

7.   See Example 29 for details of the temporary three-year carry back of trading losses arising in 2008/09 and 2009/10. Under FA 2009 Sch 6 losses are offset against profits of the most recent tax year before those from earlier years, with relief given only against trading profits so that the new relief is almost identical to terminal loss relief. However, the new rules limit relief in the years prior to the penultimate year to a total of £50,000, whereas there is no similar restriction for terminal losses. Therefore, when the final loss is significant, terminal loss relief will normally be taken in priority to relief under FA 2009 Sch 6.

Question

A.

Rodney Rogers is a single man who has been farming in England since 1970 and has interest on savings of £5,000 (gross) per year.

His recent results (after capital allowances) have been:

Year ended	Profit (loss) £
30 April 2005	40,000
30 April 2006	20,000
30 April 2007	22,000
30 April 2008	(9,000)
30 April 2009	21,000

(a)   State the original assessable profits for all relevant tax years, assuming that a general income s 64 loss relief claim was made for the first available year, and

(b)   State the amended profits for all years assuming that Rodney makes claims for 'averaging relief' wherever possible and assuming that a s 64 loss relief claim is made for the most advantageous year.

(c)   Comment on the effect of the averaging adjustments, and include a summary of Rodney's tax credit position.

B.

Harold Pendragon had farmed Tintrim Farm for many years.

In 2007 Harold moved from Tintrim Farm to Bishops Farm, but the move was unsuccessful, so he moved in April 2008 to Green Leasowes Farm.

His recent farming results (after capital allowances) were as follows, accounts always having been prepared to 30 April:

				£
9 months ended 31 January 2007	Tintrim Farm	Profit	54,200	
3 months ended 30 April 2007	Bishops Farm	Loss	(12,000)	42,200
11 months ended 31 March 2008	Bishops Farm	Loss	(11,000)	
1 month ended 30 April 2008	Green Leasowes	Profit	2,450	(8,550)
Year ended 30 April 2009	Green Leasowes	Profit		40,000

Harold, who is a single man, has savings income taxed at source of £5,000 gross per annum (none of it being dividends).

(i)   Calculate Harold's income for all years affected by the above trading results, making averaging and loss claims to the best advantage, and show the effect on Class 4 national insurance contributions.

(ii)   Show the effect of the averaging claims on payments on account, assuming claims are made to reduce such payments based upon the most favourable averaging/loss choice.

C.

Kay Connor, a single woman aged 45, is an author who has written many books.

Her income as an author fluctuates and for recent years her results have been:

Year ended 30 April 2006		Loss	(£3,650)
(Fully relieved against 2005/06 assessable profits under ITA 2007 s 64)			
Year ended 30 April 2007		Loss	(£11,760)
Year ended 30 April 2008		Profit	£90,400
Year ended 30 April 2009		Profit	£32,550

Kay has no other income. Her income from appearances and talks is included in her literary accounts.

Show the tax and Class 4 national insurance contributions payable by Kay for each year, assuming all available reliefs are claimed.

Relevant allowances and tax bands are as follows:

	Starting rate band 10%	*Basic rate threshold*	*Personal allowance*	*Income limit for higher rate tax*
	£	*£*	*£*	*£*
2005/06	2,090	32,400	4,895	37,295
2006/07	2,150	33,300	5,035	38,335
2007/08	2,230	34,600	5,225	39,825
2008/09	2,320*	34,800	6,035	40,835
2009/10	2,440*	37,400	6,475	42,875

* Starting rate applies only to savings income for 2008/09 onwards. If taxable non-savings income is above this limit the starting rate is not applicable.

Class 4 national insurance contributions are payable at the rates indicated on profits between the following limits:

2005/06	@ 8% on	£4,895 to £32,760 and 1% thereafter
2006/07	@ 8% on	£5,035 to £33,540 and 1% thereafter
2007/08	@ 8% on	£5,225 to £34,840 and 1% thereafter
2008/09	@ 8% on	£5,435 to £40,040 and 1% thereafter
2009/10	@ 8% on	£5,715 to £43,875 and 1% thereafter

Answer

A.   Rodney Rogers

(a)   Original assessable profits for 2005/06 to 2009/10 assuming s 64 claim made for first available year

		£	£
2005/06	(yr to 30.4.05)		40,000
2006/07	(yr to 30.4.06)		20,000
2007/08	(yr to 30.4.07)	22,000	
	Less s 64 claim re loss of yr to 30.4.08	(9,000)	13,000
2008/09	(yr to 30.4.08) Loss, therefore		–
2009/10	(yr to 30.4.09)		21,000

(b)   Amended assessments for 2005/06 to 2009/10 assuming averaging relief claimed wherever possible and assuming s 64 claim made for most advantageous year

Assessments before loss claims are:

		£		£
2005/06	(7/10ths = £28,000)	40,000	becomes	30,000
2006/07		20,000	becomes	30,000
		60,000		60,000
2006/07	(7/10ths = £21,000, 3/4 = £22,500)	30,000	becomes	28,500
2007/08		22,000	becomes	23,500
	Difference	8,000		
	× 3 =	24,000		
	Less 3/4 × £30,000	22,500		
	Deduct from higher and add to lower	1,500		
2007/08	(7/10ths = £16,450)	23,500	becomes	11,750
2008/09		–	becomes	11,750
		23,500		23,500
2008/09		11,750	becomes	16,375
2009/10	(7/10ths = £14,700)	21,000	becomes	16,375
		32,750		32,750

It will be better to claim loss relief in 2008/09 rather than 2007/08 (see part (c)). Assessments after loss claims will therefore be as follows:

		£	£
2005/06			30,000
2006/07			28,500
2007/08			11,750
2008/09		16,375	
	Less s 64 claim re loss of yr to 30.4.08	(9,000)	7,375
2009/10	(subject to any averaging claim re 2010/11)		16,375

(c)   **Effect of averaging adjustments**

Where an averaging adjustment decreases the income of an earlier year, this does not result in any change to the self-assessment of that year, because although the *tax saving* is calculated according to the tax position of the earlier year, the claim is *given effect* for the later year (see explanatory note 7).

Averaging 2005/06 and 2006/07 is worthwhile because it eliminates the higher rate tax in 2005/06. However, as the original profits exceeded the Class 4 national insurance contributions threshold of £32,760 for 2005/06, it increases the NIC liability. The profits over the threshold without averaging are charged at 1% whereas averaging causes profits each year to be below the relevant thresholds and therefore charged to NIC at 8%.

Averaging 2006/07 and 2007/08 does not, in fact, achieve any immediate tax saving because no higher rate tax was payable in either year.

Without an averaging claim for 2007/08 and 2008/09, there would be no trading income in 2008/09 because of the loss. There is £5,000 of non-trading income. Averaging brings income into 2008/09 to cover the balance of the personal allowance. Claiming relief for the 2008/09 loss in 2007/08, however, would reduce the trading income of that year to only £2,750, thus wasting most of the nil-rate Class 4 band. It would be better to make the loss claim for 2008/09, at the same time making an averaging claim for 2008/09 and 2009/10 to increase the 2008/09 trading income to £16,375 (time limit for loss claim 31 January 2011). After setting off the loss of £9,000, there is then sufficient income remaining (trading income £7,375 plus savings income £5,000) to cover the personal allowance and nil-rate Class 4 national insurance contributions. If 2008/09 and 2009/10 were not averaged, the trading income of £11,750 plus savings income of £5,000 would be reduced to £7,750 after the loss claim, so that part of the Class 4 nil-rate band would be wasted.

The effect of averaging on Class 4 contributions payable by Rodney is as follows:

Class 4 national insurance contributions payable:

	No averaging		*Averaging*	
	Profit	*Class 4*	*Profit*	*Class 4*
	£	*£*	*£*	*£*
2005/06	40,000	2,302	30,000	2,008
2006/07	20,000	1,197	28,500	1,877
2007/08	13,000	622	11,750	522
2008/09	–	–	7,375	155
2009/10	21,000	1,223	16,375	853
		5,344		5,415

From 2005/06 to 2009/10 there is a net increase of £71.

Tax credits

For tax credits the farming income is before averaging. For 2006/07 that would amount to £20,000 and a nil award would be made. Assuming Rodney had made a protective claim by 7 July 2008 he would be entitled to tax credits in 2008/09 of:

Eligibility – working full-time and aged over 25. Yes.

	£	£
Income: Investment income	5,000	
Less:	300	4,700
Trading loss (y/e 30.04.08)		(9,000)
Unrelieved trading loss carried forward		(4,300)

WTC (per day)

Basic	4.94	
30 hours	2.02	
365 days ×	6.96	£2,540

For 2009/10 his provisional claim will be based upon the income of 2008/09, ie nil, and Rodney Rogers would receive a tax credit award of:

WTC claim (per day)

Basic	5.18	
30 hours	2.13	
365 days ×	7.31	£2,668

His actual income for 2009/10 for tax credits would be:

		£
Investment income (as above)		5,000
Trading income (y/e 30.04.09)	21,000	
Loss brought forward	(4,300)	16,700
Tax credits income for 2009/10		21,700
Provisional income for 2009/10 (based on 2008/09)		nil
Disregard first £25,000 of increase		21,700
		21,700
		nil

Rodney will keep the WTC paid in 2009/10 of £2,668 but in computing a claim for 2010/11 his income will be provisionally based upon the 2009/10 income of £21,700 and therefore no award is due for 2010/11.

B.   Harold Pendragon

(i)   Total income and Class 4 national insurance contributions

(a)   Assessable profits, subject to averaging (see explanatory note 9)

		£
2007/08	yr to 30.4.07	42,200
2008/09	yr to 30.4.08 (Loss of £8,550)	–
2009/10	yr to 30.4.09	40,000

Relief for the loss of £8,550 for 2008/09 may be claimed under s 64 in 2008/09 or 2007/08, or the loss may be carried forward to 2009/10.

(b)   Possible farmer's averaging adjustments

		£		£
Profits if all three years	2007/08	42,200	becomes	21,100
are averaged	2008/09	–	becomes	21,100
		42,200		42,200
	2008/09	21,100	becomes	30,550
	2009/10	40,000	becomes	30,550
		61,100		61,100

		£	£
Profits if only 2007/08	2007/08		21,100
and 2008/09 are averaged	2008/09		21,100
	2009/10		40,000

(c) Total income, taking into account averaging and loss claims

Averaging all three years will eliminate the higher rate tax for 2007/08 and 2009/10. Relief for the loss should then be claimed in 2008/09, thus reducing the tax of that year and reducing the payments on account required for 2009/10. If losses are carried back, the tax saving from the loss claim does not reduce payments on account for *any* year (see explanatory note 7).

Higher rate tax could be substantially eliminated by averaging only 2007/08 and 2008/09, and carrying the loss forward to reduce the profits of 2009/10. This would, however, result in more tax being paid at an earlier stage and increase the payments on account required for 2009/10. The best overall position is achieved by averaging all three years and claiming relief for the 2008/09 loss against the income of that year. This gives the following results:

	2007/08 £	2008/09 £	2009/10 £
Farm profits (a)	42,200	–	40,000
Averaging adjustments (b)	(21,100)	30,550	(9,450)
Case I assessable profits	21,100	30,550	30,550
Savings income	5,000	5,000	5,000
	26,100	35,550	35,550
Loss relief under s 64		(8,550)	
Total income	26,100	27,000	35,550

(d) Effect on Class 4 national insurance contributions

			2007/08 £	2008/09 £	2009/10 £
Profits before averaging, with 2008/09 loss set against 2007/08 profits (i)			33,650	–	40,000
Profits after averaging and with loss set against 2008/09 profits (ii)			21,100	22,000	30,550
Contributions payable					
(i)	33,650 – 5,225	@ 8%	2,274		
(ii)	21,100 – 5,225	@ 8%	1,270		
(i)	–			–	
(ii)	22,000 – 5,435	@ 8%		1,325	
(i)	40,000 – 5,715	@ 8%			2,743
(ii)	30,550 – 5,715	@ 8%			1,987
Increase/(decrease)			(1004)	1,325	(756)

There is thus a net decrease in national insurance contributions of £435.

(ii)   **Effect of averaging claims on payments on account**

(a)   **Before averaging claims**

				£	Tax £
2007/08	Trading income			42,200	
	Savings income			5,000	1,000
				47,200	
	Personal allowance			5,225	
				41,975	
Tax thereon:	34,600		@ starting and basic rates	7,344	
	7,375		@ 40%	2,950	
	41,975			10,294	
Class 4 NIC	(34,840 – 5,225)		@ 8%		
	(42,200 – 34,840)		@ 1%	2,443	12,737

Tax due by payments on account 31.1.08

and 31.7.08 with balancing payment 31.1.09   11,737

Note

It is not possible to reduce this amount because of the loss/averaging claim to be made for 2008/09. The amount will be repayable in part when the 2008/09 return is filed.

2008/09	Payments on account due on each of 31.1.09 and 31.7.09	
	– half of £11,737	5,869

(b)   **Following averaging claims re 2007/08 and 2008/09 and s 64 loss claim**

			£	Tax £
2007/08	Trading income		21,100	
	Savings income		5,000	1,000
			26,100	
	Personal allowance		5,225	
			20,875	
Tax thereon:	Non-savings income –			
	2,230	@ 10%	223	
	13,645	@ 22%	3,002	
	Savings income 5,000	@ 20%	1,000	
			4,225	
Class 4 NIC (21,100 – 5,225)	@ 8%		1,270	5,495
				4,495
Paid for year (as in (a))				11,737
Repayment given effect for 2008/09 on filing 2008/09 return				7,242
2008/09	Trading income		21,100	
	Savings income		5,000	1,000
			26,100	
	Less: s 64 claim re loss of year		(8,550)	

			£	Tax £
			17,550	
Personal allowance			6,035	
			11,515	

Tax thereon:

	11,515	@ 20%	2,303	
Class 4 NIC (21,100 – 8,550 – 5,435)		@ 8%	569	2,872
				1,872
Payments on account due 31.1.09 and 31.7.09 as in (a)			11,737	
Reduced to actual following claim on Form SA303			9,865	1,872
2009/10	Payments on account due on each of 31.1.10 and 31.7.10 – half of £1,872			936

(c) Following averaging claim re 2008/09 and 2009/10

2008/09	Trading income		30,550	
	Savings income		5,000	1,000
			35,550	
	Less s 64 claim re loss of year		(8,550)	
			27,000	
	Personal allowance		6,035	
			20,965	

Tax thereon:

	20,965	@ 20%	4,193	
Class 4 NIC (22,000 – 5,435)		@ 8%	1,325	5,518
				4,518
Paid for year (as in (b) above)				1,872
Due with 2009/10 liability				2,646

			£	Tax £
2009/10	Trading income		30,550	
	Savings income		5,000	1,000
			35,550	
	Personal allowance		6,475	
			29,075	

Tax thereon:

	29,075	@ 20%	5,815	
Class 4 NIC (30,550 – 5,715)		@ 8%	1,987	7,802
				6,802
Payments on account per (b)				1,872
				4,930
Due for 2008/09 re averaging claim as above				2,646
Payable re 2009/10 on 31.1.11				7,576

		£	Tax £
2010/11	Payments on account due on each of 31.1.11 and 31.7.11 – half of £6,802		3,401
	Total payable 31.1.12		10,977

Summary of payments due

		£	£
2007/08	Total due by 31.1.09		11,737
2008/09	Due 31.1.09 (1st payment on account)	5,869	
	Reduced by claim	4,933	
	Revised amount due 31.1.09		936
	2nd payment on account due 31.7.09		936
2009/10	Due 31.1.10		936
	Due 31.7.10		936
	Balance due 31.1.11	7,576	
2010/11	1st payment on account due 31.1.11	3,401	10,977
Repayable re 2007/08 by claim with 2008/09 tax return			(7,242)

Tax Credits

As trading results are always taken before farmer's averaging Harold would be entitled to a payment of tax credits for 2008/09 of £2,540 (see above in part A(c) for computation) providing a protective claim was made by 7 July 2008. This is based upon a trading loss for 2008/09 of £8,550 and savings income of £5,000. There would be no claim for 2009/10 as trading profits for year ended 30 April 2009 (2009/10) amounted to £40,000 before averaging. Any provisional tax credits paid for 2009/10 between 6 April 2009 and date of notifying actual income for 2009/10 would be repayable.

C.Kay Connor

Tax and Class 4 national insurance contributions payable

Assessable profits

	£	£	£
2006/07			
Year ended 30.4.2006			Nil
(Loss carried back to 2005/06)			
2007/08			
Year ended 30.4.07 – Loss	(11,760)		
2008/09			
Year ended 30.4.08 – Profit	90,400		
Claim for averaging with 2007/08 made by 31.1.11:			
Year ended 30.4.07		–	
Year ended 30.4.08		90,400	
Average		45,200	
Revised assessments:			
2007/08			
Average profits		45,200	
Less: s 64 loss claim re: year to 30.4.07		(11,760)	33,440
2008/09			

	£	£	£
Average profits	45,200		
2009/10			
Year ended 30.4.09	32,550		
Difference	12,650		

Averaging by claim made by 31.1.12:

75% of higher profit =	£33,900		
70% of higher profit =	£31,640		
Averaging adjustment is:			
3 × 12,650		37,950	
Less 75% × 45,200		33,900	
Deduct from higher and add to lower		4,050	

Revised assessments:

2008/09	(45,200 – 4,050)		41,150
2009/10	(32,550 + 4,050)		36,600
(subject to any claim to average with 2010/11)			

Tax payable

			£	£	£
2006/07					Nil
2007/08 Income from profession				33,440	
Personal allowance				5,225	
Taxable income				28,215	
Tax thereon:	2,230	@ 10%		223	
	25,985	@ 22%		5,717	
	28,215			5,940	
Class 4 NIC	(33,440 – 5,225) @ 8%			2,257	
				8,197	8,197
2008/09					
Income from profession				41,150	
Personal allowance				6,035	
Taxable income				35,115	
Tax thereon:	34,800	@ 20%		6960	
	315	@ 40%		126	
	35,115			7,086	
Class 4 NIC	(40,040 – 5,435)	@ 8%	2,768		
	(41,150 – 40,040)	@ 1%	11	2,779	9,865

2009/10

Income from profession			36,600	
Personal allowance			6,475	
Taxable income			30,125	
Tax thereon:	30,125	@ 20%	6,025	
Class 4 NIC	(36,600 – 5,715)	@ 8%	2,471	8,496

Explanatory Notes

Averaging claims

1.   ITTOIA 2005 s 221 gives averaging relief for individuals and partnerships who are farmers or creative artists who make a claim in their tax return or an amended return. It need not be claimed unless required. Profits to be averaged are taken into account *after* capital allowances. The amount of capital allowances *claimed* may be varied using the disclaimer provisions (see Example 19). The profits taken into account for averaging are before deducting losses.

Creative artists

2.   A 'creative artist' is someone whose profits are:

(a)   derived wholly or mainly from literary, dramatic, musical or artistic works, or from designs, created by the taxpayer personally or by someone in partnership with the taxpayer, and

(b)   chargeable to income tax as trading income.

'Artistic works' would include paintings and sculpture. The inclusion in profits of appearance fees and speaking fees would not prevent a claim for averaging.

Time limits for claims

3.   The time limit for making averaging claims is 12 months from the 31 January following the end of the second tax year (eg by 31 January 2010 for an averaging claim for 2006/07 and 2007/08).

The averaging adjustment

4.   The averaging rules provide that if, in respect of consecutive years of assessment, profits in either year do not exceed 7/10ths of the other year or are nil, a claim may be made for the profits of each year to be adjusted so that one-half of the profits for the two years taken together, or for the year for which there are profits, is assessed in each year.

Where profits are nil because there is a loss, any independent claim for loss relief is not affected and in calculating available losses the original results and not the averaged results are used.

5.   Marginal relief is available where profits for either year exceed 7/10ths but are less than three-quarters of the profit for the other year. Profits for each year may then be adjusted by adding to those that are lower and deducting from those that are higher three times the difference between them less three-quarters of the higher profits. This is illustrated in part A(b) of the example in relation to the 2006/07 and 2007/08 assessments.

Once an averaging calculation has been done, the average itself is the figure to use if the next year's profits are to be averaged.

No claim can be made for the first and last years of assessment.

6. A claim is nullified if profits for either year are adjusted for any other reason (for example because of a change of accounting date, or cessation of trade), but any further claim in respect of the profits as adjusted is not out of time if made before one year from 31 January following the tax year in which the adjustment is made.

Carry-back claims under self-assessment

7. The treatment under self-assessment of claims that affect an earlier year is that although the effect of the adjustment is *calculated* by reference to the tax position in the earlier year, the adjustment is *given effect* in the later year (TMA 1970 Sch 1B). The adjustment does not, however, affect the tax *assessed* for the later year. For taxpayers who are calculating their own tax, the amount of any tax underpaid for the earlier year is shown in box 13 on the Tax Calculation Summary accompanying the tax return and any overpayment is shown in box 14.

   Carried back amounts do not affect payments on account for the first of the two years that are averaged, because the tax of the earlier year is not adjusted. The payments on account for the second of the averaged years will initially be based on the unaveraged profits of the first year. Once the liability for the second year can be accurately ascertained, based on the averaged profits, a claim can be made to reduce payments on account if appropriate. The change to the assessable profit of the second year affects the payments on account for the next following year, which are based on the tax *assessed* for the second year.

   The treatment of averaging claims under self-assessment means that even if an averaging adjustment which reduces the profits of the current year does not save any tax overall, because it is balanced by an increase of the same amount in the tax payable for the previous year, a cash flow advantage will still arise. This is because the reduction in the current year's tax reduces the payments on account for the next following year. Furthermore, if the reduction of the current year's liability reduces the amount payable below the payments on account made for that year, repayment supplement will be payable on the overpaid amounts as at 31 January in the tax year and 31 July following, even though the overpayment will be balanced by an underpayment for the previous year, that underpayment being payable by 31 January following the current year.

   Thus in part B(ii) of the example, the repayment based on 2007/08 does not alter the payments for that year, or payments on account for 2008/09, but is repayable after any outstanding tax (and tax due within 35 days) is settled. Once the revised liability for 2008/09 is known, a claim may be made to reduce payments on account for that year to the revised liability, repayment supplement being paid where appropriate. Following the next claim to average 2008/09 with 2009/10, this increases the liability for 2008/09, the increase being added to the tax due for 2009/10 (ie on 31 January 2011) but the adjustment does not affect the payments on account for any year, nor does it affect the tax *assessed* for 2009/10, so that the payments on account for 2010/11 are based on the 2009/10 tax due of £7,402 less the tax of £1,000 deducted at source.

   Interest on overdue or overpaid tax is charged from 31 January following the second year. There is therefore no interest benefit from an adjustment that reduces the tax of the earlier year as in 2007/08 in B(ii) above. On the other hand there is no interest disadvantage from an averaging adjustment that increases the tax of the earlier year as in 2008/09 in B(ii) above. And where the tax of the second year is reduced as a result of the adjustment, then interest will be paid on overpaid payments on account for the second year as indicated above. For detailed notes on carry-back claims see Example 43.

Partnerships

8. Under the current year basis, averaging claims are made by individual partners in respect of their shares of the profit and not in respect of the partnership as a whole.

Farming treated as one trade

9. In part B of the example, Harold's trade is treated as continuing notwithstanding his change of farms, since all farming carried on by any particular person is treated as one trade (ITTOIA 2005 s 9).

Where the trade is carried on by a firm then that trade is separate from any farming trade carried on by an individual who is a partner of the firm (s 859).

Restrictions on relief for farming losses

10.   The farmers in both parts of this example have made intermittent profits and losses. There are special rules where farmers sustain losses over a long period. Relief for a loss against general income (ITA 2007 s 64) in a trade of farming and market gardening is not available if a loss (calculated without reference to capital allowances) has been made in each of the five tax years preceding the loss-making year in question. Certain exceptions are made to this rule (ITA 2007 s 67). One such exception applies where the trade is carried on with 'a reasonable expectation of profit'.

Similar rules apply to a loss in a company accounting period following a five-year run of losses (ICTA 1988 s 397).

Losses prevented from being relieved against general income (s 64) under the above provisions can be carried forward (under s 83) against later profits from the same trade.

Although under the current year basis rules, capital allowances are treated as trading expenses, and are thus part of a trading loss, losses are still calculated before capital allowances for the purpose of s 67.

National insurance contributions

11.   For detailed notes on national insurance contributions see Example 48.

Tax Credits

12.   For detailed notes on tax credits see Example 7 and for interaction with losses Example 29.

Question

(a)   Somerton, Tiverton and Dulverton have been trading in partnership for many years sharing profits and losses after charging interest on capital and salaries in the proportions of one-half, one-fifth and three-tenths respectively, drawing up accounts to 30 April annually. Interest on capital amounts to £3,200, £2,260 and £940 respectively. Dulverton is entitled to a salary of £16,000 and Somerton to a salary of £8,000.

The partnership results for the years to 30 April 2009 and 2010 are as follows:

		Profit (loss) £
Year to 30 April	2009	18,600
	2010	(9,600)

Show the tax allocation of trading profits and losses for the two years, and show what ITA 2007 s 64 claims may be made assuming that the partners have substantial other income.

(b)   John, Paul and George have been partners in a firm of turf accountants for many years, making up accounts annually to 31 July and sharing profits and losses in the ratio 40:35:25. The accounts for recent periods, as adjusted for tax purposes, have shown the following profits and losses:

	£
Year to 31 July 2008	53,200
Year to 31 July 2009	11,800
Period to 31 January 2010	(43,920)
Total of partners' overlap profits for 8 months from 1 August 1996 to 5 April 1997	19,867

On 31 January 2010 John retired due to ill health.

Calculate the assessable profits for 2008/09 and 2009/10 and show the allocation of these profits among the partners. Show also how the loss to 31 January 2010 is treated and indicate the loss claims available to each partner.

Ignore capital allowances.

(c)   Greely is a limited partner in a partnership and under the partnership agreement his share of the profits or losses of the business is 25%. His capital introduced was £10,000.

During the year to 31 March 2010 the partnership suffered a loss of £60,000.

Calculate Greely's share of the loss for income tax purposes.

(d)   Victoria became a member of Posh LLP, a trading limited liability partnership, on 6 April 2006, introducing capital of £10,000 into the LLP. The LLP makes up accounts annually to 5 April. During the year ended 5 April 2010 Victoria made a further capital contribution of £27,000 for the purposes of the partnership's trade. Victoria has sufficient other income to claim full loss relief under ITA 2007 s 64 in all years.

The profit/losses attributable to Victoria are as follows:

	£	
Year to 5 April 2008	(6,000)	Loss
Year to 5 April 2009	(6,000)	Loss
Year to 5 April 2010	(30,000)	Loss
Year to 5 April 2011	34,000	Profit

Set out the amounts of sideways loss relief available for each year.

(e) Richard and Judy commence trading as property developers on 6 April 2009. The partnership is funded by capital introduced of:

Richard   £500,000
Judy   £10,000

It is agreed that Richard be entitled to a salary of £50,000 and profits and losses be divided equally. Richard works full time in the business but Judy only works five hours per week, on average, for the partnership.

The results for the first three years are:

	Profit (loss) £
Year to 5 April 2010	(100,000)
Year to 5 April 2011	(30,000)
Year to 5 April 2012	80,000

On 31 March 2012 Judy contributes further capital of £20,000 for the purpose of the partnership's trade. Both Richard and Judy have sufficient other income to utilise their share of losses for all relevant years. They have made no capital withdrawals from the partnership.

Set out the amount of ITA 2007 ss 64 or 72 loss relief available for Richard and Judy for each year and the amount of loss relief carried forward after making maximum claims against other income.

Answer

(a) **Somerton, Tiverton and Dulverton**

Profit of year to 30 April 2009

	Total £	Somerton £	Tiverton £	Dulverton £
Interest on capital	6,400	3,200	2,260	940
Salaries	24,000	8,000	–	16,000
Balance ½, 1/5, 3/10	(11,800)	(5,900)	(2,360)	(3,540)
	18,600	5,300	(100)	13,400
Eliminate Tiverton's 'loss' 5,300:13,400		(28)	100	(72)
Division of assessable profit	18,600	5,272	–	13,328

The partners are individually assessable on their profit shares in 2009/10.

Loss of year to 30 April 2010 available for relief under s 64

	Total £	Somerton £	Tiverton £	Dulverton £
Interest on capital	6,400	3,200	2,260	940
Salaries	24,000	8,000	–	16,000
Balance ½, 1/5, 3/10	(40,000)	(20,000)	(8,000)	(12,000)
	(9,600)	(8,800)	(5,740)	4,940
Eliminate Dulverton's 'profit' 8,800:5,740		2,990	1,950	(4,940)
Final division of loss	(9,600)	(5,810)	(3,790)	–

Each partner's share of the loss is a loss of 2010/11 for ITA 2007 s 64 claims, relief for which may be claimed against total income of 2010/11 and/or 2009/10 (see explanatory note 2). Since they have substantial other income, they will be able to obtain full relief in either year. If relief is claimed against 2009/10 income, Somerton's share of £5,810 would eliminate his profit share of £5,272 and the balance of £538 would be set against his other income. Since Tiverton's 2009/10 profit share was nil, his share of the loss, ie £3,790, would all be set against his other income. (The losses set against non-trading income would still be available to reduce the partners' later profit shares for calculating Class 4 national insurance contributions.)

Carrying back losses does not, however, reduce the tax of the earlier year (see Example 42 for details). Relief is *calculated* by reference to the earlier year but is *given effect* in relation to the loss year. Furthermore, the tax saving through the carryback claim does not affect the calculation of payments on account for any year (although the refund flowing from the loss claim may enable payments on account to be discharged or repaid). Somerton and Tiverton may prefer to claim relief against their 2010/11 income, providing the rate of tax saved was the same. This would then reduce the tax *assessable* for that year, enabling 2010/11 payments on account to be discharged or repaid and affecting the calculation of payments on account for 2011/12.

(b) **Assessments on John, Paul & George 2008/09 and 2009/10**

Under the current year basis, each partner is treated as if he carried on a separate notional trade, which ceases when he leaves the partnership, unless he continues the business on his own, in which case the actual date of cessation is taken. When John retires on 31 January 2010, therefore, his business is treated as having ceased and he can claim terminal loss relief if appropriate.

The accounting date has been changed by making up accounts to 31 January. Unless the partnership choose to notify the change to HMRC, the accounts to 31 January 2010 could be regarded as interim (see Example 28). The next accounts could be made up for the six months to 31 July 2010 and the two sets of results amalgamated as far as Paul and George are concerned. On the assumption that the accounting date is in fact changed permanently, the position would be as follows:

Individual assessments 2008/09

The 2008/09 assessments are based on the profit of the year to 31 July 2008, which is divided as follows:

	Total £	John (40%) £	Paul (35%) £	George (25%) £
	53,200	21,280	18,620	13,300

Position for 2009/10

There will be nil assessments in 2009/10, since the basis period runs from 1.8.08 to 31.1.10 and the combined result of the accounts of that period shows losses for each partner as follows:

	Total £	John (40%) £	Paul (35%) £	George (25%) £
Yr to 31.7.08	11,800	4,720	4,130	2,950
6 mths to 31.1.09	(43,920)	(17,568)	(15,372)	(10,980)
Loss in basis period		(12,848)	(11,242)	(8,030)

Division of overlap profits

	Total £	John (40%) £	Paul (35%) £	George (25%) £
	19,867	7,947	6,953	4,967

As indicated in the example, the overlap relief covers the eight months from 1 August 1996 to 5 April 1997. John's share of the overlap relief would be taken into account in full on the cessation of his business. Since the 2009/10 basis period spans 18 months, Paul and George would include in their allowable losses for 2009/10 a six months' proportion of their overlap relief, ie 6/8ths = £5,215 and £3,725 respectively, leaving overlap profits carried forward of £1,738 and £1,242 respectively.

Share of 2009/10 losses for ITA 2007 s 64 claims

Under the current year basis, losses are calculated for the same periods as profits for ITA 2007 s 64 claims. Available losses are therefore as follows.

	John (40%) £	Paul (35%) £	George (25%) £
Loss as above	12,848	11,242	8,030
Overlap relief	7,947	5,215	3,725
	20,795	16,457	11,755

Relief is available against the *total* income of 2009/10 and/or 2008/09. Although the partners' other income is not known, each has sufficient *trading* income in 2008/09 to obtain full relief for his loss share, although unless there is other income some of their personal allowance would be wasted. In addition to the tax saving, the loss claim would eliminate the 2008/09 Class 4 national insurance contributions. If loss relief was claimed against other income in 2009/10, John would lose the benefit of reducing Class 4 contributions, but Paul and George would be able to set the losses against later *trading* income for Class 4 purposes. If Paul and George did not wish to claim relief under ITA 2007 s 64 their shares would be carried forward under ITA 2007 s 83 to set against later trading profits.

John's loss for ITA 2007 s 89 terminal loss claim

John's terminal loss is the loss from 1.2.09 to 31.1.10, excluding any loss for which relief has already been obtained, and including the *whole* of any available overlap relief. John had a loss of £12,848 in the 18 months' basis period for 2009/10, and the whole of his share of the profit of the year to 31 July 2009, ie £4,720, was taken into account in arriving at that amount. His loss of £17,568 has therefore been relieved to that extent, so that only £12,848 can be included in the terminal loss claim. This is then augmented by the overlap relief of £7,947 to give a terminal loss of £20,795, which is the same as under ITA 2007 s 64. Since John has no trading income in 2009/10, this could be fully relieved against his 2008/09 trading profit. Had the loss been larger it could have been carried back against his 2007/08 profits and then his 2006/07 profits.

Effect of carry-back claims

As indicated in part (a), carry-back claims are *calculated* by reference to the tax position of the earlier year but are *given effect* for the later year (see Example 43 for details).

(c) Greely

Greely's share of the loss of £60,000 for the year to 31 March 2010 is £15,000. Since his capital contribution is only £10,000, however, and he is a limited partner, he may not claim loss relief against income other than from the business on any amount in excess of £10,000, plus the amount of his undrawn profits, less any part thereof that has been offset by earlier losses.

(d) Victoria, partner in Posh LLP

As a member of Posh LLP, Victoria is entitled to ITA 2007 s 64 relief for her share of losses arising, subject to maximum loss claims not exceeding her subscribed capital. This restriction would not apply if the LLP carried on a profession.

Her s 64 loss claims are as follows:

2007/08	£6,000	(capital remaining £4,000)
2008/09	£4,000	(capital remaining nil, loss carried forward £2,000)
2009/10	£25,000	(capital contributed £27,000 of which £25,000 used, leaving £4,000 (£2,000 + £2,000 from 2008/09) carried forward)

In 2009/10 her actual loss of £30,000 can be increased by the unrelieved loss of £2,000 brought forward, making £32,000 available for relief against future profits of the partnership trade, or partially at relievable against other income subject to restrictions of ITA 2007 Chapter 3. Since Victoria contributed £27,000 for the purposes of the trade, her sideways loss relief is limited to the lower of £32,000 available losses, £27,000 capital contribution and £25,000 annual cap ie £25,000, leaving £7,000 available to carry forward.

(e)   **Richard and Judy**

Loss of year to 5 April 2010

	Total £	Richard £	Judy £
Salary	50,000	50,000	
Balance equally	(150,000)	(75,000)	(75,000)
	(100,000)	(25,000)	(75,000)

The 2009/10 assessments will be *nil* for both partners. Relief will be available under s 64 in 2009/10 or 2008/09 or under s 72 in 2006/07 against other income as follows:

	Richard £	Judy £
Loss as above	25,000	75,000
ITA 2007 s 64/ s 72		
Restricted to contribution to trade	25,000	10,000
Restricted loss carried forward	–	65,000

Loss of year to 5 April 2011

	Total £	Richard £	Judy £
Salary	50,000	50,000	–
Balance equally	(80,000)	(40,000)	(40,000)
	(30,000)	10,000	(40,000)
Element of Richard's profit	–	10,000	10,000
	(30,000)	–	(30,000)

The 2009/10 assessments will be *nil* for both partners. Richard does not have a share of loss to use in an ITA 2007 ss 64 or 72 claim.

Judy has fully used her 'contribution to trade' and therefore can only add the loss of £30,000 to the amount of restricted loss brought forward of £65,000 to carry forward £95,000 to 2010/11.

Profit of the year to 5 April 2012

	Total £	Richard £	Judy £
Salary	50,000	50,000	–
Balance equally	30,000	15,000	15,000
	80,000	65,000	15,000

Richard will be assessed on profits of £65,000 in 2011/12.

Judy for 2011/12 has:

	£
Profits	15,000
Restricted loss brought forward	95,000
Available restricted loss	80,000

	£
s 64 / s 72 loss claim (being contribution to trade)	20,000
Restricted losses carried forward	60,000

Her assessment will be nil with relief for £20,000 given under s 64 in either 2011/12 or 2010/11, or under s 72 in 2008/09.

Had the £20,000 been contributed for purposes of obtaining loss relief, not for purposes of the trade, no sideways relief would be due.

Explanatory Notes

Commencement and cessation

1.   Each partner is treated as starting a new business when he joins a partnership (unless he previously carried on the business as a sole trader) and as ceasing business when he leaves, unless he continues the business on his own, in which case he will not be treated as ceasing until that business is permanently discontinued (ITTOIA 2005 s 852).

As and when a partner is treated as ceasing business, he may claim terminal loss relief if appropriate (ITA 2007 s 89) (see part (b) of the example, and also Example 32).

Losses are personal to the partners, so if anyone retires or dies with unrelieved losses, the losses cannot be transferred to the other partners.

Losses for ITA 2007 s 64 claims

2.   Under the current year basis rules, loss relief under s 64 is given against the income of the current and/or previous tax years.

Losses carried forward

3.   In calculating a loss available to carry forward under s 83, any loss that has been relieved in some other way must be excluded. This includes not only relief by way of another loss claim but also relief by aggregating the loss with a profit in arriving at the assessable result for a year. Hence the restriction on the losses available to be carried forward by Paul and George in part (b) of the example.

Extended carry back

4.   Although not relevant to any of the examples considered, Finance Act 2009 Sch 6 introduces an extended loss carry-back for both income and corporation tax. For income tax, losses in the fiscal years 2008/09 and 2009/10 may be carried back by three years. In order to claim relief, at least one claim under ITA 2007 s 64 must be made. The new relief then provides relief against profits of the same trade by a single claim affecting all relevant years. For 2008/09 losses, the claim under section 64 might be made in 2008/09, in which case the new relief would then be a three-year claim affecting 2007/08, 2006/07 and 2005/06 in that order. If a claim was made under s 64 in respect of 2007/08, then the new claim would provide relief only in 2006/07 and 2005/06.

The additional relief is restricted so that only £50,000 of the loss can be carried back by more than one year. If the business ceases so that the loss is incurred in a short period, this restriction is reduced pro rata.

The relief is quite attractive as it allows the claimant to leave other income in charge to tax, so that personal allowances can cover it, thus providing more relief than might otherwise be available.

For more details see Example 29.

Unusual profit/loss allocations

5. It is not possible for one partner to show a loss for tax purposes whilst there is an overall profit, and vice versa.

    Hence the elimination of Tiverton's minus share in the year to 30 April 2009 and Dulverton's plus share in the year to 30 April 2010 in part (a) of the example. The amount that has to be eliminated is split between the other partners in the ratio of their shares of the original allocation.

    If, exceptionally, the partnership agreement provides that losses are to be shared in a different proportion to profits and the accounting results show a profit whereas the taxable amount is a loss then the partnership agreement applies to the accounting results even if the effect is to divide the loss for taxation in a different proportion to that provided for by the partnership agreement.

    In both of the above cases it would be possible to provide in the partnership agreement for a tax indemnity for any tax costs arising to a partner due to the taxable division being different to that provided for by the profit share in the partnership agreement.

Non-active partners'/limited partners' loss relief restriction

6. The provisions of the Income Tax Act 2007 restrict loss relief for limited or non-active partners in traditional partnerships (ss 103–106) and LLPs (ss 107–114). Loss relief is limited to a maximum of capital contributed (provided it is not contributed for the purposes of obtaining a tax advantage), but from 2 March 2007 this is capped to a maximum of £25,000 per tax year.

    These restrictions apply to ITA 2007 s 64 'sideways relief' for losses against general income, s 72 losses in the early years of the trade, and set off against capital gains (TCGA 1992 s 261B). These restrictions were introduced to counter tax avoidance schemes using partnership losses to reduce income tax liabilities. These restrictions do not apply to general partners, and losses continue to be available for offset against profits arising from the partnership trade.

    The definition of 'limited partner' is widely drawn and covers any person in partnership who acts in substance as a limited partner, who is not entitled to take part in the management of the trade, and whose liability for debts incurred for the purposes of the trade is limited. A 'non-active partner' is an individual who does not devote a significant amount of time to the trade specified as an average of at least ten hours per week personally engaged in activities for the purposes of the trade. This applies both to LLPs and traditional partnerships. Finance Act 2008 inserted a further requirement that the activities are carried out on a commercial basis with a view to the realisation of profits as a result of those activities. This additional condition applies to relevant periods ending on or after 12 March 2008.

    Capital contributions specifically include any share of profit added to capital, as well as funds contributed. However, ITA 2007 s 113A disallows amounts contributed for the purposes of obtaining tax relief. Capital contributions are reduced by amounts paid back at any time (five years for an LLP) while the individual is in partnership, unless the withdrawal gives rise to an income tax charge as profits of the trade.

    The additional restrictions of the £25,000, and test of purpose of the capital contribution, were introduced with effect from 2 March 2007. There are transitional provisions for periods straddling this date. There are exclusions and alternative restrictions for Film Relief.

Film partnership

7. The provisions of ITA 2007 ss 115–116 restrict loss relief in film making partnerships. They are targeted at individuals using such partnerships for the purposes of obtaining loss relief, and apply particularly to individuals who do not devote a significant amount of time to the trade.

Limited liability partnerships

8.   For detailed notes on limited liability partnerships see Example 26 part (b) and explanatory notes 12 and 13.

National insurance contributions

9.   For detailed notes on national insurance contributions see Example 48.

Question

A.

Mr Harding, a married man born in 1955, is a British subject who is not resident in the UK.

His income for 2009/10 is:

	£
UK rental income (net amount after basic rate tax)	3,816
Interest (gross) from 3½% War Loan	1,500
Earnings from employment abroad	60,000
Interest from Canada (gross)	150

His employment is with a company resident outside the UK for whom he has worked for seven years and none of the duties are performed in the UK. The country in which he works is outside the European Community and he is not a servant of the Crown.

His wife accompanied him abroad, but is not working there, and she returns to their UK home for the main school holidays when their children aged 17 and 14 are home from boarding school (approximately two months each year). Both husband and wife are regarded as neither resident nor ordinarily resident in the UK. Mrs Harding has UK building society interest of £5,000 per annum (received in full), an annuity from a family trust of £4,770 per annum (from which basic rate tax is deducted), and interest of £250 on a foreign bank account.

Compute the amount of UK income tax payable by or repayable to Mr and Mrs Harding for the year 2009/10 assuming that any available relief is claimed.

Ignore double taxation.

B.

Mr Carey, a single man, is a British subject who is domiciled, resident and ordinarily resident in the United Kingdom. He is taking up employment in France on 1 August 2009 and plans to make his permanent home there.

Relevant details of his tax position are as follows:

	2009/10 (to 31.7.09) £
Salary	7,200
Tax paid under PAYE	1,008
UK bank interest – amount received (April to July)	24

The following additional information is available:

(a)   He will retain the bank account and expects the interest credited on 31 December 2009 to be £100.

(b)   He is renting out his house furnished and will get £180 per week (for twenty-eight weeks in 2009/10), which will be collected by an agent. The agent will deduct tax at the basic rate from the net rents and pay it over to HMRC.

Expenses are estimated at £1,500 for 2009/10, including mortgage interest from 1 August 2009.

(i)   State what action Mr Carey should take in relation to his UK tax position before he leaves.

(ii) Show Mr Carey's estimated tax position for 2009/10, indicating the amount of tax refund which is likely to arise.

(iii) Show how Mr Carey's tax position would alter if he did not settle in France and returned to live in England in February 2011.

Answer

A. **United Kingdom income tax position 2009/10**

	UK income £	UK tax paid £
Mr Harding		
UK rental income (3,816 + 954)	4,770	954
Personal allowance (part)	(4,770)	
Taxable income	–	
Tax repayable		954
Mrs Harding	£	£
UK annuity	4,770	954
UK building society interest	5,000	–
	9,770	954
Personal allowance	6,475	
Taxable income	3,295	
Tax thereon: 2,440 @ 10%*	244	
855 @ 20%	171	415
Tax repayable		539

> * Since Mrs Harding's taxable income is all savings income (the annuity being set off against her personal allowance), she remains entitled to the 10% starting rate.

B.

(i) **Action to be taken by Mr Carey before emigration**

(a) Arrange for agent to receive rental monies and pay tax quarterly to HMRC on the net rental income.

(b) Write to notify HMRC that he is emigrating and asking for a self-assessment return to be sent in due course to enable him to claim a tax refund.

(c) Inform bank of his change in status so that he can then receive interest gross.

(ii) **Estimated income tax position for 2009/10**

	£	UK income £	Tax deducted £
Salary		7,200	1,008
Rental income (see explanatory notes 6 and 8)*		3,036	607
Bank interest**			
To 31.7.09 (24 + tax deducted 6)	30		6
December 2009	100	130	
		10,366	1,621
Personal allowance		6,475	
Income chargeable to tax		3,891	
Tax thereon: @ 20%			778

	£	UK income £	Tax deducted £
Refund due			843
* Rental income (28 weeks at £180)			5,040
Less: Estimated expenses		1,500	
Wear and tear allowance 10% of £5,040		504	2,004
Amount assessable			3,036

* The deduction of tax at source may be applied to the profits after deductible expenses (20% × £3,036) = £607.

** £24 bank interest received to 31.7.09 is after deduction of 20% tax. £100 interest in December 2009 is received gross.

(iii) **If Mr Carey resumed UK residence in February 2011**

If Mr Carey is absent from the UK only from 1 August 2009 to January 2011 his absence will not have spanned a tax year and he will be regarded as having remained resident and ordinarily resident in the UK throughout. He will be liable to UK tax on his earnings in France, subject to double tax relief for tax suffered in France. Since his UK income will have been fully charged to tax (see explanatory note 6) there will be no other change to his tax position (unless other income had arisen to him while he was in France). Tax will again be deducted at source from his bank interest.

Mr Carey should have submitted his 2009/10 tax return by 31 January 2011 (or by 31 October 2010 if submitting on paper), but may not have received the calculated refund at the time he returns to the UK. He will need to notify an amendment to the return to bring the French earnings into charge and the tax position will need to be recalculated. Depending on the tax deducted by the French authorities he may still have overpaid tax for 2009/10. If not, however, he will be charged interest on any underpayment from 31 January 2011.

Explanatory Notes

Personal allowances for non-residents

1. Non-residents are not entitled to UK personal allowances unless they qualify under the provisions of either ITA 2007 s 56(3) or ICTA 1988 s 278, or under the terms of a double taxation agreement. The main categories of qualifying non-resident are citizens of the UK, Commonwealth or Republic of Ireland, residents of the Isle of Man or Channel Islands and EEA nationals (the EEA covers the European Union plus Iceland, Liechtenstein and Norway). Non-residents will not normally be able to register as blind and will not therefore be entitled to blind person's allowance. The available allowances may be set against any of the person's income which is liable to tax in the UK (ITA 2007 ss 34(2) and 42(4) and ICTA 1988 s 278). From 6 April 2010 no personal allowance will be available to those who qualify only on grounds of being citizens of former Commonwealth countries, but many affected individuals will qualify in any event under Double Taxation Agreements (FA 2009 Sch 1).

To qualify for tax credits Mr or Mrs Harding have to be 'in the UK' (physically present here) and ordinarily resident within the meaning of the Tax Credits legislation (see TCTM02003 of the HMRC's Tax Credit Technical Manual as to how HMRC interpret ordinary residence for this purpose). It is unlikely that either Mr Harding or Mrs Harding would qualify as ordinarily resident under the tax credits tests so no entitlement to CTC will arise. If Mrs Harding was able to establish ordinary residence for the future she would make a claim for tax credits as a single person based on the number of days she was 'in the UK' (ignoring certain periods of temporary absence – see SI 2003/654 reg 4). Only her income would count in the tax credits claim.

Government 'FOTRA' securities

2.   Government securities are not liable to UK income tax whilst in beneficial ownership of persons not ordinarily resident in the UK (ITTOIA 2005 s 713). Such securities are referred to as FOTRA securities (Free Of Tax to Residents Abroad). The exemption does not, however, apply where the interest is received as part of a trade carried on in the UK.

UK dividend tax credits

3.   Non-residents are not automatically entitled to a tax credit on UK dividends (ITTOIA 2005 s 397). A person who claims UK personal allowances under ITA 2007 Pt 3 (in accordance with s 56) or ICTA 1988 s 278 is, however, entitled to a tax credit (s 397(4)). Sometimes a double tax agreement may provide for income that is not exempt from UK tax to be charged at a reduced rate, for example interest may be taxed only at 10%. Tax credits for non-residents are provided for in most double taxation agreements (ICTA 1988 s 788) and the agreement may provide that the UK tax is not to exceed 15% of the tax credit inclusive amount. Now that the UK tax credit rate is only 10% such a restriction is not relevant.

Although UK dividend tax credits are not repayable to UK residents, non-residents are still entitled to repayment under double tax agreements if the credit exceeds the rate under the agreement, but the reduction of the UK tax credit rate to 10% means that repayments will rarely arise.

Where a dividend is received by a non-resident who is neither within the categories entitled to UK allowances as in note 1, nor entitled to relief under a double tax agreement, he is liable to tax only on the tax credit exclusive amount and then only to the extent, if any, of higher rate tax over lower rate tax (ITTOIA 2005 ss 399 and 400).

Working/living abroad

4.   Someone who is working full-time abroad for a period spanning a complete tax year is treated as non-resident from the date of leaving the UK to the date of return, providing that UK visits during the absence are less than 183 days in any tax year, and average less than 91 days in a tax year (taken over a maximum of 4 years). However, recent cases have emphasised that the individual must first effect a proper departure from the UK.

For the purposes of the 183-day rule (and 91-day rule below), days are counted as spent in the UK if the individual is present in the UK at midnight at the end of that day with effect from 6 April 2008. There are limited exceptions for individuals whose presence at midnight is merely because they are in transit and their functions carried out whilst in the UK are not substantial.

The 91-day rule is not statutory but, provided that the other criteria are complied with, HMRC will honour it. However, given that the 91-day rule is not statutory, the Courts will not necessarily follow this methodology. This can work both to the advantage of and against taxpayers.

The residence status of spouses and civil partners is determined independently. Where, however, someone who satisfies the above conditions is accompanied or later joined abroad by his/her spouse/civil partner, the same treatment applies to the accompanying/joining spouse/civil partner, whether or not he/she works full-time abroad.

See Example 12 part A(i) for the treatment of those who leave the UK without taking up full-time employment abroad.

New guidance on establishing non-residence has been issued as booklet HMRC 6, which is available on HMRC's website.

Split-year treatment

5. Strictly the question of whether a person is resident or not resident in the United Kingdom ought to be decided for the tax year as a whole. By Concession A11, however, HMRC split the year for a person either coming to the UK for permanent residence, or leaving the UK for permanent residence abroad. This concession also applies to someone going to take up full-time employment abroad, providing they are away for a complete tax year, the employment lasts throughout that tax year, and interim UK visits during the absence do not amount to 183 days or more in any tax year or an average of 91 days or more in a tax year (taken over a maximum period of 4 years). A further concession (A78) extends the same treatment to a non-working spouse or civil partner accompanying or later joining his or her spouse or civil partner who is working full-time abroad. For the split-year rules in relation to capital gains tax see Example 73 part (c).

    Where the tax year is split under Concession A11, the limit on income chargeable on non-residents outlined in note 6 does not apply for that tax year. Even though income for each part of the year is calculated according to whether the individual is, or is not, resident, full personal allowances are available for that tax year.

    As Mr Carey emigrates in 2009/10 in part B of the example, therefore:

    (a) His income arising in 2009/10 after the date of emigration will be assessed as if he were not resident, ie no liability on his foreign income (his French salary) but liability on income arising in the UK (his rental income and bank interest).

    (b) Full personal allowances will be available for 2009/10.

    (c) From 2010/11 the provisions in note 6 will apply.

Taxation of non-residents

6. There is a general requirement for tax at the basic rate to be deducted from interest paid to a person whose usual place of residence is outside the UK (ITA 2007 s 874), but this is subject to various exceptions (see Example 5 part (a)). One of the exceptions covers banks and building societies, who will pay interest gross to deposit holders who provide them with a declaration that they are not ordinarily resident in the UK, and give their address abroad (ITA 2007 s 858).

    Since 6 April 2001 banks, building societies etc have been required to provide information to HMRC on interest paid to depositors whether or not ordinarily resident in the UK. Paying and collecting agents who handle interest and dividends from abroad are included in the provisions.

    In addition, FA 2006 replaced the existing arrangements for exchange of information with overseas jurisdictions with more extensive arrangements that will cover not only the exchange of information with overseas tax authorities in both directions, but will also allow for enforcement of foreign taxes in the UK, and of UK taxes abroad.

    In April 2006, HMRC were successful in obtaining a disclosure order requiring Barclays Bank, and subsequently other UK banks to provide details of accounts held overseas by customers with UK addresses. This led to a disclosure programme inviting taxpayers to make a voluntary disclosure of undeclared income with penalties fixed at 10%. A second disclosure opportunity was launched from 1 September 2009, following the acquisition of more information from foreign banks, using information powers in the Finance Act 2008 Sch 36.

    In addition to being exempt from tax on interest on government stocks, and possibly on other sources of income under a double tax agreement (see notes 2 and 3), non-residents may receive social security benefits and investment income other than rents in full, even though such income is not exempt. The *maximum* tax payable by a non-resident is the tax, if any, deducted at source from such income plus the tax on any other income, calculated as if personal allowances were not available (ITA 2007 s 811). If a claim is made for UK personal allowances, however, any non-exempt income is taken into account, which effectively means that the allowances are set against the untaxed social security benefits and investment income first.

Thus in part A of the example, both Mr and Mrs Harding have taxed UK income of £4,770. Mr Harding's only other UK income is *exempt* interest on government stocks, so his tax refund following his claim for UK allowances is the full amount of tax deducted, ie £954. Mrs Harding's building society interest, on the other hand, although received gross and not in itself chargeable to UK tax, has to be taken into account in the repayment claim, so she can reclaim only £539 of the £954 deducted from her annuity.

By comparison, if Mrs Harding's UK building society interest had amounted to £10,000, it would have been beneficial for her to forgo personal allowances and exclude the interest from her tax computation, thus having a repayment of:

	UK income £	UK tax paid £
UK annuity	4,770	954
Tax thereon: @ 20%		954
Further tax payable		Nil

Had personal allowances been claimed the computation would have been:

	UK income £	UK tax paid £
UK annuity	4,770	954
UK building society interest	10,000	
	14,770	
Personal allowance	6,475	
	8,295	
Tax thereon: 2,440 @ 10%	244	
5,855 @ 20%	1,171	1,415
Further tax payable		461

In part B of the example, if Mr Carey remained non-resident, the bank interest would escape tax from 2010/11 if he did not claim allowances under ITA 2007 Pt 3 or ICTA 1988 s 278. In view of the level of his rental income, however, it is probable that he would make a claim for allowances, so that the bank interest would be taken into account in arriving at the UK tax payable.

A non-resident who carries on a trade in the UK (on his own or in partnership) is taxed on his profits that relate to the UK trade, measured on an arm's length basis.

This example sets out the basic principles of the taxation of non-residents. Reference must always be made to any relevant double tax agreements, the provisions of which override the tax legislation of the respective countries.

Temporary absences

7. If the absence abroad is not permanent and does not span a complete tax year, a person is regarded as remaining resident and ordinarily resident in the UK throughout. In part B(iii), Mr Carey's French salary would therefore be taxable as earnings, for details of which see Example 12.

Income from property letting

8. Although Mr Carey is letting furnished accommodation in his own home, the rent is not exempt under the rent a room relief provisions of ITTOIA 2005 part 7 Chapter 1, because the property will

not have been his main residence at any time during the rental period (see Example 97 explanatory note 14). If, however, Mr Carey had shared occupation with the tenant before 1 August 2009 then a claim under the rent a room provisions would be available for 2009/10 only.

Where rent is paid to someone who usually lives abroad, tax is normally deducted at the basic rate, as shown in the example, although tax need not be deducted in certain circumstances. For further details see Example 97 explanatory note 11.

Self-assessment

9.   HMRC sometimes makes a provisional repayment to someone who emigrates if they have no continuing sources of UK income. This does not apply to Mr Carey in part B of the example, who will receive UK rents and bank interest.

The self-assessment return contains a non-residence section which is aimed at enabling individuals to work out their own residence status. For further details see Example 12 part A(i). Using the form, Mr Carey would have worked out that he was entitled to split-year treatment for 2009/10, ie to be treated as non-resident from his date of departure, since he intended to be away until after 5 April 2011. He would therefore have excluded his French earnings from the return, and based on his expected liability for 2009/10 a repayment would have been due to him. If he returned in February 2011, however, the liability would change and he would need to notify an amendment to the return, as indicated in the example. The time limit for notifying an amendment is one year from the filing date for the return, ie by 31 January 2012 for the 2009/10 return.

HMRC Residency

10.   There is a separate unit within HMRC which deals with operational and technical work (including compliance) relating to non-resident individuals, non-resident trusts and certain non-resident companies. Its operations include dealing with non-resident landlords and double tax relief claims, and providing advice to individuals on their residence and domicile status.

Payment of tax or national insurance in Euros

11.   Any tax or national insurance can be paid in Euros. There is a helpline on 01274 539630 or 01236 783500. The payment is converted at the current rate of exchange. Any overpayment is repaid in sterling.

Question

(a)   During 2009/10 Johnson, a single man who is resident and ordinarily resident in the UK, has the following income:

	£
Salary from employment	41,035
UK bank interest (tax deducted £348)	1,740
Dividends	
From UK companies	810
From Ruritanian company	255
From Utopian company	315
The following foreign tax had been deducted from the overseas dividends before receipt:	
Ruritanian company	45
Utopian company	315
and additionally the following underlying (indirect) tax had been suffered:	
Utopian company	50

No double taxation agreements exist between either country and the United Kingdom and relief is given unilaterally. Johnson owns 10% of the shares in the Ruritanian company and 5% of the shares in the Utopian company. There is no tax charge on company profits in Ruritania.

Showing the workings of overseas credits, compute the amount of United Kingdom income tax remaining to be paid by Johnson for the year 2009/10 presuming that his salary had been subject to deduction of tax under PAYE of £6,912.

(b)   In 2009/10 Boswell, a married man aged 75 who is resident and ordinarily resident in the UK, had UK income comprising state pension £7,519, UK building society interest (gross) of £5,371, gross foreign interest from Ruritania of £2,000 on which the foreign tax was £300 and gross foreign interest from Narnia of £1,000 on which the foreign tax was £100.

Show his liability to UK tax if he claims double tax relief where appropriate. His wife is aged 67.

Answer

(a)   **Income tax payable by Johnson for 2009/10**

						£
Salary						41,035
Bank interest						1,740
Dividends –	United Kingdom	(810 + 90)				900
	Ruritania	(255 + 45)				300
	Utopia	(315 + 315) ÷ 90%				700
						44,675
Personal allowance						6,475
						38,200

Income tax thereon:					
On non-dividend income	36,300	@ 20%		7,260	
On dividends (part)	1,100	@ 10%		110	
	37,400				
On dividends (balance)	800	@ 32½%		260	7,630
	38,200				

Less: PAYE deductions				6,912		
Tax credit on United Kingdom dividends				90		
Tax credit on foreign dividends						
(treating Utopian dividend as top slice of income)						
Utopian company						
Lower of: Foreign tax			315			
UK tax	700	@ 32½%	228	228		
section 397A credit				70		
Ruritanian company						
Lower of: Foreign tax			45			
UK tax	100	@ 32½%	32			
	200	@ 10%	20	52	45	7,345
	300					
Tax remaining to be paid						£285

(b)   **Boswell's income tax liability for 2009/10**

Claiming double tax relief on dividends and interest

		£
State pension		7,519
UK interest		5,371
Foreign interest	– Ruritania	2,000
	– Narnia	1,000
	– Narnia	1,000
		15,890

	£
Personal allowance (over 75)	9,640
Taxable income	6,250

		£
Tax thereon:	2,440 at starting rate of 10%	244
	3,810 at basic rate of 20%	762
		1,006
Less: age-related married couple's allowance 6,965 @ 10%		696
		310

Less: double tax relief:			
On interest – Ruritania			
Lower of foreign tax	300		
and UK tax 2,000 @ 20% = £400 restricted by allowances to	310	300	
On interest – Narnia			
Lower of foreign tax	100		
and UK tax (310 – 310)	Nil	–	300
UK tax payable			10

Claiming double tax relief only on interest from Ruritania

	£
State pension	7,519
UK interest	5,371
Foreign interest – Ruritania	2,000
Foreign interest net of foreign tax – Narnia	900
	15,790
Personal allowance (age 75)	9,640
Taxable income	6,150

		£
Tax thereon:	2,440 @ 10%	244
	3,710 @ 20%	742
	6,150	986
Less: age-related married couple's allowance 6,965 @ 10%		696
		290
Less: double tax relief on interest – Ruritania:		
Lower of £300 and £290		290
UK tax payable		Nil

Tax payable is £10 less through not claiming double tax relief on foreign interest from Narnia.

Explanatory Notes

Tax on savings income

1. The tax rate on both UK and foreign savings income, excluding dividends, is 20% if the savings income, as the top slice of income, does not exceed the basic rate limit, and 40% on any excess over

the basic rate limit. Any unused starting rate at 10% is also available against savings income (ITA 2007 s 10). The tax rate on both UK and foreign dividend income is 10% if the dividend income, when treated as the top slice of savings income, does not exceed the basic rate limit and 32½% on any excess (ITA 2007 s 13).

These rates do not apply to foreign savings income that is charged on a remittances basis (ie where it is received by someone who is not ordinarily resident and/or not domiciled in the UK). Such income is taxed at non-savings rates.

Double tax relief

2.	Where the same income and capital gains are liable to tax in more than one country, relief for the double tax is given either under the provisions of a double tax treaty or unilaterally (ICTA 1988 ss 788–791, TCGA 1992 s 277).

	Where there is a double tax treaty, it may provide for certain income and gains to be wholly exempt, or for tax to be deducted at a reduced rate (see Example 35 explanatory note 3). Income that is not exempt is charged to UK tax, but a credit is given for the lower of the overseas tax and the UK tax.

	Where there is no treaty, unilateral relief may be claimed against the UK tax at the lower of the overseas tax and the UK tax.

	To counter tax evasion both nationally and internationally, HMRC have the power to obtain relevant tax information from taxpayers and third parties and for such information to be exchanged with, or obtained for, other EU states and countries with whom the UK has made either a double taxation agreement or a tax information exchange agreement (ICTA 1988 ss 815C and 816). FA 2006 contains powers to cancel existing arrangements, and replace them with more comprehensive information exchange arrangements, and also powers to recover tax in overseas courts.

3.	Double tax relief is available only for direct foreign taxes on the income and where the income is dividend income, no credit is available for the underlying tax on the profits out of which the dividend is paid (ICTA 1988 s 790). Where the overseas country operates a similar system to the UK imputation system of corporation tax, under which dividends have tax credits attached and withholding tax is not deducted, the tax credits represent underlying tax and are not eligible for double tax relief unless specifically provided for by the double tax agreement. Where the treaty does not so provide, the net dividend paid is the amount charged to UK tax.

4.	Sources of overseas income may be taken in the order most advantageous to the taxpayer (ICTA 1988 s 796); if the Ruritanian dividend had been regarded as the top slice of income in part (a) of the example, the credits would have been less advantageous, as follows:

	Ruritanian company
	Lower of:	Foreign tax					45
				UK tax		300	@ 32½%		97		£45		(same)

	Utopian company
	Lower of:	Foreign tax					315
				UK tax		500	@ 32½%	163
							200	@ 10%	20	183		£183	(compared with £228)
							700

5.	If following a double tax claim, the amount of foreign tax payable is later adjusted, the amount of double tax relief claimed must be similarly adjusted. If an adjustment to foreign tax results in too much relief having been claimed, HMRC must be notified within one year after the adjustment (ICTA 1988 s 806).

Not claiming double tax relief

6.   If double tax relief is not claimed, the income or gain is charged to UK tax net of the overseas tax suffered (ICTA 1988 s 811, TCGA 1992 s 278). This will rarely be more beneficial, except where the net overseas income is covered by allowances, or tax arising is reduced by other deductions, such as age-related married couple's allowance, as shown in part (b) of the example in relation to the foreign interest. If double tax relief is claimed on both sources of foreign interest, then after treating the Ruritania interest as the top slice of the income, attracting tax of £400, but restricted by claim for age-related married couple's allowance to £310, no UK tax relates to the Narnia interest, so that the double tax relief on that interest is nil. By not claiming double tax relief on the Narnia interest, the tax payable of £290 relates wholly to the Ruritania interest and no tax is suffered on the UK income and the Narnia interest. Although the UK tax on the Ruritania interest is reduced from £310 to £290, this does not reduce the double tax relief because the credit is limited to the foreign tax of £300 in any event.

Basis of assessment of foreign income

7.   For notes on the basis of assessment of foreign income, see Example 5 for saving income and Example 12 for employment income. Where income is charged on the basis of the amount arising abroad, and the income has not been brought into the UK, it is converted into sterling at the exchange rate on the date it arises. Where there are frequent items, an average exchange rate for the year may be used, using rates published by HMRC, providing it is used consistently and does not materially affect the taxable amounts. Income chargeable on the remittances basis should be converted at the rate on the date the income is received in the UK.

UK tax credits in respect of foreign income

8.   From 6 April 2008, individuals who receive dividends from shareholdings of less than 10% in foreign companies are entitled to the equivalent tax credit that they would have had, had the companies been UK-resident. From 6 April 2009 this is extended to all shareholdings of whatever size provided the company is based in a country where there is a double taxation agreement which contains a non-discrimination provision – essentially one which imposes a tax on company profits. Thus Johnson in part A was entitled to the credit for the Utopian company dividend but not that from the Ruritanian company (ITTOIA 2005 s 397A(2) as amended by FA 2009 Sch 19).

The credit is in addition to any foreign tax credit and increases the gross income treated as received. Therefore, Johnson's actual income is £630 (the amount received plus the tax withheld in Utopia. However, it is treated for income tax purposes as £700 with an attached tax credit of £70.

9.   As with UK dividend tax credits, the credit is not repayable. Furthermore, the credit is reduced by any deductions reducing the amount brought into charge (s 397A(3)). Similarly, as is the case in Johnson where the overseas tax credit covers the tax liability on the dividend, no additional credit is available.

Question

Summarise the legislation relating to pension contributions giving brief details of the limits on contributions and the options and benefits available on retirement and death.

Answer

Pension contributions

The legislation covering the taxation treatment of pension contributions was re written with effect from 6 April 2006. Registered pension schemes operate under the rules introduced by Finance Act 2004 Part 4, Finance Act 2005 Part 5 and related regulations.

Where taxpayers had better rights under the previous legislation than under the new rules then existing rights, as at 6 April 2006, were broadly preserved (FA 2004 Sch 36).

An individual can belong to, or contribute to, as many schemes as they wish at any time (FA 2004 s 188). Previously there was a problem of interaction between the varying sets of rules.

The legislation gives tax relief on pension contributions paid to a registered pension scheme in a fiscal year. There are no carry back or carry forward rules. The way in which tax relief is given for contributions made by individuals depends upon the method of payment. This is set out in detail at note 5 below. In the case of contributions paid by an employer tax relief will be given in the accounting period in which contributions are paid (FA 2004 s 196(2)).

Two tests apply to restrict tax relief in any tax year.

Annual allowance (FA 2004 ss 227 to 238)

The first test compares the 'total pension input' for a pension input period ending within a tax year with its annual allowance. The annual allowance was fixed for the first five years at (FA 2004 s 228)

2006/07 – £215,000

2007/08 – £225,000

2008/09 – £235,000

2009/10 – £245,000

2010/11 – £255,000

It was expected that a further five years of allowances would be announced. However, the 2008 Pre-Budget Report announced the annual allowance will be frozen from 2011/12 for five years to 2015/16 at £255,000.

Total pension input (FA 2004 s 229)

In order to be able to have one set of rules it is necessary to compute in each year 'total pension input'. This is the sum of the contributions made to pension policies plus the increase in value of defined pension. See note 3 below as to period that is a 'pension input period' and as to the method of computing the value of pension input from defined benefits schemes.

If exceptionally an individual has 'total pension input' in excess of their annual allowance then there will be a tax charge on the individual of 40% on any amount of pension inputs over the annual allowance (s 227(4)).

Tax relief (FA 2004 ss 186 to 203)

The second test restricts the tax relief available to an individual to:

– Contributions paid by an individual in the fiscal year, to the higher of

  • 100% of UK earnings chargeable to tax, or

  • £3,600 (provided relief at basic rate is given at source)

(FA 2004 s 190).

The interaction between the two tests means that tax relief is effectively limited to the lower of the annual allowance and earnings or if higher £3,600.

Contributions are normally paid net of basic rate tax. However, if contributions are paid in excess of the above limits the excess amount will be allowed to remain within the pension fund, but the excess will be deemed to be a gross contribution. For example, John, who is normally a higher rate tax payer earning approximately £70,000 pa, makes a pension contribution of £8,000 pa each year being a gross contribution of £10,000 less tax relief of £2,000. In 2008/09 John's UK earnings only amounted to £3,000. He will, therefore, have a tax deductible premium of (£2,880 net + £720 tax =) £3,600 being the maximum allowed plus a non-tax allowable contribution of (£8,000 – £2,880) = £5,120 giving a total increase in his pension fund of £8,720.

The rate of tax relief has been restricted from 22 April 2009 for those with income of more than £150,000. See explanatory note 2 for further details.

An individual is entitled to tax relief on pension contributions paid in a tax year provided they are a 'relevant' UK individual (s 188(1)). A relevant UK individual is defined in s 189 as an individual who

–   has UK earnings chargeable to UK income tax, or

–   was resident in the UK at some time during the tax year, or

–   was resident in the UK when they joined the pension scheme and has been resident in the UK during part of the last five years, or

–   the individual or their spouse (or civil partner) has earnings from overseas Crown employment subject to UK tax.

The contributions may be paid directly to the pension provider or paid via an employer sponsored scheme. Relief is also available where the contribution is in the form of a transfer of eligible shares, ie those acquired under a SAYE option scheme or approved share incentive plan (s 195). Such transfers must be made within 90 days of exercising the SAYE option (when the shares are appropriated to the employee). The shares will be treated as a contribution equal to their market value at the date of transfer. Normally contributions are made net of tax and therefore tax relief is given on the grossed up value.

Where pension contributions are made by the employer then the full amount paid in the accounting period may be allowed subject to the usual restriction that the deduction must be for a payment made 'wholly and exclusively' for the purpose of the trade (FA 2004 s 196). (See HMRC manuals at BIM 46001 for further guidance).

In order for pension contributions paid to be allowable they must form part of a normal remuneration package. They are not considered as a stand-alone amount. It follows that a salary sacrifice will not prevent a tax deduction. Contributions will be allowable if the overall salary package is a normal commercial amount.

It is likely that HMRC will disallow any amount identifiable as relating to a non-trade purpose, for example, as part of arrangements to dispose of a business where the payment represents part of the sale proceeds, or of exceptional size. This would be of issue if the employer was not carrying on a trade eg a property holding company. The main focus of disallowance is likely to be in respect of directors who are controlling shareholders or their relatives/friends, and where the salary package has been significantly increased, eg where funds previously taken as dividends are now taken as a pension contribution.

Where exceptionally the employer makes special contributions and those contributions are in excess of £500,000 then the special contribution will be spread over two, three or four years. (FA 2004 s 197). (See Example 38, part A as to the calculation of the special contribution and detailed rules on spreading.)

Where an individual has UK earnings in excess of the annual allowance then tax relief will be granted upon all the contributions made, but the actual tax relief will be limited by the annual allowance charge (FA 2004 s 227). In so far as the contributions are in excess of the annual allowance, an 'annual allowance charge' of 40% will apply to the excess. This will effectively restrict relief to the lower of:

– taxable earnings; or

– contributions,

subject to a maximum of the annual allowance (2009/10 – £245,000).

Lifetime allowance (FA 2004 ss 214–226)

Benefits from money purchase schemes are based upon amounts paid in plus the growth in value of the fund. However defined benefit schemes have benefits based upon final salary and years of service. Both of these principles are restricted by a lifetime limit.

A fund will not be tested during its accumulation periods. The member can have as many different funds as he wishes. The lifetime limit only applies when withdrawals are made. If the fund value on which a withdrawal is to be made exceeds the remaining lifetime allowance then there will be a tax charge. The lifetime allowance was fixed for the first five years at

2006/07	£1,500,000
2007/08	£1,600,000
2008/09	£1,650,000
2009/10	£1,750,000
2010/11	£1,800,000

Again, it was expected that a further five years of allowances would be announced in 2009. However the 2008 Pre-Budget Report announced the lifetime allowance will be frozen from 2011/12 for five years to 2015/16 at £1.8m.

(FA 2004 s 218.)

Benefit crystallisation event (FA 2004 s 216 and Sch 32)

When a withdrawal is made from any fund, other than a transfer to another registered pension scheme or pension splitting, this is known as a 'benefit crystallisation event'. (FA 2004 s 216.)

At that stage the withdrawal is valued and if it exceeds the available lifetime allowance then the excess will be subject to a lifetime allowance charge. If the amount to be used is lower than the remaining lifetime allowance then no tax charge arises but that proportion of the lifetime allowance that has been used will be noted and only the remaining percentage will be available on subsequent benefit crystallisation events (s 219).

Where the amount being used for a benefit crystallisation event exceeds the lifetime allowance then the excess is subject to a lifetime allowance charge (s 215) of

– 25% if the balance is used to buy a pension, or

– 55% if taken as a lump sum.

Pension benefits (FA 2004 ss 164 to 171 and Sch 28 and 29)

Benefits can be taken from most pension schemes from age 50, however from 6 April 2010 the minimum pension age is raised to 55.

Subject to the rules of the pension scheme, which must allow early retirement, there is no requirement for the employee to leave service when starting to draw a pension.

Part of the benefit crystallisation can be taken as a tax free lump sum, to a maximum of 25% of the fund being crystallised, restricted by the lifetime allowance and the scheme rules. This gives an effective maximum for 2009/10 of 25% × £1.75 million = £437,500. Under the legislation all funds have lump sum availability. (Subject to the rules of the specific scheme.)

In the case of a money purchase scheme the lump sum is up to 25% of the fund. In the case of a defined benefit scheme, the scheme pension is multiplied by 20, and any entitlement to a lump sum added, to give a notional value, 25% of which is the maximum lump sum (FA 2004 Sch 29 para 3(6)).

Where a member of a money purchase scheme uses the fund to buy a scheme pension (defined benefits rules then apply) shortly before retirement, then the tax free lump sum is restricted to 25% of the original fund. (FA 2006 Sch 23(22).)

The tax free lump sum cannot be recycled into pension funds, any such recycling will constitute an unauthorised payment (see note 23 as to the tax consequences). This provision applies even if the pension contribution is made before the lump sum is drawn. It does not apply if the total lump sums received in a 12 month period does not exceed 1% of the lifetime limit (2009/10 £17,500) or where the increase in pension contributions do not exceed 30% of the lump sum (Sch 29 para 3A).

The balance of the fund must be used to buy a pension for the life of the member, or this can be provided by the fund. The annuity can be written for the joint lives of the member and spouse (including civil partner) and for a term certain not exceeding ten years.

The pension may be:

– level;

– increasing (including one-off increases);

– linked (eg to RPI or based upon a with profit fund);

– with lump sum death benefits.

Where a pension is purchased with a death benefit then the death benefit must be payable on a death before age 75 and will be subject to a tax charge of 35%. The death benefit must represent the difference between the amounts paid in lifetime and the original amount paid for the annuity policy. Such a policy is known as a 'value protected annuity'.

Where the pension is drawn before aged 75 it may be provided by

– an unsecured pension, or

– part of the fund being used to buy a short-term annuity (up to five years).

By age 75 the fund must have been used to buy a pension, or, where the member has a particular aversion to buying an annuity, to provide an 'alternatively secured pension' (ASP).

An ASP has the attributes of an unsecured pension (income withdrawal). That is to say the fund is not used to buy an annuity but instead the annuity is paid from the fund. However the balance of the 'alternatively secured pension' fund is not available for withdrawal on death. At that time the fund must be used to provide an unsecured pension for spouse, civil partner or dependant, if any, (or ASP if spouse/civil partner is aged 75 or older).

On the death of the spouse, civil partner or dependant or on the death of the member (if no dependants) the remaining alternatively secured pension fund must be gifted to a nominated charity.

A transfer to another member of the same pension scheme is permitted but is treated as an unauthorised payment (FA 2004 s 172BA) subject to a 70% unauthorised payment charge. In addition the payment, net of unauthorised payment charge, may also be subject to inheritance tax. This can increase the total tax charge to 82%. The tax is payable by the pension scheme administrator.

Death benefits (FA 2004 s 167 and Schs 28 and 29)

Where a death occurs before age 75 the whole of the fund, including contributions and growth in value and any insured or uninsured benefits payable on death, may be paid as a death benefit, with no tax, provided it is before crystallisation and the total of all of the funds do not exceed the lifetime allowance. Similar provisions apply to the proceeds of tax registered overseas pension schemes.

Any amount in excess of the lifetime allowance is subject to tax of 55% (25% if taken as a pension by a surviving spouse).

After benefits have crystallised in an unsecured pension any remaining amounts on death drawn as cash will be subject to a tax charge of 35%. Such payments can only be made providing death occurs before age 75.

After age 75 the fund must have been used to buy an annuity or to have changed to an ASP which cannot pay a death benefit.

Overseas pension schemes (FA 2004 s 150(7))

Payments to recognised overseas pension schemes will also attract tax relief. If payments are not made by way of a deduction from pay (before tax) then the contributions are included on the tax return and full relief given subject to the same restrictions as for UK based schemes. To check whether a scheme is recognised see www.hmrc.gov.uk/pensionschemes/qrops.pdf.

Further details

See notes 1 to 13 below for examples of maximum pension contributions, annual allowance charge and lifetime allowance charge. The notes also give more details on how tax relief will be given, transitional provisions, unsecured pension, alternatively secured pensions and term assurance.

Notes 13 to 26 give details of the interactions with other legislation, such as national insurance, losses, divorce and tax credits.

Explanatory Notes

1. From 6 April 2006 the previous tax provisions relating to occupational and personal pension schemes were replaced by a single scheme for all registered pension schemes.

    Pension providers are able to invest in many types of investment, excluding residential property, and certain tangible moveable property where the policy holder can influence investment decisions (FA 2004 Sch 29A). The borrowing limits are restricted, normally to a maximum of 50% of the fund value. The minimum pension age will rise from 50 to 55 on 6 April 2010 (earlier retirement still being permitted on ill health grounds).

Restriction of higher rate tax relief for pension contributions

2. The government intends to restrict higher rate tax relief for pension contributions for those with income of £150,000 or more from 6 April 2011 (2011/12). Relief will be tapered away so that those with income over £180,000 will only receive basic rate (20%) tax relief for their pension contributions. Draft legislation in respect of the new proposed rules for 2011/12 has not yet been issued.

    New rules have been introduced to prevent individuals taking advantage of the delayed introduction of the restriction in relief. FA 2009 Sch 35 introduces a special annual allowance charge which limits tax relief for contributions made in 2009/10 and 2010/11 for those with income of £150,000 or more and who change their normal pattern of regular pension contributions after 22 April 2009. Where total (including employer or third party) pension contributions in a tax year exceed £20,000 the new charge of 20% may be levied and collected via self-assessment. For 2009/10 the £20,000 limit applies in effect to the period 22 April 2009 to 5 April 2010.

Normal ongoing pension savings that qualify are not tested against the new special £20,000 annual allowance and higher rate tax relief continues to be available. To qualify, pension contributions must be paid under existing contracts at 22 April 2009 and must be paid at least quarterly or more often. Annual contributions do not qualify as regular contributions, but the special annual allowance is varied for those with irregular contributions. Any qualifying existing contributions reduce the amount of allowance available as shown below.

Example

David has income of £170,000 in 2009/10 and makes pension contributions of £50,000. The contributions reflect a regular monthly policy of £2,000 pm and a single payment of £26,000. Higher rate tax relief is available on the regular contributions of £24,000 even though they exceed £20,000, whereas the additional contribution of £26,000 is subject to the new special annual allowance charge in full.

If David's regular contributions had been £1,000 per month his special annual allowance limit would be £8,000 (£20,000 – £12,000). Any single contribution in excess of this limit would be subject to the new charge.

Where an individual has not made contributions on at least a quarterly basis, but has an established pattern of contributions in excess of £20,000, then the special annual allowance is increased to the lower of the average contributions in 2006/07 to 2008/09 and £30,000.

Individuals affected by the changes may be able to claim a refund of contributions paid with the refund cancelling the special annual allowance tax charge. However the refund is subject to a 40% tax charge.

Points to note regarding the income limit of £150,000:

–   The special allowance only applies where relevant income is £150,000 or more in the current tax year or in either of the previous two tax years.

–   The calculation of relevant income for the £150,000 limit is set out in a six-step process, which starts with total income and deducts pension contributions (subject to £20,000 maximum), losses and gross gift aid payments, but adds salary sacrifice in favour of pension contributions since 22 April 2009.

Example

Louise has been employed for many years as a management consultant. In 2009/10 she is paid a salary of £160,000 pa. Her employer makes monthly contributions into a defined contribution registered pension scheme on her behalf equal to 15% of net earnings, which is £24,000 in 2009/10. Louise paid a donation to charity of £2,000 gross in 2009/10. Her employer has had a very successful year and Louise is due to receive a bonus of £40,000, and it has been agreed that the bonus will be paid as a contribution to Louise's pension.

Louise's relevant income for the purpose of Sch 35 is £158,000. There is no deduction for pension contributions as they are not paid by Louise. Louise is therefore within the scope of the special annual allowance charge.

The effect of the pension payments by Louise's employer are therefore:

	£
Regular pension input amount – protected under Sch 35	24,000
Special annual allowance – base amount	20,000
Less: regular contributions treated as protected pension input	24,000

	£
Special annual allowance	Nil
Extra contribution by employer	40,000
Tax charge on Louise @ 20%	8,000

Example

Pili is a successful self-employed consultant. In 2009/10 his profits are £173,000, which is at least £30,000 more than they have been previously. Pili makes annual contributions to a number of pension providers, normally totalling £25,000 pa, but in view of his success this year he has made a contribution of £50,000. The effect of this is as follows.

		£
Total profits 2009/10		173,000
Less: pension contributions paid in year	50,000	
Subject to a maximum of		(20,000)
Relevant income for Sch 35		153,000

Pili has no regular pension input amount for the purposes of Sch 35 so his protected pension input is nil. He does, however, benefit from the increased special annual allowance.

	£
Regular pension input amount	Nil
Average irregular contributions 2006/07, 2007/08 and 2008/09	25,000
Between £20,000 and £30,000 so:	
Special annual allowance = average contributions	25,000
Contributions 2009/10	50,000
Special annual allowance	(25,000)
Amount on which special annual allowance charge due	25,000
Tax charge on Pili @ 20%	10,000

Pili has the option to change his mind once this fact becomes clear, and in 2010/11 he could ask for repayment of the £25,000 excess contribution, which would reverse all of the tax impact – being charged at 40% and cancelling the special annual allowance charge.

As an alternative, and as Pili is so close to the relevant income limit, and has not been above it in the preceding two tax years, he might consider making a donation to charity of £2,800 in 2010/11 and carrying it back to 2009/10. The gross payment would be £3,500 and would reduce the relevant income for Sch 35 to £149,500, thus eliminating the £10,000 tax charge. The total saving by making this donation would be £10,000 + higher rate relief on the donation of £1,050, making the effect of the donation a saving of £8,250.

Pension inputs (FA 2004 s 229)

3.   A pension input is the amount contributed to a pension policy in a pension input period plus the increase in value of defined pension benefits. Where the amounts contributed are in cash or equivalent they are easily valued. Where the pension scheme provides a defined benefit then the scheme administrator will compute the increase in value of the pension benefits using the formula

(Opening Benefits × 10) + Lump Sum =	X
(Closing Benefits × 10) + Lump Sum =	Y

Increase $\qquad$ Z

If a member does not accrue any rights under the arrangement during the pension input period (typically because the member is no longer an employee of the sponsoring employer) then the opening value (X) is to be increased by the greater of 5% or RPI inflation for the year.

The administrator of each fund will produce a figure for each member. Where exceptionally the difference is a decrease the amount will be deemed to be nil. Therefore all positive increases are aggregated with the contributions paid by the member, or others (eg his employer) to the defined contribution fund. The sum is known as 'total pension input'. This is used to test against the annual allowance (see note 4 below).

There is no pension input if, before the end of the tax year, the member has died, or taken all of the benefits available from that fund, ie the benefits have crystallised.

A 'pension input period' is defined in FA 2004 s 238. A 'pension input period' commences for a registered pension scheme when the individual's rights begin to accrue, or in the case of a money purchase scheme, the date of payment of the first premium. The period ends on the date nominated by the scheme administrator, however the period cannot exceed one year. This is to allow maximum flexibility to scheme administrators. Typically, the nominated date will be the end of the tax year, or the scheme accounting year end. Each subsequent pension input period is for twelve months until all benefits have been provided under the pension arrangements.

Example

John is entitled to a pension on 1/60th of final salary plus 3/80ths lump sum. He has 5 years service as at 6 April 2009, the commencement of the pension input period, and a salary of £210,000 per annum. By 6 April 2010 his salary has increased to £240,000 per annum. His P60 shows salary for the year of £230,000. John's pension input is

		£	£
Opening value	5/60ths × £210,000 × 10	175,000	
	15/80ths × £210,000	39,375	214,375
Closing value	6/60ths × £240,000 × 10	240,000	
	18/80ths × £240,000	54,000	294,000
Pension input			79,625
Annual limit			245,000
Maximum other contributions in year before 'Annual allowance charge' applies			165,375

John is entitled to obtain tax relief on contributions paid to all schemes to the maximum of his earnings for the year chargeable to UK tax (£230,000). However, if his contributions exceed £165,375 (excluding contributions to the defined benefit scheme) he will attract an annual allowance charge of 40% on the excess.

In practice John may not wish to pay a premium greater than the amount chargeable at 40% tax (see below), or an amount that would exceed his pension input maximum. Because the calculation of pension inputs cannot be made until after the end of the pension input period John will have to estimate his pension input from defined benefits scheme to determine the amount he wishes to contribute.

The tax charge under FA 2009 Sch 35 does not apply to any normal, regular ongoing pension savings that were in place before 22 April 2009, regardless of value. Assuming the scheme qualifies, the pension input of £79,625 should be treated as made under an existing obligation. However regular does not include cases such as John who makes one-off contributions annually based upon earnings. Any additional pension contribution made by John will therefore be subject to a special annual allowance charge in full.

Annual allowance – excess contributions (FA 2004 s 227)

4.   Where 'total pension inputs' are in excess of the annual allowance for the fiscal year, then the excess is subject to the 'annual allowance charge' of 40%. This is entered on to the self-assessment tax return additional information pages at box 8 on page Ai 4.

Example

Jill has paid £80,000 in 2009/10 to a registered pension scheme via regular monthly contributions. The policy was set up before 22 April 2009.

Subsequently she is notified by the scheme administrators of her defined benefits pension scheme that the 'pension input' for the year 2009/10 is £180,000.

When Jill completes her Self-Assessment Tax Return for 2009/10 she will have to enter an annual allowance charge computed as

	£
Total pension input (£80,000 + £180,000)	260,000
Annual allowance	245,000
Excess chargeable @ 40%	15,000

However, when she completes her self-assessment tax return, she will claim tax relief on the £80,000. (Jill does not suffer any restriction to her 2009/10 tax relief under FA 2009 Sch 35 as her contributions qualify as regular paid to a pension scheme.) This will be allowable providing she has sufficient taxable earnings. Assuming her earnings were £250,000 her tax return would show

			£
Relief for pensions paid	80,000	@ 40%	32,000
Less annual allowance charge	15,000	@ 40%	6,000
Actual relief	65,000	@ 40%	26,000

It should be noted that the total pension input on which tax relief is being granted then equals the annual allowance ie value of pension inputs on increase in defined benefits £180,000 plus tax relief on £65,000 = £245,000.

Where there is a charge under FA 2009 Sch 35, the amount which is liable to the annual allowance charge is deducted from the amount charged under Sch 35 so that it is not liable to a tax charge twice.

The way tax relief is given (FA 2004 ss 190 to 201)

5.   The way in which tax relief is granted depends upon the way in which the contributions are paid.

Members' own contributions are normally paid net of basic rate tax (s 192). Relief is therefore granted as follows:

Basic rate – at source

Higher rate – self-assessment tax return (or PAYE coding notice). See explanatory note 2 above for changes to higher rate relief from 2009/10 onwards. For those unaffected by FA 2009 Sch 35 (either because their income is below the threshold of £150,000, they have qualifying existing contributions, or their total contributions do not exceed £20,000) higher rate relief continues to be available.

Higher rate relief is obtained by increasing the basic rate band for income tax by the gross pension contribution (s 192(4)). When calculating income for age allowance purposes only, the gross pension payment is deducted from income (s 192(5)).

If a member pays a contribution via the employer then the contribution is paid to the insurance company gross. Tax relief is effectively given to the member by the net pay scheme (s 193). This means that the gross pension contributions are deducted from earnings for PAYE (but not NI) and relief given by taxing pay net of pension contributions.

Because employer-deducted contributions are excluded from earnings, relief for higher rate tax is given automatically. If an employer-deducted contribution cannot be relieved by deduction from earnings (eg payment made after month 12 payroll has been processed) or where earnings are not liable to PAYE, such as benefits, then the employee makes a claim on the self-assessment tax return, and earnings are reduced by the unrelieved premiums paid.

Retirement annuity premium (RAP) contributions, that is policies effected prior to 1 July 1988, continue to be paid gross (s 194).

Relief for premiums paid gross is given by reducing earnings by the pension contributions made when computing total income (s 194(1)). The claim is normally made in the tax return.

Where a member contributes up to £3,600 pa (gross) to a pension scheme but has no taxable income then tax relief is given because the pension premium is paid net. There is no recovery of the tax deducted at source.

If contributions in excess of the annual allowance are paid then the excess is clawed back by the 'annual allowance charge' of 40%. This charge does not apply when all pension benefits for the scheme crystallise in the same year as the contribution is made. In that final year 'pension input' for that scheme will be nil. However the maximum tax relief obtainable will of course be restricted to the amount of tax due.

Where tax is deducted at source on an amount in excess of £3,600, and earnings are nil (or less than £3,600 pa), then the first £2,880 of the payment will be deemed to be a net pension contribution and the excess will be deemed to be a gross pension payment on which no tax relief is available. The following example illustrates how such a situation can occur.

Jack, a self-employed builder, pays a net pension contribution of £500 per month. His accounts for the year ended 31 January 2010 show a tax adjusted net profit of £2,800. He has no other earnings.

Jack is entitled to tax relief in 2009/10 on the higher of	
– 100% earnings =	2,800
– or	3,600
In 2009/10 Jack has paid pension contributions (net) of	
12 × 500 =	6,000
Maximum allowable (£3,600 × 100/80 =)	2,880
Gross pension contribution (no relief available)	3,120
Total pension contribution paid by Jack (net)	6,000
Tax repaid to pension scheme (£3,600 × 20%)	720
Amount added to Jack's pension scheme	6,720

Lifetime limit (FA 2004 ss 214 to 226)

6. When pension benefits, other than State Pensions, are drawn there is a 'benefit crystallisation event'. At that time it is necessary to check the amount of pension funds used against the lifetime limit. If the amount is below the lifetime limit then full benefits can be paid with no additional tax charge. If a previous 'benefit crystallisation event' has used part of the lifetime limit then only the remaining percentage of the limit for the current year can be applied.

Example of one fund and one crystallisation

George has a pension fund of £2 million and is aged 75 next week. He wishes to take the maximum amount as a lump sum using the balance to buy a pension. The lifetime limit for 2009/10 is £1.75 million. Ignore transitional rules.

	£	£
Value of fund	2,000,000	
Maximum tax-free lump sum		
25% × £1.75 million	437,500	437,500
	1,562,500	
Balance of lifetime limit used to		
buy a pension (75% × 1.75 million)	1,312,500	
Excess	250,000	
Lifetime allowance charge		
Taken as lump sum – 55%	137,500	112,500
Maximum lump sum		550,000

If George had not wished to take the excess as a lump sum but instead wished to buy a pension then the tax charge would be as follows:

	£
Excess of fund	250,000
Lifetime allowance charge – 25% of £250,000	62,500
Available to buy pension	187,500

Effectively the tax charge will be identical as when the pension is taken it will be taxable income liable at say 40% therefore the tax due on the pension will be:

	£
40% × £187,500 (assumed pension received)	75,000
Lifetime allowance charge @ 25% of £250,000	62,500
Giving total of	137,500

Thus the total tax collected by HMRC is 55% of £250,000 in each instance.

In practice very few members will have only one fund, or will draw the whole of their fund on one occasion. Where there are multiple withdrawals then the test has to be done each time benefits crystallise. The percentage of the fund that has been used is calculated and only the remaining percentage of the later year lifetime allowance will be available for later benefits.

Example of two crystallisations

William has a 'benefit crystallisation event' in 2006/07 using £1 million of his pension funds.

He has a further 'benefit crystallisation event' in 2010/11 using £700,000 of his pension fund. The lifetime allowance limit in 2010/11 is £1,800,000

2006/07 Lifetime limit	£1.5 million
'Benefits crystallisation event' fund used	£1 million (ie 66.67% of lifetime limit)

	£
2010/11 Lifetime limit	1,800,000
Used in 2006/07 66.67% × £1.8 million	1,200,000
Available lifetime allowance	600,000

Crystallised 2010/11	700,000
Lifetime allowance excess chargeable	100,000

There will be no charge on any other pension funds held until they have a 'benefit crystallisation event'. Then, as the whole 100% of the lifetime allowance has been used, the fund value on crystallisation will be chargeable.

It should be noted that William may believe that he does not have any charge to pay as his total crystallisation is £1 million plus £700,000 and the lifetime allowance in 2010/11 is £1.8 million whereas in reality there will be a deduction of £55,000 from funds taken in cash or £25,000 from funds taken used to buy a pension.

Pensions in payment as at 6 April 2006

If an individual had a pension in payment as at 6 April 2006 then immediately before the first 'benefit crystallisation event' occurring there is a deemed 'benefit crystallisation event', the amount of the lifetime limit used is

25 × existing annual pension in payment

If the individual has a pre 6 April 2006 income withdrawal then the existing pension is deemed to be 120% of the standard annuity (see note 7) regardless of the amount actually drawn.

If the individual has taken a tax free lump sum prior to 6 April 2006 then that amount when aggregated with the lump sum to be taken must not exceed 25% of the lifetime allowance.

In practice many individuals with existing vested policies or pensions in payment will use the transitional provisions (see note 9 below). Enhanced protection is available if no pension contribution, or increases in benefit rights, occur after 5 April 2006 even if the 'A day value' of the funds is below £1,500,000. This enables the benefits to be taken after 5 April 2006 without consideration of the lifetime allowance. The maximum tax free lump sum may still be restricted.

Unsecured pensions (FA 2004 s 165)

7.   The rules are very similar to the previous income withdrawal rules. Unsecured pension withdrawal will be available from age 50 (55 from 2010) until the pensioner is aged 75. On commencing withdrawal there is a benefit crystallisation event. At that time tax free cash can be taken up to 25% of the fund. The amount designated as available to pay the unsecured pension plus the tax-free cash taken is treated as the amount crystallised (s 216(1b)(1)). When the balance of the fund is used to buy an annuity, to convert to an alternatively secured pension or on death, the funds then available must also be tested against the remaining lifetime limit as a 'benefit crystallisation event' has occurred (s 216(1b)(1)(4)(7)). However, the amount crystallised is reduced by the amount previously tested against the lifetime limit (Sch 32 paras 3 and 4, as amended).

The balance of the fund must then be used to pay a pension each year. The pension will be taxable and subject to PAYE. There is no minimum withdrawal and the maximum withdrawal is 120% of the government standard annuity. The amount taken can be varied each year.

At five yearly intervals the standard annuity will be revalued thereby giving a new maximum amount.

Alternatively the fund can buy a short term annuity for a period not exceeding five years (and ending before the pensioner is aged 75).

If the pensioner dies before age 75 and before a pension is bought then the fund can be used

–   to buy a pension for spouse or other dependant, or

–   to provide an unsecured pension for spouse, if they are under age 75, or

–   35% of the fund can be paid as tax with the balance taken as a lump sum.

Alternatively secured pension ('ASP') (FA 2004 Sch 28)

8.   These are available from 6 April 2006 for pensioners aged 75. They are designed for those who have conscientious objections to buying annuities. Instead of buying an annuity the member crystallises their benefits as for unsecured pensions. If the fund has not previously been used to take a tax free lump sum then up to 25% of the fund (subject to lifetime limit) can be used to provide a cash sum.

The balance of the fund must be used to provide a taxable pension. The maximum amount that can be drawn is 90% of the standard annuity payable to an annuitant aged 75 of the same sex. The minimum pension drawn must be 55% of that standard annuity.

In the case of alternatively secured pensions the pension must be reviewed every year using an annuity rate for an annuitant aged 75 applied to the then fund value.

On the death of the alternatively secured pensioner the remaining fund must be used to provide a pension for their spouse, civil partner or other dependant. If the recipient is under 75 unsecured pension rules will apply. From aged 75 the alternatively secured pension rules will apply.

When the last recipient dies then the balance of the fund will be gifted to a nominated charity. If the member has not nominated a charity then the scheme administrator may select the charity. There is no tax to pay on the donation to a charity.

If the fund is not gifted to a charity but transferred to another member of the same pension scheme then it is liable to an unauthorised payment charge of 70%. In addition the amount, net of charge, is treated as the top slice of value in the estate of the original member and is liable to inheritance tax thus giving a potential charge of 40% × (100% − 70%) = 12% and an overall tax charge of 82%. The liability to pay the tax rests with the pension scheme administrator.

Transitional provisions (FA 2004 Sch 36)

9.   Existing pension rights, as at 6 April 2006, may be preserved by using the following provisions from Finance Act 2004. The freezing of the standard lifetime allowance for five years may have implications for those seeking to benefit from transitional relief. Some individuals may consider drawing benefits earlier than previously planned to avoid future growth causing a charge.

Primary protection (Sch 36 para 7)

(a)   Primary protection is given to any pension member who has a fund valued in excess of £1.5 million as at 6 April 2006. The pension member is required to give notice to HMRC. Notice must have been given by 6 April 2009.

Where notice has been given then there will be an enhancement to the lifetime limit. This is calculated as

$$\frac{\text{Fund value @ 6 April 2006} - £1.5\ \text{million}}{£1.5\ \text{million}} \times \text{Lifetime Limit}$$

For example if Alison has a fund of £2 million as at 6 April 2006 then the lifetime limit enhancement will be

$$\frac{£2\ \text{million} - £1.5\ \text{million}}{£1.5\ \text{million}}$$

= 33⅓% (expressed as a percentage)

Therefore in a later year, say 2010/11, the lifetime limit for Alison would be the actual limit of £1.8 million × 133⅓% = £2.4 million.

Enhanced protection (Sch 36 para 12)

(b)   Where a pension fund member has relevant pension arrangements that became registered pension schemes on 6 April 2006 and had ceased active membership of all registered pension schemes then enhanced protection is available from 6 April 2006. There is no minimum fund value to claim enhanced protection.

If the member has **any** pension input then the value of enhanced protection is lost and only primary protection is available. This applies to contributions made or benefits uprating received on or after 6 April 2006.

Where the member has elected for enhanced protection then there will be no lifetime charge when a pension and tax-free lump sum are drawn. The tax-free lump sum is still restricted to 25% (or a lower specified percentage) of the fund value.

If the member makes any contribution, or his benefits are enhanced or the member wishes to withdraw his notice then enhanced protection may be replaced by primary protection.

Valuation of funds at 6 April 2006 for protection

(c)   In order to compute the value of a pension fund as at 6 April 2006 it is necessary to add the value of all uncrystallised funds, ie the monetary value of defined contribution funds, plus the annual rate of pension to which the member is entitled × 20, plus the lump sum to which the member is entitled. To which is added the value of all crystallised pensions ie pensions in payment (for this purpose the annual pension is multiplied by 25 to take into account the lump sum already taken) plus an amount equal to the value of benefits that have been taken prior to 6 April 2006 wholly or mainly in the form of a tax free lump sum. Where the taxpayer is making income withdrawals the pension used is the maximum available under the arrangements.

Retirement before age 50 (Sch 36 paras 21–23)

(d)   If the pension member has the right to draw their pension because of their profession before age 50 (eg sportsmen) then that right will be preserved providing it is in place as at 6 April 2006.

Lump sums (Sch 36 paras 24–36)

(e)   Protection is provided for an accrued right to a lump sum in excess of £375,000 as at 6 April 2006.

This right is preserved by increasing the maximum lump sum accrued as at 6 April 2006 by the pro-rata increase in the lifetime limit.

Justin is entitled to a lump sum as at 6 April 2006 of £600,000. He crystallises his pension in 2010/11 when the lifetime limit is £1.8 million. His maximum lump sum would then be

$$\frac{\text{£1.8 million (2010/11 limit)}}{\text{£1.5 million (2006/07 limit)}} \times £600,000 = £720,000$$

A further protection is available if under an occupational pension scheme the member is entitled to a lump sum that exceeds 25% of the uncrystallised rights as at 6 April 2006. This protection works by computing the accrued lump sum as at 6 April 2006 and increasing that figure in line with the increasing lifetime limit as above. To that amount may be added 25% of the value of benefits that have accrued since 6 April 2006. If benefits are transferred from the scheme then protection is lost and only 25% of the fund is available as a lump sum.

Funded unapproved retirement benefit scheme (FURBS)

10. Where contributions to an existing FURBS (funded unapproved retirement benefits scheme) have been taxed on the employee and the income and gains of the scheme have been taxed on the trustees *and* no further contributions are added from 6 April 2006 then any amounts paid out as a lump sum will be tax free.

   If contributions are added to the FURBS after 5 April 2006 only the value on 5 April 2006 increased by RPI will be tax free.

Unfunded unapproved retirement benefit schemes

11. It would appear that promised benefits under unfunded unapproved retirement benefit schemes do not constitute a pension input and do not give rise to a benefits in kind charge (because no payments are made into the scheme). When any benefits are drawn they will be taxable as pension income immediately. The employer (or former employer) only obtains tax relief when taxable benefits are paid.

   Employer contributions to non-registered pension schemes are not tax deductible until the benefit is paid out to the employee.

Term assurance

12. Tax relief for term assurance written under pension rules has been withdrawn. Relief continues on policies taken out before 6 December 2006 provided the sum insured is not increased or the term extended (FA 2007 Sch 18). Where relief is available the premiums will be pension inputs counting towards the annual limit. Because those policies are registered pension schemes the proceeds will count towards the lifetime limit. Tax will be charged if the total proceeds plus other pension fund values exceed the lifetime limit (at 55% of the excess).

Commutation of trivial pensions

13. To reduce the possibility of very small pension funds having to buy annuities at poor rates because of the administrative costs involved it is possible, from 6 April 2006, to withdraw the whole amount on vesting. The amount taken in excess of the tax-free sum is treated as pension income and is liable to income tax. This facility is only available where

   – the total value of *all* pensions for that individual is less than 1% of the Lifetime Allowance (£17,500 for 2009/10),

   – the individual is aged between 60 and 75,

   – the whole of all funds are withdrawn within a 12-month period,

   – all rights are extinguished by the payment from the fund.

   In addition regulations are to be introduced to enable small 'stranded pension pots' to be vested without the purchase of an annuity. This will apply to 'pots' of less than £2,000. Up to 25% will be available as a tax free lump sum with the excess taxed as pension income of the year of withdrawal.

National insurance contributions

14. Registered pension premiums are not deducted from profits for Class 4 national insurance purposes (SSCBA 1992 Sch 2.3). Nor do they reduce earnings for employers' and employees' Class 1 contributions (SI 2001/1004 para 24), although an *employer's* pension contributions to an employee's policy do not count as earnings for Class 1 purposes (see note 19).

Losses

15. Where relief for losses is claimed under trade loss relief against general income (ITA 2007 s 64) or early trade loss relief (ITA 2007 s 72), the loss is set against total income, and no set-off order is

specified. A s 64/s 72 claim may therefore be regarded for pension purposes as reducing non-trading income in priority to trading income, thus enabling relevant earnings of the claim year to be left at a higher level.

Contracting out of S2P

16.   Unless an employee is already in a registered scheme that is contracted out of the State Second Pension Scheme (S2P – see note 17), he may elect to contract out, whilst continuing to contribute for a basic retirement pension. The fund accumulated with such contributions is known as a protected rights fund and benefits can be taken from age 60 onwards and must be drawn by age 75. The fund can normally be commuted for a lump sum and the pension must include provision for widows'/ widowers' pensions. Employees and employers still pay full national insurance contributions, and HMRC pays the combined employer/employee contracting-out rebate plus tax relief at the basic rate on the gross equivalent of the employee's share of the rebate to the pension provider after the end of the tax year (see Example 48 part (e)(i)). The employee may contract out in this way whether or not the employer has a non-contracted-out registered scheme. Where there is no registered scheme, any premium paid by the employee is paid net of basic rate tax and HMRC pays the tax into the plan.

The state pension age is to be equalised for men and women at 65, the change being phased in from 2010 to 2020. Women born before 6 April 1950 will still qualify at 60 but those born on or after 6 March 1955 will be subject to the 65 age limit. Women born between those dates will have a retirement age between 60 and 65 depending upon their date of birth.

Replacement of SERPS by S2P

17.   From 6 April 2002 the State Earnings Related Pension Scheme (SERPS) was replaced by the State Second Pension Scheme (S2P). All existing benefits under SERPS are retained and the new scheme provides a better pension for those earning under £31,000 pa (for 2008/09) (SI 2006/1009).

The S2P scheme gives enhanced benefits to the lower paid (under £13,900 pa (Social Security Pensions (Low Earnings Threshold) 2009/10)), certain carers and those with long term disabilities. Contributions continue to be a percentage of earnings above the earnings threshold.

The change to the funding basis makes the decision whether or not to contract out very evenly balanced. The treatment of national insurance and rebates to S2P is set out in note 16 above.

Upper accruals point

18.   As part of pension restructuring the new upper accruals point (UAP) has been introduced from 2009/10. This is now separate from the upper earnings limit (UEL), which previously marked the limit of accrual of earnings related benefits under S2P. The UEL increased quite significantly in 2009/10 from £770 per week to £844 per week to align with the higher rate tax threshold. The UAP, introduced in 2009/10 is the new point at which no further earnings related pension entitlement is accrued, and for 2009/10 this is £770 per week.

Employer contributions

19.   An employer can contribute to the registered pension plan of an employee. As with employers' contributions to company schemes, the employer's contribution to an employee's registered pension scheme is not treated as the employee's earnings (ITEPA 2003 s 308), nor is it liable to employer's national insurance contributions (Social Security (Contributions) Regulations SI 2001/1004 para 24 and Sch 3 Part VI).

In view of the fact that employers' pension contributions are not liable to national insurance, whereas there is no national insurance saving on an employee's pension contributions, it could be tax-efficient for a salary sacrifice to be made by the employee, and for the employer to pay a pension contribution of the sacrificed amount boosted by the employer's national insurance saving. The cost to the employer would be the same. For example if a basic rate taxpayer paid £80 a month into his personal pension the gross pension contribution would be £100. If he made a salary sacrifice of £116 per month, his net pay would reduce by the same amount, ie:

Gross pay			116	
Tax	@ 20%	23		
Class 1 NI	@ 11%	13	36	£80

His employer could then contribute £116 plus the employer's NI of £116 @ 12.8% = £15, giving a gross pension contribution of (116 + 15 =) £131 per month.

It is likely that employer contributions in relation to employees with income in excess of £150,000 will be taxed in some way from 2011/12 when pension contributions are restricted to basic rate relief. See explanatory note 2 above regarding the impact of employer contributions under the anti forestalling measures introduced by FA 2009 Sch 35.

Commissions on pension policies

20. HMRC have issued a statement of practice SP 4/97 on their view of the tax treatment of commission, cashbacks and discounts. As far as pension policies are concerned, care must be taken to ensure that commission arrangements do not jeopardise the tax approval of the fund (as to which see note 22). The main point is that the commission arrangements must be under a separate contract. The pension contribution will be treated as the net amount paid if the commission is deducted from the contribution or a discounted premium is paid. If the contribution is paid in full and the commission is received separately, tax relief will be given on the full amount. A pension scheme's tax approval may be withdrawn if commission paid as a result of transfers between schemes represents an unauthorised payment.

The income position for the recipient of the commission is that it does not count as income if it is received by an ordinary member of the public. Commission passed on to customers by agents or employees of pension providers will count as part of the agent's or employee's income, but there will usually be an offsetting expenses deduction. Commission on an employee's own contracts will not count as employment income if it is available on the same basis to the general public. Similar treatment will apply by concession to the self-employed.

Transfers between funds

21. Someone with a registered pension plan who enters pensionable employment may transfer his pension fund to the new employer's scheme or to another registered scheme without tax consequences.

Missold personal pension plans

22. Some employees were wrongly advised to opt out of their employers' schemes and take out personal pension plans funded by their own contributions. Where compensation is received for such wrong advice, the compensation is exempt from tax.

Unauthorised payments

23. Tax is charged at 40% on any unauthorised payments including recycled tax free lump sums, non-arm's length transactions with a member, or employer (s 208), or on deregistration of the fund by HMRC (s 242). The tax is payable by the member (or employer) or, on deregistration, by the scheme administrator.

Where the total unauthorised payments in any twelve-month period exceeds 25% of the value of member's rights in the fund a further surcharge of 15% will apply (ss 209–213).

A further penalty known as a 'Sanction Charge' will be imposed on the administrator at the rate of 40% of the relevant transaction. This applies where a fund borrows more than 50% of the fund value, or makes unauthorised payments (other than benefits in kind chargeable to income tax by FA

2004 s 173). Where the sanction charge applies as well as the unauthorised payment charge then the charge is reduced by the lower of the unauthorised payment charge or 25% of the chargeable figure, giving an effective rate of 15% (ss 239–241).

If Alan's pension fund was valued at £1,000,000 and the administrator made an unauthorised payment of £50,000 to Alan the charges would be:

		£
– On Alan 40% × £50,000 (s 208)		20,000
– On the Administrator		
40% × £50,000 (s 239)	20,000	
Less tax paid by Alan restricted to		
25% × £50,000	12,500	7,500
Effective rate of tax is 55%		27,500

If the payment had been £251,000 to Alan then there would be a surcharge on Alan of 15% (£5,209) giving a total charge of 70% (ie £251,000 × 70%=) £175,700.

All of the above charges apply where the whole of the remaining fund in an alternatively secured pension (ASP) is transferred (other than to a qualifying charity) giving an effective rate on the ASP of 70%.

Pension splitting on divorce

24. A pension fund can be split on divorce without affecting the tax approved status of the fund. A divorcing couple will not be *required* to share pensions, but all schemes (whenever they were registered or approved) are regarded as including pension sharing provisions. Where the pension is shared, the spouse/civil partner in a pension scheme will get reduced pension rights (a 'pension debit') and rights will be allocated to the other spouse/civil partner (a 'pension credit'). The pension credit received will count towards the lifetime allowance at a benefits crystallisation event. If the pensions credit is a pension in payment then that pension will already have been applied against the other party's lifetime allowance. To prevent double counting, the recipient's lifetime allowance will be increased by an appropriate factor to reflect the value of the pension arising from the pension credit (FA 2004 s 220). The pension credit to the transferee spouse/civil partner must be administered in the same way as for any other registered pension scheme. Benefits may be taken between ages 50 and 75 with the usual options for a lump sum, unsecured pension etc. The pension splitting legislation applies to all types of pension arrangements other than the basic state pension.

Stakeholder pensions

25. From 6 April 2001 a further type of registered pension known as a stakeholder pension was introduced. For a pension to qualify as a stakeholder pension, the costs must be restricted to 1% of the fund per annum. For those joining from 6 April 2005 the charges can be up to 1.5% of the fund value per year for the first 10 years and 1% thereafter. The investment fund can be chosen by the policyholder or be the default investment. That default may have a lifestyle feature allowing the insurer to move funds into low risk products as retirement approaches (SI 2005/577). The premiums must be able to be started or stopped at will and the minimum premium cannot exceed £20. From 8 October 2001 all employers with five or more employees must provide employees with access to a registered stakeholder scheme, except as indicated below. Those who operate a qualifying salary-related occupational scheme that all relevant employees are eligible to join within one year of starting work, and those who offer a group registered pension to all relevant employees which has no exit charges, that is available after no more than thirteen weeks' service and to which the employer contributes at least 3% of earnings, will not have to offer a stakeholder scheme. Relevant employees are all employees employed in the UK except those whose earnings were below the lower earnings limit (£95 per week in 2009/10) at any time in the previous three months, those under 18 or within

five years of normal pension age, employees who have been offered membership of an occupational pension scheme and have declined to join and non-residents without UK net relevant earnings. If employees of non-exempt employers join a scheme, employers must deduct the net contributions from net pay if the employee so requests and forward them to the scheme provider by the 19th of the following month.

Waiver of premiums

26.   From 6 April 2001 new policies that provide for waiver of premium contributions will not obtain tax relief on the cost of that benefit. If a claim is made on such a policy the proceeds may be used to buy a pension net of basic rate tax.

Non-cash contributions to schemes from 6 April 2001

27.   Under the pension scheme rules applicable from 6 April 2001, a provision may be made for contributions to be made not only in cash but by way of transfer of shares received under SAYE share option schemes, approved share incentive plans (previously called all-employee share ownership plans) and approved profit sharing schemes (as to which see Example 85). Such transfers must be made within 90 days of exercising the SAYE option or of shares being appropriated to the employee. The shares will be treated as contributions equal to their market value at the date of the transfer. Tax relief will then be given on the contributions in the same way as for cash contributions.

Tax credits

28.   Income for tax credits is reduced by tax deductible pension contributions paid by the claimant or partner. The amount of the deduction is the gross allowable premium paid.

Question

A.

Woodhouse Eaves Ltd is a manufacturing company preparing accounts to 31 March, but its system of management accounting enables it accurately to predict its result for the year after the result shown by the three quarters' accounts to 31 December is known.

Harold and Frank are the only two directors, owning between them the entire issued share capital. There are no associated companies.

The company has a money purchase pension scheme for the directors and a designated stakeholder pension scheme for the workforce.

The trading profit for the year ending 31 March 2010, after deducting capital allowances, is expected to be £450,000, and to be higher in the following year.

Earlier profits have been depleted by the capital allowances resulting from a substantial plant investment programme, but the profits for corporation tax purposes for the year to 31 March 2009 were £130,000. The company has not paid any dividends for that year and does not anticipate paying a dividend in 2010. The company paid £20,000 to the pension scheme for the directors in the year to 31 March 2009. A sum of £60,000 was paid in the year ended 31 March 2008, and £85,000 in 2007.

It has been suggested to Harold and Frank that substantial increased payments could be made to the pension scheme for the directors.

There is not expected to be any lack of cash within the company following the completion of the plant investment programme and the directors feel that this would be a good opportunity to make up for the years where they have not been contributing significant amounts to a pension scheme, by not only paying the first of the intended regular annual contributions but also a substantial additional amount.

Illustrate how relief for the contributions in the year to 31 March 2010 will be given, assuming the payment of an annual premium of £275,000 and an additional contribution of £247,000.

Harold's and Frank's total income for 2007/08, 2008/09 and 2009/10 is constant at £75,000 each.

Make brief comments on the position if the pension premiums of £470,000 were paid during the year ended 31 March 2010 after 22 April 2009 and the director's total income exceeds £150,000.

B.

Dr Jolly is a medical practitioner who is in general practice. He makes his accounts up to 31 December in each year. In the year to 31 December 2009 his profits, adjusted for taxation (except for superannuation payments made) amounted to £112,500. He has other income in 2009/10 of:

Bank Interest Received	£480
Dividends Received	£270

He made a donation under Gift Aid to a national charity of £1,000 and paid (net) a pension contribution of £8,000.

Dr Jolly's staff are members of the NHS superannuation scheme. The employer's contribution for the year to 31 December 2009 amounted to £11,900.

As well as receiving NHS income, Dr Jolly is a police surgeon, has a consultancy with a leading engineering firm, undertakes insurance and HGV medical examinations and signs death certificates, passport applications, etc.

Your examination of Dr Jolly's superannuation account within his records provides the following information:

		£	£
01.01.09	Creditors – superannuation due		7,486
31.01.09	Quarterly payment	2,965	
30.04.09	Quarterly payment	2,965	
20.05.09	Settlement for 2008/09	3,983	
31.07.09	Quarterly payment	3,113	
30.10.09	Quarterly payment	3,113	
31.12.09	Creditors – superannuation due	6,221	
	Charged in accounts		
	Employers Contribution		10,424
	Employees Contribution		4,468
		22,360	22,360
01.01.10	Creditors – superannuation due		6,221
31.01.10	Quarterly payment	3,113	
02.04.10	Settlement for 2009/10	3,975	
30.04.10	Quarterly payment	3,113	

In May 2010 the NHS scheme administrator informs Dr Jolly that his pension input for the year 2009/10 amounted to £33,483.

You are required to:

(a)   adjust the taxable profits for the year ended 31 December 2009 for superannuation paid;

(b)   indicate how relief is given for superannuation paid by Dr Jolly; and

(c)   compute Dr Jolly's 2009/10 tax liability.

Answer

A.

Provided a pension scheme is registered by HMRC through the HMRC Savings, Pensions, Share Schemes (IR SPSS), a contribution paid by the employer is deductible in computing the trading profits of the chargeable period in which it is paid (FA 2004 s 196).

In addition to normal contributions, companies may make special contributions to a registered scheme, for example to provide benefits for back service, to augment benefits already secured or to make up an actuarial deficiency in the fund. Where large contributions are paid, HMRC may require that the deduction in computing profits is to be spread forward over a period of years (FA 2004 s 197). Forward spreading is not, however, required for excess contributions that, in total, are less than £500,000 or that do not exceed 210% of the amount contributed in the previous chargeable period. Any amount in excess of 110% of the amount contributed in the previous chargeable period is known as the 'relevant excess contribution'. Relevant excess contributions are normally spread evenly over a period of up to four years as follows, commencing in the year of payment:

Relevant excess contributions	*Spread over*
£500,000 or more but less than £1,000,000	2 years
£1,000,000 or more but less than £2,000,000	3 years
£2,000,000 or more	4 years

(See note 2 below for periods of other than one year)

Once determined, the period of spread will not be varied because of subsequent fluctuations in contribution(s) or the payment of further large contributions in later years. If the trade ceases relevant excess contributions that have not been allowed by the time the trade ceases will normally be allowed in that period, or by election re-apportioned over the period since they were paid. (FA 2004 s 198).

The position if a regular contribution of £275,000 and an additional contribution of £247,000 is paid in the year to 31 March 2010 will be:

	£	£
Anticipated profit for the year		450,000
Pension scheme contributions:		
Normal	275,000	
Additional	247,000	522,000
Resulting trading loss		(72,000)
Carry back against profits of year to 31 March 2009		72,000

If the additional contribution was more than £247,000, the amount allowed against the profits of the year to 31 March 2009 would be reduced to one half of the relevant excess contribution plus 110% of the amount contributed in the previous year. For example a pension contribution of (£275,000 + £275,000) £550,000 would give an allowable deduction of:

			£
Paid in year to 31 March 2009			20,000
Paid in year to 31 March 2010			550,000
Less: 110% of year to 31 March 2009			22,000
'relevant excess contribution' which exceeds:			528,000
210% of year to 31 March 2009	£42,000		
And	£500,000		
Allowed in year to 31 March 2011 – one half			264,000
			264,000
110% of year to 31 March 2009			22,000
Allowed in year to 31 March 2010			286,000

In order to qualify for relief, the pension contributions must be paid in the relevant period and not merely provided for in the accounts.

The tax saved as a result of making the contribution would be:

Year to 31 March 2010		£	£
300,000	@ 21%	63,000	
150,000	@ 29.75%	44,625	107,625
Year to 31 March 2009			
Tax on original profit, 130,000	@ 21%	27,300	
Tax on revised profit, 58,000	@ 21%	12,180	
Repayment			15,120
Total saving			122,745

giving effective rate of tax relief on £522,000 of 23.51% (122,745/522,000).

The company needs to consider the anticipated marginal tax rates in deciding when to make additional contributions as the small companies rate is expected to increase to 22% for the year ended 31 March 2011. For the year ended 31 March 2010 the 21% band runs to £300,000 with a marginal rate of 29.75% on the next £1,200,000. See Example 53 for comparisons of different loss claims.

Although a premium of £522,000 is tax efficient for Woodhouse Eaves Ltd the same cannot be said when considering the tax position of the two directors, Harold and Frank.

Assuming that neither director makes any other pension contribution in the year to 5 April 2010 and that the payments are allocated equally between the two directors then each will have a 'pension input' in respect of the Woodhouse Eaves Ltd scheme of:

		£
½ × £522,000	=	261,000
Annual limit for 2009/10		245,000
Excess		16,000
Liable to an 'annual allowance charge' of 40%	=	£6,400

Which would require a bonus (assuming the director is liable to tax at 40%) of:

	£
Gross bonus	10,847

				£
Less: tax at	40%	4,339		
NI at	1%	108		4,447
Net to meet tax liability				6,400

and the employer would have a further liability to employer NI of 12.8% × £10,847 = £1,388 giving a cost to the company of (£10,847 + 1,388 =) £12,235 for each director, reduced by the value of the corporation tax relief.

	£
Cost of bonus (2 × £12,235)	24,470
Loss carried back to y/e 31 March 2009 – relief at 21%	5,139
Net cost	19,331

It would be more sensible to restrict the additional pension contributions so that the 'total pension input' for each director does not exceed £245,000 (ie maximum additional contribution of £215,000 when added to normal contribution of £275,000 and divided between the two directors).

On total contributions of £490,000 the corporation tax position would be:

		£
Anticipated profit for the year		450,000
Pension scheme contributions		490,000
Resulting trading loss		(40,000)

The tax then saved would be:

Year to 31 March 2010			£	
300,000	@ 21%		63,000	
150,000	@ 29.75%		44,625	107,625
Year to 31 March 2009				
40,000	@ 20%			8,000
Total saving				115,625

giving effective rate of tax relief on £490,000 of 23.60%, without giving £12,800 of additional tax liability in the hands of the directors or the costs of extracting funds from the company to meet that additional liability.

Frank's and Harold's total income for 2009/10 and two earlier years is below £150,000, therefore no charge arises under FA 2009 Sch 35 special annual allowance charge.

Director's income exceeds £150,000

If income in the current (2009/10) tax year, or in either of the two previous tax years, exceeds £150,000 it is necessary to consider the special annual allowance charge in FA 2009 Sch 35. This imposes a tax charge at 20% (collected via self-assessment) on the pension contributions paid by an individual's employer on their behalf above the special annual allowance of £20,000. The tax charge does not apply to any normal ongoing pension savings that were in place before 22 April 2009, whatever their value. However, although the scheme is in existence at 22 April 2009 there does not appear to be any arrangements to make regular fixed contributions.

As there have been irregular contributions Sch 35 para 17 permits the special annual allowance to increase slightly, where these have exceeded £20,000 (using the average of preceding three years).

		£
Contribution paid in year ended 31 March	2009	20,000
	2008	60,000
	2007	85,000
		165,000
Average annual irregular contributions (two members)		55,000
Average annual irregular contributions – each director		27,500

The special annual allowance charge therefore increases to the lower of the average annual irregular contributions and £30,000, in this case £27,500 each. The tax charge for each director therefore will be:

	£
Pension contribution	245,000
Less: special annual allowance	(27,500)
Amount on which special annual allowance charge is calculated	217,500
Tax @ 20%	43,500

B.   (a)   Dr Jolly adjusted profits of year to 31 December 2009

	£	£
Profits before superannuation adjustments		112,500
Add: Charged in accounts for Dr Jolly		
Employers contribution	10,424	
Employees contribution	4,468	14,892
Net profit for tax purposes		127,392

Note

No adjustment is required for staff superannuation provided the amount charged in the accounts is equal to the amount paid in the accounting period (FA 2004 s 196).

(b)   Relief for superannuation paid

Dr Jolly is a member of the National Health Service Pension Scheme, which is a registered pension scheme. Relief is, therefore, available for contributions paid within the fiscal year.

In the year 2009/10 the amount paid was:

		£
30.04.09	Quarterly payment	2,965
20.05.09	Settlement for 2008/09	3,983
31.07.09	Quarterly payment	3,113
30.10.09	Quarterly payment	3,113
31.01.10	Quarterly payment	3,113
02.04.10	Settlement for 2009/10	3,975
Claim in 2009/10 tax return (box 3 on page TR4)		20,262

(c)   Tax Liability of Dr Jolly for 2009/10

			£	
Self-employed earnings			127,392	
Bank interest received (480 + 120)			600	
Dividends (270 + 30)			300	
			128,292	
Superannuation paid			20,262	
			108,030	
Personal allowance			6,475	
Taxable income			101,555	
Tax thereon:				
	37,400	@ 20%	7,480	
	11,250	@ 20%*	2,250	
	52,605	@ 40%	21,042	
	300	@ 32½%	97	
	101,555			30,869
Class 4 national insurance				
On 43,875 – 5,715	@ 8%		3,053	
On 127,392 – 43,875	@ 1%		835	3,888
Total Liability				34,757

* Basic rate band is extended by:
Gross pension contributions (paid net)
8,000 × 100/80 10,000
Gross Gift Aid payments
1,000 × 100/80 1,250
11,250

Explanatory Notes

Employer provided pensions

1.   From 6 April 2006 the previous tax legislation relating to occupational and personal pension schemes was replaced by a single scheme for all registered pension schemes. See Example 37 for the new provisions.

Individuals are now able to contribute to as many schemes as they wish. Pension providers are able to invest in most types of investment, excluding residential property and tangible moveable property if the policyholder or member can influence the investment decisions of the fund (FA 2004 Sch 29A). The minimum pension age will rise from 50 to 55 on 6 April 2010 (earlier retirement still being permitted on ill health grounds).

Deductible contributions

2. The limit on contributions by employers is the requirement that the expenditure is incurred wholly and exclusively for the purpose of the business. This will normally mean that all contributions paid in the chargeable period will be deductible (FA 2004 s 196). (See HMRC manuals at BIM 46001 for further guidance.)

In order for pension contributions paid to be allowable they must form part of a normal remuneration package. They are not considered as a stand-alone amount. It follows that a salary sacrifice will not prevent a tax deduction. Contributions will be allowable if the overall salary package is a normal commercial amount.

It is likely that HMRC will disallow any amount identifiable as relating to a non-trade purpose, for example as part of arrangements to dispose of a business where the payment represents part of the sale proceeds, or of exceptional size. This would be of issue if the employer was not carrying on a trade eg property holding company.

The main focus of disallowances is likely to be in respect of directors who are controlling shareholders or their relatives/friends, and where the salary package has been significantly increased, eg where funds previously taken as dividends are now taken as a pension contribution.

In the case of Harold and Frank they run a highly profitable trading company. HMRC would normally accept a remuneration package of any amount that could be funded by the efforts of the controlling directors. It follows that a total package, that includes a bonus for earlier years, even though paid mainly as a pension will be a commercial amount incurred 'wholly and exclusively' for the purpose of the business. It is unlikely that a pension contribution of £550,000 or less would be challenged in this set of circumstances.

Where large contributions are made the relief may be spread. This applies where contributions are made in two consecutive chargeable periods and the amount paid in the current period exceeds 210% of the amount in the previous period. The excess over 110% is known as the 'relevant excess contribution' and is then subject to the following rules (FA 2004 s 197)

(1) If the excess is less than £500,000   no restriction applies.

(2) If the excess is between £500,000 and £999,999   – ½ allowed in current period
       ½ allowed in following period.

(3) If the excess is between £1,000,000 and £1,999,999   – ⅓ allowed in current period
       ⅓ allowed in next period
       ⅓ allowed in following period.

(4) If the excess is £2,000,000 or more   – ¼ allowed in current period
       ¼ allowed in each of the following three periods.

Where the previous and current chargeable periods are not of equal length the amount paid in the previous chargeable period is adjusted by applying the fraction

$$\text{Contribution in previous period} \times \frac{\text{Days in current chargeable period}}{\text{Days in previous chargeable period.}} = \text{relevant contribution}$$

If the employer ceases trading before relief has been fully given for the spread contributions then the unrelieved contributions are deductible in the period of cessation or spread evenly over the period that starts on the first day of the current chargeable period (ie the period of actual payment) and ends on the date of cessation (FA 2004 s 198).

For detailed notes on pension contributions and benefits and the transitional rules to preserve existing rights see Example 37.

Self-administered schemes

3.   Employers may use an insurance company to provide a registered pension scheme.

Employers can instead (or also) establish under trust a registered self-administered scheme receiving the pension premiums into a fund under the control of trustees, one of whom must be an appropriately qualified person, referred to as the pensioneer trustee. This may be done in conjunction with an insurance company, actuary or professional trustees.

This gives the employers flexibility over the investment of the fund pending its being required to pay the retirement benefits, but the employer must always remember that the fund is under the control of the trustees and that it must be sufficiently liquid at the right time to provide the retirement benefits.

The insurance company in the first case, and the pensioneer trustee in the second, will structure the scheme and register it with HMRC.

Pension splitting on divorce

4.   The legislation enables a share of pension rights to be transferred on a divorce (FA 1999 s 79 and Sch 10). See Example 37 explanatory note 24 for details.

Self-assessment

5.   Trustees of registered pension schemes, other than insured schemes, are within the scope of self-assessment, and trustees are required to notify HMRC by 5 October following the tax year if they have a liability to tax and do not receive a return. The same self-assessment rules and time limits apply to trusts as for individuals. Pension fund trustees may complete returns on an accounting year basis and accounts should accompany the return. The return must be filed electronically.

Self-assessment does not apply to scheme administrators (although they may be the same people as the trustees), who have separate responsibility for notifying liability on various chargeable events. HMRC will issue assessments to collect the tax due.

Pension inputs: annual allowance charge

6.   To confirm that Dr Jolly is not liable to an annual allowance charge it is necessary to compare total pension inputs with the annual allowance for 2009/10.

	£
Pension inputs	
Defined benefits scheme (NHS)	
– per administrator	33,483
Defined contribution scheme	
– own pension (gross)	10,000
	43,483

As £43,493 is less than the annual allowance for 2009/10 of £245,000 no annual allowance charge is payable.

It should be noted that the pensions input on a defined benefits scheme is calculated by reference to the increase in the benefits accruing, not on the amount paid into the scheme. See Example 37 at note 3 for details of the calculation. In practice such calculations are undertaken by the pension scheme administrator.

Relief for contributions paid

7.   Tax relief is available for contributions paid, restricted to earnings of the year (see Example 37 at note 5). Where contributions are paid net of basic rate tax the basic rate band is extended by the grossed up pension contribution.

Normally contributions to a defined benefits scheme are paid via the employer and the net pay scheme is used to give relief (FA 2004 s 193). However, a GP doctor is self-employed and, therefore, relief cannot be given in that way. Instead the contributions actually paid in the fiscal year are deducted in arriving at taxable income. Relief is claimed on the self-assessment tax return by way of an entry into box 3 on page TR4. No deduction is permitted for any pension contribution of the taxpayer in computing the Class 4 national insurance contributions.

Restriction of higher rate tax relief for pension contribution

8.   See Example 37 explanatory note 2 for details of the restriction of higher rate tax relief for pension contributions.

     The restrictions do not apply to Harold, Frank and Dr Jolly as their income does not exceed the threshold of £150,000.

Contributions by retired GP's

9.   Tax relief is only due provided the payer has UK earnings. Because GP's make payments on account in respect of superannuation with a settlement when the annual return is submitted it is possible for payment of the final superannuation contribution to be made in the fiscal year after retirement. Insofar as the contribution exceeds earnings in that year, no relief will be given.

     Should the final adjustment be a refund of contributions that should be credited against the actual payments made and an amended tax return filed, normally for the year of retirement.

Question

(a)   In December 2004 Joe Friend, who is a widower, attained the age of 65 and retired from his employment. He received from his superannuation fund a lump sum of £100,000 and a pension of £13,680 per annum. PAYE deducted at source for 2009/10 amounts to £2,238. He immediately invested £20,000 in a single premium insurance company bond with a life of five years and the other £20,000 in a similar bond but with a life of ten years. For both bonds the compound growth had been 15% pa for the first two years and nil since. Joe has taken annual withdrawals of 5% of the initial investment in each bond. In 2009/10 Joe's other income was the state retirement pension of £7,000 and building society interest of £2,000 (gross).

Calculate Joe's tax liability on the gain arising in 2009/10.

(b)   Show what the position in (a) above would have been if Joe Friend's taxable income after allowances had been £37,000 including dividend income of £2,000 (being net dividend of £1,800 plus tax credit of £200).

(c)   Show the effect on the position in (a) and (b) if, after receiving the proceeds from the five year bond, Joe had made a gift aid donation to charity of £1,600 in February 2010.

Answer

(a) **Joe Friend – tax liability on gain on single premium bond in 2009/10**

There is no liability on annual withdrawals from single premium bonds providing they do not exceed 5% of the initial investment.

The annual amounts withdrawn are taken into account in calculating the gain when the bond is finally cashed.

Joe Friend therefore has no liability in 2009/10 in relation to the ten year bond which he still holds. The position on the five year bond that matured in December 2009 is as follows:

		£
2005/06	Initial investment in December 2004	20,000
	15% growth in value	3,000
		23,000
	Less 5% of £20,000 withdrawn	(1,000)
		22,000
2006/07	15% growth	3,300
	5% withdrawn	(1,000)
		24,300
2007/08	0% growth	–
	5% withdrawn	(1,000)
		23,300
2008/09	0% growth	–
	5% withdrawn	(1,000)
		22,300
2009/10	0% growth	–
	Value on maturity	22,300
	Add annual withdrawals (4 × £1,000)	4,000
		26,300
	Less original investment	(20,000)
	Profit on bond	6,300

The bond profit is only liable to tax on the excess, if any, at higher rate tax less basic rate tax. But it counts as part of income for age allowance, so a tax charge may indirectly result.

Joe's income tax position in 2009/10, taking into account the bond profit, is as follows:

	£	
State pension	7,000	
Occupational pension	13,680	2,238
Savings income – building society	2,000	400
Profit on bond	6,300	
	28,980	2,638
Personal allowance (age allowance not available if income exceeds £28,930)	6,475	
Taxable income	22,505	

				£
Tax thereon:	22,505	@ 20%		4,501
Less basic rate tax deemed to have been paid on bond profit				
£6,300		@ 20%		1,260
Tax				3,241
Tax paid at source				(2,638)
Tax payable				603

Without the bond profit tax on Joe's income would have been as follows:

	£
State pension	7,000
Occupational pension	13,680
Savings income	2,000
	22,680
Age allowance	9,490
Taxable income	13,190
Tax thereon: 13,190 @ 20%	2,638
Tax paid as above	(2,638)
Tax due	–

The bond profit has therefore resulted in a tax charge of = £603 (representing the loss of tax relief at 20% on (9,490 – 6,475)).

Top slicing relief is available to reduce the rate of tax charged on the bond profit as indicated in (b) below. This is of no benefit in the above computation, because the relief applies only where a different tax rate would apply to the 'appropriate fraction' (one fifth in this example) of the bond profit. The bond profit of £6,300 falls wholly within the income charged at the basic rate (and no tax arises since the tax on the bond profit is covered by the notional tax treated as deducted) and the appropriate fraction would similarly fall within the basic rate band.

(b) **Joe Friend – tax liability on gain on single premium bond in 2009/10 if taxable income after allowances was £37,000**

To the extent that the bond profit falls within the basic rate band tax it is charged at 20%. The tax thereon is covered by the notional credit. The tax payable on the excess is (40 – 20) = 20%. The position is therefore as follows:

	£
Basic rate threshold	37,400
Income	37,000
Basic rate band remaining	400
Bond profit	6,300
Bond profit in higher rate band	5,900
Tax thereon @ 20%	1,180
Less: Top slicing relief (see below)	320
	860

	£
Annual equivalent of bond profit:	
1/5 × 6,300	1,260
Within basic rate band	400

			£
Taxed	@ 20%		860

Tax on annual equivalent (860 × 20% =) £172, multiplied by 5 (policy years) = £860, therefore top slicing relief is (1,180 – 860 =) £320.

Tax on income of (37,000 + 6,300 =) £43,300:

			£
Non-dividend income	35,000	@ 20%	7,000
Dividend income	2,000	@ 10%	200
	37,000		7,200
Bond profit (part)	400	@ 20%	80
	37,400		
Bond profit (balance)	5,900	@ 40%	2,360
	43,300		9,640
Less: Top slicing relief			(320)
Basic rate tax deemed to have been paid on bond profit	6,300	@ 20%	(1,260)
Tax credit on dividend	2,000	@ 10%	(200)
Tax payable			7,860

(c)   **If Joe Friend made gift aid payment of £1,600 net, £2,000 gross, in February 2010**

With taxable income before allowances of £28,980 as in (a)

For the purpose of computing age-related personal allowances only, taxable income may be reduced by the gross gift aid payment. Joe Friend would therefore have a revised liability of:

	£	£
Taxable income before allowances	28,980	28,980
Less: Gift aid payment (gross)	2,000	
	26,980	
Age allowance income limit	22,900	
Excess	4,080	
Personal allowance (65 to 74)	9,490	
Less: One half of £4,080	2,040	7,450
Taxable income		21,530
Tax thereon: 21,530 @ 20%		4,306
Less: Basic rate tax deemed to have been paid on bond profit		(1,260)
		3,046
Tax paid at source as in (a)		(2,638)
Tax payable		408
Amount previously payable as in (a)		603
Additional tax saving		195
Tax treated as deducted from gift aid payment £2,000 @ 20%		400
Total saving (effective rate 30%)		595

With taxable income before allowances of (37,000 + 6,475 =) £43,475 as in (b)

Clearly no age allowance is due and therefore income is not reduced by gift aid payments. Instead the basic rate band of £37,400 is increased by £2,000 to £39,400. The increase does not apply, however, when computing top slicing relief on life insurance bonds, so that the top slicing relief remains at £320 as calculated in (b). The position would therefore be:

				£
Taxable income before allowances				43,475
Bond profit				6,300
				49,775
Personal allowance				6,475
Taxable income				43,300
Tax thereon:				
Non-dividend income	35,000 @ 20%		7,000	
Dividend income	2,000 @ 10%		200	
	37,000			
Bond profit (part)	2,400 @ 20%		480	
	39,400			
Bond profit (balance)	3,900 @ 40%		1,560	9,240
Less: Top slicing relief as in (b)	43,300			(320)
Basic rate tax deemed to have been paid on bond profit				(1,260)
Tax credit on dividend				(200)
				7,460
Amount previously payable as in (b)				7,860
Additional tax saving				400
Tax treated as deducted from gift aid payment	2,000 @ 20%			400
Total saving (effective rate 40%)				800

Paying a registered pension scheme premium in place of gift aid

The tax liability on the bond in (b) above could be eliminated by Joe Friend paying an allowable pension premium in 2009/10 of £713 gross, £570 net. For the net cost of £570 the tax of £860 on the bond profit would be eliminated and there would be £713 in a pension fund. Although the treatment of pension payments is the same as for gift aid payments, ie the basic rate band is increased by the gross payment, there is no provision denying that increase when computing top slicing relief.

If Joe Friend in (a) had paid a pension premium of £1,600 net instead of a gift aid payment then exactly the same relief would be obtained, as total income for age allowance is reduced by gross pension contributions by ICTA 1988 s 256A.

Explanatory Notes

Qualifying policies

1. Although life assurance premium relief is not available for policies taken out after 13 March 1984, there are still tax advantages for qualifying policies, in that the proceeds are tax free unless the policy is surrendered less than ten years after the policy was taken out (or, for endowment policies, before the expiry of three-quarters of the term if that amounts to less than ten years).

The definition of qualifying policy is broadly that the policy must be on the life of the policyholder or his spouse/civil partner, it must secure a capital sum on death, earlier disability or not earlier than ten years after the policy is taken out, the premiums must be reasonably even and paid at yearly or shorter intervals and there are various requirements as to the amount of the sum assured and sometimes as to the surrender value (ICTA 1988 s 267 and Sch 15).

If the policy is surrendered before the end of the ten year period (or three-quarters of term), any profit arising is charged to tax in the same way as that on a non-qualifying policy (ITTOIA 2005 s 485) (see note 2 below).

Non-qualifying policies

2. If a policy is not a qualifying policy, the proceeds are free of capital gains tax, but any profit is charged to income tax at the excess, if any, of higher rate tax over the basic rate (ITTOIA 2005 s 530) subject to top slicing relief (see note 3 below).

    The most common form of non-qualifying policy is a single premium bond, as in this example. In each year (ending on the anniversary of the policy) withdrawals of not more than 5% of the initial investment may be made without attracting a tax liability at that time (to a maximum of 20 years). Any excess over the 5% limit is charged to tax at the excess of higher rate tax over the basic rate, amounting to 20% in 2009/10 as indicated in part (b) of the example. The 5% limit is, however, a cumulative figure and amounts unused in any year swell the tax-free withdrawal available in a later year. Any annual withdrawals that are not taxed when made are taken into account as part of the profit when the bond matures.

Top slicing relief

3. In calculating the tax on the bond profit, top slicing relief is available (ITTOIA 2005 s 535). The surplus on the bond is divided by the number of complete policy years that the bond has been held (or since the last chargeable event), and the amount arrived at is treated as the top slice of income to ascertain the tax rate, which is then applied to the full profit.

    If there are two chargeable events in one year, top slicing relief is calculated by working out the appropriate fractions for each policy and adding them together to arrive at the amount charged as the top slice of income.

    Part (c) of the example shows the effect on top slicing relief of paying gift aid donations and pension premiums. The provision preventing a gift aid donation from reducing income for top slicing purposes is in ITTOIA 2005 s 535(7). See Examples 37 and 90 for detailed notes on gift aid payments and pension premiums respectively.

Age allowance

4. Although in many instances it is possible to cash in a bond when no higher rate tax is payable, there is a possible tax charge as a result of the withdrawal of age allowance, as illustrated in part (a) of the example. Note that age allowance for a man aged between 65 and 74 exceeds the normal personal allowance by £3,015. Since the excess is withdrawn at the rate of £1 for every £2 by which income exceeds £22,900, the age allowance ceases to be available when income exceeds £22,900 + (2 × £3,015) = £28,930.

Losses on single premium bonds

5. If there should be a loss on a single premium bond, tax relief is not available, but if such a loss occurs in a year when the taxpayer is chargeable at higher rates and earlier withdrawals have been charged to tax, the lower of the amount of the deficiency on the bond and the total amount previously charged to tax on the bond will be allowed as a deduction in calculating the taxpayer's liability to tax

at excess rates. The saving will be at the excess of higher rate over basic rate tax for non-dividend income and the excess of the dividend upper rate of 32½% over the dividend ordinary rate of 10% for dividend income (ITTOIA 2005 s 539).

Dividend income

6. Dividend income is normally treated as the top slice of income (ITA 2007 s 16). This is, however, subject to ITTOIA 2005 s 535(4) dealing with giving relief for higher rates of tax on life policy gains, which provides that life gains are taken into account *after* dividend income to compute the relief. Hence in Joe Friend's case in part (b) of the example the life policy gain was taxed as the top slice of the income regardless of how much of the income was dividend income.

Shares in life policies

7. Except for transfers of shares in life policies between spouses/civil partners living together, where a policy is changed from joint to single names or vice versa it will be treated as a part assignment and therefore subject to the 'chargeable events' rules outlined in this example. Any gain arising will be taxed on the transferor. No tax charge will be made if the transfer is made for no consideration (ITTOIA 2005 ss 505–514).

Personal portfolio bonds

8. There are anti-avoidance provisions in ITTOIA 2005 ss 515–526 and SI 1999/1029 relating to personal portfolio bonds. Personal portfolio bonds are broadly investment linked or index-linked policies that enable the policyholder to select the underlying investments or index. For policy years ending on or after 6 April 2000, other than the last year, there is an annual taxable gain (yearly charge) amounting to 15% of a deemed gain equal to the total of the premiums paid and the total deemed gains in earlier years, less any taxable amounts withdrawn in earlier years. The yearly charge is taxed in a similar way to the normal chargeable events rules, but top slicing relief is not relevant. The total amount of gains taxed under the yearly provisions is deducted from any gain arising when the policy terminates. If gains arising during the life of a policy are reversed when the policy comes to an end, a compensating deduction will be made from taxable income.

    Most bonds taken out before 17 March 1998 are excluded from the provisions, and those who needed to change the terms of the policy to benefit from this exclusion had until the end of the first policy year after 5 April 2000 to do so. Policyholders who were not UK resident on 17 March 1998 will have at least 12 months after becoming resident to make the change.

Commissions and discounts

9. On 27 November 1997 HMRC published a detailed statement of practice (SP 4/97) about the taxation of commission, cashbacks and discounts and comments about the statement were published in Tax Bulletin dated February 1998.

    In general, commissions on a policyholder's own policies that would otherwise form part of trading profits or employment income are not taxed if a member of the general public would have received an equivalent amount.

    In relation to a policyholder's own life policies, where commission is received, netted off or invested, the qualifying status of the policy is not affected if commission is paid under a separate commission contract. If a discounted premium is paid, it is the net premium that is taken into account to decide whether the policy qualifies.

    In relation to life policy chargeable events, if commission is paid separately, the gain is calculated by reference to the gross premium. Commission invested in the policy counts as part of the premiums paid. Where a premium is paid net of commission, or a discounted premium is paid, the gain is calculated using the amount paid.

FA 2007 introduced anti-avoidance provisions to stop the exploitation of the commission rules. The scheme involved the policyholder taking out a large single premium life policy, typically linked to an interest bearing cash deposit fund. A large proportion of the commission received by the adviser was passed to the policyholder as a tax-free payment. The bond was then cashed when its value returned to the original premium value, ie at the point that there was no chargeable event gain. Thus the actual increase in value, ie the rebated commission, avoided a tax charge.

The legislation only applies where the premiums paid in a year exceed £100,000 and the policy is held for less than three years. Where the provisions apply only the net premium, after any commission rebate, is deducted in computing the chargeable event gain. The provisions apply to individuals, companies and trusts (ITTOIA 2005 s 541A and 541B and ICTA 1988 s 548A and 548B). The deduction of commission from the premium does not apply if the chargeable event is the death of the policyholder.

The insurer will produce a certificate of chargeable event gains without reference to any rebated or reinvested commission and it will be the responsibility of the taxpayer to compute the taxable chargeable event gain taking into account the commission adjustment if required by this legislation.

Tax credits

10. The profit on a bond is counted as investment income for tax credits. No top slicing relief is available. Assuming that the claimants have used their £300 deduction against other investment income this could mean that a taxpayer, only liable at basic rate, would have a significant withdrawal of tax credits.

Say the claimant's tax credit details for 2009/10 were as follows:

Employment income (both full-time)	£31,200
Investment income	£300

The couple have two qualifying children (aged 3 and 5) and pay eligible childcare costs of £180 per week. Their tax credits income in 2008/09 was £37,230 and they have received £4,506 in tax credits in 2009/10. Because their income has dropped they cashed a bond giving a chargeable event gain of £5,000 (number of complete years – 5) with notional tax credit of £1,000. No income tax liability arises, however for tax credits the cost would be:

			Income with Chargeable Event Gain £	Income without Chargeable Event Gain £
Employment			31,200	31,200
Investment income (less £300)			5,000	nil
Tax credits income 2009/10			36,200	31,200
Maximum claim (per day)	£			
WTC – Basic	5.18			
– Second adult	5.10			
– 30 hours	2.13			
– 2 children £6.13 × 2	12.26			
– Family element	1.50			
Total	26.17			
Annual figure × 365	9,552			
Childcare £180 × 80% × 52	7,488		17,036	17,036
Restricted by 39% × (36,200 – 6,420)			11,614	
(31,200 – 6,420)				9,664

	Income with Chargeable Event Gain £	*Income without Chargeable Event Gain* £
	5,422	7,372
Tax credits – received	4,506	4,506
– now payable	916	2,866

Effective cost of chargeable event gain is £5,000 × 39% = £1,950 (2,866 – 916).

In the same way a claimant liable to higher rate tax and a tax credits withdrawal at 6.67% would find that the effective cost of a chargeable event gain in 2009/10 will be 20% + 6.67% = 26.67%, where income for tax credits including chargeable event gain has increased by more than £25,000 over base year.

Non-UK life insurance bonds

11. Gains made on foreign life assurance policies are liable to UK income tax if the holder is UK resident when the policy is encashed. There is no notional tax credit available unless the policy has suffered a comparable European Economic Area tax charge (ITTOIA 2005 s 532), or a similar foreign tax charge (ITTOIA 2005 s 534).

   Top slicing relief is available (see note 3 above).

   If the policyholder was resident outside the UK for part of the period since the policy was taken out then the gain is reduced as follows

   $$\text{Gain} \times \frac{\text{No of days non-resident}}{\text{No of days policy held}} = \text{Chargeable Event Gain}$$

(ITTOIA 2005 s 528)

Many overseas bonds are written in jurisdictions with favourable tax regimes, such as the Channel Islands or the Isle of Man. No tax is charged on the income or gains of the policy during its life thus allowing gross roll-up of most income. Note that if the income received has borne a non-repayable withholding tax or has a notional tax credit (eg UK dividends) then the benefit of that tax will be lost.

On encashment the whole of the gain is subject to income tax without any credit. By use of top slicing relief, and careful timing, it may be possible to restrict the tax charge to basic rate only thus saving the higher rate charge that would have applied had the income been chargeable on the taxpayer when it arose.

Question

Mr and Mrs Norton, who are resident, ordinarily resident and domiciled in the United Kingdom, have previously dealt with their own tax affairs. In May 2009 they instructed you to prepare their income tax returns, and compute all tax liabilities, for the year ended 5 April 2009.

You have not received any documents from them other than their tax return forms for 2008/09 but at your initial meeting you were informed that their personal circumstances were as follows:

(1)   They are married and Mrs Norton has one child, James, from a previous marriage. Mr Norton was born on 11 May 1964 and Mrs Norton on 5 October 1968. James was born on 7 June 1996.

(2)   Mr Norton is the overseas purchasing manager of Rumwell plc, a London department store, and receives gross remuneration of approximately £45,000 per annum. A car is provided by his employer.

(3)   He has a bank deposit account.

(4)   He pays an annual subscription to his professional association and gift aid payments to his local church.

(5)   He has a mortgage of £80,000 on their private house in London.

(6)   Mrs Norton is a director (working part time only) of Priddy Ltd, undertakers. She receives gross remuneration of between £2,500 and £10,000 per annum, depending upon results, and receives mileage allowance for use of her own car. As this is her family company, she also receives a dividend on her shareholding based upon the tax planning requirements of the company.

(7)   She has stock exchange investments and building society deposits.

(8)   She paid a premium under a personal pension plan in the year ended 5 April 2009.

  (i)   Prepare schedules to be sent to Mr and Mrs Norton listing documents and information that you will require for completion of their tax returns and computation of tax liabilities for the year ended 5 April 2009.

  (ii)   It is your office policy to undertake a review of the file of each personal taxation client before the end of each tax year. Explain why this is advisable and outline the matters which you would include in your review in February 2010.

Answer

(i) **Schedules to be sent to Mr and Mrs Norton listing documents and information required to complete tax returns and to compute liabilities for year to 5 April 2009**

Schedule to be sent to Mr Norton

1. **Earnings**

    (a) The following are required in respect of Rumwell plc for 2008/09:

    P60 year-end certificate of pay and tax deducted

    Coding notices issued for 2008/09 (and also coding notice for 2009/10) (Form P2), together with details of any underpayments brought forward from 2006/07 or 2007/08 to 2008/09, or amounts carried forward to 2009/10 in respect of 2008/09

    Form P11D (details of benefits and expenses received), together with any additional schedules provided by the employer

    Details of any expense payments received from the employer not included on Form P11D (eg those covered by a dispensation or by a PSA)

    Expenses incurred in performance of duties of the employment to be itemised for expenses claim

    Details of car, including list price when new, CO_2 emissions figure, whether any capital contribution made or accessories provided after the car was made available to him and whether private fuel provided

    Details of share options and incentives, with particulars of any options exercised during 2008/09

    Details of any amounts received, other than from Rumwell plc in respect of the employment

    Confirmation of whether Mr Norton is a member of Rumwell's pension scheme.

    (b) Confirmation that there are no earnings from other sources. If there are any such earnings, details required of amount, source and date of payment. If employment changed in the year, Form P45 (part 1A) is required.

    (c) National insurance number (if not shown on P60 or tax return).

2. **Bank deposit account**

Details of the interest credited during the year to 5 April 2009. The name of the deposit taker and account number. Confirmation that the account is a UK based account and that interest is after deduction of basic rate tax. Tax vouchers for such interest.

3. **Professional subscription**

Amount paid and name of professional association.

4. **Details of gift aid payments**

Amounts actually paid to church in year with confirmation that Mr Norton has signed a gift aid declaration.

Confirmation that Mr Norton did not make any other covenanted payments or charitable gifts from which he deducted basic rate tax during the year ended 5 April 2009.

Details of any gift aid payments made since 5 April 2009, so that consideration may be given to a claim to carry such payments back to 2008/09.

5. Information for tax credits

Child's full name, confirmation that James's father cannot make any child's tax credit claim in respect of James. If he could make such a claim, consider surrendering the child's tax credit to him if Mr and Mrs Norton are unable to make a full claim because of the level of their income.

Confirmation that Mr & Mrs Norton have made a claim for tax credits for 2008/09. This claim is based upon income for 2007/08 and then adjusted to actual income for 2008/09. It is possible that a claim will be due for 2008/09 as their joint income after deduction of professional subscription, gift aid payments, pension premiums and the £300 disregard for non-earnings, could be less than £58,170. If their income in 2007/08 was lower their final entitlement will also benefit from the £25,000 disregard. Their income is probably too high to qualify for childcare credit.

6. Other income and outgoings, and capital transactions

Details of any other income and outgoings, or changes therein, and capital assets acquired or disposed of. (Details of capital assets acquired are not required for the tax return, but are essential for the adviser's file.) Details of any capital gains tax losses brought forward.

Confirmation that no investments in James's name were provided by Mr Norton.

7. 2007/08 tax calculation working sheet

Copies of the working sheet for 2007/08, or of HMRC's calculation of liability, together with a copy of the 2007/08 self-assessment tax return.

8. 2008/09 payments on account

Copies of any payments on account notices and summary of payments statements already issued for 2008/09. Details of any claim made to reduce payments on account (Form SA303).

9. Form 64–8

Signed Form 64–8 giving authority to HMRC to issue copies of formal notices to agent and to discuss all taxation, national insurance and tax credit issues.

10. Electronic filing

Confirmation that electronic filing of the return will be acceptable.

Schedule to be sent to Mrs Norton

1. Earnings

P60 from Priddy Ltd for 2008/09, together with coding notices issued for 2008/09 and 2009/10 (Form P2) and details of any benefits and expenses received (Form P11D, together with any additional schedules provided by the employer, and details of any expenses or benefits received not included on P11D).

Expenses incurred in performance of duties.

Details of business mileage undertaken in her own car and the amount paid by her employer.

Amount, source and date of payment of any earnings in the year other than those included on Form P60.

National insurance number (if not shown on P60, code notices, or tax return).

2. Investments

Dividend vouchers for dividends paid by Priddy Ltd during 2008/09.

Dividend and interest vouchers on stock exchange investments and contract notes covering any purchases and sales of securities.

Details of original acquisitions of investments and whether any capital gains tax elections are in force. Details of any capital gains tax losses brought forward.

Details of building society accounts including account numbers and interest credited in the year. Confirmation that they are UK based accounts and interest is credited net of basic rate tax. Tax vouchers for such interest.

3. Personal pension policy

Name of insurance company to which personal pension premium paid and amount thereof, Form PPCC or other evidence of payment, and confirmation that the premium was paid net of basic rate tax.

Confirmation that Priddy Ltd has not included her in a company pension scheme.

4. Covenants and gifts

Confirmation that no covenanted payments or gifts under deduction of basic rate tax were made during the year to 5 April 2009 or since 5 April 2009.

5. Provision for James

Details of any investments in James's name provided by Mrs Norton.

6. Self-assessment details for 2007/08 and payments on account for 2008/09

Copies of any payments on account notices and summary of payments statements already issued for 2008/09, and of the tax calculation working sheet, or HMRC calculation of liability, for 2007/08, together with a copy of the 2007/08 tax return.

7. Other income and outgoings, and capital transactions

Details of any other income and outgoings or changes therein, and capital assets acquired or disposed of.

8. Form 64–8

Signed Form 64–8 giving authority to HMRC to issue copies of formal notices to agent and to discuss all taxation, national insurance and tax credit issues.

9. Electronic filing

Confirmation that electronic filing of the return will be acceptable.

(ii) **Year end review to be undertaken in February 2010**

Need for annual review

An annual review is essential in order that opportunities for tax mitigation are considered and any necessary action may be taken before the end of the tax year.

A record of the review should be kept in the file of each personal taxation client, and also those for whom one prepares accounts and agrees business taxation liabilities in so far as the personal taxation aspect of their affairs is concerned.

The main areas to be covered in the review are:

Areas relevant to Mr and Mrs Norton

1.   Pension provision

The schedule received from Mr Norton re 2008/09 will confirm whether Rumwell plc operates a pension scheme of which he is a member. Assuming that this is the case, consider whether any additional pension contributions are appropriate.

Mrs Norton's pension provision should similarly be reviewed, including the possibility of paying £3,600 pa even if that is more than her earnings.

Check that Mr and Mrs Norton have not exceeded the lifetime limit (unlikely). Also, it is possible if Mr Norton is a member of an occupational pension scheme that he has rights to a lump sum in excess of 25% of the fund. If so that right will be preserved providing he does not transfer funds from that scheme before drawing benefits.

2.   Is income sufficiently large to utilise personal allowances, loss etc claims, and the basic rate bands of each spouse and child?

Mr Norton clearly uses his available allowances. The position for Mrs Norton and her child should be checked. If allowances etc are not being used there may be nothing that can be done. If possible Mrs Norton should receive salary and benefits of an amount which, together with her savings income other than dividends, equals at least her personal allowance before receiving dividends from Priddy Ltd and other investments, as the tax credit on dividends is not repayable.

3.   Gifts to charities

As well as ensuring that a gift aid declaration has been made for all charities to whom amounts are given, should additional gifts be made in favour of charities and a payment made before 6 April, relief at the higher rate then being available if appropriate? (Payments made after 5 April but before filing the tax return and before 31 January may also be carried back to the previous year.)

Check that gifts are made by the spouse with the highest marginal rate of tax, ie Mr Norton unless Mrs Norton's investment income is substantial. If gifts were made by Mrs Norton, and she was a non-taxpayer, she would have to account for basic rate tax if insufficient tax credits were available on her dividend income to cover the amount deemed to be deducted (see Example 90).

4.   Potential capital gains tax position

Has Mrs Norton made sufficient gains to utilise the annual exemption (£10,100 for 2009/10)? If gains above that level have already been realised, are there assets standing at a loss which should be sold before 6 April 2010 in order to reduce the chargeable gains? Remember that the contract date is the date of disposal for capital gains tax. It should be borne in mind that in later life state aid for nursing care will be affected by the resulting holdings of assets.

5.   Transfers between spouses and inheritance tax planning

It appears that Mr Norton has no investments. Consider whether it would be appropriate for Mrs Norton to transfer some investments to him to utilise his annual exemption for capital gains tax, or into joint ownership (see explanatory note 4). Such transfers must be absolute gifts to be effective.

When reviewing the investment position, a review of current wills could be made, incorporating a calculation of the potential inheritance tax liability. Consideration should be given to the FA 2008 changes enabling the transfer of nil-rate bands between spouses effective from October 2007. Any necessary advice about new wills and mitigation of potential inheritance tax liabilities by insurance, use of trusts, or other means could then be given.

If appropriate, Mr and Mrs Norton should be made aware of the inheritance tax provisions for small gifts, gifts out of income and annual exemptions, and the facility to make potentially exempt transfers.

Areas for consideration generally

6.   Maximising allowances, basic rate band and reliefs

Consider whether justifiable payments for one spouse assisting in the other's business can be made before 6 April where appropriate. This is relevant not only for trades, professions and vocations but also in relation to a UK property business and for occupations such as clergymen and examiners. PAYE regulations (completion of Form P46, deduction at source if appropriate etc) must be followed. The national insurance implications should also be considered. In 2009/10 a spouse could be paid £110 a week without attracting national insurance contributions. Pay at or above £95 makes the year a qualifying year for benefits purposes (including state pension). On the other hand, if a spouse's pay was at a much higher level (in order to use the basic rate band) the national insurance cost would be substantial.

In the case of discretionary trusts or deceased's estates, should a distribution be made before 6 April?

Where there is a family company, should a dividend be paid by the company before 6 April rather than after 5 April? Conversely would the tax position of the recipient be improved by delaying a dividend or indeed other income until a later tax year if that is possible? Since tax credits on dividends are not repayable, dividends are not effective in enabling personal allowances to be used.

For those near or over 65, the effect of bunching of income on age-related allowances should be borne in mind.

Explanatory Notes

Notifying HMRC of agent's appointment

1.   Upon receiving instructions the agent should file Form 64–8 with the Central Agent Authorisation Team at Longbenton, Newcastle-upon-Tyne, NE98 1ZZ. It would be usual to write to the Area Office informing them of the instructions to act for Mr and Mrs Norton, asking them to supply copies of formal notices etc, and asking for:

(a)   Copies of the last tax returns of Mr and Mrs Norton.

(b)   Copies of the notice of calculation of tax liability for 2007/08.

(c)   Confirmation that there was no outstanding correspondence requiring attention, open appeals, or contentious matters under discussion or enquiry.

(d)   Details of any PAYE coding adjustments affecting 2008/09 or 2009/10.

HMRC will usually supply this information/documents upon processing the Form 64–8, but otherwise they will do so on receipt of a letter from Mr and Mrs Norton.

It should be noted that Form 64–8 is not sent to CAAT for

–   Cases dealt with by Claims Offices,

–   Complex personal returns,

–   Expatriates,

–   Companies, or

–   Where there was also a CIS registration card application to accompany the Form 64–8.

These 64–8 Forms should be sent to the appropriate area office. If the agent files electronically, or uses a computer produced tax return, then the client will no longer receive a tax return for completion, but a formal notice requiring the submission of a completed return by the relevant date.

Pension provision

2. Mrs Norton will pay personal pension premiums net of basic rate tax. Her employment income is low, but if her investment income is high enough to take her income above the basic rate limit, further relief will be due on the premiums.

    As an alternative, it may be possible to get Mrs Norton's employer (Priddy Ltd) to make the payments to the personal pension. Employer contributions are paid gross. The pension contribution is deductible for trading income purposes to the extent that it is incurred wholly and exclusively for the purpose of the trade. However, it is the remuneration package in total that must be wholly and exclusively for the purposes of the trade. HMRC have stated that the proportion that the pension contribution bears to salary will not affect the deduction, but the total amount must be justified by the work done.

    The pension contribution is paid from funds that have not been reduced by national insurance contributions. It is, therefore, possible to effect a salary sacrifice of an amount that would have been liable to national insurance contributions, and enhance the contribution (and, therefore, total remuneration) by the amount of the national insurance saved. This can increase the value of the amount invested into the pension by up to 31%.

3. All files should be reviewed each year in time for appropriate action to be taken in relation to pension contributions before 6 April 2010. If Mr Norton is not a member of an occupational scheme, a personal pension plan would be appropriate.

Transferring assets between spouses

4. Rather than transferring assets outright, spouses may prefer to put them into joint ownership. In that event the income will be divided 50:50 for tax purposes regardless of the actual ownership proportions (ITA 2007 s 836). This provision does not apply to close company shares (from 6 April 2004). In that case the division of income always follows the actual ownership.

    If the taxpayers prefer, a declaration may be made of the true beneficial ownership of the investment. Provided HMRC is notified (on Form 17) within 60 days of the date of the declaration, the true division of income will apply from the date the declaration was made (ITA 2007 s 837). In Tax Bulletin 63 (February 2003) HMRC made it clear that joint bank and building society accounts are held equally and cannot be the subject of a s 837 election unless the parties have changed the legal basis on which the account is held, for example, by way of deed.

5. Where action is being contemplated to reduce the income of the main earner from a family company full regard must be given to the anti-avoidance legislation relating to settlements in ITTOIA 2005 part 5 chapter 5. If an element of bounty is provided, then the income remains taxable on the main earner. The decision in *Young v Pearse, Young v Scrutton* (1996) should be noted. In this case, preference shares without voting rights were issued to wives, entitling them to dividends of 30%. It was held that the preference dividends remained assessable on the husbands under ITTOIA 2005 s 626 since the property given was wholly or substantially a right to income. HMRC have given its view as to when the settlement provisions will apply in Tax Bulletin 64 (April 2003).

    HMRC will review cases where it appears that:

    –   the main earner draws a low salary leading to enhanced dividends paid to other family members or friends

    –   dividends represent disproportionally large returns on capital investments

    –   there are different classes of shares enabling dividends to be directed to shareholders only paying the lower rate of tax

–   there are dividend waivers in favour of shareholders who only pay at the lower rate of tax

–   there is income transferred from the earner to other members of the family or friends who pay tax at a lower rate.

Commonly, the settlements legislation will be considered to apply where:

–   shares are subscribed for that carry only restricted rights

–   shares are gifted that carry only restricted rights

–   shares are subscribed for at par in a company where the income is derived mainly from the earnings of a single employee

–   a share in a partnership is transferred at below market value

–   there are dividend waivers

–   dividends are only paid on certain classes of share

–   dividends are paid to a settlor's minor children.

In the case of *Jones v Garnett* (Arctic Systems), the main earner was paid a salary well below the going rate, which provided funds that could be distributed equally between husband and wife by a way of a dividend. A decision in 2005 confirmed that taking a salary below the market rate provided bounty, and therefore the dividend declared to the wife was taxable on the husband. This decision was reversed, and upheld by the House of Lords. Draft legislation known as 'income shifting' which 'reversed' the Arctic decision was then published. The rules were widely drafted and caught a number of 'commercial' situations, eg businesses involving spouses, siblings, parents and children. The 2008 Pre-Budget Report confirmed that these rules are to be deferred although the issue remains 'under review'.

National insurance

6.   A client's national insurance position needs to be considered when a business commences or any additional activities are undertaken. Notification of commencement of business should be made by telephone or on Form CWF1 within three calendar months of the calendar month of commencement.

A certificate of deferment should be applied for if a client is expected to pay more than the overall maximum contributions under Classes 1, 2 or 4. The first application should normally be made by *14 February* before the relevant tax year (see Example 48). Renewal forms will be sent by the National Insurance Contributions Office for later years. If a deferment certificate is not held, a repayment should be applied for.

Those with small earnings from self-employment (under £5,075 for 2009/10) may apply for a certificate of exception from Class 2 contributions. Exception must be claimed no later than 31 December following the end of the relevant tax year. The certificate needs to be renewed each year. It may well be thought advisable for a client to pay the contributions in any event, in order to maintain a contributions record (the alternative voluntary Class 3 contributions being £9.65 a week higher).

Employees have entitlement to benefits if their earnings exceed the lower limit (£95 per week in 2009/10). Their contributions are 11% of earnings over £110 per week to a maximum of the upper earnings limit of £844 per week and 1% thereafter. Employers' contributions of 12.8% commence at earnings above £110 per week. Accordingly an employee could have earnings of £5,720 per annum without attracting any national insurance contributions. A PAYE scheme would be needed to establish the employee's entitlement to benefits. From 2009/10 the upper accruals point is £770. Earnings above this limit up to the upper earning limit are still charged to national insurance at 11%, but they do not accrue any further social security benefits such as S2P.

Inheritance tax and taxation of trusts and estates

7.   For detailed provisions see companion book Tolley's Taxwise II 2009/10.

Tax credits

8.   All taxpayers with a qualifying child, or who work 30+ hours per week and are aged 25 or over should consider making a protective claim for tax credits by 6 July in a tax year. Any later claim can only be backdated by three months. Because an award is eventually based upon income for the actual year it will not be known, by 6 July, whether or not an amount will be payable. If the claimant waits until the award can be quantified it will often be too late to make any claim. See Example 7 for full details. This is especially relevant in the current economic climate where many businesses are making unpredicted losses and employees are surprised by redundancy.

Question

Outline the self-assessment provisions that apply to individuals.

Answer

Outline of self-assessment provisions for individuals

1. General

(a) Requirement to send in a return

The filing deadline varies depending on whether a taxpayer uses an electronic method of filing the tax return (TMA 1970 s 8 (1D) from 2007/08). On receipt of a notice from HMRC requiring a return to be made, those taxpayers who wish to work out their own tax must send in their return, together with supporting schedules by:

- 31 October following the end of the tax year if the return is non electronic, (ie, by 31 October 2010 for 2009/10); or

- 31 January following the end of the tax year for an electronic return (ie, by 31 January 2011 for 2009/10).

If a notice is given after 31 July following the tax year the return must be filed by:

1. three months from the date of notice (for a non-electronic return); or

2. 31 January, if later than 1 (for an electronic return).

Taxpayers may produce returns using a computer if they wish and appropriate software is commercially available. HMRC cannot accept a return on disk. Filing via the internet is available to those who register with HMRC's online services (accessible from www.hmrc.gov.uk).

The Government accepted Lord Carter's recommendation that to encourage online filing, computer generated substitute returns should no longer be accepted. This applies from 2007/08 onwards for SA individual returns, SA partnership returns and SA trust returns. However, there are a small number of SA taxpayers who cannot file online because of their particular circumstances. HMRC allow this small minority to file on paper up to 31 January. The solution is only intended for the small minority but they have confirmed they will accept 'other' paper returns filed up to 31 October provided they are identical. HMRC have threatened to withdraw this option for all if the solution is used inappropriately by those who could file online.

If precise figures are not available when the return is submitted, best estimates should be used. Where provisional figures are used, box 20 should be ticked and an acceptable explanation for the delay, together with an estimated date by which the final figure will be provided, entered in the additional information box. If the figures are not available within the one year time limit for taxpayer amendments or HMRC enquiries (see notes 6 and 13), HMRC will accept an 'error or mistake' claim (see Example 43) to reduce the tax payable, or will issue a discovery assessment under TMA 1970 s 29 (see note 15) to recover any additional tax payable. Error or mistake claims will be replaced by the wider statutory relief in FA 2009 Sch 52 from April 2010.

If HMRC receives an unsatisfactory return it will be rejected. This includes:

- non-standard return form;

- unsigned return;

- relevant supplementary pages not enclosed with the return;

- a return containing unjustified provisional figures.

If HMRC sends back an unsatisfactory return between 18 January and 31 January following the tax year, then in cases of genuine oversight 14 days are allowed for the return to be resubmitted without incurring a penalty.

Where a taxpayer starts a business or joins a partnership, it may not be possible to submit accurate information relating to the business as the first year-end is after the relevant 5 April. The procedure for provisional figures set out above should be used. For partnerships see Example 42 note 9.

(b) Calculation of tax payable

Taxpayers do not have to work out their own tax and HMRC will make the calculations if the return is sent in by 31 October (eg by 31 October 2010 for 2009/10). A tax calculation is provided automatically as part of filing on-line. Calculations of amounts on which the tax is based must, however, be done by the taxpayer, for example capital allowances and capital gains. Taxpayers may ask HMRC to check valuations used in calculating their capital gains before they send in their returns.

HMRC will still calculate the tax for returns received after 31 October if required, but will not guarantee to advise the amounts due in time for the taxpayer to avoid interest (and possibly a surcharge). As far as employees are concerned, even if they are working out their own tax, for 2008/09 they must meet the 31 October (or 30 December if filed online) deadline if there is a tax underpayment of up to £2,000 that they wish to have collected through the PAYE scheme rather than being required to pay it on 31 January following the end of the tax year. If the 31 October deadline is missed but HMRC receives the paper return by the end of November, they will still try to collect the underpayment through PAYE but cannot guarantee to do so, although submission of a paper return at this point could attract a penalty.

Where a taxpayer with employment income settled an underpayment in excess of £500 by payment in the previous year then the HMRC system will not code out underpayments in excess of £500 in the current year. Care should be taken to warn clients of this problem if they fail to file their return by 31 October and therefore have to pay the balance of tax due on 31 January following.

Taxpayers need not include pence on the return, and income and gains may be rounded *down* and tax paid/dividend tax credits rounded *up*. If an entry in a particular box covers several different items, it is the *total* figure that should be rounded. The tax calculation may also be rounded, although not the resulting payments on account. If the tax is calculated either by HMRC or by commercial software, it will be calculated in pounds and pence, and software packages also show income and gains in pounds and pence.

Several errors have been identified in HMRC's computer program for calculating tax and interest, so it is advisable to check the figures.

(c) Trust and estate returns

To minimise delays in winding up estates and trusts and distributing estate or trust property, HMRC will, on request, issue tax returns before the end of the tax year of death, or of winding up an estate or trust, and will give early confirmation if they do not intend to enquire into the return.

The death of the taxpayer does not automatically cancel the payments on account due for that year based upon the previous year's liabilities. It is necessary to compute the likely liabilities to the date of death, then make a claim on Form SA303 to reduce the payments on account to the expected liability.

(d) Partnerships

In addition to partners completing their own self-assessment returns, a partnership is required to file a partnership return, together with a partnership statement (TMA 1970 ss 12AA and 12AB). A partner's individual return shows only the partner's share of income and gains, the details being in the partnership return. See Example 42 for the detailed provisions.

HMRC free software for internet filing does not cover partnerships. Third party software exists, but where this is not being used, it is necessary to hand write the paper form and file by the paper deadline of 31 October.

(e)   No tax liability for year

If a taxpayer receives a return, and he has no tax liability, HMRC takes the view that the return must even so be completed. Since most penalties under self-assessment currently cannot exceed the tax payable, the only penalty which would be effective in securing the return would be the £60 daily penalty, only payable after a direction which was previously given by the Commissioners, but would now be given by the First-tier Tribunal (TMA 1970 s 93(3)). See note 12 for more detail on the future changes to penalties. If the return is not completed it would be advisable to notify HMRC that there was no income.

(f)   Part-year residents

Where an individual leaves the UK and becomes non-resident part-way through the tax year, HMRC will accept a return made after the departure date but before the end of the tax year if it is accompanied by Form P45.

2.   Self-employment

When completing the self-employment pages of the tax return, the profit or loss is required to be shown on the self-employment pages in standard layout, which differs for smaller businesses with turnover of below the VAT limit (£68,000 for 2009/10) (see Example 15 for an illustration). For taxpayers who have a balance sheet, the balance sheet details must also be provided. For 2008/09 returns this does not apply to those whose turnover is less than £30,000, who are not required to submit a balance sheet and need only show their turnover, and tax deductible total expenses, and net profit.

For 2009/10 tax returns onwards the three line account threshold for self-employment and property businesses will be aligned with the VAT registration threshold.

Where more than one accounting period relates to the basis period for the year (for example where the accounting date has changed), a separate set of self-employment pages must be completed for each account.

Accounts need not be sent in with returns (with the exception of very large partnerships and partnerships with only corporate partners – see Example 42 note 5). Taxpayers may send whatever supporting information with their returns they consider is necessary in order to make a full disclosure, but unless the relevance of any additional material is pointed out, this will not stop HMRC later trying to make a discovery assessment (see Example 44). The return forms include various blank spaces for additional information (known as 'white space'), and it would be sensible to use the white space to refer to any additional information that is being sent with the return.

3.   Retaining records

Even though accounts etc need not be submitted with returns, taxpayers must retain their records for a statutory period. Traders and those with letting income must keep the records until the fifth anniversary of the 31 January next following the relevant tax year. Other taxpayers must retain records until the first anniversary of that 31 January date. So for 2008/09 the time limit for traders and landlords is 31 January 2015 and for other taxpayers 31 January 2011. If HMRC enquires into the return (see note 13), the records must be retained until the enquiry is completed if later than the normal retention date (TMA 1970 s 12B).

Where a claim is made other than in a return (see Example 43), records relating to the claim must similarly be retained until any HMRC enquiry into the claim is completed, or until HMRC is no longer able to start such an enquiry (TMA 1970 Sch 1A para 2A).

A penalty of up to £3,000 per tax year may be charged for non-compliance.

Finance Act 2008 allows HMRC to expand the definition of statutory records contained within s 12B by way of regulations and also by notice. There is as yet no idea of how HMRC may apply this new power, and no Regulations have yet been issued. However, statutory records have a specific identity under the new inspection powers, see note 13 below.

4.   Information from employers

Employers must provide employees with appropriate information relating to their earnings to enable the employees to complete their tax returns. Form P60 (pay and tax details) must be supplied by 31 May, and Forms P11D/P9D (details of expenses payments and benefits, including calculations of cash equivalents) by 6 July.

Employers sometimes make PAYE 'tax equalisation' arrangements for foreign national employees (see Example 8 explanatory note 19). There is a special Help Sheet IR 212 to assist such employees and their advisers in the completion of their tax returns, and see also Revenue Tax Bulletins of October 1997, June 1998, June 2002 and February 2006.

5.   Notification of liability if no return received

Anyone who is liable to income tax or capital gains tax and does not receive a notice under TMA 1970 s 8 must notify HMRC that he is so chargeable within six months from the end of the tax year, ie by 5 October 2010 for 2009/10 (TMA 1970 s 7). There is a penalty of up to the amount of tax payable as at 31 January following for non-notification. Penalties for failure to notify liability will be aligned from April 2010, with a behaviour based tax geared penalty of increasing amount depending on whether the failure was deliberate or not.

There is no liability to notify if the individual has no capital gains or liability to higher rate tax, and tax on all income has been accounted for under PAYE, or by deduction at source, or by tax credits on dividends. Employees will not usually have received their coding notices by 5 October, but if they have a copy of Form P11D they may assume HMRC is aware of its contents unless they have reason to believe otherwise.

Tax returns will not normally be issued unless income exceeds £2,500, providing the tax due can be dealt with through PAYE.

6.   HMRC corrections and taxpayer amendments

HMRC have nine months from the date a return is received to correct obvious errors in the return (TMA 1970 s 9ZB), and taxpayers may make amendments within a year from the filing date (TMA 1970 s 9ZA), but if the return is selected for further enquiry – see note 13 – amendments made between the time HMRC gives notice that they intend to enquire into the return and the time the enquiries are completed only take effect on the completion of the enquiry (TMA 1970 s 9B). HMRC will accept an amendment from a taxpayer's agent unless they believe the taxpayer may not have authorised it. HMRC's right to correct a return extends to making consequential corrections within nine months after a taxpayer amendment.

The taxpayer has an explicit right under TMA 1970 s 9ZB to reject an HMRC correction to a return, providing notice of rejection is given within 30 days (similar rights being given in relation to partnership returns by s 12ABB – see Example 42 note 8). In practice any rejection outside that period will be accepted if it is as a result of an HMRC error.

If an amendment results in extra tax payable, the due date of payment for the extra tax is 30 days after the amendment or, where relevant, the date of completion of an HMRC enquiry (TMA 1970 Sch 3ZA), although interest on overdue tax runs from the original due date for the return.

7.   Payments on account

Under TMA 1970 s 59A, provisional payments on account are due half-yearly on 31 January in the tax year and 31 July following. The payments on account are equal to half of the *net* income tax and Class 4 national insurance liability of the previous tax year (ie after deducting PAYE tax relating to that year, tax deducted from interest etc, dividend tax credits and tax deducted from subcontractors' payments and excluding student loan repayments). Payments on account are not required where more than 80% of the previous year's tax liability was covered by tax deducted at source and dividend tax credits, or where the previous year's net tax and Class 4 national insurance was less than £1,000 (£500 for 2008/09).

At any time before the 31 January filing date for the return, a taxpayer who believes he would otherwise overpay tax may make a claim (on Form SA303) for the payments on account not to be paid, or to be reduced. Care needs to be taken in working out appropriate payments on account for a taxpayer whose PAYE coding includes a previous year's underpayment or, in the future, a recovery of overpaid tax credits. The tax return provides for claims to reduce payments on account to be made in the return itself.

Following a claim, if either or both of the payments on account have already been made, the appropriate amount will be repaid, with repayment supplement from the payment date. If, however, the final tax figures for the year show that all or part of the reduction in the payments on account should not have been made, interest will be charged on the shortfall from the original due dates. In addition to being charged interest, a taxpayer who fraudulently or negligently reduces his payments on account is liable to a penalty not exceeding the shortfall in payment (TMA 1970 s 59A(6)). HMRC will calculate payments on account for taxpayers who do not calculate their own tax. Taxpayers receive regular statements of account (Form SA300) showing amounts due, amounts paid, and interest charges/repayment supplement where relevant. Statements will be issued when a new charge will become due within 35 days, every two months where an overdue amount is between £32 and £500 and every month where an overdue amount is £500 or more.

HMRC previously provided summary information, excluding interest on unpaid tax, on a client's statement of account at key dates in the year to agents for whom HMRC have the taxpayer's authority (on Form 64–8) to send copy information. This facility was withdrawn during 2008, although taxpayer's account information is available online. Taxpayers' statements of account can be sent to agents instead of the taxpayer by ticking the relevant box on the Form 64–8.

8.   Balancing payments/repayments

Under TMA 1970 s 59B, the total income tax, Class 4 national insurance and capital gains tax due for the tax year is compared with the amount already paid and the balance is payable or repayable on or before the following 31 January. If, however, a taxpayer had given notice of liability by 5 October following the tax year as indicated in note 5, and did not receive a notice to complete a return until after 31 October, the balancing payment is due three months from the date of the notice. In either case, the first payment on account for the next tax year is due at the same time.

Although the balancing payment for a tax year is due for payment at the same time as the latest date for sending in the return, the payment is sent to the HMRC accounts office and the return to the tax office.

Where a return shows an overpayment, it will be refunded if the appropriate box is ticked in the return, but overpaid payments on account are not refunded automatically. A letter requesting a refund of the payments on account should be sent or a refund requested online.

9.   Interest on overdue tax/Class 4 national insurance and repayment supplement

Interest on overdue payments on account and balancing payments runs from the due date of payment to the date the tax is paid (TMA 1970 s 86), and repayment supplement from the payment date to the date the repayment order is issued (ICTA 1988 s 824) (see Example 44 part B note 11 for the date when payment is regarded as having been made). There is no liability to tax on repayment supplement (ITTOIA 2005 s 749). At the time of publishing due to the fall in interest rates the current (since 27 January 2009) rate of repayment supplement is 0%.

Class 4 national insurance contributions and student loan repayments that are collected along with income tax also attract interest and repayment supplement as appropriate. Where a taxpayer has deferred Class 4 contributions (see Example 48), any amount that ultimately becomes payable is collected by the national insurance contributions office (NICO) and interest is not payable. If a taxpayer has overpaid Class 4 contributions because of exceeding the annual maximum, the refund is made by NICO and no adjustment is made to the amount self-assessed, so there is no effect on payments on account, interest etc.

The provisions in note 7 for charging interest in relation to payments on account apply where the payments have been reduced below half the previous year's liability. Except in relation to such a reduction, interest is not charged on any amount by which the payments on account fall short of the final net income tax liability for the year. If, however, the payments on account *exceed* the final income tax liability, repayment supplement is paid from the dates the payments were made. Since the first payment on account for the following year is due at the same time as the balancing adjustment, there will not usually be a repayment, but this does not affect the entitlement to repayment supplement. If a surcharge or penalty is repaid, repayment supplement is added to that repayment. For further points relating to interest and supplement calculations see Example 44.

Legislation has been introduced in FA 2009 Schs 53 and 54 to harmonise the interest regimes for income tax, VAT, PAYE, NIC and CIS. Corporation tax is currently excluded although parallel legislation is expected in the Finance Bill 2010. The change removes some of the differences in taxes which were formerly administered separately by the Inland Revenue and Customs and Excise prior to their merger. The rules provide for two single rates of simple interest on sums due and overpaid to HMRC based on Bank of England base rates. For income tax the rules do not contain any major changes, and interest on late paid income tax will remain disallowed in computing trading profits.

10. Surcharges

Surcharges currently apply as follows (in addition to interest) if the balancing payment for a year is more than 28 days late (TMA 1970 s 59C):

5% of the unpaid amount if the balance of tax due is not paid by 28 February.

A further 5% if not paid by 31 July.

The taxpayer may appeal against a surcharge, and the Appeal Commissioners may set the surcharge aside if the taxpayer has a reasonable excuse. HMRC have the power to mitigate or remit the surcharge.

Where additional tax is payable following an amendment to a return, the tax is due 30 days after the amendment, and surcharge arises only if the tax is paid more than 28 days after the 30-day period, and further surcharge only if the payment is not made within a further 5 months.

Surcharge is due for payment within 30 days after the date on which it is imposed, and it attracts interest from that date in the same way as the tax itself if it is paid late (s 59C(6)).

The penalty regime for late payment of taxes is being reformed. FA 2009 Sch 56 introduces new late payment penalties across the range of taxes (IT, CT, PAYE, NIC, CIS, SDLT, SDRT, IHT, pension and petroleum tax) excluding tax credits. Taxpayers have a right of appeal against all penalties and no penalty can be charged if they have a reasonable excuse. Penalties can be suspended where the taxpayer agrees a time to pay arrangement (subject to meeting the terms of the arrangement). Implementation of the new penalties requires changes to HMRC's computer systems and so will be introduced in stages from April 2010.

For income tax and capital gains tax the following late payment penalties arise:

- penalties of 5% of the amount of tax unpaid one month after the payment due date;

- further penalties of 5% of any amount of tax still unpaid at six and twelve months after the payment due date.

11.   Penalties for incorrect returns

Finance Act 2007 Sch 24 included a new framework for assessing penalties on incorrect tax returns. These covered income and corporation tax, PAYE, NIC and VAT. The new rules take effect for returns due to be filed after 31 March 2009. FA 2008 extends this framework to all other taxes and duties (inheritance tax, environmental taxes, stamp duties etc) except tax credits.

The penalty for submitting a return or other document which contains an inaccuracy which leads to an understatement of the tax liability is determined (as a percentage) by the amount of potential lost revenue, the nature of the behaviour giving rise to the understatement, and the quality of the disclosure (if any). These range from no penalty for a mistake made despite taking reasonable care to 100% for deliberate and concealed inaccuracies. This is best shown in a table below:

Penalties for incorrect returns

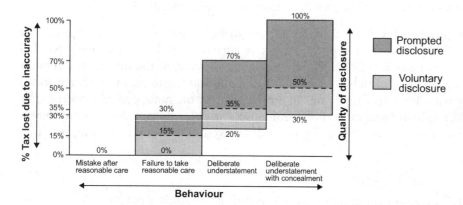

* The dotted line marks the minimum percentage for a prompted disclosure. The maximum percentage for a voluntary disclosure (unprompted) is the top of each category. For example, for an unprompted disclosure of a careless inaccuracy the penalty will be 30% (max), or 0% (min) or any amount in between.

Potential lost revenue

For a penalty to be charged two conditions must be satisfied:

1.   The document given to HMRC must contain an inaccuracy that leads to:

    ●   an understatement of tax liability;

    ●   an excessive tax loss; or

    ●   an excessive tax repayment claim; and

2.   The inaccuracy was careless or deliberate.

The list of documents covered is quite comprehensive and these penalties do not only apply to documents which are normally thought of as tax returns.

In order to arrive at the penalty it is necessary to know the amount of potential lost revenue (PLR). The basic rule is the PLR is the additional amount due as a result of correcting the inaccuracy. For the purpose of calculating PLR 'tax', NIC is included. In addition, group relief and relief given on repayment of a loan by a close company (ICTA 1988 s 419(4)) are ignored.

Special rules apply to losses, groups, multiple errors and delayed tax, so that the legislation prescribes an amount to be potential lost revenue in some cases, for example, where no relief for an overstated loss has yet been given.

Behaviour

The new penalties focus on behaviour. They are designed to educate and support those who try to comply and penalise those who deliberately evade. They therefore include the concept of no penalty for errors/omissions where the taxpayer took reasonable care plus substantially higher penalties in all other cases. Taxpayer's behaviours are divided into four separate groups shown above. An inaccuracy made by a person in a document or return may be:

- made despite taking reasonable care (**no penalty**); or

- careless; or

- deliberate but not concealed; or

- deliberate and concealed.

HMRC have published considerable material including their Compliance Handbook Manual, e-learning packages, various leaflets and frequently asked questions (www.hmrc.gov.uk/about/new-penalties/index.htm). These contain examples of the various behaviours.

Error despite taking reasonable care – No penalty

What is 'reasonable care' will be different for every taxpayer and depends on their ability and circumstances. HMRC have confirmed they do not expect the same level of knowledge from a self-employed un-represent individual, as from a plc.

An example of an error despite taking reasonable care is an arithmetical or transposition inaccuracy that is not so large (either in absolute terms or relative to overall liability) as to produce an obviously odd result or be picked up by a quality check, eg transposing a figure when filing a SA tax return – car benefit shown as £5,190 instead of £5,910.

It is important, when completing documents (tax returns etc) to fully disclose any contentious positions as this shows reasonable care and may protect the taxpayer from a penalty if the tax treatment is subsequently changed.

If an inaccuracy was made despite taking reasonable care at the time the document was submitted (normally no penalty), it can be treated as careless (ie, potential penalty) if the person discovered the error at some later time and did not take reasonable steps to inform HMRC of the inaccuracy.

Penalties can be raised where an adviser makes an error, however, no penalty can be charged if the taxpayer took reasonable care to ensure the document was correct.

Failure to take reasonable care 'careless' – penalty 0% to 30%

Careless is likened to the previous long-standing concept of 'negligence' which was the basis for a penalty under the old system for direct taxes. This includes omitting to do something a reasonable person would do or doing something a reasonable person would not do. For example, a plumber failing to keep accurate records to prepare his SA return.

HMRC expect taxpayers to take their tax affairs seriously and seek advice on unfamiliar transactions. If failing to seek such advice leads to an error it would be considered 'careless'. For example, Jack the trade electrician changes from using a van to a car to facilitate personal use (at weekends) but continues to claim all input tax on fuel without seeking advice from HMRC or his accountant. If advice is sought but subsequently found to be wrong (after disclosing all facts and from a reliable source) the taxpayer would have shown reasonable care and no penalty applies.

To encourage taxpayers to improve their systems and procedures, the careless penalty can be suspended for a maximum of two years provided the taxpayer complies with various conditions. The conditions relate to compliance with a view to preventing further problems. Provided such conditions are met, the penalty will be cancelled at the end of the suspension period.

Failure to notify an under-assessment within 30 days is a separate offence but subject to the same maximum penalty of 30%.

Deliberate but not concealed – penalty 20% to 70%

The key word here is 'deliberate' which implies the person knew what they were doing. An inaccuracy can arise by deliberately not doing something or deliberately getting something wrong. For example, knowingly failing to record all sales such as taking £50 'pocket money' or entering an inflated input figure on the VAT return and hoping the return would not be checked.

Deliberate and concealed – penalty 30% to 100%

The distinction between this category and the previous one can be a fine line, as almost any deliberate inaccuracy is likely to have some element of concealment. HMRC guidance states the person has taken active steps to cover their tracks by making arrangements. For example, taking 'pocket money' of £50 or entering the wrong input tax figure on the VAT return AND creating false paperwork to support.

Disclosure

A disclosure is unprompted if it is made at a time when the person making it has no reason to believe that HMRC have discovered, or is about to discover, the error.

A disclosure can be treated as unprompted even if:

- The full extent of the disclosure is not known, as long as full details are provided within a reasonable time.

- Made following a national campaign highlighting an area of the trading community.

- Exceptionally during a visit/compliance check *if* the disclosure is about something the officer has not discovered or is about to discover. For example, during a compliance check on a capital gain, the taxpayer discloses a car benefit or during a PAYE audit they disclose transfer pricing errors.

For VAT purposes, self-correcting errors on a subsequent VAT return (as under de minimis limit) does not count as a voluntary disclosure of the inaccuracy. Therefore all mistakes other than those made after reasonable care (and under the de minimis limit) should be disclosed in full.

Quality of disclosure

All of the penalties can be substantially reduced depending on the 'quality' of the disclosure. Quality is defined to include the timing, nature and extent of three elements. These elements are:

Telling: admitting, disclosing and explaining in full.

Helping: helping to quantify inaccuracies by volunteering information; actively engaging and providing positive assistance.

Giving access: responding positively to requests for information; allowing access to relevant documents.

For example, Mel has been systematically diverting taxable receipts into an undisclosed bank account and covering the traces. He is willing to make a full disclosure and is sure HMRC have no knowledge of his wrong doings. The maximum penalty for this type of behaviour is 100%. This can be reduced to 30% if the quality of Mel's disclosure warrants such a reduction.

The disclosure is to be seen as a continuous process involving much more than the initial contact. This means that in order to secure the maximum possible reduction (ie, reduce the penalty to 30%), Mel needs to make a reasonably full initial disclosure at the earliest possible stage and to cooperate fully with HMRC's subsequent enquires as required.

12. Penalties for late returns

If returns are made late, automatic penalties are currently charged as follows (TMA 1970 s 93):

£100 if the return is not made by 31 January (or the filing date for the return if later), plus a further £60 a day if HMRC have applied for and received a direction from the First-tier Tribunal to charge the daily penalty. Following the case of *Steeden v Carver* (1999) a late filing penalty will not be charged for returns received up to midnight on 1 February.

Further £100 if the Tribunal has not imposed the daily penalty and the return is not made by 31 July (or six months from the filing date if later).

Further penalty of an amount equal to the tax that would have been payable under the return if it is not made by next 31 January, or by one year from the filing date if later (not applicable to partnership returns).

The *fixed* (but not *daily*) penalties cannot exceed the amount of tax that remains outstanding at the return due date, and cannot be charged if a repayment is due. Where this applies, any fixed penalty already paid, or the appropriate part thereof, will be refunded (TMA 1970 s 100). This does not apply to late partnership returns.

The taxpayer may appeal against a penalty, and the First-tier Tribunal may set it aside if the taxpayer has a reasonable excuse. Interest is charged on unpaid penalties as it is on unpaid tax (TMA 1970 s 103A).

In a reasonable excuse case the onus is on the taxpayer to show that the excuse should be considered reasonable and that excuse must exist throughout the period of default. A reasonable excuse for late filing of a tax return could include:

- Fire or flood at the Post Office that handled the return, or prolonged industrial action within the Post Office.
- Loss of records through fire, flood or theft.
- Very serious illness such as coma, stroke, major heart attack or serious mental or life threatening illness.
- Death of a close relative or domestic partner.

Although HMRC does not consider reasonable excuse cases for VAT relevant for direct tax, such cases may well influence the decision of the Tribunal.

The following reasons are unlikely to be acceptable:

- Pressure of work.
- Failure of a tax agent, although this excuse was held to be reasonable in an appeal against a surcharge (*Rowland v HMRC*, 2006).
- Lack of information, unless due from a third party and actively pursued.
- Considering the tax form too difficult.

HMRC previously imposed penalties in some cases not only where a return was late, but where a return filed on time was not correct and complete (for example, where the return contained estimated figures). Following an appeal against their practice, they now accept that the inclusion of provisional or estimated figures does not enable them to impose a late filing penalty (unless reasonable care was not taken with the figures, or final figures could have been obtained before the return was sent in), although it will be a factor to take into account in deciding whether to open an enquiry.

HMRC have introduced an advance claim procedure for reasonable excuse against a potential late filing penalty for those unable to file their returns online due to technical constraints. The new single page Reasonable Excuse Claim form is submitted with the return where it is filed after 31 October and the return could not be filed online; there are several categories of taxpayer who are affected by this, including Members of Parliament and those with losses on foreign lettings. Details can be found on the online services pages of HMRC's website.

The penalty regime for late filing of returns is also being reformed. Finance Act 2009 Sch 55 introduces new late filing penalties across the range of taxes (IT, CT, PAYE, NIC, CIS, SDLT, SDRT, IHT, pension and petroleum tax) excluding tax credits. Taxpayers have a right of appeal against all penalties and no penalty can be charged if they have a reasonable excuse.

For income tax and capital gains tax the following late filing penalties will apply to income tax returns filed late:

- a £100 penalty, IRRESPECTIVE of whether the tax has been paid;

- daily penalties of £10 per day up to a maximum of 90 days once the return is three months late;

- penalties of 5% of tax due (tax payable for period not tax outstanding) for prolonged failures (over six and at twelve months);

- higher penalties of 70% of the tax due where a person fails to submit a return for over twelve months and has deliberately withheld information necessary to assess the tax due (100% penalty if deliberate with concealment).

It is important to note that when the new late filing penalty regime commences, the fixed £100 penalty for a late return will always apply, even when the taxpayer has no liability or is owed a repayment.

13. HMRC enquiries and compliance checks

The enquiry period is linked to the date a return is filed. For returns made on time, HMRC have a year after the day on which a return is delivered to open an enquiry, eg to 31 May 2011 for a 2009/10 return filed on 31 May 2010. If the return or an amendment to it is made after the due date, then the time limit is a year from the time the return or amendment is delivered plus the period to the next quarter day, ie the next 31 January, 30 April, 31 July or 31 October) (TMA 1970 s 9A). Otherwise the tax as calculated will normally stand unless there has been inadequate disclosure or failure to take reasonable care or deliberate understatement (previously fraudulent or negligent conduct). (Similar rules apply to partnership returns – see Example 42.)

Following completion of the enquiry, HMRC will issue a closure notice informing the taxpayer of their conclusions and any amendments they have made to the return. The taxpayer has 30 days to appeal against the conclusions stated and amendments made by HMRC, and the appeal and postponement procedures dealt with in Example 44 apply. (TMA 1970 ss 28A, 31.)

HMRC have similar powers to enquire into claims made separately from the return (TMA 1970 Sch 1A.5) (for claims procedures see Example 43). The time limit for opening an enquiry into such a claim is the same as for an enquiry into an amendment to a return, and the same procedures apply for the taxpayer to appeal against HMRC amendments when the enquiry is completed. There is, however, no provision for tax to be postponed.

HMRC may select cases for enquiry at random, and are not required to state whether the enquiry is a random one or whether they suspect something is wrong. There is no statutory relief for accountancy fees, although HMRC have confirmed that if an enquiry results in no addition to profits, or only in an adjustment to the year of enquiry that does not arise out of negligent or fraudulent conduct, accountancy expenses relating to the enquiry will be allowed (see Example 15 explanatory note 3). If it is considered that an enquiry has been unnecessarily prolonged, taxpayers may ask the First-tier Tribunal to direct that it should be closed, and they may also complain to the Adjudicator or Ombudsman, each of whom has the power to recommend compensation.

FA 2008 Sch 36 introduced new rules for checking that businesses and individuals have paid the correct amount of IT, CGT, CT, VAT and PAYE known as 'compliance checks'. These apply from 1 April 2009 and include more stringent record keeping, a power to look at records 'in real time' and visit business premises.

There has been widespread unease about the new powers and whether applying the 'real time' concept to income tax returns gives HMRC too much power. A forum has been created including members from HMRC, accountancy/tax bodies, industry, law society etc to report to the Treasury on matters arising from the implementation of the new powers.

Finance Act 2008 repeals TMA 1970 ss 19A and 20 (but not the enquiry rules in s 9A). In their place is a far broader set of powers under FA 2008 Schedule 36 part 1. No enquiry is required, instead HMRC can issue new information notices to any person requiring the production of information and or documents provided it is reasonably required to check a person's tax position (Sch 36 part 1 para 1 taxpayer notices and para 2 third party notices). The notice may be appealed against unless it relates to the production of statutory records which the taxpayer is obliged to keep or the First-tier Tribunal has approved the issue of the notice.

Schedule 36 part 2 (para 10) provides the power to inspect a person's business premises including vehicles and parts of homes used for business purposes and inspect documents on those premises provided reasonably required for the purposes of checking that person's tax position. They cannot search premises and as stated in HMRC Compliance Handbook manual at CH25650 'the person ... has the right to refuse you entry.' Therefore even when an officer has been given access to the premises he can be asked to leave at any time and HMRC's instructions make it clear that the officer must leave straight away.

The power of inspection does not extend to a person's home used solely as a dwelling, unless invited.

Business records become statutory records when they are created. As stated at note 3 above the normal time limit for a trader to retain their statutory records is over five years. For example, on 1 July 2009 a sole trader, with a 31 March year end, who has filed all tax returns on time and has not been subject to an enquiry in the last six years will hold statutory records for the period 1 April 2003 to 1 July 2009.

Non-business records which must be kept for tax purposes only become statutory records after the end of the chargeable period to which they relate. For example, Joanne gifts a precious ring to her sister on 1 July 2009 and on that date has an independent valuation carried out to calculate the gain arising. The valuation does not become a statutory record until after 5 April 2010 and assuming she files her return on time and no enquiry is opened must be retained until 31 January 2012.

An information notice or inspection may only be issued where it is 'reasonably required to check a person's tax position.' However, when a return has been made for the period, the notice must be issued within the enquiry window, unless a discovery has been made. Notices may, however be issued in respect of periods for which no return has yet been made, and the enquiry window principle does not apply to PAYE and VAT compliance checks.

HMRC have agreed to introduce a Charter for taxpayers by 31 December 2009. A draft charter was issued in February 2009 and HMRC is undertaking a consultation process on the final form of the Charter. FA 2009 s 91 introduces a statutory basis for the HMRC Charter.

HMRC have significantly (and successfully for some) changed its approach to compliance for large businesses. Some of these changes are expected to be rolled out to small and medium-sized enterprises by 2011. One target is to reduce the administrative burden around audits and inspections for businesses considered to be tax compliant. This works with large businesses where a business risk review is carried out and a low / high risk rating is given. Obtaining a low risk rating has considerable benefits. Due to the number of SME's the business risk review would be quite different and it is not clear exactly how it will be carried out but meeting all filing and payment deadlines and having effective reliable systems and processes in place seem obvious factors in a business's favour.

14.   HMRC determinations of tax due

HMRC have the power to determine the amount of tax due if a return is not submitted and their determination is treated as a self-assessment until superseded by an actual self-assessment (TMA 1970 s 28C). A determination under s 28C cannot be made more than five years after the filing date for the return, and a superseding self-assessment can only be made within the time limit, or if later within twelve months after the determination.

15.   HMRC assessments

Under self-assessment, HMRC will not normally issue assessments except for 'discovery assessments' under TMA 1970 s 29 to prevent a loss of tax in cases of 'failure to take reasonable care and deliberate understatement' or for returns due to be filed up to 31 March 2009 where there has been 'fraudulent or negligent conduct', or where there has been inadequate disclosure (see Example 44). There are still some other limited occasions when assessments will be raised outside the self-assessment system, for example:

Under ITA 2007 s 424 to recover tax deemed deducted from a gift aid payment to charity where the payer has insufficient income tax or capital gains tax chargeable to cover the tax – see Example 90.

Under ICTA 1988 s 307 to withdraw relief under the enterprise investment scheme – see Example 93.

Under TCGA 1992 s 153A to withdraw capital gains rollover relief provisionally given in respect of business assets – see Example 82.

Under FA 2004 s 192(9) to recover basic rate or other tax relief on excessive pension contributions.

Tax under HMRC assessment is due for payment thirty days after the issue of the assessment (TMA 1970 s 59B(6)). Interest is, however, payable from 31 January following the tax year to which the assessment relates, regardless of when the assessment is issued (TMA 1970 s 86).

The appeal and postponement procedures outlined in Example 44 apply to all HMRC assessments.

16.   Electronic submission of returns

Accountants and tax agents approved by HMRC may submit tax returns in respect of individuals, partnerships and trustees electronically (TMA 1970 s 115A & Sch 3A), where the taxpayer or agent has registered with HMRC online services.

For agents initial registration is via the HMRC website using the agent's code. Then the agent registers via the Government gateway at www.gateway.gov.uk. The agent is required to keep a copy of the filed tax return and accompanying schedules which must have been approved by the client before submission. The approval must authorise the electronic submission of the return.

Users of SA Online have the facility to view the client's self-assessment statement of account and perform basic housekeeping tasks online. The online account facility enables agents to see the same information as HMRC staff in respect of liabilities and allocation of payments, and to expand details relating to the current and earlier years. Agents can also check when repayments are issued, view the previous year's tax account and check the filing status (ie which returns have been filed for self-assessment and when) online.

It is government policy to increase electronic filing, and HMRC have been recommended to aim for electronic filing by computer literate groups by 2012. In FA 2002 ss 135 and 136, HMRC have been given power to make regulations *requiring* taxpayers to use electronic communications for the delivery of information, subject to a penalty of up to £3,000 for failing to do so. Initially this power has been used in relation to PAYE returns (see Example 8 part A note (11)), but the legislation paves the way for a much wider use of internet filing in the future. The SA return will not be brought within the mandatory online rules, but use of online filing is encouraged through the extended filing deadline for online returns.

Draft regulations to require online filing for both corporation tax and VAT have been issued. The regulations are subject to comment but propose:

- For VAT, returns and payments to be made online from April 2010 for all businesses with turnover in excess of £100,000 and all new businesses.

- For corporation tax, returns and payment online for all companies for returns delivered on or after 1 April 2011 relating to periods ending on 1 April 2010 or later. The returns will require the use of XBRL.

17. Non-statutory clearances

From 1 April 2008, HMRC will provide clearance across all business taxes where there is a material uncertainty. For direct tax older than the last four Finance Acts there is an additional requirement that the uncertainty relates to a commercially significant issue. HMRC aim to respond to applications within 28 days although reserves the right for longer in complex cases.

18. Certificates of tax deposit

Individuals, partnerships, personal representatives, trustees or companies may purchase certificates of tax deposit, subject to an initial deposit of £500, with minimum additions of £250. The certificates may be used to pay any tax except PAYE, VAT, tax deducted from payments to subcontractors and corporation tax. The only purpose for which companies may use tax deposit certificates is to pay income tax due under the quarterly accounting system. A certificate purchased in the name of a partnership can only be used against partnership liabilities.

Interest at a variable rate accrues daily for a maximum of six years. A lower rate of interest applies if the deposit is withdrawn for cash rather than used to cover tax liabilities. The interest accrued at the time the deposit is used or cashed is charged to tax as savings income.

The certificates are a way of ensuring that funds are available to meet tax payments when due. They also prevent interest charges on tax in dispute, because interest on overdue tax is not charged when the certificates are used to pay tax, except to the extent if any that the deposit was made after the due date of payment for the tax.

19. Short tax return

From 2004/05 the short tax return has been used nationally for taxpayers whose affairs are straightforward. These include employees and pensioners with limited investment income and those self-employed with turnover below £30,000 (to be raised to the VAT threshold for 2009/10 returns). The return does not include the facility to self-calculate so needs to be completed by 31 October for HMRC to perform the calculations before the following 31 January. There is an option to file the short return over the telephone using voice recognition software. A short tax return cannot be used by a company director, those receiving trust income or those who require supplementary pages. A short return will not be issued on demand or to taxpayers who failed to file on time in the previous tax year. A taxpayer whose affairs have changed such that they are not eligible for a short return must request a full return.

20. Disclosure of use of tax avoidance schemes

Taxpayers who use tax avoidance schemes are required to include on their tax return the registration number of the scheme. If the scheme has been implemented offshore or developed in-house then taxpayers will be required to provide details of the scheme directly to HMRC.

21. Student loans

Where an individual is self-employed, their student loan repayment is made together with their tax payment, ie, by 31 January after the end of the year of assessment. Student loan repayments are calculated as 9% of the income over the starting limit of £15,000. Student loan repayments are not included in the payments on account for the following year.

For example, Jo's 2009/10 profits amounted to £30,000 and her tax calculation is:

Income					30,000
Less personal allowance					(6,475)
					23,525
Tax thereon	23,525		@ 20%	4,705	
Class 4 NIC	30,000	– 5,715	@ 8%	1,943	
Student loan	30,000	– 15,000	@ 9%	1,350	
Total					7,998
Less payments on account for 2009/10 say					6,000
Balancing tax payment due 31 January 2011					1,998
First payment on account for 2010/11 due 31.1.11					3,324
Second payment on account for 2010/11 due 31.7.11					3,324

The payments on account are half the total excluding the student loan, ie, £7,998 – £1,350 = £6,648/2 = £3,324.

Where an individual is an employee, student loan deductions are made by the employer each pay day, ie, normally monthly or weekly. Each pay day is treated separately and therefore varies based on earnings. If earnings are below the starting limit for that period (ie, £15,000/12 or 52) the employer should not make a deduction.

Student loan repayments can be affected by large savings income (over £2,000 pa) and can be made voluntarily direct to the Student Loans Company.

22. Internal review

From 1 April 2009 all tax appeals are heard by either the First-tier Tribunal or the Upper-tier Tribunal. From that date for direct taxes the role of case reviewer was created within HMRC. The primary role of the review officer is to review the decision made by the case worker; objectively checking whether the disputed decisions are in line with HMRC's legal and technical guidance, policy and current practice (Appeals reviews and tribunals guidance (ARTG)).

The review may conclude that the decision should be:

– Upheld – the taxpayer can appeal within 30 days and proceed to a tribunal.

– Varied – the original decision is changed in some way. The taxpayer has the right to appeal within 30 days.

– Cancelled – HMRC back down and accept the taxpayer's argument.

The internal review is not part of the appeal procedure. It is not intended as a substitute for tribunal hearings, but rather to avoid unnecessary and costly hearings. A review can be offered by HMRC or requested by the taxpayer. Where requested by a taxpayer, HMRC will provide their view of the matter. HMRC must then carry out a review within 45 days (unless a different period is agreed).

23. Business Payment Support Service (BPSS)

The BPSS was introduced in November 2008 to help viable businesses having difficulty in paying their tax liabilities due to the economic climate. The service formalises the previous time to pay arrangements which were provided informally. Upon making contact with the service it is usual to agree a time to pay arrangement. These typically allow a business to repay accrued tax debts over a period which meets the taxpayer's individual needs (often six to twelve months). Interest is normally charged on the late payment of liabilities but surcharges and penalties can be avoided where a taxpayer complies with the agreement. The business support telephone number is 0845 302 1435, and most decisions can be given within ten minutes.

A business which is incurring losses in the current period of trade can ask for relief for the loss to be taken into account in negotiating the time to pay arrangement. Strictly, relief for losses cannot be given until the accounting period producing the loss has come to an end. This arrangement allows a time to pay arrangement to bridge the period from when a tax liability falls due to when relief for the loss can formally be claimed. If the BPSS does take current period losses into account it will ask the business to undertake to submit the return for the current year on time.

Finance Act 2009 s 110 introduces managed payment plans (MPP) which will be effective from April 2011. These allow taxpayers to choose to pay their income and or corporation tax (but not groups or those making quarterly payments) liabilities by equal monthly instalments over a period of twelve months spaced equally, either side of the normal due dates. While in a plan taxpayers will be protected from the interest and penalty consequences of payments made after the due date.

24. Collection of small debts through PAYE

Finance Act 2009 s 109 provides for the collection of small debts through the PAYE system from April 2012. 'Small' is defined as less than £2,000. Currently HMRC can, with the taxpayer's agreement, collect small underpayments of income tax and capital gains tax by an adjustment to their PAYE code (often referred to as coding out). Similarly, HMRC can recover overpayments of tax credits in this way. The new legislation allows HMRC to collect other small debts by an adjustment to the tax code.

Any amount recovered through an adjustment to a taxpayer's code will be treated for interest purposes as having been paid on the first day of the tax year in which the coding out is applied. For example, the effective date of payment for amounts successfully recovered by coding out during 2012/13 will be 6 April 2012. Interest will be calculated and collected once the debt has been fully paid.

Question

Outline the self-assessment provisions that apply to partnerships.

Answer

Requirement to send in partnership returns

1. Self-assessment applies to partnerships as well as to sole traders in that partnerships must complete partnership returns (TMA 1970 s 12AA). There is, however, no assessment on the partnership itself, and each partner brings his profits into his own personal self-assessment.

2. The responsibility for completing the return is usually that of a representative partner to whom it is sent, but it may be issued in the name of the partnership, in which case the partners may nominate a partner to complete it. If the partner originally responsible for filing returns is no longer available, provision is made for a successor to be nominated by the partners, or if they do not do so, by HMRC.

    The filing deadline (from 2008/09 onwards) varies depending on whether a partnership uses an electronic method of filing the tax return (TMA 1970 s 12AA sub-s 4). On receipt of a notice from HMRC requiring a return to be made, a partnership must send in their return, together with supporting schedules by:

    ●   31 October following the end of the tax year if the return is non-electronic (ie, by 31 October 2010 for 2009/10); or

    ●   31 January following the end of the tax year for an electronic return (ie by 31 January 2011 for 2009/10).

    If a notice is given after 31 July following the tax year the return must be filed by:

    1.   three months from the date of notice (for a non-electronic return); or

    2.   31 January, if later than 1 (for an electronic return).

Penalties for late partnership returns

3. Automatic penalties are charged for late returns as follows, the penalties being charged on the partners themselves and not on the partnership (TMA 1970 s 93A):

    Fixed penalty of £100 for *each partner* who was a member of the firm during the period covered by the return;

    Unless HMRC have applied for a daily penalty, a further fixed penalty of £100 per partner if the return is still outstanding six months after the filing date.

    For more substantial delays, HMRC may apply to the Commissioners for a daily penalty of up to £60 per relevant partner, which will be charged from the date the Commissioners issue the relevant direction.

    Appeals against the imposition of penalties may be made by the representative partner.

    The penalty provisions are similar to those relating to personal returns. There is, however, no tax geared penalty since no tax is payable by the partnership as such. On the other hand, there is no provision as there is for individual returns for fixed penalties to be restricted where the tax due on the partnership profits is minimal.

    Finance Act 2009 Sch 55 introduces new late filing penalties across a range of taxes. The new penalties will be introduced in stages from April 2010, see Example 41 note 12.

Business profits

4. Partnership returns show details of trading or professional profits for the accounting period ended in the tax year to which the return relates. If more than one account was made up to a

date in that tax year, separate sets of trading pages should be completed for each account, unless there was a temporary change in the accounting date such that the two sets of accounts together added up to the normal 12-month period. In that event the figures could be combined and shown as a single set of figures (see note 9). As far as changes of accounting date are concerned, the same rules apply for partnerships as for individuals (see Example 28), and the individual partners are bound by the accounting periods adopted by the partnership. See Example 25 explanatory note 3 for the particular problems of self-assessment where there is a partnership merger.

5. Accounts details must normally be shown in the partnership return in 'Standard Accounts Information' (SAI) format (see Example 15). Where the annual partnership profits are below £30,000,however, only the turnover, expenses and net profit need be shown. For 2009/10 returns this threshold will be aligned with the VAT registration limit. If profits are above £15 million (or all members of the partnership are companies), accounts must be submitted (and the SAI need not be completed). Otherwise accounts need not be sent in unless HMRC asks for them. As for individual traders, records relating to returns must be kept until the fifth anniversary of the 31 January next following the relevant tax year (TMA 1970 s 12B).

Any expenses paid personally by partners and capital allowances on partners' own cars *must* be included in the *partnership* return and cannot be separately claimed in the partners' own personal returns. Such items must be included before apportioning the profit between the partners, with the share of the relevant partner then being adjusted appropriately. If expenses incurred individually are not shown in the partnership accounts, it will be necessary to reconcile the accounts figures with those shown in the partnership return. To avoid the possibility of discrepancies leading to an HMRC enquiry, it would be appropriate to file both the accounts and the details of the adjustments with the partnership return.

Charges from which tax is deducted are shown under 'Other expenses' in the SAI and are disallowed in calculating the trading profit. From 6 April 2007 patent royalties are allowed as a deduction in calculating profits if they meet the wholly and exclusively test. If they are *trade* charges, however, such as an annuity to a former partner, they are shown in the partnership statement (see note 7) and allocated between the partners, each individual partner then being able to claim a deduction for his share in his personal return. It is provided in TMA 1970 s 12AB(1)(a)(iv) and (b) that the partnership statement should show charges and the division thereof in relation to *periods of account*. The self-assessment partnership tax return, however, states that the amount to be shown in the return is the amount paid in the *tax year*, the partnership statement then showing the allocation between the partners. This is, in fact, the information required by each partner in order to claim the appropriate relief in his own personal return.

Non-trading income

6. The return includes details of income other than from the trade or profession and of disposals of partnership chargeable assets. The details provided normally relate to the accounting year ended in the tax year. Details of *taxed* income and of disposals of chargeable assets (and charges on income – see explanatory note 5) are, however, shown for the tax year itself rather than for the accounting year ended in the tax year, in order that the partners have the information they need to complete their own returns.

The return states that the taxed income of the relevant accounting periods should be apportioned to arrive at the figure for the tax year. A straight time apportionment would, however, give anomalous results if tax rates changed. It is acceptable, and probably more appropriate, to enter the taxed income actually received in the tax year itself. Similarly, where profit shares change, the partners' actual shares of the taxed income may be shown rather than time apportioning the total for the tax year.

Partnership statement

7. The partnership return must be accompanied by a statement showing the names, addresses and tax references of everyone who was a partner at some time in the year, the dates of joining or leaving where relevant, each partner's share of profits, losses and charges on income, and tax deducted or credited (TMA 1970 s 12AB). There is a short version of the partnership statement for partnerships with only trading or professional profits and taxed interest and a full version for partnerships with other types of income and/or capital gains. In the latter case, the statement shows each partner's share of the proceeds for chargeable assets, each partner calculating his gain or loss according to his own circumstances.

Amendments and HMRC enquiries

8. The rules for amending individual returns broadly apply to partnership returns and statements, ie the partners may notify amendments within 12 months (TMA 1970 s 12ABA) and HMRC may correct obvious errors within nine months, the partnership having the right to reject the correction (TMA 1970 s 12ABB) (see Example 41 for further details). The enquiry period is linked to the date a return is filed from 2007/08 tax returns onwards. For returns made on time, HMRC have a year after the day on which a return is delivered to open an enquiry. For example, to 31 May 2011 for a 2009/10 return filed on 31 May 2010. For 2006/07 and earlier years, the enquiry period (for returns filed on time) was one year after the filing due date, eg 31 January 2009 for a 2006/07 return filed on 31 May 2007. For late returns, a year from the time the return or amendment was filed plus the period to the next 31 January, 30 April, 31 July or 31 October as the case may be. As with individual returns, the partnership return may be amended within the permitted twelve-month period while an enquiry is in progress, but amendments that affect amounts stated in the return will not take effect until the enquiry is completed, and only then if they are accepted by HMRC (TMA 1970 s 12AD).

    If HMRC enquire into a partnership return, this automatically means that the enquiry extends to partners' personal returns, since the personal returns must reflect any changes to the partnership return. An enquiry into a personal return relating to non-partnership matters does not affect the other partners. HMRC will notify each partner when they open and close an enquiry, but the partner responsible for the return must keep the other partners aware of how the enquiry is progressing.

    Under TMA 1970 s 30B, HMRC may amend a partnership statement outside the twelve-month enquiry period if they discover that profits have been understated because of the fraudulent or negligent conduct of a partner, or because of inadequate information (see Example 41 for the new penalty provisions).

    Under TMA 1970 s 31, the partnership may appeal within 30 days of receiving a closure notice from HMRC against the conclusions stated and amendments made in the notice, or within 30 days of being notified of an HMRC 'discovery' amendment under s 30B.

    See Example 41 note 13 for the new compliance checks.

Partners' personal returns

9. Each partner is required to complete supplementary partnership pages in his personal return. As with the partnership return, the personal return contains a short version of the partnership pages if the partnership has only trading profits and taxed interest. The income shown in the personal return must agree with that shown in the partnership statement. In some circumstances, however, the partner will not receive the relevant information in time to give the correct figures in his personal return.

    For example, if an established partnership makes up accounts to 31 December and a new partner joins on 1 January 2010, the new partner will be taxed in 2009/10 on his profit to

5 April 2010, but his profit share will form part of the profit shown on the 2010/11 partnership statement. In these circumstances, he would have to include an estimate of the relevant figure in his 2009/10 return, and notify the exact figure as soon as it was known.

Say that following the admission of the new partner, an existing partner left the partnership on 31 March 2009. He would have a basis period for 2009/10 covering the 15 months from 1 January 2009 to 31 March 2010, and he would similarly have to include an estimate of the three months' profits to 31 March 2010 in his 2009/10 return. (He would be entitled to deduct any available overlap relief from the profits of the 15 months' period to the date he left the firm.)

It would be possible for the partnership to prepare intermediate accounts to 31 March 2010 without permanently changing its accounting date, because a change of accounting date does not take effect unless notice is given to HMRC (see Example 28). It might then be possible for the partnership to let the incoming/retiring partner know his exact profit share for the three months to 31 March 2010. If this were done, the accounts to 31 March 2010 would even so not be shown in the 2009/10 partnership statement but would be combined with those of the nine months to 31 December 2010 and shown as a single set of figures in the 2010/11 partnership statement.

10.   Class 4 national insurance contributions are included in partners' personal returns. The personal tax return makes provision for a partner to indicate that he is excepted from contributions or that contributions have been deferred. See Example 48 for detailed notes on national insurance contributions.

11.   Partners are individually responsible for paying their own tax. If a partnership pays the bill on behalf of the partners, the partners' names, tax reference numbers and amounts applicable to each partner must be provided. HMRC would prefer the partners' individual payslips to be forwarded as well.

Limited liability partnerships (LLPs)

12.   An LLP is taxed as a partnership and will receive a partnership tax return as if the members were partners carrying on a business in partnership. Accordingly all of the rules set out above apply to an LLP which carries on a trade.

Where an existing partnership incorporates as an LLP during an accounting period, then a single partnership return can be made for the tax year. This will apply even if there is a change of accounting date.

Question

Outline the procedure for making claims and elections, both for individuals and companies.

Answer

Claims procedure for income tax and capital gains tax

The procedure for making claims and elections and for giving notices was formalised with the introduction of self-assessment. Taxes Management Act (TMA) 1970 s 42 provides that where notice to submit a return has been given, claims must normally be made in the return or an amendment to the return, which means that the time limit for making the claim is normally twelve months from the filing date for the return. Section 42(1A) requires claims to be quantified when made.

Where it is not possible to include a claim in a return, a separate claims procedure is laid down in TMA 1970 Sch 1A, under which similar provisions apply as for entries in returns, ie HMRC have nine months from the date of the claim to correct obvious errors and the taxpayer has twelve months to amend it. HMRC may enquire into a claim made outside a return, or amendment to such a claim, within the period ending 12 months after 31 January following the tax year to which the claim relates, or if later, the quarter day (31 January, 30 April, etc) next following 12 months after the date of the claim. Unless another time limit is stipulated in the legislation, the time limit for claims made outside the return is five years from the 31 January filing date for the return (TMA 1970 s 43), which will reduce to four years from the end of the tax year from April 2010.

Section 42 and the Schedule 1A claims procedures do not apply to capital allowances claims by traders, which are still required by CAA 2001 s 3(3)(a) to be made in a return or amendment to a return.

Where HMRC enquire into a return or claim, as a result of which they make amendments to the return or claim, the taxpayer may appeal against the amendments within 30 days of being notified of them (TMA 1970 ss 31, 31A and Sch 1A para 9).

Claims for relief involving two or more years

Schedule 1B to TMA 1970 deals with claims that involve two or more years. It provides that references to claims include references to elections and notices. It does not apply to claims to treat payments made under gift aid to be deemed paid in the preceding tax year under ITA 2007 s 426 (see Example 90).

Where relief is claimed for a loss incurred or payment made in one tax year to be set against the income of an earlier year, then although the tax adjustment resulting from the claim is calculated by reference to the tax position of the earlier year, the claim is treated as relating to the later year and is given effect in relation to that later year.

These provisions also apply to carrying back post-cessation receipts (see Example 16 part (c)(ii) and claims for averaging farming profits and creative artists (see Example 33)).

For claims to carry back losses, the recalculated tax will be lower than that originally payable. Farmers' and creative artists' averaging claims may result in the earlier year's tax being reduced or increased. Claims to carry back post-cessation receipts result in the tax of the earlier years being increased. Since the claim is *given effect* in relation to the later year, however, it is the view of HMRC that interest on underpaid tax or supplement on overpaid tax runs from the balancing payment date for the later year, ie 31 January following that later year. In relation to repayment supplement this has now been made explicit in the legislation (ICTA 1988 s 824).

When recalculating the tax position of the earlier year following a carryback claim, any relevant claims for allowances, reliefs etc, may be made or revised, for example transferring surplus married couple's allowance.

Claims for coding adjustments under PAYE

Taxpayers may make claims for coding adjustments (for example claim for higher rate relief for personal pension contributions) either in their tax returns or separately from the return. A claim made in-year may subsequently be reflected in a tax return. Where no such return is issued the claim will normally become final 22 months after the end of the tax year (for example by 31 January 2012 for a 2009/10 claim) and cannot be reopened by HMRC unless there has been deliberate understatement or incomplete disclosure. HMRC have confirmed that they will apply the same time limits where coding claims are carried forward automatically, or are implemented on the basis of preliminary information from the taxpayer, even though HMRC may strictly enquire into such claims at any time up to 5 years 10 months after the end of the tax year (Tax Bulletin October 1996).

FA 2008 introduced new rules for IT, CGT, CT, VAT and PAYE changing the assessment time limits to four years for mistake/discovery, six years (except VAT which is four) for failure to take reasonable care and 20 years for deliberate understatement. The new rules apply to failures after 1 April 2009, with a transitional period making them fully operative after 1 April 2010.

Claims procedure for companies

Under corporation tax self-assessment, (applies APs after 30 June 1999), the provisions for claims and elections are similar to those for income tax self-assessment. The general provisions are in FA 1998 Sch 18 Part VII. Unless there is a specific provision giving a longer or shorter period, the time limit for making claims is six years from the end of the accounting period. Where a discovery assessment is made, other than one arising from the taxpayer's deliberate understatement, provision is made for claims, elections, notices etc to be made, revoked or varied within one year after the end of the company accounting period in which the assessment is made.

Where possible claims must be included in the corporation tax return (CT 600) or in an amended return and the claims will be given effect in the company's self-assessment. This means that claims must normally be made within two years from the end of the accounting period.

For accounting periods ending after 31 March 2008, the enquiry period for companies that are not members of large groups is linked to the date a return is filed. For returns made on time, HMRC have a year after the day on which a return is delivered to open an enquiry, eg to 31 August 2011 for a 31 May 2010 year end return filed on 31 August 2010. Previously, the enquiry period (for returns filed on time) was one year after the filing due date, eg 31 May 2010 for a 31 May 2008 year end return filed on 31 August 2008. The position for large groups has not been changed on the basis the different returns from such groups need to be looked at together.

If HMRC enquire into the return the time limit is extended to thirty days after the time when the profits or losses of the period are finally determined. The provisions of TMA 1970 Sch 1A mentioned under the income tax self-assessment provisions above also apply to companies in respect of claims that cannot be included in a return. The time limit for an HMRC enquiry into a claim made outside a return is the quarter day (31 January, 30 April, etc) next following 12 months after the date of the claim.

Also see Example 41 note 13 regarding HMRC's new compliance checks.

The group relief claims provisions are in FA 1998 Sch 18 Part VIII. The provisions enable group relief claims to be made without being accompanied by copy notices of consent to surrender, and enable one company to act on behalf of the group in making claims and surrenders and amending returns where the group is dealt with mainly within one tax district.

The current six-year time limit for claims does not apply. Group relief claims must be made by the latest of one year after the filing date for the return, 30 days after the completion of an HMRC enquiry into the return, thirty days after notice of HMRC amendments to the return following an enquiry, and 30 days after the final determination of an appeal against such an amendment.

The order in which claims are treated as made for the purpose of determining amounts previously surrendered or claimed in respect of group or consortium relief for overlapping periods is dealt with in ICTA 1988 s 403A(6)(7).

Capital allowances claims are dealt with in FA 1998 Sch 18 Part IX and CAA 2001 s 3(3)(b). The current six-year time limit does not apply and claims are subject to the same time limits as stated above for group relief. If the effect of a claim following an enquiry is to reduce the allowances available for a later period for which a return has been submitted, the company has 30 days from the settlement of the enquiry to make any necessary amendments to that return, failing which amendments will be made by HMRC.

Late claims

HMRC have discretion to admit late claims by companies. They have stated that this will only be done in exceptional circumstances, for example where the delay was due to circumstances beyond the company's control, or where an HMRC error was a major reason for the delay, and not where claims are late because the company has changed its mind or because a different combination of claims would be more advantageous.

Error or mistake claims

A taxpayer can currently claim a repayment of tax under the 'error or mistake' provisions of TMA 1970 s 33 (individuals) or FA 1998 Sch 18 para 51 (companies), where an error or mistake has been made in a *return*. Relief is not available in respect of mistakes in claims included in the return, for which the normal time limits apply. Nor is it available where there has been an error as to the basis on which tax ought to have been computed if the return was made in accordance with the practice prevailing at the time. This prevents the error or mistake procedure being used to reopen assessments where there is a court decision against HMRC. There are similar provisions enabling claims to be made in respect of errors or mistakes in partnership statements (TMA 1970 s 33A). Where the partnership statement is amended, HMRC will notify partners of the changes to be made to their self-assessments.

The current time limit for an error or mistake claim by individuals is five years from 31 January following the relevant tax year. The current time limit for companies is six years from the end of the company accounting period. See above regarding the new time limits introduced by FA 2008.

Whereas prior to June 2003 HMRC regarded any interest, surcharge or penalty for the claim year as unaffected by the claim, they now accept that these charges too should be mitigated, in line with the relief granted under the claim.

From 1 April 2010 the error or mistake rules will be repealed and replaced by statutory relief for overpaid tax in FA 2009 Sch 52. Part 1 applies to income tax and capital gains tax, and Part 2 to corporation tax. The new rules relax the requirement for an error or mistake. Instead the taxpayer has a statutory right to repayment where tax has been overpaid. Repayment claims will be subject to a self-assessment style regime with HMRC rights of enquiry. The time limit for claims is reduced to four years.

Explanatory Notes

Time limits and late claims

1.   There are many exceptions to the normal time limits for claims and it is essential that the time limit for the relevant claim is complied with. Although HMRC usually has discretion to admit late claims, they will only exercise that discretion in exceptional circumstances. See SP 5/01 for HMRC's approach to late company claims for loss relief, capital allowances and group relief.

Requirements for valid claims

2.   The requirements for making a valid claim have often not been clear-cut, and it was only as a result of losing a case on what a group relief claim needed to contain that HMRC specified the minimum information required. Group relief claims are now made in accordance with specific statutory provisions.

As far as income tax loss claims are concerned, a loss claim may be made by indicating the source of the loss, the year of loss and either the year of claim or the statutory reference under which the relief is claimed. Providing that claim is made within the relevant time limit, the supporting accounts may follow later.

3.   Many claims are required by the provisions of the legislation to be made in writing. This has been varied by FA 1998 s 118, which enables HMRC to direct that specified income tax claims may be made by the use of a telecommunications system. This applies to claims by individuals or their agents (but not to claims by partners, trustees or personal representatives). Statements of practice SP2/03 and SP3/03 give details of claims that may be made and information that may be given by telephone. Claims can be made by internet in so far as they are included within a tax return filed online. There is the possibility of allowing further claims to be made by internet at a later stage (and claims and elections are included within the information that HMRC may require to be made electronically at some future time under the provisions of FA 2002 s 135 – see Example 41 note 16).

Error or mistake claims

4.   See Example 41 note 1(a) regarding the use of error or mistake claims when provisional figures have been included in a return.

Question

A.

Explain the procedure for making assessments in respect of income tax and capital gains tax and the extent to which an assessment (including a self-assessment) is capable of being amended, and whether an assessment, once determined, is capable of being re-opened either by the taxpayer or by HMRC.

B.

Outline the provisions for charging interest on overdue income tax and capital gains tax and paying repayment supplement on overpayments of those taxes.

C.

Bill has taxable income for 2009/10 as follows:

	£	£
Business profits		56,508
Untaxed interest	1,470	
Taxed interest (tax deducted £1,800)	9,000	10,470
		66,978
Less: 100% initial allowance: conversion of flat over shop		(20,000)
		46,978
Less: Personal allowance		(6,475)
		40,503

Bill paid a personal pension premium of £2,000 (net) during the year.

The investment on the conversion of the flat was made on 31 March 2010, and no rental income was receivable for 2009/10. On 15 January 2011, before filing his 2009/10 tax return, he made a gift aid donation of £1,600 (net), having made an election to carry the gift back to 2009/10.

Bill made payments on account of his 2009/10 tax and Class 4 national insurance liability of £7,450 each by BACS transfer on 15 February 2010 and 30 September 2010, based on the net tax and Class 4 liability for 2008/09 of £14,900.

He electronically submitted his 2009/10 tax return at the end of January 2011, claiming relief for the initial allowance of £20,000, and including the claim to carry back to 2009/10 the January 2011 gift aid payment. The repayment due to Bill was made on 21 April 2011.

(a) Calculate the tax and Class 4 national insurance contributions due for the year 2009/10, indicating the net amount repayable after taking into account the first payment on account for 2010/11 due on 31 January 2011.

(b) Calculate the interest on overdue tax originally chargeable, and the interest and repayment supplement adjustments following the submission of the return.

Interest on overdue tax and repayment supplement are to be taken as 4% and 1% respectively throughout.

D.

Petersen's original net tax payable for 2006/07 was £25,000, so that 2007/08 payments on account of £12,500 each were payable on 31 January 2008 and 31 July 2008. A discovery assessment relating to 2006/07 was issued on 1 December 2010 for additional tax of £15,000.

State the consequences of the issue of the discovery assessment on tax payable for 2006/07 and 2007/08, and the position relating to interest on overdue tax, on the assumption that on 31 January 2009 a balancing payment had been made for 2007/08 amounting to:

(a)   £20,000

(b)   £5,000.

Answer

A. Assessments

Self-assessment

1. Under self-assessment, it is the responsibility of the taxpayer to assess his own tax liability. Although HMRC will make the calculations for him, this still counts as a self-assessment. If a taxpayer does not submit a return, HMRC have the power to determine the tax payable, but this determination is still treated as a self-assessment until superseded by the taxpayer's own self-assessment. For details see Example 41 note 14.

2. HMRC have the absolute right, without giving any reason, to enquire into any return within twelve months of its submission (TMA 1970 ss 9A and 12AC) (and for large companies within twelve months of the filing deadline, if later). The enquiry procedure does not, however, enable HMRC to issue *assessments* if they consider the taxpayer's self-assessment to be insufficient. Their remedy is to make amendments to the return (see Example 41 note 13).

HMRC assessments

3. There are only limited circumstances in which HMRC will issue assessments themselves, other than under the TMA 1970 s 29 'discovery' procedure dealt with in note 9 below (see Example 41 note 15 for the main occasions when such assessments will be issued).

4. The provisions of s 29 enable HMRC to issue an assessment if they discover that profits have escaped assessment, or an assessment has become insufficient, or excessive relief has been given. If a return has been submitted, HMRC's powers under s 29 may only be used in cases of failure to take reasonable care or deliberate understatement (previously fraudulent or negligent conduct), or where they could not reasonably have been expected to be aware of the situation in time to deal with it under the enquiry procedures. See Example 41 note 1(a) for the use of the discovery procedure when provisional figures have been included in a return. Similar 'discovery' provisions apply under TMA 1970 s 30B to enable HMRC to amend partnership statements. The time limits for discovery assessments are currently five years from 31 January following the tax year to which the assessment relates (s 34), extended to 20 years from that 31 January date in cases of failure to take reasonable care/deliberate understatement (previously fraudulent or negligent conduct) (s 36). FA 2008 introduced new rules for IT, CGT, CT, VAT and PAYE changing the assessment time limits to four years for mistake / discovery, six years (except VAT which is four) for failure to take reasonable care and 20 years for deliberate understatement. The new rules will apply to VAT-related failures after 1 April 2009, with a transitional period making them fully operative for all other taxes after 1 April 2010.

Appeals and postponement applications

5. Under TMA 1970 ss 31 and 31A, a taxpayer has thirty days to appeal against any HMRC conclusions stated or amendments made at the end of an enquiry, jeopardy amendments made during the course of an enquiry (see Example 47 explanatory note 6), 'discovery' amendments to partnership statements (see Example 42 note 8) and any assessments which are not self-assessments. Appeals may be made within the same 30-day period against HMRC amendments to claims made outside the return (TMA 1970 Sch 1A).

   The officer (previously known as an Inspector) may accept a late appeal made without unreasonable delay after the 30 days if he is satisfied that there was a reasonable excuse for not bringing the appeal within the time limit. If the officer is not prepared to do so, the taxpayer can ask for his late appeal to be admitted by the First-tier Tribunal (TMA 1970 s 49).

An appeal against a national insurance issue may be made, within 30 days of the decision, to the First-tier Tribunal or, if the tribunal rules so determine, the Upper Tribunal (Social Security Contributions (Transfer of Functions etc.) Act 1999 Part II).

There is no prescribed form of appeal, although a tax assessment is usually accompanied by a form on which an appeal and, if appropriate, postponement application may be made.

6.   An appeal does not alter the due date of payment of tax unless an application is made for postponement (TMA 1970 s 55). Under self-assessment the postponement provisions apply only to amendments to self-assessments made by HMRC as a result of an enquiry into the return and to HMRC assessments.

The time limit for making a postponement application is also within thirty days after the date of the assessment/amendment as the case may be. Late applications for postponement may be made if changed circumstances since the original postponement application or lack of it result in the taxpayer having grounds for believing that he has been overcharged. It is not sufficient in a postponement application to say that the tax may be excessive. The application must state by how much the taxpayer believes he has been overcharged and the specific reasons for that belief (TMA s 55(3)).

Where application is made for tax to be postponed, the due date for that *not postponed* becomes thirty days after the Tribunal's decision on the postponement and against which no appeal is pending. If the officer agrees the postponement without recourse to the Tribunal, the due date for the tax not postponed becomes thirty days after the officer's agreement to the postponement provided that no appeal is made against the postponement decision (TMA 1970 s 55).

7.   When the appeal is settled, any tax and, if relevant, Class 4 national insurance contributions found to be due but previously postponed and any additional amounts become payable 30 days after the officer issues to the appellant notice of the total amount payable (TMA 1970 s 55).

8.   If an assessment or HMRC amendment to a self-assessment is not appealed against within the time limit (or within any further time allowed by HMRC), the assessment will stand. Where an appeal is made, it is most likely to be heard by the First-tier Tribunal, although the Tribunals Service may allocate the case under its own rules to the Upper Tribunal, whose decisions on questions of fact are normally binding on both parties, but with a right of further appeal on a point of law. Appeals from the First-tier Tribunal are made to the Upper Tribunal, and from there to the Court of Appeal (Court of Session in Scotland) and, where leave is granted, the Supreme Court (formerly the House of Lords). To assist appellants the Tribunals Service has a website which explains how the appeals procedure works. See www.tribunals.gov.uk/tax/ formsguidance.htm. Once an appeal has been determined, it is final and conclusive (TMA 1970 ss 46(2) and 56). TMA 1970 s 54 provides that an appeal can be settled by agreement between the taxpayer and HMRC before going to the Tribunal, in which case the agreement is treated as if the appeal had been determined by the Tribunal.

The case of *Pepper v Hart* (HL 1992) led to a change in the way legislation may be interpreted by the courts. The House of Lords held in that case that the intentions of Parliament in introducing the legislation could be looked at where the legislation was obscure, or led to an absurdity, providing the material relied on consisted of clear ministerial statements and other parliamentary material relevant to understanding those statements.

HMRC published their Appeals handbook in 2007. The manual covered appeals to the General Commissioners, Special Commissioners, and judicial review, which heard tax and NIC appeals before the tribunal reform under the Tribunals, Courts and Enforcement Act 2007. The handbook was replaced from 1 April 2009 by a new online handbook entitled 'Appeals, Reviews and Tribunals Guidance' (ARTG).

Most appeals are normally now to the First-tier Tribunal, but review by HMRC will be offered to anyone notifying an appeal before the Tribunal is involved. Appeals are not now managed by HMRC, and the appellant deals directly with the Tribunal once notice of appeal has been sent to HMRC.

Discovery assessments

9. Following the introduction of self-assessment, HMRC can make a 'discovery' where there has not been full disclosure and

    (a) the loss of tax is the result of a failure to take reasonable care or deliberate understatement by the taxpayer or his agent, or

    (b) the officer could not reasonably be expected to have been able to identify the circumstances giving rise to the loss of tax either before the end of the normal enquiry period, or by using the information made available to him

    (TMA 1970 s 29(4) and (5)).

    Information is treated as made available if

    (a) it is contained in the tax return or supporting accounts, statements or documents supplied; or

    (b) it is contained in any claim made; or

    (c) it is contained in any document, accounts or particulars supplied in relation to an enquiry into a return or claim; or

    (d) it is information which could reasonably be expected to be inferred from the above; or

    (e) it is information notified in writing by the taxpayer.

    References to a return mean the return under review and either of the two previous returns. Information supplied by an agent is deemed to be supplied by the taxpayer (TMA 1970 s 29(6) and (7)).

    Accordingly HMRC cannot make a discovery if the relevant information has been supplied to them with the tax return (or the previous two returns) and, based upon the Olin Energy Systems Ltd case mentioned below, a reasonably competent officer would have been aware of the relevant matter from the information supplied. It is thought that this will apply whether or not the taxpayer has brought the specific point to the attention of HMRC.

    As far as discovery assessments are concerned, a discovery can be made by a different officer from the one who made the assessment, and can apply where it is decided that the law has been incorrectly applied, as well as when new facts emerge. It was held in the case of *Cenlon Finance Co Ltd v Ellwood* (1962), however, that a discovery cannot be made in respect of a specific point which has been dealt with in reaching an agreement on an appeal under TMA 1970 s 54. It was further held in the case of *Scorer v Olin Energy Systems Ltd* (1985) that even where there has been no specific agreement, HMRC cannot make a discovery where the information provided and on which an agreement under s 54 was based was such as to bring home to an ordinarily competent officer the nature of what had been claimed. In the Olin case, brought forward losses of a ship-chartering trade were clearly shown in the computations submitted as being set against profits of a manufacturing trade. It was, however, held in the case of *R v HM Inspector of Taxes, ex parte Bass Holdings Ltd* (QBD 1992) that the Olin decision does not apply if a written agreement does not reflect what the parties actually agreed. In the Bass case group relief had mistakenly been deducted twice.

    It has also been held, in the case of *Gray v Matheson* (ChD 1993), that a s 54 agreement is not binding where *incorrect information* has been supplied, even though there was no culpability on the taxpayer's part. The facts of the case were that there had been an investigation of two years' accounts, and in the next two years a significantly lower gross profit percentage was shown, reverting to the previous level in the following year. The Court held that it was consideration of the events both before and after the two 'low' years that led the inspector (now known as officer) to make a discovery, and that the Olin decision was not relevant.

HMRC issued a detailed statement of practice (SP 8/91) covering discovery assessments, in which they indicated that they do not consider the Olin decision applies where:

(i) Profits or income have not been charged because of fraudulent or negligent (now failure to take reasonable care or deliberate) conduct

(ii) The officer has been misled or misinformed

(iii) There is an undiscovered arithmetical error in a computation

(iv) There is an error which cannot be claimed to be unintended, such as a double deduction of a particular item.

The principles established by the Olin and Cenlon cases strictly only apply where there has been an appeal against an assessment, or an appeal against a decision relating to a claim under TMA 1970 s 42 (see Example 43) but HMRC stated in SP 8/91 that they will stand by an agreement on a specific point, even where there was no appeal. Where a point was not specifically agreed, or was not fundamental, they will still not make a discovery assessment providing all relevant facts were disclosed and the taxpayer could reasonably have believed that the officer's view was correct. Nor will they seek adjustments where their view of the law is changed as a result of a Court decision.

In the case of *Langham v Veltema* (2004) the taxpayer was advised by a professional valuer that the value of a house transferred to him in 1998 by his employer was £100,000. He used this figure in his self-assessment tax return which was received and acknowledged by HMRC as needing no correction on 9 September after the tax year. Later the issue of valuation was raised by HMRC and a revised amount of £145,000 was agreed with the taxpayer's agent. HMRC raised a discovery assessment on the taxpayer for £45,000. The courts upheld HMRC's appeal. Given the facts it would not have been reasonable to expect the inspector (now officer) to have been aware that the valuation of the property in September 1998 was unreliable.

By HMRC statement of 23 December 2004, updated in January 2006, it is recommended that taxpayers who use a valuation in completing their tax return should state in the Additional Information box

–   that a valuation has been used, and

–   who carried out the valuation giving the name and qualification and stating that they are an independent suitably qualified valuer.

If a taxpayer has adopted a different view of the law from that published by HMRC the Additional Information space should state that HMRC guidance has not been followed.

If the return includes exceptional items the entry in the Additional Information space should give full details of the exceptional entries.

If this guidance is followed then the return should become final at the end of the twelve-month enquiry period if HMRC does not open an enquiry (or open and close an enquiry). A 'discovery' would not then arise unless the information provided was incorrect because of fraud or negligent conduct by the taxpayer.

HMRC have been proposing a new Management Act (to rewrite the old Inland Revenue and Customs & Excise administrative provisions in TMA 1970 and CEMA 1979) to harmonise the rules relating to the assessment of different taxes. However, the 2007 budget confirmed that this is not being pursued at this time except as is needed by the overall review of powers.

Penalties for incorrect returns

10.   The FA 2007 included a new framework for penalties on incorrect tax returns. These covered income and corporation tax, PAYE, NIC and VAT. The new rules take effect for returns due for filing after 31 March 2009. The FA 2008 extends this framework to most other taxes (inheritance tax, environmental taxes, stamp duties etc) except tax credits with effect from 1 April 2010.

      The penalty for submitting a return or document containing an inaccuracy which leads to an underpayment of tax is determined (as a percentage) by the amount of tax potentially lost, the nature of the behaviour giving rise to the understatement, and the quality of the disclosure (if any). These range from no penalty for a mistake despite taking reasonable care to 100% for deliberate and concealed inaccuracies. This is best shown in the table shown in Example 41 note 11.

Equitable liability

11.   Once the time limits for appealing against assessments, or for substituting a taxpayer's own self-assessment for an HMRC determination under self-assessment, have expired, the tax assessed or determined becomes legally due. HMRC have, however, stated that where income tax (including PAYE tax) or capital gains tax is higher than it would have been if all the relevant information had been submitted at the proper time, they may be prepared to accept an amount equal to what the correct liability would have been, providing the taxpayer's affairs are brought fully up to date, although this should rarely be necessary under the self-assessment system. This practice is known as 'equitable liability' (see HMRC's Tax Bulletin August 1995). HMRC now proposes to remove the practice, regarding it as unnecessary, and consultation is ongoing on this issue.

National insurance contributions

12.   HMRC consider that there is no time limit on their power to *assess* Class 1, 1A and 2 national insurance contributions, although they usually only go back six years. (Class 4 contributions are subject to the income tax rules (SSCBA 1992 s 16).)

      The Limitation Act 1980 prevents any action to enforce recovery of amounts due after six years from the date on which the liability arose. It does not, however, apply to Crown proceedings to recover 'any tax or duty or interest on any tax or duty'. It is accepted by HMRC that national insurance is not a tax or duty, so that the Limitation Act places a time-bar on an action for recovery of national insurance contributions. HMRC have been known to argue, however, that the six years run from the date the liability is discovered rather than from when the contributions fell due, although they will usually accept that the six years began at the date the liability arose if there has been no deliberate concealment of an underpayment.

      If the person liable to pay the alleged contributions acknowledged the liability or made any payment in respect of it, a new six-year period would start from that time. Any payment made on account of arrears should therefore always specify to which years it relates, without referring to the earlier years, since that would constitute an 'acknowledgment' and, in the absence of specific allocation, would allow HMRC to set the payment against the oldest, potentially out-of-time, debts first.

      HMRC may still *assess* and endeavour to collect arrears for all years, but they would not be able to enforce the assessments in proceedings once the six-year limit had elapsed.

B.   Interest on overdue tax and repayment supplement

Due date of payment of tax

1.   The dates on which tax is payable under self-assessment are dealt with in Example 41. In most cases, equal payments on account are due on 31 January and 31 July in the tax year, based on the net tax, Class 4 national insurance liability and student loan repayments of the previous year, and a balancing payment, which includes any capital gains tax payable, is due on 31 January following the tax year (or three months after receiving notice to complete a return for certain late issued notices – see Example 41 1.(a)).

2.   Where a self-assessment is amended after, or less than 30 days before, the due date for the balancing payment for the year, tax is payable or repayable 30 days after the notice of amendment is given.

3.   Where HMRC issues an assessment, the due date of payment for the tax is 30 days after the issue of the assessment (TMA 1970 s 59B(6)). Most HMRC assessments will be discovery assessments under TMA 1970 s 29 (see part A).

4.   The payments on account that are regarded as being due for any tax year take into account any subsequent amendments to the previous year's tax liability resulting from taxpayer amendments, or amendments following HMRC enquiries, or HMRC discovery assessments (TMA 1970 s 59A(4A)(4B)(5)). If a non-discovery HMRC assessment is made, it does not affect payments on account.

5.   Special provisions apply where a claim is made that involves more than one tax year (TMA 1970 Sch 1B). These are dealt with in Example 43. See note 10 below re the effect on interest and repayment supplement.

Interest on overdue tax

6.   Under TMA 1970 s 86, interest is normally charged on SA tax and (by SSCBA 1992 Sch 2 para 6) Class 4 national insurance paid late, from the date the payment was due to the date the tax is paid, ie from 31 January in the tax year and 31 July following for payments on account, and from 31 January following the tax year for the balancing payment.

Interest also runs from 31 January following the tax year to which the assessment relates for assessments issued by HMRC (unless otherwise provided) regardless of when the assessment was issued (see Example 41 note 15). For amendments to self-assessments, interest runs from 31 January following the relevant tax year. Note that the tax itself is payable by a different date (see notes 2 and 3 above).

It is understood that when calculating interest on overdue tax, a denominator of 366 days is always used regardless of whether or not a leap year is involved. A denominator of 365 days is understood to be used for repayment supplement calculations. This practice works in favour of the taxpayer. Repayment supplement is dealt with in note 9 below.

7.   In addition to being charged on unpaid tax, interest is payable on late paid surcharges and penalties (see Example 41 notes 10 and 11).

Any interest charged under these provisions is not an allowable deduction for tax purposes (TMA 1970 s 90).

8.   Discovery assessments, in addition to carrying interest as indicated in note 6, also affect payments on account. TMA 1970 s 59A(4B) provides that the payments on account that should have been made for the next following year are increased accordingly, subject to a claim under TMA 1970 s 59A(3)(4) to eliminate or reduce them because they exceeded the tax payable for that following year. The effect is that if, even after taking into account the revised payments on account, a balance of tax would remain payable for the following year, interest would be payable on the increase in each payment on account from the due date to 31 January

following the later year. If the revised payments on account would produce an overpayment for the following year, the taxpayer could apply for them to be reduced so as to prevent the overpayment occurring, and the interest chargeable would be reduced or eliminated accordingly. This is illustrated in part D of the example.

Repayment supplement

9. Tax-free repayment supplement under ICTA 1988 s 824 (income tax), SSCBA 1992 Sch 2 para 6 (NIC) and TCGA 1992 s 283 (capital gains tax) is paid to both residents and non-residents on overpaid tax and Class 4 national insurance contributions relating to payments made direct to HMRC (and also on any overpaid surcharge and penalties) from the date the amount was paid until the date the repayment order is issued. If, however, a taxpayer pays more than the amount that is legally due at the payment date, the overpayment does not attract supplement.

    Where there is a refund of tax deducted at source, supplement runs from 31 January following the relevant tax year. Tax deducted at source includes PAYE tax, except that amounts deducted in respect of previous years are excluded.

    As indicated in note 6 above, a denominator of 365 is used in making supplement calculations even if a leap year is involved.

Claims involving more than one year

10. Special provisions apply to claims involving more than one year (see Example 43). Where such claims result in an *increase* in tax for the earlier year (for example through farmers' averaging), any additional tax payable is regarded as relating to the later year and is due for payment on 31 January following that later year. Where a claim *reduces* the tax for the earlier year (for example through farmers' averaging, or where losses or gift aid donations are carried back), *effect is given* to the claim in relation to the later year, by repayment or set-off, or by an increase in the amount to be deducted in arriving at the balancing payment for the year under s 59B, or 'otherwise'. HMRC takes the view that this enables amounts repayable to be offset against tax that has not yet been paid for the earlier year. They used to do this regardless of whether the payment for the earlier year was already due, or due at some time in the future. Following representations they have agreed to relax this position for claims to carry back losses. Now if the earlier year's tax is not yet due, the set-off need not be made and repayment can be claimed up to the amount of the earlier year's tax. This treatment must be specifically requested, through the self-assessment account. Effectively the 35-day rule no longer applies (see Tax Bulletin June 1997). Interest due on the tax for earlier years will cease from the date of the claim. Thus an early claim can stop interest accruing against a taxpayer even if no supplement would be due if the same amount was repaid. Supplement will only be relevant if the claim is given effect after the 31 January following the later year, supplement then running from that 31 January date (ICTA 1988 s 824).

Date when payments regarded as made

11. Payments of SA tax and national insurance contributions have historically been treated as made as follows for the purpose of calculating interest or repayment supplement:

    Tax payments made at local offices are credited on the date of payment.

    The payment date for postal payments is the day they are received by HMRC, except those received following a day when the HMRC office was closed, which are treated as received on the first day the office was closed (see below re cheques).

    Payments by electronic funds transfer (BACS/CHAPS) are treated as paid one working day before HMRC receive them.

    Payments by bank Giro or Girobank is the date payment is made at the bank or post office.

PC and telephone banking payments are treated as made on the day before the date on which the bank makes the transfer of cleared funds.

From 19 July 2007 HMRC have had the power to make regulations to deem all payments made by cheque to have been made only when funds have cleared HMRC's account, but no such regulations have yet been made, although they are expected when e-payment is made compulsory. (FA 2007 s 95.)

Tax/national insurance payable by employers

12. As far as late payments by employers of tax, NI and other amounts due under PAYE are concerned, interest is charged from 19 April after the end of the tax year if the amount due is not paid by that date (ITEPA 2003 ss 684–685 and SI 2003/2682).

Large employers (250 or more employees) are required to make their monthly payment of PAYE/NIC and subcontractors' tax electronically (SI 2003/2682 Part 10 Chapter 3). The full amount must reach HMRC by the last bank working day before the 23rd of the month. Thus for November 2009 the payment due on 22 November 2009 (Sunday) must reach HMRC as cleared funds by 20 November 2009.

Electronic payments include BACS direct credit, CHAPS (Clearing House Automated Payment System), Internet banking, BillPay and telephone banking. The extended payment date also applies to medium/smaller employers who pay electronically. CHAPS is a same day transfer facility whereas most other electronic methods require three bank working days for clearance (Revenue directions 5 April 2004).

If a large employer fails to pay by the due date then a default notice will be issued. A surcharge will then be payable from the third default notice within the surcharge period. The surcharge period starts with the due date for payment for the first period in default and ends at the end of the year in which the taxpayer has not been in default in respect of any payment. The surcharge applies to the net total of tax due for the year and is at the following rate per default:

No of defaults within surcharge period	%
1 – 2	Nil
3 – 5	0.17%
6 – 8	0.33%
9 – 11	0.58%
12 or more	0.83%

The surcharge is payable 30 days after the issue of the surcharge notice (SI 2003/2682 regs 199–204).

Class 1A contributions on employee benefits are due for payment by 19 July (22 July if paid online) following the tax year to which they relate (eg contributions re 2008/09 should be paid by 19 July 2009). Interest is charged on late payments (SI 2001/1004 reg 76). The amount due is shown by the employer on Form P11D(b).

Where Class 1B contributions are payable under a PAYE Settlement Agreement (as to which see Example 8 explanatory note 9), they are due for payment by 19 October (22 October if e-paid) following the tax year in respect of which the payment was due and interest runs from that date (SI 2001/1004 Sch 4 para 17).

FA 2009 includes a penalty regime for late payment of tax, including in-year PAYE and NIC for all employers. For income tax and capital gains tax the new penalties will follow the existing surcharge arrangements, imposing a 5% surcharge on payments which are at least a month late, with a further 5% for payments which are six months late. The rules differ slightly for corporation tax, with the first penalty arising when the payment is three months late. The new regime is expected to commence from April 2010. The penalty for late payment of in-year PAYE and NIC will initially be imposed on a risk-assessed basis but will eventually become automatic, once IT system development has been completed.

Fixing interest and repayment supplement rates

13.	The process for setting interest rates on late paid tax and repayment supplement was revised during 2008/09. Finance Act 2009 s 103 gave the Treasury power to set interest rates across all of the taxes, while ss 101–102 set new harmonised rules for late payment interest and repayment interest. These changes are expected to be implemented in April 2010. In the meantime, interest rates on late paid tax are varied when the Bank of England rates change, and the minimum repayment supplement is subject to a collar of 0%. Rates set on 24 March 2009 were a 2.5% charge on late payment and a 0% repayment supplement. For the purpose of this example specimen rates have been quoted for use.

C.	**Bill – tax position for 2009/10**

(a)	**Tax and Class 4 national insurance contributions due**

				£	£
Tax on income of £40,503:	39,900	@	20%	7,980	
	603	@	40%	241	
	40,503			8,221	
* Basic rate limit increased by gross pension contribution of £2,500					
Class 4 NICs (43,875–5,715)		@ 8%		3,053	
(56,508–43,875)		@ 1%		126	3,179	11,400
Less: Tax deducted at source					1,800
Tax due for direct payment					9,600
Less: Payments made on account (2 @ £7,450)					14,900
Tax repayable					5,300
Further repayment due in respect of gift aid donation carried back to 2009/10 by extending the basic rate tax band by £605 (being less than the gross donation of £2,000), saving tax on £603 at 20%					121
					5,421
Less: Used to cover first payment on account for 2009/10 due 31.1.10 (half of £9,600)					4,800
Net amount repayable 21 April 2010					621

Notes

1.	The conversion of redundant space above business premises entitles Bill to an initial allowance of 100% of the expenditure, subject to a number of conditions. If the building had already been let, the allowance would have been given primarily against the letting income and then against other income. Since the building is not tenanted in 2009/10, Bill can claim relief for the UK property loss against his income of that year. For the detailed provisions see Example 21.

2.	Class 4 national insurance contributions are calculated on trading income after taking into account balancing charges and capital allowances relating to the trading activities, but not allowances on non-trading activities, or the personal pension premium .

(b) Interest on overdue tax and repayment supplement

				£
Interest originally charged on payments on account:				
On 1st instalment of £7,450 from 31.1.10 to 12.2.10 =	12	days		
On 2nd instalment of £7,450 from 31.7.10 to 29.9.10 =	60	days		
	72	days	@ 4%	58.62

		£
Payments on account actually @ 4%		37.77
due were (½ × 9,600) =		
£4,800 each, with interest for		
(12 + 60) days		
Interest repayable		20.85

				£
Repayment supplement on overpaid payments on account of (7,450– 4,800) = £2,650 each:				
On 1st instalment – 15.2.10 to 21.4.11 =	430	days		
On 2nd instalment – 30.9.10 to 21.4.11 =	203	days		
£2,650 for	633	days	@ 1 %	45.96

	£
Offset by part of repayment @ 1% for 79 days from	10.39
used to cover 31.1.11 1.2.11 to 21.4.11	
payment on account =	
£4,800	
Repayment supplement due	35.57

No repayment supplement is due in respect of the refund of £121 relating to the carried back gift aid donation (see part B note 9). Nor does it reduce the 2009/10 or 2010/11 tax for the purpose of calculating payments on account. If tax relief for the payment would be at higher rates in 2010/11, it would probably have been better to claim relief for the donation in that year, thereby reducing the 2011/12 payments on account.

D. Petersen – discovery assessment and interest on overdue tax

Before the discovery assessment was made, the position was:

		£
2006/07	Net tax payable	£25,000
2007/08	31 January payment on account	£12,500
	31 July payment on account	£12,500
(a)	Balancing payment	£20,000
	(giving total 2007/08 tax of £45,000)	
(b)	Balancing payment	£5,000
	(giving total 2007/08 tax of £30,000)	

The tax of £15,000 under the 2006/07 discovery assessment would be due for payment on 31 December 2010, but interest would run from 31 January 2008 to the date the tax was paid. The revised tax for 2006/07 is £40,000.

In the case of (a) (ie 2007/08 balancing payment of £20,000), the amounts that should have been paid by way of payments on account for 2007/08 would be increased by £7,500 to £20,000 each, and interest thereon would run from the half yearly due dates of 31 January 2008 and 31 July 2008 to 31 January 2009 (the underpayments of £7,500 each being effectively paid as part of the balancing payment of £20,000).

In the case of (b) (ie 2007/08 balancing payment of £5,000), the effect of increasing the payments on account to £20,000 each would be to give an overpayment of £10,000 for the year, so that a claim could be made to reduce the additional amounts payable to £2,500 each. As with (a), interest thereon would run from the half yearly due dates of 31 January 2008 and 31 July 2008 to 31 January 2009.

Question

Your firm has recently been appointed as advisers to Sparks Manufacturing Ltd. Following your appointment the accountant of the company has informed you that HMRC is shortly to carry out a PAYE inspection and he has asked that your firm review the procedures in operation prior to the HMRC visit. The following information is relevant:

(1)   The company has 36 full-time and ten part-time workers. These include three full-time office staff, one sales representative and the directors, who are Mr and Mrs Sparks. Mr and Mrs Sparks own all the shares in the company.

(2)   The manufacturing workers are paid weekly in cash, and earnings are variable depending on hours worked. Any production bonuses are paid on a month-by-month basis.

(3)   The office staff are paid monthly by cheque. The sales representative is paid gross on a commission basis and is treated as self-employed. His commission is in excess of £44,000 per annum.

(4)   Mr and Mrs Sparks receive monthly standing order payments of £500 each. Any additional amounts for expenses are drawn by cheque on a monthly basis.

(5)   The accountant applies PAYE and national insurance to the wages and bonus payments made to the full-time employees with the exception of Mr and Mrs Sparks and the salesman.

(6)   Part-time employees are all production workers, who each receive £94 per week gross. The production bonus for part-time workers in April 2008 amounted to £110 each and was paid gross.

(7)   The company does not hold signed Forms P46 for the following part-time workers:

     (a)   Mrs Acorn (aged 35) – a married lady with no other employment.

     (b)   Mrs Beech (aged 63) – in receipt of a state pension based upon her husband's contributions and with no other employment.

     (c)   Mr Chestnut (aged 19) – a student who only works during vacations.

     (d)   Mr Dallow (aged 40) – a milkman.

     It is understood that all part-time workers were first employed on 6 April 2007 when the evening shift commenced.

(8)   The company pays £18 per week to each of its full-time employees and £10 per week to each of its part-time employees as subsistence payments. These amounts do not appear on the deductions working sheets (P11) and the full-time employees have received them since 6 April 2004 and the part-time workers since they joined the company.

(9)   The company provides a car first registered 1998 (1,298 cc) with fuel to the foreman, who travels 10,000 business miles per year. The list price of the car when new was £23,200, although it is now worth only about £1,000. The foreman's salary in 2008/09 was £18,000.

(10)   Miss Fallow, secretary to the managing director, also has a car provided for her own use with all fuel paid for by the company. The current car is two years old (1,298 cc) and had a list price of £10,200 when new and a CO_2 emissions figure of 149. In 2008/09 she travelled approximately 1,000 business miles. Her salary in that year was £8,400.

(11)   Mr Sparks, whose salary is shown in the company accounts as £45,000 per annum, is provided with a 2,500 cc car which had a list price of £26,000 and a CO_2 emissions figure of 272 when new in 2007. He travels 25,000 business miles each year. Mrs Sparks only attends directors' meetings and is paid £4,700 per annum. She is provided with a two-year-old car (1,988 cc, CO_2 figure 249) which had a list price of £19,500 when new. Business mileage is minimal. Fuel is provided for both cars.

Mr Sparks has a mobile telephone with 'hands free' operation in his car. The telephone bills in 2008/09 amounted to £1,200 plus VAT. From the bills it would appear that 40% of the calls are non-business.

(12) Mr Jones, the accountant, uses his own car (1,998 cc) for business purposes and is paid 75p per mile.

(13) Miss Fallow prefers to buy her own petrol, which is reimbursed to her through petty cash.

The other car users and the sales representative have obtained petrol on company credit cards, the amounts for 2008/09 being as follows (amounts excluding VAT):

	£
Foreman	1,480
Sales representative	2,040
Mr Sparks	3,880
Mrs Sparks	300

As car parking is limited at the factory, five season tickets for the car park in the next street are purchased by the company for £2,000 per annum plus VAT each for use by the above.

All VAT on the above items has been recovered in full without any adjustments for private usage.

(14) The following expenses have been drawn in the year 2008/09 (amounts shown net of VAT where appropriate):

	Subsistence £	Entertaining £	Round Sum £	Motoring £	Home telephone £
Sales representative	2,460	428	–	–	940
Foreman	820	–	–	–	280
Mr Sparks	–	–	10,500	–	770
Mrs Sparks	–	–	4,300	–	–
Mr Jones	–	1,842	–	1,452	320
Miss Fallow	–	–	–	460	–

(15) Forms P11D have been completed only for Mr Sparks and Mr Jones showing the figures above and Mr Sparks's car.

(16) Sparks Manufacturing Ltd arranged a golf weekend for its customers in 2008/09 and invited ten managing directors to join Mr Sparks and the sales representative for the event. The total cost was £12,000.

The firm also gives its suppliers Christmas hampers, the size of which reflects the value of transactions undertaken in the year. At Christmas 2008 the cost of the hampers varied from £50 to £500.

Set out the implications of the above in respect of PAYE, national insurance, VAT and corporation tax as regards Sparks Manufacturing Ltd, and the effect on the individual's taxable earnings under the following headings:

(a) Part-time employees

(b) Directors' remuneration

(c) Cars and fuel

(d) Other benefits

(e) Sales representative

Without calculating precise figures, indicate the possible basis on which a settlement with HMRC might be negotiated for the period to 5 May 2009, and any steps which could be taken to minimise the liability.

Answer

(a) **Part-time employees**

Part-time employees are subject to PAYE and national insurance in the same way as other staff. For those employees for whom Form P46 is held showing that this is the main or only employment, no PAYE or national insurance liability or reporting requirement arises unless their weekly pay equals or exceeds the following limits:

| | Thresholds | | Lower earnings limit |
| | PAYE | NI | |
	£	£	£
2006/07	97	97	84
2007/08	100	100	87
2008/09 to 6 September	105	105	90
2008/09 from 7 September	117	105	90
2009/10	125	110	95

Note that from 7 September 2008 the tax threshold was increased to £117 per week but the National Insurance threshold (at which contributions become payable) remained £105 per week.

Their current weekly pay inclusive of subsistence payments is £104 a week, and they receive a variable monthly bonus. The cumulative pay inclusive of bonuses needs to be checked to ensure that the PAYE limit has not been exceeded. The same check needs to be made for national insurance, but on a non-cumulative basis. As far as national insurance is concerned, there is clearly a liability in the weeks when bonus payments are made, and a reporting requirement throughout, as P46 must be submitted if the employee's pay exceeds the lower earnings limit (LEL) in any week. For those employees who have not signed Form P46, or where it is not possible to obtain a signed P46 certifying that this is the main or only employment, income tax at the basic rate of tax should be deducted from all remuneration (see below re Mrs Beech). Failure to do so could result in HMRC assessing the tax not deducted on the company by way of a determination under the PAYE regulations.

It would appear that the company has been in breach of its obligations under the PAYE/NI scheme since April 2007. It will be necessary to agree a settlement with HMRC for that period. The penalty for failing to submit Form P46 is the same as that for not submitting or not giving employees copies of Form P11D and Form P9D, ie, an initial penalty of up to £300 per form, plus up to £60 a day if the form is still not submitted or copy provided (TMA 1970 s 98(1)). There is a penalty of up to £3,000 for fraudulently or negligently submitting incorrect Forms P11D, P9D and P46 (TMA 1970 s 98(2)) for years up to 2007/08. For returns due for submission after 31 March 2009, the new penalties for incorrect returns set out in FA 2007 Sch 24 apply where there has been failure to take reasonable care or deliberate understatement. With regard to any tax and national insurance underpaid, HMRC may issue a determination of the amount due under SI 2003/2682 reg 80. For underpayments before April 2009, interest is charged on unpaid tax and national insurance from 14 days after the end of the tax year (except to the extent that the collector has required an amount to be paid by an employee) without the need for a formal determination. From April 2010, interest becomes chargeable from the 19th of each month when the deductions should have been paid to HMRC, although HMRC's systems are not yet able to calculate liabilities automatically.

It is probable that the HMRC auditors would compute the liability for the month of April 2009 and then apply that amount for the previous two years.

The company should compute the actual liability for the 25-month period. It is possible that for a number of weeks the actual remuneration (inclusive of subsistence) would be under the lower earnings limit for national insurance and therefore no liability to employer's or employees' contributions would arise. The company should also obtain signed Forms P46 wherever possible. In the case of Mr Chestnut a Form P38(S) should be obtained and retained for three years as he is a student. Again, it is unlikely that any income tax liability would arise. Since Mrs Beech receives a pension, if the company obtains a Form P46 from her now, it will have to be sent to HMRC in any event and tax at the basic rate deducted from her pay. Mrs Beech is over state pension age so no employee's national insurance would be payable, although employer's contributions would still be due. The company should ask her to apply for a formal certificate of age exception from NICO in Newcastle upon Tyne, but this merely evidences the fact of exception: provided the company is certain of her age, it cannot be liable for employee contributions, whether or not a certificate has been issued. It seems almost certain that basic rate tax and appropriate national insurance contributions will be applicable to Mr Dallow.

If this matter is disclosed to HMRC and correct procedures are put in place, then it is possible that a settlement could be negotiated based upon the correct liability plus interest and penalties. For returns due for submission after 31 March 2009, the new penalties for incorrect returns set out in FA 2007 Sch 24 would apply. The penalties in respect of this enquiry largely relate, however, to returns already filed, so the old penalty provisions apply. In relation to the type of errors here, under the new system, disclosing the inaccuracies in full at the commencement of the visit would not count as an unprompted disclosure, but if the company could show that the failure was through a lack of reasonable care rather than deliberate, with the full discount for disclosure the penalty should be only 15%. It may also be possible to have the penalty suspended for up to two years, as these failures might be regarded as systemic. This would give the company the opportunity to restructure payroll and reporting procedures with the aim of future compliance.

(b)   **Directors' remuneration**

It is not clear whether the monthly standing order is intended to be remuneration or withdrawals from directors' current accounts, or such current accounts are running in credit.

PAYE and national insurance are not relevant unless the amounts are on account of remuneration (see Example 58 explanatory note 12).

In the case of Mr Sparks it would appear that the remuneration of £45,000 per annum, when credited to his director's current account net of PAYE/NI, would be sufficient to provide funds for his withdrawals. If, however, the round sum drawings by Mr Sparks have not been charged to his director's current account, they would give rise to a liability. In that event, the amount drawn should be grossed up and PAYE applied to that gross figure. As Mr Sparks will already have paid the maximum higher rate employee's national insurance contributions, only employer's liability will apply to that grossed up figure, plus 1% employee's contributions since 6 April 2003.

Similar comments apply to Mrs Sparks. However, it is almost certain that Mrs Sparks will not have a credit balance on her director's current account and therefore if the round sum drawings are not in anticipation of earnings and they have been charged to her director's current account, the beneficial loans rules and the provisions of ICTA 1988 s 419 will apply (see below). If the round sums have not been charged to the account, PAYE and national insurance must apply on each and every withdrawal. Unless there is evidence that the payment to Mrs Sparks is made by Mr Sparks as part of their personal relationships, it is not likely that HMRC would treat the withdrawal by Mrs Sparks as coming from the remuneration of Mr Sparks.

Directors' national insurance contributions are computed on a yearly pay period basis and liability strictly only arises when the cumulative drawings for the tax year exceed the earnings threshold. National insurance liability will of course arise on the total amount when the annual earnings threshold is reached, thus giving a material liability in that month for employer and director.

Should the company pay the PAYE liability due in respect of Mr and Mrs Sparks in any settlement, then that amount will be treated as a further benefit in kind taxable on the director unless it is charged to the director's loan account (ITEPA 2003 s 223). Any settlement by the company of a national insurance liability in respect of employee contributions applicable to the director will again be treated as a benefit in kind giving rise to further tax liabilities, again unless charged to the director's loan account.

If a director's account becomes overdrawn, then there will be a potential benefit in kind liability in respect of the interest due on that loan under ITEPA 2003 Part 3 Chapter 7. In addition, the company will have a charge to tax at 25% on the loan under ICTA 1988 s 419. If drawings are made in anticipation of their being cleared later by voting a bonus, and those drawings make the account further overdrawn, the drawings must be treated as payments of earnings for NI purposes and Class 1 contributions accounted for. Later voting of the bonus to clear the account would then be subject to PAYE but not NI, because the NI has already been paid.

To avoid the problems with s 419 and the beneficial loans rules (and also possible contravention of the Companies Acts), it is suggested that regular monthly salaries should be drawn which are subject to PAYE and national insurance contributions. All round sum allowances should be stopped. Mr and Mrs Sparks should draw actual expenses against vouchers.

The VAT position of round sum allowances should be checked. If any input tax has been recovered because of purported VAT-inclusive expenditure in the round sum allowances this must be declared to HMRC and repaid.

If the above was put into force then it is possible that Mrs Sparks would receive remuneration under the national insurance limit and contributions would not be payable. In addition, it should be suggested to her that fuel should not be provided for her car as the benefit in kind cost appears to be greater than the value of fuel provided (a similar comment will apply for VAT and Class 1A national insurance contributions – see (c)).

A Form P11D should have been completed for Mrs Sparks as she is a director. The penalty for failure to provide that information is as stated in part (a). If the company had sent in Form P11D(b), which confirms that Forms P11D have been submitted for all relevant employees, this will probably be regarded as fraudulent or negligent conduct triggering the penalty of up to £3,000 in addition to the penalty for not sending in the Form P11D. For returns due for submission after 31 March 2009, the new penalties for incorrect returns set out in FA 2007 Sch 24 apply.

HMRC may contend that the car provided to Mrs Sparks is in fact provided by reason of Mr Sparks's employment. Such a contention should be disputed on the grounds that ITEPA 2003 s 169 applies, ie, that the car was provided to Mrs Sparks by reason of her directorship and that it is normal commercial practice for a director to be provided with a motor vehicle. Although the charge is the same amount as would be charged on Mr Sparks, it is likely that Mrs Sparks's tax rate will be lower than her husband's.

It is possible that HMRC could argue that the remuneration paid to Mrs Sparks is excessive for her duties as a director. The remuneration for 2008/09 could be considered to be:

Salary		4,700
Round sum allowance		4,300
Benefit in kind –	Car 35% × 19,500	6,825
	Fuel 35% × 16,900	5,915
		£21,740

unless any of it is charged to Mrs Sparks's director's account.

It is therefore possible that a disallowance will occur in the taxable trading profit computation of the company.

The company should have paid Class 1A national insurance contributions in respect of the directors' cars (see (c)).

(c) **Cars and fuel**

Clearly, both the foreman and Miss Fallow are employees not excluded from the benefits code (they are not in lower-paid employment by virtue of ITEPA 2003 s 217) when the benefits charges for cars are added to their respective salaries.

Again Forms P11D should have been provided to HMRC in respect of the foreman, Miss Fallow and probably the sales representative (see (e)), so penalties may arise.

The company should have paid Class 1A national insurance contributions each year in respect of the cars and fuel provided to employees, including the directors' cars. Records should be available in respect of the business mileage travelled to 5 April 2009 to show that the correct contributions have been paid.

It would appear that no VAT adjustments have been made for private fuel. The company should apply the scale charges in respect of private fuel at the relevant rate. Up to 30 April 2007 it would appear that there would be two cars at the lower rate (foreman and Miss Fallow), one car at the middle rate (Mrs Sparks) and one car at the higher rate (Mr Sparks). From 1 May 2007 the VAT scale charges are based on the CO_2 emissions using the benefit in kind tables to set the emission bands. In addition, there will be a scale charge in respect of the sales representative if he is an employee. If he is not, VAT will be due on the full value of the supply to him.

Providing the company makes a voluntary declaration to HMRC of the underpaid VAT there will currently be no penalties. (For returns due for submission after 31 March 2009, the new penalties for incorrect returns set out in FA 2007 Sch 24 apply.) Interest will be chargeable where appropriate.

The company should consider the financial viability of providing cars. The combined tax, VAT and national insurance charges on employer and employee may well be greater than the benefits actually obtained, particularly for Miss Fallow.

Similar comments apply to the provision of fuel to all employees and directors. For Mr and Mrs Sparks the fuel charge for 2009/10 is 35% of £16,900 = £5,915 each. If free fuel is to be withdrawn, the charge for a tax year will be reduced according to the period for which fuel is provided (unless free fuel is provided again later in the same tax year).

Mr Jones is paid a mileage allowance. If that amount exceeds the mileage allowance payment in ITEPA 2003 s 230 then it should be treated as remuneration. The figure of 75p per mile exceeds 40p per mile and therefore NI should have been applied to the excess of 35p per mile (ie, in total 1,936 miles @ 35p = £677, but accounted for monthly as mileage allowances were paid) and the excess of £677 should have been reported on Mr Jones's P11D. From 2002/03 the authorised mileage allowance rate for tax for Mr Jones's car has been 40p per mile up to 10,000 miles and 25p thereafter, the 40p rate applying to all miles for NI. If Mr Jones's mileage allowance was restricted to the authorised rate, it would no longer have to be taken into account for income tax and NI.

(d)   **Other benefits**

Telephones

The provision of a mobile phone to Mr Sparks and private use thereof is not subject to an income tax charge. However, VAT is payable on the non-business use of the mobile. This would appear to be 40% × (1,200 × 17.5%) = £84 in a normal year, with a slightly smaller figure due for the temporary period during which VAT has been reduced to 15%. This amount must be declared to HMRC and repaid assuming full input tax deduction had occurred.

The home telephone expenses for Mr Sparks and Mr Jones have already been shown on Forms P11D. An income tax charge could apply to the mobile phone if the company provides more than one per employee.

They should also be shown for the foreman and the sales representative (if he is an employee). It is then up to the individual employee to make an ITEPA 2003 s 336 claim for actual business calls. The balance will be liable to tax – if the company pays the bills directly to the telephone provider, the bills are reported on P11D, but if the company gives cash to the employees for them to pay their personal bills, the identified private element (rental and private calls) should be paid through payroll. For national insurance purposes, it does not matter whether the employer pays the bill or gives the employee the cash to do so: the same private element should be subject to Class 1 national insurance through the payroll. Identified business calls (but not part of the rental) may be excluded from the amount on which contributions are payable, or alternatively if there is an agreement with HMRC as to the business proportion for tax purposes, it is acceptable for NI purposes. The required adjustment for the telephones will be applied for all relevant years. Although the income tax liabilities are technically those of the individual employees it is possible that the company will wish to settle them, as it has been in breach of its obligations under ITEPA and the PAYE and NI regulations in not submitting Forms P11D. The penalties and interest within any such settlement would not be an allowable deduction for the company, but the tax and national insurance would be allowed in the year of payment if the amounts paid by the company in respect of the telephone bills had been grossed up to calculate that tax and national insurance.

Entertaining

The amounts to be shown on Forms P11D should be inclusive of VAT. If any input tax has been recovered on such sums then it must be repaid to HMRC. Interest will be charged but, for errors until 31 March 2009, no penalties if voluntary declarations are made to HMRC. For returns due to be submitted after 31 March 2009, the new penalties for incorrect returns set out in FA 2007 Sch 24 apply. No deduction is allowed in calculating the business trading profits.

Car parking

As the cost of the car parking near the factory is borne by the company, there will be no PAYE or national insurance liabilities on these amounts.

Subsistence

Subsistence will be an important part of the settlement. Subsistence payments in cash to employees who are not at a temporary workplace are pay, and PAYE and NI are due at the appropriate rates. Similar payments are due for earlier years back to 2004. For example, 36 employees × £18 per week × 48 weeks = £31,104 per annum which at 22% + NI of 23.8% = £14,245 for each of 2004/05, 2005/06, 2006/07, 2007/08 and 2008/09. The tax, NI, interest and penalties will fall on the company, which could in theory recover the PAYE, and some of the NI from the most recent year, from workers who are still employed, but this is unlikely in practice because of the damage to employee relations. If it was the company's intention that the amounts should be gross, the tax and NI liabilities should be calculated on normal PAYE lines, with no grossing up (ECH19005). The company could, however, agree that the amounts were net payments and therefore should be grossed up. In either case, it would normally be agreed that the whole of the PAYE and NI would be deductible in calculating trade profits of the accounting period when it was paid, as the payment is an employer payment wholly and exclusively in respect of employing staff. The fact that it is not necessary for the company to agree to bear the employees' tax and NI liabilities is irrelevant.

It should be noted that if the company, instead of paying a subsistence allowance, had an in-house canteen with subsidised or free meals or arrangements had been made with a local caterer to provide similar meals then no liability would arise. No dispensation would be needed from HMRC as the benefit is not taxable. Although VAT would be due on amounts paid by employees, any costs involved would give rise to deductible input tax. A reasonable subsistence allowance may be paid tax- and NI-free to workers who work away from their normal permanent workplace on any particular day. This could be covered by a dispensation. With effect from April 2009 HMRC provides benchmark scale rates which employers may adopt, but a dispensation would still be needed. For more details see the Employment Income Manual at EIM 05200

To minimise the costs in this case, calculations should be made to ensure that the actual liabilities are applied rather than global calculations, eg, go back and exclude days for which allowances were not paid to employees because of illness, holidays etc. Also confirm any days for which subsistence allowance was genuinely due, eg, days out of the factory. Check if any employee was lower paid or on lower national insurance rates, thus avoiding liability or having a lower liability.

The treatment of the subsistence paid to the sales representative depends on whether he is classified as employed or self-employed. If he is an employee the position is as described above. In the unlikely event that HMRC agrees that he is self-employed (see (e)), the subsistence payments to him will represent part of his fees. Unless he is VAT-registered and has submitted a VAT invoice, no VAT input tax should have been recovered on the subsistence, and if any has been, it should be repaid to HMRC. Any subsistence provided and paid for directly by a business for self-employed agents, etc, is disallowed as entertaining expenditure (*C & E v Shaklee International* (1981)).

Third party benefits

Where an employer has *arranged* for a third party to provide benefits to employees the employer is required to include the benefits on Forms P11D. If third party benefits are provided other than by arrangement with the employer, the third party is required to provide written details of the cash equivalent of the benefits to the employees concerned by 6 July following the relevant tax year, ie, by 6 July 2009 for 2008/09 (SI 2003/2682 reg 95). The third party is treated as the employer in respect of the benefits and is required to provide details to HMRC for Class 1A national insurance purposes, and to pay the NI liability (SI 2001/1004, Regs 70–80). The Incentive Award Unit in Salford will issue the third party Class 1A return on request, but no return is required for income tax purposes unless HMRC calls for a return under TMA 1970 s 15.

The third party benefits provisions do not apply to corporate hospitality, ie, entertainment or hospitality provided by someone who is not the employer or a person connected with the employer, where the employer or connected person has not arranged or procured the provision of the benefit, and it is not provided in return for particular services performed or anticipated to be performed by the employee in the course of his employment (ITEPA 2003 s 265).

Nor do they apply to benefits covered by ITEPA 2003 s 324. This excludes gifts from third parties that do not exceed a VAT-inclusive value of £250 to any individual in a tax year.

The golf weekend will be covered by the corporate hospitality provisions unless HMRC argues that the benefit was provided as a result of specific services performed or to be performed by the managing directors in their companies, eg, to give special favour to contracts with Sparks Manufacturing.

The provision of Christmas hampers up to a value of £250 would normally be covered by ITEPA 2003 s 324. Suppliers receiving hampers would only be chargeable if they received them as employees. In this case hampers in excess of that value would need to be notified, and the company should consider entering into a taxed award scheme for the future. The same penalties apply for not notifying third party benefits as for not reporting the annual Class 1A liability on Form P11D(b).

If Sparks Manufacturing do not wish the recipients to pay tax on the benefit, they may arrange with the Incentive Valuation Unit of HMRC to pay tax on the grossed-up value of the award under the Taxed Award Scheme. In that event the recipients would receive information under the Taxed Award Scheme rules rather than the third party benefits reporting requirements and the company would pay tax and NI on the benefits.

Sparks Manufacturing will not be able to claim a deduction for VAT or in calculating trade profits for the golf weekend or the hampers.

Any amounts paid or reimbursed to Mr Sparks (and the sales representative if an employee) in respect of the golf weekend should be included on Forms P11D. A s 336 claim can then be made in respect of the whole amount, since it represents a specific payment for entertaining carried out in the performance of the director's duties (which has been disallowed in calculating trade profits).

National insurance on benefits in kind

Employer's Class 1A national insurance contributions are payable on all taxable benefits (except those subject to Class 1 contributions, and certain childcare provision). The rate of Class 1A contributions has been 12.8% since 2003/04. Benefits are shown separately from expenses on Form P11D. No liability arises for non-directors who are lower paid, for whom P9D is used. The liability is computed for all relevant directors/employees and summarised on Form P11D(b). A separate payslip is then used to pay the Class 1A liability by 19 July following the tax year. Interest is charged on late payments and a penalty may be levied of £100 per 50 employees (or part thereof) for each month (or part thereof) the return is late.

The employer is liable to Class 1A national insurance on any benefits received by an employee from a third party if the benefit has been arranged by the employer. However, HMRC will not impose that charge on the employer provided the third party has paid the Class 1A liability. As noted above, the third party is liable if the employer did not arrange the award of the benefit. Meeting the Class 1A liability can be done as part of the provision of a Taxed Incentive Award.

Sparks Manufacturing Ltd should carefully check the completion of Forms P11D to ensure that benefits are shown separately from expenses, and that Class 1 national insurance has been paid on round sum payments and the settlement of employees' pecuniary liabilities. No Class 1A liability arises on any amount liable to Class 1, or exempt from tax (eg, one mobile telephone per employee). Liability is as follows:

Subsistence	Class 1 on profits
Cars and fuel	Class 1A on scale charges
Mileage payments	Class 1 on profit
Mobile telephones	No charge (one per employee)
Reimbursed petrol	Class 1 (on profit if business usage identified)
Car parking	No charge
Entertaining	No charge
Round sums	Class 1 on full amount
Home telephone	Class 1 (on rent and private calls provided business calls identified)

Sparks Manufacturing Ltd will be liable to pay the employers' Class 1A national insurance due on the golf weekend if HMRC succeeds in treating the amount as a taxable third party benefit for the guests.

(e)   **Sales representative**

The status of this worker should be clarified. The information provided suggests at point 1 that he is an employee, but at point 3 that he is treated as self-employed. The facts suggest that he is under the control and direction of the company. He would appear to be an integral part of the business and does not appear to be taking commercial risks. He draws all expenses from the company and is provided with benefits such as subsistence allowance, car parking space, etc. He would appear to work only for the company. It is therefore most likely that he will be treated as an employee throughout (see Example 94 for a full discussion of employment status).

Reclassification can strictly take place from the date of the commencement of the employment, but if the position has been clearly disclosed to HMRC in earlier years, reclassification from a later date may be negotiated, particularly if the sales representative has prepared and submitted accounts and agreed and paid all of his tax and NI liabilities to date. In computing the liability HMRC should take into account the personal allowances of the employee and any potential s 336 expenses claims. The Class 2 national insurance contributions paid by the sales representative should be credited against his Class 1 employee's national insurance liability. Any Class 4 national insurance contributions and trading income tax paid may be repaid to the employee. As the sales representative still works in the business, negotiations should take place with him for part or all of the tax to be repaid to the company, or indeed set off in the settlement by agreement between the sales representative and the company. Strictly the company has no legal right to recover from the sales representative national insurance contributions for previous years. Following the *Demibourne* case, new PAYE regulations were introduced from 6 April 2008 which potentially apply where an employer is required to account for PAYE but fails to do so and the employee has paid tax under self-assessment as though self-employed. These allow a direction to be made to transfer the PAYE liability from an employer to an employee. HMRC have published some FAQs on this new legislation at www.hmrc.gov.uk/employers/faq-transfer-paye.htm.

If he were to be classified as an employee, the sales representative would be assessed on benefits in kind in the normal way.

The provision of personal services through a limited company or partnership became liable to PAYE/NI on a deemed salary from 6 April 2000. If the sales representative attempts to retain his self-employed status by use of a partnership (or limited company) it is likely to lead to his partnership or service company being liable to account for PAYE and NI on a notional payment of most of his profit deemed to happen on 5 April each year, so such an arrangement would probably be ineffective. However, in those circumstances Sparks Manufacturing Ltd would have no liability for any PAYE/NI arising on a reclassification. The case of *Cable & Wireless plc v Muscat* found there to be a continuing contract of employment between the company and an individual working via both his own limited company and an employment agency after he was forced to transfer into that structure after having been an employee for some time. It is unlikely that the sales representative's self-employed status can be maintained.

Generally

The company clearly has material liabilities to HMRC in respect of failure to operate PAYE and national insurance in earlier years. These amounts should be quantified as soon as possible and declared to HMRC before the commencement of the visit. The company should regularise its position as follows:

(i) account for PAYE in respect of payments to the sales representative unless it can be specifically established with HMRC that he is self-employed;

(ii) cease paying subsistence and replace with canteen facilities (or add subsistence to pay for payroll purposes);

(iii) apply PAYE and NI to part-time staff;

(iv) regularise the position of Mr and Mrs Sparks and their monthly drawings;

(v) prepare and submit outstanding Forms P11D for all relevant employees, also providing the directors and employees with copy P11Ds for 2008/09;

(vi) give third parties written details of benefits provided in 2008/09;

(vii) obtain signed Forms P46/P38S for all part-time workers;

(viii) use the Authorised Mileage Allowance Payment rate for the accountant's business mileage.

In addition, the VAT implications of all transactions mentioned above should be reviewed. A voluntary disclosure should be made to HMRC as soon as possible. If the net disclosure is under the greater of £10,000 or 1% of turnover in box 6 of the return on which the error is to be corrected, subject to an upper limit of £50,000, the adjustment can be made in the next VAT return. If the figure is in excess of these limits a written declaration must be made to HMRC showing the liability divided between VAT accounting periods so that interest may be calculated for the last three years.

The company should cease paying round sum allowances and should only reimburse expenses against actual vouchers. VAT input tax can then be recovered with the exception of that on entertaining. In the case of motoring, VAT will only be recoverable on the petrol element of the allowance paid to Mr Jones, using the VAT fraction applied to the current advisory mileage rate. It should be confirmed that VAT has only been recovered on the business proportion of telephone bills, not the total bill.

Note that the European courts have ruled that the recovery of input VAT by an employer on company expenses where the expense was incurred by the employee is against EU rules. In Notice 700/64 HMRC states that input tax may be recovered in respect of business use if supported by a VAT invoice. Output tax must be accounted for in respect of private use.

It is probable that there will be significant settlements to be agreed with HMRC in respect of past breaches. Full co-operation and correction of past errors will be strong mitigating factors when negotiating the level of liability and penalties thereon.

Explanatory Notes

PAYE inspections

1. HMRC have power to visit employers' premises to undertake PAYE tax and national insurance inspections (Income Tax (PAYE) Regulations 2003 (SI 2003/2682 reg 97) and Social Security (Contributions) Regulations 2001 (SI 2001/1004 Sch 4)). FA 2008 Sch 36 extends HMRC powers to visit in other circumstances – see Example 41 explanatory note 13.

    Employers are required to produce to HMRC investigators all records relating to the calculation of PAYE income, and the deduction of tax and national insurance therefrom. It is common for an inspection to reveal areas of non-compliance with the regulations by the employers, and in that event HMRC will typically require settlement for the current and previous six years, with the addition of interest and penalties depending on the nature of the irregularities. Where there has been no lack of care, the assessing time limit is reduced by FA 2008 Sch 39 to four years, although the six-year limit is otherwise unchanged, except for where understatements are found to have been deliberate, when the limit becomes 20 years. These new time limits apply in full from April 2010.

    HMRC may agree to accept the amount due by instalments. The example illustrates many of the typical points to be considered in a PAYE/NI investigation.

2. Where HMRC consider that the employer has been guilty of fraudulent or negligent conduct, a penalty of up to 100% of the underpayment could be charged, but this will be subject to mitigation along the lines indicated in Examples 46 and 47. HMRC factsheets EC/FS3 and EC/FS4 indicate their approach to negotiating PAYE settlements. For returns due for submission after 31 March 2009, the new penalties for incorrect returns set out in FA 2007 Sch 24 apply. Penalties for understatements over the last six years will be calculated separately according to the penalty regime that applied to the return which contained an inaccuracy. See Example 41 for more details on the penalty regime from April 2009.

Year-end returns

3. As far as employers' returns are concerned, year-end Forms P35 and P14 are due to be submitted by 19 May after the end of the tax year (ie, within 44 days), although the tax is due for payment by 19 April (22 April for e-payers). TMA 1970 s 98A imposes penalties in respect of late submission (although by Revenue Concession B46 a penalty will not be charged if the forms are received on or before the last business day within the seven days following 19 May). It is possible for HMRC to proceed instead under TMA 1970 s 98, in which case the penalties are the same as for Forms P11D etc as outlined in part (a) of the example.

    Under s 98A, there are automatic penalties for late year-end Forms P35 and P14 as follows:

    (a)   A non-mitigable amount of £100 a month or part month for every 50 employees (and an additional £100 where the number of employees is not a multiple of 50), for up to 12 months, plus

(b)   If the returns are outstanding for more than 12 months, an amount not exceeding the amount unpaid at the original due date (ie, 19 April following the year to which the returns relate).

These penalties are imposed by a determination made by an officer under TMA 1970 s 100 and no proceedings before the First-tier Tribunal are necessary.

Similar penalties apply for late year-end Forms P11D(b) (SI 2001/1004 Sch 4 para 22).

Where the statutory penalty exceeds the total tax and national insurance due, it will normally be reduced to that amount or to £100 whichever is greater.

The s 98A penalties based on number of employees cover both tax and national insurance. Where the returns are outstanding for more than twelve months, a penalty may be imposed up to the amount of national contributions unpaid at the original due date, in addition to the penalty on the unpaid tax (Social Security Contributions and Benefits Act 1992 Sch 1 para 7).

4.   The time limit for sending in Forms P11D, P11D(b) and P9D is 6 July after the end of the tax year. The penalties outlined above will normally be imposed if the forms are not filed with HMRC by 19 July. Employers must provide employees with copies of Forms P11D and P9D by 6 July following the tax year (see Example 8), and the penalties that apply for failing to provide such copies are outlined in part (a) of the example. HMRC will not normally impose penalties for failure to provide copy Forms P11D unless the amount involved is significant or the employer persists in failing to comply. As indicated in part (d) of the example, similar penalties apply for not notifying third party benefits.

Penalties for late submission of returns are subject to new legislation included in Finance Act 2009 Sch 55, but implementation is to be delayed at least until 2010 while HMRC systems are prepared.

Determinations of tax due

5.   Under SI 2003/2682 reg 78 HMRC have power to estimate the monthly payments due if no payment is made or they are not satisfied with the tax paid. The specified amount must be paid within seven days of the issue of the notice unless the employer can satisfy HMRC that a lower amount is due.

6.   Where an officer considers that tax and national insurance due under PAYE has not been paid, he may issue a formal determination of the amount due (SI 2003/2682 reg 80). Under the pre-Finance Act 2009 rules, where a regulation 80 determination is made, interest automatically runs on late paid tax and national insurance from 19 April after the end of the tax year (income tax SI 2003/2682 reg 82, national insurance SI 2001/1004 Sch 4 para 17). FA 2009 s 101 introduced provision for interest to run from the actual due date of the original payment until actual payment to HMRC, but HMRC announced in 2009 Budget Note 91 that it will apply these rules on a limited basis only, from April 2010.

Employees' national insurance position on PAYE settlements

7.   Where an employer negotiates a settlement with HMRC and pays a sum representing tax that should have been deducted from the employees' earnings it is sometimes contended by HMRC that the employer is thereby meeting a pecuniary liability of the employee and that contributions are due on the payment as if a PAYE settlement agreement had been reached. There is no PSA (see Explanatory note 8), and the cases of *CIR v Woollen* (1992) and *CIR v Nuttall* (1990) suggest that this approach is not correct, since the employer is statutorily liable to make the payment, the employee is not party to such an agreement and HMRC's right to recover the amounts from the employee has been subsumed within the overall amount payable by the employer.

PAYE Settlement Agreements (PSAs)

8.   Some employers negotiate annual voluntary settlements with HMRC in respect of the tax liability on certain expenses payments and benefits to employees, which are referred to as PAYE settlement agreements (ITEPA 2003 Part 11 Chapter 5). Class 1B national insurance applies to PSA's, under

which contributions are payable on the benefits, etc, taxed under a PSA plus the tax thereon, to the extent that there would have been a national insurance liability under Class 1 or Class 1A. For details see Example 8 explanatory note 9.

Recovery of underpaid tax and national insurance from employee

9. Where an employer has to account for tax and national insurance contributions that he has failed to deduct, his rights of recovery from the employee are limited. However, the case of *Kleinwort Benson Ltd v Lincoln City Council* (1998 4 AER 513) now allows recovery where money was wrongly paid under a mistake of law, such as incorrectly treating an employee as self-employed. For other recoveries from an employee the case of *Bernard and Shaw Ltd v Shaw* (1951) held that recovery of PAYE was restricted to later payments of remuneration. As far as national insurance is concerned, the regulations provide that recovery of an underpayment that arose from an error made in good faith can be made only by deducting it from pay in the same year or the next following year, and then not exceeding an extra amount in each pay period equal to the normal deduction for that period (SI 2001/1004 Sch 4 paras 6 and 7). In any event, most employers would find it difficult to recover amounts from their employees, and may well suffer all or most of the payment themselves.

10. Following the *Demibourne* case, new PAYE regulations were introduced from 6 April 2008 which potentially apply where an employer is required to account for PAYE but fails to do so and the employee has paid tax under self-assessment as though self-employed. These allow a direction to be made to transfer the PAYE liability from an employer to an employee. HMRC have published some FAQ on this new legislation at www.hmrc.gov.uk/employers/faq-transfer-paye.htm.

(See Example 94 for a full discussion and recent court case on employment status.)

Childcare vouchers

11. See Example 9 explanatory note 24 for details of the income tax and national insurance treatment of childcare vouchers provided by an employer.

See also Example 7 explanatory note 7 for the interaction of tax credit claims with the provision of childcare vouchers.

Personal service companies

12. This legislation is covered in detail in Example 86.

Question

Grenville is an antique dealer, and he has accounts professionally prepared to 31 October each year. The accounts for the year ended 31 October 2008, forming the basis of his self-assessment return for the tax year 2008/09, were submitted to HMRC, together with the return, on 30 September 2009.

Grenville is married, his wife assisting minimally in the business, for which she has consistently received a wage just below the income tax threshold. She has no other income.

On 28 February 2010 Grenville received a formal notice from HMRC under TMA 1970 s 9A(1) stating that they had decided to enquire into his 2008/09 self-assessment, and calling for the following documents and information:

1. The business records for the accounting year to 31 October 2008.

2. Grenville's private bank statements and building society account books covering the tax year ended 5 April 2009.

3. An explanation of the source of £20,000 described in the accounts as capital introduced.

4. An analysis of the deduction in arriving at the accounts profits for wages, casual labour and porterage.

Grenville is concerned at the apparent extent of HMRC's powers in pursuing its enquiry and in particular the implied ability of the officer to examine his private financial records.

He says that he can explain and prove the capital introduced, since it was from his wife's bank current account, but confides in you that when the officer sees his own private bank and building society accounts he is bound to be curious about large deposits and withdrawals, which Grenville acknowledges are for business transactions which have not been recorded in the business books and hence not reflected in the profits.

Advise Grenville:

(a) of the consequences of failing to comply with the officer's request for information and documents, and what protection he has if he finds that request unreasonable;

(b) given that the information and documents are provided, how the officer's enquiry is likely to proceed; and

(c) to what extent the officer may extend his enquiry to cover the self-assessment for 2007/08 (which was filed on 31 December 2008, tax having been paid appropriately) and to 2006/07 and earlier years.

(d) state what action you, as a tax adviser, must take to comply with money laundering regulations.

Answer

(a)   **HMRC's request for information and documents**

If Grenville fails to comply with the request for information and documents, HMRC is able formally to demand these under FA 2008 Sch 36 para 1 by the issue of a taxpayer notice, the initial request to Grenville with the formal notice of enquiry being an opportunity for him to provide what HMRC requires without their using their formal powers.

Grenville cannot object to the officer enquiring into the return, but if he finds the request for information and documents unreasonable, he has the right to appeal to the First-tier Tribunal within 30 days from the date of the taxpayer notice. If the Tribunal confirms the notice, the taxpayer will have a further period allowed to produce the information and documents required, normally specified by the Tribunal, but alternatively such period as is reasonably specified by the officer in writing. There is no right of appeal against a request to produce documents which form part of the taxpayer's statutory records. If during the progress of the enquiry the taxpayer feels that HMRC have no reasonable grounds for continuing it and that it should therefore be concluded, he can ask the Tribunal to direct HMRC to issue a closure notice (TMA 1970 s 28A(4)).

(b)   **Enquiry procedure**

Upon seeing Grenville's bank and building society accounts, HMRC will undoubtedly come to the conclusion which Grenville predicts, and he would be advised at the time of submitting them to point out to HMRC the irregularities in his business records and accounts.

Despite Grenville's ability to explain the £20,000 capital introduced and to prove the source from which it has come, HMRC can also be expected to question how his wife, given her evident income, could have accumulated that amount of money in her current account.

They cannot directly ask Grenville about this unless his wife gives her specific permission for them to do so and for Grenville to disclose such information about her affairs to them, but they can serve a formal notice (a third party notice) on her under FA 2008 Sch 36 para 2, which empowers HMRC to ask for documents in the possession or power of one person which might affect the taxation liability of another. Normally HMRC would do so with the agreement of the taxpayer concerned, but the officer can seek prior approval of the Tribunal where it is appropriate (FA 2008 Sch 36 para 3). The taxpayer will have a right to make written representations to the Tribunal in most cases.

The implication here is that the wife's current account, like Grenville's own personal bank and building society accounts, had been used for business transactions and Grenville and his wife should be advised to agree a way forward with HMRC under which the omitted profits can be ascertained.

Although the business records have been discredited, they may still be useful in piecing together what has happened, for example by seeking to match the recorded expenditure on purchases, restoration costs, hotels, credit card payments showing where petrol and meals have been purchased, with sales and stock records.

An overall reconsideration of personal and business finances over an agreed period, embracing the accounts results, those of the specific matching exercise referred to in the previous paragraph, and the transactions through Mrs Grenville's account, will go a long way to calculating meaningful profits.

In the course of its investigation, HMRC will be concerned to prove the veracity of the recorded business expenditure, particularly in the areas highlighted by their request for information, there being a danger that amounts paid away for casual labour and porterage should really have gone through the payroll or otherwise have been reported to HMRC under the procedures for providing information about monies paid to the employees of others.

When the enquiry is completed Grenville will be invited to make an offer to HMRC in consideration of its not taking proceedings against him, the amount of the offer comprising the tax and interest plus a penalty.

Where income or gains have been understated, the penalty regime in FA 2007 would be relevant to this year, as the return was due for filing after 31 March 2009. The size of the penalty is determined by taxpayer behaviour giving rise to the penalty, and by the degree and type (whether prompted or unprompted) of disclosure. In this case, if the understatement of tax was considered to be as a result of a careless error, the maximum penalty would be 30% of the potential lost revenue. However, it is likely that HMRC would seek to argue that the understatement is deliberate, and therefore a penalty of 70% would apply, unless steps had been taken to conceal the inaccuracy, which would command a penalty of 100% of the potential lost revenue. Where disclosure has been made during the course of the enquiry the penalty could be reduced to 15% in the case of careless error, 35% for deliberate understatement or 50% if the understatement was concealed. (The exact details of how the discounts are calculated are in the HMRC Compliance Handbook.) (For returns due for submission before 1 April 2009, the penalties for incorrect returns would be based on 100% of the tax, mitigated for size, gravity, disclosure and co-operation.)

If HMRC accepts the taxpayer's offer, a binding contract is concluded, breach of which through non-payment by the taxpayer enables HMRC to take action for recovery of the amount outstanding.

(c) **Extending enquiry to earlier years**

Except where a return is filed late, for 2006/07 and earlier years HMRC could only open an enquiry under TMA 1970 s 9A into the amount of a taxpayer's self-assessment within the period ending 12 months after the filing date (31 January next but one after the tax year – and hence 31 January 2009 for Grenville's 2006/07 assessment). For 2007/08 onwards, the enquiry period for returns made on time is one year after the day on which the return is delivered. When the time for opening an enquiry has expired, however, HMRC have the power to issue an assessment themselves (under TMA 1970 s 29) in cases of fraudulent or negligent conduct (for 2008/09 returns this becomes failure to take reasonable care or deliberate understatement), or where there has been inadequate disclosure by the taxpayer. The time limit for such assessments in cases of inadequate disclosure is currently five years from 31 January following the tax year (TMA 1970 s 34), extended to 20 years where there is fraudulent or negligent conduct (TMA 1970 s 36) (FA 2008 changes these time limits from April 2010 to four years for mistake/discovery, six years for failure to take reasonable care and 20 years for deliberate understatement).

If, therefore, their enquiries into the 2008/09 self-assessment indicate that the self-assessments for 1999/00 to 2007/08, and the assessed profits for earlier years, are likely to have been inadequate, they can raise discovery assessments for those years to the best of the officer's judgment under TMA 1970 s 29.

Grenville and his advisers should agree with HMRC a suitable way of attempting to calculate the profits for a mutually acceptable number of years working back from 2008/09.

(d)

Tax practitioners, whether qualified or not, are bound by the money laundering regulations which came into force on 1 March 2004. These regulations require them to make reports not only of money laundering transactions, but also of the existence of any proceeds of crime. By under-declaring income, Grenville has obtained a monetary advantage in retaining funds that he otherwise would not have, and these are the proceeds. The proceeds of crime include the proceeds of tax evasion, bribery or any costs saved by failure to comply with regulatory requirements where failure to comply is a criminal offence – in this case the failure appears to be deliberate, and could be the subject of prosecution if HMRC so chose.

The fact that the tax authorities are aware of the matter does not obviate the need to make a report as soon as possible. The tax practitioner must report the matter to the firm's Money Laundering

Reporting Officer (MLRO). The MLRO must then consider whether to report, and whether to make a full report or a Limited Information Value Report (LIVR).

There is no indication that these omissions were unintentional, or particularly small (there is no de minimis limit for reporting), so clearly a report must be made. As there is good evidence for the identity of the person holding the proceeds of crime, and the whereabouts of the proceeds of crime themselves, a full report must be made.

The report must, therefore, be made as soon as reasonably possible to SOCA on a Suspicious Activity Report (SAR). This can be done online, or mailed by first-class post.

Explanatory Notes

Conduct of an enquiry

1.   Example 47 deals with the method of computing overall income or income omitted from tax returns, and the way in which a settlement will usually be concluded with HMRC. In making that calculation, allowance must be made for VAT on additional sales for which a liability exists.

HMRC's sources of information

2.   HMRC might already be in possession of information about Grenville and his affairs, and some of the documents or information called for may be to test that he is being completely open in providing them following the officer's challenge.

3.   There are a number of statutory provisions requiring persons to disclose income or transactions of others.

Those producing most information to HMRC are the requirements for banks and building societies to provide details of interest credited to depositors; for those paying commissions to provide details of the payee and amount, for example insurance and finance companies; for insurance companies to provide details of chargeable events arising out of the surrender or partial surrender of life assurance policies; and returns by solicitors and others of income arising on funds under their control. Government Departments, public bodies, and National Savings and Investments are also required to provide information. Under FA 2008 Sch 36 para 5 with the approval of the First-tier Tribunal, HMRC is able, where serious tax default is suspected, to require information without naming the suspected individuals, eg asking sponsors of tax avoidance schemes that are not legally effective to give details of those who used the scheme.

Information is also obtained from other government departments such as HMRC Capital Taxes, Department for Work and Pensions, Companies House, the Land Registry and in respect of holdings of government stocks. The exchange of information between government departments is strictly controlled, but FA 1997 s 110 extended the rules relating to the disclosure of information by the Department for Work and Pensions to HMRC, so that there are now general powers for information to be exchanged between both departments.

4.   In addition to the persons that are required to provide information mentioned in note 3, HMRC have a general power under FA 2008 Sch 36 para 3 to obtain information from third parties, with the approval of the taxpayer, or the consent of the First-tier Tribunal, and under this provision an accountant may be required to make available his working papers relating to a client's tax affairs, except for audit papers and tax advice (FA 2008 Sch 36 paras 24 and 25). HMRC used the predecessor to this power to require the major banks to disclose details of offshore accounts held by customers with UK addresses. This led to the introduction of an amnesty for those holding assets abroad to disclose non-reported income and assets in return for a nominal 10% penalty. The amnesty applied for disclosures made from 17.4.07 to 26.11.07. Some 60,000 taxpayers made a disclosure. In April 2008 HMRC announced they were pursuing those who didn't come forth to make a voluntary

disclosure. A further amnesty was announced, beginning on 1 September 2009, before which HMRC used the third party information notices to obtain such information as they deemed necessary. To do this, approval of the First-tier Tribunal was required and was duly given.

Finance Act 2008 extended HMRC's powers from 1 April 2009 to visit business premises, but not people's homes, and review records in 'real time'. Section 109 also allows an officer access to any computer used in relation to any relevant document – essentially part of anybody's statutory tax records.

In Grenville's case, HMRC could have obtained information on Grenville's affairs as a result of looking at working papers relating to someone else.

5.   A considerable amount of information available to the public generally is also used by HMRC to check the accuracy of returns, such as share registers, planning applications, press and media coverage, the Internet, entries in telephone and trade directories, and details of new company formations, not only in so far as the new company is concerned, but the other business activities of the personnel involved, which may be apparent from the documents submitted to Companies House. HMRC are also known to use various technologies such as Xenon, a data-mining tool which explores the Internet looking for unregistered (with HMRC) businesses or trading websites.

HMRC also have a vast amount of information at their disposal from the files of other taxpayers, for example, loans, capital acquisitions and disposals, and they glean considerably more in meetings with taxpayers and in examining their business records, when the affairs of others with whom they have been concerned are bound to come under scrutiny and comparisons are made between the records of businesses which deal with each other.

In Grenville's case, HMRC might well have been alerted to the apparent irregularities in his affairs through investigating the affairs of another trader with whom he has done business, or indeed by having had a concentrated look at his particular trade in his geographical area. For example, they might have seen the records of an auction house and, by a combination of those and other means, have formed the view that declared profits were inadequate.

Finally, HMRC, like other authorities, receive information from informants and someone suspecting Grenville's under-declarations might well have provided HMRC with information which has assisted them in formulating their views.

Completion of enquiry

6.   In addition to examining bank and building society accounts, HMRC will require a certified statement of assets and liabilities before agreeing Grenville's liabilities, to ensure that all of these have been included in considering the calculation of profits.

Grenville will also be asked to sign a certificate of full disclosure and of bank and building society accounts operated.

7.   From a combination of the certified statements at note 6 above, the independent information which they hold and the detailed workings, HMRC will be as satisfied as in the circumstances it is possible to be that all income and gains have been taken into account.

8.   The enquiry will usually be settled by HMRC accepting an offer from the taxpayer (contract settlement), or for some self-assessment enquiries, by HMRC issuing a closure notice under TMA 1970 s 28A setting out HMRC's conclusions and the amendments to the self-assessment. For details of the settlement procedure see notes 20 to 22.

Criminal proceedings

9.   Whilst the usual practice of HMRC is to seek a pecuniary settlement with the taxpayer, it should always be borne in mind that they could take criminal proceedings in the case of provable fraud, being quite distinct from the civil proceedings for the recovery of unpaid tax, interest and penalties.

Furthermore, the Court of Appeal held in *R v W and Another* (1998) that the Crown Prosecution Service could prosecute a taxpayer even where HMRC had decided not to do so. The Revenue stated, however, in their Tax Bulletin of June 1998 that this will ordinarily only occur where tax evasion is incidental to allegations of non-fiscal criminal conduct, which was the case in *R v W*.

Fraudulent evasion of income tax has been a specific criminal offence since 1 January 2001 (FA 2000 s 144). It applies in relation to things done or omitted where someone is knowingly concerned in the fraudulent evasion of income tax by himself or someone else.

The Human Rights Act 1998 introduced further rights and protections (from 2 October 2000) for a client in criminal matters. The definition of 'criminal' includes offences that can give rise to a penalty which is punitive. It is thought by some that any case where HMRC imposes a penalty, as opposed to only recovering the unpaid tax plus interest, could be classified as criminal under the Human Rights Act 1998.

It may be argued in such cases that HMRC needs to prove its case beyond all reasonable doubt (instead of on the basis of the balance of probability), that the taxpayer is not required to incriminate himself, that the onus of proof is on HMRC and that only admissible evidence may be used to prove the case.

In practice taxpayers may prefer to negotiate a settlement rather than risk the possibility that HMRC may take a criminal prosecution.

Any appeal to the First-tier Tribunal could be considered a civil matter, eg determining the facts of a case such as employment status, or a criminal matter. In the latter case it would be best practice for the matter to be fully discussed with HMRC to get them to disclose their skeleton arguments and to give the taxpayer's advisers full access to any evidence.

In the matter of a deceased taxpayer, the Human Rights Act confirms that criminal liability ceases at the date of death. This will prevent HMRC imposing tax-geared penalties on the personal representatives for actions of the taxpayer prior to death.

Enquiries under self-assessment – income tax and capital gains tax

10. The time limit for submitting an electronically filed return is 31 January following the end of the tax year (eg 31 January 2011 for 2009/10). HMRC have an absolute right, without giving any reason, to enquire into any return within 12 months after the date it is filed, ie by 31 May 2011 for a 2009/10 return filed on 31 May 2010 (TMA 1970 ss 12AA(4) and 9A(2). Under TMA 1970 s 28C, HMRC are able to 'determine' the tax due where a return is not submitted, and this is treated as a self-assessment unless and until superseded by an actual self-assessment. The time limit for the determination is five years from 31 January following the tax year, and a superseding self-assessment can only be made within that period or, if later, within twelve months after the determination.

11. HMRC assessments will still be issued (under TMA 1970 s 29) in cases of fraudulent or negligent conduct, or where there has been inadequate disclosure by the taxpayer, as indicated in part (c) of the example. In cases of fraudulent or negligent conduct HMRC have the power to issue a discovery assessment even though the time limit for opening an enquiry into a return has not expired. See HMRC's Tax Bulletin August 2001 for the circumstances in which this might be done.

12. As far as interest on overdue tax is concerned, interest automatically runs from the due dates of the payments on account and balancing payments and there is no provision for interest to be mitigated (TMA 1970 s 86). (For years before self-assessment, ie 1995/96 and earlier, interest is also charged under s 86 and runs from 31 January following the relevant tax year.) Where there is an HMRC discovery assessment under TMA 1970 s 29, the provisional payments required for the following tax year will be regarded as being increased accordingly (TMA 1970 s 59A(4B)). Interest will therefore be charged not only on the underpaid tax for the tax year to which the discovery assessment relates but also on the amounts by which the next year's provisional payments fell short of what they should

have been. The interest on the shortfall in the provisional payments will run to the date when the balancing payment fell due (ie normally 31 January following the end of the tax year).

13. A taxpayer can only amend his self-assessment within twelve months after the 31 January filing date for the return. Generally speaking a voluntary amendment of a return should qualify for the maximum discount for unprompted disclosure, bringing the penalty down to zero for a careless understatement, 20% for a deliberate inaccuracy and 30% when the inaccuracy has been concealed. See Example 41 for more details on the structure of the penalty system.

    Taxes Management Act 1970 s 28A provides that returns are not amended by a taxpayer on completion of an HMRC enquiry. Amendments required by HMRC are made by them in a closure notice issued to the taxpayer (see note 22).

14. Most HMRC enquiries under self-assessment are based on the risk of understatement on the return, an approach that will be refined from April 2009 onwards with the introduction of new powers. It is likely in the early days of new powers that checks (the new term for compliance interventions) will be carried out on a single aspect of a return, not unlike an aspect enquiry under the old regime. It remains to be seen whether HMRC will continue to open 'full' enquiries as they did previously, and indeed what part random enquiries play in the new risk-assessed process. It should be borne in mind that the new powers allow a check on a period for which a return has not yet been submitted, and this may lead to 'breaking the records', which in turn could lead to a discovery assessment. There is no doubt that HMRC will concentrate to a significant extent on the adequacy of records for smaller businesses. The opening of an enquiry does not mean that HMRC have already identified a reason for dissatisfaction with the return, but the vast majority of enquiries will be opened because of the potential risk that the returns concerned are incorrect or incomplete. The scale of the enquiry will, however, reflect the circumstances of the case and the degree of risk of error or omission. Trivial or remote risks will not be pursued, nor will HMRC seek information that can be verified from their own records.

Enquiries under self-assessment – corporation tax

15. Self-assessment applies to companies for accounting periods ending after 30 June 1999.

    The same provisions apply as for income tax for the company to amend the return and HMRC similarly have the power to enquire into the return. For accounting periods ending after 31 March 2008, the enquiry period for companies that are not members of large groups is linked to the date a return is filed. For returns made on time, HMRC have a year after the day on which a return is delivered to open an enquiry. For example, to 31 August 2010 for a 31 May 2009 year end return filed on 31 August 2009. For companies which are members of large groups, the enquiry period (for returns filed on time) remains as one year after the filing due date, eg 31 May 2011 for a 31 May 2009 year-end return filed on 31 August 2009. There is a practical relaxation of this rule which allows a group to be subject to enquiry from twelve months after the date that the last company member of the group filed its return for the relevant accounting period. HMRC may also issue determinations of the tax due if no return is submitted, such determinations being superseded by an actual self-assessment if it is made not later than five (see below re: FA 2008 changing this to three) years after the filing date for the return or 12 months after the determination if later. HMRC may still make discovery assessments, and they may also make 'discovery determinations' where a return incorrectly states an amount that affects another period or another company.

    HMRC may only make discovery assessments and discovery determinations where there is fraudulent or negligent conduct (for returns due on or after 1 April 2009, failure to take reasonable care or deliberate understatement) or HMRC was given inadequate information.

    The time limits for assessments in respect of accounting periods ending on or before 30 June 1999 are six years after the end of the accounting period (TMA 1970 s 34), extended to 20 years where there is fraudulent or negligent conduct (TMA 1970 s 36). Under corporation tax self-assessment, the six-year time limit remains the same but the 20-year time limit is increased to 21 years, both provisions being contained in FA 1998 Sch 18 para 46. Finance Act 2008 introduced new rules for IT, CGT, CT, VAT and PAYE changing the assessment time limits to four years for mistake / discovery, six years (except VAT which is four) for failure to take reasonable care and 20 years for deliberate understatement. The new rules will apply to VAT failures after 1 April 2009, and will be fully operative for the other taxes after 1 April 2010.

Level of penalties and interest

16. In all cases HMRC have power to determine penalties at less than the maximum levels (FA 2007 Sch 24 para 11), by applying a special reduction. However this must be applied in special circumstances, which does not include an inability to pay the tax concerned. The interest element will rarely be less than the maximum, except where HMRC have caused serious delay in reaching a settlement.

    How much interest is payable then depends upon the dates of the issue of assessments and when tax payments have been made.

17. HMRC will normally indicate to a taxpayer in Grenville's position that his full disclosure in establishing the amount of unpaid tax will be to his advantage in determining the amount eventually required from him and in the circumstances he should be advised to make a complete disclosure to HMRC and to co-operate fully in ascertaining the tax underpaid for earlier years. The penalty discount will be determined by the degree of 'telling', 'helping' and 'allowing access' in the disclosure. That is:

    • telling HMRC that there is an inaccuracy on a return, and how the inaccuracy arose;

    • helping HMRC to quantify the amount of the understatement of tax; and

    • allowing HMRC full access to the records (if requested) to enable the tax authority to establish that the understatement has been correctly rectified.

    Where HMRC does not request access to the records, the full discount for the 'allowing' aspect is given.

    Depending upon the level of profits there might also be liability for Class 4 national insurance contributions, and if so, this will have to be included in the amount due to HMRC and will be treated like tax due for the purposes of calculating interest and penalties.

18. Interest will run at the prescribed rate on the unpaid tax (and Class 4 national insurance contributions) for the years concerned, and in order to restrict it, Grenville should be advised to make a meaningful payment on account to HMRC.

Appeals against estimated assessments

19. It is usual for the taxpayer to lodge appeals against estimated assessments raised by HMRC. HMRC will usually resist any application to postpone the charge for tax and Class 4 national insurance unless a meaningful payment on account of liabilities to be agreed is made.

Contract procedure for settlement of enquiry

20. When the unpaid tax and Class 4 national insurance contributions have been ascertained, Grenville will be invited to make an offer to HMRC in consideration of their not issuing formal assessments or additional assessments for its recovery and not formally determining the interest and penalties, and upon his doing so and the Board of HM Revenue and Customs accepting that offer, there is a legally binding contract upon which HMRC can rely if Grenville does not make payment.

    The amount of the offer will usually have to be for at least the unpaid tax and national insurance contributions plus interest and an appropriate uplift to cover the penalty element.

21. The amount of penalty added to the agreement will be determined by applying the new penalty rules in FA 2007. There is very little room for the officer to vary the penalty by subjective judgement as the

discounts for disclosure are all included in primary legislation. The Compliance Handbook includes examples of how penalties are calculated under the new rules.

Settlement of self-assessment enquiry by s 28A notice

22. The legislation provides that at the end of an enquiry HMRC will issue a closure notice stating their conclusions and showing the revisions to the taxpayer's self-assessment and the additional tax due (TMA 1970 s 28A). The taxpayer then has thirty days in which to appeal in writing against conclusions stated or amendments made by the closure notice, giving the grounds of appeal (TMA 1970 ss 31, 31A).

    Where penalties are being sought HMRC will usually look for a contract settlement rather than using the s 28A procedure.

Taxpayer amendments notified in the course of an enquiry

23. A taxpayer may give HMRC notice of an amendment to the self-assessment return (within the permitted twelve months after the filing date for the return) whilst an enquiry is in progress. The amendment will not restrict the scope of the enquiry but may be taken into account in the enquiry. If it affects the tax payable, it will not take effect unless and until it is incorporated into the s 28A closure notice issued to the taxpayer (see note 22 above) (TMA 1970 s 9B).

Referral of questions to the Tribunal during enquiry

24. At any time during an enquiry, any question in connection with the subject matter of the enquiry may be referred to the Tribunal for determination. To do so, the referral must be made in writing jointly by the taxpayer and HMRC. Either party may withdraw from the referral process providing they give notice before the first hearing of the matter by the Tribunal. The determination will be binding on both parties as if it were a decision on a preliminary issue under appeal (TMA 1970 ss 28ZA–28ZE and ss 31A–31D for companies).

Class 4 national insurance contributions

25. Class 4 national insurance contributions are included for interest and penalty purposes where they arise because of failure to supply information or the supply of erroneous information. From 6 April 1999, criminal proceedings may be taken for fraudulent evasion of national insurance contributions (SSAA 1992 s 114).

Acceptance of offer at local level

26. The tax office dealing with the enquiry has power to accept an offer by a culpable taxpayer up to certain limits of size and gravity, but above those limits the offer has to be referred to a head office department who will consider it, taking into account the recommendations of the tax office and endeavouring to preserve national consistency.

Civil Investigation of Fraud

27. The civil procedure for dealing with cases of suspected serious fraud is set out in HMRC's Code of Practice 9 (COP9), from 1 September 2005. Following the merger of Inland Revenue and Customs and Excise, the separate powers of each of the original departments were retained, and then replaced by new powers. As a temporary measure, FA 2007 s 81 extended Customs' previously ring fenced powers of arrest (albeit in limited circumstances) to the merged HMRC. The powers were also aligned with the Police and Criminal Evidence Act (PACE). New powers have been introduced by FA 2008 and have effect from 1 April 2009.

    In the case of suspected serious fraud the procedure adopted by HMRC covers both direct and indirect taxes. It is very similar to the old 'Hansard' regime that it replaced, with the exception that the threat of prosecution for the original offence (but not necessarily offences coming to light during the course of the procedure) was removed, and interviews are not tape-recorded.

The Board of HMRC reserves complete discretion to pursue criminal investigations, and will refer cases to the Revenue and Customs Prosecution Office (RCPO) before commencing the COP9 'Civil Investigation of Fraud' procedure. The COP9 procedure will not lead to prosecution for the original offence, but other related offences might be reported to SOCA and lead to prosecution. The procedure gives the taxpayer the opportunity to make a complete disclosure of all irregularities in direct and indirect taxes. In the case of direct taxes, HMRC will propose a settlement covering tax, interest and penalties, which will form part of a legal contract if accepted. In the case of indirect taxes, an assessment will be issued. If the disclosures are found to be materially incorrect, then prosecution can follow.

The previous 'Hansard' procedure was carried out by the former Special Compliance Office. This was replaced by Special Civil Investigations Office, now renamed Specialist Investigations, but the COP9 procedure will not be restricted to SI investigators. It is possible that the disclosure orders obtained against banks will result in wider use of this procedure.

Amending claims on completion of enquiries

28. Where an assessment is issued to make good any loss of tax, the taxpayer can make, revise or withdraw claims which would otherwise be out of time. That right is extended (by Finance Act 2003) to situations where a return is amended at the end of an enquiry. Claims affecting another person's liability will require the written consent of that other person. The ability to amend claims does not extend to rebasing elections for capital gains tax, surrender of married couple's allowance or children's tax credit, and is restricted to the additional tax payable by the assessment or amendment.

Tax Credits

29. Any adjustment to income (from 2003/04 onwards or 2001/02) may have a corresponding effect upon the income for tax credits. The fact that tax credits are based on joint income will complicate the enquiry procedures in the event of a joint claim. The Tax Credits Act 2002 ss 19 and 20 give HMRC appropriate enquiry and discovery powers. It is understood that where a taxpayer under enquiry has made a tax credits claim that both enquiries will be undertaken at the same time by the same officer. Separate opening and closing letters and 'offer' letters will be required. Normally enquiries for the years 2002/03 or earlier years will not affect tax credits. Where the enquiry is for 2003/04 or later years, as for Grenville, then any adjustment to income will affect the tax credits claim made for 2003/04, 2004/05, 2005/06, 2006/07, 2007/08, 2008/09 and the provisional awards for 2009/10. The tax credit cost of any settlement could be higher at 39% (for 2009/10, 37% for years before 2008/09) than the combined income tax (20% for 2009/10, 22% for years before 2008/09) and national insurance (8%) liabilities. The tax credits settlement would not attract interest (unless the claim was fraudulent) and any penalties are not tax-based. The maximum penalty is £3,000 for providing incorrect information fraudulently or negligently, or £300 for failure to provide information. In both instances the penalty can be reduced depending upon the seriousness of the issue, amounts involved, co-operation and disclosure. For further details see factsheets WTC/FS1, FS2 and FS3, leaflet WTC7 Tax Credits Penalties and HMRC Manual CCM 10380 in respect of Penalties and Interest.

The Money Laundering Regulations – Tax Practitioners

30. Money laundering regulations, which had long applied to banks and other financial institutions, were extended to accountancy and tax advice activities on 1 March 2004. The Consultative Committee of Accountancy Bodies (CCAB) issued Anti-Money Laundering guidance in December 2007. Supplementary Anti-Money Laundering Guidance for the Tax Practitioner was issued by The Chartered Institute of Taxation (and others) in April 2008. These documents aim to assist in complying with the Proceeds of Crime Act 2002 and Money Laundering Regulations 2007.

The purpose of the regulations is to require relevant businesses to make reports to SOCA of any knowledge or suspicions of money laundering activity. However, this is limited to knowledge or suspicions acquired in the course of business or employment, not knowledge acquired through personal social connections.

Firms affected must appoint an individual as the Money Laundering Reporting Officer to receive money laundering reports from staff, and to make reports to SOCA. All staff must be trained in the recognition and reporting of potential money laundering transactions, and how to verify the identity of new clients. The firms must establish appropriate internal procedures to detect and prevent money laundering. There are a number of further important requirements, and significant criminal penalties for principals and employees for breaching money laundering regulations. The CCAB guidance has recommendations on complying with the regulations, which can be downloaded from www.c-cab.org.uk.

Firms, and their staff, are affected by money laundering regulations if they provide accountancy services, insolvency services, tax advice, or the services of formation or management of a company. This applies as much to unqualified accountants and tax advisers as to qualified individuals, applies outside the UK as well as within the UK, and applies to accountants generally, not just within the profession.

The form of identification to be obtained is not specified by the Act, but is determined by the firm's own policies via a risk-based approach. The guidance given to them by the Joint Money Laundering Steering Group (originally intended for banking and financial services), is often followed.

The offences to be reported include any criminal activity giving rise to proceeds, and, in particular, these are not limited to terrorism or drug dealing. The proceeds of crime, termed 'criminal property', include the proceeds of tax evasion, bribery, or costs saved by failure to comply with regulatory requirements (where the failure to comply is a criminal offence). There is no de minimis limit for the value of the proceeds of crime to be reported, so even the smallest transactions may require a report.

Reports must be made as soon as reasonably possible to SOCA on a Suspicious Activity Report (SAR), and can be made online at www.soca.gov.uk/financialintel/suspectactivity.html#forms. The details to be reported are specified on this site.

A Limited Intelligence Value Report (LIVR) may be made where, individually, the information in the report is likely to be of limited value (the report is required in case correlation of many such reports yields useful information). A LIVR is never appropriate for serious crimes such as terrorism or drugs offences, but might be used for small discrepancies arising from mistakes rather than dishonest behaviour, or where the identity of the criminal is not known.

Accountants and tax advisers in practice are expected to make reports on clients in circumstances where failure to comply with tax regulations has led to underpayment of tax, or late payment. A professional should never indicate to a client that they are making a report, or they may be guilty of the offence of tipping off. HMRC indicate that around a fifth of SARs received identify a new subject of interest and a quarter lead to new enquiries in relation to direct taxation matters.

The 2007 regulations require all businesses to be supervised by an appropriate anti-money laundering supervisory authority. For many businesses the supervisory authority will be the professional body to which they belong, e g The Chartered Institute of Taxation (CIOT). Those businesses that are not members of, or otherwise regulated by one of the approved bodies will be supervised by HMRC. For advice on how to register see www.hmrc.gov.uk/mlr/register.htm.

The 2007 regulations expanded on the original 2003 regulations and:

- provided more detailed obligations regarding customer due diligence, for example ongoing monitoring of business relationships and identification of the beneficial owner as well as the customer;

- varied customer due diligence and monitoring according to money laundering risk, requiring enhanced due diligence in high risk situations;

- allowed firms to rely on certain other firms for undertaking customer identification.

Legal privilege

31. In a relatively narrow range of circumstances, such as litigation or giving legal advice where making a report to SOCA would compromise the client's rights to legal privilege, qualified accountants have the same legal privilege as the legal profession allowing them to claim protection from reporting suspicious transactions. An example of a circumstance where an accountant would enjoy legal privilege would be where he is working as an expert witness for a firm of lawyers. This applies only to money laundering, not offences under the Terrorism Act 2000.

Question

Feckless, a married man with three children all born between 1992 and 1998, has been in business on his own account as a retailer of fruit and vegetables at shows, carnivals and race meetings since May 2003. HMRC had sent him self-assessment forms for the years 2003/04 onwards, but he had not submitted them, and in their absence HMRC had determined the tax for each tax year up to 2007/08 in amounts which increased each year, Feckless having paid the tax and the fixed penalties for failing to make returns.

As a result of reading in the press in May 2010 that some £50,000 had been stolen from Feckless's house, HMRC wrote to him pointing out that although the determinations for earlier years had been made in amounts which were HMRC's then best estimates of what he should have paid, they were entitled to increase such estimates if they were discovered to be inadequate, the reported theft of such a large cash hoard suggesting that they were. The officer invited Feckless to provide HMRC with a statement showing his overall financial position, seeking thereby to ascertain his trading profit since he commenced in business, and enabling assessments in correct amounts for all years to replace the determinations.

A friend who had limited experience in this area produced for Feckless the following statement which purported to calculate the profits figures covering the period to 30 April 2009 and resulting tax position for the tax years 2003/04 to 2009/10:

'Assets at 30 April	2003 £	2004 £	2005 £	2006 £	2007 £	2008 £	2009 £
Cash hoard	50,000	50,000	50,000	50,000	50,000	50,000	–
Cash at bank – current account	100	3,900	7,600	11,300	13,900	19,900	47,100
Stock (minimal since everything sold at the end of a day)	–	10	10	15	15	20	20
Wife's jewellery (received from deceased relative) at original value	6,000	6,000	5,000	3,000	–	–	–
Freehold house at cost net of £150,000 mortgage	–	–	–	–	20,000	20,000	20,000
	56,100	59,910	62,610	64,315	83,915	89,920	67,120
At previous 30 April		56,100	59,910	62,610	64,315	83,915	89,920
Increase/(Decrease)		3,810	2,700	1,705	19,600	6,005	(22,800)
Expenses							
Rent (before buying house)		4,338	4,338	4,338	4,169	–	–
Mortgage interest		–	–	–	720	10,440	10,440
Housekeeping		5,156	5,156	5,156	5,156	5,156	5,156
Miscellaneous		1,200	1,200	1,200	1,200	1,200	1,200
		10,694	10,694	10,694	11,245	16,796	16,796
Total of wealth increase + expenses		14,504	13,394	12,399	30,845	22,801	(6,004)
Income							
Sale of jewellery		–	(1,000)	(2,000)	(3,000)	–	–
Betting winnings		(650)	(800)	(1,000)	(1,200)	(1,500)	(2,000)
Net increase/(decrease)		13,854	11,594	9,399	26,645	21,301	(8,004)

Total increases over the five trading years to 30 April 2008 are £82,793, giving an average income over that period of £16,558 per annum.

Loss of £8,004 for the year to 30 April 2009 establishes a nil profit for the tax year 2009/10 and the loss may be deducted from the 2008/09 profit of £16,558, reducing it to £8,554.'

Feckless submitted this statement to HMRC accompanied by completed self-assessments for 2003/04 to 2008/09 in which estimated figures of turnover, purchases and business expenses were included to net off to the averaged profit figures.

HMRC have issued formal notices of enquiry into the self-assessments for all years, saying that there are many anomalies and areas which the statement does not properly or sufficiently address, setting out their areas of concern and listing the information and documents that they require in order to resolve them.

(i)   Without preparing an amended statement, set out what you believe HMRC's reaction to the content of the statement will have been and say what further information and evidence you feel will have been asked for.

(ii) Apart from an amended statement, amended self-assessments for 2003/04 to 2008/09 and eventually the self-assessment for 2009/10, what other certificates etc will HMRC require at the conclusion of its enquiry?

(iii) Since Feckless had not put in false returns, as distinct from accepting HMRC determinations, is HMRC correct in suggesting in the summer of 2009 that it can amend the tax payable for 2003/04 when the time limit for replacing a determination for that year expired on 31 January 2010 (five years after the filing date for 2003/04, which was 31 January 2005)?

(iv) How might the statutory procedure for amending the self-assessments be adapted in the present circumstances?

Answer

(i)   **Officer's reaction to statement, and information etc required to take matter forward**

Cash hoard

1.1   Whilst the theft might be evidence of the cash stolen, what evidence is there that it was consistent over the years?

1.2   How did a hoard of £50,000 arise in 2003 before business commenced? It is far more likely to have arisen over the trading period.

1.3   What evidence is there that the stolen cash hoard represented all the cash? Certificate required of present cash count. Was it kept in one place and in what sort of container? What is the result of insurance company investigations if a claim for loss was made?

1.4   The amount stolen should be included in the statement for 2009. Its omission accounts for the apparent decrease in wealth for that year and before considering any other points, turns the loss of £8,004 into a profit of £41,996, which makes a nonsense of the figures Feckless has used for turnover, purchases and expenses in the calculation of the result for the year to 30 April 2009 contained in the self-assessment for 2009/10.

Bank accounts

2.1   Banker's certificate required, not only to confirm current account balances but also as a check on other transactions and matters included by banks in the standard certificate required by HMRC, eg accounts at other branches (including abroad), securities held etc.

Bank statements required for examination. Particular deposits, withdrawals, indications of transfers to/from other accounts, and the pattern of transactions may lead to other relevant points.

Trading stock

3.1   Stock very low despite the nature of the trade. More information required on how the trade is operated.

3.2   Are purchase invoices and dates of shows etc available? If so this will give some idea if stocks are, albeit exceptionally, carried.

3.3   Such invoices will also give some idea of the potential profit achievement if, for example, a trading pattern, attempted profit margin, wastage etc, can be established.

Jewellery

4.1   What evidence is there that jewellery was inherited or received by way of gift, as distinct from being purchased, for which funds would be required?

4.2   If purchased, then as with the cash at 1.2, how could it have been accumulated before trading started? HMRC is likely to suggest that it did not exist, or if it did, that it was acquired after trading started. Also, what evidence of sales?

4.3   Contents insurance policy required to confirm/contradict the point.

4.4   It has, in any event, been included twice – once as a movement in assets and once more as income.

4.5   Alternatively the income figure may represent the profit on sale. Determine actual cost and sale proceeds, profits and likely gain, or exceptionally does this constitute a further trading source?

House mortgage etc

5.1 Consistent mortgage interest implies that house purchase was financed on a fixed mortgage. Confirm by reference to statements or adjust for capital repayments.

5.2 Copy of mortgage application form required since this may indicate the level of income reported to the lender. How was that income calculated?

5.3 Costs of buying house and of furnishing it to be incorporated.

5.4 The fixed mortgage suggests that capital repayments may be being dealt with by an endowment or personal pension policy. No premiums are indicated in the yearly expenditure. Has Feckless had a long-term fixed-rate mortgage?

5.5 Has there been any house improvement expenditure and how financed? Was the property previously occupied as a 'sitting tenant'?

Living expenses

6.1 Housekeeping is low for a family of this size.

6.2 Further, it will have risen over the years with the cost of living and will not have been consistent.

6.3 Sample costs required at present time, which will then be worked backwards using appropriate index and taking into account known changes in circumstances.

Miscellaneous expenses

7.1 What is covered under miscellaneous expenses?

7.2 What should be covered, given the habits of the family; such as smoking, drinking, gambling, entertaining and holidays?

Betting winnings

8.1 Absolute proof required of betting winnings.

8.2 In absence of absolute proof, the inclusion of the winnings has admitted the activity and since it usually costs money, an additional expense instead of an item of income will arise.

8.3 The Officer will in all probability contend that proved winnings have, in any event, been cancelled by undisclosed losses, thus cancelling the winnings and involving further cash payments.

Wife and children

9.1 Child benefit will have been received in respect of the children, mitigating the position.

9.2 The statement includes certain items relating to wife, eg jewellery. It does not include wife's income or expenses (eg personal expenditure, hairdresser, clothes, motoring costs of her vehicle). Although the officer has not opened an enquiry into the wife's affairs, clearly they interlink with those of Feckless. In practice the officer may ask for voluntary disclosure of the assets, liabilities, income and expenses of Mrs Feckless, only resorting to issuing a tax return to her (so that a formal enquiry notice may be issued) if she will not cooperate.

National insurance and tax payments

10.1 Self employed Class 2 national insurance contributions have not been included as an outgoing.

10.2 The tax and Class 4 national insurance paid on the determinations have not been included as outgoings.

Arriving at increases/decreases

11.1 The increases/decreases cannot be averaged. Each year must stand on its own.

11.2 The only decrease in this case has already been eliminated (see 1.4), but should one arise it may suggest further expenditure on assets, extraordinary items or living expenses, in the latter case with persuasive influence on other years.

11.3 An increase may be used as an indication that other years should show a similar increase, or be persuasive as to profitability.

The 2007 increase arises directly as a result of the house purchase. It is undoubtedly not applicable solely to that year. Where were the funds previously held and did any of them arise before the business started?

Fixed assets of the business

12.1 The statement does not include anything for fixtures, fittings or vehicles. Presumably there will be some. When acquired and for how much?

(ii) **Other certificates etc required**

Apart from a new statement and (subject to (iv) below) amended self-assessments, reflecting the above points, HMRC will require from Feckless a certificate of complete disclosure, a certified statement of assets and liabilities at a date approximating to that on which the officer concluded his enquiry and a certified list of bank and building society accounts operated throughout the period covered by the enquiry.

(iii) **HMRC's position re 2003/04**

In order to replace the determination for 2003/04 which is outside the normal statutory time limit, HMRC would have to prove negligent or fraudulent conduct. They would undoubtedly succeed in their contention that the acceptance of determinations lower than what would be compatible with living standards and accumulation of wealth amounts to negligent conduct, their grounds being that the reasonable man must have known that his trading was more successful than the profits which would have been necessary to produce the tax and Class 4 national insurance contributions payable under the determinations. As a result, not only will Feckless have to pay the additional tax and Class 4 national insurance contributions for those years, but the unpaid amounts will attract interest from 31 January following the relevant tax year, with a consequential effect on the payments on account for the next tax year and hence interest thereon from those earlier dates.

For 2008/09 onwards the new penalty terms of 'failure to take reasonable care' and 'deliberate understatement' replaced 'negligent and fraud', and this year would be considered separately for the purpose of penalties (see Explanatory note 4 for more details regarding the penalty calculation).

FA 2008 also changed the time limits for income tax (and other major taxes) to four years for discovery, six years for failure to take reasonable care and 20 years for deliberate understatement or failure to notify liability. As the new time limits come fully into force in April 2010, and the enquiry started after that date the issue regarding 2003/04 would be covered by the new rules, as these provide for a 20-year time limit for an assessment where the underpayment relates to deliberate action by the taxpayer.

(iv) **Adaptation of the statutory procedure for amending the self-assessments**

In consideration of their not taking proceedings against him, Feckless will be invited by HMRC to make an offer to them embracing tax, interest and a penalty loading for the tax years 2003/04 to 2008/09. A binding contract ensues upon acceptance by HMRC, hence the expression a 'contract settlement'.

Feckless is making a settlement for years up to 2008/09. See Example 46 note 18 for details of the new penalties for incorrect returns that apply for 2008/09 tax returns onward. These are substantially higher but can be reduced based on the quality of a disclosure. Explanatory note 4 provides more details.

The amendments to the original 2003/04 to 2008/09 self-assessments will then be dealt with by HMRC internal procedures without any action from Feckless.

The self-assessment for 2009/10 will be able to be made in the correct amount and filed under the normal procedures by 31 January 2011 (31 October 2010 if filed on paper).

Explanatory Notes

National insurance and VAT

1. If Class 2 national insurance contributions have not been paid (see (i) 10.1 above), Feckless will have an additional liability for the unpaid amount. He will be required to pay the contributions at the highest rate applicable over the relevant period plus a penalty of £100 for failure to notify. New penalties for failure to notify tax liabilities were introduced by FA 2008, and NIC regulations were amended to introduce similar penalties for failure to notify Class 2 liability. These are effective for obligations commencing after 31 March 2009 for tax and VAT and 6 April 2009 for NIC. These mirror the new penalty provisions for incorrect returns as penalties are calculated as a percentage of the tax lost, determined by behaviour and extent of disclosure. As a result the penalty for failure in future is expected to be significantly lower than £100. There is no provision for charging interest on unpaid Class 2 contributions.

    As far as VAT is concerned, any amount due to HMRC is available to reduce the calculated trading profits so long as the VAT liability is agreed before the settlement of the direct tax with HMRC. Since all sales may well have been zero-rated, Feckless may have registered for VAT as all returns would give rise to refunds. In that event, copies of VAT returns submitted may assist in allocating income and expenditure to accounting periods.

    If incorrect VAT returns have been submitted, a further settlement will be necessary under civil fraud procedures, with turnover and expenditure figures being estimated using similar techniques to those for calculating trading profits.

Negligence assessments

2. Under the self-assessment provisions, a taxpayer's self-assessment is final unless HMRC enquire into the return (see explanatory note 3 below), except where there is fraudulent or negligent conduct (for 2008/09 failure to take reasonable care or deliberate understatement) or inadequate disclosure, in which case HMRC may issue assessments under TMA 1970 s 29. The time limit for HMRC assessments is currently five years from 31 January following the tax year, extended to 20 years in cases of fraudulent or negligent conduct.

    FA 2008 introduced new rules for IT, CGT, CT, VAT and PAYE changing the assessment time limits to four years for mistake/discovery, six years (except VAT which is four) for failure to take reasonable care and 20 years for deliberate understatement. The new rules will apply to VAT failures after 1 April 2009, with the remainder fully operative after 1 April 2010.

3. Under self-assessment, HMRC may serve formal notice on the taxpayer that they are enquiring into the accuracy of his tax return within twelve months after the date the return is filed (that is by 31 May 2011 for a 2009/10 return filed on 31 May 2010), extended appropriately where, as in this example, the self-assessment is filed late.

Penalties

4. The 2008/09 disclosure is governed by the penalty legislation in FA 2007. As such the amount would be separate from the amounts for earlier years as the penalty treatment is quite different. The penalty applies where either the taxpayer has submitted an incorrect document or return which contains an inaccuracy which leads to an underpayments of tax, or where the taxpayer has received an assessment from HMRC which shows an understatement and does not take adequate steps to notify HMRC of the under-assessment.

   Feckless has not submitted a return for 2008/09 so he cannot be liable to the higher penalties for making a dishonest return – which could be either 70% or 100% if the dishonesty is compounded by his concealing it. Instead, he is liable to the lower penalty of 30% for failure to notify an incorrect assessment (FA 2007 Sch 24 para 2). This amount may be subject to discount for disclosure, but as HMRC had to approach Feckless the disclosure would be prompted, and the minimum penalty would be 15% of the understated tax. To achieve a full discount, Feckless would need to have told HMRC that there is an understatement, given help in quantifying the understatement and provided full access to HMRC, allowing the authorities to check the position. From the facts it is likely that the penalty would be somewhere between 15% and 30%, and at the higher end of this range as full discount for disclosure may not apply, but Feckless is now co-operating with the officer.

2009/10 self-assessment

5. Given that the taxable profits are calculated on the basis of a comparison of assets and liabilities, taking into account other sources of income and personal/private expenditure, it is unrealistic to require the inclusion of individual figures in the self-assessment, since they could only be estimated and would serve no purpose.

Jeopardy amendments

6. HMRC have the power to issue 'jeopardy amendments' to a self-assessment to create an additional tax charge during the course of an enquiry if they think there is likely to be a loss of tax if they do not make an immediate amendment (TMA 1970 s 9C). This power should only be used when HMRC believe or suspect that the taxpayer intends to dispose of assets, or become non-resident or bankrupt, or is about to go to prison.

   A well advised taxpayer will normally make a substantial payment on account at an early stage in the enquiry, thus negating the need for HMRC to consider a jeopardy amendment to the self-assessment.

Tax credits

7. If Feckless has made a claim for tax credits for the years 2003/04 to 2009/10 then the tax credits office should be notified that the declared profits are incorrect and amended details for 2005/06 (year to 30 April 2005) to 2009/10 (year to 30 April 2009) filed with them. This may not affect the tax credit claim if payment had been at the family rate of £545 for each year and the amended joint tax credit income does not exceed £50,000 for each year. Otherwise an overpayment will arise and possibly penalties for incorrect returns. In those circumstances an enquiry should be opened by the tax credits office and a settlement agreed at the same time as for income tax.

Question

(a) There are various classes of contributions for national insurance purposes. Indicate the circumstances in which a liability arises under each class.

(b) State how earnings are defined for national insurance purposes, the payments that may be excluded and the way in which benefits in kind are treated.

(c) J Bond is a Member of Parliament and his salary is £66,000. He also carries on business as a management consultant and for the year ended 30 June 2008 his taxable profits were £22,000. His wife is employed by him as a research assistant for his Parliamentary duties and receives a salary of £5,400 per year. She is also employed by him in his management consultancy business for which she receives a salary of £5,400 per year.

Advise him and his wife of their national insurance position and calculate their national insurance liabilities for 2009/10.

(d) Mrs Williams and her son are the directors of Tation Ltd, which trades as a restaurant employing four waitresses. She has asked you to explain how contributions are charged on directors' earnings and also to state whether the following items must be included in gross pay for the purposes of Class 1 contributions of the waitresses:

 (i)   Tips and gratuities

 (ii) Benefits in kind

 (iii) Payment of bills.

Draft a memorandum to answer the points raised by Mrs Williams.

(e) (i)   Set out the national insurance consequences for the employer and employee of contracting out of the State Second Pension (S2P).

 (ii) Set out how national insurance contributions are collected.

Answer

(a) **Classes of national insurance contributions**

National insurance contributions are payable under six categories as follows:

Class 1 contributions (SSCBA 1992 ss 5–9)

These relate to employed persons and are subdivided into primary contributions (payable by employees) and secondary contributions (payable by employers). A liability arises whenever earnings exceed the relevant limit in any earnings period (SSCBA 1992 s 5). For 2009/10 the relevant limit is known as the earnings threshold (ET), and the annual figure is fixed at £5,715. For employees there is also a lower earnings limit (LEL), with a 'nil contributions' band for earnings between that limit and the ET. Even though no contributions are payable on that band of earnings, employers are required to report earnings at or above LEL in order that the employee may retain entitlement to social security benefits.

There is an upper earnings limit (UEL) for employees' contributions charged at 11%, but no upper limit for employers' contributions, which are paid at 12.8% on all earnings over the ET. On earnings above the UEL employees pay 1% contributions. From 6 April 2009, there is also an upper accruals point (UAP) for the second state pension, which is below the UEL. Earnings between the UAP and the UEL always attract the 11% contribution rate, but earnings below the UAP attract a lower, rebated rate of contribution where the employee is contracted out of the second state pension (S2P).

The employees' contributions are deducted by the employer from earnings and paid with the employer's contributions and the PAYE tax to the HMRC Accounts Office. Payment must be received by HMRC by the 19th of the following month, unless payment is made quarterly.

Payment may be deferred until the 22nd of the month (or the last working day before that date if the 22nd is a non-working day) if payment is made electronically.

The current (2009/10) earnings limits are:

	Weekly	Monthly	Annual
Lower earnings limit (LEL)	£95	£412	£4,940
Earnings threshold (ET)	£110	£476	£5,715
Upper accruals point (UAP)	£770	£3,337	£40,040
Upper earnings limit for employees (UEL)	£844	£3,656	£43,875

An earnings period is the interval at which earnings are normally paid. Thus if pay is paid weekly the first limits apply, if two-weekly twice the first limits and so on. If pay is paid at intervals of less than one week then the weekly limit applies. If the employee is a director then the annual limit applies (except in the year of appointment, where a pro rata limit applies, based on the weeks from the week of appointment to the end of the tax year). Contributions for directors may, however, be payable provisionally according to the normal pay period, with an annual adjustment if necessary (SI 2001/1004 reg 8(6) – see part (d)).

Contributions are payable by employees on or after their 16th birthday until they are of retirement age (normally 65 years for a man and 60 for a woman). An employer has no liability to pay contributions for an employee under 16 but full secondary contributions are payable for persons over retirement age. In some circumstances, employees' contributions are credited rather than paid, such credits counting towards satisfying the contribution conditions for certain benefits, in particular the basic state pension (see under Class 3).

Married women who elected on or before 11 May 1977 pay reduced rate (Table B) contributions in exchange for limited benefits. The employer still pays full secondary contributions. If a reduced rate election lapses or is revoked it cannot be revived (see explanatory note 11).

The liability is calculated on the earnings of a given pay period from a given employer (subject to anti-avoidance rules relating to uneven payments and pay from another business which is 'in association' with the employer – see explanatory note 10). There is now no maximum Class 1 national insurance liability for employed earners. Those earning over £43,875 in one or more employments generally have to pay 1% on that excess. For those with more than one employment (or with employment and self-employment) there are complex rules to ensure that they do not pay excessive contributions (see below under Maximum contributions payable). There is no maximum for employers' secondary contributions. 'Earnings' broadly means amounts paid in cash/cheques or paid on the direction of the employee, but it also includes some non-cash payments, such as credits to a director's loan account, employee shares in quoted companies and payment in the form of vouchers (eg shopping vouchers). Payments in kind do not count as pay for Class 1 contributions unless the asset concerned is specifically included (see part (b)). The assets included are mainly assets that can be readily converted into cash. Employers' Class 1A contributions are payable on virtually all taxable benefits that are not within the Class 1 charge (see below).

The rates of contributions for 2009/10 are:

Employer's contributions

Earnings up to earnings threshold (ET)	–	Nil
Excess above ET	–	12.8%

Employee's contributions

The employee's contributions (full rate) are:

Earnings up to earnings threshold (ET)	–	Nil
Earnings between ET and upper earnings limit (UEL)	–	11%
Earnings above UEL	–	1%

Married women's reduced rate contributions are:

No liability if earnings do not exceed ET.

Earnings between ET and UEL	–	4.85%
Earnings above UEL	–	1%

The rebate for contracted-out contributions on earnings between the LEL and the UAP is:

Salary-related schemes (COSR)	1.6%	Employees
	3.7%	Employers
Money-purchase schemes (COMP)	1.6%	Employees
	1.4%*	Employers

*   HMRC pays an age-related rebate into the scheme – see part (e)(i).

Any contracted-out rebate due to an employee is first deducted from any primary national insurance liability of that employee for that period. In so far as the rebate exceeds the national insurance liability of the pay period it is retained by the employer. The rebate due to the employer is recovered by deduction against any national insurance payable for the tax year or is paid to the employer by HMRC.

Class 1A contributions (SSCBA 1992 s 10)

Class 1A national insurance contributions are payable by employers (not by employees) in respect of the provision of any taxable benefits except those specifically exempted (eg certain childcare provision) or already charged under Class 1 to a P11D employee or director.

The amounts on which the contributions are payable are the cash equivalents of the benefits as measured for income tax purposes, reduced by any employee contribution. For 2009/10 the contributions are at the rate of 12.8% of the cash equivalents and are payable annually in arrear by 19 July (22 July if paid electronically), after the taxable benefits have been calculated by the employers for P11D purposes. The summary of the Class 1A amounts shown on P11Ds plus the calculation of the contributions due is shown on Form P11D(b). The payment is sent to the Accounts Office using a special payslip.

If the business ceases, then the liability for Class 1A contributions arises 14 days after the tax month of succession or cessation, eg, if an employer ceases in October 2009 then Class 1A contributions for the period 6 April 2009 to the date of cessation will be payable with the October national insurance payment on 19 November 2009. If the date of cessation is any day up to 5 July then the liability includes the Class 1A amount due for the preceding tax year. The same provisions apply to a predecessor employer if a business changes hands, but only in respect of employees not continuing with the successor. The successor takes over the liability for employees who continue in the business and includes them in the normal end-of-year return.

No Class 1A liability arises on any amount already charged to Class 1 or 1B, or not liable to income tax as general earnings, or benefits provided exclusively for business use. However Class 1A contributions are due on the full amount of benefit where there is mixed business and private use, and the benefit is not liable under Class 1 (ie reimbursed personal bills with business and private elements are shown on the P11D but lead to a Class 1 charge on the private element, but no Class 1A charge). Insignificant private use is ignored for this purpose.

The main benefits chargeable to Class 1A contributions are:

- Cars and fuel
- Vans
- Beneficial loans
- Living accommodation
- Private medical insurance
- Gifted assets
- Taxable gifts from third parties (chargeable on the provider)
- Goods and services provided for private use
- Taxable relocation benefits provided by the employer (note: taxable reimbursed expenses are within Class 1, not Class 1A).

Class 1B contributions (SSCBA 1992 s 10A)

Employers are able to settle the tax and national insurance liability on minor and irregular benefits by making a lump sum payment under a PAYE Settlement Agreement (PSA) (see Example 8 explanatory note 9). Class 1B contributions are payable on all items in the PSA that would otherwise be liable to Class 1 or Class 1A contributions and on the tax payable under the agreement. The rate of contributions is the employers' secondary rate of 12.8%. The Class 1B contributions are payable with the tax on the agreement on 19 October (22 October for e-payment) following the relevant tax year, eg 19 October 2010 for 2009/10.

Class 1B contributions are not credited to an individual's national insurance contribution records even when paid in lieu of Class 1 contributions. However, an employee who has cash earnings just below the LEL may require earnings in the PSA to be taken into account for the purpose of qualifying for SSP, SMP, SAP or SPP.

Class 2 contributions (SSCBA 1992 ss 11, 12)

Class 2 contributions are payable by 'self-employed earners', which means those who are gainfully employed other than as employed earners (SSCBA 1992 s 2). The Class 2 net is wider than for Class

4, because it relates to 'businesses', whereas Class 4 is restricted to trades, professions and vocations. Class 2 contributions are due at the flat rate of £2.40 per week for 2009/10. Contributions are payable within 28 days of receiving a bill for the previous quarter from the HMRC National Insurance Contributions Office (NICO), or by monthly direct debit. A liability arises whenever a person is self-employed in any week if they are over 16 and under pension age. A person who is also employed is liable to pay both Class 1 and Class 2 (and possibly also Class 4) contributions.

Liability to Class 2 must be notified no later than 31 January after the end of the tax year in which liability arises due to the commencement of trading. A penalty applies for failure to notify. The penalty may be 100% of the lost contributions if the failure is deliberate and concealed, 70% if deliberate but not concealed, or otherwise 30%. This will not be imposed if the contributor has a reasonable excuse or a successful claim for exemption is made (see below).

If the earnings from self-employment are expected to be below £5,075 in 2009/10 or were below the limit of £4,825 in 2008/09 and circumstances have not materially altered, then application may be made for a certificate of exception by telephoning 0845 915 4655 or applying online at www.hmrc.gov.uk/selfemployed. Exception cannot apply from a date earlier than 13 weeks before the date of the application but waiver of Class 2 contributions may be granted by concession. The certificate needs to be renewed each year.

If exception has not been granted, and earnings prove to be below the exception limit then application for repayment of Class 2 contributions must be submitted before the next following 31 January, ie 2009/10 refund applications must be made by 31 January 2011.

Earnings for this purpose are the net earnings from self-employment shown in the accounts. If any income from *employment* is included in the accounts figures it is disregarded (SI 2001/1004 reg 45), but care should be taken to exclude any other non-trading income (such as rents) from the accounts, otherwise HMRC may contend that it is part of the earnings.

If no Class 2 contributions are paid in a year then state retirement pension may be reduced and entitlement to short-term benefit when unable to work through sickness (employment and support allowance) will be lost for two years. A voluntary Class 3 contribution could be paid to safeguard the state pension benefits but state pension and sickness benefits can be safeguarded at a Class 2 cost of only £2.40 a week. As with Class 1 contributions, in some circumstances contributions are credited rather than paid, such credits counting towards satisfying the contribution conditions for certain benefits, in particular the basic state pension (see under Class 3). Neither Class 2 nor Class 3 contributions give rise to an entitlement to jobseeker's allowance.

A woman with a valid reduced rate contribution certificate (see Class 1 above) need not pay Class 2 national insurance contributions but will receive no contributory state benefits.

Class 3 contributions (SSCBA 1992 ss 13, 14)

Class 3 contributions are voluntary so there is no obligation to pay them. The contributions give an entitlement to basic retirement pension and widow's benefits. Payment could be made by those not liable for other contributions, eg, non-employed, self-employed with small earnings, persons taking early retirement or moving abroad etc, to maintain a full national insurance record. Anyone who is registered as unemployed or is receiving jobseeker's allowance is credited with Class 1 contributions at the lower earnings limit and does not have to pay Class 3 contributions to maintain a full contributions record. An unemployed man aged 60 to 64 is credited with Class 1 contributions whether or not he is registered as unemployed. Class 1 credits are also usually given to those aged 16 to 18 who would otherwise not have paid enough contributions, and also for certain periods of full-time training lasting up to 12 months, but not for longer courses such as university degree courses. Credits are also given to those claiming employment and support allowance, maternity allowance, invalid care allowance or disability working allowance.

The Class 3 rate for 2009/10 is £12.05 per week. This should be compared to £2.40 per week Class 2 contributions which can also be paid voluntarily to protect benefits and protect short-term as well as long-term benefit entitlement. Payment is as for Class 2, that is by quarterly bill or monthly direct debit, although most Class 3 contributions are paid after the end of a tax year when the need to make up a deficiency in order to protect benefits can be ascertained.

Class 4 contributions (SSCBA 1992 ss 15–18)

These contributions do not provide any benefits. The liability is calculated on trading profits, as agreed for income tax, after adjusting for capital allowances, balancing charges, trading losses and trade charges but before deducting registered pension scheme premiums. Where trading losses have been relieved against non-trading income for income tax purposes, they still reduce the first available current or later trading profits for Class 4 contributions (SSCBA 1992 Sch 2 para 3(4)).

Class 4 contributions are paid as part of payments on account and balancing payments under self-assessment. The rates for 2008/09 are:

Profits up to	£5,715	@	Nil
Profits between	£5,715 and £43,875	@	8%
Profits in excess of	£43,875	@	1%

The Class 4 contributions relate to a tax year, so the limits remain the same where more than one account is made up to a date within the tax year, or where the trader is involved in more than one business. Husband and wife are charged separately. A liability does not arise in any tax year in which the taxpayer is aged under 16 (and holds a certificate of exception) or over state pension age at the commencement of the year, or in which he is not resident in the UK for income tax.

If income taxed as trading income is also liable to Class 1 national insurance contributions (eg, sub-postmasters, actors, self-employed supply teachers) then the amount liable to Class 4 contributions is reduced by the amount on which Class 1 contributions have been paid.

Maximum contributions payable

Maximum Class 1 and 2

Where a person has more than one 'employment' (and in this context that includes self-employment) the annual maximum of Class 1 and Class 2 contributions depends on the number of jobs, and how much is earned in each of those jobs. Each earner will therefore have his, or her, own individual maximum.

The computations are complex, involving eight steps, but basically each earner will be required to pay at 11% on 53 times the difference between the primary earnings threshold and the upper earnings limit (£734 (£844 − £110) × 53 = £38,902 @ 11% = £4,279.22), plus 1% of the *aggregate* of all 'employed earner's' earnings which fall between the primary and upper earnings limits insofar as they exceed £38,902, plus 1% of all 'employed earner's' earnings above the upper limit. (The fact that the regulations take 53 times the difference between the upper earnings limit and the primary threshold means that the normal annual upper limit (£43,875) is effectively superseded.

Employees who think that they may have overpaid should complete a Refund Claim Form CA 5610 by applying to NICO, Refunds Group, Benton Park View, Newcastle-upon-Tyne, NE98 1ZZ. The provisions determining the annual maxima are in SI 2001/1004 and work as follows:

An individual has three 'employments', A, B and C, receiving salaries of £52,000, £22,000 and £5,000. Steps 1 and 2 of Reg 21 of SI 2001/1004 require the calculation of the £4,279.22 as above (Step 1 calculates the £38,902, Step 2 takes 11%). Step 3 aggregates the earnings of each employed earner's employment which fall between the primary earnings threshold and the upper earnings limit, in this case:

A	38,160	(43,875 – 5,715)
B	16,285	(22,000 – 5,715)
C	–	(all below 5,715)
	54,445	

Step 4 deducts from this figure 53 times the difference between the upper limit and the earnings threshold (that is the £38,902 of Step 1) leaving 15,543 (54,445 – 38,902). Step 5 takes 1% of this figure, giving £155.43.

Step 6 takes the earnings of each employed earner's employment in so far as it exceeds the upper earnings limit, in this case just employment A, £52,000 less £43,875 = £8,125 and Step 7 takes 1% of that figure £81.25. The annual maximum for Class 1 for this individual becomes £4,515.90, the sum of Steps 2, 5 and 7 (£4,279.22 + £155.43 + £81.25).

Where an individual has Class 2 liability, and therefore more than one 'employment' the same procedure applies but the maximum calculated will be compared with the sum of their Class 1 and 2 payments, see the main example below and Example X in the Table below. Note that, in most years, 52 Class 2 contributions will be paid, but the annual maximum calculation is based on 53 weeks' contributions.

Maximum Class 1, 2 and 4

Where a person has employment and is also self-employed and paying Class 4, there is also a maximum amount of contributions to be paid at the main Class 1 and Class 4 rates (11% and 8%).

Contributors should apply for a refund if they pay more than:

- £3,180.00 at the Class 1 (11%) rate, Class 2 and Class 4 (8%) rate in 2009/10, or

- £4,279.22 at the Class 1 (11%) rate and Class 2 in 2009/10.

The computation of the Class 4 refund is even more complex than the calculation for Class 1. It is a nine step process with three different 'Case' scenarios applying after the fourth step (see Reg 100 of 2001/1004). The method is best demonstrated by working through the steps in one main example and then giving summary figures for three further examples (X, Y and Z) in a Table below.

Take the situation of someone employed on a salary of £45,000, with self-employed profits of £48,000. Their national insurance liability before applying any annual maxima will be:

			£
Class 1, assumed paid monthly,	(3,656 – 476)	@ 11% × 12	4,197.60
	(3,750 – 3,656)	@ 1% × 12	11.28
			4,208.88
Class 2, £2.40 × 53			127.20
			4,336.08
Class 4	(43,875 – 5,715)	@ 8%	3,052.80
	(48,000 – 43,875)	@ 1%	41.25
			7,430.13

Steps 1, 2 and 3 involve computing the £3,180.00 maximum of Class 2 and 4 (53 × £2.40 = £127.20 plus (43,875 – 5,715) 38,160 × 8% = £3,052.80). Step 4 then requires the deduction of the Class 1 contributions at the main rate plus the total Class 2 contributions actually paid, in this case a total of £4,322.40 (£4,197.60 + £124.80).

	£
Steps 1, 2 and 3	3,180.00
Step 4	(4,322.40)

£

(1,142.40)

If a negative figure is achieved, the result of this step is nil, the maximum amount of Class 4 payable at the main rate is nil and four more steps have to be applied to compute the 1% liability. This is a Case 3 scenario. (See below for Case 1 and 2 scenarios.)

Step 5 involves taking the figure at Step 4 and multiplying it by 100/8. In this case the answer is still nil. Step 6 involves deducting the lower profits limit from the smaller of the actual profits and the upper profits limit. In this case, the latter applies:

£

Step 6	43,875
Lower profit limit	(5,715)
	38,160

Step 7 requires Step 5 to be deducted from Step 6, in this case leaving £38,160 and Step 8 takes 1% of that figure ie £381.60.

Step 9 calculates the extra Class 4 that is due on profits over £43,875 (48,000 – 43,875 @ 1%), in this case £41.25 and the maximum Class 4 payable by this taxpayer is the sum of Steps 4, 8 and 9 ie £422.85 (Nil + £381.60 + £41.25). This is, of course, 1% of all the profits over the lower profits limit ((48,000 – 5,715) @ 1% = £422.85). This taxpayer should apply for a refund of Class 4 of £2,671.20 (£3,094.05 less £422.85).

This individual would also be entitled to a refund of some of the Class 2 as the following application of the eight step process shows:

£

Steps 1 and 2		4,279.22
Step 3, Employment income (43,875 – 5,715)	38,160	
Step 4	(38,902)	
	–	
Step 5, 1% of		Nil
Step 6, Employment income (45,000 – 43,875)	1,125	
Step 7, 1% of £1,125		11.25
Step 8		4,290.47
Class 1 and 2 paid (latter for 52 weeks)		4,333.68
Refund due of Class 2		43.21
Refund of Class 4 as above		2,671.20
Total refund		2,714.41

The Table below shows three further examples:

- Another case 3 scenario but where the Class 4 is only paid at the main rate (Example X);

- A Case 1 scenario – that is where the result at Step 4 is positive and exceeds the aggregate of Class 1 (11%) rate plus Class 2 plus Class 4 (8%) rate. For Case 1 the Steps 5 to 9 are unnecessary (Example Y); and

- A Case 2 scenario where the surplus at Step 4 does not exceed the NI paid at main rates, and Steps 5 to 9 become necessary to determine the total Class 4 maximum.

The Table assumes all salaries paid monthly.

	X (Case 3) £		Y (Case 1) £		Z (Case 2) £
Class 1, salary £43,700	4,178.64	Class 1, salary £10,000	471.72	Class 1, salary £25,476	2,174.04
Class 2 paid (× 52)	124.80		124.80		124.80
Class 4, profits £10,000	342.80	Class 4, profits £15,715	800.00	Class 4, profits £29,715	1,920.00
Total NIC paid	4,646.24		1,396.52		4,218.84
Steps 1, 2 and 3	3,180.00		3,180.00		3,180.00
Main rate Class 1 + Class 2	4,303.44		596.52		2,298.84
Step 4	Nil		2,583.48		881.16

Y (Case 1), after Step 4: This figure exceeds all the NI paid at the main rates (£1,396.52) so the computation ends and the max Class 4 NI is £2,583.48

	X (Case 3)	Y (Case 1)	Z (Case 2)
Step 5	Nil	881.16 × 100/8	11,014.50
Step 6, deduct lower profit limit	10,000.00		29,715.00
	5,715.00		5,715.00
	4,285.00		24,000.00
Step 7, deduct Step 5	–		11,014.50
	4,285.00		12,985.50
Step 8, take 1% of Step 7	42.85		129.85
Step 9 not applicable	–		–
Max Class 4 sum of Steps 4, 8 and 9	42.85	2,583.48	1,011.01
Class 4 refund due	299.95	Nil	908.99

Example X would also give rise to a refund of Class 1 or 2 as the following application of the eight step process shows:

		£
Steps 1 and 2 (11% × 53 weeks of UEL–ET)		4,279.22
Step 3, Employment income (43,000 – 5,715)	37,285	
Step 4	(38,902)	
Step 5, 1% of	Nil	Nil
Step 6, Employment income (43,000 – 43,875)	Nil	
Step 7, 1% of	Nil	Nil
Step 8		4,279.22
Class 1 and 2 paid		4,303.44
Refund due		24.22

An overpayment will normally be notified to the taxpayer by HMRC where the amount due exceeds £38.50. They will invite an application for a refund. A claim for a Class 1 or 2 refund is made to HMRC, NICO Refunds Group, Benton Park View, Newcastle upon Tyne, NE98 1ZZ. A Class 4 refund (minimum 50p) is made to Deferment Services at the address below.

Where contributions are paid at the contracted-out rate or married woman's reduced rate then they are recomputed at the standard rate in order to compare with the above limits.

If self-employed earnings are expected to be below the exemption limit of £5,075 then exception should be claimed. For information re exception contact the Class 2 Self-Employment Contact Centre on 0845 915 4655.

It is possible to apply for deferment of Class 1, 2 and 4 contributions.

If an individual has more than one employment and expects to pay primary Class 1 contributions on earnings of at least £844 per week (£3,656 per month) throughout the whole tax year in any one employment, or earnings of at least £954 per week (£4,132 per month) in two jobs, then they can apply for deferment. If Class 1 deferment is granted then NI of 1% of all earnings above the earnings threshold will be payable on each employment to which the deferment applies.

The position is complex and reference should be made to HMRC's leaflets CA72A (in respect of deferral of Class 1 contributions) or CA72B (in respect of deferral of Class 2 and 4 contributions).

A person who is both employed and self-employed may apply to defer payment of Class 2 and/or Class 4 contributions. If successful in the application for deferment, assessment and collection of Class 2 and Class 4 contributions will be made by Deferment Services who will do their calculations after the end of the year, taking into account the profits and gains and the contributions already made. 1% Class 4 will be paid with income tax through the self-assessment form on all self-employed income above £5,715 for 2009/10.

Leaflets CA72A and CA72B contain the necessary deferral forms which can also be downloaded from HMRC's website. Another useful form is:

SE1 Are you thinking of working for yourself?

The address for Deferment Services is HMRC NICO Deferment Services, Benton Park View, Newcastle upon Tyne, NE98 1ZZ. Telephone: 0845 915 7141.

Interest on late paid contributions

Late paid Class 1 contributions attract interest from 19 April after the end of the tax year in which the contributions were due for payment. Late paid Class 1A contributions attract interest from 19 July after the end of the tax year. Late paid Class 1B contributions attract interest from the due date of payment, ie 19 October following the tax year in respect of which the contributions were due. (SI 2001/1004 Sch 4 para 17.)

There is no provision for charging interest on late-paid Class 2 contributions.

Penalties

Failure to notify liability to Class 1A by 19 July on Form P11D(b) gives rise to a penalty of £100 per month (or part thereof) per 50 employees (or part thereof), restricted to the Class 1A liability.

With effect from 1 April 2010 a unified penalty regime applies to most taxes including NI. The former fixed £100 penalty for failure to notify liability to Class 2 within three months has been dropped and replaced by a penalty based upon all NI not paid as a result of the notification failure.

If the failure is due to an innocent error no penalty will be charged provided the contributor makes an unprompted disclosure of the facts to HMRC within twelve months of 31 January after the end of the tax year in which liability to register arose. If the disclosure is made later, the penalty will be between 10% and 30%.

If the error is due to carelessness then a penalty of up to 30% of the unpaid revenue will be due. That amount will not be charged if the taxpayer had a reasonable excuse for the failure (eg they had reasonable grounds for believing that no liability arose). If the late notification was unprompted and within twelve months of end of the tax year in which the first day fell on which a liability became payable, then the penalty can be mitigated to Nil. If notification was prompted the maximum mitigation is to a 10% penalty. If prompted notification is over twelve months late, as above, the reduction is to not less than 20%.

For an unconcealed deliberate failure to notify the penalty is 70% of the tax unpaid with mitigation for an unprompted disclosure to not less than a 20% penalty (35% if prompted).

For a concealed deliberate failure to notify the penalty is 100% with discount for unprompted disclosure to not less than 30% (50% if prompted) (Finance Act 2008 Sch 41 and SI 2001/1004 regs 87B–87G).

Various breaches of the national insurance legislation may lead to criminal proceedings.

(b) **Earnings for Class 1 national insurance contributions**

Meaning of earnings

Earnings for Class 1 national insurance contributions are defined in s 3 of the Social Security Contributions and Benefits Act 1992 as including 'any remuneration or profit derived from an employment'. The amount of a person's earnings for any period is computed in accordance with Part 2 of the Social Security (Contributions) Regulations SI 2001/1004. That statutory instrument provides that a liability arises on earnings paid, or treated as paid, in an earnings period (reg 2). The amount paid is the gross earnings from the employment.

Payments that do not count as earnings

SI 2001/1004 Sch 3 lists certain payments that do not count as earnings, with a vast number of exclusions from the provisions, and with the Schedule running to ten separate parts. This represents a minefield for employers struggling to know what does and what does not constitute earnings, and there are even longer lists in the Employer's Further Guide to PAYE and NICs (CWG2). Most of the exclusions, however, relate to items that are exempt from income tax. Some particular exclusions are as follows:

Payments in kind, unless specifically included – see below. (Virtually all taxable benefits that escape Class 1 liability are liable to employers' Class 1A contributions where they are provided to P11D employees and directors – see part (a).)

Tips or gratuities not paid directly or indirectly by the employer or where the payment is not directly or indirectly allocated by the employer to the earner, providing the payments are not from a trust where the beneficiaries are employees or of an amount in excess of the amount that a non-connected person might give if from a connected person (SI 2004/173).

Any payments by way of a pension, other than certain lump sums.

An employer's contribution to an employee's personal or occupational pension.

A payment by shares or options over shares which form part of the ordinary share capital of the employer company or its holding company, where the shares or options are either obtained under an approved scheme or are not readily convertible assets.

Any value added tax chargeable on earnings.

Redundancy payments.

Any specific and distinct payment of, or contribution towards, expenses actually incurred by an employed earner in carrying out his employment.

Payments in kind treated as earnings

The following are exceptions to the 'payments in kind' exclusion and are treated as earnings (SI 2001/1004 reg 25 & Sch 3 Parts II, III and IV):

Stocks and shares, and warrants and options in respect of stocks and shares, that are readily convertible assets (other than as indicated above) (see Example 8 explanatory note 12 and Example 85).

Unit trusts and units in collective investment schemes (eg enterprise zone trusts, interests in investment LLPs)

Commodity futures and other futures and hedging contracts

Options to acquire or dispose of:

> an asset falling under any other heading
>
> currency
>
> gold, silver, palladium or platinum

Assets capable of being sold on a recognised investment exchange (ie an investment exchange recognised under the Financial Services and Markets Act 2000) or on the London Bullion Market

The value of certain payments from tax avoidance planning transactions (after 2 December 2004) which involve employment-related securities

Money debts

Gemstones and certain fine wines

Assets (including vouchers) which are readily convertible assets (see Example 8 explanatory note 12)

Any voucher capable of being exchanged for any of the assets listed above and any other non-cash vouchers other than those falling within SI 2001/1004 Sch 3 Part V (see below).

Certain life insurance policies including

> Life and annuity policies
>
> Linked long term policies
>
> Capital redemption policies
>
> Other policies with any of the foregoing elements

Benefits received by an employee who makes a restrictive covenant with his employer (SSCBA 1992 s 4 – see Example 11 part (a)).

The exceptions from the voucher charging rules mainly mirror income tax provisions. They include transport vouchers for non-P11D employees working for passenger transport undertakings, vouchers exchangeable for sports or recreational facilities, vouchers exchangeable for meals on the employer's premises, the first 15p per day of luncheon vouchers, and childcare vouchers up to £55 per week for children up to age 16. Non-cash vouchers are valued as for tax purposes, but unlike the tax position, they must be dealt with on a weekly or monthly basis (with a limit of £243) basis rather than at the year-end.

In addition to Class 1 contributions, employers (but not employees) have to pay Class 1A national insurance contributions at 12.8% on taxable benefits provided to P11D employees and directors that are not within the Class 1 or Class 1B charge.

(c) **Mr and Mrs Bond – national insurance position**

J Bond has employment liable to Class 1 contributions and self-employment liable to Class 2 and 4 contributions. As the total payments exceed the likely maxima, application should be made in advance for deferment of Class 2 and 4 liabilities. The small technical liability that will arise because the maximum is based on 53 weeks' contributions may not then be collected, giving a total liability of £4,418.88 under Class 1 paid monthly rather than £4,500.47 paid after refunded Class 2 (see computation below).

If deferment is not applied for then the payments would have been:

			£
Class 1, salary paid monthly,	(3,656 – 476)	@ 11% × 12	4,197.60
	(5,500 – 3,656)	@ 1% × 12	221.28
			4,418.88
Class 2 × 52			124.80
Class 4, profits (22,000 – 5,715)		@ 8%	1,302.80
Total NIC			5,846.48

Class 4 refund computation

Steps 1, 2 and 3	3,180.00
Main rate Class 1 + Class 2	4,322.40
Step 4	Nil
Step 5	Nil
Step 6,	22,000.00
Deduct lower profit limit	5,715.00
	16,285.00
Step 7, deduct Step 5	–
	16,285.00
Step 8, take 1% of Step 7	162.85
Step 9 not applicable	–
Max Class 4, sum of Steps 4, 8 and 9	162.85
Class 4 paid	1,302.80
Class 4 refund due	1,139.95

Mr Bond would also be entitled to a refund of Class 2 as the following application of the eight step process shows:

		£
Steps 1 and 2 ((844–110) × 53 × 11%)		4,279.22
Step 3, Employment income (43,875 – 5,715)	38,160	
Step 4	(38,902)	
Step 5, 1% of	Nil	Nil
Step 6, Employment income (66,000 – 43,875)	22,125	
Step 7, 1% of	22,125	221.25
Step 8		4,500.47
Class 1 and 2 paid		4,543.68
Refund due		43.21
Total refund (43.21 + 1,139.95)		1,183.16

Mrs Bond has two employments, but both are with J Bond. The earnings must therefore be aggregated (unless it would be impracticable to do so, because for example earnings were worked out at different pay points), giving a liability for primary (employee's) Class 1 contributions (assuming paid equally throughout the year) of:

£

5,715 @ nil	–	
5,085 @ 11%	559.35	(if CA37 tables are used £562.32)
10,800		

J Bond will have a liability as employer to pay secondary contributions of £10,800 – £5,715 = £5,085 @ 12.8% = £650.88 (£654.36 using tables), which will be allowed in computing his earnings/profits in the year of payment.

(d) **Memorandum for Mrs Williams re national insurance liabilities**

Treatment of directors' earnings

Contributions are charged on directors' earnings whenever they are drawn but on a cumulative, annualised basis. An employer may, however, use the normal pay period rules to compute the weekly or monthly contributions provided that the liability is recomputed at the end of the year (or when a director leaves) by reference to the annual limits. There is a facility on the Employers CD-Rom to undertake the Annual Earnings Review for directors.

This special treatment prevents irregular payments of bonuses, commissions etc, being used to give reduced contributions because of the monthly upper limit. Where a regular salary is paid, the overall amount will be the same.

For example, if an employee is paid £45,000 at £3,750 a month, his monthly contributions will be (349.80 + 0.94 =) £350.74, making £4,208.88 in the year and the employer will pay contributions on the excess of the monthly pay of £3,750 over the earnings threshold of £476, ie £3,274 @ 12.8% = £419.07, giving £5,028.84 for the year. If a director is paid the same amount and the annual basis is used, the *total* amount payable is the same, but the position will be as follows:

Cumulative pay Mth	£	Employee's contribution	£		£	Employer's contribution	£
1	3,750		–				–
2	7,500	5,715 @ nil	–		5,715 @ nil		–
		1,785 @ 11%	196.35		1,785 @ 12.8%		228.48
3	11,250	3,750 @ 11%	412.50		3,750 @ 12.8%		480.00
4 to 11	41,250	30,000 @ 11%	3,300.00		30,000 @ 12.8%		3,840.00
12	45,000	2,625* @ 11%	288.75		3,750 @ 12.8%		480.00
		1,125 @ 1%	11.25				
Total contributions payable			4,208.85				5,028.48

* 1% contributions on (45,000 – 43,875) = £1,125, therefore 11% contributions due on (3,750 – 1,125) = £2,625.

Treatment of payments/benefits for waitresses

(i)   **Tips and gratuities**

If Tation Ltd collects the tips and divides them between the employees or controls the way in which they are divided, then they are earnings liable to Class 1 national insurance (providing the total earnings exceed the lower limit in an earnings period). If Tation Ltd does not control the division of the tips but leaves that to the employees, the amounts are not liable to national insurance, even if collected in the main till with other takings. Any amount paid directly from the customer to staff does not attract national insurance provided the employer does not influence the division of the tips. This also applies if the donor is connected to the employer provided that the tip does not exceed an amount an unconnected person might have given.

Any amounts collected by the employer and paid to staff under a legal obligation are liable to NI. Amounts paid as part of the national minimum wage can still be gratuities and not liable to national insurance provided they are paid by the employer through its own payroll, albeit at the direction of the troncmaster or staff committee.

For further details and examples on tips etc see HMRC booklet E24 (2008). To determine the tax, national insurance and VAT treatment it is necessary to divide tips into the following categories

- mandatory service charges,

- discretionary service charges,

- gratuity paid to the employer (eg by debit/credit card),

- gratuity put into a staff box, or

- cash gratuity handed directly to a member of staff.

A tip, freely given, is outside the scope of VAT. If a customer is required to pay a service charge that amount is standard-rated.

For PAYE the employer must deduct tax from all amounts paid to the employee. If a member of staff distributes the tips, this is known as a tronc and the troncmaster is responsible for deducting PAYE.

The individual member of staff is responsible for declaring tips received, and paying tax on amounts received. This may be done by way of a code number adjustment or direct payment of tax due.

For mandatory service charges, and where an employer has control over tips distributed by an employee, PAYE and NIC must be deducted by the employer.

(ii) Benefits in kind

The basic rule for national insurance is that Class 1 contributions are not payable on benefits in kind. Instead they are chargeable to Class 1A contributions of 12.8% payable by the employer. However, where a benefit can be converted to cash merely by surrendering the asset (see explanatory note 6), or represents the settlement of a debt of the employee (see (iii)), or is a round sum payment or expense with a profit element, then Class 1 contributions are due. The provision of free meals to waitresses, provided all members of staff are entitled, in a staff dining room or a designated staff area of the restaurant, would be free of tax and NI. If Mrs Williams occasionally books and pays for a taxi home for a waitress who exceptionally has to work after 9pm, that should also be tax- and NI-free.

(iii) Payment of bills

If an employer pays bills relating to the employee, the treatment depends on who made the contract. If the employer made the contract it is a payment in kind; if the employee made the contract the employer's payment is the settlement of a pecuniary liability of the employee and is therefore earnings for Class 1 national insurance.

For example, if Tation Ltd paid an employee's telephone bill the payment would be earnings (because the contract was between the employee and the telephone company) whereas if Tation Ltd was the subscriber for the telephone installed at the employee's home, Class 1 contributions would not be payable. However, because there is both private and business use of the line Class 1A contributions would be due on the total bill if the employee is a P11D employee or director.

If the company reimbursed an employee for the cost of parking near the restaurant, Class 1 contributions would not be payable, whether or not the company contracted directly with the car parking company. In that event there would also be no Class 1A charge, as the benefit is not taxable. If the company contracted with a supplier for the supply of meat and then gave the meat to its employees the gift would not be earnings for Class 1 but would be a taxable benefit liable to Class 1A contributions if provided to a P11D employee or director. Whereas if the employee went to the same supplier and ordered meat, giving the bill to the company for settlement, it would be earnings for Class 1.

Reimbursements of expenses incurred in the course of the employment are not earnings or benefits provided the expenses are identified and quantified. Round sum allowances are earnings and are fully liable to Class 1 national insurance unless they represent no more than a reasonable estimate of actual costs incurred and the employer has a written agreement with HMRC to enable them to make such payments free of tax and national insurance. An advance may be made against expenses providing the actual expenses are identified and any surplus repaid (or treated as earnings).

HMRC may grant a dispensation to enable certain payments to be regarded as covering expenses incurred by the employee in carrying out his duties, and such a dispensation is also accepted for national insurance purposes. Where an employee is away from home overnight on business, contributions are not chargeable on payments or reimbursements of personal expenses up to £5 a night (£10 if outside the UK).

(e)

    (i)   An employee may be contracted out of the State Second Pension scheme (S2P) in one of two ways: –

        An employer may provide a registered approved salary-related or money-purchase pension scheme to replace the additional earnings-related component of the state pension and, in return for removing a burden from the state scheme, pay reduced national insurance contributions on employees' earnings between the lower and upper earnings limits. From 6 April 1997 (for the purposes of contracting out of S2P or SERPS (which applied until 5 April 2002) salary-related schemes must broadly provide retirement benefits that are equivalent to or better than the earnings-related component of the state scheme. (Pension rights built up before that date had to provide a 'guaranteed minimum pension' for each individual member.) Under a money-purchase scheme, employers must make guaranteed minimum contributions.

    –   Alternatively, the employee may take out a registered personal or stakeholder pension plan and elect to contract out of S2P. In that case, full contributions are paid by both employee and employer and the HMRC National Insurance Contributions Office (NICO) makes a rebate payment directly to the pension provider. NICO also pays in an additional amount equivalent to tax relief on the employee's share of the contracting-out rebate, grossed up at the basic rate of tax.

All contracting-out rebates of Class 1 contributions for both personal pension plans and contracted-out money purchase schemes (but not final-salary schemes) are age-related. The minimum rebate is 3.0%. The age at which the maximum rebate of 7.4% is reached is currently 49 in 2009/10 and 2010/11 and 50 and over in 2011/12. The rebate for contracted-out salary-related schemes is 5.3% (employer 3.7%, employee 1.6%). Employers with a contracted-out money-purchase scheme pay a rebated national insurance contribution for scheme members based on the lowest age-related rebates level of 3.0% (employer 1.4%, employee 1.6%). The payroll 'rebates' are deducted from the normal contributions payable and retained by the employer for payment into the pension scheme.

For personal pension plans, the rebates are biased to give lower earners a higher rebate. This is done by applying different percentages to different bands of earnings. For 2009/10 the first band covers earnings between the lower earnings limit and a stipulated 'low earnings threshold' of £13,900 (SI 2009/610) per annum, the next covers earnings between £13,900 and £31,800 and the third covers earnings between £31,800 and the upper accruals point of £40,040. The rebate rate on the first band of earnings is double that on the third band. This is offset by a reduced rebate rate on the second band. The overall effect for those earning above £31,800 is to give a rebate of 4.7% for those under 17, increasing to 7.4% at age 43 or over.

The relevant information is recorded on year-end Forms P14 and HMRC pays the age-related rebate top-up when they receive and successfully process the Forms P14.

(ii)   National insurance contributions are normally collected as follows (subject to what is said in part (a) about deferment of contributions):

Class 1	Employees' (primary) contributions are deducted from earnings when paid, and together with the employers' (secondary) contributions, they are paid over to HMRC by the employer with the PAYE deductions either monthly or, if total payments average less than £1,500 a month and the employer so wishes, quarterly.
Class 1A	Employers' contributions on taxable benefits are paid to HMRC annually in arrears by the 19 July (22 July for e-payment) following the tax year.
Class 1B	Employers' contributions payable under a PAYE Settlement Agreement (PSA) on benefits liable to NI plus the tax thereon are paid to HMRC together with the tax on the PSA annually in arrear on 19 October (22 October for e-payment).
Class 2 and *Class 3*	Direct to NICO by quarterly bill payable within 28 days after the bill is issued, or by direct debit monthly in arrears. Class 3 may be paid annually after the issue of a deficiency notice showing how much is needed to make a year qualify.
Class 4	Provisional half yearly payments are made to HMRC on 31 January and 31 July in respect of all income tax and Class 4 national insurance due, with any remaining balance on the following 31 January.

Explanatory Notes

Liability to pay national insurance contributions

1.   HMRC frequently assess arrears of contributions for several years where, for example, someone has been reclassified as employed rather than self-employed. Although they have the right to assess arrears for as many years as they wish, their rights to *enforce payment* for more than six years may be restricted by the Limitation Act 1980, providing liability has not been admitted in writing within the six-year limitation period.

See Example 13 explanatory note 2 for the special rules regarding the employment status of entertainers and explanatory note 3 for the treatment of contributions paid in the mistaken belief that a worker was an employee.

2.   Where there is a dispute about national insurance contributions, there is a right of appeal to the First-tier Tribunal on a question of fact or law relating to a decision of HMRC, with further rights of appeal on points of law to the Upper Tribunal, Court of Appeal and House of Lords (Supreme Court from 1 September 2009).

Structural changes to state pension scheme

3.   The State Second Pension (S2P) replaced the State Earnings Related Pension Scheme (SERPS) from 6 April 2002. The scheme gives enhanced benefits to lower earners (below £13,900 per annum), carers and long-term disabled. As a consequence the rebate payable on contracting out by way of a personal pension plan (but not by way of a money purchase scheme) has been biased to give lower earners a higher rebate as indicated in part (e)(i) of the example (SI 2006/1009). These rebates are to be abolished for money-purchase pensions (occupational and personal schemes) from April 2012, although final-salary schemes are unaffected.

Alignment of tax and national insurance legislation

4. There are already many areas where the national insurance legislation has been aligned with the income tax legislation, and this process is continuing. There are still some differences in treatment, however, for example where an employee receives a mileage allowance for business use of his own car, national insurance contributions are not payable on allowances that do not exceed the Mileage Allowance Payment Rates for up to 10,000 miles (40p), whatever the mileage (for details see Example 9 explanatory note 20).

    For details of HMRC dispensations and the treatment of incidental personal expenses see Example 9 explanatory notes 11 and 12. For the national insurance position on relocation allowances see Example 9 explanatory note 7.

5. Following the transfer of the Contributions Agency to HMRC, the Department for Work and Pensions has retained responsibility for benefit entitlement including pension credits, but not for tax credits, statutory sick pay, statutory maternity pay or contracted-out pension schemes. Appeals on those matters are, however, to a different chamber of the Tribunal from appeals about NI contributions.

Benefits that can be surrendered for cash

6. The employer's further guide to PAYE and NICs CWG2 Chapter 5 (included on the Employers CD-Rom) gives detailed notes on what is included in pay both for tax and national insurance.

    It is the view of HMRC that even where a benefit is transferred from the employer to the employee it does not come within the definition of a benefit in kind if it can be converted into cash by mere surrender, rather than requiring to be sold, and they give as an example premium bonds (CWG2 page 76). Class 1 national insurance contributions would therefore be payable on such benefits.

Cars – benefits or cash

7. Where an employee has a choice between the use of a car and additional salary, the employee's tax and national insurance position is based on what he actually gets – either salary or the use of the car (ITEPA 2003 s 119).

Directors and other special classes of employees

8. Special rules apply for certain classes of employees – for example see booklet:

Directors	(on CD-Rom)	CA 44
Foreign-going mariners and deep sea fishermen	(on CD-Rom)	CA 42
Social Security abroad		NI 38

    See part (d) of the example for the special annual earnings period rules for directors.

9. Where payment by a company of a director's personal bills is charged to the director's loan or current account, the payment does not count as earnings for national insurance unless the payment represents drawings in anticipation of earnings and the credit balance in the account is insufficient to meet the cost or the account is overdrawn. This will occur where the overdrawn loan account is settled by way of a bonus. The liability then arises at the time the loan account became overdrawn.

Associated employers etc

10. Class 1 national insurance contributions are payable on earnings from one employment in one earnings period without regard to any other payment of earnings (Social Security Contributions and Benefits Act 1992 s 6(4)). However where two or more employers 'carry on business in association' or where more than one job is held with the same employer, earnings are aggregated to compute the

liability for that earnings period unless it is not reasonably practical to do so (Social Security Contributions and Benefits Act 1992 Sch 1 para 1). See the Revenue's Tax Bulletin of August 2000 for their views on the meaning of 'not reasonably practicable'. It has been assumed that the two employments of Mrs Bond in part (c) of the example would be aggregated as both jobs are with J. Bond. If however the research post was with her husband's political party then her liability in respect of each employment would be:

£

5,400 @ nil   —

giving a reduction of £559.35, and the employer's liability would also be reduced to nil compared with £650.88.

Married women's reduced rate contributions

11.   Married women who pay reduced contributions cannot claim contributory benefits, but they can claim retirement pension (at a reduced level) and widow's benefit, both based on their husband's contributions. A woman widowed after 5 October 2010 will, however, inherit only half of her late husband's SERPS/S2P entitlement. Those widowed between 6 October 2002 and 5 October 2010 will inherit between 60% and 90% of the spouse's SERPS/S2P entitlement. Women lose the right to pay reduced contributions on divorce (effective immediately after the decree absolute) or widowhood (effective from the end of the tax year, or if the husband died between 1 October and 5 April, from the end of the next tax year). The right is also lost if a married woman neither pays Class 1 contributions nor has self-employed earnings for two consecutive tax years. A woman with a valid reduced rate election is not permitted to pay voluntary contributions without first permanently revoking the election.

Contracted-out contributions

12.   When contributions are paid at contracted-out rates the actual contributions are revalued to their full rate equivalent in order to test whether the maximum contribution levels have been exceeded. The order of repayment of excess contributions is:

Class 4
Class 2
Class 1   (full rate)
Class 1   (contracted-out rate, contributions in respect of salary-related schemes being refunded before contributions in relation to money purchase schemes)

therefore contracted-out contributions will not normally be repaid unless there is more than one such employment. In that case the appropriate actual excess will be refunded (not the full-rate calculated contribution).

Liability for outstanding national insurance contributions of employees

13.   A culpable company director or other culpable officer (including any shareholder who exercises management powers) will be personally liable under SSA 1992 s 121C for the arrears of a company in respect of national insurance contributions if a notice is issued under this section. The arrears must arise through the officer's fraud or neglect and the amount payable will include interest. The officer may appeal against the notice to the First-tier Tribunal, with the burden of proof on HMRC as agent for the Secretary of State.

From 6 August 2007 this power is extended to the NI debts of a managed service company (MSC) by ITEPA 2003 s 688A (added by FA 2007). For this section recovery is against a director, other office holder or an associate of the MSC, or a provider or person who directly or indirectly encouraged, facilitated or was actively involved in the provision by the MSC of the services of the individual.

Employer's liability to Class 1 contributions re unapproved share option schemes

14. When an employee exercises an unapproved share option in a company where the shares are marketable (ie, a readily convertible asset), then a PAYE/NI liability arises on the taxable value realised by exercise of the option. This gives the employer a liability on an amount that cannot be determined in advance by the employer and the timing of the liability depends on the actions of the employee. To prevent unexpected national insurance costs affecting the employer, in respect of unapproved options granted on or after 6 April 1999 that have not yet been exercised, the employer and employee may jointly elect that the secondary NIC liability will be that of the employee. Furthermore, in computing the income tax payable by the employee the national insurance Class 1 secondary contributions paid by the employee on behalf of the employer will be deductible from the taxable amount (ITEPA 2003 s 478), for example: Gain on exercise of option liable to income tax £10,000. Employer's NIC paid by employee £1,280. Tax due (10,000 − 1,280) = £8,720 @ say 40% = £3,488, giving the employee an effective marginal rate of tax of 47.68% (ie 1,280 + 3,488 = £4,768 paid out of £10,000).

For general enquiries regarding NI and Individuals there is a helpline at 0845 302 1479.

Question

Holsworthy Ltd, which has no associated companies, commenced trading as a manufacturer of adhesives in 1960. It has always drawn up its accounts to 31 December and prepares its accounts under UK GAAP. It is not a close company.

For the year to 31 December 2009 the net profit before taxation was £5,467,185. The following information has been provided (VAT having been adjusted appropriately in the figures given):

1. The following items of investment income have been included in the profit:

    Interest receivable

	£
Lundy Building Society	85,000
Interest on 10% loan note (issued by Worth plc)	68,000
	153,000

    The amounts actually received in the year to 31 December 2009 were building society interest of £87,000 in March 2009 and interest on Worth plc loan note of £65,000 on 31 May 2009.

    UK dividends of £18,000 (£20,000 including tax credits of £2,000) were received in November 2009, and are reported in the accounts in accordance with FRS 16.

    Rent

    Rent received is shown as £24,800. £12,800 of this amount was rent received from a house behind the factory which is let furnished. The company paid £1,200 insurance premium for the house on 1 January 2009 and this has been included in the general charge for insurance. The tenant pays the council tax and water rates.

    The remaining £12,000 was received in respect of a block of garages let on tenant's repairing leases. In the accounts a deduction has been made for £2,000 of rent arrears on the garages. The company has not yet taken any steps to recover the overdue rent.

2. In January 2009 the company had sold its 6% stake in an unquoted trading company which it had acquired in October 1992, resulting in a chargeable gain (after indexation allowance) of £5,330. A freehold investment property which cost £117,762 (including legal costs of purchase) in March 1991 was sold for £289,370 in March 2009. Indexation allowance for the period March 1990 to March 2009 was 74.1%. The profit figure of £5,467,185 is before taking these transactions into account.

3. On 30 August 2009 Holsworthy Ltd acquired leasehold factory premises at Milford Parva to be used in its trade. The term of the lease is 30 years. No premium was payable. In June 2009, the company had vacated its former leasehold factory premises at Milford Parva. The lease still had four years to run from the end of June 2009 and the company was likely to find it difficult to assign the lease in the foreseeable future. The annual rent was £100,000. In addition to the annual rent, a provision of £200,000 was made at 31 December 2009 and charged against profits (in accordance with FRS 12) for the company's future rental obligations under the lease (less its estimated income from sub-letting).

4. An analysis of the salaries and wages account shows that the following payments were made during the year:

	£
Removal expenses of new employee	8,700
Expenses of employee seconded to Housing Charity	15,400

	£
Misappropriation of funds by former employee	12,000
Ex gratia payment to former director to settle claims made by him on the company	20,000
Statutory redundancy payments	70,000

5. An analysis of legal charges shows that the following amounts have been expended:

	£
Debt recovery	3,200
Sale of property March 2009	10,360
Lease of factory at Milford Parva	15,780
Fine for breach of Health and Safety at Work Regulations	3,700
Penalty for infringement of a patent	12,800
Legal costs of (successful) defence of action for breach of contract	3,890
Preparation of service agreement for sales manager	1,600

6. The entries in the bad debts account may be summarised as follows:

	£
Debts written off	35,000
Debts recovered	(15,000)
Decrease in specific bad debt provision	(8,000)
Increase in general bad debt provision	9,000
Charge to profit and loss account	21,000

7. Sundry expenses include the following items:

	£
Fees for apprentice training course at technical college	2,500
Contribution to Milford Parva Enterprise Agency	3,000
Donation to Political Party	4,000
Gift Aid donation to Oxfam June 2009	5,000
Gift Aid payment to local charity (gross amount – paid January 2009)	2,000
Trade association subscription	400
Debit interest on quarterly instalments of corporation tax for 2008	4,360

8. Entertaining and gifts were made up as follows:

	£
Entertaining and gifts – UK customers	138,940
– Foreign customers	24,480
Staff dinner	42,460
Pocket diaries for UK customers (company's name embossed thereon) costing £3.75 each	13,125
	219,005

9. Depreciation charged for the year on the factory and plant and machinery amounted to £521,000. In addition, amortisation of goodwill of £300,000 was written off to profit and loss account. This related to goodwill costing £1,500,000 that was acquired on the purchase of the Sven Glue Co Ltd business and assets in January 2007. The company is amortising the goodwill equally over five years. Capital allowances of £456,400 are available on assets used in the factory.

10. Loan interest payable charged against the profit was £200,000. The loan was £2,000,000 borrowed from the trustees of the company's self-administered pension fund to provide additional finance for the trade on 1 October 1999, on which interest at 10% per annum was payable half yearly on 31 March and 30 September.

11. Patent royalties of £42,000 per annum (gross) were charged against the profit. These were paid to Barmouth plc half yearly in June and December.

12. A final dividend of £800,000 for the year ended 31 December 2008 was paid in June 2009 and an interim dividend of £500,000 for the year to 31 December 2009 was paid in January 2010.

    (a) Compute the corporation tax liability for the year to 31 December 2008.

    (b) Show how the company would account for the taxation liabilities arising out of the information given. (Note: The company was liable to pay its tax under the quarterly payment regime in 2008.)

Answer

(a) **Computation of Corporation Tax liability for year to 31 December 2009**

		£	£
Net profit per accounts			5,467,185
Less:	Interest receivable	153,000	
	UK dividends	18,000	
	Rent (24,800 income less 1,200 expenses)	23,600	
	Capital allowances on plant and machinery	456,400	651,000
			4,816,185
Add:	Legal expenses re sale of property		10,360
	Legal expenses re lease of factory		15,780
	Fine for breach of Health and Safety at Work Regulations		3,700
	Penalty for infringement of patent		12,800
	Increase in general bad debt provision		9,000
	Donation to Political Party		4,000
	Gift Aid donation to Oxfam		5,000
	Gift Aid payment to local charity		2,000
	Entertaining and gifts (other than staff dinner and diaries) (219,005 – 42,460 – 13,125)		163,420
	Depreciation and amortisation of goodwill (521,000)		521,000
Trading income			5,563,245
Property business income (footnote 1)			22,320
Non-trading loan relationship credits			
	Worth plc 10% loan note interest		68,000
	Building society interest		85,000
Chargeable gains (footnote 2)			79,317
Total profits			5,817,882
Less charges on income (gross amounts paid):			
	Gift aid donations (paid gross) (5,000 + 2,000)		(7,000)
Profits chargeable to corporation tax			5,810,882
Corporation tax thereon			
	@28%		1,627,047

Footnotes

1.	Property business income – rental income (12,800 + 14,000)			26,800
	Less: insurance (house)		1,200	
		wear and tear allowance (house – 10% of 12,800)	1,280	
		provision for rent arrears (garages)	2,000	4,480
				£22,320

	£	£
2. The chargeable gains are (see explanatory note 10):		
On sale of unquoted trading company shares January 2009		5,330
On sale of freehold investment property March 2009:		
Sale proceeds	289,370	
Less: Costs of sale	10,360	
	279,010	
Cost of property – March 1991	117,762	
Gain before indexation allowance	161,248	
Less: Indexation allowance £117,762 × 74.1%	87,261	73,987
		79,317

(b)   Accounting for taxation liabilities arising out of information given

(i)   Treatment of dividends

As the tax credit of £2,000 is a notional amount rather than an actual amount of tax deducted from the dividend, FRS 16 requires the accounts to report the amount received of £18,000.

For purposes of calculating marginal rates of corporation tax, the dividend is treated as a tax-credit inclusive amount of £20,000 (10% × 20,000 =) £2,000.

(ii)   Accounting for corporation tax on profits

As the company paid its 2008 tax liability under the quarterly instalment payment ('QIP') regime and its profits chargeable to corporation tax for the year ended 31 December 2009 exceed £1,500,000, the corporation tax payable of £1,627,047 per part (a) will be accounted for under the QIP regime. Thus 25% of the estimated liability is payable on each of 14 July 2009, 14 October 2009, 14 January 2010 and 14 April 2010 (see explanatory note 15).

During 2009, the company paid tax on account of its 2008 corporation tax liability. The last two 25% instalments of the 2008 liability were paid on 14 January 2009 and 14 April 2009. The debit interest of £4,360 on the QIPs arises due to insufficient tax being paid on the QIP basis compared with the relevant proportion of the final liability which should have been paid. Such interest is an allowable deduction against profits for corporation tax purposes.

Explanatory Notes

Scope of corporation tax

1.   Corporation tax is charged on the *profits* of *companies* (CTA 2009 s 2(1)). Profits means both income and chargeable gains (see explanatory note 10 below). Corporation tax is not, however, charged on dividends and other distributions received from other UK companies (known as franked investment income), subject to what is said in explanatory note 4(ix) about share dealers (CTA 2009 s 1285).

The definition of company for corporation tax purposes is 'any body corporate or unincorporated association'. This would include a members' club, which is liable to corporation tax on its income from non-members, such as investment income and guests' fees. (Income from members, eg subscriptions, is not taxed under the 'mutuality' principle.) Registered community amateur sports clubs, broadly amateur sports clubs open to the whole community which require their surpluses to be reinvested in the club, enjoy a number of special tax exemptions (see Example 90 for the detailed provisions).

The definition specifically excludes a partnership, a local authority or a local authority association. Most unit trusts fall within the definition (ICTA 1988 ss 468 and 832). LLPs carrying on a trade are treated as partnerships unless and until they go into formal liquidation, from which time they are taxed as companies. See Example 26 part (b) for details.

UK resident companies are charged on their worldwide profits. Non-resident companies carrying on a trade in the UK through a permanent establishment are charged on income arising from the permanent establishment and on capital gains on the disposal of assets in the UK used for the purposes of the trade or attributable to the permanent establishment.

Certain companies, called close companies, are subject to special restrictions. A close company is broadly one under the control of five or fewer shareholders or of its directors. See Example 56 for details.

Chargeable accounting periods

2.   The basis of the charge to tax is the profits of a 'chargeable accounting period'. This normally means the period for which a company makes up accounts, as in the case of Holsworthy's year to 31 December 2009. Where a period of account exceeds twelve months, however, it has to be split into one or more chargeable accounting periods of twelve months, and a chargeable accounting period comprising the remainder of the period. For detailed notes on chargeable accounting periods see Example 52.

Calculation of profits

3.   In computing a corporation tax liability, the Corporation Tax Act (CTA) 2009 and the remainder of ICTA 1988 set out the basis on which profits are calculated. CTA 2009 s 2(2) defines profits as income and chargeable gains, and ss 3 and 4 exclude both income tax and capital gains tax from applying to company profits. CTA 2009 abandons the principle that profits are computed along income tax lines, and further abolished Schedules and cases, prescribing both a method of calculation and a descriptor for each income type, not unlike the changes made by the income tax law rewrite in ITTOIA 2005 and ITA 2007. Corporation tax has a number of special computational aspects, among these interest paid and received, profits and losses on a company's capital transactions relating to loans, foreign exchange and certain financial instruments (see explanatory note 5) and expenses and gains on most intangible fixed assets including goodwill (see explanatory note 4(vii) and (viii)).

CTA 2009 s 46 requires that the profits of a trade are calculated in accordance with generally accepted accounting practice (GAAP), subject to any adjustment required or authorised by law. Losses must be calculated on the same basis as profits (CTA 2009 s 47). GAAP is defined in ICTA 1988 s 832(1) as modified by FA 2004 s 50(1) which extends the definition to companies and groups following International Financial Reporting Standards (IFRS).

See explanatory note 16 for introduction of International Financial Reporting Standards.

4.   The general rule in CTA 2009 s 54 for dealing with trading expenses in computing trading profits is that, unless they are covered by a specific statutory provision, expenses must be wholly and exclusively for the purposes of the trade. In addition they must not involve committing a criminal offence, such as paying a bribe or protection money (including payments overseas that would be illegal if paid in the UK), nor be paid in response to threats, menaces, blackmail and other forms of extortion (CTA 2009 s 1304). Any VAT input tax on legal expenses in court proceedings relating to illegal acts may, however, be recovered providing the criminal payment relates directly to the business (*C & E v Rosner* (1993)). Applying the rules to this example:

    (i)   *Rents and provision for lease rental obligations*

        Rent is clearly expenditure incurred for trade purposes, even after a company has vacated its premises. *CIR v Falkirk Iron Co Ltd* (1933) held that rent payable on premises which had ceased to be occupied was an allowable deduction as the rent obligation arises from the lease which is taken out for trading purposes. Furthermore, it was decided that provision for future rental obligations on vacated premises was acceptable under GAAP in *Herbert Smith (a Firm) v Honour* (1999).

Following the High Court's decision in that case, HMRC conceded that there was no longer a (judge-made) rule which prevented provision being made for future expenditure in accordance with GAAP, and this has now been made statutory as indicated in explanatory note 3 above. In particular, accounting provisions required under FRS 12 are accepted for tax purposes. Broadly, FRS 12 requires provision to be made where the business has a current (legal or constructive) obligation as a result of a past event; it is probable that expenditure will be required to satisfy it; and the provision can be reliably estimated. FRS 12 would require provision to be made for future net rental obligations where the company is unable to assign the lease or can only sub-let it at a lower rent. By entering into the lease, the company has incurred the legal obligation to pay the rents – the lease becomes an onerous contract since the unavoidable costs of meeting the obligations exceed the benefits to be received under it. This applies to Holsworthy's rent provision in this example.

(ii) *Salaries and wages, loss of money lent to staff, redundancy payments*

The basic requirement is that the payments must be wholly and exclusively for the purposes of the trade. The removal expenses for the new employee satisfy this rule and are allowable. For the tax treatment of the employee see Example 9 explanatory note 7.

The expenses of an employee seconded to a charity would not usually satisfy the 'wholly and exclusively for the trade' rule, but they are specifically allowable by CTA 2009 s 70.

The loss of money lent to directors and employees would normally be allowed as a non-trading debit under the 'loan relationship' rules (as the lending would not be connected with or arising out of the trade). No relief would be given if the debtor was a connected person (CTA 2009 s 354 – see Example 63 explanatory note 7). The amount written off would normally be charged on the employee under the general charging provisions of employment income or under ITEPA 2003 s 188 for employees earning £8,500 or more and directors, s 188 applying to such employees even after they have left, or under the special provisions for close companies (see Example 58). The ex gratia payment will be allowed as a deduction by the company providing it is wholly and exclusively for the trade, and will be charged on the director under the 'golden handshakes' provisions (see Example 11).

Misappropriations of funds by staff are an allowable expense provided they are the sort which one might expect to be an ordinary risk of the trade. Such losses are distinguished from those arising as a result of misappropriations by persons in controlling positions such as directors, which have been held in various cases to be not allowable – eg *Curtis v Oldfield Ltd* (1925), *Bamford v ATA Advertising Ltd* (1972).

In the case of an ongoing business, redundancy and other termination payments would normally be incurred as part of a rationalisation programme and would be allowed under general principles as expenditure incurred wholly and exclusively for the purposes of the trade (CTA 2009 s 54). Statutory redundancy payments are specifically deductible as a trading expense (CTA 2009 s 77). HMRC also allow *contractual* redundancy payments made on cessation of trade, following the Privy Council's decision in *Hong Kong CIR v Cosmotron Manufacturing Co Ltd* (1997). The rationale is that such payments are made under a pre-existing obligation to employees taken on for the purposes of the trade (HMRC Tax Bulletin February 1999, and now CTA 2009 s 76).

The Cosmotron decision does not cover ex-gratia or non-contractual redundancy payments made on cessation. Under CTA 2009 s 79, however, an amount of up to three times the statutory redundancy payment is specifically allowed provided it would otherwise have satisfied the 'wholly and exclusively' rule.

(iii) *Legal charges*

Capital items, ie the charges on the sale of the property and the acquisition of the lease, are not allowable (CTA 2009 s 54). Fines and penalties for breaches of the law, and costs connected therewith, are not allowable. The costs of defending a civil action for breach of contract are wholly and exclusively for the purposes of the trade and are allowable, whether the action is successful or not.

In the case of *McKnight v Sheppard* (1999), the House of Lords held that legal expenses incurred by a stockbroker in an (unsuccessful) defence against Stock Exchange disciplinary proceedings for gross misconduct were to avoid the destruction of his business and satisfied the 'wholly and exclusively' rule, although the fines imposed by the Stock Exchange were not allowable, since they represented a loss which did not arise out of the trade.

(iv) *Bad debts*

In relation to ordinary trading transactions with customers and suppliers, bad debts written off and specifically provided for are allowable (CTA 2009 s 54). A general bad debts provision, or increase therein, is not. (Bad debt provisions are not covered by FRS 12 (see note (i) above) as they reduce the value of an asset (the debtors).) Bad debts which do not relate to ordinary trading transactions are dealt with under the rules for 'loan relationships' (see explanatory note 5).

(v) *Sundry expenses*

Where expenses of training courses are met by the employer, they are allowable as part of the benefits provided to staff, and they are not assessable on the employees providing certain conditions are met (see Example 9 explanatory note 33). Employers may also deduct the cost of retraining employees who are about to leave or have just left their present jobs (CTA 2009 s 74).

Contributions to approved local enterprise agencies, training and enterprise councils, Scottish local enterprise companies and 'business link' organisations are specifically allowable (CTA 2009 s 82).

Charitable and political donations are not allowable as trading expenses, unless exceptionally they satisfy the 'wholly and exclusively' rule. Charitable donations can be claimed, under the Gift Aid rules as deductions from *total* profits (see explanatory note 11).

As far as trade association subscriptions are concerned, most trade associations have agreed with HMRC to pay tax on the excess of their receipts over their allowable expenditure and the subscriptions are accordingly allowed to the payer. Any other subscriptions would be considered under the 'wholly and exclusively' rule.

Under corporation tax self-assessment (CTSA), interest on overdue and overpaid tax is taken into account in calculating taxable profits (see Example 53 explanatory note 7).

(vi) *Entertaining and gifts*

With regard to entertaining and gifts, all expenditure in relation to customers, both home and overseas, is disallowed, except for gifts that are not food, drink, tobacco or gift vouchers, that carry a conspicuous advertisement and that cost not more than £50 per person in each accounting period, which applies to the pocket diaries in this example (CTA 2009 s 1300) (see Example 15). The disallowance does *not* apply to anything provided for staff, unless it is incidental to entertaining customers. The cost of staff entertaining is allowed in calculating taxable profits providing it is wholly and exclusively for the trade. Staff entertaining may, however, result in a tax and national insurance charge on employees earning £8,500 per annum or more and directors under the benefits provisions (see Example 9 explanatory note 31), unless the conditions for staff entertaining are fulfilled and the expenditure in a tax year does not amount to more than £150 per head.

Relief may be claimed for gifts of machinery, plant and trading stock to schools and other educational establishments (CTA 2009 s 105). Similarly, relief is available under CTA 2009 s 1300(5) for gifts in kind to a charity or heritage body (within ICTA 1988 s 507(1)).

Under these provisions, nothing has to be brought into account either as a trading receipt if the item is from trading stock or as disposal proceeds for capital allowances if it has been used in the donor's trade. Relief is also given for trading stock consisting of medical supplies donated for humanitarian purposes to developing countries (together with transportation and delivery costs) (CTA 2009 s 107). These provisions are accompanied by an anti-avoidance provision which excludes the donor from receiving any benefit in return for the gift. (CTA 2009 s 108.)

VAT-registered traders donating used or obsolete items have to account for VAT only on the current value of such items, not on their original cost.

See explanatory note 11 regarding relief as a charge on income for gifts of stocks and shares and land.

(vii) *Depreciation of factory and plant etc and amortisation of goodwill*

Depreciation is a capital item and is disallowed. (Most but not all assets qualify instead for capital allowances.)

Amortisation of purchased goodwill is deductible as a trading expense under the intangible fixed assets regime (CTA 2009 Part 8 starting at s 711). Thus no adjustment should be required for the £300,000 goodwill amortisation charge. See Example 66 for details of the intangible fixed assets rules.

(viii) *Patent royalties*

Patent royalties were brought within the intangible fixed assets rules by FA 2002 , and are therefore also dealt with by CTA 2009 Part 8. The broad effect of these rules is to provide tax relief for all expenses, losses, profits etc relating to such assets, normally based on the amounts reflected in the accounts as part of the profits of the trade. This means that patent royalties are deductible as a trading expense instead of as a charge on income. Thus, in this example, full relief can be taken for the patent royalties of £43,000 already charged against Holsworthy's profits, with no further tax adjustment being required.

(ix) *Non-trading income*

Non-trading income is excluded from the trading profits computation. It is then brought in appropriately elsewhere, except dividends received from other UK companies, which are not chargeable to corporation tax. From 1 July 2009 foreign dividends are similarly exempt from corporation tax.

For share dealers, dividend income and manufactured payments that are treated as dividends are trading income rather than investment income and are included in trading profits (exclusive of tax credits).

UK property business income of companies is computed as a single figure under the 'UK property business rules' with separate computation for an overseas property business. Allowable deductions are broadly those that apply to business profits, hence a provision may be made for unpaid rents as indicated in the example. Rent from sub-letting *part* of business premises (not land) that is *temporarily* surplus to requirements may for convenience be included in the trading income providing it is comparatively small. For detailed notes on the treatment of rents see Example 97.

Interest from banks and building societies is received by companies in full without deduction of tax (ICTA 1988 s 481 and CTA 2009 s 498). The same applies to interest on UK government stocks, unless application is made for net payment (ICTA 1988 s 50). Companies receive most interest in full but in the rare cases where investment income is received net of income tax, the gross amount is nonetheless included in the profits chargeable to corporation tax. The income tax suffered is taken into account in the Schedule 16 quarterly income tax accounting (see explanatory note 13) or set off against the corporation tax payable. The corporation tax treatment of interest is dealt with in explanatory note 5 below.

Loan relationships

5.   Special rules apply to a company's 'loan relationships', which essentially means all money debt except where it relates to amounts outstanding on trading transactions for goods and services (CTA 2009 Parts 5 and 6). Interest payable that relates to a trade is brought into account in calculating the trading profits. Non-trading interest payable and all sources of interest receivable both in the UK and abroad (and any profits/losses on non-trading loans) are aggregated and an overall profit is charged as a non-trading profit on loan relationships (previously a profit under Schedule D Case III). Where the company's trade includes moneylending the relevant amounts are trading profits. If there is an overall loss (a non-trading deficit) relief is available similar to that for trading losses (see Example 64) (CTA 2009 Part 5 Chapter 16 starting at s 456).

Under the loan relationships rules, interest is brought into account according to the amounts payable and receivable.

For detailed notes on the loan relationships provisions see Example 63.

Pre-trading expenditure

6.   Pre-trading expenditure, other than interest (and elected research and development (R&D) expenditure – see below), incurred by a company within seven years before the start of the trade that would have been allowable if incurred after commencement is treated as paid on the first day of trading (CTA 2009 s 61).

Where interest is paid before the trade starts, it is deducted on an accruals basis in calculating the non-trading profit or loss. This does not apply if the company makes a claim, within two years after the end of the period in which the deduction was given, to bring the interest in as a trading expense of the first trading period. In order to be deductible in that period the trade must start within seven years after the end of the accounting period in which the interest would otherwise have been deducted as non-trading debits (CTA 2009 s 330).

Where a small/medium-sized company incurs qualifying R&D expenditure before it begins to carry on the relevant trade, it may elect to treat 175% of the expenditure as if it were a trading loss (see Example 52 explanatory note 9). Where an R&D election is made, the amount cannot be treated as a pre-trading expense.

Capital allowances

7.   When the trading profit has been ascertained using the above principles, capital allowances are then deducted as a trading expense and balancing charges included as a trading receipt (CAA 2001 s 2).

Value added tax

8.   For a fully VAT-registered company, VAT does not normally enter into the profits and expenditure for corporation tax, except as follows:

(a)   Non-recoverable VAT on cars forms part of the allowable cost for capital allowances.

(b)   Scale VAT charges for private fuel provided to employees are included in motoring expenses.

There may be other non-recoverable VAT, for example on repairs, refurbishments and other expenses relating to domestic accommodation provided for directors, and it will form part of the allowable expense against the profit (subject to the normal rules for allowable expenses). Non-recoverable VAT on entertaining is disallowed along with the entertaining expenditure itself (but see Example 15 explanatory note 7 re staff entertaining).

A partly exempt or non-VAT registered company includes VAT as part of allowable expenses or capital costs, subject to the disallowance of VAT on business entertaining. Some approximation may be necessary for partly exempt companies in allocating the VAT to the various items of expenditure, and this will be accepted by HMRC providing it is reasonable.

National insurance contributions

9. Companies are required to pay Class 1 secondary national insurance contributions at 12.8% in respect of their employees' earnings in excess of £110 a week (from 6 April 2009). (Employees' Class 1 primary contributions are also payable on earnings in excess of £110 a week. For 2009/10 the main charge runs out at the upper earnings limit of £844 a week, £43,875 a year, and a charge of 1% applies to earnings above this limit.) Earnings for Class 1 contributions comprise cash pay and certain benefits in kind that can be readily converted into cash. Employers (but not employees) also pay Class 1A contributions at 12.8% on most taxable benefits in kind that do not attract Class 1 contributions, and also Class 1B contributions at 12.8% in relation to PAYE settlement agreements (see Example 8 for details). The contributions are an allowable expense against the profits.

See Example 48 for the detailed provisions on national insurance.

Chargeable gains

10. Company chargeable gains are calculated using capital gains tax principles, but are then charged to corporation tax rather than to capital gains tax (CTA 2009 s 2(2), TCGA 1992 ss 1 and 8). References in the capital gains legislation to years of assessment are treated as references to accounting periods. If losses exceed gains, the excess is carried forward to set against later gains (see Example 95 explanatory note 11).

For companies indexation relief continues to apply in the calculation of chargeable gains. However, companies have seen an increasing amount of capital assets being removed from the capital gains regime (where they are only broadly taxed on a 'realisation' basis) and taxed instead in accordance with profits and losses recognised in the accounts.

Charges on income and interest

11. Charges on income are deductible from total profits (both income and capital profits) so far as paid in the chargeable accounting period (ICTA 1988 s 338). There is an exception to the rule that charges must be paid in the accounting period for companies who are wholly owned by a charity that donates the whole of their taxable profits to the charity (see Example 90 explanatory note 7 for details).

Charges on income used to comprise many types of transaction commonly found in corporation tax. They now principally comprise the following.

- Qualifying donations made by companies under gift aid, including covenanted payments.

- The market value (plus incidental costs) of certain gifts of stocks and shares or qualifying interests in land to charities (ICTA 1988 s 587B).

Annuities and other annual payments are treated as management expenses (see companies with investment business, Example 64). Companies will rarely make any payments within the 'annuities or other annual payments' category.

Companies and local authorities pay patent royalties and annual interest on a gross basis (without deducting tax) where they believe the recipient to be a UK-resident company, local authority or a UK permanent establishment of a non-resident company (ICTA 1988 ss 349A–349D). Interest is also paid gross on quoted Eurobonds which means interest-bearing securities issued by a company and listed on a recognised stock exchange (ICTA 1988 s 349(4)).

In other cases, such as where the recipient is an individual, a non-exempt trust or a non-resident company, the amounts continue to be subject to deduction of tax at the relevant rate. (If the payment is made overseas with the benefit of a double tax treaty, a 'nil' or reduced rate of withholding may apply.)

Companies may still *receive* patent royalties net of tax where the payer is an individual.

Corporation tax rates

12. The rate of corporation tax is fixed for years ended 31 March which are called financial years. Financial years are identified by the calendar year in which they start. Thus the year ending 31 March 2010 is called the financial year 2009. The rates for the financial year 2009 are a small companies' rate of 21% (2008: 21%) where profits do not exceed £300,000 and a full rate of 28% (2008: 28%) where profits exceed £1,500,000.

    It has been announced that the small companies' rate will rise by 1% to 22% for FY 2010.

    Where company accounting periods do not coincide with financial years, the profit for corporation tax is apportioned over the years concerned to determine the rates at which tax is payable (CTA 2009 s 8), unless the rate is the same for both years. This apportionment is done in days rather than months.

Quarterly income tax returns (ICTA 1988 Sch 16)

13. A company has to make a return under ICTA 1988 Sch 16 to account for any income tax it has deducted in each relevant calendar quarter from payments to individuals or non UK residents. If the company has suffered income tax on any of its income (for example if it has received patent royalties from an individual), the income tax suffered will be set off against the income tax to be accounted for. Where tax is deducted, the rate of tax deducted from interest is 20%. The return under Sch 16 must be made within fourteen days after the end of the return period on Form CT61.

    If the income tax suffered exceeds income tax to be accounted for and income tax has been paid over to HMRC on an earlier return in the same accounting period, a repayment will be made, but not exceeding the amount of the earlier payments.

    At the end of an accounting period, if income tax suffered on relevant payments received exceeds income tax to be accounted for on relevant payments made, the excess is deducted from the corporation tax payable for that accounting period. If the excess of income tax suffered should *exceed* the corporation tax payable, the excess is *repayable*.

Corporation tax self-assessment (CTSA)

14. Under the CTSA system companies are required to send in a statutory corporation tax return CT600, together with full accounts and computations, within twelve months after the end of the accounting period, and are liable to penalties if they do not (FA 1998 Sch 18 paras 3, 11, 14 and 17).

Payment of corporation tax

15. Although the corporation tax self-assessment return CT600 must be filed within twelve months of the year end, corporation tax must be paid within nine months and one day of the end of the accounting period (except for large companies that must pay by instalments). Interest on corporation tax unpaid after nine months was 7.5% from 6 January 2008 until 5 November 2008, and then fell rapidly over the next three months until it was set at 2.5% on 24 March 2009 under new rules introduced in January 2009. The new rules will make the rate more responsive to bank base rate changes, but mean that the rate will change at a variety of dates rather than only on 6th of the month.

    Quarterly instalments

    In Holsworthy's case the company qualifies as large and the tax must be paid in four equal instalments as follows:

Instalment	Due	Date	Percentage
Instalment 1	6 months + 13 days after start of AP	14/07/09	25%
Instalment 2	3 months after instalment 1	14/10/09	25%
Instalment 3	3 months after instalment 2	14/01/10	25%
Instalment 4	3 months plus 14 days after end of AP	14/04/10	25%

The number of instalments will be reduced if the accounting period is less than nine months in length. A company qualifies as large if its profits (including non-group franked investment income) exceed £1.5 million, as scaled-down for shorter accounting periods and for the number of associate companies (see Example 50 explanatory note 3).

A company is not large if:

(a)   its tax liability does not exceed £10,000 (as scaled-down for shorter accounting periods); or

(b)   its profits for the accounting period do not exceed £10 million (as adjusted for shorter accounting periods), *and* it was not large (disregarding the £10 million exclusion) in the previous accounting period.

Holsworthy's profits were below £10 million, but it was large in the previous year, and its profit is above £1.5 million so quarterly payments are required. A company will not be large in the previous period if it did not exist or have an accounting period in any part of the previous 12 months, or if it was not a large company for an accounting period that fell within or ended in the previous 12 months.

Estimating quarterly instalment payments (QIPs)

It is the company's responsibility to state on the self-assessment return CT600 that it is liable to make QIPs. It is also its responsibility to estimate the amount of the QIP, which involves estimating the profit for the year before the year has ended. Because the instalments are estimated the amount paid will rarely match the final liability, and interest is charged or paid on underpaid or overpaid instalments. Interest runs from the date of the first instalment, and is currently charged at 1.5% on underpayments, and credited at 0.25% on overpayments (from 16 March 2009; the rates are changed frequently).

Interest on unpaid instalments is deductible, and interest on overpaid instalments is assessable in calculating profits for tax.

Payments can be made at any time, and a system exists for reclaiming overpayments made during the year. Group payment arrangements can be made by groups of companies, with the effect that over and underpayments by a group member can be offset.

Introduction of International Financial Reporting Standards (IFRS)

16.   For accounting periods commencing after 1 January 2005, publicly-traded companies have been required to prepare consolidated accounts in accordance with IFRS. However, the individual company accounts may still be prepared in accordance with UK GAAP. All companies (not charities) may adopt IFRS, but must then apply it consistently. FA 2004 s 51 paved the way for the introduction of IFRS in the UK, followed by further details in the 2005 Finance Acts.

IFRS for SMEs has undergone consultation, and its implementation is expected to be supported by the UK accounting profession.

This legislation made it clear that accounts prepared under UK GAAP, full IFRS or EC-adopted IFRS will be acceptable for UK tax purposes. It amended existing legislation to accommodate IFRS terminology, specified that any prior year adjustments on transition would be dealt with in the period to which the accounts related, and provided detailed rules on debits and credits arising from IFRS valuations.

UK GAAP and IFRS are likely to give broadly similar results for trading, but there can be significant differences on goodwill and financial instruments. The trend is to align UK GAAP with IFRS, so it is likely that all businesses will prepare accounts under IFRS in the foreseeable future.

There is also a move to align profits for tax with accounting profits, with HMRC relying on more closely defined and regulated accounting standards to produce fair and consistent results.

The adoption of IFRS caused special problems for securitisation companies, where a mismatch in methods for valuation of financial assets and matching financial liabilities might have produced tax liabilities out of all proportion to profits or cash flow generated. In this case, a special regime for securitisation companies was provided for by FA 2006 s 101, which for tax purposes matches assets against liabilities, as had been done by UK GAAP.

Question

A.

Able Ltd, a company with no associated companies, has been trading for ten years and has always prepared accounts annually to 31 March. The accounts for the year to 31 March 2010 show profits chargeable to corporation tax of £310,000. There is no franked investment income.

Compute the corporation tax payable.

B.

Baker Ltd, a UK trading company with no associated companies, produced the following results for the year ended 31 March 2010:

Income and gains:	£	£
Adjusted trading profit		244,000
Rental income		15,000
Bank deposit interest receivable		5,000
Capital gains:　　25 September 2009	35,000	
28 March 2010	7,000	42,000
(There were capital losses of £8,000 bf at 1 April 2009)		
Dividends from UK companies (13,500 + tax credits 1,500)		15,000
Charges paid (gross):		
Gift Aid donation to charity		7,000
Dividend paid:		
24 July 2009		52,000

(a)　Compute the corporation tax payable by Baker Ltd for the above accounting period.

(b)　Comment on the effect on the company's tax liability of the sale of the asset on 28 March 2010, resulting in the capital gain of £7,000.

C.

Cakes Ltd, a company supplying food products to supermarkets, has traded for several years, making up accounts to 30 September each year.

David Eccles, the sole owner and controlling director of Cakes Ltd entered into a partnership with two other individuals, Mr Jaffer and Mr Tigh, who are the sole owners and controlling directors of their own profitable companies, one in the plant hire industry, the other in the IT consultancy field. The partnership – Happy Days Ventures – is owned in equal shares and provides golf and fishing facilities.

Mrs Eccles has recently set up her own business, which provides interior design services. Mr Eccles does not own any shares in the company, Designed 4U Ltd, nor is he a director. The company was formed on 1 April 2010 and expects to make a small loss in the first accounting period to 31 March 2011.

The balance on Cakes Ltd's plant and machinery pool at 1 October 2008 was £100,000. Its profits in recent years and projected profits, both before capital allowances are as follows:

Trading profits to 30 September 2009	£190,000
Chargeable gain on trade investment 17 October 2008	10,000
Year ended 30 September 2009	£200,000
Year ended 30 September 2010	£250,000

Cakes Ltd expects capital expenditure on moveable plant and machinery to amount to £25,000 per half calendar year.

The partnership is expected to make a profit of around £35,000, and has a year end of 5 April. It expects to incur regular capital expenditure on machinery.

The companies owned and controlled by the other partners also make profits of around £200,000 per year, and incur substantial capital expenditure.

Cakes Ltd qualifies as a small company.

Estimate Cakes Ltd's corporation tax for the years ending 30 September 2009 and 30 September 2010, stating due dates of payment.

Corporation tax rates and marginal relief limits and fractions from 1 April 2005 to 31 March 2010 are as follows:

Year ended 31 March

	2006 & 2007	2008	2009 & 2010	2011
Full rate	30%	30%	28%	28%
Small companies' rate (marginal relief limits £300,000 to £1,500,000 throughout)	19%	20%	21%	22%
marginal relief fraction	11/400	1/40	7/400	6/400

Answer

A.   **Able Ltd**

Corporation Tax Computation – year ended 31 March 2010

	£
Profits chargeable to corporation tax (and also for small companies' rate since there is no franked investment income)	310,000
Corporation tax thereon @ 28%	86,800

$$Less : (1,500,000 - 310,000) \times \frac{300,000}{310,000} \times \frac{7}{400} \qquad 20,825$$

	£
Corporation tax payable	£65,975

Looked at in marginal rate terms, this represents:

300,000 @ 21%	63,000
10,000 @ 29.75%	2,975
	£65,975

B.   (a)   **Corporation tax payable by Baker Ltd for year to 31 March 2010**

	£
Trading income	244,000
Property business income	15,000
Loan relationship non-trading credits	5,000
Chargeable gains net of allowable losses (42,000 – 8,000)	34,000
Total profits	298,000
Less charges on income:	
Gift Aid donation	7,000
Profits chargeable to corporation tax (I)	291,000
Add franked investment income (tax credit inclusive dividends)	15,000
Profits for small companies' rate (P)	306,000
Corporation tax payable on £291,000 @ 28%	81,480

$$Less : (1,500,000 - 306,000) \times \frac{291,000}{306,000} \times \frac{7}{400} \qquad 19,871$$

	61,609

(b)   **Corporation tax effect of the sale of the asset on 28 March 2010**

The sale of the asset on 28 March 2010 at a gain of £7,000 took the company's profits above the small companies' rate lower limit of £300,000 and thus attracted tax to the extent of the excess, ie £6,000, at over 29%. If the gain had not been made, the profits for small companies' rate would have been £299,000 and the corporation tax on the profits of £284,000 would then have been @ 21%, ie £59,640, compared with £61,609, a reduction of £1,969. The overall rate of tax on the gain of £7,000 therefore works out at just over 28%. In addition, deferring the gain to 1 April 2010 would have given a cash flow advantage because corporation tax would then have been payable one year later.

C.   Corporation tax payable by Cakes Ltd

Year ended 30 September 2009

As the company's accounting period spans two financial years, the profits must be apportioned and taxed at the rates applicable in the appropriate financial year.

Capital Allowances

Entitlement to allowances on plant and machinery depends on when the expenditure was incurred, and the legislation applicable to that period, as below.

Capital allowances 1 October 2008 to 30 September 2009

	Plant and machinery pool £	£ *Pool*	*Total allowances* £ *Allowances*
01/10/08–30/09/09			
Pool at 1/10/08		100,000	
Additions	50,000		
AIA	(50,000)	–	50,000
WDA @ 20%		(20,000)	20,000
		80,000	
Additions – balance – all incurred after 1/4/09	10,000		
FYA @ 40%	(4,000)	6,000	4,000
Pool at 30/09/09		86,000	
Allowances			74,000

- Capital allowances are calculated on the basis of expenditure incurred and the tax regime applicable to this part of the accounting period. The balance of expenditure over and above the £50,000 can qualify for FYA's if it was incurred on or after 1 April 2009. As the expenditure is £30,000 in each calendar half year, this will be the case.

Capital allowances 1 October 2009 to 30 September 2010

	Plant and machinery pool £	£ *Pool*	*Total allowances* £ *Allowances*
01/10/09–30/09/10			
Pool at 1/10/09		74,000	
Additions	50,000		
AIA	(50,000)	–	50,000
WDA @ 20%		(14,800)	14,800
		59,200	
Additions – balance – all incurred before 31/3/10	10,000		
FYA @ 40%	(4,000)	6,000	4,000
Pool at 30/09/10		65,200	
Allowances			68,800

A single allowance is apportioned between all the members of a group, but businesses under common ownership can each obtain a separate AIA subject to separate activities (NACE classification), and not sharing premises. A single company is entitled to only one AIA per year irrespective of how many trades it may contain. As Cakes Ltd is controlled by one director, it is entitled to full AIA as an unrelated business.

The partnership's entitlement is governed by separate rules (CA 2001 51(H) to 51(J)), and a separate allowance is available to both the company and the partnership, as they carry out quite different trades.

Summary of profits chargeable to corporation tax

Accounting period	Profit before CAs	Capital allowances	Profits for corporation tax
1 October 2008 – 30 September 2009	200,000	74,000	£126,000
1 October 2009 – 30 September 2010	250,000	68,800	£181,200

Chargeable gains are apportioned on a time basis between financial years.

Estimate of corporation tax due:

Year ended 30 September 2009

	£
Profit for the year	126,000
Tax at 21%	26,460

The tax of £26,460 is due on 1 July 2010

Year ended 30 September 2010

Again, the company's accounting period spans two financial years, so profits must be apportioned, and taxed at the rates applicable in the appropriate financial year. Designs 4U Ltd was formed during this accounting period, so this must be taken into account in determining the limits, and is treated as associated for the whole accounting period.

	£
Profit for the year ending 30 September 2010	181,200
Profit – 6 months ended 31 March 2010	90,600
Lower limit £300,000 × (6/12) ÷ 2	75,000
Upper limit £1,500,000 × (6/12) ÷ 2	375,000
Tax at 28%	25,368
Small companies relief (375,000 – 90,600) × (1/40)	(4,977)
Corporation tax due (75,000 @ 21% + 15,600 @ 29.75%)	20,391
Profit – 6 months ended 30 September 2010	90,600
Lower limit £300,000 × (6/12) ÷ 2	75,000
Upper limit £1,500,000 × (6/12) ÷ 2	375,000
Tax at 28%	25,368
Small companies relief (375,000 – 90,600) × (6/400)	(4,266)
Corporation tax due (75,000 @ 22% + 15,600 @ 29.5%)	21,102

The tax of £20,391 + £21,102 = £41,493 is due on 1 July 2011

Explanatory Notes

Small companies' rate

1. Corporation tax is payable on both capital profits and income profits (other than franked investment income).

    A reduced rate of corporation tax known as the 'small companies' rate' (ICTA 1988 s 13) applies to a UK resident company where the *profits* (as defined below) were less than what is called the lower relevant maximum amount. A lower 'starting rate' applied from 1 April 2000 to 31 March 2006 where profits fell below the 'first relevant amount' of £10,000, with marginal relief where profits were between £10,000 and £50,000 (s 13AA) (but see explanatory note 7 where there are associated companies). The starting rate was 10% for the financial years 2000 and 2001, but it was reduced to 0% for the financial years 2002, 2003, 2004 and 2005. The small companies' rate does not (and the starting rate did not) apply to the profits of a 'close investment-holding company' (see Example 56 for definition of close investment-holding company). The small companies' rate and full corporation tax rate are fixed for financial years, the financial year 2009 being the year to 31 March 2010. The full rate reduced from 30% to 28% for the year to 31 March 2009.

    The small companies' rate was 20% for the year ended 31 March 2008, rising to 21% for the years ending 31 March 2009 and 2010, and to 22% for the year ending 31 March 2011.

Meaning of 'profits'

2. 'Profits' for starting and small companies' rates means corporation taxable profits (including chargeable gains) plus franked investment income.

    Franked investment income is not, however, included in profits for the small companies' rate if it comes from a UK-resident 51% subsidiary or from a fellow UK 51% subsidiary of a parent company (s 13 and s 13ZA).

Marginal small companies' rate relief

3. Marginal small companies' rate relief is available where profits are above the lower limit but below an upper limit. Since financial year 1994 the lower and upper limits have been £300,000 and £1,500,000, with marginal relief fractions varying with corporation tax rates accordingly.

    The limits are scaled down pro rata where there are associated companies and for accounting periods of less than 12 months (see explanatory note 7). Where there are different relevant maximum amounts and/or different rates of tax for different parts of the same accounting period, the profits are apportioned between those parts. If the marginal relief fraction changes, the same proportions are applied in calculating the marginal relief, as shown in part B(b) of the example.

    Where an accounting period is split in this way because of a change in the upper and lower limits (not rates), it is treated as two separate periods in applying the rules outlined below for associated companies (ICTA 1988 s 834(4)). After the starting rate was abolished, the accounts straddling 1 April 2006 were treated as two separate accounting periods (FA 2006 ss 26(9) to (11)). The accounting period is not, however, regarded as two separate periods where the rate changes, the legislation merely requiring profits to be apportioned as necessary (CTA 2009 s 8(5)).

4. Where marginal relief applies, tax is calculated at the full rate on the corporation taxable profits, but is then reduced by:

$$(M - P) \times \frac{1}{P} \times \text{relevant fraction}$$

where M is the upper limit for marginal relief, I is the 'basic profits', which means profits chargeable to corporation tax, and P is profits as defined for small companies' rate purposes, ie including franked investment income (see explanatory note 2).

5. The effect of the marginal relief is to charge *all* of the corporation tax profits at a gradually increasing rate, which reaches the full tax rate at the upper limit. Looked at in terms of marginal rates, the effective tax charge on each £1 of income and/or chargeable gains between the lower and upper limits is 29.75% for the financial years 2008 and 2009 and 29.5% for the financial year 2010. This marginal rate applies where profits do not include franked investment income.

    Thus Able Ltd in part A of the example, would have paid tax at 21% if profits had been £300,000, amounting to £63,000. The tax payable on its profits of £310,000 is £65,975, so the extra £10,000 of profits has resulted in extra tax of £2,975, ie 29.75%.

6. If profits include franked investment income, the marginal rates on income and/or chargeable gains are somewhat lower.

    Thus in the year to 31 March 2010:

	£	£
Profits (P):		
Income and/or chargeable gains (I)	290,000	
Franked investment income (FII)	10,000	
	300,000	
Tax on I £290,000 @ 21%		60,900
Profits (P):		
I	300,000	
FII	10,000	
	310,000	
Tax on I £300,000 @ 28%	84,000	
Less: $(1,500,000 - 310,000) \times \dfrac{300,000}{310,000} \times \dfrac{7}{400}$	20,153	63,847
Tax on extra £10,000 of income and/or chargeable gains (= 29.47%)		2,947

Associated companies

7. If a company has associated companies, the lower and upper limits are reduced proportionately and they are also reduced proportionately if the accounting period is less than twelve months. An associated company (including a non-resident associated company) is counted even if it is associated for only part of the accounting period. One way of avoiding the adverse effect of this rule would be to commence a new accounting period before a new associated company was acquired.

    An associated company that has not carried on any trade or business throughout the accounting period is ignored. In *Jowett v O'Neill & Brennan Construction Ltd* (1998), an associated company that had substantial money on deposit on which it received interest was held not to be carrying on business. However, in *Land Management Ltd v Fox* (2002), a company which let property, made and held investments, advanced an interest-bearing loan to a connected company, as well as placing funds on deposit at the bank, was held to be carrying on a business. As far as holding companies are concerned, HMRC will disregard a non-trading holding company only if it has no assets other than shares in 51% subsidiaries, it has no income or gains other than group income that it has distributed to its own shareholders, and it has no expenses entitling it to a deduction for charges on income or management expenses (SP 5/94).

Companies are 'associated' for small companies' rate purposes if one has control of the other or both are under the control of the same person or persons (ICTA 1988 s 13(4)). 'Control' is defined in ICTA 1988 s 416 – see Example 56 explanatory notes 3 and 4.

The definition of associated companies was amended with effect from 1 April 2008, for purposes of small companies' rate relief only. From 1 April 2008, business partners are not automatically associates for purposes of small companies relief.

The partnership exemption for associated companies is intended to address a problem arising from the fact that partnerships may have an indefinite number of partners. Prior to this change, other companies controlled by business partners also counted towards associated companies limits, so the marginal limits had to be reduced for the number of companies owned by partners. In large partnerships or private equity structures, partners might have no knowledge of their fellow partners, and no means of knowing how many associated companies existed.

If a person or group of persons can control one company, but cannot control another company without the addition of another person or persons, the companies are not associated. If, for example, A owns 51% of company X and 40% of company Y, and B owns 20% of each of X and Y, the companies are not associated, because A controls X on his own, but controls Y only with B.

Although the rights of defined relatives are taken into account in deciding whether two companies are controlled by the same persons (see Example 56 explanatory note 4(b)(ii)), HMRC ignore relatives other than the spouse/civil partner see Example 56 explanatory note 4) and minor children for small companies' rate purposes unless there is substantial commercial interdependence between the companies (HMRC extra statutory concession C9). Extra statutory concession C9 also indicates other circumstances in which the strict definition of 'control' will not be applied for small companies' rate purposes. The House of Lords decision in *R v IRC ex parte Newfields Development Ltd* (2001) confirmed that HMRC can attribute any shares held by associates to an individual irrespective of whether that individual is a shareholder in the company. For an illustration of the associated companies rules see Example 62 part A.

Planning points

8.   The effect of profits lying in the marginal tranche for small companies' rate purposes should be borne in mind, particularly:

    (i)   Where there are alternative ways of obtaining relief, such as carrying back or carrying forward losses, or transferring losses to another group company.

    (ii)   When considering at what time capital expenditure qualifying for capital allowances should be incurred.

    (iii)   When considering the timing of large items of revenue expenditure.

    (iv)   When considering the timing of capital disposals.

Every £1 by which profits are increased or reduced within the *marginal tranche* presently costs or saves tax at 29.75% reduced to some extent where there is franked investment income. This is shown in part B of the example in relation to the capital disposal by Baker Ltd.

Claims for relief

9.   HMRC issued Statement of Practice 1/91 stating that small companies' rate and marginal relief are not applied automatically and the company must make a claim. The claim may be made merely by an appropriate indication on the corporation tax computation or return, the return including a box for this purpose. Except for unincorporated associations the claim should state the number of associated companies in the accounting period, or that there are none, as the case may be.

Non-corporate distribution rate

10.   During financial years 2003 to 2005 there was an additional rate of corporation tax known as the non-corporate distribution rate, which was intended to ensure that the minimum rate of corporation tax of [then] 19% was charged when a company made distributions to non-company shareholders, while lower rates of corporation tax continued to apply where profits were retained. Following its abolition, all profits in the range £1–£300,000 are taxed at the small companies' rate. As the combined rate of tax and national insurance is 28% on profits in the range of £6,475 – £43,875 for an unincorporated business (which also has to make payments on account), trading through a limited company still remains an attractive option. The increase in the small companies' rate to 21%, rising to 22% for the year 2010/11 narrows this differential.

Question

Your firm has acted for Captain H. Blower for many years, preparing rental income computations and personal tax returns. After a distinguished career in the forces, he started trading in executive cars in April 2008, under the name EEC (Extremely Expensive Cars). Accounts prepared by the bookkeeper, showing a profit of £40,000, have proved remarkably accurate, and give rise to a tax and NIC bill of £13,400 in respect of the car dealing business, after taking into account £20,000 of other income.

The following note of 12 December 2009 addressed to the senior partner who is on holiday, has just been found amongst the accounting records, and passed to you on 15 December 2009 to deal with.

'Jim, what a great round of golf last weekend – I'll get even with you next time!

I had a fantastic first year, not just because of good profits, but I just love driving those wonderful cars. The hard bit is parting with them when I get to the customer. I have a good customer base now, although some of them make my jaw drop. One customer bought an old Audi from me for £14,995 in cash, which was a pretty steep price, and then I saw it advertised for sale at £7,500 a week later. And then he gave me an unbelievable price on my Aston Martin! Well, it takes all types to make a world. Anyway, I feel the time has come to transfer the business to a limited company. It does not have much in the way of assets, other than the Aston Martin, but I hope to buy a transporter next summer. Apparently, I can save tax by transferring the goodwill of EEC to the company, and closing it after a couple of years, and pay tax at only 10%. The rental income business is paying the bills, so I could put as much money as you advise from the car business into a pension. I set up the company myself on 3 February 2008, and immediately put £5,000 into a company deposit account, so it receives trivial amounts of interest every month. I put a couple of cars deals through it on 3 November 2009 to start it trading, and then on 10 November 2009 issued a second share to my wife, who is also a director. I have just put in Form 225 to extend the year end to get extra time for filing the accounts and I am changing the name to European Executive Cars Ltd. You probably do not know the answer to this, or would not know how to do it, but should my company adopt the new International Accounting Standards if it is allowed to? I would like to do so if it saved any tax. So, this will wait until you have recovered from your holiday. Have a good trip.

Rodney'

Research on Companies House website shows that the directors are indeed as stated, and that the company was formed on 3 February 2008.

(a) Draft notes for a meeting with the captain, explaining the compliance and tax issues that the note raises for the limited company.

(b) State what action you, as a tax adviser, need to take to comply with statutory requirements.

Disregard VAT & Excise Duty.

Answer

(a) **Notes for a meeting with Captain H. Blower**

Money laundering

The captain has been a client for many years and has met the firm's procedures for existing clients. However, existing money laundering obligations were replaced by SI 2007/2157, effective 15 December 2007. These regulations have enhanced obligations, including ongoing monitoring of the business relationship, and risk assessment. Examples of instances where ongoing due diligence methods may be applied are a change in business strategy or profile, as here. The firm must ensure that it holds evidence of the identity of the client and the ultimate owners and that it has knowledge of the purpose of the business relationship. As the level of due diligence is based on risk, the firm should perform a risk assessment.

Company filing dates

As the captain's private company was formed on 3 February 2008, its accounting reference date (ARD) will be 28 February. For a newly formed company, the accounts must be filed within 22 months of the date of incorporation (not ten months from the ARD – see below for accounting periods commencing after 6 April 2008), that is by midnight on 3 December 2009. The accounts are therefore already overdue.

Extending the company's year end will not extend the date of filing of the accounts. Furthermore, the application must be made within the timescale for filing the accounts. As the application to extend the year end will be received after the due date for filing the accounts, it will be rejected. The company's ARD remains 28 February.

Company name

Companies House controls the use of 'sensitive words and expressions'. Examples are words such as 'British', 'International' or 'European' which may imply greater size and scope than the company actually possesses. A list can be found in the guidance section on company names in the Companies House website. The change of name application will be rejected unless the company can show that their scope of trading within Europe is sufficient to justify it.

Charge to corporation tax

The company must give notice to HMRC within three months of coming into charge to corporation tax, in this case of the company acquiring the deposit account which earns interest. If this has not been done, the company faces a penalty of at least £300. Notification should be made as soon as possible.

As the company receives interest, it is within the charge to corporation tax, and not dormant. The normal tax payment and tax filing deadlines apply to it. As a period of account for corporation tax cannot exceed one year, there are two periods of account: 3 February 2008 to 2 February 2009; and 3 February 2009 to 28 February 2009. Any tax on these accounting periods should have been paid by 3 November 2009 and 29 November 2009 respectively, after which interest would run, but after costs and fees it is unlikely that any tax would fall due. Although the payment deadline is nine months, the filing deadline for the tax return CT600 (of which two are required, one for each accounting period) is twelve months. A tax return is required for each period, failing which a penalty of £100 each will apply. The filing deadline is 28 February 2010 for both returns (see note 5(b)), so these penalties can easily be avoided.

Consideration should be given to shortening the current accounting period (year ending 28 February 2010). The due date for filing the accounts for this year will be 28 December 2010 (not 31 December

2010), so an application to shorten the accounting period may be made at any time up to that date. An accounting period may not be less than six months in length, so it would be possible to shorten the accounting period to 31 October 2009, which would give an eight-month period.

The amount of tax for this period will be minimal, as trading does not commence until November 2009. The effect of shortening the non-trading accounting period to 31 October 2009 will be to place the trading activity and profits into a year ending 31 October 2010. The due date for filing accounts will be 31 July 2011 (filing deadlines are reduced by one month for accounting periods commencing on or after 6 April 2008), and deferring the due date of corporation tax to 31 July 2011. It would also allow the company to claim capital allowances for any capital expenditure it incurred up to 31 October 2010.

Form 42

Guidance issued by HMRC in April 2006 does not require a report of the issue of shares to the founder before commencement of trade. This guidance clarifies that a report still needs to be made on issue to directors after commencement of trade. A report must therefore be made by 6 July 2010 of the issue shares to Mrs Blower on 10 November 2009. We recommend making the report immediately, to avoid having to diary this date, as the report may be made annually or on issue by issue basis.

Transfer of goodwill

The recognition of goodwill in the accounts at fair market value is a proper transaction for both tax and accounting purposes. Achieving an acceptable valuation is a matter of extreme uncertainty.

Because the goodwill introduced generates a liability as a credit to the director's loan account it has no effect on the value of the company, nor are there tax implications in extracting the fair value.

Goodwill can be classified into three kinds (see HMRC Manual):

(i)   Personal goodwill – the trader's name and reputation.

(ii) Inherent goodwill – the location of the business.

(iii) Free goodwill – the brand name, customers, business reputation and super-profits.

Personal goodwill cannot be transferred as it is personal to the individual. Inherent goodwill goes with the property, and can only be transferred if an interest in the property is transferred. HMRC accept that free goodwill of a sole trader business may be transferred to the owner's new limited company. If EEC cars has contracts, premises, salesmen and a business separable from the proprietor himself, then there may be goodwill to transfer. If the whole process of buying, selling and delivery is done by the captain himself, this may be regarded as evidence that goodwill is not separable from him as an individual. The fact that a couple of deals can easily be put through another legal entity is unlikely to be helpful, unless there is some special reason for singling out these particular transactions.

It seems unlikely on the face of it that goodwill can be valued at a substantial figure. If it is placed on the company at over-value, HMRC may seek to treat the excess as a dividend, or even to tax it under PAYE as an inducement to take up employment.

It is possible to agree the value of goodwill with HMRC, via a post-transaction valuation check, but by definition this happens only after the transaction has been completed. The request for a post-valuation check should be made well before the deadlines for filing the personal or corporation tax returns, to allow them to reflect the agreed figure.

The value for goodwill that is agreed will be the disposal value for capital gains tax. That amount will be credited to Director's Current Account and can be withdrawn with no further tax liability. To minimise the CGT payable, the goodwill should not be transferred until EEC has been trading for a full year and is therefore able to take advantage of entrepreneur's relief to reduce the effective rate of tax to 10%.

Even if goodwill is transferred, there is no tax advantage to the company. The intangible fixed assets rules do not allow depreciation for tax purposes of assets acquired from a connected person. The capital gain on disposal by the sole trader will suffer tax whether or not the company can claim relief. If the business has independent goodwill, which can later be sold, then the initial value of goodwill forms the base cost which will reduce the chargeable gain in the company on a sale of trade and assets out of the company.

Tax avoidance

The UK has no General Anti-Avoidance Rule (GAAR), and the captain may arrange his tax affairs in such a way as to minimise his tax liability, subject to specific laws.

However, the client believes that he could save tax by transferring goodwill in the company, taking very low remuneration, and then liquidating the company to take advantage of the lower rate of tax applicable to capital gains. The anti-avoidance rule of ICTA 1988 s 703 (cancellation of tax advantages in transactions in securities) is likely to allow HMRC to cancel such an advantage. There is also the danger that surplus assets in the company would cause it to lose business property status for entrepreneur's relief, in which case any gain would be taxed at 18%.

FA 2009 also introduces rules to prevent the transfer of income into gains, transfers of income streams that would need to be reviewed. See capital gains tax examples.

If the issue of one share to the captain's wife is to divert income to her by means of dividends, then care must be taken with the settlements legislation (as described in Example 59). The settlements legislation involves a bounteous transfer, and in this context a high value placed on goodwill as a result of future earnings would be unhelpful. If the transfer of the business to the limited company goes ahead, the shareholdings and a dividend policy will have to be examined with great care.

Pension payments

Pension payments are deductible against company profits in the same way as salary. If contributions are made by the company to an individual registered pension scheme they will be treated as the settlement of a pecuniary liability and will be liable to tax and NIC. The premiums will then be limited to 100% of remuneration and are paid net of basic rate tax. Higher rate tax relief will be available to the individual (Captain Blower will not be subject to any restriction on his higher rate tax relief on the assumption his income does not exceed £150,000 in any relevant year).

If the company sets up a registered pension scheme, then contributions are not limited and are paid gross. If the amount added to the benefits of an individual exceed the annual limit, £245,000 for 2009/10, then the excess is liable to the annual allowance charge of 40%, payable by the individual. Although the company may pay exceptionally high pension contributions, it will obtain tax relief only on the amount that is expended wholly and exclusively for the purposes of the trade. This is measured in the same way as other deductions, which are also deductible only insofar as they are expended wholly and exclusively for the purposes of the trade. One informal guideline is that an amount that would have been taxed as profit on a sole trader will generally be allowable as remuneration for a controlling director. HMRC guidance on the deductibility of pension payments states that the proportion of pension to salary in the overall remuneration package will be disregarded. On this basis, it would appear that the captain's remuneration could be paid entirely as pension, and the company would still obtain a tax deduction for the remuneration.

The guidance also states that large or exceptional pension contributions are likely to attract attention, particularly if they were made on behalf of a controlling director. It is likely that such a high proportion of pension would attract scrutiny.

Other matters

As a sole trader, the captain has to make tax payments on account on 31 January 2010 and 31 July 2010. The payment on 31 January 2010 will therefore be £20,100, being £13,400 for 2008/09 plus the first payment on account of 2009/10. The payment on account system accentuates the fluctuations in tax liabilities for sole traders with uneven profits. The transfer of a trade to a limited company will reduce the tax liability for 2009/10. Care should be taken to make payments on account of an amount sufficient to cover the tax liability on the income retained in the captain's own name. The reduction should be claimed by completing Form SA303, and submitting it to HMRC. At these income levels, it is likely that the overall tax liability of European Executive Cars Ltd and Captain Blower will be reduced following incorporation of the business provided that the balance between salary and dividends is carefully managed. However, payment of salary will be subject to PAYE and higher payroll NIC burdens. The fact that PAYE is paid during the tax year can prevent the build-up of unmanageable tax liabilities.

The Aston Martin should not be brought into the limited company since the scale charges, which are based on its list price when new and not the advantageous price paid for it, are likely to be prohibitive. A claim of 40p per mile (25p after 10,000 miles per annum) should be made for actual business miles travelled by the captain for the company. As a sole trader, the captain receives a tax deduction on the proportion of motor expenses related to business use, and bears the actual cost of private mileage out of taxed profit.

High value dealer

As EEC does not have a clear policy of not accepting cash for sales of €15,000 or over, it is classed as a high value dealer, and should have registered with HMRC which monitors compliance with money laundering regulations for money service businesses and high value dealers. There are requirements to observe policies on identification and record keeping, to check Bank of England 'financial targets' for MSBs, and to make reports to SOCA on suspicious transactions.

EEC should have registered as soon as practicable after commencing trade, and both it and the company must now register as soon as possible. Penalties for non-compliance with these regulations are up to £5,000 for each failure to comply, and there are clearly major failures.

Accounting Standards

UK GAAP is converging with IFRS, and the two standards are treated as equal as a basis for preparing accounts for UK tax. For a company without intangibles, financial assets or derivatives, the differences are likely to be small. All companies are entitled to adopt IFRS for accounting periods beginning after 1 January 2005. Our firm is of course able to prepare IFRS accounts, but IFRS has no equivalent to the Financial Reporting Standard for Smaller Entities (FRSSE) at present, so adoption will involve additional work, and a higher level of fees. The IASB (International Accounting Standards Board) currently estimates that the International Financial Reporting Standard for Small and Medium-Sized Entities (IFRS SME) will be issued in July 2009, and it is expected that UK accountancy bodies will back implementation in the UK from an early date. This standard would be available for the use of all companies other than those will a public reporting requirement.

(b) **Money laundering/Disclosure of Tax Avoidance Schemes (DOTAS)**

Disclosure of tax avoidance schemes

The DOTAS rules are aimed principally at marketed tax avoidance schemes, and are specifically not intended to apply to routine advice. The advice that our firm will be giving will be aimed at allowing the taxpayer to benefit from the reliefs intended by tax legislation and will not involve any abuse of artificial transactions intended to exploit loopholes in the law. The captain can be reassured that there is no requirement to make a disclosure under the DOTAS rules in respect of our advice.

Money laundering

Money laundering regulations have applied to accountants since 22 March 2004, so our firm has identification details on file, and has set up procedures for identifying clients, for training staff to detect signs of money laundering, for reporting to the Money Laundering Reporting Officer (MLRO) and for the MLRO to report to SOCA.

The 2003 Money Laundering Regulations were replaced by the Money Laundering Regulations 2007, SI 2007/2571, with effect from 15 December 2007. These extended obligations to an ongoing monitoring of the business relationship, and a requirement to vary due diligence in higher risk situations.

Even though we have identity on file, this change in business relationship requires a risk assessment, possibly followed by further due diligence. We must, therefore, ensure we have details of the identity of the business and its beneficial owners, and ensure that we know the purpose of the business relationship. We are also required to obtain identification details of the ownership of the limited company and of its directors. There is an obligation to retain the records of identification for five years after the business relationship ceases.

The training the firm has received in money laundering enables us to detect the likelihood of serious incidences of money laundering. It would appear that the captain's customers have bought cars for cash, both in the case of the Audi and the Aston Martin, and then resold them (accepting a loss) in exchange for bankable funds from a reputable source, a classic form of money laundering. This must be reported immediately to the MLRO, who will probably wish to make a report to SOCA as a matter of urgency.

It is an offence under the money laundering regulations to 'tip off' a suspect, subject to a maximum term of imprisonment of five years, or a fine, or both. The captain is not the suspect, but under no circumstances must any member of our staff let him, or anyone else, know that a report may be/has been made to ensure compliance with this regulation. We may continue to act for him as normal, indeed there is an obligation on us to do nothing to tip him off that our suspicions have been aroused.

The captain's failure to register as a high value dealer is a compliance failure that could potentially lead to prosecution. As such, it should be reported to the MLRO, who will probably decide to make a report – particularly since, had he registered, the HMRC guidelines supplied with the registration pack would have alerted the captain to what was going on. This makes it all the more important that he notifies HMRC voluntarily as soon as possible, before an enquiry is opened in response to information from SOCA.

Explanatory Notes

Company formation

1.   A company is formed by registration with Companies House, website http://www.companieshouse.gov.uk/ from whom full details and statutory forms may be downloaded.

A new company must:

- file a Memorandum and Articles of Association, showing its objects and authorised share capital;
- give names, addresses and other details of its directors, company secretary and members;
- specify a registered office. The registered office of the company will be either in England and Wales, or in Scotland, and the country cannot subsequently be changed.

Details of limited companies, and their accounts, are placed in the public domain by filing with Companies House, and can be obtained on payment of a fee. There are procedures and forms for changing the details, and an annual return confirming that details remain unchanged must be filed each year. Many forms, documents and returns can be filed on-line.

A new company comes into existence when the Registrar of Companies issues a certificate of incorporation, which may be achieved within 24 hours for a private company. There are a number of restrictions on names.

The types of private company available are:

- limited by shares;

- limited by guarantee; or,

- unlimited.

These companies may have only one member. From 6 April 2008, the company is not required to appoint a company secretary, and may have a sole director as the single company officer. From 1 October 2008 the sole director must be a natural person, not a legal entity.

A public limited company (plc) has a higher level of regulation and cost commensurate with access to financial markets. It must have at least two members, two directors, and a qualified company secretary. The minimum issued share capital is £50,000.

A Societas Europeae (SE), is a European company. These have been available since 8 October 2004, but very few have been formed in UK. They have regulations similar to those of the plc, and a special tax regime to facilitate trading within Europe. They may be formed by merger, as a holding company or as a subsidiary, and can also be formed by a plc transforming into an SE. There are requirements for worker participation.

Accounting reference date

2. The company must specify its accounting reference date, which must be not be more than 18 months, nor less than six months after formation. As the accounting period for corporation tax may not exceed one year, longer periods of account will have to be split.

An accounting reference date may not be extended more than once in every five years unless specific circumstances apply.

Companies House filing deadlines

3. The Companies Act 2006 amended the due dates for filing accounts with effect from 6 April 2008, generally shortening the filing deadline by one month and increasing penalties for late filing.

Under company law, for accounting periods beginning on or after 6 April 2008, public companies must normally file accounts with the Registrar of Companies not later than six (previously seven) months after the end of the accounting period, the time limit for private limited companies being nine months (previously ten). There are automatic penalties for late filing, the penalties for public companies ranging from £750 (previously £500) if accounts are up to three months late, to £7,500 (previously £5,000) if accounts are more than twelve months late, and for private companies from £150 (previously £100) to £1,500 (previously £1,000). The Companies Registry interpretation of six or nine months is that the accounts are due by the same day of the month as that in which the company's account ends, eg accounts to 28 February 2010 should be filed by 28 August/ 28 November 2010.

Duty to give notice of coming within charge to corporation tax

4. Under FA 2004 s 55, a company must give notice to HMRC of the start of its first accounting period, or of a period in which it becomes chargeable to corporation tax after a period of dormancy. The notice must specify the date the accounting period began, and the following.

(a) the company's name and its registered number;

(b) the address of the company's registered office;

(c) the address of the company's principal place of business;

(d) the nature of the business being carried on by the company;

(e) the date to which the company intends to prepare accounts;

(f) the full name and home address of each of the directors of the company;

(g) if the company has taken over any business, the name and address of that former business and, the name and address of the person from whom it was acquired.

Notice must be given within three months of coming into charge. In practise, Companies House will inform HMRC of the formation of a new company and HMRC will then normally issue the Form CT41G which requests the above information. However if HMRC fail to issue the Form CT41G or the company comes into charge after a period of dormancy it is still the company's responsibility to supply the information.

For tax periods commencing prior to 1 April 2008 the original self-assessment penalty regime remains in force and late notification is subject to a penalty of £300 plus £60 daily penalty and up to £3,000 for fraudulently or negligently providing incorrect information. For accounting periods commencing on or after 1 April 2008, the new penalty regime in FA 2008 Sch 41 applies. Under this legislation, different levels of penalty apply depending upon the potential loss of tax (Sch 41 para 7) and behaviour of the taxpayer: careless, deliberate but not concealed or deliberate and concealed. See Example 41 note 11.

This duty applies to companies only, not to partnerships or unincorporated associations.

Corporation tax self-assessment

5. The Tax Law Rewrite project are in the process of amending the corporation tax legislation. They have issued CTA 2009 which applies to all corporation tax accounting periods ending after 31 March 2009. A second bill is being written to cover rules currently found within ICTA 1988 such as computation of a company's tax liability, loss and group reliefs and close company provisions. A third bill is also expected to cover international and miscellaneous provisions.

Corporation tax is administered on the self-assessment system, and a guide to HMRC's views is found at http://www.hmrc.gov.uk/ctsa/index.htm.

The self-assessment provisions are contained in FA 1998 s 117 and Sch 18, with minor and consequential amendments in Schedule 19 and also in FA 1999 Sch 11 and FA 2001 Sch 29. The provisions relating to payment dates and interest are in TMA 1970 ss 59D, 59DA, 59E, 87 and 87A, and ICTA 1988 ss 826 and 826A and new FA 2009 ss 100–103.

Returns for corporation tax must be made on prescribed forms within time limits, and must be accompanied by accounts and computations. A company only satisfies its filing obligation when it delivers the completed corporation tax return form (and relevant supplementary pages) together with a copy of its accounts and tax computations.

The most important supplementary pages are:

CT600A	For loans made to participators of close companies.
CT600B	For tax liabilities of controlled foreign companies.
CT600C	For claims to and surrenders of group and consortium relief.
CT600E	Charities and Community Amateur Sports Clubs.
CT600G	Corporate Venturing Scheme.
CT600J	Disclosure of tax avoidance schemes.

Corporation tax returns may be filed on-line, in which case it is possible to view the filing and payment status on-line. Draft regulations have been published to make it compulsory for all returns to be filed online for returns delivered on or after 1 April 2011 relating to periods ending on 1 April 2010 or later.

The return must be made on the standard Form CT600, or for small companies, may be made on the short form if it contains boxes for all the entries that the company requires. It does not contain boxes for group reliefs or reporting of CFCs, but will be sufficient for many small standalone companies trading within the UK.

The company tax return CT600 contains a self-assessment of the amount of tax payable, including the tax on loans or advances by close companies' participators and tax relating to controlled foreign companies. This self-assessment creates the charge to tax.

Filing dates

6.   HMRC issue a notice to deliver a corporation tax return (CT603) between three and seven weeks after the end of the return period. This is accompanied by a return Form (CT600), unless the company's agents use an approved substitute form. (Tax agents receive a monthly listing (CT603A list) detailing their client companies to whom a CT603 has been sent.) The CT603 notice should be for the period that HMRC believes to be an accounting period of the company. Where the period specified in the notice does not correspond with the company's accounting period, a return is usually required for any period that ends within the specified notice period.

Dormant companies do not usually receive a notice to complete a corporation tax return, but if they do, then technically a nil return is required. The company should write to inform the inspector that the company is dormant and ask whether the return is required. It is important not to ignore the notice, otherwise penalties may arise.

A notice to deliver a corporation tax return might specify a period that does not coincide with the company's accounting period. If so, the company has to make a return for any accounting period(s) ending in the specified period. If a period of account started but none ended within the specified period, a nil return has to be made for the period up to the date the period of account started. If the specified period is less than twelve months and falls wholly within an accounting period of the company, a return does not have to be made but the inspector should be notified. If the company is outside the scope of corporation tax throughout the specified period (eg because it is non-resident and not trading in the UK, or because it is dormant), a nil return should be filed.

The return must usually be filed within one year of the end of the accounting period for corporation tax, failing which penalties will be incurred.

If a *period of account* exceeds twelve months but does not exceed 18 months, the due date for filing the returns for the accounting periods within that period of account is twelve months from the end of the period of account, if later than the normal due date. If a period of account exceeds 18 months, the due date is 30 months after the beginning of the account, or the normal due date if later. For example, if accounts are made up for the 18 months from 1 October 2007 to 31 March 2009, the returns for the accounting periods to 30 September 2008 and 31 March 2009 are both due by 31 March 2010. If the accounts were made up instead for the 21 months from 1 October 2007 to 30 June 2009, the return for the accounting period to 30 September 2008 would still be due by 31 March 2010 (30 months after the start of the account). The return for the nine months to 30 June 2009 would be due by 30 June 2010 (twelve months after the end of the account).

A flat rate penalty of £100 is charged if the return is no more than three months late, and £200 if more than three months, but these rise to £500 and £1,000 if the returns are late for more than three accounting periods in a row.

In addition, if the company does not file a return within 18 months of the end of the accounting period and has not paid the right amount of tax, a tax related penalty of 10% is imposed. This rises to 20% if the return is late by 24 months or more.

The penalty regime for late filing of returns is being reformed. FA 2009 s 105 introduces new late filing penalties across the range of taxes (IT, CT, PAYE, NIC, CIS, SDLT, SDRT, IHT, pension and petroleum tax) excluding tax credits. Taxpayers have a right of appeal against all penalties and no penalty can be charged if they have a reasonable excuse. Penalties can be suspended where the taxpayer agrees a time to pay arrangement (subject to meeting the terms of the arrangement). Implementation of the new penalties requires changes to HMRC's computer systems and so will be introduced in stages from April 2010.

For corporation tax the following late filing penalties apply to corporation tax returns filed late:

- £100 penalty;

- daily penalties of £10 per day up to a max of 90 days;

- penalties of 5% of tax due (tax payable for period) for prolonged failures (over six and at twelve months);

- higher penalties of 70% of the tax due where a person fails to submit a return for over twelve months and has deliberately withheld information necessary to assess the tax due (100% penalty if deliberate with concealment).

Payment of tax

7. Companies with profits below the small companies' rate upper limit (£1,500,000) pay corporation tax nine months and one day after the end of the accounting period (TMA 1970 s 59D).

    Large companies (for this purpose meaning companies with profits at or above the upper limit for small companies' relief, ie £1.5 million) are required to pay their corporation tax by equal quarterly instalments (under SI 1998/3175 issued under TMA 1970 s 59E). The upper limit is reduced pro rata where there are associated companies and for accounting periods of less than twelve months – see Example 50.

Claims and elections

8. General provisions on claims are in FA 1998 Sch 18 paras 9 and 10 and Part VII. All claims must be for a specified amount and must be made where possible in a return or amendment to a return, although there is an overall time limit for most claims of four years (six years prior to 2008/09) from the end of the accounting period. Claims for group relief (Part VIII) and capital allowances (Part IX) can only be made in a return or amendment to a return. Where it is not possible to make claims on a return the provisions of TMA 1970 Sch 1A apply (see Example 43).

    Unless HMRC otherwise allows, the time limit for capital allowances claims is the latest of twelve months after the filing date for the return, 30 days after the completion of a HMRC enquiry, 30 days after the issue of a HMRC amendment following an enquiry, and 30 days after the date when any appeal against such an amendment is finally determined. See Example 64 explanatory note 8 regarding group relief claims.

HMRC corrections and taxpayer amendments

9. HMRC have nine months from the date a return is received to correct obvious errors in the return, and companies can make amendments within a year from the filing date. If the return is selected for further enquiry, amendments within the permitted twelve-month period will not restrict the scope of the enquiry but may be taken into account in the enquiry. If an amendment affects the tax payable for the current or another period, or by another company, it will not take effect unless and until it is incorporated in the closure notice issued to the company at the end of the enquiry (see explanatory note 12).

    From 1 April 2010 the error or mistake rules are repealed and replaced by FA 2009 s 99. The new rules relax the requirement for an error or mistake. Instead the taxpayer has a statutory right to repayment where tax has been overpaid. Repayment claims will be subject to a self-assessment style regime with HMRC rights of enquiry. The time limit for claims is reduced to four years.

HMRC enquiries

10. Under FA 1998 Sch 18 para 24, unless a CT600 return is filed late, HMRC must initiate an enquiry into the return by the first anniversary of the filing date, ie within two years after the end of the relevant accounting period. Thus, for a period ending on 31 December 2007, the filing date is 31 December 2008 and the enquiry window closes on 31 December 2009. For accounting periods ended after 31 March 2008, the time span for which HMRC may give notice of an enquiry into a single company or a company that is a member of a small group is shortened to 12 months from the date when the return was delivered to HMRC. Thus for a small company with an accounting period ended 31 December 2009, return filed 31 March 2010 the enquiry window closes on 31 March 2011.

   See Example 46 explanatory note 24 regarding referring questions to the Tribunal during an enquiry, and see Example 43 regarding HMRC enquiries into claims made separately from the return.

Keeping records and compliance checks

11. Companies are required to keep sufficient records to make a correct and complete return. These records must be kept until the sixth anniversary of the end of the period for which the company may be required to deliver a tax return, and there has been a penalty of up to £3,000 per accounting period for failing to comply. For tax periods commencing on or after 1 April 2008 that are due to be filed on or after 1 April 2009 the new penalty regime may override. The records, or the information in them, may be preserved in any form or by any means.

   Submitted CT600 returns are subject to a detailed checking system. HMRC are likely to start an enquiry where there is a potential risk of the return being incorrect, or where additional information is needed to satisfy them that the tax treatment adopted is correct. A small number of enquiries are made on a random basis. An enquiry may either be an aspect enquiry raising one or more specific queries in relation to the return, or it may be a full enquiry including a comprehensive review of the accounts and underlying records. HMRC have wide powers to request further information, documents etc for the purpose of their enquiry.

   HMRC Code of Practice 14 (COP 14) provides useful information about HMRC's approach to enquiries under CTSA. For example, it states that where relevant records are required for examination by HMRC they should be provided within a reasonable time. A request may be made to examine them at the company's premises, as this may be more convenient. Similarly, HMRC may request a meeting with relevant officers or employees of the company and their professional adviser. The company may be asked to comment on HMRC's notes of the meeting (noting any disagreement) and sign them. However, HMRC officers have powers to enter any business premises to inspect the premises and/or the records, if this is reasonably required for the purpose of checking the tax return. They are required to give 24 hours' notice, or to obtain authorisation from a senior officer.

   A company may be invited to make a payment on account during the enquiry process to mitigate its potential interest exposure, although it is not legally obliged to pay any additional tax until HMRC invite it to amend its self-assessment.

   A closure notice will be issued by HMRC when they conclude their enquiry, together with their findings. HMRC undertake to agree their findings with the company before inviting an amended return in accordance with their proposed adjustments. If the company disagrees and does not amend the return within the relevant 30-day window, HMRC make their own amendments, which can then be subject to the appeals process. (If the return or an amendment to it is made after the due date, the enquiry window runs from a year from the time the return or amendment is delivered plus the period to the next quarter day, ie the next 31 January, 30 April, 31 July or 31 October.) If an enquiry is not opened within the time limit, the tax as calculated will normally stand unless there is a HMRC 'discovery assessment' (see explanatory note 13 below).

FA 2008 introduced new rules for checking that businesses and individuals have paid the correct amount of IT, CGT, CT, VAT and PAYE known as 'compliance checks'. These apply from 1 April 2009 and include more stringent record keeping, a power to look at records 'in real time' and visit business premises.

FA 2008 repeals TMA 1970 ss 19A and 20 (but not the enquiry rules in s 9A). In their place is a far broader set of powers under FA 2008 Sch 36 part 1. No enquiry is required, instead HMRC can issue new information notices to any person requiring the production of information and or documents provided it is reasonably required to check a company's tax position (Sch 36 part 1 para 1 taxpayer notices and para 2 third party notices). The notice may be appealed against unless it relates to the production of statutory records which the taxpayer is obliged to keep or the First-tier Tribunal approved the issue of the notice.

Schedule 36 part 2 (para 10) provides the power to inspect business premises including vehicles and parts of homes used for business purposes and inspect documents on those premises provided reasonably required for the purposes of checking that company's tax position. They cannot search premises and as stated in HMRC Compliance Handbook manual at CH25650 'the person ... has the right to refuse you entry.' Therefore even when an officer has been given access to the premises he can be asked to leave at any time and HMRC's instructions make it clear that the officer must leave straight away.

The power of inspection does not extend to a person's home used solely as a dwelling, unless invited.

Business records become statutory records when they are created. As stated above the normal time limit for a company to retain their statutory records is six years. (as part of their new powers HMRC may reduce this period below the six year limit) For example, on 1 July 2009 a company with a year end of 31 December who has filed all tax returns on time and has not been subject to an enquiry in the last six years will hold statutory records for the period 1 January 2002 to 1 July 2009.

An information notice or inspection may only be issued where it is 'reasonably required to check a person's tax position.' However, when a return has been made for the period, the notice must be issued within the enquiry window, unless a discovery has been made. Notices may, however, be issued in respect of periods for which no return has yet been made, and the enquiry window principle does not apply to PAYE and VAT compliance checks.

There has been widespread unease about the new powers and whether applying the 'real time' concept to corporation tax returns (and income tax) gives HMRC too much power. A forum has been created including members from HMRC, accountancy/tax bodies, industry, Law Society, etc to report to the treasury.

HMRC have significantly (and successfully for some) changed its approach to compliance for large businesses. Some of these changes are expected to be rolled out to small and medium-sized enterprises by 2011. One target is to reduce the administrative burden around audits and inspections for businesses considered to be tax compliant. This works with large businesses where a business risk review is carried out and a low / high risk rating is given. Obtaining a low risk rating has considerable benefits. Due to the number of SMEs the business risk review would be quite different and it is not clear exactly how it will be carried out but meeting all filing and payment deadlines (unless under business payment support scheme etc) and having effective reliable systems and processes in place seem obvious factors in a business's favour.

Senior accounting officers

12.   Although not relevant in this example, senior accounting officers of large companies are annually required by FA 2009 s 92 to personally certify that their company's accounting systems are adequate

for the purposes of accurate tax reporting. Failure to comply make the officer personally liable to a penalty of £5,000. It is intended that the new rules will apply to financial years beginning on or after the finance bill 2009 receives royal assent.

Interest and penalties regarding overdue and overpaid tax

13.   Interest on overdue and overpaid corporation tax (including tax on close company loans to participators) is deductible/taxable as non-trading interest under the 'loan relationships' provisions (see Example 63). If interest on overpaid tax is received or receivable by a company in liquidation in its final accounting period, however, the interest is not included in taxable profits if it does not exceed £2,000. The rates of interest are adjusted to reflect the fact that the interest is taken into account in computing taxable profits, but the rate on underpaid tax is still much higher than that on overpaid tax.

It is understood that regardless of when leap years occur HMRC use a denominator of 366 in all calculations of interest on overdue tax and a denominator of 365 for interest on overpaid tax, which in each case gives a slight benefit to the taxpayer company.

Legislation has been introduced to harmonise the interest regimes for the different taxes in FA 2009. This currently excludes corporation tax although parallel legislation is expected in next year's Finance Bill.

The penalty regime for late payment of taxes is being reformed. S 106 FA 2009 introduces new late payment penalties across the range of taxes (IT, CT, PAYE, NIC, CIS, SDLT, SDRT, IHT, pension and petroleum tax) excluding tax credits. Taxpayers have a right of appeal against all penalties and no penalty can be charged if they have a reasonable excuse. Penalties can be suspended where the taxpayer agrees a time to pay arrangement (subject to meeting the terms of the arrangement). Implementation of the new penalties requires changes to HMRC's computer systems and so will be introduced in stages from April 2010.

For corporation tax the following late payment penalties arise:

- penalties of 5% of the amount of tax unpaid one month after the payment due date;

- further penalties of 5% of any amount of tax still unpaid at six and twelve months after the payment due date.

HMRC determinations and assessments

14.   As with income tax self-assessment, HMRC are able to determine the tax payable in the absence of a return, and this will count as a self-assessment until superseded by an actual self-assessment. HMRC may still make discovery assessments under the self-assessment regime (FA 1998 Sch 18 para 41). Note that losses and other negative amounts are subject to self-assessment and are thus incorporated within the figure of tax payable under HMRC determination. They may also make 'discovery determinations' where a return incorrectly states an amount that affects another period or another company, see Example 44 explanatory note 9.

Penalties

15.   The tax-based penalty regime introduced by FA 2007 Sch 24 applies to accounting periods beginning on or after April 2008 with a filing date on or after 1 April 2009.

Penalties for inaccurate documents are based on a scale of percentages depending on the taxpayer's behaviour, and are applied to tax lost or delayed.

Behaviour	Maximum penalty % Potential Lost Revenue	Minimum penalty % Potential Lost Revenue
Mistake after reasonable care	0%	0%
Careless	30%	0%
Deliberate not concealed	70%	20%

Deliberate and concealed   100%   30%

HMRC are required to mitigate penalties for co-operation, broken down into prompted/unprompted disclosure, providing HMRC with reasonable help and with access to records.

The new penalty provisions are covered in more detail in Example 41.

Form 42 – employment-related securities – reportable events

16.   Finance Act 2003 Sch 22 introduced rules requiring a report to be made to HMRC of securities issued in connection with employment. These details must to be returned on Form 42 or a suitable alternative.

The circumstances under which a report is required have been the source of much confusion. At the time the legislation was originally enacted, it was thought to affect complex unapproved share schemes, in which employees were remunerated by shares or securities. HMRC then issued guidance making it apparent that, in their view, the reporting requirement was of far wider scope, and affected the routine transactions of ordinary trading companies, flat management companies, and clubs that issue shares. The regulations apply to all companies including those with simple shareholding structures.

Revised guidance was issued in April 2006 (available from HMRC website at www.hmrc.gov.uk), reducing the number of situations in which a report was required, particularly in the case where founder shareholders acquire shares from a formation agent.

Reportable events must be notified to HMRC, on Form 42, by 6 July following the year in which the securities were issued, failing which penalties commencing at £300 per reportable event per employee may be charged.

Reportable events include acquisitions, transfers and disposals of securities, rights issues or alteration in the values and rights of securities. Securities include shares, debentures, loan stock, bonds, certificates of deposit, warrants, futures, units in collective investment schemes and rights under contracts for differences, all in connection with employment.

A report of the issue of such securities is required unless one of the exemptions applies. It is emphasised that Form 42 is concerned with the transfer of shares in connection with employment. Transfers of shares in the normal course of domestic, family or personal relationships do not have to be reported. However, it is up to the transferor to determine whether the transfer is being made for purely personal reasons, and to be able to demonstrate this. HMRC specifically states that it will accept that shares passing to children involved in the business will be considered as being made in the normal course of family relationships. However, if any element of remuneration is shown to be present, a report would be required (and the transfer would be liable to income tax and national insurance).

The transfer of founder shares to the owners of the new company need not be reported provided:

- all the initial shares are obtained at nominal value; and
- the shares are the only form of security that is obtained; and
- their shares are not acquired by reason of another employment; and
- the shares are acquired by a person who is to be a director of the company, or by somebody with a family relationship with the director (provided the transfer is in the normal course of family relationships, rather than by reason of employment).

Similarly, if prospective directors or other family members acquire additional shares before trading commences, Form 42 will not be required. However, if additional shares are issued after the company commences trading, then Form 42 is required but only for the shares issued after commencement of trade.

A report is only required if a reportable event occurs in the tax year, unless HMRC have issued a Form 42 return, in which case it must be filed whether there was a reportable event or not. A Form 42 report is not required for HMRC approved share schemes and options, as these have their own specific reporting requirements. For Enterprise Management Incentives (EMI), the grant of options up to the EMI limit of £100,000 will be reported on a special scheme form, while the excess over £100,000 must be reported on Form 42.

The requirement affects not just current employees but directors and office holders, prospective employees, and former employees where the event was within seven years of the ex-employee leaving.

Forms may be filed on-line, or can be completed on-screen using HMRC's employers' CD-Rom. Paper versions can still be obtained.

For unrestricted shares, the information required is the name of the employee, the employer's name, the description of the shares, date of transfer, number of shares, market value, price and whether PAYE was applied.

It is important to consider Form 42 reporting requirements whenever a security is transferred.

Goodwill on incorporation

17. The goodwill attaching to a business at the date of incorporation may have substantial tax consequences for capital gains tax, income tax, and corporation tax, in the year of incorporation and in subsequent years.

Where a sole trader or partner disposes of goodwill to a company that they control, the transfer is one between connected persons, so takes place at market value for tax purposes. A capital gain arises in this case for the individual (which may be sheltered by reliefs, such as entrepreneur's relief (see Examples 78 and 87), while an intangible asset and director's loan account will be established in the company's records. The transfer of goodwill is exempt for stamp duty purposes.

The key difficulty is establishing the value of goodwill and to what it is attributable. In view of the reliefs available, it is desirable to place as high a value as can be justified on goodwill, but excess valuation may be challenged by HMRC. The overvalue may give rise to income tax, national insurance contributions, or corporation tax, depending on the circumstances.

Where, as in the case of the skills of individual tradesman, the goodwill is inseparable from the individual, it is not capable of being transferred to the company. It is essential to demonstrate that goodwill attaches to the business rather than the owner, using the evidence of location of business premises, an organisation separate from the owner, brands, contracts or customer lists.

The disposal of goodwill must be reported in the capital gains tax section of the individual's self-assessment return, where it may well qualify for entrepreneur's relief, and where the annual exemption of £10,100 may be available.

The company's balance sheet will show an intangible asset but, because it was acquired from the connected person, no tax relief will apply to amortisation. The company may pay for the goodwill, but often will credit its value to a director's loan account. The cost recorded for goodwill can in future be used as the base cost in the event of sale of the trade, while the corresponding director's loan may provide a means of extracting funds without incurring a tax liability.

Sale of goodwill at overvalue

18. HMRC offers a free post-transaction value check service, but as its name implies it can only be requested after the event.

If it proves that goodwill was transferred at overvalue, under exceptional circumstances it is possible to unwind the transaction, and have the individual repay the company or reduce the directors' loan account. This is only possible where goodwill was formally valued by a named qualified valuer, who was given adequate information. If the reduction in the loan account causes it to become overdrawn, income tax will be due on the benefit, and tax may become payable under ICTA 1988 s 419. In most cases it is likely to give rise to a tax charge, either as income of employment, or as a distribution.

If excess goodwill is shown to be an inducement for the individual to join the company, or to represent payment for future services, it will be treated as income of employment under ITEPA 2003 s 62. The company is required to account for income tax and national insurance contributions under PAYE regulations, failing which penalties and interest will apply. It may, under certain circumstances, represent a benefit reportable on Form P11D.

Where there is no evidence that the excess goodwill represents earnings from employment, particularly when transferred before the company commences trade, the excess will be treated as a distribution. If the distribution does not cause the individual to exceed the higher rate band, no further tax will arise on the individual.

The money laundering regulations – tax practitioners

19. With effect from 15 December 2007, the Money Laundering Regulations 2007 replaced the Money Laundering Regulations 2003, as the means of applying the Proceeds of Crime Act 2003 and the Terrorism Act 2000 to regulating affected businesses.

The purpose of the regulations is to require relevant businesses to make reports to SOCA of any knowledge or suspicions of money laundering activity. However, this is limited to knowledge or suspicions acquired in the course of business or employment, not knowledge acquired through personal social connections.

Firms affected must appoint an individual as the money laundering reporting officer (MLRO) to receive money laundering reports from staff, and to make reports to SOCA. All staff must be trained in the recognition and reporting of potential money laundering transactions, and how to verify the identity of new clients.

The Money Laundering Regulations 2007 (SI 2007/2157) set out number of specific requirements, including 'due diligence', and record keeping:

Due diligence:

'Customer due diligence measures' (approximately equivalent to 'know your customer' procedures) involve identifying the customer and verifying the customer's identity on the basis of documents, data or information obtained from a reliable and independent source, and identifying the beneficial owner, if this is not the customer, and taking measures to establish their identity, and obtaining information on the purpose or intended nature of the business relationship.

Ongoing monitoring

There is a requirement for ongoing monitoring of the business relationship, which is defined as meaning:

– scrutiny of transactions undertaken throughout the course of the relationship, including the source of funds, to ensure that the transactions are consistent with the firm's knowledge of the customer, the business and the risk profile;

– retention of documentation obtained for the purpose of customer due diligence;

– enhanced customer due diligence must be applied on risk-sensitive basis, for instance where the customer is not physically present for identification.

Record-keeping:

The records, which must be kept for at least five years, are:

– a copy of the customers identity documentation;

– supporting records in respect of the business relationship which is the subject of customer due diligence and ongoing monitoring.

Businesses may rely on others for due diligence purposes, but they must have the agreement of the person being relied upon, and they are responsible for ensuring that the person can provide the necessary documentation.

HMRC have issued revised Money Laundering Regulations 2007 (MLR 2007) which are intended for businesses registered with HMRC, and which are considered to form guidance for POCA 2004 and the Terrorism Act 2000.

These regulations summarise money laundering obligations as follows:

'**MLR 2007 Regulation 20** sets out the requirement for relevant businesses to establish and maintain appropriate and risk-sensitive policies and procedures relating to:

- customer due diligence;

- reporting;

- record keeping;

- internal control;

- risk assessment and management;

- the monitoring and management of compliance; and

- the internal communication of such policies and procedures, in order to prevent activities related to money laundering and terrorist financing.

These policies and procedures must include policies and procedures that:

- Identify and scrutinise

  - complex or unusually large transactions,

  - unusual patterns of transactions which have no apparent economic or visible lawful purpose,

  - any other activity which could be considered to be related to money laundering or terrorist financing,

- specify the additional measures that will be taken to prevent the use of products and transactions that favour anonymity for money laundering or terrorist financing;

- determine whether a customer is a politically exposed person (person holding a prominent public function outside the UK, or their associates);

- nominate an individual in the organisation to receive disclosures under Part 7 of POCA and Part 3 of TA;

- ensure employees report suspicious activity to the Nominated Officer; and

- ensure the Nominated Officer considers such internal reports in the light of available information and determines whether they give rise to knowledge or suspicion or reasonable grounds for knowledge or suspicion of money laundering or terrorist financing.'

The CCAB guidance on money laundering, issued in December 2007, applies to accountancy and tax businesses, including those that are supervised by HMRC. Treasury approval of this guidance has been sought, which would give it the status of guidance that courts would be obliged to consider for POCA 2004 and the Terrorism Act 2000 purposes. This guidance is essentially similar to Money Laundering Regulations (MLR) 2007, being based on the same SI, but is applied to the circumstances of accountancy businesses.

The form of identification to be obtained is not specified by the Act, but is determined by the firm's own policies via a risk-based approach, and specific details and circumstances relating to acceptable identity are set out in MLR 2007. Furthermore, a firm's customer due diligence procedures need not be standard for all clients, but may vary on a risk-based approach. The guidance given them by the Joint Money Laundering Steering Group (originally intended FSA supervised businesses), is often followed, and this guidance was used in the preparation of MLR 2007. The offences to be reported include any criminal activity giving rise to proceeds, and in particular are not limited to terrorism or drug dealing. The proceeds of crime, termed criminal property, include the proceeds of tax evasion, bribery, or costs saved by failure to comply with regulatory requirements (where the failure to comply is a criminal offence). There is no de minimis limit for the value of the proceeds of crime to be reported, so even the smallest transactions may require a report. Reports must be made as soon as is reasonably possible to SOCA on a suspicious activity reports (SAR), and can be made online at www.soca.gov.uk/financialIntel/index.html. The details to be reported are specified on this site. The client should never be made aware of the adviser's suspicions because tipping off is a criminal offence.

A Limited Intelligence Value report (LIVR) may be made where, individually, there is likely to be limited intelligence value in the report (the report is required in case correlation of many such reports yields useful information). A LIVR is never appropriate for serious crimes such as terrorism or drugs offences, but might be used for small discrepancies arising from mistakes rather than dishonest behaviour, or where the identity of the criminal is not known.

Accountants and tax advisers in practice are expected to make reports on clients in circumstances where failure to comply with tax regulations has led to underpayment of tax or late payment.

Legal privilege

20.   In a relatively narrow range of circumstances, such as litigation or giving legal advice where making a report to SOCA would compromise the client's rights to legal privilege, qualified accountants have the same legal privilege as the legal profession allowing them to claim protection from reporting suspicious transactions. This applies only to money laundering, not offences under the Terrorism Act 2000.

Money laundering – HMRC responsibilities

21.   HMRC have the responsibility for administering the money laundering regulations in respect of:

- money service businesses (MSB);

- high value dealers (HVD);

- trust and company service providers (TCSP);

- accountancy service providers (ASP).

Members regulated by specified recognised legal, accountancy or bookkeeping professional bodies are supervised by those bodies. All other businesses within the scope of the regulations are required to register with HMRC.

Accountancy service providers (ASPs)

Members of designated professional tax, accountancy and bookkeeping bodies continue to be regulated by those bodies, not by HMRC.

Unlike other businesses supervised by HMRC for money laundering regulations, ASPs:

–   MLR 2007 requires ASPs to follow CCAB guidance rather than the MLR 2007 guidance;

–   ASPs are not required to complete the 'fit and proper' test.

Existing ASPs should have applied for registration by 1 July 2008, and may not trade legally if not registered by 1 October 2008. Registration costs £95.

Accountancy service providers are businesses providing external accountancy, bookkeeping, payroll, and tax services. Internal providers are specifically excluded.

Trust or company service providers

Services such as company formation, trustee, nominee, or representation services are not covered by the ASP designation, but by the trust or company service provider (TCSP) designation. HMRC have, however, stated that firms providing such services that are members of specified recognised legal, accountancy or bookkeeping professional bodies do not need to register with HMRC, but continue to be governed by those bodies.

TCSPs that are not governed by a specified professional body are required to complete a 'fit and proper' test at a cost of £50 per test, and should have applied for registration by 31 May 2008.

MSBs and HVDs

Failure to register or to comply with money laundering regulations may lead to prosecution by HMRC, or civil penalties. Businesses must register as soon as possible on commencing the above activities, which need not be their sole or main activities.

A money service business (MSB) is a business that carries out the activities of:

● bureau de change; or

● transferring a customer's money (money transmission); or

● third party cheque cashing.

Banks and businesses regulated by the FSA do not need to be registered under the MSB scheme.

The registration number issued to the MSB forms part of its identity, which it will use in its dealings with banks and other MSBs. A register is kept of all businesses not covered by the FSA register covering bureaux de change, money transmitters and third party cheque cashers.

A high value dealer (HVD) is any business that does not have a clear policy of not accepting payments over €15,000 per transaction in cash.

MSBs and HVDs are required to complete 'fit and proper' tests as well as registering. Specific additional requirements apply to them and to money transmission businesses, but basic requirements are essentially the same.

Penalties

Civil Penalties

HMRC have the power to impose civil penalties on businesses that fail to comply with the requirements of the Money Laundering Regulations in respect of:

● notification and registration requirements;

● customer due diligence measures;

● ongoing monitoring of a business relationship;

● enhanced customer due diligence and ongoing monitoring;

● record-keeping;

● policies and procedures to prevent money laundering and terrorist financing;

● appointing a Nominated Officer and internal reporting procedures;

● training of employees.

Penalties will be for an amount that is considered appropriate for the purposes of being effective, proportionate and dissuasive, with no upper limit.

Penalty and registration decisions can also be appealed to the VAT and Duties Tribunal.

Criminal offences

The Money Laundering Regulations 2007 provide for criminal sanctions for failure to comply with the detailed requirements of the regulations, by fine or prison sentence of up to two years. This includes failures relating to registration, customer due diligence, ongoing monitoring, verification, ceasing transactions, enhanced due diligence, record keeping and training. These are in additions to offences under POCA 2002 or the Terrorism Act 2000.

Countering tax avoidance

22.　　There is currently no general anti-avoidance rule in the UK although a consultative document on GAAR was published in 1998. Historically, taxpayers have been entitled to rely on a strict interpretation of tax law to minimise their taxes, and professional advisers have been entitled to assist them in doing so.

　　This principle has been changed by the decision of the European Court of Justice on 21 February 2006 concerning a VAT repayment claimed by the Halifax Bank, which had set up a separate company to maximise a claim to VAT on the construction of a call centre. The court confirmed that it was not permissible to exploit the VAT provisions abusively, but instead that the purpose of the legislation had to be established and taken into account. As this decision affects indirect taxes, its application to direct taxes is yet to be clarified.

　　In the *Halifax* case, however, the court stated that the fact that a company was trying to minimise tax was not in itself a sufficient reason to look through the arrangements. In an opinion dated 2 May 2006, an advocate general of the European Court of Justice gave the opinion that establishing a subsidiary in another EC state so as to take advantage of a more favourable tax regime was legitimate, and anti-avoidance provisions such as the UK's CFC rules should be targeted at 'wholly artificial arrangements'.

　　There are many measures addressing non-compliance with existing tax law, which are covered in context throughout this publication. The government's and HMRC's anti-avoidance campaign is concerned with situations where weaknesses or anomalies in the law are exploited abusively to give unintended advantages, particularly where artificial transactions are concerned.

　　Tax avoidance is addressed in two main ways:

- specific anti-avoidance rules;
- the disclosure of tax avoidance schemes (DOTAS).

　　However, a principles-based anti-avoidance approach is being considered for tax-privileged returns on financial products.

　　FA 2009 introduces two new anti avoidance provisions that include a principles based approach. Section 49 disguised interest and s 49 transfers of income streams. It will be interesting to see how the courts interpret these provisions and whether they mark the beginning of a principles based rewrite of much more tax legislation.

　　HMRC have introduced a system of online alerts as part of the attempts to counter avoidance. The spotlight service will identify examples of avoidance schemes that the Revenue has reason to believe are ineffective and that they would challenge when encountered.

Specific anti-avoidance rules

23.　　There are a very large number of specific anti-avoidance provisions throughout tax legislation, designed to prevent exploitation of specific rules to give unintended tax advantages. It is not possible to give a comprehensive list, but examples include: the dividend stripping rules; the transfer pricing rules; rules concerning transactions in land; and the controlled foreign companies (CFC) rules.

　　Tax avoidance seeks to remain within the existing law, while manipulating or abusing it to obtain tax advantages that it was not intended to confer, and often involves artificial transactions or entities whose main purpose is to obtain tax advantages. Because anti-avoidance law is intended to ensure that existing law achieves its purpose, it may be brought to bear on transactions carried out for purely commercial reasons, or on persons who believed they were complying fully with the law.

Avoidance and anti-avoidance gives rise to considerable uncertainty for many taxpayers who are not seeking to abuse the tax system.

In the *Garnett v Jones* case, the company was acting in a way that most of the tax and accountancy profession believed to be fully compliant with tax law. HMRC used the anti-avoidance provision of s 660A, originally dating back to the 1930s, to seek to cancel the tax advantage obtained by paying dividends. See Example 59 explanatory note 12 for comments on the *Garnett v Jones* case.

Taxpayers are advised to bear anti-avoidance legislation in mind, to ensure that they do not fall foul of it even with structures or transactions that have no tax avoidance purpose. For example, in the field of personal taxes, the setting up of any trust is likely to have tax consequences, gifts made to assist relatives may well fall foul of the pre-owned assets charge.

Disclosure of Tax Avoidance Schemes (DOTAS)

24. The Disclosure of Tax Avoidance Schemes rules aim to deter the use of schemes that are abusive or involve artificial transactions, or exploit loopholes that parliament did not intend, by allowing HMRC to detect and close them down more quickly, perhaps with retrospective effect.

     The provisions are not intended to prevent tax advisers from advising their clients of the tax reliefs intended by legislation, nor to prevent taxpayers minimising their taxes within the framework of the tax legislation, provided that by sticking to the letter of the law they are not abusing the purpose of the law.

     The Disclosure of Tax Avoidance Schemes regime began on 1 August 2004, when it was limited to financial products and arrangements connected with employment. There is a requirement to disclose schemes providing a tax advantage in income tax, corporation tax, capital gains tax, VAT, SDLT and, from 1 May 2007, national insurance contributions (NICs).

     ● The definitions of arrangements and tax advantage are very widely drawn: an arrangement includes any scheme, transaction or series of transactions;

     ● an advantage includes increases in relief or repayment, reduction or avoidance of amounts assessable, deferral of tax, or any avoidance of the obligation to account for or deduct tax.

     For corporation tax, income tax and capital gains tax, schemes must fall within prescribed conditions, or 'hallmarks' to be disclosable. The hallmarks for a promoter's scheme, which are found in The Tax Avoidance Schemes (Prescribed Descriptions of Arrangements) Regulations 2006 (SI 2006/1543), are as follows.

     ● Hallmark 1: Confidentiality from other promoters.

     ● Hallmark 2: Confidentiality from HMRC.

     ● Hallmark 3: Premium fee.

     ● Hallmark 4: Off-market terms (involving financial products).

     ● Hallmark 5: Standardised tax products.

     ● Hallmark 6: Loss schemes.

     ● Hallmark 7: Leasing arrangements.

     If arrangements exist that provide a tax advantage, and one or any of these hallmarks apply, the promoter must notify HMRC within five days of the scheme becoming available. The scheme will be issued with an eight-digit reference number, which users must show on their tax returns. If the scheme is not disclosed by the promoter, for example if the promoter is offshore, the user must make the disclosure within 30 days. The maximum penalty for initial failure to disclose is £5,000, plus £600 per day thereafter.

Schemes meeting the hallmark tests may not constitute avoidance, but may still need to be disclosed, and it may be necessary to disclose schemes of which HMRC are already aware. HMRC guidance, together with appropriate forms, is found at http://www.hmrc.gov.uk/aiu/index.htm.

FA 2007 s 108 gives HMRC the power to enquire into reasons for non-disclosure, and increases HMRC's powers to police the scheme.

The advice provided to the client in this example is in reaction to specific circumstances, and is not a scheme. It does not cause any hallmarks to apply, and is therefore not notifiable. The legislation is aimed at schemes of far wider scope, and larger potential tax saving.

The rules for an in-house scheme are different, with the following hallmarks.

- Hallmark 2: Confidentiality from HMRC.

- Hallmark 3: Premium fee.

- Hallmark 7: Leasing arrangements.

An in-house scheme is only notifiable if it is intended to give a tax advantage to a business that is not a small or medium-sized enterprise.

Additional exemptions from disclosure apply to the leasing hallmark, one of which is that schemes providing an advantage to SMEs need not be disclosed.

The budget 2009 announced a review and further consultation regarding DOTAS with a view to extending the number of situations in which HMRC have to receive notification of planning.

International information and gathering powers

25.   FA 2006 ss 174–177 provide for the cancellation of existing agreements to exchange information with overseas tax authorities, and replace them with arrangements giving increased powers to collect and disclose information. In addition, it provides for the possibility of recovery of foreign tax debts through UK courts, and therefore the recovery of UK tax debts in foreign courts.

These powers will probably have a greater effect on tax fraud rather than tax avoidance. Furthermore, HMRC obtained disclosure orders against banks, requiring them to disclose details of all offshore accounts held by customers with UK addresses and details of holders of credit cards linked to offshore accounts. This move does not change existing law, but has the effect of policing it more stringently.

Accounting Standards, tax law and IFRS

26.   The relationship between accounting practice and law is stated in FA 1998 s 42: 'the profits of the trade, profession or vocation must be computed in accordance with generally accepted accounting practice subject to any adjustment required or authorised by law …'

Generally Accepted Accounting Practice (GAAP) is defined in FA 2004 s 50 as follows: 'UK generally accepted accounting practice means generally accepted accounting practice with respect to accounts of UK companies (other than IFRS accounts) that are intended to give a true and fair view …' The same section specifies that this definition applies to individuals, non-UK companies and entities other than companies.

As GAAP is increasingly codified and becoming more uniform, there is a trend to align profits for tax with accounting profits. Furthermore, it is the intention of the ASB to align UK GAAP with IFRS, which is already similar to it in many respects. The International Accounting Standards Board (IASB) is working with the US FASB on the global convergence of accounting standards. The European Commission has adopted most international accounting standards, with some exceptions from IFRS 39. FA 2004 s 50 makes it clear that accounts will be regarded as complying with generally accepted accounting practice whether full IFRS standards, or EEC approved standards, are used.

European law required listed companies to use IFRS for accounting periods commencing on or after 1 January 2005 for their consolidated accounts. However, all UK companies and limited liability partnerships may adopt IFRS for their consolidated and individual accounts from that date. Listed companies will have to adopt IFRS under European law, larger companies may choose to adopt IFRS, while other companies will continue to comply with GAAP, which is actively being aligned with IFRS.

It is the intention of the legislation that companies drawing up their accounts under either set of standards should receive broadly equivalent tax treatment. This will of course be increasingly achieved as IFRS and GAAP converge in the next few years.

While it is government policy to align tax and accounting profits, there will continue to be departures from the accounting rules, whether from IFRS-based accounts or from UK GAAP. There are a great many departures, arising from public policy, in the areas of anti-avoidance, the distinctions between capital and revenue, fiscal incentives or valuation rules. Examples are given in context throughout the publication, and particularly in Example 49.

Question

Tweeters Ltd has traded as a manufacturer of specialist hi-fi speakers since 1968 and has no associated companies. Accounts have previously always been prepared for years ended 31 March. The following information relates to the period of account for eighteen months ended 30 September 2009.

(a) Trading profits as adjusted for tax purposes but *before* making any adjustment for capital allowances are summarised as follows:

	£
Trading profits after finance costs	2,391,770
Add: Depreciation	160,000
Disallowable legal costs	5,780
Charitable donations to CAFOD (see (e) below)	36,000
Entertaining	15,250
	2,608,800
Less: Investment income	(77,600)
Additional 75%* on research and development expenditure of £80,000	(60,000)
Adjusted trading profits before capital allowances	2,471,200

As research and development (R&D) expenditure of £80,000 (all eligible under Chapter 2 of Part 13 of CTA 2009) has been written off in the period, a further £60,000 deduction has been made to bring the overall R&D tax credit up to 175% of the qualifying R&D expenditure, as all of the expenditure was incurred after 1 August 2008. Tweeters Ltd qualifies as a medium-sized enterprise for R & D purposes (CTA 2009 s 1119).

(b) The written down value of the plant and machinery allowances pool at 31 March 2008 was £300,000. On 21 February 2009 plant which had cost £100,000 in August 1989 was sold for £196,800 and plant costing £80,000 was acquired on 10 September 2009. Tweeters Ltd qualifies as a medium-sized company for Companies Act purposes.

(c) Investment income was:

			£
(i)	Bank deposit interest received		
	30 June 2008	3,000	
	31 December 2008	2,500	
	30 June 2009	5,500	11,000
(ii)	Building society interest received 1 January 2009		2,000
(iii)	Gross debenture interest receivable from Dovedale plc (£100,000 at 8.4% per annum) (received half yearly on 1 March and 1 September)		12,600
(iv)	Dividends from UK companies		
	May 2007 (27,000 + tax cr 3,000)	30,000	
	May 2008 (18,000 + tax cr 2,000)	20,000	50,000

The opening and closing accruals in respect of (i) to (iii) were as follows:

	At 1.4.08 £	At 30.9.09 £
Bank interest	1,100	3,000
Building society interest	1,400	1,500

	At 1.4.08 £	At 30.9.09 £
Debenture interest	700	700

(d)   Interest at 10% per annum is paid on 1 July each year on a loan of £200,000 from Mr Woofer. Mr Woofer is a controlling shareholder of Tweeters Ltd and lent the money to provide additional working capital for trading purposes.

(e)   Gift Aid donations were paid to CAFOD (a UK charity) on 30 April each year amounting to £25,000 per annum (gross amounts).

(f)   A dividend of £800,000 was paid on 1 March 2009.

(g)   Indexation allowance for the period August 1989 to February 2009 is 82.6%.

(h)   Calculate the company's corporation tax liability for eighteen months ended 30 September 2009.

(i)   State the main conditions required for an R&D tax relief claim under CTA 2009 Part 13 Chapter 2.

(j)   Calculate the corporation tax payments due for that period (based on the final liability), stating the relevant due dates of payment. (In recent years Tweeters Ltd has always paid tax at the main rate.)

(k)   Show any amount required to be reported on Form CT 61 (quarterly return of income tax) for the eighteen months to 30 September 2009.

Answer

(1) Corporation Tax Liability

		12 months to 31.3.09	6 months to 30.9.09
Schedule D Case I	£	£	£
Trading profits (see note 3) (365:183 days)		1,645,910	825,210
Less: Capital allowances: plant and machinery			
Year to 31 March 2009			
WDV at 31 March 2008	300,000		
Sale proceeds 21 February 2009			
(elimination from pool is limited to cost)	(100,000)		
	200,000		
WDA 20%	(40,000)	(40,000)	
	160,000		
6 months to 30 September 2009			
Addition 10 September 2009 (part)	25,000		
AIA @£50,000 × (6/12)	(25,000)		(25,000)
WDA 20% x 6/12		(16,000)	(16,000)
Addition 10 September 2009 (balance)	55,000		
FYA 40%	(22,000)	33,000	(22,000)
WDV cf		177,000	
		1,605,910	762,210
Schedule D Case III (see explanatory note 7)			
Bank deposit interest		8,600	4,300
Building society interest		1,400	700
Debenture interest		8,400	4,200
Chargeable gain:			
Plant sale proceeds (February 2008)	196,800		
Less: Cost	100,000		
Unindexed gain	96,800		
Less: Indexation allowance			
100,000 @ 82.6%	82,600		
Gain after indexation allowance		14,200	
		1,638,510	771,410
Less: charges on income:			
Gift Aid donations paid		(25,000)	(25,000)
Profits chargeable to corporation tax		1,613,510	748,410
Corporation tax thereon:			
FY 2008 1,613,510 at 28%		451,783	
FY 2009 748,410 at 28%*			209,555
Mainstream corporation tax liability		451,783	209,555

* Profits for small companies' rate are £748,410 plus FII £20,000 = £768,810, therefore marginal small companies' rate does not apply.

(2)   **Main conditions for a research and development tax relief claim under Chapter 2 of Part 13 CTA 2009**

Small and medium-sized companies (see below) are able to claim special research and development (R&D) tax relief equal to 175%, capped at €7.5 million per project, (150% in respect of expenditure incurred before 1 August 2008) of their qualifying research and development expenditure provided they spend more than £10,000 in an accounting period (reduced pro rata for periods of less than 12 months). This means, in effect, that an additional 75% trading deduction is given, making 175%, in all (previously 150%). For these purposes, R&D is as defined in accordance with generally accepted accounting practice (particularly SSAP 13) as qualified by the BERR guidelines on the topic entitled 'Guidelines on the meaning of Research and Development for Tax Purposes', adopted by SI 2004/712.

The R&D tax relief is given as a deduction in arriving at the trading profits for the accounting period. In the example, the deductions given in the 12 months to 31 March 2009 and 6 months to 30 September 2009 represent 175% of the amounts allowable as a deduction in computing Tweeters Ltd's trading profits (the trading deductions in each period being the time-apportioned amounts of the R&D expenditure).

The main conditions for the special R&D relief for SME's on their own R & D expenditure under CTA 2009 Part 13 Chapter 2 are as follows:

- The claimant company is a small or medium-sized enterprise under the EU regulations. This means that the company (together with any company in which it controls more than 25% of the capital or voting rights) has:

  –   fewer than 500 employees *and*

  –   annual turnover not exceeding €100 million (approx £86 million), *or*

  –   gross balance sheet totals not exceeding € 86 million (approx £74 million).

  These limits were half the amounts stated above prior to 1 August 2008 (FA 2007 s 50 and SI 2008/1880).

  A company ceases to qualify as a small or medium-sized enterprise if it fails the above definition for two consecutive periods, although if the limit is exceeded by virtue of takeover on or after 1 December 2008, the change takes effect from the beginning of the accounting period , not the end (Revenue & Customs Brief 55/08).

- The R&D expenditure is of a revenue nature (ie not capital expenditure, although 100% R&D capital allowances may be available on capital expenditure, but relief is not denied by virtue of the cost being capitalised for accounting purposes.

- The expenditure relates to the company's trade, an extension of that trade, or a trade that will be derived from the R&D.

- The expenditure relates only to staffing costs (as defined in CTA 2009 s 1123), and to software or consumable items (as defined by CTA 2009 s 1125) or to R&D contracted out to someone else.

- Any intellectual property created from the R&D, such as know-how, patents etc, vests in the company or jointly with the company and others.

- The R&D does not relate to activities that have been contracted out to the company by any person (but see explanatory note 10 re separate relief for work contracted out by a qualifying large company).

- The R&D spending is not subsidised by the State or any other party (the R&D tax relief being ignored for this purpose).

To assist companies not yet in profit, companies may 'surrender' their unused relief to obtain a cash tax credit equal to up to 24% of the actual R&D cost. See explanatory note 9 for further details.

The definition of R&D expenditure is complex. Essentially R&D requires that the company undertook a project to resolve a scientific of technological uncertainty where the answer is not readily deducible or available to a competent professional working in the field. Claimants need to be sure that their expenditure falls within it before making a claim. The claim should be supported by a brief written statement explaining this scientific or technological advance. Claims must be made, amended or withdrawn on the company's corporation tax return, within one year of the anniversary of the filing date.

(3) **Corporation tax payments**

	Year to 31.3.08 £	6 months to 30.9.08 £
Mainstream corporation tax payable as in (1)	451,783	209,555
Due dates of payment:		
14 October 2008	112,946	
14 January 2009	112,946	
14 April 2009	112,946	
14 July 2009	112,945	
14 October 2009	–	104,778
14 January 2010	–	104,777
	451,783	209,555

In practice, Tweeters Ltd would make instalment payments based on its *estimated* tax liability for the relevant periods, making appropriate adjustments to the payments when it had finalised its self-assessed liability. HMRC would compare the estimated payments with the payments which should have been made based on the final liability and calculate the appropriate (underpaid) debit interest or (overpaid) credit interest up to the normal nine month due date when the normal interest rates apply. The interest will be reflected on the company's statement.

(4) **Accounting for income tax (ICTA 1988 Sch 16)**

Period	Date due	£	Tax deducted from interest etc paid Tax rate	£	Payable to Inland Revenue £
Year ended 31.3.09					
Qr to 30.6.2008 no return required					
Qr to 30.9.2008	14.10.2008	20,000	20%	4,000	4,000
Qr to 31.12.2008 no return required					
Qr to 31.3.2009 no return required					
					4,000
6 months ended 30.9.09					
Qr to 30.6.2009 no return required					
Qr to 30.9.2009	14.10.2009	20,000	20%	4,000	4,000

Explanatory Notes

Chargeable accounting periods

1. Full notes on the computation of profits for corporation tax are in Example 49.

2. (a) Corporation tax rates are fixed for financial years (defined as the year beginning 1 April), but corporation tax assessments are made by reference to chargeable accounting periods, and the profits arising in an accounting period are apportioned on a time basis between the financial years in which the accounting period falls in order to determine the rate of corporation tax applicable (CTA 2009 s 8(5)).

    (b) An accounting period of a company begins whenever:

    (i) the company, not then being within the charge to corporation tax, comes within it, whether by the company becoming resident in the UK or acquiring a source of income, or otherwise, or

    (ii) an accounting period of the company ends without the company then ceasing to be within the charge to corporation tax (CTA 2009 s 9(1)).

    (c) An accounting period of a company ends on the first occurrence of any of the following (CTA 2009 ss 10(1) and 12):

    (i) twelve months after the beginning of the accounting period

    (ii) an accounting date of the company or, if there is a period for which the company does not make up accounts, the day before the date from which accounts are made up

    (iii) the company beginning or ceasing to trade or to be, in respect of the trade or (if more than one) of all the trades carried on by it, within the charge to corporation tax

    (iv) the company beginning or ceasing to be resident in the UK

    (v) the company ceasing to be within the charge to corporation tax

    (vi) the commencement of winding-up of the company (following which accounting periods end at twelve monthly intervals until the completion of the winding-up).

    Since the period for which Tweeters Ltd has made up accounts exceeds twelve months, the eighteen month period ended 30 September 2009 must be divided into two chargeable periods, the year to 31 March 2009 and the six months to 30 September 2009.

Allocating profits and losses to accounting periods

3. CTA 2009 s 52(2) provides that where it is *necessary* in order to arrive at profits or losses of an accounting period to apportion profits/losses to specific periods, the apportionment is made according to the days in the respective periods (S 52(3)). In exceptional circumstances, a more accurate measure of profits may be obtained other than by time-apportionment, in which case time-apportionment is not *necessary* (*Marshall Hus & Ptnrs Ltd v Bolton* (1981)).

4. Except for interest, in respect of which there are special rules (see explanatory note 7) and income from intangible fixed assets, such as patent royalties (see Example 66), a company's other sources of income are dealt with in the chargeable period in which they arise, using income tax principles. Capital gains and losses are dealt with in the chargeable period in which the disposal is made (TCGA 1992 s 8). Where gains and losses on disposal relate to a company's 'loan relationships' they are included in calculating income rather than capital gains (see Example 63). The same applies to gains and losses on intangible fixed assets, although a special rollover relief applies where intangible fixed assets are replaced.

5.   For capital allowances purposes, additions and disposals are dealt with in the chargeable accounting period in which they occur.

6.   Charges on income (the charitable Gift Aid donations in this example) are deducted in the chargeable period in which they are paid, not as they accrue (ICTA 1988 s 338(1)).

Treatment of interest paid and received

7.   Interest paid and received is normally taken into account on an accruals basis (see Example 63 for details). If the interest relates to the trade (which, except for financial businesses, will usually apply only to interest *payable*), it is incorporated within the Schedule D Case I result of the period of account, which is time apportioned over the chargeable accounting periods if the period of account exceeds twelve months. As far as non-trading interest is concerned, the same treatment would normally be used to arrive at the amounts included in the Schedule D Case III profit or deficit, unless the amounts involved were material and time-apportionment would not give a fair result.

      In this example, the loan interest paid will already be deducted in arriving at the trading profits. The non-trading interest received over the period to 30 September 2009 is arrived at as follows and has been time-apportioned as shown:

	£	To 31.3.09 £	To 30.9.09 £
Bank interest (11,000 – 1,100 + 3,000)	12,900	8,600	4,300
Building society interest (2,000 – 1,400 + 1,500)	2,100	1,400	700
Debenture interest (12,600 – 700 + 700)	12,600	8,400	4,200

Research and development (R&D) tax reliefs

8.   Where *any* trader either incurs revenue expenditure on research and development related to his trade, or pays a sum to an approved scientific research association, university, college or research institute to be used for that purpose, the expenditure is deductible as a trading expense of the accounting period in which it is incurred (CTA 2009 ss 87 and 88).

9.   The special 175% enhanced tax deduction for R&D revenue expenditure by small/medium-sized (SME) companies summarised in part (2) of the example was introduced by FA 2000 s 69 and Sch 20. Tax law rewrite has now included R & D relief at CTA 2009 Part 13.

      The SME scheme differs from the large company scheme in that it can lead to repayable tax credits. Losses attributable to qualifying revenue R&D expenditure may, subject to conditions, be surrendered for a tax credit equating to 16% of the loss enhanced at 150%, or 14% of the loss enhanced at 175%.

      HM Treasury wished to extend eligibility for the enhanced tax deduction to a wider range of companies, so FA 2007 s 50 doubled the criteria for qualifying as an SME to 500 employees and €100 million turnover or €86 million net assets, with effect from 1 August 2008. Furthermore, FA 2008 s 24 increased the rate of relief from 150% to 175% in relation to expenditure incurred on or after that date. The maximum relief available under this scheme and the vaccines research scheme is capped at €7.5 million per project in relation to relief claimed on or after 1 August 2008 with the balance claimable under the large companies scheme (CTA 2009 Part 13 Chapter 8, at s 1113).

      Relief is available only to a claimant that is a going concern (CTA 2009 ss 1046 and 1057). A company is a going concern if the latest accounts were published on a going concern basis, and expectation of tax credits was not the only reason for adopting the going concern basis.

      For pre-trading R&D expenditure, the company may elect to treat the 175% deduction as a trading loss for that pre-trading period and it will not then be treated as incurred on the first day of trading under the normal rules (CTA 2009 s 1045) (see Example 49 explanatory note 6).

Where the effect of the deduction is to give a trading loss, the normal company loss reliefs will apply. Where a trading loss is attributable to the 175% R&D relief, this part of the loss can be 'surrendered' for a tax repayment (ie R&D credit) from HMRC equal to 14% of the surrendered loss. However, the R&D credit is restricted to the total amount of the company's PAYE and Class 1 national insurance payments for the relevant accounting period. For this purpose the PAYE/NI for the tax months (to 5th of each month) ending in the accounting period would be taken. Say, for example, a company spent £120,000 on R&D (on revenue account) so the R&D tax deduction at 175% was £210,000. The PAYE/NI for the period was £21,000. In this case the maximum potential R&D tax refund would be £29,400 (= 14% of £210,000) but the R&D tax credit repayment would be restricted to £21,000. The repayment represents a trading loss of £150,000, leaving an unused loss available to carry forward of £60,000 (£210,000 less £150,000).

10. A similar R&D tax relief is available for 'large' companies (ie non-SME companies – see explanatory note 9 above). Large companies may claim an enhanced R&D tax deduction equal to 130% (125% prior to 1 April 2008) of qualifying R&D expenditure (the rules are contained in CTA 2009 Part 13 Chapter 5, starting at s 1074). Although similar to the SME provisions, the relief for large companies is given at a lower rate and there is no corresponding provision allowing for a cash repayment in loss-making situations.

   Where a company carries out R&D on its own behalf, the qualifying rules include the same provisions as for SMEs in relation to the qualifying threshold of £10,000 per 12-month period, the requirement for the expenditure not to be capital in nature and to be incurred on staffing costs, consumables, software or utility costs, and for the company to be a trading company.

   The principal difference from the SME relief relates to subcontracted R&D, as it is possible for a subcontractor to claim under the 'large' company rules even where it will not be the owner of the intellectual property developed, and also for the relief to be claimed by a small/medium-sized subcontractor working for the large company. There are also provisions giving the enhanced relief where a large company makes contributions to special defined bodies or individuals conducting R&D which is relevant to the trade of the company concerned.

11. A special 40% relief (50% before 1 August 2008) is available to companies, over and above the normal or enhanced R&D deductions dealt with in notes 8 to 10 above, in respect of qualifying expenditure on research and development relating to vaccines and medicines for TB, malaria, HIV and AIDS, and contributions to independent research into such vaccines or medicines (CTA 2009 Part 13 Chapter 7).

Quarterly accounting for income tax

12. A company has to make a return under ICTA 1988 Sch 16 to account for any income tax it has deducted in the return period from patent royalties (see Example 49 explanatory note 13), interest and any charges on income (such payments being referred to as 'relevant payments'), subject to a set-off for any income tax suffered on taxed income. The return must be made within fourteen days after the end of the return period on Form CT 61.

   The return periods are the calendar quarters to 31 March, 30 June, 30 September and 31 December. If a company's accounting period does not end on one of those dates, however, the company must make up returns to each of those dates and also a return ending on the last day of the accounting period.

   Taxed receipts and payments are brought into the quarterly accounting system according to when they are received and paid. Where, looking at the cumulative position during a chargeable accounting period, too much income tax has been accounted for owing to later receipts of taxed income, the excess payments to HMRC are repayable upon completion of the appropriate CT 61 return form. HMRC will not, however, repay sums in excess of those already paid to them in the accounting period. Such excesses can be used to cover the company's liability on later payments in the same accounting period, any balance being treated as indicated in note 13. The rate of tax deducted from interest is 20%. The rate of tax deducted from other taxed amounts such as patent royalties is the basic rate, presently also 20% (22% prior to 6 April 2008).

As demonstrated in part (4) of the example, considerably fewer CT61 returns are now required, as a result of changes made in recent Finance Acts (see Example 49 explanatory notes 11 and 13 for details). Thus in the example Tweeters Ltd receives its debenture interest from Dovedale plc gross, but must withhold 20% tax from its loan interest payments to Mr Woofer, since tax must still be deducted from interest payments to individuals (other than on quoted Eurobonds). Companies are still required to deduct tax on payments of annual interest, patent royalties and any annual payments where they are made to individuals, trustees (other than trustees of exempt bodies), or non-residents (such as overseas group or associate companies), and will suffer tax if they receive payments such as patent royalties from individuals.

Excess income tax suffered

13.   If at the end of an accounting period more income tax has been suffered on taxed income than the company is liable to account for in respect of its taxed payments, the excess income tax is set off against the corporation tax bill for the relevant accounting period (see explanatory note 14). If it should *exceed* the corporation tax bill, then the balance will be *repaid to the company*. Since the majority of UK source investment income is now paid on a 'gross' basis, such situations are likely to be rare. However, in such cases, companies claim repayment of excess income tax suffered when they submit corporation tax returns (ICTA 1988 s 7).

14.   Companies are not *required* to set off income tax suffered against income tax payable under the Schedule 16 quarterly return procedure, and may if they wish set the whole amount against the corporation tax payable for the relevant accounting period (ICTA 1988 s 7(2) and Sch 16 paras 5 and 7). In most cases, it will only be *excess* income tax suffered that is set against corporation tax payable. The relevant accounting period in which excess income tax suffered is set off is that in which the related income is taken into account (ICTA 1988 s 7(2)).

Payment of corporation tax

15.   Corporation tax self-assessment applies to both accounting periods in this example. As Tweeters Ltd is a 'large' company paying tax at the full rate for both periods, it is liable to pay its (self-assessed) corporation tax for these periods under the quarterly instalment payment (QIP) regime.

For the twelve months to 31 March 2009, the company must pay its corporation tax in four equal instalments on 14 October 2008, 14 January 2009, 14 April 2009 and 14 July 2009.

For the following accounting period (six months to 30 September 2009), the company must pay the full amount of tax in two equal instalments as follows:

1st instalment	(6 months and 13 days after 1.4.2009)	14 October 2009
Final instalment	(3 months and 14 days after 30.9.2009)	14 January 2010

In practice, Tweeters Ltd would pay instalments based on its *estimated* liability at the due dates, with interest being charged or credited on underpayments or overpayments as compared with the final liability.

Capital gains rollover relief

16.   If the plant sold in this example is fixed plant, the company may claim rollover relief in respect of the chargeable gain if the proceeds are reinvested in other business assets acquired within one year before and three years after the date of disposal (see Example 82 for details).

If, on the other hand, the plant sold (or the replacement plant) is not fixed plant but moveable plant, then rollover relief is not available.

Research spin-out companies

17. FA 2005 ss 20–22 introduced into statute provisions relating to research spin-out companies, but unfortunately Tweeters Ltd is unable to make use of this very specialised relief. It applies in the context of scientific research organisations (SROs) (which may comprise universities, NHS trusts, or the Ministry of Defence), who share intellectual property (IP) with their employees by setting up spin-out companies to exploit the IP. Employees receive shares in the newly formed company, which constitute remuneration from employment liable to income tax and NIC. The relief serves to defer the tax charge to the time of disposal of the shares, when the value will be known, and funds will have been generated. The relief works by deeming the value of the IP to be nil provided the employee receives shares before the transfer of the IP or within 183 days of the transfer.

Question

Streetfield Ltd, which has no associated companies, had made up its accounts to 30 September since its incorporation in 1978, but decided after the accounting year to 30 September 2007 to make up a six-month account to 31 March 2008.

The results of recent periods were:

	Year ended 30.9.05	Year ended 30.9.06	Year ended 30.9.07 £	6 mths ended 31.3.08 £	Year ended 31.3.09 £
Adjusted trading profit (loss)	210,000	32,000	15,000	84,500	(210,000)
Loan relationship non trading profit – interest on debenture stock of Lane plc	2,000	2,000	2,000	1,000	2,000
Capital gains	–	–	–	–	20,500

Having reorganised the business following its difficult trading period, the company has recently secured a major new contract and a (taxable) trading profit of some £320,000 is anticipated for the year to 31 March 2010. The company will continue to receive the debenture interest.

Corporation tax rates during the period have been as follows:

Year ended 31 March

	2006	2007	2008	2009 & 2010
Full rate on profits over £1,500,000	30%	30%	30%	28%
Small companies' rate on profits up to £300,000	19%	19%	20%	21%
Effective marginal rate on profits between £300,000 and £1,500,000	32.75%	32.75%	32.5%	29.75%
Starting rate on profits up to £10,000	0%	19%	20%	21%
Effective marginal rate on profits between £10,000 and £50,000	23.75%	N/A	N/A	N/A

(a) Illustrate the alternative ways in which relief may be obtained for the trading loss of the year to 31 March 2009, stating the time limits within which any claims must be made.

(b) Indicate what the position would be if the company had made a Gift Aid donation to a charity of £1,000 gross on 31 March each year.

Answer

(a) **The loss claims available in respect of the loss of the year to 31 March 2009 are as follows:**

1. The adjusted trading loss of £210,000 can be carried forward under ICTA 1988 s 393(1) to set against future profits of the *same trade* (not any other income nor chargeable gains). If the anticipated trading profit of £320,000 is made in the year to 31 March 2010, relief for the loss will be obtained in that year, reducing the corporation tax payable on 1 January 2011.

   If this alternative is adopted, Streetfield Ltd will have profits chargeable to corporation tax for the year ended 31 March 2009 of £22,500 taxable at the small companies' rate of 21%.

2. Alternatively a claim may be made under s 393A to set the loss against the *total profits* of the same accounting period, viz.

Trading loss for year ended 31 March 2009	210,000
Set against total profits before charges of same accounting period	22,500
Leaving a balance unrelieved of	£187,500

   which may be carried forward under s 393(1).

   On its own, there would only be a small tax saving from this claim, because there is only £22,500 profit chargeable to corporation tax in the year to 31 March 2009, the tax on which amounts to £4,725 (22,500 @ 21%). The claim against any current profits is, however, a prerequisite if the company wishes to claim under the provisions of note 3 below.

3. After a claim has been made under 2 above, then alternatively to carrying the unrelieved trading loss of £187,500 forward it may be carried back to set against the *total* profits of accounting periods ending wholly or partly within the previous three years, latest first. Results are apportioned where, as in this example, an accounting period falls only partly within the three year period. Any unrelieved balance is then carried forward. Section 393A provides that when losses are carried back, the set-off in the earlier period(s) is restricted so as not to interfere with relief for *trade* charges (but non-trade charges are not protected). There is a limit, however, to how much loss can be carried back by more than twelve months. Of the loss only £50,000 may be carried back against profits in the 24 months preceding the twelve months before the loss.

   The carryback claim is as follows:

	£	£
Unrelieved loss of year to 31 March 2009 as above		187,500
Set against total profits of six months to 31 March 2008:		
Trading profits	84,500	
Loan interest	1,000	
		(85,500)
Set against total profits of year to 30 September 2007:		
Trading profits	15,000	
Debenture interest	2,000	
		(17,000)
Set against total profits of year to 30 September 2006		
Trading profits	32,000	
Debenture interest	2,000	

	£	£
		(34,000)
Set against one half of total profits of year to 30 September 2005		
Trading profits	105,000	
Debenture interest	1,000	
	106,000	
Loss set off (see explanatory note 5)	7,500	(7,500)
Leaving taxable profits of	98,500	
Loss carried forward under s 393(1)		43,500

4. Losses that are carried forward under s 393(1) are set off automatically against later trading profits without the need for a claim. The time limit for making current and carryback claims under s 393A is two years after the end of the loss period, ie by 31 March 2011 or within such further period as HMRC may allow.

5. (i) The anticipated results for the year to 31 March 2010 are:

Trading profits	320,000
Profit on non trading loan relationship (say)	2,000
	£322,000

The company therefore expects to have £22,000 profits in the marginal small companies' rate tranche. Since there would be a loss carried forward of £43,500 after the carryback claim, the benefit of setting off losses against profits chargeable at the higher marginal corporation tax rate shown on page 53.1 would be available whichever loss claim is made, and the balance of carry forward loss relief would be at the then small companies' rate of 21%. The rate of tax saved through the carryback loss claims varies, although some of the loss will be relieved against profit within the nil-rate band in 2006.

Although there is a small tax liability for the current year to 31 March 2009 of £4,500, the maximum tax saving of £46,025 is made by carrying the loss forward, to relieve tax at the marginal rate and at the increased small companies' rate applicable in the future.

If the loss is carried back under s 393A, usage will be as follows:

	Profit/ (Loss)	Loss Relief		Tax Saving
01.04.05 to 30.09.05	105,000	7,500	@ 19%	1,425
1.10.05 to 31.3.06	5,000	5,000	@ 0%	0
	12,000	12,000	@ 23.75%	2,850
01.04.06 to 30.09.06	17,000	17,000	@ 19%	3,230
01.10.06 to 31.03.07	8,500	8,500	@ 19%	1,615
01.04.07 to 30.09.07	8,700	8,500	@ 20%	1,700
01.10.07 to 31.03.08	85,500	85,500	@20%	17,100
01.04.08 to 31.03.09	(210,000)			
	22,500	22,500	@ 21%	4,725
01.04.09 to	322,000	22,000	@ 29.75%	6,545

	Profit/ (Loss)	Loss Relief		Tax Saving
31.03.10		21,500	@ 21%	4,515
		210,000		43,678

If the loss is carried forward under s 393(1):

	Profit/ (Loss)	Loss Relief		Tax Saving
01.04.08 to 31.03.09	(210,000) 22,500	0 0		
01.04.09 to 31.03.10	322,000	22,000	@ 29.75%	6,545
		188,000	@ 21%	39,480
		210,000		46,025

The saving arises largely because small companies' rates rose through this period.

(ii)   The other factors to be considered in relation to the loss claims are the time when the tax saving will occur and whether any repayments will be boosted by tax-free interest.

Given that the carryback claim avoids payment of the 2009 liability of £4,500, and brings a cash advantage of £43,678 forward by about a year, the Streetfield directors are likely to give the carryback option serious consideration. There is an obvious cash flow advantage in a carryback claim, and it may be possible to bring forward the date of repayment by prompt filing of the tax return and the claim.

(iii) To the extent that the loss is carried forward, the relief will reduce the corporation tax payable on 1 January 2011. Relief against current or earlier profits will either result in tax not yet paid being discharged, or in tax being repaid.

(iv)   Any repayment for the earlier years would attract interest, if any, from 1 January 2010, except for the six months to 31 March 2008, for which interest would run from 1 January 2009 (see explanatory note 7).

(b)   **If Streetfield Ltd had paid £1,000 gross annually on 31 March to a charity under Gift Aid**

A Gift Aid donation to charity is a charge on a company's income, but can only be deducted where there are profits available to cover it. (Excess charges may, however, be surrendered under the group relief provisions whether they are trade charges or non-trade charges – see Example 64 explanatory note 5.) Where losses are carried back, it is only trade charges that are protected, not non-trade charges. Few payments are treated as trade charges, so they will be encountered very infrequently.

Streetfield Ltd would obtain full relief for the Gift Aid donations if it made the carry forward claim, sufficient profits being available in both the loss year to 31 March 2009 and the following year to cover the non-trade charges. If the loss was set against the current and previous profits as indicated above, there would be £1,000 unrelieved in the loss year to 31 March 2009 and in the six months to 31 March 2008; relief would also be lost for the donation in the years ended 30 September 2006 and 2007. In the year to 30 September 2005, the donation would be covered by the profits remaining after the loss claim.

Explanatory Notes

Loss relief against current and previous profits under ICTA 1988 s 393A

1.   This example outlines the reliefs available to a single company in a continuing business in respect of trading losses and excess charges on income. Under corporation tax self-assessment, all 'negative

amounts', including trading losses, included in the CT 600 return become final in the same way as a self-assessment, subject to HMRC's ability to enquire into a return or make a discovery, although FA 2008 s 114 provides that an officer of HMRC may amend a tax return that appears to be incorrect.

2. Relief for trading losses may be claimed under ICTA 1988 s 393A against profits of whatever description in the current and carryback period of three years. The extension to the normal one year carry back period applies to losses in accounting periods ending between 24 November 2008 and 23 November 2010, and is dealt with by FA 2009 Sch 6. The relief is given by a single claim affecting all three years, giving relief in the later years before earlier years.

    There is a cap on the profits which can be carried back by more than one year. For accounting periods ending between 24 November 2008 and 23 November 2009 no more than £50,000 of the loss may be carried back by more than one year, and similarly for accounting periods ending later than this but up to 23 November 2010. The existence of this cap on relief may mean that some companies will still wish to claim terminal loss relief, with a similar carryback period of three years for losses of the last twelve months' trading but no cap on relief (see Example 54). The loss is set against the profits of accounting periods ending wholly or partly within the carryback period of three years preceding the loss period, latest first. Where an accounting period falls only partly within the carryback period, relief is given against a proportionate part of the profits (see explanatory note 5). The length of the loss period does not affect the carryback period.

    Current and carryback claims under s 393A must be made within two years after the end of the loss period, or within such further period as HMRC may allow. See Statement of Practice 5/01 for the circumstances in which HMRC may accept late claims.

Carrying losses forward under ICTA 1988 s 393

3. Where relief is not claimed under s 393A, or part of a loss remains unrelieved, the loss is carried forward automatically under s 393(1) without the need for a claim.

Unrelieved charges

4. In respect of the accounting period in which a trade ceases, s 393A(7) provides that any unrelieved trade charges of that accounting period may be included in the loss available to be carried back. For an illustration of loss claims on cessation of trading see Example 54. F(No 2)A 2005 provided that only qualifying charitable donations and gifts of assets to charities may be deducted as charges. Annuities and other annual payments that would previously have been deducted as charges are treated as management expenses.

5. Where there is a change of accounting date during the carryback period, as shown in this example, s 393(2) provides that the reduction to be made in the profits of a period falling only partly within the carryback period shall not exceed the appropriate proportion of those profits, as indicated in explanatory note 2 above.

    In this example, the time apportionment must also reflect the capping rule referred to in explanatory note 2 above. The relief given in periods prior to 1 April 2007 must be computed to ensure that no more than £50,000 of the loss gains relief before that date.

	Relief given
Six months ended 31.03.07	8,500
Year ended 30.09.06	34,000
	42,500
Balance – allowed in six months ended 30.09.05	7,500
Maximum amount to be carried back more than one year	50,000

Where there are charges on income, s 338 provides that they are allowed as a deduction against the total profits for the period as reduced by any other relief from tax, other than group relief.

Section 393A(8) provides that relief is not to be given for a trading loss in the carryback period 'so as to interfere with any relief under s 338 in respect of payments made wholly and exclusively for the purposes of that trade'.

Other loss claims

6. Losses may be the subject of a group relief claim for a company that is a member of a 75% group – for details see Example 64. That example also deals with the treatment of excess charges on income and excess management expenses of an investment company.

Interest on repayments

7. Where tax is repaid following a loss claim, interest on the repayment normally runs from nine months and one day after the loss period (except for a repayment relating to an account falling wholly within the 12 months before the loss period, for which interest runs from nine months and one day after that earlier period).

Hence in this example, interest on repayments would run from 1 January 2010, except for any repayment for the six months to 31 March 2008, on which interest would run from 1 January 2009, as indicated in the example at part (a) note 5(iv).

A 'large' company which is subject to the quarterly instalment payment rules may also generate repayments following the carryback of losses. However, even in such cases, interest will accrue only from the relevant nine months and one day due dates (ICTA 1988 s 826(7D) and (7E)).

Interest on underpaid and overpaid tax is taken into account in calculating profits chargeable to corporation tax.

Relief for non-trading losses

8. Companies may generate non-trading losses on other activities. The relief available for such losses depends on the nature of the loss, as summarised below for the most important categories:

   (a) Capital losses – offset against capital gains of the same accounting period, with any unrelieved loss being carried forward to reduce capital gains in future periods (see Example 73 explanatory note 1).

   (b) Non-trading foreign exchange/loan relationships deficit – a claim can be made to relieve such deficits in various ways (see Example 64 part A).

   (c) Property business losses on leased UK property – ICTA 1988 s 392A provides that losses on a UK property leasing business can be offset against the company's total profits of the same period and/or included in a group relief claim under ICTA 1988 s 403ZD. Any surplus property business loss is carried forward against future total profits (provided the property business continues). A company with investment business can carry forward an unrelieved property business loss (*after* the property business has ceased) as a management expense under ICTA 1988 s 75 (ICTA 1988 s 392(3)). See Example 97.

   (d) Overseas property letting business losses must be carried forward for future offset against profits of the same overseas property business (ICTA 1988 s 392B) (see Example 97).

   (e) Schedule D Case VI losses can only be relieved against current or future Schedule D Case VI income.

Question

Calamity Ltd, a family-owned close company that had operated in an enterprise zone, ceased trading on 30 June 2009.

It was incorporated many years ago and the company has had no income other than from the trade. The company has paid a charitable Gift Aid donation of £1,000 per annum. The last payment under Gift Aid was made in December 2008. A summary of recent adjusted trading results is as follows:

		£
Year ended		
31.12.05	Profit	150,000
31.12.06	Profit	143,000
31.12.07	Profit	35,000
31.12.08	Loss	65,000
6 months to 30.6.09	Loss	53,500

On 31 August 2009 the company's factory (on which enterprise zone allowances had been claimed) was sold, a balancing charge of £48,000 and a chargeable gain of £15,000 arising. The final accounting period is to 31 December 2009.

Assuming that the company claims relief for losses in the most appropriate way:

(a) Show the tax position in relation to the balancing charge and chargeable gain.

(b) Show the final amounts chargeable to corporation tax for each of the chargeable periods shown, after loss relief claims, together with the amounts of unrelieved losses and charges, if any.

(c) Give the latest dates by which the loss claims could be made by Calamity Ltd.

Answer

(a) **Tax position on balancing charge and chargeable gain**

The balancing charge of £48,000, together with the chargeable gain of £15,000, totalling £63,000, will be taxed at 28% (see explanatory note 4), giving tax payable of £17,640. The balancing charge is, however, treated in the same way as a post-cessation receipt under CTA 2009 ss 196 and 285 (formerly ICTA 1988 s 105) (CAA 2001 s 354), so that brought forward losses may be set against it.

Taking into account the rate of tax payable on the balancing charge, and the other circumstances of the period concerned, as shown in part (b) below, it would be better to carry forward the loss of the six months to 30 June 2009 against the balancing charge than claiming carryback relief under ICTA 1988 s 393A, ie:

	£
Relief under ICTA 1988 s 393A Loss of 6 months to 30.6.09 of £53,500, set against profits of year to 31.12.06, saving tax of £53,500 @ 19% (profits of year to 31.12.07 having been eliminated by loss carried back from the year to 31.12.08)	10,165
Relief wholly under CAA 2001 s 354 Unrelieved loss £53,500 carried forward and set against balancing charge, saving tax of £48,000 @ 28% and leaving unrelieved loss of £5,500	13,440
Additional saving with CAA 2001 s 354 relief	3,275

(b) **Final amounts chargeable to corporation tax, after loss claims:**

Taking into account (a) above, the position is as follows:

Accounting period to	Case I profit £	Chargeable gains £	Trading losses* £	Non-trade charges** £	Chargeable to corporation tax £
31.12.09	48,000	15,000	(48,000)	–	15,000
30.6.09	–		–	–	–
31.12.08	–		–	–	–
31.12.07	35,000		(35,000)	–	–
31.12.06	143,000		(30,000)	(1,000)	112,000
31.12.05	150,000			(1,000)	149,000

*   *Losses are relieved as follows:*

**   *Unrelieved non-trade charges*

Non-trade charges are deducted after trade losses and, if there are no profits to cover them, no relief is available. The payments under Gift Aid for the years to 31 December 2007 and 31 December 2008 are therefore unrelieved.

	1.1.07 – 30.6.07	1.7.07 – 31.12.07
Year to 31.12.08 (see explanatory notes 1 and 2)	£	£
Trading loss (£65,000)	32,500	32,500
Set against profits of previous year/three years, net of trade charges (s 393A):		
Year to 31.12.07 (£35,000)	(32,500)	(2,500)
Year to 31.12.06 (balance)		(30,000)
6 months to 30.6.09		
Trading loss		53,500
Set against balancing charge of period to 31.12.09		48,000
Leaving loss unrelieved of		5,500

(c)   **The latest date for making the s 393A claim** to carry back the loss of the year ended 31 December 2008 is 31 December 2010 (or such further period as HMRC may allow) (TA 1988 s 393A). The loss carried forward is automatically set against the balancing charge without the need for a claim.

Explanatory Notes

Terminal loss relief

1.   Relief for losses in the final period of trading is claimed under the normal rules and there is no separate provision for claiming relief for terminal losses as there is for income tax. Although the normal loss carryback period under ICTA 1988 s 393A is one year, there are two provisions that extend the relief available for the loss of the last twelve months of trading.

First, losses in that twelve months may be carried back for a full three years (ICTA 1988 s 393A subsections (2A) and (2B)). Where an accounting period falls partly within the last twelve months, the three year carryback applies to the appropriate proportion.

2.   In Calamity Ltd's case, the loss of the twelve months ended 31 December 2008 must be apportioned between:

–   6 months to 30 June 2008, which is available for carryback against the previous year only (ICTA 1988 s 393A(2))

–   6 months to 31 December 2008, which falls within twelve months of the cessation date, and can therefore be carried back against the previous three years' profits (s 393A(2)–(2B)).

The loss for the final 6 months to 30 June 2009 could also be carried back for up to three years (as part of the loss of the last twelve months), but it is more beneficial to carry the loss forward to relieve the balancing charge.

3.   The carryback provisions of ICTA 1988 s 393A restrict the set-off in an earlier accounting period so as not to interfere with earlier relief for *trade* charges, but relief for non-trade charges is not protected, as shown in the example. Most payments that used to be treated as trade charges are now tax deductible, and they will be encountered very rarely.

Capital gains and balancing charges after cessation of trade

4.   The capital gain after the cessation of trading illustrates the possible danger of disposing of capital assets after the cessation of a trade.

Trading losses of the *same accounting period only* are available for set-off against capital gains. Since the cessation of trade marks the end of an accounting period (CTA 2009, s 10(1), formerly ICTA 1988 s 12), any losses of the final trading period are automatically prevented from being allowed against gains arising on the subsequent disposal of the company's assets, resulting in practical difficulties since invariably the assets have to be retained until after the cessation of trading. It was common before 21 March 2007 for balancing charges to arise on disposals of industrial buildings, but balancing adjustments on industrial buildings were withdrawn from that date. Balancing adjustments on pooled items arise at the end of the final trading period, so are automatically offset against profits or losses. Adjustments on single pool assets, or enterprise zone buildings arise on sale of the asset, and therefore may fall outside the final trading period. Under CAA 2001 s 354 unrelieved trading losses may be set against such a balancing charge, as shown in the example. But there can be no set-off against capital gains.

Furthermore, once the trade has ceased, Calamity Ltd becomes a close investment-holding company and must therefore pay tax at the full corporation tax rate of 28% regardless of the level of its profits. The protection available for the *first* accounting period during a company's liquidation is not applicable here (see Example 60, explanatory note 5).

If, however, the *contract* for sale of the assets was made prior to the cessation of trading, with *completion* taking place after the cessation, the date of disposal would be the contract date (TCGA 1992 s 34), so that the chargeable gains would then arise in the final trading period and be available to offset any trading losses of that period and the close investment-holding company problem would also be avoided.

Although a balancing charge effectively represents delayed trading profits, and is treated in the same way as a post-cessation receipt under CTA 2009 ss 196 and 285, (formerly ICTA 1988 s 105), enabling unrelieved amounts to be set against it (see Example 16 part (c)(ii)), the provisions of ITTOIA 2005 s 257 which enable post-cessation receipts of an unincorporated trader to be carried back and treated as received on the date the trade ceased do not apply. There is also no provision for regarding the trade as being carried on in the period in which the balancing charge is received, so that the balancing charge suffers tax at 28%.

Because of this anomaly, more tax is saved in the example by not claiming s 393A relief for the final period to 30 June 2009 and instead carrying forward the loss of £53,500 in the period to 30 June 2009 to set against the balancing charge. The greater tax saving is achieved despite the fact that £5,500 of the loss remains unrelieved.

Company reconstructions without a change of ownership

5.   Under ICTA 1988 s 343, where a trade is transferred from one company to another, and at some time within one year before the transfer and two years after the transfer the same persons have a 75% ownership, the trade is treated as being transferred to the successor company rather than being discontinued for the purposes of carrying forward capital allowances. This prevents the predecessor carrying trading losses back three years, and enables the successor to take over the unrelieved losses of the predecessor. Where, however, the successor does not take over all the predecessor's assets and liabilities, and the liabilities of the predecessor immediately after the transfer exceed the market value of its assets (including any consideration received or receivable for the transfer of the trade), the trading loss transferred to the successor is reduced by the excess.

The successor also takes over the predecessor's capital allowances computations. First-year allowances on plant and machinery are claimed by whoever incurred the expenditure and balancing adjustments are made on the company carrying on the trade at the time of the disposal. Writing down allowances are split on a time basis.

Question

A.

Domo Ltd is a UK trading subsidiary of a large multinational group, which has over twenty active UK and overseas trading companies. The majority of Domo Ltd's business is carried on from the UK but it also has a branch in Norland, a country which imposes taxation at the rate of 35% on the profits of companies resident there and profits arising there. Domo Ltd also has a number of trade-related investments.

The following information relates to Domo Ltd for the year ended 31 March 2010:

	£
Trading income – UK trade	180,000
– Norland branch (before deducting tax suffered in Norland)	30,000
Investment income	
Dividend received in May 2009 on a holding of 15% of the ordinary (voting) shares in Fiord Norland Ltd	
(after deducting 15% withholding tax)	11,050
Interest receivable on a holding of 12% of the debentures of Lake Norland Ltd	
(after deducting 20% withholding tax)	12,000
Dividend received in May 2009 on a holding of 8% of the ordinary shares of Valley Norland Ltd	
(after deducting 15% withholding tax)	10,200
Net capital profit on land in Norland bought for £20,000 in 2001, sold in March 2010 for £37,000 – tax suffered in Norland £5,950	
(UK indexation allowance to be taken as 25%)	11,050
Gift Aid donation paid to NSPCC	5,000
Dividend paid – January 2010 – final for year ended 31 March 2009	152,000

The company did not have any unrelieved amounts brought forward at 1 April 2009.

Compute the corporation tax payable by Domo Ltd for the year ended 31 March 2010 after all reliefs.

B.

Jones Ltd is a member of an international group of 30 companies and its only investment is a 40% holding in Shelley SA, a company resident in Ruritania. This is a country with which the UK does not have a double taxation agreement. In June 2009, Jones Ltd received in cash a dividend of 108,000 Ruritanian Dollars (R$), which had suffered a 10% Ruritanian withholding tax. The rate of exchange is R$1 = £1.25.

The dividend resolution did not indicate the accounting period for which it was paid. The Ruritanian accounts of Shelley SA for the three years to 31 October 2007, 2008 and 2009 are set out below.

Shelley SA – trading and profit and loss account

	Year ended 31.10.07 R$	Year ended 31.10.08 R$	Year ended 31.10.09 R$
Operating profit before tax	205,000	350,000	400,000
Unrealised exchange gain/(loss) on investments	100,000	(80,000)	70,000
Taxation			
Current tax	(40,000)	(60,000)	(80,000)
Deferred tax	(15,000)	(20,000)	(20,000)
(Under-)/over-provision for previous year	10,000	(5,000)	(5,000)
Profit after taxation cf	260,000	185,000	365,000

		Year ended 31.10.07 R$		Year ended 31.10.08 R$		Year ended 31.10.09 R$
Profit after taxation bf		260,000		185,000		365,000
Unrealised exchange items transferred (to)/from non-distributable capital reserve		(100,000)		80,000		(70,000)
Transfer to statutory non-distributable reserve for contingencies		(30,000)		(30,000)		(30,000)
Transfer to general reserve		(25,000)		(45,000)		(60,000)
Dividend paid in the year		–		–		(300,000)
Retained profit/(loss) per accounts	R$	105,000	R$	190,000	R$	(95,000)
Actual tax paid for the year	R$	45,000	R$	65,000	R$	80,000

For its year ended 31 March 2010, Jones Ltd has adjusted trading income profits taxable of £200,000 (before deducting (non-trade) interest payable of £150,000). It also paid a dividend of £80,000 in January 2010. There were no unrelieved amounts brought forward at 1 April 2009.

(a)   Compute the foreign income assessable arising from the dividend, and

(b)   Calculate the corporation tax payable by Jones Ltd for the year ended 31 March 2010.

C.

How would the position alter in parts A and B if the dividends had been received after 1 July 2009?

Answer

A.   Domo Ltd – Mainstream Corporation Tax for year ended 31 March 2010

			Trading Income	Loan Relation-ship	Foreign Income		
	Total	UK	Norland Branch (Note 1)	Non-Trade Profits Lake Norland (Note 2)	Fiord Norland (Note 3)	Valley Norland (Note 4)	Foreign chargeable gains (Note 5)
	£	£	£	£	£	£	£
Trading profit	210,000	180,000	30,000				
Debenture interest	15,000			15,000			
Foreign dividends	32,000				20,000	12,000	
Chargeable gains	12,000						12,000
	269,000	180,000	30,000	15,000	20,000	12,000	12,000
Less charges – Gift Aid donation (see note 6)	(5,000)	(5,000)					
Profits chargeable to CT (and also for small companies' rate since no FII)	264,000	175,000	30,000	15,000	20,000	12,000	12,000
Corporation tax payable @ 28% (see note 7)	73,920	49,000	8,400	4,200	5,600	3,360	3,360
Less double tax relief * restricted to UK tax	(23,400)		(8,400)*	(3,000)	(5,600)*	(1,800)	(3,360)*
Corporation tax payable	50,520	49,000	–	1,200	–	1,560	–
Foreign tax unrelieved							2,590
Unrelieved foreign tax carried forward (or carried back in relation to the Norland branch)			2,100		3,350		

Notes

1.

Norland branch profits foreign tax – 30,000 @ 35% =	£10,500

The excess double tax of £2,100 suffered on the Norland branch income (ie £10,500 less £8,400 maximum offset) can be carried back for set-off against UK tax suffered on the Norland branch income of the three years to 31 March 2009, any balance being carried forward to set against future Norland branch income.

2.

Debentures in Lake Norland – 12,000 + (20/80) 3,000 withholding tax =	£15,000

3.   *Related qualifying foreign dividend (QFD)*

Shares in Fiord Norland (holding carries at least 10% voting power):

	£
Dividend (net)	11,050
Withholding tax (15/85)	1,950
	13,000
Underlying tax (35/65)	7,000
Foreign income	20,000

The calculation of foreign income includes all foreign taxes, whether relievable or not. The maximum relievable foreign tax (known as the 'mixer cap') is 28% of the sum of the dividend plus the underlying tax.

Calculation of eligible unrelieved foreign tax credit

The tax suffered on the Fiord Norland dividend exceeds the 28% mixer cap restriction, and gives rise to eligible unrelieved foreign tax (EUFT). However, the amount of foreign tax which is eligible for relief cannot exceed 45% of the gross dividend (the 45% restriction applying to both underlying and withholding tax). The EUFT is the amount by which the 45% cap on the dividend (or, if less, the actual foreign tax suffered) exceeds the double tax relief offset, as shown below.

	£	£
Lower of:		
45% cap		
Foreign income – £20,000 × 45% (upper limit)	9,000	
Total foreign tax suffered		
Withholding tax	1,950	
Underlying tax	7,000	
	8,950	
Foreign tax suffered on dividend		8,950
Less: Actual DTR restriction		(5,600)
EUFT		3,350

This EUFT could be used to offset the UK tax suffered on any other qualifying foreign dividends (QFDs) in the same period (year ending 31 March 2010), but in this case there are none. The excess EUFT may be carried back for offset against the UK tax on QFDs for the years ended 31 March 2009, 2008 and 2007. Otherwise it must be carried forward for future offset. It should be noted that the excess EUFT on the Fiord Norland dividend cannot be applied against the residual UK tax on the dividend from Valley Norland, since this must be held in a separate EUFT pool as it attracts relief for withholding tax only (the Valley Norland shares carrying less than 10% voting power).

4. *Unrelated qualifying foreign dividend*

   Shares in Valley Norland
   10,200 + withholding tax (15/85) 1,800 =   £12,000

5.

Chargeable gain:	Sale proceeds March 2010		37,000	
	Cost – 2001	20,000		
	Indexation allowance 25%	5,000	25,000	£12,000

6. Gift Aid donations are treated as a charge on income and paid gross.

7. The small companies' rate is not available to Domo Ltd as it is associated with twenty active companies (active non-resident companies count for the purpose of this test).

B. (a) **Jones Ltd – Foreign income arising from June 2009 dividend**

Jones Ltd's dividend from Shelley SA before withholding tax is

$$108,000 \times \frac{100}{90} = R\$120,000$$

The total dividend paid by Shelley SA is

$$120,000 \times \frac{100}{40} = R\$300,000.$$

Since the dividend is not paid out of a specified period (see explanatory note 4), it is treated as coming first out of the distributable profits of the year to 31 October 2008 (being the last accounts before June 2009 when the dividend was received) then the previous year as follows:

	Year to 31.10.08 R$		Year to 31.10.07 R$
Retained profits per accounts	190,000		105,000
Add transfer to general reserve	45,000		25,000
	235,000		130,000
Attributable to dividend (R$ 300,000) (1st)	235,000	(balance)	65,000
Actual tax paid	65,000		45,000

			R$	
Underlying tax:				
Year to 31.10.08	40% ×	65,000	26,000	
31.10.07	40% × (	$\frac{65,000}{(130,000}$ × 45,000)	9,000	
			35,000	
Dividend inclusive of withholding tax			120,000	
			155,000	
Overseas tax borne (35,000 + 12,000)			47,000	
Converted to sterling at R$1 = £1.25 =				58,750
Dividend received R$108,000 converted at R$1 = £1.25 =				135,000

	Year to 31.10.08 R$	Year to 31.10.07 R$
Foreign income (including overseas tax £58,750)		£193,750

(b)   Corporation tax payable by Jones Ltd for year to 31 March 2010

	Total £	Trading Income £	Foreign Income £
UK and foreign profits	393,750	200,000	193,750
Non-trading deficit (interest payable)	(150,000)	(150,000)	
Profits chargeable to corporation tax	243,750	50,000	193,750
Corporation tax payable @ 28%*	68,250	14,000	54,250
Less double tax relief (restricted to UK tax)	(54,250)		(54,250)
Mainstream corporation tax	14,000	14,000	–

The excess foreign tax suffered on the dividend from Shelley SA of £4,500 (£58,750 – £54,250) represents EUFT relievable against the UK tax on future dividends received from Shelley SA (see explanatory notes 6 and 7).

> * Small companies' rate not applicable in view of the number of associated companies, overseas companies counting for this purpose.

Dividends received after 1 July 2009

A major reform of the corporation tax rules on foreign profits is effective from 1 July 2009. This exempts dividends from overseas companies in most instances.

Domo Ltd is a large company and so it would be necessary to consider the new exemption contained in CTA 2009 s 930D. The dividends from Fiord Norland Ltd and Lake Norland Ltd should qualify under CTA 2009 s 930F.

Jones Ltd is also a large company and similar considerations to Domo Ltd will apply.

A further change is that for accounting periods commencing after 1 January 2010, it may be necessary to restrict loan interest paid by Domo Ltd or Jones Ltd. This is in accordance with FA 2009 Sch 15.

Explanatory Notes

Interest received

1.   Interest received from abroad by individuals is taxed as income from foreign securities as interest income under ITTOIA 2005 Part 6 Chapter 2. This does not apply to companies, for whom both UK and foreign interest is taxed according to the 'loan relationships' provisions (see Example 63). Unless received by a financial business as trading profits, it is taxed under loan relationships non-trading profits, as shown in part A of the example.

The 'loan relationships' rules provide for interest received to be brought into account on an accruals basis rather than on the amount arising in the period. As a result, foreign tax may be apportioned to an earlier accounting period than that in which it was suffered. Thus in part A of the example, the debenture interest receivable from Lake Norland Ltd of £12,000 after 20% withholding tax may include interest accrued but not received at 31 March 2010. The withholding tax taken into account for double tax relief would include the tax suffered on the accrued amount.

Double taxation relief

2. Where a company suffers tax twice on the same profits, whether they are income profits or capital profits, relief may be claimed either under the provisions of a double tax treaty (ICTA 1988 s 788) or unilaterally (s 790) for a credit against the UK tax charged. Double tax treaties specify which taxes are covered by the agreement. Most treaties are based on the OECD model agreement, but each is separately negotiated between the respective countries, and there are often points specific to the particular treaty. HMRC have issued Statement of Practice 7/91 concerning their approach to identifying relevant foreign taxes where unilateral relief applies.

3. FA 2000 s 103 and Sch 20 introduced far-reaching changes to the double tax relief system. These changes targeted the use of offshore mixer companies which were previously used to ensure that maximum double tax relief was obtained on a UK company's various sources of overseas income, also enabling lowly taxed income from Controlled Foreign Companies (CFCs) to be repatriated with little or no extra tax, thus avoiding a UK tax charge on undistributed profits. Extensive detailed anti-avoidance legislation of a very technical nature exists, and continues to be issued, to combat schemes giving a UK tax advantage in this area.

    Double tax relief is computed on a 'source by source' basis. For each source, the relief given is at the lower of the UK tax (based on the most beneficial allocation of losses etc) and the overseas tax attributable to the income or gain.

    A measure of relief has been available for unrelieved foreign tax relating to *overseas branch income* and for *dividends received from overseas companies* (see explanatory notes 6 and 7). The relief enables any unused double tax relief credit to be carried back against the UK tax on the same source of foreign income for up to three years and then carried forward indefinitely against future UK tax from the same foreign source (ICTA 1988 ss 806A to 806M).

    Section 806C provides that the relief may be claimed by a non-resident company in respect of foreign tax suffered on dividends by a UK branch or agency other than in the non-resident company's home state. A claim to relieve unused foreign tax must be made within six years (reduced to four years from 1 April 2010) after the end of the accounting period in which the amount arose.

    Clearly, if the overseas tax rate suffered on the foreign income is consistently higher than the UK rate, these rules are likely to be of little assistance.

Relief for underlying tax and relevant profits

4. Normally, only direct overseas taxes are taken into account, but underlying tax on overseas *dividends* may be taken into account if the UK company controls not less than 10% of the voting power in the foreign company. Relief may also be claimed for underlying tax paid by other companies in a chain where the 10% control test is met at each stage in the chain and dividends are paid by one company to the other (ICTA 1988 s 801). There are anti-avoidance provisions to prevent companies exploiting these provisions (see explanatory note 8).

    The underlying tax is that part of the foreign tax on the relevant profits that is attributable to the dividend. The relevant profits are as follows:

    (a)   If the dividend is paid for a specified period, the profits of that period, or

    (b)   The profits of the last set of accounts ended before the dividend became payable.

    If (a) or (b) applies, but the total dividend exceeds those profits, the excess is treated as coming out of earlier undistributed profits, latest first (ICTA 1988 s 799).

Thus, in part B of the example, the dividend (being for an unspecified accounting period) is treated as being paid out of the last accounting period (31 October 2008) which *ended* before it was paid in June 2009. The balance of 'unmatched' dividend is then allocated to the prior accounting period to 31 October 2007.

5. The relevant profits are the foreign company's *distributable* profits, not profits for tax purposes (*Bowater Paper Corporation Ltd v Murgatroyd* (1970)). This ruling has now been codified into ICTA 1988 s 799(5) and (6), which provides that the distributable profits are based on the foreign company's accounts drawn up under the law of that country. Those accounts must only include reserves, provisions for bad debts or contingencies permitted under the law of the company's home State. HMRC take the view that:

(i) Realised gains on exchange differences are distributable profits. Unrealised exchange gains are not, unless they are in fact used for a dividend or are treated by the foreign company as distributable profits.

(ii) Realised capital profits are also distributable profits.

(iii) Deferred tax, and any under- or over-provisions for tax in earlier years may be taken into account in computing distributable profits (but not in computing the actual rate of underlying tax).

Some countries, including Jersey and Guernsey, operate a system under which tax is accounted for when a dividend is paid ('company tax deducted'), and is thus shown on the dividend voucher, but that tax may then be refunded depending on the company's ultimate tax position. HMRC require the actual underlying tax to be computed and relief is restricted to that amount (SP 12/93).

System of double tax relief for overseas dividends prior to 1 July 2009

6. Broadly, relief for tax on underlying profits and withholding tax is available up to certain limits for qualifying foreign dividends (QFDs), subject to any double tax treaty.

Firstly, underlying and withholding taxes may be offset against UK tax liability, up to the rate of UK corporation tax (currently 28%), as for trading profits. The maximum offset is calculated source by source, by a formula known as the 'mixer cap' (ICTA 1988 s 799). Application of the source by source limit may result in unrelieved foreign tax for some sources, while for other sources UK tax may be higher than foreign taxes, in which case further relief may be available.

Secondly, the amount of foreign underlying and withholding tax that exceeds the rate of UK corporation tax (currently 28%), but does not exceed 45% becomes eligible unrelieved foreign tax (EUFT). This amount may, subject to conditions, be relieved against other sources of dividend for the same period for which foreign taxes amounted to less than 28%, or may be carried back three years or forward indefinitely.

This may be illustrated as follows:

	H Co	L Co	Total
Net dividend	53	82	135
Underlying tax	47	18	65
'Gross' dividend	100	100	200
Maximum UK tax creditable 28%	28	28	56
Limited to lower of foreign tax and 28%(mixer cap)	(28)	(18)	(46)
H Co's EUFT (max 45%) set against L Co		(10)	(10)
UK Tax liability	nil	nil	nil

Total foreign taxes were 65 (47+18), of which 2 (47–45) are unrelievable because of the 45% EUFT cap, giving maximum potentially relievable foreign tax for the year of 63 (65–2), and a maximum capacity for relief at 28 % in the year of 56 (200 × 28%).

H Co is able to offset 28 of the 45 EUFT cap, resulting in a nil UK liability, and generating 17 (45–28) in EUFT.

Of the EUFT of 17, L Co is able to utilise 10, bringing its offset up to the maximum of 28%.

The surplus EUFT of 7 (17–10) may be carried back for three years, or forward without limit, against H Co source dividends only.

See explanatory note 7 below for further details.

Eligible unrelieved foreign tax (EUFT)

7.   Where an overseas company (or overseas intermediate holding company) pays a dividend which has suffered withholding tax and/or underlying tax at a total rate exceeding 28% of the 'gross' dividend, an amount of EUFT arises.

The EUFT can then be applied to relieve the overseas tax on other eligible overseas dividends in the same period under the so-called 'onshore pooling' calculation. For this purpose only certain dividends can be pooled (referred to as qualifying foreign dividends – QFDs). A QFD will broadly be a dividend from any overseas resident company *except* dividends that have been paid by a controlled foreign company in pursuance of an acceptable distribution policy.

Having calculated the EUFT on all dividends (this will be the amount of £3,350 included in note 3 to part A of the example), the respective amounts are included in a single pool of EUFT and effectively used against QFDs. The EUFT pool must be split between separate *underlying tax* and *withholding tax* pools. Dividends will enter the withholding tax pool if they do not attract relief for underlying tax (broadly dividends from companies in which less than 10% of the voting rights are held).

The total EUFT is initially offset against the pooled QFD (ICTA 1988 s 806D). Any excess EUFT can be carried back for up to three years on a last in first out basis (ICTA 1988 s 806E) or carried forward indefinitely. EUFT that cannot be carried back may be surrendered to another company in the same 75% group (ICTA 1988 s 806H and SI 2001/1163). The claimant company may treat the surrendered EUFT as its own EUFT for the purposes of the carry back/carry forward rules. The group relief option is available only in respect of unrelieved foreign tax on dividends and not for unrelieved foreign tax on overseas branch income.

Anti-avoidance provisions

8.   There are anti-avoidance provisions in ICTA 1988 s 801A to prevent group companies, particularly financial companies, artificially increasing the amount of underlying tax they are entitled to by means of an avoidance scheme. The provisions limit relief for underlying tax by reference to the rate of corporation tax payable by the UK company on the dividend which it receives.

There are also rules in ICTA 1988 ss 798, 798A, 798B and 803 to prevent banks and other financial traders getting excessive relief for foreign tax paid on overseas interest that is part of their trading profits. A number of detailed technical anti-avoidance provisions exist, targeted at schemes notified under DOTAS.

System of taxation of overseas dividends from 1 July 2009

9.   The rules for dividends received by small companies differ from those for medium and large companies but in each case, the result is that the great majority of dividends will be exempt from corporation tax.

CTA 2009 Part 9A provides detailed rules including detailed anti-avoidance provisions in respect of artificial structures and CFCs.

It is possible to elect out of the exemption in respect of a specific dividend (CTA 2009 s 930Q).

Treatment where double tax relief not claimed

10. Where no credit is claimed for the overseas tax, the foreign profits are taken into account net of the overseas tax (s 811).

If, for example, profits, including overseas profits, were to be reduced to nil by trading losses, so that no UK tax was payable, there would be no credit available for the foreign tax. By including the foreign profits net of overseas tax, the offset of losses would be reduced, leaving the losses available to set against other profits as shown below:

	£
UK profits	60,000
Overseas branch profits (£50,000 less foreign tax paid £20,000)	30,000
	90,000
Trading losses (part of £130,000)	(90,000)
Profits chargeable to corporation tax	–
Losses available against other profits	40,000

If the overseas branch profits had been brought into account before overseas tax, giving total profits of £110,000, no foreign tax credit would have been available since no corporation tax is payable, and the unrelieved losses would be only £20,000 instead of £40,000.

Treatment of charges on income etc

11. Where there are charges on income, management expenses, group relief, or other amounts which can be offset against profits of more than one description, the company is able to use them in the most advantageous manner for double tax relief (s 797(3)). Domo Ltd in part A can accordingly offset the charges paid against UK profits in priority to foreign income and gains, leaving a higher amount of foreign profits to absorb double tax credits. The non-trade interest (loan relationship non-trading 'deficit') can be set against the UK trading profits rather that the overseas trading profits, as shown for Jones Ltd in part B of the example.

Later adjustments to foreign tax paid

12. If the amount of foreign tax payable is later adjusted, the amount of double tax relief claimed will be similarly adjusted. If an adjustment to foreign tax results in too much relief having been claimed, HMRC must be notified within one year after the adjustment (ICTA 1988 s 806).

Question

A.

Bray Motors plc has an authorised and issued share capital of 10,000,000 ordinary shares of £1 each, and its shares are listed and regularly dealt in on the Stock Exchange.

The present shareholdings in the company are as follows:

	Shares
John Bray (the company's founder, now retired)	2,550,000
Colin Rawson (a private investor)	1,000,000
Lawrence Jones (the company's managing director)	600,000
Globe Autos Ltd (a close company)	470,000
Alan Brooks (a private investor)	460,000
James Baker (the company's financial director)	370,000
Ace Car Hire Ltd (not a close company)	370,000
Brian Pritchard (a private investor)	360,000
Edward Hay (a private investor)	340,000
340 private investors, none of whom own more than 20,000 shares	3,480,000
	10,000,000

All the shares are beneficially owned.

None of the shareholders is related to or associated with any other shareholder.

The company owns a trade investment of 5,000 shares in Marsh Alternators Ltd, an unquoted trading company with an authorised and issued share capital of 100,000 ordinary shares of £1 each.

The other shares in the company are currently owned as follows:

	Shares
Norman Marsh	8,000
Trustees of a settlement made by Norman Marsh for his grandchildren	19,000
Henry Simpson (Norman Marsh's cousin)	3,000
Gerald Black (no relation to any of the above)	5,000
Ellen Black (Gerald's wife)	1,000
Tom Black (Gerald's son)	4,000
Nigel Clement (Gerald Black's nephew)	3,000
Walter Metcalfe (Nigel Clement's partner in an unrelated antiques business, and sole owner of the wholly independent company Metcalfe Motors Ltd)	3,500
Richard Court (no relation to any of the above)	3,500
Keith Court (Richard's brother)	1,000
35 other shareholders, none of whom owns more than 2,000 shares and none of whom is related to or associated with any other shareholder	44,000
	95,000

All the shares are beneficially owned.

The directors of Marsh Alternators Ltd are Gerald Black and Richard Court.

Set out the reasoning as to whether the close company provisions are applicable to:

(i)   Bray Motors plc

(ii)   Marsh Alternators Ltd.

B.

Indicate the circumstances in which a close company is within the definition of a 'close investment-holding company' and state the consequences.

C.

Cook is about to acquire shares in a publicly quoted company for £350,000 out of his own funds, giving him around a 2% equity stake. The shares currently yield a dividend of £28,000 pa and the prospects of significant capital appreciation in the future are excellent. At the end of 10 years, Cook may decide to sell some or all of the shares. It has been suggested to Cook by a friend, Dodge, that instead of buying the shares himself he should form a new investment company, Cook Ltd. Cook would subscribe for 350,000 £1 shares in Cook Ltd, which would then use the cash to buy the shares. Dodge has told Cook that he could draw out director's remuneration of up to £10,000 pa and that Cook Ltd could deduct this against the dividend income and that the balance of £18,000 would only attract a small amount of tax because of the 'nil' starting rate of corporation tax. Dodge has also said that Cook could save tax on his director's earnings by paying premiums into a personal pension scheme.

State whether the advice which Cook has received from Dodge is correct.

Answer

A.

(i)   **Bray Motors plc,** whilst controlled by five participators, is a quoted company in which 35% of the shares are held by the public and not more than 85% are held by the principal members, viz:

Name	Shares	Control Test 5 largest participators	Public ownership Test 35%	Principal Members Test 5 largest over 5% (500,000 shares)
John Bray	2,550,000	2,550,000		2,550,000
Colin Rawson	1,000,000	1,000,000		1,000,000
Lawrence Jones (director)	600,000	600,000		600,000
Globe Autos Ltd (close company)	470,000	470,000	470,000	
Alan Brooks	460,000	460,000	460,000	
James Baker (director)	370,000			
Ace Car Hire Ltd (open company)	370,000		370,000	
Brian Pritchard	360,000		360,000	
Edward Hay	340,000		340,000	
340 private investors	3,480,000		3,480,000	
Total Shares	10,000,000	5,080,000	5,480,000	4,150,000
Percentage	100%	50.8%	54.8%	41.5%

Therefore Bray Motors plc is *not* a close company.

(ii)   **Marsh Alternators Ltd** is controlled by five participators together with their associates, viz:

5 largest holdings		Holding including associates
Norman Marsh	8,000	
Trustees of settlement for grandchildren	19,000	27,000
Gerald Black	5,000	
His wife	1,000	
His son	4,000	10,000
Nigel Clement	3,000	
Walter Metcalfe, Nigel Clement's partner	3,500	6,500*
Richard Court	3,500	
His brother	1,000	4,500
Bray Motors Ltd		5,000
		53,000
Others: H Simpson	3,000	
35 other shareholders	44,000	47,000
		100,000

* From 6 April 2008, for purposes of the small companies' rate only, business partners are not automatically associates, unless there is a tax avoidance purpose. This change has no effect on determining close company status however, and the shareholding of Nigel Clement's business partner continues to be attributed to Nigel Clement for this purpose.

Marsh Alternators Ltd is therefore a close company.

B.

A close company is a close investment-holding company in an accounting period *unless* throughout that period it exists wholly or mainly for one or more of the following purposes:

(i) Carrying on a trade on a commercial basis (including dealing in land, shares or securities)

(ii) Investing in land or buildings for letting to third parties (ie other than to persons connected with the company or their spouses or relatives)

(iii) Acting as a holding company for one or more companies each of which qualifies under (i) or (ii) above.

A company that makes loans to qualifying companies in the same group, or holds property or provides other services for those companies, qualifies for exclusion, as does a holding company that itself carries on a trade, or acts as the top company in a group and merely holds shares in a subsidiary that has qualifying subsidiaries (ICTA 1988 s 13A(1)–(3)).

Where a close company goes into liquidation, it is not treated as a close investment-holding company for the accounting period commencing with the winding-up if it was a qualifying company in the previous accounting period (but this may not help if the company ceased trading some time before going into liquidation – see Example 60 explanatory note 5).

The main consequence of being a close investment-holding company is that, regardless of the level of the company's profits, corporation tax is charged at the full rate, ie it is not entitled to the benefit of the corporation tax small companies' rate, or marginal relief (ICTA 1988 ss 13(1)(b) and 13AA(8)).

A further important restriction is that interest relief on loans taken out to acquire ordinary share capital of a close company is not given if the company is a close investment-holding company or becomes such a company (ICTA 1988 s 360(1) and (2)).

C.

Since Cook Ltd would be controlled by Cook, it would be a close investment-holding company. As such it is not able to take advantage of the small companies' rate, regardless of the level of its profits. The full rate of 28% (until 31 March 2008 this was 30%) is payable. If, however, the only source of profits was the dividends on the shares, that income would be franked investment income which is not chargeable to corporation tax. There would therefore be no taxable profits out of which to deduct any director's fees paid.

As far as director's remuneration is concerned, the remuneration would have to be wholly and exclusively for the purposes of the company's business. If the only activity of the company was to hold the shares in the public company it is clear that Cook's directorship would not involve much commitment and it is unlikely that anything more than a nominal amount would be allowed as director's fees. Any amounts that were paid would be subject to payment of national insurance contributions by the company and also by Cook.

From 6 April 2006, pension contributions paid by the company have been limited for practical purposes by the individual's annual and lifetime allowances (see Example 37). As an individual, Cook may contribute the higher of £3,600 or 100% of earnings, and if a higher rate taxpayer he may claim higher rate tax relief subject to the restrictions on higher rate tax relief for those with income over £150,000. See Example 37. He would retain basic rate tax relief at 20% out of the payment, the pension provider recovering that amount from HMRC, and if Cook is a higher rate taxpayer, he would claim the extra higher rate relief in his self-assessment return. However, the amount that the company can claim for a tax deduction is limited by the wholly and exclusively test, and is likely to be nominal.

In the long term, the capital appreciation on the shares may lead to double taxation, if the company is liquidated when the shares are sold. The capital gain on the disposal of the shares would be charged to tax at the full corporation tax rate. (Given that Cook Ltd would only hold a 2% interest in the shares, it would not be entitled to the substantial shareholdings exemption on the disposal – see Example 66.) Cook could either extract the company's chargeable gain as a dividend prior to the liquidation, receiving the balance of the proceeds by way of capital distribution, or leave the gain as part of the funds paid out on the liquidation. If the company sold the shares for, say, £550,000 and, assuming indexation allowance of £50,000 for the company, with entrepreneur's relief not applying as this is not a trading company, the comparative position using the current corporation tax rates is set out below. (It is assumed that there is no retained income in the company at this point.)

If accounting profit (reserves) paid out as dividend prior to liquidation

	£
Gain (£550,000 less cost £350,000)	200,000
Corporation tax @ 28% on capital gain of £150,000 (£200,000 less indexation)	42,000
Cash dividend (= reserves)	158,000
Tax credit 1/9	17,556
Cook's income for tax purposes	175,556
Tax thereon @ say 32½%	57,056
(of which £39,500 is payable after deducting tax credit)	
Balance of proceeds paid out in liquidation (= share capital)	
(550,000 less tax and dividend amounting to 200,000)	350,000
Cost of Cook's shares in Cook Ltd	350,000
Chargeable gain	–
Surplus on share sale, net of tax (£508,000 – £350,000 – £39,500)	118,500

Note

It has already been announced that the higher rate on dividends is to be increased to 42½% from 6 April 2010 for those with incomes over £150,000. The actual tax due on the large dividend will depend on Cook's other income in the year in which the distribution is made.

If investment shares sold and company liquidated

	£
Sale proceeds for investment shares	550,000
Corporation tax on gain	42,000
Capital distribution to Cook	508,000
Cost of Cook's shares in Cook Ltd	350,000
Chargeable gain	158,000
Capital gains tax @ 18% (assuming annual exemption already used)	28,440
Surplus on sale of shares net of tax (£508,000 – £350,000 – £28,440)	129,560

If Cook held the investment shares personally, his surplus on sale would be £164,000, calculated as follows:

	£
Sale proceeds	550,000
Cost of investment shares	350,000
Chargeable gain	200,000
CGT @ 18% (assuming annual exemption used elsewhere)	36,000
Surplus on sale (£550,000 – £350,000 – £36,000)	164,000

This demonstrates the impact of the 'double taxation' which arises where appreciating assets are held within an (investment) company.

Explanatory Notes

Definition of close company

1. A close company is one under the control of five or fewer participators or of participators who are directors (ICTA 1988 s 414).

2. A *participator* is a person having a share or interest in the capital or income of the company (ICTA 1988 s 417(1)), the most common form of participator therefore being a shareholder although the legislation does not restrict the definition to a shareholder. The word 'person' includes both an individual and a company.

3. *Control* means exercising, or able to exercise, or entitled to acquire control over, the company's affairs, and in particular, but without prejudice to the general meaning of the foregoing, possessing or entitled to acquire the greater part of the share capital, or issued share capital, or of the voting power in the company (ICTA 1988 s 416(2)).

    An entitlement to receive now or in the future the greater part of the income if the whole income were to be distributed, or the greater part of the assets of the company that were available for distribution among the participators on a winding-up, also denotes control.

Participator's associates etc

4. In determining whether five or fewer participators (or participators who are directors) control a company, the rights of certain other persons must be regarded as those of the participator, namely:

    (a) His nominee (ICTA 1988 s 416(5))

    (b) His associates, being (ICTA 1988 ss 416(6) and 417(3) and (4))

         (i)   a business partner (but not for purposes of application of the small companies rate)

         (ii) his spouse or civil partner, parent or remoter forebear, child or remoter issue, brother or sister

         (iii) trustees of any settlement made by the participator or the relatives in 4(b)(ii) above

         (iv) where the participator has an interest in shares or obligations of the company that are in a trust or deceased's estate, the trustees and personal representatives and, if the participator is a company, any other company interested in those shares or obligations. (This provision covers, inter alia, trusts for occupational pensions and employee benevolent funds.)

    (c) Any company or companies of which the participator or he and his associates have control (ICTA 1988 s 416(6)).

Close company exclusion where public holdings are 35% or more

5.   There is an exclusion from close company status if shares in the company carrying not less than 35% of the voting power (and not carrying a fixed rate of dividend with or without further rights to participate in profits) are *held by the public* (see explanatory note 6 below) and such shares have within the preceding twelve months been listed on and the subject of dealings on a recognised stock exchange (ICTA 1988 s 415(1)). This exclusion does not, however, apply where the voting power possessed by the principal members exceeds 85%, the principal members being the five persons possessing the greatest percentage of the voting power, each owning over 5% (ICTA 1988 s 415(2) and (6)). Where there are no such five persons, because two or more possess equal percentages, all those with equal percentages are counted, eg two with 20% and five with 10% = seven principal members together holding 90%.

6.   Shares are regarded as held by the public if they satisfy one of the following tests (unless they are excluded by the next following paragraph):

(a)   If held by a non-close company

(b)   If held on trust for an approved superannuation fund

(c)   If not held by a principal member.

Public holdings *exclude* a holding by a director or his associate or by a company under their control, or by a company associated with the company concerned, or a holding by certain funds for the benefit of past and present employees, directors or their dependants (for example occupational pension funds, employee share trusts and benevolent funds). Companies are 'associated' if, within twelve months previously, one has control of the other or both are under the control of the same person or persons (ICTA 1988 s 416(1)). See Example 50 explanatory note 7 for further details.

The holding of a non-close company counts as a public holding and is included in the 35% rule, but if the non-close company has one of the five largest vote carrying holdings it also counts as a principal member and is therefore included in the 85% rule.

eg voting power in quoted company held as follows:

	(a)	(b)
Two directors equally	60%	60%
Non-close company	10%	30%
Members of public (none holding over 5%)	30%	10%
	100%	100%

In both cases the public holdings are 40%.

In example (a) the principal members hold 70% and the company is accordingly *not* a close company.

In example (b) the principal members hold 90% and the company *is* a close company.

Other exclusions from close company status

7.   There are certain other exclusions from close company status:

(a)   a non-resident company

(b)   a registered industrial and provident society within the meaning of ICTA 1988 s834(1) (formerly s 486(12))

(c)   a building society

(d)   a company controlled by the Crown, unless it could be treated as a close company on the ground of being under the control of persons acting independently of the Crown

(e)   a company controlled by a company which is not a close company (other than by reason of non-residence), or by two or more companies none of which is a close company, where it cannot be treated as a close company except by taking as one of the five or fewer participators requisite for its being so treated a company which is not a close company

(f)   a company which could only be close by taking as a participator entitled to receive the greater part of its assets on a winding-up, a loan creditor which is a non-close company (other than by reason of non-residence).

(ICTA 1988 s 414.)

Consequences of being a close company

8.   Where a company is within the definition of a close company, the following provisions apply:

(a)   Any benefits derived by a participator, other than an employee earning £8,500 per annum or more, or a director, are regarded as distributions of profits rather than deductions from trading profits (see Example 58).

(b)   If a close company makes a loan to a participator, the company has to pay tax at 25% on the amount of the loan, subject to certain exceptions (ICTA 1988 s 419 – see Example 58 and also (e) below).

(c)   The small companies' rate is not available if the company is also a close investment-holding company (ICTA 1988 ss 13(1)(b) and 13AA(8)).

(d)   If the company transfers an asset at undervalue, the shareholders will suffer an appropriate reduction in the capital gains base cost of their shares, unless the shortfall has already been taken into account for income tax (TCGA 1992 s 125 and HMRC concession D51).

(e)   Under the 'loan relationships' rules for companies (see Example 63), where the parties to a loan are a close company and a participator or associate of a participator, the following provisions apply:

(i)   The company is denied a deduction for a loan written off if the loan is to a controlling shareholder (see Example 63 explanatory note 7). See Example 58 explanatory note 11 for the treatment of individuals where loans to them have been written off.

(ii)   Where the company has borrowed from a participator or his associate, or from a company controlled by a participator, or in which a participator has a 40% or greater holding, interest paid by the company more than twelve months after the period in which it would otherwise be treated as accruing cannot be deducted until it is paid, unless the participator or associate is a company that has included the interest in its profits on an accruals basis (FA 1996 Sch 9 para 2).

(iii)   Where the close company has borrowed from the participator or associate on a deeply discounted security (ie where the difference between issue price and redemption price is more than 0.5% per year or more than 15% overall), relief for the discount is not given until the security is redeemed (FA 1996 Sch 9 para 18), unless the holder of the security is within the loan relationships rules, ie is taxed on the discount.

See also Example 71 note 4 re the apportionment of gains of non-resident companies that would have been close companies if they had been UK resident.

Other points

9.   For detailed provisions on personal pension scheme contributions see Example 38. Capital gains tax is dealt with in Examples 73 to 83.

Question

You have been appointed to act professionally for Morrissey Ltd, a close company which was formed a month ago and which has an issued share capital of £50,000 divided into 50,000 ordinary shares of £1 each. The funds for the set-up of the company and subscription to share capital were provided by a substantial gain on sale of the whole of Mr Morrissey's previous business, which took place in January 2006.

The managing director, Mr Morrissey, has only a general knowledge of corporation tax and is particularly anxious that you should explain to him:

 (i)   what is meant by a 'distribution';

 (ii)   whether the fact that it is not intended that the company should declare any dividends during the first few years of its existence, but rather to retain any profits in the business, would have any taxation effects;

(iii)   whether the granting of a loan by the company to any of its shareholders would be affected by taxation;

(iv)   how the company might be affected from a taxation point of view if it had to go into liquidation.

Mr Morrissey stresses to you that it should be borne in mind that the company's operations will be confined to the UK, its income will only be derived from its trading profits and from the letting of property owned by it and it is not intended that the company's issued share capital should be altered in any way nor any other shares or securities issued. The profits are not expected to exceed the upper limit for small companies' rate.

Write to Mr Morrissey setting out the information requested by him.

Answer

10 Upping Street
Downtown
21 July 2009

Mr Morrissey
Morrissey Ltd
Downtown Industrial Estate
Downtown

Dear Mr Morrissey,

Thank you for your letter of 1 July asking me for information on the taxation treatment of certain matters affecting your company. The answers to the points raised by you are as follows:

(i) *Meaning of the term distribution*

The term distribution has a very wide meaning for corporation tax, and that meaning is extended in the case of companies controlled either by their directors or by five or fewer participators (broadly shareholders). Such companies are termed close companies and Morrissey Ltd falls within the definition.

Many of the provisions relating to distributions are concerned with share issues, redemptions etc, and since your company is not contemplating any changes in its share capital they will not apply. The term distribution in your case will therefore cover:

(a) Any dividends paid in cash

(b) Any distribution of assets in a non-cash form, and any benefit provided for shareholders or their associates (such as the use of cars, provision of living accommodation, entertainment etc). This will not usually apply where the assets or benefits are provided to a director, or to an employee earning £8,500 per annum or more. Directors and employees earning £8,500 per annum or more are charged to tax on the provision of assets and benefits as employment income and the company suffers a Class 1A national insurance contributions charge of 12.8%. The expense of the provision is deductible by the company in arriving at its profits so long as it can be shown to be wholly and exclusively for the purposes of the trade.

(ii) *Effect of retaining profits rather than paying dividends*

The fact that the company does not intend to make any distributions within the first few years will not have any immediate taxation effects and will undoubtedly assist with your cash flow and working capital requirements.

Some companies are required to pay corporation tax in instalments, but only where their profits exceed a specified limit, presently £1,500,000 (which is not expected to apply in your case). It should be mentioned that, as and when dividends are paid, the shareholders will receive a tax credit equal to one-ninth of the dividend (ie 10% on the grossed up amount of the dividend). Shareholders will only suffer an additional tax liability if they are higher rate taxpayers, the additional tax currently (until 6 April 2010) being equal to 25% of the cash dividend received (22.5% on the grossed up amount). After 6 April 2010 for those liable at the new higher rate of 50% (income over £150,000) the additional tax will be equal to 36.1% of the cash dividend or 32.5% of the grossed up amount.

If the company's profits can be retained and subsequently taken in a 'capital' form, this is likely to prove more beneficial for tax purposes. You will be aware of the benefits of the former taper relief from the sale of your previous company in January 2006, but taper relief was abolished with effect from 5 April 2008. The top rate for capital gains tax was 40%, which could be reduced to 10% through the effect of taper relief. From 6 April 2008, all capital gains are taxed at 18%, unless entrepreneur's relief applies, in which case the gain is reduced by 4/9ths, resulting in an effective rate of 10%.

Entrepreneur's relief was introduced with effect from 6 April 2008. It is of more limited scope than taper relief, as it applies only to significant disposals of business assts, and relief is limited to the first £1 million of net gains per lifetime realised since 6 April 2008. The gain from the sale of the previous business therefore does not count towards the £1 million limit, but if that gain would have qualified, certain held-over gains realised after 5 April 2005 could now qualify for relief.

Enterpreneurs' relief applies only to the disposal of the whole or a substantial part of a business, and also to associated business assets. Subject to a number of conditions, gains on sales of shareholdings in personal trading companies (companies in which the seller owned a holding of at least 5% for at least a year, and in which they were an officer or director), qualify for a reduction of 4/9ths of the gain.

The fact that the company receives letting income may, however, prevent it qualifying as a trading company, and therefore qualifying for entrepreneur's relief. Both taper relief, and the earlier retirement relief upon which entrepreneur's relief is to some extent modelled, contained provisions to prevent non-business assets being 'parked' in businesses to qualify for tax reliefs on sale of those businesses. For some purposes HMRC have stated that they consider that the principles of retirement relief apply to entrepreneur's relief, and this would have denied relief for non-business assets.

For taper relief purposes it had to be shown that any non-trading purposes had no substantial effect on the extent of the company's activities, then interpreted as letting receipts exceeding 20% of the combined trading and letting income, depending on the company's particular circumstances. Any substantial ownership of properties acquired with the intention of letting (other than holiday lets until 5 April 2010), is likely to disqualify the company from entrepreneur's relief. It may however be borne in mind that the difference in rate between business and non-business assets is now 8% (18%–10%), while previously the difference was up to 30% (40%–10%).

In the company's case, the opportunities for shareholders to take capital profits are relatively limited, for example, on receiving a capital sum on a liquidation (see (iv) below) or on selling shares back to the company on retirement (provided they have been held at least five years and certain other conditions are satisfied), in which case entrepreneur's relief should be available. Such considerations would not usually be expected to dictate the company's dividend policy during its early years, although reduction of surplus cash balances by payment of dividend may prove to some extent beneficial in establishing trading company status.

Under the taper relief regime, if the assets did not qualify as business assets, it was frequently beneficial to pay dividends rather than receive capital where non-business rates of taper relief applied to assets that had been held for significantly less than ten years. From 6 April 2008, capital gains treatment at either 10% or 18% is preferable to income tax treatment at an effective rate of 40%/50%.

(iii) *Loans to shareholders*

If the company makes loans to shareholders (other than loans of £15,000 or less to full-time directors or employees who do not own more than 5% of the share capital) the company will have to pay tax at 25% of the loan, repayable by HMRC as and when the loan is repaid by the shareholder to the company. This is a 'stand-alone' tax charge and is not deductible from the corporation tax payable on profits.

If the company should release or write off such a loan, the company can reclaim the tax paid. However, a shareholder who controls the company is connected with the company under the special rules for loans. As far as the shareholder is concerned, any amount released is grossed up at the dividend tax credit rate of 10%, ie by 100/90, and treated as income. It would, however, only be liable to the current higher dividend tax rate of 32½% (less the lower rate credit of 10%) where taxable income exceeded the basic rate limit (currently £37,400). Any higher rate liability is effectively 22½% of the gross amount released.

There will be no other effect on a shareholder who receives a loan from the company unless he earns £8,500 or more, or is a director. In that event he will be charged to tax under the employment-related loans provisions. This means that he will be deemed to have received extra remuneration equal to interest on the loan at the prevailing official rate less any interest which he actually pays to the company (which will be computed and returned on his P11D Form). This will not apply if the total loans outstanding in a tax year to that shareholder or anyone connected with him do not exceed £5,000. If the loan is one on which interest (if charged) would have been available for income tax relief, no taxable benefit arises.

You should also note that the company will have to pay Class 1A national insurance contributions at 12.8% on the deemed taxable benefit arising from the notional interest charge on non-qualifying loans. If a loan to a director-shareholder or other employee-shareholder is written off or released, HMRC will expect Class 1 national insurance contributions to be accounted for through the payroll on the amount written off as if cash had been paid to the shareholder.

Where loans to employees or directors are written off or released, there is ordinarily a deemed employment benefit to the value of the write-off or release that the employer must report on the P11D for income tax purposes. Where the loan is to a shareholder, however, the amount is treated for income tax purposes as a distribution as described above instead.

(iv)   *Tax consequences of liquidation*

If the company goes into liquidation, the commencement of the winding-up will denote the end of an accounting period and commencement of another for corporation tax. If the company ceases trading prior to the commencement of liquidation the cessation of trading also triggers the end of a corporation tax accounting period.

The cessation will require balancing adjustments to be made in respect of capital allowances claimed and if trading losses arise in the final twelve months that are not covered by other profits of the same period, relief may be claimed against the total profits of the three previous years, latest first. Profits may arise in the final trading period in the form of chargeable gains on the disposal of assets, but it would be necessary for the contract for the disposal to be made before the cessation of trade to enable trading losses in the final accounting period to be set off against those gains. Brought forward trading losses cannot be set against other sources of income or gains.

To the extent that the company retains income and capital profits, a double tax charge will inevitably occur on liquidation. The company will have paid corporation tax at the time the profits were made, and unless they have been distributed to the shareholders as a dividend before the liquidation, the retentions will swell the amounts received by the shareholders in the winding-up. Amounts paid out to the shareholders during the liquidation will be chargeable to capital gains tax, after deducting their base value for the shares, any capital gains tax reliefs, including entrepreneur's relief if applicable, and any available personal annual exemption. Where entrepreneur's relief applies, the capital distribution should be made within three years of cessation of trade to ensure the conditions for relief are met.

I shall be happy to provide any additional information you require, or to discuss further with you the matters dealt with above.

Yours sincerely,

John Smith

Explanatory Notes

Distribution – general meaning

1.   For companies in general the term 'distribution' means (ICTA 1988 ss 209–211):

   (a)   Any dividend paid by the company, including a capital dividend

   (b)   Any other distribution out of the company's assets, whether in cash or not, except a repayment of capital or an amount for which new consideration is given

   (c)   Any bonus issue of securities or redeemable shares issued in respect of shares or securities of the company (excluding scrip dividends – see explanatory note 6)

   (d)   Any excess of market value of benefit received where assets or liabilities are transferred to shareholders over any new consideration given (except for intra-group transfers)

   (e)   Where share capital (other than fully paid preference share capital) is repaid, bonus issues made at the same time or subsequently. This does not apply to non-close listed companies where the bonus issue is not redeemable share capital and takes place more than 10 years after the repayment of capital

   (f)   Interest payments on securities in certain circumstances, eg where the interest exceeds a normal commercial rate or varies with the company's profits. This does not, however, catch interest on 'ratchet loans' (ie loans where the rate increases as profits deteriorate and vice versa). The legislation is intended only to apply where interest effectively represents a share in profits. The provisions are complex and are subject to anti-avoidance provisions in ICTA 1988 s 212 which prevent interest payments from one company to another being artificially turned into franked investment income in the receiving company's hands because of the distribution provisions.

2.   Distributions in a winding-up do not count as income distributions and are subject to capital gains tax (as a 'deemed' disposal of shares under TCGA 1992 s 122).

3.   The distribution provisions are relaxed in relation to demergers (see Example 68) and the purchase by a company of its own shares (see Example 61).

Qualifying and non-qualifying distributions

4.   Non-qualifying distributions are bonus issues of redeemable shares or securities, either issued directly or issued out of bonus redeemable shares or securities received from another company (ICTA 1988 s 14). The shareholder is liable where appropriate to the excess of the dividend rate upper rate of 32½% over the dividend income ordinary rate of 10% on the grossed up amount of the distribution. The company is required to notify HMRC within fourteen days after the end of the quarter in which the non-qualifying distribution is made (ICTA 1988 s 234). When the shares are redeemed the redemption is a qualifying distribution but tax paid at excess rates on the non-qualifying distribution may be set against any tax due at excess rates on the later qualifying distribution (ICTA 1988 s 233).

Distribution – extended meaning for close companies

5.   For close companies the term distribution has an extended meaning (ICTA 1988 s 418). It covers the provision of benefits to participators and their associates, except those provided to directors and employees earning £8,500 or more, which are already assessable as employment income (see Example 9). The calculation of the amount of the distribution in respect of benefits to participators is made in the same way as for benefits to directors and employees earning £8,500 or more (ICTA 1988 s 418(4)). For further details on directors' loans see Example 58. Close company liquidations are dealt with in Example 60.

Scrip dividends

6.   As indicated in note 1(c), scrip dividends, ie dividends taken in the form of shares rather than in cash, are not treated as distributions.

   Where an individual takes a scrip dividend, he is deemed to have received income equal to the 'appropriate amount in cash', grossed up at the dividend income rate of 10%. The 'appropriate amount in cash' means the amount of the cash option, unless it is substantially different from the market value of the shares, 'substantially' being interpreted by HMRC as 15% or more either way (Statement of Practice A8). In practice HMRC will ignore a difference of up to 17% in any case not involving avoidance. If the difference is substantial, the appropriate amount in cash is the market value of the shares on the first day of dealing. Basic rate taxpayers have no liability on the scrip dividend, but the notional credit is not repayable. Those liable to higher rate tax pay tax at 22½% (32½% less 10%) on the grossed up amount as for cash dividends (ITTOIA ss 409–414).

   The gross equivalent of scrip dividends is income of a deceased's estate when such shares are issued to personal representatives. It is also income of discretionary and accumulation trusts (other than trusts in which the settlor has retained an interest), the trustees being liable to tax at the same 32½% rate as individuals (less the 10% credit).

   Where scrip dividends are issued to a company, or a trust in which the settlor retains an interest, they are capital rather than income, with a capital gains base cost of nil.

   Companies have to make separate quarterly returns of any scrip dividends issued (ICTA 1988 s 250).

Loans written off

7.   See Example 56 explanatory note 8 part (e) for the treatment of loans written off for companies and Example 58 note 11 for the treatment of individuals.

Capital gains tax taper relief

8.   For detailed notes on entrepreneur's relief see Example 78.

Question

Misses Stiff and Starch are the only directors of Oaks in Charnwood Ltd, which owns a large country property from which it carries on the business of a rest home for the elderly.

They live on the premises in order properly to attend to the residents, sharing with their lifelong friend Miss Gentle (who is employed as resident matron) a private suite, the annual rental equivalent of which has been agreed with HMRC at £15,000 for the whole suite. The suite was fully refurnished at the company's expense on 7 April 2009 at a cost of £6,000 and the cost of lighting, heating, cleaning, repairs and maintenance in 2009/10 was £3,000 for the whole suite. Neither the directors nor Miss Gentle make any contribution to the company for this accommodation.

The equal shareholders are Misses Stiff and Starch together with Miss Stiff's brother, Donald. Although Donald does not live at the rest home he has his meals there daily, the cost of the meals being £2,000 in the year ended 31 March 2010. Donald has not contributed anything towards this cost. Misses Stiff and Starch each pay to the company an amount representing the cost of their own meals.

Miss Gentle is paid a salary of £9,000 per annum. As well as living on the premises, she has the use of a 1,900 cc company car with an original list price of £12,000 (CO_2 emissions figure 164 grams per kilometre) and the annual running expenses borne by the company amount to £1,200. Miss Gentle reimburses to the company the cost of petrol provided for her private motoring. The annual mileage is 10,000, of which 2,600 relates to private motoring.

Miss Gentle has an interest-free loan from the company of £4,300, the whole amount of which was outstanding during 2009/10. On 6 April 2009 the company had released her from repaying £700, the original loan having been £5,000 in 1999, to help her to furnish a seaside cottage which she intends to use as a retirement home.

The directors each receive a salary of £24,000 per annum under the PAYE system.

No dividends have been paid during the year.

During the year ended 31 March 2010, the company made private payments for the directors which were charged to their current/loan accounts, as follows (there being nil balances on the accounts at the beginning of the year):

	Stiff £	Starch £
30 June 2009	3,600	–
30 September 2009	2,500	950
31 December 2009	1,000	600
31 March 2010	2,500	450
	9,600	2,000

The directors have the use of company cars. Miss Stiff's is a Volvo 70 series (CO_2 emissions figure 240 grams per kilometre), that had a list price when new of £24,320, and Miss Starch's is a Volkswagen Golf (petrol CO_2 emissions figure 159 grams per kilometre) list price when new £19,270. Miss Stiff travels extensively on the business of the company and in 2009/10 recorded 20,000 business miles. Miss Starch's total mileage was 15,000, of which 5,000 was for business purposes. The company provides all the motor running expenses.

The corporation tax adjusted profit for the year ended 31 March 2010, before any adjustment arising out of Donald's meals, was £20,650.

Apart from her income from Oaks in Charnwood Ltd, Miss Gentle has gross building society interest of £6,000 per annum.

(a) Calculate the corporation tax payable by the company for the year ended 31 March 2010.

(b) State the amounts of directors' assessable emoluments for 2009/10 in respect of each of Miss Stiff and Miss Starch and calculate the national insurance contributions liability payable by the company on their emoluments.

(c) Calculate the total income tax payable by Miss Gentle for 2009/10.

(d) State the taxation position resulting from the balances on the directors' current/loan accounts with the company from time to time.

(e) State what the consequences and procedure would be if it was discovered that, during the year to 31 March 2010, Misses Stiff and Starch had each irregularly retained for themselves company income of £7,500, which had not been reflected in the company accounts.

The official rate of interest is set at 4.75% for 2009/10.

Answer

(a)   **Corporation tax computation – year ended 31 March 2010**

	£
Profit chargeable to corporation tax (20,650 + 2,000 for Donald's meals)	22,650

(The cost of the directors' and employees' benefits will already have been charged in arriving at the profit and is allowable)

	£
Corporation tax thereon: 22,650 @ 21%, payable 1 January 2011	4,757

(b)   **Directors' assessable emoluments – 2009/10**

	Miss Stiff £	Miss Starch £
Remuneration for year ended 31 March 2010	24,000	24,000
Use of company car:		
car benefit –		
Volvo 70 (CO_2 = 240) 24,320 × 35%	8,512	
Volkswagen Golf (CO_2 = 159) 19,270 × 19%		3,661
car fuel benefit –		
Volvo (£16,900 × 35%)	5,915	
Volkswagen (£16,900 × 19%)		3,211
Annual rental equivalent of accommodation		
(1/3rd each × 15,000)	5,000	5,000
Value of furnishings (20% × 6,000 × 1/3)	400	400
and services (3,000 × 1/3)	1,000	1,000
Beneficial loan interest (see (d))	205	–
	45,032	37,272

Company's national insurance liability re directors – 2009/10

	£	£
Employer's Class 1 NIC (24,000 – 5,715) @ 12.8%	2,340	2,340
Employer's Class 1A NIC 21,032/13,272 @ 12.8%	2,692	1,699
Total employer's NIC	5,032	4,039

(c)   **Miss Gentle – tax payable 2009/10**

	£
Salary – Oaks in Charnwood Ltd	9,000
Use of company car (CO_2 = 164) 12,000 × 20%	2,400
Amount of loan released	700
	12,100
Benefit of furnishings, heating and lighting etc	
(1,000 + 400, but limited to 10% of other emoluments)	1,210
Emoluments from Oaks in Charnwood Ltd	13,310
Building society interest	6,000
	19,310
Less: Personal allowance	6,475
Taxable income	12,835

		£
On savings and earned income	12,835 @ 20%	2,567

The savings starter rate band of £2,440 applies only to the extent that non-savings income does not exceed £2,440, as savings income is treated as the higher slice of income.

Miss Gentle will not be charged to tax on the benefit of the interest-free loan, since it does not exceed £5,000. She is, however, charged on the loan released, as indicated above.

(d)   **Tax position on directors' loans**

Tax charge under ICTA 1988 s 419

The company will have to pay tax on the amount of the directors' overdrawn accounts at 31 March 2010 amounting to 25% × £11,600 = £2,900. The tax is payable by 1 January 2011, interest being charged from that date if the tax is not paid (ICTA 1988 s 419). The tax is not payable if the loan is repaid within that time (see explanatory note 9).

The company must report the loans made during the year ended 31 March 2010 on supplementary page CT 600A on its self-assessment corporation tax return for the year. If it fails to do so, it will have made an inaccurate return. Because the return is due after 1 April 2009, the new behaviour-based penalty regime applies, under which penalties from 0% to 100% are applied, depending on the category of the inaccuracy, and co-operation provided. The categories of inaccuracy are: mistake without carelessness (no penalty); careless (maximum 30% of potential lost revenue, minimum 0%); deliberate not concealed (maximum 70%, minimum 20%); and deliberate and concealed (maximum 100%, minimum 30%). The minimum percentages noted here would apply only if the company disclosed the omission of the amounts without being prompted by an HMRC enquiry. For prompted disclosures, the minimum rates would be 15%, 35% and 50% respectively.

For these purposes no account is taken of s 419 tax which is refundable or relievable due to the loan being repaid (FA 2007 Sch 24 para 5(4)).

To fall into the 'careless' category, the directors would have to demonstrate that they took reasonable care, based on their circumstances and abilities, after seeking suitable advice. There is no likelihood of HMRC accepting the behaviour described in part(e) as merely careless. Indeed HMRC states that 'deliberately withdrawing money for personal use from an incorporated business and not making any attempt to make sure it is treated correctly for tax purposes' is an example of a deliberate inaccuracy. If the loans were declared in the accounts, but not properly declared in the corporation tax return as loans to directors, then penalties under the 'deliberate but not concealed' category might be expected as a minimum, although HMRC might even argue for 'deliberate and concealed' on the basis that the directors would have known that the failure to show the drawings in the accounts would hide them from scrutiny by an inspector.

There would be no assessment on the directors, but if the company released or wrote off the loans or any part of them, then that part released or written off would be included in the director's taxable income, grossed up at 10%. Basic rate taxpayers would have no liability, but higher rate taxpayers would have to account for tax at the difference between the dividend income upper rate, currently 32½% and the dividend income ordinary rate of 10% on the grossed up equivalent of the loan (ITTOIA 2005 s 416). The effective rate is therefore currently 22½% of the 'gross' amount released, ie 25% of the cash amount. (This charge takes priority over the release of loans taxed as a benefit under ITEPA 2003 s 188.) HMRC believes that loan write-offs must be treated as payments of earnings for Class 1 national insurance purposes, although there is no specific statutory provision to this effect. The s 416 charge is relevant only to tax, so although the write-off is taxed as a distribution rather an employment benefit, Class 1 contributions remain payable.

If the directors repay all or part of the loans *after* the s 419 tax falls due, the company may claim repayment of the appropriate part of the tax paid (ICTA 1988 s 419(4)). The tax will be due for repayment nine months after the end of the accounting period in which the loan is repaid, and the repayment will attract interest from that date (see explanatory note 10). If the loan is released or written off, the company may reclaim the tax in the same way as for loans repaid (see explanatory note 11).

Charge on directors under employment-related loans rules

Notwithstanding the operation of ICTA 1988 s 419 HMRC will also apply the employment-related loans rules contained in ITEPA 2003 ss 173–191 by calculating the notional interest chargeable as a benefit.

There will be no charge on Miss Starch, since the total amount outstanding at any time in the year did not exceed £5,000 (ITEPA 2003 s 180). There will, however, be a charge on Miss Stiff. The normal method of calculation (ITEPA 2003 s 182) is to take the average of the opening and closing overdrawn balances at the beginning and end of the tax year (or from the date the account was overdrawn to the date the loan was repaid, as the case may be), multiply by the complete months for which the loan was outstanding and divide by 12, then multiply by the official rate of interest. This gives the following result:

Average balance for period 1 July 2009 – 5 April 2010

$$\frac{3,600 + 9,600}{2} = £6,600$$

6,600 × 9/12 (9 months) @ 4.75% = £235

The 'alternative' method shows a lower amount of interest payable, ie £205 (see explanatory note 6). Miss Stiff may elect to be assessed on the lower figure.

(e) **Irregular extractions of company funds**

The profits of the company would be increased by £15,000, and the tax payable adjusted accordingly.

Misses Stiff and Starch would also be treated as having had an advance of £7,500 each from the company, totalling £15,000, on which a tax charge at 25% amounting to £3,750 would be payable to HMRC (ICTA 1988 s 419). This £3,750 would be repayable by HMRC to the company following the repayment by Misses Stiff and Starch to the company of the £15,000 irregularities (ICTA 1988 s 419(4)). The underpaid corporation tax and tax under s 419 would attract interest and penalties. Because the due date for filing the return is after 1 April 2009, the new penalty regime applies. Where a corporation tax return is shown to understate the true tax liability the company is subject to a tax-related penalty, the amount of which depends on the nature of the inaccuracy, and cooperation given. For these purposes, any understated s 419 tax is treated as a full tax liability (with no credit offset given for any repayment of the loan after the nine months due date) (FA 2007 Sch 24 para 5(4)).

Penalties under the new regime are based on tax lost: 30% for careless action, 70% for deliberate but not concealed action, and 100% for deliberate and concealed action. HMRC have powers of mitigation, firstly to recognise whether the taxpayer makes an unprompted disclosure and, secondly, for co-operation and disclosure, with a minimum penalty for unprompted disclosures of 0% for careless behaviour, 20% for deliberate not concealed understatements, and 30% for deliberate but concealed understatements. For prompted disclosures, the minimum rates are 15%, 35% and 50%. Mitigation from the relevant maximum down to the relevant minimum is based on the quality of disclosure, which in HMRC's view is broken down into the three elements of: (1) telling HMRC about the inaccuracy; (2) helping to sort out the discrepancies; and (3) giving access to records/IT.

As the loans are not reflected in the accounts the inaccuracy is very likely to be considered as 'deliberate and concealed'. The 'deliberate and concealed' category includes inaccuracies that have been concealed by creating false documents, falsifying documents, recording understated sales/ overstated deductible expenditure, destroying records or using undisclosed bank accounts.

HMRC's technical guidance gives a number of examples, including

– 'systematically diverting takings into undisclosed bank accounts and covering the traces',

– 'creating sales records that deliberately understate the value of the goods sold, the balance of the full price being paid separately to the person'.

Whether the inaccuracy is considered as 'deliberate and concealed' as opposed to 'deliberate not concealed' depends on the exact circumstances of the case. Whichever category applies, the penalties will be mitigated very substantially for unprompted disclosure, co-operation and access to records. The company should provide the help and access required by HMRC.

Because of the irregularities which had been discovered, HMRC would undoubtedly seek to satisfy themselves that no other irregularities, extractive or otherwise, had occurred. They would do this by an in-depth examination of the company records and of the personal finances of the directors, in the latter case satisfying themselves in particular that all personal bank/building society lodgements, asset purchases and personal and private expenditure were properly explained and accounted for.

HMRC are strictly entitled to assess Misses Stiff and Starch on employment-related loan interest under ITEPA 2003 s 175 in respect of the advances of £7,500 each. They have announced they will not do so where the extractions also involve liabilities to corporation tax and under s 419 with interest and penalties thereon.

Explanatory Notes

Close company benefits in kind to participators

1. The provision of Donald's meals is a distribution and thus cannot be deducted in computing trading profits (ICTA 1988 s 418(4)). Whilst the benefits in kind treatment extends to services provided for the family or household of a director (or employee earning £8,500 or more), family or household for this purpose is defined as spouse or civil partner; sons and daughters and their spouses/civil partners; parents; and servants, dependants and guests; the term does not therefore include a brother or sister (ICTA 1988 s 168(4)). Hence in this example the meals are treated as a distribution to Donald as a shareholder and not as a benefit to his sister.

Provision of living accommodation

2. Miss Gentle is not assessable on the value of the benefit arising from her living accommodation since she is a representative occupier, ie, one whose duties require her to live on the premises for their proper performance (ITEPA 2003 s 99(1)). Directors are not entitled to the representative occupier exemption unless they are full-time directors owning not more than 5% of the shares. Misses Stiff and Starch do not come within this exemption and are chargeable (ITEPA 2003 s 99(3)). The legislation now covers the position where directors/employees share the use of living accommodation – by virtue of ITEPA 2003 s 108, the total benefits charges will not exceed the amount that would have been chargeable on a single employee.

    The value of living accommodation is based on the old gross annual value for rating purposes. Employers are asked to estimate rateable values for new property and also where there are significant changes to existing property, and their estimates will be agreed by HMRC with assistance from the District Valuer.

    There is specific legislation to prevent salary sacrifice schemes being used to reduce the tax charge for the provision of living accommodation (ITEPA 2003 s 109).

    Residential care homes are classed as domestic dwellings for council tax, with the liability for payment of the tax being that of the owner, ie, Oaks in Charnwood Ltd in this example, rather than the residents. Had the property been mixed business/private property instead of a care home, with Misses Stiff, Starch and Gentle having to live there to do their jobs, and the company had paid the council tax on the domestic accommodation, Misses Stiff and Starch would have been assessable on the benefit relating to them, but Miss Gentle would have escaped tax under the representative occupier provisions.

3. For a P11D employee, the representative occupier exemption does not extend to the provision of furnishings and the cost of lighting, heating, cleaning, repairs and maintenance. The normal calculation of the benefit is the expense of providing the services and where an asset like furniture is made available, 20% of the cost (ITEPA 2003 s 205(3)(b)), but for a representative occupier the assessable benefit is limited to 10% of the earnings excluding the expenditure in question (ITEPA 2003 s 315). Earnings for this purpose are after deducting mileage allowance relief, capital allowances given by way of a deduction from earnings, and contributions to registered pension schemes.

    The provision of care in residential homes for the elderly is exempt from VAT (although those that have been trading since before 2002 can register and charge VAT so that they can recover input tax). If Oaks in Charnwood had been registered for VAT following the *Kingscrest* decision, it would not have been able to claim a set-off for input tax on repairs, refurbishments and other expenses relating to domestic accommodation provided for directors and their families (VATA 1994 s 24(3)). Any such non-recoverable input tax would be deducted as an expense in computing profit. As a non-registered business, Oaks in Charnwood will have included any VAT it has suffered in all its expenditure taken into account for tax purposes, any VAT relating to business entertaining being disallowed along with the entertaining expenditure itself.

Provision of cars and fuel

4. Directors and employees earning £8,500 or more are assessable on the benefit of private use of a motor car (ITEPA 2003 s 120).

    The assessable benefit is based on a percentage of the relevant car's list price, the percentage being graduated according to the carbon dioxide (CO_2) emissions rating of the relevant car (the emissions figure for a car being rounded down to the nearest 5 grams per kilometre). The relevant CO_2 ratings for the various company cars are given in the example. In practice, details of CO_2 ratings can be obtained from the New Car Fuel Consumption and Emission Figures booklet published by the Vehicle Certification Agency – also found on the Internet at www.vcacarfueldata.org.uk. For detailed notes on the company car benefit regime (including the relevant CO_2 ratings tables) and the related VAT and national insurance position, see Examples 9 and 10.

Where employees have private petrol paid for by their employer (whether directly or by reimbursement), the same percentage which applies to the car's list price is also applied to a statutory figure of £16,900 from 6 April 2008 (previously £14,400) (ITEPA 2003 ss 149–153).

Benefit charge on interest-free or cheap loans

5.   Where a company makes a loan either interest-free or at a rate below the 'official rate' to an employee earning £8,500 per annum or more or to a director (or to their relatives, meaning spouse, parents and remoter forebears, children and remoter issue, brothers and sisters, and the spouses of any of these relatives) the benefit is charged to tax under ITEPA 2003 ss 173 –191 on the shortfall of the interest charged compared with the official rate. The official rate is normally set in advance for the whole of the tax year: it was set at 6.25% for 2008/09, although the drastic changes to base rate and mortgage rates in late 2008 led to the official rate being reduced to 4.75% from 1 March 2009, which was the first mid-year change for many years. The average rate for 2008/09 became 6.1%.

There is no tax charge on loans made to employees on commercial terms by employers who lend or supply goods and services on credit to the general public. No employment-related loan charge arises if the loan is a qualifying loan, ie, where the interest on the loan (irrespective of whether it is actually paid) would qualify for income tax relief (for example, a loan taken out to buy shares in a close company or a loan used for trading purposes – see Example 1 explanatory note 13) (ITEPA 2003 s 178). Nor is there any charge if the total of all non-qualifying loans to any person or those connected with him do not exceed £5,000 at any time in the tax year (ITEPA 2003 s 180). If there are qualifying loans and non-qualifying loans, there is no charge on the non-qualifying loans if they do not exceed £5,000 in total at any time in the tax year.

If the loan is for a qualifying purpose for interest relief (see Example 1 explanatory note 13), the tax relief due on the interest paid reduces the tax chargeable.

6.   The normal method of calculation of the beneficial loan interest is shown in part (d) of the example. An employee may elect for the interest to be calculated using the alternative method. The alternative method may also be used if the inspector so requires (ITEPA 2003 s 183). The time limit for the employee or inspector to make such an election is one year from 31 January following the relevant tax year. To calculate the interest under the alternative method, the amounts outstanding for each day in the tax year for which the interest rate is the same are added together, divided by 365 (or 366 in the case of a leap year) and multiplied by the official rate. The amounts arrived at for each rate are then added together. The interest for Miss Stiff on the alternative method is therefore calculated as follows:

1.7.09 – 30.9.09	3,600 × 92 days	=	331,200
1.10.09 – 31.12.09	6,100 × 92 days	=	561,200
1.1.10 – 31.3.10	7,100 × 90 days	=	639,000
1.4.10 – 5.4.10	9,600 × 5 days	=	48,000
			1,579,400

$$\frac{1,579,400}{365} \times 4.75\% = £205$$

7.   Employers must show the cash equivalents of employment-related loans on Forms P11D, a copy of the P11D being given to employees (see Example 8). Where there are several loans, the loans are not aggregated to calculate the benefits. Employers who are close companies may, however, elect to aggregate non-qualifying employment-related loans in the same currency that are outstanding at the same time in the tax year (ITEPA 2003 s 187).

Class 1A NIC charge on taxable benefits

8. Employer's Class 1A national insurance contributions are chargeable on all taxable benefits in kind provided to P11D employees and directors (except for certain childcare benefits and apart from those already subject to the normal Class 1 charge, such as loans written off, readily convertible assets and the payment of personal bills). The Class 1A national insurance contributions charge is based on cash equivalents calculated under the taxable benefits provisions. See Example 48 for details.

Loans by close companies to participators

9. If a close company makes a loan or advances any money to a participator, there are tax implications for the company under ICTA 1988 s 419, as indicated in part (d) of the example. These are, in addition to the employment-related loans, rules where the participator is a director or £8,500+ employee. A loan is treated as made where the participator incurs a debt to the close company, or to a third party who assigns the debt to the close company. The provisions of s 419 do not apply to:

    (a) a loan made in the ordinary course of a moneylending business;

    (b) a debt for goods or services unless more than six months' credit or a longer credit period than normal is given; and

    (c) a loan of up to £15,000 to a full-time employee/director owning not more than 5% of the ordinary share capital.

    As indicated in part (d) of the example, under self-assessment, loans to participators are reported on the supplementary Form CT 600A with the corporation tax return CT 600, which must be submitted within twelve months from the end of the company's accounting period.

    The 25% tax charge on the loan is due nine months and one day after the end of the accounting period in which the loan is made (ICTA 1988 s 419), and interest is charged from that date if the tax is not paid on time. Tax is not payable if the whole of the loan is repaid within the nine month period. Companies show the tax on s 419 loans in their tax returns as part of the total tax due, but can claim an offsetting deduction if the loan has been repaid before the return is filed.

Repayment of loans after tax paid

10. When all or part of the loan is repaid after the tax has been paid, the company may claim repayment of the appropriate amount of tax, the time limit for the claim being six years after the end of the accounting period in which the loan is repaid (ICTA 1988 s 419(4)). However, this tax is not repayable until nine months after the end of the accounting period in which the loan is repaid and interest on the repayment runs from that date (ICTA 1988 s 826(4)).

    Thus in part (d) of the example, if the directors repaid the loans on or before 1 January 2010 the company would not have to pay tax on the loans under ICTA 1988 s 419. If the loans were repaid in (say) February 2011, ie, in the year to 31 March 2011, the company should have paid the tax by 1 January 2011 (interest being charged from that date if it had not) and would not be entitled to repayment until 1 January 2012, interest on the tax repayable running from that date.

Loans written off

11. If a loan or overdrawing is written off by a company, the effect on both the lender and the borrower needs to be considered.

    As far as the lender company is concerned, writing off loans is normally allowable under the 'loan relationships' rules unless the parties are connected, the 'connected' test does not apply to *all* participators, only to controlling shareholders (see Example 63 for the detailed provisions). The company may recover the tax paid on loans written off in the same way as for loans repaid (ICTA 1988 s 419).

The release of a loan due to a 'non-connected' company gives rise to a taxable credit in the borrower's books, except where the release is part of a relevant compromise or arrangement (FA 1996 Sch 9 para 5(3)). A released debt for expenditure previously deducted against the borrower's trading profits produces a taxable receipt under CTA 2009 s 94. (This debt would fall outside the loan relationship regime as it represents an amount due for the supply of goods and services and not the lending of money (FA 1996 s 81)).

For close companies, the treatment for a shareholder of loans written off (including a shareholder who is a director or employee) is as indicated in part (d) of the example. Thus s 419 loans written off are treated as being net of the dividend income ordinary rate of 10% (ITTOIA 2005 s 416), effectively being taxed in the same way as dividends, but (in the opinion of HMRC) nevertheless subject to Class 1 national insurance contributions if the shareholder is an employee or director.

If the write-off of the loan is not caught by the close company rules for loans to shareholders, and it has been obtained by reason of the borrower's employment (such as the loan to Miss Gentle, who is not a shareholder but is an employee), then whether the employee is a P11D employee or not, and whether or not the loan is at a rate of interest below the 'official rate', the director or employee is treated as having received an equivalent amount of remuneration at that time (which also attracts Class 1 national insurance contributions). This does not apply to loans written off on death. Nor does it apply if the write-off occurs after the employee has left, except for P11D employees. Any such loan write-off on termination of the employment cannot benefit from the £30,000 exemption under s 403 because it is already taxable under the benefits code.

Irregular extraction of company funds

12.   Extractive irregularities are not treated as additional remuneration. They are not subject to tax on the directors. Instead, the directors are accountable to the company for their repayment, corporation tax then being payable on the additional profit if the extractions arise from suppressed income or overstated expenses. Tax at 25% is also payable by the company pending repayment by the directors to the company of the amounts extracted. Since interest and penalties are calculated on both the corporation tax and the s 419 liabilities which arise out of the same irregularities, the interest and penalty cost is that much greater than in the case of identical irregularities by sole traders and partners.

Question

Tank Engines Ltd trades as a manufacturer of toy train and railway sets, and draws up accounts to 31 March each year. It has a dormant subsidiary company, Toby Ltd. There are no other associated companies. Following a successful advertising campaign, the company is making substantial profits and expects that its profits for the current year to 31 March 2010 will be around £1,200,000. (Its total asset value at the year end is expected to be around £6,000,000.)

Mr Thomas (aged 52) is the company's managing director and owns 800 of the company's 1,000 £1 ordinary shares. The other 200 shares are held by the trustees of an accumulation and maintenance trust set up for the benefit of Mr Thomas's children, Annie and Clarabel.

Following this year's exceptional trading performance, Mr Thomas wishes to extract £200,000 for himself either as a bonus or dividend. He already draws a monthly salary of £4,000. Mr Thomas is a member of the company's pension scheme (which he joined in July 1984).

Mr Thomas also plans a £50,000 bonus for each of his other directors, Mr Gordon and Mr Toby. Both directors have intimated that they would like a small shareholding in Tank Engines Ltd as they have both worked for the company for over 10 years and would welcome a sense of proprietorship. Mr Thomas is agreeable to this provided they take no more than 5% of the company's total shareholding.

Mr Thomas also wishes to pass some income to his wife, who does not work for the company and has little personal income. He realises that he cannot pay her a significant salary and therefore wishes the company to issue her with sufficient non-voting preference shares to provide her with an annual dividend of £10,000.

Mr Thomas has asked you to comment on his proposals at a meeting before the company's year end on 31 March 2010. Prepare a detailed briefing paper for Mr Thomas to consider at the meeting.

Answer

Mr Thomas – Bonus v dividend

1. The decision to take £200,000 either as a bonus or dividend depends on a number of factors. A key consideration is usually the combined tax and national insurance (NIC) cost for each option. In this case, the company's anticipated profits fall within the marginal small companies' rate band of £300,000 to £1,500,000 for the year to 31 March 2010 and so the marginal rate is 29.75%.

    The marginal limits are not reduced by reference to the dormant subsidiary company. Although this is an associated company, it is disregarded as it is not carrying on a trade or business in the relevant accounting period (ICTA 1988 s 13(4)).

    As Mr Thomas draws a salary of £48,000 per annum, he is a higher-rate taxpayer and above the upper earnings limit for NIC purposes (£43,875 for 2009/10). Thus he will only be liable for the additional 1% charge on any bonus. Employer's NIC would be paid on the bonus at the rate of 12.8%.

2. A comparison between the *bonus v dividend* routes shows the following:

	Bonus £		*Dividend* £
Profits to be extracted	200,000		200,000
Less: Employer's NIC 200,000 × 12.8/112.8	(22,695)		
Corporation tax 200,000 @ 29.75%			(59,500)
Bonus/dividend payment	177,305		140,500
Less: PAYE/NIC on bonus 177,305 @ 41%	(72,695)		
Dividend		140,500	
Tax credit 1/9th		15,611	
		156,111	
Dividend income tax @ 32.5%		50,736	
Tax credit		(15,611)	(35,125)
Net cash available	104,610		105,375

    Extraction of the profits by dividend rather than bonus would leave Mr Thomas with (105,375 – 104,610 =) £765 additional cash.

3. PAYE is deducted at the time of the bonus payment. If the bonus was paid in March 2010, the PAYE tax would be due by 19 April 2010 (or 22 April if paid electronically). In the case of a dividend, the tax would be paid in accordance with Mr Thomas's self-assessment payment position. Assuming Mr Thomas's only income for the previous year was his salary, the dividend upper rate tax on a dividend paid in March 2010 would not fall due until 31 January 2011, and the corporation tax on the profits out of which the dividend is to be paid would not be due until 31 December 2010. A dividend would thus also offer a small cash flow saving.

    If the bonus is provided in the accounts and paid (or made available) within nine months after the year end (ie by 31 December 2010), it can still be deducted against the company's taxable profits for the year ended 31 March 2010. However, delaying the payment of the bonus until 2010/11 would make some of it suffer the proposed 50% maximum income tax rate, rather than the current maximum of 40%.

4.   From 6 April 2006, pension contributions may be made based on the lesser of the cumulative lifetime limit of £1,750,000 or the annual limit of £245,000 for 2009/10. These are contribution limits, not the limits for tax relief, which are lower for practical purposes. Where contributions are paid by an individual rather than an employer, tax relief will be obtained on an amount of the greater of £3,600 or 100% of earnings. The payment of a bonus will therefore increase the potential amount of higher rate tax relief available to Mr Thomas on additional pension contributions, although both dividend and bonus could take Mr Thomas's income over £150,000 for the year, which will trigger the anti-forestalling provisions in FA 2009 Sch 35, thereby limiting tax relief to basic rate on any contributions in excess of £20,000 by means of the special annual allowance charge. If contributions are paid by an employer, they will be tax-deductible provided they are expended wholly and exclusively for the purpose of the trade.

5.   Other factors to consider would include the following:

(i)   The fact that dividends are payable rateably to all shareholders may not provide a fair basis for rewarding the 'working' shareholder, Mr Thomas. If, for example, a dividend of £200,000 was declared, 20% would be received by the trustees of the accumulation and maintenance trust, leaving Mr Thomas with only £160,000. As an alternative, a dividend of £250,000 could be proposed, with the trustees of the accumulation and maintenance trust waiving their entitlement to the trust's dividend of £50,000 (20% × £250,000) before it becomes payable, but waiver of dividends may be perceived as a form of income shifting, and could give rise to an HMRC enquiry.

(ii)   Share valuations – while dividend payments may influence *minority* share valuations for capital tax purposes, they would not usually be a factor in determining *controlling* shareholding valuations, which tend to be based on earnings and/or net asset values.

(iii)   The income shifting proposals were put forward in 2007/08, but have been deferred indefinitely. These were broad enough to affect Tank Engines, even though the profits are earned by the company as a whole rather than being attributable to identifiable individuals. Payment of bonus would avoid any likely problems with future income shifting legislation.

(iv)   The pension anti-forestalling rules should not apply to an employer pension contribution that is made in 2009/10 where there is no salary sacrifice arrangement and Mr Thomas's total income remains below £150,000 for the year and has not exceeded that figure in the previous two years.

6.   Although the dividend route gives an additional £765 in post tax funds, it limits Mr Thomas' options on additional contributions to his individual registered pension scheme, and may cause difficulties with future income shifting legislation. Because of the comparatively small monetary difference, the non-monetary factors must be explained fully to Mr Thomas

Mr Gordon and Mr Toby – bonus

7.   The net cost to the company of paying £100,000 out as bonuses (£50,000 each) to Mr Gordon and Mr Toby would be:

	£
Bonuses (50,000 × 2)	100,000
Employer's NIC @ 12.8%	12,800
Gross cost	112,800
Corporation tax relief @ 29.75%	(33,558)
Net cost	79,242

The bonuses would rank for tax relief if paid during the year ended 31 March 2010 or if provided in the accounts to 31 March 2010 and paid within nine months of the year-end.

Mr Gordon and Mr Toby – shares in Tank Engines Ltd

8. Any issue or transfer of shares in the company to Mr Gordon and Mr Toby would be regarded as obtained by virtue of their employment. Each director would have an amount of employment income equal to the difference between the market value of the shares less the amount they paid for them. In this instance, the market value of the shares would be based on the value of a very small minority holding and hence would be heavily discounted. Assume that, based on its past maintainable earnings, Tank Engines Ltd is worth £4,000,000. A shareholding of (say) 2½% might be valued at (say) £25,000 (ie £4,000,000 × 2½% × 25% (75% discount)). Each director would have to pay around £25,000 for his shares in order to avoid any taxable benefit.

    If the shares constitute 'readily convertible assets' (ie where there are trading arrangements in existence enabling the director, or likely to enable him, to obtain cash for his shares now or at a future date), the tax would be payable through the PAYE system (ITEPA 2003 s 696) and NICs would also be chargeable (see explanatory notes 7 and 8). If the shares are not readily convertible assets, no NICs would be due.

    In addition, the company would have to complete Form 42 which is headed 'Employment-related securities and options: reportable events under s 421J ITEPA 2003' and submit to HMRC Employee Shares & Securities Unit before 7 July 2010.

9. Consideration should be given to granting share options under the enterprise management incentive (EMI) scheme. This would enable the directors to be granted options to acquire shares exercisable at any time (within ten years). No income tax (or NIC) charge arises if the option enables the shares to be acquired at an amount equal to their market value at the date the option is *granted*. The total initial market value of the shares (based on the value at the date of the grant) held under EMI options granted by the company cannot exceed £3 million at the date of any grant (see Example 85 for details). Tank Engines Ltd will therefore not have any difficulty in meeting this requirement. Tank Engines Ltd should also satisfy the various qualifying conditions for establishing an EMI scheme. It is an independent (non-controlled) company and carries on a qualifying manufacturing trade. The balance sheet total of its gross assets is well within the maximum permissible amount. The EMI scheme is much more attractive than an approved company share option plan as it gives complete flexibility with regard to the timing of the exercise of the options, and the procedure enabling the value of shares to be agreed with HMRC Shares & Assets Valuation (promptly) at the time of the grant gives certainty of tax treatment. EMI share option agreements must be notified to HMRC within 92 days of the option grant. The clear disadvantage of granting options rather than awarding shares is that the two directors have no ownership interest until they exercise their options (and cannot be paid dividends), but this also means that they will have no shares to be bought back if they leave the company before they exercise.

    EMI options need not be granted at full market value, but if the exercise price is discounted so that the directors can buy shares at low cost the discount is subject to income tax at exercise. Whether the exercise price is set at or below market value, the company should be able to claim a corporation tax deduction for any discount to current (rather than initial) market value when the options are exercised.

Providing a dividend income of £10,000 for Mrs Thomas

10. As a 75% plus controlling shareholder, Mr Thomas could arrange for Tank Engines Ltd to issue non-voting preference shares carrying the relevant dividend coupon to give Mrs Thomas a dividend of £10,000. However, following the case of *Young v Pearce* (1996) (see Example 2 part (b)(iii)), it is likely that such arrangements would be treated as a settlement by

Mr Thomas in favour of his wife. This would mean that the dividend income on the shares would be taxed on Mr Thomas as settlor (ITTOIA 2005, ss 624–626).

11. If, however, shares which carried substantive rights (such as voting rights and an entitlement to capital surpluses on a winding up, as well as dividend income) were issued or transferred to Mrs Thomas, this would escape the settlement provisions, since the shares would be an outright gift which carried other significant rights apart from a right to income (s 626).

    Mr Thomas could transfer part of his existing (ordinary) shareholding to his wife. Alternatively, he could arrange for the company to create another class of ordinary shares (but carrying virtually the same rights as the existing ordinary shares). This would provide greater flexibility with regard to future dividends, for example enabling dividends to be declared on the new class of shares. Mr Thomas could provide the necessary funds to enable his wife to subscribe for the new class of shares, although this would involve injecting capital in a non-distributable form.

12. Over a number of years, HMRC sought to apply the settlements legislation contained in ICTA 1988 s 660A(1)(2) now ITTOIA 2005 s 624 to dividends paid to the spouse of the main earner in certain circumstances. HMRC issued guidance, and a number of illustrations of their view, in Tax Bulletin issues 64 (April 2003) and 69 (February 2004). The case of *Jones v Garnett* (the Arctic Systems case) confirmed that the inter-spouse exemption applied in the case of company ordinary shares – although the settlements legislation is still in point in all other cases.

    In the Arctic Systems case, HMRC targeted the situation where profits derived principally from the work of the main earner, and where the main earner took remuneration at less than the market rate, thereby allowing funds to accumulate, to be paid subsequently as dividend, resulting in income being transferred to the other spouse in proportion to shareholding. Having lost the argument, HMRC proposed income shifting rules that went well beyond this, and did not exclude income generated by a substantial business (rather than the earnings of an individual), but these were shelved. Future income shifting proposals may affect a much wider range of companies than were potentially affected by the settlements legislation.

Explanatory Notes

Bonus v dividend

1. The detailed comparisons between bonus and dividend payments are set out in notes 1 to 6 of the example. Even if substantial dividends are being contemplated, it is recommended that a basic level of remuneration is paid following the National Minimum Wage Act 1998 unless a director does not have an 'explicit' contract of employment with the company. If he does have an explicit contract he would fall within the minimum wage rules and must pay himself at least £5.73 per hour (£5.80 per hour from 1 October 2009). See HMRC's Tax Bulletin of December 2000 for their detailed comments on the minimum wage legislation. Dividends are disregarded for minimum wage purposes. Similarly, benefits in kind are ignored, except living accommodation, subject to a limit. Regular remuneration also builds up an NIC contribution record (to secure full state benefits), provides the basis for any redundancy entitlement, and assists with mortgage applications etc.

2. Where the shareholder's marginal rate of tax is 40%, in years prior to 2008/09 the overall tax/NIC cost of paying a bonus was lower if the company paid tax at the marginal small companies' rate of tax which was 32.5% for the year ended 31 March 2008. If the company paid tax at the full or small companies' rate (then 30% and 20% respectively for the year ended 31 March 2008), greater tax/NIC savings were obtained by paying a dividend. In 2008/09 the marginal rate of corporation tax dropped from 32.5% to 29.75%, reflecting the decrease in the full rate from 30% to 28%, and the increase in the small companies rate from 20% to 21%. For 2008/09 onwards, the overall tax/NI cost is less for a dividend than for paying bonus at all rates of corporation tax, even when the

maximum income tax rate rises to 50% and the higher dividend rate to 42.5% from 6 April 2010. If the company pays tax at the marginal rate, the difference in cost is small, and any non-monetary factors may outweigh the saving.

Taking £200,000 as the amount to be extracted (as in the example) but assuming the company paid tax at 21%, the net cash available from a bonus would still be £104,610, as in note 2 of the example.

The net cash available by paying a dividend would be £118,500 (a saving of £13,890 over the bonus) calculated as follows:

	£ CT 21%	£ CT 28%	£ CT 29.75%
Profits to be extracted	200,000	200,000	200,000
Corporation tax at 21%/28%/29.75%	(42,000)	(56,000)	(59,500)
Cash dividend	158000	144,000	140,500
Tax credit 1/9th	17,556	16,000	15,611
	175,556	160,000	156,111
Dividend income tax at 32.5%	(57,056)	(52,000)	(50,736)
Net cash available	118,500	108,000	105,375

If the company paid tax at 28%, the net cash available by paying a dividend would be £108,000, giving a saving of £3,390, while at the marginal rate of 29.75% the saving of £765 is relatively small.

While accrued bonus is tax-deductible if paid within nine months of the year end, pension contributions cannot be accrued. If a combination of bonus and pension is considered, it must be considered well before the year end, and the company must pay the contribution before the year end. The potential impact of the special annual allowance charge where income exceeds £150,000 must also be considered.

3. For shareholders paying tax at the basic rate, and liable to additional employees' NIC, separate calculations are required in each case to determine whether a bonus or dividend should be paid, although the comments in note 1 regarding payment of a basic level of remuneration are likely to be particularly appropriate.

Pension contributions

4. The maximum tax relief for pension contributions is based on a lifetime limit, with an annual maximum personal contribution equal to earnings for the year. The company will therefore be able to make very substantial contributions.

If Mr Thomas agreed to take £100,000 subject to PAYE (keeping his income below £150,000 and thereby avoiding the special annual allowance charge), and £100,000 as a pension contribution, the situation would be:

	Bonus £200,000	Bonus £100,000 Pension £100,000
Earnings subject to PAYE	200,000	100,000
Employer's NIC @ 12.8/112.8	(22,695)	(11,348)
Bonus payment	177,305	88,652
PAYE and NIC @ 41%	(72,695)	(36,347)
Net cash available	104,610	52,305
Contribution to pension fund		100,000
Value received	104,610	152,305
Tax borne immediately	95,390	47,695

The reduction in current year taxes would be £47,695, but the pension will be subject to PAYE when drawn (although perhaps at a lower rate, and no NICs will be due as the law currently stands). To be tax-deductible for Tank Engines Ltd, the pension contribution, as other remuneration or costs, must be expended wholly and exclusively for the purpose of the trade. HMRC guidance specifically states that the contribution is looked at in the context of the overall remuneration package, not a stand-alone amount. The proportion of pension contribution to other remuneration is not considered for this purpose.

The normal situation is that contributions will be tax-deductible, unless there is an identifiable non-trade purpose. As Tank Engines Ltd is a profitable trading company, and paying this remuneration out of profit, there should be no objection from HMRC, in spite of the tax saving arising from the salary sacrifice.

From 2011/12, tax relief will be restricted on pension contributions made by or for those earning more than £150,000 per annum, and it is also expected that company contributions will produce a tax charge on employees earning more than £150,000. The relief will be given at a tapered rate from £150,000 to £180,000, after which relief will be available only at basic rate. To prevent high earners from partially circumventing this legislation, anti-forestalling legislation was included in Finance Act 2009, which will prevent those with income in excess of £150,000 from increasing their contributions in either 2009/10 or 2010/11 from the normal amount they pay. This may interfere with the ability of Tank Engines Ltd to significantly increase the pension contributions this year unless Mr Thomas has not drawn income in excess of £150,000 in any of the years 2007/08 to date.

Dividend waivers

5.   To be effective for income tax purposes, dividend waivers must be made before the dividend becomes due and payable. For this purpose, an interim dividend does not become due and payable until it is actually paid – the directors could rescind the dividend at any time before it is paid. However, a final dividend becomes payable at the company's annual general meeting when it is declared, unless the resolution specifies a later date (*Hurll v CIR* (1922); *Potel v CIR* (1970)).

6.   A dividend waiver would only be treated as a settlement for income tax purposes where the necessary element of bounty was present (*CIR v Plummer* (1979)). HMRC would argue that 'bounty' would have been conferred if the company's distributable profits could not have supported the dividend without the waiver, ie where the waiver enables one or more shareholders to receive a greater dividend than would otherwise be the case. In such cases, HMRC would only apply the settlements legislation where dividends are waived to increase the dividend payable to the settlor's spouse, children or the trustees of an accumulation and maintenance trust for the settlor's children (ITTOIA 2005 s 624). There is no transfer of value for inheritance tax purposes, provided a dividend waiver is made within twelve months before the right to the dividend accrues (IHTA 1984 s 15). The detailed inheritance tax provisions are in the companion to this book, Tolley's Taxwise II 2009/10.

Giving shares to employees

7.   Except for shares acquired under HMRC-approved schemes (as to which see Example 85), a tax charge arises on shares given to employees unless full market value is paid for them. The taxable amount is the market value of the shares less the amount (if any) paid for them and this is chargeable under the normal 'money's worth' provisions of ITEPA 2003 s 62, although as it is not a payment in cash it is not chargeable through PAYE unless the shares are readily convertible assets. Since it is chargeable under s 62, it is outside the 'cash equivalents' benefits charging provisions for P11D employees and directors. The employer is, however, required under SI 2003/2682 reg 85 and ITEPA 2003 s 421J to make a return before 7 July after the end of the tax year. Employees need to report the relevant details in their tax returns. Gifts of shares in an employer company that are not readily convertible assets are not chargeable to either Class 1 or Class 1A national insurance contributions (SI 2001/1004 reg 40 and Sch 3 Part IX para 2).

8. Unquoted shares are unlikely to be readily convertible assets unless there are arrangements which exist or might in future exist enabling them to be realised in cash. This might be the case where there is a planned sale or flotation of the company or where an employee share trust is available to buy the shares. The wide subjective nature of the definition can be difficult to apply.

Question

The Steamdriven Computer Co Ltd has faced a declining market in recent years. It is expected to make a net *unadjusted* trading loss, including interest income, of £17,750 in the six months ending on 31 March 2010. Results for the previous three years (*before* any adjustments for tax purposes) have been as follows:

	Trading Profits £	Bank Interest receivable £
Year ended 30 September 2007	10,000	–
Year ended 30 September 2008	3,000	–
Year ended 30 September 2009	4,000	400

The projected balance sheet at 31 March 2010 on a going concern basis is as follows:

Fixed assets	£	£
Office premises (at valuation)		120,000
Fixed plant and machinery	50,000	
Less: Depreciation	(35,000)	15,000
		135,000
Current assets		
Trading stock		39,000
Cash		500
		39,500
Less: Creditors (excluding any corporation tax of year to 30 September 2009, which will be discharged by loss claim)		(4,000)
Net current assets		35,500
Total assets		170,500
Financed by:		
Share capital		10,000
Retained profits		135,500
		145,500
10% Debenture		25,000
		170,500

The projected profit and loss account for the six months to 31 March 2010, again on a going concern basis, is as follows:

	£	£
Sales		91,000
Opening stock	42,000	
Purchases	60,000	
Less: Closing stock	(39,000)	(63,000)
Gross profit		28,000
Less: Staff and administrative costs	42,200	
Depreciation	2,500	
Debenture interest	1,250	
Bank interest	(200)	(45,750)
Net loss		(17,750)

Mr Ludd, who owns 99.9% of the company's issued share capital, proposes that the company should sell all of its assets on 31 March 2010 for cash to an unconnected third party for a total amount of £143,000, attributable as follows:

	£
Goodwill	–
Office premises	107,000
Plant and machinery	2,000
Trading stock	34,000
	143,000

Immediately after the assets are sold, the company would cease trading and the liquidation of the company would commence. The company would pay all of its liabilities at cessation and the liquidator would distribute the balance of cash to its shareholders shortly afterwards. Mr Ludd is unsure whether the cash should be distributed before or after 6 April 2010.

The company is expected to receive any repayments of corporation tax, including any arising out of its trading loss, by 7 June 2010. It is estimated that these amounts will just be sufficient to cover the liquidator's fees so that no further cash will be distributed to the company's shareholders.

The following information is also available:

(i) The 10% Debenture was issued in March 1975 to finance the company's trading activities. Interest is payable and has always been paid half yearly on 30 September and 31 March. The interest has been deducted in arriving at the profit figure shown.

(ii) All of the plant and machinery was acquired on 1 April 2003. The company has claimed maximum writing-down allowances (but no other allowances) in respect of this expenditure.

(iii) In computing depreciation for accounts purposes, the company uses a straight-line basis of 10% per annum and applies the same depreciation rate to all of the plant and machinery.

(iv) The company has no associated companies and has not paid dividends for several years.

(v) The disposal of the office will give rise to a nil gain/nil loss position for capital gains purposes.

(vi) Mr Ludd inherited his shares in the company in March 1982, when they had a probate value of £10,000.

(vii) Mr Ludd, who is single and aged 46, will have total income of £60,000 in 2009/10 and around £10,000 in 2010/11. He plans to retain all of his existing capital assets (except his shares in the company) for the foreseeable future.

Assume that all staff and administrative expenses are fully allowable. Indexation allowance from March 1982 to April 1998 was 104.7%.

On the basis of the estimated figures:

(a) Compute the final corporation tax liabilities of the company in respect of the periods commencing 1 October 2006 and ending 31 March 2010.

(b) Compute the total amount which should be repaid to the company by HMRC on 7 June 2010.

(c) Advise Mr Ludd as to which method of distributing cash by the company is preferable.

Answer

A. Final corporation tax liabilities for periods from 1 October 2006 to 31 March 2010

	Yr to 30.9.07 £	Yr to 30.9.08 £	Yr to 30.9.09 £	6 mths to 31.3.10 £
Profit per accounts	10,000	3,000	4,000	
Add: depreciation (see workings)	5,000	5,000	5,000	
Less: capital allowances (see workings)	(3,955)	(2,670)	(1,839)	
Trading income	11,045	5,330	7,161	–
Loan relationships				
Bank interest			400	200
Total profits	11,045	5,330	7,561	200
Less: loss relief under s 393A				
(totalling £24,136)	(11,045)	(5,330)	(7,561)	(200)
Profits chargeable to corporation tax	–	–	–	–
Unrelieved loss (25,806 per workings – 24,136)				£1,670

There are no charges on income in this example. Debenture interest is treated as a trading expense (see note 4). Had there been any charges in the final trading period, the loss would have been set off *before* those charges.

Workings

Capital allowances computation:

		£
WDV at 30.9.06 (50,000 less 25% pa on reducing balance for four years)		15,820
Yr to 30.9.07	WDA 25%	3,955
		11,865
Yr to 30.9.08	WDA 22.5% (effective rate)	2,670
		9,195
Yr to 30.9.09	WDA 20.0%	1,839
		7,356
6 mths to 31.3.10	Sale proceeds	2,000
	Balancing allowance	5,356

Loss to 31 March 2009:

	£
Net loss per accounts	(17,750)
Depreciation	2,500
Bank interest	(200)
Capital allowances	(5,356)
Loss on sale of stock (39,000 – 34,000)	(5,000)
Loss available for relief under ICTA 1988 s 393A	(25,806)

Depreciation:

Cumulative figure of £35,000 on balance sheet represents £5,000 per annum on a straight-line basis from 1 April 2003 to 31 March 2010.

B. **Amount repayable to company on 7 June 2010**

No tax is payable for the six months to 31 March 2010, so interest is not relevant. Interest on the repayment for the year to 30 September 2009 runs from 1 July 2010, and for the years to 30 September 2008 and 30 September 2007 from 1 January 2011 (the payment date for the loss period). Since the repayment is made on 7 June 2010, it does not attract any interest.

	£
Year to 30 September 2007:	
Financial Year 2006	
11,045 × 183/365 = £5,538 @ 19%	1,052
Financial Year 2007	
11,045 × 182/365 = £5,507 @ 20%	1,101
	2,153

The corporation tax on the profits of £5,330 for the year to 30 September 2008 was £1,093 at 20/21%, and on the profits of £7,561 for the year to 30 September 2009 was £1,588 at 21%. The loss claim of £200 for the six months to 30 March 2010 would result in only a minimal tax saving of £42.

C. **Advice to Mr Ludd on how cash should be distributed**

If all the cash is distributed before 6 April 2010, Mr Ludd will have a chargeable gain in 2009/2010 as follows.

	£
Available funds in company:	
Proceeds of sale of assets	143,000
Add cash in hand	500
Less: amounts used to pay creditors and	
debenture holders (4,000 + 25,000)	(29,000)
Distributable to shareholders	114,500
Mr Ludd's share of distributions (99.9%)	114,386
Cost of shares March 1982	(10,000)
Gain before entrepreneur's relief	104,386
Entrepreneur's relief @ 4/9	(46,394)
Gain before annual exemption	57,992
Less: Annual exemption	(10,100)
	47,892

The gain of £47,892 would be taxed at 18%, giving rise to a tax liability of £8,621.

There is little advantage to delaying the capital distribution following the introduction of entrepreneur's relief and the 18% rate of tax on capital gains other than a small increase to the annual exemption and a delay in the payment of tax. Previously there could have been a disadvantage with the period after the cessation of trade only attracting the non business asset rate of taper relief. For entrepreneur's relief to apply, the distribution has to be within three years of the cessation of trade. However, a small initial distribution in the earlier tax year may be considered if the annual exemption has not been utilised followed by the balance of the distribution in the subsequent tax year.

Explanatory Notes

Chargeable accounting periods

1.   CTA 2009 ss 10 and 12 provide that a chargeable accounting period ends on the earliest of the following (see Example 52 explanatory note 2(c)):

Twelve months from its commencement

An accounting date of the company

Cessation of trading

Immediately before the commencement of a winding-up.

Trading losses

2.   Trading losses carried forward are only available against future profits of the *same trade* (ICTA 1988 s 393(1)). If any chargeable gains had arisen in the liquidation period, therefore, the losses could not have been set against them. See Example 54 for the rules for including trade charges of the last twelve months of trading in the loss available for relief under ICTA 1988 s 393A. Trading losses are normally extinguished on the cessation of trade. However, they may be utilised under CTA 2009 s 196 against any post cessation trading receipts arising in the liquidation.

Interest on overpaid tax

3.   For detailed notes on the dates from which interest runs when tax is repaid following loss claims, see Example 53 explanatory note 7.

Under self-assessment, interest on underpaid and overpaid tax is taken into account in calculating taxable profits. If interest on overpaid tax is received or receivable by a company in liquidation in its final accounting period, however, the interest will not be included in taxable profits if it does not exceed £2,000. (ICTA 1988 s 342A(4)). The actual tax repayments in this example did not attract any interest.

Loan interest payable

4.   Interest on a loan for the purposes of the trade is deducted on an accruals basis in arriving at the trading profit. For detailed notes see Example 63.

Close investment-holding companies

5.   Where a company is a close investment-holding company, it is liable to tax at the full corporation tax rate, no matter how small its profits are (ICTA 1988 s 13A). (For detailed notes see Example 56.) If the company was not close before liquidation, it will not become close as a result of the liquidation.

Companies that are trading or property investment companies are excluded from the definition of close investment-holding company, but clearly there is a problem when a company goes into liquidation following the cessation of its trade. Section 13A(4) provides that a company that is wound up will not be treated as a close investment-holding company in the accounting period commencing with the winding-up if it was outside the definition in the previous accounting period. But the cessation of a trade itself triggers the end of an accounting period, and there will often be an interval between that cessation and the passing of the winding-up resolution, in which case the company in liquidation will not be helped by this provision. It would be relevant, however, if a company's trade had been continued by a Receiver or Administrator up to the date of the winding-up resolution, or if a company had let properties and the lettings continued after the cessation of the trade, enabling the company to escape close investment-holding company status in the period leading up to the winding-up resolution.

In this example, the disposal of the assets after the cessation of trading does not give rise to any chargeable gains, nor is any income received, so that the problem of being a close investment-holding company does not arise. For an illustration see Example 54.

Liquidation distributions

6.   Once a liquidation has commenced, sums can only actually be paid to shareholders by the liquidator as a capital distribution payment in respect of their shares. Any surplus over the indexed cost of the shares (or indexed 31 March 1982 value as the case may be) is subject to capital gains tax, after taking into account available reliefs and exemptions, including entrepreneur's relief and the annual exemption, as shown in the example.

Any distributions before the commencement of the liquidation carry a tax credit equal to 10% but with no tax liability for the shareholders unless their income exceeds the basic rate limit, and then only at the excess of dividend income upper rate tax of 32.5% over 10%. This represents an effective tax rate for a shareholder liable at the higher rate of 25% of the cash dividend.

Entrepreneur's relief will be available providing the shares in the trading company (or holding company of a trading group) had been held throughout a period of one year ending with the date on which the company ceases to be a trading company or a member of a trading group and that date is within the period of three years ending with the date of disposal and the individual was:

●   an officer or employee of the company: and

●   owned at least 5% of the share capital and that holding enables the individual to exercise at least 5% of the voting rights.

	No entrepreneur's relief	Entrepreneur's relief	Dividend
Distribution available	1,000,000	1,000,000	1,000,000
Entrepreneur's relief	N/A	4/9	
Capital gain/income	1,000,000	555,556	1,000,000
Tax rate (after credit)	18%	18%	25%
Tax	180,000	100,000	250,000

Under the new capital gains tax regime a capital gain would be more tax-efficient than a dividend.

7.   In the case of a formal liquidation ICTA 1988 s 209(1) provides that distributions received in respect of share capital are treated as capital receipts. If instead application is made for the company to be struck off under Companies Act 1985 s 652A, this provision would not apply. However, under HMRC Extra Statutory Concession C16 the distribution of assets to shareholders will be treated as a capital sum in the hands of the shareholders, providing appropriate assurances are given to HMRC by the company and the shareholders. This is a useful way of proceeding when the company is not insolvent. The procedure for voluntary striking-off is in the Companies Act 1985 ss 652A to 652F; (these sections are superseded by the Companies Act 2006 ss 1003 to 1011 with effect from 1 October 2009, but the substance remains largely the same).

Share capital and other non-distributable reserves cannot strictly be repaid as a precursor to dissolution, although HMRC and the Treasury Solicitor accept this happening in practice where the amount involved does not exceed £4,000. A voluntary liquidation also offers greater protection for directors and shareholders, as a Court can only restore a dissolved company after liquidation within two years after an application by the liquidator or any other interested person (Companies Act 1985 s 651). In contrast, where a company has been struck-off, an 'aggrieved' member or creditor can apply to the Court to restore the company, which can normally be done at any time within 20 years from the publication of the striking off notice (s 653). These periods for restoration are unified at six years by the Companies Act 2006 with effect from 1 October 2009.

Administrations and Voluntary Arrangements

8. Under the Insolvency Act 1986, Administrations and Voluntary Arrangements may be used (among other purposes) to obtain a more advantageous realisation of a company's assets than would occur on a winding-up. HMRC have a unit to handle voluntary arrangements, known as the Voluntary Arrangements Service.

    When a company goes into administration, this marks the start of a new accounting period. Thereafter, the normal rules apply so that an accounting period ends on cessation of trade or the normal accounting date. The date when a company comes out of administration will represent the end of an accounting period (CTA 2009 s 10(1)(j)). Liabilities for corporation tax, PAYE/NIC and other taxes arising in the course of an administration are payable as an expense of the process.

    A Voluntary Arrangement may be agreed, based on 'a proposal to the company and its creditors for a composition in satisfaction of its debts or a scheme of arrangement of its affairs'. A compromise in satisfaction of debts would constitute a release of each debt to the extent specified by the terms of the Voluntary Arrangement, but the debtor does not have to treat the amount released as a taxable receipt (CTA 2009 ss 94 and 322) and the creditor may claim a deduction for the release of the debt provided that the parties are not connected (see Example 63 explanatory note 6).

    The definition of 'statutory insolvency arrangement' is found in ICTA 1988 s 834(1). A statutory insolvency arrangement is an arrangement under British insolvency laws or the Companies Act, or a corresponding arrangement in countries outside the United Kingdom.

Question

A.

Fitzwilliam Ltd is an unquoted trading company in which 80% of the share capital is owned by members of one family. The remaining shares are currently owned by Hilton, who is not related in any way to the other shareholders.

Hilton, a longstanding employee, now wishes to retire from work and to dispose of all or a part of his shareholding. The other members do not have funds which they could use to purchase his shares, but the company has sufficient funds and distributable reserves to purchase at least part of his shareholding.

Consider whether capital or income tax treatment would apply to the purchase of shares from Hilton by the company in 2009/10 together with the respective tax implications.

B.

You act as tax adviser for Bliss Ltd (which operates a successful marriage bureau) and its managing director, Mr Crippen. The company has made tax-adjusted trading profits in excess of £250,000 pa over the previous five years. It has now built up a substantial reserve of cash, since its policy has been not to pay out any dividends. The company has not made any chargeable gains in recent years and has always made up its accounts to 30 April. Mr Crippen informs you that he and Mr Bluebeard, his fellow shareholder, are in serious disagreement about the future strategy of the company and that this is having a very harmful effect on the running of the business. It has therefore been decided that Mr Bluebeard should no longer be involved in the management of the company and that the company will purchase all of his shares from him.

Further relevant information is as follows:

(a)   Mr Bluebeard is 66 years old and has worked in the company as a full-time director since it was incorporated on 1 January 1988, when he acquired 30% of the ordinary shares at par for £50,000. The company has agreed to buy the shares back at their market value of £662,000 on 7 April 2009.

(b)   All of Bliss Ltd's assets are in use for the purposes of its trade.

(c)   Mr Bluebeard, who is single, has a private income of £55,000 pa and has made no capital disposals in 2009/10.

Set out the amounts and dates of payment of the tax liabilities which would be incurred by both Bliss Ltd and Mr Bluebeard in respect of the share purchase, on the assumption that:

(i)   the purchase does not qualify for the special treatment in ICTA 1988 ss 219–229,

(ii)   the purchase does qualify for the special treatment.

Answer

A.

Fitzwilliam Ltd – consideration of whether capital or income tax treatment would apply to the share buy back and the respective tax implications.

Treatment of share purchase as capital gains disposal

1. Under the provisions of ICTA 1988 ss 219–229, the purchase of its own shares by an *unquoted* trading company will not be treated as a distribution but as a capital gains tax disposal by the shareholder providing certain conditions are satisfied, as follows:

    (a) Hilton must be resident and ordinarily resident in the UK.

    (b) He must have owned his shares for at least five years.

    (c) The company must either acquire the whole of Hilton's shareholding or his holding must be 'substantially reduced', which means that the holding *after* the purchase as a fraction of the reduced share capital must not exceed 3/4 of the corresponding fraction before the purchase. In Hilton's case this means that he must not be left with more than 15% of the reduced share capital.

    (d) The purchase must be made wholly or mainly to benefit the company's trade and not to enable Hilton to participate in profits without receiving a dividend or for tax avoidance reasons.

    (e) The purchase must not be part of a scheme or arrangement under which, although Hilton's shareholding is initially substantially reduced, his interest at a later stage will be such as to breach the 'substantially reduced' requirement.

2. The company may apply for a pre-transaction clearance from HMRC to confirm that HMRC agrees that the conditions for capital treatment will be met such that the proposed purchase will not be treated as a distribution. It is also usual to apply for clearance under ITA 2007 s 701 (transactions in securities).

3. Within 60 days of paying for the shares the company must provide details to the company's tax office.

4. If the purchase is treated as a disposal for capital gains tax, it may be possible to reduce any gain if the conditions for entrepreneur's relief are met and by the annual exemption of £10,100 unless Hilton has already used these reliefs. Any balance will be taxable at 18%.

Treatment of share purchase as income distribution

5. If the purchase does not satisfy the requirements in 1 above, the excess of the price paid by the company over the amount originally subscribed for the shares will be treated as a distribution. Hilton will receive a tax credit equivalent to the dividend income ordinary rate (10%) and will be liable if applicable at the excess of the dividend income upper rate (32.5%) over the dividend income ordinary rate (10%) on the amount of the distribution plus the tax credit. For capital gains purposes, Hilton would effectively be regarded as having disposed of his shares for the amount originally subscribed for them, since the price he receives will be reduced by the net distribution amount on which he pays income tax. Assuming the base cost of the shares was equal to their subscription price, there would be no capital gain and no allowable loss. Care should be taken if there has been a reorganisation of the share capital of Fitzwilliam Ltd.

B.

Amounts and dates of payment of tax liabilities which would be incurred by Bliss Ltd and Mr Bluebeard in respect of the share purchase

(i)   If the purchase does not satisfy the provisions of ICTA 1988 ss 219–229

The excess of the payment of £662,000 by Bliss Ltd on 7 April 2009 over the amount subscribed for the shares of £50,000, ie £612,000, is treated as a distribution.

Mr Bluebeard is regarded as having received dividend income of £612,000 + (1/9th) £68,000 = £680,000 on 7 April 2009. This will form part of his taxable income for 2009/10. The tax credit will cover Mr Bluebeard's dividend income ordinary rate liability and he will be liable to tax at a further 22.5% (32.5% – 10%), amounting to £153,000, which will be payable with his balancing payment under self-assessment on 31 January 2011.

Since the tax credit of £68,000 is not repayable, Mr Bluebeard cannot recover it by making tax-efficient investments, although, if he uses the cash from the share purchase to make such investments, he may be able to recover other tax paid.

He will also be treated as having disposed of his shares for capital gains tax purposes, the position being:

	£
Disposal proceeds April 2009	
(£662,000 less £612,000 charged as income)	50,000
Cost January 1988	50,000
	–

No gain or loss therefore arises.

(ii)   If the purchase does satisfy the provisions of ICTA 1988 ss 219–229

Bliss Ltd will be treated as having bought the shares from Mr Bluebeard for £662,000. The purchase will not result in a tax liability for the company.

Assuming all the conditions for entrepreneur's relief are met and neither this relief nor the annual capital gains tax exempt amount have been used elsewhere, Mr Bluebeard will be liable to capital gains tax for 2009/10 on:

	£
Sale proceeds April 2009	662,000
Cost January 1988	(50,000)
	612,000
Less: entrepreneur's relief (4/9ths reduction of gain)	(272,000)
	340,000
Annual exemption	(10,100)
Chargeable gains for 2009/10	329,900
Capital gains tax thereon @ 18%	£59,382

Due for payment 31 January 2011

Explanatory Notes

Purchase of own shares by unquoted company

1. The provisions of ICTA 1988 ss 219–229 enable the purchase by an unquoted trading company of its own shares to be effectively treated as a disposal by the shareholder subject to capital gains tax rather than the receipt of a distribution attracting an income tax liability provided certain conditions are met.

2. Where an unquoted trading company or the unquoted holding company of a trading group (75% subsidiaries) buys back its own shares (or redeems them or makes a payment for them in a reduction of capital) in order to benefit a trade (excluding dealing in shares, securities, land or futures), the transaction will *not* be treated as a distribution (attracting dividend income upper rate tax where appropriate). Instead, there is a disposal for capital gains tax. (Where there is an arrangement the main purpose of which is simply to get undistributed profits into a shareholder's hands without incurring the 'distribution' tax liabilities, capital gains treatment will be denied.)

3. In order for the transaction to be treated as a capital gains tax disposal and not a distribution the very detailed requirements of the legislation must be complied with. These are broadly as follows:

    (i)   The company must be an unquoted trading company or holding company of a trading group (companies on the Alternative Investment Market being treated as unquoted). The company does not qualify if its trade is dealing in shares, securities, land or futures.

    (ii) The shareholder must be resident and ordinarily resident in the UK.

    (iii) The shares must normally have been owned by the shareholder for at least five years but where the shares are in an estate (or have been inherited) the period is reduced to three years, and ownership by the deceased (and the estate) counts towards the three years. If during the five years the shares had been transferred to the shareholder by his spouse with whom he still lives, the spouse's ownership is treated as the shareholder's ownership.

    (iv) The shareholder must either dispose of his entire interest in the company or his interest must be 'substantially reduced'. This means that the fraction he owns of the (reduced) issued share capital immediately after the purchase must not exceed 75% of the corresponding fraction he owned immediately before the purchase and also that he would not be entitled to more than 75% of the share he was previously entitled to of the company's distributable profits. HMRC have indicated that a purchase would rarely be regarded as for the benefit of a company's trade unless virtually the whole of the shareholder's interest was disposed of. Furthermore, in order to ensure the 'trade benefit' test is satisfied, any existing directorship with the company must be severed and a director cannot continue to act for the company in a consultancy capacity. The 75% rule would permit a purchase to be made in stages, or a small number of shares to be retained for sentimental reasons. (HMRC Statement of Practice 2/82.)

    (v)   The shareholder must not immediately after the purchase be connected with the company (ie be able to control it, or be in possession of more than 30% of the voting power, share capital, combined share capital and loan capital etc).

    (vi) There are provisions dealing with cases where the company is a member of a group, and interests held by associates after the purchase have to be taken into account. Associates include husband or wife, civil partners, minor children, trustees of a settlement created by the shareholder and a wide range of other relationships.

    (vii) The capital gains treatment is not applied if there are arrangements under which certain of the tests could cease to be satisfied.

    (viii) The company must send a return to HMRC within 60 days after the purchase stating that the payment has not been treated as a distribution.

4. The redemption, repayment or purchase of its own shares by an unquoted trading company or unquoted holding company of a trading group is also not treated as a distribution where the payment (net of any capital gains tax arising) is used to pay inheritance tax charged on a death, but only where the inheritance tax cannot otherwise be paid without undue hardship and is paid within two years of the death.

5. A company may apply for clearance under ICTA 1988 s 225, before a transaction is undertaken.

6. If the above provisions do *not* apply, then part of a payment for the purchase by a company of its own shares will be treated as a dividend income distribution. The amount of the distribution is the excess of the payment over the amount originally subscribed for the shares (even though the vendor may not be the original subscriber) (ICTA 1988 s 209(2)(b)).

7. Insofar as the company is concerned, the purchase of the shares must be covered by the proceeds of a new issue or by a transfer from distributable reserves (although any premium on the redemption must be taken from reserves). Any legal costs and other expenditure incurred by a company in purchasing its own shares will not be allowable against the company's profits.

Capital gains and entrepreneur's relief

8. A flat rate of capital gains tax of 18% was introduced in the UK from 6 April 2008 and at the same time many of the previous reliefs, such as taper relief, were removed. Under the previous regime, many people with full business asset taper relief would have had an effective capital gains tax rate of 10%. Entrepreneur's relief was introduced from 6 April 2008 to provide an effective rate of tax of 10% on certain 'qualifying business disposals' by reducing the gain by 4/9ths. However, unlike taper relief, entrepreneur's relief only applies to the first £1 million of qualifying lifetime gains.

Given that a buy-back of shares which is treated as a distribution is effectively taxed at 25% of the net distribution for higher rate taxpayers, many shareholders will wish to ensure that their sale back to the company is structured as a capital gains transaction within ICTA 1988 s 219 so far as this is practicable.

Question

A.

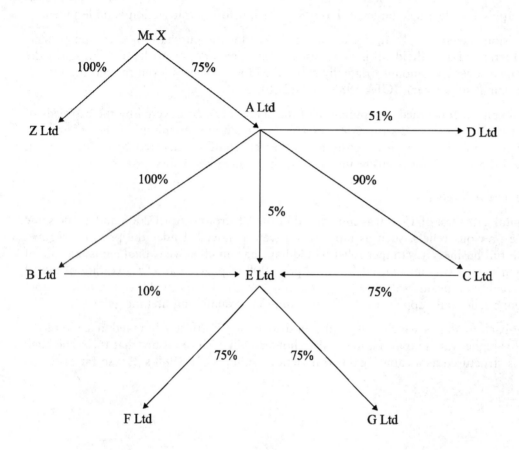

This diagram outlines ownership of various companies. They are resident in the United Kingdom and none deals in shares. The remaining 10% shares of E Ltd are owned by unconnected parties.

From the diagram above calculate the percentage ownership in each case and explain the relationship for taxation purposes amongst the companies and the taxation position in regard to:

(i)   small companies' rate of corporation tax;

(ii)   deduction of tax from payments passing between them;

(iii)   assets transferred for the purposes of capital gains.

B.

The directors of Spitch Ltd, the parent company of a trading group, intend that the company should purchase an interest in Wick Ltd, a manufacturing company, in the autumn of 2009. The proposal is that Spitch Ltd will acquire either 70% or 80% of the issued share capital of Wick Ltd.

Wick Ltd has accumulated unrelieved trading losses brought forward, and it is expected that the company will continue to incur losses for the next few years. Wick Ltd also has unused surplus ACT of £150,000 carried forward.

It is intended that, after the purchase, freehold property owned by Wick Ltd, which is surplus to that company's requirements, will be transferred to Spitch Ltd at market valuation (which is substantially above cost) and used subsequently by Spitch Ltd for the purpose of its trade.

Draft a memorandum in note form of the taxation consequences (including stamp duty taxes) of the proposals.

Answer

A. Relationship for tax purposes among group of companies

D Ltd is a 51% subsidiary of A Ltd.
B Ltd is a 100% subsidiary of A Ltd.
C Ltd is a 90% subsidiary of A Ltd.
E Ltd is owned as follows:

Directly by A Ltd	5.0%
Through B Ltd 100% × 10%	10.0%
Through C Ltd 90% × 75%	67.5%
	82.5%

Therefore E Ltd is the 82.5% subsidiary of A Ltd.

F Ltd and G Ltd are each 75% owned by E Ltd, who in turn is 82.5% owned by A Ltd, therefore F Ltd and G Ltd are 75% × 82.5% = 61.875% subsidiaries of A Ltd.

Mr X controls:

100% of Z Ltd
75% of A Ltd
Through A Ltd –

75% of 51%	= 38.25% of D Ltd
75% of 100%	= 75% of B Ltd
75% of 90%	= 67.5% of C Ltd
75% of 82.5%	= 61.875% of E Ltd
75% of 61.875%	= 46.4% of F Ltd and G Ltd

(i) Taxation position in relation to small companies' rates

The upper and lower limits for small companies' rate are scaled down according to the number of 'associated companies' in the accounting period, including companies who have been associated for only part of the period as well as overseas associated companies, but excluding dormant companies.

For small companies' rate purposes, two companies are associated if one controls the other or the same person or persons control both (ICTA 1988 s 13(4)). See Example 50 explanatory note 7 for further details. The rights of a company controlled by a person are attributed to that person. Although Mr X indirectly owns only 38.25% of the share capital of D Ltd, and 46.4% of each of F Ltd and G Ltd, the rights of A Ltd are attributed to him, because he controls A Ltd. Since all of the six companies D Ltd, B Ltd, C Ltd, E Ltd, F Ltd and G Ltd are controlled by A Ltd, they are regarded as controlled by Mr X. Mr X therefore controls Z Ltd plus the other seven companies for small companies' rate purposes, so that the upper and lower limits are divided by eight for each company.

(ii) Taxation position in relation to deduction of tax from intra group payments

As all the companies in the group are UK-resident, tax will not be deducted from any payments of interest and patent royalties between them. Tax is still required to be deducted from some payments in other circumstances, although there are now very few payments to which this applies. For the detailed provisions see Example 49 part (b) and explanatory note 11.

(iii) Taxation position in relation to assets transferred for the purposes of capital gains

Assets transferred between connected persons (which includes companies in a group) are normally deemed to be transferred at open market value for capital gains purposes (TCGA 1992 ss 17 and 18).

Assets are, however, transferred on a no loss/no gain basis in a group of companies between a UK-resident parent company and its 75% UK-resident subsidiaries and also any UK resident 75% subsidiaries of those 75% subsidiaries, but excluding a company that is not an 'effective 51% subsidiary' (ie where the parent company is not entitled both to more than 50% of any profits available for distribution to equity shareholders and more than 50% of the assets available to equity shareholders on a winding-up) (TCGA 1992 s 170). A company is a 75% subsidiary of another company if the other company owns, directly or indirectly, not less than 75% of its ordinary share capital (ICTA 1988 s 838).

A non-UK resident parent or subsidiary company can be included in establishing the required group relationship for chargeable gains purposes. A non-UK resident company can also be the principal company of the chargeable gains group. (Previously the chargeable gains group could only comprise UK-resident companies and required a UK-resident principal company at the 'top' of the group ownership structure.) However, despite the removal of the UK residence requirement, companies can only benefit from the reliefs provided they are UK-resident or in relation to assets that would be chargeable to UK corporation tax under TCGA 1992 s 10B (ie capital assets that have been used or will be used for the purposes of a UK trade carried on by a non-resident through a permanent establishment). For example, the no gain no loss transfer rule under TCGA 1992 s 171(1) (dealt with below) would only operate on a transfer between UK-resident companies or in relation to assets used for the purposes of a UK permanent establishment trade carried on by a non-resident company (TCGA 1992 s 171(1) and (1A)). F(No 2)A 2005 ss 51–65 introduce reliefs facilitating formation of a Societas Europaeas by merger on or after 1 April 2005.

The inclusion of 75% subsidiaries of 75% subsidiaries means that the group relationship between a parent and a sub-subsidiary can be less than 75%. In this example B Ltd, C Ltd and E Ltd are 75% subsidiaries of A Ltd, and F Ltd and G Ltd are 75% subsidiaries of E Ltd. All these companies are also effective 51% subsidiaries of A Ltd. Hence, all the companies controlled by A Ltd except D Ltd form a 75% group for chargeable gains purposes.

In the case of a transfer to which TCGA 1992 s 171(1) applies, the transferee takes over the base cost of the transferor, inclusive of any indexation allowance due at the date of transfer, but not so as to create or increase a loss when the transferee disposes of the asset (TCGA 1992 s 56). The rule about indexation allowance not creating or increasing a loss does not apply to indexation allowance already incorporated into base cost as a result of no gain/no loss transfers made before 30 November 1993 (TCGA 1992 s 55(7) and (8)).

For disposals on or after 6 April 1988, an irrevocable election may be made for all assets that were owned on 31 March 1982 to be treated as acquired at their market value on that date. Where the election is made, indexation allowance is given on that 31 March 1982 value. Where the election is not made, the asset is still treated as acquired at its 31 March 1982 value in calculating the gain or loss on disposal unless using original cost (or 6 April 1965 value for assets acquired before that date) would give a lower gain or lower loss. (For most taxpayers, the time limit for making the election will have expired.) Indexation allowance in this event is always given on the higher of 31 March 1982 value and cost (or 6 April 1965 value if that value is used to calculate the gain or loss under the pre-31 March 1982 rules) (TCGA 1992 ss 35 and 55).

Where an asset acquired before 31 March 1982 is transferred on or after 6 April 1988 to another group company, then when the acquiring company disposes of the asset outside the group, the indexation allowance is still calculated using the 31 March 1982 value where this is beneficial, but the indexation allowance included in the base cost on the intra-group transfer is excluded from the allowable cost on the eventual disposal (TCGA 1992 s 55). If the intra-group transfer was made before 30 November 1993, indexation allowance up to the date of the transfer may be used to create or increase an allowable loss when the transferee company disposes of the asset, as indicated above.

Unless a 31 March 1982 rebasing election had been made, however, the value of the asset on the intra-group transfer would be its original cost plus indexation allowance to the date of the transfer. On a subsequent disposal outside the group, the transferee company is treated as holding the asset on

31 March 1982 (TCGA 1992 Sch 3 para 1) and can use the 31 March 1982 value of the asset with full indexation based thereon. The transferee company would therefore do two computations, using the deemed acquisition cost (as adjusted for indexation) and 31 March 1982 value, and take the lower gain or lower loss. In practice, this intermediate step would usually be ignored as 31 March 1982 value will normally give a lower gain or loss – the transferee company will simply calculate the gain by reference to 31 March 1982 value with full indexation from March 1982 to date.

Example:

	£
Asset cost 1980	100,000
31.3.82 value	120,000
Irrevocable election for 31 March 1982 value not made.	
Transferred intra-group May 1989 when asset valued at	170,000
Deemed to be transferred at cost of £100,000 plus indexation	
allowance of 44.8% calculated on 31.3.82 value of £120,000	
= £53,760, giving	153,760
Sold April 2009 by transferee company for	350,000

Assume indexation allowance from March 1982 to April 2009 – 166.2%.

The position on sale is as follows (based on 31.3.82 value since using cost would clearly give a higher gain):

	£	£
Sale proceeds April 2009		350,000
Value at 31 March 1982	120,000	
Indexation allowance 166.2% × £120,000 31.3.82 value	199,440	319,440
Gain		£30,560

If the sale proceeds had been £110,000, then the indexation allowance of £53,760 accrued up to the time of the intra-group transfer in May 1989 would be allowed as part of the cost in computing the allowable loss, but the lower loss would in fact be arrived at by using the 31 March 1982 value as follows:

	Using cost £	Using 31.3.82 value £
Sale proceeds	110,000	110,000
Deemed cost	(153,760)	
31.3.82 value		(120,000)
Giving loss of	(43,760)	(10,000)
Allowable loss would therefore be		£10,000

The provisions of s 171 deeming intra-group transfers to be on a no loss/no gain basis do not apply where there is a share for share exchange between group companies (s 171(3)). However, from 1 April 2002, the disposal may be eligible for the substantial shareholdings exemption (SSE) in TCGA 1992 s 192A and Sch 7AC (introduced by FA 2002), even though the disposal is to a fellow group company. Where the share for share exchange rules disapply s 171, the transferor's chargeable gains position is protected by the SSE (assuming all the relevant conditions are met) since Sch 7AC para 4(1)(b) also overrides the application of the capital gains 'no disposal' treatment under the reorganisation provisions of TCGA 1992 s 127. Thus the transferor's base cost for the new 'replacement' shares is market value (and *not* the original cost of the 'transferred' company's shares).

Where the SSE is not available (for example, where the transfer occurred before 1 April 2002 or where the transfer does not satisfy all the relevant SSE conditions), the transferor company is treated as acquiring the replacement shares at the original cost of the shares for which they were exchanged (TCGA 1992 ss 127 and 135), and the transferee company is treated as acquiring the transferred shares at market value (s 17(1)). This, of course, assumes that HMRC accepts that the share exchange was motivated by bona fide commercial reasons, for which clearance may be obtained in advance under TCGA 1992 s 138, if appropriate. Nor do the no gain/no loss rules apply if shares are exchanged for a new issue of loan notes which constitute qualifying corporate bonds. The provisions of TCGA 1992 s 116 require the gain or loss at the time of such an exchange to be calculated and held over until the bonds are disposed of (see Example 80 explanatory note 4), but the exchange is not treated as a disposal of the shares (s 116(10)). For s 171 to apply there must be both a disposal and an acquisition (TCGA 1992 s 171(1) – see Revenue's Tax Bulletin December 1996). Once again, as noted above, the SSE can override the 'no disposal' rule in appropriate cases (TCGA 1992 Sch 7AC para 4(1)(a)).

There are anti-avoidance provisions where a company leaves a group within six years after acquiring an asset from another group company on a no loss/no gain basis (TCGA 1992 s 179).

There are wide-ranging anti-avoidance provisions in TCGA 1992 ss 177A, 184A–184F and Sch 7A to eliminate the benefit of 'capital loss' buying or 'capital gain' buying. The provisions effectively prevent group companies deriving a tax benefit by bringing together gains and losses that have accrued while the relevant assets were in unrelated ownership. For further details see Example 65 explanatory note 3(b).

B. Taxation consequences of proposal for Spitch Ltd to acquire 70% or 80% of issued share capital of Wick Ltd

(1) Unless Spitch Ltd acquires at least 75% of the share capital of Wick Ltd it will not be able to take advantage of either the group relief provisions for trading losses or the group chargeable gains provisions.

(2) If Spitch Ltd acquires 75% or more of Wick Ltd's share capital and is entitled to 75% of Wick Ltd's profits and 75% of its assets on a winding-up, trading losses of Wick Ltd arising after the acquisition will be able to be transferred to Spitch Ltd under the group relief provisions, providing Spitch Ltd has sufficient profits in the relevant corresponding accounting period to cover the losses it wishes to claim.

(3) Similarly, 75% share capital ownership and entitlement to more than 50% of profits and of assets on a winding-up will enable Spitch Ltd to acquire by transfer the freehold property from Wick Ltd on a no loss/no gain basis for capital gains purposes (TCGA 1992 s 171). This will also enable any capital losses realised by Wick Ltd or Spitch Ltd after the takeover to be offset against capital gains made by the other company provided a joint election is made under TCGA 1992 s 171B. This election is changed slightly from Royal Assent to the Finance Act 2009 (on 21 July 2009) and enables a 75% group member disposing of a chargeable asset to transfer a gain or loss arising to a fellow 75% group member provided that prior to the disposal, TCGA 1992 s 171(1) would have applied to a disposal of the asset from the one group company to the other immediately prior to the gain or loss accruing. For corporation tax purposes, the effect of the election to transfer the gain or loss from company A to company B is that the gain or loss is treated as accruing to company B at the time that it would have accrued to company A and company B will record the chargeable gains computation on its tax return even though the actual disposal is made by company A.

(4) A similar 'tax neutral' basis applies for intangible fixed assets transferred between group companies under the intangible fixed assets regime (FA 2002 Sch 29 para 55 and para 140). For these purposes, the 'group' definition is based on 75% ownership of subsidiaries and is very closely modelled on the one used for capital gains purposes (see FA 2002 Sch 29 paras 46 to 54). These rules enable intangible fixed assets, such as goodwill, intellectual property etc.

acquired by the *group* after 31 March 2002 to be transferred at their original cost to the group company, irrespective of the actual consideration passing between the companies (and recorded in their accounts).

(5)   Previously, assets normally passed between group members in a 75% ownership relationship without attracting stamp duty under FA 1930 s 42. (The stamp duty 'group' requirements were satisfied where the parent company (directly or indirectly) held at least 75% of the ordinary share capital (as well as *at least* 75% of the profits available for distribution to equity holders and assets available on a winding up).) There were anti-avoidance rules in FA 1967 s 27 which prevented stamp duty intra-group transfer relief being given in certain specified cases, such as where there were arrangements for the transferee company to leave the group at the date of the intra-group transfer. Furthermore, for transfers after 15 April 2003, a stamp duty degrouping charge applied where land was transferred (or a lease had been granted or surrendered) and the transferee company left the group within three years after the transfer. In effect, the stamp duty relief obtained on the intra-group transfer was clawed back (FA 2002 s 111 and FA 2003 s 126). Note that the clawback avoidance device of dropping property into a subsidiary and then selling the *parent* company of that subsidiary has been stopped. In large part, the provisions of FA 2003 s 62 and Sch 7 have continued the group relief exemption for stamp duty land tax where land and buildings are transferred although the clawback provisions have become increasingly complex over time.

(6)   As far as Wick Ltd's brought forward trading losses are concerned, it will not be possible for these to be carried forward for use against profits subsequently made by Wick Ltd, unless the change of ownership can steer clear of the 'blocking' provisions of ICTA 1988 ss 768 and 769.

(7)   Where there is a change in ownership of a company, s 768 prevents losses being carried forward to a period after the change, and s 768A prevents losses being carried back to a period before the change, if either:

(a)   within a period of three years during which a change of ownership occurs there is also a major change in the nature or conduct of the trade; or

(b)   the change in ownership occurs after the scale of activities of a company has become small or negligible and before any considerable revival.

Similar provisions apply to prevent surplus ACT being carried forward under the post-5 April 1999 shadow ACT rules (SI 1999/358 reg 16).

(8)   Although a major change in the nature or conduct of the trade is widely defined and includes a major change in the types of property dealt in, the services or facilities provided, or customers and outlets, it is sometimes possible to steer clear of the three year rule in 7(a) by keeping the trade ticking over at its current level for three years and not making any significant changes in customers, outlets etc during that time. But there is no three-year time limit for 7(b) and so if Wick Ltd's scale of activities has already sunk to a low level, a revival at any time would bring the provisions of ss 768 and 768A (and the shadow ACT rules) into effect.

(9)   As Wick Ltd has surplus ACT brought forward, it will be subject to the shadow ACT regulations (SI 1999/358). Care will therefore need to be taken with reg 16, which prevents surplus ACT being carried forward (and therefore used to obtain a reduction of corporation tax) if a major change in the nature of Wick Ltd's trade occurs within three years (either side) of its acquisition by Spitch Ltd, or there is a considerable revival in its trade in the circumstances noted in (7) above.

Provided Wick Ltd can avoid the above anti-avoidance rule, it may offset its actual surplus ACT against corporation tax under the shadow ACT rules. It will only obtain an offset, however, if it can generate taxable profits and its consequential ACT offset capacity (ie 20% of its taxable profits) is not covered by shadow ACT allocated by Spitch Ltd on its own dividends.

None of the surplus ACT in Wick Ltd can be offset against the tax arising on a gain attributable to the disposal of the freehold property (transferred from Spitch Ltd) within three years of the acquisition of Wick Ltd by Spitch Ltd (SI 1999/358 reg 18).

(10) Any dividends paid by Wick Ltd to Spitch Ltd do not give rise to shadow ACT (unless Wick Ltd has franked investment income and an election is made to treat an identical amount of any dividend it makes as a franked payment).

(11) For small companies' rate purposes, the relevant upper and lower limits are divided by the number of associated companies and Spitch Ltd and Wick Ltd will be associated companies for this purpose, since Spitch Ltd will control Wick Ltd. The companies are treated as associated from the time when 'arrangements' are in place for the acquisition of Wick Ltd.

Explanatory Notes

Statutory provisions relating to groups

1. The main provisions relating to groups of companies and the required group relationships are as follows:

Group relief for losses etc	75% groups	(ICTA 1988 ss 402 to 413)
Group capital gains	75% groups	(including 75% sub-subsidiaries) (TCGA 1992 ss 170 to 184)
Group intangible fixed assets	75% groups	(including 75% sub-subsidiaries) (FA 2002 Sch 29 paras 46 to 71)
Group stamp duty land tax relief	75% groups	FA 2003 Sch 7
Group stamp duty relief	75% groups	FA 1930 s 42

Change in ownership of a company

2. There are various anti-avoidance provisions that apply when there is a change in ownership of a company coupled with a major change in the nature or conduct of the trade or business, as follows:

TA 1988

ss 767A & 767AA	Avoiding payment of corporation tax (see explanatory note 6)
ss 768 & 768A	Carrying trading losses forward and back (see part B note (7))
s 768B	Carrying excess management expenses etc forward (see explanatory note 4)

TCGA 1992

ss 177A, 184A–184F & Sch 7A	Set-off of pre-entry losses and use of pre-entry gains when a company joins a group (see Example 65 explanatory note 3(b))

Shadow ACT regs (SI 1999/358)

Reg 16	Carrying ACT forward on a change of ownership after 5 April 1999
Reg 17	Carrying forward ACT surrendered to a subsidiary on a change of ownership after 5 April 1999
Reg 18	Setting off ACT carried forward on a change in ownership against tax on a gain on an asset transferred intra-group

The shadow ACT rules in SI 1999/358 regs 16, 17 and 18 replicate the original statutory provisions of ICTA 1988 ss 245, 245A and 245B which applied in relation to ACT offsets under the pre-6 April 1999 regime.

The rules for deciding whether a change of ownership has occurred are in ICTA 1988 s 769, which provides that true economic ownership is taken into account. Revenue Statement of Practice SP 10/91 indicates their interpretation of 'a major change in the nature or conduct of a trade or business'.

Small companies' profits

3. When calculating a company's profits for small companies' rate purposes, dividends received from a 51% subsidiary company (or from a fellow 51% subsidiary of the same holding company) or by a member of a consortium from its consortium (trading or holding) company are left out of account (ICTA 1988 s 13). See Example 50 explanatory note 7 for the treatment of group holding companies in calculating the number of associated companies for small companies' rates.

Change in ownership of company with investment business

4. Provisions similar to those in ICTA 1988 s 768 outlined in note (7) of part B to the example apply to companies with investment business (for accounting periods beginning before 1 April 2004, investment companies only comprised those companies whose business consists wholly or mainly of making investments and whose income is mainly derived therefrom – CTA 2009 s 1218). Unrelieved management expenses, interest and charges of a company with investment business and, from 1 April 2002, unrelieved non-trading losses on intangible fixed assets, may not be carried forward where, within the six years beginning three years before the change of ownership, there is a major change in the nature or conduct of the business; or the business revives at any time, after having become small or negligible; or after the change there is a significant increase in the company's capital.

    Similarly, unrelieved management expenses, interest etc of an acquired company with investment business cannot be used to reduce capital gains arising on the disposal of an asset routed through that company by a member of the purchasing group. This restriction only applies to disposals within the three years following the takeover of the company with investment business. (ICTA 1988 ss 768B, 768C, 768E and Sch 28A).

Relieving surplus ACT under the shadow ACT regime

5. Where a group company buys a company with unrelieved ACT and transfers assets to it shortly before they are sold, ACT in respect of distributions made before the company is purchased cannot be set against tax on gains on assets transferred intra-group on a no gain no loss basis if they are disposed of within three years of the change in ownership, as noted in part B(9) of the example (SI 1999/358 reg 18). These rules mirror those of ICTA 1988 s 245B which prevented the set-off of ACT in the same circumstances on a pre-6 April 1999 takeover.

Schemes to avoid corporation tax liabilities

6. ICTA 1988 s 767A contains provisions to counteract schemes under which a company's trading assets are transferred to another group company prior to the sale of the company and the new owners strip the company of the remaining cash assets, leaving the company unable to pay its corporation tax. (Such action may result in criminal proceedings on the basis that it may involve conspiracy to defraud HMRC.)

    Corporation tax liabilities arising before the sale of the company may in prescribed circumstances be collected from the previous owners. There are also provisions in ICTA 1988 s 767AA which enable unpaid corporation tax liabilities arising after a sale to be collected from the previous owners if it could reasonably have been inferred at the time of the sale that the tax liabilities were unlikely to be met. HMRC have specific powers in ICTA 1988 s 767C to obtain information re changes in ownership.

Capital gains

7. Part B of the example indicates that Wick Ltd is still incurring losses. If it transfers its freehold property to Spitch Ltd *before* it becomes its 75% subsidiary, a chargeable gain will arise, but trading

losses of the *same accounting period* will be able to be set off against the gain, and the cost of the property to Spitch Ltd will be the higher market value at the time of transfer. This would enable some of the Wick Ltd current trading losses to be utilised more quickly and put Spitch Ltd in a better position on a future sale of the property.

Had the property been standing at a loss at the time of the intra-group transfer, the loss could not be used to offset a capital gain made by Spitch Ltd after the transfer. For details see Example 65 explanatory note 3(b).

8. See Example 83 part (2) and explanatory notes 1 and 2 for further notes on the capital gains position on intra-group no gain no loss transfers, including a potential problem where the transfer was made between 31 March 1982 and 5 April 1988.

Cross references

9. For detailed notes on group relief and on management expenses see Example 64. Other examples deal in detail with the computation of the various reliefs. See Example 65 for group capital gains (including the election for group companies to be *deemed* to have transferred assets between them and the provisions of TCGA 1992 ss 178–180 where a company leaves a group within six years of acquiring an asset from another group company). The group aspects of rollover relief for replacement of business assets are dealt with in Example 82 explanatory note 9.

Question

A.

You have received the following letter from Mr Wilkins, Finance Director of Systems Holdings plc, one of your major clients.

Systems House
97 Commercial Road
Birmingham
21 July 2009

J S Lower Esq
Carter, Sons & Co
Chartered Accountants
19 South Street
Birmingham

Dear Mr Lower,

Group Borrowings

The above matter was discussed at our last Board Meeting. I have been asked by the Board to prepare a report on current and future borrowing requirements of the group. The report will include a section on taxation, covering the occasions on which income tax has to be deducted at source from interest, the deductibility of interest for corporation tax purposes and the reliefs available for a loss attributable to interest payments. It would be helpful if you could provide an analysis of these tax aspects to enable me to draft the tax section of the report.

As you know, we have a number of trading and investment companies in our group all based in the United Kingdom. Our current financing comes mainly from three sources:

(1)   overdrafts and short, medium and long-term loans from United Kingdom banks;

(2)   short, medium and long-term loans from other United Kingdom based institutions;

(3)   intra-group loans.

It is envisaged that the same sources will supply the necessary funds in future.

I should be grateful if you would let me have your comments on the taxation implications as soon as possible.

Yours sincerely,

T.M. Wilkins

Finance Director

Reply to Mr Wilkins setting out, with reference to the relevant legislation, the taxation implications of the above.

B.

Baikal Ltd, a UK-resident company which is an unlisted company that is not a close company, has been engaged in the manufacture of agricultural equipment since the company was incorporated in 1956. It owns 60% of the share capital of Ladoga Ltd, another UK resident company, but is not connected with any other company.

In the summer of 2009, the directors of Baikal Ltd wish to borrow funds to expand the trade and are considering the methods shown below.

(1)   A mixture of long-term loans and overdrafts from UK banks.

(2)   An issue of debentures, of which 70% would be taken up by a UK merchant bank and 30% by the directors. The debentures would be redeemable in 2010.

(3)   A loan for 2 years from Ladoga Ltd, which has surplus funds.

(4)   A loan by a director. This would be repayable in 11 months' time.

Indicate how interest on each of the above types of borrowing would be relieved for corporation tax, also indicating the extent to which income tax is deductible at source.

Answer

A.

Carter, Sons & Co
Chartered Accountants
19 South Street
Birmingham
11 August 2009

T M Wilkins Esq
Finance Director
Systems Holdings plc
Systems House
97 Commercial Road
Birmingham

Dear Mr Wilkins,

Group Borrowings

In reply to your letter of 21 July 2009, the treatment of interest for corporation tax purposes is part of wider provisions in CTA 2009 Part 5 (ss 292–476) and Sch 2 (paras 53–71) dealing with a company's 'loan relationships'. The term 'loan relationships' essentially means all money debt (for the lending of money) except where it relates to trading transactions for goods and services. The provisions cover not only interest payable and receivable but also capital profits and losses on loans. The basic rules are as follows:

(1)   *Deductibility of interest for corporation tax purposes*

The trading companies in your group deduct interest payable from their trading profits (CTA 2009 s 297(1) and (3)). In general, the deductions are arrived at on an accruals basis rather than on the basis of the payments made.

The group's companies with investment business aggregate all non-trading interest receivable and payable (and also any profits and losses on the disposal of loans) and are taxed on the overall profit as non-trading profits (CTA 2009 s 299(1)). As with interest relating to the trade, the interest is usually taken into account on an accruals basis. If there is an overall loss (a non-trading deficit) the rules in (3) below apply.

For both trading and non-trading loans, the amounts allowable include any expenses relating to the loans, including incidental costs of raising the loans, or of attempting to raise them even if unsuccessful (CTA 2009 s 329(1) and (2)).

As far as intra-group payments are concerned, they are treated in the same way as other payments, providing the amounts have been fully taken into account (under the UK loan relationships rules) on the accruals basis by both borrower and lender.

Transfer pricing applies to transactions between UK resident companies. The basic principle of the transfer pricing legislation is that all transactions involving connected persons must use arm's length prices. An adjustment is required where a transaction departs from an arm's length price and confers a tax advantage. Interest therefore needs to comply with the transfer pricing legislation to be deductible.

FA 2009 contains provisions designed to potentially restrict interest deductions in the UK for groups (referred to as the 'Debt Cap'). These rules affect only large groups, ie groups in which any member has 250 or more employees or less than 250 employees if both the member's turnover exceeds €50 million and the gross balance sheet exceeds €43 million.

If the group is large, the Debt Cap applies where the sum of the net debt of each group company with a UK tax presence (calculated on an entity-by-entity basis, excluding companies with debt of less than £3 million) exceeds 75% of the worldwide gross debt of the group. In such a case detailed calculations must be performed to calculate any restriction. As your group is a UK group, the UK debt will be the same as the worldwide debt and therefore we expect the need to perform calculations and submit returns. However, no net disallowance should result.

(2) *Deduction of income tax at source*

Interest may be either short interest or annual interest. Short interest is interest on loans for a fixed period of less than twelve months, and it includes overdraft interest, since overdrafts are usually repayable on demand. Annual interest is interest payable on loans capable of exceeding twelve months.

Income tax is never deducted at source from short interest, nor from annual interest paid to banks. As far as other annual interest is concerned, since 1 April 2001 companies do not have to deduct tax from interest payments where they reasonably believe the recipient company to be a UK corporation taxpayer, ie where the lender is either a UK-resident company or a UK permanent establishment of a non-resident company (ITA 2007 ss 930–938). This will, of course, include interest paid to other UK-resident group members. Since 1 October 2002, companies have not had to deduct tax from interest paid to local authorities or certain tax-exempt bodies including pension funds (ITA 2007 s 936).

Following the changes outlined above, the distinction between short and annual interest only remains important for interest paid to non-UK resident lenders, non-corporate lending institutions other than local authorities and exempt bodies, or individuals. In such cases, tax must still be deducted at source from annual interest but not short interest. Where any such interest is paid, all companies should deduct 20% income tax therefrom and account for it to HMRC (ITA 2007 s 901). The tax is accounted for on Form CT 61 within 14 days after each calendar quarter end, ie by 14 April, 14 July, 14 October and 14 January, and also within 14 days after the end of the company's accounting period if it does not coincide with one of the calendar quarter ends (ITA 2007 ss 946–950). If payment to HMRC is not made on the due dates, interest is payable thereon.

(3) *Reliefs available for a loss attributable to interest payments etc*

Interest that has been deducted by trading companies in arriving at trading income as indicated above will be incorporated within any trading loss the company makes, and the normal reliefs for trading losses may be claimed. These are that the loss may be the subject of a group relief claim (see below), and any part of the loss not included in such a claim may be set against *any* profits (including chargeable gains) of the same accounting period, then against any profits of the previous year (ICTA 1988 s 393A). Any remaining balance may be carried forward to set against later trading income from the same trade (ICTA 1988 s 393(1)).

As far as companies with investment business are concerned, any loss relating to interest will be incorporated within an overall non-trading deficit on loans (see (1) above). Under CTA 2009 Part 5 Chapter 16 ss 456–463, relief for all or part of the deficit may be claimed against any other profits (including capital gains) of the deficit period (CTA 2009 s 459), or by way of group relief (see below), or against loan relationship profits of the previous year (CTA 2009 s 463(1)). Any part of the deficit for which relief is not claimed as indicated above will be carried forward to set against the *total* non-trading profits (including capital gains) of later accounting periods. A claim may, however, be made for all or part of any carried forward amount not to be set against the non-trading profits of the accounting period immediately following the deficit period (CTA 2009 s 458). Such a claim may be desirable in order to maximise taxable overseas income and its corresponding double tax relief.

Where losses that are attributable to interest payments arise in groups of companies (in which there is a minimum 75% parent/subsidiaries relationship), they may be surrendered to other companies in the group who have profits available in the corresponding accounting period to cover the amount surrendered (ICTA 1988 ss 402–413). The available amount may be split between two or more companies in the group.

If a loan between companies in your group was written off, no relief would be available to the lender. Conversely the borrower would not have to bring any credit into account.

(4)   *Documenting transfer pricing policies*

Under corporation tax self-assessment, it is necessary to keep and maintain adequate records to support a correct and complete return. In relation to transfer pricing with connected companies, the documentation must demonstrate that carefully considered arm's length transfer pricing policies were adopted and applied. The payment of interest between group companies should therefore be reviewed together with any other group transactions as part of a transfer pricing exercise.

It will be seen from the foregoing that the tax treatment of interest is fairly complex, particularly in relation to non-trading interest and where losses are involved. If there are any points on which you would like further information or which you would like to discuss with me, please let me know.

Yours sincerely,

J S Lower

B.   **Baikal Ltd – treatment of interest paid**

1.   Interest on overdrafts and long-term loans from UK banks is paid gross and deducted as a trading expense in arriving at the trading profit, the amount allowable being arrived at on the accruals basis.

2.   Interest paid on the debentures is paid gross to the merchant bank as the bank is a UK-resident company. The interest paid to the directors is subject to deduction of tax, with the tax being accounted for on the normal quarterly basis. The gross amount of the interest is allowed on the accruals basis in arriving at the trading profit.

3.   Interest on the loan from the subsidiary company, Ladoga Ltd, is paid gross and deducted from trading profits on the accruals basis as in 1 and 2.

4.   Since the loan from the director is for less than a year, it is 'short' interest and tax is not deducted at source. The interest is allowed as a trading expense on an accruals basis.

Explanatory Notes

Loan relationships rules

1.   The provisions of CTA 2009 Part 5 (ss 292–476) and Sch 2 paras 53–71 deal with profits, gains and losses (including exchange gains and losses (CTA 2009 s 328)) on a company's 'loan relationships', which essentially means all money debt (both UK and foreign), except where it relates to trading transactions for goods and services. The provisions therefore cover both simple debts and securities such as government stocks and corporate bonds. Where a company has guaranteed a debt, however, a payment under the guarantee is outside the loan relationships rules (see Example 95 explanatory note 5). Interest may not be deducted from profits other than under the loan relationships rules (ICTA 1988 s 337A). Certain interest is, however, treated as a distribution rather than as interest and such interest is outside these rules (CTA 2009 s 465). For notes on such interest see Example 57 explanatory note 1.

Shares are not loan relationships (CTA 2009 s 303(4)). Building society permanent interest bearing shares (PIBS) are excluded from the definition of shares, and are therefore within the loan relationships rules for all purposes. (For individuals and trusts, PIBS are an exempt asset for capital gains tax as they are treated as a qualifying corporate bond in their hands (TCGA 1992 s 117(A1), (4), (5)).)

Non-resident companies who have UK income that does not arise through a UK permanent establishment pay *income tax* on that income (see Example 72). The loan relationships provisions only apply for corporation tax. The income tax provisions for interest paid and received are dealt with in the income tax examples.

References in the following notes are to the CTA 2009 provisions unless otherwise stated.

2. A company's income profits include not only interest payable and receivable but also profits and losses on the disposal of loans and fees and expenses incurred. Guarantee fees incurred in connection with loan relationships are considered by HMRC to be allowable where the loan would not be granted without the guarantee being given (as is frequently the case). The basic rules are subject to various special provisions, particularly in relation to unit trusts, investment trusts and insurance companies. There are also special rules for stock market transactions such as manufactured payments and stock 'repos' (sales and repurchases of stock).

Under s 328 foreign exchange gains and losses on loan relationships are brought within the loan relationships rules.

Authorised accounting methods

3. There have traditionally been two statutory authorised accounting methods for bringing amounts of interest into the corporation tax computation – the accruals basis, under which adjustments are made for amounts in arrears and advance, and the 'mark to market' basis under which amounts are brought into account in each period at fair value (FA 1996 s 85, repealed for accounting periods beginning on or after 1 January 2005). Where the accruals basis is used, interest that has been capitalised in the company's accounts is still deducted as it accrues (s 320).

Accounts for tax must be prepared in accordance with UK GAAP, or in accordance with IFRS, which was made the full equivalent of UK GAAP by FA 2004. The trend is for UK GAAP to align with IFRS. The new terminology is amortised cost (which is broadly equivalent to accruals) and fair value (which is broadly equivalent to mark to market). For the vast majority of loans on standard terms by commercial providers of finance, the amortised cost (or accruals method) will continue to be used. There are special rules for derivatives, and there is a special regime for securitisation companies.

Bringing amounts into account

4. Amounts that relate to a trade are brought into account in calculating the profits of a trade (s 297). See Example 53 for details of the relief available for trading losses. Non-trading profits and losses, including foreign exchange gains and losses, are aggregated. An overall non-trading profit is charged to corporation tax on income (s 299). If there is an overall loss (a 'non-trading deficit'), relief is available similar to that available for trading losses. The reliefs for deficits are outlined in part A of the example. For detailed notes see Example 64.

Except for moneylending businesses such as banks, the amounts brought into the computation of trading profits comprise interest payable on loans for the purposes of the trade and expenses relating thereto. The non-trading amounts for non-moneylending businesses comprise interest payable on loans re investments, such as the purchase of shares in an associate/subsidiary or let property (other than qualifying furnished holiday lettings, for which the interest is treated as relating to the trade – see Example 97), interest receivable, expenses relating to non-trading loans, and any profits and losses on the disposal of loans.

In the case of indexed gilts held for non-trading purposes, taxable income is reduced each year by the index increase (or increased if the index decreases) (s 400). Other indexed securities (except those linked to a share index – see explanatory note 5) are treated in the same way as other loan stock.

Some companies may be neither trading companies nor companies with investment business (for example housing associations). Such companies were previously only able to get relief for interest in restricted circumstances. They are now entitled to relief under the provisions for non-trading profits and losses.

Financial instruments

5. There are a number of provisions clarifying the treatment of certain financial instruments, and extensive technical anti-avoidance provisions.

   (a) Derivative contracts – CTA 2009 Part 7 ss 570–710 set out the rules for derivative contracts which are options, futures and contracts for differences, as disclosed in accounts prepared according to relevant accounting standards.

   'Debits' and 'credits' (all revenue gains and losses recognised by accounting standards) are treated in one of two ways: if the company entered into the contract for trading purposes, they are income or expenses of the trade; if entered into for non-trading purposes, they are within the loan relationship rules. Where derivatives are embedded in a host loan contract, and split into separate contracts in accordance with accounting standards, s 415 provides that the host contract is taxed under loan relationship rules, while the derivative contracts are taxed under the derivative rules (s 585). Special rules for embedded derivatives are in ss 639–673.

   (b) Securitisation companies regime – SI 2006/3296 'The Taxation of Securitisation Companies Regulations 2006' defines securitisation companies, and sets out the basis of taxation for those securitisation companies that elect to use it. Securitisation companies typically involve financial assets generating an income stream, matched by liabilities by which these assets were acquired. For example, a batch of commercial property mortgages generating rents receivable may be transferred to a securitisation company, which funds the purchase price by issuing marketable bonds, allowing the transferor company to raise further borrowings for further productive assets. The margin between the income receivable and the costs of funding the borrowings may be very fine.

   Under IFRS, there is a danger of mismatch if the financial assets are valued at fair value, while the corresponding funding liabilities are valued at amortised cost. This might produce unpredictable tax liabilities which the company would have no means of paying out of its narrow margin. The regulations are intended to ensure that a major source of finance is not destabilised.

   The effect of the regulations is to tax only the retained profits (as defined) of the company, avoiding the potential fluctuations in fair value arising from application of accounting standards, particularly IAS 39.

   Treasury stock

   Schedule 2 para 69 provides that the income to be taken into account in respect of holdings of 5.5% Treasury Stock 2008/2012 shall be confined to the interest, unless the stock is held as an integral part of the trade.

Loss of money lent

6. Writing off or releasing debts covered by the loan relationships provisions is allowed (except for loans between connected persons – see explanatory note 7). Any subsequent recoveries must be brought into account. If the borrower is a company, that company is required to bring a credit into account for the amount released, unless the release is part of a compromise or arrangement with

creditors (for notes on such arrangements see Example 60 explanatory note 8). The loan relationships rules effectively extend to all companies the treatment that previously applied only to moneylending companies.

7. Special rules apply where the parties to a loan relationship are connected in an accounting period. A person (including a company) is connected with a company only if they are able to secure that the company's affairs are conducted in accordance with their wishes, by reason of their shareholding, voting power, or rights under the company's Articles etc in the accounting period (s 472).

(a) Where a company lender writes off or releases a loan to a connected person, a deduction is not allowed (s 354). If the borrower is a company, that company does not have to bring a credit into account (s 358). See Example 57 for further points relating to close company loans, including the income tax treatment of the release of loans made to close company participators.

(b) The rules in respect of late paid interest are amended by FA 2009.

The old rules

Interest paid more than twelve months after the period in which it would otherwise be treated as accruing cannot be deducted until it is paid, unless the other party to the transaction is a company that has brought the full amount into account on the accruals basis under the loan relationships rules (s 373). This 'late interest' rule applied where one of the parties had control of the other (s 374 as defined in s 466 – see above), or where one had a major (ie 40%) interest in the other (s 377), or in most cases where the loan was made by trustees of a retirement benefits scheme (s 378). These provisions also extended to cover loans to *close* companies where the lender was a participator, associate of a participator, or a company in which that participator had a major interest (s 375).

The new rules (amendments are in FA 2009 Sch 20)

The rules are relaxed such that relief is available for interest on an accruals basis if the loan is from any company and that company is taxable in its own country by reason of domicile, residence or place of management and the UK has a double tax treaty with that country which includes a non-discrimination article (in practice this means an accruals basis deduction is available on most overseas corporate loans to the UK).

(c) The rules which disallow deductions for certain discounted securities until payment are similar to the late paid interest rules. They are also relaxed by FA 2009.

The old rules

Relief to the borrower for discount accruing on deeply discounted securities was only allowed if the lender was taxed on the amount accrued. Otherwise relief was given when the security was redeemed (s 407). This rule broadly operated where one of the companies controls or has a major interest in the other during the relevant period (using the s 466 definition of control for this purpose). For close company borrowers, relief was given only at redemption even if the participator who made the loan was a company except where the lender was within the loan relationships rules (s 409 – see Example 56 explanatory note 8(e)(iii)). Securities are discounted securities where the difference between issue price and redemption price was more than 0.5% per year or more than 15% overall (ITTOIA 2005 s 430).

The new rules (amendments are in FA 2009 Sch 20)

The rules are relaxed such that relief is available for discount on an accruals basis if the loan is from any company and that company is taxable in its own country by reason of domicile, residence or place of management and the UK has a double tax treaty with that country which includes a non-discrimination article (in practice this means an accruals basis deduction is available on most overseas corporate loans to the UK).

Groups of companies

8.   Prior to F(2)A 2005 changes transfers of loan relationships between companies in a 75% group were ignored, however it is now necessary to treat the transfer as being at the notional carrying value (s 340).

Anti-avoidance provisions

9.   There are anti-avoidance provisions covering transactions not at arm's length (s 444, although in most cases the ICTA 1988 Sch 28AA transfer pricing provisions will take priority) and loans for unallowable purposes (s 441). See also Example 62 explanatory note 4 for the provisions dealing with losses on change of ownership of a company with investment business.

Short interest

10.   The meaning and treatment of short interest is outlined in part A of the example. Where statutory interest is payable on late paid commercial debts, HMRC regard it as short interest, so that tax is not deducted at source. As interest on a money debt it will be taken into account by companies under the loan relationships rules (see Revenue Tax Bulletin August 1999).

Deduction of tax from interest payments

11.   The ITA 2007 s 933 provisions re paying interest (and charges on income) gross between UK companies from 1 April 2001 are dealt with in Example 49 explanatory note 11. For the detailed treatment of the way tax deducted from other interest and charges is accounted for see Example 52.

Transfer pricing

12.   See Example 70 note 13 for the FA 2004 changes for more details on transfer pricing.

Alternative finance arrangements

13.   Certain finance arrangements are structured so as to avoid giving rise to the receipt or payment of interest, principally for reasons of observance of Islamic law. These arrangements often involve contracts of agency, partnership, co-ownership or rent, which can have an effect similar to that of conventional financial products.

       Provisions in the Finance Acts of 2005, 2006 and 2007 provide that the alternative finance arrangements covered shall be treated in the same way for tax as equivalent conventional products.

       The products include savings products, asset finance, and Islamic bonds. These are brought within the loan relationship rules for all purposes, in the same way as their conventional counterparts are.

       This provides certainty on the tax treatment of the products, facilitating their use, and removing disadvantages facing institutions trading in the UK financial markets.

Question

A.

What reliefs may be obtained for excess interest and expenses of management incurred by a company with investment business and for interest and charges in excess of profits from which they can be deducted by any company, if it is:

(i) an unconnected company

(ii) a member of a group.

B.

Cribbon Holdings Ltd owns 75% of the equity share capital of Cribbon Inks Ltd and 90% of the equity share capital of Cribbon Travel Ltd. Both subsidiaries undertake trading activities but the parent does not trade. All three companies started business on 1 April 2001 and accounts are made up annually to 31 March.

The adjusted results for the year ended 31 March 2010 are as follows:

	Cribbon Holdings Ltd £	Cribbon Inks Ltd £	Cribbon Travel Ltd £
Trading income		55,500	488,000
Loan relationship credits		750	1,000
Chargeable gains		12,000	20,000
Non-trading deficit on loans	(10,000)		
Charges on income (qualifying charitable donations)	(3,000)	(2,000)	(4,000)
Management expenses	(6,850)		
Dividends received	10,800		9,765

No intra-group dividends have been paid during the year.

There were no unrelieved amounts brought forward from the year to 31 March 2009 and Cribbon Holdings Ltd did not have a Schedule D Case III loan relationship credit for that year.

Calculate the corporation tax payable by each of the three companies in respect of the year ended 31 March 2010 on the assumption that the group wishes to minimise its taxation liability.

C.

X Ltd has four wholly owned subsidiaries, A Ltd, B Ltd, C Ltd and D Ltd, each of which makes up accounts to 31 March annually and each of which made profits of £500,000 in the year to 31 March 2010.

X Ltd makes up accounts to 31 December and made a trading loss of £400,000 in its year to 31 December 2010.

Show the maximum amounts X Ltd may surrender to each subsidiary by way of group relief in respect of its trading loss, and the most efficient way of using group relief.

D.

The issued share capital of Z Ltd is 80,000 £1 ordinary shares. In its year to 31 July 2009 it had a trading profit of £50,000. Its shares are owned by the following companies, whose trading results for the year to 31 July 2009 were:

		£	Shares in Z Ltd
A Ltd	Profit	40,000	48,000
B Ltd	Loss	(60,000)	24,000
C Ltd	Profit	10,000	8,000
			80,000

All companies are resident in the United Kingdom.

Explain what consortium relief is available in respect of B Ltd's loss.

Answer

A. (i) Interest payable

Under the loan relationships provisions of CTA 2009 Parts 5 and 6 (see Example 63), interest payable that relates to a trade is taken into account in arriving at the trading result, so that it forms part of a trading loss for which the normal loss reliefs are available ie the loss may be set off under ICTA 1988 s 393A against the total profits of the same accounting period, then the total profits of the previous year, with any remaining loss carried forward against later trading income under ICTA 1988 s 393. The time limit for a s 393A claim is two years from the end of the loss period.

The treatment of unrelieved interest that does not relate to a trade is the same for both trading companies and companies with investment business. Non-trading interest payable is netted off against interest receivable together with any profits and losses on non-trade related loans, *including* foreign exchange or financial instruments losses and gains (see Example 63 explanatory notes 2 and 4).

If there is an overall loss, ie a 'non-trading deficit', then all or part of the loss may:

(a)   be claimed against other profits (including capital gains) of the deficit period;

(b)   be the subject of a normal group relief claim;

(c)   be carried forward against total non-trading profits of subsequent periods;

(d)   be carried back against loan relationship credits (formerly Schedule D Case III) income arising in the twelve-month period prior to the beginning of the deficit period (CTA 2009 s462).

The company may, however, make a claim for all or part of the carried forward amount not to be set against the non-trading profits of the accounting period *immediately* following the deficit period. The time limit for the claim is two years after the end of that next following accounting period (CTA 2009 s458).

See explanatory note 2 for the interaction of relief for non-trading deficits with other claims for relief, and also for points on restricting claims.

Excess charges on income and management expenses (other than interest)

Interest payable is excluded both from charges on income and from the management expenses of a company with investment business. Charges on income now almost invariably comprise qualifying charitable donations. From 16 March 2005 annuities and other annual payments are dealt with as trading expenses or management expenses, so trade charges now rarely arise.

Charges on income are deducted from profits *after* all other reliefs except group relief (ICTA 1988 s 338). To the extent that *trade* charges arise, carried back trading losses and carried back non-trading loan relationship deficits do not displace relief for them. (Losses ICTA 1988 s 393A(8), deficits CTA 2009 s 463(5)). The deduction of management expenses under CTA 2009 s 1219 is mandatory.

Neither excess charges nor excess management expenses can be carried back against earlier profits (with the exception of excess *trade* charges of the last twelve months when a trade ceases, which may be included in a loss carryback claim under ICTA 1988 s 393A and for which the carryback period is three years – see Example 54 explanatory note 1). Excess charges relating to a continuing trade are incorporated within a loss carried forward under ICTA 1988 s 393(9) and set against future *trading* profits. Excess management expenses of a company with investment business), together with excess charges paid wholly and exclusively for the company's business, are carried forward in accordance with CTA 2009 s 1223 and treated as though they were management expenses of the subsequent year, so that they are set off against any profits chargeable to corporation tax.

Anti-avoidance provisions

For companies with investment business, there are anti-avoidance provisions relating to amounts carried forward in respect of non-trading deficits, charges on income and management expenses if there is a change in ownership of the company (see Example 62 explanatory note 4).

There are similar provisions that potentially apply in respect of trading losses on a change of ownership.

(ii)

Where a company is a member of a 75% group, trading losses, non-trading deficits on loans, charges on income, property business losses and management expenses may be the subject of a claim for group relief under ICTA 1988 s 402. In the case of charges on income, management expenses, property business losses and non-trading losses on intangible fixed assets, they can only be surrendered to the extent that in aggregate they exceed the surrendering company's profits for the relevant period (ICTA s 403(3)). However, trading losses, excess capital allowances and non-trading loan relationship deficits can be surrendered irrespective of the surrendering company's profits against which losses could be set (see s 403(2)).

Excess management expenses (within a ICTA s 403ZD claim) of a company with investment business may be surrendered whether or not the *claimant* company is a company with investment business.

Group relief claims may be made only in respect of the unrelieved amount of the *current* period, and cannot include unrelieved amounts brought forward.

B.   Cribbon Holdings Ltd

Since there are three companies in the group, the lower and upper limits for small companies' rate for the financial year 2009 are £100,000 and £500,000.

Before any claims are made, the position of each company for the year to 31 March 2010 is as follows:

	Cribbon Hold-ings Ltd £	Cribbon Inks Ltd £	Cribbon Travel Ltd £
Trading income	–	55,500	488,000
Loan relationship credits	–	750	1,000
Chargeable gains	–	12,000	20,000
	–	68,250	509,000
Less: Charges on income	(3,000)	(2,000)	(4,000)
Management expenses	(6,850)		
Profits chargeable to corporation tax	–	66,250	505,000
Non-trading deficit on loans	(10,000)		
Management expenses	(6,850)		
Charges on income	(3,000)		
Excess amounts for surrender (ICTA 1988 s 403ZD)	(9,850)		
Corporation tax payable:			
66,250 @ 21%		13,913	
505,000 @ 28%			141,400
Franked investment income (10,800 + (1/9) 1,200)	12,000		

	Cribbon Hold- ings Ltd £	Cribbon Inks Ltd £	Cribbon Travel Ltd £
(9,765 + (1/9) 1,085)			10,850

Cribbon Holdings Ltd cannot carry back any part of the non-trading deficit on loans of £10,000 to the year to 31 March 2009, since it did not have a Schedule D Case III loan relationship surplus for that year. Nor can it carry back excess management expenses and charges totalling £9,850 (see part A(i) of the example). Relief could, however, be obtained by a group relief claim, under which these amounts, totalling £19,850, could be surrendered to Cribbon Travel Ltd or Cribbon Inks Ltd or partly to one company and partly to the other.

Since the rate of tax saved on any surrender to Cribbon Inks Ltd would be only at the small companies' rate, the full excess amounts should be surrendered to Cribbon Travel Ltd, which will save tax partly at the full rate and partly at the marginal small companies' rate.

The revised tax payable by Cribbon Travel Ltd after the group relief claim will be as follows:

	£
Profits before group relief claim	505,000
Less: Amounts surrendered by Cribbon Holdings Ltd (see explanatory note 1):	
Non-trading deficit on loans (ICTA 1988 s 403ZC)	(10,000)
Excess charges on income and excess management expenses (ICTA 1988 s 403ZD)	(9,850)
Profits chargeable to corporation tax (I)	485,150
Add franked investment income	10,850
Profits for small companies rate (P)	496,000
Corporation tax payable: 485,150 @ 28%	135,842
Less: Marginal relief	

$$(500,000 - 496,000) \times \frac{485,150}{496,000} \times 7/400 \qquad (68)$$

	135,774
Compared with tax originally payable of	141,400
Tax saved through group relief claim (approx 30.5%)	£5,626

The corporation tax payable by each company for the year to 31 March 2010 after group relief claims is as follows:

	£
Cribbon Holdings Ltd	Nil
Cribbon Inks Ltd	13,913
Cribbon Travel Ltd	135,774

In view of the minority interest, a payment from Cribbon Travel Ltd to Cribbon Holdings Ltd for the tax value of the amount surrendered would be appropriate.

C.   **X Ltd and its subsidiaries – maximum group relief claims**

X Ltd's loss period corresponds as to three months with the accounting periods to 31 March 2010 of each of its four subsidiaries, the remaining 9/12ths of the loss period corresponding with the subsidiaries' accounts to 31 March 2011. X Ltd cannot surrender more *in total* than 3/12ths of its loss, ie £100,000, for use by its subsidiaries in the year to 31 March 2010. Each of the subsidiaries has more than enough profit in the corresponding part of the accounting period to 31 March 2010 to cover the amount available for surrender. If £100,000 were surrendered, say, to A Ltd, there would be no further loss available to surrender to the other subsidiaries. If less than £100,000 were surrendered to A Ltd, the remainder could be surrendered to one or more of B Ltd, C Ltd and D Ltd.

The remaining £300,000 of X Ltd's loss would be similarly treated in relation to the accounts of the subsidiaries for the year to 31 March 2011.

D.

(i) Consortia are often appropriate to specific projects and joint venture structures and the group relief provisions extend to them in defined circumstances. A claim under these provisions is called a consortium claim (ICTA 1988 s 402(3)).

(ii) A company is owned by a consortium if three-quarters or more of its ordinary share capital is beneficially owned between them by companies, including , non-resident companies, of which none beneficially owns less than one-twentieth of that ordinary share capital.

These companies are called the *members* of the consortium (ICTA 1988 s 413(6)).

(iii) Prior to April 2006 (see explanatory note 4) consortium relief claims or surrenders could only be made by UK-resident companies or by non-resident companies in relation to the losses of a UK permanent establishment trade (and only if they were not relievable in the overseas country against non-UK profits). Similarly, a UK-resident company can also obtain relief for trading losses of an overseas permanent establishment (provided those losses cannot be deducted for overseas tax purposes against the profits of another person) (ICTA 1988 ss 402(3A) and (3B), 403D and 403E).

Group relief for consortia which satisfy the above criteria is available where *either* the surrendering company *or* the claimant company is a *member* of a consortium and the other is:

(a) a trading company which is owned by the consortium and which is not a 75% subsidiary of any company, or

(b) a trading company:

   (i) which is a 90% subsidiary of a holding company which is owned by the consortium; and

   (ii) which is not a 75% subsidiary of a company other than the holding company, or

(c) a holding company which is owned by the consortium and which is not a 75% subsidiary of any company.

A holding company is defined for these purposes as a company whose business consists wholly or mainly in holding shares in 90% trading subsidiaries, irrespective of where they are resident (ICTA 1988 s 413(3)(b)).

Losses surrendered to a consortium company member are limited according to the percentage of ordinary share capital the member company owns, and losses surrendered by a consortium company member to a consortium-owned company are similarly limited to the fraction of the profits of the consortium-owned company that the loss making consortium member owns (ICTA 1988 s 403C).

Where a company is both a member of a group and is either a consortium-owned company or one of the joint owners of a consortium, a loss may be surrendered partly as group relief and partly as consortium relief, and consortium relief can flow through the consortium member to and from other companies in the consortium member's group (ICTA 1988 ss 405 and 406).

ICTA 1988 ss 403A to 403C prevent companies obtaining relief earlier than would otherwise be available by having different year-ends for the various group/consortium companies (see part C of the example and explanatory note 7).

Where a surrendering company is owned by a consortium, the trading loss available for surrender is deemed to be reduced to the extent that the surrendering company has profits chargeable to corporation tax in the same accounting period against which a s 393A claim *could* be made, regardless of whether such a claim is actually made (ICTA 1988 s 403ZA(3)).

(iv)   In the example Z Ltd is owned as to:

A Ltd	48,000	Shares
B Ltd	24,000	Shares
C Ltd	8,000	Shares
	80,000	

A Ltd, B Ltd and C Ltd are members of a consortium and Z Ltd is owned by the consortium. As a member of the consortium, B Ltd may surrender its trading loss of £60,000 in the year to 31 July 2009 against the profits of a trading company owned by the consortium (Z Ltd) in the proportion which it owns the shares of Z Ltd.

The position is therefore:

Loss of B Ltd   £60,000
Available for set off against profit of Z Ltd:

$$\frac{24,000}{80,000} \times \text{the profit of Z Ltd } (£50,000) \qquad\qquad £15,000$$

The balance of B Ltd's loss after the surrender of whatever amount up to £15,000 is chosen will be carried forward against its own future trading profits under ICTA 1988 s 393(1) or relieved against its own other profits under s 393A, or under the group relief provisions if B Ltd itself is a group member.

Had the companies had different year-ends, the amount that B Ltd could have surrendered would have been restricted to the *lowest* of the *unused* part of its available loss for the overlapping period, the *unused* part of Z Ltd's profits for the overlapping period and the proportion of the loss of the overlapping period equal to the proportion B Ltd owns of Z Ltd's shares (ICTA 1988 s 403C). Similar provisions apply where a loss is surrendered *by* a consortium owned company *to* a consortium member. (See explanatory note 7 for the meaning of the *unused* part of a profit or loss.)

As the accounting period is for the year ended 31 July 2009, the claim for consortium relief must normally be made within one year after the filing date for the claimant company's tax return for the year ended 31 July 2009 (unless a later date is appropriate – see explanatory note 8), and requires the consent of each member of the consortium as well as that of the surrendering company.

Explanatory Notes

Reliefs available for losses and deficits

1.   The reliefs available to a single trading company in respect of trading losses and excess charges on income are outlined in Example 53. This example deals additionally with non-trading deficits on a

company's loan relationships and excess management expenses of companies with investment business, and with the loss relief available to groups and consortia.

ICTA 1988 s 403(3) requires charges on income, property business losses and management expenses to be aggregated and only the *excess* amount over the surrendering company's profits of the same period can be group relieved. (For these purposes, profits are *before* deducting any current trading losses, excess capital allowances and any other losses or deficits (ICTA 1988 s 403ZE).) On the other hand, s 403(2) allows trading losses, excess capital allowances and non-trading deficits on loans to be surrendered whether or not the surrendering company has profits against which they could be set.

In part B of the example, therefore, Cribbon Holdings Ltd could not have surrendered the management expenses and charges on income totalling £9,850 if it had had any other profits. In contrast, the non-trading deficit of £10,000 could be surrendered even if the company had profits against which it could have been set.

Non-trading deficits

2.   The provisions for dealing with a non-trading deficit on a company's loan relationships are outlined in part A of the example. Where there are other claims for relief, relief for the deficit against the other profits of the *same* accounting period is given *after* relief for brought forward trading losses but *before* relief for current or carried back trading losses, carried back non-trading loan relationship deficits or for charges on income. The fact that partial claims may be made, however, enables profits to be left in charge where appropriate, for example to cover non-trade charges or to maximise double tax relief.

The carry-back relief for non-trading loan relationship deficits is given against the loan relationship credits of the set-off period *after* relief for any non-trading loan relationship deficits incurred in the set-off period or in an earlier period, relief for trade charges, group relief, and current or carry-back relief for trading losses.

3.   Interest is excluded from the management expenses of a company with investment business and is instead brought into account in calculating loan relationship profits and losses.

Group and consortium relief

4.   The group relief provisions are contained in ICTA 1988 ss 402–413.

Two companies are members of a group if one is a 75% subsidiary of the other or both are 75% subsidiaries of a third company. (75% subsidiary means holding, directly or indirectly, 75% of the ordinary share capital, entitled to 75% or more of any profits available to equity holders and of any assets available to equity holders on a winding-up (ICTA 1988 ss 413(7) and 838).) There are extensive provisions on the measurements of equity ownership in ICTA 1988 Sch 18. The group relationship can be traced through any company (irrespective of its residence), although as indicated in part D(iii) of the example, before April 2006 only UK-resident companies or UK permanent establishments of non-resident companies could benefit from group relief claims and surrenders. This is beneficial to multinational groups as they do not have to ensure that any UK subsidiaries acquired (perhaps through the purchase of another group) have to be located in a UK sub-group relationship. It is therefore possible, for example, for two or more UK-resident subsidiaries owned directly by a US holding company to make group relief claims between themselves. FA 2006 Sch 1 sets out arrangements for a limited form of group relief for EEA-resident subsidiaries and consortium companies.

Group relief where the surrendering company is not resident in the UK

Relief is given for qualifying overseas losses. The surrendering company must be in charge to tax under the law of another EEA territory. It need not be resident in these countries, but it may instead be chargeable to tax through a permanent establishment. The claimant company must be UK resident. The surrendering company must be a 75% subsidiary of the UK-resident claimant company, or both the surrendering and claimant companies must both be subsidiaries of a third UK-resident company.

Losses are not available for surrender by way of group relief unless they meet four conditions, which are:

- The equivalence condition,

- The EEA tax loss condition,

- The qualifying loss condition, and

- the precedence condition.

The equivalence condition

The loss must be equivalent in all material respect to an amount of a kind that, for purposes of s 403, would be available for surrender for UK group relief.

The EEA tax loss condition

The loss must first be calculated in accordance with the tax law of the country in which the subsidiary is resident for tax purposes. The loss must not be attributable to a UK permanent establishment of the subsidiary..

The qualifying loss condition

UK tax relief is only available if all possibilities for overseas tax reliefs for the current period, previous period and for subsequent periods have been exhausted, after every effort has been taken to secure them.

The precedence condition

The loss must be offset against all available profits of group companies in any overseas territory in priority to being group relieved against UK profits.

If the loss meets these four conditions, and is potentially available for group relief, it must be recalculated in accordance with UK tax law. ICTA 1988 Sch 18A (Part 2) gives details of the basis on which it is to be recalculated.

The amount available for group relief is the lower of the loss computed according to UK tax principles, and the loss computed according to overseas tax principles. If either computation yields a profit, then there is no loss for group relief.

The provisions for consortia are outlined in part D of the example.

5.   The items eligible for a group or consortium relief claim are as follows:

(a)   Trading losses (providing trade is conducted on a commercial basis with a view of profit).

(b)   Excess capital allowances on plant and machinery leased other than in the course of a trade or Schedule A letting business (see Example 18 part (b) (s 403ZB)).

(c)   Non-trading deficits on loan relationships (s 403ZC).

(d)   Charges on income (trade and non-trade charges), property business losses, and management expenses to the extent that the aggregate amount exceeds the surrendering company's gross profits (ss 403(3) and 403ZD).

As indicated in part A(ii) of the example, group relief cannot include any unrelieved amounts brought forward.

6.   Group relief is given as a deduction from the claimant company's total profits *before* reduction by any relief derived from a later accounting period (eg by carry-back of losses under s 393A) but *after* reducing by any other relief, including relief for charges.

Overlapping accounting periods

7.   Where the accounting periods of the surrendering and claiming companies do not coincide, the amount that may be surrendered to any company is the lower of the *unused* part of the surrendering company's available loss for the overlapping period and the *unrelieved* part of the claimant company's profits for the overlapping period (ICTA 1988 s 403A). (For consortium claims, a further limit is imposed by s 403C based on the proportion of the trading company's shares owned by the consortium member, as indicated in part D of the example.) The 'unrelieved' or 'unused' part of the profit or loss is the amount remaining after taking previous group relief (or consortium relief) claims into account. Apportionments are normally made on a time basis, but may be made on a 'just and reasonable' basis, if appropriate (s 403B).

Group relief claims

8.   All claims, or changes to claims, for group relief must be made in the corporation tax return (CT 600) or in an amended return and the amount claimed must be quantified (ie not formulaic) at the time of the claim. Claims need not be for the full amount available. They must be preceded or accompanied by written notice of consent from the surrendering company (and for consortium claims, the consent of each consortium member as well). Notices of consent may only be amended by a 'withdrawal notice' and replaced by a new notice of consent. Such notices must be made where the surrendering company has previously consented to surrender more than it has available. Any changes must be made on an amended return if the tax return has already been filed.

If all, or substantially all, of a group's tax returns are made to the same HMRC office, the group may make special arrangements whereby all group relief claims are deemed to include surrenders (ie there is no need to provide copy notices of consent to surrender), and amendments to returns may be made by a single joint amended return, although individual group companies must each make a separate return initially.

The time limits for group relief claims are the latest of one year after the filing date for the return, thirty days after the completion of an HMRC enquiry into the return, thirty days after the notice of HMRC amendments to the return following an enquiry, and thirty days after the final determination of an appeal against such an amendment.

The order in which claims are treated as made for the purpose of determining amounts previously surrendered or claimed in respect of group or consortium relief for overlapping periods is dealt with in ICTA 1988 s 403A(6)(7).

HMRC will only consider late group relief claims in exceptional circumstances, for example where the delay was due to circumstances beyond the company's control, or where a HMRC error was a major reason for the delay (Statement of Practice 5/01).

Payment for group relief

9.   No payment for group relief amounts need be made by the claimant company to the surrendering company. However, payment can be made up to the full amount surrendered without it being taken into account in computing profits or losses of either company for corporation tax purposes, nor is it regarded as a distribution (ICTA 1988 s 402(6)).

In some cases, a payment will clearly be appropriate, for example where subsidiaries are not wholly owned or in the case of consortia.

There are provisions to deny or restrict an allowable loss for capital gains purposes to the extent there has previously been a 'depreciatory transaction' within a group of companies (TCGA 1992 s 176). The amount of a payment, or lack of a payment, for group relief could constitute a depreciatory transaction, but HMRC will not usually seek to apply the provisions so long as any payments do not exceed the tax advantage obtained.

Anti-avoidance provisions

10.   There are various anti-avoidance provisions in relation to groups, including those in ICTA 1988 ss 403A to 403C outlined in explanatory note 8. Other rules include provisions to prevent companies forming groups on a temporary basis to take advantage of the group relief provisions (ICTA 1988 s 410), and denying group relief where the surrendering company is a dual resident investing company (s 404).

Group relief is also not available for that part of any accounting period during which arrangements exist under which one of the companies could leave the group (ICTA 1988 s 410). See Statement of Practice SP3/93 and extra statutory concession C10 for the way HMRC interpret and apply the provisions relating to 'arrangements'.

Question

Ivon Products plc is a quoted engineering company with an issued share capital of £2,380,000 in ordinary shares of £1 each. It has two subsidiary companies, being the owner of the whole of the issued share capital of Dylan (RGW) Ltd and 65% of the issued share capital (which consists solely of ordinary shares) of Terrence Supplies Ltd. Dylan (RGW) Ltd is a property letting business, letting commercial units to third parties. Terrence Supplies Ltd is a wholesale supplier.

The accounts of Ivon Products plc for the year ended 31 March 2010 show a trading profit of £576,190 and investment income of £39,260. Further information available is shown below.

1. Expenses charged in arriving at trading profit include the following:

	£
Depreciation	41,350
Health club subscriptions –	
re managing director of Ivon Products plc	450
re managing director of Dylan (RGW) Ltd	380
Architect's fees for proposed new factory	2,400
Cost of levelling adjacent ground for use as company car park	2,265
Patent application fees re new patent	250
Legal fees – Debt collection	955
New service agreements	1,045
Planning application for new factory	4,160
Patent royalties	25,880

2. The capital allowances for the year were £16,160 on plant and machinery (including £10,000 on acquisitions during the year) and £21,900 on industrial buildings.

3. The amount shown for patent royalties takes into consideration accrued royalties of £5,380 on 31 March 2009 and £3,605 on 31 March 2010.

4. Investment income consists of the following items, all of which were received during the year:

	£
Interest on government stocks (received gross) 30 September 2009 and 31 March 2010 (no interest accrued due at 31 March 2009 or 2010)	5,760
Dividend from Terrence Supplies Ltd	21,450
Dividends from other United Kingdom companies (excluding tax credit) received 1 January 2010	8,100
Building society interest received 31 March 2010 (no interest accrued due at 31 March 2009)	3,950
	39,260

5. During the year ended 31 March 2010, Ivon Products plc paid a final dividend of 5p per share for the year ended 31 March 2009 on 1 July 2009, and an interim dividend of 4p per share for the year ended 31 March 2010 on 1 December 2009.

6. On 31 March 2009, Ivon Products plc had surplus advance corporation tax to carry forward of £300,000.

7. On 1 February 2010, the managing director of Ivon Products plc exercised an option under the company's approved share option plan. He acquired 20,000 shares in Ivon Products plc for 150p each at a time when the share price was listed at 625p. The company's results have not been adjusted to reflect this transaction.

The following figures relate to the subsidiaries for the year ended 31 March 2010:

	Dylan (RGW) Ltd £	Terrence Supplies Ltd £
Profit from property income	24,610	
Profit from trading income		103,150
Interest on local authority stocks (gross amount) (£2,425 received 30 September 2009 and £2,425 received 31 March 2010)		4,850
Dividend paid 1 December 2009 (including that to Ivon Products plc)		33,000

The directors of Ivon Products plc are currently negotiating the sale of the company's shares in Dylan (RGW) Ltd and it is expected that the transaction will be completed in December 2010. The principal asset of Dylan (RGW) Ltd is a freehold building originally bought by Ivon Products plc for £72,000 in 1981 and transferred to Dylan (RGW) Ltd for £100,000 in December 2004, when its market value was £220,000. The market value of the building was considered to be £80,000 at 31 March 1982 and its current value is approximately £285,000. (The building has always been let to third parties.) Assume indexation allowance from March 1982 to December 2004 was 139%.

(a)   Calculate the mainstream corporation tax payable by Ivon Products plc for the year ended 31 March 2010.

(b)   Calculate the mainstream corporation tax payable by each subsidiary for the same year.

(c)   Explain how the surplus advance corporation tax brought forward in Ivan Products plc is dealt with, also showing how the dividends paid in the year to 31 March 2010 are treated.

(d)   Explain the taxation implications of the proposed sale of shares in Dylan (RGW) Ltd and suggest an alternative transaction which might be more efficient for corporation tax purposes.

Answer

(a)   **Mainstream corporation tax payable by Ivon Products plc for year to 31 March 2010**

	£	£
Trading profit per accounts		576,190
Add: Depreciation		41,350
Health club subscription re managing director of Dylan (RGW) Ltd		380
Architect's fees for proposed new factory		2,400
Cost of levelling adjacent ground for use as company car park		2,265
Costs of planning application		4,160
		626,745
Less: Managing director's share acquisition (see explanatory note 2)	(95,000)	
Capital allowances – Plant and machinery pool	(16,160)	
Industrial buildings	(21,900)	(133,060)
Trading profit		493,685
Interest on government stocks	5,760	
Building society interest	3,950	9,710
Profits chargeable to corporation tax		503,395
Corporation tax payable thereon @ 28%		140,951
(small companies' rate not applicable since upper limit for a company with two associated companies is £500,000 for financial year 2009)		
Less: ACT offset (see workings in (*c*) below)		(49,154)
Mainstream corporation tax payable		91,797

(b)   **Mainstream corporation tax payable by Dylan (RGW) Ltd for year to 31 March 2010**

Property income profit	£24,610
Corporation tax payable thereon @ 21%	£5,168

Mainstream corporation tax payable by Terrence Supplies Ltd for year to 31 March 2010

	£
Trading profit	103,150
Interest on local authority stocks	4,850
Profits chargeable to corporation tax	108,000
Corporation tax payable thereon (marginal small companies' rate applies, lower limit being £100,000 and upper limit £500,000 for financial year 2009)	
108,000 @ 28%	30,240
Less: (500,000 – 108,000) × 7/400	(6,860)
Mainstream corporation tax payable	£23,380

(c)   **Treatment for Ivon Products plc of surplus ACT brought forward of £300,000 and shadow ACT arising on dividends paid in year to 31 March 2010**

The surplus ACT brought forward of £300,000 must be recovered under the shadow ACT regulations. Broadly, this means that it can only be offset (and hence repaid) after the shadow ACT on current dividends paid (net of non-group dividends received) has been fully deducted in Ivon Products plc (within the normal 20% set-off limit) (see explanatory note 4).

The position relating to the shadow ACT arising in the period to 31 March 2010 is as follows:

			£	£
Final dividend	2,380,000 × 5p			119,000
Interim dividend	2,380,000 × 4p			95,200
				214,200
Dividend received				8,100
Net distributions				206,100
Shadow ACT @ 25%				51,525
Maximum ACT offset for period:				
£503,395 @ 20%				100,679
Less: Shadow ACT offset				(51,525)
Surplus ACT brought forward		300,000		
Offset in year – balance		(49,154)		49,154
Surplus ACT carried forward		250,846		

Thus, at 31 March 2010, Ivon Products plc has a surplus of actual ACT carried forward for future offset of £250,846, with no surplus shadow ACT carried forward.

(d)   **Taxation implications of proposed sale of shares in Dylan (RGW) Ltd**

The substantial shareholdings exemption (SSE) is potentially available in respect of gains on post-31 March 2002 disposals of subsidiaries and associated companies provided the investing company holds at least a 10% equity stake for a minimum period of twelve months within the two years before the disposal. The detailed provisions are in Example 66. However, in this example, Ivon Products plc would not be entitled to the SSE on the disposal of its 100% shareholding in Dylan (RGW) Ltd because Dylan (RGW) Ltd would not satisfy the 'trading company' requirement in TCGA 1992 Sch 7AC para 19.

Furthermore, when Dylan (RGW) Ltd ceases to be a subsidiary of Ivon Products plc in December 2009, this will trigger a TCGA 1992 s 179 'degrouping' charge, ie Dylan (RGW) Ltd will be deemed to have sold the freehold building acquired from Ivon Products plc in December 2004 when it was acquired from that company, the deemed sale proceeds being the market value at that time. A gain of (220,000 – 80,000 =) £140,000 less indexation allowance @ 139% of £80,000, ie £111,200 = £28,800 will therefore be deemed to be made by Dylan (RGW) Ltd in December 2004. Although computed as if the asset had been disposed of in December 2004, the gain is regarded as arising at the beginning of the accounting period in which Dylan (RGW) Ltd leaves the group, and will be charged at the corporation tax rate applicable to that accounting period (see explanatory note 5).

It is possible for the degrouping 'gain' to be allocated to the parent company and its 75% subsidiaries under TCGA 1992 s 179A. The departing subsidiary and the group member(s) to whom the gain is allocated must make a joint election under s 179A within two years after the end of the departing subsidiary's accounting period in which the degrouping gain arose. The ability to reallocate degrouping gains in this way enables the degrouping charge to be allocated to other (75%) group members that may have available capital losses etc to shelter the degrouping gain. In this example, the only prospective recipient of the potential degrouping gain is Ivon Products plc but it does not have any reliefs available to reduce it, although it might agree to take over the liability as part of the sale negotiations. (Terrence Supplies Ltd is only a 65% subsidiary and is not eligible for any s 179A allocation.)

FA 2002 also allowed degrouping gains to be eligible for business assets rollover relief under TCGA 1992 s 152 where the subsidiary leaves the group after 31 March 2002 (TCGA 1992 s 179B and Sch 7AB). However, TCGA 1992 s 152(1) as modified by Sch 7AB provides, amongst other things, that the relevant asset giving rise to the degrouping charge must have been used for trading purposes by the degrouped subsidiary and by the group transferor company. In this example, the freehold property has always been used for letting (the rents being taxed as property income) and hence rollover relief is not possible.

Thus, if no s 179A allocation is made, Dylan (RGW) Ltd will have to pay the tax, and the s 179 liability is likely to be taken into account in determining the sale price of the shares.

The market value of the premises less an allowance for the potential tax liability (appropriately discounted) on an eventual sale of the premises may also no doubt be reflected in the sale price of the shares, so that Ivon Products plc would effectively have borne tax on the increase in value of the premises through a reduction in the price it receives for its shares in Dylan RGW Ltd. Since Ivon Products plc will also have a tax liability on any profit on sale of its shares in Dylan (RGW) Ltd, it is effectively bearing tax twice on the increase in value of the premises.

Explanatory Notes

Adjustments to trading profits and treatment of interest

1. The subscription paid by Ivon Products plc on behalf of the managing director of its subsidiary, Dylan (RGW) Ltd, does not relate to the company's own trade and is therefore not allowable.

    Both managing directors would have the subscriptions included in their employment income and it is irrelevant that the managing director of the subsidiary did not have the subscription paid by his own employer. It arises from his employment and is taxable as part of his emoluments.

    Whilst the architect's fees and car park levelling costs are capital expenditure and thus not allowed in calculating trading profits, they would qualify as expenditure for industrial buildings relief purposes when the factory and car park are brought into use, although IBAs will be phased out by April 2011.

    The costs of the planning application, on the other hand, while similarly disallowed as capital expenditure, will not be taken into account for capital allowances purposes since they are not expenditure on the *construction* of the building.

    These costs would, however, be allowable costs for deduction in calculating any future chargeable gain arising on a disposal.

Corporation tax relief for employee share acquisitions

2. For accounting periods beginning on or after 1 January 2003, FA 2003 Sch 23 allows companies to claim, subject to various qualifying conditions, a statutory corporation tax relief for amounts equivalent to:

    (a) the difference between market value and the consideration given (if any), where shares are awarded to employees; and

    (b) the difference between market value and the consideration given, where there has been the exercise of an approved, unapproved or EMI share option.

    The company's deduction is given against its profits for the accounting period in which the employee acquires the shares.

    The underlying policy objective of the provision is to recognise the increasing use of shares as part of an employee's remuneration package. The aim is to match relief for the company with the taxation of the income on the employee. In order to achieve this, eligibility for the relief is dependent on the employee being liable to income tax on his acquisition (or that he would be were it not for the fact that the acquisition is from a tax-relieved share scheme), he must be resident and ordinarily resident in the UK and the share award must be in respect of duties performed in the UK.

The shares acquired must meet the following requirements:

(a)   They must be part of the company's ordinary share capital.

(b)   They must be fully paid-up.

(c)   They must not be redeemable.

(d)   They must be:

    (i)   shares of a class listed on a recognised stock exchange; or

    (ii)   shares in a company which is not controlled by another company; or

    (iii)   shares in a subsidiary of a listed company.

The reduction is computed as follows:

	£
Market value of shares acquired (20,000 at 625p each)	125,000
Less: Consideration given for shares (20,000 at 150p each)	(30,000)
	£95,000

Group provisions available to Dylan (RGW) Ltd and Terrence Supplies Ltd

3.   The main provisions in relation to groups of companies are outlined in Example 62. The group capital gains provisions apply between a parent and its 75% subsidiaries and also any 75% subsidiaries of those 75% subsidiaries (TCGA 1992 ss 170 and 171), whereas the group relief provisions for trading losses apply only to a parent and its own 75% subsidiaries (subject to the rules relating to a consortium) (ICTA 1988 ss 402–413). From 1 April 2000, shares in 75% non-resident companies are included in determining whether a group relationship exists for both group loss relief and capital gains purposes. UK-resident companies or UK permanent establishments that are subject to corporation tax can benefit under these rules and, following the case of *Marks and Spencer plc v Halsey* (2005), certain EU subsidiaries may also be able to surrender their losses for group loss relief purposes although only in limited circumstances.

The percentage share ownership in the subsidiaries in this example enables the group to take advantage of the following provisions:

Wholly owned subsidiary – Dylan (RGW) Ltd:

(a)   *Shadow ACT*

Under the shadow ACT rules (see explanatory note 4 below), dividends paid by Dylan (RGW) Ltd to Ivon Products plc do not give rise to shadow ACT.

(b)   *Transfer of chargeable assets*

Either company can transfer a chargeable asset to the other without incurring a liability to corporation tax on the chargeable gain which would arise if a sale were made outside the group. Instead, the transferee company is treated as acquiring the asset from the transferor company at the base cost to the transferor company plus the indexation allowance thereon (TCGA 1992 ss 56, 170 and 171), but not so as to create or increase a loss when the transferee company disposes of the asset (TCGA 1992 s 56). Indexation allowance already built into cost on a no gain no loss transfer *before* 30 November 1993 is not affected.

As a 75% subsidiary, Dylan (RGW) Ltd can enter into an election to allocate degrouping gains under the TCGA 1992 s 179A arrangements as described in part (d) of the example.

As Dylan (RGW) Ltd is not a trading company, it is unlikely to be party to a group business assets rollover relief claim or be able to roll over any degrouping gains under TCGA 1992 s 179B and Sch 7AB. Such reliefs would, however, normally be available to a 75% *trading* subsidiary.

FA 2000 effectively introduced a system of group relief for capital losses. From 1 April 2000, a group company can treat the disposal of a capital asset to a third party as though it had been made by another group member. These provisions are relaxed in FA 2009 allowing group companies to transfer chargeable gains or allowable losses to elect to transfer gains or losses between one another with effect from 21 July 2009, the date of Royal Assent. TCGA 1992 s 171A as originally enacted enabled the two group members jointly to elect that the relevant asset is first *deemed* to be transferred from one to the other on a no gain no loss basis, with the transferee group member being treated as selling the asset to the third party purchaser. For s 171A purposes, it is possible to elect that appropriate (fractional) parts of the asset are deemed to have been transferred through one or more companies, thus enabling the capital losses held in such companies to be fully accessed. The conditions for a valid actual intra-group transfer must be satisfied. Both companies must make a joint election for the deemed intra-group/onward sale rule to apply within two years after the end of the chargeable accounting period of the transferor group member in which the actual sale is made. FA 2009 simplifies this rule. The election can apply where there is no disposal to a third party and the effect of the election is no longer a deemed intra-group transfer prior to a disposal. Instead, the effect is simply to treat the gain or loss (or a proportion thereof) as belonging not to the company making the disposal but to the other company that is party to the election.

The deemed transfer rule is generally used to obtain relief for the group's capital losses and eliminates the administrative burden and potential increased stamp duty and stamp duty land tax costs of routing disposals through a group company with capital losses. Alternatively, if it wishes to do so, the 'disposing' company can still make an actual transfer of the asset to a group 'capital loss' company first, which then makes the onward disposal to the third party purchaser. There are, however, provisions in TCGA 1992 s 177A and Sch 7A to prevent 'capital loss buying'. Where a company with realised or unrealised capital losses joins a group, those losses cannot be used against gains of another group company. The loss company may use the losses against gains on its own assets held when it entered the group or on assets acquired later from outside the group that are used in its pre-existing trade.

Further anti-avoidance rules were introduced in Finance Act 2006 and Finance Act 2007, aimed at 'continued schemes or arrangements to obtain a tax advantage' from capital losses.

(c) *Capital gains rollover/holdover relief on replacement of business assets*

If one group company makes a disposal of an asset within the classes attracting rollover/holdover relief and this disposal attracts corporation tax on a chargeable gain, and another group company makes an acquisition of an asset within those classes within the permissible rollover/holdover period, the chargeable gain of the company disposing can be rolled/held over against the acquisition by the other company (TCGA 1992 s 175). See also (b) above and part (d) of the example for the rollover relief provisions in relation to degrouping gains. For detailed notes on rollover relief see Example 82.

(d) *Group relief*

Trading losses of either parent or subsidiary can be surrendered under the group relief provisions for use by the other against profits of the corresponding accounting period (ICTA 1988 s 402). For details see Example 64.

65% subsidiary – Terrence Supplies Ltd:

The chargeable gains provisions at (b) and (c) and the group relief provisions at (d) do not apply, so only (a) is relevant.

Shadow ACT

4. If a company had actual surplus ACT carried forward at 6 April 1999, it is recoverable under the shadow ACT regulations (SI 1999/358).

A company cannot offset its actual surplus ACT until its available ACT set-off has first been regarded as used up by shadow ACT, and if the available set-off has been fully covered by shadow ACT, no actual set-off is possible. Shadow ACT is treated as having been paid at the rate of 25% on the value of net distributions paid (after deducting distributions received).

In part (c) of the example, the shadow ACT is less than the maximum ACT offset in Ivon Products plc, hence the remaining offset capacity of £49,154 can be applied against the actual surplus ACT brought forward. The company can therefore recover this amount by deduction against its corporation tax liability. On the other hand, if the shadow ACT had exceeded the available offset, the surplus *shadow ACT* would be carried back against the previous six years on a last in first out basis, but only to accounting periods beginning from 6 April 1999. (Accounting periods straddling 6 April 1999 are treated as two separate periods for ACT offset purposes.) Thus prior year offsets are confined to periods dealt with under the shadow ACT rules. Any actual ACT offset in the previous year only is displaced by a carryback of shadow ACT – the company would have to repay the tax offset and it would be resurrected as surplus ACT carried forward (SI 1999/358 reg 12).

For a parent company and its 51% subsidiaries, any remaining surplus shadow ACT must be allocated between those subsidiaries. In this example, Ivon Products plc has fully offset its current shadow ACT of £51,525 against its tax liability and hence there is no shadow ACT to be carried back or allocated to its 51% subsidiaries.

Intra-group dividends do not give rise to shadow ACT in the paying company and are not taken into account as franked investment income in the recipient company. This is subject to an exception where a group company has received franked investment income from outside the group. The group company may elect (within two years after the end of the relevant accounting period) to pay an intra-group dividend of an equivalent amount as a franked dividend. This would not give rise to shadow ACT in the paying company but the recipient company would have franked investment income to reduce shadow ACT on its own dividends.

Any surplus shadow ACT remaining after the carryback and maximum group surrender is carried forward to the next accounting period in the company generating the shadow ACT.

Capital gains position when company leaves a group

5. Where a company leaves a group and continues to hold an asset which it acquired from another group member within the previous six years, the company leaving is treated as having sold the asset when it was acquired from the other group member at its market value at that time and immediately reacquired it at that value. A chargeable gain or allowable loss is deemed to arise accordingly. The time when the gain or loss is deemed to arise under these provisions is either at the beginning of the accounting period in which the company leaves the group, or, if later, at the time the asset was acquired from the other group member (TCGA 1992 s 179). If, for example, Dylan (RGW) Ltd had left the group on 15 December 2010, the gain on the asset transferred intra-group within the six years to 15 December 2010 would be worked out according to the actual transfer date of December 2004, but would be deemed to arise on 1 April 2009.

Although the legislation provides that the liability falls on the subsidiary acquiring the asset (ie Dylan (RGW) Ltd in this example), as noted in part (d) of the example, following FA 2002 an election may be made to allocate all or part of post-31 March 2002 s 179 gains to one or more members of the 'vendor' group (TCGA 1992 s 179A). Also from 1 April 2002, degrouping gains on business assets can be rolled over under the normal rollover relief rules against qualifying expenditure by the vendor group or the departing subsidiary (TCGA 1992 s 179B and Sch 7AB).

In the absence of a s 179A reallocation election or s 179B rollover claim, the gain will arise on the acquiring company in the normal way. However, in all cases, following the s 179 charge, the base cost of the relevant asset is uplifted to market value by virtue of the deemed reacquisition.

31 March 1982 rebasing and share pooling elections for capital gains

6.   TCGA 1992 s 35 provides that for disposals on or after 6 April 1988, taxpayers may make an irrevocable election within a two year time limit to treat all chargeable assets they owned on 31 March 1982 (other than plant and machinery) as having been acquired at their market value on that day. If the election is not made, the 31 March 1982 value is still used to calculate the gain or loss unless using the previous computational rules would show a lower gain or loss, in which case the lower figure is taken.

7.   In relation to a group of companies, an irrevocable rebasing election under TCGA 1992 s 35(5) (to treat all chargeable assets as acquired on 31 March 1982 at their market value on that day) may normally only be made by the parent company, and it applies to all companies in the group, the time limit of two years from the end of the accounting period of disposal applying to the first relevant disposal on or after 6 April 1988 by any group company (TCGA 1992 Sch 3 para 8). A company that had already made a disposal and for which the two year time limit had already expired before the company joined the group is not covered by the election. A company that joins the group after the group election has been made may still make its own election in respect of its first post 5 April 1988 disposal if the time limit has not expired.

Similar provisions apply in relation to share pooling elections under TCGA 1992 Sch 2 para 4 to bring pre-6 April 1965 acquisitions of quoted shares into the 1982 holdings (see Example 79 explanatory note 4 and Example 83 explanatory note 3). The two-year time limit runs from the end of the company accounting period in which a disposal is made after 31 March 1985 by any company in the group.

8.   To obtain greater certainty with 31 March 1982 valuations of land and buildings for self-assessment, companies and groups holding a substantial property portfolio at that date (ie current total valuation of all relevant properties more than £30 million or 30 relevant properties or more) can ask HMRC's District Valuer to agree the valuations in advance for rebasing purposes. For further details on this scheme, see HMRC's Capital Gains Manual.

Further anti-avoidance provisions

9.   Group relief cannot be claimed for that part of an accounting period in which arrangements exist whereby one of the companies could leave the group during or after the end of the accounting period (ICTA 1988 s 410). This would have restricted a group relief claim between Ivon Products plc and Dylan (RGW) Ltd in the year to 31 March 2010 if the sale offer had been accepted in that year, group relief only being available for the part of the accounting period up to the date that the acceptance of the offer brought 'arrangements' into existence. (See Example 64 explanatory note 10.)

10.   In this example, Ivon Products plc cannot claim the valuable benefit of the substantial shareholdings exemption (SSE) on the disposal of its wholly owned subsidiary, Dylan (RGW) Ltd, for the reason given in part (d) of the example. This means that the normal raft of anti-avoidance provisions that potentially bite on a sale of a subsidiary must be considered. Broadly, these provisions prevent companies reducing or eliminating capital gains on the sale of a subsidiary by reducing its value before the sale. If the subsidiary distributes what are effectively unrealised gains to the parent company, the parent company will be deemed to have received additional consideration up to the amount attributable directly or indirectly to the 'chargeable' value-shift. There will be no adjustment in respect of distributions that could be made wholly out of normal distributable profits and reserves (TCGA 1992 ss 31–33). Thus a normal pre-sale dividend will still be effective in reducing the capital gain arising on the sale of a subsidiary (since the 'taxable' sale price will be reduced by the amount of

the 'tax-free' dividend). The special value-shifting rules broadly apply to dividends paid out of profits which have not been taxed – for example, the book profit arising on an intra-group transfer of an asset under TCGA 1992 s 171.

Before 9 March 1999, multinationals could also circumvent the special 'value-shifting' charge by arranging to transfer the subsidiary to an *overseas* group company before it was sold on to the ultimate purchaser. TCGA 1992 s 31A counters such arrangements for subsidiaries transferred after 8 March 1999. If the subsidiary is sold by the overseas group company (within six years of its transfer from the UK group company) a charge now arises in respect of the value stripped out of the subsidiary.

11. The ownership definitions for groups to be entitled to group relief and group capital gains treatment are drawn so as to prevent advantage being taken of those provisions when the subsidiary company is in reality under different ownership.

Question

The Hogwarts Group manufactures and sells pharmaceutical products and develops potential drugs, making up accounts to 31 December each year. All companies in the group pay tax at the main rate (currently 28%) and there are no brought forward trading or capital losses.

The corporate structure of the Hogwarts Group shown below (indicating the relevant percentage of ordinary share capital and voting rights held for each holding) has remained the same for many years.

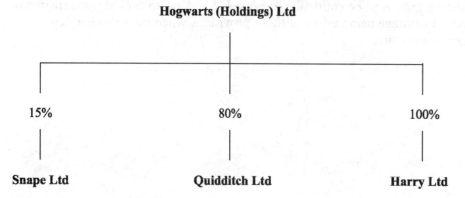

All the above companies carry on pharmaceutical trades except Harry Ltd, which specialises in the development of herbal remedies. The remaining 85% of Snape Ltd's ordinary share capital is held by Leviosa Spa, a listed Italian resident company. 20% of Quidditch Ltd is owned by Rowling plc.

The group is currently considering an offer to sell the entire share capital of Harry Ltd to Wizard plc. Harry Ltd was incorporated as a subsidiary of Hogwarts (Holdings) Ltd in 1975 with 100,000 £1 ordinary shares (issued at par). It is estimated that Harry Ltd's shares were worth about £500,000 at 31 March 1982. At that date, the value of Harry Ltd's goodwill was £300,000. Harry Ltd has never acquired capital assets from other members of the group.

The sale of Harry Ltd is likely to take place on 31 December 2009 with legal Heads of Agreement for a share sale to be finalised some weeks earlier. The expected sale consideration is £4 million. The current balance sheet value of Harry Ltd's net assets is around £1.5 million, which effectively places around £2.5 million on the value of Harry Ltd's goodwill, patents and other intellectual property.

However, Wizard plc have just indicated that they would now prefer to buy Harry Ltd's trade and assets (including goodwill) and would be willing to pay an additional £200,000 (ie total consideration of £4,200,000) to secure this deal structure. Mr Dumbledore, the finance director of Hogwarts (Holdings) Ltd, still believes, however, that the disposal should proceed as a sale of the entire share capital of Harry Ltd.

(a) As tax adviser to the Hogwarts Group, you have been asked by Mr Dumbledore to prepare a brief memorandum for him, indicating the most advantageous method of sale for the group. He has also requested that the memorandum explain why the purchaser is likely to prefer to buy the trade and assets from Harry Ltd. (Assume that the rise in the retail prices index from March 1982 to December 2009 is 170%.)

Answer

To: Mr Dumbledore – Finance Director, Hogwarts (Holdings) Ltd

From: Ron Weasley

Re: Sale of Harry Ltd

Date: 31 October 2009

1. *Introduction*

    You have asked me to consider the most advantageous method of structuring the sale of the business carried on by Harry Ltd. The basic choice is whether the deal should be structured as a sale of the group's 100% shareholding in Harry Ltd or a disposal of Harry Ltd's trade and assets (including goodwill etc).

2. *Recommendation*

    In my view, for the reasons given below, the group should sell the shares in Harry Ltd for £4 million and should not accept Wizard plc's current proposal for the group to sell Harry Ltd's trade and assets (including goodwill) for £4.2 million.

3. *Substantial shareholdings exemption (SSE)*

    TCGA 1992 Sch 7AC provides a valuable capital gains exemption for *companies* that sell their substantial shareholdings in trading companies – this is known as the substantial shareholdings exemption (SSE). For these purposes, substantial means at least 10% of the ordinary share capital (and other economic rights such as at least a 10% entitlement in profits available for distribution) (Sch 7AC para 8).

    Based on my understanding of Harry Ltd's and the group's activities etc, the proposed sale of Harry Ltd's shares should qualify for the SSE. This avoids a potential tax liability on a share sale of around £742,000, calculated as follows:

	£'000
Sale proceeds (estimated)	4,000
Less: 31 March 1982 value	(500)
Indexation (March 1982 to date) £500,000 × 170%	(850)
Capital gain	2,650
Corporation tax thereon at 28%	742
Net proceeds (£4,000,000 less £742,000)	3,258

    On the basis that the SSE is available, the group should expect to receive the £4 million free of tax. There are no other tax charges to consider as Harry Ltd has not received any chargeable assets by way of intra-group transfer within the previous six years.

    It is clearly important to ensure that the relevant conditions for obtaining the SSE will be satisfied. Briefly, these are:

    (a) The investing company (ie Hogwarts (Holdings) Ltd) must be a sole trading company or a member of a trading group throughout the 'qualifying period' which *begins* at the start of the relevant twelve-month 'substantial shareholding' period (see (b) below) and *ends* when the substantial shareholding is sold. It must also be a sole trading company or trading group member immediately after the disposal.

(b)   The relevant shareholding investment must qualify as a 'substantial shareholding' held *throughout* a twelve-month period starting not more than two years before the shares are disposed of. (It is possible to 'look through' any no gain/no loss transfer (such as an intra-group transfer) and include the *transferor's* period of ownership for the purpose of satisfying this test.)

(c)   The company in which the shares are held (ie Harry Ltd) must be a qualifying trading company or qualifying holding company of a trading group throughout the 'qualifying period' defined in (a) above and immediately after the disposal.

4.   *Trading group requirement*

For the purpose of the above rules, a trading company or trading group is one whose activities do *not* to any 'substantial' extent include *non-trading* activities. Based on my understanding of the group's activities, I do not see any particular difficulty here. Taken together, all the activities of the group relate to trading. Although the shareholding in Snape Ltd might appear to be treated as an investment activity, it should qualify as a 'trading' activity under the special rules for joint venture companies (TCGA 1992 Sch 7AC para 23). Broadly, these provisions enable the corporate shareholder of a trading joint venture company to be treated as carrying on an appropriate part of the joint venture company's trading activity. This beneficial treatment is only available where the relevant shareholding is at least 10% *and* at least 75% of the shares in the joint venture company are held by five or fewer persons (irrespective of their tax residence status), which is the case in relation to the group's holding in Snape Ltd.

5.   *Wizard plc's preference for an asset-based deal*

Given that the value placed on Harry Ltd includes a substantial premium for its goodwill and related intellectual property, I suspect that Wizard Ltd is keen to benefit from the tax reliefs available for post-31 March 2002 purchases of intangible fixed assets.

Broadly, under the intangible fixed assets regime (CTA 2009 Part 8), Wizard plc would obtain a tax 'write-off' on the £2.7 million (£2.5 million plus additional £0.2 million) it would pay for Harry Ltd's goodwill and intellectual property. The value of this tax relief would depend on the timing of the amortisation of the goodwill/intellectual property in Wizard plc's accounts. For example, if such assets were written off over five years, the value of Wizard plc's tax relief is likely to be £151,200 each year (being £540,000 at 28%), some £756,000 in total (before discounting for the timing of the related cash flow). Furthermore, the purchase of such assets would be free of stamp duty, whereas Wizard plc would be liable to stamp duty at 0.5% on the entire amount paid for the shares in Harry Ltd.

Clearly, an asset deal would be very attractive to Wizard plc and would provide them with a significant financial advantage, even allowing for their proposed 'sweetener' payment of £200,000. On the other hand, an asset deal would be expensive for Harry Ltd. At the very least, Harry Ltd would incur a tax charge on the sale of its goodwill/ intellectual property of just over £529,000 calculated as follows:

	£'000
Sale proceeds (estimated)	2,700
Less: 31 March 1982 value	(300)
Indexation (March 1982 to date) £300,000 × 170%	(510)
Capital gain	1,890
Corporation tax thereon at 28%	529

In addition, it is likely that Harry Ltd would incur further tax liabilities, for example due to a clawback of capital allowances and profit on the sale of its trading stock.

As the group would be able to sell the *shares* in Harry Ltd on a tax-free basis, this remains the best deal structure. This would also be sensible from a commercial viewpoint since all pre-sale contingent risks and liabilities associated with Harry Ltd's business and tax affairs would, in effect, be assumed by Wizard plc (subject to the negotiated warranties and indemnities). Under an asset-based deal, these risks would generally remain with the group.

Explanatory Notes

Substantial shareholdings exemption (SSE)

1. FA 2002 Sch 8 introduced an important capital gains exemption enabling companies to sell their shareholdings in qualifying companies (where they hold a substantial interest) on a tax-free basis. Similarly, as the gains are not chargeable, where the relevant conditions are met, no tax recognition is given for capital losses realised in such cases. The substantial shareholdings exemption (SSE) is not restricted to shareholdings in UK-resident companies and applies equally to gains arising on the sale of non-resident subsidiaries and other eligible investments. The Government's main policy objective was to increase the UK's attractiveness as a location for multinational groups, since the SSE enables them to restructure and sell their subsidiaries without triggering a tax charge.

2. Companies wishing to rely on the substantial shareholdings exemption (SSE) must pay careful attention to the numerous qualifying conditions and various anti-avoidance provisions in TCGA 1992 Sch 7AC. The main conditions are stated in paras 7–9, 18 and 19 of the Schedule, which are summarised in note 3 of the example.

Trading company and trading group requirements

3. It will be seen from note 3 in the example that both the investing company/group and the company being sold must satisfy the strict 'trading company/group' definitions laid down in the legislation. This means that, in the case of a singleton company, it must be 'a company carrying on trading activities whose activities do not include to a substantial extent activities other than trading activities' (TCGA 1992 Sch 7AC para 20). A company is treated as carrying on trading activities if it is carrying them on in the course of, or for the purposes of, its trade. This also includes an intended acquisition of a significant interest in the share capital of a trading company/group (from a third party). Activities carried out for the purposes of preparing to trade also count.

   In practice, HMRC apply a 20% 'benchmark' for determining whether a company has a *substantial* level of non-trading activities. Where a company has 'non-trading' activities or investments, HMRC may look at a range of possible measures depending on the facts of the particular case, such as contribution to profits, assets employed, expenses and management time.

4. A 'trading group' is defined in much the same way as a sole trading company (TCGA 1992 Sch 7AC para 21). The definition of 'group' follows TCGA 1992 s 170 (see Example 62, part A), except that the qualifying holding requirement is 51% (as opposed to 75%).

   A trading group is one where, taking all the activities of the group together, it carries on trading activities, ignoring any non-substantial non-trading activities. The legislation requires all the activities of the group to be taken together. This ensures that any intra-group transactions are effectively ignored. For example, property leased to another 51% group member is not regarded as an investment/non-trading activity.

   The special rule for joint venture companies referred to in note 4 of the example is covered by Sch 7AC paras 23 and 24.

Interaction of SSE with other exemptions

5. The SSE takes priority over the normal capital gains reorganisation provisions, such as TCGA 1992 s 127. This means that the normal 'no disposal' treatment is disapplied, and that, for example, the SSE applies (where the relevant conditions are met) on a share-for-share exchange. This is particularly helpful if the shares received on the exchange do not qualify for SSE (for example, they represent a holding of less than 10%). The new shares would be treated as being acquired for market value at the date of sale, so the benefits of the SSE would be 'locked-in' at that point (Sch 7AC para 4). On the other hand, corporate no gain no loss transfers (such as intra-group disposals under TCGA 1992 s 171 or corporate reconstruction transfers under TCGA 1992 s 139) take priority over the SSE (Sch 7AC para 6).

Secondary SSE

6. Where the vendor company satisfies the conditions for the main SSE referred to above, and owns an 'asset related to shares' (ie options over or securities convertible into such shares), any gain arising on such a related asset is tax-exempt (Sch 7AC para 2). Sch 7AC para 3 also permits relief to be claimed in circumstances where the trading company/holding company requirement is not satisfied at the time of sale but would have been met at any time in the previous two years.

Anti-avoidance

7. A special anti-avoidance rule is contained in Sch 7AC para 5 to prevent the SSE being abused in certain prescribed cases.

Intangible fixed assets regime

8. Before 1 April 2002, the capital cost of most intangible fixed assets did not attract any tax relief against trading profits, although capital allowances were available on patents and know-how. From that date, a new regime applies for companies in respect of goodwill, intellectual property and other intangible assets, including fishing and agricultural quotas. For the treatment of computer software see Example 20 explanatory note 6.

Scope of the intangible fixed assets regime

9. As indicated in explanatory note 8, the intangible fixed assets regime in CTA 2009 Part 8 applies from the 1 April 2002 'commencement date'. However, the transitional provisions are designed to ensure that only intangible fixed assets which were acquired from an unrelated third party or internally created after 31 March 2002 qualify for relief under the regime. Special rules apply where the intangible fixed assets were owned before 1 April 2002 but additional expenditure is incurred on them after that date.

    The effect of the 1 April 2002 commencement date is that intangible fixed assets held on 1 April 2002 (or acquired from a related party who held them on that date), known as 'old regime' assets, continue to give rise to capital gains on their subsequent sale. For example, if a company that started trading in 1990 sells its trading goodwill, this will generate a capital gain (with indexation relief).

    The related party provisions are in CTA 2009 ss 834–851. Companies are related where one controls the other or the same person controls both. In the case of a close company, a person will be related to the company if the person is a participator or associate of a participator in that company.

10. In broad terms, companies can generally obtain tax relief for intangible fixed assets purchased (other than from related persons) or created from 1 April 2002 onwards, referred to as 'new regime' assets. This means that expenditure on qualifying purchased goodwill, patents, trade marks, copyrights, know-how, licences, brands, names, logos, customer lists, designs, commercial formats etc now qualifies for tax relief. These rules only apply for corporation tax purposes and thus to UK-resident companies and UK permanent establishments. (The existing capital gains tax rules continue to apply to individuals.)

11.   The tax relief for intangible assets will be given against trading profits for trading companies, property income for property businesses or as non-trading amounts (CTA 2009 ss 745–753). If there is a non-trading loss, relief may be claimed within two years after the end of the accounting period to set the loss against the total profits of the same period. Any loss not relieved in that way and not surrendered by way of group relief will be carried forward to set against later non-trading profits (CTA 2009 s 753).

Alignment with accounting treatment

12.   The intangible assets rules follow the increasing trend of aligning the tax treatment with that adopted in the accounts. The timing of the tax relief for new regime assets will therefore follow the rules in Financial Reporting Standard (FRS) 10, which deals with goodwill and other intangibles, including intellectual property. FRS 10 requires such assets to be amortised or written off against profits based on the useful working life of the asset. An appropriate goodwill 'write-off' may also be made where its value has been 'impaired'. Thus overall these rules provide the advantage of tax-deductible amortisation and 'impairment review' write-downs where none existed before. It should be noted that for companies adopting International Financial Reporting Standards (IFRS), International Accounting Standard 38 (IAS 38) prohibits the amortisation of goodwill, although impairment reviews are permissible under IAS 36.

The accounting treatment adopted will therefore influence the timing of the tax relief for purchased goodwill or intellectual property, being based on the amount amortised in the accounts, as illustrated in note 5 of the example (CTA 2009 ss 726–729). However, as an alternative, companies may elect to claim tax relief at the rate of 4% of the goodwill/ intellectual property cost per year (CTA 2009 s 730).

Where the accounting treatment does not properly reflect generally accepted accounting practice (GAAP), it will be replaced for tax purposes by a treatment that accords with that practice. This is most likely to apply to UK permanent establishments of companies incorporated outside the UK, since they are not required to comply with UK GAAP. However, for accounting periods beginning on or after 1 January 2005, accounts drawn up in accordance with IFRS, whether those adopted by the European Commission or full IFRS, will be accepted as the equivalent of UK GAAP. (FA 2004 s 50.)

Profits on sale of intangible fixed assets and 'income' rollover relief

13.   Any profits on the sale of goodwill and other intangible property will be treated as income rather than capital gains (CTA 2009 ss 720–721). However, the tax can be deferred under an 'income' style rollover relief, provided the proceeds are reinvested into other new regime intangible fixed assets within the normal 'reinvestment window' starting one year before and ending three years after the gain arises (CTA 2009 ss 754–763).

The rollover relief for intangible fixed assets is modelled on the existing capital gains rollover relief, and is extended to cover intangible fixed assets transactions by 75% group members (CTA 2009 s 777). Profits arising on the disposal of such assets are deferred to the extent that the proceeds are reinvested in intangible fixed assets. The relief is reduced where only part of the proceeds are reinvested. The base cost of the 'replacement' intangible fixed asset is reduced by the original profit. Thus, as the relief reduces the base cost for tax deduction purposes, there will be a mismatch with the accounting treatment. Separate computations will be required to calculate the tax deduction for each period and keep track of the post-rollover relief base cost applying for tax purposes.

There is a special rule designed to give some neutrality between asset and share-based acquisitions. In such cases, profits on intangible fixed assets may be rolled over against any new regime intangible fixed assets *owned by an acquired 75% subsidiary*. The broad effect of this special rule is therefore to look through the shareholding investment in the 75% subsidiary to its underlying *new regime* intangible fixed assets. The profits will be deducted from the carrying values of the relevant intangible fixed assets owned by the subsidiary at the date of its acquisition.

Under transitional rules, capital gains on old regime goodwill and fishing and agricultural quotas will qualify for the rollover relief when reinvested into new regime intangible fixed assets (CTA 2009 s 898). Under further transitional rules in TCGA 1992 s 156ZA, old regime goodwill and quotas disposed of on or after 1 April 2002 may be rolled over under the capital gains rules against certain pre-1 April 2002 acquisitions of goodwill or quota or under the intangibles rules or partly under the capital gains rules and partly under the intangibles rules.

Treatment of groups

14.   Intra-group transfers of new regime assets are made on a no gain/no loss ('tax-neutral') basis in broadly the same way as the capital gains rule in TCGA 1992 s 171 (CTA 2009 s 775). The same 75% group definition also applies (CTA 2009 ss 764–773).

15.   An income-based degrouping charge applies if new regime intangible fixed assets are transferred on a tax-neutral basis between group companies and the transferee company leaves the group within six years, still owning the transferred asset (CTA 2009 ss 780–794). The mechanics of the intangible fixed assets degrouping charge and the related exemptions are identical to those used for group capital gains purposes. Thus, for example, the degrouping charge can be rolled over or reallocated within the group (see Example 65 part (d) for detailed coverage of the capital gains rules).

Treatment of royalties etc

16.   The intangible fixed assets regime applies equally to payments made for the use of both old and new regime intangible fixed assets. Hence, royalties payable and receivable are taxed on the amount reflected in the accounts. Special transitional rules ignore any royalties previously recognised for tax purposes (see Example 49 explanatory note 4(viii)).

Question

Fred Nietz, the managing director of Chase Ltd, has approached your firm for advice.

Chase Ltd, a UK company that has been trading for 30 years making up accounts annually to 31 March, is a subsidiary of a large UK-resident company. The present market conditions have hit Chase Ltd particularly hard and it is essential that substantial investment in new machinery be made. The directors of the parent company are unwilling to authorise this expenditure and instead propose to sell the company.

Fred and his colleagues are interested in acquiring the business of Chase Ltd and have arranged the necessary finance for the acquisition and for the new machinery.

Chase Ltd has unrelieved trading losses of £200,000 and a property worth £440,000 which was acquired from the parent company in July 2003 at its cost price of £220,000 when its market value was £370,000. The parent company had bought the property in February 1992. Assume indexation from February 1992 to July 2003 was 30.3%.

Write a memorandum to the Tax Partner, outlining the tax matters to be considered in effecting the buy-out either:

(a)   through a direct purchase of the shares held by the parent company, or

(b)   by forming a new company which would acquire the trade and assets of Chase Ltd,

and indicating any income tax points that should be brought to the attention of Fred Nietz and his colleagues.

Answer

1 June 2009

To: Tax Partner
From: Alan White

Chase Ltd – Proposed management buy-out

I have considered the proposed buy-out of Chase Ltd by Fred Nietz, managing director, and his colleagues and outline below the tax matters to be considered.

Acquisition by direct purchase of shares held by parent company

1. The parent company would almost certainly favour a sale of the shares in Chase Ltd, since any capital gain should be entirely exempt under the substantial shareholdings exemption (SSE) rules in TCGA 1992 Sch 7AC. (All the relevant SSE conditions appear to be satisfied.) Furthermore, the parent company would not have any balancing charge on the sale of the assets, and any contingent commercial and tax liabilities will effectively be assumed by the purchaser. The latter is subject to any limitations imposed by warranties and indemnities under the share sale agreement, but these are often restricted in management buy-out situations as managers are assumed to be aware of the company's previous commercial and financial obligations and possibly its tax compliance history (see 2(c) below).

    On the other hand, the parent company might consider an asset sale if this would facilitate the acquisition provided there were no material tax costs. For example, the trading losses brought forward are available against any balancing charges and the proceeds could be paid up to the parent as a 'tax free' intra-group dividend or, alternatively, loaned by Chase Ltd (which would of course in those circumstances still be a group member) to other group companies. The transfer pricing implications of such loans would, of course, require examination.

2. A share purchase/sale has several disadvantages for the buy-out team:

    (a) It may be more difficult to raise finance for the purchase of the shares than it would be for the purchase of machinery, for example through hire purchase.

    (b) There would be a crystallisation of the held-over gain on the property acquired from the parent company in July 2003 (the degrouping charge), as Chase Ltd is leaving the group with the property within six years of the acquisition. Chase Ltd would be deemed to have made a gain of (£370,000 – £220,000) = £150,000 less indexation allowance of 30.3%, (ie £66,660) = £83,340, in July 2003. The gain would be regarded as arising at the beginning of Chase Ltd's accounting period in which the shares were purchased (likely to be 1 April 2009).

    Such degrouping gains can be allocated to the parent company or any of its 75% subsidiaries by making a TCGA 1992 s 179A election. This would enable the gain to be sheltered by any capital losses etc in those companies. Alternatively it can be rolled over under the business assets rollover rules – either against qualifying expenditure in the parent company's group (under TCGA 1992 s 179B) or within Chase Ltd itself (for example, to the extent that the new machinery qualified as *fixed* plant or machinery). The replacement qualifying assets must be purchased within the normal reinvestment period beginning one year before and ending three years after the gain occurs. (Note that post-31 March 2002 acquisitions of goodwill do not count as a qualifying business asset for capital gains regime rollover relief.)

    If the gain (and hence the liability) remains within Chase Ltd, it would be necessary to ensure that the purchase price of the shares was reduced to take account of this tax charge. The gain cannot be reduced by brought forward trading losses, but if losses were still being made, the losses of the same accounting period could be offset against it.

(c)   There may be other latent capital gains and other liabilities of which Fred Nietz is not aware, because of decisions taken at parent company level and because of statutory non-compliance or HMRC making an enquiry under corporation tax self-assessment, which may extend to earlier years.

Whilst the buy-out team should seek to obtain suitable warranties and indemnities from the parent company as part of the agreement to purchase, these are often restricted (for the reasons outline in 1 above). Furthermore, the transaction is inevitably far more complicated, costly in legal fees and time-consuming.

(d)   There is a possibility that the brought forward losses plus any further losses not relieved against other profits may be forfeited because of the provisions of ICTA 1988 s 768. This section prevents losses being carried forward following a change of ownership if either:

(i)   Within a period of three years there is both a change of ownership and also a major change in the nature or conduct of the trade, or

(ii)   The change in ownership occurs after the scale of activities of a company has become small or negligible and before any considerable revival.

In the particular circumstances of this buy-out, Fred Nietz and his colleagues could argue a strong case against the application of s 768, since it appears unlikely that the trade has sunk to a negligible level. Furthermore, the injection of new machinery should be held not to constitute a major change in the nature or conduct of the trade, particularly having regard to SP10/91, under which HMRC confirm that the section will not be applied to investment necessary to keep pace with new technology etc. HMRC apply this particular section very harshly, however, and the carry forward losses may be vulnerable to forfeiture. If any (discounted) payment is sought for the losses (as part of the share price), this should only be paid on a deferred basis as and when the future loss offsets are effectively agreed.

There would, however, be no possibility at all of the losses being available for carry forward if the trade and assets were purchased instead of the shares.

Acquisition by forming new company to acquire trade and assets of Chase Ltd

1.   This method will probably be the preferred method for the buy-out team because it is more straightforward and does not have the disadvantages of the share purchase which have been indicated. Although it is unlikely that a significant amount would be paid for Chase Ltd's goodwill (owing to its recent trading losses etc), it is worth noting that the new company can now secure a trading deduction for goodwill (along with intellectual property), based on the amount amortised in its accounts each year or, alternatively, at 4% per annum on a straight-line basis. The company is required to make an irrevocable election to claim this treatment within two years of the end of the accounting period in which the asset is acquired. The stamp duty land tax on the chargeable assets purchased may, however, be more expensive than a share purchase. (Shares only attract stamp duty at 0.5% and would effectively be based on the *net* value of the company (ie reduced by debt).) If the consideration (which includes assumed liabilities) allocated to land and property assets, such as property (£440,000) and fixed plant, exceeds £500,000, stamp duty land tax will be levied at 4%. Chargeable consideration between £250,000 and £500,000 attracts stamp duty land tax of 3%. Stock and moveable plant should not attract a stamp tax charge. Goodwill and intellectual property transfers (such as trade marks, patents, etc) are specifically exempt from stamp duty.

2.   The buy-out team would be able to claim capital allowances on the plant transferred, as well as on the new purchases. The current writing down allowance for qualifying plant and machinery is 20% pa. Furthermore, the annual investment allowance (AIA) may be available, which provides 100% relief for the first £50,000 of qualifying additions. Any new expenditure

that does not qualify for the AIA may qualify for a 40% first-year allowance in the 2009/10 tax year instead. Industrial building writing down allowances (IBAs), if available, should not be clawed back on the vendor where the disposal occurs after 21 March 2007. The purchaser may be able to claim IBAs based on the vendor's written down value, although relief is being phased out and will be withdrawn in 2011.

3. The sale of assets as far as the parent company is concerned may be more difficult to achieve, bearing in mind that a 'share sale' of Chase Ltd is exempt from tax under the SSE rules noted above. However, the following points may be relevant in trying to negotiate an 'asset deal':

   (a) Although there would be a balancing charge on the disposal of the assets on which capital allowances had been claimed, this could be offset by the brought forward trading losses of £200,000; if not used before sale, these losses may have to be discounted on a share sale because of the provisions of ICTA 1988 s 768 mentioned above. If a profit still remained, the tax thereon would be at a maximum rate of 28% if it occurred in the year to 31 March 2010 (unless profits fell in the marginal small companies' rate band, in which case the tax rate on profits within the band would be 29.75%).

   (b) There would be a capital gain on the disposal of the property but a large part of this will crystallise in any event on a share sale (under the degrouping rules) and would have to be taken into account in the price for the shares. There may be the possibility of rolling over the gain (on a direct disposal) against other acquisitions of the group. Alternatively, the property could be retained and leased to the new company formed by the purchasers.

   (c) The parent company would be able to extract the book profit on the sale of the assets (less any corporation tax thereon) by way of a tax-free intra-group dividend. The overall tax arising on the sale may therefore be minimal if the balancing charge on the assets can be mitigated by the brought forward trading losses and the property gain can be rolled over.

   Overall, the parent company is likely to seek to sell the shares in Chase Ltd because of the SSE exemption and the much greater commercial protection. In practice, it would only accede to sale of Chase Ltd's trade and assets if it can be structured on a broadly 'tax-neutral' basis.

Other considerations

If the parent company sold Chase Ltd to an outside party, then unless the staff were taken over (under the transfer of undertakings rules on an asset sale) it would be involved in heavy redundancy payments and possibly union problems. If staff transfer under TUPE, as will almost certainly be the case in an asset sale, both seller and buyer are vulnerable to unfair dismissal and other staff claims. This favours share sale unless indemnities are obtained from the buyer.

Income tax points to be brought to the attention of Fred Nietz and his colleagues

1. It appears that the new venture, whether through Chase Ltd or a new company, will be a close company. Fred Nietz and his colleagues should therefore be able to obtain interest relief on money borrowed to buy their shares or lent to the company for the company to buy the assets, providing they either each own more than 5% of the share capital, or own some share capital and work full-time in the management of the company (ITA 2007 s 383).

   Funds provided as share capital will be locked into the company, whereas money provided on loan can be withdrawn when the company is able to repay it. If money is borrowed to lend to the company, interest relief is restricted if the loan is repaid by the company without a corresponding reduction in the loan to the buyout team.

2. HMRC take the view that where employees buy out the company or business for which they previously used to work, they do so in pursuance of an opportunity offered to them as

employees of that company or of a new company formed to take over the business. There is a contrary argument that where a new company is formed to purchase the target company or its assets and trade, the management buy-out team acquire the shares in the new company as founders.

Clearly, the risk exists that HMRC will look for any 'benefit' derived from the managers' employment. This would arise where the parent company has sold the company or business to the management team below an arm's length price. There are likely to be practical difficulties in demonstrating that a commercial price has been paid by the management team in the absence of comparable bids for the company from third parties. A discount may be appropriate on a management buy-out if the deal can be completed quickly and with fewer warranties (see above).

Many buy-out teams typically form a new company to acquire the shares or trade and assets, as this is more efficient for financing and facilitates bank and institutional lending and investment. If management acquire their shares in the new company on preferential terms (for example, compared with shares issued to institutions etc), it may be argued that an employment income charge arises.

This is a notoriously difficult area in practice. Under self-assessment, appropriate disclosure is required (to avoid any accusation of negligence). A fully justified case should be disclosed on the return where no taxable amount is being reported.

3.   If a new company is formed, and at some future date the shares are disposed of at a loss, the capital loss may be available to be set off against income of the year of disposal or the previous year (or both years, if the loss is large enough) (ITA 2007 s 131). This relief is only available where shares have been subscribed for and so would not be available if the management team directly purchased the existing shares in Chase Ltd from the parent company.

4.   Whether the existing shares are purchased or new shares subscribed for, any new capital could be raised from non-working shareholders through the enterprise investment scheme. On an assets purchase, all the share capital put up by non-working shareholders would qualify whereas only new capital would qualify on a share purchase (but see explanatory note 4).

If the management team formed a new company to acquire the *shares* in Chase Ltd, then the non-working shareholders could subscribe for shares in the new company and obtain enterprise investment relief, provided that all qualifying conditions were met and the trade and assets of Chase Ltd were hived-up to the new company on acquisition (under ICTA 1988 s 343 and TCGA 1992 s 171).

For EIS shares in a close company, it is not possible to get tax relief on interest paid on a loan to buy the shares. Another possible source of funding is a venture capital trust (see explanatory note 4).

Explanatory Notes

Different forms of management buy-out

1.   The example describes the features of two of the main forms of management buy-outs.

Although a direct purchase of Chase Ltd's shares is contemplated here by the management team, it is more common for the acquisition to be made by a new company formed by the management team. This makes for easier and more efficient financing. Bank borrowing etc is through the new company, which can be repaid out of the post-acquisition cash flows of the acquired trade. If the managers borrowed personally to finance the acquisition, they would have to pay tax on monies taken out to finance the repayment of the bank borrowing.

A third possibility where the buy-out team already owns shares in the company is to utilise the provisions enabling a company to purchase its own shares without the payment being treated as a distribution. The provisions are covered in Example 61. Yet another variation is for assets to be hived down into a new company, using the reorganisation provisions of ICTA 1988 s 343, and for the shares in the new company to be sold to the buy-out team.

Substantial shareholdings exemption

2. From 1 April 2002, groups can sell their trading subsidiaries (or indeed any shareholding investment in a trading company in which they hold at least 10% of the equity) free of tax under the substantial shareholdings exemption (SSE) rules. This means that they will invariably be seeking to structure their 'business' disposals as a sale of shares. On the other hand, if a significant amount is being paid for goodwill (which is *not* the case in this example), a corporate purchaser would clearly prefer an asset deal. This is because, from 1 April 2002, they can usually claim tax relief on the cost of the goodwill (and any intellectual property), normally based on the amount amortised in the accounts under generally accepted accounting practice (see CTA 2009 Part 8). These tax rules mean that the 'fiscal tension' between vendors and purchasers is probably greater than ever and the structure of each transaction will have to be negotiated on a case-by-case basis. The relative negotiating strength of each party usually determines the outcome.

Entrepreneur's relief

3. The management team are likely to want to ensure that they meet the relevant conditions to allow them the potential to benefit from entrepreneur's relief, to the extent that they have not already utilised it, on an exit, for example, on a trade sale of the business or the company buying back their shareholding on retirement. Entrepreneur's relief was introduced from 6 April 2008 to provide an effective rate of tax of 10% on certain 'qualifying business disposals' by reducing the gain by 4/9ths. However, unlike taper relief, entrepreneur's relief only applies to the first £1 million of qualifying lifetime gains. The company's activities should be regularly reviewed to ensure that no investment activities are started which could jeopardise the shareholders' entrepreneur's relief (see Example 78 for the detailed provisions).

Sources of finance

4. Financing a buy-out can be a major problem. It may be helped by the provisions of the enterprise investment scheme linked with the provisions enabling a company to buy its own shares. This means that the company may buy back an investor's shares after the five-year period has elapsed, but it is not possible for guaranteed exit arrangements to be provided at the outset (ITA 2007 s 177).

    A newly formed company may qualify under the enterprise investment scheme (EIS) rules where it is formed to buy the trade and assets *or* the shares in Chase Ltd. (HMRC normally accept that the share subscription proceeds were applied for trading purposes if the trade and assets of Chase Ltd were transferred to the new company on acquisition – see below.) The management team could not, however, obtain any EIS relief as they would be 'connected' with Chase Ltd and the new company under ITA 2007 s 166.

    Bank borrowing and any institutional finance may be conveniently structured through a new company, which then makes the acquisition.

    A direct purchase of the existing shares in Chase Ltd would not qualify for EIS relief but the subsequent issue of new shares (for new assets and new working capital) should attract relief.

    Another possible source of funding is from a venture capital trust. HMRC commented in their Tax Bulletin of August 1995 on the circumstances in which such a trust may provide funding for a management buyout. Even where the buyout company acquires shares in the existing company rather than its assets, HMRC will accept that shares issued by the buyout company to the venture capital trust will be a qualifying holding if the trade of the acquired company is hived up to the buyout company as soon as possible after the buyout.

For details of the enterprise investment scheme and venture capital trusts see Example 93.

Other points

5.   See the Revenue's Statement of Practice 10/91 for their interpretation of a 'major change in the nature or conduct of a trade'.

Question

Pluto Ltd owns 100% of Socrates Ltd and 100% of Aristotle Ltd. All companies are UK-resident, and each company carries on a different trade associated with the chemical industry.

The shareholding in Pluto Ltd is held equally by three families, each of which has a different view as to how the group could be more effectively controlled and managed. Owing to the differing views of the families, it is clear that the companies in the group could be better managed by each of the families taking control of one particular trade currently carried on by the companies in the group.

This objective may be achieved through a reorganisation at the end of December 2009 by either:

(i) Pluto Ltd distributing the shares in the subsidiary companies directly to the family shareholders interested in gaining control of that particular company's trade, or

(ii) Pluto Ltd transferring the shares in the subsidiary companies to new companies especially formed for that purpose. These new companies would then issue shares to the respective shareholders of Pluto Ltd.

Under either alternative, the shares held in Pluto Ltd by the families who are to acquire Socrates Ltd and Aristotle Ltd will be cancelled, leaving the members of the third family as the only shareholders in Pluto Ltd.

State what reliefs (if any) are available to the shareholders of Pluto Ltd if the proposals at (i) or (ii) above were implemented and what conditions must be satisfied for those reliefs to apply.

Comment on any other tax implications.

Answer

(a) **Reliefs available to shareholders of Pluto Ltd and conditions to be satisfied for those reliefs to apply**

There are various tax problems associated with a company break-up such as that planned for Pluto Ltd, and some of the problems are dealt with under the demerger provisions of ICTA 1988 ss 213–218, as follows:

(1) Distributions that are exempt distributions as defined are not treated as income in the hands of the shareholders. An exempt distribution is defined as (s 213(3)):

   (a) a distribution consisting of the transfer by a company to *all or any* of its members of shares in one or more companies that are its 75% subsidiaries; or

   (b) a distribution consisting of the transfer by a company to one or more other companies of a trade or trades, or of shares in one or more companies which are its 75% subsidiaries, and the issue of shares by the transferee company or companies to *all or any* of the members of the distributing company.

(2) Both the distribution of the subsidiaries' shares directly to the individual shareholders as proposed in Pluto Ltd's alternative (i) and the transfer of the subsidiaries' shares to the relevant new companies as proposed in alternative (ii) would come within the definition of exempt distributions (s 213(3)). The distributing company will often be a holding company distributing one or more trades or shares in 75% subsidiaries. In some cases, a singleton trading company may distribute one or more of its trading divisions via a demerger distribution. The shares in the new companies would be issued to the requisite family shareholder groups in Pluto Ltd. Since the distributions would be exempt distributions, there would be no income tax implications for the shareholders.

(3) An exempt distribution under part (a) of the definition is also not treated as a capital distribution for capital gains purposes, but as a company reorganisation under the provisions of TCGA 1992 ss 126–131 (TCGA 1992 s 192). This covers the distribution of the subsidiaries' shares in alternative (i), so that no capital gains tax consequences should arise for the shareholders as a result of the demerger. Under the second alternative, the issue of shares in the new companies in exchange for the Pluto Ltd shares should not be treated as a CGT disposal under the shareholder reconstruction provisions in TCGA 1992 s 136 (reconstruction involving issue of securities) – the shareholders would effectively retain their existing base cost.

(4) As far as corporate gains are concerned, Pluto Ltd will make a capital gains disposal when it distributes its 100% holdings in Socrates Ltd and Aristotle Ltd. From 1 April 2002, it is important to note that the substantial shareholdings exemption (SSE) could apply to the disposal of a qualifying shareholding (see Example 66 explanatory notes 1 to 7). However, where the disposal falls to be dealt with under the TCGA 1992 s 139 corporate capital gains reconstruction relief provisions (which provide for 'no gain/no loss' treatment), these will prevail over the SSE (TCGA 1992 Sch 7AC para 6(1)(a)). The SSE should be available to exempt any gain arising on the direct 'demerger' disposal of the shares to the individual shareholders under alternative (i) as this would not rank for s 139 relief. This is because one of the pre-conditions for s 139 relief is that the disposal is to another *UK-resident company* (or of an asset which is to be used in a UK permanent establishment trade carried on by a non-resident). Alternative (ii) should meet this requirement as the transfer of the shares in the 100% subsidiaries (treated as the transfer of a business for TCGA 1992 s 139 purposes) is to the relevant two new *companies*. Thus, under this route, the shares in the subsidiaries should be transferred on a no gain/no loss basis (ie at their indexed base cost) under s 139 and not under the SSE provisions.

(5) The provisions in TCGA 1992 s 179 for the crystallisation of capital gains on a company leaving a group do not apply when a company ceases to be a member of a group as a result of an exempt demerger distribution. There will therefore be no charge on Aristotle Ltd and Socrates Ltd when they leave the group under either alternative (i) or (ii), in respect of any assets that have been transferred to them on a no gain no loss basis by any group company within the previous six years. Similarly, a 'degrouping charge' under the intangible fixed assets provisions (see Example 66 explanatory note 15) will not apply to an exempt distribution (CTA 2009 s 787).

In order for the above treatment to apply the following conditions must be satisfied:

(i) All the companies concerned must be UK-resident at the time of the distribution.

(ii) The distributing company must be a trading company or member of a trading group and each subsidiary must be either a trading company or the holding company of a trading group.

(iii) The shares transferred by the distributing company and, where relevant, issued by the transferee company, must be non-redeemable and must constitute all or substantially all (considered by HMRC to mean around 90% or more) of the ordinary share capital, and confer all or substantially all of the voting power in the company concerned.

(iv) The distributing company must remain a trading company or member of a trading group unless the demerger involves two or more 75% subsidiaries and the parent company is wound up without there being any net assets available for distribution (other than to cover liquidation costs and any negligible share capital remaining – Revenue concession C11).

(v) Where a trade is transferred the distributing company must not retain more than a minor interest in the trade (which HMRC interpret as around 10% or less).

(vi) The only or main activity of any transferee company must be to carry on the trade or hold the shares transferred to it.

(vii) The distribution must be wholly or mainly to benefit some or all of the trading activities previously carried on by a single company or group and subsequently by two or more companies or groups.

(viii) The distribution must not be part of a tax avoidance scheme, or a scheme to enable other persons to obtain control of one of the companies, or a scheme for the purpose of the cessation or sale of a trade. Where a payment other than a bona fide commercial payment is made to the shareholders within five years after an exempt distribution it is treated as miscellaneous income in their hands, the paying company may not deduct it for corporation tax and the 'demerger' capital gains reliefs (such as protection from the TCGA 1992 s 179 de-grouping charge but not the general TCGA 1992 ss 136 and 139 reconstruction reliefs) are withdrawn.

It appears, from the information available, that either of the alternatives proposed by Pluto Ltd would satisfy the required conditions, but there is provision for advance clearance of a demerger transaction and it is obviously sensible for the clearance to be obtained. Furthermore, the shareholder capital gains tax relief under TCGA 1992 s 136 and the company reconstruction capital gains relief under TCGA 1992 s 139 are dependent on the transaction being for bona fide commercial purposes, for which advance clearance can be sought under TCGA 1992 s 138 and s 139(5) respectively. (A statutory clearance is not required for SSE disposals under TCGA 1992 Sch 7AC.)

The demerger provisions do not provide relief for all the tax consequences of a demerger. Under both routes, the anti-avoidance rules that prevent the carry forward of trading losses or shadow ACT on a change of control may be triggered if there is a major change in the nature or conduct of the trades (ICTA 1988 s 768 and shadow ACT rules in SI 1999/358 reg 16). HMRC have, however, indicated in Statement of Practice 13/80 that these matters will be given sympathetic treatment. Pluto Ltd's disposal of the shares in the subsidiaries to the shareholders under the first alternative should be exempt under the SSE provisions (as indicated above).

Stamp duties must always be considered when structuring a demerger. A direct demerger distribution to shareholders (first alternative) should not give rise to any stamp duty or stamp duty land tax liability. An indirect demerger distribution by a holding or 'stand alone' company should obtain relief under FA 2003 Sch 7 para 8, restricting the tax to 0.5% on the dutiable assets transferred. This relief is particularly beneficial if chargeable assets (such as property) are being transferred as a demerger distribution of a trade (where the shareholdings are being split). Goodwill was exempted from charge with effect from 23 April 2002. Since alternative (ii) involves the transfer of shares which only attract a 0.5% stamp duty charge, there would be no need to rely on the FA 2003 Sch 7 para 8 transfer of undertaking relief in this case.

There is the possibility of problems occurring under both alternatives by reason of ITA 2007 s 684 (cancellation of tax advantage from transactions in securities). A clearance procedure is, however, available (s 701).

Explanatory Notes

Aim of demerger provisions

1. The aim of the demerger legislation, according to the then Chancellor, was to enable businesses grouped inefficiently under a single company umbrella to be run more dynamically and effectively by being demerged and being allowed to pursue their separate ways under independent management. It is accordingly not relevant where the aim is for a company to be liquidated or sold.

Company reconstructions

2. The shareholder and company reconstruction reliefs in TCGA 1992 ss 136 and 139 respectively both require a 'scheme of reconstruction'.

    Under the statutory rules, of TCGA 1992 Sch 5AA a scheme of reconstruction contains the following key elements:

    ●   Only the ordinary shareholders of the relevant business must receive ordinary shares under the scheme, ie no one else must be entitled to receive new shares

    ●   The proportionate interests of the shareholders before and after the reconstruction must remain the same

    ●   The business previously carried on by the 'original' company or companies must be carried on by one or more successor companies *unless* the scheme is carried out under a compromise or arrangement under Companies Act 1985 s 425 (or equivalent). Companies Act 2006 s 834(5) defines a 'scheme of reconstruction' as being that given in TCGA 1992 Sch 5AA.

Other statutory demerger routes

3. A further type of statutory demerger covered by the 'exempt distribution' provisions involves the transfer of a trade or trades to one or more new companies in consideration of the transferee company/companies issuing shares to all or any of the distributing company's shareholders. Such a demerger would normally be covered by the TCGA 1992 s 139 corporate reconstruction provisions, so that the relevant assets such as 'old regime' goodwill (see Example 66 explanatory notes 9 and 13) and property would be transferred on a no gain no loss basis (see note (4) in the example). A similar 'tax neutral' treatment applies to the transfer of goodwill under the intangible fixed assets regime in CTA 2009 Part 8 (CTA 2009 s 818). It is possible to have a variant of this basic transaction, since ICTA 1988 s 213(12) enables the demerger distribution of the trade and assets to be made by a *75% subsidiary company* to the new company (although this would not qualify for the FA 2003 Schs 7–8 stamp duty reduction). Where the subsidiary makes a demerger distribution of the trade and assets,

this must be followed by a further demerger distribution by the parent company of that subsidiary company's shares (their value would invariably be minimal due to the prior demerger distribution).

It should be noted that it is not possible to transfer the trade and assets directly to the shareholders, although, as seen in alternative (i) in the example, this is permissible for a transfer of shares in a 75% subsidiary. The general thrust of the demerger rules requires the trades and underlying assets to remain in the corporate sector.

Where a demerger proceeds as a transfer of a trade and assets, the distributing company will be treated as ceasing to carry on the relevant trade, with the normal tax consequences, such as the forfeiture of brought forward trading losses and the potential crystallisation of balancing charges on the transfer of plant. These particular adverse effects could be eliminated if the transfer of the trade fell within the scope of the ICTA 1988 s 343 corporate trade succession provisions, which require, amongst other things, that there is 75% common ownership at shareholder level before and after the transfer.

Non-statutory demerger using Insolvency Act 1986 s 110

4.   It is possible to demerge businesses or 75% subsidiaries without using the statutory demerger provisions in ICTA 1988 ss 213–218. This route would involve winding up the relevant company, with the liquidator then distributing the businesses or subsidiaries under the procedure laid down in s 110 of the Insolvency Act 1986. These are often known as 'non-statutory' demergers and may be used where it is not possible to satisfy a particular condition in the statutory demerger code, for example where an investment business (such as property letting, which is not a trade) is being demerged by way of a partition between different groups of shareholders. It is necessary for the transfers (which are generally for no consideration other than the assumption of liabilities) to take place in the course of a winding up to prevent the shareholders from suffering an income tax charge under the distribution provisions (ICTA 1988 s 209(1) proviso). The shareholders' and corporate capital gains reconstruction reliefs under TCGA 1992 ss 136 and 139 should also apply here.

Demergers and trusts

5.   Although, as indicated in the example, demergers usually have neither income tax nor capital gains tax consequences for shareholders, there are particular problems for trustees. For details see Example 80 explanatory note 3.

Question

Harrison Group Ltd is considering making an offer for the whole of the ordinary share capital of Jayes Ltd (a close company making electrical components).

The finance director of Harrison Group Ltd has asked you to write a memorandum indicating the various taxation indemnities and warranties which should be incorporated in the purchasing agreement.

Draft a reply to the finance director, explaining the thinking behind the inclusion of these aspects in the agreement, the meaning of each of the terms, their purpose and significance.

Incorporate into your reply five areas that you consider should be the subject of a tax warranty and five areas that would be dealt with by a deed of indemnity.

Answer

Memorandum to the finance director of the Harrison Group Ltd (Harrison) in connection with the possible offer for the whole of the ordinary share capital of Jayes Ltd (Jayes)

Since Harrison proposes to acquire the share capital of Jayes as distinct from purchasing its assets on a going concern basis and continuing the trade, any actual or contingent liabilities and potential claims against Jayes will not be affected by the sale of shares.

In the event of claims of whatever nature arising against Jayes, Harrison will be affected in that the price which it is proposed to pay for the Jayes shares may, with the benefit of hindsight, be thought excessive, quite apart from the effect on the continuing trading of Jayes, depending upon the nature, seriousness and size of the claim.

The known liabilities and defined contingent liabilities will of course be taken into account in fixing the purchase price for the shares, but it is the unknown claim in respect of which care has to be exercised in a transaction of this sort.

Such claims are not limited to taxation matters, and can arise for example through product guarantees, breach of trade descriptions, property liabilities (such as contaminated land), employee matters and so on. Together with those relating to taxation, they will be the subject of a series of indemnities and warranties in the purchase agreement. The objective is to ensure that Harrison, as the new owner of the shares, is protected against claims which are made against Jayes relating to a period before the shares were acquired.

It should be remembered that the value of the indemnities and warranties is only as good as the ability of the vendors of the shares to make payment in the event of a claim, quite apart from the considerable professional costs which are usually involved. The vendor may therefore take out appropriate insurance to cover the potential liability (although it can be relatively costly). This arrangement would be beneficial to Harrison as it would have the comfort of knowing that in the event of a claim being necessary, the funds will be forthcoming if the claim is proved. If the vendor refuses to take out insurance cover, the purchaser may insist on a proportion of the sale proceeds being retained for (say) a year to meet potential liabilities. (There is a view that most problems surface after the first audit by the purchaser's auditors.)

There is usually a de minimis provision in the purchase agreement so that insignificant claims are not raised, and an overall ceiling on the liability of the vendors which is normally no greater than the price paid to them for their shares.

The indemnities and warranties in the purchase agreement will be drafted so as to be as wide and comprehensive as possible. There will be a blanket tax indemnity covering diminution in the value of the Jayes shares as a result of any unprovided tax liability arising from the period prior to the purchase of the shares.

Having said that, it is usual in the purchase agreement to set out specific points on which indemnities and warranties are given.

Defining the terms:

The deed of indemnity (also known as the 'tax covenant') is an undertaking to compensate for loss or expense flowing from the matters contained in the deed.

A *warranty* is something contractually guaranteed, breach of which justifies a claim for damages but from which loss will not necessarily flow so that no claim will arise under the deed of indemnity.

Drawing attention to the matters which the purchaser wishes to cover by warranties does, however, minimise the risk of a claim eventually arising, since the vendor of the shares is alerted to possible areas where a loss may arise because of events before the share sale. Most vendors will take the opportunity to take any appropriate corrective action before the sale. They will invariably make appropriate disclosure to the purchaser (in the 'letter of disclosure'). The purchaser is then deemed to take that point into account in negotiating his purchase, no claim then arising under the warranties for a loss flowing from that point. It will normally be difficult for the 'disclosure' to protect the vendor against any liability under the deed of indemnity.

Typical tax areas to be dealt with by the deed of indemnity are:

1. That there is no liability for corporation tax (including tax payable under ICTA 1988 s 419 (loans to participators)) for periods of account ended prior to the share sale, beyond that provided in the accounts.

2. That there is no liability for PAYE, national insurance (or tax deductions from subcontractors, if appropriate) for periods of account ended prior to the share sale, beyond that provided in the accounts.

3. That there is no liability for VAT for periods of account ended prior to the share sale, beyond that provided in the accounts.

4. That, except as provided in the accounts for the latest period ended before the share sale, no liability arises under ICTA 1988 Schedules 13 and 16 (accounting for advance corporation tax (to 6 April 1999) and for income tax on company payments which are not distributions).

5. That the company has not caused any diminution of its assets which is such that an apportionment of that diminution could be made amongst its participators for inheritance tax purposes, with the liability to pay falling on the company (IHTA 1984 s 94).

The share sale will inevitably not coincide with the last available accounts. The indemnity will have to be extended to cover the period from those last accounts to the date of completion of the share sale but will not apply to tax liabilities arising on transactions in the ordinary course of the business since the accounts date (other than interest, penalties, or a surcharge). (Many standard 'deeds of indemnity' specify certain tax 'anti-avoidance' provisions and capital asset disposals as *not* being in the ordinary course of business.) Alternatively, if completion accounts are being drawn up, the deed of indemnity will be aligned to cover liabilities not provided for in the completion accounts.

Typical areas covered by the warranties will be:

1. That there has been proper compliance with PAYE, national insurance (and subcontractors tax deduction if appropriate) regulations. (If not, a liability may arise which is not covered by the creditors in the accounts.)

2. That the accounts, tax computations and returns submitted to HMRC have been correct. That no disagreement exists between the company and HMRC. That all pre-self-assessment returns and computations including (where relevant) those on the last prepared accounts prior to the share sale have been agreed. That no disclosure which should have been made has not been made, and that there are no outstanding appeals or enquiries.

    That the correct tax has been paid by the due date. Where the company is paying tax in instalments, that tax has been paid in the appropriate instalments and there are no circumstances which could give rise to penalties for deliberately failing to pay instalments.

3. That the VAT regulations have been properly complied with, and that no dispute exists with HMRC as to the rate and incidence of output tax and the eligibility to claim input tax (again, a liability not provided in the accounts may arise).

4. That the base value for capital gains purposes of any assets appearing in the accounts is not less than the figure in the balance sheet. (It will be if there has been business assets rollover relief, giving a potentially higher tax liability than the commercial profit on sale.)

5.   That there is no potential capital gains liability arising from the investment of asset proceeds in wasting assets and thus having given rise to capital gains holdover relief, the tax on which will become payable at latest ten years from the earlier sale unless replaced by rollover relief.

Question

Chiltern Tools (UK) Ltd is a small company resident in the UK. It holds:

(a)   80% of the ordinary shares in Paradise Measuring (West Indies) Ltd, which is resident in a Caribbean country with which there is no double tax treaty. (HMRC have agreed that control is not exercised from the UK so as to make it a UK resident company.)

(b)   100% of Chiltern Tools (Europe) Ltd which is UK resident. This company is primarily engaged in retail distribution world-wide of precision scientific measuring instruments. The parent company charges rent and management charges to the subsidiary.

The stock-in-trade of each company is manufactured in various countries. Each company finds its own markets but various transactions take place between them. In the year to 31 August 2008, Chiltern Tools (UK) Ltd bought 8,000 items from Paradise for sale in UK markets.

The amount paid by Chiltern was based on the ultimate selling price of the items in the UK, which ranged between £75 and £200, subject to an agreed deduction to reflect Chiltern's profit margin.

Chiltern's corporation tax computation and return for the year ended 31 August 2008 was submitted in July 2009 reflecting the above purchases from Paradise without any further adjustment.

In December 2009, HMRC opened an enquiry into the return for the year ended 31 August 2008 and queried the basis on which the transfer price of the items purchased from Paradise had been determined.

(a)   State whether each company is within the scope of the transfer pricing rules, and outline their tax obligations.

(b)   Detail the procedure for HMRC's enquiry and the specific information which Chiltern requires to satisfy HMRC's queries.

(c)   State how Chiltern may obtain greater certainty on the acceptability of the transfer pricing used on its future transactions with Paradise.

(d)   Explain how HMRC could extend its enquiries to earlier periods if they felt that non-commercial transfer pricing was operated by the two companies in those years.

Answer

(a)

Under the provisions of ICTA 1988 Sch 28AA para 5B small and medium-sized companies are exempt from transfer pricing rules in respect of transactions with related businesses that are based in the UK or in any country with which the UK has a double taxation treaty containing a suitable non-discrimination article. As there is no such treaty between the UK and the Caribbean country in which Paradise Measuring (West Indies) Ltd is resident, the UK transfer pricing rules apply to Chiltern Tools (UK) Ltd's transactions with Paradise Measuring (West Indies) Ltd. In determining whether a company qualifies for the small or medium status, all connected companies (including 'linked' and 'partnership' enterprises – see explanatory note 5) must be aggregated. Provided that the companies are not large when aggregated, Chiltern Tools (Europe) Ltd will not be caught by transfer pricing rules in respect of transactions with its parent company. Chiltern Tools (Europe) Ltd will be caught by the transfer pricing rules in respect of any transactions it may enter into with Paradise Measuring (West Indies) Ltd in the future.

Of course, the usual rule that expenses are deductible from profit only in so far as they are expended wholly and exclusively (CTA 2009 s 54) for the purposes of the trade will apply to both UK companies.

Chiltern Tools (UK) Ltd must declare its profit for tax after making any adjustments necessary to bring its transactions with Paradise Measuring (West Indies) Ltd onto an arm's length basis to the extent that Chiltern Tools (UK) Ltd has enjoyed a UK tax advantage. Chiltern Tools (Europe) Ltd, if the group qualifies as small, will tick the box on page one of the company tax return Form CT600 that it qualifies for the SME exemption for transfer pricing. In the event that its profits would be reduced by the compensating adjustment under transfer pricing, it would be able to irrevocably waive the exemption (ICTA 1988 Sch 28AA para 5B(3)).

(b) **HMRC enquiry procedure and specific information required to satisfy HMRC**

HMRC have the right to make an enquiry into the company's tax return without giving any reason. A notice must be issued by HMRC, indicating their intention to enquire into the return, within the 12-month period following the filing date (for returns submitted on time) (FA 1998 Sch 18 para 24). The enquiry can extend to anything contained in the return.

Transfer pricing enquiries into company tax returns are subject to the normal rules of FA 1998 Sch 18. So all of the normal rules regarding the opening and conduct of enquiries and the 'enquiry window' apply. In Chiltern's case, the enquiry is specifically in relation to its application of the transfer pricing provisions of Sch 28AA (given that Chiltern has direct control of Paradise – see ICTA 1988 Sch 28AA paras 1(1) and 4(1)).

The determination of an arm's length transfer price is based on 'OECD Transfer Pricing Guidelines for Multinational Enterprises and Tax Administrations' and Chiltern is required to show that the amount paid for the items purchased from Paradise is justifiable on this basis. Given that no adjustment was made in the return, the amount paid to Paradise must be an arm's length price not giving rise to a UK tax advantage. A UK tax advantage would only occur if the amount actually paid exceeded the arm's length price, reducing Chiltern's UK taxable profits. (HMRC could also attack the transaction under CTA 2009 s 54 on the grounds that the excess amount was not laid out wholly and exclusively for the purposes of the trade – although in practice this is rare.)

A vital part of Chiltern's defence is to demonstrate that a reasonable and honest attempt has been made to apply a commercially justifiable arm's length price and, furthermore, good quality documentation has been prepared and retained to support this. Chiltern should have the following information to support the transfer pricing policy with regard to its purchases from Paradise:

- Full details of the nature of the transactions between the two companies, showing the terms, amounts, unit prices and payment terms. Transactions of the same or similar nature can be aggregated.

- The transfer pricing methodology used, demonstrating how an arm's length transfer price was arrived at. As Chiltern is primarily acting as distributor, the Resale Price Method could easily be applied by the parties in this case. For each line item, the ultimate UK sale price would be taken, reduced by an appropriate 'gross margin' for Chiltern.

If Chiltern adds little value to the product, the gross margin would be determined by its selling and other costs, stock and bad debt risks, and its expected profit. Chiltern's gross profit margins earned on similar items purchased from third party suppliers would be useful here. If Chiltern had 'third party' comparable information for similar transactions undertaken by competitors and gross profit margins for similar distributorships, this would give additional support. However, care should be taken to ensure that the third party comparable information is either truly comparable to the transaction between Chiltern and Paradise Measuring (West Indies) Ltd or that reasonable adjustments can be made to the data so as to be a useful benchmark for the pricing between the connected parties.

HMRC would expect the 'connected' companies to have used their commercial knowledge and judgement to apply an arm's length transfer pricing policy on their transactions. The documentary evidence should indicate that a considered effort was made to satisfy the arm's length requirements of ICTA 1988 Sch 28AA.

Obviously, there may be a range of prices which may be reasonably justifiable. HMRC may disagree that the price charged for certain items meets the arm's length standard. However, transactions between the same connected companies may be evaluated together to determine whether a UK tax advantage arises. If an adjustment is conceded, HMRC would do this as part of its 'closure notice' procedure, inviting Chiltern to amend its return on completion of its enquiry. Provided that the company has prepared appropriate documentation that supports its filing position, then Chiltern should be able to show that it has taken 'reasonable care' and so not be regarded as negligent and thus should not be liable to any penalty under FA 1998 Sch 18 para 20. However, an additional tax charge and an interest charge on the late payment of tax would arise. It will also be necessary to consider whether a corresponding adjustment is required by Paradise Measuring (West Indies) Ltd, if permissible under its own domestic tax rules.

(c) **Obtaining greater certainty on the acceptability of transfer prices set on future transactions**

Chiltern could apply to HMRC for an advance pricing agreement (APA) under FA 1999 s 85. The APA would cover the transfer pricing basis to be used on its future transactions with Paradise. Provided the transfer prices are set in accordance with the APA, they are treated as satisfying the arm's length standard in ICTA 1988 Sch 28AA and will be accepted by HMRC while the APA remains in force. This therefore provides Chiltern with certainty about its transfer pricing position before it files its return.

In practice, the company would approach HMRC Policy International to discuss how an APA would apply to the relevant transactions. Chiltern's formal application to HMRC would then deal with the transfer pricing basis which would be applied to the purchases from Paradise so as to satisfy the arm's length requirements of the legislation, the issues on which clarification is sought from HMRC and Chiltern's understanding about how they should be implemented.

HMRC can revoke an APA from a particular time or where the company fails to comply with one of the conditions laid down in the APA, such as the requirement to provide information and reports.

Companies considering applying for an APA need to bear in mind that the process is designed to offer assistance in resolving complex transfer pricing issues. HMRC's policy is that entering into APAs on less complex matters is not a sensible use of its resources in the absence of significant doubt as to the manner in which the arm's length principle should be applied. It may therefore decline to accept applications that do not satisfy those criteria. Depending on the complexity of Chiltern's submitted fact pattern, HMRC will decide whether to participate in the APA process with the Group.

(d) **Statutory powers of HMRC to extend their enquiries to earlier years**

If the results of HMRC's enquiry in (a) revealed significant problems, they may raise discovery assessments under TMA 1970 s 29 (FA 1998 Sch 18).

HMRC's 'discovery' powers enable them to raise estimated assessments on companies where they believe tax to be understated, and the onus is then on the taxpayer company to dispute the assessment through the appeal procedure.

In practice, many Inspectors raise a transfer pricing enquiry in one year and then try to 'roll back' their conclusions to the previous six years on the basis of discovery. It is possible for HMRC to go back more than six years in cases of negligent conduct or fraud.

HMRC should not, however, extrapolate conclusions about the arm's length price drawn from its current enquiry into other years where the economic and commercial factors in previous years are very different from the year under enquiry. If HMRC still has concerns about the transfer pricing in previous years then it may seek to open enquiries into those years too. For international transactions involving parties in states with which the UK has a double tax agreement, any resolution must be defensible in front of both competent authorities as taxpayers may seek to avoid double taxation under the terms of the relevant double tax treaty.

Explanatory Notes

1. The UK's transfer pricing regulations, as they currently stand, are set out in ICTA 1988 Sch 28AA and were introduced by FA 1998 s 108(2) and Sch 16. The rules took effect for accounting periods ending on or after 1 July 1999.

    The transfer pricing legislation applies where a provision is made between two connected entities by the means of a transaction, or series of transactions (including arrangements, understandings and mutual practices whether or not they are or are intended to be legally enforceable). A provision includes transactions in goods and services as well as the making available of intellectual property, financing facilities and guarantee arrangements, to mention a few. Businesses are connected if one business is in a position to directly or indirectly participate in the management, control or capital of the other, or if the same person participates in the management, control or capital of a number of businesses. The rules will also apply to businesses which are under the control of a number of 'major participants'. A major participant is defined as one who has at least 50% of the holdings of the enterprise.

    The regulations equally apply to transactions between two UK entities and between a UK resident and a non-UK resident entity. Transactions between a joint venture enterprise controlled by two participants (each having at least a 40% interest) are also caught.

    The basic principle of the transfer pricing legislation is that all transactions involving connected persons must use arm's length prices. An adjustment to the potentially advantaged person's taxable profits or losses (ICTA 1988 Sch 28AA para 5) is required where any part of the arrangements involving a transaction or series of transactions departs from the arm's length standard and confers a tax advantage (ie where the price charged gives a lower taxable profit or a higher allowable loss than would have resulted if an arm's length price had been used). An arm's length price requires business to be undertaken on terms and conditions which independent parties would have adopted.

    If the actual provision (ie terms of the contract) made between the 'connected' parties creates a tax advantage (when compared with the arm's length provision), the enterprise must compute its profits for corporation tax using arm's length prices (ICTA 1988 Sch 28AA para 1). Any difference giving rise to a tax advantage should be corrected by making an appropriate adjustment in the tax return. It is not necessary for any actual contractual arrangements to be adjusted, other than to the advantaged party's tax return. There is no provision to adjust a disadvantaged party's tax return, ie to reduce taxable profits or increase tax losses.

The UK transfer pricing rules require taxpayers to construe the arm's length principle in accordance with the 'OECD Transfer Pricing Guidelines for Multinational Enterprises and Tax Administrations' (the OECD Guidelines).

2. The OECD Guidelines set out five transfer pricing methods but they state a preference for using the three transactional methods, namely:

    (i)   Comparable Uncontrolled Price (CUP) – using evidence of prices in similar transactions between independent parties dealing at arm's length;

    (ii) Resale Price Method – applying a discount from the end selling price of the goods to determine the transfer pricing;

    (iii) Cost-plus approach – applying an arm's length mark-up to the value added costs of the selling party to identify the transfer price (with bought-in goods and services on which no risk is taken or value added being recharged at cost as disbursements incurred on behalf of the other company).

Evidence of prices on comparable transactions between unconnected buyers and sellers is often hard to come by. The companies may have no near competitors selling similar products. Even where there are similar transactions the question is complicated by such matters as the terms of the transaction, after sales service, warranties, discounts etc. Often the information will be unavailable because it is confidential to the parties concerned. Whilst CUP is the preferred method in most cases, the difficulty of obtaining reliable information available in the public domain makes it difficult to apply the CUP method in practice.

The discounted resale price approach has the advantage of starting from the actual price at which the goods are sold, but the determination of an appropriate discount (known as a gross margin) can be difficult because different accounting approaches between entities can impact on the gross margins they report and because they may bear risks, or perform functions, to a different extent.

The cost-plus approach is similarly fraught with all sorts of difficulties relating to the manner in which the companies operate their allocation of central and other costs, and the identification of the value added nature of those costs.

3. As mentioned above, the transfer pricing rules apply to all forms of provision, including non-trading and financial transactions. Thus, where a UK-resident company makes an interest-free loan to a non-resident subsidiary, the loan would be the provision and a commercial rate of interest would have to be charged on the loan. However, where a UK subsidiary pays excessive interest on a loan from an overseas group company, the excess interest is disallowed. (Interest may be deemed to be excessive not simply because of the rate charged but also in terms of the size of the loan, for example where the UK company is thinly capitalised.)

4. HMRC's specialist transfer pricing team deals with large and complex cases involving multinationals. Other transfer pricing enquiries are dealt with at area level, with appropriate support.

Documenting transfer pricing policies

5. Under CTSA, taxpayers must keep and maintain adequate records to support a correct and complete return. In relation to transfer pricing with connected companies etc, the documentation must demonstrate that carefully considered arm's length transfer pricing policies were adopted and applied. The precise form of the documentation would depend on the complexity of the transactions involved. The HMRC manuals suggest that whilst the exact form of a business' documentation is for it to decide, it should:

- identify the associated businesses with which the relevant transactions took place and the nature of the association;

- describe the nature of the business in the course of which the relevant transactions took place, and the property (tangible and intangible) used in that business;

- set out the contractual or other understandings between the associated businesses and the risk assumed by each party;

- describe the method used to establish an 'arm's length' result and explain why that method was chosen;

- not have to provide evidence about associations or transactions between businesses where those associations or transactions are not within the scope of UK transfer pricing rules;

- not have to provide evidence related to each relevant transaction, but may provide aggregated evidence related to a class of similar transactions;

- not have to create new evidence in relation to transactions that occur after evidence has been created in relation to transactions that are similar and for which there have been no material changes in the circumstances for determining an 'arm's length' result;

- not have to commission the production of evidence from a professional adviser if the business is able to produce appropriate evidence itself;

- choose to explain its general commercial and management strategy, or that of the group of businesses of which it is a member, as well as the current and forecast business and technological environment, competitive conditions, and regulatory framework;

- choose to make documentation in relation to relevant transactions available to HMRC before the tax return in which those transactions are reflected is due to be made.

To reduce or eliminate the administrative burden, most small and medium-sized businesses will largely be exempt from the new transfer pricing rules. The adjectives 'small' and 'medium-sized' are defined using EU criteria. These definitions apply to an employee headcount ceiling and a financial ceiling to a business or, where that business is part of a group, to the group. The thresholds are set out in the Annex to the Commission Recommendation 2003/361/EC of 6 May 2003.

A small business is one with fewer than 50 employees and either an annual turnover or a balance sheet asset total not exceeding €10,000,000.

A medium-sized business is one with fewer than 250 employees and either an annual turnover not exceeding €50,000,000 or a balance sheet asset total not exceeding €43,000,000.

The thresholds are applied on a group-wide basis and the definition of a group is widely drawn to include 'linked and partnership enterprises'.

Small and medium-sized businesses benefit from the transfer pricing exemption in respect of transactions with related businesses which are based in the UK or in any country with which the UK has a double taxation treaty containing a suitable non-discrimination article. Tax treaties drafted on the OECD model contain such a clause, but each treaty must be checked individually.

Notwithstanding the exemption, HMRC have power to require transfer pricing adjustments to be made in exceptional cases involving medium-sized businesses. Such an instruction will only be issued where the amount of tax involved is 'significant'. There is no equivalent power for HMRC to issue a similar notice to a small business.

6.   The documentation should exist at the latest by the time the corporation tax return is made. It is not necessary to prepare fresh documentation for each return period, provided the original information supports a correct and complete return. If significant transactions are not documented, the taxpayer may be found negligent and penalties would be applied to any adjustment made under FA 1998 Sch 18 para 20.

7. The normal self-assessment rules for retaining records apply (see Example 41 explanatory note 3 for income tax).

Use of Advance Pricing Agreements

8. As noted in part (b) of the example, Advance Pricing Agreements (APAs) under FA 1999 ss 85 to 87 can be used to achieve greater certainty about the transfer pricing policies used in transactions between connected companies. APAs are particularly useful for very complex transactions where there are considerable difficulties or doubts in determining the method by which the arm's length principle should be applied. An APA is likely to be much more efficient than a retrospective examination of transfer pricing policies.

    An APA is a binding written agreement between the company and HMRC for determining the transfer pricing method before the return is submitted. HMRC's detailed policy and procedures relating to applications for APAs are set out in SP 3/99. Provided the terms of the APA are complied with, it will be binding on HMRC and the company for the period covered by the APA. The company is expected to propose the initial term for the APA over which the relevant transfer pricing method(s) will remain appropriate – this is expected to be between three and five years. The APA will apply to accounting periods beginning after the application has been made, but may also be effective for a period which has ended before agreement has been reached.

9. An APA may be used to determine:

    (a) transfer pricing between separate companies where issues arise as to the determination of the arm's length provision under the legislation;

    (b) transfer pricing between parts of the same company operating in different countries where it is necessary to determine the taxable income arising in each country, as follows:

    – The attribution of income to a UK permanent establishment (where there is no double tax treaty)

    – The attribution of income arising outside the UK within a UK-resident company (where there is no double tax treaty)

    – Income attributable to any permanent establishment where a double tax treaty is in force.

10. A 'bilateral APA' enables the transfer pricing basis to be agreed by the UK HMRC and the relevant overseas tax authority and is therefore preferred. This can only be obtained where there is a double tax treaty between the UK and the relevant overseas country which contains a mutual agreement procedure (see explanatory note 12).

    UK companies providing the same service or facility (for example, licensing know-how or brand names) in several countries may wish to seek APAs with the various overseas tax administrations using a so-called multilateral APA. There is no formal mechanism for negotiating multilateral APAs and this will strictly represent a series of bilateral APAs. In some cases, whilst the arrangements may appear to be the same, there can be individual variations requiring a different transfer pricing basis to be adopted. Multilateral APAs are especially useful for allocating the profits of a global activity or operation carried out in various UK and overseas permanent establishments so as to avoid double taxation.

11. A 'unilateral APA' only provides agreement with HMRC on the UK tax treatment of transfer pricing. It does not necessarily provide an agreed basis with the overseas tax jurisdiction and may therefore give rise to double taxation. A UK company would, however, choose a unilateral APA where it considers the 'bilateral APA' process to be unnecessarily long or complicated or there is no double tax treaty with a mutual agreement procedure.

    It should be noted that HMRC only intend to enter into APAs to resolve difficult transfer pricing problems which involve significant doubt and may decline applications where the transfer pricing can be readily established (such as where reliable market comparables exist). Consequently, Chiltern Tools (UK) Ltd may not be successful in obtaining an APA on its UK distributorship of precision tools as there should be comparable 'benchmark' transactions within the industry etc.

Once the policies have been agreed by HMRC, then provided the relevant transactions are priced in accordance with the APA, they will be accepted by HMRC as satisfying the arm's length requirement.

An APA is nullified if the taxpayer fraudulently or negligently provides false or misleading information when negotiating an APA and a penalty of up to £10,000 can also be imposed (FA 1999 s 86(8)).

Procedures for corresponding transfer pricing adjustments

12.   Transfer pricing adjustments in one country clearly could have consequences in relation to tax charged in the other country, and consequently transfer pricing is one of the matters dealt with in double taxation agreements. The OECD model agreement and various guidelines provide for a profits adjustment where transfers between associated enterprises result in profits that are not at arm's length. Countries in the European Union have established a mechanism for resolving transfer pricing disputes between member states, following the ratification by member states of the Arbitration Convention, which came into force on 1 January 1995. ICTA 1988 s 815B requires effect to be given in the UK to agreements and decisions under the Convention. See also the HMRC Tax Bulletin of October 1996 for their transfer pricing procedures in the light of the OECD Guidelines and the Arbitration Convention and the mutual agreement procedure enabling countries with double tax treaties to consult one another to resolve transfer pricing issues and if possible to prevent any adjustments resulting in unrelievable double taxation.

The intention is that transfer pricing should not cause double taxation of the same profits. As far as cross-border transactions are concerned, double taxation treaties already contain procedures for addressing this. For domestic transactions, a compensating reduction in the profits of one party to a transaction is allowed where there has been a transfer pricing adjustment to increase the taxable profits of the other party. The legislation provides for 'balancing payments'. These enable a business with the benefit of a compensating reduction in profits to pass the cash effect of the benefit back to the related business which suffered the disallowance.

Payments of interest

13.   The transfer pricing rules perform the same function as the 'thin capitalisation' rules in force in many countries to counter excessive amounts of interest being charged between parent companies and other group members funding subsidiaries with higher levels of debt than would have been available on an arm's length basis. In determining whether the interest payment is greater than that which would have been made in the absence of a special relationship or connection, the following criteria should be considered:

(a)   the extent of the borrowing company's overall indebtedness;

(b)   whether the loan or the amount of the loan would have been made to the borrowing company if arm's length conditions had applied; and

(c)   whether the rate of interest charged and the other terms of the loan were on a commercial basis.

Interest on loans which are made between companies under common control, whether UK-resident or not, will be subject to restrictions. Where a loan exceeds the amount that would have been provided by an unconnected lender, the interest on the 'excessive' part of the borrowing is disallowed as a tax deduction. Similarly, the lending company is only taxed as if it had received an arm's length amount of interest. F(No 2)A 2005 Sch 7 para 13 introduced the definition of 'a commercial rate of interest' into FA 1996 s 103(3A).

The anti-avoidance provisions of F(No 2)A 2005 s 40 counter tax advantages derived from financing arrangements set up by parties acting in concert up to six months before a control relationship exists. This is intended to counter coordinated avoidance action by investors who (although not connected parties according to the normal definition) share control of the company. Although any of the parties concerned may be minority owners, if interest paid to any or all of them is not considered to be at an arm's length rate, relief for excessive interest can be denied.

Since late 2007 it has been possible for companies to make a unilateral agreement (known as an Advance Thin Capitalisation Agreement (ATCA)) with HMRC to agree the arm's length borrowing capacity and interest rates to apply to lending to the company from connected parties.

Historically, thin capitalisation issues were addressed through applications under Double Tax Agreements by non-resident entities. The introduction of the ATCA process has meant that it is now possible to negotiate a thin capitalisation agreement outside the treaty route. Although based on the same statutory provisions, the negotiation of APAs and ATCAs are separate processes. ATCAs are available to companies brought into transfer pricing legislation by virtue of the 'acting together' legislation set out in ICTA 1988 Sch 28AA para 4A and introduced by F(No 2)A 2005 s 40, referred to above.

Question

The directors of your company have decided to set up a trading operation in a country outside the European Economic Area where the rate of corporation tax is 10%. They are considering two alternative approaches:

(a)   To run the overseas operation as a permanent establishment of the UK company

or

(b)   To run it as a foreign-registered subsidiary of the UK company.

Prepare detailed notes on the UK taxation implications of each of the alternative proposals as a basis for a report to the directors.

Answer

A. **UK tax implications of operating as an overseas permanent establishment compared with operating through an overseas subsidiary**

Setting up an overseas permanent establishment or an overseas subsidiary

1. The establishment of either an overseas permanent establishment or an overseas subsidiary will involve foreign tax being suffered on the profits, because the company will be moving from trading *with* the country concerned to trading *in* it. Overseas countries generally impose tax where business is carried on through a permanent establishment in their country. Most double tax treaties have a similar definition to the OECD model, which states that a permanent establishment includes a place of management, a branch, an office, a factory, a workshop and a mine, oil or gas well, quarry or any other place of extraction of natural resources (subject to certain exclusions). The way in which the foreign tax may be relieved is dealt with below.

UK corporation tax liability re overseas permanent establishment

2. If a trade is carried on through an overseas permanent establishment of a UK-resident company, the company is liable to corporation tax on all the profits of the permanent establishment.

    For accounting periods ended on or after 1 April 2000, any trading loss etc incurred by such an overseas operation can only be group 'relieved' provided it is *not* relievable against taxable overseas profits of any other company under the law of the relevant foreign jurisdiction (ICTA 1988 s 403E). This would exclude, for example, any loss which is offset in a consolidated tax return or surrendered under foreign group relief provisions. Under the group relief provisions as amended by FA 2000, the loss can be surrendered to a 75% UK-resident holding company, or any 75% UK-resident subsidiary (irrespective of whether the requisite 75% ownership is traced through a UK or foreign resident company), or against the profits of a UK permanent establishment of a non-resident 'group' member.

UK corporation tax liability re overseas subsidiary

3. If a trade is carried on through a non-UK resident subsidiary, the parent company would be liable to tax on amounts received from the subsidiary by way of interest, dividends etc. Profits that are accumulated in the overseas country would be subject to overseas tax. Furthermore, there are provisions in ICTA 1988 ss 747–756 and Schs 24 to 26 relating to 'controlled foreign companies'. These rules enable UK companies to be taxed on the profits of a foreign company if it is (broadly) under overall UK control and pays tax in its country of residence of less than three-quarters the amount that a UK-resident company would pay, which would clearly apply in this case. The provisions will not be applied if the foreign company satisfies one or more of certain tests (for example it carries on exempt activities or was established for genuine commercial reasons and not tax avoidance). Furthermore, the CFC rules do not apply if the foreign company's profits for a twelve-month period were less than £50,000. In order to avoid being caught by these provisions it would be necessary to ensure that the overseas company met one of the various CFC 'let-out' provisions (and even then the company may still be subject to the CFC provisions if the country in which the company is located has been specified in regulations as being one in relation to which the CFC exemptions do not apply – see explanatory note 9).

    If the overseas subsidiary makes losses rather than profits, these generally cannot be relieved against the UK company's profits. UK transfer pricing legislation operates to ensure that transactions between the companies must take place at arm's length value. If the subsidiary is operating in the EEA area (that is the European Community plus Iceland, Liechtenstein and

Norway), and a 75% group relationship exists, then losses may in certain circumstances be group relieved against UK profits. All foreign tax relief for tax credits must be sought and used in priority to group relief against UK profits, and other restrictions apply. Losses made by a subsidiary outside the EEA area cannot be group relieved against UK profits, and would only attract relief under the tax provisions of that overseas country.

Capital gains

4. Capital gains made by an overseas permanent operation are chargeable to corporation tax. Gains made by a non-resident subsidiary are not so chargeable, except where they come within the provisions of TCGA 1992 s 13 (which apply where the company would be 'close' if it had been UK resident). This section provides for a non-resident company's gains to be apportioned to the UK-resident 'participators' as defined in ICTA 1988 s 417 (participators mainly being shareholders, but the term is more widely defined – see Example 56 explanatory note 2) and charged to UK capital gains tax, unless the apportioned gain is not more than 10% of the total gain. For gains arising after 6 March 2001 the section does not apply to gains attributed to an exempt approved pension scheme. Nor does it apply if the gains relate to UK PE or overseas business assets (subject to certain provisions).

    Where the gain is distributed within the *earlier* of three years from the end of the accounting period in which it arose or four years from when the gain arose, the capital gains tax suffered on the apportionment is deducted in calculating income tax or capital gains tax liabilities on the distribution.

    Any amount not so relieved forms part of the capital gains cost of the shares (whether or not the gain was distributed within the prescribed period). If the overseas subsidiary is resident in a country whose double tax treaty with the UK exempts residents from a UK capital gains charge, this may prevent s 13 applying.

5. There would be no disposal for capital gains on the transfer of assets to a permanent establishment (being an 'internal' transfer), whereas a chargeable disposal would arise on the transfer to a non-resident subsidiary (as the assets are being removed from the charge to UK tax). The no loss/no gain provisions of TCGA 1992 s 171 (transfers within a 75% group) would not apply, because they do not cover transfers to non-resident companies (except where they are to be used for the purposes of a UK permanent establishment trade).

Establishing non-resident status

6. There may be a problem with an overseas subsidiary in establishing that it is actually not resident in the UK.

    If the parent company exercised control of its activities in a management rather than a shareholding sense then the subsidiary could be held to be UK resident. The subsidiary must in any event be incorporated abroad since if it is incorporated in the UK it will be regarded as UK-resident no matter where it is managed and controlled (unless held to be non-resident under the provisions of a double tax treaty) (TMA 1970 s 109A).

If the company established a permanent establishment initially and then incorporated it

7. The conversion of a permanent establishment into an overseas subsidiary would result in a notional discontinuance of the trade for the parent company (CTA 2009 s 41) and stock would accordingly have to be valued at open market value. There would also be balancing adjustments for capital allowances purposes on the relevant assets transferred to the subsidiary, which may result in significant balancing charges.

8. The parent company could make a claim to defer the charge to tax on the net capital gains arising on the transfer of assets to the subsidiary if the following conditions were satisfied (TCGA 1992 s 140):

(a) All the assets of the permanent establishment (other than cash) used for the trade (or part of the trade, if the whole trade is not transferred) must be transferred.

(b) The consideration must be wholly or partly shares or loan stock in the transferee company, and the parent company must hold at least 25% of the ordinary share capital of the transferee company (which in a holding/subsidiary relationship it will). If the consideration is only partly shares and loan stock, only part of the gain may be deferred.

The deferred gain would crystallise as and when the parent company disposed of the shares or stock. It would also crystallise if the transferee company disposed of the assets within six years after the transfer.

9. Before 1 July 2009, Treasury consent was required if the subsidiary issued shares or debentures, or if the UK company transferred some of its shares in the subsidiary. However, the Treasury Consent rules were repealed and replaced by a post transaction reporting regime for certain transactions having a value exceeding £100 million and taking place on or after 1 July 2009.

B. Reportable events – replacing Treasury Consents

From 1 July 2009 a new reporting requirement was introduced targeted at high value transactions (FA 2009 Sch 17). This replaces Treasury Consents and applies where the value of a reportable transaction exceeds £100 million. A reportable event must be reported to an officer of HMRC within six months of the event. The Commissioners will then consider whether the event or transaction resulted in a tax advantage.

C. Relief available in respect of foreign tax paid and shadow ACT offset

Relief for foreign tax paid by a permanent establishment is available against the UK corporation tax paid on the permanent establishment, subject to the overriding restriction that it cannot exceed the amount of UK corporation tax payable. In arriving at that UK tax, charges on income and interest payable may be deducted in the most favourable manner to leave foreign income as high as possible (ICTA 1988 s 797). (From 1 April 2000, any unrelieved foreign tax relating to an overseas permanent establishment may be carried back for up to three years and then carried forward indefinitely against the UK tax on the same source of income. This requires a claim to be made within six years of the end of the relevant accounting period (ICTA 1988 ss 806L and 806M).)

Most dividends paid on or after 1 July 2009, which are received by a UK resident parent company are exempt from UK tax. Dividends received from 'small' companies are exempt if received from a company that is resident in a tax treaty country with which the UK has a tax treaty that contains a non-discrimination provision (CTA 2009 s 930C). In broad terms this means that it is not tax efficient to have a branch of a UK company carrying on an active business in a low taxed country. This is because the additional UK tax payable would mean the company's tax rate on those profits would be at least 28%. In contrast if the business was operated in a company in a low tax country there would be no further UK tax on the repatriation of the dividend to the UK and the tax rate would be that of the low tax country and not 28%.

In the unusual circumstances that the dividend exemption does not apply then double tax relief should be available in respect of the underlying tax on the profits out of which the dividend is paid, in addition to the withholding tax on the dividend, providing the parent company owns at least 10% of the voting power in the subsidiary (ICTA 1988 ss 799, 800 & 801). (For further details of double tax relief, see Example 55.) Where relief is not claimed by way of tax credit, foreign tax suffered may be deducted in arriving at the income chargeable to UK tax, which may be more beneficial if there are UK trading losses (ICTA 1988 s 811).

Dividends paid by companies after 5 April 1999 do not give rise to ACT. This is of considerable benefit where the company is distributing dividends received from an overseas subsidiary or foreign branch profits, as no surplus ACT can arise. Surplus ACT remaining at 6 April 1999 can only be recovered under the shadow ACT rules. Post-5 April 1999 dividends give rise to shadow ACT which is (notionally) offset before actual surplus ACT. The normal ACT offset limit is 20% of profits but there is an exception for foreign income. The shadow ACT regulations mirror the pre-6 April 1999 ACT offset rule for foreign income – so that the ACT offset is restricted to the residual UK tax on the foreign income *after* double tax relief (or if lower, 20% of the foreign income). These rules therefore still pose a problem for companies trying to recover structural surplus ACT built up by the previous distributions of foreign income.

Explanatory Notes

Factors affecting choice between overseas permanent establishment and overseas subsidiary

1. The main UK tax considerations in the choice between an overseas permanent establishment and an overseas subsidiary are explained in the example. The UK position must be considered alongside the taxation position in the overseas country. There are also many commercial factors, such as the local 'commercial' perception of dealing with a local company rather than a permanent establishment of a UK company.

    Following the introduction of the substantial shareholdings exemption (SSE) from 1 April 2002, UK companies may prefer operating their overseas business through a separate subsidiary, if it is likely to be sold at some stage. The SSE is available on the sale of shares in a trading subsidiary etc and the exemption is available on shareholdings in both UK and overseas resident companies (see Example 66). Also, there is no requirement that the subsidiary's trade is carried on in the UK. In contrast, the sale of the trade and assets (including goodwill) of an overseas permanent establishment would be subject to UK (and possibly overseas) tax. (Some protection of the UK tax base from possible exploitation of the exemption has been introduced by FA 2002 s 90, amending ICTA 1988 s 747 – see explanatory note 6.)

    Other overseas taxes must be considered, such as indirect (VAT or sales type) taxes, property taxes (which can be expensive), employee taxes and social security.

    Many overseas tax authorities have thin capitalisation and/or earnings stripping type rules which prevent excessive debt being used to finance the overseas company (to secure as much tax deductible interest as possible). From the UK company's viewpoint, it would not be efficient for interest charged on debt (fully taxed in the UK) to create surplus losses overseas.

    The method of financing the overseas permanent establishment or company also requires careful consideration, for example local 'third party' borrowing is tax-efficient for a permanent establishment of the UK company (as 'interest' on internal funds from the UK head office would not be tax-deductible).

Residence of a company

2. CTA 2009 s 14 provides that companies incorporated in the UK on or after 15 March 1988 are resident here, no matter where they are managed and controlled (subject to what is said in explanatory note 6).

3. The following general principles have been established from case law:

    (a) A company resides where its real business is carried on, ie where the central management and control is situated (*De Beers Consolidated Mines v Howe* (1906)).

    (b) The place of incorporation is a factor to be considered but is not conclusive (*Calcutta Jute Mills v Nicholson* (1876)).

(c)   The place where directors meet is an important indicator (*Cesena Sulphur v Nicholson* (1876)) but again it is not conclusive.

(d)   Control as a shareholder does not amount to management and control (*Kodak Ltd v Clark* (1901)). (But where a parent company usurped the functions of its subsidiary company's board, or the subsidiary's board merely rubber stamped the parent company's decisions without independently considering them, HMRC would draw the conclusion that the subsidiary's residence was the same as that of the parent company.)

(e)   A company may have dual residence, but this requires some substantial business operations in each country (*Bullock v Unit Construction Co Ltd* (1959)).

Where dual residence is concerned, many double tax treaties provide that the company is deemed to be resident where its place of effective management is situated. The treaty may also have a 'tie breaker' clause under which a company is held to be resident in only one of the two countries (see explanatory note 6).

(f)   In cases where management decisions are extended and/or devolved to non-directors and third parties, the residence of those 'dictating' decisions to management are also taken into consideration when deciding the residence of the company (*Wood v Holden* (2006)). This is of particular significance when interpreting the role and influence of professional advisers in management decisions.

(g)   The place of effective management is considered a more accurate measure of residency to that derived from the place where the centre of top level management is located (*Smallwood v Revenue & Customs* (2008)). Effective management is decided given consideration to points (a) to (f) above, and is generally where key management and commercial decisions necessary for the conduct of the business are in substance made and given. This case was overturned by the High Court in 2009, but on the basis that there was not reason to invoke the tie breaker in the treaty.

It is worthy of note that given the increasing sophistication of communication systems, it is no longer necessary for a group of people to meet in one location to make decisions. This may have a significant impact on the incidence of dual residence and the application of effective management tie breakers.

4.   The case law provisions outlined in explanatory note 3 (a) to (e) are still relevant to decide where companies incorporated abroad are resident (subject to what is said in explanatory note 6). If they are regarded as UK-resident and if they wish to migrate, they will have to give HMRC notice of their intention and make HMRC-approved arrangements for payment of tax (FA 1988 s 130 – see SP 2/90). This will include tax on unrealised gains, except on UK assets of a permanent establishment which remains here (TCGA 1992 s 185). Deferment is possible in respect of foreign assets of a foreign trade if the company is a 75% subsidiary of a company remaining resident in the UK and the two companies so elect within two years. The parent company is then charged to tax on the net gains on the deemed disposal as and when the subsidiary disposes of the assets (within six years), or ceases to be a subsidiary (at any time) (TCGA 1992 s 187).

5.   Certain UK incorporated companies were treated as non-resident at 15 March 1988 or had applied to be so treated at that date and obtained Treasury consent subsequently. Such UK companies will not be treated as UK-resident unless they cease business or cease to be liable to overseas tax, in which case they will be treated as UK-resident from that time. If, however, they transfer their central management and control to the UK, they will be treated as resident from the time of the transfer (CTA 2009 Sch 2 Part 5).

Dual resident companies

6.   Where there is a tie-breaker clause in a double tax agreement that provides for a company to be resident in another country and *not* in the UK, CTA 2009 s 18 provides that the company is

non-resident for the purposes of the Corporation Tax Acts (preventing, for example, the surrender of losses by way of group relief). From 1 April 2002, these provisions are disregarded in deciding whether a company is a 'person resident in the UK' for the controlled foreign company rules dealt with in explanatory notes 9 and 10. This exception does not, however, apply to companies treated as not resident in the UK immediately before that date (ICTA 1988 s 747 as amended by FA 2002 s 90).

Dual resident companies that are *not* regarded as non-UK resident under a tie-breaker clause are not within CTA 2009 s 18. However, if they are *investing* companies they are subject to some specific anti-avoidance provisions, the main ones being the following:

(a)   The company cannot surrender losses, non-trading deficits on loans, charges etc under the group relief provisions (ICTA 1988 s 404 and Sch 17).

(b)   Where an asset is sold to such a company by a company under the same control, the sale may not be treated as being at written down value for capital allowances (CAA 2001 s 570).

(c)   An asset may not be transferred intra-group to such a company on a no loss no gain basis for capital gains purposes (TCGA 1992 s 171).

(d)   Rollover relief on replacement of business assets cannot be claimed within a group where the new asset is acquired by such a company (TCGA 1992 s 175).

Capital gains on transfer of business within EU

7.   For businesses operating in the European Union, TCGA 1992 s 140C provides an alternative to the relief available under s 140 outlined in note 8 of the example. Under the EU Mergers Directive, local tax is not payable on a transfer of a business between companies resident in member states. TCGA 1992 s 140C provides for a UK-resident company to claim relief on the transfer of a non-UK trade carried on through a permanent establishment located in a country in the EU to a company in another member state in exchange for shares or securities in the other company. The transfer must be for bona fide commercial reasons and not part of tax avoidance arrangements (s 140D). Where the conditions are satisfied, the net capital gains are charged to tax, but the tax is reduced by the local tax that would have been paid in the country where the permanent establishment is located had it not been for the Mergers Directive (s 140C(5) and ICTA 1988 s 815A).

Under the provisions of the Distributions Directive (90/435/EEC), most EU companies do not deduct withholding tax from dividends to parent companies in other EU countries, although many countries have imposed a minimum time for the parent to have held shares in the subsidiary before this applies ('subsidiary' in this context requiring not more than 25% ownership by the 'parent'). F (No 2) A 2005 ss 51–58 introduce reliefs to facilitate the tax neutral formation of the Societas Europaeas (SE) from 1 April 2005.

Where a permanent establishment was converted into a subsidiary before 6 April 1988 and capital gains tax was deferred under the provisions of TCGA 1992 s 140, then if the deferred gain related wholly or partly to an asset acquired before 31 March 1982, and it crystallises on or after 6 April 1988, one half of the gain is exempt from tax (TCGA 1992 Sch 4 para 4). If the conversion took place on or before 31 March 1982, however, and the date when the liability would crystallise is on or after 6 April 1988, the deferred gain is wholly exempt from tax (TCGA 1992 Sch 4 para 4(5)).

Controlled foreign companies

8.   The controlled foreign company legislation of ICTA 1988 ss 747 to 756 is aimed at preventing UK companies diverting profits to overseas tax havens or preferential tax regimes. The rules are particularly intended to counter the establishment in low tax areas of companies interposed between UK supplier and foreign customer, or vice versa, captive finance and insurance companies, and companies established to accumulate dividends from other foreign subsidiaries. Where the low tax area is an EU country, the UK provisions may well conflict with EU law.

As a general rule, if the local corporation tax rate is 10%, it would be efficient for the overseas trade to be run through a separate overseas company, as those profits would be insulated from the higher UK tax rate. However, this would be subject to the application of the controlled foreign company rules noted below.

A controlled foreign company (CFC) is a company which is resident outside the UK, controlled by persons resident in the UK, and subject to a 'lower level of taxation'. (See explanatory note 6 for the provisions treating a company that is non-resident under a 'tie breaker' clause in a double tax agreement as a 'person resident in the UK' for the CFC rules.) This broadly means less than 75% of the tax that a UK resident company would pay. (However, the use of 'designer-rate' schemes which permit potential CFCs to pay just the right amount of overseas tax to avoid the 'lower level of tax' condition is prevented by ICTA 1988 s 750A.) A non-resident company can only be a CFC if the UK company has at least a 25% 'interest' in it, which normally coincides with voting shares (see ICTA 1988 s 749B – loan creditors do not have an interest).

The UK 'control' definition includes joint venture 'CFC' companies where at least 40% of the shares etc are held by a UK company and at least 40% (but not more than 55%) are held by a foreign person.

9.   A controlled foreign company is not subject to a CFC tax liability under ICTA 1988 s 747 if it satisfies one of certain specified exemptions for the relevant accounting period. In order to protect the UK from harmful tax practices, however, ICTA 1988 s 748A enables HMRC to issue regulations preventing any of the exemptions applying to controlled foreign companies operating in specified overseas jurisdictions, so that all such companies would be within the provisions. Such regulations cannot take effect without the express consent of Parliament. Section 748A applies to accounting periods beginning on or after 24 July 2002. The specified exemptions were as follows:

(a)   the company pursues an acceptable distribution policy (note: this exemption does not apply for accounting periods commencing on or after 1 July 2009), the distributions being made at a time when the company is not resident in the UK, or

(b)   the company is engaged in exempt activities (broadly trading activities with third parties, but subject to various conditions), or

(c)   the company's profits do not exceed £50,000 (proportionately reduced if the accounting period is less than twelve months), or

(d)   the company does not exist wholly or mainly to reduce UK tax by diverting profits from the UK, and any reduction was either minimal or incidental (the 'motive' test).

The acceptable distribution level was 90% of *taxable* income profits, ie excluding capital gains and foreign tax. (For these purposes, the taxable income was calculated using UK tax principles.) The dividend from the CFC must have been paid within 18 months after the end of the CFC's accounting period (and, in HMRC's view, received by the UK company within the 18-month period). This exemption is, however, not available for accounting periods commencing on or after 1 July 2009, although there are special provisions that deal with the straddle period.

Companies are excluded from the CFC provisions if they are resident and carrying on business in a country listed in the 'Excluded Countries' regulations (SI 1998/3081).

Following the case of *Cadbury Schweppes* (C-196/04) (2006), the UK was forced to make several changes to the CFC regime. It was thought by many people that the decision in that case threatened the validity of the UK CFC rules, and that they would need to be widely reformed, or even abandoned.

Instead, rules were introduced in FA 2007, to enable companies to apply to HMRC to disregard profits of CFCs arising from genuine economic activity in other EU and certain EEA countries, with effect from 6 December 2006. There is a right of appeal if an application is refused.

Rules were also introduced to amend the exempt activities test which state that the conditions for exemption shall not be regarded as fulfilled in relation to a company which is resident in an EEA territory unless there are sufficient individuals working for the company in the territory who have the competence and authority to undertake all, or substantially all, of the company's business. In other respects, the new rules confirm that the Exempt Activities exemption applies in the same way to all CFCs – resident inside or outside the EEA.

There are questions as to whether these changes go far enough to comply with EU law as defined by the Cadbury Schweppes judgement, and this has yet to be fully resolved.

FA 2008 introduced a number of changes to the CFC legislation to counter tax avoidance. One of the key changes is that gross income of a CFC shall now also include trust income for which the CFC is either a settlor or a beneficiary.

Self-assessment provisions

10. For accounting periods ending after 30 June 1999, UK (holding) companies must 'self-assess' their corporation tax liabilities in respect of CFCs. Where the UK company pays its tax in instalments (as will often be the case) the tax relating to CFCs must also be included in the estimated tax payable.

    Full details of all CFCs must be disclosed on the supplementary page CT 600B of the corporation tax return CT 600. If the CFC's profits are covered by an acceptable distribution policy or satisfy one of the other exemptions (see below), an appropriate note is made. For each *non-exempt* CFC, the company must report its chargeable profits (less creditable tax) and the UK tax due.

    Companies which *may not* be CFCs (for example, because they are not subject to a lower level of tax) but would clearly be covered by an exemption can also be shown on the return. This saves the UK company the cost of working out whether the company is, in principle, a CFC and preserves its disclosure position.

    Under self-assessment, the UK corporation tax payable in respect of a non-exempt CFC is based on the UK company's share of the CFC's income profits (which must be at least 25% as indicated in explanatory note 9), as computed for UK corporation tax purposes. If the CFC is carrying on a trade, it is treated as though it were a UK resident carrying on a trade wholly abroad, using Schedule D Case V rules. The UK corporation tax on the CFC's income is then reduced by the appropriate share of 'creditable tax', which comprises double tax relief for overseas tax, including local tax payable in the CFC's country of residence and any actual UK tax charged on any part of the CFC's profits.

    To give companies greater confidence in determining their self-assessment position and liabilities in respect of CFCs, HMRC introduced a comprehensive CFC clearance system for companies and their advisers. Clearances generally apply indefinitely provided the underlying facts and the law remain the same. HMRC work to a 28-day turnaround target provided all the necessary information is included in the clearance application. Full details are given in HMRC's CFC guidance notes.

Transfer pricing

11. Transactions between UK-resident and non-resident companies under common control are subject to the self-assessment transfer pricing provisions. Transactions for goods, services, financing etc between the UK company and its overseas subsidiary company must be based on arm's length prices or consideration. The UK company's tax computation and return must incorporate arm's length income and expenditure on transactions with 'connected' overseas companies (with an appropriate transfer pricing adjustment if necessary to reflect this). If the UK company fails to reflect arm's length transfer pricing on its return, it is likely to be liable to significant penalties and interest. (The UK transfer pricing legislation is based on OECD principles and most overseas jurisdictions have similar tax rules.) See Example 70 for the detailed provisions.

The profits of an overseas permanent establishment would be fully liable to UK tax. The overseas jurisdiction would normally have powers to ensure that the profits arising in the permanent establishment are established on an arm's length basis, for example under the 'associated enterprises' article of a double tax treaty.

Double tax relief

12.   The calculation and application of double tax relief is dealt with in Example 55. However, as mentioned above most dividends required by UK companies after 1 July 2009 should be exempt from UK tax and consequently will not need to claim double tax relief on such income.

Anti-avoidance

13.   The interaction of rules of different jurisdictions has provided an opportunity for many tax-avoidance schemes of a technical nature, and many have been notified under the avoidance disclosure regime. Many of the CFC and DTR regulations are the subject of detailed technical anti-avoidance provisions, contained in FA 2005 and F(No 2)A 2005.

International Tax Enforcement Arrangements

14.   FA 2006 ss 173 and 174 pave the way for a major strengthening in international tax enforcement arrangements. At present a number of agreements, for instance under double tax treaties, allow for the exchange of information between the UK and overseas tax jurisdictions, typically limited to direct taxes.

The Act increases the United Kingdom's ability to make agreements with other territories concerning mutual assistance on the enforcement of taxes, and also enables the UK to ratify the 1988 Council of Europe – OECD convention on Mutual Administrative Assistance in Tax Matters. HMRC and other government departments are empowered to collect information on liabilities to income tax, corporation tax and capital gains tax, for the purposes of assisting with quantifying the liability to foreign taxes.

As well as facilitating the exchange of information relating to foreign taxes, FA 2006 s 175 also empowers HM Treasury to make regulations to facilitate the recovery in the UK of foreign tax debts. The rules specifying the procedure for recovery of foreign tax debts will be made by statutory instrument at the date to be announced.

Question

Bergplatz SA, a company resident in Austria for tax purposes, has decided to set up a business in the UK manufacturing plastic food containers under the name Boris. The anticipated profits of the branch are likely to be around £100,000 for the first few years.

Draft notes briefing the tax partner as to the major UK tax considerations that should be borne in mind in determining whether to operate through a permanent establishment or subsidiary company, and consider whether a European Company (SE) would be possible or advantageous.

(Comment on the specific provisions of the UK/Austria double tax agreement is not required.)

Answer

31 August 2009

To: Tax partner
From: A D Viser

Bergplatz SA: UK permanent establishment or subsidiary – major UK tax considerations

Operating through UK permanent establishment

1. If the Boris manufacturing operation is carried on through a UK permanent establishment, Bergplatz SA will be liable to corporation tax on the permanent establishment's trading profit and on any income from property or rights used or held by the permanent establishment. It will also be liable to corporation tax on any capital gains on the disposal of property or rights held by the permanent establishment and assets situated in the UK used for the trade or by the permanent establishment (CTA 2009 ss 5 and 19 and TCGA 1992 s 10B). If there are any sources of UK income that are not connected with the permanent establishment the company will be liable to income tax at the basic rate thereon.

    There will be no tax consequences when the permanent establishment makes remittances to Bergplatz.

    Assuming Bergplatz SA has no UK subsidiaries, the legislation enabling UK permanent establishments of non-resident companies to take advantage of the group relief provisions for losses and the capital gains provisions for tax neutral intra-group transfers and group rollover relief on replacement of business assets is not relevant.

2. It is provided by ICTA 1988 s 13 that a non-resident company is not entitled to the benefit of the small companies' rate of corporation tax, and must pay the full rate, currently 28% for financial year (FY) 2009 commencing 1 April 2009. This will not apply, however, if the UK/Austria double tax treaty contains a non-discrimination clause. Even if it did not, there is a strong possibility that an Austrian resident company (being an EU resident) could argue that the UK's restriction of the small companies' corporation tax rate is in breach of EU law (especially following the taxpayers' success in *Metallgesellschaft Ltd v CIR* and *Hoechst AG v CIR* (2001), where the UK's exclusion of groups with non-resident parent companies from the provisions enabling subsidiaries to pay dividends without accounting for ACT was held to be discriminatory). If s 13 did apply, the whole of Bergplatz SA's profits would be taken into account in deciding whether the small companies' rate was available on the branch profits.

3. Where a permanent establishment pays interest for the purposes of the trade, it is deductible as a trading expense (on an accruals basis) (CTA 2009 ss 296–301). The borrowing would be taken out by Bergplatz for the purpose of the UK permanent establishment's trade. In contrast any interest charged to the permanent establishment by Bergplatz as a result of an internal transfer of funds would not be allowable since a permanent establishment is not a separate entity. As a general rule, third party borrowing is advised in order to ensure that competent interest deductions can be made by non-banks.

    There will be no deduction for royalties paid by the permanent establishment to Bergplatz SA – see explanatory note 1 for the treatment of royalty and interest payments.

4. If the permanent establishment suffers any foreign taxes, double taxation relief may be claimed for both direct and underlying foreign tax paid other than in Bergplatz SA's home state, ie Austria (ICTA 1988 s 794).

5. A permanent establishment of a non-resident company is outside the definition of close company in ICTA 1988 s 414. Close trading companies do not, however, suffer any major tax disadvantages, so this exclusion has little practical importance.

Operating through UK subsidiary

6. If Boris is set up as a UK subsidiary, then in order for the subsidiary to be regarded as UK-resident, it must either be incorporated in the UK (CTA 2009 s 14) or its place of central management and control must be in the UK. Unless this applies, the subsidiary would be treated as a non-resident company and its tax treatment would be the same as that described above for a permanent establishment.

7. If the subsidiary is regarded as UK-resident, then it will be fully liable to UK corporation tax on its worldwide profits in the same way as any other resident company. It should therefore be able to take advantage of the small companies' rate of corporation tax on its anticipated profits (21% for FY 2009 on profits up to £150,000 if the subsidiary's only associated company is Bergplatz SA).

8. The general right to repayment of dividend tax credits to non-residents ceased on 6 April 1999, but this does not affect tax credits repayable under some of the UK's double tax treaties (F(No 2)A 1997 s 30(5) and (9)). Dividends paid by a UK subsidiary may continue to enjoy repayment of part of the tax credit in certain countries (for example under the UK/Switzerland double tax treaty, but not under the UK/Austria treaty). However, with the lower tax credit of 10%, the amount refunded is now only 0.278% of the net cash dividend (before 6 April 1999, the amount repaid was 6.875% of the dividend paid). The treaty refund must be claimed direct from HMRC's Centre for Non-Residents (CNR).

9. Interest paid by a UK subsidiary for the purposes of a trade is normally deductible as a trading expense. In order to prevent thin capitalisation, interest paid to a non-resident parent company by a UK subsidiary is not, however, deductible to the extent that it exceeds the amount that would have been paid between unconnected companies.

Converting a branch to a subsidiary

10. If Boris is set up in the first place as a permanent establishment, it may subsequently be converted into a UK-resident subsidiary. The transfer of the trade from the non-resident parent to the UK-resident subsidiary will not have any adverse effect on trading results because the acquiring company will take over the losses, capital allowances etc (ICTA 1988 s 343). Stock can be transferred at the amount paid rather than open market value, providing that amount is taken into account in the subsidiary's profit computation and an election is made by both companies under CTA 2009 s 167 within two years after the transfer.

11. As far as capital gains are concerned, where a non-resident company transfers the whole or part of a UK permanent establishment business to a UK resident company in the same group (as defined in TCGA 1992 s 170), the chargeable assets are automatically transferred on a no loss no gain basis (TCGA 1992 s 171).

Societas Europaeas (SE)

12. Societas Europaeas (SE) must have their head office in an EU member state. The purpose of the SE is to allow businesses operating in several member states to combine their operations into a single entity without tax cost. The resulting SE would be subject to the tax regime of the country in which its head office is registered. An SE has corporate governance obligations similar to a plc, and is required to make provision for employee participation. The minimum issued share capital for an SE is €120,000 including at least £50,000 in sterling in the UK.

It should be noted that Bergplatz SA can only group activities into an SE to the extent that the commercial bodies forming an SE have their registered offices in the EU.

Explanatory Notes

Taxation of non-UK resident companies

1.   The basis of charge to corporation tax in respect of accounting periods beginning on or after 1 January 2003 is found in FA 2003 ss 148–156 and Schs 25–27 and is as follows:

   (a)   A non-UK resident company is to be subject to corporation tax by reference to a 'permanent establishment' in the UK rather than a branch or agency in the UK.

   (b)   There are specific rules for quantifying the profits attributable to a permanent establishment. For this purpose, the permanent establishment must be treated as a separate enterprise dealing independently with the non-UK resident company.

   (c)   Mechanisms in the UK tax system for the assessment, collection and recovery of tax, as well as for interest on unpaid tax, will apply to the permanent establishment as a representative of the non-UK resident company.

   As was previously the case, a non-UK resident company carrying on a non-trading business in the UK (eg property investment) will not be subject to corporation tax, but may remain liable to income tax on any UK source profits.

What is a permanent establishment?

   Non-UK resident companies are chargeable to corporation tax if they carry on a trade in the UK through a permanent establishment. A non-UK resident company will have a permanent establishment in the UK if:

   (a)   there is a fixed place of business in the UK through which the company's business is carried on; or

   (b)   company business is carried on in the UK by an agent acting on the company's behalf.

   Some examples of a fixed place of business are:

   (a)   a place of management;

   (b)   a branch;

   (c)   an office;

   (d)   a factory or workshop;

   (e)   an installation or structure for the exploration of natural resources; and

   (f)   a building site or construction project.

   However, a non-UK resident company will not be treated as having a permanent establishment if its UK activities are 'only of a preparatory or auxiliary character'. This includes:

   (a)   the use of facilities for the purpose of storage, display or delivery of goods or merchandise belonging to the company;

   (b)   the maintenance of a stock of goods or merchandise belonging to the company for the purpose of storage, display or delivery;

   (c)   the maintenance of a stock of goods or merchandise belonging to the company for the purpose of processing by another person; and

   (d)   purchasing goods or merchandise, or collecting information, for the company.

   Where a non-UK resident company previously had a UK branch or agency, it will almost certainly have a permanent establishment under the revised rules. Since the definition of a permanent establishment is somewhat wider than that of a branch or agency, a number of non-UK resident companies not previously subject to corporation tax may subsequently be caught by the revised regime.

In contrast to the view taken by other OECD member states, the UK does not consider that a server, either alone or together with websites, could in itself constitute a permanent establishment of a business. This view, as published on 11 April 2000 (press release 84/00) is taken by the UK regardless of whether the server is owned, rented or otherwise utilised by the business.

Determination of profits attributable to a permanent establishment

One of the difficulties with the previous rules for UK branches or agencies was the absence of clear guidelines for the determination of attributable profits. The revised legislation provides a specific basis for the calculation of such profits. However, it should be noted that this can be overridden where there is a treaty between the UK and the non-UK resident company's home jurisdiction which contains a business profits article – ICTA 1988 s 788(3) specifies that treaty provisions take precedence over domestic law.

Under CTA 2009 s 19 (2) and (3), the profits attributable to a permanent establishment for corporation tax purposes are:

(a)   trading income arising directly or indirectly through, or from, the permanent establishment;

(b)   income from property or rights used or held by the permanent establishment; and

(c)   chargeable gains arising on the disposal of assets used in, or for the purposes of, the trade carried on through the permanent establishment or on the disposal of assets used or held by the permanent establishment.

The main assumption to be made in the determination of the relevant profits is to treat the permanent establishment as though it were a separate and distinct enterprise, engaged in the same activities under the same conditions and dealing independently with the rest of the non-UK resident company of which it is a part. This is referred to as the 'separate enterprise principle' and it reflects the wording of Article 7(2) of the OECD Model Tax Convention.

In applying this principle, transactions between the permanent establishment and any other part of the non-UK resident company are deemed to take place on an arm's length basis, unless the non-UK resident company provides the permanent establishment with goods or services which it does not supply to third parties in the ordinary course of its business. In that case, the arm's length rule is not applicable and the quantum of the permanent establishment's expense is the actual cost incurred by the non-UK resident company. In addition, expenses incurred for the purposes of the permanent establishment (even if not incurred or reimbursed by the permanent establishment itself) are deductible, as long as they would have been allowable if incurred by a company resident in the UK.

Two further assumptions underlying the separate enterprise principle are that the permanent establishment is to be treated as having:

(a)   the same credit rating as the non-UK resident company; and

(b)   such equity and loan capital as it could reasonably be expected to have if it were an independent enterprise.

The law then prohibits deductions in arriving at profits chargeable to corporation tax in excess of those which would have arisen on those assumptions.

No deduction is available to a permanent establishment for royalties and similar payments made to any part of the non-UK resident company for the use of intangible assets held by the non-UK resident company (although contributions to the costs of creating such assets are allowable). It is difficult to reconcile this stipulation with the separate enterprise principle – in particular, it is unclear why a permanent establishment, which is treated for tax purposes as an independent entity, should not be allowed to deduct an arm's length charge for the use of an intangible asset.

Similarly, no deduction is available for payments of interest or other financing costs by a permanent establishment to other parts of the non-UK resident company, unless they are payable in respect of borrowings by a permanent establishment in the ordinary course of a financial business such as banking or money-lending carried on by it. On the other hand, a permanent establishment should be entitled to tax relief in respect of interest incurred on its own external borrowings.

There are a number of other special rules for the permanent establishments of overseas banks.

Assessment, collection and recovery of corporation tax (FA 1995 s 126 and Sch 23)

The UK representative of a non-UK resident company is required to deal with all matters connected with the payment of corporation tax (including interest on unpaid tax) as if any obligations and liabilities of the non-UK resident company were its own.

The UK representative is defined as the permanent establishment in the UK through which the non-UK resident company carries on its trade. Should the permanent establishment cease to trade in the UK, it will continue to be the non-UK resident company's UK representative in relation to the profits attributable to the permanent establishment. The UK representative is treated as a distinct and separate person from the non-UK resident company.

Factors affecting choice of UK business medium

2.   The main points to be taken into account are explained in the example or in note 1 above, but see notes 7 and 8 below re group relief and no loss no gain transfers for capital gains purposes.

3.   For notes on the country of residence for a company see Example 71.

4.   Transactions between Bergplatz and a UK-resident subsidiary will be subject to the transfer pricing provisions. Similarly, transactions between Bergplatz and its UK branch must take place on an arm's length basis. For details see Example 70.

5.   The decision on whether to operate through a permanent establishment or subsidiary needs to take into account the taxation position in Austria. If a permanent establishment makes losses, it may be possible to offset them against the profits of Bergplatz in Austria. Permanent establishment profits, on the other hand, may suffer further tax in Austria. In contrast, the profits of an Austrian subsidiary would be insulated from tax in the UK when the CFC rules applied.

6.   From a company law point of view, there is very little difference in that a UK subsidiary would be subject to the accounts and filing provisions of the Companies Acts, whilst a foreign company with a UK permanent establishment would have to register with the Registrar of Companies and supply information, including the company's accounts, on a regular basis.

Group provisions

7.   Where a non-resident company carries on a trade in the UK through a permanent establishment and is itself a member of a group which includes other UK-resident companies or UK branch activities, then it may participate in various 'group reliefs'. It may surrender to other UK-resident members of the group its trading losses etc attributable to its UK trading activities under ICTA 1988 s 402(3A)(3B). However, any part of a trading loss that is relievable against non-UK profits (not chargeable to UK corporation tax) for foreign tax purposes is excluded from the loss available for surrender (ICTA 1988 s 403D). This rule applies irrespective of whether an actual foreign tax offset has been claimed – the fact that a loss is potentially relievable is sufficient. Similarly, the UK permanent establishment may claim group relief from other UK-resident members of the group against its profits which are chargeable to UK corporation tax. It is important to note that, following the relaxation in the UK residence requirement for certain group relationships, it does not matter if the non-resident company holding the UK permanent establishment is owned by another non-resident company.

8.   A UK permanent establishment can also transfer chargeable assets used in the UK trade to other 75% UK resident subsidiaries and vice versa under the no gain no loss rule in TCGA 1992 s 171. The normal degrouping charge under TCGA 1992 s 179 will arise if the recipient company leaves the group within six years of the intra-group transfer while still holding the asset. The UK permanent establishment can also participate in group rollover relief in respect of assets which have been or are to be used for the purposes of the UK trade under the provisions of TCGA 1992 s 175.

See Example 55 explanatory note 3 re double tax relief in respect of foreign tax suffered by a UK permanent establishment of a non-resident company.

Treatment of permanent establishment's income

9.   Where interest is paid by any UK resident to a UK permanent establishment and the permanent establishment's profits are liable to UK tax, tax does not have to be deducted at source from the interest under ITA 2007 s 874, even though the permanent establishment is operated by a non-resident company.

10.   Where income is charged to income tax rather than corporation tax, for example where a non-resident company's only UK income is property income, it is not subject to the 'loan relationships' provisions of CTA 2009 and interest may be deducted where appropriate, despite the ICTA 1988 s 337A prohibition of a deduction for interest other than under the loan relationships provisions.

Capital gains

11.   There are various capital gains provisions relating to non-residents.

Non-residents are charged on gains if they carry on a trade, profession or vocation through a UK permanent establishment (TCGA 1992 s 10B).

Rollover relief for replacement of business assets is available only where the replacement asset is within the charge to UK tax, ie acquired for the purpose of the UK trade (TCGA 1992 s 159). Group rollover relief may also be available (see explanatory note 8) and assets can be transferred to other UK-resident companies or UK permanent establishments under the no gain no loss rule in TCGA 1992 s 171.

Where an asset ceases to be a chargeable asset, either because the UK permanent establishment's business ceases, or because the asset is removed from the UK charge to tax, the asset is treated as disposed of and reacquired at market value, thus triggering a tax charge (TCGA 1992 s 25).

TCGA 1992 s 25 does not apply to the transfer of a UK permanent establishment by a non-resident company to another company under TCGA 1992 s 171 (intra-group disposal) or s 139 (company reconstruction). Nor does it apply to the transfer of a UK trade from one company resident in an EU country to another EU resident company in exchange for securities (including shares). Providing the conditions are satisfied, such transfers are made on a no loss no gain basis (TCGA 1992 s 140A).

Similarly, the provisions under TCGA 1992 s 25 do not apply to the transfer of assets to a non-resident company under TCGA 1992 s 140 and the gain so arising can be deferred in proportion to the consideration given in the form of shares and loan stock until:

(a)   the shares and loan stock are disposed of; or, if earlier

(b)   the date when the assets (or any part thereof) are disposed to a third party (if disposed of within six years of the transfer),

provided that the following conditions are satisfied:

(a)   the trade (or part of the trade transferred) and all the assets of the trade (other than cash) must be transferred,

(b)   the shareholding in the transferring company immediately after the transfer must be at least 25% of the ordinary share capital.

Recovery of unpaid tax from other group companies etc

12.   There are provisions in TCGA 1992 s 190 to the effect that if a non-resident company operating through a UK permanent establishment fails to pay the corporation tax on a chargeable gain within six months after the due date, the tax may be recovered from another company in the same 51% group or from a controlling director.

There are separate provisions in FA 2000 s 98 and Sch 28 enabling *any* corporation tax due from a non-resident company that remains unpaid after six months to be collected from another company in the same group or (to the appropriate extent) from a member of a consortium owning the non-resident company.

Societas Europaeas (SE)

13.   The concept of the European company was created by Council Regulation (EC) No 2157/2001 of 8 October 2001, and made possible in the UK by SI No 2326/2004. The effective date of this was 8 October 2004, and it has been possible to set up this new legal entity since December 2004. Most of the tax provisions relating to it have effect from 1 April 2005.

The SE is intended for large organisations with operations in a number of member states. The legislation covering the formation and governance of SEs has many parallels with that of plc's, and accounting requirements are the same as a plc. The SE is required to have a minimum amount of subscribed share capital to the equivalent of at least €120,000 (including at least £50,000 in the UK). Its accounts can be kept in any currency.

An SE cannot be registered and brought into existence until either an agreement has been reached for employee involvement in company decisions, or until it is confirmed that the standard rules of the jurisdiction for employee involvement apply. It will be possible for an SE registered in one member state to move to another, unlike a plc.

It is envisaged that SEs will be formed by merger of the existing companies in different member states, by transformation of a plc into an SE, or by the formation of subsidiaries by companies registered in the EC. The commercial bodies forming an SE must have their registered offices in the EU, and a presence in more than one member state.

F(No 2)A 2005 ss 51–65 amended existing tax legislation to ensure that a UK company's decision to merge with a company in another member state to form an SE is not disadvantaged or driven by tax considerations. These sections deal with chargeable gains, intangibles, loan relationships, derivative contracts, capital allowances and stamp duty reserve tax, giving certainty to the tax treatment of a number of transactions, and making them tax neutral. They are designed to allow UK businesses to take advantage of the new corporate vehicle if they so wish.

Question

(a)   Give a brief outline of the basis of charge to capital gains tax, stating:

    (i)   the main persons chargeable to capital gains tax, and how it is charged;

    (ii)   how gains are measured;

    (iii)   what events trigger a charge to tax.

(b)   Explain the effect of a UK-domiciled taxpayer's country of residence on his liability to capital gains tax.

(c)   Explain how the remittance basis applies with respect to capital gains tax.

(d)   Explain the tax treatment of an individual who is temporarily resident outside the UK.

(e)   Connected persons.

    (i)   State, in the context of capital gains tax, what is meant by the term 'connected persons'.

    (ii)   Explain what special considerations apply when computing the chargeable gain or allowable loss arising on a disposal between a brother and his sister (both being adult).

(f)   Capital gains tax is assessed on chargeable gains accruing to a person on the disposal of assets.

    (i)   Indicate which assets are exempt from capital gains tax.

    (ii)   Explain, where an asset is disposed of under a contract, how the date of the disposal is determined.

    (iii)   Explain how the date of a capital gains tax chargeable event is fixed where there is not a disposal under a contract.

(g)   Explain how relief is given for capital losses:

    (i)   in respect of UK-domiciled individuals;

    (ii)   in respect of non-UK domiciled individuals.

Answer

(a) **Basis of charge to capital gains tax**

   (i) **Who is liable to tax**

Individuals, personal representatives and trustees are liable to capital gains tax. This is a separate tax from tax on income, although for individuals it is calculated by adding taxable gains as the 'top slice' of the income tax calculation.

Charities are exempt from tax on gains, provided that they use the money for charitable purposes. Pension funds are exempt from tax on gains realised for the benefit of pensioners.

Certain investment vehicles such as authorised unit trusts and investment trusts, open-ended investment companies and venture capital trusts are exempt from tax on gains made on their investment assets.

Companies pay corporation tax on gains, not capital gains tax. For details of the differences, see Example 83.

   (ii) **How gains are measured**

Capital gains tax (or corporation tax on chargeable gains) is a tax on increases in value, not on cash profits. If a disposal or acquisition is made other than as a bargain at arm's length, the market value of the asset is used instead of any actual consideration (TCGA 1992 s 17). This means that the gain which has accrued during a person's ownership is charged when they dispose of the asset, even if they paid nothing for it (on a gift or inheritance) or receive nothing for it (on a gift).

Taper relief was given to relieve gains for periods after 5 April 1998. But this was withdrawn with effect from 6 April 2008. Also removed from that date was indexation allowance which applied where the asset was acquired prior to April 1998. Once all gains have been computed (netted off by any allowable losses), the amount remaining chargeable is then reduced by an annual exemption.

   (iii) **Chargeable events**

The following events trigger a charge to tax on gains:

1. Disposal or part disposal of the asset by sale at arm's length, sale at undervalue, or gift (s 21).

2. Exchange of one asset for another.

3. Capital sums derived from an asset (s 22), for example insurance proceeds arising when an asset is damaged.

4. Creation of rights over an asset (s 21(2)(b)).

The following events do not trigger a charge to tax on gains:

1. Disposal of an asset which is exempt.

2. Disposal by an exempt person.

3. Gifts to charity and registered community amateur sports clubs (from 6 April 2002) (s 257 and FA 2002 s 58 and Sch 18).

4. Disposals between spouses and civil partners (s 58) or companies within a 75% group (s 171). Strictly, such disposals are recognised by the legislation, but the proceeds are fixed so as to eliminate any chargeable gain (or loss) arising.

5. Disposals on death (s 62).

6. Reorganisation of share capital (ss 127–136).

In addition, many reliefs apply to reduce or defer the charge in certain circumstances.

(b) Effect of residence on capital gains tax liability

An individual is liable to capital gains tax if resident or ordinarily resident in the UK (TCGA 1992 s 2). Taxpayers who are domiciled in the UK are liable on all gains wherever they arise. For the meaning of residence, ordinary residence and domicile see Example 12.

Non-residents who are not ordinarily resident in the UK are not liable to capital gains tax unless they carry on business in the UK through a permanent establishment. In that event they are liable to tax on gains arising on the disposal of business assets in the UK (s 10), and they are also liable if the assets are removed from the UK, or if the permanent establishment business ceases (s 25) (see Example 72).

(c) The remittance basis and capital gains tax

If domiciled abroad a taxpayer might be entitled to limit liability to gains arising in or remitted to the UK (s 12). The remittance basis will apply equally for income tax purposes.

The general provision giving rise to the remittance basis is found in ITA 2007 s 809B. That requires a claim to be made. Where the individual has spent at least 7 of the previous 9 tax years as a resident in the UK and is an adult, then the claim for the remittance basis will require a £30,000 charge to be paid in addition to the tax payable on any amount remitted to the UK.

The remittance basis will also be available without a claim if either:

- the individual's overseas unremitted income and gains are less than £2,000 (s 809D); or

- the individual has no UK income or gains, no remittances of overseas income or gains and either:

  – has spent 6 or fewer of the previous 9 tax years resident in the UK; or

  – is aged 18 or under throughout the tax year (s 809E).

Taxpayers who claim to be taxed on the remittance basis (under ITA 2007 s 809B) will cease to be entitled to the annual exemption (s 3(1A)). The annual exemption will therefore continue to be available to taxpayers on the remittance basis if no claim has been made under s 809B and non-remitted income and gains fall below the de minimis threshold in ITA 2007 s 809D.

For the rules concerning losses, see (g)(ii) below.

(d) Temporary non-residence

Special rules apply to those who become 'temporarily' non-resident (TCGA 1992 s 10A). Someone who has been resident or ordinarily resident in the UK for any part of at least four of the previous seven tax years, and becomes not resident and not ordinarily resident for less than five tax years, will be liable to tax on gains on assets owned before they left the UK. All such gains in the tax year of departure will be taxed for that year, and assessments in respect of such gains may be made up to two years after the 31 January following the tax year of return. Later gains on such assets during the period of absence will be taxed in the year when the person again resumes UK residence. Losses will be allowed on the same basis as gains are taxed. Gains on assets acquired while the individual was resident abroad that are realised in the years between the tax year of departure and the tax year of return are exempt (subject to certain anti-avoidance provisions). With effect from 16 March 2005, F(No 2)A 2005 introduced anti-avoidance measures which counter the use of double tax treaties to establish CGT non-residence for short periods of absence. However, the avoidance scheme which prompted that legislation was held by the Special Commissioners not to be effective (*Smallwood* (2008)).

Under Revenue Concession D2, it is possible in certain circumstances to split the tax year, and to regard the taxpayer as resident for part and not resident for part. Where this treatment applies, gains in the non-resident part are not charged, and losses in the non-resident part are not allowed. Split year treatment applies:

- to those leaving the UK, only if they have been not resident in the UK for four of the last seven years (ie they are not caught by the provision on gains realised abroad, as described above);

- to those coming to the UK, only if they have been not resident in the UK for the whole of the five tax years up to the tax year of return.

This means that the split year treatment is generally available (on both arriving and leaving) to foreign people coming to the UK and leaving after a brief period; but it is not generally available (on either leaving or arriving) to UK residents who go abroad for a brief period and then return. Such a person must wait until 6 April following departure to make a disposal on which the gain will be exempt (albeit possibly subject to a charge on re-entry), and must make disposals by 5 April before returning (and will then escape tax if the assets disposed of were not owned at the time of departure).

The re-entry charge was introduced for taxpayers who became non-resident on or after 17 March 1998. Revenue Concession D2 was also more generous before that date.

(e) **Connected persons**

(i) **Connected persons in context of capital gains tax**

The term 'connected persons' for capital gains tax is defined as follows (TCGA 1992 s 286):

A person is connected with his or her spouse/civil partner, with his or his spouse's/civil partner's close relatives (ie brothers, sisters, ancestors, lineal descendants) and relatives' spouses/civil partners, and with business partners and their spouses/civil partners and relatives (except in relation to normal commercial acquisitions and disposals of partnership assets).

If a person is trustee of a settlement, he is connected with the settlor (if an individual) and with any person connected with the settlor. The transfer of property into settlement is a connected persons transaction, because the trustees become connected with the settlor at the time the settlement is created. After the settlor's death, the trustees are no longer connected with those who were connected with the settlor.

Companies under the same control are connected with each other and with the person controlling them.

(ii) **Special considerations**

In computing the chargeable gain or allowable loss arising on a disposal between adult brother and sister, the disposal is deemed to be at open market value (TCGA 1992 ss 17 and 18).

If the disposal is by way of gift and it gives rise to a chargeable gain, and either the asset is a qualifying business asset or the gift is a transfer which is immediately chargeable to inheritance tax, a claim may be made for the gain not to be charged, but to be treated as reducing the acquisition cost of the donee, so that the donee's base cost is the cost to the donor plus the indexation allowance to date or to April 1998 if earlier. (This relief is not confined to connected person transactions (TCGA 1992 ss 165 and 260 – see Example 82 for details and certain restrictions introduced by Finance Act 2004).)

If the disposal gives rise to an allowable loss, the loss may not be set against general gains, but only against a gain made on a later transaction with the same connected person (see Example 95 explanatory note 11 for the order in which losses may be used up) (TCGA 1992 s 18).

(f)   **Exemptions; date of disposal**

(i)   **Assets exempt from capital gains tax**

Assets which will not give rise to capital gains tax on disposal (and for which no relief is available for capital losses) are as follows (references are to TCGA 1992):

1.   Private motor cars (s 263) (see explanatory note 10).

2.   Foreign currency for an individual's own spending and maintenance of assets abroad (s 269).

3.   British Government securities and qualifying corporate bonds (s 115).

4.   Life policies in the hands of the original holder or beneficiaries (s 210).

5.   Chattels (ie tangible movable property) with a predictable useful life not exceeding fifty years, except where they are used in a business and capital allowances have been or could have been claimed (s 45). Plant and machinery is always regarded as having a predictable life of less than 50 years (even if it is a collector's item that is in fact much older) (s 44) (see explanatory note 10).

6.   Decorations for valour acquired otherwise than for money or money's worth (s 268).

7.   Bettings, pools and lottery winnings and winnings from games with prizes (s 51).

8.   Compensation or damages for personal or professional wrong or injury (s 51) (see explanatory note 13).

9.   Compensation for mis-sold personal pensions (FA 1996 s 148).

10.   National Savings Certificates and premium bonds (s 121). (The terminal bonus under a Save As You Earn contract is also exempt from all taxation (s 271(4) & ITTOIA 2005 ss 702–703).)

11.   The taxpayer's only or main residence (ss 222–226). Part of the gain may be chargeable in certain circumstances – for details see Example 81.

12.   Gifts of assets that are considered by the Treasury to be of pre-eminent national, historic or scientific interest, but breach of any conditions imposed will nullify the exemption (s 258).

13.   Gifts to charities and registered community amateur sports clubs (from 6 April 2002) (s 257 and FA 2002 s 58 and Sch 18) (see Example 90).

14.   Gifts of land to registered housing associations (s 259).

15.   Shares in respect of which business expansion scheme relief has been given and not withdrawn (s 150).

16.   Shares which qualified for enterprise investment scheme relief which have been held for three years (five years where shares issued before 6 April 2000), although losses remain allowable (s 150A).

17.   Investments held through a Personal Equity Plan or Individual Savings Account (s 151).

18.   Shares in a qualifying venture capital trust (s 151A).

(ii)   **Determining date of disposal**

Where an asset is disposed of under a contract, the date of disposal is the contract date, unless the contract is conditional, in which case the date of disposal is the date when the condition is satisfied (TCGA 1992 s 28).

(iii) Where gain is charged on a capital sum

Where a gain is charged on a capital sum derived from an asset, the time of disposal is the date of receipt of that sum (s 22(2)).

If an asset is destroyed without compensation, the disposal occurs on the date of destruction (s 24(1)).

An estate duty case (Re *Rose*) established that a gift of shares takes place when the donor has done everything necessary to make the gift happen (in this case, handing over a signed transfer form and the share certificate).

(g) Relief for capital losses

(i) UK-domiciled individuals

Losses are calculated in precisely the same way as gains, with three exceptions. So, for example, supposing an individual bought a second home for £500,000 (plus associated costs of £30,000) in year 1 and sold it in year 2 realising sale proceeds of £500,000 (but incurring sale costs of £10,000), the individual would have an allowable loss of £40,000.

Exception to the basic rule

Loss relief is restricted in respect of chattels sold for less than £6,000 but costing more than that. In such cases, the loss is calculated as if the disposal proceeds were £6,000 (so that the loss is limited to the amount by which the acquisition costs exceed £6,000) (TCGA 1992 s 262(3)).

How loss relief is given

Losses are relieved by deducting them from any gains in the tax year.

If there are net gains for the year, then no further calculations are made even if the gains (without the benefit of the loss relief) fall within the annual exemption.

If, however, the total losses exceed the total gains, then the excess is carried forward to be available for set off against gains in future years. These losses are set off against gains until such time as the losses are fully utilised. However, losses from other years are utilised only so far as is necessary to reduce a person's gains to the annual exempt amount.

Losses are generally not carried back. However, unrelieved losses arising in the year of a taxpayer's death may be carried back up to three years (s 62). In addition, where the value of an earn-out must be ascertained under the *Marren v Ingles* principle, losses on the actual disposal of the earn-out can now be related back to the year of the original disposal (ss 279A–279D).

See also Example 74(a).

Restriction on use of losses

In FA 2006, rules were inserted to prevent companies from realising losses artificially and claiming relief thereon.

These have now been rolled out for capital gains tax purposes as well and are now found in s 16A.

The general effect of the rules is that a loss ceases to be 'an allowable loss' (and is therefore unavailable to be set off against capital gains) if it arises as a result of any arrangement for which the (or a) main purpose is to secure a tax advantage (widely defined). The rules apply to any loss accruing on a disposal on or after 6 December 2006.

The difficulty with these rules is that they are broadly drafted and will catch almost every loss ever realised. However, HMRC have published guidance (http://www.hmrc.gov.uk/budget2007/ avoidance.pdf) as to the situations in which they will apply the legislation. This guidance (as well as the use of such widely drafted legislation) has attracted a lot of criticism.

(ii)   Non-UK domiciled individuals

Until the reforms of the remittance basis with effect from 6 April 2008, non-domiciled individuals were given no relief for overseas losses (former s 16(4)). Now that the remittance basis will not always be attractive to taxpayers, a new set of provisions has been introduced.

Elections regarding losses

Section 16ZA provides that an election may be made by taxpayers in respect of the first year in which they are not domiciled in the UK and claim to be taxed on the remittance basis (under ITA 2007 s 809B).

Where an election is made, it is irrevocable.

If an election is made:

- gains which:

  - arise in a tax year on or after the first in which the remittance basis is claimed under s 809B (and the taxpayer is not UK-domiciled), but

  - are remitted in a subsequent year (and are so taxed in that later year),

  do not qualify for loss relief and (assuming that the remittance basis is not claimed in that later tax year under s 809B) cannot be offset by the annual exemption. (TCGA 1992 s 16ZB). This applies whether or not the taxpayer is subject to the remittance basis in this later year.

- In years for which the remittance basis applies (whether or not claimed), loss relief is available but such losses must be set off against:

  - first, foreign gains of that tax year to the extent that they are remitted to the UK in that year;

  - next, foreign gains of that tax year to the extent that they are not remitted to the UK tax year;

  - finally, UK gains of that year (s 16ZC).

  When setting off losses against unremitted foreign gains special rules apply if the losses are not sufficient to exhaust all such gains:

  - first, losses are deducted from the latest such gains before any earlier gains;

  - however, where the gains of a particular day exceed any remaining loss relief available, the losses are apportioned (s 16ZC(2)).

Consequences of not making an election

Where no election is made, the taxpayer will not be entitled to loss relief in respect of any overseas assets for that year or any subsequent tax year (s 16ZA(3)). The legislation appears to prevent such loss relief in respect of overseas assets even if the taxpayer were subsequently to acquire a UK domicile.

Explanatory Notes

Scope of capital gains tax

1.   Capital gains tax was introduced on 6 April 1965 to charge tax on gains arising on the disposal of assets on or after that date. Companies are charged to corporation tax on their gains rather than capital gains tax as indicated in part (a) of the example (see Example 49 explanatory note 10).

Technically, the charge covers all assets unless the *gain* is specifically exempt, and the assets themselves are not classified as either chargeable or exempt. It is, however, more usual and convenient to use the terms chargeable assets and exempt assets. The main body of capital gains legislation is the Taxation of Chargeable Gains Act 1992 (TCGA 1992) and references are to that Act unless otherwise stated.

In general the same rules apply for calculating allowable capital losses as for chargeable gains (ss 15, 16). Where losses exceed gains of the same chargeable period the excess is carried forward to set against later gains. Special rules apply to losses on transactions between connected persons, as indicated in part (e)(ii) of the example. See also Example 95 explanatory note 11.

2. Where an asset is not a chargeable asset, then neither a chargeable gain nor allowable loss can arise (ss 15, 16). All forms of property, including options, debts and intangible property, any currency other than sterling, and assets created by the person disposing of them, eg goodwill, are chargeable assets unless they are specifically exempt, either wholly or in part (s 21) or, in the case of companies, are covered by the loan relationships rules (see Example 63) or intangible assets rules (see Example 66). Special provisions apply to taxpayers other than companies in respect of the loss of money lent. For details see Example 95 explanatory note 5.

3. In FA 1998, a separate regime was introduced for taxpayers other than companies. This was subsequently abolished with effect 6 April 2008. However, such taxpayers now have a 'simplified' system whereas the pre-1998 regime continues to operate for companies. Most notably, companies are able to deduct indexation allowance to reflect the inflationary effects on their costs since the time of acquisition. (See Example 83.)

Meaning of 'disposal'

4. A gift of an asset is normally treated as a disposal at open market value (see Example 82 explanatory note 17). A disposal includes a part disposal, and there is also a disposal when a capital sum is derived from an asset even though no asset is acquired by the person paying the capital sum, the time of disposal being the time when the capital sum is received (s 22). This particularly applies to compensation, including insurance proceeds, for loss of or damage to an asset (subject to what is said in Example 95 explanatory notes 6 and 7), and to compensation for surrendering rights. Where, however, *statutory* compensation is paid, for example to business tenants under the Landlord and Tenant Act 1954, it is exempt (see Revenue's Tax Bulletin April 1996 for the circumstances in which such an exemption will apply). Certain other compensation is exempt (see items 8 and 9 of part (f)(i) of the example and explanatory note 13).

Cashbacks

5. HMRC have stated its view on the treatment of 'cashbacks' offered as inducements to purchase goods, services or financial products (for example in connection with a mortgage or car purchase). Such payments are not regarded as deriving from an asset and are exempt from capital gains tax. An income tax liability may, however, arise if the payments are received by a business, or by an employee by reason of his employment (SP 4/97).

Building society and other mergers, conversions etc

6. Payments to account holders on building society *mergers* are regarded by HMRC as being income payments and are paid net of 20% tax. Following the cases of *Foster v Williams* and *Horan v Williams* heard by the Special Commissioners in 1997, HMRC accepts that the treatment of cash payments on building society *takeovers and conversions* is that amounts received by *depositors* (and presumably by borrowers) are wholly exempt from tax, and gains on amounts received by *shareholders* are taxable. Calculations are not, however, necessary, where the payment is covered by the annual exemption (taking into account any other capital gains in the tax year).

Where *shares* are received in a building society conversion or takeover, there is no capital gains liability at that time and they are treated as acquired for the amount paid for them. Where they are issued free, there is no allowable cost for a future disposal (s 217).

Some mutual insurance companies have also converted into companies, and the tax treatment depends on the facts of the particular case (see Revenue's Tax Bulletin April 1998). For both building society and insurance company conversions, it was possible to avoid future capital gains tax on shares issued on the conversion by transferring the shares to a personal equity plan, but only up to 5 April 1999. Shares cannot be transferred in this way into an Individual Savings Account – see Example 92 part (a) note 8.

Where shares are issued to the members of the mutual organisation, and are then exchanged for loan notes, the capital gain is 'frozen' at the date of the exchange and deferred until the loan notes are encashed. However, the encashment of the loan notes over a period of years enables the holder to set several annual exemptions against the capital gain.

Connected persons

7.   All transactions between connected persons, or not at arm's length, are regarded as being made at open market value. This does not apply to transactions between spouses/members of a registered civil partnership which are not normally chargeable (see Example 76), nor to normal commercial transactions between partners, where HMRC will accept the value placed thereon by the partners, eg goodwill on admission of a new partner, where this is dictated by commercial terms and not because of the family relationship between the partners.

8.   In general, market value means the price that might reasonably be expected on a sale in the open market (s 272). Quoted securities are valued at the *lower* of one-quarter up from the lower of the quoted prices and halfway between the lowest and highest recorded bargains. Unit trust holdings are valued only at the bid price, not 'quarter up' (s 272(5)). In valuing unquoted securities it is assumed that all relevant information is available to the prospective purchaser (s 273). Where the value of an asset has been ascertained for inheritance tax on a death, that value is regarded as the market value at death for capital gains tax (s 274), and whoever acquires the asset acquires it at that value. See Example 76(c) for further consideration of this rule.

9.   Where someone disposes of assets on different occasions within a period of six years to one or more persons connected with him, and their value taken together is higher than their separate values, then the disposal value for each of the transactions is a proportionate part of the aggregate value, and all necessary adjustments will be made to earlier tax charges (ss 19 and 20).

See Example 95 explanatory note 11 re the possible effect on connected persons of the self-assessment rules for setting off losses brought forward.

Exemptions

10.   The exemption for private motor cars applies to 'a mechanically propelled road vehicle constructed or adapted for the carriage of passengers, except for a vehicle of a type not commonly used as a private vehicle and unsuitable to be so used'. It therefore covers veteran and vintage cars (except one-seater models), and is available whether or not the cars are used in a business. So profits on the disposal of cars are either trading profits if the seller is carrying out 'an adventure in the nature of trade' or are exempt. A one seater car that is not covered by the 'cars' exemption, and also any other 'plant or machinery', would be exempt as a wasting chattel if it was disposed of by an investor rather than a trader, even if it was a collector's item (ss 44 and 45). The chattels exemption therefore covers items such as antique clocks and watches.

11.   For details on British Government securities and qualifying corporate bonds see Example 80.

12.   Where chattels are used in a business, and/or are non-wasting chattels, gains are exempt if the chattel is sold for £6,000 or less (s 262). For details see Example 77 explanatory note 5.

13.   There is a complete exemption for 'compensation or damages for any wrong or injury suffered by an individual in his person or in his profession or vocation'. HMRC considers that 'in his person' has a wide definition extending beyond physical injury, so that damages or compensation for 'distress, embarrassment, loss of reputation or dignity' such as unfair discrimination are not chargeable. The same exemption applies to wrong or injury suffered in a professional capacity, such as libel or defamation.

      Where compensation is for personal injury, and it is received by way of periodical payments, or where interest is payable on the compensation, such payments are income rather than capital, but they are similarly exempt from income tax – ITTOIA 2005 ss 731, 732 and 751.

      Strictly, any right to compensation or damages not covered by the exemption is taxable. By Concession D33, however, damages are treated as derived from any underlying assets (and therefore exempt, taxable or partly taxable depending on the extent to which the underlying asset is exempt or taxable). For example, compensation for professional negligence that resulted in damage to a building would be treated as outlined in Example 95 explanatory note 6. By Concession D50, certain compensation from foreign governments for property lost or confiscated is exempt.

Contracts

14.   In the case of *Jerome v Kelly* (HL 2004), the House of Lords had to examine the effect of the contract disposal rule in TCGA 1992 s 28. Mr Jerome made a disposal of land which, for the purposes of illustration, can be simplified as follows:

      ●   in tax year 1, J signed a contract to sell the land, for delivery in tax year 3;

      ●   in tax year 2, J assigned the land (subject to the contract for sale) to a foreign trust;

      ●   in tax year 3, the trustees completed the sale and received the consideration.

      HMRC assessed the gain on disposal on J in tax year 1. He appealed, contending that s 28 could only fix the time of disposal, but it could not change the identity of the person who made that disposal – in this case, the trustees. In the High Court, Park J agreed with this argument, and suggested that HMRC should have assessed J on his disposal to the trustees in year 2.

      The Court of Appeal restored the traditional understanding of the effect of s 28. The asset was disposed of under a contract; the signing of that contract fixed not only the time of disposal, but also the identity of the seller.

      The House of Lords' view was that s 28(1) was no more than a timing provision and did not deem the contract to be a disposal. Furthermore, Parliament should not be attributed as having intended to impose a liability on someone who would not be treated as having made a disposal under the scheme for taxing the disposal of assets held on trust. They allowed the taxpayer's appeal and held that the disposal was made by the foreign trust.

      Subject to further legislative changes, this may leave scope for some limited post-transaction planning in cases where there is a period between entering into a contract for disposal and the executing of the contract (completion). For example, a husband agrees a contract and then realises that his wife has unrelieved losses brought forward. The husband could transfer the land subject to the uncompleted contract.

15.   However, a mere cancellation of a binding contract will not constitute a disposal and subsequent re-acquisition (*Underwood v R&C Commrs* (2008)).

Date of disposal

16.   A Special Commissioner's hearing, *A & S Smith v CIR SpC 388* (2003), considered whether a contract was conditional on giving vacant possession. Mr & Mrs Smith owned a farm where they carried on their business as farmers. They received an offer and payment for the farm in 1991. However they remained in occupation until 31 October 1999. They paid rent from 1 February 1992.

The letter of offer placed an obligation on the sellers 'to flit and remove from the subjects (ie farm property) at 1 February 1992 or such other date on which the sellers are entitled to take occupation of their new farm ...'. The taxpayers tried to argue that this made the contract conditional, so the time of disposal was when the condition (the purchase of the new farm) was satisfied. The Commissioner rejected this argument.

Question

(a) Indicate the annual exemption available for 2009/10 and how it interacts with the rules allowing taxpayers not to make returns of their capital gains.

(b) Explain how the loss relief is used in the following situations:

    (i) In 2009/10, Abigail has realised a £15,000 loss and a gain of £20,000. Explain how the loss relief is used.

    (ii) Brenda has £15,000 unused losses brought forward from an earlier year. In 2009/10, she makes a disposal of an asset, realising a gain of £20,000. Explain how the loss relief is used.

(c) Show the treatment of the following gains and losses (which are after taking indexation allowance into account) for a taxpayer who had no losses brought forward at 6 April 1998:

	Gains £	Losses £	Annual exemption £
2007/08	3,000	6,000	9,200
2008/09	7,200	1,000	9,600
2009/10	14,500	1,200	10,100

What would the position in 2009/10 have been if the losses brought forward had been £7,000?

Answer

Annual exemption

(a)   Outline of legislation

Annual exemption

Individuals, except those who make a claim under ITA 2007 s 809B to be taxed on the remittance basis, are entitled to an annual exemption. This exemption is £10,100 for 2009/10. Personal representatives are entitled to an exemption of the same amount on disposals in the tax year of death and the next two tax years (but not thereafter). Trustees are entitled to an annual exemption of £5,050 or £10,100 if the trust is a trust for the disabled. The annual exemption is divided equally between trusts created by the same settlor, subject to a minimum exemption of £1,010 for each trust (except for pre-7 June 1978 trusts, or pre-10 March 1981 disabled trusts). No annual exemption is available to companies.

If chargeable gains for a fiscal year do not exceed the annual exemption, and total proceeds from chargeable disposals do not exceed four times the annual exemption (£40,400 for 2009/10), it is not necessary to complete the detailed capital gains pages of the personal tax return. These limits were substantially increased to this level in FA 2003 as a simplification measure. Although it is obvious how this will benefit HMRC, the taxpayer will only know whether they do not need to report a gain if they know how much the total is, so the benefits seem especially weighted towards HMRC. Personal representatives and trustees also potentially benefit from these rules.

(b)   Allocation of loss relief

(i)   Abigail

Abigail must use her entire loss even though this will take her net gains to £5,000 (below the annual exemption).

(ii)   Brenda

Brenda will reduce the gain by £9,900 so as to match the net figure to her annual exemption of £10,100. Brenda will have no capital gains tax to pay for the year and her losses brought forward will be reduced to £5,100.

(c)   Treatment of losses brought forward

		£
2007/08	Net losses for the year carried forward	(3,000)
2008/09	Net gains for the year of £6,200 are covered by the annual exemption, leaving losses carried forward as before	(3,000)
2009/10	Gains (14,500 – 1,200)	13,300
	Less: losses brought forward	(3,000)
		10,300
	Less: annual exemption	(10,100)
	Chargeable gains	200

If losses brought forward had been £7,000, ie £4,000 higher:

		£
2008/09	Losses brought forward	(7,000)
2009/10	Gains (14,500 – 1,200)	13,300
	Less: losses brought forward	(3,200)
		10,100
	Less: annual exemption	(10,100)
	Chargeable gains	Nil
	Losses available to carry forward	
	Brought forward	7,000
	Used in 2009/10	(3,200)
	Carried forward to future years	3,800

Explanatory Note

Interaction of loss relief and annual exemption

Losses are relieved by deducting them from any gains in the tax year.

If there are net gains for the year, then no further calculations are made even if the gains (without the benefit of the loss relief) fall within the annual exemption.

If, however, the total losses exceed the total gains, then the excess is carried forward and to be available for set off against gains in future years. These losses are set off against gains until such time as the losses were fully utilised. However, losses from other years are utilised only so far as is necessary to reduce a person's gains to the annual exempt amount.

Question

(a) Calculate the capital gains tax payable in the following circumstances all relating to the tax year 2009/10:

   (i) Chloë is a higher-rate taxpayer with income of in excess of £200,000. She makes gains of £20,000 and realises no losses in the year.

   (ii) Zoë, aged 90, has no income. In order to meet living expenses, she sells a family heirloom realising a gain of £20,000. She realises no losses in the year.

   (iii) A discretionary trust (not settlor-interested) makes gains of £94,000 and losses of £1,200. The settlor had not made any other settlements.

(b) On 10 April 2010, Leo disposes of an asset for £400,000, creating a chargeable gain, after the annual exemption, of £350,000. Assuming no change in the law, state how the tax will be paid if:

   (i) the contract was dated 31 March 2010,

   (ii) the contract was dated 6 April 2010,

   (iii) the contract was dated 31 March 2010, and the consideration will be payable in four instalments of £100,000 each on 31 March 2010, 31 March 2011, 31 March 2012 and 31 March 2013.

(c) Beatrice sold her company on 30 September 2009 in a deal which gave her £1m in cash immediately, with a promise of 20% of the profits earned over the next four years, payable on 31 March 2014. The company had been set up in 1990 for £1. Set out the capital gains tax consequences if the following figures apply to the right to receive more proceeds as valued in 2009, and the amount of the further proceeds actually received:

	2009 value	Received
(i)	£200,000	£900,000
(ii)	£900,000	£900,000
(iii)	£900,000	£200,000

Assume that Beatrice does not wish to claim (or does not qualify for) entrepreneur's relief.

(d) What (in principle, without calculations) would the situation be if Beatrice was instead given £1m of shares in the purchasing company in 2009, with a promise of more shares to the value of 20% of the profits over the next four years, so she received further shares in 2014?

What would the situation be if the right to more consideration was in the form of loan stocks rather than shares? Would it make a difference if Beatrice continued to be employed by the company?

Answer

Rates of tax

(a) Since 6 April 2008, capital gains tax has been charged at a flat rate of 18%. The type of taxpayer makes no difference. Nor is the taxpayer's income level of any significance (TCGA 1992 s 4).

    (i) Net gains £20,000. Less annual exemption of £10,100. Chargeable gain is £9,900. Tax payable £9,900 @ 18% = £1,782.

    (ii) Net gains £20,000. Less annual exemption of £10,100. Chargeable gain is £9,900. Tax payable £9,900 @ 18% = £1,782.

    (iii) Net gains £94,000 – £1,200 = £92,800.

    Less:

    Annual exemption £5,050.

    Chargeable gains £87,750.

Tax payable £87,750 @ 18% =£15,795.

Payment of tax, including payment by instalments

(b) The disposal is deemed to occur on the date on which the contract is agreed (or, if later, becomes unconditional). The timing of the actual conveyance is not relevant.

    (i) Disposal in 2009/10: tax payable in one sum on 31 January 2011. Capital gains tax has no effect on payments on account for the following year, which are only based on income tax liabilities.

    Capital gains tax unpaid at 31 January 2011 will, however, attract interest from that date; any tax remaining unpaid at 28 February 2011 will attract surcharge. See Example 40 for further details on payment of tax, interest and surcharge under self-assessment.

    (ii) Disposal in 2010/11: tax payable in one sum on 31 January 2012. A delay of 6 days in executing the contract delays payment of the tax by 12 months.

    (iii) Ordinarily, tax payable will be £350,000 @ 18% = £63,000 due on 31 January 2011. However, by that date, Leo would have received only £100,000 of the proceeds.

    Since the instalments are payable over a four-year period, the taxpayer may opt to pay the tax by such instalments as HMRC allow (see explanatory note 3). Interest is charged only on instalments paid late. HMRC's practice is to set the instalments at 50% of the consideration received to date, although the taxpayer may be able to negotiate better terms depending on the circumstances. Otherwise it is likely in this example that the instalments will be £40,000 due on each of 31 January 2011 (the normal due date) and the balance of £23,000 on 31 March 2011 when the second instalment is paid.

Earn-outs

(c) The earn-out deal is treated as two separate disposals. The 'right to more' is valued and forms part of the proceeds for the first disposal, and this value is then the base cost for the second disposal.

The three scenarios produce the following gains and losses:

	(i) £'000s	(ii) £'000s	(iii) £'000s
2009/10			
Proceeds: cash plus right	1,200	1,900	1,900
The initial cost is ignored as negligible.			
2013/14			
Proceeds: more cash	900	900	200
Cost	(200)	(900)	(900)
Gain/(loss)	700	Nil	(700)
Total chargeable	1,900	1,900	see below

Under TCGA 1992 s 279A, Beatrice could make an election in respect of the 2013/14 disposal to treat the loss of £700,000 as realised instead in 2009/10. This would have the effect of reducing the gain of that year to £1,200,000. This would ensure that Beatrice is not prejudiced by her over-optimistic valuation of the earn-out right (on which she paid tax up-front). The election is complicated if there are other reliefs which have already been used against the gain in the earlier year. See explanatory notes 7 and 8.

(d)   If Beatrice was given securities and a right to more in 2009/10, she would be treated as receiving two different securities, unless she elected to be treated as making a disposal. The transaction would be a 'share-for-share exchange' within TCGA 1992 s 135. Strictly, the base cost should be split between the actual shares received and the deemed security, so that the cost of the 'more shares' relates to the amount allocated to the deemed security. In this case, the cost is insignificant, so this is not important.

If the right to more was in the form of a right to qualifying corporate bonds, it would again in theory be necessary to value that right so that the base cost could be split between the shares and the deemed security. When the QCBs are issued in satisfaction of the deemed security, a gain must be calculated on the basis of the value of the loan stocks at that time, and the gain will be attached to the loan stocks and charged when they are disposed of. In this case, because the cost is insignificant, the 'frozen gain' on issue of the loan stocks will simply be equal to their value.

See explanatory note 10 for the implications of Beatrice continuing to be an employee.

Explanatory Notes

Rates of tax – individuals

1.   For all taxpayers liable to capital gains tax, gains are charged at a flat rate of 18%. This is a marked change from the regime that applied between 1988 and 2008 when capital gains tax was charged on individuals at the rates which would have applied if the gains were the top slice of income (and, latterly, were savings income other than dividends, ie 10%, 20% or 40%) (TCGA 1992 s 4). Personal allowances, charges on income etc cannot be set against chargeable gains. This is illustrated in part (a) of the example.

Rates of tax etc – trustees and personal representatives

2.   The capital gains tax rate for all trusts and for personal representatives is similarly 18% (TCGA 1992 s 4) from 6 April 2008 (previously 40%).

3.   TCGA 1992 ss 77–79 contained provisions to assess capital gains made by trustees, for which a settlor had retained an interest and where both a settlor and the trustees were resident or ordinarily resident in the UK on the settlor.

     The provisions were introduced to prevent a tax advantage being obtained through the use of a settlor-interested trust. With the introduction of the single rate of capital gains tax for both the settlors and the trustees of 18%, these provisions were rendered redundant.

Payment by instalments

4.   Where the consideration, or part of the consideration, is payable over a period exceeding 18 months from the date of disposal, then at the taxpayer's option, capital gains tax may be paid by such instalments as HMRC allow over a period not exceeding eight years and ending not later than the time of the last instalment (TCGA 1992 s 280). No specific provision is made for interest on overdue tax, so interest would be payable on any instalment that was paid late. HMRC's practice is illustrated in part (b) of the example.

     Capital gains tax may also be paid by instalments on certain gifts where gains on the gifts cannot be deferred under the gifts relief provisions. The gifts concerned are gifts of land, or a controlling holding of shares or securities in a company, or minority holdings of shares or securities in a company that is not quoted on a recognised stock exchange. Companies whose shares are traded on the Alternative Investment Market (AIM) are treated as unquoted. Tax may be paid by ten annual instalments. Interest is, however, charged on the full amount outstanding, the interest being added to each instalment (TCGA 1992 s 281).

5.   For a further illustration of the instalment option and for the detailed provisions on gifts relief, see Example 82.

6.   Where consideration is due after the time of disposal, provision is made for a gain to be adjusted if part of the consideration becomes irrecoverable (TCGA 1992 s 48). It was held by the Court of Appeal in *Goodbrand v Loffland and Bros North Sea Inc* (1998) that where the consideration was in foreign currency (in this case American dollars) payable by instalments over several years, s 48 did not cover a loss arising as a result of the sterling equivalent of the consideration being much lower than expected because of exchange rate fluctuations.

     In effect, the company made a chargeable gain based on the sterling equivalent of the contract price, as calculated on the date of the contract; it then made a separate loss on realisation of the contract debt (an exempt asset, not being a 'debt on a security') in later years.

Earn-outs

7.   An 'earn-out' is the usual expression used to describe the type of deal in part (c) of the example, which involves 'contingent variable' consideration. This is dealt with in accordance with the decision in the case *Marren v Ingles* (1980) 54 TC 76, HL:

     ●   the initial disposal is treated as a sale for consideration in two parts – the 'right to more' has to be valued as at the date of the contract (ie building in estimates of the likelihood of receiving something, the likely amounts, and the timing);

     ●   the receipt of further consideration is a further disposal for CGT – the base cost of the 'right to more' is the value brought into account on the first disposal, and the 'more' is the proceeds.

     This can have unfortunate results. The most basic problem is the difficulty of valuing the contingent right, which is by its nature speculative. Strictly, the value of the earn-out right does not constitute 'consideration receivable by instalments', so there is not a clear right to payment of tax by instalments, but this may be negotiated with the inspector, as the situation is very similar to the receipt of fixed instalments and may cause the same hardship. Nevertheless, if a high value is placed on the earn-out right, it may create a cash-flow difficulty for the vendor.

If an over-optimistic value is placed on the 'right to more', it is possible to pay extra CGT on the first disposal and then incur a loss on the second. Before the Finance Act 2003 this could not be offset against the gain in the earlier year.

8. Finance Act 2003 introduced a significant relief to reduce the disadvantage of overvaluing the earn-out right. Where the 'second disposal' takes place on or after 10 April 2003, it will be possible to elect for a loss on the second disposal to be treated as if it had been realised in the same year as the first disposal, so allowing offset against the gain on that first disposal. The rules, in TCGA 1992 ss 279A to 279D, are very complicated, because they determine the interaction between this loss and gains, other losses of the year of the first disposal, losses brought forward and relieved in that year, and all the other details of CGT. But the essence of the relief is that the loss on the second disposal will reduce the gain on the first disposal, so that it will be charged to tax as if exactly the right value (without any discounting for time) was placed on the earn-out right at the time of the first disposal. It should be noted that this special loss carry-back relief is only available to individuals and trustee vendors (not companies).

9. Where the 'right to more' is only a right to securities (of a variable amount) in the purchaser, the first and second disposals are treated as 'share-for-share exchanges' (provided normal rules in TCGA 1992 s 135 are met). It is recommended that advance clearance is obtained on this point. The 'right to more' being treated as if it were a security itself. This is not available if there is any possibility that the further consideration could be taken in cash.

The first disposal still requires a valuation of the 'right to more', because the original cost has to be split between the immediate consideration (whether shares or cash) and the deemed security. The portion of the cost which is allocated to the deemed security is then carried forward and transferred to the shares which are issued in satisfaction of the earn-out right.

Prior to FA 2003 it was necessary to elect for 'security treatment'. It is now automatic unless the vendor chooses for it not to. It is most likely to be beneficial.

If the vendor continues to work for the company, entrepreneur's relief might continue to be made available (see Example 78 for further details).

If the earn-out right is eventually exchanged for qualifying corporate bonds, a charge to CGT is calculated at that point and attached to the bonds (as described in Example 80 explanatory note 4). Even if the eventual consideration will be exempt qualifying corporate bonds (QCBs), the deemed security is not a QCB and is regarded as chargeable to CGT. See also FA 2003 s 161.

Employment related securities

10. The introduction of the complex employment related securities regime in FA 2003 Sch 22 has created some uncertainties in relation to the tax treatment of earn-outs satisfied by loan notes and/or shares in the acquirer. Where the right is obtained by reason of employment or prospective employment, the receipt of the earn-out loan notes or shares would be subject to an income tax charge and, where appropriate, national insurance contributions.

HMRC have confirmed that where an earn-out fully represents consideration for sale of the target company's shares (as it will normally do) the income tax charges above will not apply. However, where all or part of an earn-out relates to value provided to an employee as a reward for services over a performance period, this remuneration element would constitute taxable earnings.

HMRC have issued guidance on the key factors for determining whether an earn-out is further sale consideration rather than remuneration. Where the earn-out is a mixture it is necessary to make a just and reasonable apportionment. Where certainty is required an application can be made under Code of Practice 10 to Employee Shares & Securities Unit, HM Revenue and Customs, Room G52, 100 Parliament Street, London, SW1A 2BQ (see Example 41 note 17).

Loss on unquoted shares in trading company

11.   Where an individual makes a loss on the disposal of shares he has *subscribed for* in money or money's worth in an *unquoted* qualifying *trading* company (and see below re quoted companies), he may claim *income tax relief* under ITA 2007 s 131 instead of relief against capital gains. (The relief does not apply to shares acquired some other way, for example by transfer from another shareholder, unless the transferor subscribed for the shares and the transfer is a lifetime transfer to his or her spouse/civil partner.) Relief may be claimed against the net total income of the tax year in which the disposal is made or the previous year (or both, if the loss is large enough). Relief for the capital loss takes priority over a claim under ITA 2007 ss 64 or 72 in respect of an income loss. The *tax saving* flowing from carrying back the loss against an earlier year's income is computed by reference to the tax position of the earlier year, but the claim is *given effect* in the tax year of loss (see Example 43).

The time limit for the claim is one year from 31 January following the tax year of loss.

The rules for identifying which shares have been disposed of are the same as those that apply for the enterprise investment scheme (EIS) and venture capital trust scheme (VCT). For details of those schemes see Example 93.

Under the rules which have applied since 6 April 1998, a qualifying trading company is a UK resident company none of whose shares, stocks, debentures or other securities are marketed to the general public and which

(a)   either

    (i)   is an eligible trading company at the time of disposal, or

    (ii)   has ceased to be an eligible trading company within three years of that time and has not since been an excluded company, an investment company or a trading company that is not an eligible trading company; and

(b)   either

    (i)   has been an eligible trading company for a continuous period of six years up to the time in (a) above, or

    (ii)   has been an eligible trading company for less than six years but has not previously been an excluded company, an investment company or a trading company that is not an eligible trading company.

An eligible trading company is defined by reference to the EIS definition in ITA 2007 Pt 5 (ITA 2007 s 137). Furthermore, in line with the revised conditions for EIS shares (see Example 93 part (a) note 3), s 131 relief will be available for a loss on *quoted* shares, providing they were unquoted at the time they were issued and there were no arrangements at that time for the company to cease to be unquoted. This applies to shares issued on or after 7 March 2001, and shares issued before that date but after 5 April 1998 where the company ceases to be unquoted on or after 7 March 2001.

An excluded company is a company dealing in land, in commodities or futures or in shares, securities or other financial instruments, or a company not operated on a commercial basis, or a company that is the holding company of a non-trading group, or a building society or registered industrial and provident society.

Although the company itself must qualify as an EIS company, the shares disposed of do not have to be shares on which EIS relief was given. It is therefore possible for a person to qualify for s 131 relief even if they are connected with the company, or even on a share subscription of over the EIS subscription limit of £500,000 (before 2008/09, £400,000). The EIS-based conditions do not apply to shares subscribed for before 6 April 1998.

A disposal does not qualify for relief under these provisions unless it is:

(a)   at arm's length for full consideration, or

(b)   a distribution in a winding up (or when the disposal occurs on the dissolution of a company without a distribution being made), or

(c)   a deemed disposal under TCGA 1992 s 24(2) where the shares have become of negligible value.

(ITA 2007 ss 131–151.)

In relation to (c), HMRC will accept a loss claim of less than £100,000 without referring the case to its Shares Valuation specialists if the company is UK registered, is not a plc and is either in liquidation or has ceased trading (see CG13131).

12.   The use of s 131 relief means that the full value of any loss is relieved.

Cross references

13.   For the detailed provisions relating to the private residence exemption, see Example 81 and for gifts holdover relief Example 82. The taxation of trusts and estates is dealt with in detail in the companion to this book, Tolley's Taxwise II 2009/10.

Question

(a)   (i)   Explain the special capital gains tax rules which affect spouses and civil partners.

      (ii)   Explain how these rules apply to other cohabiting couples.

(b)   Indicate the position in respect of the following:

    1.   Husband runs his business from premises owned by his wife, who does not work in the business. She acquired the premises in 1991. In May 2009 she transfers the premises to her husband and in June 2009 he sells them at a substantial gain.

    2.   The facts are as above but the wife transferred the premises to the husband in March 2008.

    3.   Husband has been a full-time working director for twenty years of an unquoted trading company in which he owns 4% of the voting shares. His wife, who does not work in the business, has also owned 4% of the voting shares for a similar period. The couple is now considering selling their shareholding, realising a gain of about £1,000,000.

(c)   Explain the capital gains tax implications of a taxpayer's death.

(d)   On 30 September 2009 Mr McCarthy, who works for Mack plc, a quoted company, acquired 5,000 shares in the company for £25,000 with the proceeds of an approved SAYE share option scheme run by the company. The market value at the date of acquisition was £37,500. He and his wife (who does not work for the company) already had a joint holding of 20,000 shares in the company which had cost £128,000. Mr and Mrs McCarthy decide to sell half the joint holding on 31 October 2009, realising £76,800. Show the capital gains treatment of the sale.

Answer

(a)

Capital gains tax position of spouses and civil partners

Following a statutory instrument under the provisions of Finance Act 2005 s 103, members of a registered civil partnership have been subject to capital gains tax in the same way as married couples since 5 December 2005.

Thus, within any couple, each partner is entitled to the annual exemption, which is £10,100 for 2009/10.

Where property is owned jointly by a couple, gains and losses are calculated according to the underlying beneficial ownership. (See Example 2 part (b)(iii) for the different forms of joint ownership, ie as joint tenants or tenants in common.) Where a couple have a joint holding of shares in a company, and either or both also own shares individually, HMRC does not regard one partner's share in the joint holding as being held in a different capacity from the individually owned shares. This is important when applying the special rules for matching disposals with acquisitions (see part (d) for an illustration).

Transfers between the couple if living together are not chargeable to capital gains tax (unless the asset is disposed of or acquired as trading stock, in which case the transfer is deemed to be at open market value (TCGA 1992 s 58)). In order to give effect to this provision there is deemed to be such consideration that gives rise to neither a gain nor a loss. This will almost invariably mean that the transferee spouse/civil partner inherits the transferor's base cost.

However, prior to 6 April 2008 (and in respect of assets originally acquired after 31 March 1982 but before 1 April 1998), the transfer triggered an unindexed gain equal to the available indexation allowance, so that the net result is no gain/no loss and the transferee acquires the asset at original cost plus indexation allowance to date or to April 1998 if earlier.

When the abolition of the (then-frozen) indexation allowance was announced with effect from 6 April 2008, HMRC accepted that this method would allow couples to bank indexation allowance provided that the transfer between them occurred before 6 April 2008. However, the legislation would have had the effect of denying this to couples where the asset had been acquired before 1 April 1982. To remedy this, FA 2008 inserted TCGA 1992 s 35A to ensure that indexation could be banked in respect of all pre-April 1998 acquisitions. (Section 35A(2) provides that s 56(2) applies to the nil-gain, nil-loss transfer whereas, previously, it did not actually apply in such cases.)

If, for example, an asset that had cost £10,000 was transferred from husband to wife in September 1993 at an indexed cost of £13,000, and the wife disposed of it in June 2009 for £21,000, the position would be as follows:

Sale proceeds June 2009		21,000
Cost	10,000	
Indexation allowance to September 1993	3,000	13,000
Gain		£8,000

The nil-gain, nil-loss rule applies throughout the year of separation, but not in later years. Since the partners are connected persons up to the date of divorce or dissolution (as appropriate) (TCGA 1992 s 286), transfers between them after 5 April following separation but before divorce (or dissolution) are deemed to be made at open market value (TCGA 1992 s 17). The gifts holdover relief (see Example 82) is usually available on transfers of qualifying assets.

Tax Bulletins 66 and 68 revise HMRC's views on transfers between spouses on divorce. Prior to this, they viewed transfers as part of a divorce settlement being for money or money's worth and therefore hold-over relief was not available. *Following G v G* [2002] EWHC 1339 (Fam) (and effective for claims made after or unsettled at 31 July 2002 in cases where there is recourse to the courts and a court makes an order):

- for ancillary relief under the Matrimonial Causes Act 1973 or Civil Partnership Act 2005 which results in a transfer of assets from one partner to another, or

- formally ratifying an agreement reached by the parties dealing with the transfer of assets.

They now accept that the transfer is not for consideration and therefore a claim for hold-over relief should not be restricted on the grounds that actual consideration has been given.

One consequence is that transferring ownership of the rights conferred by a life insurance policy under a court order is not for money or money's worth and no gain can arise. In the past insurers may have issued chargeable event certificates reporting gains as a result of assignments on divorce and the 2002/03 self-assessment tax guide was incorrect. It may therefore be possible to amend earlier self-assessment tax returns to reflect the change and further details about which returns can be amended are given in Bulletin 68.

Married couples and civil partners may have between them at any time only one residence that qualifies as their main residence for relief under the rules in TCGA 1992 ss 222 to 226B.

How the rules apply to other cohabiting couples

Other couples are not subject to any of the above rules. In particular, transfers between such couples can generate chargeable gains and/or losses (subject to the rules in TCGA 1992 s 17 concerning transactions otherwise than at arm's length). Each member of such couples can own their own main residence.

An attempt for non-married couples to obtain the same taxing rights as married couples failed in the Special Commissioners (*Holland v CIR* (2002) SpC 350) on the basis that the difference in rules did not interfere with a couple's human rights. It remains to be seen whether the tax 'penalties' of being married are more susceptible to a similar challenge.

(b) **Inter-spouse transfers**

1. The acquisition by the husband in May 2009 is treated as a nil-gain, nil-loss transfer by his wife. Therefore, her disposal proceeds are simply the same as her original acquisition cost (plus any subsequent enhancement expenditure reflected in the value of the property at the time of the transfer). Therefore, the husband is liable to capital gains tax on the difference between his net proceeds and his wife's qualifying expenditure.

2. The facts are almost identical. However, because the transfer took place before April 2008, the wife's allowable expenditure (in her nil-gain, nil-loss disposal calculation) is increased by reference to the indexation between 1991 and April 1998. This additional relief increases the husband's base cost and therefore reduces the chargeable gain arising in June 2009.

3. Shares can qualify for entrepreneur's relief which will cover gains of up to £1m (lifetime allowance). However, throughout the year before the disposal, the person making the disposal must:

    (a) have 5% or more of the shares of the company; and

    (b) be an officer or employee of the company (TCGA 1992 s 169I).

    Consequently, the wife cannot qualify for the relief. However, the husband can, provided his wife transfers her shares to him at least a year before the disposal.

(c)   **Capital gains tax implications of a taxpayer's death**

No capital gains tax charge arises on death (TCGA 1992 s 62). If prior to his death the deceased has made losses in excess of gains in that tax year, they may be carried back and set against gains assessable in the three previous tax years, latest first. As with brought forward losses, the set-off is made only against any gains not covered by the annual exemption in the carryback years (s 62).

Following the reduction of earlier gains, tax will be refunded accordingly, with interest if appropriate. Although the repayment is *calculated* by reference to the tax position of the earlier year(s), interest on the repayment runs from 31 January following the tax year of death (TMA 1970 Sch 1B).

If the gains of the year of death exceed the losses of that year they are taxable in the usual way and the full annual exemption is available.

The personal representatives or legatees are treated as acquiring the assets at the market value at the date of death (TCGA 1992 s 62). If an asset qualifies as a business asset by reference to the deceased's personal representatives, it will qualify as a business asset by reference to a legatee of the deceased during the period from the date of the deceased's death and the assets being assented to the legatee. Market value normally means open market value (s 272). Where, however, the probate value has been *ascertained* for inheritance tax, that value is taken as the market value for capital gains tax (s 274). Inheritance tax will not be ascertained where no tax is payable on the estate, for example because of exemptions and/or the inheritance tax nil-rate band. When personal representatives dispose of assets at values in excess of the values at death, gains arising are charged to CGT, but the personal representatives may claim the annual exemption in respect of disposals by them in the tax year of death and in each of the two following tax years (TCGA 1992 s 3(7)). If any losses arise, they may only be set against gains of the personal representatives and cannot be transferred to the beneficiaries. Personal representatives pay tax on gains at the rate of 18% from 6 April 2008 (previously 40%).

For inheritance tax, where land is sold within three years after death, a claim may be made by those liable to pay the tax to substitute the sale proceeds for the value at death (IHTA 1984 ss 190 and 191). A similar claim is available in the fourth year after death if the property is sold at a lower value than its value at death (IHTA 1984 s 197A). Such a claim is normally relevant where land is sold at a loss. In the case of *Stonor & Mills (Dickinson's Executors) v CIR* (SpC 288, 2001), no inheritance tax was payable on the estate because of the nil-rate band and exemptions. The executors sold freehold properties from the estate for significantly more than the probate value. They tried to claim under IHTA 1984 s 191 to substitute the sale proceeds for the probate value, thus increasing the capital gains tax base cost and eliminating the gains. It was held that, since no one was liable to pay any tax on the estate, no one was entitled to make a s 191 claim.

Personal representatives are allowed to treat a proportion of the costs of obtaining probate as allowable expenditure. SP 2/04 sets out HMRC's policy on this and a simplified calculation using a sliding scale.

If the personal representatives distribute assets to the legatees, this is not treated as a disposal, and the legatee is deemed to take over the base cost at the date of death.

Where within two years after a death the persons entitled to the estate vary the way in which it is distributed, and include a statement in the deed of variation that it is to take effect for capital gains tax, the variation is not regarded as a disposal by those originally entitled but as having been made by the deceased at the date of death so that no capital gains tax charge arises on any increase in value between the dates of death and variation for those who give up all or part of their entitlement (TCGA 1992 s 62(6)–(9)) and the beneficiary receiving the chargeable asset does so for tax purposes at the value at the date of death. In *Marshall v Kerr* (1994), the House of Lords decided that this deeming provision only has the effect of exempting gains on the variation itself. A trust established by a variation is treated for capital gains tax as settled by the person who made the variation, not by the deceased. Before 1 August 2002 it was necessary to make a separate election to HMRC within six months after executing the deed of variation for it to be ignored for capital gains tax (and, if desired, for inheritance tax).

For disposals before 10 December 2003, personal representatives did not enjoy the benefit of private residence relief unless they qualified under ESC D5. Since this date, the concession has been given statutory effect. The concession/new legislation is necessary as personal representatives are not trustees and do not enjoy the benefit of the relief in TCGA 1992 s 226 (trust disposal of a property occupied by beneficiary).

Personal representatives can now claim private residence relief if any persons who lived in the property both before and after the relevant death were entitled to at least 75% of the net proceeds of sale. A specific claim for relief is required by the personal representatives.

For example, Mr X owned a house and following his death his widow and children occupied the house until it was sold by the personal representatives. Mrs X and children were entitled to over 75% of the net proceeds (proceeds less costs allowable under TCGA 1992 s 38(1)(c)). Any gain arising between date of death and the sale of the house would be exempt under the private residence rules.

(d)   **Mr & Mrs McCarthy – joint and separate holdings**

Even though Mr and Mrs McCarthy owned some of the shares held jointly, for capital gains purposes HMRC does not regard Mr McCarthy as holding his 50% proportion of those shares in a different capacity from those he owns individually. Therefore, the shareholdings will be pooled as follows:

	No. of shares	Base cost £
Half joint shareholding	10,000	64,000
Cost September 2009	5,000	25,000
	15,000	£89,000

The position on the sale of 10,000 shares is therefore as follows:

Mr McCarthy

Sale proceeds 5,000 shares October 2009 (½ × 76,800)	38,400
Cost 5,000/15,000 × 89,000	29,667
Chargeable gain (reduced by annual exemption if available)	£8,733

Mrs McCarthy

Sale proceeds 5,000 shares October 2009	38,400
Cost (¼ × 128,000)	32,000
Chargeable gain (subject to annual exemption if available)	£6,400

The remaining 15,000 shares will be regarded for capital gains purposes as owned as to 10,000 by Mr McCarthy and 5,000 by Mrs McCarthy with base costs of (£89,000–£29,667 =) £59,333 and £32,000 respectively.

Explanatory Notes

Transfers between spouses and civil partners

1.   Disposals between spouses/civil partners are not charged to capital gains tax because they are treated as made at a 'no loss, no gain' price. In effect, the transferee takes over the original owner's base cost, plus indexation to April 1998 if the asset was owned before that time (TCGA 1992 s 58).

2.   As a result of these provisions, it is common practice to regard the transferee as simply taking over the transferor's original acquisition cost and acquisition date. However, this is not correct, and will give a misleading answer where the rules for share identification apply.

Example

H has owned 1,000 shares in ABC plc since 1988. They cost £5,000. W acquired 2,000 shares in the same company for £18,000 on 10 June 1998. H gave his shares to W on 15 June 2009. Five days earlier, W had sold 1,000 shares for £20,000.

Because W is selling shares within 30 days of her acquisition from H, W's disposal is deemed to be of the shares acquired (albeit subsequently) from H rather than the shares acquired by W in 1998. Thus:

- the shares have a base cost of £5,000 (rather than £9,000);

- the gain is £15,000 (rather than £11,000).

Cross-references

3.   For detailed provisions on inheritance tax and the taxation of personal representatives see the companion to this book, Tolley's Taxwise II 2009/10.

Question

(a)   A acquired a chargeable business asset in April 1983 at a cost of £10,000. In September 1983 the value of the asset was increased by enhancement expenditure of £5,000 and the value was further increased in June 1996 by enhancement expenditure of £15,000. Show the capital gain or loss arising on the asset, assuming that the asset was sold on 10 May 2009 for (a) £50,000 or (b) £28,000, and that no claim to rollover or holdover relief is available.

Without making calculations, indicate what the position would have been if the facts had related to A Ltd rather than an individual.

(b)   (i)   On 1 January 1988 D purchased an antique for £2,600 and on 20 April 2009 sold it at auction for £7,200, incurring selling expenses of £720.

(ii)   On 1 January 1988 E purchased a picture for £7,000 and sold it on 20 April 2009 for £4,850.

(iii)   On 1 January 1995 F purchased a set of antique candlesticks for £5,400 and sold part of the set to a collector on 20 April 2007 for £2,600. On 20 April 2009 he sold the remainder to the same person for £4,600.

D, E and F are private collectors. Show the capital gains or losses arising in each case.

(c)   Explain what determines wasting assets (other than short leases) for capital gains tax purposes, and state the taxation implications on the disposal of such assets.

(d)   G, a property owner, acquired a 51-year lease for £60,000 on 16 March 2006. On 16 March 2010 he assigned the lease to Y for £77,000. Show the capital gain or loss arising.

(e)   John Gregory owned a farmhouse which had been let to tenants for many years. On 1 January 2009 he granted an option to Jack Price, on payment of £10,000, to acquire the property for £215,000. The option could be exercised at any time between 1 May 2009 and 31 December 2009. Finding himself unable to finance the purchase, Jack sold the option to Jimmy Matthews on 30 June 2009 for £15,000. Jimmy exercised the option on 31 December 2009.

(f)   C sold an investment property on 10 April 2009 for £150,000 which had cost £1,000 on 10 April 1940. The costs of purchase and sale were £185 and £3,000 respectively. The value was £15,000 at 6 April 1965 and £48,200 at 31 March 1982.

(g)   H purchased a house for £44,000 on 5 January 1974 and on 5 July 1977 paid £12,000 to convert the house into two self-contained flats. On 27 April 2009 he sold the upper floor flat for £65,000 but declined an offer of £77,000 for the ground floor flat. He recognised that £77,000 was the market value, but preferred to let that flat in the expectation that the value would increase during the next few years. At no time did H live in the house. The market value of the whole at 31 March 1982 was considered to be £60,000.

Set out the taxation implications of the transactions described above.

Answer

(a) **A – treatment of enhancement expenditure (see explanatory notes 1 and 4)**

(a)			
Sale proceeds 10 May 2009			50,000
Less: Cost April 1983		10,000	
Enhancement expenditure September 1983		5,000	
Enhancement expenditure June 1996		15,000	30,000
Chargeable gain 2009/10			£20,000

The gain of £20,000 would be aggregated with A's other gains and losses and then be reduced by the annual exemption of £10,100.

(b)			
Sale proceeds 10 May 2009			28,000
Less: Cost April 1983		10,000	
Enhancement expenditure September 1983		5,000	
Enhancement expenditure June 1996		15,000	30,000
Allowable loss 2009/10			£2,000

If the facts had related to A Ltd, indexation allowance would have been available. This would have enabled A Ltd to claim additional deductions to reflect the increase in the retail prices index between the date of expenditure (April 1983, September 1983 and June 1996) and the date of disposal (May 2009).

Indexation allowance, however, cannot be used to create a loss. Therefore, in (a) the maximum indexation allowance would be limited in any case to a maximum of £20,000. Nor can indexation allowance be used to increase a loss. Therefore, in (b) the situation would be unchanged from that shown above for A.

Companies are not entitled to an annual exemption.

(b) **2009/10 gains on sales of chattels in April 2009 (see explanatory notes 5 and 6)**

(i)		(ii)		(iii)	
	£		£		
Sale by D (7,200 – 720)	6,480	Sale by E		F's two transactions are treated as	
Cost Jan. 1988	2,600	deemed to be	6,000	one since the set has been sold to	
		Cost Jan. 1988	7,000	the same person	
				Thus:	£
Gain	3,880			1st sale	2,600
				2nd sale	4,600
					7,200
				Cost Jan. 1995	5,400
				Gain	1,800
Limited to (7,200 – 6,000) =				This is less than 5/3 × £1,200	

(i)		(ii)		(iii)	
	£		£		
£1,200 × 5/3	£2,000	Allowable loss	£1,000	= £2,000, so gain is	£1,800

HMRC manuals state (Capital Gains Manual 76637–8) that the gain in (iii) is apportioned between the two tax years of disposal in proportion to the sale proceeds, so 26/72 = £650 would be assessed in 2007/08 (with 40% taper) and the remaining £1,150 would be assessed in 2009/10. See explanatory note 6.

(c) Wasting assets

Wasting assets are defined in TCGA 1992 s 44 as assets with a predictable useful life not exceeding fifty years, subject to the following:

(a)   Freehold land is never a wasting asset.

(b)   Plant and machinery is always treated as a wasting asset.

The cost of a wasting asset is deemed to waste away on a straight line basis over its useful life (TCGA 1992 s 46), unless the asset has been used in a trade, profession or vocation and capital allowances have been or could have been claimed on it, in which case the rules for straight line depreciation do not apply (TCGA 1992 s 47).

Where the wasting asset is a chattel, ie tangible movable property, then unless it is used in a business it is not a chargeable asset for capital gains purposes, so that no chargeable gain or allowable loss can arise (TCGA 1992 s 45). Gains on business chattels are exempt if the chattel is sold for £6,000 or less. (For further points on business chattels see explanatory note 5.)

Since wasting chattels are either exempt or are business chattels to which the straight line rules do not apply, the provisions of s 46 will apply only to intangible property, such as options (see part (e) of the example and also explanatory note 9). (Special rules apply to short leases – see part (d) of the example and explanatory note 7.)

(d) G – assignment of short lease (see explanatory note 7)

	£
Sale proceeds – 16 March 2010	77,000

$$\text{Cost March 2006 } £60,000 \times \frac{\text{Years unexpired on sale 47}}{\text{Years unexpired on acquisition 51}}$$

	£
$\text{Substituting percentages } 60,000 \times \dfrac{98.902}{100}$	59,341
Chargeable gain 2009/10	17,659

(e) Tax implications of option transactions

John Gregory

Since the option was exercised in a later tax year than that in which it was granted, John Gregory will initially have been liable to tax on the option proceeds of £10,000 in 2008/09 (less the annual exemption if available).

The option then being exercised, the price paid for the option is incorporated with the proceeds for the farmhouse to form a single transaction. (The tax originally charged will be taken into account in the amount of tax payable on the second transaction.)

John Gregory will therefore be liable to capital gains tax on the disposal in December 2009, his proceeds being the £10,000 received on granting the option plus the proceeds of £215,000 for the farmhouse. This will be reduced by the cost of the farmhouse plus any enhancement expenditure which is reflected in the value of the property when sold. Any capital allowances given to Gregory will not be deducted from the cost in computing the gain (whether or not they have been withdrawn by means of a balancing charge).

Jack Price

Since Jack Price did not exercise the option, the disposal of it is treated as a separate chargeable transaction. The option is a wasting asset and its cost wastes away on a straight line basis over its life, ie from 1 January 2009 to 31 December 2009. The allowable cost is restricted according to how much of that life has expired. The depreciated cost is set against the disposal proceeds of £15,000. The position is therefore as follows:

	£
Sale proceeds 30 June 2009	15,000
Depreciated Cost $10,000 \times \dfrac{6}{12}$	5,000
Chargeable gain 2009/10	10,000

Jimmy Matthews

Since Jimmy Matthews exercised the option, the purchase of the option and of the farmhouse will be treated as a single transaction.

(f) **C – asset acquired before 6 April 1965**

The gain must be calculated using the 31 March 1982 value:

Net sale proceeds – 10 April 2009	147,000
Less: 31 March 1982 value	48,200
Gain	98,800

(g) **H – part disposal**

	£
The gain using 31 March 1982 value is:	
Sale proceeds – 27 April 2009	65,000
31 March 1982 MV $£60,000 \times \dfrac{65,000}{65,000+77,000} =$	27,465
Gain	37,535

Explanatory Notes

Introduction and application of capital gains tax legislation

1. Capital gains tax was introduced on 6 April 1965 to charge tax on gains arising on the disposal of assets on or after that date by individuals, trustees and personal representatives. The gains of companies are computed under capital gains principles but are then charged to corporation tax rather than capital gains tax. The law was consolidated in the Taxation of Chargeable Gains Act 1992, to which all references in this example relate. For details of exempt assets see Example 73.

Major structural changes were made by FA 1998 but these were substantially reversed by FA 2008 with some further 'simplification measures'. Those changes did not affect companies, for whom there are no plans at present to change the rules.

Before FA 1998 the broad effect of the legislation was to calculate gains and losses on each chargeable asset, allowing an indexation allowance for inflation as detailed in notes 4 and 5 (but since 30 November 1993 not so as to increase allowable losses), aggregating the results and reducing net chargeable gains by an annual exemption, which was not, however, available to companies.

For individuals, trustees and personal representatives, FA 1998 froze indexation allowance at April 1998 and introduced a taper relief instead. Gains and losses were calculated on each chargeable asset, taking indexation allowance into account to April 1998 if the asset was acquired before 1 April 1998. The results were then aggregated to give the net chargeable gains or allowable losses for the tax year. Net chargeable gains were then reduced by any available taper relief, and finally by the annual exemption. Taper relief was given on the disposal of business assets that had been owned for at least one complete year and on the disposal of non-business assets that had been owned for at least three complete years after 5 April 1998. For assets acquired before 17 March 1998 an extra year was added, but this extra year did not apply to disposals of business assets from 6 April 2000 onwards. Unlike indexation allowance, taper relief was based on the time the asset had been owned, regardless of the dates of any later enhancement expenditure.

From 6 April 2008, taper relief has been abolished with all gains on all assets being taxed on all persons at a flat rate of 18% (after any annual exemption). At the same time, any frozen element of the indexation allowance was lost with the exception of disposals of assets previously transferred between spouses before 6 April 2008 (see Example 76). In those cases, indexation allowance is available up to the date of the spousal transfer. Whilst the headline rate of capital gains tax has fallen in many cases (from a top rate of 40%), the 'simplification' has led to an increase of taxes in many cases.

Example

Suppose Aida, a higher-rate taxpayer, disposes of an asset in April 2008, which she had held since April 1982. Aida's actual cost was £10,000 and her disposal proceeds are £36,700.

Indexation allowance would have reduced any subsequent gain by approximately £16,700 had she sold the asset before 6 April 2008. Aida would have also been entitled to taper relief of 40% (if the asset was a non-business asset throughout the period 6 April 1998 until the date of disposal) or 75% (if the asset was a business asset throughout that period) or a figure between those extremes if the status of the asset changed during the period.

Thus the gain before taper relief would be £10,000 and the gain before any annual exemption would range from £2,500 to £6,000.

Assuming that no annual exemption is available, this would have meant a capital gains tax liability of between £1,000 and £2,400 (and less if Aida had not been a 40% income taxpayer).

Had Aida sold the asset after 5 April 2008, her gain would be simply £36,700 less £10,000 (ie £26,700). Ignoring annual exemption, this leads to a tax bill of £4,806.

If losses exceed gains the excess is carried forward to set against later chargeable gains, subject to anti-avoidance provisions in relation to groups of companies (see Example 65 explanatory notes).

For further details on the annual exemption see Example 75.

Allowable expenditure

2.   The allowable expenditure that may be taken into account in computing gains and losses is (s 38):

(i)   Cost of the asset plus incidental costs of acquisition.

(ii)   Enhancement expenditure, ie additional capital expenditure reflected in the asset at the time of disposal.

(iii)   Incidental costs of disposal.

Incidental costs of acquisition or disposal are fees etc for services of surveyors, valuers, auctioneers, accountants, agents or legal advisers, costs of transfer or conveyance (including stamp duty), advertising to find a seller or a buyer, and costs of making valuations or apportionments, including expenses of ascertaining market value, but not, in HMRC's view, any costs incurred in *agreeing* a valuation. (Under self-assessment, individuals, trustees and companies may ask HMRC to check valuations used to calculate gains and losses before they send in their returns, and any values agreed in this way will not later be challenged unless information relating to the valuations has been withheld.)

No loss no gain disposals

3.   Married couples and civil partners are taxed independently on their capital gains, with separate annual exemptions, and losses of one spouse/civil partner may not be netted off against gains of the other. Assets may, however, be transferred from one spouse/civil partner to the other on a no gain/no loss basis (see Example 76). Certain other disposals may also be made on a no loss/no gain basis.

Indexation allowance

4.   No allowance was made for the effects of inflation until 1982, when an *indexation allowance* was introduced for individuals, trustees and companies to reduce the gain that would otherwise arise. There have been various changes to the rules over the years and historic indexation allowance may still be incorporated within the base cost of certain assets.

The position since April 2008 is that indexation allowance is only available for companies. The indexation allowance is calculated by applying to each item of expenditure the increase in the retail prices index between the month when the expenditure was incurred, or March 1982 if later, and the month of disposal of the asset, or, when relevant, April 1998 if earlier.

The formula used for this calculation is

$$\frac{RD - RI}{RI}$$

where RD is the index for the month of disposal and RI the index for the month in which the expenditure was incurred (or March 1982 if later). If the index for the month of disposal is less than that for the month the expenditure was incurred, the indexed rise on that item of expenditure is nil. The index increase is expressed as a decimal and rounded (up or down) to three decimal places (s 54).

The retail prices index was established at base 100 in January 1974. It was re-referenced to base 100 again at January 1987 (January 1987 on the old base being 394.5). In most published tables of indices (including the one in this book) the figures for months before January 1987 have been re-referenced to the new base, so that the standard formula may be used in all cases.

Chattels

5. Chattels (ie tangible movable property) that are wasting chattels (ie with a predictable life of fifty years or less) are exempt from capital gains tax unless they are business chattels on which capital allowances have been or could have been claimed (s 45). Where capital allowances have been claimed but then withdrawn because the taxpayer was not entitled to them, plant and machinery qualifies for exemption from capital gains tax as a non-business wasting chattel (*Burman v Westminster Press Ltd* (1987)). The main examples of non-wasting chattels are antiques, works of art and collectors' items (subject to what is said in Example 73 explanatory note 10 about collectors' items that are machinery).

    Gains on business chattels and non-wasting chattels are exempt if the sale proceeds (before deducting any selling expenses) are £6,000 or less (s 262). Where the proceeds exceed £6,000 the chargeable gain is not to exceed 5/3rds of the excess of the proceeds (before deducting selling expenses) over £6,000 (s 262(2)).

    Where a loss arises on the disposal of business or non-wasting chattels, then if the proceeds are less than £6,000 they are deemed to be £6,000 in calculating the allowable loss (s 262(3)). Hence in part (b)(ii) of the example, although E's actual loss is (7,000 – 4,850) = £2,150, his allowable loss is only £1,000.

    Note that it is only *movable* plant and machinery that is within the chattels rules. Fixed plant and machinery is fully chargeable to capital gains tax if sold at a capital profit, but the gains arising qualify for rollover relief if the assets are replaced (rollover relief not being available on movable plant and machinery). In the more usual case where fixed plant and machinery is sold for less than cost, an allowable loss will not arise. For further details on plant and machinery and rollover relief see Examples 82 and 95.

6. Where two or more assets which have formed part of a set owned by one person are disposed of by him to the same person or connected persons, then for the purpose of applying the chattels rules in explanatory note 5, the transactions are regarded as one transaction, as illustrated in part (b)(iii) of the example (s 262(4)).

    The guidance in the HMRC CGT Manual states that the resulting gain is then apportioned between the tax years concerned in proportion to the sale proceeds of each part of the set, increasing the gains of an earlier year. However, the legislation states only that 'any necessary apportionments' are required to treat the transaction as the disposal of a single asset. Therefore, a treatment similar to that used for options may be a more correct approach. The HMRC Manual on this issue does seem very dated. The legislation contains no time limit on its operation, although it is perhaps unlikely that a set would be sold piecemeal to the same person over a very long period.

    HMRC have commented on the position regarding fine wines and shotguns in their bulletins. While a pair of shotguns may or may not be a set depending upon circumstances, bottles of wine would constitute a set if they are from the same vineyard and vintage year. Manuscripts and collections of books are likely to form a set where they are 'similar, complementary and worth more together than separately' (CG 76632).

    The chattels exemption is relatively generous. Where a collection of goods represents a number of separate assets that are individually exempt (proceeds below £6,000) there will be no tax to pay even if the total proceeds are much higher. Care is required to ensure that the collection does not constitute a set.

Short leases

7. Where a lease with 50 years or less to run is disposed of, part of the cost is deemed to have wasted away. Wasting assets generally are deemed to waste away on a straight line basis, as stated in part (c) of the example, but where the wasting asset is a lease, the part of the expenditure that is deemed to have wasted away is determined on a curved line basis according to the Table in Schedule 8

(reproduced on page (x)). The allowable expenditure for the purpose of calculating the indexation allowance is the depreciated amount. For a detailed illustration see Example 99.

Part disposals

8.   Where part only of an asset is disposed of, the cost of the part disposed of is the proportion of the overall cost that the sale proceeds bear to the sale proceeds plus the market value of what remains unsold (s 42). Any available indexation allowance is calculated on the apportioned part of the cost and not on the cost of the whole asset.

Any expenditure which is, on the facts, wholly attributable to what is disposed of, or wholly attributable to what is retained, is not apportioned. If, for example, conversion expenditure was incurred on a property in order to divide it into two self-contained flats, and it could be shown that some part of the expenditure was properly relevant only to the first flat or only to the second flat, that part of the expenditure would be attributed to the relevant part and would not be apportioned.

Special provisions apply to a part disposal of land. For details see Example 95 explanatory note 3.

Options

9.   Special rules apply to options connected with employment (see Example 85). For companies, currency or interest rate options and options relating to loans (for example re government securities and qualifying corporate bonds) are dealt with in calculating the company's income under the rules for derivative contracts in FA 2000 Sch 26 (see Example 63 explanatory notes 2 and 4). Options to acquire or dispose of intangible fixed assets are dealt with for companies in calculating income under the intangible assets rules (see Example 66).

There are anti-avoidance provisions in ICTA 1988 s 127A and Sch 5AA and ITTOIA 2005 ss 555–569 imposing an income tax or corporation tax charge on profits realised from schemes involving commodity or financial futures or options that effectively produce a *guaranteed* return. The provisions do not apply if the profits are already taxed as trading income, or to a company's transactions if they are within the derivative contracts legislation referred to above, or to authorised unit trusts.

The capital gains rules apply to other options, and the treatment depends on the type of option (ss 143–148). The following options are not treated as wasting assets:

(a)   Quoted options to subscribe for new shares.

(b)   Traded options to buy or sell shares or other financial instruments quoted on a recognised stock exchange or futures exchange and 'over the counter' financial options.

(c)   Options to acquire assets for use by the option holder in his business.

When such options are disposed of or abandoned, therefore, the full cost is taken into account in calculating the chargeable gain or allowable loss.

Other options are treated as wasting assets, so that their cost wastes away on a straight line basis over their life (s 46). If such options are abandoned no allowable loss can arise. The forfeiture of a deposit is treated as the abandonment of an option.

Whether an option is treated as a wasting asset or not, it is generally treated as a separate chargeable asset, so that the full amount of the consideration for the option is treated as a chargeable gain. This separate treatment does not apply if the option is exercised. In that case the consideration for the option is incorporated with that of the underlying asset to form a single transaction both as regards the seller and the buyer, as shown in the example for John Gregory and Jimmy Matthews.

Where a call option is exercised and settled in cash, rather than by delivery of the asset, the grantor of the option is treated as having disposal proceeds equal to the price paid by the grantee for the option, less the cash payment made by the grantor, and the grantee is treated as having disposal proceeds equal to the cash received from the grantor less the indexed cost of the option (but with indexation limited to companies, so restricted so as not to create or increase a loss) (s 144A).

In *Garner v Pounds Shipowners & Shipbreakers Ltd* (HL 2000), a company received some £400,000 for the grant of an option over land it owned, and applied £90,000 in removing a restrictive covenant over the land. Although the prospective purchaser had requested this, the option was not exercised, and the £400,000 was assessed as a gain. The House of Lords held that this was correct: the £90,000 was a cost of improving the land which was still owned, and was neither an allowable cost nor a deduction from proceeds in the computation of the gain on the option.

10. In relation to shares the above provisions are modified to bring options within the rules for matching disposals with acquisitions. The rules that apply to companies are that purchased options of the same series will be pooled if an acquisition is not matched with a disposal on the same day or within the next nine days, and indexation allowance will then be available. If an option is exercised, the shares acquired merge with any existing pool of shares of the same class in the same company, and the indexed cost of the option will form part of the pool cost. For disposals by individuals, the matching rules are outlined in Example 79 explanatory note 7.

For individuals, the disposal of an option to buy or sell gilt-edged securities or qualifying corporate bonds is exempt (subject to what is said in explanatory note 10). For companies, such options are taken into account in calculating profits under the 'loan relationships' rules (see Example 63).

11. The case of *Mansworth v Jelley* (2002) STC 53, CA led to a major revision of the way in which shares acquired by employees under share option schemes are treated, and a change in the law. The changes operate by disapplying the market value rule in s 17 in relation to transactions with options (TCGA 1992 s 144ZA–s 144ZD).

Agricultural buildings

12. For the interaction of agricultural buildings allowance and capital gains tax see Example 23 explanatory note 21.

Assets acquired before 31 March 1982

13. The original capital gains tax base date of 6 April 1965 has been generally moved forward to 31 March 1982 so that only gains or losses accrued since 31 March 1982 are brought into account (TCGA 1992 s 35 and Sch 3), and, for companies, inflation is recognised from that time by indexation allowance. The position of companies is considered further in Example 83.

Question

(a)   Brown makes gains of £630,000 on 20 January 2009 and £1,700,000 on 15 April 2011.

Suppose Brown claims entrepreneur's relief in respect of both gains, calculate the capital gains tax due in respect of the two gains.

Assume that the annual exemption is fully used in both years and ignore other reliefs. Assume also that there is no change in the rules before 2011/12.

(b)   Cooper is a farmer with 100 acres of land. If she sells ten of the acres, could she qualify for entrepreneur's relief?

(c)   Kennedy is a beneficiary of the Sunshine Trust. The trustees own a factory which has been occupied and used for the purposes of Kennedy's manufacturing business. Kennedy is considering retirement and the sale of the business. Advise the trustees the extent to which they might qualify for entrepreneur's relief on the disposal of the factory and, if they might qualify, explain which timing conditions need to be satisfied.

(d)   (i)   Eagle sold the shares of his personal company on 1 June 2008 realising a gain of £250,000. The company used premises which Eagle owned personally which were sold at the same time at a gain of £500,000. Is Eagle entitled to entrepreneur's relief on the disposal of the premises?

(ii)   To what extent would the answer differ if the shares were disposed of on 1 June 2007?

(iii)   Assuming that the shares were disposed of on 1 June 2007, identify how the gain on the shares might accrue in 2008/09 and qualify for entrepreneur's relief.

(e)   Identify which disposals qualify for entrepreneur's relief:

(i)   Osborne has held 4% of the ordinary share capital of a trading company for two years. He had originally acquired 10% of the shareholding but transferred 6% to his wife to reduce exposure to higher rate tax. He retires from the business and sells his shares realising a capital gain of £400,000. Osborne's wife sells the shares at the same time realising a gain of £600,000.

(ii)   Cameron has held 6% of the ordinary share capital of a trading company for two years. He retires from the business and sells his shares realising a capital gain of £400,000. Six months before the disposal, his voting rights increased from 4% to 6%.

(iii)   Cable owns a manufacturing business. It operates two factories. However, on 19 September 2009, Cable closes down and sells one factory (realising a gain of £¼ m) and transfers production to the other site. However, on 25 January 2010, Cable receives an offer for the business which he accepts, realising a gain of £½ m, and retires.

Answer

(a) **Brown – calculating the relief**

2008/09

Brown can reduce the 2009 gain by 4/9. Thus the gain becomes 5/9 × £630,000 = £350,000.

Tax @ 18% = £63,000 (thus an equivalent 10% tax rate).

2011/12

The gain of £1,700,000 must be aggregated with previous qualifying gains so as not to exceed the lifetime allowance of £1m.

Lifetime allowance		1,000,000
Use in 2008/09		630,000
Available in 2011/12		£370,000
Gain made in 2011/12		1,700,000
Entrepreneur's relief		370,000
Subject to full tax rate		1,330,000
Taxed at reduced rate	370,000	
Reduction @ 4/9	(164,444)	
Remaining taxable		205,556
Total taxable gain		1,535,556
Taxed @ 18%		£276,400

(b) **Cooper – disposal of part of farm**

Cooper will not generally be entitled to entrepreneur's relief on the disposal of a number of fields. The key test will be whether or not she has disposed of a part of her business and the case law suggests that selling a number of fields represent merely a disposal of some assets used in the business.

A different result may emerge if it can be shown that the fields disposed of represented an identifiable part of the business. For example, were those fields dedicated to crops and sold so that Cooper could focus on her cattle production?

(c) **Kennedy – trust business assets disposal**

Trustees' disposals of assets might qualify for entrepreneur's relief. The first hurdle is to ensure that Kennedy is a qualifying beneficiary.

That first requires Kennedy to have an interest in possession in the trust (or the part of the trust which includes the factory) and not be merely a member of the class of discretionary beneficiaries.

Secondly, that interest in possession must not be a fixed interest. However, it can be a defeasible interest.

If that condition is satisfied, the trustees must take care to satisfy the timing requirements.

First Kennedy must have carried on the business throughout a full year ending no more than three years before the date on which the factory is to be disposed of.

Secondly, Kennedy must cease to carry on the business during or at the end of that three-year period.

(d)   Eagle – associated disposal

(i)   Sale of shares on 1 June 2008

Under s 169K, there are three conditions to establish entitlement for entrepreneur's relief in respect of associated disposals.

- The principal disposal must be a material disposal of business assets – being shares (or securities) or an interest in a partnership.

- Secondly, that disposal must be part of the individual's withdrawal from participation in the business carried on by the company or partnership.

- Thirdly, the asset on which the relief is claimed must have been used throughout the year ending with the earlier of the principal disposal or the cessation of the business.

However, it is also necessary to consider the various ways in which the relief can be restricted (see explanatory note 19).

First condition – material disposal of business assets

Eagle sold the shares of his personal company on 1 June 2008. Given that the company is a personal trading company, this 'principal disposal' would be a material disposal of business assets if it qualified as a personal trading company throughout the year from 1 June 2007 to 1 June 2008 (s 169I(6)).

Alternatively, the 'principal disposal' would be a material disposal of business assets if the company so qualified throughout a year ending on any date between 2 June 2005 and 31 May 2008 (s 169I(7)).

Second condition – withdrawal of participation

Secondly, the share disposal must have been part of Eagle's withdrawal of participation in the company's business. Whilst the legislation appears to be restrictive, the practice of HMRC is to interpret this condition very broadly.

Third condition – use of the asset

It is stated that the premises were used for the company's trade. It must be ensured that the company so used the premises throughout the year ending with the disposal of the shares (or, if the business ceased before that date, the year ending with the cessation). However, if the property has not been in business use throughout the entire period of ownership, then the relief is available but is restricted to the period used in the business.

(ii)   Sale of shares on 1 June 2007

A share sale in 2007/08 would not qualify for entrepreneur's relief (FA 2008 Sch 3 para 5). However, the rules for associated disposals do not require the principal disposal to have qualified for entrepreneur's relief. The test is that the principal disposal would have qualified for relief had the relief been available at the time.

Entitlement to relief on the associated disposal also depends on how the premises have been used since 1 June 2007. If the premises became vacant on the sale of the shares and have been marketed for sale since that time, then the second condition will be satisfied.

(iii)   Claiming relief on the sale of shares on 1 June 2007

Although the share sale might have taken place during 2007/08, Eagle might have entered into an arrangement that would have permitted the deferral of any gain arising. For example, Eagle might have sold the shares in exchange for qualifying corporate bonds (QCBs).

(QCBs are considered in more detail in Example 80, notes 9–11.)

A specific transitional provision (FA 2008 Sch 3 para 7) ensures that entitlement to entrepreneur's relief is available to the extent that the QCBs are disposed of on or after 6 April 2008. This partly compensates some of the taxpayers who had originally expected to be entitled to taper relief when they disposed of the QCBs.

(e)

(i)   Osborne – 4% shareholding; Mrs Osborne – 6% shareholding

As Osborne has held only 4% of the ordinary share capital, it is not a personal company and therefore entrepreneur's relief is not available.

Mrs Osborne's ownership would qualify for relief if:

- she acquired the shares more than a year before their disposal; and

- she is for that year an employee or officer (full or part-time).

(ii)   Cameron – 6% shareholding

The company was not a personal company in relation to Cameron for the year before the disposal because for some of that year he held less than 5% of the voting rights.

(iii)   Cable – two factories

The disposal of the first factory does not on its own qualify for entrepreneur's relief as there is at the time no disposal of a business. It is important to make enquiries to establish whether this is the case.

The subsequent disposal of the business will qualify provided that the business had been carried on by Cable since 25 January 2009.

Explanatory Notes

Introduction

1.   Entrepreneur's relief was introduced on 6 April 2008 and is largely based on the old rules for retirement relief. Indeed, some retirement relief cases will once again become relevant under the new regime.

The key elements of entrepreneur's relief

2.   Where entrepreneur's relief is validly claimed, it has the effect of reducing eligible gains by 4/9 (TCGA 1992 s 169N(2)). The effect of this is to ensure that gains are taxed at an effective rate of 10%.

3.   Entrepreneur's relief is available on up to £1m of gains (s 169N(3)). That amount operates as a lifetime limit.

4.   Claims for relief must be made by the second 31 January following the end of the tax year in which the qualifying disposal was made (s 169M(3)).

Qualifying for entrepreneur's relief

5.   There are, broadly, three types of disposal qualifying for entrepreneur's relief:

    (a)   'material disposals of business assets'

    (b)   disposals of 'trust business assets'

(c)   associated disposals.

6.   Relief can be reduced where part of the disposal represents non-trading assets.

Material disposals of business assets

7.   A material disposal of business assets is:

- a disposal by an individual

- of business assets (as defined)

- which is material (as defined) (s 169I(1)).

8.   A disposal is of business assets if it is a disposal of:

- the whole or part of a business

- an asset or assets in use for the purposes of the business at the time at which the business ceases to be carried on

- an interest or interests in such assets

- one or more assets consisting of shares in or securities of a company or

- interests in such shares or securities (s 169I(2)).

9.   Where the disposal is of the whole or part of the business, the disposal is material if the business had been owned throughout the year ending with the date of the disposal (s 169I(3)).

10.   Where the disposal is of assets (or interests in such), the disposal is material if:

(a)   the business had been owned throughout the year ending with the date on which the business ceased and

(b)   the disposal takes place within three years of that cessation (s 169I(4)).

11.   Where the disposal is of shares or securities (or interests in such), the disposal is material if either:

(a)   throughout the year ending with the disposal:

–   the company is the individual's personal company;

–   the company is either a trading company or the holding company of a trading group; and

–   the individual is an officer or employee of the company (or, if the company is a member of a trading group) of one or more companies within the group (s 169I(6)); or

(b)   throughout the year ending with the date on which either:

1.   the company ceases to be a trading company without continuing to be or becoming a member of a trading group or

2.   the company ceases to be a member of a trading group without continuing to be or becoming a trading company,

the following three conditions are met

–   the company is the individual's personal company,

–   the company is either a trading company or the holding company of a trading group, and

–   the individual is an officer or employee of the company (or, if the company is a member of a trading group) of one or more companies within the group (s 169I(7)).

Part disposals of business assets

12.   The requirement for there to be a disposal of a business or part of a business is reminiscent of the retirement relief rules. This was an issue that arose in a number of High Court cases – in particular *Purves (HM Inspector of Taxes) v Harrison* (2000); *Barrett (HM Inspector of Taxes) v Powell* (1998); *Wase (HM Inspector of Taxes) v Bourke* (1995); *Jarmin (HM Inspector of Taxes) v Rawlings* (1994); *Pepper (HM Inspector of Taxes) v Daffurn* (1993); *Atkinson (H.M. Inspector of Taxes) v Dancer* (1988); *Mannion (H.M. Inspector of Taxes) v Johnst* (1988) and *McGregor (HM Inspector of Taxes) v Adcock* (1977).

13.   The key point is that there is a difference between a business and a mere asset used in the business.

14.   In addition, the statute (s 169I(8)) ensures that in the context of partnerships:

-   disposals of interests in assets used for the purposes of an individual's business on entering into a partnership which will carry on the business is to be treated as a part disposal of the business;

-   similarly, disposals by individuals of the whole or part of the individual's interest in a partnership's assets will be treated as a disposal of the whole or part of the business carried on by the partnership

-   at any time when a business is carried on by a partnership it is treated as owned by each individual who, at the time, is a member of the partnership.

Disposals of trust business assets

15.   Trustees are treated as making disposals of trust business assets if:

-   they make a disposal of assets that are settled property and either

    -   consist of shares in or securities of a company or

    -   assets used or previously used for the purposes of a business

-   an individual is a qualifying beneficiary (as defined) and

-   in the case of a disposal of shares or securities, throughout a year ending within three years before the disposal:

    -   the company is the qualifying beneficiary's personal company

    -   the company is either a trading company or a holding company of a trading group and

    -   the qualifying beneficiary is an officer or employee of the company (or, if the company is a member of a [trading] group of companies, of one or companies within the trading group) and

-   in the case of a disposal of assets:

    -   the assets are used for the purposes of the business carried on by the qualifying beneficiary throughout a one-year period ending during the three years before the disposal and

    -   the qualifying beneficiary ceases to carry on the business on the date of disposal or within the three previous years (s 169J(1), (2), (4) and (5)).

16.   Again the statute provides that businesses carried on by the qualifying beneficiary can include businesses carried on in a partnership of which the qualifying beneficiary is a partner (s 169J(6)(a)). Cessations of businesses by a qualifying beneficiary include the qualifying beneficiary ceasing to be a member of the partnership or the partnership ceasing to carry on the business (s 169J(6)(b)).

17.   To be a qualifying beneficiary, an individual must have an interest in possession (other than for a fixed term) in the whole of the settled property or a part of it which consists of or includes the assets disposed of (s 169J(3)).

Associated disposals

18.   The third route to entrepreneur's relief arises if there is an 'associated' disposal. That arises if:

- an individual makes a material disposal of business assets consisting of either:

    - the whole or part of the individual's interest in the assets of a partnership or

    - shares in or securities of a company or

    - interests in such shares or securities;

- that disposal is made as part of the individual's withdrawal from participation of the business (which in the case of a disposal of company shares or securities can be carried on by a company which is a member of the same trading group as the company concerned); and

- the assets disposed of (in the material disposal of business assets) are in use for the purposes of the business throughout the year ending with the earlier of:

    - the date of the material disposal of business assets and

    - the cessation of the partnership or company's business (s 169K).

19   Relief is restricted where the use of the asset in the business:

- has been for only part of the period of ownership; or

- has been only partly used; or

- the individual has only been involved in the business for part of the period of ownership;

or

- has been dependent upon the payment of rent.

Rent paid prior to 6 April 2008 is ignored (FA 2008 Sch 3 para 6).

Business

20.   Although the statute refers to business assets, as was the case with taper relief, the term 'business' is narrowly defined to cover only trades, professions or vocations (as defined in the Income Tax Acts). Furthermore, the activity has to be conducted on a commercial basis *and* with a view to the realisation of profits (s 169S(1)). Therefore, hobby farms, for example, will not qualify.

Personal company

21.   For a company to be a personal company, an individual must hold 5% or more of both the ordinary share capital and the voting rights in the company (s 169S(3)). It is not possible to aggregate shareholdings of connected parties. Thus, suppose a husband and wife owned 4% each of a trading company, neither would qualify for entrepreneur's relief in respect of that shareholding. One would have to transfer a minimum 1% shareholding to the other at least a year before the earlier of the cessation of the business or the disposal of the shares. For entrepreneur's relief to be available in respect of the combined shareholding then one spouse would have to transfer the entire shareholding to the other at least a year before the earlier of the cessation of the business or the disposal of the shares.

Question

(1) Explain the share identification rules with effect from 6 April 2008 for the purposes of capital gains tax. Identify the exceptions to the general rule and briefly explain the extent to which the pre-2008 rules remain relevant.

(2) Jeremy sold 5,500 shares in Penny Pincher plc (a quoted company) on 15 August 2009 for £41,250, his previous dealings in the shares having been as follows:

10 November 1986	bought	3,000	shares for	£6,100
16 July 1988	bought	1,000		£3,060
25 May 1990	sold	2,000		£9,125
15 July 1993	bought	3,500		£14,210
25 March 2008	bought	500		£2,675
30 March 2008	sold	2,000		£12,700
15 June 2009	bought	3,000		£18,000

Calculate his chargeable gains on the disposals on 30 March 2008 and 15 August 2009. Jeremy is not and has never been an employee of the company.

(3) Pickles had the following dealings in the shares of Chutney plc:

10 May 1983	Bought	2,000	shares for	£8,000
14 July 1983	Bought	1,000		£5,300
18 October 1984	Bought	500		£2,300
21 February 1985	bought	500		£2,250
13 June 1996	sold	2,500		£16,500
17 July 1996	bought	1,000		£9,500
19 September 2009	sold	2,000		£17,700

(a) Calculate the gain or loss on the September 2009 disposal.

(b) State how the computation would be affected if Pickles bought another 1,000 Chutney plc shares for £8,950 later in September 2009.

(4) In July 1983 Kevin bought 2,000 ordinary shares in Collins plc for £12,000. Collins plc made a scrip issue of one ordinary share for every four held in December 1985 and a further scrip issue of one for one in May 2005. In July 2009 Kevin sold 2,500 of his shares for £20,840.

Calculate the chargeable gain or allowable loss arising.

(5) On 27 June 2009 Julian sold 5,000 quoted ordinary shares in Verdon plc for £31,250. Before the sale he owned 14,600 such shares, the history of his holding being as follows:

		£
March 1979	Bought 4,500 shares for	3,520
September 1980	Bought 1,500 shares for	3,050
November 1982	Bought 2,000 shares for	4,130
April 1984	Received a 1 for 2 scrip issue	
May 1988	Rights offer of 1 for 5 at £2 a share. One half of the rights sold nil paid for proceeds of £3 a share and other half of rights shares taken up. Ex rights price was £4.80 a share.	
July 1989	Bought 2,400 shares for	12,000
March 1994	Sold 1,000 shares for	3,500

The market value of the shares in issue at 31 March 1982 was £2.10 per share.

Calculate the chargeable gain or allowable loss arising on the sale of the rights shares in May 1988, the 1,000 shares in March 1994 and the 5,000 shares in June 2009.

Answer

(1) Introduction to share pooling and identification

Share pooling and identification provisions are required to provide a set of rules that determine how gains (and losses) are to be calculated when part-disposals of shareholdings are made. Without prescriptive rules, it would be possible to argue that shares acquired on a particular acquisition have been disposed of so as to minimise the gain arising (or to maximise the loss arising or to ensure that the annual exemption is not unduly wasted).

Example

Suppose Byron acquires 500 shares in Fairfax plc for £1 each on 1 May 2009 and a further 200 shares for £1.50 each on 13 May 2009.

If Byron then sells 350 shares for £1,000, without special rules, it would be arguable that either:

(a)   Byron has sold 350 of the shares originally acquired on 1 May 2009 (realising a gain of £650);

(b)   Byron has sold the shares acquired on 13 May 2009 plus 150 of the shares acquired on 1 May 2009 (realising a gain of £550); or

(c)   Some combination of the two.

Summary of the operation of the rules

Different rules apply for corporation tax. The rules below relate only to capital gains tax.

Until 5 April 2008, different rules applied to the identification of shares and other securities depending on when the securities were acquired. In particular, in the era of taper relief, it was necessary to identify the acquisition date of assets acquired on or after 6 April 1998.

From 6 April 2008, however, shares and securities are pooled so as to form a single asset which increases or decreases as and when individual shares are acquired or disposed of (TCGA 1992 s 104).

Thus, applying the facts of the above example:

Byron is treated as holding an asset (containing 700 shares) with a base cost of £800 (500 × £1 + 200 × £1.50).

So, when the 350 shares are disposed of, Byron will be treated as making a gain of £1,000 – (£800 × 350/700 = £400) = £600. (Byron's remaining shareholding of 350 shares will have a base cost of £400.)

When share identification rules apply

The share identification rules apply whenever a taxpayer acquires:

- shares of the same class

- in the same capacity (TCGA 1992 s 104(1)).

Thus, if a father owns shares for himself and also as trustee for his infant daughter, the two holdings are not treated as the same for the share identification rules.

Similarly, different classes of shares are kept separate (even if the underlying rights are the same).

This rule is subject to the following exceptions:

- shares acquired and disposed of on the same day (TCGA 1992 s 105(1)) – these shares are matched to each other so far as is possible;

- shares acquired under an approved share scheme (TCGA 1992 s 105A) if an election is made;

- shares acquired in the 30-day period following the disposal (TCGA 1992 s 106A(5)). This rule was introduced to prevent 'bed and breakfast transactions' in which taxpayers made disposals on one day only to reacquire the shares the next (at negligible net cost) (to create a loss or to take advantage of the annual exemption by increasing the shares' base cost).

In addition, s 105(2) provides a fallback option for shares disposed of yet not covered by any of the above. Given the introduction of the 30-day rule in FA 1998, it is highly unlikely that this rule will be applied in practice. However, where it does, it ensures that earlier acquisitions are matched to disposals before any later acquisitions.

Other assets subject to the rules

They do not apply only to shares. They apply also to company securities and any other asset which might be dealt in without identification of the particular assets involved. For example, suppose Max and Dan were to buy a house jointly and then Max subsequently bought Dan's share. If Max were then to sell a share of his interest to John, the share identification rules would be in point.

Relevance of pre-2008 rules

The pre-2008 rules continue to be relevant because the pools formed on 6 April 2008 (made up of shares owned before that date) will acquire their base costs from the shares not previously deemed to have been disposed of.

The key differences are:

- shares acquired after 5 April 1998 are not pooled;

- shares acquired pre-31 March 1982 form a pool separate from those acquired between 31 March 1982 and 5 April 1998;

- shares acquired pre-6 April 1965 could also be kept in a separate pool.

(2)   **Jeremy: pooling pre- and post 6 April 2008 – chargeable gains on disposals in 2007/08 and 2009/10**

500 of the 2,000 shares sold on 30 March 2008 are identified with the purchase on 25 March 2008 (acquisitions since 6 April 1998, most recent first). The remaining 1,500 shares come out of the post-1982 pool.

The sale on 15 August 2009 is identified with the s 104 pool. The position is therefore as follows:

Post-1982 pool

		Shares	Unindexed Pool value £	Indexed Pool value £
November 1986	Bought	3,000	6,100	6,100
July 1988	Bought	1,000		
Indexed rise				
$\dfrac{106.7-99.29}{99.29}$				455
Add new expenditure to both pools		___	3,060	3,060
		4,000	9,160	9,615
May 1990	Sold	(2,000)		
Indexed rise				
$\dfrac{126.2-106.7}{106.7}$				1,757

					11,372
Proportion applicable to sale					
$\dfrac{2,000}{4,000}$				(4,580)	(5,686)
			2,000	4,580	5,686
July 1993	Bought		3,500		
Indexed rise					
$\dfrac{140.7-126.2}{126.2}$					653
Add new expenditure to both pools				14,210	14,210
			5,500	18,790	20,549
March 2008	Sold		(1,500)		
Indexed rise to April 1998*					
$\dfrac{162.6-140.7}{140.7}$					3,198
					23,747
Proportion applicable to sale					
$\dfrac{1,500}{5,500}$				(5,125)	(6,476)
			4,000	13,665	17,271
Pool renamed s 104 pool					Indexation ceased to be relevant
June 2009	Bought		3,000	18,000	
			7,000	31,665	
August 2009	Sold		(5,500)		
Proportion applicable to sale	5,500/7,000			(24,880)	
Pool values cf			1,500	6,785	

* The rounded percentage from the table, 15.6%, may also be used.

	£	£
Disposal on 30 March 2008		
Sale proceeds 500 shares (500/2,000 × 12,700)	3,175	
Cost 25 March 2008	(2,675)	500
Sale proceeds 1,500 shares (1,500/2,000 × 12,700)	9,525	
Indexed pool cost as above	(6,476)	3,049
Total chargeable gain on disposal		3,549

40% taper relief will be available on the gain of £3,549 on the indexed pool in 2007/08 (ten-year qualifying period, including the 'bonus year' for pre-17 March 1998 ownership) reducing the gain to £2,129 (subject to other reliefs being available).

Disposal on 15 August 2009		
Sale proceeds	41,250	
Pool cost as above	(24,880)	
Chargeable gain		16,370

(3) **Pickles: gain or loss on September 2009 disposal**

(a) Holding at 6 April 1985, which provides the opening figures for the post-1982 pool, comprised:

		Shares		Cost £
May 1983	Bought	2,000		8,000
July 1983	Bought	1,000		5,300
October 1984	Bought	500		2,300
February 1985	Bought	500		2,250
		4,000		17,850

Post-1982 pool			*Shares*	*Pool value £*
At 6 April 1985			4,000	17,850
June 1996	Sold		(2,500)	

Proportion applicable to sale

$$\frac{2,500}{4,000}$$

				(11,156)
Cf			1,500	6,694

Post-1982 pool			*Shares*	*Pool value £*
Bf			1,500	6,694
July 1996	Bought		1,000	9,500
			2,500	16,194

Pool renamed s 104 pool

September 2009	Sold		(2,000)	

Proportion applicable to sale

$$\frac{2,000}{2,500}$$

				(12,955)
Pool values cf			500	3,239

September 2009	Sale proceeds 2,000 shares			17,700
	Less: Cost			(12,955)
	Chargeable gain			4,745

(b)   The disposal of 2,000 shares would be identified first with purchases of the same class in the next 30 days.

Thus the disposal of 1,000 shares (realising £8,850) would be identified with the acquisition costing £8,950 (giving an allowable loss of £100).

The remaining 1,000 shares disposed of would come from the s 104 pool with a base cost of £6,478 giving rise to a gain of £2,372.

This would leave a balance of 1,500 shares in the s 104 pool.

(4)   **Kevin – scrip issues (see explanatory note 13)**

Kevin's shares would be pooled as follows:

	Number of shares	Pool value £
July 1983	2,000	12,000
December 1985 scrip issue 1 for 4	500	
May 2005 scrip issue 1 for 2	2,500	
(no indexation adjustment since pool value not increased)		
	5,000	
Sold July 2009	(2,500)	
Applicable to sale		
$\dfrac{2,500}{5,000}$		(6,000)
Carried forward	2,500	6,000
Sale proceeds		20,840
Less: cost		(6,000)
Chargeable gain		14,840

(5)   **Julian – Part sale of rights shares in May 1988, sales of 1,000 shares in March 1994 and 5,000 shares in June 2009**

At the date of the rights issue in May 1988 the holding comprises:

Pre-1982 pool (*non-statutory method*)	Shares	Unindexed 31.3.82 value £	Indexed 31.3.82 value (£2.10) £
March 1979 Bought	4,500		
Sept 1980 Bought	1,500		
	6,000	12,600	12,600
April 1984 Scrip issue 1 for 2	3,000	–	–
	9,000	12,600	12,600
Indexed rise to May 1988 33.7%			4,246
	9,000	12,600	16,846

Post-1982 pool	*Shares*	*Unindexed pool value* £	*Indexed pool value* £
Nov 1982 Bought	2,000	4,130	4,130
April 1984 Scrip issue 1 for 2	1,000		
Indexation allowance to April 85			

$$\frac{94.78-82.66}{82.66} = 14.7\%$$

			607
At 6 April 1985	3,000	4,130	4,737
Indexed rise to May 1988			

$$\frac{106.2-94.78}{94.78}$$

			571
	3,000	4,130	5,308

Value of holdings in May 1988:	*Pre-1982 pool* £	*Post-1982 pool* £
9,000/3,000 shares @ ex rights price of £4.80 each	43,200	14,400
1,800/600 rights shares worth £3 each nil paid,		
half sold, half retained	5,400	1,800
	48,600	16,200

5% of (48,600 + 16,200) £64,800 = £3,240, which is less than rights sale proceeds of (1,200 @ £3) = £3,600, so sale of rights is treated as part disposal. Cost of part disposed of is:

Pre-1982 pool

$$\text{Unindexed value } 12,600 \times \frac{2,700}{48,600} = £700. \text{ Indexed value } 16,846 \times \frac{2,700}{48,600} = £936$$

Post-1982 pool

$$\text{Unindexed value } 4,130 \times \frac{900}{16,200} = £229. \text{ Indexed value } 5,308 \times \frac{900}{16,200} = £295$$

The sale of 1,000 shares in March 1994 is identified with the post-1982 pool.

The sale of 5,000 shares in June 2009 is identified with the s 104 pool, .

The sale and acquisition of rights shares in May 1988 and sales in March 1994 and June 2009 are therefore dealt with as follows:

Post-1982 pool at May 1988 as above

	Shares	*Unindexed pool value* £	*Indexed pool value* £
	3,000	4,130	5,308
Applicable to sale of rights		(229)	(295)
Rights shares purchased	300	600	600
Cf	3,300	4,501	5,613

	Shares	Unindexed pool value £	Indexed pool value £
Bf	3,300	4,501	5,613
July 1989 Bought	2,400		
Indexed rise			
$\dfrac{115.5-106.2}{106.2}$			492
Add new expenditure		12,000	12,000
	5,700	16,501	18,105
March 1994 Sold	(1,000)		
Indexed rise			
$\dfrac{142.5-115.5}{115.5}$			4,232
			22,337
Applicable to sale (1,000/5,700)		(2,895)	(3,919)
	4,700	13,606	18,418

Indexation ceases to be relevant post-6 April 2008

	Shares	Unindexed pool value £	Indexed pool value £
Carried forward to single s 104 pool	(4,700)	(13,606)	
	Nil	Nil	

	Shares	31.3.82 value £
Pre-1982 pool at May 1988 as above	9,000	12,600
Applicable to sale of rights		(700)
Rights shares purchased	900	1,800
	9,900	13,700
Amalgamated with s 104 pool (6 April 2008)	4,700	13,606
	14,600	27,306
June 2009 Sold	(5,000)	
Applicable to sale (5,000/14,600)		(9,351)
Cf	9,600	17,955

On sale of 1,200 rights shares May 1988 (sold for more than indexed cost):

Sale proceeds 300 shares in post-1982 pool	900
Indexed cost as above	295
Gain	£605
Sale proceeds 900 shares in pre-1982 pool	2,700
Indexed cost as above	936
Gain	£1,764
Total gain on May 1988 sale of rights	£2,369

On sale of 1,000 shares March 1994 (proceeds between unindexed and indexed cost):

Sale proceeds 1,000 shares in post-1982 pool	3,500
Unindexed cost as above	2,895
Unindexed gain	605
Indexation allowance (3,919 – 2,895) = 1,024, but restricted to	(605)
No gain no loss	–

On sale of 5,000 shares June 2009:

Sale proceeds	31,250
Cost as above	(9,351)
Gain	21,899

Explanatory Notes

Basic rules re shares and loan stock

1. All references in this example are to TCGA 1992 unless otherwise stated. The treatment of corporate shareholders differs in some respects from that for other shareholders. The position of corporate shareholders is dealt with in Example 83.

   The general principles of capital gains tax dealt with in other examples apply to all chargeable assets, including quoted securities, but because of the special problems of frequent purchases and sales, scrip and rights issues, takeovers etc, there are additional provisions relating only to securities. The rules for shares are different from the rules for interest bearing stocks, although from 6 April 1998 the same rules are used for matching disposals with acquisitions in the case of non-corporate shareholders, as indicated in note 7.

   In general, references to 'quoted' securities have been replaced by references to 'listed' securities (FA 1996 Sch 38) and shares referred to as unquoted shares are normally those that are not listed on a recognised stock exchange. The terms quoted and unquoted are, however, still retained in some parts of the legislation and for convenience they are used in this publication. Securities on the Alternative Investment Market (AIM) are unquoted.

   Foreign stocks and shares are broadly subject to the same provisions as UK stocks and shares, and any provisions relating to quoted securities apply to foreign securities that are listed on a stock exchange recognised by HMRC (ITA 2007 s 1005). In 2001, HMRC adopted a new interpretation of the expressions 'listed' and 'quoted' (IR Press Release 28 November 2001). This mainly affects foreign securities, and will not change the status of AIM shares.

   FA 2007 Sch 26 modified the definition of 'recognised stock exchange'. It permits HMRC to designate any recognised investment exchange (as defined in FISMA 2000) – in the UK as well as any market outside the UK – to be a recognised stock exchange.

Securities held on 6 April 1965

2. The treatment of shares (and loan stock) that had quoted market values on a recognised stock exchange at 6 April 1965 was different from the treatment of shares (and stocks) that were unquoted at that date (Sch 2). For later share acquisitions the same rules apply to all shares of the same class in the same company (s 104).

Stamp duty and stamp duty reserve tax

3. Transactions in securities are subject to stamp duty or stamp duty reserve tax. See Example 84 for details.

Share pooling for non-corporate shareholders – before 6 April 2008

4. Before FA 1998, shares of the same class in the same company were subject to a pooling system, except for certain pre-6 April 1965 acquisitions. There are two separate pools for each class of shares, one relating to shares acquired between 6 April 1965 and 5 April 1982, referred to in the legislation as the 1982 holding (s 109) but referred to in this book as the pre-1982 pool, and the other relating to shares acquired between 6 April 1982 and 5 April 1998, now referred to in the legislation as the s 104 holding but referred to in this book as the post-1982 pool.

Shares acquired under an employee share scheme and subject to restrictions are treated as shares of a different class from unrestricted shares until the restrictions are lifted. See Example 80 explanatory notes 1 to 3.

Shares acquired on or after 6 April 1998, except for scrip and rights shares, were not pooled until 6 April 2008. Previously, they are treated as separate, free-standing assets (s 104).

The way in which the legislation developed (which may still be relevant if a share history has to be reconstructed from a list of transactions) was as follows:

(a) *6.4.65 to 5.4.82*

Shares of the same class in the same company were pooled, ie treated as a single asset, growing with purchases and diminishing with sales, so that an average price was used as the cost of disposals.

The pool excluded shares already owned on 6 April 1965, but in respect of *quoted* shares the taxpayer could make an election (under what is now Sch 2 para 4) to include them in the pool at their quoted price on that day. Two pooling elections could be made, one in respect of all 6 April 1965 holdings of fixed interest securities and preference shares, and the other in respect of all other quoted securities held on that day. If such pooling elections were not made, the shares were dealt with as separate, free-standing assets according to the date they were acquired. This separate treatment still applies unless a rebasing election is made.

(b) *6.4.82 to 5.4.85*

Indexation allowance was introduced, but because it was subject to various restrictions, shares acquired between 6.4.81 and 5.4.85 were treated as separate free-standing assets.

(c) *6.4.85 – 5.4.98*

Following the removal of the original restrictions on indexation, the shares referred to in (b) were merged to form the post-1982 pool, except for shares acquired between 6.4.81 and 5.4.82, which were merged with the pre-1982 pool.

No shares are added to the pre-1982 pool, other than as a result of scrip or rights issues (see explanatory note 13) (or as a result of a pooling election after 5 April 1985 to include pre-6 April 1965 shares in it).

From 6.4.88 a 'rebasing' election could be made to use only 31 March 1982 value, and ignore original costs, for virtually all assets held on that day.

(d)   *6.4.98 – 5.4.08*

Shares acquired on or after 6 April 1998 are treated as separate, free-standing assets, except for scrip and rights shares (see explanatory note 13).

(e)   *6.4.08 onwards*

All shares are pooled in a single pool.

Freezing of indexation allowance and introduction of taper relief

5.   Indexation allowance is not given to non-corporate shareholders on any acquisitions on or after 6 April 1998 and no further indexation allowance is given after April 1998 on earlier acquisitions (s 110A). Until 5 April 2008, taper relief was given instead of indexation according to the complete years the shares have been owned, with an extra year added for shares acquired before 17 March 1998, unless the shares qualify as business assets. As indicated in part (4) of the example, the pre- and post-1982 pools are regarded as single assets, with the post-1982 pool treated as acquired when it first came into being (s 106A), so that providing this was before 17 March 1998 acquisitions between 17 March 1998 and 5 April 1998 still counted for the extra year's taper relief.

See Example 77 explanatory note 4 for the changes in the rules for indexation allowance that have taken place since 6 April 1982.

Abolition of taper relief and indexation allowance

6.   From 6 April 2008, taper relief has ceased to be available. Furthermore, indexation allowance that had accrued in respect of periods of ownership before April 1998 has ceased to be available. This will cause difficulties with records where only the records of the indexed cost were kept. However, a note of the actual cost (as well as indexed cost) did become necessary from 30 November 1993 when the indexation of losses ceased to apply.

Matching disposals with acquisitions

7.   Disposals of shares before 6 April 2008 of the same class in the same company by non-corporate shareholders on or after 6 April 1998 (17 March 1998 in relation to heading (b)) are matched with acquisitions as follows (s 106A):

(a)   Acquisitions on the same day as the disposal

(b)   Acquisitions within 30 days after the disposal, earliest first (but see notes below)

(c)   Previous acquisitions after 5 April 1998, latest first

(d)   The post-1982 pool

(e)   The pre-1982 pool

(f)   Pre-6 April 1965 acquisitions that are not included in the pre-1982 pool, latest first

(g)   Acquisitions more than 30 days after disposal, earliest first.

For disposals after 5 April 2008, the following matching rules apply:

(a)   Acquisitions on the same day as the disposal

(b)   Acquisitions within 30 days after the disposal, earliest first (but see notes below)

(c)   All previous acquisitions (as pooled)

(d)   Acquisitions more than 30 days after disposal, earliest first.

All acquisitions on the same day are normally treated as a single asset. This is subject to special rules where some of the acquisitions are acquired under an approved employee share scheme – see Example 80 explanatory note 8.

The above matching rules apply despite the fact that some of the shares were otherwise identified by the disposal, but shares disposed of by a person in one capacity are not identified with shares held in another capacity (s 106A). This means that shares held by trustees or personal representatives are not identified with shares they own personally. It does not, however, in the view of HMRC, treat shares held by a husband and wife/civil partners jointly as held in a different capacity from shares held by them separately. See Example 76 for an illustration of this point.

Where shares are held in an individual savings account (ISA) they are regarded as held in a different capacity from other shares held (see Example 92).

The 30-day rule in (b) above prevents 'bed and breakfast' transactions, where shares are sold and bought back on the following day in order either to use the capital gains exemption or to produce losses to reduce chargeable gains. For married couples (or civil partners) it would, however, be possible for the spouse to repurchase the shares on the market (but not directly from the other spouse).

In the case of *Davies v Hicks* (2005), the 30-day rule was successfully used by a trust which was about to become non-resident in the UK. To avoid an exit charge on the trust, the trustees sold its shareholding shortly before ceasing to be UK resident. When it had become non-resident (and within 30 days of the original disposal), the shares were reacquired by the non-resident trustees. The shares disposed of were then matched with the shares subsequently reacquired and so a considerable gain was eliminated. The non-resident trustees consequently acquired the original base cost of the shares.

This scheme was blocked with effect from 22 March 2006 by FA 2006 which provides that the 30-day rule does not apply in respect of any acquisition by a person who is not UK resident (and not treated as resident under a tax treaty).

The Revenue's Tax Bulletin of April 2001 contains a review of their understanding of the identification rules, and comments on a number of published planning schemes which make use of the 'bed and breakfasting' rule. HMRC does not believe that the identification of 'same day share transactions' overrides the many provisions of TCGA 1992 which trigger a gain or loss by deeming a 'disposal and immediate reacquisition' of an asset.

The Tax Bulletin of August 2001 included further examples of how HMRC resolves the difficult interaction of share identification, inter-spouse disposals (now also relevant for civil partners) and taper relief. This is analysed in two articles in Taxation, 18 October 2001, which point out a number of difficulties which HMRC's approach leaves unresolved. More recently this issue is touched upon in 'merging and diverging interests' (Taxation, 22 May 2003).

Calculating gains and losses for non-corporate shareholders – pre-6 April 2008

8.   Gains and losses are calculated as follows:

Post-1982 pool

(a)   There are two pool values, one representing the actual qualifying expenditure and the other an indexed pool of expenditure, no further indexation being added, however, after April 1998 (s 110). To arrive at the initial figures for shares already on hand at 6 April 1985, indexation allowance was calculated on each separate acquisition from the month of purchase to April 1985, and the indexed pool of expenditure at 6 April 1985 was the total qualifying expenditure plus the total of all the calculated indexation allowances.

Where a post-1982 pool first came into being after the April 1985 date, the unindexed pool value and the indexed pool value were initially the same amount.

Every time there is an 'operative event' on the holding (ie an event which results in the qualifying expenditure being reduced or increased), then before dealing with that event, the indexed pool value is increased by:

$$\frac{RE - RL}{RL}$$

where RE is the retail prices index for the month in which the event occurs, and RL is the retail prices index for the month when the last event occurred (or the month the pool was created if there have been no previous acquisitions or disposals).

The first operative event after 5 April 1998 is the last occasion on which the indexation adjustment will be made, indexation being given only up to April 1998 as shown in the example. Thereafter the unindexed and indexed pool figures will be adjusted only for disposals and for scrip and rights issues. It is possible to calculate the final indexation in anticipation of that operative event. However, it is still necessary to identify separately the cost and indexed cost, because indexation cannot create or increase a loss.

The index increase is expressed as a decimal (and unlike the normal indexation allowance calculation, there is no stipulation for this to be rounded to three decimal places. (HMRC would probably not object if rounded figures from published indexation tables were used.) If RL exceeds RE the indexed rise is nil and the indexed pool value remains the same. When the next purchase or sale occurs, however, RL in that calculation is the index for the month of the previous operative event, even though no index adjustment took place.

After the index adjustment has been made to the indexed pool, the new expenditure is then added to both pool values.

Where a disposal occurs, a proportionate deduction is made from both pools, the indexation allowance on the disposal being the difference between the two pool values.

If a receipt is not treated as a disposal (eg on a capital distribution or sale of rights), the amount received is deducted from both pool values.

The operation of the indexed pool is shown in part (2) of the example, and the treatment of capital distributions and rights issues is dealt with in parts (4), (6) and in Example 80.

Partly paid shares

9.   Where a company issues partly paid shares, the subsequent calls qualify for any available indexation allowance from the date the shares were issued, unless they are paid more than 12 months later, in which case they qualify from the date they are paid (s 113). This does not apply where the shares are already fully paid, but are then sold with the price payable by instalments, as in the case of the privatisation issues, which qualified for indexation allowance on the full purchase price from the date of issue even if sold when some instalments had not been paid, providing any unpaid instalments were added to the disposal proceeds in the computation on the sale. Any privatisation issue vouchers that were used to reduce bills were deducted from the allowable cost. Any free shares acquired later were added to the holding and treated as acquired at market value on the first day of dealing in them.

Unit trusts, investment trusts and open-ended investment companies (OEICs)

10.   Authorised unit trusts and investment trusts are exempt from tax on their gains (s 100). Disposals by those who invest in such trusts are usually chargeable to tax in the normal way. Those who invest in unit and investment trusts through monthly savings schemes used to be able to simplify the post-1982 pool calculations by being treated as if they had made a single annual investment in the seventh month of the trust's accounting year, but this no longer applies. Each monthly contribution must now therefore be separately identified.

The 2003 Budget Press Releases included a statement that the rules are unwieldy when applied to savings plans, and a promise that a clearer explanation of how to operate them is being developed. Presumably it will use some of the simplifying effects of the post-indexation regime. Under taper relief, when units were disposed of, the monthly acquisitions could be grouped together in bands of 3 years (no taper) and single years after that (5%, 10% etc). The effect of separate identification will therefore be quite similar to the previous rule. However, if any individual month's acquisition shows a loss, that should be separately identified for offset against gains with the lowest taper.

From 28 April 1997, open-ended investment companies (OEICs) are permitted under UK law. The shares in OEICs may be continuously created or redeemed, depending on investor demand. They are treated in essentially the same way as unit trusts, and existing unit trusts may convert into OEICs if they wish.

Negligible value

11. See Example 95 explanatory note 8 for the treatment of shares that have become of negligible value.

Stock lending, repos, etc

12. In line with the Government's intention to maintain the competitiveness of the UK in world financial markets, there are various special rules designed to facilitate stock market transactions such as stock lending, manufactured payments and 'repos' (ie sale and repurchase transactions where the repurchase price is fixed, fluctuations in market value being borne by the original holder) (ITA 2007 ss 601–614, 653–655, ICTA 1988, s 736A, TCGA 1992 ss 263A to 263C, FA 2003 Sch 38).

Scrip and rights issues

13. A reorganisation of a company's capital (eg by scrip or rights issue) is not treated as a disposal of the original shares or acquisition of a new holding. The new shares stand in the shoes of the old as regards acquisition date and cost, but for indexation purposes any payment for rights shares is regarded as incurred on the date when it was actually incurred and not when the original shares were acquired (TCGA 1992 ss 126–131), so that indexation allowance is not given on rights shares acquired after 5 April. On the other hand, when such rights shares form part of pre-6 April 1998 acquisitions and the shares do not constitute business assets, for disposals before 6 April 2008 their cost was taken into account in computing the gain eligible for the extra year's taper relief.

If on the reorganisation the shareholder receives any cash from the company, that cash is regarded as a capital distribution and is accordingly dealt with as detailed in explanatory note 14 (s 128(2)). The value of the holding is worked out by taking the ex rights value of the existing shares plus the proceeds of the sale of rights. Where a shareholder sells some of his rights and takes up the balance, the value of the holding at the time of the sale includes the 'nil paid' value of the rights retained (see part (5) of the example). Part (5) of the example illustrates rights proceeds that are not 'small'.

Capital distributions

14. Where a company makes a capital distribution it is treated as a disposal of an interest in the shares (TCGA 1992 s 122) and a chargeable gain or allowable loss arises accordingly, unless the distribution is regarded as 'small'. HMRC will accept a distribution as small if it is *either* not more than 5% of the value of the shares *or* not more than £3,000, and they will consider on their merits cases where the taxpayer wants an amount to be treated as small even though it exceeds both these limits. Where the capital distribution is small then instead of being treated as a part disposal it is regarded as reducing the base cost of the holding. HMRC will not, however, object if someone wants to treat the receipt as a part disposal, which may be to their advantage if a gain would be covered by the annual exemption, or if a loss would reduce an existing chargeable gain. A small capital distribution must be treated as a part disposal if it exceeds the allowable expenditure, or if the allowable expenditure is nil (as is the case with demutualisation shares). Where there is allowable expenditure that is less than the 'small' capital distribution, the amount chargeable may be reduced by that expenditure, leaving the holding with no allowable cost for future disposals.

If the 'small' capital distribution relates to a pre-1982 pool or to pre-6 April 1965 shares, the legislation provides that the original cost of the holding (or 31 March 1982 value where appropriate) is indexed from March 1982 and the reduction from base cost is indexed from the date the capital sum is received (TCGA 1992 s 57). These adjustments are not necessary, however, if the pre-1982 pool is maintained in the same way as the post-1982 pool.

Some companies return capital to shareholders by linking the payment to a consolidation of the shares in order to avoid a reduction in earnings per share. The cash received in such instances represents a capital distribution that is subject to the rules outlined above. Other companies have merely paid special dividends to shareholders, such dividends being treated as income and having no capital gains consequences.

Some companies have carried out a reorganisation of share capital into 'ordinary shares' and 'B shares', followed by a purchase of the B shares through a broker or redemption of the B shares by the company. Although this seems to be a transparent scheme to circumvent the treatment of a purchase of own shares as a dividend, it appears that HMRC generally allow the share split to be treated as a capital reorganisation, and the redemption of the B shares to be a pure capital disposal for the shareholders.

Scrip dividend options

15. Where scrip shares are offered by a UK resident company as an alternative to a cash dividend, the capital gains tax cost for an individual, personal representatives, or trustees of a discretionary trust (other than one in which the settlor retains an interest) is the 'appropriate amount in cash'. That means the amount of the cash option, unless it is substantially different from the market value of the shares (TCGA 1992 s 142), 'substantially' was previously interpreted by HMRC as 15% or more either way (Statement of Practice A8). HMRC also ignored differences of up to 17% in any cases not involving deliberate avoidance. SP A8 also stated that the 15% calculation was based on the market value of the shares, but in fact HMRC accepted calculations based on the cash dividend instead. From 6 April 2005, however, SP A8 has been legislated for and its provisions are now found in ITTOIA 2005 s 412. That refers to a 15% figure and this is applied to the market value. However, it remains to be seen whether HMRC will continue to relax the rules in accordance with former SP A8 in certain cases. If the difference is substantial, the appropriate amount in cash is the market value of the shares on the first day of dealing.

For shares acquired before 6 April 1998, the 'appropriate amount' is treated in the same way as a purchase of rights shares, ie the shares increase existing holdings proportionately, and the deemed cost attracts indexation allowance from the month of issue. This does not apply to a 'bare trust', ie where someone is absolutely entitled as against the trustees (or would be but for being an infant or a person under a disability). For bare trusts, the scrip shares are treated as acquired for the 'appropriate amount in cash' by the beneficiary directly, so that they are not treated as an addition to an existing holding (TCGA 1992 s 142).

For shares acquired on or after 6 April 1998, scrip option shares are treated as a separate, free-standing acquisition in all cases where the shares are taxed as income (see Example 57 explanatory note 6), and not just for bare trusts (s 142).

Where scrip option shares are issued to a corporate shareholder or to a discretionary trust in which the settlor retains an interest, they are capital rather than income, with a capital gains base cost of nil (because the 'income' treatment in ICTA 1988 s 249 only applies where an *individual* is beneficially entitled to the shares, or when the shares are issued to personal representatives or trustees of discretionary trusts – see Example 57 explanatory note 6). This means that the whole of their value will be reflected in a capital gain on disposal, with no cost or indexation allowance.

The position of life interest trusts is not clear, and the offers by many companies some years ago of enhanced scrip options led to particular problems for such trusts. The Revenue issued a Statement of Practice (SP 4/94) giving their views. They consider that it is up to the trustees, taking into account trust law and the position of the particular trust, to decide whether the scrip shares constitute capital or income. They will not seek to challenge what the trustees have done if they have treated the scrip dividend in one of the following ways:

(a)   The scrip dividend belongs to the income beneficiary;

(b)   The scrip dividend belongs to the trust capital;

(c)   The scrip dividend is added to capital, but the income beneficiary is compensated for the loss of the cash dividend he would have had.

The effect of alternative (a) would be that the trustees would be treated as holding the shares as bare trustees, the beneficiary thus being treated as having acquired the shares directly. Under alternatives (b) and (c) the treatment would be the same as for a corporate shareholder, ie there would be no income tax implications and the shares would be treated as acquired at nil cost for capital gains tax. Different provisions apply to Scottish life interest trusts.

Some companies have replaced scrip dividend options with dividend reinvestment plans (DRIPs), under which shareholders may use their dividends to acquire shares bought on the stock market by the company on their behalf. Such schemes avoid the reduction in value of existing shares caused by issuing scrip dividend shares. Shareholders taking DRIPs have higher costs than for scrip dividends, because they have to pay brokers' fees and stamp duty reserve tax. Since the abolition of the repayable tax credit in April 1999, and the treatment of scrip dividend options as market purchases from April 1998, DRIPs are now taxed in exactly the same way as scrip dividend options (higher rate income tax on the cash dividend forgone, and a purchase of shares for CGT at the same amount).

Part sale of rights

16.   Part (5) of the example illustrates the treatment of a rights issue where the shareholder sells some of the rights nil paid and takes up the balance. The value of the unsold holding at the time of the sale includes the 'nil paid' value of the rights retained as well as the ex rights value of the existing shares.

17.   Rights shares are sometimes issued partly paid. In that event, the unpaid amount is added both to the sale proceeds when the shares are sold and to the cost (s 128). The unpaid amount is indexed from the date of acquisition of the rights shares unless it is due more than 12 months later, in which case it is indexed from the payment date (s 113). If therefore partly paid shares are sold more than 12 months before the balance is due, the balance would not qualify for indexation allowance even though it is included in the allowable expenditure. Indexation allowance is not available on rights shares acquired by non-corporate shareholders after 5 April 1998.

Question

(1) On 1 May 1981 Larkin purchased 6,000 ordinary shares in Maine plc at a price of £2 each. On 1 November 1981 there was a scrip issue of 1 for 2. The market value of the shares at 31 March 1982 was £1.30 each, giving £11,700.

On 1 March 2004 there was an offer of £0.50 cash plus two ordinary shares of Street plc for each Maine plc share held.

The offer was accepted and following acceptance Street plc's shares were quoted at £2.50 each.

Calculate the chargeable gain, and show the position if Larkin then disposes of the Street plc holding in December 2009 for £49,500.

(2) Pamela bought 2,000 shares in Fielding plc for £3,300 in February 1984. In November 1986 Fielding plc made a rights issue of 1 preference share for every 10 ordinary shares held, at £1.20 each. Pamela took up her rights in full. The opening market values on the first day of dealing ex rights were £2 for the ordinary shares and £1.40 for the preference shares. The ordinary shares were sold for £8,000 in September 2009.

Calculate the capital gain or allowable loss on the disposal of the ordinary shares.

(3) Victoria owned 20,000 shares in Forum Follies plc which she purchased in May 1998 for £50,000. In November 2006 Exciting Enterprises plc acquired all the share capital of Forum Follies plc. Under the terms of the takeover shareholders in Forum Follies received 3 ordinary shares and 1 preference share in Exciting Enterprises plc plus £1 cash for every 2 shares previously held in Forum Follies plc. Immediately after the takeover the ordinary shares in Exciting Enterprises were quoted at £3 each and the preference shares at £1.50 each. Victoria then sold the preference shares, receiving £15,000, in June 2009.

Calculate Victoria's gains for 2006/07 and 2009/10.

(4) On 31 March 2002, Neville bought 10,000 ordinary shares in Bateman plc at a cost of 310p per share. On 10 January 2004 a demerger took place in which shareholders received 1 Newbee plc ordinary share for each Bateman plc share. First day prices were Bateman plc ordinary 630p, Newbee plc ordinary 625p. On 15 June 2009 Neville sold his Newbee plc shares for £65,000. He retained his holding of Bateman plc shares.

Show the treatment of the demerger and of the sale of the Newbee plc shares.

(5) Michael Stewart received £250,000 on 10 July 2009 from Big plc when that company repaid all its issued 9% loan stock at par. Mr Stewart had received the loan stock (which is a qualifying corporate bond) in June 1987 in exchange for his 100,000 shares of £1 each in Small Ltd when Big plc acquired Small Ltd. Mr Stewart had acquired his shares in Small Ltd for £125,000 in November 1983. The shares were worth £250,000 in June 1987.

Show Mr Stewart's tax position at the time of the takeover and at the time of the repayment of the loan stock.

(6) Alex acquired shares in his employer's company (a quoted trading company) as follows:

		Number of shares	£
June 1998	Allocation from approved profit sharing scheme (APSS)	800	3,200
June 1999	Allocation from APSS	750	3,600
June 2000	Allocation from APSS	650	4,000
August 2000	Exercised share options	1,000	4,100
June 2001	Allocation from APSS	560	5,000
June 2002	Allocation from new approved Share Incentive Plan (SIP)	500	5,200
June 2003	Allocation from SIP	400	6,000
June 2004	Allocation from SIP	500	5,000
August 2004	Exercised share options	1,500	9,000
June 2005	Allocation from SIP	450	4,500
June 2006	Allocation from SIP	550	5,500
June 2007	Allocation from SIP	600	7,000
		8,260	

The company's approved profit sharing scheme released each allocation of shares to Alex three years after the allocation date. The value shown is the market value on each allocation date. The SIP shares will be restricted for five years.

The company's SAYE-related share option scheme enabled Alex to buy shares in 2000 and 2003 at the prices shown. The values of the shares on the exercise dates were £6,200 in 2000 and £25,000 in 2003.

On 31 December 2007, Alex transferred 1,500 shares to his civil partner, Chris, and on 1 January 2010 they each sold 1,500 shares for their full market value of £22,500.

Set out the capital gains tax position of Alex and Chris (who does not work for the company).

(7)   In what circumstances will an investment by an individual constitute a 'qualifying corporate bond'?

The following retail price indices may be used:

Nov 83 86.67; Apr 85 94.78; June 87 101.9

Answer

(1)   Larkin – takeover (see explanatory note 1)

Maine plc

		£
6,000	shares purchased 1981 @ £2	12,000
3,000	scrip issue 1 for 2 in 1981	–
9,000		12,000

Takeover by Street plc March 2004

	£
18,000 Street plc shares (2 for 1) @ £2.50	45,000
Cash (50p per share for 9,000 shares)	4,500
Total value received	49,500

Since the cash of £4,500 exceeds £3,000 and also exceeds 5% of the total value received (£2,475) it is likely to be treated as a part disposal as follows:

		Using cost £	Using 31.3.82 value £
Proceeds March 2004		4,500	4,500
Cost	$\dfrac{4,500}{49,500} \times 12,000$	1,091	
31.3.82 value	$\dfrac{4,500}{49,500} \times 11,700$		1,064
		3,409	3,436
Indexation allowance to April 1998 on cost (being higher than 31.3.82 value) £1,091 × 104.7%		1,142	1,142
		2,267	2,294
Chargeable gain in 2003/04 is the lower of the two (eligible for 20% taper relief unless reduced by losses)			£2,267

	£
Sale of Street plc shares December 2009	
Sale proceeds	49,500
Use of 1982 value obligatory post 5/4/08	
31.3.82 value (11,700 – 1,064 allowed on takeover by Street plc	10,636
Chargeable gain in 2009/10	38,864

(2)   **Pamela and Fielding plc – rights shares of a different class**

Where rights shares of a different class are acquired, the respective pool values are then split according to the ex rights values of the different classes of shares on the first day that prices are quoted, as follows:

The respective values of the shares ex rights are:

10 ordinary shares @ £2	20.00
1 preference share @ £1.40	1.40
	£21.40

The pool values are therefore split in those proportions, ie .93458 to the ordinary shares and .06542 to the preference shares. The treatment of the transactions is as follows:

Fielding plc	Ord shares	Pool value £
Feb 1984	2,000	3,300
Nov 86		
Rights 1:10	200	240
	2,200	3,540
Exclude re pref .06542	(200)	(232)
Leaving re ord .93458	2,000	3,308
Sold September 2009	(2,000)	
Re sale		(3,308)
Sale proceeds September 2009		8,000
Cost		(3,308)
Chargeable gain 2009/10		£4,692

Fielding plc	Pref shares	Pool value £
At Nov 86	200	232

(3)   **Victoria: takeover – gain on Forum Follies shares 2006/07**

Value received on takeover by Exciting Enterprises plc is:

Ordinary shares 30,000 @ £3	90,000
Preference shares 10,000 @ £1.50	15,000
Cash	10,000
	£115,000

Since the cash of £10,000 exceeds 5% of £115,000 (£5,750), it is likely to be treated as a part disposal of the holding.

The holding's base cost of £50,000 is split 90:15:10 as follows:

Ordinary shares	39,130
Preference shares	6,522
Cash	4,348
	£50,000

The new shares stand in the shoes of the old as follows:

Forum Follies plc		*Shares*	*Cost* £
May 1998 Bought		20,000	50,000
Nov 2006 takeover			
Cost of part disposal (cash)			(4,348)
Balance to Exciting Enterprises holdings:			45,652
Being: Ordinary			39,130
Preference			6,522
			45,652

Exciting Enterprises ord	*Shares*	*Base cost* £
November 2006 from Forum Follies	30,000	39,130

Exciting Enterprises pref		*Shares*	*Base cost* £
November 2006 from Forum Follies		10,000	6,522
The cash treated as a part disposal gives a chargeable gain (eligible for 30% taper relief) of (10,000 – 4,348) =			£5,652

2009/10	
Proceeds	15,000
Base cost	(6,522)
Gain	8,478

(4)   **Neville – demerger of Bateman plc and Newbee plc**

Subject to some special rules for trusts (see explanatory note 3), the demerger is treated in a similar way to a scrip issue of a different class, and since there is no cash element there is no indexation uplift at the time of the demerger. The value of the holding is split according to first day prices, as follows:

$$\text{Bateman plc} \frac{630}{1,255} = .501992$$

$$\text{Newbee plc} \frac{625}{1,255} = .498008$$

Original cost was 310p. Therefore respective base costs following demerger are:

Bateman plc 310p ×.501992 = 155.62p

Newbee plc 310p ×.498008 = 154.38p

Neville's tax position is as follows:

		Shares	*Base cost* £
At 31.3.02		10,000	31,000
10.1.04 To Newbee plc	(.498008)		(15,438)
Bateman plc cf	(.501992)	10,000	15,562
Pre-1982 pool Newbee plc		*Shares*	*Base cost* £
10.1.04 From Bateman plc demerger		10,000	15,438

June 2009 sold	(10,000)	
Applicable to sale		(15,438)
Sale proceeds		65,000
Cost		15,438
Gain		49,562

(5) **Michael Stewart – Tax position in relation to Big plc loan stock received on takeover**

Position at time of takeover

Deemed proceeds, being value of Small Ltd shares June 1987 (see explanatory note 4)		250,000
Cost of shares November 1983	125,000	
Indexation allowance to April 1985 to establish post-1982 pool:		

$$\frac{94.78-86.67}{86.67} = 9.4\%$$

	11,750	
	136,750	
Indexation allowance to June 1987		

$$136{,}750 \times \frac{101.9-94.78}{94.78}$$

	10,273	147,023
Gain held over until disposal of loan stock		£102,977

On the repayment of the loan stock on 10 July 2009 the held over gain is chargeable, so that there is a chargeable gain in 2009/10 of £102,977. Even though the gain is treated as realised in 2009/10 it was calculated on the basis of the pre-2008/09 rules and thus takes into account indexation allowance.

(6) **Alex and Chris**

Shares held within an employee share scheme trust are not identified with 'unrestricted' shares (TCGA 1992 s 104(4)). The allocations in June 2003, 2004, 2005, 2006 and 2007 are therefore not identified with the disposal on 31 December 2007. The shares which have been released from the APSS are treated as acquired on the allocation date for their market value; shares acquired under an approved option scheme are treated as acquired on the date the option is exercised for the amount paid for them.

Alex's holding on 31 December 2007 is therefore:

	Number of shares	Cost £
June 1998	800	3,200
June 1999	750	3,600
June 2000	650	4,000
August 2000	1,000	4,100
June 2001	560	5,000
June 2002	500	5,200
August 2004	1,500	9,000

Transfer to Chris 31 December 2007

For identification purposes, the transfer to Chris is treated as any other disposal. He therefore acquires the latest shares acquired by Alex, ie the August 2004 shares.

Disposals 1 January 2010

		£
Chris's gain is:	Proceeds	22,500
	Cost	9,000
	Gain	13,500

Alex's own gain is based on the pool of shares created on 6 April 2008.

	Number of shares	Cost £
June 1998	800	3,200
June 1999	750	3,600
June 2000	650	4,000
August 2000	1,000	4,100
June 2001	560	5,000
June 2002	500	5,200
June 2003	400	6,000
Pool created on 6 April 2008	4,660	£31,100

The gain is calculated as follows:

Proceeds	22,500
Less: cost	
1,500/4,660 × £31,100	(10,011)
	£12,489

(7) **Qualifying corporate bonds**

Qualifying corporate bonds (QCBs) are defined in TCGA 1992 s 117 as sterling loan stock purchased or issued on commercial terms after 13 March 1984, including bonds that are convertible into other qualifying corporate bonds but excluding bonds that are convertible into shares or other kinds of securities and securities linked to a share index. The interest bearing stocks that are outside the definition, therefore, are those denominated in a foreign currency, those that are convertible into shares or linked to a share index, and non-commercial loans. Corporate bonds purchased before 14 March 1984 are also outside the definition.

QCBs are exempt from the charge to CGT. Profits on some QCBs (relevant discounted securities) are chargeable to income tax; on most other QCBs, an income tax accrued income scheme charge has to be calculated on disposal.

A loan stock which is a 'debt on a security' and which is not a QCB is a chargeable asset for CGT, and will give rise to gains and losses in the normal way. A loan stock which is a 'simple debt' may not be chargeable to CGT. Various points on non-exempt loan stocks are set out in explanatory notes 11 and 12.

Explanatory Notes

References in these notes are to TCGA 1992 unless otherwise stated.

Takeovers

1.   Where shares or debentures in a new company are received for shares or debentures held in a company which has been taken over, the takeover is treated as if the two companies were the same company and the exchange were a reorganisation of its capital (TCGA 1992 s 135) (known as 'paper for paper' treatment). Any cash received is therefore treated as a capital distribution as explained in Example 79 explanatory note 14. The part disposal element in Larkin's case in part (1) of this example is accordingly £4,500 and the gain is calculated by reference to the ratio that the cash bears to the cash plus market value of the shares received in exchange for the original shares (TCGA 1992 s 129). Since the cash is more than £3,000 and more than 5% of the value received, it is not 'small' and is not therefore treated as reducing the base cost of the holding, although HMRC have indicated that they will negotiate if the taxpayer considers that a larger receipt should be treated as 'small' in the circumstances.

See Example 75 explanatory notes 8–10 for consideration of 'earn-out' elements in a paper-for-paper takeover.

See part (5) of the example for the position where part of a takeover package takes the form of qualifying corporate bonds and see explanatory note 14 below for further comments.

Reorganisations: rights and scrip shares of a different class

2.   The treatment of rights shares of a different class from the existing shares is shown in part (2) of the example. An indexation uplift is made to the holding before the cost of the rights is added in (but not after April 1998 for non-corporate shareholders), and, provided that there was an ultimate disposal before 6 April 2008, the unindexed and indexed figures were then split between the different classes of shares according to the market values on the first day that prices are quoted following the issue (TCGA 1992 s 130).

Similar treatment applies where different classes of shares are received as a result of a takeover, as illustrated in part (3) of the example.

For a scrip issue of a different class the treatment is the same as for a rights issue, except that no indexation uplift is made because no additional expenditure is incurred.

Demergers

3.   Demergers that are 'exempt distributions' normally do not have either income tax or capital gains tax consequences for the shareholders, although there may be a taper relief problem in some circumstances (see Example 68). The capital gains tax treatment is shown in part (4) of the example. Effectively the demerger is treated like a scrip issue of a different class of shares, the unindexed and indexed values of the shares being split between the demerged holdings according to market values on the first day that prices are quoted after the demerger.

Demergers can cause problems for trusts. In relation to the demerger of ICI and Zeneca, it was held in the case of *Sinclair v Lee* (1993) that the demerger represented a capitalisation by ICI of part of its distributable profits and thus the Zeneca shares were a capital distribution in the hands of the trustees.

This is not necessarily the case for all demergers. Where shares in a 75% subsidiary are distributed direct to the shareholders (a 'direct demerger'), the HMRC view is that although the shares are exempt from income tax under the 'exempt distribution' rules, they are nonetheless income of the trust, because under company law they are a dividend paid out of accumulated profits. The treatment then differs according to whether the trust is a discretionary trust or a life interest trust (see Revenue's Tax Bulletin October 1994). The tax consequences for trusts of the different types of demerger are dealt with in the companion to this volume, Tolley's Taxwise II 2009/10, at Example 50.

Reorganisations: qualifying corporate bonds

4.   For details of the rules relating to QCBs, see notes 8 to 10. Sometimes on a reorganisation of share capital or on a takeover, QCBs may be converted into, or exchanged for, shares or vice versa. If QCBs are exchanged for shares, the normal reorganisation provisions dealt with in note 1 above do not apply, and the shares are deemed to be acquired at their market value at the date of the exchange. If shares are exchanged for QCBs, the shares are treated as disposed of for their market value immediately *before* the exchange, the gain or loss at that date is calculated and is then 'frozen' until the QCBs (or part thereof) are disposed of, when the frozen gain or loss crystallises accordingly, as illustrated in part (5) of the example (TCGA 1992 s 116). The same applies where a security changes its status from non-qualifying to qualifying corporate bond. The frozen gain or loss does not crystallise on a transfer between spouses, or intra-group (see also Example 62 part A), but it is 'inherited' by the person acquiring the bonds, so that it will crystallise on disposal by that person. Where a frozen gain crystallises, it is possible for an individual to defer it again by subscribing for shares in a qualifying unquoted trading company under the enterprise investment scheme provisions (see Example 93).

For companies, under the rules for 'loan relationships', any gain or loss arising on the disposal of QCBs in exchange for shares on or after 1 April 1996 is brought into account in calculating income. Where shares are exchanged for QCBs, either before or after 1 April 1996, the 'frozen gain or loss' treatment applies, with the frozen gain or loss on the shares being brought in as a *capital* gain or loss when the bonds are disposed of (s 116(16)).

If the QCBs fall in value, the effect of the 'frozen gain' treatment may be that the taxpayer is charged on a gain even though in fact he has made a loss. This problem can be overcome by giving the bonds to a charity. The frozen gain will not then crystallise, nor are there any tax consequences for the charity when it disposes of the bonds (TCGA 1992 s 257, Revenue Interpretation 23).

If a frozen gain on QCBs has not crystallised by the time the taxpayer dies, the gain escapes tax. It is not chargeable on the personal representatives, nor on any beneficiary. If, however, there is a frozen gain accruing to the personal representatives themselves, the gain crystallises on disposal (but not on transfer to a beneficiary, the crystallisation in those circumstances being further deferred until the beneficiary disposes of the loan stock).

Shares acquired under HMRC approved schemes

5.   Unless they are subject to any special restrictions, shares acquired under approved SAYE and discretionary share option schemes are treated in the same way as other acquisitions. They are regarded as acquired on the date the option is exercised for the amount paid for them, plus the amount, if any, paid for the option. The amounts paid attract indexation allowance from the date of payment, but not after April 1998.

6.   Shares acquired under an approved profit sharing scheme (APSS) or approved share incentive plan (SIP) are in each case regarded as being of a different class from other shares held by the employee while they are retained by the trustees (s 104(4)). APSS shares are treated as acquired by the employee at market value at the date they are allocated to him and indexed from that date (until April 1998). After the three year period of retention, the shares are no longer kept separate from the employee's other holdings and are either added to pre-6 April 1998 holdings or treated as free-standing acquisitions depending on the date they were allocated to the employee, the acquisition value being cost plus any available indexation allowance. They are effectively inserted into the acquisitions record retrospectively, even though disposals may have already occurred which would have been identified with them if they had not been kept separate. SIP shares are treated as acquired

at market value on the date they are withdrawn from the plan (as long as they have remained within it for at least five years), so if they are disposed of immediately after withdrawal no capital gains tax arises.

7. The rules for matching disposals of shares with acquisitions are dealt with in Example 79 explanatory note 6. Part (6) of this example illustrate the application of the rules to disposals between married couples and civil partners, and also the identification rules for shares acquired under employee share schemes. Example 79 explanatory note 7 indicates that all acquisitions of shares of the same class in the same company on one day are normally treated as being a single asset. This rule has been varied for shares acquired by employees on or after 6 April 2002 under an approved share option scheme (TCGA 1992 ss 105A and 105B) (see Example 85 parts (1), (2) and (6) for details of such schemes). Where some of the same day acquisitions are from an approved share option scheme they may have a lower capital gains cost than the other acquisitions, which would reduce the average cost of any shares disposed of, and if there was a part disposal of the holding the capital gain would be correspondingly higher. In respect of scheme shares acquired on or after 6 April 2002 on the same day as other shares, the taxpayer may make a written election, on or before 31 January in the next but one tax year after the tax year in which he first makes a disposal of any of the same day acquisitions (eg by 31 January 2012 in respect of a disposal in 2009/10), to have the scheme shares and the other shares treated as two separate assets, the non-scheme shares being treated as disposed of first. The effect of the election could be to reduce immediate gains on a part disposal, although the remaining shares would have a lower capital gains tax cost. For detailed notes on the various share schemes see Example 85.

Qualifying corporate bonds

8. Most interest bearing stocks issued by UK companies come within the definition of QCBs. Before FA 1996, both individual and company investors were exempt from tax on gains (and could not normally claim relief for losses) on QCBs and government stocks. For corporate investors, then subject to one or two special provisions, all profits and gains on a company's 'loan relationships' are brought into account along with interest payable and interest receivable in arriving at the company's income profits. For the detailed provisions see Example 63. The *capital gains* exemption still applies and is extended as far as companies are concerned to any securities that would previously have been outside the definition of qualifying corporate bond, subject to what is said below (s 117(A1)).

9. A company's gains and losses on the disposal of convertible securities and securities linked to a share index are still dealt with under the capital gains rules (such securities being outside the definition of qualifying corporate bond and therefore within the capital gains charge).

    A company's holdings of 3½% Funding Stock 1999/2004 and 5½% Treasury Stock 2008/12 are still covered by the capital gains exemption, although interest on the stocks is within the loan relationships rules (FA 1996 s 96).

10. The exemption from CGT for investors other than companies still applies, so that there are neither chargeable gains nor allowable losses on government securities and QCBs.

Non-exempt loan stock

11. Where interest bearing stocks were not exempt as QCBs, the post-1982 pooling provisions did not apply, and each acquisition on or after 6 April 1982 was treated as a separate asset (s 104). If a rebasing election had been made to treat all assets owned on 31 March 1982 as acquired at the market value on that date, all securities of the same class in the same company owned on that date could be regarded as a single asset. Even if the rebasing election had not been made, the same treatment applied for quoted securities if an election was made for acquisitions before 6 April 1965 to be pooled with later acquisitions (s 109). If there has been neither a rebasing election nor an election to pool pre-6 April 1965 quoted securities, those securities are treated as separate assets.

Before FA 1998, disposals were not matched with acquisitions according to the rules for shares. They were matched with acquisitions in the following order (s 108), subject to provisions for matching securities bought for delivery on or before the delivery date for the disposal:

- those acquired in the previous 12 months on a first in first out basis

- earlier acquisitions since 5.4.82, on a last in first out basis

- the pool of acquisitions from 6.4.65 to 5.4.82

- non-pooled pre 6.4.65 acquisitions, last in first out.

No indexation allowance was available if the securities were disposed of within the nine days after the date they were acquired (s 54(2)).

12. These matching rules still apply for companies in respect of those securities that remain within the capital gains charge. Where securities are dealt with under the loan relationships provisions, there are no special rules for matching disposals with acquisitions and any consistent basis adopted for accounting purposes is acceptable. For individuals the matching rules for disposals of non-exempt loan stock after 5 April 1998 are the same as those for shares.

An instance where the rules for non-exempt loan stock apply is on the disposal of stock bought before 14 March 1984. It is not possible to circumvent the rules by making a no gain no loss transfer after 13 March 1984, for example from husband to wife.

Unusual loan stocks

13. Increasingly, corporate financiers are designing unfamiliar financial instruments with which to carry out transactions. The terms of the instrument need to be compared carefully with the legislation to determine the correct tax treatment.

For example, a 'special stock unit' with a set redemption date and premium was issued as part of the Royal Bank of Scotland takeover of National Westminster Bank. This was treated as a share; it was chargeable if the shareholder sold it, but the premium on redemption would be charged to income tax as a dividend.

An index-linked government stock is exempt from CGT, but an index-linked stock issued by a company is an 'excluded indexed security' rather than a 'relevant discounted security'. It is therefore chargeable to capital gains tax rather than to income tax.

Some building societies have issued permanent interest bearing shares (PIBS), which are treated as QCBs for the purposes of capital gains tax, and are therefore exempt in the hands of an individual or trustee. For corporation tax purposes, since PIBS are shares, they were previously outside the 'loan relationships' rules (except in relation to interest received), so a gain or loss on disposal was within the scope of corporation tax on gains (s 117(A1), (4) and (5)). For accounting periods beginning on or after 1 October 2002, the loan relationships definition of shares excludes building society shares (FA 1996 s 103 as amended by FA 2002), so PIBS are wholly within the loan relationship rules from that date and the capital gains rules do not apply (see Example 63 explanatory note 1).

14. Because of the different treatment of takeovers where QCBs and non-QCBs are received in exchange for shares, close attention has to be paid to the following choice:

- exchange shares for QCBs: calculate the gain at the date of exchange, 'freezing' it until the QCB is disposed of, and fixing the taper relief at that date; or

- exchange shares for non-QCBs: no disposal at the date of exchange; a gain is only calculated when the bonds are disposed of, and the whole ownership period counts for taper relief.

The non-QCB route is preferable if the loan stocks become worthless, because the gain is never charged and the loss is allowable.

As can be seen in the case of *Weston v Garnett (Inspector of Taxes)* [2005] EWCA Civ 742, it is important that the loan note is really a QCB. In this case the loan notes were found to be non-QCBs as they carried the right (albeit indirect) to conversion into shares.

Question

(1)   Show the capital gains position in the following instances:

(a)   Miss Fielding sold a freehold house in Southampton on 28 March 2010 for net proceeds of £752,220. She had bought the house for £15,000 on 1 October 1970 and immediately occupied it as her sole residence; between 1 October 1972 and 1 April 1986 the house was let while she was employed in Suffolk, where she lived in rented accommodation. She resumed occupation of the house on 1 April 1986 but moved to a different permanent residence on 27 March 1988, the house then being let until the date of sale. The value of the house at 31 March 1982 was £70,000.

(b)   Galsworthy bought a freehold house on 1 April 1984 for £27,000 including expenses of purchase. He lived in the house until 30 September 2003 when he took a job as a caretaker and had to live on his employer's premises. He therefore let the house until he sold it on 30 June 2009 for £352,100 after deducting expenses of sale, his employer moving him to a branch in another part of the country so that he could not resume residence.

(c)   On 1 January 1971 Hardy purchased for £4,000 a flat which he used as his only residence. On 30 June 1975 he purchased a house which became his main residence and from that date his widowed mother occupied the flat free of any consideration. His mother vacated the flat on 31 March 1986 and he let it continuously at a commercial rent from that date until he sold it for £240,000 on 30 September 2009. The value on 31 March 1982 was considered to be £26,000.

(d)   On 30 June 2009 Compton sold a freehold house in Hampshire for net proceeds of £973,260. He had bought the house for £20,800 on 1 October 1974 and the history of his ownership is summarised below:

1.10.74	Occupied house as sole residence.
1.04.80	House let on taking up employment abroad. He returned to England on 1 January 1983, but started his own business in Liverpool and lived in rented accommodation, continuing to let his own house.
1.07.87	Resumed occupation of own house on retiring from business.
1.01.89	Moved to Sussex and purchased a house which became his main residence from this date, the Hampshire house being let until it was sold.

The market value of the Hampshire house was £90,000 on 31 March 1982.

(e)   Harold married Georgina on 6 April 1996. Both had been married before, and both owned houses. Harold had bought his house in April 1984, and lived in it with his first wife, who died in 1991. Georgina and her first husband bought their house in June 1988, but divorced in 1996, after the husband had moved out in January 1993. The house was subject to an order along the lines of *Mesher v Mesher*, which provided that it would be held on trust for Georgina and her former husband until their children reached the age of 18 (in October 2009), when it would be sold, and the proceeds divided equally.

Harold moved into Georgina's house in April 1996, and they have lived there ever since, during which time Harold's own house has been let out. In October 2009, they sold both houses, and bought a third. The gain on Harold's house was £400,000; the gain on Georgina's house was £200,000, of which her share was £100,000. Harold had kept his own house in his own name.

(f)   Stanley's father died in 1990, and Stanley decided to provide a home for his mother. He bought a house for £160,000 and placed it into a trust in which his mother had a life interest, with reversion to Stanley on her death. In 1998, the trustees sold the first house for £260,000, and bought another for the same sum. In 2009, Stanley's mother died, when the second house was worth £440,000. It will be sold as soon as possible and the proceeds returned to Stanley.

(g)   Gordon sold his house for £500,000 on 30 September 2009. He bought it for £220,000 in April 2000. He has always used 20% of his house exclusively for business purposes, and has made claims for income tax relief for that proportion of the running costs (including council tax and mortgage interest). Calculate the chargeable capital gain on disposal.

(h)   On 31 January 2003, James transferred a house to the trustees of a discretionary trust and claimed to hold over the gain of £200,000 that would otherwise accrue. The beneficiaries of the trust are his children, Gemma and Sue. The terms of the settlement permit the trustees to allow certain persons to occupy the house. The trustees allow Gemma to do so, and she occupies the house as her only residence on 31 January 2003.

On 31 August 2009, Gemma vacates the house. The trustees then sell the property on 30 September 2009 giving rise to a gain (including the held over gain) of £250,000. Calculate the trustees' entitlement to private residence relief.

(i)   Fiona sells her main residence at a gain of £400,000 in July 2009. It has been lived in by Fiona throughout her period of ownership as her only or main residence but she also teaches typing and administrative skills to students who lodge in the property whilst undergoing tuition. It has been agreed that 30% of the property has been used for teaching, 7.5% has been used as the students' lodgings and 62.5% has been used as the residence of the owner. Calculate the chargeable gain, ignoring any entrepreneur's relief that may be due.

(2)   In addition to his London house (which he has owned and occupied since 1992) Nash has just bought a house in the country. Nash has stated that it is his intention in approximately five years to give his London house to his nephew and then live solely in his new house in the country. He now divides his time equally between the two houses and expects this arrangement to continue until he gives his London house to his nephew. The London house is currently worth about 20% more than he paid for it. Nash has a substantial part of his income charged at 40% and regularly makes gains in excess of the annual exempt limit. Advise Nash what he should do.

Answer

(1)

(a) **Miss Fielding**

Property was occupied from 31.3.82 as follows:

31.3.82–31.3.86	4	yrs	Let while working away (resident before and after)
1.4.86–27.3.88	2	yrs	Owner occupied
28.3.88–28.3.10	22	yrs	Let up to sale
	28	yrs	

Exempt proportion:

Owner occupation	2	yrs
Allowable period of absence while working elsewhere in UK	4	yrs
Last 3 yrs	3	yrs
	9	yrs

	£
Sale proceeds March 2010	752,220
31 March 1982 value	70,000
Gain	682,220
Less: exempt proportion 9/28	219,285
	462,935
Less: residential lettings exemption	
Lower of £40,000 and exempt gain of £219,285	(40,000)
Chargeable gain	422,935

(b) **Galsworthy** has no chargeable gain. Either actual (to September 2003) or deemed (3 years for place of work, last 3 years) owner occupation throughout. See explanatory note 4.

(c) **Hardy**

		£	£
Flat sale proceeds 30 September 2009			240,000
31 March 1982 value			26,000
			214,000
Less:	Exempt re dependent relative occupation		
	(31.3.82 to 31.3.86) 4/27.5 × 214,000	31,127	
	Exempt re last three years' ownership		
	3/27.5 × 214,000	23,345	
	Residential lettings exemption	40,000	94,472
Chargeable gain			119,528

The exemption for the let period is the smaller of £40,000 and the amount exempt through *qualifying* occupation. It was previously asserted by HMRC that occupation by a dependent relative did not qualify. However, this view was challenged and HMRC revised its guidance as stated at paragraph CG64718 of their Capital Gains Tax Manual.

(d) **Compton**

Property was occupied from 31.3.82 as follows:

	Period of ownership on and after 31.3.82		Note	Actual or deemed owner occupation		Chargeable period	
	Yrs	Mths		Yrs	Mths	Yrs	Mths
31.3.82–1.1.83		9	(i)		9		
1.1.83–1.7.87	4	6	(ii)	4	6		
1.7.87–1.1.89	1	6	(iii)	1	6		
1.1.89–30.6.09	20	6	(iv)	3		17	6
	25	25		8	21	17	6
Total	27	3		9	9	17	6

(i)   Employed abroad, house let, resident before and after.

(ii)   Working away from home, house let, resident before and after, therefore covered for first four years because of absence through working away in UK and for remaining 6 months as part of period of up to 3 years for any reason.

(iii)   Owner occupied.

(iv)   Let prior to sale (partly covered by exemption for last three years of ownership).

$$\text{Chargeable proportion of gain is therefore} \frac{17.5 \text{ years}}{27.25 \text{ years}}$$

The gain using 31.3.82 value is:

	£
Net sale proceeds – 30 June 2009	973,260
31 March 1982 value	90,000
Gain	£883,260
Chargeable proportion of gain 17½/27¼ × £883,260	567,231
Residential lettings exemption is lower of £40,000 and amount equal to gain exempt through owner occupation	
	(40,000)
Chargeable gain	£527,231

(e)   **Harold and Georgina**

Harold's house has been his only or main residence at some point during his ownership. While he is married to Georgina, only one of the two houses can be the exempt residence, and his house has been let out since the marriage; accordingly, that house is chargeable. However, the last three years of ownership qualify for exemption, and the additional lettings relief is also available. The chargeable gain on Howard's house is therefore:

Actual occupation: 12 years; deemed occupation: 3 years; total ownership: 25.5 years

	£
Chargeable gain: 10.5/25.5 × £400,000	164,706
Lettings exemption: lowest of £164,760; £235,294; £40,000	40,000
Taxable gain 2009/10	124,706

The Mesher order results in a transfer into trust. Any gain on this transfer is normally covered by TCGA 1992 s 225. The sale of Georgina's house is therefore exempt from CGT, because the house has been occupied throughout as the only or main residence by a beneficiary of the trust

(Georgina and the children) and there has been no previous transfer subject to gift relief. The shares of the proceeds paid out to both Georgina and her former husband are exempt from CGT.

(f) **Stanley**

The sale in 1998 is exempt under TCGA 1992 s 225, provided that a claim is made by the trustees. The trust is one in which the settlor retains an interest (as Stanley is entitled to the reversion), but this means only that Stanley is assessable on any gains that would normally be assessed on the trustees. As the trustees would not be assessed on a gain on the disposal of the house, neither is Stanley.

The reversion to settlor on the death of the life tenant is exempt from inheritance tax (IHTA 1984 s 54) (because her interest was created before 22 March 2006), so the return to his own estate does not create an inheritance tax charge for Stanley. However, TCGA 1992 s 73 provides that the normal 'uplift to probate value' does not apply on such a reversion to settlor, so the base cost of the second house to Stanley is the trustees' deemed cost of £260,000, not the current market value of £440,000. The gain is realised by Stanley. Therefore, subject to selling costs, a gain of £180,000 will be realised.

(g) **Gordon**

	£
Sale proceeds September 2009	500,000
Cost April 2000	(220,000)
Gain before private residence relief	280,000
Private residence relief: 80%	(224,000)
Chargeable Gain	£56,000

(h) **James**

Anti-avoidance legislation was introduced from 10 December 2003 to prevent exploitation of the interaction between private residence and hold-over relief to avoid CGT. Therefore because the trustees' allowable expenditure was reduced as a result of the claim to gift relief, they cannot cover the whole gain by private residence relief. But because the gift relief related to a transfer before 10 December 2003 the transitional rule applies.

31.1.03 to 9.12.03 = 313 days

31.1.03 to 30.9.09 = 2,435 days

Entitlement to private residence relief:

$313/2,435 \times 250,000 = \underline{32,136}$

Private residence relief is not available in respect of the 2,122 days from December 2003 to September 2009. The transitional rule specifically prevents any period on or after 10 December 2003 from qualifying for relief as part of the final three years' exemption.

(i) **Fiona**

	£	£
Net gain		400,000
Private residence relief at 62.5%		(250,000)
		150,000
Relief under s 223(4) limited to the lowest of		
Private residence relief	250,000	
£40,000	40,000	
Gain arising by reason of the letting (7.5%)	30,000	

	£	£
Section 223(4) relief		(30,000)
Chargeable gain (before any entrepreneur's relief that may be due)		£120,000

(2)

Nash needs to elect which of his two residences is his main residence qualifying for exemption from CGT. The election must be made within two years from the date of acquisition of the second property. The election can subsequently be varied, and any variation will take effect not earlier than two years before HMRC is notified that Nash wishes to vary the election.

The gift to the nephew of the London house will be treated for CGT as a sale at open market value. If Nash elects for the London house to remain as his exempt house for CGT, then no chargeable gain or allowable loss will arise when he disposes of it, but the intervening period will result in a chargeable gain or allowable loss on the country property when it is disposed of, for the part of the period of ownership for which it is not Nash's main residence for CGT (unless it is not disposed of in Nash's lifetime).

If Nash elects for his country property to be his main residence, then no chargeable gain or allowable loss will arise on its eventual disposal. As a result, a proportion of any eventual gain on the London house may become chargeable. The last three years of ownership will, however, always be counted as a qualifying period of residence, which will make the chargeable fraction quite small (perhaps 2/22).

Depending on the likely date of disposal of the country house and the probable gain, Nash might wish to elect for the London house to be his main residence for two further years (ie until three years before its likely sale) and then elect for the country house to be his main residence.

It is also worth ensuring that the country house is treated as Nash's main residence for some period in the period of ownership (as little as one day). This will ensure that the last three years of ownership will qualify for the exemption.

Explanatory Notes

More than one residence

1. References in this example are to TCGA 1992. The gain on the disposal of an individual's only or main residence is exempt from tax, wholly or in part. Where an individual has two or more residences he may *elect* which is to be his exempt residence for CGT and this need not be the residence which is in fact his main residence. (It must, however, be or have been his *residence*. An investment property in which he had never lived would not qualify.) If no election is made the matter is determined by the facts of the case. The right to make an election would revive if a taxpayer had a change of residence, or acquired a third residence, but the period covered by the election would only date from the time that the new or additional property was acquired if the time limit had previously expired. If householders realise losses rather than gains when selling properties, such losses are not allowable losses unless and to the extent that there is a non-exempt period of ownership.

    Following *Griffin v Craig-Harvey* (1993), it is generally taken to be the case that an initial election must be made within two years of a taxpayer acquiring a second residence. If this time limit is missed, no election may be made at all unless there is a subsequent change in the taxpayer's number of residences. Whilst it is therefore advisable for tax advisers to make protective elections within the two-year period, it has since been suggested that *Griffin v Craig-Harvey* was wrongly decided (see the *Personal Tax Planning Review*, 2005, 10(1), 27–38 and *Taxation*, 24 January 2008). If this view is correct it would mean that elections might be made at any time backdated (if necessary) by up to two years whether or not one was owned during the initial two-year period.

The provisions enabling a main residence election to be varied with retrospective effect for two years could be beneficial to someone who has had two residences for some years and plans to sell the one that is not the elected main residence. An election could be made for the property that is to be sold to be the main residence with effect from two years before the date HMRC was notified of the change. A further election could then be made one week after the first election reverting back to the original main residence, again with retrospective effect for two years. The effect would be to obtain the exemption for the last three years' ownership of the property that is being sold (see note 3), and possibly the extra lettings exemption as well, at the cost of only one chargeable week in respect of the original main residence. This is confirmed in the HMRC's Capital Gains Tax Manual.

Nash's gift to his nephew in part (2) of the example would be regarded as made at open market value, since it would not be an arm's length bargain (s 17). If the nephew had been a connected person, then under s 18 any loss arising could have only been set against a gain on a later transaction with the nephew, but a nephew is not within the definition of relative in s 286 (see Example 73 part (e)(i)).

An election is not required where someone owns a residence and has a second residence that he/she neither owns nor leases (eg accommodation with relatives, or a hotel room). A tenancy of a property would, however, need to be taken into account even if the right of occupation had no capital value (see Revenue's Tax Bulletin October 1994).

2.   For a married couple or civil partners living together, there can be only one main residence for both, and if they own two or more residences between them (either jointly or separately) the main residence election must be made by both (s 222(6)). If only one member of the couple is the property owner, only that person would make the election. If on marriage/registration of a civil partnership each owned a residence, the two year period for electing which was the main residence would start at the date of marriage/registration. No election is necessary in the case of Harold and Georgina in part (e) of the example, because Harold does not live in his house following his marriage. When one spouse/civil partner inherits the residence on the other's death, then although the survivor's acquisition value for capital gains is the market value at death, the period of ownership of the other (since 31 March 1982), and therefore any non-residence during that period, is taken into account to compute any chargeable gain on disposal by the survivor (s 222(7)).

Periods of non-residence

3.   Where there have been periods of non-residence then the non-resident fraction of the total period of ownership since 31 March 1982 is the chargeable part of the gain (or allowable part of the loss).

Where there is a delay of up to a year (extended in some circumstances to not more than two years) in taking up residence, because land has been bought on which a house is being built, or because of alterations or redecorations, or because of completing the arrangements to sell a previous property, the period of non-residence will count as a period of residence by Extra Statutory Concession D49, and the exemption on any other qualifying property during that period will not be affected.

Provided a property has been an individual's only or main residence at some time during his total period of ownership (whether before or after 31 March 1982), the last three years of ownership always count as a period of residence (s 223(1)). Certain other absences also count as residence, if preceded and followed (not necessarily immediately before and after) by a period of actual residence and providing relief is not being claimed for another main residence during the absence. These are (ss 222 and 223):

(a)   Up to three years for any reason

(b)   Any absence throughout which the individual is employed abroad

(c)   Up to four years during which the individual is prevented from living in the house because of the distance from his place of work or because his employer requires him to live elsewhere. 'Place of work' covers both employment and self-employment, hence the exemption for Compton in part (d) of the example covering four years of the period from 1.1.83 to 1.7.87 when he was working too far away to live in his own house.

By Extra Statutory Concession D4 absences under headings (b) and (c) do *not* require a later period of actual residence if an individual cannot resume residence because the terms of his *employment* require him to work elsewhere. The concession does not apply to an absence under (c) where the individual is self-employed, so a later period of actual residence is necessary for such an absence to qualify.

If someone is going to occupy rented accommodation while away, then the rented property would be treated as a residence (see note 1). HMRC would probably be prepared to accept a main residence election for the owned property, so that the rules for allowable periods of absence would apply.

Job-related accommodation

4.   If a person who lives in job-related accommodation (eg caretaker, like Galsworthy in part (b) of the example) owns a house that he intends in due course to occupy as his only or main residence, he is regarded as being in occupation of his house during the time he lives in the job-related accommodation (s 222(8)). This provision also applies to self-employed people living in job-related accommodation.

Galsworthy either lived in the property himself or lived in job-related accommodation throughout the period from 31 March 1982 to the date of sale. Providing he had intended to live in the house again after taking the caretaker's job, his period of non-residence would count wholly as a period of residence. Even if he had not intended to resume residence at some later date the period of non-residence would still have counted as residence, because it is covered by the allowance of the last three years of ownership plus up to four years of absence while required by one's employment to live elsewhere. (A later period of actual residence is not necessary for an employment-related absence –see note 3.)

Residence occupied by a dependent relative

5.   The exemption for owner occupied property extends to one residence occupied *rent free* by a dependent relative as his/her sole residence, but only where the relative occupied the property on or before 6 April 1988. The exemption is not available where a dependent relative first occupies a property on or after 6 April 1988. If there are periods of non-residence, the same rules apply as outlined in note 3. But if the property ceases to be the sole residence of the dependant, either before or after 6 April 1988, subsequent periods of residence on or after that date by that or any other relative do not qualify for relief (s 226).

The legislation defines a dependent relative but imposes no income restriction, so that the relative need not be financially dependent on the owner of the residence. By Extra Statutory Concession D20 HMRC do not regard payments of council tax by the relative or payments towards the upkeep of the property as breaching the 'rent free' requirement providing the owner is not left with a surplus over his outgoings.

Divorce and separation

6.   When spouses or civil partners separate, the matrimonial home ceases to be the main residence of the party who leaves it. His or her share of any calculated gain on a subsequent sale is therefore chargeable to the extent that it relates to the period of non-residence, subject to any available exemptions or reliefs. The last three years of ownership always count as a period of residence, even if a new qualifying residence has been acquired. If the property is disposed of more than three years after an individual leaves it, part of the calculated gain is assessable, but only in the proportion that the excess period over three years bears to the total period of ownership since 31 March 1982,

against which any available and annual exemption (currently £10,100 for 2009/10) may be used. There is an Extra Statutory Concession (D6) covering absences exceeding the final three-year period, but only where the property is eventually transferred to the spouse/civil partner remaining in it as part of the financial settlement, and an election for a new qualifying residence has not been made by the individual moving out in the meantime.

A better arrangement for CGT purposes is by using a Court Order and the rule for settlements, is illustrated in part (e). However, after 22 March 2006, such an arrangement can give rise to an inheritance tax charge.

Residential lettings exemption

7. There is a further relief for owner-occupiers who at any time during their period of ownership have let all or part of the property as residential accommodation (s 223(4)). The gain attributable to the letting is reduced by the lower of:

    (a) An amount equal to the part of the total gain that is exempt because of the owner occupation,

    (b) £40,000

    (c) The gain arising by reason of the letting.

         In a simple case, where the property has only been used as the only or main residence, or has been let as residential accommodation, then the gain remaining after deducting private residence relief will be the gain arising by reason of the letting. However, if for example there has been a part of the property used exclusively for the purpose of a trade, the gain remaining after deducting private residence relief will not only be due to the letting. In such a case, s 223(4) can only relieve part of the gain remaining after private residence relief has been deducted.

    The relief is illustrated in parts (a), (c), (d) , (e) and (i) of the example.

    This relief in relation to letting residential accommodation also applies where a residence is occupied under the terms of a settlement but not where a residence is occupied by a dependent relative. Hence in part (c) of the example the part of the gain attributable to the dependent relative's occupation is not taken into account in the calculation of the residential lettings relief.

    'Residential letting' is not defined in the legislation. HMRC took the view that the letting must have some degree of permanence, but they lost a case on the point in the Court of Appeal (*Owen v Elliott* (1990)), where it was decided that the exemption was available to the owners of a small private hotel who occupied the whole of the property during the winter months, with one or two guests, but moved to an annexe during the summer.

    The exemption can be claimed only if the property qualifies as the CGT exempt residence for at least part of the period of ownership, so it cannot be claimed on a property which, although the taxpayer lives in it sometimes, has never been his only or main residence for CGT. Subject to that, it can be claimed where all of the property has been let for part of the period of ownership, or part of the property has been let for all or part of the period of ownership.

Property acquired before 31 March 1982

8. Where the residence was acquired before 31 March 1982, it is only periods of residence and non-residence on and after that date that determine how much, if any, of the gain is chargeable (although the last three years' ownership is exempt in any event providing there has been owner occupation at any time during the full period of ownership). The period of non-residence after 31 March 1982 as a fraction of total ownership after that date is then the chargeable part of the gain, as shown in parts (a), (c) and (d) of the example.

Sale of land after sale of residence

9.   The private residence exemption includes land that is for 'occupation and enjoyment with the residence as its garden or grounds up to the permitted area' (s 222(1)(b)), the permitted area being (inclusive of the site of the house) up to half a hectare, which is approximately 1¼ acres, or such larger area as is appropriate to the size and character of the house. The exemption applies even if some of the land is sold separately. But the land must satisfy the conditions *at the time of disposal*, so that in *Varty v Lynes* (1976) it was held that land sold *after* the sale of the house did not qualify since it did not form part of the residence at that time.

Meaning of 'residence'

10.   There have been several cases on what constitutes a residence. In *Batey v Wakefield* (1981) a caretaker's bungalow physically separate from the main house was included within the exemption. In *Markey v Sanders* (1987) the court held that for a group of buildings to be treated as a single residence they must be capable of being regarded as a single building, so a large, separate staff bungalow some distance from the main house did not qualify. But in *Williams v Merrylees* (1987) a staff lodge even further away from the house than the *Markey v Sanders* bungalow was held to be part of a single entity and included within the private residence exemption. The High Court in the case of *Lewis v Rook* (1990) similarly held that a gardener's cottage some distance away from the house occupied by the elderly woman owner was part of the main residence, but this was overruled in the Court of Appeal in 1992. There are clearly very fine distinctions in some of these decisions, and the way in which questions of fact are presented to and decided by the Commissioners is very important. HMRC issued a statement in their Tax Bulletin of February 1992 indicating what they take into account in arriving at the exempt area of land with a dwelling house, and how they deal with buildings separate from the main house. They have made further comments in their Tax Bulletins of August 1994 and August 1995.

       In the case of *Longson v Baker* (2000) the taxpayer appeared to convince the inspector that an area of just over 1 hectare was 'reasonably required' for a person who bought a house for its stables and riding opportunities. However, his claim for 7½ hectares was rejected by the inspector, Special Commissioners and High Court. The High Court judge stated that 'reasonably required' was an objective test, and the taxpayer's subjective liking for horses was irrelevant. This suggests that the inspector may have been too generous in allowing more than the minimum.

11.   A different point was at issue in *Goodwin v Curtis*, in which the Court of Appeal decided in 1998 that a short period of occupation of a property while it was up for sale did not constitute residence, even though it was accepted that there was no trading motive (as to which see note 15). The Court held that the General Commissioners were entitled to conclude that the occupation did not have a sufficient degree of permanence to have the quality necessary for residence.

Part use for business

12.   Where part of a residence is used exclusively for business purposes, the provisions for exempting all or part of the gain relating to the only or main residence (including the exemption for the last three years of ownership) do not apply to the business proportion of the gain, but rollover relief is available on the business proportion if the property is replaced.

13.   An article in Taxation (7 August 2003 – Splitting up the home) argues that it may be possible to obtain the benefit of the last three years exemption if say the business ceases one year before the property is sold or if say a doctor was able to move his surgery to a different part of the property for the last six months before sale. This is on the basis that the last three years exemption applies in any case except where part has been used throughout for business purposes.

Relocation of employee

14.   Where an employee is relocated and sells his home either to his employer or to a relocation company, with a right to share in any profits when the employer or relocation company later sells the home,

then by Extra Statutory Concession D37, the employee is exempt from CGT on the later amount to the same extent as he was exempt on the original sale, providing the later sale occurs within three years. (Part of the original gain may have been chargeable because the home had not always been the main residence, or had been let, etc, in which case the same proportion of the later amount will be chargeable.) See Example 9 explanatory note 7 for the income tax position in relation to employee relocation.

Intention to resell at a profit

15. The CGT exemption does not apply if the residence was acquired with the intention of reselling at a profit, or if expenditure has been incurred on the property wholly or partly to make a gain on sale, an appropriate part of the gain is not exempt (s 224(3)). In practice HMRC ignores costs of obtaining planning permission or of removing restrictive covenants. A series of profitable sales may in exceptional circumstances be challenged as trading, as in the case of *Kirkby v Hughes* (ChD 1992), where a builder had bought and sold three houses that he had renovated while living in them (see Example 13 for the criteria for deciding when a trade is being carried on).

Restriction of private residence relief where holdover relief is claimed

16. Where the base cost of a property is reduced by an earlier holdover relief claim under s 260 (whenever made), no private residence relief can be claimed on a subsequent disposal (by the trustees or an individual) after 9 December 2003. The rules only apply where the gain is affected by an earlier holdover relief claim.

    Transitional rules permit a claim for private residence relief for disposals after 10 December 2003 in respect of the period before this date on a time apportioned basis. Therefore, in part (h) of the question, had the trustees triggered a disposal for CGT on say 1 January 2004 they would have suffered the disallowance of relief for only 22 days and the qualifying gain would have increased to 313/335 × 250,000 = £233,582 thus reducing the taxable gain.

    If the holdover claim is withdrawn in respect of an earlier disposal, it is treated as if it had never been made (new s 226A(6)). Also, if a holdover claim is made subsequently, the gain on disposal is recomputed. All necessary adjustments are made to the assessments.

    In the future, the transferor could refrain from claiming holdover relief on the transfer and pay tax on any gains up to that point. Private residence relief could then apply to any subsequent gains during the period in which the property was a beneficiary's or donee's main residence. If the property does not show any significant taxable gain it may be worth paying tax on this transfer if that enables subsequent gains to be sheltered by the valuable residence relief.

Trustees of settlements

17. For disposals on or after 10 December 2003 it is necessary for trustees to make a claim for private residence relief when they dispose of property which has been occupied by a beneficiary under the settlement as that person's qualifying residence.

Question

(a) Murray Ltd purchased a freehold building for £40,000 in June 1982 for use in the hotel trade and sold it in October 1986 for £60,000. At the same time, the company acquired another hotel for £56,000, claiming rollover relief appropriately. The new hotel was sold in January 2010 for £300,000. Assume the retail price index in January 2010 is 214.0.

    (i) Calculate the chargeable gains arising as a result of these transactions.

    (ii) Calculate the chargeable gains that would have arisen if the freehold building had been acquired in 1972 instead of in June 1982, the market value being £54,000 at 31 March 1982, and all other particulars remaining the same. From 6 April 1985 to 5 April 1988, gains on pre-March 1982 purchases were calculated using original cost, with the company having the right to elect to calculate indexation allowance on the March 1982 value.

(b) Your client, Medway Ltd, has been offered £1,200,000 for a freehold factory it is considering disposing of in October 2009. It acquired the factory in October 1943 for £40,000 and it had been valued for insurance purposes at £136,000 in April 1965 and £380,000 in March 1982. The factory site does not have any development value. The company has not made a 31 March 1982 rebasing election.

    1. Compute the chargeable gain which will arise if Medway Ltd disposes of the factory (assuming indexation allowance from March 1982 to October 2009 to be 170%).

    2. Indicate to the company the capital gains consequences of each of the following alternative courses of action it is considering taking following the sale, and give any advice you consider to be relevant:

        (i) acquiring a larger freehold factory in 2010 for £1,400,000.

        (ii) acquiring a smaller freehold factory in 2010 for £900,000 and using the remainder of the proceeds as working capital.

        (iii) using the proceeds to pay a premium of £1,400,000 for a 40 year lease of a new factory (it is possible that a freehold warehouse will be bought in about five years' time for an estimated cost of £1,480,000).

        (iv) acquiring a 40 year lease of a new factory for a yearly rental of £56,000 and a nil premium and loaning the sale proceeds to Newtown Ltd (a subsidiary in which Medway Ltd holds between 70% and 80% of the ordinary share capital) to be used by Newtown Ltd to acquire a freehold shop costing £1,220,000.

        (v) acquiring a new lease for a nil premium (as in (iv) above) and investing the proceeds in working capital. A 100% subsidiary, Parkland Ltd, that was acquired by Medway Ltd in 1985, will dispose of a holding of shares giving rise to an allowable loss for capital gains purposes of £180,000. Medway Ltd wishes to set the loss of Parkland Ltd against its chargeable gain.

(c) On 30 March 2010 Rochester disposed of his property in Darke Road, comprising a house and workshop in the garden, for £225,150. He purchased the property on 1 May 1975 for £5,000 and its value at 31 March 1982 was £58,000. Throughout his period of ownership the house was his principal private residence and the workshop was used for his printing business. 20% of the value of the property relates to the workshop.

On 20 April 2009 Rochester had purchased a house, with a workshop annexe, in Howells Road for £250,000. Both the house and workshop were kept empty until 30 March 2010 when his family and the printing business occupied the premises. 15% of the value of this property relates to the workshop.

Calculate the chargeable gain arising, assuming that Rochester had made a 31 March 1982 rebasing election and that he claims rollover relief on the gain on the workshop.

(d)   On 1 March 2003 Fordwich, aged 57, acquired a 20% shareholding in a trading company. 85% of the company's chargeable assets are chargeable business assets. He gave 5% of the shares to his son on 1 May 2009, and the gain arising before taking any available reliefs into account was £80,000.

Show how much of the gain, if any, is chargeable to tax assuming all available reliefs are claimed.

(e)   Quincey invested £35,000 in April 1987 in unquoted shares in his friend's trading company (the shares representing a 4% holding). On 5 July 2009 Quincey sold the shares to his sister for £55,000. She agreed to pay the purchase price in ten equal annual instalments commencing July 2009. The market value in July 2009 was £85,000. Quincey had made other chargeable disposals in 2009/10 which used the annual exemption, and he had no allowable losses brought forward.

Show the capital gain arising and state how this may be treated.

(f)   In January 2010 Harry transfers a painting to a discretionary trust and claims gifts relief. The asset was bought in March 2002 for £200,000 and was worth £500,000 at the date of transfer. Harry does not have an interest in the settlement at the date of transfer.

The asset is sold by the trustees in March 2010 for £502,000. The trustees also dispose of another asset realising a loss of £275,000.

Calculate the trustees' capital gain.

Explain what the consequences would be if Harry acquired an interest in the settlement in May 2010.

Answer

(a) **Murray Ltd – rollover relief**

(i)

	£	£
Sale proceeds – freehold building – October 1986		60,000
Cost June 1982	40,000	
Indexation allowance $\dfrac{98.45-81.85}{81.85} = 20.3\%$	8,120	48,120
		11,880
Less: rollover relief claimed re amount reinvested in replacement assets		7,880
Chargeable gain (assuming no other acquisitions of business assets within rollover period; £60,000 proceeds less £56,000 reinvested)		4,000
Second sale proceeds – hotel premises – January 2010		300,000
Cost October 1986	56,000	
Indexation allowance $\dfrac{214 - 98.45}{98.45} = 117.4\%$	65,744	
Less: Rolled over gain	(7,880)	113,864
Chargeable gain (assuming no other acquisitions of business assets within rollover period)		186,136

The gains on the two assets are therefore £4,000 in 1986/87 and £186,136, in 2009/10.

(ii)

	£
Sale proceeds – freehold building – October 1986	60,000
Cost 1972	40,000
Unindexed gain	20,000
Less: Indexation allowance on election for 31 March 1982 value £54,000 × 23.9%	12,906
	7,094
Less: roll-over relief claimed re amount reinvested in replacement assets	3,094
Chargeable gain (assuming no other acquisitions of business assets within rollover period; £60,000 proceeds less £56,000 reinvested)	4,000

	£	£
Second sale proceeds – replacement hotel – January 2010		300,000
Cost – October 1986	56,000	
Indexation allowance 117.4%	65,744	
Less: Rolled over gain after halving relief (see explanatory note 10) 3,094 × ½ =	(1,547)	120,197
Chargeable gain (again assuming no other acquisitions of business assets within rollover period)		179,803

(b)   **Medway Ltd – alternatives for deferring gains**

(1)   **Chargeable gain that will arise on disposal of factory**

	Using cost £	Using 31.3.82 value £
Sale proceeds October 2009	1,200,000	1,200,000
Cost October 1943	(40,000)	
31 March 1982 value		(380,000)
	1,160,000	820,000
Indexation allowance (on 31.3.82 value) 170%* × 380,000	(646,000)	(646,000)
Overall gain	514,000	

* Assumed figure given in example
Time proportion

$$\frac{6.4.65 - \text{October } 2009 \quad 44\frac{1}{2}}{6.4.45 ** - \text{October } 2009 \quad 64\frac{1}{2}} \times 514,000 \qquad 354,620 \qquad 174,000$$

** Earliest date for time apportionment
The chargeable gain will be   £174,000

If a general 31.3.82 rebasing election had been made the gain would have been the same, ie £174,000. The election for 6.4.65 value would clearly give a higher gain than 31.3.82 value, so it is not considered. Companies still enjoy indexation allowance after April 1998 and April 2008.

(2)

(i)   If a larger freehold factory were acquired in 2010 for £1,400,000, the gain of £174,000 need not be charged and could instead be rolled over to reduce the base cost of the new factory for capital gains purposes to (1,400,000 – 174,000 =) £1,226,000 (ie indexed 31 March 1982 value £1,026,000 plus £200,000 further expenditure).

(ii)   If a smaller freehold factory were acquired for £900,000 in 2010, with the remainder of the proceeds used as working capital, then the whole of the gain would be realised and included in the profit for corporation tax purposes.

The rolled over gain would thus be reduced to nil giving a base cost for the replacement factory of £900,000.

(iii)   If the proceeds were used to pay a premium of £1,400,000 for a 40 year lease of a new factory, then since the replacement asset would be a depreciating asset (life 60 years or less at the time of acquisition) the gain could not be rolled over, but it would be held over and assessment deferred until the earliest of:

A   Date of disposal of the leasehold factory

B   Time when leasehold factory ceased to be used for the purposes of the trade

C   Ten years from the date of acquisition of the leasehold factory

unless another qualifying non-depreciating asset, such as the freehold warehouse that may be purchased in about five years' time, was acquired at or before the time that one of these three chargeable occasions occurs. In that case the deferred gain could be deducted from the acquisition cost of the third asset for capital gains tax purposes.

(iv)   If the proceeds were not used by Medway Ltd to acquire qualifying assets but were instead loaned to its subsidiary Newtown Ltd, which in turn used the loan to acquire a freehold shop costing £1,220,000, the capital gains treatment would depend on how much of Newtown's ordinary share capital Medway owns. If Medway owns 75% or more of Newtown's ordinary share capital then Medway's gain could be rolled over against Newtown's acquisition, so that Newtown's base cost for capital gains tax would be (1,220,000 − 174,000 =) £1,046,000 (ie £1,026,000 indexed 31 March 1982 value of old factory plus £20,000 further expenditure). If Medway does not own 75% of Newtown's share capital then rollover relief would not be available and the gain of £174,000 would be immediately assessable (subject to the acquisition of qualifying assets by Medway within three years after the sale of its factory, in which event rollover relief could be claimed).

(v)   Since the requisite 75% or more parent/subsidiary relationship exists between Medway and Parkland, they form a group for capital gains purposes. Parkland could therefore transfer the shareholding to Medway on a no loss no gain basis under TCGA 1992 s 171 and Medway could then make the disposal outside the group, so that Medway would be able to set the loss arising of £180,000 against the chargeable gain of £174,000 on the sale of the factory, provided Medway disposes of the shareholding before the end of the accounting period in which it disposes of the factory.

Under TCGA 1992 s 171A, there is no need for actual transfer of the shareholding from Parkland to Medway. Section 171A provides that Parkland may make the disposal of the shareholding and the two companies may elect, within two years after the end of the accounting period in which the asset was disposed of outside the group, to be treated as if the shareholding had been transferred by Parkland to Medway immediately before the disposal, and s 171 is deemed to have applied to the deemed transfer, so that the gain would be regarded as made by Medway. This virtually amounts to the group surrender of capital gains or losses. See Example 65 explanatory note 3(b) for more detailed comments.

Additional points to note in relation to the various alternatives are as follows:

1.   Rollover relief has the effect of reducing the capital gains base cost of the replacement asset, so that when the replacement is sold, indexation allowance is effectively forfeited on the rolled over amount for the intervening period. This does not apply where gains are held over as a result of acquiring depreciating assets, because the capital gains cost of the replacement is unaltered. On the other hand the maximum deferral time is ten years, so the point when tax becomes payable may be much sooner. (If the depreciating asset is a lease, the cost of the lease will be depreciated once the unexpired life is 50 years or less, reducing the indexation allowance accordingly if the lease is disposed of.)

2.   If alternative (iv) were adopted (Medway owning 75% or more of Newtown's share capital), then a larger gain would be charged on Newtown when it disposed of the shop. Since Newtown is not a wholly owned subsidiary a compensating financial adjustment would need to be made between the companies in respect of any additional tax arising.

3.   The claim for 'deemed transfer' in (v) above can transfer the loss or the gain. It is therefore possible to match the gain and loss in the same company, and also to choose which of the two will pay the tax. If one would have a lower marginal corporation tax rate, this would give a further advantage.

(c)   **Rochester – business use of private residence**

			£
Sale proceeds 30 March 2010 Darke Road house			225,150
31 March 1982 value			58,000
Gain before reliefs			167,150
Less: private residence exemption 80%			133,720
Gain on workshop 20%			33,430
Less rolled over against replacement acquired within previous year:			
Proceeds relating to old workshop			
20% × 225,150		45,030	
Amount reinvested in new workshop			
15% × 250,000		37,500	
Amount not reinvested		7,530	
Total gain on workshop		33,430	
Rolled over gain		25,900	25,900
Chargeable gain			£7,530

It is assumed that the workshops are used exclusively for business purposes.

It seems likely that the workshop and house are treated, both on the old property and on the new, as a single asset. If this is the case, the base cost of the new house for CGT purposes will be (£250,000 – £25,900 =) £224,100. When the new house is sold, a gain calculated using this base cost will be 15% chargeable by reason of business use.

If the new workshop could be regarded as a separate asset which cost 15% × £250,000 = £37,500, that separate asset would have a base cost of (£37,500 – £25,900 =) £11,600.

(d)   **Fordwich – gift of shares to son 1 May 2009**

Since 15% of the company's chargeable assets are not business assets, only 85% of the gain qualifies for gifts relief under TCGA 1992 s 165. The test followed that for taper relief purposes and, following the abolition of taper relief, is now found in s 165A. If the existence of that level of non-business assets means that the company is not regarded as 'substantial', gifts relief is not available at all after 5 April 2004 (but 15% is unlikely to be regarded as 'substantial' on its own – further information is required about the importance of the non-business assets to the operations of the company).

The chargeable gains therefore become:

	£
Gain before reliefs	80,000
Gifts relief (85%)	(68,000)
Chargeable gain	12,000

The son's base cost of the shares would be the market value at the date of gift, less the £68,000 held over.

(e) **Quincey – sale of shares at undervalue to sister, payment by instalments**

Quincey's sister is a connected person, therefore sale is deemed to be at open market value (see note 1).

	£	£
Deemed sale proceeds – July 2009 (replacing £55,000 received)		85,000
Cost April 1987		35,000
Chargeable gain		50,000

£20,000 of the gain, ie the £55,000 consideration less £35,000 cost, relates to the actual consideration received and £30,000 to the 'gift' element of the deemed consideration.

Quincey and his sister may elect for the 'gift' element of the gain, ie £30,000, to be treated as reducing the sister's acquisition cost (see explanatory note 19). If the annual exemption is not available and tax is due, there are two alternative provisions enabling the tax on this gain to be paid by instalments.

Since part of the consideration is due more than 18 months after the date of disposal, Quincey may opt to pay the tax by such instalments as HMRC allows over a maximum of eight years (TCGA 1992 s 280). Interest will be charged only on instalments paid late.

Alternatively, he may elect to pay the tax by ten annual instalments, but with interest on the full amount outstanding being added to each instalment. Furthermore, if the shares were later disposed of for valuable consideration (whether by the sister or by someone else) the full amount of tax outstanding at that time would be payable immediately (TCGA 1992 s 281). See explanatory note 25.

Of course, as the tax on £20,000 is only £3,600 (if Quincey's annual exemption is not available), it may be simpler to pay all the tax on the normal due date.

(f) **Trustees' capital gain 2009/10**

Asset from Harry

	£	£
Proceeds – March 2010		502,000
Less: trustees' base cost		
MV January 2010	500,000	
Less: gain held over	(300,000)	(200,000)
Gain		302,000
Less: loss		(275,000)
Capital gain		27,000

Tax due thereon is payable by 31 January 2011.

Harry acquiring an interest in the settlement in May 2010

Holdover relief is no longer available for gifts to settlor interested trusts from 10 December 2003. This applies where the trust is settlor interested at the date of the gift or within the claw-back period (see explanatory note 26).

Harry is therefore assessed to tax on the gift in January 2010 in the tax year 2010/11 (the year he acquired an interest in the settlement) as follows:

	£
Market value (January 2010)	500,000
Less: cost	(200,000)
Gain	300,000

The trustees' gain is recomputed on the basis that gifts relief was not due on Harry's transfer to them.

		£
Proceeds		502,000
Less: trustees' base cost		
MV January 2010	500,000	
Less: gain held over	–	(500,000)
Gain		2,000
Less: loss		(275,000)
Capital gain		–

The excess losses of £273,000 would be carried forward and any tax paid in January 2011 would be repaid.

Explanatory Notes

Assets qualifying for rollover/holdover relief

1.   References in this example are to TCGA 1992 unless otherwise stated. Traders may claim rollover/holdover relief for business assets under s 152 when both the assets disposed of and those acquired are within the following classes (s 155):

Land, buildings and fixed plant and machinery ('fixed' is considered to mean fixed on a permanent or semi-permanent basis to the premises)

Ships, aircraft, hovercraft, satellites, space stations and spacecraft

Goodwill*

Milk and potato quotas* (see note 11)

Ewe and suckler cow premium quotas*

Fish quota*

Lloyd's syndicate rights

*   Since 1 April 2002 these assets have been dealt with for companies under the intangible assets rules – see explanatory note 15.

The acquisition must be made within one year before or three years after the disposal. The fact that the replacement may be acquired up to one year before the disposal does not, however, permit a gain on the sale of part of an asset within 12 months after its acquisition to be rolled over against the acquisition cost (*Watton v Tippett*, CA (1997)). HMRC have discretion to extend the time limits, and would probably exercise their discretion where there was a firm intention to acquire qualifying assets within the stipulated period but the taxpayer was prevented from doing so by circumstances beyond his control (Tax Bulletin November 1991). However, as shown in *R v CIR ex p Barnett* the discretion to allow a late claim was solely in the hands of the Revenue (now HMRC) and the Commissioners (although making certain helpful findings in the taxpayer's favour) had no jurisdiction to review it. The disposal and acquisition do not have to be within the same class of asset, and the replacement asset need not be used in the same trade where one person carries on two or more trades either successively or at the same time. HMRC regards two trades as having been carried on successively if there is an interval between them not exceeding three years (SP 8/81). Disposals during the interval qualify for relief, appropriately adjusted for the period of non-business use. Gains may be rolled over or held over by reference to acquisitions during the interval, providing the assets acquired are not used or leased for any purpose during that time and are brought into use in the successor trade on its commencement.

The relief is not confined to a single disposal and a single acquisition. The gain on one asset could be rolled over or held over against several replacement assets, or gains on several assets could be rolled or held over against a single replacement. Concession D22 provides that capital expenditure on improvements to existing qualifying assets may be treated as expenditure on new assets. (The initial cultivation costs of short rotation coppice (net of any woodland grants) count as improvement expenditure under this heading.)

To prevent abuse of the concession, and other concessions deferring gains, ss 284A and 284B provide that where a gain has been deferred under a concession first published before 9 March 1999, or a later replacement concession with substantially the same effect, then if, when the asset is disposed of, the person disposing of it seeks to avoid bringing the gain into charge on a disposal on or after 9 March 1999, he is treated as having made a chargeable gain equal to the deferred gain in the tax year or company accounting period in which the disposal takes place. The person on whom the charge arises could be the same taxpayer or another taxpayer to whom the asset had been transferred with the benefit of capital gains deferral.

Reinvesting the proceeds

2.   (i)   To get full relief the full amount of the proceeds must be reinvested. Where only part of the proceeds is reinvested, the chargeable gain is deemed to be reinvested last (s 153). This means that if the amount paid for the replacement asset is less than the sale proceeds for the old asset, the difference represents a realised gain, in respect of which relief is not available. If the difference exceeds the chargeable gain then rollover/holdover relief is not available at all. Where several disposals take place at the same time but the total proceeds are not fully reinvested, the disposals in respect of which relief is claimed may be chosen so as to maximise the benefit of the claim. For example if two assets were sold for a total of £200,000, being £130,000 and £70,000 respectively, showing total gains of £70,000 (£25,000 and £45,000 respectively) and replacement assets were acquired costing £120,000, relief could be claimed in respect of the second asset, the proceeds of £70,000 having been reinvested, even though looking at the combined position it appears that no part of the gains has been reinvested.

   (ii)   The relief is available if a gain arises on a gift of a qualifying asset, providing the deemed proceeds are matched by reinvestment in qualifying assets.

Rollover relief

3.   The rolled over gain on the disposal is deducted from the cost of the new asset(s). Indexation allowance is available for companies up to the date of disposal. For individuals, indexation allowance is only given on disposals before 6 April 2008, and the allowance is given up to 6 April 1998. Where available, it is taken into account in arriving at the gain and thus effectively forms part of the base cost of the replacement asset, as shown in part (a)(i) of the example, where the base cost of the building is £48,120, being £40,000 original cost of the freehold building plus £8,120 indexation allowance on its disposal. In part (a)(ii) the building has a base cost of £54,453, being £40,000 cost of the freehold building plus indexation allowance of £12,906 plus the half of the deferred gain, £1,547, that is excluded under the provisions of Sch 4 (see explanatory note 10).

The effect of the rollover relief is to give a lower base cost for the replacement asset(s), which means that indexation allowance is effectively forfeited on the rolled over amount for the intervening period to the time the replacement asset is sold, as shown in parts (c) and (d) of the example.

4.   If, exceptionally, the gain on a qualifying asset acquired before 6 April 1965 is arrived at by using time apportionment rather than 6 April 1965 value or 31 March 1982 value, and the full proceeds are not reinvested in qualifying replacement assets, the whole of the non-reinvested gain would not be chargeable because it would be restricted by time apportionment (s 153(1)).

If, for example, in part (b)1. of the example the time apportioned gain of £354,620 had been the lowest gain, and £100,000 of the proceeds of sale had not been reinvested as in 2(ii), only 44½/64½ × £100,000 = £68,992 would be immediately chargeable and the remainder of the chargeable gain would be rolled over.

Holdover relief on depreciating assets

5.   If the replacement asset is a wasting asset (ie with a life of 50 years or less), or an asset that will become a wasting asset within ten years (called a depreciating asset), the gain cannot be deducted from the cost thereof, but a claim may be made for it to be held over and deemed not to arise until the earliest of the following three dates, thus deferring calculation of the tax (and payment) to that time:

(i)   The date of disposal of the replacement asset

(ii)   The time when the replacement asset ceases to be used for the purposes of the trade

(iii) Ten years from the date of acquisition of the replacement asset.

If, however, another qualifying non-depreciating asset is purchased not later than the earliest of the three dates, the gain may instead be deducted from that purchase (s 154). The rules are illustrated in part (b)2.(iii) of the example.

Rollover/holdover relief claims

6.   Because of the length of time that may elapse before an asset is replaced, the position for corporation tax for accounting periods ended on or before 30 June 1999 (which also applied for capital gains tax for years before 1996/97) was that gains should be assessed at the normal time, but with the company having the opportunity to claim to postpone the tax on production of satisfactory evidence of its intention to acquire a qualifying replacement. Should the intended replacement then not materialise, interest on the tax that should have been paid would be charged from the normal due date. Corporation tax claims should be made within six years from the end of the company accounting period to which the claim relates (TMA 1970 s 43).

Under s 153A, applicable from 1996/97 for non-corporate taxpayers and for accounting periods ending after 30 June 1999 for companies, provisional claims for rollover relief may be made in tax returns before reinvestment takes place, the provisional claims being replaced by actual claims when the conditions are satisfied. If the reinvestment does not take place, the provisional claim ceases to have effect three years from 31 January following the tax year of disposal, or four years from the end of the accounting period of disposal for companies, and all necessary adjustments will then be made to earlier assessments. Where a holdover claim is being replaced by a rollover claim as a result of the later acquisition of a non-depreciating asset (which could in fact be up to thirteen years after the disposal giving rise to the gain that has been held over), it is thought that the claim to switch from holdover to rollover relief would need to be made at or soon after the time of acquisition of the non-depreciating asset, and in any event in the next tax return. The capital gains tax time limit for claims from 1996/97 is five years from 31 January following the relevant tax year.

Death of taxpayer

7.   If a taxpayer dies before a rolled over gain crystallises, the gain escapes tax as a result of the death. The same does not strictly apply where a gain has been held over, but by Extra Statutory Concession D45 the death of the taxpayer does not trigger the held-over gain.

Groups of companies

8.   Where two or more companies form a 75% group (parent company and subsidiaries in which the parent owns 75% or more of the ordinary share capital), all the trades in the group are treated as a single trade for rollover/holdover relief and the relief may be claimed no matter which group company makes the disposals and which the acquisitions (s 175). (A non-trading company that holds assets for trading companies in its group is included in these provisions under s 175(2B).)

Disposals from one group company to another are made on a no loss/no gain basis, as indicated in part (b)2.(v) of the example. Where, however, a company joined a group after 31 March 1987, and had realised or unrealised capital losses at 16 March 1993, the losses cannot be used against gains of another group company arising on or after 16 March 1993. In part (b)2.(v) of the example, therefore, Medway Ltd would not have been able to use an intra-group transfer (whether actual under s 171 or deemed under s 171A) to obtain the use of Parkland Ltd's loss on the shareholding if Parkland had joined the group after 31 March 1987 and the shareholding had been standing at a loss at 16 March 1993.

Further anti-avoidance provisions deny rollover relief where the replacement asset is acquired on a no loss no gain basis (s 175(2C)). These provisions would prevent Medway Ltd in part (b) of the example avoiding the gain on the disposal of the factory by acquiring a qualifying business asset from Parkland Ltd on a no loss no gain basis. To obtain the relief, a new asset must be brought into the group.

For detailed notes on the group capital gains provisions see Examples 62 and 65. See also note 13 to this example re compulsorily purchased land.

Assets owned personally and used by company

9.   Rollover/holdover relief is also available on the disposal and replacement of an asset owned personally and used in the owner's partnership or personal trading company (ie a trading company in which he owns 5% or more of the voting rights). The payment of rent does not affect the position (s 157).

Where personally owned assets are used in a personal company, the old and new assets must be acquired by the same individual, and used by the same personal company (and not for example by a new company following the liquidation of the first company). If the personal company is a holding company, use of an asset by a subsidiary does not qualify, because the subsidiary does not qualify as a personal company.

Effect of 31 March 1982 rebasing provisions on rolled over and heldover gains

10.   If a qualifying asset was disposed of at a gain before 31 March 1982 and a replacement asset was acquired before that date against which the gain was rolled over, the effect of the FA 1988 rebasing provisions is that the rolled over gain escapes tax, because it is not taken into account in arriving at the 31 March 1982 value of the replacement asset. The same result would not occur if the pre 31 March 1982 disposal had produced a gain to be held over as distinct from rolled over, but it is provided by Sch 4 para 4(5) that any such gain also escapes tax (see below in last paragraph of this note).

If a qualifying asset acquired pre 31 March 1982 is disposed of on or after 6 April 1988, the 31 March 1982 value may be used to calculate the gain to be rolled over or held over.

But if a rollover or holdover had occurred after 31 March 1982 and before 6 April 1988 (as in part (a)(ii) of the example, where the building acquired in 1972 was disposed of in 1986), then only the cost of the asset and not the March 1982 value was deducted in calculating the gain (despite the indexation allowance being calculated on the March 1982 value if the taxpayer had made an appropriate election). In these circumstances, any increase in value at 31 March 1982 of the asset giving rise to the deferred gain forms part of the deferred amount, since the gain has not been reduced by the increase in value up to 31 March 1982.

It is accordingly provided in Sch 4 that a claim may be made two years after the end of the company accounting period in which the relevant event occurs for only one half of any deferred amount to be charged to tax in these circumstances, where the deferred amount is attributable directly or indirectly, in whole or in part, to a gain on the disposal before 6 April 1988 of an asset acquired before 31 March 1982. This is known as halving relief. Halving relief was withdrawn for individuals, trusts and estates from 5 April 2008 with no further claims possible after that date. The claim under Sch 4 is still available to companies and this applies in the following situations:

(a) Under the following provisions, where the deduction made in the base cost of a replacement asset acquired after 31 March 1982 and before 6 April 1988 is halved:

    (i) Where a replacement asset is acquired after receipt of compensation or insurance money (s 23(4) and (5))

    (ii) Where a replacement asset is acquired on the disposal of a business asset, as in this example (see (a)(ii)) (s 152)

    (iii) Where shares are acquired on transfer of a business to a company (s 162)

    (iv) Where a gain is held over on a business asset acquired by gift (s 165)

    (v) Where replacement land is acquired on compulsory acquisition of other land (s 247)

    (vi) Where a gain is held over on an asset acquired by gift under the former general gifts relief (FA 1980 s 79).

(b) Under the following provisions, where gains that have been postponed on a disposal before 6 April 1988 are halved when they crystallise (or, in the case of the first four items, possibly exempted altogether, as indicated in the last paragraph of this note):

    (i) Where securities are acquired in exchange for a business acquired by a non-resident company (s 140)

    (ii) Where gilts are acquired on compulsory acquisition of shares (s 134)

    (iii) Where a depreciating asset is acquired on compulsory acquisition of land (ss 247 and 248(3))

    (iv) Where a depreciating asset is acquired as replacement for a business asset, as in part (d)2.(iii) of this example (s 154)

    (v) When a company leaves a group, in respect of an asset acquired from another group company (s 178)

    (vi) Where there is a reorganisation involving the acquisition of qualifying corporate bonds (s 116(10) and (11)).

By Sch 4 para 4(5) where a gain (or loss) would otherwise crystallise on or after 6 April 1988 in relation to any of the items (i) to (iv) above, and it is *directly* attributable to the disposal of an asset on or before 31 March 1982, then it is not brought into account at all.

Milk quota

11.   Milk quota was introduced in 1984. HMRC considers that quota is a separate asset from the land to which it relates, and if the owner had the quota allotted in 1984 he will have no base cost (Tax Bulletin February 1993). See explanatory note 15 for the treatment of quota in the hands of companies from 1 April 2002.

       Where compensation is paid to producers (called SLOM producers) as a result of their not being allocated milk quota in 1984, HMRC consider it to be income, and that it should be taken into account when the legal entitlement arises and when the amount payable can be quantified with reasonable certainty (Tax Bulletin May 1994).

Capital allowances

12.   The reduction of the base values of assets for capital gains tax does not affect the income tax figures. Capital allowances would still be available, for example, on the amount of £1,400,000 (less the cost of the land) paid for the freehold factory in part (b)2.(i) of the example, whereas the base figure for capital gains tax is £1,226,000. And in (b)2.(iii), Medway would be able to claim a deduction against its profit each year for the part of the £1,400,000 premium that was assessed on the landlord as extra rent. For details see Example 99 part (h).

Rollover relief and compulsory purchase

13.   Although rollover relief is not normally available on investment property (except for furnished holiday lettings – see Example 97 explanatory note 25), s 247 allows relief to be claimed where property is disposed of under a compulsory purchase order, and a replacement is acquired within one year before and three years after the disposal. The relief is not available if the replacement property is the taxpayer's capital gains tax exempt dwelling at any time within six years after acquisition (s 248). Companies in a 75% group can claim this relief if one company makes the disposal and another company acquires the replacement. 'Compulsory purchase' includes purchase of the freehold by a tenant exercising his right to buy (SP 13/93).

       Where *part* of a holding of land is compulsorily purchased, small proceeds may be treated as reducing the capital gains cost of the holding rather than being treated as a part disposal (s 243). 'Small' is not defined but is taken by HMRC to mean not more than 5%.

Rollover relief and grants towards replacement assets

14.   Where a grant is received towards the cost of an asset, it is generally required to be deducted from the expenditure allowable for capital gains tax (TCGA 1992 s 50). The case of *Wardhaugh v Penrith Rugby Union Football Club* (Ch D 2002) considered whether this had any effect on a rollover relief claim. The club sold some land for £315,000, realising a gain of £204,000; it bought a new clubhouse for £600,000, and received a grant of £409,000 from the Sports Council towards this expenditure. The Revenue argued that the grant should reduce the expenditure on the new asset to £191,000 for rollover purposes, which would leave £124,000 of the gain in charge to tax. The High Court held that s 50 operates only in calculating the gain on a disposal, and is independent of s 152 which restricts rollover relief for partial reinvestment. Accordingly, the full gain could be held over against the expenditure of £600,000. This has the surprising effect of establishing a negative cost for the asset (as it would be reduced by the rollover claim and by the s 50 deduction). The Revenue did appeal this decision, but the appeal was dismissed in June 2003.

Rules for intangible fixed assets

15.   From 1 April 2002, companies receive deductions from revenue profits for the cost of goodwill and fish and agricultural quotas purchased. Accordingly, goodwill and quotas purchased from that date cease to be a capital gains rollover asset for companies (unless acquired from related parties) and the sale of such goodwill and quota is subject to taxation as a trading profit. There is a separate rollover

relief for that trading profit where the proceeds are used to buy other intangible assets: this operates in a similar way to capital gains rollover, but is independent of it, and there is no interaction between the two reliefs.

There was a transitional period during which a disposal on or after 1 April 2002 of goodwill or quota acquired before 1 April 2002 could be rolled over:

- under the capital gains rules against a purchase of goodwill or quota before 1 April 2002, and within the 12 months before the sale (ie the normal reinvestment time limit), or

- under the intangible assets rules (see Example 66), or

- partly under the capital gains rules and partly under the intangible assets rules.

Apart from this transitional provision, capital gains will not be rolled over against the purchase of intangible assets, and gains on intangible assets will not be rolled over against property within the capital gains rollover classes.

Goodwill and quotas purchased by a sole trader or partnership remain chargeable assets for CGT, and remain eligible for rollover relief.

For the detailed provisions of the intangible assets legislation see Example 66.

Gifts and disposals to connected persons

16. A gift of a chargeable asset is regarded as a disposal at open market value (except for transfers between spouses/civil partners) (s 17), and the chargeable gain or allowable loss is computed in the usual way. Where the parties are connected persons, then not only gifts but all transactions between them are deemed to be at market value (except for transactions between spouses and civil partners who are living together). For detailed notes on connected persons and how market value is arrived at see Example 73. See also Example 56 explanatory note 8(d) for the effect of a transfer at an undervalue by a close company.

Holdover relief on pre-14 April 1989 gifts

17. Before FA 1989, where a gain arose on a gift, then provided that the gift was made by an individual or trustees, and the donee was either an individual resident or ordinarily resident in the UK, or trustees who on a subsequent disposal would be liable to UK capital gains tax, a claim could be made for the gain which would otherwise be chargeable to be held over and treated as reducing the base acquisition cost of the donee (FA 1980 s 79). The relief applied to gifts from and to individuals after 5 April 1980, extended to include gifts to trustees after 5 April 1981 and to gifts by trustees after 5 April 1982. This general gifts relief was abolished by FA 1989 for disposals on or after 14 March 1989, but many assets will still be owned against which such gains have been held over.

18. For disposals on or after 14 March 1989 more restricted gifts relief provisions are now contained in ss 165 and 260. Company donors do not qualify for gifts relief, but the donee of a s 165 gift may be a company (except for gifts of shares).

Holdover relief for gifts of business assets under s 165

19. S 165 broadly provides for individuals to claim that gains on gifts of the following assets be held over and treated as reducing the base acquisition cost of the donee:

(a) Assets used in the donor's business or in his personal trading company (ie a company in which he holds not less than 5% of the voting rights), or used by a company in a trading group of which the holding company is the donor's personal trading company.

(b) Farm land and buildings that would qualify for inheritance tax agricultural property relief (broadly all farming land providing certain conditions as to length of ownership and occupation are satisfied, including farm land held as an investment providing it has been owned for seven years and occupied for agriculture throughout that period).

(c)   Shares or securities in unquoted trading companies, or unquoted holding companies of trading groups. (Shares on the Alternative Investment Market qualify for relief.)

(d)   Shares or securities in the donor's personal trading company or personal holding company of a trading group.

A gift of shares or securities to a company does not qualify for s 165 relief (s 165(3)(b)).

Where agricultural property has development value, the gain qualifying for relief under (b) is not restricted to the agricultural value, even though inheritance tax agricultural property relief is so restricted.

It should be noted that heading (d) enables relief to be claimed on a gift out of a 5% holding of shares in a *quoted* company. A holding of *any* size qualifies for relief under (c). If the holding (of quoted or unquoted shares) is 5% or more, however, relief is restricted to the business assets proportion of the gain (Sch 7 para 7). In part (e) of the example, Quincey owns only 4% of the shares, so his relief is not restricted. In part (d) of the example, the relief *is* restricted, because Fordwich owns 20% of the shares in his company.

Relief under s 165 is also available for disposals by trustees, heading (a) above being amended so as to relate to assets used in a trade carried on by the trustees or a life tenant and heading (d) relating to holdings in quoted companies carrying at least 25% of the voting power.

Claims for s 165 relief are made jointly by the donor and donee, unless the *donees* are trustees, in which case the claim is made by the donor alone.

Holdover relief under s 260

20.   S 260 provides for holdover relief on gains on the following gifts by individuals or trustees:

(a)   Certain gifts of heritage property (works of art, historic buildings etc)

(b)   Gifts to funds for the maintenance of heritage property

(c)   Gifts to political parties

(d)   Gifts that are *immediately* chargeable to inheritance tax, or would be apart from the annual exemption or nil-rate threshold. This mainly covers gifts to trusts and close companies.

As with claims for relief under s 165, claims for relief are made by the donor and donee jointly, unless the *donees* are trustees, in which case the claim is made by the donor alone.

Effect of gifts relief on inheritance tax

21.   For both ss 165 and 260, any inheritance tax payable on the gift is deductible in arriving at the chargeable gain on a later disposal (but not so as to create a loss), and this applies where inheritance tax is payable at some later time, for example because the donor dies within seven years. All necessary adjustments will be made to the earlier computation. But if a gift does not qualify for gifts relief and capital gains tax is payable, there is no direct inheritance tax relief for the capital gains tax paid if the gift becomes chargeable to inheritance tax because of the donor's death within seven years (although the capital gains tax paid has reduced the wealth of the donor and therefore the amount liable to inheritance tax on his death). The detailed inheritance tax provisions are in the companion to this book, Tolley's Taxwise II 2009/10.

Assets disposed of at an undervalue

22.   Gifts relief under both ss 165 and 260 is also available where assets are not given outright but are disposed of for less than their value, but if the actual consideration is greater than the original cost of the assets, so that the donor has in fact realised some of the gain in cash, then the chargeable gain which may be held over is restricted by the excess of the actual proceeds over cost, as shown in part (e) of the example.

Effect of non-residence

23. Gifts relief is not available if the donee is not resident and not ordinarily resident in the UK, or would not be chargeable to tax on a gain as a result of being regarded as non-resident under a double tax treaty (ss 166 and 261). Relief under s 165 is not available if the donee is a foreign controlled company (s 167).

    The held-over gain is charged to tax if the donee becomes not resident and not ordinarily resident in the UK within six years after the end of the tax year in which the gift was made (s 168). This could have had significant implications since the abolition of taper relief. Assume Georgie gave a long-held business property to her son Sam in May 2006 and the gain of £180,000 was held over. In March 2010 Sam emigrated to Australia. The held-over gain of £180,000 would crystallise in 2009/10 with tax due on 31 January 2011. No taper relief is available in these circumstances (even though it might have been due had Georgie not held over the gain). If Sam did not pay this tax within 12 months, it can be collected from the donor, ie Georgie. This compares with the situation if no hold-over claim had been made. Georgie would have been charged the tax on only:

	£
Gain (2006/07)	180,000
Taper (75%)	(135,000)
	45,000

Gifts relief claims

24. No specific time limit is stipulated for the gifts relief claims, so that the normal time limit of five years ten months in TMA 1970 s 43 will apply.

    HMRC have stated that in most circumstances it will not be necessary to agree market values at the time of a gifts relief claim. Establishing the market value at the date of the gift can normally be deferred until the donee disposes of the asset (Statement of Practice 8/92 and *Tax Bulletin* April 1997). There is a standard claim form for holdover claims. The form is included in HMRC Helpsheet IR 295. Under self-assessment the claim is separate from the return, although it will often be sent in with the return.

Paying tax by instalments

25. Where gifts relief is not available, or does not cover the full amount of the gain, any tax arising may be paid by ten annual instalments on gifts of land, a controlling holding of shares or securities in a company, or minority holdings of shares or securities in an unquoted company. Interest is, however, charged on the full amount outstanding and is added to each instalment (s 281). The other instalment option outlined in part (e) of the example is only available where the consideration is payable by instalments over a period of more than 18 months (see Example 75 explanatory note 5 for details).

FA 2004 restriction of gift relief to settlor interested trusts

26. Prior to 10 December 2003, gift relief was often used to restart the taper relief clock to avoid apportionment provisions, as part of an IHT avoidance arrangement and to use tax reliefs within a trust (eg other losses or entitlement to main residence relief) to eliminate a chargeable gain.

    As shown in part (f) above, holdover relief is no longer available where the trust is settlor interested either at the date of the gift or any time before the sixth anniversary of the start of the tax year following the one in which the disposal was made (the claw-back period). This applies to gifts under both s 165 or s 260.

    For the holdover claim to fail, the following conditions must be satisfied (new TCGA 1992 s 169B onwards):

    (a)   The disposal must be to a trust;

 (b) The disposal can be from a trust to a trust or from an individual to a trust and either

  (i) the trust is settlor interested or there is an arrangement (which is widely defined) under which an interest could be acquired by the settlor; or

  (ii) the trust is one which benefits an individual who in the past (whenever) has made a holdover claim in respect of which that asset thereby now has a reduced base cost.

Interest is widely defined at new TCGA 1992 s 169F and includes where either the settlor or spouse (s 169F(4)) obtains a benefit directly or indirectly from such property. Subsection (5) provides that an interest of a settlor (or spouse/civil partner) can be ignored in limited circumstances involving the death of particular parties.

Point (b) above is intended to prevent the rules being avoided using a chain of transfers, eg Connor settles assets on trust A from which he is excluded (claiming holdover relief) which then transfers the asset to trust B from which he is not excluded.

The claw-back provisions provide that a chargeable gain arises at the time the settlement becomes a settlor interested settlement equal to the held-over gain, and the trustees' allowable expenditure is increased by the amount of the held-over gain.

There are limited exclusions from these rules for certain disabled trusts and historic buildings.

Question

(1) (a) Outline the principal differences between the tax treatment of capital gains made by individuals and those made by companies.

     (b) Kaput Ltd owns a 100% subsidiary, a 60% subsidiary and a 40% stake in a consortium company. All the companies are UK resident. Comment on the implications of these shareholdings for the taxation of Kaput Ltd's capital gains, including the implications of transactions between the companies.

(2) Fancy Trading Ltd has a UK subsidiary, Plain Trading Ltd, in which it holds 80% of the issued share capital. Both companies make up accounts annually to 31 December. No general 31.3.82 rebasing election has been or is being made in respect of the group.

On 30 May 2009 Plain Trading Ltd sold 10,000 50p ordinary shares in Twisty Ltd, a non-quoted company, for £51,000. It had acquired the shares in May 1986 from Fancy Trading Ltd for £1.50 each. Fancy Trading Ltd had acquired the shares at par in January 1980, and they were valued at £1.55 each on 31 March 1982.

Show the capital gains position on the sale in May 2009 and indicate what the position would have been if the proceeds had been only £6,000.

The following indexed rises may be used:

March 1982 – May 1986: 23.2%

March 1982 – May 2009: 165%

Answer

(1)

    (a)   **Principal differences between the tax treatment of capital gains made by individuals and companies**

        (i)   Individuals are charged separately to capital gains tax on gains, while companies treat chargeable gains as another source of profits chargeable to corporation tax. For individuals, the rate of tax is a flat 18% on any chargeable gain, irrespective of the individual's other income levels. For corporation tax, the chargeable gains can affect a company's marginal tax rate.

        (ii)   Individuals enjoy an annual exemption for gains (£10,100 for 2009/10), but companies do not.

        (iii) Companies are entitled to indexation allowance to reflect the effect of inflation between:

- the later of:
  - the acquisition date, and
  - 31 March 1982, and
- the date of disposal.

Individuals are not entitled to indexation allowance.

        (iv) For assets held before 31 March 1982, individuals are required to treat the assets as having been acquired on that date for the then market value. Companies may opt into this treatment (either globally or on an asset-by-asset basis). If they do not, two sets of calculations are necessary. Where the two calculations yield two gains or two losses, the lower of the two gains or losses is used. Where one calculation gives a gain and another a loss, then the disposal is deemed to be for neither a gain nor a loss. For companies, a third option applies in respect of assets owned before 6 April 1965. They can be rebased to that date or have time-apportionment of gains reflecting the period of ownership after 6 April 1965 (but with any period of ownership before 6 April 1945 completely ignored).

        (v)   For capital gains tax, all shares and securities of the same class, held by a taxpayer in the same capacity, are pooled in a single pool (subject to some limited exceptions – see Example 79). For companies, different pools operate for shares acquired before 1 April 1982 and before 6 April 1965 (except where a rebasing election has been made).

        (vi) Many capital gains reliefs and exemptions are not relevant to companies (eg only or main residence, incorporation relief, entrepreneur's relief, gifts relief).

        (vii) Where an individual is an officer or employee then part or all of a gain may be taxed as income under the employment-related securities rules.

        (viii) There is no 'exit charge' when an individual becomes non-UK resident, but a company becoming non-UK resident is deemed to dispose of all its chargeable assets at their market value on the date it becomes foreign resident (unless the assets remain within the charge to corporation tax through being used by a UK permanent establishment of the company).

        (ix) The tax treatment of loan stocks and foreign currencies is different for companies. Under the 'loan relationships' provisions, most loan stocks and currency exchange differences are dealt with for companies as income under Schedule D Case III. Individuals and trustees would pay:

- income tax on the whole profit on a 'deeply discounted security';

- capital gains tax on some loan stocks which are non-qualifying corporate bonds (non-QCBs) (eg stocks redeemable in a foreign currency);

- income tax on accrued income on disposal of most qualifying corporate bonds (QCB)s;

- capital gains tax on exchange profits on foreign currency assets (but foreign currency liabilities are outside the scope of capital gains tax).

For the detailed corporation tax provisions on loan relationships see Example 63.

(x) For acquisitions on or after 1 April 2002 from unrelated parties, goodwill and fishing and agricultural quotas are not chargeable assets for companies. Gains and losses on such assets are taken into account under the 'intangible assets' provisions. For the details see Example 66.

(xi) For disposals on or after 1 April 2002, companies are exempt from tax on the disposal of a substantial shareholding (broadly 10% of ordinary share capital) in a trading company. For details see Example 66.

(xii) On 5 December 2005, companies became subject to specific anti-avoidance measures. For capital gains tax these became relevant with effect from 6 December 2006. These measures are intended to prevent taxpayers from claiming relief in respect of capital losses:

1. that arise in the course of a transaction where the realisation of the loss was a main or the main purpose;

2. where there is a change in the ownership of a company and a main or the main purpose for the change in ownership is to secure a tax advantage; or

3. where a capital gain has arisen but it would ordinarily have been charged as income but for a tax avoidance scheme entered into in order to convert the income into a gain so as to offset capital losses.

(b)

Kaput Ltd and its 100% subsidiary are a group for capital gains purposes. This means that any assets chargeable to tax on gains are transferred between them on a 'no loss no gain' basis (see explanatory note 1), and a gain on the disposal of a business asset by one can be rolled over against the acquisition of a qualifying asset by the other (see Example 82).

Kaput Ltd and its 60% subsidiary do not qualify for the above treatment. They are connected persons, so transactions between them are routinely taxed at open market value. A loss on a disposal by one to the other can only be offset against gains on disposals to the same person.

Kaput Ltd is not connected with the consortium company. A transaction which is not at arm's length would have to be adjusted to market value, but losses on disposal should be allowed against other gains.

(2) **No gain no loss transfers – disposal of shares in Twisty Ltd 30 May 2009**

Plain Trading Ltd will be treated as having acquired the shares in Twisty Ltd at their cost to Fancy Trading Ltd, ie £5,000 plus indexation allowance to May 1986 of 23.2% × £5,000 = £1,160, giving a total acquisition cost of £6,160. (Although an election could have been made to base the indexation allowance on the intra-group transfer on the 31.3.82 value of £15,500, this would not usually have been done, since as the law then stood, it would not have affected the calculation when the asset was transferred outside the group.)

The position on the sale on 30 May 2009 is as follows:

		Using cost		Using 31.3.82 value
	£	£		£
Sale proceeds		51,000		51,000
Deemed value on intra-group transfer May 1986	6,160			
Less: indexation allowance included therein	1,160			
	5,000			
31.3.82 value – 10,000 @ £1.55			15,500	
Indexation allowance on 31.3.82 value 165% × 15,500	25,575	30,575	25,575	41,075
		20,425		9,925
Chargeable gain is the lower of the two, ie				9,925

If the sale proceeds had been £6,000

Although indexation allowance cannot normally create or increase a loss on a disposal on or after 30 November 1993, this does not apply to the indexation allowance up to the time of the intra-group transfer in May 1986. It is not clear, however, whether HMRC would be prepared to allow the calculation to be based on the 31.3.82 value of £15,500, giving indexation allowance of 23.2% of £15,500 = £3,596, since the election to use 31.3.82 value on such a transfer had to be made within two years from the end of the relevant accounting period (ie by 31.12.88) or within such further period as HMRC allows. If HMRC did allow this, the proceeds of £6,000 would be compared with an indexed cost of £8,596, giving an allowable loss of £2,596. If they will not allow 31.3.82 value to be used to calculate the indexation allowance, only 23.2% × £5,000, ie £1,160, could be added to the cost of £5,000, making £6,160, and the allowable loss would be £160 (being less than the loss using 31.3.82 value of £15,500).

Explanatory Notes

No gain no loss disposals

1.   References in this example are to TCGA 1992 unless otherwise stated. Section 56 provides that on a disposal which would be treated as a 'no gain, no loss' disposal under the normal rules, an unindexed gain equal to any available indexation allowance is deemed to arise, thus giving a net result of no gain, no loss. These provisions apply to:

(a)   Transfers on company reconstructions (s 139)

(b)   Transfers within a 75% group of companies (s 171)

(c)   Transfers between spouses/civil partners (s 58)

(d)   Replacement of business assets (s 152).

If, however, there is a loss when the asset is eventually disposed of, for corporation tax, it is reduced by any indexation allowance added at the time of the no gain/no loss transfer (s 56(3)). This does not apply if the transfer was made before 30 November 1993, indexation allowance up to the time of such a transfer being available as part of an allowable loss (s 56).

If, for example, a husband acquired an asset in January 1987 and transferred it to his wife in August 1997, the wife would be treated as having acquired the asset at the cost to the husband plus indexation allowance from January 1987 to August 1997. Current practice is that indexation allowance is incorporated and so increases the loss in respect of a disposal by the wife after 5 April 2008.

In part (2) of the example, Plain Trading Ltd is treated as acquiring the shares in Twisty Ltd at their cost to Fancy Trading Ltd in 1980 plus indexation allowance from 1982 to the time of the intra-group transfer in May 1986. This can create a loss as it occurred before November 1993.

2. The rebasing provisions of s 35 enable gains and losses on assets acquired before 31 March 1982 to be calculated using 31 March 1982 value. Where an asset owned on 31 March 1982 was transferred before 6 April 1988 under specified no loss/no gain provisions, and is then disposed of on or after 6 April 1988, Sch 3 para 1 provides that the eventual transferor is treated as having owned the asset on 31 March 1982. The gain or loss on that eventual disposal is therefore computed using either 31 March 1982 value or original cost whichever shows the lower gain or loss (unless a general 31 March 1982 rebasing election has been made). In making the calculation based on cost, indexation allowance can be given on 31 March 1982 value, but in order to prevent double counting the indexation allowance included in the acquisition cost has to be excluded (s 55(5) and (6)).

In part (2) of the example, therefore, the calculation based on cost excludes the indexation allowance made on the intra-group transfer from Fancy Trading Ltd to Plain Trading Ltd.

The provisions to prevent double counting would also apply if the original acquisition by the first person had been before 31 March 1982 and the no gain/no loss transfer had been after 5 April 1988. For an illustration see Example 62 part A.

There is a problem as indicated in part (2) of the example where intra-group transfers took place between 31.3.82 and 5.4.88. Up to 31.3.85 indexation allowance was based on cost, and from 1.4.85 to 5.4.88 it could be based on 31.3.82 value only if an appropriate election was made. Although 'rolled up indexation' on a no gain no loss transfer between those dates may be treated as part of cost under s 56, it is not clear whether the indexation calculation can be made using the 31.3.82 value where that would be beneficial to the taxpayer.

The main instances to which these provisions apply are those in (a), (b) and (c) of explanatory note 1, ie transfers on company reconstructions, within a 75% group and between spouses/civil partners.

For 75% groups of companies, the general 31.3.82 rebasing election is made by the principal company in the group, and it applies to all group companies (subject to provisions to deal with companies joining and leaving the group – see Example 65 explanatory note 5) (Sch 3 para 8 and 3 para 9).

Corporate shareholders – share matching rules

3. Disposals of securities are matched with acquisitions as follows, except for scrip and rights shares (including scrip dividend options – see Example 79 explanatory note 13), which are treated as acquired when the original shares were acquired, and loan stock (see Example 80 explanatory note 4):

(a) Acquisitions on the same day as the disposal

(b) For disposals before 5 December 2005: where the company owns 2% or more of the issued shares of a particular class, acquisitions in the previous month (latest first) then acquisitions in the following month (earliest first)

(c) Where (b) does not apply, acquisitions within the previous nine days (and no indexation allowance is available on the disposal)

(d) The post-1982 pool

(e) The pre-1982 pool

(f) Pre 6 April 1965 acquisitions that are not included in the pre-1982 pool, latest first

(g)   Acquisitions after disposal (other than those taken into account in (b)), earliest first.

The rules outlined above (except (b) and the scrip dividend option rules) applied to unincorporated shareholders as well as companies before 6 April 1998.

The abolition of rule (b) with effect from 5 December 2005 was a consequence of the introduction of the specific anti-avoidance rules referred to in part 1(a)(xii) of the example. On the basis that artificial losses do not now qualify as allowable losses, the anti-bed and breakfasting provision previously found in s 106 was thought no longer necessary.

Capital gains provisions for groups of companies

4.   The capital gains treatment of groups of companies is dealt with in more detail in Examples 62 and 65. See also Example 82 part (b) for rollover relief aspects.

Transactions not at arm's length

5.   It is necessary to use market value as the deemed proceeds for such transactions (s 17) but the restriction on the offset of losses in s 18 only applies to persons connected within s 286.

Question

A.

Briefly describe when a liability will arise to:

(a)   stamp duty land tax (SDLT)

(b)   stamp duty

(c)   stamp duty reserve tax.

B.

A wealthy client, Mr Argenton, has been involved in a number of transactions during the year ended 5 April 2010:

8 May 2009	He purchased the total issued share capital of a company from Mr Copperfield; the consideration was a £1 nominal cash payment together with the release of a loan of £50,000 which Mr Argenton had originally made to Mr Copperfield.
7 August 2009	He sold land and standing timber, with a value of £450,000, to a timber merchant.
9 September 2009	As trustee of his family's accumulation and maintenance settlement, he arranged for the transfer of trust shares having a value of £75,000 to his eldest daughter. The transfer was made upon his daughter reaching the age of 25 and was in accordance with the terms of the settlement.
10 January 2010	A gift of £350,000 cash was made to his eldest son to help with a property purchase.
15 January 2010	Mr Argenton subscribed in cash for £250,000 nominal value 5-year convertible loan stock 8%. The issue was by his wholly owned investment company.
20 March 2010	Mr Argenton had previously loaned £250,000, interest free, to a friend's property development company. As part of a reconstruction scheme for that company, he agreed to receive 2,500,000 10p shares issued by the company in satisfaction of the debt.

Provide Mr Argenton with a memorandum that sets out the stamp duty liabilities of each transaction.

C.

Briefly outline the significance of the effective date for stamp duty land tax purposes.

D.

(a)   Explain what is meant by the process known as 'adjudication' in relation to stamp duty, indicating when it is used, the consequences that flow from it and the remedies available to a dissatisfied taxpayer.

(b)   Brown Ltd is the parent company of a diverse group. As part of an exercise to rationalise the group investment structure, all shareholdings in both group and non-group companies are being transferred to Brown Ltd.

        The following transactions took place on 31 December 2009:

        (i)   Blue Ltd, a wholly owned subsidiary, transferred its shares in Black Ltd (its own wholly owned subsidiary) to Brown Ltd for £50,000.

(ii) Brown Ltd owned 70% of Colourless Ltd, which in turn owned all the capital of Rainbow Ltd. All shares in Rainbow Ltd were transferred to Brown Ltd for £100,000. (The remaining 30% of Colourless Ltd was not owned by the group.)

(iii) Rainbow Ltd contracted to sell 200 shares in Indigo plc, a quoted company, to Brown Ltd for £3,000. Before the contract was completed, Brown Ltd transferred its beneficial interest in the shares to a third party for £2,900 on 21 January 2010.

Outline the stamp duty and stamp duty reserve tax consequences of these transactions.

Answer

A.   (a)   Stamp Duty Land Tax (FA 2003 ss 42–124 and Schs 3–19)

Stamp duty land tax (SDLT) applies to transactions involving UK land and buildings. It applies regardless of where the contract is executed and is not dependent on UK residency. The charge arises when the transaction is 'substantially performed' (ie when consideration paid or the purchaser, or someone connected with the purchaser, takes possession) or on completion.

SDLT is charged on land transactions entered into in return for 'chargeable consideration'. A land transaction is defined as the 'acquisition of a chargeable interest'.

The definition of 'acquisition' is widely drawn, and encompasses the creation, surrender and in some cases, variation, of a chargeable interest. In every instance, liability to pay the tax rests with the purchaser.

In a straightforward sale of land, it is clear who fits the description of 'purchaser'. The legislation sets out rules for identifying the purchaser in all the different scenarios.

Where a chargeable interest has been *created*, the 'purchaser' is the person who becomes entitled to the interest created, for example, the buyer of a freehold property.

Where there is a *surrender* of a chargeable interest (for example, where a tenant surrenders a lease to the landlord), the 'purchaser' is the person whose benefit or interest is enlarged thereby, in this case, the landlord.

The *variation* of a chargeable interest *other than a lease* is also a land transaction, and in this case, the purchaser is the party benefiting from the variation. On the other hand, the *variation of a lease* qualifies as a land transaction for SDLT purposes in two circumstances. The first is if the variation takes effect, or is treated for SDLT purposes, as the grant of a new lease (see explanatory note 9 below; SDLT provisions on rent). The second is if the variation is such as to reduce the rent or term of the lease.

Except where explicitly provided in the legislation, a charge to SDLT arises regardless of the means by which the transaction is effected. In other words, it is generally irrelevant whether the 'acquisition' is by agreement of the parties, court order, legislative provision, or operation of law.

'Chargeable interests' are estates, interests, rights or powers in or over land in the United Kingdom. The definition also includes the benefit of any obligation, restriction or condition affecting the value of such estates, interests, rights or powers. These all qualify as chargeable interests only insofar as they are not specifically declared by the legislation to be 'exempt'.

Examples of exempt interests are security interests, tenancies at will, and licences. The position for tenancies at will is somewhat unclear. FA 2003 Sch 17A para 4 makes provision for leases for an indefinite term. Broadly, these are treated in the first instance as leases for one year, and if the lease continues beyond one year, as a lease for two years, and so on. As a result of such a continuation, SDLT may eventually become payable under the lease. The problem with tenancies at will is that paragraph 4 includes them under the ambit of leases for an indefinite term. It is therefore a possibility, on the reading of that paragraph, that a charge to SDLT could arise in relation to a tenancy at will.

SDLT applies to consideration in money or money's worth. If there is a contingency it is charged on the assumption that the full amount is payable. The tax is then adjusted when the contingency occurs or it is clear that it will not occur. VAT is included unless the vendor/ landlord has not opted to tax the land/building at the time of sale/granting of the lease (see explanatory note 3).

Where the consideration is uncertain (for example, where it is based on future turnover), or unascertained (for example, based on a set of accounts which have not been finalised), then a reasonable estimate is made. The purchaser may apply to defer payment in respect of contingent and uncertain consideration. There is no such provision for unascertained consideration.

Special rules apply where the land is acquired by a connected company (see explanatory note 5) so that SDLT is payable even when the land is gifted to the connected company.

The acquisition of land by a partnership from a partner or an incoming partner, or, the acquisition of land by a partner or former partner from a partnership or from another partner is liable to SDLT.

Land transactions on marriage breakdown, variations following death, assents and appropriations by personal representatives and certain leases granted by registered social landlords are exempt from SDLT.

The rates of SDLT are based upon chargeable consideration and are:

Effective date 3.9.08–31.12.09
Rate

	Residential	Non-Residential or Mixed
	£	£
0%	175,000	150,000
1%	175,001–250,000	150,001–250,000
3%	250,001–500,000	250,001–500,000
4%	Over 500,000	Over 500,000

Effective date before 3.9.08 or after 31.12.09

Rate	Other land in the UK		Land in disadvantaged areas	
	Residential	Non-Residential or Mixed	Residential	Non-Residential or Mixed
	£	£	£	£
0%	125,000	150,000	150,000	150,000
1%	125,001–250,000	150,001–250,000	150,001–250,000	150,001–250,000
3%	250,001–500,000	250,001–500,000	250,001–500,000	250,001–500,000
4%	Over 500,000	Over 500,000	Over 500,000	Over 500,000

On the assignment of a lease of residential property which has less than 21 years to run, the £175,000 zero rate limit above does not apply where the effective date is on or after 3 September 2008 and before 22 April 2009. In such cases, the zero rate limit is £125,000 (£150,000 if the land is in a disadvantaged area).

Where a lease is granted, there are two potential elements which are chargeable to SDLT.

The first is the premium payable on the grant. This is subject to SDLT in the same way as on a sale but the temporary increase in the zero rate limit to £175,000 does not apply to leases of less than 21 years where the effective date is on or after 3 September 2008 and before 22 April 2009. However, in the case of non-residential or mixed property, if the annual rental under the lease (or, for mixed property, the part of the annual rental which is attributable, on a just and reasonable apportionment, to the non-residential part) exceeds £1,000 per year, the zero rate band does not apply, instead the 1% rate applies to the premium (FA 2003 Sch 5.9A).

The second element is the rental payable during the term of the lease. This is subject to SDLT at the following rates

Effective date 3.9.08–31.12.09

Rate (%)	Net present value of rent	
	Residential	Non-residential or Mixed
0%	First £175,000	First £150,000
1%	Excess over £175,000	Excess over £150,000

Effective date before 3.9.08 or after 31.12.09

Rate (%)	Net present value of rent	
	Residential	**Non-residential or Mixed**
Zero	First £125,000	First £150,000
1%	Excess over £125,000	Excess over £150,000

The £175,000 limit for transactions for which the effective date is on or after 3 September 2008 and before 1 January 2010 does not apply to the grant of leases for less than 21 years. In such cases, the zero rate limit is £125,000.

Note that where the net present value of rent on a residential property exceeds the zero rate limit, the 1% rate does not apply to the whole of the rental but only applies to the excess above the zero rate limit (the 'slice' system of charging tax). This is unusual in the context of stamp duty land tax where the rate usually applies to the whole of the consideration (the 'slab' system). For the grant of leases of residential property where the effective date is on or after 3 September 2008 and before 22 April 2009, where the net present value of the rent exceeds £175,000, the 1% rate applies to the excess over £125,000.

The 'net present value of rent' is defined in FA 2003 Sch 5 para 3 and is effectively the aggregate of the rent payable over the term of the lease, discounted by the 'temporal discount rate' which has been set initially at 3.5% per year.

A land transaction is a chargeable transaction for SDLT, unless it falls within an exemption. The most important exemptions are:

(a)   transactions where there is no chargeable consideration for the disposal (ie gifts);

(b)   transactions in connection with divorce;

(c)   variations of wills etc after death.

No land transaction return is required if one of the exemptions apply.

SDLT on property with a mortgage based on unconventional principles (eg Islamic rules) will be the same as that payable on a property with a conventional mortgage.

If two pieces of land are exchanged, there will be two separate SDLT transactions. The chargeable consideration for each transaction is the market value of the land acquired by each purchaser and SDLT will be payable accordingly. There are special reliefs for certain exchanges of residential property. These include the situation where a house-building company acquires a dwelling in part exchange for the disposal of a newly constructed dwelling. The old dwelling must have been the only or main residence of the individual disposing of it and he must intend to occupy the new dwelling as his only or main residence. The effect of the relief will usually be that no SDLT is payable on the old dwelling.

A return and payment of SDLT must be made by the purchaser within 30 days of the effective date. The tax is self-assessed. A return is required for every 'notifiable transaction' even if no tax is chargeable. A return is also required within 30 days of any event altering the SDLT liability eg confirmation of consideration or contingency, withdrawal of any relief such as SDLT group relief.

In order to register a notifiable land transaction the purchaser must produce a certificate, issued by HMRC, showing compliance with SDLT.

(b)   **Stamp Duty**

Stamp duty is a duty on documents completed in the UK relating to UK transactions involving shares and marketable securities. No duty arises on transactions which are carried out orally (FA 1999 ss 112–113 and Schs 13–16).

If an instrument that is liable to be stamped is not so stamped, it cannot be used as evidence in civil proceedings. Therefore, a failure to have a document properly stamped could lead to legal problems in the case of a dispute. A company secretary will not register a transfer of shares or securities if the document has not been properly stamped.

Although stamp duty is not directly enforceable, interest and penalties can be levied for a failure to ensure that documents are properly stamped. (The interest and penalty rules are set out at explanatory note 11).

The administration and collection of stamp duty is the responsibility of HM Revenue and Customs (Stamp Taxes).

The Stamp Act 1891 s 5(a) requires that full details of the facts and circumstances relating to an instrument are provided in order to allow the correct stamp duty to be calculated. Failure to do so can lead to a fine of up to £3,000.

Duties can be 'ad valorem' which means that the duty will be a percentage of the consideration passing. Alternatively, duties can be 'fixed'. (Most fixed duties have, however, now been abolished with the exception of a limited number of cases relating to pre-SDLT land transactions.)

Some instruments – most notably instruments which transfer shares by way of a gift where no consideration is payable – are not stampable, provided that the appropriate exemption certificate is completed. These instruments are listed in SI 1987/516.

Stamp duty depends upon the heading under which a transaction falls, ie

(1)	Share and convertible loan stock transactions (including purchase by a company of its own shares, takeovers, mergers, demergers, and schemes of reconstruction and amalgamation, except where there is no real change in ownership)	½%
(2)	Shares converted into depositary receipts or put into duty free clearance systems (see part (c))	1½%
(3)	Most bearer instruments (excluding those in foreign currency – but see part (c))	1½%

Ad valorem duty is calculated as a strict percentage, and then rounded up to the nearest multiple of £5 (FA 1999 s 112). Duty is not chargeable on a transfer of stock or marketable securities where the consideration for the sale is not more than £1,000 (FA 1999 Sch 13 para 1).

Stamp duty is not payable when a company issues new shares to its shareholders, for example on the initial creation of the company or when new shares are subscribed for.

Where shares are repurchased by a company, ad valorem duty at a rate of 0.5% is payable on the Form 169 delivered to the Registrar of Companies.

The consideration payable by the purchaser to the vendor will usually be in the form of cash. However 'consideration' can take other forms such as other shares and marketable securities, the release of debt or liability or a dividend in specie.

Therefore stamp duty cannot be avoided by the purchaser paying for the new shares in non-cash form. Effectively the value of the non-cash assets offered in exchange for the shares is treated as consideration and is subjected to ad valorem stamp duty.

Sometimes the consideration for a transfer of shares may be uncertain at the time of the transaction. The stamp duty payable depends on how the deal is structured. If the contingent amount is fixed then that amount is also subject to stamp duty. The same rule applies if the variable amount has a maximum limit, stamp duty is then payable on the maximum amount. However, if the variable amount only has a minimum limit then stamp duty is only payable on the minimum amount. If the variable amount has no maximum or minimum limit then no ad valorem duty is payable in relation to the potential extra consideration.

If shares are exchanged, then two share transfers will be executed. Both will be liable for ad valorem duty. Each will be liable to stamp duty by reference to the value of the shares transferred by the other document.

In both cases, the transaction may be documented as a sale of the higher value shares. The transfer of the higher value shares will be liable to ad valorem duty but the transfer of the shares in consideration will not. To qualify as a sale of the higher value shares, there must be a cash element to the sale which is more than nominal.

There is an exemption from stamp duty where shares pass between two companies in a group. A group is where one company owns 75% of the shares of another, or both are under the 75% ownership of another company. This is sometimes referred to as 'stamp duty group relief' (FA 1930 s 42). The instrument of transfer must be adjudicated (see below at D). The exemption does not apply if, at the time the instrument is executed, arrangements are in existence which mean that any other person can gain control of the transferee company (FA 1967 s 27).

There are special exemptions from duty for financial intermediaries trading in UK securities and in connection with stock lending and sale and repurchase arrangements (FA 1986 ss 80A to 80D). Exemption also applies where a mutual insurance company transfers its business to a conventional company (FA 1997 s 96), and to transfers of units in unit trusts or shares in open-ended investment companies (FA 1999 Sch 19), although the latter are now charged to stamp duty reserve tax (see below).

A stamp duty (and stamp duty reserve tax) exemption also applies where the trustees of an approved share incentive plan transfer shares to the employees as partnership shares or dividend shares (FA 2001 s 95 – see Example 85 part (3)).

(c)   **Stamp Duty Reserve Tax**

Stamp duty reserve tax is charged under the provisions of FA 1986 ss 86 to 99 on transactions in *chargeable securities* (broadly, stocks, shares, loan capital, and units under a unit trust scheme (as to which see below) (FA 1986 s 99)) which are not charged to stamp duty, for example, sales of renounceable letters of allotment. The rate of tax is ½%. Transactions under the paperless system for transferring securities (CREST), are subject to stamp duty reserve tax on the agreement to transfer, rather than stamp duty (FA 1996 s 186). Stamp duty continues to be charged on securities transferred outside the CREST system. Stamp duty reserve tax does not apply to gilt edged stocks, traded options and futures, non-convertible loan stocks, foreign securities not on a UK register, depositary interests in foreign securities, purchases by a charity, transfers of units in foreign unit trusts, and the issue of new securities. See also part (b) for the exemption for shares transferred to employees under approved share incentive plans.

There are special exemptions for financial intermediaries (FA 1986 ss 88, 88B, and 89AA) which apply to transactions on a regulated market or multilateral trading facility (both as defined in the EU Markets in Financial Instruments Directive) or on a recognised foreign exchange or recognised foreign options exchange. If a person who has qualified for exemption then transfers securities to a fellow group member, the normal exemption on intra-group transfers does not apply and stamp duty reserve tax is payable (FA 1986 s 92).

An anti-avoidance measure charges stamp duty reserve tax at ½% on transfers of foreign currency bearer shares and of sterling or foreign currency bearer loan stock that is convertible or equity related. The charge does not apply if the securities are listed on a recognised stock exchange and the transfer is not made as part of a takeover (FA 1986 s 90).

A further anti-avoidance measure charges stamp duty reserve tax at 1½% on the issue or transfer by a UK company of foreign currency bearer instruments into a depositary or clearance service in connection with a merger or takeover of any company and on the issue or transfer into a depositary or clearance system of foreign currency bearer instruments that would otherwise be exempt from duty, unless they are subscribed for cash and carry a right to a dividend at a fixed rate or are loan capital (FA 1986 ss 95 and 97).

From 6 February 2000 stamp duty reserve tax replaced stamp duty on transfers of units in a unit trust and shares in open-ended investment companies (OEICs). The rate is ½%, but this can be reduced where within the same or following calendar month similar units are issued.

Liability to stamp duty reserve tax arises at the date of the agreement (or, if the agreement is conditional, the date the condition is satisfied) (FA 1986 s 87). For transactions via an exchange (in particular CREST transactions), the tax is payable on a date agreed with HMRC (or if there is no agreed date, the fourteenth day after the transaction). For other transactions the due date is the seventh day of the month following the date of the transaction and the person liable to pay the tax (ie the broker, dealer or purchaser) must give notice of the charge to HMRC on or before that date. If stamp duty is paid after reserve tax has been paid, the reserve tax is refunded (plus interest on refunds over £25, the interest being free of income tax).

Stamp duty reserve tax also applies to securities converted into depositary receipts or put into a duty free clearing system, and the rate of tax on these transactions is 1½% (FA 1986 ss 93–97). The tax is only payable, however, to the extent that it exceeds any ad valorem stamp duty on the transaction, and where the ad valorem duty exceeds the amount of reserve tax, no reserve tax is payable. There are exemptions for exchanges of securities between associated companies (FA 1930 s 42, FA 1986 s 88 – see explanatory note 6). Clearing systems may elect to pay stamp duty or stamp duty reserve tax in the normal way on their transactions, and in that event the 1½% charge when securities are put into the system does not apply (FA 1986 s 97A).

B.   Memorandum for Mr Argenton

8 May 2009	The true consideration for the purchase of the company's share capital is £1 plus the loan of £50,000 = £50,001. The rate of stamp duty on shares is ½% rounded up to the nearest £5. Accordingly the duty payable is £255. If the shares are actually worth less than £50,001 then the transfer may be submitted for adjudication and duty paid at the above rate on the actual value of the shares (FA 1980 s 102(2)).
7 August 2009	The sale of land and standing timber is a transfer of property valued in excess of £250,000 but less than £500,000 and therefore attracts SDLT at the rate of 3%, ie £450,000 × 3% = £13,500, unless Mr Argenton had elected to waive his exemption for VAT. If the sale was subject to VAT, the VAT would amount to 15% of £450,000 = £67,500, making total consideration of £517,500. SDLT payable is therefore £517,500 × 4% = £20,700. The purchaser is liable for the tax (FA 2003 s 85).
9 September 2009	The trustees are transferring property in accordance with the trust deed. That transaction is exempt from duty in accordance with the Stamp Duty (Exempt Instruments) Regulations 1987 (SI 1987/516) – Category F. No duty is payable providing the appropriate certificates are signed.
10 January 2010	Stamp duty is a tax on shares. SDLT is a tax on land and buildings. As cash does not fall into these categories no duty is payable.
15 January 2010	Mr Argenton is not liable to stamp duty on the issue of loan stock because it is specifically exempt under FA 1986 s 79(2). (That section also exempts the *transfer* of loan stock unless it carries a right either of conversion into shares or to more than a commercial rate of return, but see part A(c) re the charge to stamp duty reserve tax on the transfer of certain bearer loan stock.)

20 March 2010   No liability arose on the granting of the loan, and the issue of new shares to Mr Argenton in satisfaction of the debt is also exempt from duty. (The exemption from duty on issues of shares does not apply where they are issued as consideration for a sale, subject to what is said in explanatory note 6. Nor does it apply to bearer shares – FA 1963 s 60.)

C.   The effective date

The 'effective date' of a transaction is significant for many reasons. It identifies the date of the transaction for the purposes of determining, among other things, the following:

- when the land transaction return should be filed;

- when the tax should be paid;

- the date from which interest begins to run, and from which penalties may be charged; and

- the market value of the consideration, eg where non-monetary consideration is given for a land transaction, FA 2003 Sch 4 para 8 provides that its value is taken to be its market value at the effective date of the transaction.

Generally speaking, the effective date of a transaction is the date of completion. However, there are certain circumstances in which a different date applies.

In the case of a contract to transfer land where the transaction will be completed by a conveyance, the effective date is the date of completion. However, if the contract is 'substantially performed' without being completed, the effective date is the date when the contract is substantially performed. The effect of this provision is to catch attempts to avoid tax by 'resting on contract'. Without the 'substantial performance' provision, SDLT could be avoided by the purchaser, for example, taking possession of the property without the contract ever being completed.

A contract may be made between two parties, providing for a chargeable interest to be conveyed by one party (A), at the request or direction of the other party (B), to a third party. If the contract is substantially performed, B is treated as having acquired a chargeable interest at the date that the contract is substantially performed.

Where an agreement for lease is made, and is substantially performed without being completed, the agreement is treated as the grant of a lease under the terms of the agreement, with the effective date being the date of substantial performance.

Where an agreement for lease has been made, and the lessee under the agreement assigns his interest under the agreement after it has been substantially performed, the assignment is taken as a separate land transaction, the effective date being the date of assignment.

A contract is taken to be 'substantially performed' if the purchaser, or a connected person, takes possession of the whole, or substantially the whole, of the subject matter. 'Taking possession' includes the receipt of rents or the right to receive them. Also, it is immaterial whether possession is taken under the contract or under a licence or lease of temporary character.

A contract is also taken to be substantially performed if a substantial amount of the consideration is paid or provided. In a case where none of the consideration is rent, such as the outright sale of land, this condition is taken to have been met if the whole, or substantially the whole, of the consideration is paid or provided. Where the consideration includes rent and some other consideration, such as a premium, the condition is met if either the whole, or substantially the whole of that other consideration (eg the premium) is paid or provided, or when the first payment of rent is made. Where the consideration consists of rent only, the condition is met when the first payment of rent is made.

The acquisition of an option or right of pre-emption is a land transaction in its own right, distinct from any land transaction arising from its exercise. In the case of the acquisition of the option or right, the effective date is the date it was acquired.

D.   **(a)   Adjudication**

Adjudication is the process whereby HMRC (Stamp Taxes) assess the amount of stamp duty, if any, payable on a document, including adjudication as to the amount of any penalty payable for late stamping (as to which see explanatory note 11). Additionally, if after adjudication an unstamped or insufficiently stamped document is not duly stamped within 30 days, a penalty of up to £300 may be charged.

Adjudication may be voluntary or compulsory. Any person may ask HMRC to adjudicate as to whether a document is chargeable to stamp duty, and if so, to state the duty payable. If HMRC decide that no stamp duty is payable the document will be stamped to that effect. Once stamped a document is admissible in evidence (Stamp Act 1891 s 12).

The Registrar of Companies may require adjudication for an allotment of shares where the terms have not been put in writing (Companies Act 1985 s 88(4)).

Adjudication may also be required where consideration needs to be established in order to determine the duty payable, eg where shares are issued as consideration for a transaction.

If a taxpayer is dissatisfied with the decision of HMRC he may appeal against it. Appeals must be made within 30 days and the duty plus any interest or penalty must be paid first. Appeals relating to late stamping penalties go first to the First-tier Tribunal and other appeals to the High Court.

(b)   Transactions by Brown Ltd group of companies

(i)   Providing the documents are submitted for adjudication, the transfer by Blue Ltd to Brown Ltd of shares in Black Ltd will be exempt from stamp duty as Blue Ltd is a wholly owned subsidiary of Brown Ltd (FA 1930 s 42).

(ii)   Stamp duty of ½% of £100,000, ie £500 will be payable as Brown Ltd owns only 70% of Colourless Ltd.

(iii)   The agreement to sell shares in Indigo plc is not itself dutiable, and therefore the transfer of the beneficial interest in that contract by Brown Ltd will avoid stamp duty but not stamp duty reserve tax. This will be charged on Brown Ltd, ie ½% × £3,000 = £15.

The actual share transfer will be between Rainbow Ltd and the third party and that document will attract stamp duty of £15, ie ½% × £2,900 = £14.50, rounded up to nearest multiple of £5.

Explanatory Notes

SDLT legislation

1.   From 1 December 2003 SDLT applies to transactions in UK land and buildings and stamp duty applies to documents relating to stocks and marketable securities and the issue of bearer instruments. SDLT also applies to the acquisition of a partnership which holds UK land.

SDLT, stamp duty, and stamp duty reserve tax are dealt with by HMRC (Stamp Taxes).

Adjudication

2.   The process of adjudication is outlined in part D(a) of the example. Where a document bears an adjudication stamp this is normally conclusive evidence of stamping.

Section 12 of the Stamp Act 1891 provides for HMRC to 'adjudicate' on any executed instrument if requested to do so. HMRC can be asked to adjudicate on a number of points such as:

(a)   whether the instrument is stampable;

(b)   the amount of duty;

(c)   whether a late stamping penalty is payable;

(d)   what penalty is correct and appropriate.

If HMRC decides that an instrument is not chargeable to stamp duty, then it will be stamped to show this. Otherwise it will be stamped with the amount adjudicated and the relevant amount should be paid as appropriate. Adjudication is the only way to formally determine the amount of stamp duty due. Adjudication is compulsory for certain instruments, such as transfers of shares to charities, specifically exempt transfers (eg, intra group transfers) and transfers in satisfaction of a debt.

If a person is unhappy with the adjudication, he has 30 days to bring an appeal. However, an appeal can only be brought on payment of the stamp duty plus any penalty in conformity with HMRC's decision and any interest that would be payable following the adjudication.

Value added tax

3.   Where property that is conveyed or leased is property on which the option may be taken to charge VAT (broadly all land and buildings except domestic, relevant residential or non-business charity buildings) then SDLT is payable on the value *plus VAT* if the option is exercised. The availability of a claim to recover input tax will not alter the charge to SDLT.

Chargeable consideration does not include any VAT that may become payable as a result of an election to waive exemption after the effective date. This means that, for example, if a landlord 'opts to tax' *after* granting a lease, the VAT payable will not form part of the chargeable consideration.

The notice to waive exemption from VAT (option to tax) is not liable to SDLT, and SDLT itself is never liable to VAT.

On the sale of the land and standing timber in part B on 7 August 2009 the option to charge VAT may have been available. If Mr Argenton did not exercise the option before sale, SDLT is not payable on the VAT that might have become due. If, on the other hand, the option was exercised at any time before completion, then SDLT would be payable on the VAT inclusive value.

If the transaction is part of a sale of a business, then VAT is not chargeable under the transfer of a going concern provisions. If this is expected to be the case, it may well be that the provisions relating to contingent consideration will apply.

Mortgaged property

4.   Care must be taken with transfers of mortgaged property, as the value for SDLT is the sum of the price paid plus the outstanding loan (see *CIR v City of Glasgow Bank* (1881), a case decided under stamp duty). This also applies where there is no actual consideration; duty is payable on the value of the debt taken over (see Revenue Statement of Practice SP6/90).

This is particularly relevant where the transaction is between connected persons, eg a mortgaged property held in the name of one spouse is transferred into joint names, or into the name of the other spouse, or from joint names to a single name.

Where the transferor covenants to pay the debt and the transferee does not assume any liability for it, no consideration has been given. The transfer is then not liable to SDLT as no chargeable consideration is provided by the purchaser (FA 2003 Sch 3 para 1 and Sch 4 para 1).

If, however, the transferee agrees to pay the debt or to indemnify the transferor against his personal liability to the lender that will constitute valuable consideration liable to SDLT. A covenant or agreement may be in writing or implied.

The above rules do not affect any statutory exemption from SDLT, eg transfers to a charity or a charitable trust (FA 2003 Sch 8) and certain transfers from one party to the other in connection with a divorce or separation (FA 2003 Sch 3 para 3).

Transfer to connected company

5.   Special rules apply where the purchaser is a company and either:

(a)   the vendor is connected with the company; or

(b)   some or all of the consideration for the transaction is the issue or transfer of shares in a company with which the vendor is connected.

An example would be where land is transferred from a sole trader or partnership to a company on incorporation. In this case, the chargeable consideration is the market value of the land at the date of the transaction. This rule applies even if the land is gifted to the company, as the exemption in FA 2003 Sch 3 para 1 is disapplied (FA 2003 s 53).

Transfers between associated companies and company reconstructions

6.   Transfers of property between associated companies and on company reconstructions are exempt from SDLT (FA 2003 Sch 7). Group relief applies where one company is the parent of the other company, or both are subsidiaries of a common parent, and the parent company owns in each case not less than 75% of the ordinary share capital of the subsidiary, and is entitled to 75% or more of the profits and on a winding up 75% or more of the assets (Sch 7 para 1). Exemption also applies to the grant of a lease by one group company to another group company or an agreement for a lease between group companies. There are anti-avoidance provisions in Sch 7 para 3 to prevent these provisions being used to avoid SDLT when property, or an economic interest in it, passes out of the group.

Group relief may be withdrawn if the vendor and purchaser companies cease to be members of the same group within three years, in certain circumstances. The tax that would originally have been paid becomes chargeable. It becomes payable 30 days after the event which causes the withdrawal of the group relief. Group relief is not withdrawn where the companies cease to be members of the same group because the vendor leaves the group.

SDLT group relief must be claimed in a land transaction return and a further return made if the relief is withdrawn.

A reduced rate of SDLT of ½% applies to land transactions entered into for the purposes of or in connection with the acquisition by a company of the whole or part of an undertaking of another company in exchange for shares (Sch 7 para 8). This is subject to anti-avoidance provisions where the undertaking includes UK land (Sch 7 para 9).

As indicated in part A(c) of the example, there is an exemption from stamp duty reserve tax for certain transfers of securities between associated companies.

Transfer to a limited liability partnership

7.   There is an exemption from stamp duty land tax where land is transferred to a limited liability partnership (LLP) in connection with its incorporation.

Three conditions must be satisfied:

(a)   the effective date of the transaction is not more than one year after the incorporation of the LLP;

(b)   the partners in the old partnership and the new LLP are the same and the transferor is one of those partners;

(c)   the interests of the partners in the old and new partnerships are the same or any change in the interests is not part of a tax avoidance scheme (FA 2003 s 65).

Variable or contingent consideration

8.   Where all or part of the consideration payable on a land transaction is not in money or money's worth then market value at the effective date of the transaction is used. However, this rule only applies in the absence of any contrary provision. 'Market value' is determined using the capital gains tax rules in TCGA 1992 (FA 2003 s 118 and Sch 4 para 7). There is no discount for postponed consideration (Sch 4 para 3). Where, however, the consideration is ascertainable but not fixed, SDLT is paid on the basis that any contingent amount will be payable. Where consideration is uncertain SDLT is paid on the amount that could reasonably be certain to be received (FA 2003 s 51). Where the value is based upon an annuity payable for more than 12 years the value is restricted to the twelve highest annual payments (FA 2003 s 52).

Special rules apply to leases in the case of variable or uncertain rent (see FA 2003 Sch 17A para 7). See explanatory note 9 below.

SDLT provisions on rent

9.   Different provisions apply where the rent payable under a lease is contingent, uncertain or unascertained. If the rent payable relates to any period before the end of the fifth year of the lease, the normal rules for contingent, uncertain and unascertained consideration apply. If it relates to a period after the end of the fifth year, the 'annual amount' is taken to be the highest amount of rent payable in any consecutive 12-month period within the first five years of the lease. Finance Act 2003 Schedule 17A para 7 gives details on how to determine this figure.

For contingent, uncertain or unascertained rent payable within the first five years of the lease, an adjustment must be made, either at the end of year five, or if the rent payable ceases to be uncertain at an earlier time at that time. If, at the end of year five, the rent is still uncertain, it is calculated using the rules in the preceding paragraph. If, as a result of the rent ceasing to be uncertain, a transaction becomes notifiable, or tax (or additional tax) becomes payable, the purchaser must make a return (together with self-assessment) to HMRC within 30 days, and pay the tax due not later than the filing date for the return. The tax is calculated using the rates in force at the effective date of the transaction. This is beneficial for the taxpayer if rates have risen since then. If it turns out that the purchaser had initially paid more tax than turned out to be in fact due, a refund is given.

Where a lease is varied so as to increase the rent payable within the first five years of the term, this is treated as a grant of a new lease, in consideration for the additional rent payable. However, this rule does not apply where the increase in rent is made in pursuance of a provision within the lease itself. It also does not apply to leases under certain legislation relating to agricultural holdings and tenancies.

Where the variation of a lease resulting in an increased rent occurs after the fifth year of the term, it will only be regarded as a new lease if the increase is 'abnormal'. The new lease is taken to be granted in consideration for the excess rent, ie the difference between the new rent and the old rent. FA 2003 provides a formula to be used in order to determine whether or not the increase is abnormal.

SDLT administration

10.   Where there has been a 'notifiable transaction', the purchaser must, within 30 days of the effective date of the transaction, submit to HMRC a land transaction return. The following are notifiable transactions:

(a)   the acquisition of a 'major interest' in land, other than one falling within one or more of the exceptions listed below:

A 'major interest' means, in relation to land in England and Wales, an estate in fee simple absolute, or a term of years absolute. In relation to land in Northern Ireland it means any freehold or leasehold estate. In relation to land in Scotland, it means the interest of an owner of land, or the tenant's right over or interest in property subject to a lease.

(b)   an acquisition of a chargeable interest which is not a 'major interest' if there is chargeable consideration in respect of which SDLT would be chargeable at a rate of 1 per cent or higher, or would be so chargeable, but for a relief;

(c)   the substantial performance of a contract in circumstances envisaged by FA 2003 s 44A(3) dealing with a contract under which a chargeable interest is to be conveyed to a third party (see notes to Question C above); and

(d)   a notional land transaction under the anti-avoidance provisions of FA 2003 s 75A.

The exceptions to (a) above are:

(i)   an acquisition which is exempt under FA 2003 Sch 3;

(ii)   an acquisition (other than the grant, assignment or surrender of a lease) where the chargeable consideration is less than £40,000;

(iii)   the grant of a lease for a term of at least seven years where any chargeable consideration other than rent is less than £40,000 and the annual rent is less than £1,000;

(iv)   the assignment or surrender of a lease originally granted for a term of at least seven years where the chargeable consideration for the assignment or surrender is less than £40,000;

(v)   the grant of a lease for less than seven years where the chargeable consideration does not exceed the zero rate threshold; and

(vi)   the assignment or surrender of a lease originally granted for a term of less than seven years where the chargeable consideration for the assignment or surrender does not exceed the zero rate threshold.

Payment of SDLT must be made on or before the filing date for the return.

Interest and penalties

11.   SDLT is subject to a regime similar to income tax self-assessment with penalties for failure to deliver a return, for a fraudulent or negligent return (or, where the liability arises after 31 March 2010, for a careless or deliberate error in a return), failure to keep or preserve records, failure to comply with notices to provide documents or information and criminal sanctions for fraudulently evading SDLT. Interest is paid on overpaid tax and charged on overdue SDLT at the same rates as for income tax.

Penalties for stamp duty and stamp duty reserve tax may apply where documents are submitted late for stamping (SA 1891 s 15B). There are separate interest and penalty provisions in relation to bearer instruments.

If documents are not presented for stamping within 30 days, the maximum penalty for documents presented up to one-year late is £300 or the amount of the duty if lower. For documents submitted outside the one year period the maximum penalty is £300 or the amount of the duty if more. The penalties are subject to mitigation where there is a reasonable excuse. For documents executed abroad the 30 days and one-year periods run from the date the document is brought into the UK. There is a penalty of up to £300, or up to £3,000 in cases of fraud, for administrative offences.

Interest is chargeable where a document liable to ad valorem duty is not stamped within 30 days of execution. The interest is rounded down to a multiple of £5, and is not chargeable if it amounts to £25 or less. For documents executed abroad, the interest runs from 30 days after execution, not the date the document is brought into the UK. Where stamp duty or late stamping penalties have been overpaid, interest is payable on repayments amounting to £25 or more from 30 days after execution or from the date of payment of the duty or penalty if later. The rates of interest are the same as for income tax, ie from 24 March 2009 2.5% (previously 3.5%) on underpayments and from 27 January 2009 0% (previously 0.75%) on overpayments.

Executing a document outside the UK does not delay payment if it relates to UK shares, because the transaction is caught by stamp duty reserve tax (FA 1986 s 86(4)), even if made outside the UK between non-resident parties.

Interest is charged on overdue stamp duty reserve tax at the same rate as for income tax from 14 days after the transaction date for transactions on an exchange and otherwise from 7 days after the end of the month of the transaction, and there are various penalties for defaults, including a mitigable penalty of £100 where the appropriate notice of liability has not been given and the tax has not been paid. Interest is payable on repayments from the payment date at the same rate as for income tax.

From a date to be appointed, both stamp duty land tax and stamp duty reserve tax will fall within the cross-tax penalty for failure to make payments on time under FA 2009 Sch 56. It is also intended to align interest regimes across all taxes.

Question

Outline the provisions relating to the acquisition of shares by employees and directors and the special rules relating to the following worker participation plans:

(1)   SAYE share option schemes

(2)   Company share option plans (CSOP schemes)

(3)   Share incentive plans (SIP)

(4)   Enterprise management incentives (EMI plans)

(5)   Corporation tax relief on employee shares.

Answer

A. Acquisitions of shares and other employment-related securities by employees and directors

The legislation relating to the acquisition of securities by employees and directors is complex and wide-ranging. Although favourable tax treatment is given to participants in the HM Revenue & Customs (HMRC) approved employee share plans, there are very detailed statutory provisions that must be satisfied for each plan. The costs of establishing HMRC approved employee share plans are allowable deductions for corporation tax as are the incidental costs of running all types of employee share plans. Further corporation tax implications are considered below under **Corporation tax relief on employee shares**.

The legislation was entirely rewritten by Income Tax (Earnings and Pensions) Act 2003 (ITEPA 2003) which took effect on 6 April 2003, though the purpose of this was simply to make it more intelligible, and only minor changes were made to the law itself. Three days after this Act took effect, the 2003 Budget announced numerous changes, with much of the legislation again completely rewritten by FA 2003, this time making major changes to the law, in particular tightening up the numerous anti-avoidance provisions.

Except in relation to the approved plans and EMI, the legislation applies to 'securities' rather than just to shares. The definition of securities for these purposes in ITEPA 2003 s 420(1) is wide-ranging, including debentures, loan stock and other securities issued by companies, warrants, options (other than options over securities) as well as a range of other financial instruments, including government and local authority loan stock, and units in collective investment schemes. The approved plans deal only with 'ordinary shares' as defined in ITA 2007 s 989. The legislation applies where the securities have been acquired by reason of employment. It deems this to be the case where employees or directors acquire shares (or other securities) in their employing company unless it can be demonstrated that the acquisition was by reason of personal or family relationships or the securities were acquired in the open market on the same terms as are available to independent third parties (eg, shares are purchased by the employee independently on the Stock Market having made his own arrangements to do so). The employment by reason of which the individual acquires his shares includes prospective employment or any employment that terminated in the previous seven years. Where someone acquires securities by reason of the employment of another person, ITEPA 2003 Part 7 applies and the latter individual will be subject to the charges so arising as if he had acquired the securities or associated benefit himself.

The main provisions of the current approved plans, EMI and other relevant legislation are as follows.

Reporting requirements

Under all the approved plans, employers are required to provide annual returns to HMRC using the appropriate form. Detailed information must also be provided when chargeable events occur in relation to employment-related securities. Penalties apply if the company fails to comply. Employees must similarly ensure that appropriate details are included in their tax returns (see below under **Self-assessment**).

The legislation in ITEPA 2003 s 421J goes further and requires notification, by 6 July following the fiscal year, of *all* acquisitions of shares and securities by a director/employee by reason of employment (including past and prospective employments (s 421B)). Thus acquisition of an initial subscriber share by a company formation agent is not reportable, but generally all subsequent transfers of shares or an issue of new shares will be reportable if the shareholder is or will be a director or employee including those who are founding members of a company. The report should be on Form 42 sent to the Employee Shares and Securities Unit. HMRC will not impose penalties if the information is provided by letter to the local Inspector with the CT 41G (notification of a company coming within the charge to corporation tax (FA 2004 s 55)). In 2005, a simplified form became available for use by newly formed companies and their advisers. However, by 2006, HMRC announced that most subscriptions to shares in newly formed companies would not need to be the subject of a return, provided that trade had not commenced. The notification must be given by the responsible person. In the case of the initial subscriber share, notification is required by either the company formation agent or by the company. In the case of subsequent transfers or issues of shares ITEPA 2003 s 421L provides that notification is to be given by either the employer or the person from whom the shares were acquired.

Where a notice to file has been received there is a penalty not exceeding £300 for failure to file by the due date which can be increased by up to £60 per day for continued failure. In addition, a penalty of £300 per reportable event can be imposed by way of penalty proceedings, with further penalties not exceeding £60 per day. The penalties for failure to file returns are under review as part of a project to harmonise penalty provisions across different taxes, and new penalty provisions have been included in FA 2009 Sch 55 but the changes have not yet been implemented. They should in due course provide for:

- an initial penalty of £100;

- if the failure continues for more than three months after the due date and HMRC decides to impose it and gives notice of the fact, a further penalty of £10 per day for up to 90 days;

- if the failure continues beyond six months, a penalty of the greater of 5% of the tax that would have been shown in the return and £300; and

- for failure extending to twelve months

  – in cases of carelessness a further 5% or £300;

  – for deliberate failure the greater of 70% of the tax and £300; and

  – for failure that is both deliberate and concealed 100% of the tax or £300.

A return is not required if it can be ascertained that there was no element of remuneration and the transfer was made by an individual and the right or opportunity was made available in the normal course of the domestic, family or personal relationships of that person (s 421B(3)).

There are additionally some specific circumstances where HMRC have indicated that they will not require a report via Form 42. For example, the HMRC guidance to Form 42 states that a report may not be required in respect of shares acquired by employees or directors purchased on the open market independently of the company where the company is quoted on a recognised stock exchange. Shares acquired in a company listed on a recognised stock exchange in connection with a bonus issue, rights issue or dividend reinvestment plan may also be exempt where the right is offered to all shareholders.

Securities that are 'readily convertible assets'

Where employment-related securities are acquired by employees other than under approved plans, or are subject to a tax charge under the rules of an approved plan, employers must account for income tax and Class 1 national insurance contributions under the 'notional pay' provisions of PAYE if the securities are 'readily convertible assets', ie, they may be sold on the Stock Exchange or arrangements exist for them to be traded (see Example 8 explanatory note 12). These provisions apply to shares acquired directly and through the exercise of unapproved options that were granted on or after 27 November 1996 (5 December 1996 for NIC purposes). They also apply where there is a chargeable event arising where a securities option is assigned or released, or a restriction attached to the securities is lifted or varied or the securities are sold when still subject to such restriction (unless certain elections have been entered into – these are discussed in more detail in the restricted securities section below), or securities are converted into other forms of security (see below). The national insurance legislation for options granted on or after 6 April 1999 deems the taxable gain to be earnings for Class 1 contributions purposes when the unapproved options are exercised, although there is no provision deeming the exercise to constitute a payment of those earnings. (See Example 48 explanatory note 14 for the optional treatment of the employee paying the employer's secondary

Class 1 liability.) The tax provisions relating to convertible shares and shares liable to forfeiture are mirrored for national insurance purposes for shares or interests in shares acquired on or after 9 April 1998. If shares are not readily convertible assets, neither Class 1 nor Class 1A national insurance contributions are payable and any such income tax arising should be paid under the self-assessment system.

From 10 July 2003, shares and other securities that would not otherwise be readily convertible assets are treated as such (except for the purposes of the share incentive plan rules) unless they are shares (or stock) that attract a corporation tax deduction under the provisions at (5) below. When the major changes made by FA 2003 to the acquisition of employment-related securities (other than under the various approved plans in an approved manner) came into effect on 1 September 2003, PAYE and national insurance were extended to chargeable events within those new provisions. Where the chargeable event takes the form of a receipt of money, or of an asset that is a readily convertible asset, PAYE and NICs apply regardless of whether or not the securities subject to the plan are themselves readily convertible assets.

See Example 59 explanatory note 7 for the treatment of employment-related securities issued free or below market value to employees where the securities are not readily convertible assets.

Directors or employees with a 'material interest'

Under all approved employee share plans, employees or directors with a material interest in the company cannot participate if the company is a close company (see Example 56). 'Material interest' is determined by the percentage of the company's ordinary share capital owned or controlled by the employee and his or her associates. Associates are normally close relatives, but also include trustees of trusts under which the employee might benefit. Shares held by a trust set up for the benefit of employees will, however, usually be ignored in determining whether an employee has a material interest.

The relevant percentages are more than 30% for EMI plans, more than 25% for SIPs, SAYE share option schemes and CSOP schemes. Before 10 July 2003, the percentage for CSOP schemes was 10%. (The limit for EMI plans applies to all companies, not just close companies.) Employee Share Ownership Trusts do not constitute an approved plan (though may be used in conjunction with one), however, there is a 5% material interest test for inheritance tax purposes where a close company is the settlor, but this only applies if the amount of any benefit received by an individual with a material interest is not subject to income tax.

Restrictions on sale etc

Shares issued under approved share option plans or profit sharing schemes may be subject to a restriction in the company's articles of association requiring employees to sell them when they leave their employment, thus enabling companies to retain some control over holdings of their shares. Employee-controlled companies may use a class of shares of which the majority is held by directors or employees and gives them control of the company.

Securities options

The right to acquire shares (or other securities) is a securities option. A securities option is not itself regarded as a security for tax purposes (ITEPA 2003 s 420(5)(e) and (8)) except where certain tax avoidance schemes are used.

Favourable tax treatment is given under ITEPA 2003 Part 7 Chapter 7 and Sch 3 for HMRC approved SAYE plans and Chapter 8 and Sch 4 for approved CSOP schemes, and under ITEPA 2003 Part 7 Chapter 9 and Sch 5 for enterprise management incentives (EMI).

Where the option is not granted under an *approved* plan, an income tax charge arises at exercise on the difference between the open market value of the securities acquired at the time of exercising the right and the cost of acquiring them, including any amount paid for the option (ITEPA 2003 s 479). As indicated above, PAYE and national insurance contributions will be collected through payroll if the securities are readily convertible assets.

Where a right to acquire securities other than under an approved plan is assigned or released, an income tax charge arises on the consideration received less the cost of acquisition of the rights. A charge to income tax also arises when any benefit is received or gain is realised because the option holder allows the option to lapse, or grants someone else an option over the securities. As indicated above, income tax and national insurance contributions will be charged through the payroll if the securities are readily convertible assets.

These income tax charges apply on the exercise, chargeable assignment or release of the option by any associated person and not just by the employee (ie, the person by reason of whose employment the option was granted). 'Associated persons' include the person to whom the option was granted (if not the employee), persons connected with the employee (or with the grantee) and members of the same household as the employee (or grantee). To some extent, this was always the case but the scope of the charge is narrower before the appointed date (ie 1 September 2003) in that it applies only where the person exercising, assigning or releasing the option is connected with the employee.

A tax charge also arises on the amount or market value of any benefit received, in money or money's worth, by the employee (or an associated person) in connection with the option, which might include, for example, sums received for varying the option or as compensation for its cancellation.

Whatever the reason for a tax charge, any amount paid for the option itself is deductible in determining the taxable amount. From 1 September 2003, expenses incurred in connection with the exercise, assignment, release or receipt of benefit are also deductible, however notional costs of sale of the underlying securities are no longer deductible for income tax purposes.

For capital gains tax, the amount taxed as income on exercise of an unapproved employee share option counts as part of the cost of acquisition of the securities (as does anything paid for the option itself). The position was temporarily thrown into disarray, however, by the Court of Appeal decision in *Mansworth v Jelley* in December 2002 and, in particular, HMRC's reaction to it. It was decided in that case that the appellant could deduct for capital gains purposes the market value of the shares at the time he acquired them and not just their actual cost. In a statement on its website on 8 January 2003, HMRC announced that following this judgment, taxpayers could deduct *both* the market value of shares acquired *and* the amount charged to income tax. This was illogical and likely to result in a capital loss being incurred for tax purposes, even though in reality no such loss had occurred. For options exercised after 9 April 2003, FA 2003 restored the position to what it was understood to be before *Mansworth v Jelley*, so the price paid to exercise the option will usually constitute the CGT base cost of the shares for the future. For options exercised on or before that date though, HMRC's interpretation of *Mansworth v Jelley* still applied until mid-2009, when HMRC revised its view. The decision in *Mansworth v Jelley* did not affect options exercised under approved SAYE and CSOP schemes in accordance with the rules of those plans, but it does apply to options exercised under EMI plans in the same way that it applies to unapproved options.

For the purposes of the above provisions, no income tax liability arises on the *grant* of an option, unless exceptionally the option is granted at a discount under a CSOP scheme. Before 1 September 2003, if an option over shares (or in the case of other securities, 15 April 2003) was capable of being exercised more than ten years after it was granted, or seven years for options granted before 6 April 1998, a charge arose at the time the right was *granted* on the excess of the then market value of the option shares over the price which, under the option, had to be paid for the shares. For years before 2002/03 the *tax paid* when the option was granted was deducted from any tax arising when the option was exercised. From 2002/03 the *amount chargeable to tax* when the option is granted is deducted from the amount chargeable to tax on exercise (ITEPA 2003 s 478).

Partly-paid securities

If securities are issued at a price equal to the current unrestricted market value, with the price being paid by agreed instalments, no charge will arise under the general income tax charging provisions since full market value is being paid, and this will apply even though the market value has increased by the time the securities are paid for, unless the arrangement is being entered into for tax avoidance purposes. Any growth in value of the securities should be liable only to capital gains tax, provided that none of the other charging provisions of ITEPA Part 7 are in point.

A director or an employee who subscribes for securities other than under the approved plans where the capital is not called immediately is, however, regarded for P11D purposes (but not for s 419 purposes) as having received an interest-free loan equal to the deferred instalments, on which tax is charged at the beneficial loan interest rate, unless the total of all beneficial loans outstanding from that director or employee in the tax year, including the deferred instalments, does not exceed £5,000. Fully-paid shares sold to employees on deferred terms will give rise to a similar benefit in kind but a s 419 loan may also be created.

However, tax relief under ITA 2007 s 392 is available to offset the beneficial loan charge to individuals who acquire securities in a close company (that is not a close investment holding company) and who either hold a material interest in the ordinary share capital, or work for the majority of their time in the management or control of that (or an associated) company.

The loan is regarded as being repaid as and when the instalments are paid. Any amount written off is taxed as employment income at that time (however if at the outset there is an intention to write off the amount outstanding, HMRC will treat the securities as having been acquired at a discount, and company law will not permit the new shares to be issued for a price below their nominal value); any amount so charged is deductible for capital gains tax purposes when the securities are disposed of (ITEPA 2003 ss 192–197 and 446Q–446W). In relation to shares acquired before 16 April 2003, these charges did not apply to lower-paid employees (ie, those earning at a rate of less than £8,500 per annum).

There are a number of non-tax legal (eg, Companies Act and Financial Services & Markets Act) and accounting issues (eg, FRS20) associated with the offer of any securities to employees and these should be considered carefully when implementing any plan.

Anti-avoidance rules

Various anti-avoidance provisions apply to employment-related securities. These do not apply in relation to shares that comply with the provisions of approved plans, but it is important to note that EMI plans are not regarded as approved plans for this purpose. The FA 2003 changes mean that advantages gained not just by the employee but by 'associated persons' are brought fully within the charge to tax. 'Associated persons' include the person who acquired the securities (if not the employee), persons connected with the employee (or with the person who acquired the securities) and members of the same household as the employee (or person who acquired the securities). There are exemptions from some of the rules below where the securities are acquired under a public offer, or are shares in an employee-controlled company or where the event in question affects all the company's shares of the same class and the majority of them are held by outside shareholders; these exceptions apply in respect of restricted securities, convertible securities and post-acquisition benefits.

In addition, the Paymaster General announced on 2 December 2004 that share-related avoidance schemes discovered after that date could be blocked with retrospective effect going back to that date. This threat was carried out in Finance Act 2006 with changes being made to ITEPA 2003 s 420 that took effect from 2 December 2004.

Restricted securities

If employment-related securities have certain restrictions or conditions attached to them, including risk of forfeiture (meaning a requirement to dispose of the securities for less than their market value), their actual market value (AMV) on acquisition will be less than their true initial unrestricted market value (IUMV), which reduces the charge to income tax on acquisition if the award of shares is treated as a payment of earnings. To counter this, further chargeable events occur when the restrictions are lifted, varied or, when the securities are disposed of while still subject to any of the applicable restrictions, since this could be a method of giving the employee a gain that would otherwise be a capital gain. The charge is calculated using a complex formula that is designed to subject to income tax the effect the restriction had on the value of the securities at the time it was lifted and so charges a proportion of the value of the securities at the relevant time to income tax, whether or not there has been growth in their value.

In cases where the risk of forfeiture of the securities will lift within five years, the normal income tax charge on acquisition is removed, but income tax is still chargeable when the risk of forfeiture is lifted/varied, etc.

There is no charge once seven years have expired after the relevant employment ceases and no charge on death. These provisions apply from 1 September 2003 but only affect securities acquired on or after 16 April 2003. (ITEPA 2003 ss 422–432 and FA 2003 Sch 22 para 3.)

The previous rules are contained in ITEPA 2003 ss 422–434 as originally enacted and ss 449–452 as originally enacted and still affect shares acquired before that date but on or after 6 April 2003. Under the original ss 422–434, the charge to tax when a risk of forfeiture is lifted, or on earlier disposal, is on the market value of the shares at that time, less anything paid for them, and less amounts previously charged to tax when they were acquired or subsequently. The original ss 449–452 charged income tax where the value of shares increases because of the creation or removal of restrictions or the variation of rights relating to the shares or to other shares in the company.

Whilst the new rules might be said to be broadly comparable with the old, they can result in very different amounts being taxed at different times. They can also result in tax charges arising when the restrictions lift or are varied but there is no market for the securities on which funds could be realised to meet that liability. To avoid such issues, the employee and employer can together enter into an election to disapply, for tax and national insurance purposes, the effect of all or any of the restrictions attaching to the securities (ITEPA s 431). Hence if all restrictions are disapplied, on acquisition of the securities the employee would be charged to income tax on the difference between the IUMV of the securities (rather than their 'restricted' AMV) and the cost of acquisition. The effect is to charge amounts earlier than would otherwise be the case, possibly by reference to a lower market value if the value of the securities is rising. However, the election is irrevocable, and if share values fall rather than rise, with the result that the employee never realises a gain, there is no possibility of tax and NIC being refunded. Valid elections in such cases take the form of an agreement between employer and employee, in a form approved by HMRC, made within 14 days after acquisition or a chargeable event; there is no requirement that they be submitted to HMRC or that the approval of HMRC be sought, although evidence of the election must be retained for future reference. One such election possibility is to waive the exemption on acquisition (for securities subject to early forfeiture) in order to limit the potential charge on a subsequent chargeable event; this was not possible under the old rules.

Any amount charged to income tax forms part of the acquisition cost of the securities for capital gains tax purposes. Where the securities are held in trust until such time as the risk of forfeiture or other restriction is removed, they are usually treated as acquired at that time, rather than any earlier time, though this does depend on the exact terms of the agreement.

Convertible securities

Where securities are convertible into securities of a different class or description, or may become convertible if conditions are met, any income tax due on acquisition is computed by reference to what their market value would be without the conversion right. When they are converted, or on any other chargeable event (which could be a disposal, a release of the conversion right or a receipt of a benefit), the value of the conversion right is taxed at that time at its then value, with a deduction allowed for anything payable by the employee for the conversion itself. These provisions apply from

1 September 2003 and, except for the way tax is charged on acquisition, apply to all securities from that date regardless of when they were acquired. (ITEPA 2003 ss 435–444 and FA 2003 Sch 22 para 4.)

The previous rules were contained in ITEPA 2003 ss 435–446 as originally enacted. Under those rules, convertible securities were taxed on conversion at their value at that time, less anything paid for them on acquisition or conversion and any amounts charged to tax when they were issued. There was no special rule for computing tax on acquisition.

Amounts charged to income tax form part of the acquisition cost of the securities for capital gains tax purposes.

Post-acquisition benefits

Tax is chargeable on the amount or market value of any special benefit received in connection with employment-related securities. Apart from the extension of the charge to benefits received by associated persons (see above), the new rules, which apply from 16 April 2003, are fairly similar to the old (ITEPA 2003 ss 447–450). HMRC have stated that it will not normally argue that this provision should be used to tax dividends from employment-related securities as employment income, although the possibility exists that it will indeed do so where an avoidance scheme involving dividends has been used.

Securities with artificially depressed market value

From 16 April 2003, if the market value at the time of acquisition of employment-related securities is depressed by 10% or more by means of non-commercial transactions, the reduction in value is charged to income tax as employment income. This also applies in conjunction with the rules above for restricted securities and convertible securities to prevent the reduction of tax charges on chargeable events under those rules. In addition, in the case of restricted securities only, if any such non-commercial transaction has occurred in the previous seven years, a charge arises on 5 April in the relevant tax year as if the restrictions had been lifted on that date. For national insurance purposes, these provisions apply from the appointed date (ie 1 September 2003) (ITEPA 2003 ss 446A–446J), although again there is no provision deeming a payment to take place.

Securities with artificially enhanced market value

From 16 April 2003 provisions were introduced to ensure that where in any tax year the market value of employment-related shares is enhanced by 10% or more by means of non-commercial transactions, the increase in value is charged to income tax as employment income on 5 April in that year or, if earlier, on disposal. For national insurance purposes, these provisions also apply from 1 September 2003 (ITEPA 2003 ss 446K–446P) and again lack a provision deeming payment to take place.

Securities disposed of for more than market value

When employment-related securities are disposed of for more than their market value, the excess is chargeable to income tax rather than capital gains tax. In relation to securities disposed of before 16 April 2003, this charge did not apply to lower-paid employees (ie those earning less than £8,500 per annum) (ITEPA 2003 ss 198–200 and 446X–446Z).

Priority allocations in public offers

Where shares are offered to the public, a priority allocation is often made to employees and directors. Where there is no price advantage, a benefit will not be deemed to arise because of the right to shares in priority to other persons so long as the shares that may be allocated do not exceed 10% of those being offered, all directors and employees entitled to an allocation are entitled on similar terms (albeit at different levels), and those entitled are not restricted wholly or mainly to persons who are directors or whose remuneration exceeds a particular level (ITEPA 2003 Part 7 Chapter 10).

Where employees are offered a discount compared with the price paid by the public, the employees will pay income tax on the discount, but the benefit of the priority allocation will still escape tax. The employee's base cost for capital gains tax is the amount paid plus the discount that was charged to tax.

Approved employee share plans

More detailed points on the various approved employee share plans are as follows:

(1)   **SAYE share option schemes**

The legislative requirements of SAYE share option schemes are set out in ITEPA 2003 ss 516–520 and Sch 3. No income tax charge arises when an approved SAYE option is granted nor on exercise where the exercise price of the option is paid out of the proceeds of a linked SAYE scheme.

The SAYE contributions themselves are saved with National Savings and Investments, a building society or a bank by way of a deduction from net pay. The present maximum monthly contribution is £250 and the scheme minimum contribution may not be set above £10. There is no tax relief on the contributions, but any interest and bonuses (paid on savings at a set rate) received from the SAYE savings contract are tax-free. This applies whether or not the employee exercises the option to take up the shares.

The employee is given the option to buy shares after either three, five or seven years, at a price which must not normally be less than 80% of the market value of the shares at the time the option is granted. The total price to be paid must not exceed the proceeds of the SAYE contract. The scheme must be available to all directors and employees within a qualifying period of not more than five years' service and it must not have features that discourage eligible employees from participating or which exclude part-time employees. If an employee dies before completing the contract, his personal representatives may exercise the option within 12 months after the date of death. If an employee dies within six months of the bonus date, the option remains exercisable until the expiry of 12 months from the bonus date.

Employees who leave because of injury, disability, redundancy or retirement must be allowed to exercise the option within six months thereafter. Those who leave for any other reason will not normally be allowed to exercise the option unless the scheme allows it, and then only where the options have been held for at least three years, and are exercised within six months. An employee who has been transferred to an associated company that is not participating in the scheme may nonetheless be permitted by the scheme rules to exercise the option within six months after the date his savings contract matures, or, if he leaves because of injury, disability, redundancy or retirement, within six months of leaving. Employees may also exercise scheme options if the company or part of the business that employs them is sold or otherwise leaves the group operating the scheme, even though they have been in the scheme for less than three years, but in these circumstances any gain arising is charged to income tax. Regardless of the treatment of the option, the SAYE contract itself may be continued by an employee after he leaves, by arrangement with the savings body, so that the benefit of receiving tax-free interest and bonuses at the end of the contract is retained. Payments will then be made direct to the savings body.

(2)   **Company share option plan (CSOP) schemes**

Under the provisions of ITEPA ss 521–526 and Sch 4, shares acquired by employees under an *approved company share option plan* do not attract an income tax charge when the option is granted unless the price to be paid for the shares under the option plus the price paid for the option itself is less than the market value of a similar quantity of shares at the time the right to acquire is granted. In that event an income tax charge arises on the difference in the year the option is granted, the amount charged to income tax then forms part of the cost of the shares for capital gains tax when the option is exercised (TCGA 1992 s 120(6)). However under an approved CSOP, an option cannot be granted with an exercise price that is 'manifestly less' than the market value of the underlying shares at the date of grant (ITEPA Sch 4 para 22(1)(b)).

There is also no income tax charge when the option is exercised if the plan retains approval up to the time of exercise and the options are exercised between three and ten years after the date they were granted. (Prior to 9 April 2003, in order to be free from income tax on exercise, there was a further requirement that the option was not exercised within a three year period commencing with the date of the previous approved income tax free exercise.)

Approved options may be exercised prior to the third anniversary of grant (or prior to 9 April 2003, more frequently than every three years), however if this is done, then for income tax purposes, the option is treated as an unapproved securities option (as described above), with income tax (PAYE, and national insurance if the shares are readily convertible assets) arising on the gain on exercise of the option. This is also the case if the plan has lost its approved status.

Employees who leave because of injury, disability, redundancy or retirement will be allowed to exercise the option within the three year period without a charge to income tax, where the CSOP rules specifically permit this and where the CSOP option is exercised within six months of the termination date. This period is extended to 12 months where the plan permits exercise after the employee's death.

For directors to participate they must be full-time working directors (ie working at least 25 hours per week), but part-time employees do qualify. The value (as at the date of the grant of the option) of shares over which a person holds CSOP options must not exceed £30,000.

ITEPA 2003 Sch 3 Part 7 and Sch 4 Part 6 permit participants in a SAYE scheme or CSOP scheme to exchange existing share options for options over shares in a company that takes over the employer company, so long as an election is made within six months and certain conditions are met.

(3)   **Share incentive plans**

Under ITEPA 2003 s 488 and Sch 2 an employer can introduce a plan that enables the company to give shares to its employees and obtain a tax deduction for the market value of those shares in the accounting period in which the shares are awarded. Furthermore the plan enables an employee to buy shares in his employing company out of his gross income provided the conditions set out in the relevant legislation are met and the plan has received HMRC approval.

Such plans were previously referred to as 'all employee share ownership plans'. They are now known as share incentive plans or SIPs. A SIP must provide benefits to all employees who are eligible and liable to UK tax on employment income. An employee does not have to accept an offer to join the plan. The plan must not contain features that discourage participation (eg, loss of other rights for joining). All employees must participate on similar terms, although those terms may vary by reference to remuneration, length of service, hours worked or performance targets, but not so as to give preferential treatment to directors or higher paid employees.

The plan may contain a qualifying period for participation but this must not exceed 18 months for free and partnership shares where there is no accumulation period, or six months for partnership shares where there is an accumulation period. Where an employee within a group works for more than one group company, employment with any group company can count towards the qualifying period. The employee must not have a material interest in the employing company or receive shares under another SIP from the same or a connected company in the same year, except, where a group restructures and the employee transfers to another company within the group. Then the employee, subject to one overall limit, may receive shares under SIPs run by both companies.

The shares available under the plan can be of four types, all of which are held in a UK resident trust established for the purpose in accordance with the SIP legislation (known as a 'SIP trust'):

1. *Free shares*

An employee can be given shares worth up to £3,000 in a tax year, valued as at the date of the award. The gifted shares are held within a SIP trust and no tax liability arises on the award while the shares are so held. Free shares must normally be kept in the SIP trust for a stipulated period, which may be not less than three nor more than five years. If an employee ceases employment, the shares are removed from the SIP trust and the SIP may provide for such shares to be forfeited if this occurs within three years of the date of their award. A partial tax charge may arise if the shares are removed from the trust after three years, but before they have been held for five years. However, after five years the shares may be removed from the trust without tax charges and with the current value as the CGT base cost.

2. *Partnership shares*

An employee may be given the opportunity to buy shares (known as partnership shares) by way of a salary deduction. The maximum deduction is 10% of salary as defined by the SIP (excluding benefits in kind) subject to a limit of £1,500 in a tax year, with a minimum deduction which may be set at a level no higher than £10. The deduction reduces gross salary before PAYE/national insurance is applied. Although that does not reduce earnings for pension and tax credit purposes, HMRC have issued guidance in leaflet IR177 on the effect any such reduction in national insurance payments might have on benefits as well as the employee's entitlement to statutory sick pay (SSP), statutory maternity pay (SMP), the state pension and any means-tested benefits or tax credits, and requires employers to include relevant warnings in the scheme documentation given to employees invited to participate. The money deducted from salary must either be used to buy shares in the company establishing the SIP (or its parent company as set out in the SIP) within 30 days, or accumulated for up to one year, and then used within 30 days of the end of the accumulation period to acquire the shares. The price may then, however, be by reference to the lower of market value on the first day of the accumulation period or the date of acquisition. If the employee leaves during the accumulation period, the amount deducted (net of PAYE/NI) is returned to him. The employee may withdraw the shares from the plan at any time (although this may result in an income tax charge as indicated below).

3. *Matching shares*

An employer can offer up to two 'matching shares' for each partnership share purchased. The matching shares are awarded at nil cost. They must be awarded on the same day and on the same basis as the partnership shares and be of the same class. They are held in the SIP trust on the same terms as free shares and may be made forfeitable within a three-year period from the date of award in the event that employment is terminated (save for an excepted reason) or in the event that partnership shares are withdrawn.

4. *Dividend shares*

The SIP may provide, or an employee may elect, for dividends to be reinvested being used to purchase further SIP shares whilst the shares on which the dividends were paid are held in the SIP trust, to a maximum of £1,500 per tax year. Reinvested dividends do not carry a tax credit. The shares purchased will have the same rights as the shares on which the dividend is paid and are not subject to forfeiture but may be subject to a holding period of up to five years. Such shares must be acquired within 30 days of the payment of dividend. Any dividend so invested is not liable to higher rate tax as long as the reinvested shares are held in the SIP trust, which must be for a period of at least three years. If the shares are withdrawn within that period, eg, on leaving employment, the trustee must give the employee the relevant details and dividend upper rate tax may be payable by the recipient if he is a higher rate taxpayer (after taking into account a tax credit at the rate in force when the shares are taken out of the SIP trust).

General provisions

The shares used in the SIP must be ordinary shares that are fully paid up and not redeemable. They can be listed, or shares in a company not controlled by another company, or shares in a company that is under the control of a company listed on a recognised stock exchange and is not close. The shares may be subject to certain limited restrictions such as pre-emption, risk of forfeiture on termination of employment or on voting rights, subject to the detailed provisions of the legislation. The shares must not be in a service company.

Tax provisions

No tax charge arises on the acquisition of the shares under the terms of the SIP (and, as noted above, payroll deductions used to buy partnership shares are tax-deductible). An income tax charge (and a Class 1 national insurance charge if the shares are readily convertible assets) can, however, arise if free, partnership or matching shares are removed from the plan within three years, based on the value of the shares on the date of removal. Where shares are withdrawn from the SIP trust between three and five years, the charge is on the lower of the value on removal and, for free and matching shares, the value at the date of the original acquisition of the shares under the plan, and for partnership shares the amount of partnership share money used to acquire the shares (ie, recapturing the relief given for the payroll deductions). Dividend shares removed from a plan within three years are taxable as dividend income as indicated above, based on the original dividends reinvested. See also under Partly-paid shares and Restricted shares etc on pages 85.4 and 85.5 for the charge on directors and P11D employees where employers have guaranteed a sale price.

No tax arises on the death of the employee, or on withdrawal after five years where the shares are free of both income and capital gains tax provided that the shares are not held for any period after withdrawal from the SIP trust. Furthermore, no tax charge arises if the shares cease to be subject to the SIP because of injury or disability, redundancy, transfer under the Transfer of Undertakings (Protection of Employment) Regulations, change of control of the employing company or retirement on or after retirement age (not earlier than 50).

As far as capital gains tax is concerned, there is no liability if the shares are kept in the SIP trust until disposed of. If they are removed and held for a period before disposal, the base cost will be the value at the date of removal and the capital gain will be based on the increase in value after they are withdrawn. Partnership or dividend shares transferred to employees under the SIP are exempt from stamp duty and stamp duty reserve tax (see Example 84 part A(b) and (c)).

Capital gains tax rollover relief (TCGA 1992 s 236A and Sch 7C)

Where existing shareholders (other than companies) transfer ownership of shares they hold in an unquoted company to an approved SIP that holds (either immediately or within twelve months after the transfer) 10% of the company's shares, gains arising on the shares transferred may be treated as reducing the acquisition cost of replacement chargeable assets acquired within six months after the disposal (unless the chargeable assets are shares on which enterprise investment scheme income tax relief is given (see Example 93) and subject to some special provisions relating to dwelling houses).

(4) **Enterprise management incentives (EMI)**

A further share option plan is known as the enterprise management incentives (EMI) plan (ITEPA 2003 ss 527–541 and Sch 5, the 'EMI Code'). The plan enables employees to be awarded qualifying share options over shares worth up to £120,000 each (£100,000 for options granted prior to 6 April 2008) in a qualifying company (this limit is reduced by the value at grant of any shares under subsisting CSOP options). Subject to the EMI limits on individuals and in total (see below), each employee may be awarded a different amount without restriction. The grant and exercise of the option is tax- and NI-free (except to the extent, if any, that the exercise price of an EMI option is less than the value of the underlying shares at the time the option was granted, in which case the element of that discount on grant is subject to income tax (and national insurance if the shares are readily convertible assets) on exercise of the option). When the shares are sold, the excess of the proceeds over the price paid to acquire the shares (plus any amount charged to income tax) is a chargeable gain for CGT purposes.

In order to qualify, the EMI must satisfy the detailed requirements of the legislation. These include:

(a)   The employing company must be one that would qualify under the EMI Code in terms of the company/group having gross assets less than £30 million, the company/group must be independent and have only qualifying subsidiaries (as defined in the EMI Code) and undertake a trade that is not excluded under ITEPA Sch 5 paras 16 to 23, the rules being similar to the rules for the Enterprise Investment Scheme (EIS) (see Example 93). In addition, from 21 July 2008 there is a limit of 250 on the number of employees of the qualifying company/group.

(b)   The maximum value of shares in respect of which unexercised EMI options exist at any particular grant date must not exceed £3 million (measured at the date of each grant).

(c)   The option must be granted for commercial reasons to recruit or retain an employee and not for tax avoidance purposes.

(d)   The individual must work at least 25 hours per week for the company (or if less, 75% of his working time – in both employment and self-employment if applicable) and must not, with associates, have a material interest in the company (ie 30% or more of the ordinary share capital).

(e)   An employee may not hold unexercised qualifying options in respect of shares with a total value of more than £120,000 when the options were granted (the value of any restricted shares being taken as IUMV rather than AMV). Once that limit is reached, any further options granted within three years of the date of the last qualifying option are not qualifying options, regardless of whether the earlier options have then been exercised or released. Any unexercised options under CSOPs (see part (2)) count towards the £120,000 limit.

(f)   The general requirements relating to the option must be met, eg, notice must be given to HMRC within 92 days of the grant of the option in the form specified, together with a declaration that the information is complete and correct and that the employee is an eligible employee.

If a disqualifying event occurs after an EMI option has been granted, but before it is exercised, the holder of the option has 40 days from the date of the event in which to exercise the option without losing the EMI tax benefits. If the option is exercised after that time, then income tax is charged under ITEPA 2003 Part 7 Chapter 5 s 476 on the difference between the market value of the shares on the date of exercise and their market value immediately before the disqualifying event (s 532).

Disqualifying events include (s 533):

–   the company becoming a 51% subsidiary, or under the control of another company,

–   the company ceasing to meet the trading activities test,

–   the employee ceasing to be an eligible employee,

–   a variation in the terms of the option so that the market value of the shares is increased,

- an alteration to the share capital that affects the value of the shares to which the option relates without prior HMRC approval,

- certain conversions of shares into shares of a different class,

- the company having qualified on the basis that it was preparing to trade, but not doing so within two years of the grant of the option.

(5) **Corporation tax relief on employee shares**

Companies were encouraged to promote employee share ownership through a trust set up for this purpose known as a qualifying employee share ownership trust (QUEST). Payments made by the employer to set up the trust and to acquire shares to distribute to its employees obtained corporation tax relief so long as certain stringent conditions were met. These trusts were expensive to operate and have now been abolished, to be replaced with less restrictive arrangements.

In general, from 1 January 2003, under the terms of FA 2003 Sch 23 (now in CTA 2009 Part 12) an employer will receive corporation tax relief of an amount equal to the difference between the market value of the shares at the time the employee exercises a share option and the price the employee pays. The relief is given in the accounting period in which the option is exercised and the shares acquired. The relief applies to CSOP, SAYE and EMI options (which are tax-free) and unapproved options or outright share acquisitions, or charges arising in connection with restricted or convertible shares, where the employee is subject to income tax.

The shares must be ordinary shares, and the company either a listed company, under the control of a listed company, or a stand-alone company (or the holding company of a group).

Shares for a SIP have always given a corporation tax deduction as set out above . Relief is not, however, permitted in respect of shares forfeited back to the trust and in respect of which relief has already been given.

B. Capital gains tax

Shares acquired under approved SAYE or CSOP schemes are regarded for capital gains tax as acquired at the price paid (plus the amount, if any, paid for the option), and when they are disposed of, any gain is accordingly chargeable (subject to any available allowances and any unused annual exemption). For SAYE schemes and SIPs, shares can be transferred free of capital gains tax within 90 days of emerging from the scheme, or within 90 days after the end of the three year period, if earlier, into an Individual Savings Account (ISA) up to the annual ISA limit. Any income and gains within the ISA will then be tax-free (see Example 92). There is no similar provision for EMI shares. Shares acquired under SAYE schemes and SIPs may be transferred into personal pension schemes and tax relief obtained thereon (see Example 38 explanatory note 26). This first became possible in 2001 and has continued after A-Day (FA 2004 s 195). For the interaction of the employee share scheme provisions with the capital gains tax rules for matching disposals with acquisitions, including special rules from 6 April 2002 where shares under SAYE share option schemes, company share option plans and enterprise management incentive schemes are acquired on the same day as other shares, see Example 80 explanatory notes 6 to 8.

See above for the impact of the decision in *Mansworth v Jelley*.

C. Self-assessment

Details of taxable events in relation to employee share plans, employment-related securities and related benefits must be shown in tax returns (in the Share Schemes section) and any tax due must be included in the self-assessment. Where securities have been taxed as notional pay under PAYE (see above), the relevant amounts will be included in the pay figures in the Employment pages of the return, but they must also be included in the SA101 additional information (Ai) pages (where required). The detailed provisions are outlined in Additional Information Notes AiN 6–27.

Employees who do not get tax returns must notify HMRC by 5 October after the end of the tax year if they have income or gains that have not been fully taxed (see Example 40 note 5). If the only untaxed amounts relate to securities or share options and the total tax due is less than £2,000, employees may ask to have the tax collected through their PAYE codings. When the extra tax due is £2,000 or more tax returns must be completed. Employers do not have to give details of taxable amounts on Forms P11D, but since the scheme rules require them to give details to HMRC, they should be able to provide the relevant figures.

As noted above a return of all employment-related securities and options issued, transferred, or disposed of, is required for each fiscal year normally using Form 42. The return will be made by the employer by 6 July following the fiscal year or by the person from whom the securities or option was acquired (ITEPA 2003 s 421L). Separate forms are required for each HMRC approved share scheme, as well as EMI.

Question

A.

Explain the rules that deem remuneration to be liable to PAYE and national insurance contributions where services are provided via an intermediary and the managed service company anti-avoidance legislation does not apply. Set out who is liable to pay the tax, the relieving provisions to mitigate double tax liabilities and the restrictions on the use of any loss created.

B.

Margaret Johnson, a design engineer, provides her services to a manufacturing client, working full-time as the manager of the R&D function, via M J Engineering Ltd, a company founded and owned equally by Margaret and her partner John Allen, who are also its only directors. (Margaret and John live together as husband and wife.) They decide on pension and remuneration policy and deal with the day-to-day administration and banking transactions, but employ accountants to calculate PAYE, and to prepare accounts at the year end. M J Engineering Ltd has always made up its accounts to 31 December each year. The latest accounts, before taking into account personal services adjustments, include:

	£	Yr ended 31 Dec 2009 £	£	Yr ended 31 Dec 2010 £
Turnover		46,000		54,000
Less: Salary – John Allen (administrator)	7,210		8,100	
Travelling	5,340		5,086	
Training and courses	450		780	
Use of home as office	620		660	
Telephone, Internet and sundries	1,120		1,234	
Bank and professional costs	1,710		1,930	
Capital allowances – computers	1,240		410	
Director's salary – Margaret Johnson	6,000		7,000	
National insurance	1,730		1,950	
Pension payments	5,000	30,420	5,000	32,150
Profit for year		15,580		21,850

On 5 May 2009 M J Engineering Ltd declared a dividend of £10,800.

M J Engineering Ltd had paid PAYE/NI on a deemed payment plus employer's NI of £16,200 for the year 2008/09 in April 2009. The resulting loss had been carried back to the accounting year ended 31 December 2008. No dividend was paid in 2008/09. The deemed payment, net of employee's tax and NI, for 2008/09 was £9,844.

In the tax year 2009/10 M J Engineering Ltd received £48,200 (net of VAT) from clients in respect of work done by Margaret. In performing her duties she had travelled in 2009/10 14,800 miles in her own car and was paid 40p per mile mileage allowance by M J Engineering Ltd. Margaret's P11D for 2009/10 shows:

	£	
Use of home as office	640	
Excess mileage allowance (4,800* miles @ 15p per mile)	720	
Home telephone (bill in name of employee)	700	(one half re business)
Private medical insurance	400	
	2,460	

*   See Example 10 EN 20 authorised rates are 10,000 miles @ 40p additional miles @ 25p

M J Engineering Ltd had paid a pension contribution for Margaret of £3,000 on 6 December in each year. The use of Margaret's home as an office has been agreed as an allowable expense against her employment income. She keeps itemised bills to support the claim that half of her home telephone bill represents business calls.

Assume that PAYE tax has been paid on Margaret's salary and taxable benefits, less her personal allowance of £6,475.

As the management of the company is clearly provided by the couple, and not by a service provider, the Managed Service Company rules of ITEPA 2003 Part 2 Chapter 9 do not apply.

Compute the amount liable to PAYE/NI for Margaret Johnson in the name of M J Engineering Ltd for 2009/10, together with amounts liable to corporation tax. Set out the amount of dividend taxable on Margaret for 2009/10 if the appropriate election is made.

Answer

A. Provision of personal services through an intermediary when legislation applies

Where an individual (known as 'the worker') *personally* provides services, or has an obligation personally to perform services, for another person (known as 'the client') and the contractual arrangements are with one or more third parties (known as the 'intermediary') through which the services are provided, in such a way that if the services of the worker had been provided directly to the client the worker would be an employee of the client, then the legislation in ITEPA 2003 Part 2 Chapter 8 applies. The legislation also applies if the client is an individual who is not in business (eg, provision of care to an older person directly, and provision of services by domestic workers such as nannies or butlers). It does not normally apply to any contract where the worker does not directly or indirectly have any interest in the intermediary (eg, a non-connected employee of the intermediary).

This legislation does not apply to provision of services through managed service companies – see Example 94.

Deemed payment

Where the personal services legislation applies, a deemed payment of employment income is calculated for the work done by the worker for the client and compared with actual salary and non-cash benefits from the intermediary (net of VAT and net of allowable expenses). Any shortfall of actual salary and benefits is treated as a single payment, made on the last day of the tax year, liable to tax as employment income and to Class 1 national insurance contributions. The PAYE tax and NIC are payable by the intermediary by 19 April following the end of the tax year. The amounts are included on the worker's P14/P60 and therefore appear on the worker's personal tax return on the employment pages. The deemed payment, together with employer's Class 1 national insurance thereon, becomes a deduction from trading income for the intermediary in the period of account in which the last day of the tax year falls. The deemed payment is not included as income for tax credits.

Effect on dividend payments

In so far as the deemed payment, net of PAYE and employee's national insurance, is paid out as a dividend, the intermediary company may make a claim, by 31 January following the tax year in which the dividend is paid, for the dividend to be treated as covered by the deemed payment and not therefore liable to income tax. Such dividends would however count as income for tax credits.

Trading losses

If the deduction of the deemed payment gives rise to a loss in a trade and the intermediary is a company, then normal loss rules apply, ie the loss may be carried back one year under ICTA 1988 s 393A (the accounting period to 31 December 2010 ends outside the window for the temporary three-year extended carry-back), or carried forward, and can be used in a terminal loss claim.

If the intermediary is a partnership, then the deduction can only reduce the trading profits to nil – it cannot create a loss. Any excess is unrelieved. Furthermore, in computing the trading income of a partnership the maximum deduction for expenses relating to actual earnings is restricted to the amount deductible in computing the deemed payment (including the 5% of relevant earnings deduction – see below).

Amounts taken into account

The earnings taken into account in computing the deemed payment are the total amounts of the cash and non-cash benefits received in the tax year by the intermediary in respect of engagements to which the personal services legislation applies for that worker. The amount includes any sub-contractor's tax deducted but excludes any VAT. The exclusion of VAT applies even if the flat-rate scheme is used. Irrecoverable VAT relating to allowable expenses met by the intermediary would be allowable as part of the expenses in the same way as if the intermediary was not VAT-registered.

Computation of deemed payment

To compute the deemed payment the following formula is used:

		£
Amounts received from relevant engagements by the intermediary		X
Less: 5%		X
		X
Add: any other payments or benefits received by the worker in respect of relevant engagements, not otherwise chargeable as employment income of the worker, but which would be so chargeable if the worker had been an employee of the client		X
		X
Less: Expenses paid by the intermediary that would have been deductible against employment income if paid by the worker (as an employee of the client). This includes reimbursed expenses	X	
Capital allowances that could have been claimed by the worker	X	
Pension contributions paid by the intermediary for the worker	X	
Employer's Class 1 national insurance paid and Class 1A or 1B national insurance payable in respect of the worker	X	X
		X
Compared with amounts actually received by the worker from the intermediary in the tax year (which do not represent items for which a deduction has already been given above):		
Taxable actual salary	X	
Taxable benefits in kind and exempt mileage allowances	X	X
Maximum deduction from trading income		X

The amount computed is the deemed payment plus employer's Class 1 national insurance contributions. If the employer's NI nil band of £5,715 (for 2009/10) has already been used for the worker then the deemed payment will be:

	£
Deemed payment including employer's NIC (as above)	X
Less: 12.8/112.8 × deemed payment including employer's NIC*	X
Deemed payment to enter on worker's PAYE deductions working sheet (P11)	X

* If the nil band has not been fully used any excess is deducted from this amount first.

There is a spreadsheet template to calculate deemed payments (albeit only for full-year operations) at www.hmrc.gov.uk/ir35/ir35.xlt

More than one intermediary

If more than one intermediary exists, then all intermediaries have a joint and several liability for the PAYE/NI in so far as the intermediary has received any payment or benefit for the worker. However, the relevant earnings may be reduced by any amount included as relevant earnings by subsequent intermediaries to prevent double counting, leaving the prime liability with the last intermediary in the chain.

Benefits received directly from client

If the worker receives benefits or other amounts directly from the client (eg, provision of a company car by client to worker) then the deemed payment is increased by that amount without a 5% deduction.

Common control

Where the intermediary company and the client company are 'associated' by virtue of both being under the control of the worker, or of the worker and others, the IR35 rules do not apply to that engagement, so a shareholder-director of a holding company does not fall into IR35 when he works for a subsidiary and is paid dividends from the holding company that are partly derived from the management charges it levies on the subsidiary.

B. M J Engineering Ltd

Computation of deemed payment for 2009/10 for Margaret Johnson

				£
Amounts received				48,200
Less: 5% allowance				2,410
				45,790
Less: Expenses – Use of home as office			640	
Business use of telephone			350	
Pension contribution for M Johnson			3,000	
Employer's NI for M Johnson				
Class 1 ((7,000 + 350*) – 5,715)	@	12.8%	209	
Class 1A (on medical insurance 400)	@	12.8%	51	
Salary			7,000	
Taxable benefits and exempt mileage allowances (400 + 350 + 720 + 5,200)			6,670	17,920
Excess amount				27,870
Less: Employer's Class 1 NIC therein (12.8/112.8 × £27,870)				3,163
Deemed payment				24,707

> *   Re private element of home telephone bills – no NI on mileage allowance since permitted NI rate for 2009/10 is 40p per mile regardless of miles travelled.

PAYE/NI liability on deemed payment in name of Margaret Johnson

	£
Actual salary	7,000
Taxable benefits (2,460 – 640 – 350)	1,470
Deemed payment	24,707
	33,177
Less: Personal allowance	6,475
Total taxable earnings	26,702

Tax has already been charged on salary and benefits of (7,000 + 1,470 – 6,475 =) £1,995, leaving £35,405 of basic rate band available. Employee's and employer's NI has already been charged on excess of salary and benefits of £7,350 over the earnings threshold of £5,715, so that the employee's and employer's NI rates payable are 11% (up to upper earnings limit of £43,875) plus 1% on the excess and 12.8% respectively.

£

Tax on deemed payment:

£

24,707	@	20%		4,941

NI on deemed payment:

Employee	24,707	@	11%	2,718
Employer	24,707	@	12.8%	3,162

Payable by M J Engineering Ltd by 19 April 2009   10,821

Amounts liable to corporation tax:

	Year to 31.12.09 £	Year to 31.12.10 £
Profit per accounts	15,580	21,850
Less: Personal services (inc deemed NI)	(16,200)	(27,870)
Loss for year carried back	(620)	
Loss for year carried forward		(6,020)

Taxable dividend 2009/10:

			Margaret Johnson £	John Allen £
Dividend (50% × £10,800)			5,400	5,400
Deemed payment – 2009/10 (excluding employer's NI)		24,707		
Less: Tax	4,941			
Employee's NI	2,718	7,659		
Net		17,048		
Brought forward from 2008/09		9,844		
		26,892		
Offset after claim for relief –				
Worker		(5,400)	(5,400)	
Others		(5,400)		(5,400)
			–	–
Available to offset future dividends		16,092		

Explanatory Notes

These notes refer to the personal services legislation of ITEPA 2003 ss 48–61 only, and do not cover the managed service companies legislation of ITEPA 2003 ss 61A–61J, which is covered in Example 94.

Liability under personal services legislation

Companies

1. The legislation only applies to workers who have, together with associates, a material interest in the intermediary company or who receive or could receive payments or benefits from the intermediary company which are not employment income but could reasonably be taken to represent remuneration for services charged to the client by the intermediary.

    Material interest means the beneficial ownership or ability, alone or with associates, to control more than 5% of the ordinary share capital, or the right to receive more than 5% of any distributions, or in a close company the right to more than 5% of assets on a winding up. For this purpose the worker does not need any holding in his own name for the holdings of associates to be included. An associate is any relative or business partner. Relative means husband or wife, civil partner, parent or remoter forebear, child or remoter issue, brother or sister. A man and a woman living together as husband and wife are deemed married and are therefore associates. The interests of the associates of business partners are included with their own interest. Trustees of settlements made by the taxpayer or any relative are also included. A company is connected with another person if that person has (together with associates) control of the company.

With effect from 6 April 2007, this (IR35) legislation applies only to personal service companies/ partnerships that are not considered managed service companies, that is they are not involved with a managed service company service provider. In this case the company was founded by the individuals who actively control it, and its administration is either performed or delegated by them. It has its own bank account and PAYE registration, and no unconnected shareholders. These are all strong indicators that the company's activity is not caught by the managed service company legislation. If it were, any payment drawn from the company that was not already earnings would be deemed to be earnings, with a deduction for expenses only to the extent that those expenses would have been deductible if the worker had been directly employed by the client (eg, travel and subsistence expenses where the notional employee would have been at a temporary workplace).

The IR35 legislation applied to composite companies and managed personal service companies for tax purposes until 5 April 2007 (and for NI purposes until 5 August 2007, although HMRC appears to make no such distinction in practice), but because employment status must be ascertained on a case-by-case basis, it was difficult to enforce, and there was a perception of poor compliance. To make it easier to counter such structures that primarily avoid NI, managed service company legislation was introduced that bypasses the need to look at individual contracts. See Example 94 for further information.

Partnerships

2.   Again the legislation applies to any worker whose payments or benefits from the partnership represent the amount charged for the worker's services to the client. Otherwise a partner is only caught by the legislation if one of the following tests is satisfied:

–   the worker (together with his/her relatives) is entitled to 60% or more of the profits of the partnership, or

–   most of the profits of the partnership arise from the provision of personal services to a single client (including the client's associates), or

–   the profit share of the worker is based on the income generated by that worker in the provision of personal services.

Individuals

3.   The legislation can apply where the intermediary is an individual (but the worker cannot be an intermediary for himself). This only applies if the amount receivable by the worker from the intermediary can reasonably be taken to represent remuneration for services provided by the worker to the client.

Classification as an employee

4.   The legislation only applies if the worker would have been an employee of the client if the services had been provided directly to the client. See Examples 13 and 45 part (e) for detailed notes on the points relevant to determine status as an employee. There have been several cases specifically on the issue of whether the personal service company legislation applies, and most contain discussion on employment status. Readers are referred to *PCG v IRC* [2002] STC 165, *Hewlett Packard v O'Murphy* [2002] IRLR 4 EAT, *FS Consulting Ltd v McCaul* [2002] STC (SCD) 138, *Lime-IT Ltd v*

Justin [2002] SpC 342, *Synaptek Ltd v Young* [2003] STC 543, *Future Online Ltd v Faulds* (2004) Sp C 406 and, more recently, *Dragonfly Consultancy Ltd v Commissioners for HMRC* [2008] EWHC 2113 (Ch).

It should be noted that in the case of *Cable and Wireless v Muscat* in October 2005, an individual working through an employment agency, also using a service company, was held to be an employee of the supposed 'client', and entitled to employee rights. The facts were unusual, in that Mr Muscat had been employed by the company (ie, the client) and had been forced to switch into working through a service company to reduce employment costs, and the court was able to find that his original employment had never actually terminated.

Agency workers are not within IR35. Unless they are deliberately hired as direct employees of the agency, they work under contracts for services, and the mutuality of obligations necessary for a contract of employment do not exist (because there cannot be three parties in a master-servant relationship). Recognising this, tax and NI legislation brings their earnings into PAYE (ITEPA Part 2 Chapter 7) and Class 1 national insurance (Categorisation Regs 1978), so IR35 is irrelevant and its operation is specifically excluded for cases within the agency rules. In the case of *James v Greenwich BC* [2008] EWCA Civ 35 in February 2008, the Court of Appeal refused to imply a contract directly between an agency worker and the end user client in place of the agency contract. A contract of employment was to be implied only if the agency contract was shown to be a sham.

Exclusions

5.   The legislation does not apply to non-resident entertainers or sportsmen, who are subject to deduction of tax under ITA 2007 s 966.

6.   If the worker would not be liable to tax on UK employment income if directly employed by the client, eg, the worker is non-resident and the services are provided outside the UK, then the legislation does not apply. However, if the worker is resident in the UK, the services are provided in the UK and the client carries on business in the UK, the intermediary is treated as carrying on business in the UK wherever actually resident. See Tax Bulletin 64 (April 2003) for more detail on the service company legislation and international issues.

7.   Managed service companies: See Example 94, explanatory note 21 for managed service companies.

Where an individual's services are provided through a managed service company (eg, a composite company or managed personal service company) in which they take very little part in the management, the managed service company provider is responsible for applying PAYE and NI regulations to all remuneration.

Expenses

8.   The deductions allowable are those met by the intermediary that would have been deductible from the taxable earnings of the worker if he or she had been employed by the client and met the expenses from his or her earnings. They include all items deductible under Chapters 1 to 5 of Part 5 of ITEPA 2003 (eg expenses incurred wholly, exclusively and necessarily, allowable travel expenses, professional fees, employees' liabilities and indemnity insurance, agency fees paid by entertainers and fixed allowances). They specifically include amounts originally met by the worker but reimbursed by the intermediary (ITEPA 2003 s 54(3)) and, where the intermediary provides a vehicle which is chargeable as a benefit in kind on the worker, approved mileage allowances which the worker could have claimed if he or she had been employed by the client and used his or her own car for business (ITEPA 2003 s 54(4)). The benefit in kind itself (representing the private use of the car) would be deductible as part of the taxable salary and benefits provided by the intermediary to the worker. If the worker uses his own car in reality (as in this example) ITEPA 2003 s 54(7) preserves the relief for the approved mileage allowances by allowing the exempt amounts to be included in the amounts deducted as salary or benefits.

No deduction is allowed for training costs borne by the intermediary, as no claim is generally possible for such costs under Chapters 1 to 5 of Part 5 of ITEPA 2003. Work-related training is tax-free if funded by the employer, but the IR35 rules look at the hypothetical situation where the worker is engaged directly by the end-user, who would not be funding the training. Most employees cannot claim a s 336 deduction for training costs they bear personally.

9. Because all contracts undertaken by the worker for the intermediary relate to his/her employment with the intermediary, this means that most client premises will be temporary workplaces (see Example 13 explanatory note 6) and therefore travelling costs will be allowed from the worker's home to that temporary workplace, provided it would be a temporary workplace if he had been directly employed.

Capital allowances

10. Only capital allowances claimable by a worker can be deducted, ie, those claimable under CAA 2001 s 262, being plant and machinery necessarily provided for use in the performance of the duties. It is likely that Margaret's computer, whilst helping her to better perform her duties, would fail this test and no deduction would be allowed.

Employees of the intermediary

11. No deductions are allowed for salaries or other administrative costs in computing deemed pay. This does not prevent a deduction from trading profits for companies.

If the employee provides relevant services to the client, but does not have a material interest, etc, in the company then the amount charged to the client is excluded from the computation of deemed pay. If an invoice is rendered for the services of more than one individual, the amount must be apportioned between the individuals and only the earnings of an individual (with a material interest, etc) are taken into account.

Dividends

12. To prevent double taxation, dividends may be offset by net deemed payments if a claim is made by the intermediary company by 31 January following the tax year in which the dividend is paid. The relief is given primarily against distributions of the current year and then distributions of subsequent tax years, with relief firstly against the dividends paid to the worker and then against other dividends paid for that year.

Actual pay

13. The deduction for actual pay is the payments or benefits received in a tax year by the worker from that intermediary which are chargeable as employment income. Consequently any payments made after 5 April 2009 cannot be deducted in 2008/09, even if the amount relates to earnings in that year which have been charged to tax as a deemed payment. Instead the amount will be deducted as actual pay in the year of payment. This could result in actual pay in a subsequent year exceeding the computed deemed payment. There is no relief for the excess. Care should be taken to distribute any amount charged as a deemed payment by way of dividend, with an appropriate claim for relief being made.

Computation of deemed payment other than at 5 April

14. If a worker ceases to be connected with an intermediary during the tax year, then the deemed payment is treated as paid immediately before that event (and the deduction for the payment is based on the day before the event occurred). For partnerships this applies when a partner (or employee) ceases to hold that position. For companies it applies if the worker ceases to be a member (shareholder), director or employee. Thus if a worker resigns as a director during the tax year, a computation of the deemed payment is due to that date, with payment of the relevant PAYE/NICs. All receipts, expenses, etc to the end of the tax year will be included in the computation, even though

the payment is regarded as made at the earlier date (and the company's deduction will be based on that date). A similar provision applies where a company ceases to trade, the computation being prepared at the date of cessation with a deduction in the final accounting period.

Accounting year-end

15.   As part B of the example shows, the deemed payment deduction from income can occur in a different accounting period from that in which the earnings arise and are charged to tax. To prevent losses arising that can only be carried forward, and which might never be relieved, it is advisable to use a 5 April year-end for any intermediary caught by these rules.

HMRC opinions

16.   It is possible to get an opinion from HMRC as to whether a particular contract is caught by the IR35 provisions. The address is IR35 Unit HM Revenue & Customs, Northgate House, Sheep St, Northampton NN1 2LY, although this may change at any time with HMRC allocating work frequently and unpredictably to new offices anywhere in the country. There is also a dedicated helpline for IR35 matters 0845 303 3535, and a dedicated part of HMRC website at www.hmrc.gov.uk/ir35/index.htm, including a deemed payment calculator (and updated address details).

Question

Edzell was the sole proprietor of an aircraft maintenance business until he transferred it as a going concern to a limited company on 30 April 2009.

Since founding the business in 1980 Edzell has always made up accounts to 5 April in each year.

The profits, as adjusted for income tax purposes but before capital allowances, have been calculated as £48,753 for the year to 5 April 2009 and £3,340 for the final period to 30 April 2009.

The written down values of plant and machinery for capital allowances purposes after allowances for the year ended 5 April 2008 were as follows:

	£
Plant and equipment pool	3,506
Motor car	5,925

Subsequent plant and machinery additions have comprised a new testing machine at a cost of £2,700 on 16 June 2008 and a new aircraft tractor at a cost of £13,181 on 31 March 2009.

Edzell has always declared business use of the car at 90%, based on reasonable apportionment.

The maximum capital allowances have always been claimed as early as possible.

A freehold aircraft hangar was acquired in 1982 at a cost of £30,000 and industrial buildings allowances equal to that amount have been claimed so that the written down value is nil.

The market values of the assets at the time of the transfer of the business to the company were:

	£
Goodwill	97,500
Freehold aircraft hangar	80,800
Plant and equipment (not including any fixed plant)	20,000
Motor car	5,000
Net current assets including debtors of £15,000 (but excluding cash)	12,700
	216,000

Edzell has never made any payment for goodwill. No other asset except the aircraft hangar was transferred at a market value greater than cost, and none of the plant and equipment cost more than £6,000.

For capital allowances purposes, both Edzell and the company have elected to transfer the assets at their written down value.

The transfer was satisfied by the issue to Edzell of all of the authorised share capital of 100,000 ordinary shares of £1 each of Famosa Ltd (a company formed specifically for the purpose of the transfer) and the payment to him of £60,000 cash.

(a) Show Edzell's capital allowances and taxable profits for his last two accounting periods as a sole trader and comment on what the position would have been if Edzell had made up a final account from 6 April 2008 to 30 April 2009.

(b) Calculate Edzell's chargeable gain arising on the transfer of the business to Famosa Ltd and the capital gains tax base value of his shares in Famosa Ltd.

In this connection, the values of the goodwill and aircraft hangar at March 1982 can be taken as £25,000 and £30,000 respectively.

(c)   State the effect on both Edzell and Famosa Ltd, had the election to transfer the assets for capital allowances purposes at their written down value not been made.

(d)   State the national insurance consequences of transferring the business to the company.

Answer

(a) Edzell's capital allowances computation and taxable profits for final two accounting periods

Capital allowances computation

	£	Plant pool £	Motor car (10% private) £		Total allowances £
WDV at 6.4.08			3,506	5,925	
2008/09 (6.4.08 – 5.4.09) Additions:					
New testing machine		2,700			
New aircraft tractor		13,181			
		15,881			
AIA		(15,881)	–		15,881
WDA 20%			(702)	(1,185) (90% = 1,067)	1,769
			2,804	4,740	17,650
2009/10 (6.4.09 – 30.4.09) Deemed transfer at tax written down value (see explanatory note 9)			2,804	4,740	–

The aircraft hangar would be transferred to the company at its written down value of nil.

Taxable profits

			£
2008/09	48,753 less capital allowances 17,650		31,103
2009/10	(capital allowances nil)		3,340

If Edzell had made up a final account from 6 April 2008 to 30 April 2009, capital allowances would be computed for that period of account. Since it is the period of discontinuance of Edzell's trade, neither first year, AIA nor writing down allowances would have been available and the computation would have been as follows:

	Plant £	Motor car £	Total allowances £
6.4.08 – 30.4.09			
WDV at 6.4.08	3,506	5,925	
Additions:			
New testing machine	2,700		
New aircraft tractor	13,181		
	19,387		
Deemed transfer at tax written down value	19,387	5,925	–

The taxable profit of the final period would have been increased by £17,650 in respect of the capital allowances that would no longer be given and the written down values transferred to the company would be increased by £16,583 on the plant pool and £1,185 in respect of the motor car, a total of £17,768. This is £118 more than the capital allowances that have been claimed, because the capital allowances on the car were restricted by that amount in respect of the private use proportion. They will not be restricted in the company's computation, but Edzell will be taxed on the benefit of private use of the car under the employment income rules.

The taxable profits would be assessable as follows (see explanatory note 10):

2008/09	365/390 × (48,753 + 3,340 =) 52,093	£48,754
2009/10	25/390 × 52,093	£3,339

(b)   Edzell's chargeable gain on transfer of business to Famosa Ltd

	Goodwill £	Aircraft hangar £
Market value on transfer to company	97,500	80,800
Market value at March 1982	(25,000)	(30,000)
Chargeable gains before rollover relief	72,500	50,800

		123,300
Less: rolled over against base cost of shares in Famosa Ltd (see explanatory note 1)		89,050
Chargeable gain before entrepreneur's relief		34,250
Entrepreneur's relief if claimed at 4/9ths*		(15,222)
Chargeable gain 2009/10 (subject to annual exemption)		19,028
Tax at 18% after entrepreneur's relief (= 10% before relief)		3,425

> *   Providing the gain is not reduced by allowable losses, entrepreneur's relief is not automatic, and has to be claimed, so need not be used unnecessarily if losses or other methods of mitigating the gain are available. If entrepreneur's relief is claimed, it will apply to all gains net of losses accruing on disposal of business assets, so computed. As TCGA 1992 s 162 relief is automatic, amounts rolled over in application of this section are not gains on which entrepreneur's relief could be claimed, and so entrepreneur's relief applies only to the gain after rollover relief.

Edzell is not entitled entrepreneur's relief in respect of the gain rolled over against the base cost of the Famosa Ltd shares. As and when he disposes of the shares, entrepreneur's relief will be based on the time for which the shares have been owned.

The remaining assets do not attract a capital gains liability, since none is transferred at a value in excess of cost (and there would not have been any capital gains in any event, since both the motor car and the items of plant and equipment each valued at less than £6,000 are exempt).

The capital gains tax base value of the shares in Famosa Ltd is 156,000 − 89,050 = £66,950.

(c)   **If the election to transfer assets at written down value for capital allowances purposes had not been made**

As Famosa Ltd gives full 'market value' consideration, this would determine the disposal proceeds for plant and machinery allowance purposes (CAA 2001 s 61). For the purposes of industrial buildings allowances, on a transfer between connected persons, CAA 2001 s 568 normally deems the transfer to be made at open market value in any event, unless an election is made under CAA 2001 s 569. Famosa Ltd would therefore be deemed to have acquired the assets at market value. However, as part of phasing out Industrial Building Allowances, balancing adjustments on industrial buildings other than in enterprise zones are withdrawn. This would result in balancing charges on Edzell as follows:

	Plant	Motor car			Aircraft hangar
WDV	10,569	4,444			–
Market value 30.4.09 (but not exceeding cost)	20,000	5,000			30,000
Balancing charges	£9,431	£556	× 90% =	£500	nil

Giving an increase in 2009/10 assessable profits of   £9,931

(d) **Edzell's national insurance position**

As a sole trader, Edzell will have been liable to pay weekly flat rate Class 2 contributions of £2.30 during 2008/09. He will also have been liable to pay Class 4 contributions of 8% of his profits between £5,435 and £40,040. In addition, contributions have been payable at 1% on profits above the upper profits limit. This gave him a national insurance liability for 2008/09 of Class 2 £120 + Class 4 £2,053 = £2,173. The equivalent figures for 2009/10 are Class 2 £2.40 per week and Class 4 8% of profits between £5,715 and £43,875, together with an uncapped 1% payable on all profits above £43,875.

The national insurance position (using 2009/10 rates) if the business is transferred to the company is as follows. As a company director Edzell will be liable to pay Class 1 employee's contributions at the rate of 11% on his earnings between £110 and £844 per week, with an uncapped 1% charge on any earnings in excess of £844 per week. (Strictly a director has an annual earnings period – see Example 48 part (d).) In addition, the company, as his employer, will have to pay contributions at 12.8% on remuneration exceeding £110 per week (£5,715 per year), with no upper ceiling on the earnings on which contributions are payable. Furthermore, most taxable benefits in kind (including company cars, private fuel, living accommodation) also attract company Class 1A national insurance contributions at the rate of 12.8%. The company's contributions will, however, be allowable expenses against the profit for corporation tax.

Edzell will be able to control how much of the profit is left in the company and how much to draw as remuneration. In relation to Famosa Ltd, for the financial year to 31 March 2010 profits up to £300,000 will be taxed at the small companies' rate of 21%.

Since there is no upper limit for the employer's contributions, it is not possible to work out an overall maximum of national insurance contributions. But if Edzell had no other income and drew remuneration in 2009/10 of £43,875 to cover the basic rate band of £37,400 and personal allowance of £6,475 (and taking the position as if he had been employed for the full year for simplicity), the position would be:

Employee's contributions £734 (844 – 110) × 11% × 52 weeks			4,198
Employer's contributions £38,160 (43,875 – 5,715) × 12.8%		4,884	
Less: corporation tax relief @ say 21%		(1,026)	3,858
Net national insurance cost			£8,056
Compared with the liability of a self-employed person earning £43,875			£3,173

Clearly there is a much higher national insurance liability operating through a company than as a sole trader. A greater range of state benefits is, however, available to Edzell as an employee, particularly jobseeker's allowance and earnings-related retirement pension.

The national insurance disadvantage of operating through the company could be reduced (or avoided altogether) if Edzell drew a lower salary and received higher dividends, on which national insurance contributions are not payable. Although the corporation tax rate at 21% is 1% higher than the basic rate of income tax at 20%, it is lower than the combination of income tax and NI contributions, so payment by dividends could give a lower overall tax/national insurance bill than the sole trader format. Payment of dividend now comes under closer scrutiny, but this company is not affected by IR35, and the settlements legislation does not apply. The company may still pay dividends.

Explanatory Notes

Rollover relief under TCGA 1992 s 162 on transfer of business to company

1. Where a business is transferred to a company as a going concern, together with all assets of the business other than cash, wholly in exchange for shares in the company, the chargeable gains arising on the assets transferred are deducted from the cost of the shares.

   Partial relief is available where the consideration is only partly satisfied by shares in the new company, using the fraction:

$$\frac{\text{Value of shares in new company}}{\substack{\text{Value of whole consideration received in} \\ \text{exchange for the business}}} \times \text{Chargeable gains on assets transferred}$$

(TCGA 1992 s 162)

The relief under s 162 is automatic and a claim is not necessary. Certain reliefs take priority over relief under s 162, such as rollover relief for replacement assets under s 152, because the relief is given by reducing the *consideration* for a disposal. But s 162 relief cannot be ignored where, for example, gains would be covered by the annual exemption. To avoid the problem, the appropriate part of the consideration equal to available reliefs and exemptions could be left on director's loan account, so that a gain would be immediately realised.

Where the transfer to the company occurred between 31 March 1982 and 6 April 1988 and the deferred gains relate in whole or in part to a period before 31 March 1982, the deferred gains are halved when brought into charge on or after 6 April 1988 (see Example 82 explanatory note 10). This option was abolished for individuals from 6 April 2008, but remains available for corporation tax.

Where gains have been held over following the acquisition of a depreciating asset (see Example 82), those gains will crystallise when the depreciating asset is transferred to the company, but technically they do not arise on the disposal of the asset and cannot therefore be deferred under s 162.

The total market value of assets transferred by Edzell to Famosa Ltd in the example was:

Goodwill	97,500
Freehold aircraft hangar	80,800
Plant and equipment	20,000
Motor car	5,000
Net current assets including debtors of £15,000 (but excluding cash)	12,700
	£216,000

The chargeable gain can therefore be rolled over against the base cost of the shares in the proportion:

$$\frac{156,000 \ (\text{consideration received as shares})}{216,000 \ (\text{total consideration})}$$

which is

$$\frac{156}{216} \times £123,300 \qquad\qquad £89,050$$

Stamp duty land tax is chargeable on the market value of the land and buildings transferred under the sale of business agreement:

Freehold aircraft hangar £80,800

However, because the premises are business premises, the rate of tax is 0% where the consideration given for the hangar is £150,000 or less (FA 2003 s 55).

Electing under TCGA 1992 s 162A to disapply s 162 relief

2. The incorporation of a business can adversely affect the proprietor's entrepreneur's relief. Under s 162, the gains are rolled over and the proprietor's entrepreneur's relief clock is reset to start afresh (in relation to the shares). No entrepreneur's relief 'credit' is given for the pre-incorporation holding period of the property, goodwill etc.

    The TCGA 1992 s 162A election can recapture relief 'lost' on incorporation by removing the automatic application of s 162 relief to the various gains. The gains thus become chargeable and would qualify for entrepreneur's relief, provided the assets had been owned for one year and the other qualifying conditions had been met. If the rolled over assets were to be owned for less than one year, or if other qualifying conditions on shareholdings or employment/office-holding could not be met, this election may be considered. Calculations would normally be required in each case to determine whether a s 162A election would be beneficial.

    Where the shares acquired on incorporation are sold by the end of the tax year *following* the tax year of the incorporation, the s 162A election must be made by the 31 January after the end of that *following* tax year (the normal time limit for amending a self-assessment return), ie by 31 January 2011 for a 2008/09 disposal. In all other cases (ie where the shares are still retained at the end of the tax year following the tax year of incorporation) the time limit is extended by a further year (to 31 January 2012 for a 2008/09 disposal).

Retaining some assets and claiming gifts holdover relief under TCGA 1992 s 165 on others

3. The gain on the aircraft hangar could have been avoided if it had been retained by Edzell personally and let to the company. If rent were charged for the hangar, this would not have prevented full business asset taper relief being available if there was a gain when the hangar was finally disposed. For entrepreneur's relief however, charging rent after 5 April 2008 will cause relief to be restricted (TCGA 1992 s 169P (4)(d)). As the loss of relief would result in a CGT charge rising from 10% to 18% after annual allowance, while rent would be liable to income tax at 20% or 40% subject to personal allowances, calculations would have to be carried out on a case by case basis depending on the ownership of the property and the owners' marginal tax rates.

    If the hangar was not transferred, Edzell would have a chargeable gain on the goodwill, since the relief under s 162, described in note 1 where assets are transferred to the company is only available where the *whole assets* of the business (other than cash) are transferred.

    Even in that case, however, the gain on the goodwill could be deferred if Edzell assigned the goodwill to the company under the business gifts holdover relief provisions of TCGA 1992 s 165 for its value at 31 March 1982 (plus the unused part of his capital gains tax annual exemption if appropriate). This relief is not affected by his retaining the premises.

(A holdover election under TCGA 1992 s 165 is not available on the transfer of shares in an unquoted trading company etc to a company, although this will rarely be relevant on a business incorporation.)

Thus, if Edzell had not used his capital gains tax exemption of £10,100, he could sell the goodwill for its 31 March 1982 value of £25,000 plus the annual exemption £35,100, which would be immediately chargeable and not available for rollover. This would give him a credit of that amount to his director's account with the company and would be an exempt gain for him as follows:

		£
Deemed sale proceeds		97,500
31 March 1982 value		(25,000)
		72,500
Less:	Gain immediately chargeable, being excess of actual proceeds over 31 March 1982 value (£35,100 – 25,000 = £10,100), leaving a gain of £10,100 covered by the annual exemption	10,100
Gain held over		62,400

The company would have a base cost of £34,600 as follows:

		£
Market value on acquisition		97,500
Less:	Heldover gain	(62,400)
Being:	Paid to Edzell	£35,100

Under this arrangement, Edzell is only credited in the accounts of the company with £35,100, and the company's capital gains cost is the same amount, rather than the market value of £97,500. The company will continue to be entitled to indexation allowance on the amount of £35,100 (the removal of indexation allowance applying only to non-corporate taxpayers).

Entrepreneur's relief is not available on the gains held over under TCGA 1992 s 165 since the relief is only given on chargeable gains. It is important to note that the individual proprietor's or partner's entrepreneur's relief clock starts again based on the date the shares were acquired (or if later, when the company starts to trade). The consequential loss of the qualifying period should be taken into account when an incorporation is being considered, particularly if there is a strong likelihood of the business being sold within the next year.

Where gifts holdover relief is claimed, HMRC require the shares to be subscribed for separately from the document for the transfer of the gifted assets.

Alternative strategy of selling goodwill at its market value

4.   In many cases, the sole trader's goodwill will qualify for entrepreneur's relief as an associated disposal. Hence it should be possible to sell the goodwill to the company for its fair market value at a relatively low tax cost – ie effective CGT rate of 10% with no stamp duty. This would enable a further 'credit' to be booked to the proprietor's loan account. In this way, proprietors can use appropriate repayments of their loan account (in effect created at an effective CGT rate of 10%) to replace salary/dividends (taxed at a much higher rate, including NICs on salary payments), possibly for a number of years. Such an arrangement is likely to be beneficial, but care must be taken to avoid overvalue – see Example 51 explanatory note 16.

In this example, assuming Edzell retained the hangar, goodwill would be sold at £97,500, producing a gain of £72,500. The tax on this capital gain would be relatively modest at £5,432, while providing an amount of £97,500 on director's loan account, to be drawn without further tax effect, as follows:

	£
Capital gain	72,500
Entrepreneur's relief @ 4/9ths	(32,222)
	40,278
Annual exemption	(10,100)
Taxable gain	30,178
Tax at 18%	5,432

Deferral relief under the enterprise investment scheme

5. A possible further alternative may be to 'incorporate' using the enterprise investment scheme (EIS) provisions of TCGA 1992 s 150C and Sch 5B (although the small gain, assuming that only goodwill is transferred, would not make it practicable in this particular case). The scheme enables a taxpayer who has made a chargeable gain to defer it to the extent that he subscribes for shares in cash in a qualifying unquoted trading company within one year before and three years after the disposal of the asset giving rise to the gain. There are, however, very detailed and complex conditions in order for deferral relief to be available (see Example 93) and it is not clear that the incorporation of a business may be structured in such a way as to enable the relief to be claimed, for example, shares must be subscribed for in cash and there are restrictions on receiving value. If it was used in Edzell's case, the same gain would be deferred in respect of the goodwill as for gifts holdover relief (ie without taper relief), but the capital gains base cost of the goodwill for the company would be its full value of £97,500.

Tax relief for amount paid for goodwill

6. Goodwill is included in the 'intangible fixed assets' provisions introduced by FA 2002 s 84 and Schs 29 and 30, applicable from 1 April 2002 (see Example 66). Profits and losses on such assets are taken into account in calculating income profits, and provision is made for goodwill to be amortised in the accounts. On the incorporation of a business, where the unincorporated business held the goodwill at 1 April 2002, the company would not be entitled to any tax relief for the subsequent amortisation of the purchased goodwill in the company's books, as it would be acquired from a 'related party' (Sch 29 para 118). It should be possible for an acquiring company to obtain tax relief on the amount paid for sole trade/partnership goodwill to the extent that the goodwill arises, or is acquired by the sole trade/partnership from an unrelated third party, after 31 March 2002. The relief would be based on the amount written off in the accounts each year.

Share premium account

7. The example illustrates that, when a business is transferred to a limited company as a going concern, wholly or partly for consideration to be satisfied by shares in the company, it will usually not be possible to issue *a number* of shares corresponding exactly with that part of the consideration to be satisfied in shares, since the final value of the business will not be known until after the event. Thus in this example the part of the consideration of £216,000 to be satisfied by shares is £156,000 (MV assets £216K less cash received £60K) and the nominal value of the shares allotted is £100,000.

The remaining £56,000 will be dealt with in the accounts of the company through a share premium account.

Income tax basis periods

8. Since Edzell has always made up accounts to 5 April, his basis periods coincide with his accounting periods and there is no overlap relief. Had his annual accounts been made up to another date, any overlap relief would have been deducted from the assessable profit of the last *tax year* (see Example 32 explanatory note 5). If, instead of making up a final 25-day account to 30 April 2009 as in the

example, he had made up accounts for the period from 6 April 2008 to 30 April 2009, then under the change of accounting date rules in ICTA 1988 s 62A, the accounting date would normally have been treated as having changed in 2008/09 with the basis period for that year being 12 months to the new date, ie 12 months to 30 April 2008. A change of accounting date is not, however, effective if the taxpayer does not notify the change to HMRC. It is confirmed in the then Inland Revenue's booklet SAT 1 at paragraph 1.77 that if such an account had been made up, the 2008/09 taxable profit could be calculated by reference to the old date of 5 April. The profits of the last period of account (calculated *after* capital allowances, which because of the transfer to the company would in this case be nil, as indicated in the example) would therefore have been time-apportioned as to 365/390 to 2008/09 and 25/390 to 2009/10. Any available overlap relief would have been deducted from the 2009/10 profit, and if it created a loss the normal loss reliefs would have been available.

Capital allowances and election to transfer at written down value

9.   The capital allowances basis periods are the same as the income tax basis periods. If the final account had been made up for the period 6 April 2008 to 30 April 2009, then as indicated in the comments in part (a) of the example, this would result in no first year or writing down allowances or AIA being available in the final period (CAA 2001 ss 46, 55 and 65). Where the final accounting period to cessation includes significant capital expenditure, it may be beneficial to draw up accounts to an earlier date prior to cessation (or, as in this example, not to extend the normal accounting period to include a short final period) to enable annual investment allowance etc to be claimed. Alternatively, it may be possible to crystallise a large balancing allowance on cessation by selling the pooled plant (including the newly acquired items) at less than the tax written down value (and not making an election to transfer at tax written down value) (s 61). This treatment would not apply to non-pooled assets, such as expensive cars (s 79) and short life assets (s 88).

Where the consideration allocated to plant exceeds its tax written down value, a balancing charge would arise. This can be avoided as shown in the example by an election under CAA 2001 ss 266 and 267 (plant and machinery) or ss 569 and 570 (industrial buildings) where the purchaser and the seller are connected persons (see Example 18 part (c)). A written notice to HMRC is required not later than two years after the transfer date. The company assumes the written down values of the assets, which are treated as sold in the period to the date of transfer at an amount that gives neither a balancing allowance nor a balancing charge.

The annual investment allowance (AIA) is not available to the company on assets acquired from Edzell because it is controlled by Edzell and AIA is therefore blocked by CAA 2001 ss 214 and 217 (connected persons etc).

Relief for trading losses

10.   If there had been unrelieved trading losses, Edzell could have obtained relief in respect of them against income from the company under ITA 2007 s 86 (see Example 32 explanatory note 7). An alternative way of relieving brought forward losses may arise if no election is made to transfer assets at written down value for capital allowances, so that they would be transferred at market value. If this gave rise to balancing charges (such as those indicated in part (c) of the example), the result would be to increase the profits against which the losses could be set.

Value added tax

11.   Since the business is to be transferred as a going concern, the effect for value added tax purposes is that the transfer will not be treated as a supply of goods or services and no VAT will be payable on the assets transferred (assuming that the option to tax in respect of the building had not been exercised by Edzell, or Famosa Ltd had also made the election before the transfer). Famosa Ltd will accordingly have no input tax to reclaim.

The local HMRC office must be notified within thirty days of the transfer, and at the same time Edzell and Famosa Ltd may jointly apply for Edzell's VAT registration number to be re-allocated to the company. Edzell's personal registration will then be cancelled and the company will stand in his shoes for VAT purposes. If Famosa takes over Edzell's VAT registration, it must also keep his records. If Famosa does not take over the VAT registration, Edzell will keep the records, but must make necessary information available to Famosa. HMRC is empowered to disclose to Famosa information that it holds from prior to transfer to allow Famosa to fulfil its VAT obligations.

Question

Jefford has recently received a substantial legacy and is planning to buy an established hotel in a seaside resort. His wife will help him in running the business. He is expecting modest profits at the outset but hopes that his plans for the business will enable it rapidly to become highly successful.

He is not sure whether to operate the business as a sole trader/partnership or as a limited company.

Outline the considerations he should take into account in making his choice.

Answer

Operating as a sole trader/partnership or as a limited company

(a)   Sole trader/partnership

If the unincorporated format is chosen it would probably be appropriate for Mrs Jefford to be a partner from the outset, since she is helping to run the business. This will enable profits to be shared so as to make the best use of available allowances and lower tax rates. However, it should be borne in mind that the settlements legislation ITTOIA 2005 s 626 applies to partnerships as well as to companies, and that this legislation is still in force, notwithstanding the specific facts of the *Arctic Systems* case. It is important to be able to demonstrate the reality of Mrs Jefford's involvement in the business, to counter any challenge that the partnership constitutes a settlement and an appropriate partnership agreement should be drawn up. If she were an employee, her wages would have to be justifiable as 'wholly and exclusively for the purposes of the trade' and the national insurance cost would be significantly higher (as illustrated in (b)) if the business is run through a company. For 2009/10, sole traders and partners pay income tax at 40% on income (after personal allowances) in excess of £37,400, whether profits are retained in the business or withdrawn. Tax on income below that level is at the basic and starting rates.

National insurance contributions are payable as follows for 2009/10:

Class 2 £2.40 per week

Class 4 8% of profits between £5,715 and £43,875, with an additional 1% payable on all profits over £43,875.

The income tax and Class 4 national insurance contributions on the profits plus the tax on any other income is normally payable by half-yearly instalments on 31 January in the tax year and 31 July following (based on the net tax/Class 4 national insurance payable for the previous year), with a balancing payment on the following 31 January, eg 31 January and 31 July 2010 and 31 January 2011 for 2009/10. For someone commencing self-employment there are not normally any payments on account in the first tax year and instead all tax is due 31 January following the end of the tax year the trade commences. At the same time a profitable trader will make their first payment on account of their following year's tax liability. For example, assume Jefford was previously taxed under PAYE and commenced his new business on 1 May 2009. His business was instantly profitable and his total tax liability for 2009/10 amounted to £5,000. Tax would be payable as follows:

	£
31 January 2011	
Tax liability for year ended 5 April 2010	5,000
First payment on account 2010/11 (5,000/2)	2,500
Total due	7,500
31 July 2011	
Second payment on account 2010/11	2,500

Therefore Jefford doesn't pay any tax until 21 months after commencing trading at which time he pays 1½ years worth.

If accounts were made up to 31 March annually, the profits taxable in 2009/10 would be those of the year/period to 31 March 2010. If the accounting date was 30 April, the 2009/10 profits would be those for the year/period to 30 April 2009. Choosing a 30 April year-end means that the taxable profits of one year are broadly those of the previous year, which is an advantage if profits are rising, although there is a compensating disadvantage of bunching of profits when the business ceases (see Example 17 for further details).

(b)   Limited company

For the year ended 31 March 2010, company profits (which are after deducting directors' remuneration) below £300,000 are taxed at 21%.

Mr and Mrs Jefford would be liable to income tax as employees on any amounts drawn from the company (except to the extent that the drawings were to reduce loans made by them to the company) and the remuneration would attract employer's and employee's national insurance contributions as follows:

Employer

For 2009/10, employers pay no contributions on the first £110 per week (£5,715 per annum) but pay 12.8% on the earnings (and taxable benefits in kind) above that amount, with no upper ceiling. The contributions reduce profits chargeable to corporation tax.

Employee

For 2009/10, employees pay no contributions on the first £110 per week and 11% on earnings between £110 and £844 per week. Earnings in excess of this upper earnings limit (equivalent to £43,875 per annum) are subject to a 1% charge. Employees earning between £95 and £110 a week do not pay contributions but their rights to benefits are protected (see Example 48 part (a)).

The time lag between earning profits and paying the tax would be nine months for company profits (provided the company's profits do not exceed £1,500,000), with tax and national insurance on directors' fees being payable as and when remuneration is paid or credited. If the company did not pay the remuneration within nine months after the end of the period of account, it would be deducted in calculating corporate taxable profits in the accounting period in which it was *paid*, thus increasing the tax liability of the earlier accounting period and reducing that of the period in which paid.

(c)   Comparison of alternatives

The rates of corporation tax payable by a company tend to be lower than the rates of income tax on the same profits payable by partners or sole traders. For example, profits of up to £300,000 are taxed at 21% in a limited company in 2009/10, potentially rising to 22% in 2010/11. For 2009/10 for a sole trader with a profit of £50,000 the effective rate (excluding NIC) would also be approximately 20% but would rise to approximately 37% at £300,000, whereas the company rate would remain 21 or 22%. When NIC is taken into account the effective rates for a sole trader are 26% and 38.5% respectively. The whole profits of a sole trader or partnership are taxed, whether drawn out or reinvested, while in the limited company proprietors/employees are taxed (possibly at higher rates) on dividend/salary taken. If funds are required for reinvestment, and are not drawn as salary or dividend, then the profits retained by the company are taxed only at the rate of corporation tax (not potentially higher rate income tax), facilitating growth. However, if all funds are to be extracted, in many circumstances the tax burden will be substantially similar, while the NIC cost is very much higher on salaries taken from a company.

In the case of fluctuating profits, the sole trader/partner may waste allowances or basic rate bands in a bad year, while paying higher rate tax in a good year, although averaging arrangements exist for farmers and authors. A limited company may pay a constant justifiable salary, which is deductible for corporation tax and may generate losses, to use up bands and allowances each year. The losses may be relieved against future profits, subject to loss relief rules.

The administration of cash flow tends to be simpler in a limited company, but tax liabilities may arise earlier, as some taxes are paid by PAYE monthly or quarterly, and the corporation tax is due nine months after the year end. The sole trader/partner's situation is complicated by the requirement to make payments on account. In the case of fluctuating profits there may be no requirement to make a payment on account one year, followed by the need to pay two years' worth of tax within six months the following year. If the profits for the year ended 31 March 2009 (for example) did not give rise to payments on account, and for the year ended 31 March 2010 produced a tax liability of £10,000 (for example), £15,000 (£10,000 + POA £5,000) would fall due on 31 January 2011, and £5,000 on 31 July 2011. The difficulties of finding a large lump sum have to be compared to the advantages of any deferral of payment.

In addition, if the business is required to operate the CIS scheme, deductions suffered by a company can be offset against its PAYE liability, whereas for sole traders they are set against the year's liability unless a special claim is made.

The national insurance cost is significantly higher for limited companies than for the self-employed. If profit is drawn as salary, the NIC cost will tend to negate the potential saving offered by the difference between corporation tax rates and income tax rates.

NIC cost may be controlled by paying a relatively low salary, liable to NIC, supplemented by dividends, which are not liable to NIC, but this may be seen as aggressive tax planning. The tax credit on dividends covers the shareholder's basic rate liability (but is not tax deductible so the profit has been taxed on the company at 21%), and the higher rate of 32.5% (less tax credit of 10%) is charged only to the extent that the recipient is a higher rate taxpayer.

From 6 April 2000 the 'IR35' rules obliged certain companies to pay salary and NIC in place of dividends, see Example 86. The workers of these companies are taxed on substantially their whole income, as are the self-employed, but with fewer deductible expenses, and much higher NIC cost.

From April 2003 HMRC issued guidance on the application of the settlements legislation to dividends paid other than to the company's main earner – see Example 59. The basis of this guidance was found to be faulty in the Appeal to the House of Lords of the *Arctic Systems* case.

If the dividends can be paid according to shareholdings, the limited company format is likely to result in a lower tax cost. The simplified pensions regime, which commenced on 6 April 2006 may offer opportunities for tax efficient investment. Sole traders or employees may contribute up to 100% of salary, a much higher percentage than was previously possible. A limited company may set up a company pension scheme, contributing higher amounts still if it wishes. However, to obtain a corporation tax deduction, the amounts paid must be expended wholly and exclusively for the purposes of the trade.

Contributions paid by the self-employed save higher rate tax (see Example 37 for the restrictions of higher rate tax relief for those with income of £150,000), but not NIC. Company contributions, provided they are paid wholly and exclusively for purposes of the trade, save both NIC and corporation tax. HMRC guidance states that, in determining whether contributions are wholly and exclusively for purposes of the trade, it will look at the overall remuneration package, not the proportion that pension bears to salary. A combination of salary, pension and dividend should result in a lower tax cost for limited companies than for the self-employed.

As Jefford expects the business to become highly successful, the limited company can help control tax by ensuring higher rate tax is paid only on profits taken out of the company, which he may be able to control. As the business is a hotel, profits would derive from Mrs Jefford's efforts as well as his, so it should be possible for her to receive dividends as well as salary, using her bands and allowances, as well as controlling NIC cost (see Example 59 for considerations of the settlement legislation). The couple's willingness to make pension contributions also needs to be ascertained, as a company pension scheme would allow tax-efficient pension provision in the company. It would be advisable for both spouses to subscribe for shares before the company commences trading or acquires value.

Future changes

2010/11 will see the introduction of abatement of personal allowances for those with net income of £100,000. The mechanism and definitions are likely to be the same as those used in the abatement of the age-related personal allowance for the over 65s. However, the full allowance will be withdrawn creating a marginal rate of tax of 60% on income in the band between £100,000 and £112,950 (based on the current personal allowance), after which the marginal rate will revert to 40%.

There will also be a higher rate of tax of 50% applying to taxable income in excess of £150,000 in 2010/11. Thus, the use of a limited company to shelter income for high earners will become even more attractive in the future.

It has also been proposed that from 6 April 2011 the rate of national insurance contributions will increase by ½%. Therefore class 1 contributions would increase to 13.3%, employee 11.5% up to the cap and 1½% thereafter. Class 4 contributions would increase to 8.5% up to the cap and 1½% thereafter.

(d) Illustrative computations

The following illustrations show that the point at which the company format will give a lower tax bill than the partnership depends on the extent to which profits are left in the company or drawn as profits/dividends.

Illustration 1

Say business profits before tax and national insurance are £100,000 and there are no other sources of income. Assume Mr and Mrs Jefford each drew a salary of £43,875, which after the personal allowance of £6,475 leaves £37,400 to use the basic and starting rate bands. The comparative position for 2009/10 is:

				Partners £	Company director		£
Profits/remuneration				100,000	43,875 × 2		87,750
Personal allowances				(12,950)			(12,950)
Taxable income				87,050			74,800
	74,800	@ 20%		14,960			14,960
	12,250	@ 40%		4,900			
	87,050			19,860			
Class 2 NI				250			
Class 4 NI				6,228	Employees' NI		8,395
Total personal tax and NI				26,338			23,355
Company's tax and NI:							
Profits					100,000		
Less: Directors' remuneration					(87,750)		
Company's NI thereon @ 12.8% on (87,750–11,430)					(9,769)		9,769
Taxable profits					2,481		
Tax thereon (£2,481 @ 21%)					521		521
					1,960		
Tax				19,860			15,481
NI contributions				6,478			18,164
Total tax and NI liabilities				26,338			33,645

The partnership format shows an overall tax/NIC saving of £7,307. However, any further increase in profits would be subject to 41% in the partnership against 21 or 22% in the company up to £300,000. Thus, if profits increased by £12,000, tax under the partnership format would rise by £4,920 (= £12,000 @ 41%), whereas tax under the company format would increase by £2,640 (12,000 @ 22%).

The rate differential between the small companies' rate and the higher rate of income tax is 19% in 2009/10 (40% − 21%) and could reduce to 18% for those liable at 40% or increase to 28% for those liable at 50% in 2010/11. The small companies' corporation tax rate is being increased partly to narrow the gap and remove the differential between it and the basic rate of income tax.

For items with private usage, such as cars, the disallowance of private expenditure in the unincorporated business may be more advantageous than benefits in kind charges applicable to companies, depending on individual circumstances.

There would be further higher rate tax liabilities of £490 on the company retentions of £1,960 (100,000 − 87,750 − 9,769 − 521) if they were paid out as dividends.

Illustration 2

Say profits were only £40,000 and, under the company format, each spouse took a salary of (say) £7,500, with the balance as a dividend. The position would then be:

		Partners £	Company director		£
Profits/remuneration		40,000	7,500 × 2		15,000
Dividends (19,389 as below + (⅑) 2,154)					21,543
Personal allowances		(12,950)			(12,950)
Taxable income		27,050			23,593
27,050 @ 20%		5,410	2,050 @ 20%		410
			21,453 @ 10%		2,154
			23,593		2,564
Tax credit on dividends					(2,154)
					410
Class 2 NI		250	Employees' NI (7,500 − 5,715)		
Class 4 NI (20,000 − 5,715) @ 8% × 2		2,287	@ 11% × 2		393
Total personal tax and NI		7,947			803
Company's tax and NI:					
Profits			40,000		
Less: Directors' remuneration			(15,000)		
Company's NI thereon @ 12.8% on (15,000 − 11,430)			(457)		457
Taxable profits			24,543		
Tax thereon @ 21%			(5,154)		5,154
Profits paid out as dividend			19,389		
Total tax and NI liabilities		£7,947			£6,414
Saving through company format		£1,533			

The saving through the company format may be expected to decrease in future years, with the basic rate of income tax at 20%, and the small companies' rate of corporation tax rising to 22%.

(e)   **Other considerations**

1.   Sole traders and partners are fully liable for the debts of the business and can ultimately be made bankrupt. The liability of company shareholders is limited to the amount, if any, unpaid on their shares. This protection is not, however, as valuable as it seems because lenders, landlords and sometimes suppliers often require directors to give personal guarantees. There

are also major compliance requirements for companies under the Companies Acts. Companies whose turnover is not more than £5.6 million (and balance sheet total of not more than £2.8 million) need not have their accounts audited (although many banks may still insist on it), but there are administration costs in filing annual returns and keeping minutes of meetings. It is possible to form a limited liability partnership, which will broadly give partners the same protection as members of limited companies, although it will also involve similar accounts and filing requirements (see Example 26 part (b) for details).

2.   Certain social security benefits, in particular jobseeker's allowance and earnings-related retirement pension, are not available to the self-employed.

3.   More generous loss reliefs are available to individuals than to companies in the early years of a new business (see Example 30).

4.   Following the abolition of taper relief, and the introduction of the 18% flat rate for capital gains and entrepreneur's relief, the differential in capital gains tax cost between companies and unincorporated businesses has narrowed. Provided the conditions for entrepreneur's relief are observed, reinvested profits that have been taxed at 22% could under certain circumstances be extracted at the capital gains rate of 18%, or 10% if entrepreneur's relief applied. This could theoretically give an extraction rate of (100% – corporation tax at 22%) × (100% – CGT at 18% or 10%) = 64% or 70%. Profits of unincorporated businesses would be taxed at 41% before being reinvested, but there is no further tax on these profits at extraction, giving an extraction rate of 59%.

Because a company is likely to have higher compliance costs, and will have higher NI costs, any differential in the extraction rate is unlikely to be the deciding factor on its own.

5.   Some family companies have in the past paid remuneration at around the national insurance threshold, either just below to avoid paying national insurance at all or just above to protect entitlement to contributory benefits. (Benefits can now be protected without paying any contributions, since there is a 'nil' band of contributions on earnings between £95 and £110 a week, as indicated in part (b) of the example.) This is only possible if the family members are directors, because it is necessary for family companies to comply with the National Minimum Wage Act 1998 (see Example 59 explanatory note 1). At the post-October 2009 minimum rate of £5.80 per hour, a weekly wage of £100 represents less than 18 working hours. BERR has confirmed that proprietorial directors will only be subject to the minimum wage rules if they have an *explicit* contract of employment with the company. If they are engaged in normal work in their capacity as a director, they will not fall within these regulations, since the regulations do not apply to office holders of the company. See the Revenue's Tax Bulletin of December 2000 for further comments.

6.   Although PAYE on payment of salaries may involve higher NI contributions than apply to sole trader profits, salary payments can facilitate use of rate bands and allowances between years of fluctuating profits. Furthermore, the PAYE is paid regularly, and removes the wide swings of the payment on account system that causes difficulties to sole traders.

7.   CIS deductions paid by a company can be set against its PAYE liability monthly or quarterly, while those of sole traders cannot.

Question

A.

Joe, who has worked for many years as an employee, has recently set up his own construction company, Specialists All Aspects Ltd. He has two employees, and the plant and equipment needed for general building work, but uses subcontractors at busy times, and for electrical, plumbing and decorating work.

He has asked for a meeting to go over the construction industry scheme (CIS), which he heard about as an employee.

Compile bullet points of the main features of the CIS scheme, to prepare for the meeting.

B.

(a)   George, a part-time employee with Barchester town council, has just received a legacy, and plans to buy two flats which he will renovate at a cost of £35,000, using local tradesmen. He plans to let one flat, but to sell the other at a profit, and buy further properties for renovation/let with the proceeds. He hopes eventually to make this his full-time occupation.

(b)   Master Builder plc commenced trading on 1 January 2006, establishing a nationwide chain of DIY outlets. It has a 31 December year end, and has incurred or expects to incur the following amounts on construction expenditure (excluding land):

Y/e 31 December 2006	
Master Builder retail outlets	1.7 million
Y/e 31 December 2007	
Master Builder retail outlets	0.9 million
Master Builder corporate HQ	0.5 million
Y/e 31 December 2008	
Master Builder retail outlets	0.7 million
Master Builder sales office	0.5 million
Y/e 31 December 2009	
Master Builder retail outlets	0.4 million
Refurbishment of disused building for commercial letting	0.5 million

(c)   Patrick is a builder with electrical and plumbing skills. He builds conservatories, extensions and outhouses for householders, and occasionally carries out minor property maintenance or building on the premises of small non-construction businesses, taking about £25,000 per year plus materials.

State the obligations of each of the above as regards the construction industry scheme.

C.

Specialists All Aspects Ltd has won a contract with Luxury Leisure Lodges Ltd, a company owned by a firm of architects, for the clearance of land and construction of holiday lodges, over a period of 18 months. The company had not previously had to operate the CIS scheme.

At the end of the first month of July 2009 the director reports that he has failed to grasp what is required by CIS regulations, and has taken no action towards compliance. He requests assistance in compliance, and in preparation of the first month's return. He advises that the following transactions have taken place:

Payments/invoices for costs

(1)   £1,750+ VAT   Paid to Rayne Forestry Enterprises, a forestry contractor providing its own timber harvester, loader and labour for clearing scrub and trees. Its previous activity has been limited exclusively to harvesting timber. Fuel for the timber harvester and the loader amounted to £85.

(2)	£2,000	Paid to Heavyweight Plant Hire for the hire and transport of a roller to prepare the site, to be operated by one of Specialists All Aspects Ltd's employees.
(3)	£25,000	Invoiced by Latvian Larch Lodges Inc (a Latvian-based company operating abroad for the first time) for provision and erection of one large Larch lodge, net of customs duties and VAT. Payment was made during the month, but was subject to a 10% retention.
(4)	£1,500	Paid to John Smith, a local joinery contractor for joinery work. This payment was for a single job, but it has been agreed that in future that Mr Smith will be paid £1,500 each month during the course of the project, for working Mondays, Tuesdays and Wednesdays each week. This will include the months of July and December, when he will be on holiday for two weeks. He will provide his own hand tools and van, although it is unlikely the van will be used for project purposes.
(5)	£2,500	Paid to Mega Tile plc, a major UK-wide decorative tile supplier, for supplying and installing decorative tiles in the bathroom. The payment is made up of £750 for tiles, £1,250 for labour and £500 for travel and subsistence.
(6)	£2,500	Paid to Darren, who recently became self-employed, for ground works. The payment is made up of £1,900 for labour, £350 for plant hire at cost, £75 fuel for machinery at cost and £175 travel expenses.

Company income

Specialists All Aspects Ltd invoiced Luxury Leisure Lodges Ltd for £38,000, plus VAT, subject to 5% retention, and received payment on 27 July.

PAYE for the month to 5 August 2009 amounted to £1,237.

(a) State what action needs to be taken, and what reports must be produced, with due dates.

(b) Calculate deductions, on the basis that Darren and John Smith registered for net payment, Mega Tile plc for gross payment, and the others are not registered.

D.

Henry, director of Gross Builders Ltd, was discussing tax saving schemes with his friend Keran, a sole trader, in the pub. Both have remarkably similar construction industry businesses with a turnover of £85,000 per year, including rechargeable materials costs of about £30,000, and annual profit of around £20,000 (Henry has a low salary and pays dividends). PAYE amounts to around £1,250 per quarter, and CIS deductions withheld from subcontractors to around £600.

Both businesses have a 31 March year-end, but Keran's business is registered for gross payment whereas Gross Builders Ltd is still registered for net payment. Keran says that he has taken his wife into partnership from 1 July 2009 – she does substantial work for the business – to use both rate bands. Henry asks you why we have not provided him with similar proactive advice.

Respond, forecasting CIS payments/receipts for the next year on a quarterly basis, and state when final repayment is due.

Answer

A. **Points for preparation for meeting with Joe**

The current construction industry scheme, effective from 6 April 2007, applies where:

- a subcontractor receives payment from,
- another subcontractor, a contractor or deemed contractor,
- under a 'construction contract'.

The scheme is similar to previous schemes, but the main differences for the construction industry are:

- cards certifying status have been replaced by verification from the centralised HMRC database; and
- compliance criteria for gross payment status are defined by statute, and HMRC have fewer powers of mitigation, but the compliance period is reduced from three years to one.

'Contractors' include any businesses carrying out defined construction operations. They are required to:

- Review subcontractors' status for employment/self-employment;
- If self-employed, verify their payment status with HMRC's database. There are three types of payment status, gross, 20% withholding, or 30% withholding;
- Calculate deductions correctly, excluding defined materials expenses;
- File monthly (but not annual) CIS returns and pay over deductions monthly;
- Issue monthly payslips to subcontractors subject to deduction.

Construction operations are defined in FA 2004 s 74, and listed in HMRC's guide, CIS340, covering most construction work in the UK and within the 12-mile limit offshore.

The deductions from payment do not reduce the amount of income liable to tax, but are on account of year-end tax and NIC. A company may offset CIS deductions it has suffered against its own payroll deductions and CIS amounts that it has deducted itself, but only has a right of set-off against those within the same tax year. A sole trader or partnership does not have a right of set-off against PAYE or CIS deductions paid.

Payments for construction operations will be subject to CIS deductions, unless the subcontractor can prove compliance with strict criteria that assure HMRC that all tax and NIC will be paid on time.

B.

(a) George is engaging in the repair of buildings, which is within the definition of construction operations. The activity is clearly not carried out in the capacity of a private householder, as he does not occupy the flats. The pattern and scale of expenditure will almost certainly cause the activity to be considered as a property developing business, altering buildings to make a profit.

The fact that some flats will be let, creating a separate letting business, does not affect CIS obligations, and it is common for the CIS scheme to apply to only parts of a business.

George should register as a contractor from the start of renovation of the first flat, and verify the tradesmen's payment status, to operate CIS deductions accordingly.

(b) As a retailer, Master Builder plc is not within the construction industry, and the supply of building materials is not within the scope of construction operations.

However, as a non-construction business with an average spend on construction of over £1 million per year, Master Builder plc is a 'deemed contractor', both under the old construction industry scheme, and the current scheme.

Under the old scheme Master Builder would have been liable to make deductions from payments to its contractor(s), although it is very likely that it would have appointed only one main contractor to manage its projects, which would have been registered for gross payment.

From 6 April 2007, under the new CIS, payments made for construction operations for fixed assets used for the group's business became excluded from the scheme.

From 6 April 2007, Master Builder plc no longer makes 'contract payments' in respect of its sales office or retail sales outlets. Although because of its turnover it remains a deemed contractor, it can apply for a suspension of monthly returns.

In the year ending 31 December 2009 it expects to incur less than £1 million on construction expenditure, but as the annual average at £1.16 million still exceeds the threshold, it remains a contractor.

Payments for the retail outlets are excluded from the scheme, but payments in respect of the investment property are within the scheme and must be reported on the monthly return, together with any deductions made.

(c) Patrick's business is undoubtedly a construction business, and potentially within the construction industry scheme. However, he appears not to work for contractors within the scheme. Householders are never contractors for payments on their own properties, and small businesses are unlikely to spend an average of £1 million per year over three years. The persons paying him are not within the scheme, so no deductions will be made. Patrick is free not to register as a subcontractor, but it would be advisable to register for 20% deduction, in case he was offered subcontract work by a construction company.

If he wanted to take on subcontractors, he would be obliged to register immediately as a contractor, and make the appropriate deductions from contract payments to them. This would also require him to make monthly returns, and as the penalty for late filing of monthly returns – even nil returns – is £100 per month per 50 employees, he will probably not wish to register as a contractor.

C.

(a) Specialists All Aspects Ltd must contact HMRC immediately to register as a contractor, as it should have registered as soon as it took on subcontractors. HMRC will issue the monthly return, which must be filed by 19th of the following month.

Specialists All Aspects Ltd must then review the terms under which subcontractors work, and identify those who should be categorised as employed. These are excluded from the CIS scheme, as PAYE and NI are operated instead.

When registered, Specialists All Aspects Ltd will be able to verify the status of the subcontractors, by telephone or online, to determine whether they should be paid gross, or subject to 20% or 30% deduction. It is then necessary to calculate the deductions, and pay them over by 19th of the following month (22nd if paid electronically).

(b) Calculation of deductions

(1) Forestry operations are not within the CIS scheme, so for the bulk of its activity, Rayne Forestry Enterprises, has no need to register. However, clearing scrub on a construction site falls within the definition of construction operations, and brings the business within the scheme. As it is not registered, tax will be deducted at 30% from the payment, net of VAT, and less the *cost* of fuel of £85 = (1,750–85 × 30%) = £500. The company must give Rayne Forestry Enterprises written confirmation of the CIS deduction.

The verification reference given by HMRC must be stated on the monthly pay advice.

(2) Hire and transport of equipment without an operator is excluded from the definition of construction operations, so this cost will not be reported on the return.

(3) The CIS scheme applies only within the UK, but applies to foreign businesses operating in the UK. Latvian Larch Lodges should contact HMRC to register, and arrange for repayment of tax in line with double tax treaty arrangements, using the written confirmation of deduction as evidence. As the company is not registered, the higher rate of deduction of 30% applies. The deduction is made to the amount paid, not the amount invoiced, so will be (25,000 – 2,500 × 30%) = £6,750.

The verification reference given by HMRC must be given on the monthly pay advice.

(4) As John Smith is clearly carrying out construction operations as a contractor, he will be CIS-registered, and will be paid subject to deduction at 20% (1,500 × 20%) = £300.

Contractors must review the self-employed status of workers regularly. As John Smith's future work seems likely to meet employment criteria, he will be subject to PAYE in future. The fact that he is part-time will have no effect, but the fixed times suggest a degree of control. Paid holidays are not necessarily an indicator of employee status: under the Working Time Regulations 1998, genuinely self-employed workers who provide personal service are entitled to paid holiday, but many labour-only subcontractors who cannot send a substitute to do the work will qualify. HMRC disregards the provision of hand tools in determining status, and the van is not used for contract work.

(5) As Mega Tile plc is registered for gross payment, no deduction need be made, nor is there any requirement to analyse the payment.

Work on artistic works such as statues is outside the definition of construction operations, but anything with a function, such as tiles, is included.

(6) Ground works are clearly within construction operations, so withholding will have to be applied to the payment net of specified expenses. Hire of plant, and fuel for machinery, are deductible expenses, but travel expenses, and fuel for travel are not. The deduction will therefore be (2,500 – 350 – 75 × 20%) = £415.

As this subcontractor is paid net, the monthly return must show the gross payment, the expenses deducted, and the amount withheld. A payslip must be issued to him within 14 days of the end of the month.

The amounts withheld therefore amount to (500 + 6,750 + 300 + 415) = £7,965.

The professional services of the firm of architects that owns Luxury Leisure Lodges Ltd are not within the CIS scheme. However, when they act as property developers, as in this case, they are required to operate the scheme like any other contractor in the construction business. The amounts withheld from Specialists All Aspects Ltd are (38,000 – 5% × 20%) = 7,220. Deductions are always operated on amounts paid, not on the basis of the invoice.

As this is a company, the amount suffered can be offset against amounts due within the same tax year, against payroll liabilities first.

PAYE due for month to 5 August 2009	1,237
CIS deductions due	7,965
Less: CIS deductions suffered	(7,220)
Payable for the month	1,982

Payment is due by 19th August 2009, or 22nd if paid electronically.

D.

The cost of materials is excluded from turnover for CIS purposes, so annual turnover is £55,000, or £13,750 per quarter, subject to a quarterly CIS deduction of £2,750 if applicable.

PAYE and CIS subcontractor deductions withheld amount to (1,250 + 600) = £1,850 per quarter or £7,400 per annum.

Gross Builders Ltd

As a limited company, Gross Builders Ltd can offset CIS deduction suffered against CIS and PAYE paid, with the result that cash flow from turnover will be as follows:

Quarter Ending	Turnover	CIS deductions suffered	PAYE/CIS payable	Net flow	Cumulative cash flow
30/06/09	13,750	(2,750)	Nil (offset)	11,000	11,000
30/09/09	13,750	(2,750)	Nil (offset)	11,000	22,000
31/12/09	13,750	(2,750)	Nil (offset)	11,000	33,000
31/03/10	13,750	(2,750)	Nil (offset)	11,000	44,000
30/06/10					
30/09/10					
31/12/10	CT offset	11,000	(7,400)	3,600	47,600
	55,000	Nil	7,400	47,600	

Keran

By taking his wife into partnership at 1 July 2009, Keran breaches the conditions that qualify him for gross payment, as a partnership must have a minimum of £30,000 turnover from construction operations per partner. HMRC will issue a determination effective 90 days from date of issue, that gross payment status no longer applies. This is taken to be effective in the quarter ended 31/12/09. Keran's cash flow is therefore as follows:

Quarter Ending	Turnover	CIS deductions suffered	PAYE/ CIS payable	Net flow	Cumulative Cash flow
30/06/09	13,750		(1,850)	11,900	11,900
30/09/09	13,750		(1,850)	11,900	23,800
31/12/09	13,750	(2,750)	(1,850)	9,150	32,950
31/03/10	13,750	(2,750)	(1,850)	9,150	42,100
30/06/10	IT offset	5,500		5,500	47,600
	55,000	Nil	(7,400)	47,600	

In spite of receiving payment gross for half the year, Keran has suffered a cash flow disadvantage of (£44,000 – £42,100) £1,900 by the fourth quarter. Had gross payment status been lost at the start of the year, the difference would have been £7,400 by the fourth quarter. In an unincorporated business with a high PAYE or CIS liability, loss of gross payment status will be severely damaging. Great care must be taken to avoid breaching the conditions of the compliance test for gross payment status, which requires that all returns be filed on time and all taxes be paid by the due date. Retention of gross payment status will repay the care and commitment needed to achieve it.

It is possible that HMRC would argue that a partnership share in a construction business with its attendant book-keeping, scheduling and administrative requirements involves income shifting. Although introduction of income shifting rules has been deferred, this remains an unknown quantity, and it would be better for Keran's wife to be paid for her work through payroll, perhaps at a rate that attracted little or no PAYE or NIC contributions, so as to avoid losing gross payment status. Furthermore, as a partner, any failure in respect of her personal tax filing obligations would put the firm's gross payment status at risk.

Explanatory Notes

The construction industry scheme

1. The first construction industry scheme (CIS) was introduced in 1972 as a measure to police tax compliance in an industry which offered short-term work and often paid itinerant workers in cash. The current construction industry scheme, which came into effect on 6 April 2007, is the third of its kind. It retains many of the principles of the previous schemes, but instead of issuing certificates and cards it features control of compliance and verification by means of a centralised computerised database, without the need for cards. Stringent criteria for compliance are set and HMRC is given wide powers to cancel registration for gross payment, in which case a 20% deduction rate applies, and also to cancel registration for the 20% rate, in which case a 30% rate applies. It places a huge compliance burden upon contractors, as gross payment status can inadvertently be lost by late payment of any taxes, or delay in filing tax or Companies House returns.

    The current scheme was introduced by FA 2004 Chapter 3 and Schedule 12, with detailed regulations provided by SI 2005/2045 Income Tax (Construction Industry Scheme) Regulations 2005, and guidance provided by HMRC's publication CIS 340 on the construction industry scheme. As for previous schemes, its main purpose is to deduct tax at source, unless HMRC is satisfied that the tax will be properly accounted for by the recipient. This is achieved by requiring both payers and payees to register as contractors or subcontractors with HMRC, and to make monthly returns of payments.

Online facility

2. At present it is possible to:

    - register for payment under deduction online (but a visit to the tax office is needed for identification if a sole trader has no NI number or HMRC cannot trace the NI number used);

    - verify contractors online;

    - make monthly returns online.

    If returns are made online, the subcontractors to be paid can be selected from the HMRC database, hopefully increasing accuracy in establishing deduction status.

    The free HMRC facility is intended for small contractors with 50 or fewer subcontractors. A number of proprietary software suppliers have been approved by HMRC, and are listed on their website. As well as being able to supply up-to-date information, the system will be able to collect instances of non-compliance routinely. Given the stringent compliance conditions, it may be necessary to use reliable software if compliance is to be achieved.

Application of the scheme

3. The scheme applies where:

    - a subcontractor receives a contract payment from,

    - another subcontractor, a contractor or deemed contractor,

    - under a 'construction contract'.

Subcontractors

4. A subcontractor is a person, partnership or company under a duty to carry out operations or provide labour, or responsible for operations carried out by others (FA 2004 s 58).

Contractors

5.   Private persons not acting in a business capacity cannot be contractors, with the result that the scheme does not apply to them, and they can never be required to withhold CIS deductions.

Contractors include:

- any person carrying out a business which includes construction operations (mainstream contractors);

- local authorities, NHS trusts, housing associations and a number of specified public bodies, subject to spending an average of at least £1,000,000 annually on construction operations over the last three years;

- persons not carrying on a construction business, but whose business spends on average at least £1,000,000 annually on construction operations over the last three years. There are some exceptions to this, detailed below.

Deemed contractors

6.   Deemed contractors are persons or bodies who do not operate as construction businesses, but who are deemed contractors because they have spent £1,000,000 on construction operations annually over the last three years. If they have been in existence for less than three years, this limit is scaled down proportionately; in the event of a reconstruction, the previous history is aggregated with the new structure.

The requirement for deemed contractors to operate the CIS scheme ceases only after expenditure on construction operations has been less than £1,000,000 in each of three successive years following a year in which the average of £1,000,000 was reached. For public bodies, 'year' means the year ended 31 March, while for businesses 'year' means the period of account.

Small payments exemption

There is a small payments exemption which applies to small amounts up to a maximum of £1,000 paid by deemed contractors only, not those paid by mainstream subcontractors. The contractor must be specially approved by HMRC for the purpose. The £1,000 must cover the whole cost of the contract, not stage payments on a larger contract, excluding materials.

Construction contracts

7.   Construction contracts are contracts relating to construction operations. Certain operations are defined as being within construction operations, while other operations are defined as being excluded. The CIS scheme operates only in the UK up to the 12-mile offshore limit, but it applies to non-UK businesses operating in UK.

A summary of operations considered to be construction operations as defined in FA 2004 s 74(2) is as follows:

(a)   construction, alteration, repair, extension, demolition or dismantling of buildings or structures (whether permanent or not), including offshore installations (ie, inside the 12-mile limit);

(b)   construction, alteration, repair etc of any works forming, or to form, part of the land. This particularly includes walls, roadworks, power-lines, electric communications apparatus, aircraft runways, docks and harbours, railways, inland waterways, pipe-lines, reservoirs, water-mains, wells, sewers, industrial plant and installations for the purposes of land drainage, coast protection or defence;

(c)   installation of heating, lighting, air-conditioning, ventilation, power supply, drainage, sanitation, water supply or fire protection into buildings;

(d)   painting or decorating the internal or external services of any building or structure;

(e)   preparatory operations such as site clearance, and earthmoving, excavation, tunnelling, laying foundations, site restoration, landscaping and the provision of roadways and other access works.

A summary of operations which are excluded from the definition of construction operations as per FA 2004 s 74(3) is as follows:

(a)   drilling for, or extraction of, oil and gas;

(b)   extraction of minerals (whether by surface or underground working) and tunnelling, boring or construction works for this purpose;

(c)   manufacture or building of engineering components, equipment, materials, plant or machinery, or delivery to the site;

(d)   manufacture of components or systems of heating, lighting, air-conditioning, ventilation, power supply etc or delivery to site;

(e)   professional work of architects or surveyors, consultants in building, engineering, interior/ exterior decoration or landscaping;

(f)   the making, installation and repair of artistic works, being sculptures murals or other works which are wholly artistic in nature;

(g)   signwriting, or erecting, installing or preparing signboards and advertisements;

(h)   installation of seating, blinds and shutters;

(i)   installation of security systems including burglar alarms, closed-circuit television and public address systems (but closed-circuit television systems for non-security purposes, such as traffic monitoring, would be construction operations).

Employment status

8.   There is, however, one major exclusion from CIS subcontractor status which is crucial to compliance with CIS and PAYE regulations. A contract of employment is not within the CIS scheme: PAYE and NIC deductions must be effected instead.

In particular, the fact that a subcontractor was or is registered under the CIS scheme is no indication of self-employment status. Contractors must work out the employment status of subcontractors at the time they are taken on, and this must be reviewed regularly, certainly at any change in contract terms or working practice.

HMRC emphasises that employment or self-employment status is not a matter of labelling, but a fact derived from the terms of engagement. If a worker who had been treated as self-employed is recategorised by HMRC as an employee, the employer is liable for PAYE, NICs and penalties and interest. See Example 94 'Employment status; managed service companies'.

By the primary legislation of FA 2004 s 70, contractors must declare on each monthly return that 'The employment status of each individual included on this return, and any continuation sheets, has been considered and payments have not been made under contracts of employment.' This is a monthly reminder of the importance of implementing procedures to ensure that workers are correctly classified.

If workers are reclassified as employees, the resulting additional PAYE and NIC due but unpaid may cause the contractor to fail the compliance test, and lose gross payment status.

Mixed contracts

9.   Some contracts may include construction operations and non-construction operations. In the case of such mixed contracts, the CIS regulations apply to all operations under the whole contract.

Registration

10.   Registration is central to the centralised database system. It provides notification to contractors of whether the subcontractor is to be paid gross, after deduction of 20% from the labour element, or whether a 30% deduction may need to be applied. It provides no information on whether the individual should be classified as employed or self-employed, a matter to be considered separately at the beginning of each new project, and reviewed throughout its duration.

Both contractors and subcontractors need to register under separate schemes. Therefore, a business operating both as a contractor and subcontractor will require two registrations, one for each activity.

Contractors' obligations

11.   FA 2004 empowers HMRC to make regulations detailing the obligations of contractors, which are found in SI 2005/2045 and the HMRC publication CIS 340 'Guide for contractors and subcontractors'.

Contractor registration

Contractors are required to register when they take on their first subcontractors, irrespective of whether the subcontractor is likely to be paid gross or subject to deduction of tax. Contractors may have multiple registrations (for instance different registrations for different construction sites), but the increased number of returns required will increase the risk of penalties and non-compliance.

As a result of registration, contractors will gain access to the centralised database to enable them to 'verify' the payment status of subcontractors, and they will also be required to make monthly (but not annual) returns of contract payments.

Verification

12.   The contractor must contact HMRC to verify the registration status of subcontractors, before making any payment. The contractor must provide the name and UTR, together with the NI number for individuals and partnerships, or the company registration number for companies.

HMRC will advise the contractor of a verification number. This must be retained in all cases, and is required on the monthly return for subcontractors paid at the higher rate of deduction.

13.   Verification is not required if the payee has been included on a monthly return of contract payments within the last two years. However, HMRC are required to notify contractors of any change in the registration status of subcontractors who have appeared on the contractors' monthly returns within the last two years. The contractor must implement these changes in payment status, so it is very important that the contractor is able to manage these notifications.

The contractor may not verify the status of any subcontractor before work has been offered. The contractor may verify the subcontractor status only when a contract has been entered into, or where a tender has been formally accepted.

Contractors' monthly return CIS 300

14.   Returns are for the tax month, from the 6th of the month to the following 5th, and must be returned within 14 days, that is by the 19th of the month.

The return must include all payments and deductions made, including payments made gross and costs of materials, giving the contractor's name, the UTR and accounts office reference, the NI number or company registration number if known, and the verification number for contractors subject to the higher rate of deduction. These requirements are set out in SI 2005/2045 reg 4.

The monthly return also requires the following declarations to be made.

- The employment status of each individual included on this return, and any continuation sheets, has been considered and payments have not been made under contracts of employment.

- Every subcontractor included on this return, and any continuation sheets, has either been verified with HMRC or been included in previous CIS returns in this, or the previous two tax years.

- That the return contains all the information, particulars and supporting information, and that it is complete and accurate to the best of the contractor's knowledge and belief.

The return may be filed electronically. Payment of the deductions must be made within 14 days, or within 17 days if made electronically. E-payment is mandatory for businesses which are large payers for PAYE purposes. If average monthly payments of PAYE, NIC, CIS and student loan deductions are less than £1,500, the contractor may opt to pay quarterly.

Payment and deduction of tax

15. The contractor is required to deduct tax at the appropriate rate and remit it on a monthly basis together with the monthly return.

For details of the calculation of deductions, see note 21 below.

Subcontractor registration

If the subcontractor is newly starting up on a self-employed basis, he will of course need to complete Form CWF1, notifying the start of self-employment, to avoid a penalty. FA 2008 s 118 and Sch 41 provide for this penalty to be a behaviour- and tax-based penalty for obligations arising on or after 1 April 2009.

The subcontractors may apply to register for payment under deduction or, if they can meet the conditions described below, for gross payment.

Subcontractors should register before they are due to receive contract payments, failing which tax will be deducted at the higher rate of 30%. Registration is by telephoning the helpline 0845 366 7899, and providing name, the trading name if any, address, telephone number, UTR and NI number. A visit to an HMRC office to present proof of identity will be required for new subcontractors who cannot be identified from HMRC's systems.

Provided that the applicant supplies all documentation and details, particularly relating to identity, HMRC will register the subcontractor for payment under deduction at 20%. The legislation provides that HMRC may refuse registration under deduction if they are not satisfied with the documents and identity. In this case the individual could still work in the construction industry, but would suffer deduction at 30%.

Registration for gross payment

16. Details of the criteria for registration of the gross payment are set out in FA 2004 ss 63 and 64, which are summarised below. All businesses must meet the following three tests for the qualifying period of the 12 months prior to registration:

- the business test;

- the turnover test;

- the compliance test.

The business test

17. Applicants must provide evidence that they are carrying on business in the UK involving construction operations, substantially using a business bank account. HMRC will require evidence of business address, invoices and contracts for construction work, details of payments for construction work, the books and accounts of the business and details of the business bank account including bank statements.

The turnover test

18. The turnover threshold for an individual is £30,000 from construction operations for provision of labour, and excluding materials, to be earned in the 12 months following application.

    The turnover threshold for partnerships is the lesser of £200,000, or the individual threshold of £30,000 multiplied by the number of partners.

    The turnover threshold for companies is the lesser of £200,000, or the individual threshold of £30,000 multiplied by the number of directors, or in the case of a close company multiplied by the number of directors, plus beneficial shareholders who are not also directors.

    Evidence of future turnover is likely to derived from historic turnover.

The compliance test

19. Subcontractors must have met all their compliance obligations during the previous 12 months. This includes

    – completing and sending in all tax returns received,

    – supplying all tax-related information timeously,

    – paying all personal, business, NIC, PAYE and CIS deductions on time.

    The compliance conditions are set out in detail in FA 2004 Sch 11 and SI 2005/2045 paras 32 to 37. HMRC may, at 90 days notice, cancel gross payment status if it 'appears' that:

    ● an application for registration for gross payment, if made at this time, would be refused; or

    ● that an incorrect return or incorrect information under any provision of the CIS regulations has been made; or

    ● there has been a failure to comply with any provisions under the regulations.

    A number of breaches of conditions are considered as acceptable according to HMRC factsheet CIS 343, but the breaches include failures by the firm/company and all or any of its partners/directors. These breaches are any or all of:

    – three late submissions of the monthly CIS return – up to 28 days late;

    – three late payments of CIS/PAYE deductions – up to 14 days late;

    – one late payment of Self-Assessment tax – up to 28 days late;

    – any employer's end of year return made late;

    – any late payments of corporation tax – up to 28 days late, including where any shortfall in the payment has incurred an interest charge but no penalty;

    – any self-assessment return made late;

    – any failures classed as 'minor and technical' in relation to obligations under the old Scheme, where these fall within the 12-month period up to commencement of the new Scheme.

    In addition, in this context, from 3 June 2008, late or non-payments of amounts of less than £100 are specifically to be disregarded for purposes of compliance testing.

    HMRC have limited power of mitigation on these compliance conditions and the conditions are sufficiently stringent to be breached accidentally. The contractors' records are reviewed annually and automatically on a rolling basis (known as the 'scheduled review'), as a result of which it is expected that at least a quarter of contractors who had gross payment status at commencement of the current scheme at 6 April 2007 will lose gross payment status. The withdrawal of gross payment status is notified first to the affected subcontractor, who has a right of appeal and can advance any reasonable excuse. Contractors should be notified of the change of status of a subcontractor only after the appeal deadline has expired.

Monthly returns are pre-populated and sent by HMRC to the contractor each month. The returns must be returned to reach HMRC by the 19th of the following month, even if they are nil returns. Failure to make the return incurs a penalty of £100 per month per return for 0–50 employees, with an additional £100 per increment of 50 employees per month. If a return is made three months late, the penalty in respect of that single return is currently £300, and when twelve months late an additional £3,000. Finance Act 2009 Sch 55 introduced a revised framework for the future: after a return has been outstanding for more than three months after the filing date, it will (perhaps from April 2010) attract an additional fixed penalty of £200, then if six months late 5% of deductions due for the return period, and another 5% if twelve months late. Once more than twelve months late, the return could attract a penalty of 70% of the deductions due if the contractor's delay was deliberate but not concealed, or 100% if deliberate and concealed.

Subcontractor registration

Registration for gross payment

20. A subcontractor registered for gross payment is paid without any deductions. The amount paid, excluding VAT, must be reported monthly giving UTR plus NIC number or company registration number. There is no requirement to analyse the CIS gross payment (ie, net of VAT) between materials and labour. No payslip need be issued.

Registration for net payment

21. Where a subcontractor is registered for net payment, tax at 20% or 30% must be withheld from the CIS gross (net of VAT and CITB levy) payment, as reduced for specific defined costs which are:

   ● materials;

   ● consumables;

   ● fuel (but not fuel for travelling);

   ● plant hire;

   ● cost of manufacture of prefabricated materials.

The amount deductible is the cost to the subcontractor, plus irrecoverable VAT, if appropriate. The contractor may estimate the cost to the subcontractor in the absence of evidence. The contractor must ensure that any profit element is excluded, whether evidence is presented or not.

Expenses of travel, in particular, are not deductible from the gross payment.

For the monthly return, the costs of materials must be split from the labour element. The contractor must make a monthly report of the total of amounts paid to the subcontractor, showing name, UTR, NIC or company registration number, 'gross' payment, materials element and tax deducted. Where the subcontractor is registered for the higher rate 30% deduction, the verification number must also be shown.

Contractors must issue a payment analysis to subcontractors paid under deduction of tax (but not to those paid gross) within 14 days of payment.

Recovery/offset of deductions

22. Subcontractors liable to income tax are able to offset CIS deductions against their year-end income tax liability, and then Class 4 national insurance contributions liability. Payment slips issued by the contractor will be required, and in the case of subcontractors subject to deduction of higher rate, it is essential that the verification numbers are provided.

Regulation 17 of SI 2005/2045 provides for in-year repayments, subject to proof that deductions are excessive in relation to subcontractors' profits, contractors' profits and other income for the year to date at the time of application, after deducting proportional allowances. The applicant(s) must sign a declaration that this information is given to the best of their knowledge and belief.

Companies, but not partnerships or those who are self-employed, may offset CIS deductions withheld from their income against payroll taxes, CIS deductions withheld from other subcontractors, or against corporation tax due nine months after the year end. Where CIS deductions suffered are offset against payroll taxes or deductions withheld, they may be offset only within the same tax year. Any excess of deductions suffered by the end of the tax year cannot be used to offset subsequent payroll or CIS deductions, and will be offset against the corporation tax liability, or repaid. Only excess deductions arising before the end of the company's accounting period may be offset against the corporation tax for that period.

For example, Faith and Hope Foundations Ltd has a 30 September 2010 year end.

For the quarter ended 31 March 2010, the company suffers £4,000 surplus deductions. For the two quarters to 30 June and 30 September 2010, it has payroll and CIS liabilities of £1,200 and £1,800 respectively. In the quarter to 31 December 2010, it suffered deductions at source of £1,500 in excess of PAYE and CIS liabilities.

Its corporation tax liability for the year ended 30 September 2010 was £7,500.

Offset would be as follows:

The £4,000 surplus deductions to 31 March cannot be offset against the liabilities of June and September 2010, as these fall into a different tax year. These liabilities must be paid on time to achieve the compliance conditions for gross payment.

The £1,500 excess deductions of 31 December 2010 cannot be set against the corporation tax liability for the period ended 30 September 2010, because they arose after the end of that period. They could be offset against subsequent PAYE and CIS liabilities arising later in the 2010/11 year.

Corporation tax for the period ended 30 September 2010 will therefore be offset by the surplus at 31 March 2010 only, giving £3,500 (£7,500 – £4,000).

Offset against corporation tax could represent a delay of 19 months for deductions suffered at the beginning of the period of account.

For self-employed/partnerships, self-assessment returns may be filed online, shortly after 6 April, to speed repayment.

Collection of unpaid deductions

23.   Where contractors fail to make payments of deductions, or where it appears to an HMRC officer that the payment is insufficient, HMRC may prepare a certificate to the best of the officer's judgement for the combined amount of CIS, PAYE, NIC and student loan deductions. The amount specified on such a notice is payable in seven days, under SI 2005/2045 reg 11.

Question

A.

(a) Fred, who is a married man aged 81, has the following income in 2009/10:

	£
State pension	7,595
Occupational pension (no tax deducted under PAYE)	3,035
Building society interest taxed at source (gross amount)	2,100
Dividends (including tax credits)	3,100

He paid £1,600 net to a charity under a gift aid declaration. Show the amount of income tax repayable to Fred for 2009/10.

(b) State the value of the donation to the charity.

(c) Set out the differing ways in which tax efficient donations may be made to charities.

B.

(a) The Blackhills Rugby Club has registered as a Community Amateur Sports Club (CASC) with effect from 1 April 2002. Its income and expenditure in the year ended 31 March 2010 comprise:

			£	
Income:	Membership fees		9,800	
	Donations under gift aid (including tax)		6,000	
	Bar takings – members	18,600		
	– non-members	5,400	24,000	
	Letting of club house		2,600	
	Building society interest		200	42,600
Expenditure:	Purchases for bar		12,600	
	Expenses of running club house		8,400	
	Maintaining pitches		4,800	
	Travelling costs of teams		8,100	
	Costs of members' 'night out'		4,800	
	Other costs of running club		1,900	40,600
Net cash in flow				2,000

Compute any amounts liable to corporation tax for the year ended 31 March 2010, assuming appropriate claims for relief are made.

(b) Show the effect on part (a) if Blackhills Rugby Club had sold part of its land in the year to 31 March 2010 for £200,000, resulting in a potential chargeable gain of £63,000.

(c) John, a 40% taxpayer, was a member of Blackhills Rugby Club. He pays a membership fee of £50 per year and has made a further donation to the club of £50 under gift aid. Set out the effect on John's tax liability in 2009/10.

Answer

A. (a) Fred – Income tax repayment 2009/10

				Income £	*Income tax paid* £
State pension				7,595	
Occupational pension				3,035	–
Building society interest (gross amount)				2,100	420
Dividends (including non-repayable credits £310)				3,100	
				15,830	420
Personal allowance (75 and over)				9,640	
Taxable income				6,190	
Income tax thereon: On non-savings income					
(7,595 + 3,035 − 9,640)	990	@ 20%		198	
Savings starting rate income (non-dividend)	1,450	@ 10%		145	
	2,440				
	650	@ 20%		130	
On dividends	3,100	@ 10%		310	
	6,190			783	
Less: Age related married couple's allowance (restricted – see below)				383	
				400	
Less: Tax credits on dividends				310	90
Repayment due					330
Tax retained on gift aid payment 1,600 + (20/80) = 2,000 @ 20%					£400

Personal allowances, including married couple's allowance, are restricted to ensure that the amount of income tax (and capital gains tax) charged is no less than the amount deducted from the gift aid donation. See explanatory note 1.

Surplus married couple's allowance available for transfer to wife:

	£	*Tax saving @ 10%* £
Allowance due	6,965	697
Used	3,830	383
Transfer to wife	3,135	314

(b)

Qualifying donations made to charities are grossed up for the basic rate of income tax (ITA 2007 s 414), so the gross value of the donation depends on the basic rate of tax, which is 20% for 2009/10. Because of the decrease in the basic rate of tax from 22% in 2007/08 to 20% in 2008/09, the amount of tax on the net gift reduced, and the gross payment received by the charity fell. To compensate for this, for the years 2008/09 to 2010/11, FA 2008 s 50 and Sch 19 provide for a supplement amounting to 2% to be paid as a gift aid supplement from public funds to recipient charities.

Amount of gift paid	Tax at basic rate	Gross payment
2007/2008		
1,600	22%	451	2,051
2008/2009 and subsequent years		
1,600	20%	400	2,000

Gift aid supplement is calculated by grossing up the gift at the notional rate of tax of (20% + 2%) 22% for 2009/10. The difference between this and the gross gift at the actual rate of 20% is the amount of gift aid supplement. The charity therefore receives an additional £51 (2,051–2,000) in gift aid supplement, bringing the gross value to the charity to £2,051 in 2009/10.

(c)   **Tax-efficient giving to charity**

Gifts to charity by individuals

Where an individual wishes to make a donation to a charity, tax relief can be obtained provided certain steps are taken. The gift can be made in a number of ways:

(i)   Payroll giving

(ii)   Direct gift to charity with an appropriate declaration (gift aid)

(iii)   Gift of stocks and shares or land and buildings.

A company can also make tax allowable gifts to a charity, including gifts of stocks and shares or land and buildings, without completing a declaration.

Payroll giving

Employees can authorise their employer to deduct an amount from their pay to be given to charity (ITEPA 2003 ss 713–715). This reduces their pay for tax and tax credit purposes (but not for national insurance contributions). Tax relief is therefore given at the employee's highest marginal rate on the donation. The payroll deduction is passed to an HMRC approved payroll giving agency, who will pay the amount to the nominated charity (after deducting an administration fee, typically 5%). Voluntary payments to the agency by the employer to cover running costs are allowed against the employer's taxable profits (ICTA 1988 s 86A).

Gift aid donations by individuals (ITA 2007 ss 413–446)

A gift to charity by an individual qualifies for relief at the payer's highest tax rate if a gift aid declaration is made, providing the donor is within the scope of UK tax, ie a UK resident, or a Crown employee serving overseas, or a non-resident making the payment out of income or capital gains chargeable to UK tax. The gross gift is also deductible in computing income for tax credits.

The declaration can be made for the specific gift, or for all gifts to that charity, and can be made in writing or orally. Declarations may also be given in relation to donations made prior to the date of the declaration. A donor giving orally need only give his name and address. The charity must, however, then keep an auditable record of the declaration, retaining a copy for inspection by HMRC. A written declaration must contain (SI 2000/2074):

- the donor's name and home address

- the charity's name

- a declaration that the donation is to be treated as a gift aid declaration

- a note explaining that the donor must pay income tax or capital gains tax equal to the tax deducted from the donation

- date of declaration

- donor's signature.

A written record of an oral donation needs to contain the same information as a written declaration (except the donor's signature) and must in addition state that the donor may cancel the declaration within 30 days. Such a cancellation would be retrospective. Donors may cancel a declaration at any time, and all subsequent donations are not then gift aid payments.

Payments under a gift aid donation are treated as being net of basic rate tax. The charity can recover the tax deducted providing it can show an audit trail between the gift and the donor. This can be a cheque, standing order, direct debit or by physical evidence of cash giving, eg an envelope.

Higher rate relief is obtained by increasing the basic rate band by the gift plus the tax thereon. The tax on a cash gift of £4,000 is 20/80 × 4,000 = £1,000, giving a gross gift of £5,000. The basic rate band would be (34,800 + 5,000 =) £39,800. The rate of tax saved depends on the rate payable on the top slice of the taxpayer's income. For illustrations of the various marginal rates see Example 4 part (c). The basic rate band is not extended when computing top slicing relief on life policy gains (see Example 39).

Where necessary, personal allowances are restricted to ensure that sufficient tax is paid to cover the tax on the donations, as illustrated in part (a) of the example. If there is still insufficient tax, HMRC will issue an assessment to recover the shortfall.

In computing the tax that has been charged on the donor's income, notional tax on scrip dividends and on life policy gains is excluded, but the tax taken into account is before deducting relief for married couple's allowance or relief for maintenance payments (see Example 1 explanatory note 1). Any unused married couple's allowance can be surrendered to the spouse.

With the prospect of income tax rates of 50% and even 60% effective rate in 2010/11 the carry back of gift aid donations will permit income taxed at these higher marginal rates to be relieved by subsequent gifts. The proposals to abate personal allowances in 2010/11 will take effect at net adjusted income of £100,000, after deducting losses, the gross amount of gift aid donations and the gross amount of pension contributions made. The personal allowance will then be reduced by half of the excess over £100,000 until it has been removed completely.

The carry back election is explained in detail at explanatory note 8.

Tax credits

A gift which obtains relief under ITA 2007 s 416 is deductible from income for tax credits. For claimants who are within the threshold taper of 39% this increases the value of reliefs and reduces the net cost of a gift of £100 to £41. To achieve this result the taxpayer makes an actual gift of £80 (which is net of £20 tax, ie £100 gross).

Income for tax credits is reduced by the gross gift of £100 giving an increase in tax credits of £100 × 39% = £39.

	£
Gift to charity	80
Increase in tax credits	39
Actual cost	41

If the claimant is within the threshold taper of 6.67% a similar effect occurs. However as income may be liable to the higher rate the net cost of a gross gift of £100 would then be £53.33 again with an actual payment of £80 ie:

	£	£
Gift to charity		80.00
Higher rate relief (40–20)	20.00	
Increase in tax credits	6.67	26.67
Actual cost		53.33

See Example 7 for details of tax credits.

The relief for a gift carried back for tax purposes, but relieved on a current year basis for tax credit purposes can be even more dramatic. The carryback to 2008/09 could give relief at the higher rate whereas relief in 2009/10 could give tax credits relief at 39%.

	Net cost if 39% taper applies in 2009/10 £
Gift to charity	80
Higher rate relief 2008/09	(18)
Increase in tax credits 2009/10	(39)
Actual cost	23

Benefits from charities

A charity may make a token gesture to show its appreciation for a donation. The maximum benefits that a donor can receive are set out in ITA 2007 s 418 and ICTA 1988 s 339:

Aggregate donations in tax year £	*Maximum aggregate value of benefits*
0 – 100	25% of aggregate donations
101 – 1,000	£25
1,001 – 10,000	5% of aggregate donations
10,001 +	£500

The provision of free or reduced price admission for the donor (or family) to the property of a heritage or wildlife conservation charity (such as the National Trust) is disregarded provided the right applies for at least one year or the gift is at least 10% more than the normal admission price (FA 1990 s 25(5H) as added by F(No 2)A 2005).

Transactions with substantial donors

To counter perceived abuses of the charities' exemptions involving benefits provided to substantial donors, from 22 March 2006, ITA 2007 ss 549–554 restricts tax reliefs for charities and individuals in certain circumstances.

The legislation targets payments made by a charity to substantial donors or persons connected with them. A substantial donor is a person donating gifts on which tax relief was received of at least £25,000 in a year, or £150,000 (£100,000 before 22 April 2009) over a period of six years. The donor remains a substantial donor for tax purposes for five years after making such donations.

The transactions affected are sales or leases of property, provision of services, and loans or investments between the charities and the donors. Transactions of the type that truly independent parties would have entered into are not affected, nor are arm's length transactions, provided they do not form part of an arrangement to avoid tax. A company wholly owned by the charity cannot be a substantial donor.

The value or monetary equivalent of such transactions will be treated as non-charitable expenditure, and the charity's reliefs will be restricted, according to the method shown in part B.

Gift aid donations by companies (ICTA 1988 s 339)

Companies may make tax-efficient gift aid donations in a similar way to individuals, although they are not required to make gift aid declarations. The same limits apply as for individuals where the company receives a benefit from the gift. Company donations will not be relieved if they are conditional or the company or a connected person receives one or more benefits from the donation and their value exceeds the relevant limits in ICTA 1988 s 339(3DA). Companies do not deduct tax from gift aid donations, including covenanted payments. Tax relief is obtained by treating the payment as a charge against profits for corporation tax (see Example 49 explanatory note 11).

Gifts of shares or land and buildings

Under ICTA 1988 s 587B and ITA 2007 Part 8 Chapter 3, tax relief is available for gifts to charity by individuals or companies of shares or securities listed or dealt in on a recognised stock exchange (which includes shares on the Alternative Investment Market), units in authorised unit trusts, shares in open-ended investment companies and interests in offshore funds and gifts of a freehold or leasehold interest in UK land (s 587C). The relief is equal to the market value of the security or land on the date of disposal plus costs, less any consideration received. This relief is in addition to the capital gains relief, which treats the disposal as giving rise to neither gain nor loss. An individual deducts the relief from his total income, saving tax at his top tax rate (see Example 4(c)), and a company deducts the relief as a charge against profits (see Example 49 explanatory note 11). Care must be taken if relief is given only against dividend income, as the top rate of tax includes the non-repayable tax credit of 10%. Relief for a higher rate taxpayer may therefore be restricted to 22½%, with a non-repayable credit of 10%.

No deduction is given for tax credits for gifts of shares or land and buildings.

Gifts in kind by traders

See Example 49 explanatory note 4 for the allowance of salary payments for employees seconded to charity and business gifts to charity of trading stock and plant and machinery.

Tax-efficient giving

An individual who wishes to give to charity needs to consider the tax implications of the gift. If he has quoted securities pregnant with gains, then a gift of such securities will not give rise to a capital gains liability (saving up to 18%) and in addition will attract relief at his highest rate (say 40%/42½%, but possibly only 22½% if the only income is dividend income, as indicated above).

Alternatively, for cash gifts if the individual can get his employer company to make the donation then the amount is paid out of funds that have not borne national insurance contributions.

For regular giving an indefinite gift aid declaration should be made to the charity. All gifts should be recorded and entered on the individual's tax return, so that the charity may recover the basic rate tax and the donor may obtain higher rate relief if appropriate. For one-off gifts the charity should be able to provide a gift aid declaration in the form of an envelope into which the gift is placed. Donors should maintain a record of the gift and report it on their tax return.

B. (a) **Blackhills Rugby Club – corporation tax liability year ended 31 March 2010**

As Blackhills Rugby Club is a registered Community Amateur Sports Club (CASC) under FA 2002 s 58 and Sch 18, its income is exempt from corporation tax as follows, the exempt amount being restricted to the extent that its expenditure of £40,600 includes non-qualifying expenditure (see explanatory note 10):

	£
Trading income (exempt limit £30,000 – mutual trading with own members ignored)	5,400
Property income (exempt limit £20,000)	2,600
Gift aid income	6,000
Building society interest	200
	14,200

Less: Restriction re non-qualifying expenditure
     on members' night out

$$14,200 \times \frac{4,800}{42,600}$$

	£
	1,600
Exempt income	12,600

Corporation tax is not payable on membership fees, so the only chargeable profits are the proportionate amount of non-qualifying expenditure of £1,600 and tax thereon at 21% is £336.

(b)   **Effect on (a) of sale of land with gain of £63,000**

If Blackhills Rugby Club has a potential chargeable gain of £63,000 from the sale of land, which is used for qualifying purposes, this would be added to the amount on which exemption is claimed in (a) above, but the restriction of the exemption because of the non-qualifying expenditure would increase to:

$$\frac{(14,200 + 63,000 =)\ 77,200}{(42,600 + 63,000 =)\ 105,600} \times 4,800 = £3,509$$

The chargeable amount of £3,509 would be taxed at 21%, resulting in a tax charge of £737.

(c)   **Tax treatment of John in respect of payments to Blackhills Rugby Club**

Membership fees cannot be treated as gifts for gift aid, so John will only be eligible for higher rate tax relief on £63, being £50 gift aid payment plus basic rate tax retained of £13. This will reduce John's higher rate tax liability by £63 @ 40% = £25, less tax retained £13 = £12.

Explanatory Notes

Paying sufficient tax to cover tax on gift aid payments

1.   A taxpayer may offset allowances and reliefs against income of different descriptions in the most advantageous way unless the legislation provides otherwise (ITA 2007 s 25). See Example 4 explanatory note 5.

    A taxpayer is entitled to retain the basic rate income tax deducted from gift aid payments providing he pays at least that much tax. Fred in part (a) of the example must therefore have £400 of tax chargeable. Income tax or capital gains tax charged in the year can be used to cover that amount. If, however, the tax charged would otherwise be lower than the tax retained, personal allowances are restricted to keep a sufficient amount in charge (ITA 2007 ss 423–425).

    If Fred had not made a gift aid payment, he would have claimed full married couple's allowance as follows:

	£	£
Tax as at 90.2 above	783	420
Less: MCA (36,965 @ 10%)	697	
	86	
Less: Tax credits on dividends (restricted)	86	–
Repayment due		420

The effect of the payment to charity has been to decrease Fred's repayment, but to fully utilise the tax credits on dividends and to enable surplus married couple's allowance to be transferred to his wife:

	£
Value of transferred married couple's allowance (£3,135@ 10%)	314
Less: Reduction in repayment (420 – 330)	90
Further dividend tax credits now used (310 – 86)	224

Without the charitable payment Fred would be required to offset his married couple's allowance of £697 before using non-repayable tax credits (see Example 4 explanatory note 5) and as the resultant tax would be less than the tax credits, an amount would be unrelieved. If, however, Fred was aware of that position before the commencement of the tax year he could elect jointly with his wife for her to claim married couple's allowance of £2,670, ie:

	£	£
Tax at 90.2 above	783	420
Less: MCA (6,965 – 2,670 to wife =)		
4,294 @ 10%	430	
	353	
Less: Tax credits on dividends	310	43
Repayment due		377
MCA claimed by wife 2,670 @ 10%		267
		644

The effect would be that none of the dividend credits would then be wasted.

2. If restricting personal allowances still leaves insufficient tax in charge to cover the charitable payments, HMRC will issue an assessment to recover the shortfall. For example if Fred's net gift had been £16,000, with tax retained of (20/80 =) £4,000, his tax position would be:

			Income	*Income tax paid*
			£	£
Income as before			15,830	420
Tax thereon:				
Savings starting rate	Nil	@ 10%		
Basic rate	12,730	@ 20%	2,546	
	3,100	@ 10%	310	
	15,830		2,856	
Less: Tax credits on dividends			310	2,546
Tax payable under self-assessment				2,126
Tax retained on gift aid payment				4,000

	Income £	Income tax paid £
Tax charged		2,856
Tax to be collected by HMRC assessment		1,144

Full married couple's allowance of £6,965 would be available for transfer to Fred's wife.

3. The tax available for offsetting tax relief under the enterprise investment scheme or venture capital trust scheme, or foreign tax credits, is after the deduction of the tax deemed to be retained on charitable payments.

4. If, after restricting personal allowances to nil, insufficient tax has been paid, then in computing the amount of the excess to be assessed, the tax charged does not include notional tax (on non-qualifying distributions, scrip dividends and life policy gains), tax at the basic rate on patent royalties and other annual payments, and tax treated as deducted when a loan to a close company participator is released.

Settlor-interested trusts

5. Where a trust is caught by the anti-avoidance legislation in ITTOIA 2005 part 5 Chapter 5, the trust income is deemed to be that of the settlor in certain circumstances. If such a trust gives money to a charity, ITTOIA 2005 s 628 provides that the amount taxable on the settlor is reduced by the amount (plus tax) given to the charity. The rate of tax recoverable by the charity depends on the tax payable by the trust. A charge on a settlor is also prevented where an interest free loan is made to a charity (ITTOIA 2005 s 620).

For detailed notes on the taxation of trusts see the companion to this book, Tolley's Taxwise II 2009/10.

Exemption for trading activities

6. Where a charity carries on a trade as part of its charitable purpose (for instance, employing beneficiaries of the charity in producing goods) any profits will usually be exempt from tax. Before 22 March 2006, such charities risked losing tax relief on all profits if some of its activities did not qualify as charitable. From that date, profits may be apportioned between those generated by the primary purpose of the charity, and those generated by other activities.

Where trading is to raise funds, the profits are taxable unless the turnover does not exceed £5,000 or, if greater, the lower of £50,000 and 25% of the charity's gross income (FA 2000 s 46; now ITA 2007 s 526 in respect of charitable trusts).

ITA 2007 s 529 exempts from tax the profits of fundraising events which are exempt for VAT purposes under Group 12 of VATA 1994 Sch 9. Essentially the events must be organised by the charity or qualifying body and must meet the qualifying conditions for VAT purposes, which include a restriction of no more than 15 events in one location in one year.

Trading subsidiaries

7. If the trading activities are likely to exceed the above limits, it is advisable to set up a wholly owned trading subsidiary, which will be liable to corporation tax on its profits. Any gift aid payments to the charity parent will, however, be deductible as a charge before computing the corporation tax due. (This arrangement effectively converts trading profits which would fall to be taxed in the hands of the charity into tax exempt investment income (see ICTA 1988 s 505).) A gift aid payment made by a wholly owned trading subsidiary to its charity parent can be treated as paid in an accounting period falling wholly or partly within the nine months before the payment was made (ICTA 1988 s 339).

Before 22 March 2006 this did not apply to payments made by a company wholly owned by more than one charity. These were treated as distributions, and so did not achieve corporation tax relief for the paying company. ICTA s 339 is amended from 22 March 2006 to ensure that such payments benefit from gift aid relief.

Gift aid donations and carry back

8. Where an individual makes a gift aid donation before 31 January in the tax year and before the tax return for the previous tax year has been filed, an election may be made to deem the donation to be made in the previous tax year. In 2010/11 the highest rate of income tax will be 50%, with an effective marginal band of 60% tax where personal allowances are abated at relevant net income of £100,000 or more. The carry back of gift aid donations will therefore allow potentially improved relief for wealthy taxpayers in future years, and is particularly relevant to those affected by the 60% marginal band as it is really the only effective way of reducing the impact of this rate after the tax year has ended (and once income is known).

    The carryback is not effective for tax credit purposes. The gift aid payment will still be deducted from the tax credits income on a current year basis. This is *not* treated as a claim affecting the earlier year under TMA 1970 Sch 1B but as a payment of the earlier year. The tax liability of the earlier year is reduced accordingly, as well as the payments on account for the current year.

    For example a taxpayer who was a higher rate taxpayer in 2008/09 makes a gift aid payment of £800 on 31 May 2009. This is included, by election, in his 2008/09 tax return filed on 30 September 2009. The effect on his tax liability and payments will be:

	£
Reduction in 2008/09 higher rate tax	
$800 \times 100/80 = 1,000$ @ $(40 - 20)\%$	200
Reduction in 2008/09 payment on account	100
Saving on payment due 31 January 2010	300
Saving on payment due 31 July 2010	10,090
Additional amount due 31 January 2011 (being savings in payments on account)	200

9. Taxpayers may nominate a charity to receive all or part of any tax repayment due to them. To nominate a charity the taxpayer must enter its charity code. This is available by ringing 0845 9000 444 or from the HMRC website at www.hmrc.gov.uk/charities/charities-search.htm. That repayment will itself be a gift aid donation to be included for tax relief on the tax return for the year in which the payment is made to the charity. Any election made by a taxpayer will not affect the timing of any repayment due to the recipient charity.

Amateur sports clubs

10. Under FA 2002 s 58 and Sch 18, tax exemptions are available to registered community amateur sports clubs (CASCs) similar to those available for charities. In order to register as a CASC, a club must be open to the whole community without discrimination, have reasonable membership fees, be organised on an amateur basis and have as its main purpose the provision of facilities for and promotion of participation in one or more eligible sports.

    This requires the club to be non-profit making, providing ordinary benefits for its members and their guests and using surplus funds for the purposes of the club. On dissolution any surplus must be paid to another CASC or eligible sports ruling body or a charity. Ordinary benefits are:

    –   provision of sporting facilities;

    –   provision and maintenance of sports equipment;

-       provision of suitably qualified coaches or coaching courses;

-       insurance and medical cover;

-       reimbursement of travel expenses of players and officials for away matches;

-       post-match refreshments for players and match officials;

-       sale of food and drink associated with the sporting activities.

The club may pay staff, who may be members of the CASC, on an arm's length basis.

Once registered, a club is exempt from tax on trading income (before expenses) not exceeding £30,000, property income (before expenses) not exceeding £20,000, interest and gift aid income, and capital gains, providing in each case the whole of the income or gains as the case may be is applied for qualifying purposes (ie providing facilities for, and promoting participation in, one or more eligible sports, as designated by statutory instrument) and claims for the exemptions are made.

If expenditure is incurred for non-qualifying purposes, the total amount of exempt income and gains is reduced by the proportion of non-qualifying expenditure to total income and gains. The effect on exempt income is illustrated in part B(a) of the example, where the cost of the members' night out is non-qualifying expenditure, as its main purpose is not that of providing facilities for participating in sport, resulting in part of the exempt income becoming chargeable income. Where there are exempt gains, as in B(b) the non-exempt amount is increased.

11.   Registered CASCs are treated as charities for gift aid payments by individuals, and can recover the basic rate tax on donations but not membership fees. The reliefs for gifts of shares and land and buildings (see part A of the example) and business gifts of stock or plant (see Example 49 explanatory note 4) also apply, as do the capital gains tax and inheritance tax charitable gifts exemptions.

12.   If a CASC ceases to hold an asset for qualifying purposes (without disposing of it), or ceases to be registered, the club will be treated as having disposed of and reacquired the asset at market value. The resultant gain will be chargeable to corporation tax.

Question

Your notes of a meeting with new clients Mr Powell and Mrs Powell, both aged 48, include the following points:

(i)   Your new clients have two children aged 15 and 19 (both in full time education – no income).

(ii) Mr Powell owns 60% of the share capital of P Transport Ltd, the remainder being held by Mrs Powell. The company was formed four years ago, and specialises in continental transport and storage. Its profits for the year ending 31 March 2010 are expected to amount to £330,000 after remuneration of:

	Mr Powell £	Mrs Powell £
Salary	22,000	3,000
Bonus (to be paid August 2010)	38,000	–
	60,000	3,000

Both Mr and Mrs Powell work full time in the business. Mr Powell is a director and Mrs Powell is a book-keeper and also company secretary. The business is estimated to be worth £1,500,000 as a going concern. Although the company normally has a small credit balance at the bank, it has overdraft facilities of £100,000.

P Transport Ltd is based in a designated disadvantaged area. The company anticipates needing additional storage facilities in the near future. A suitable site in the zone would cost in the region of £160,000 and the required building £500,000. Bank finance would be available for this project.

Your clients have suggested that the new building could be held either:

- by the company for its own use, or

- by Mr and Mrs Powell personally, but let to the company, or

- by a self-administered pension fund, again let to the company.

(iii) Mr Powell has a retirement annuity policy with an annual premium of £2,000. He does not have any life assurance cover.

(iv) Mr and Mrs Powell have a joint building society account containing £2,000, a house in joint names worth £440,000 (with a £75,000 mortgage) and no other assets except a director's account with the company to which Mr Powell's bonuses have always been credited and which currently stands at £60,000.

(v)   Both Mr and Mrs Powell have made wills leaving their estate to the other or, if there is no surviving spouse, equally to their children.

They have changed their adviser because they are unhappy with the lack of tax planning advice they have been receiving.

Prepare, giving reasons for the points chosen, a memorandum of tax planning points to discuss with Mr and Mrs Powell.

Answer

(a) **Children**

Both

Could they be paid by the company for legitimate services rendered in holidays, weekends etc? Watch the national insurance cost and compliance with PAYE and employment regulations. Could the amount be enhanced by the company making pension contributions for them, contributing up to £3,600 each per year?

Elder aged 19

See (b) below for possible transfer of shares to the elder child, the dividends on which would be covered by the available basic rate band.

Younger aged 15

Any income produced on funds provided by parents (but not capital gains in a bare trust) would be taxed on the parent, not on the child, until the child reaches age 18 or marries before that date (ITTOIA 2005 s 629). This is subject to a de minimis exemption whereby each parent can provide funds to produce income of up to £100 per annum. This de minimis exemption is only available if the child's total income from that parent does not exceed that amount. It does not cover the first slice of a larger sum.

If money is being provided by the parents for savings, invest in sources that do not produce income, eg investment bonds, or are not liable to income tax, such as national savings certificates including children's bonus bonds. Share transfers could be made as in (b), which would be effective for inheritance tax, but income from dividends would for the time being be treated as the parents' income. Premiums of up to £270 per annum may be paid by the parents for a qualifying friendly society policy for the child without breaching the parental settlement rules. If this has not already been done, a child trust fund should be opened for each child. Parents may contribute up to £1,200 each year (based on the child's birthday), and the income will not be taxed as the parents' income (see Example 92).

(See Example 2 part (c)(ii) for notes on bare trusts.)

(b) **Shareholdings in P Transport Ltd**

Any transfer of shares by Mr or Mrs Powell should take into account the following:

(i) They need to retain control of the company between them if they are to continue to qualify for 50% business property relief for inheritance tax purposes on any property owned by them and rented to the company. The shares themselves qualify for 100% business property relief, no matter how small the holding.

(ii) For capital gains tax, any chargeable gains on the transfer of shares could be held over by the use of business assets gifts holdover relief (TCGA 1992 s 165 – see Example 82), or by use of deferral relief under the Enterprise Investment Scheme (EIS) (TCGA 1992 Sch 5B – see Example 93). Their shareholdings should not, however, fall below the required level for the gifts relief (which is not less than 5% of the voting power). This could give rise to capital gains tax on a subsequent sale after all such relief has been used (see Example 82).

(iii) As P Transport Ltd is an unquoted trading company, the shares in the company should qualify for entrepreneur's relief from April 2008 up to a lifetime limit of £1 million of gains per individual (see Example 78). Any building owned by Mr and Mrs Powell and used for the purposes of the business would also be eligible, but no relief will be available if they are let to the business at a full market rent. Entrepreneur's relief has to be claimed, but gift relief could be claimed without using any entrepreneur's relief. Provided that both Mr and Mrs Powell work in the business and have a shareholding of at least 5%, both can claim entrepreneur's relief, making two £1 million lifetime allowances available.

(iv) Mr and Mrs Powell need to be aware of the HMRC view's on transfer of shares to children, and its interaction with the anti-avoidance legislation in ITTOIA 2005 Part 5 Chapter 5 (see Tax Bulletin 64). This legislation applies if the purpose of the transfer is to divert income to another and tax is saved. For the rules to apply the transfer must be:

– bounteous, or

– not commercial, or

– not at arm's length, or

– in the case of a gift between spouses wholly or substantially a right to income.

The provisions are unlikely to apply in this case if the gift of shares to a child is part of a strategy of involving the child in the business with a view to eventual succession to the company, provided that no dividend waivers occur to increase the income on the child's shares, and the shares are given absolutely. Although HMRC lost the *Arctic Systems* case in respect of husband and wife ordinary shares with rights to capital, the legislation is still fully effective for other situations. Income shifting legislation was to be introduced in 2009/10 however this has now been deferred. The issue remains 'under review' while the settlement legislation remains effective and should be considered. See also explanatory note 1 in Example 27 on HMRC's current view on husband and wife companies and the settlement provisions.

Subject to the above, share transfers to the children will ensure that future growth is in the hands of the next generation, that dividends are at once treated as the income of the elder child and in three years' time will be treated as that of the younger child, and that the children are given some incentive within the business.

A return of the issue of shares in connection with employment is normally required on Form 42 by 6 July following the tax year in which it is made. HMRC guidance makes it clear that the return is not required in the cases of transfers arising through personal or family relationships, and cites the example for the shares being transferred to children working in the business as an illustration of this.

Transfers now rather than later will avoid any risk that the 100% business property relief for inheritance tax is reduced by subsequent legislation, and if the shares cease to qualify for business property relief, the seven year period during which a transfer is only potentially exempt will have begun that much sooner. On the other hand, lifetime transfers are subject to capital gains tax and although the gains may be deferred they would not arise at all if the shares were still held when the parents died. However, providing each child holds at least 5% of the company's share capital, and is an employee of the company, entrepreneur's relief should be available, resulting in an effective rate of tax of 10%. Failing this, gains will be taxed at a fixed rate of 18%, avoiding the higher rate band, and their own annual exemptions (£10,100 for 2009/10) will still be available. Note that provided 100% inheritance tax business property relief remains available, there would be no charge either to capital gains tax or inheritance tax if the shares were held until death.

A shareholding by a self-administered pension fund could also be considered, subject to the same considerations and also depending upon what other involvement the fund is to have with the company (since HMRC imposes limits on the fund's participation in company shares/loans back). Furthermore the trustees of the fund may not be happy with a holding of unquoted shares which they may find difficult to realise. For further comments on self-administered schemes see (e) below.

(c)   **Profits of P Transport Ltd**

The projected profits are within the marginal tranche for small companies' rate (ICTA 1988 s 13). The anticipated £30,000 excess over £300,000 would therefore attract corporation tax @ 29.75% = £8,925, compared with the small companies' rate of 21%, giving additional tax on that slice of the profits of £2,625.

If profits could be sensibly reduced by £30,000 or more, the tax saved on the £30,000 would be £8,925. (See (e) and (f) below for ways in which profits might be reduced, in addition to the possibility of paying increased remuneration.)

(d)   **Remuneration to Mr and Mrs Powell**

Although charged in arriving at the company's taxable profits in the accounting periods to which they relate, any bonuses to Mr and Mrs Powell are taxed on them in the tax years when they are received. The August 2010 bonus of £38,000 would therefore be taxed on Mr Powell in 2010/11, and the bonus paid to him in 2009/10, if any, would be taxed in 2009/10. For the purpose of the calculations which follow it has been assumed that a similar bonus was paid in August 2009. Care must be taken if total income in 2010/11 is likely to be near to £100,000 to ensure that the restriction of 'personal allowances' does not apply otherwise a marginal rate of 60% could apply to the top slice of income.

Increasing Mrs Powell's remuneration

Since Mrs Powell works full time in the company and is also company secretary, a substantial increase in her remuneration could be justified and is in any event necessary to satisfy the requirements of the national minimum wage. If her earnings were substantially increased and Mr Powell's correspondingly reduced, then higher rate tax would be saved. The saving in higher rate tax would, however, be partly offset by increased employee's national insurance contributions at 11%, since Mr Powell is only paying contributions of 1% on his earnings above £43,875 for 2009/10, whereas his wife would pay contributions on the extra remuneration above £5,715. (Employer's contributions are at 12.8% whether remuneration is paid to husband or wife, on earnings above £110 per week (£5,715 per annum).) Increased remuneration could be used to support a personal pension contribution (see (f) below). See also (e) below re the alternative possibility of the company starting a self-administered pension scheme.

Paying dividends instead of remuneration

The company could consider paying dividends. In 2009/10 the dividends would be taxable at Mr and Mrs Powell's respective dividend rates of 32½% and 10% (less 10% tax credit) unless substantially increased remuneration were paid to Mrs Powell in 2009/10. The comparative amounts of tax and national insurance on remuneration and dividends depend on whether the company had taken steps to reduce its profits to within the small companies' rate limit of £300,000 (see (c) above). Assuming that Mr Powell was taking remuneration of £43,875 or more and thus paying national insurance contributions of 1% on his earnings above £43,875 as an employee, the comparative position for him in 2009/10, using a profit figure of £1,000 and a marginal tax rate of 40% for illustration, would be:

		£	£
Paying extra remuneration:	Company profit		1,000
	Remuneration	886	
	Employer's national insurance 12.8%	114	1,000
	Profits chargeable to corporation tax		–
	Gross remuneration		886
	Income tax at 40%	354	
	Employee's NIC @ 1%	9	363

		£	£
	Net of tax amount		£523
		£	£
Paying dividend:	Company profit	1,000	1,000
	Corporation tax at 21%/29.75%	210	298
	Dividend to shareholders	790	702
	Tax credit at 1/9	88	78
	Shareholders' income	878	780
	Income tax at 32½%	285	254
	Net of tax amount	593	526

It is therefore more tax efficient for Mr Powell to receive additional dividends, but at the marginal rate the saving is very small, and other considerations such as the basis for pension contributions might outweigh the saving. See Example 59 explanatory note 2.

Any dividends paid would be taxed separately on each of Mr and Mrs Powell, so the amount saved through paying dividends instead of remuneration to Mrs Powell would be the employer's and employee's national insurance contributions plus the saving in Mr Powell's higher rate liability unless her revised income exceeded the basic rate threshold. Mrs Powell would receive a net of tax dividend of £790 out of £1,000 company profits if the profits were taxed at the small companies' rate and her income was wholly within the basic rate limit.

Depending upon the tax rates in future years and other planning considerations (eg need to have remuneration to be able to make desired level of pension payments), dividends could be a suitable method of using the basic rate band available to Mrs Powell without having to justify services provided by her in order to substantiate her level of remuneration. She should, however, receive a salary that is sufficiently high to satisfy the national minimum wage (eg 35 hours per week @ £5.73 (£5.80 per hour from October 2009) minimum wage rate = £10,429 per annum) and also to fully utilise her personal allowance. The tax credits on dividends are not repayable. The payment of dividends would normally affect the value of the company's shares, but where a company is closely controlled by the family, other bases of valuation would also be considered, such as assets or earnings.

(e) **Acquisition of new storage facilities**

The cost of renovating, repairing or converting a qualifying building will attract a 100% FYA in the period in which the expenditure is incurred. To qualify, the building must be in a designated disadvantaged area, must previously have been used for business purposes, must have been unused for at least one year, and may not have been used wholly or partly as a dwelling. If such a building can be found, and the conditions are met, then the 100% allowance can be set against current periods profits, and if a loss is generated it can be carried back one year, or carried forward. If the full allowance is not claimed, a 25% allowance can be claimed annually, until the allowance is exhausted (FA 2005 Sch 6).

If Renovation of Business Premises in disadvantaged Area (RBPA) is not available, IBA at 2% will still be available in 2009/10, although this will be phased out by 2011.

In neither case would there be any relief for the land (CAA 2001 s 272).

Mr and Mrs Powell could acquire the building personally and obtain the same allowances, firstly against rent income and then other income of the tax year of purchase and then the following tax year (ITA 2007 s 120). If they acquired the building and let it to the company, inheritance tax business property relief of 50% would be available on an eventual transfer of ownership, so long as between them they continued to control the company. The charging of rent would reduce or remove entitlement to entrepreneur's relief in respect of the building.

The rental income arising is free of NI contributions, and taxed on Mrs Powell in proportion to her ownership of the property. If eventually a capital gain arises, although companies are still entitled to indexation, the CGT regime for individuals at a flat rate of 18% is likely to prove more effective than routing a gain through the company, where it will be subject to corporation tax before the remaining funds can be extracted subject to CGT net of reliefs.

Acquisition through self-administered pension fund

If renovation in a designated assisted area is not practicable, purchase by a self-administered pension fund could be considered. The contributions to the fund from company profits would be allowable in calculating the company's corporation tax, provided they are accepted as incurred wholly and exclusively for the purposes of the trade. Furthermore, the rent paid to the pension fund by the company would be allowable in computing company profits but not taxable in the pension fund so long as the fund had HMRC approval, and the ability of the pension fund to acquire the land effectively gives tax relief on the land purchase, since the pension fund first has to be put in funds out of pre-tax company profits.

From 6 April 2006, the amount that the fund may borrow is limited to 50% of the fund value for new loans, but the effective maximum that the company can contribute to the fund in the 2009/10 year is £245,000. However, it is unlikely that the company would obtain a tax deduction on an amount as large as £245,000, as discussed under paragraph (f) below. Any excess over £245,000 would result in an annual allowance charge of 40% on the excess on Mr Powell.

The fund could take out appropriate life assurance cover on Mr and/or Mrs Powell in order to provide a capital sum with which to pay death in service benefits to the dependants in the event of the death of one or the other whilst they were still working for the company. This could be an important consideration in view of the present lack of life cover. The restrictions on personal term assurance in FA 2007 do not affect employer contributions to group pension schemes.

One difficulty of purchasing property through a self-administered pension fund is the need to provide liquid funds to acquire an annuity on retirement. This can be minimised by deferring the purchase of an annuity until an age not later than 75 and paying the pension from the income produced by the scheme assets until that age. In addition, it might be that the children will have joined the firm and become members of the pension fund. From their contributions liquid funds could be available to purchase the annuities for Mr and Mrs Powell, so that the need to sell the property at a later date is removed. Anti-avoidance legislation exists to ensure that Mr and Mrs Powell cannot make excessive contributions to provide funds to be inherited by the children.

(f) **Pension provision for Mr and Mrs Powell (ICTA 1988 ss 618–655)**

See (e) above for the possibility of the company starting a self-administered pension scheme to provide pensions for Mr and Mrs Powell.

Mr Powell already has a retirement annuity policy but neither Mr nor Mrs Powell has a registered individual pension plan. Points to consider in relation to each of them are as follows.

If Mrs Powell's remuneration is increased as suggested in (d) above, any increased remuneration could be used to support a individual pension contribution of £3,600, or 100% of her earnings of 2009/10, if greater. There is no limit on the amount that the company may contribute, but a deduction is only available against profits if paid wholly and exclusively for the benefit of the trade. Individuals who make contributions within the limits will obtain tax relief, normally by deduction of tax at source

From 6 April 2009 consideration must be given to whether FA 2009 Sch 35 will affect any new additional pension contributions. This section restricts higher rate tax relief on new pension contributions taken out after 22 April 2009 for those with income of £150,000 or more in the relevant years. Mr and Mrs Powell are not expected to have this level of income in the relevant years (for further details see Example 38).

Thus, Mr Powell may make a personal contribution to an individual registered pension scheme of up to 100% of his gross earnings by 5 April 2010, possibly by drawing out the balance on his director's loan account to fund it. The contributions will be paid net, but will attract higher rate tax relief.

The relatively high statutory contribution limits mean that many small businesses have been able to contribute as much as they can afford to the company schemes (individual schemes' contributions are limited to 100% of salary). The restrictions in FA 2009 s 21 may impact on future pension decisions. Unlike salary, pension contributions do not involve the payment of PAYE or NI contributions, and unlike dividends they are under certain circumstances (see below) deductible for corporation tax.

If a bonus of £30,000 were paid for Mr Powell, to reduce corporation tax by £8,925 (£30,000 @ 29.75%), the relative tax implications of salary and pension contribution would be:

	Salary	Pension contribution
Salary/pension	26,596	30,000
Employer NIC	3,404	nil
Cost to company	30,000	30,000
Income tax @ 40%	10,638	
Employee NIC @ 1%	266	
Cash available	15,692	
Payroll taxes cost	(14,308)	nil
Corporation tax saving	8,925	8,925
Total tax (cost)/saving	(5,383)	8,925

If Mr Powell is not in need of funds, he may well find a pension contribution of £30,000, at a cost of £21,075 (£30,000 – £8,925), extremely attractive. He might be tempted to make pension contributions for other family members instead as FA 2007 s 69 and Sch 19 contain provisions effectively blocking pension schemes as a way of passing funds down the generations without an inheritance tax charge after age 75.

The pension contribution must be paid by the year-end, whereas an accrued bonus may be paid up to nine months after, to obtain a tax deduction.

If his salary level was determined by remuneration-related limitations to pension contributions that applied before 6 April 2006 ,when the limits were a specified percentage of earning, he may now be tempted to reduce the salary and corresponding NI contributions, and increase dividends instead without NI contribution cost.

Where statutory contribution limits do not limit the payment of contributions, HMRC's refusal to allow a full tax deduction may do so instead. The fact that there are high allowable limits for contributions does not necessarily mean that contributions paid by businesses will be deductible against profits. Contributions paid by businesses are deductible only if expended wholly and exclusively for the purposes of the employer's trade.

However, HMRC guidance specifies that it is the remuneration package in total that is considered for the wholly and exclusively test, and that the proportion of pension contributions to salary will not be relevant in the case of ordinary employees.

In the past there has been no objection to salaries at any level paid to owner-directors out of annual profits of their company, and no indication has been made that this attitude will change. Indeed, it would be hard to reconcile (for example) the IR35 rules with any limitation on payment of annual profits as remuneration.

Large or unusual contributions by controlling directors are likely to be the subject of HMRC scrutiny, and uncertainty on the part of the taxpayer and tax adviser. Although the proportion of contribution to salary should not be an issue, a particularly high proportion will presumably raise the question as to whether it was paid for purposes of the trade, or for purposes of saving tax.

HMRC have published in its Business Income Manual in BIM46001: Specific Deductions: Registered Pension Schemes, which provides guidance on deductibility of contributions in various circumstances, and the following paragraphs summarise the key points of this guidance.

Contributions, if tax deductible, are deductible in the period they are paid only, unless spread by tax law (which occurs if there is an increase of over 210% in contributions and the contribution exceeds £500,000, see Example 37). If the accounts charge is different to the contribution paid, the computation must be adjusted to make it reflect the amount paid.

Contributions will always be treated as revenue expenditure, not capital expenditure.

Contributions forming part of a normal remuneration package will be tax deductible. The contribution is looked at in the context of the overall remuneration package, not a stand-alone amount. The proportion of pension contribution to other remuneration is not considered for this purpose, so salary sacrifice schemes for ordinary employees should not jeopardise the tax deduction. The annual contribution limits must be borne in mind, and individuals who are able to sacrifice a material amount of salary may be controlling directors, in which case the circumstances will be scrutinised separately.

The normal situation is that contributions will be tax deductible, except if there is an identifiable non-trade purpose, or a contribution of exceptional size.

One example would be a contribution made as part of arrangements for going out of business. It will be important to demonstrate that payments made towards cessation of a business are for the purposes of the trade. The guidance clearly specifies that payments made to fund shortfalls in company schemes under Pensions Act 1995 s 75 arise from obligations of the trade, and if made after cessation of trade are deductible as post-cessation expenses. If such a payment is made in the accounting period following cessation of trade, it will be treated as an expense of the final trading period.

The main focus of HMRC scrutiny is likely to be on directors, who are also controlling shareholders, or employees who are close relatives or friends (not defined) of the business proprietors or controlling directors.

If their total remuneration package (of which contributions are part) is similar to that of unconnected employees in genuinely similar work, then the contributions will be accepted as wholly and exclusively for the purposes of the trade. If not, the existing guidelines on amounts purporting to be remuneration of directors in BIM47105 will be followed, seeking to disallow all or some of the contribution.

Amongst the considerations to be borne in mind, according to HMRC's BIM46001, are:

'To find out whether the payment was made for the purposes of the taxpayer's trade it is necessary to discover the taxpayer's object in making the payment. The general rule is that establishing the object behind making the payment involves an inquiry into the taxpayer's subjective intentions at the time of the payment.

The "purposes of the trade" means "to serve the purposes of the trade".

The "purposes of the trade" are not the same as "the purposes of the taxpayer".

The "purposes of the trade" does not mean "for the benefit of the taxpayer".

The "purpose for making the payment" is not the same as "the effect of the payment".'

Company contributions to individual registered pension schemes

An alternative possibility is for the company to make payments into individuals' registered personal pension policies for Mr and Mrs Powell. Provided such payments are made within the accounting year, ie by 31 March 2010, a corporation tax deduction is available. The payments would save both employer's and employees' national insurance contributions.

(g)   Personal investment

The company apparently has adequate cash resources taking into account its overdraft limit. The withdrawal of the £60,000 standing to the credit of Mr Powell's loan account would involve the company paying additional bank interest, but this would be tax relievable against its corporate profits, and Mr and Mrs Powell could personally use the £60,000 for tax-efficient investment, including utilising available retirement annuity/personal pension premium limits.

With tax relief for mortgage interest on house purchase loans no longer being available, it would also be sensible to consider reducing the house mortgage.

(h)   Wills

Leaving their estates to the other and failing that to the children ensures that no inheritance tax is payable on the first death (IHTA 1984 s 18), subject to any chargeable transfers within the seven years before death). FA 2008 s 8 provides for a claim to be made to transfer the unused portion of the nil-rate band of the first spouse to die to that of the surviving spouse, civil partner, so that the nil-rate band, currently £325,000, will not be wasted.

A survivorship clause is recommended, denying the entitlement of the surviving spouse unless he/she survives the other by a stipulated period not exceeding six months (IHTA 1984 s 92). There is no point in the survivor inheriting the estate of the other in the unfortunate event of deaths in quick succession.

In considering both the wills and the proposed lifetime transfer of shares in P Transport Ltd for the benefit of the children, it is important to emphasise to the clients the practical dangers if a surviving parent were left with a minority interest in their own company.

Care should also be taken to determine the possible source of any bequest to a discretionary fund or child on the first death. If that legacy were to include shares then a specific bequest is advisable to ensure that the relevant business property relief is given in full against that bequest. If the gift were to be part of residue with the balance to the spouse then the provisions in IHTA 1984 s 39A would apply to restrict the available relief. For detailed notes on inheritance tax see the companion to this book Tolley's Taxwise II 2009/10.

(i)   Pre-owned assets

Although not immediately of concern to Mr and Mrs Powell, they should be made aware of the income tax implications of inheritance tax planning involving the gift of property and the subsequent use or enjoyment of that property by the donor. The provisions are contained in FA 2004 Sch 15.

With effect from 6 April 2005 a free-standing income tax charge applies to the benefit of using a property, chattel or intangible asset that was formerly owned by the taxpayer. A similar charge applies to the use of such property at low cost or to the use of such assets purchased with funds provided by the taxpayer.

The income tax charge does not apply

   (i)   To property given away before 18 March 1986 (FA 2004 Sch 15 paras 3(2), 6(2) and 8(2)).

(ii) If the property was transferred to a spouse or civil partner (or to a former spouse/civil partner under a Court Order) (Sch 15 para 10(1)(c)). This also applied where the property is held in trust and the spouse/civil partner or former spouse/civil partner has an interest in possession (Sch 15 para 10(1)(d)).

(iii) If the property remains within the estate of the former owner for inheritance tax, or the 'Gift with Reservation' rules apply, then the income tax charge does not apply (Sch 15 para 11).

(iv) If the property was sold by the taxpayer at an arm's length price (Sch 15 para 10(1)(a)).

(v) Where the assets of an estate have been redirected by a deed of variation (IHTA 1984 ss 142–147) then the deed of variation applies to the asset from date of death for the pre-owned asset rules (Sch 15 para 16).

(vi) To property transferred into an interest in possession trust prior to 22 March 2006 for the benefit of the former owner. This is excluded from the income tax charge because the property remains in the estate of the donor for inheritance tax purposes. However the exemption ceases when the interest in possession comes to an end (Sch 15 para 10).

(vii) Where the gift is of property and the former owner has given part of their interest to someone with whom they share occupation or the former owner needs to move back into the gifted property following changes in circumstances (Sch 15 para 11(1)). These rules are the same as gift with reservation rules for inheritance tax.

(viii) Where the gift was in money and the gift had been made at least seven years before the donor first had use or enjoyment of the property acquired with the funds (Sch 15 para 10(1A)(c)).

(ix) If the disposal was an outright gift covered by an annual exemption, small gifts exemption or was for the maintenance of the family (Sch 15 para 10(1)(d) and (e)).

(x) To the use of property that has been used in a commercial equity release scheme.

The pre-owned asset charge does not apply in any fiscal year

(a) Where the former owner is not resident in the UK, or

(b) Where the former owner is resident in the UK but domiciled elsewhere for inheritance tax purposes, the charge then applies only to UK property, or

(c) Where the former owner was previously domiciled outside the UK for inheritance tax purposes the charge does not apply to property disposed of before becoming domiciled in the UK (Sch 15 para 12).

The income tax charge applies to the use of land or enjoyment of land, chattels and intangible assets. For the charge to apply to land the taxpayer must occupy the land (wholly or with others) and either the disposal condition, or the contribution condition must apply (Sch 15 para 3(1)).

Occupation is a very wide term and could even include usage for storage or sole possession of the means of access linked with occasional use of the property. Incidental usage is not considered to be occupation. This could include:

– Stays not exceeding two weeks each year (one month if the owner is present and it is the owner's residence).

– Social visits that do not include overnight stays.

– Domestic visits eg babysitting the owner's children.

– Temporary stays eg for convalescence after medical treatment or to look after the owner whilst they are convalescing.

However if the property is a holiday home which is only used on an occasional basis by the owner then even occasional visits by the donor could be deemed to be occupational.

The disposal condition is that after 17 March 1986 the taxpayer owned the relevant property or property the disposal of which has directly or indirectly funded the relevant property and has disposed of all or part of that interest otherwise than by an excluded transaction (see above).

The contribution condition is that the taxpayer has since 17 March 1986 contributed directly or indirectly to the purchase of the relevant property otherwise than by an excluded transaction. The charge for land is calculated by taking the appropriate rental value less any amount that the chargeable person is legally obliged to pay the owner of the relevant land in the period in respect of its occupation. The appropriate rental value is

$$R \times \frac{DV}{V} \text{ where}$$

R is the rent that might reasonably be expected to be obtained on a year-to-year letting where the tenant pays all rates, charges and council taxes and the landlord bears the cost of repairs, maintenance and insurance.

DV is the contribution that can reasonably be attributed to the cost of the relevant property. If the property, or a property that this property replaced, was previously owned by the taxpayer, its value on valuation date. If the taxpayer only owned, or disposed of, a part of the land, the relevant proportion of its value.

Example — gift of property

For example, John gave a property worth £100,000 to his son Peter in 1994. Peter sold the property for £350,000 in 1999 buying a further property for £400,000. John moves into the relevant property in 2009 when it had an annual rental value of £36,000. The contribution that could reasonably be attributed to the gifted property would be

$$\frac{350,000}{400,000}$$

(being the proportion of the cost of the relevant property funded by John's gift).

That proportion is then applied to the annual rental value of the property as at the valuation date of £36,000.

$$\frac{350,000}{400,000} \times 36,000 = 31,500 @ 40\% = £12,600 \text{ pa tax payable.}$$

Contrast this with an example where cash was given.

Example — gift of cash

Mrs Jones, a wealthy widow, wishes to reduce her estate's liability to inheritance tax. In order to do so she gives Catherine, her only daughter, £500,000 in cash in May 2007. Her daughter then buys a property in Cornwall in February 2008 for £700,000. Mrs Jones visits this property and in 2009 decides that she would like to live there each summer, taking up residence on 6 April 2010. For the remainder of the year Mrs Jones continues to live in her London residence. Although Mrs Jones is aged 72 she is in good health and would be expected to live for another 15+ years. She is a 40% income taxpayer. For 2010/11 the annual rental value of the Cornwall property would be £36,000 pa and its open market value on 6 April 2010 is £900,000. Mrs Jones has no legal obligation to contribute towards the costs of that property.

Mrs Jones has provided funds of £500,000 which have been used to buy the Cornwall property she now occupies. The appropriate rental value is

$$£36,000 \times \frac{500,000}{900,000} = £20,000$$

which gives an income tax liability of

£20,000 @ 40% = £8,000 per annum from 6 April 2010.

In this example the gift of cash is compared with the value of the property at the valuation date, whereas it would appear that if property is given then the numeration value is increased by the increase in value of the property between gift and purchase of the current property. Although the legislation is unclear in the case of a cash gift it is difficult to see how any increase in the value attributed to the investment decisions of the recipient can be said to be reasonably attributed to the donor of the cash.

The denominator is the value of the relevant land at the valuation date.

Valuation date is set out in SI 2005/724 para 2 as being 6 April in the relevant year, or if later the first day in the year on which enjoyment of the asset occurs.

The first valuation date occurs when use commences, and thereafter the valuation date is the first valuation date for a further four years. The subsequent valuation date is the fifth anniversary date, five years then the tenth anniversary date and so on.

The income tax payable is calculated by adding the appropriate rental value to the taxable income of the donor.

In the case of chattels the charge is based upon 5% pa of the value of the chattel at valuation day with similar rules to land applying to replacement chattels and cash.

For intangibles a charge only arises where they are held within a settlement and the settlor retains an interest. Again the liability is based upon 5% pa of the value at valuation date.

Where the asset is only enjoyed for part of a year the charge is reduced accordingly. There is no charge if open market rent is paid for use of the asset, and the charge is reduced by payments made under a legal obligation for the use of the asset.

If the aggregate notional value of the benefit before contribution does not exceed £5,000 then there is no charge (Sch 15 para 13).

Although the legislation provides that the value of the property shall be the price which the property might reasonably be expected to fetch if sold in the open market at that time (Sch 15 para 15) under SI 2005/724 valuations will take place when use commences and on each fifth anniversary.

There are provisions preventing a double charge to income tax under both the benefit in kind rules and the pre-owned asset rules (Sch 15 para 18).

Where a taxpayer is potentially chargeable to income tax by reference to their enjoyment of any land, or chattels, or intangible property for the first time, then they may make an election, the effect of which is that the asset is deemed to be in their estate for inheritance tax and therefore no income tax charge arises. This is a deeming provision, the asset does not actually form part of their estate and therefore there is no uplift in value for capital gains tax when death occurs (Sch 15 para 20).

If the taxpayer permanently ceases to have occupation or use and enjoyment of the asset then the gifts with reservation rules apply so that a potentially exempt transfer is deemed to have occurred at the cessation of use. On death, if more than seven years have elapsed since last enjoyment of the asset then no charge arises.

The election is required by 31 January following the end of the fiscal year of first use or such a later date as a Revenue officer may allow (FA 2007). If use first commenced in 2005/06 or earlier the election was required by 31 January 2007 (Sch 15 paras 21–23). The election must be made on Form IHT 500 (SI 2007/3000).

Where the whole of the asset would not be attributed to the donor then a similar restriction will apply to the chargeable amount ie chargeable proportion of asset value is

$$\text{Value} \times \frac{DV}{V}$$

where DV is the value provided by the donor and V is the value at the valuation date.

Value is at death (if use continues) or at cessation of use if within seven years of death.

The charge is intended to penalise users of inheritance tax avoidance schemes, such as the double trust home loan scheme (the intention of which is to remove the value of the principal private residence from the donor's estate but to enable continued use of the property), or, where the full consideration for the use of the asset is negligible as compared with the open market value of the asset.

However, the charge will also apply to situations where a taxpayer would not expect a charge to arise: for example where a donor gives away assets, eg cash, and then in the future uses property acquired with those assets without paying a full commercial consideration, and does not fall within any of the exceptions for inheritance tax or pre-owned asset exceptions. Previously if the gift was in cash then provided it was made at least seven years before the death of the donor there were no tax consequences. Now an income tax charge can arise.

Example

John gave £300,000 in cash to his daughter, Wendy, on the occasion of her marriage in 2003. She used £200,000 to buy a picture. In May 2009 Wendy moves to Australia on a temporary contract for three years. She leaves the picture with John who hangs it in his hall. The open market value as at May 2009 is £500,000. Wendy returns in May 2012 reclaiming possession of the picture. John is still alive in 2020. Assume an Official Rate of 5% throughout, and that John pays tax at 40%.

There will be a pre-owned asset charge on John of

Valuation day is May 2009.

The picture was funded by John's gift of £200,000.

The charge for 2009/10 is

$$11/12 \times 5\% \times 500,000 \times \frac{200,000}{500,000} \left(\frac{DV}{V} \right) = 9,166 @ 40\% = £3,666$$

The charge for 2010/11 and 2011/12 will be

$$5\% \times 500,000 \times \frac{200,000}{500,000} = 10,000 @ 40\% = £4,000$$

For 2012/13 the calculation is

$$1/12 \times 5\% \times 500,000 \times \frac{200,000}{500,000} = 834 \text{ ie Nil}$$

(Amounts below £5,000 are not charged)

There is no inheritance tax charge. John had a potential exempt transfer in respect of the cash gift for seven years, ie until 2012. Wendy took full bona fide possession and enjoyment of the cash in 2003. The picture cannot be included in John's estate, he does not and never did own that asset. Because the picture is not included in the estate of John for inheritance tax it is not excluded from the pre-owned asset charge. An income tax charge arises because John has the use of property purchased with funds provided by him (and used by him within seven years of the gift of cash).

The charge could be avoided by John electing, by 31 January 2011, to include the picture in his estate for inheritance tax. Providing John is still alive seven years after the picture is returned (May 2019) then there will be no charge to tax. FA 2007 s 65 allows HMRC to accept late elections. SI 2007/3000 provides that the election must be made on Form IHT 500.

Alternatively, John could pay full rental value for the case of the picture. If he is responsible for insurance this could be very low.

See also companion book, Tolley's Taxwise II 2009/10, for inheritance tax provisions.

Question

Outline the taxation treatment of individual savings accounts (ISAs) from 6 April 2009 and child trust funds and also the taxation treatment of existing personal equity plans (PEPs) and TESSA only Individual Savings Accounts (TOISAs).

Answer

(a)   **Individual Savings Accounts (ISAs)**

1.   Individual Savings Accounts (ISAs) were introduced from 6 April 1999 to replace TESSAs and PEPs. Taxpayers were not required to switch TESSAS and PEPs into the new ISAs. TESSAs opened before 6 April 1999 were allowed to run their course and the capital from a maturing TESSA could be transferred to a TOISA (TESSA only Individual Savings Account). ISA legislation was simplified by SI 2007/2119 from 6 April 2008, and PEPs and TOISAs reclassified as ISAs. The terms 'maxi' and 'mini' ISA cease to exist, and ISAs are distinguished between cash ISAs and stocks and shares ISAs. Only one ISA each per cash or per stocks and shares component may be held per year.

2.   ISAs are available to individuals aged 18 or over who are resident and ordinarily resident in the UK. Someone who becomes non-resident may retain the tax-exempt benefits of existing ISAs but no further investments may be made. Joint accounts are not permitted. ISAs are available indefinitely, with no set end date, although there is no statutory minimum period for which the accounts must be held. There is no lifetime limit on the amount invested.

A person aged 16 or 17 can open a cash ISA, but care must be taken to ensure that the funds to open such an ISA did not originate from the child's parents. In that case the income from the ISA would be taxable on the parent under the settlements provisions if, with other such income, it exceeded £100.

3.   The ISA regulations are in SI 1998/1870. The annual investment in an ISA may be split into two components:

(i)   cash

(ii)   stocks and shares.

Cash

The following investments qualify for the cash component:

(a)   Bank and building society deposit or share accounts (or European equivalent);

(b)   Units in a money market fund;

(c)   Units in a money market only fund of funds;

(d)   Designated National Savings;

(e)   Alternative finance arrangements equating to the above.

Stocks and shares

The qualifying investments for the stocks and shares component can be:

(a)   Shares issued in any country and quoted on a recognised stock exchange;

(b)   Securities with at least five years to run (when acquired by the ISA) issued in any country and quoted on a recognised stock exchange;

(c)   Government Securities of UK or European Economic Area countries (or strips thereof) with at least five years to run when acquired by the ISA;

(d)   Units in authorised unit trusts or OEICs (open-ended investment companies) which do not hold more than 50% of value of their investments in securities with less than five years to run;

(e)   Shares in qualifying investment trusts (again the 50% rule in (d) above applies);

(f)   Units or shares in UCITS (undertakings for collective investments in transferable securities), subject to the 50% rule in (d);

(g)   Depositary interests, including CREST depositary interests;

(h)   Bonds issued by multilateral institutions. These are organisations to which core contributions may be reported as official development assistance, eg the United Nations Development Programme or the African Development Fund.

(i)   Cash held pending investment.

Investments must pass the 5% test, whereby the investor must not be certain or virtually certain of receiving 95% of the unit purchase price at any time in the following five years. If such guarantees exist, then most units qualify as a component of cash ISA.

4.   The maximum investment before 6 April 2009 was £7,200, of which not more than £3,600 could be invested in cash. The ISA limit is being raised by statutory instrument to £10,200 of which up to £5,100 can be saved in cash. The commencement date depends upon the age of the investor. For those aged 50 and over in 2009/10 the new limit applies from 6 October 2009. For those aged under 50 the new limit applies from 6 April 2010. (The whole amount can be invested in stocks and shares if the saver wishes – see explanatory note 5.) There is no minimum subscription. Although there is no minimum holding period for the ISA, it is not possible to withdraw and reinvest at will. Once the investment in a component reaches the limit for the year, no further investment in the component may be made in that year, regardless of withdrawals.

5.   Savers may hold only one stocks and shares ISA and one cash ISA per year, which may be with different managers. Transfers of the whole balance of an ISA may be made to another manager during the year. A cash ISA may be transferred to another cash ISA or to a stocks and shares ISA, but a stocks and shares ISA may be transferred only to another stocks and shares ISA. An amount of up to £5,100 / £3,600 (depending upon age of investor – see explanatory note 4 above) can be invested in a cash ISA, and the balance up to £10,200 / £7,200 may be invested in a stocks and shares ISA.

6.   The annual investments in TESSAs taken out before 6 April 1999 did not affect the ISA limits and the capital (but not interest) from TESSAs maturing after 5 April 1999 could be paid into the cash component of an existing maxi ISA, or into an existing cash mini ISA, or into a separate TESSA only ISA, within six months of maturity. From 6 April 2008 these accounts are reclassified as cash ISAs.

7.   ISAs are free of income tax and capital gains tax, where ISA investments are in shares, but tax credits on dividends are not reclaimable. Where the ISA investment is in securities rather than shares, the 20% tax deducted is reclaimable by the ISA manager. Where interest arises on cash held for reinvestment in a stocks and shares ISA, the account manager has to account for tax at 20% to HMRC (this applies to PEP funds reclassified as ISAs from 6 April 2008). There is, however, no effect on the investor, who is neither treated as having received taxable income nor entitled to a tax refund.

If tax relief on an ISA is found to have been wrongly given, HMRC may make an assessment on either the account manager or the investor.

8.   Shares received from savings-related share option schemes and share incentive plans (see Example 85) may be transferred within 90 days into the stocks and shares component of the ISA free of capital gains tax, so long as, together with any other investments, they are within the annual subscription limit. This applies even where the shares would not otherwise be qualifying investments (for example, because they are not listed on a recognised Stock Exchange).There is no separate single company limit, and there is no facility to transfer shares acquired under a public offer or following demutualisation of a building society or insurer. The

shares component of an ISA is kept separate from any other holdings of the investor for the purpose of the capital gains rules for matching disposals with acquisitions.

9. Stakeholder ISAs offer terms that meet minimum criteria for charges, access and terms set by the government. The main terms are:

	Cash	*Shares*
Charges	None	1½% for first 10 years of net assets plus stamp duty and dealing charges
Access	Withdrawal within 7 days; minimum amount £10 or less	Minimum £500 a year or £50 a month
Terms	Interest no lower than 1% below base rate, upward changes to be reflected within one month, no other restrictions	Units/shares to be single priced, and at least 50% to be invested in EU shares/securities

In addition the component must:

–   use plain English

–   not link with any other product (no bundling)

–   undertake to maintain the CAT standard for existing customers.

10. An investor in an ISA can transfer his investment to another manager. The transfer must be of the whole of the current year's subscription and/or the whole or any part of a previous subscription.

11. From 6 April 2008, maxi ISAs, mini ISAs, PEPs and TOISAs ceased to exist. PEPs and the stocks and shares component of maxi ISAs are reclassified as ISAs, and contributions can be made to them, subject to annual limits. Mini ISAs, the cash element of maxi ISAs and TOISAs become cash ISAs. Amounts on prior year cash ISAs may be transferred to stocks and shares ISAs, in addition to the current year £10,200 / £7,200 investment limits.

12. Savers who withdrew ISAs from Northern Rock between 13 and 19 September 2007 were able to redeposit the amount of the withdrawn ISAs in a new ISA by 5 April 2008. Similarly Icesave cash ISA savers were allowed to reinvest some or all of their ISA compensation payment with another ISA provider by 5 April 2009.

(b)   Child Trust Fund

The arrangements for the Child Trust Fund (CTF) were established by SI 2004/1450, 2422, and 3369, and apply to children born on or after 1 September 2002.

Every child born on or after 1 September 2002 is eligible for the Child Trust Fund, provided:

–   Child Benefit has been awarded for them;

–   they are living in the United Kingdom (or are children of Crown Servants or personnel in the Armed Forces); and

–   they are not subject to immigration controls.

Special arrangements exist for children in care, where child benefit is not awarded, to ensure that they can benefit from the child's trust fund accounts.

There is no requirement to claim for CTF. Eligibility for the CTF follows the award of child benefit. When the child benefit award has been made, a voucher for £250 is sent to the parent or guardian. The voucher should be presented to a CTF provider (accounts are offered by many banks, building societies, friendly societies and other investment companies), who will open an account on behalf of the child. Accounts available are:

– savings accounts, investing contributions in cash, earning interest;

– accounts investing in the equity of listed companies, which participate in the risks and rewards of the stock market, and which are subject to various levels of fees; and

– stakeholder accounts, offered by all providers, investing in the equity market, but limited in risk and limited to charges of 1.5% of funds.

Universal age seven (the first qualifying children will be seven on or after 1 September 2009) payments of £250 are made shortly after the child's seventh birthday. The additional (low income families / children in care) age seven payments are made after the end of the tax year in which the child's seventh birthday falls, with awards linked to the tax credit and care systems (Child Trust Funds (amendment) Regulations 2009).

If an account is not opened by the time the voucher expires (January 2009 figures show one in four qualifying children failed to open an account) a stakeholder account will be opened by HMRC on the child's behalf.

Only one account may be opened, there is no facility to open multiple accounts to spread types of investment.

Where the parents' or guardians' income is below the Child Tax Credit threshold of £16,040 (£15,575 for 2008/09) the government will contribute a further £250 on opening the account, and on the child's seventh birthday. Tax credits should normally be claimed within three months. To prevent disadvantaged children missing out because a tax credit claim was not made within this period, for Child Trust Fund purposes only the three months is extended to one year by the amended 2009 Regulations.

Starting in April 2010 the government will also contribute £100 every year for all disabled children (those in receipt of disability living allowance) born on or after 1 September 2002. Where the child is severely disabled (those who receive the high care element of disability living allowance) this is increased to £200 per year. These payments do not count towards the £1,200 yearly contribution limit.

The account is administered by the parent or guardian until the child is 16, when the child must take over the administration, partly to achieve the financial education aims of CTF.

The funds in the account belong to the child. Interest arising on the account will not be taxed on the parents, even if they provided the funds, in contrast to other sorts of investment that they might make on the child's behalf. Parents or others may make contributions to the child's trust fund to the limit of £1,200 a year. For purposes of the CTF a year begins with the child's birthday, except the first period of which runs from the opening account to the child's birthday. In the first period, the amount that may be contributed is not apportioned according to the length of the period, so full £1,200 may be contributed.

There is no access to the funds until the child is aged 18, at which time the child (and no one else) has access to them. There is then no restriction as to the use of the money.

The income generated within the CTF will have no affect on family benefit or tax credits during the time that the CTF account is open.

Early access to funds is allowed in the case of terminal illness of the child, on which HMRC have issued guidance.

Explanatory Notes

ISAs

1. The legislation relating to ISAs is now contained in ITTOIA 2005 Part 6 Chapter 3 and related regulations. SI 2007/2119 introduced significant changes effective 6 April 2008. Only one cash ISA,

and one stocks and shares ISA may be opened per year, and may be with different providers. The overall annual subscription limit is £10,200 / £7,200 depending upon the age of the investor, with a maximum of £5,100 / £3,600 available for a cash ISA, and the balance for a stocks and shares ISA. For those aged 50 and over in 2009–10 the new higher limits apply from 6 October 2009. For those aged under 50 the new higher limits apply from 6 April 2010. Maxi and mini ISAs are abolished. PEPs and the stocks and shares component of maxi ISAs become stocks and share ISAs. TOISAs, mini ISAs and the cash component of maxi ISAs become cash ISAs. Prior year cash ISAs, including the TOISA element can be transferred to stocks and shares ISAs in addition to the current year investment limit.

2. The aim of ISAs is to encourage more people to save. The low level of the cash component will not, however, enable substantial tax-exempt amounts to be built up and stocks and shares are inappropriate investments for those who do not already have a firm base of low risk investments. Non-taxpayers cannot benefit from a tax-free account, and as far as the stocks and shares component is concerned, basic rate taxpayers receive no income tax savings from April 2004 and have their investment reduced by account charges. The capital gains exemption is not relevant to those with modest portfolios whose gains would be covered by the annual exemption.

3. ISAs can, however, be an alternative to a personal pension plan where the ISA investment could be funded by taking income from a company by way of a dividend rather than remuneration, thus saving national insurance contributions (see Example 91 part (d)). The advantage is most marked where the taxpayer is a basic rate payer only. Although no tax relief is obtained on the ISA investment, the fund is tax-free (apart from non-repayable dividend tax credits), and withdrawals may be made tax-free and without any restrictions.

4. Care must be taken with investors who use a cash ISA as a current account. Although the balance in the fund may be below the maximum of £3,600, investments into the fund in any year must not exceed the yearly limit. This is particularly relevant in the first year, because any withdrawals will be of that year's investment.

5. Those who are resident in the Channel Islands or Isle of Man are not UK resident for tax purposes. Those employed by the Crown overseas are, however, treated as performing duties in the UK and are eligible to invest in ISAs as are their spouses. If an investor becomes non-resident he may retain the ISA but cannot make any further contributions unless and until he becomes resident again. Account managers should be notified immediately when an account holder dies, as the investments are no longer exempt.

Question

(a)   Compare the tax reliefs available under the provisions relating to enterprise investment schemes and venture capital trusts.

(b)   Outline the tax reliefs available to a company under the corporate venturing scheme.

(c)   Set out the relief available for qualifying investments in disadvantaged communities.

Answer

(a) **Enterprise investment schemes and venture capital trusts**

The enterprise investment scheme (EIS) rules are contained in ITA ss 156–161 (income tax) and TCGA 1992 ss 150A to 150D and Schedules 5B and 5BA (capital gains tax). The rules for venture capital trusts (VCTs) are in ITA ss 258–273 (income tax) and TCGA 1992 ss 151A, 151B and Schedule 5C (capital gains tax). Both schemes give income tax relief and EIS gives capital gains tax relief where gains are reinvested.

Main provisions applying to both schemes

Qualifying conditions

1. The provisions for both enterprise investment schemes and venture capital trusts require investment in qualifying unquoted trading companies, the first being by direct subscription in the company and the second by acquiring shares in a venture capital trust, which is a quoted company which invests in qualifying unquoted trading companies. Shares on the Alternative Investment Market (AIM) are regarded as unquoted shares for these provisions. From Royal Assent, FA 2007 s 109 gives HMRC the power to designate any investment exchange recognised by the Financial Services Authority (FSA), or foreign equivalents, as a recognised stock exchange. The Alternative Investment Market is not directly regulated by the FSA, but operates through the London Stock Exchange (LSE), so there is unlikely to be any change, but the possibility should be borne in mind.

2. Both schemes are available to non-residents, but relief is given only against UK tax liabilities.

3. The respective definitions of a qualifying company are broadly the same, and in each case the definitions exclude companies that deal in land, leasing companies, companies that provide finance, legal or accountancy services, property development, farming and market gardening, forestry and timber production, hotels and nursing or residential care homes, shipbuilding and the production of coal and steel (ICTA 1988 s 297 and Sch 28B, TCGA 1992 s 164I). The total gross assets of the company (and, where relevant, other companies in the same group) must not exceed £7 million immediately before the issue of the shares, nor £8 million immediately afterwards. Before 6 April 2006, these limits were £15m and £16m respectively.

   In relation to groups of companies, a parent company qualifies providing the group's activities *as a whole* are qualifying activities. The test does not have to be satisfied by each group company. A subsidiary company can be a qualifying subsidiary if it is a 51% subsidiary except for property management or research and development subsidiaries which have to be 90% owned.

   ITA 2007 ss 190 and 301 allow the trade to be carried out by a 90% subsidiary of the qualifying investee company, or by a 100% subsidiary of a 90% subsidiary. In addition, from that date, provisions allow relevant intangible assets (intellectual property created by the EIS company) to be transferred between qualifying group companies.

4. In 2007, further restrictions required by EU state aid rules for risk capital were introduced and apply to VCT funds raised after 5 April 2007, and to EIS and CVS share issues after Royal Assent of FA 2007.

   Number of employees restriction

   The companies or groups being invested in may have no more than 50 employees at the date of share issue (ITA 2007 ss 186A and 297A).

Value of funds restriction

Companies being invested in may receive no more than £2 million annually from the VCTs, EIS, CVS or other risk capital schemes (ITA 2007 ss 173A and 292A).

For EIS, at the time of the issue of the shares there must not be any arrangements for the company to become quoted, or to become a subsidiary of a quoted company. The VCT provisions allow a VCT to continue to include shares in a company that becomes quoted in its qualifying holdings for a period of five years.

A clearance procedure is available to enable companies to obtain *provisional* approval from HMRC that their shares qualify for EIS relief.

Guaranteed exit arrangements and guaranteed loans

5. EIS relief is denied where there are arrangements at the time of an individual's investment that protect or guarantee the investment, or set up disposal arrangements for the benefit of the investor.

    Similarly, loans or securities that are guaranteed are excluded from a VCT's qualifying holdings (see note 20), and at least 10% of the total investment in any company must be ordinary, non-preferential shares. The VCT shares must be acquired for bona fide commercial purposes and not as part of a scheme or arrangement whose purpose is tax avoidance (ITA 2007 s 261(3)).

Income tax reliefs

6. EIS gives income tax relief at 20% on shares *subscribed for* up to £500,000 (prior to 6 April 2008 £400,000). The relief is withdrawn if the shares are not held for at least three years unless this occurs through the death of the holder.

    VCT gives income tax relief at the rate of 30% on shares *subscribed for* up to £200,000. The 30% rate has applied since 2006/07. Previously, the rate was 20% although it was temporarily increased to 40% for the two tax years 2004/05 and 2005/06. The relief is deducted from the total bill for income tax. It is not a requirement to have income in to charge at 40%. In addition dividends on VCT shares *acquired* not exceeding £200,000 are exempt from tax (the tax credits are not repayable). The shares must be held for at least five years. For shares issued before 6 April 2006, the waiting period was three years (as for EIS).

    See also notes 7, 9 and 22.

Shares acquired by subscription or otherwise

7. The difference between subscribing for shares and acquiring them some other way, for example by purchase from another shareholder or as a gift, should be noted. The income tax relief for EIS and VCT shares and capital gains deferral relief for EIS only apply to shares *subscribed for*, and the capital gains exemption only applies to shares on which income tax relief was given (although income tax relief is regarded as having been given even if the individual's income tax liability was insufficient to enable him to benefit from the full income tax reduction available). The VCT dividend exemptions apply to shares *acquired* up to the £200,000 limit in any year.

Claims

8. Claims for EIS income tax or capital gains tax deferral relief cannot be made until a certificate EIS 3 has been received from the company, issued on the authority of an officer of the board, stating that the relevant conditions have been satisfied. A company applies for such authority on Form EIS 1, but this cannot be done until at least four months after the relevant trade has commenced (which may be up to two years after the company obtains the share subscriptions).

The officer's authority will be given on Form EIS 2. The claim by the investor may be included in tax returns or amendments to returns if the certificate is received in time. Otherwise claims are made on the form incorporated in the EIS 3 certificate from the company. The overall time limit for claiming the relief is five years from 31 January following the tax year in which the shares are issued.

Claims for VCT relief may similarly be made in tax returns and are subject to the same time limit.

EIS and VCT certificates should be retained as part of the taxpayer's records.

Further points relating to EIS shares

Conditions for income tax relief

9. EIS income tax relief is given where a 'qualifying individual' subscribes for 'eligible shares' in a qualifying company carrying on or intending to carry on a qualifying business activity, as outlined in note 3 above. The subscription must be wholly in cash and all the shares must be issued to raise money for a qualifying business activity. 80% of the money raised needs to be used for the qualifying activity within twelve months of the issue of the shares or of the commencement of the trade, with the remainder being used within a further twelve months.

   A qualifying individual is one who is not *connected* with the company (connected broadly meaning having 30% or more control, or being or having been a director or employee). The investor may, however, become a paid director after the shares are issued. The connected persons rules do not apply to the EIS deferral relief (see note 19).

   Eligible shares are new ordinary shares that are not redeemable for at least three years. If any of the requirements for a 'qualifying individual' or 'qualifying company' are breached during a 'relevant period' – broadly, in the three years after the issue of the shares or commencement of trading if later – the relief is withdrawn. The relief is subject to detailed anti-avoidance provisions, including the 'guaranteed exit' provisions in note 5. If the anti-avoidance provisions apply and relief has already been granted, it will be withdrawn and interest will be charged from the end of the tax year in which it took effect if given through PAYE and otherwise from the date on which it was granted.

Minimum subscription

10. The minimum subscription to any one company is £500, except where the investment is made through an investment fund approved by HMRC.

Carryback to previous year

11. A claim may be made to carry back amounts invested for relief in the previous tax year. Any amount invested after 5 April 2009 may be carried back, provided the limit of relief in the previous year is not exceeded. There were previously more complex rules governing carry back, which in particular limited relief to a maximum carry-back of £50,000; carry back was also only possible in respect of half the amount invested in the first half of the tax year. This was abolished by FA 2009 Sch 8. The relief in relation to the carried back investment is then given by reference to the tax payable for the earlier year, but it will be *given effect* in relation to the later year (TMA 1970 Sch 1B – see Example 43).

Withdrawal of income tax relief

12. Income tax relief is not available (or if already given, is withdrawn) if an individual is or becomes connected with the company within the two years before or three years after the shares were issued or trading commenced if later.

There are provisions for withdrawing relief if value is received from the company within the period of one year before the shares are issued or trading commenced if later than three years after that date. It is provided that receipts of insignificant value are ignored. Amounts not exceeding £1,000 will normally be regarded as insignificant. The relief withdrawn where value (other than an insignificant amount) is received is equal to basic rate tax on the lower of the value received and the amount on which relief was given. 'Value received' includes the repayment of loans that had been made to the company before the shares were subscribed for, provision of benefits, purchase of own shares from other shareholders, and purchase of assets for less than market value. It does not, however, include dividends that do not exceed a normal return on the investment. If a shareholder waives his dividend, thus increasing the dividend of an EIS shareholder, that waiver will cause the EIS shareholder to have received value in excess of a normal return.

The cessation of trade will trigger a withdrawal of relief, unless the company commences winding up at the time of the cessation, or as promptly as the circumstances permit, and the winding up is for bona fide commercial reasons and not for tax avoidance purposes. Similarly, the appointment of an Administrative Receiver does not cause the relief to be lost, providing this is done for bona fide commercial reasons and not for tax avoidance purposes.

Income tax relief is also withdrawn if the shares are disposed of within three years after the shares are issued or after trading commenced if later. Where shares are sold at arm's length the clawback of income tax relief is restricted to the lower of the relief originally given or tax at the lower rate on the sale proceeds. If the disposal is not at arm's length the relief is withdrawn completely. Interest on overdue tax normally runs from the date on which the conditions are broken.

13. ITA 2007 ss 234–236 provides for the withdrawal of income tax relief to be effected by an assessment for the tax year for which the relief was given (see Example 41 explanatory note 15 for the issue of assessments outside the self-assessment system).

Capital gains deferral relief

14. All or part of the gains on the disposal of *any* assets (and gains triggered after 5 April 1998 under the now withdrawn reinvestment relief provisions) may be deferred to the extent that qualifying EIS shares are *subscribed* for. There is no limit on the amount that may be deferred under the EIS (although the shares must be eligible shares – see note 9). The period during which the shares must be issued is between one year before and *three* years after the gain arises.

Deferred gains become chargeable on the disposal of the shares, other than to a spouse/civil partner (the gain or loss on the disposal itself being dealt with separately). Deferred gains also become chargeable if the investor becomes non-resident within three years of acquiring the shares. Deferred gains are not triggered if the investor (or spouse to whom the shares have been transferred) dies. EIS deferred gains are triggered if the shares cease to be eligible shares, or the company ceases to qualify within three years. Shares are treated as ceasing to be eligible shares if the investor receives value (other than an insignificant amount) from the company within one year before or three years after the shares are issued or trading commenced if later.

When deferred gains are triggered, further deferral is possible into qualifying EIS shares.

15. Where gains which would have been subject to taper relief have been deferred by reinvesting in EIS shares, the abolition of taper relief from 6 April 2008 meant that the reinvested gains will resurface without the benefit of any taper relief – ie at the gross gain.

However, under the transitional rules in relation to entrepreneur's relief, gains which have been reinvested in either EIS or VCT investments, which would have attracted entrepreneur's relief on the original disposal (had the relief existed at that time) will attract entrepreneur's relief on the disposal of the EIS or VCT investment which causes the gain to resurface. Thus, those holders of EIS or VCT investments who had rolled gains potentially subject to 75% taper relief into their new investments will largely benefit from a similar relief on the disposal of the subsequent investment. However, as with any case of entrepreneur's relief, gains on commercial lettings will lose the benefit of the taper they would have attracted on a pre-April 2008 disposal, as such a gain would not have attracted entrepreneur'ss' relief when it arose. Such gains will resurface in full.

Entrepreneur's relief also includes arrangements under which the gain deferred by reinvestment in EIS shares will be the net gain after entrepreneur's relief, rather than the gross gains, as was previously the case under taper relief.

Capital gains exemption on disposal of shares

16. Gains on disposal of EIS shares *subscribed for* up to the £500,000 (£400,000 to 5 April 2008) limit per year (as distinct from deferred gains held over by reference to those subscriptions/acquisitions) are exempt, but only after three years. Relief is available for losses on EIS shares (see note 17).

    Where gains are chargeable, they are eligible for deferral in the same way as any other gains (see note 14).

17. If the disposal results in a loss, relief is available for the loss whether the disposal is within or outside the three-year period, but in calculating a loss, the allowable cost is reduced by the amount of EIS income tax relief that has not been withdrawn. A loss may be relieved either against chargeable gains, including deferred gains triggered by the disposal, or against income (see Example 78 explanatory note 10).

18. Where shares have been acquired at different times and some or all of the shares attract EIS relief, disposals are matched with shares acquired earlier rather than later. Where shares were acquired on the same day, disposals are identified first with shares to which neither EIS income tax relief nor capital gains deferral relief is attributable, then with shares to which deferral relief but not income tax relief is attributable, then with shares to which income tax relief but not deferral relief is attributable, and finally shares to which both reliefs are attributable. The normal capital gains tax identification and pooling rules do not apply.

Capital gains deferral relief

19. As indicated in note 14, gains may be deferred whether or not income tax relief was available on the EIS shares (thus enabling owner/directors to obtain deferral relief where they subscribe for shares). In order for deferral relief to be available the subscription for the shares must be wholly in cash, the issue must not be part of arrangements to avoid tax, and the shares must be issued to raise money for a qualifying business activity and must be used for that purpose within twelve months. Deferral relief is not available where there are guaranteed exit arrangements (see note 5).

    Unlike the income tax provisions (see note 12), where a deferred gain is triggered because an individual receives value (other than an insignificant amount) from a company, the whole of the deferred gain is brought into charge (less any available taper relief pre-6 April 2008), regardless of how much value is received.

Further points relating to VCT shares

Qualifying holdings for VCTs

20. The venture capital trust (VCT) provisions apply from 6 April 1995. To be eligible for VCT relief an investor needs to be aged 18 or over.

    VCTs are quoted companies holding at least 70% of their investments in shares or securities that they have subscribed for in qualifying unquoted companies (see note 3) trading wholly or mainly in the UK, at least 30% of the VCT's total investments being in ordinary shares and no single holding being more than 15%. From 6 April 2007, ITA 2007 s 280A relaxes the 70% qualifying holdings rule on disposals of holdings, effectively by allowing qualifying holdings to fall below 70% for six months after disposal, without loss of VCT relief. For six months after disposal the company is treated as if it continued to hold the holding disposed of, and the money received from the holding is excluded from the company's assets for the same period. Furthermore, HMRC are given powers to make regulations that provide discretion on withdrawal of VCT relief in the event that conditions are breached as a result of events outside the company's control. See also note 5 regarding guaranteed loans and the requirement for at least 10% of the total investment in any company to be ordinary, non-preferential shares.

The VCT must not retain more than 15% of its income from shares and securities and companies in which it invests must satisfy the gross assets test in note 3.

To be a qualifying holding the company in which the VCT has invested must use 80% of the money invested for the purpose of the company's trade within twelve months of the issue of the shares to the VCT or of the commencement of its trade if later, with the remainder being used within a further twelve months. FA 2009 relaxed this requirement to allow for all of the funds to be invested within the two-year period, removing the 80% within one year requirement.

VCT's capital gains exemption

21. VCTs are exempt from tax on their capital gains. Accordingly there is no relief for capital losses. There are anti-avoidance provisions to prevent the exemption being exploited by means of intra-group transfers, or by transferring a company's business to a VCT or to a company that later becomes a VCT (TCGA 1992 ss 101A–101C).

Withdrawal of income tax relief

22. The income tax relief will be withdrawn to the extent that any of the shares in the VCT are disposed of within five (for shares acquired before 6 April 2006, three) years (other than to the holder's spouse/civil partner, or after the holder's death). Where shares are acquired from a spouse/civil partner, the spouse/civil partner is treated as if he or she had subscribed for the shares. The relief will also be withdrawn if the VCT loses its qualifying status within the five (or three) year period. As with EIS relief, the legislation provides for relief to be withdrawn by an assessment (ITA 2007 ss 269–270).

Investors' capital gains exemption

23. The capital gains exemption on the disposal of VCT shares applies to shares acquired up to the £200,000 limit in any year, whether acquired by subscription or otherwise. There is no minimum period for which the shares must be held. Relief is not available for capital losses.

24. Any disposals of shares in a VCT are matched first with any shares acquired before the trust became a VCT. To decide whether other disposals relate to shares in excess of the £200,000 limit in any year, disposals are identified with shares acquired earlier rather than those acquired later. Where shares are acquired on the same day, shares in excess of the limit are treated as disposed of before qualifying shares. Any shares not identified with other shares under these rules qualify for the VCT capital gains exemption on disposal, and they are not subject to the normal capital gains rules for matching disposals with acquisitions.

If a VCT loses its qualifying status, shares eligible for the CGT exemption are treated as disposed of at market value (any gain being covered by the exemption) and immediately reacquired at market value. They are then brought within the normal capital gains rules for matching disposals with acquisitions.

Capital gains deferral relief prior to 6 April 2004

25.   VCT investment attracted capital gains tax relief on reinvested gains until 5 April 2004. The rules were similar to the EIS relief set out at notes 14–18 above except the VCT shares must have been issued within the period of one year before to one year after the date on which the gain arose. Any gain so deferred will be triggered if the VCT loses its approval.

(b)   Corporate venturing scheme (CVS)

FA 2000 s 63 and Sch 15 introduced a corporate venturing relief aimed at encouraging companies to invest in small, unquoted, higher risk trading companies and to form wider corporate venturing relationships. HMRC have produced a booklet IR2000 giving details of the scheme. Financial companies that invest by way of business are not eligible to claim the relief. The relief applies to qualifying shares issued on or after 1 April 2000 and before 1 April 2010 in a qualifying company (defined as for EIS and VCT). The company must not be a 51% subsidiary of another company except where the holding company is itself a CVS company. Companies may obtain advance clearance that their shares will qualify.

As with EIS and VCTs, the companies invested in must have gross assets before the investment no greater than £7 million and £8 million afterwards.

Restrictions required by EU state aid rules for risk capital apply from Royal Assent of FA 2007.

Number of employees restriction

The companies or groups being invested in may have no more than 50 employees at the date of share issue (FA 2000 Sch15(22A)).

Value of funds restriction

Companies being invested in may receive no more than £2 million annually from the VCTs, EIS, CVS or other risk capital schemes (FA 2000 Sch 15(35A).

Investing companies are entitled to 20% corporation tax relief on amounts invested in new ordinary shares of a qualifying small company providing the investing company has received from the small company a certificate of compliance that the requirements for investment relief are met. The relief will be given against the corporation tax payable for the accounting period in which the shares are issued. The relief will be withdrawn if the company disposes of the shares within three years, or in certain other circumstances.

It is provided that 80% of the money invested in the small company has to be used for the purposes of the company's trade within twelve months of the issue of the shares or of the commencement of the trade if later, with the remainder being used within a further twelve months. The activities must be carried on by the company that issued the shares or a 90% subsidiary of that company.

When the shares are disposed of, then whether or not the corporation tax relief is withdrawn as a result of the disposal, tax on any capital gain arising may be deferred to the extent that the gain is reinvested in another corporate venturing scheme holding within one year before or three years after the disposal. If capital losses arise on disposals, then instead of setting the losses against capital gains, relief may be claimed for the amount of the loss (net of the corporation tax relief obtained) against the corporate venturer company's income of the current or previous accounting period.

Relief is not available if the corporate venturer company, alone or with connected persons, controls the small company. Connected persons include the corporate venturer's directors but not its employees. The corporate venturer company's holding must not exceed 30%, and at least 20% of the small company's share capital must be held by individuals. There is no minimum investment requirement.

Relief is not lost if the small company becomes quoted during the three year qualifying period providing there were no prior arrangements to do so.

(c)   **Community investment tax relief**

Community investment tax relief was introduced by FA 2002 s 57 and Schedules 16 and 17 now ITA 2007 ss 340–343 for income tax. The relief applies where an individual or company makes an investment in a Community Development Finance Institution (CDFI) accredited under the scheme. The CDFI must use its funds to finance small businesses and social enterprises working in or for disadvantaged communities. The investment may be by loan or by subscription for shares or securities in the CDFI. The relevant conditions have to be satisfied for five years from the date of investment.

Loans to CDFIs

A loan must be for at least five years, but the amount can be advanced over the first 18 months. No repayments can be made in the first two years following the investment date and repayments cannot exceed 25% of the loan by the end of the third year, 50% by the end of the fourth year and 75% at the end of the fifth year. There cannot be any pre-arranged protection against risk other than normal commercial banking conditions.

The amount eligible for relief in the year of investment will be the average balance outstanding over the first twelve months. For the second year it will be the average balance between twelve and 24 months, and for the remaining three years the lower of the average balance for the investment year or for the 18 to 24-month period. Thus in the fourth year it would be the lower of the average balance for the periods 36–48 months or 18–24 months.

Investment in shares and securities

A subscription for shares or securities must be fully paid in cash, with no rights for redemption within five years. Again there cannot be any pre-arranged protection against loss.

Conditions to obtain tax relief

The investor will require a tax relief certificate. The investor must not control the CDFI, or if a partnership, be a partner in the CDFI. Investments must be held by investors in their own names for their own beneficial interest and not as part of a scheme or arrangement to avoid tax.

Relief for individuals

Tax relief is given for five tax years commencing in the tax year in which the investment is made. The relief in each year is the smaller of 5% of the invested amount and such amount as reduces the investor's tax liability to nil. The relief is deducted from the investor's tax liability after giving relief for chargeable event gains on life policies and EIS/VCT relief. Sufficient tax must, however, be left in charge to cover gift aid payments.

Relief for companies

Tax relief for companies is available for the accounting period in which the investment is made and the accounting periods in which the next four anniversaries of the investment date fall. The relief in each period is 5% of the invested amount, restricted to the corporation tax liability of the period. The relief is given after marginal small companies' rate or starting rate relief and corporate venturing relief but before double tax relief.

Withdrawal of relief

If a loan is disposed of, or repaid in excess of the allowable amount, then no claim can be made for that tax year or accounting period. In the case of shares and securities, they must be held on the relevant anniversary date. The CDFI must have accreditation at each of the anniversary dates, otherwise relief is not available for that year/period.

A disposal after the death of the individual investor does not cause the withdrawal of relief. In all other circumstances the disposal of a loan (or part thereof) within the five-year period causes withdrawal of relief granted on the whole amount, unless it is a permitted disposal. Permitted disposals include the repayment of the loan by the CDFI, a negligible value or total loss claim under TCGA 1992 s 24 or loss of the CDFI's accreditation. The disposal of shares or securities within five years will also cause all the relief to be withdrawn unless it is after the death of the investor, a permitted disposal (as for loans) or is a sale at arm's length for full consideration. In the latter case the relief granted will be reduced by 5% of the sale proceeds for each year of claim. A sale for more than the subscription amount would therefore result in full withdrawal of relief granted.

Relief is also withdrawn if the investor receives value (other than an insignificant amount) in the six years commencing one year before the investment date. 'Value' is exhaustively defined but it does not include a dividend on shares providing it does not exceed a normal return.

Question

A.

Kit Cadbury and Terry Thornton are both directors of Galaxy Marine Engineering Ltd. Kit retired a number of years ago, but still attends board meetings, which are short, infrequent and at irregular intervals. He receives £500 per meeting for attendance.

Terry has many business interests, and never attends board meetings due to pressure of work. He works for many companies worldwide as a marine engineer on a self-employed basis, but rarely for Galaxy. However, in 2009/10 his personal service company will undertake Galaxy's marine audit project in Korea for about four months, for a fixed fee of £30,000. He will in practice work almost exclusively for Galaxy, although he will continue other work for other clients as time and practicality of communications allows.

Advise Galaxy on employment status, and its obligation to deduct PAYE and NIC from both individuals.

B.

Derrick Field is a geophysicist, and his wife Magma Field is a petroleum reservoir engineer. After a number of years working as employees of oil companies, they plan to set up their own consultancy, specialising in projects that interest them, and that pay a premium for their expertise. They intend to charge a day rate of around £500 per day, but will not work continuously, generally averaging three months per project with considerable variation.

For reasons of data confidentiality, both will often be required to work on the client's premises in various parts of the world. The company also expects to produce consultancy reports, for fixed fees of between £10,000 and £25,000, winning this work because of the complementary skills of both its directors. The work on these reports may be done concurrently with other projects.

Magma's work will require her to work almost entirely in the clients' premises, although the work will be exclusively confined to the area of hydrocarbon deposit that she is contracted to evaluate, and with flexible hours provided that she meets her deadlines. Derrick will usually be able to choose his place of work for at least some of his working days. To bring in initial revenue, he has agreed to act as a sales consultant to his ex-employer, promoting a geophysical software application in which he is expert, using business cards, letterhead and stationery provided by the ex-employer.

They plan to set up their own company, both acting as directors, contributing share capital of £3,000 each to provide funds for promotion and additional office equipment. They plan to engage staff, occupy office space and offer additional services in a year or two as funds allow. They intend to set up and trade through their own company, but before doing so they ask you whether there is any merit in considering alternatives, such as:

- composite companies;

- managed personal service companies;

- umbrella companies.

Advise them

(a)   first considering the likely employment status issues affecting their activities;

(b)   recommend a type of company with reasons;

C.

Smith and Jones are both working at the rate of £1,000 per week on the roll-out of the Tangled Web Inc integrated management system in Cardiff, a project expected to last three months. Both live in London, and usually work in or around the City, and both incur travel and accommodation expenses of £400 per week while in Cardiff.

Smith is employed by his own company JA and JB Smith Ltd, to which he considers IR35 applies. He had the company set up by a firm of accountants, with himself as director. The accountants prepare the payroll and annual accounts, but Smith operates the company bank account, and does all other administration. Jones works through Tax Efficient Wealth Creation Ltd, a company that falls within the scope of the Managed Service Companies' legislation.

Calculate the deemed employment payment income for Smith and Jones.

D.

Peter Porter runs a small accountancy practice, specialising in limited companies working in the IT and engineering sectors. Peter has many clients who work through their own companies, and to whom Peter has been able to give detailed advice about the best way to set up and run a small limited company and how best to extract profits to minimise the tax liability on earnings. Many of Peter's clients work exclusively for large organisations which recruit their services through agencies, but all in this position work through the medium of a limited company. Peter performs all bookkeeping services for his clients, and has automated invoicing software which his clients can use to generate their sales invoices. Peter also automates the preparation of dividend minutes and vouchers for his clients. The firm prepares annual accounts for each company, and files all of the necessary tax returns. Most clients pay a flat monthly fee for the services Peter provides.

Explain how the managed service company provisions in Finance Act 2007 could apply to Peter's clients.

Answer

A.

There is no need to consider employment status for Kit Cadbury, since he is the holder of an office for tax purposes. Payment for attendance at board meetings arises directly from holding the office of director, and ITEPA 2003 s 5 and SSCBA 1992 s 2(1) equate the holding of an office to employment. Galaxy must operate PAYE and Class 1 national insurance contributions on remuneration for attendance at board meetings.

Although Terry is a director, the work he is to undertake is not related to that office, and not covered by the office-holder provisions. However, because Terry is a director of the company, HMRC will hold that all work done for the company derives from the directorship, and is liable to PAYE and NIC. As he works through his own service company, employment status should be considered to evaluate whether the provision of services through intermediaries legislation applies. Employment status must be considered according to the usual criteria. The fact that this is project-related, and that he is paid at a fixed rate, point toward self-employment. If this work fits in with the pattern of the business that he conducts with other clients, a good case can be made for self-employment status.

B. Derrick and Magma Field

(a) Consideration of employment issues – a number of approaches are possible.

    (1) Providing services personally

        The reality of the situation is that in most cases the client will hire each individual for his or her individual expertise, and not hire the consultancy to provide personnel. As this involves providing services personally, it has the potential to bring the 'IR35' provision of services through intermediaries legislation into play, so it is necessary to determine whether they might be deemed to be working as employees of the clients if they were not working through the medium of their own company.

        The fact that the company has two working directors is not in itself relevant to employment status if they cannot freely substitute for one another. If work need not be carried out personally, this would prevent the notional direct relationship being one of employment, but the fact that work is carried out personally does not by itself determine an employment relationship.

        The preparation of reports, which require specialist skill from more than one person would form part of self-employed status activity. However, this will not by itself cause all activity in the company to be considered as self-employed.

    (2) Mutuality of obligations

        HMRC is likely to take the view that the mutual obligations of an employment exist throughout the duration of each project, and that their absence between projects is not relevant. The courts appear to give relatively more weight than does HMRC to the concept of mutuality of obligations – the obligation of the employer to offer work, and the employee to accept it on a continuing basis. If status were in dispute, concurrent contracts, working hours under the contractor's control, and work on individual contracts not leading to further work, would be taken into account as evidence against mutuality of obligations of the type required to constitute an employment contract, and against employee status. Again, they would not be conclusive.

    (3) Control

Control, or the right to control, is perhaps the single element that HMRC give the greatest weight to. The day rate of both individuals suggests specialised skills that the client would be unable to control, but this by itself is not conclusive. In this context, the right to control would refer to the right to switch the individual from one project to another. In Magma's case she is required to work on the client's premises using the client's equipment. However, there is a good security reason for this, reducing its importance on balance. More significant is the fact that the client does not have the right to move her from the evaluation of one reservoir to another. If each job is undertaken in isolation and does not lead onto further work immediately, particularly if successive jobs are with different clients, it is unlikely that she would be found to be an employee through the control test.

Similar considerations apply for Derrick. Having multiple clients is not in itself significant – it is possible to have multiple concurrent and consecutive employments – but it indicates a lower level of control, and possibly the lack of continuing mutuality of obligations in the contracts affected. It is not conclusive, and is unlikely to help with the sales manager job, which would also be considered under the 'part and parcel' test below.

(4)   In business on own account

Having considered mutuality of obligations, control, and whether services are performed personally, other points of the relationship will be considered for pointers to employment or self-employment.

(5)   Financial risk

The possibility of making a loss and the ability to profit from taking that risk, or from good management, point to self-employment. The £6,000 is partly spent on marketing, which will not necessarily produce any return, but could put them in a position to profit from their skills. The amount of equipment that this investment will provide is probably insufficient to point either way. The move to office premises, when it happens, will be a clear indication of taking financial risk. Their investment and intentions point to a self-employed relationship.

(6)   Part and parcel of organisation

The test of whether an individual was integral to the organisation was a key test in the past, but is now regarded as a pointer. If Derrick holds himself out as an employee of his former employer, he will find it difficult to argue that he is not an employee. Using letterhead and business cards of the ex-employer are likely to show that this is what he is doing, and would constitute a very strong pointer to employment. The detail on the stationery, and the terms of any written contract might make a difference here. Accepting employee status for this activity has minimal effect on the status of the other activities, and may even be helpful, by demonstrating that employment status has been properly considered.

(b)   (1)   Composite companies, managed personal service companies and umbrella companies

The details of each company will be individual to it, and there may be no clear cut division.

Umbrella companies are employment businesses. They operate in a similar way to employment agencies, supplying temporary staff, but unlike typical agencies they take on the workers as their employees. Both umbrella companies and agencies operate payroll on the wages they pay to the workers, the former because the workers are employees and the latter because their wages are deemed to come from employment. Umbrella companies supply the personal services of their employees to the umbrella companies' customers, and make a margin on charging the customers for the employment costs. They have some expenses advantage over agencies supplying temporary workers: agency workers are held to have a separate permanent workplace for each assignment, but umbrella company employees have a single continuous contract of employment and the workers typically have a series of temporary workplaces. This means that, unlike agency workers, they can be paid tax- and NIC-free travel expenses for travel to and from work. This is often backed up by obtaining detailed P11D dispensations. Umbrella companies therefore typically pay lower wages than agencies (but which must be at least at the rate of the national minimum wage), but make up the net pay with tax-free expenses so that the workers are better off (because of the tax and NIC savings) and the clients save costs (because of the employer NIC savings being passed on).

Umbrella companies are not caught by the managed service company legislation of FA 2007, because they pay all remuneration subject to payroll taxes. Paying genuine travel expenses is permitted because they are expenses of employment. HMRC's main areas of interest with umbrella employers are, firstly, that the travel expenses are paid only in accordance with the dispensation and qualify under ITEPA 2003 ss 337–339 and, secondly, that the wage is not reduced below the NMW rate. Workers typically hold no shares in umbrella companies.

Composite and managed personal service companies (collectively managed service companies or MSCs) advertise tax-efficient methods of remuneration. The companies are set up and managed by a managed service company provider (MSCP), with the input of the worker perhaps limited to signing up, and providing a timesheet and expenses claim at the appropriate interval. The worker would normally buy a share in the company so that he could receive dividends out of the taxed profits of the MSC. Having paid the small companies rate of corporation tax in the MSC, a basic or higher rate taxpayer taking a dividend would ordinarily save tax compared with taking remuneration subject to PAYE and NIC.

Since 6 April 2007, all remuneration, including dividends, paid by these companies to the temporary workers who own and work through them, has been subject to PAYE, and from 6 August 2007 to NIC. They differ from IR35 personal service companies, where there is no MSCP involved, in that the deemed payment of earnings takes place whenever salary or dividend is paid out, rather than on 5 April at the end of the tax year.

There is also no requirement for the work through the MSC to involve disguised employment before these rules apply: it is sufficient for the MSC business to consist wholly or mainly of the provision of a worker's services, and pay to that worker (whether as wage or dividend) more than half of the money charged to customers for his services, with the worker paying less tax than he would as an employee, and for an MSCP to be involved.

Companies of this sort are suitable only for charging labour, and do not offer the Fields the flexibility they need to manage a business.

An overview of the Fields' proposed activity and methods of trading suggests that most activity and contracts will be classed as being carried out on self-employed status. As a result, IR35 will not apply, and the directors will be free to pay salary, dividends, pensions, or to retain profits to fund the proposed developments in company business.

The fact that self-employed status is accepted for some activity is not necessarily a severe disadvantage, as some remuneration should be paid through PAYE to qualify for minimum NI contributions and thereby state benefits, and pension contributions paid by the company qualify as payments for employment.

At this level of day rate, they are likely to be well into higher rate bands. If they retain the top slice of profit in the company, it will suffer corporation tax of 21% (2009/10) against income tax at 40%. If the non-IR35 profits are paid as dividends, NI contributions at the rate of at least 13.8% (12.8% + 1%, or 12.8% + 11% if below the upper earnings limit) will be saved. The additional commitment to administration and management required by a company that they manage and control will bring substantial financial reward, and contribute to the success of their plans. The best option is clearly to set up their own company.

C.   Smith and Jones

The IR35 legislation of ITEPA 2003 ss 48–61 continues to apply to personal service companies, provided they do not fall under the MSC provisions. As Smith controls and administers his company, MSC legislation will not apply.

A deemed employment payment has to be calculated for both, but the main differences between personal service companies and managed service companies are illustrated below.

	Smith (IR35) £	Jones (MSC) £
Income from work	1,000	1,000
5% deduction of expenses	(50)	–
	950	1,000
Temporary workplace travel and accommodation expenses	(400)	
	550	1,000
Employer's national insurance at 12.8%	(62)	(113)
Deemed payment	488	887

Under the IR35 legislation, the individual is considered to be an employee of his own company, not an employee of the end client. As a result, the temporary workplace rules apply, and the expenses of working in temporary workplaces are deductible from the deemed payment.

Under the MSC legislation, although the individual is an employee of the MSC, and theoretically could have a series of temporary workplaces (like an employee of an umbrella company), relief under the temporary workplace rules of ITEPA 2003 s 339 is denied in calculating the deemed payment, unless a worker directly employed by the client for that particular project could have claimed a deduction for the expense in question. In this example, Jones's expenses are for home-to-work travel, so they are non-deductible. If the project in Cardiff had involved his travelling from there to Tangled Web Inc's HQ in the US, and TEWC Ltd had bought the tickets and billed the client, the costs of that trip would have related to a temporary workplace for *any* employee based in Cardiff and would therefore have been excluded from the deemed payment.

D.   Peter Porter's accountancy practice

The managed service company legislation at Chapter 9 Part 2 of ITEPA 2003 was introduced by Finance Act 2007 to deal with the widespread marketing of managed service companies as a tax- and NIC-saving device, exploiting as they did the lower tax rate of dividends from small companies and the tax- and NIC-free payment of expenses of travel to temporary workplaces.

Managed service companies are subject to stringent rules regarding the tax treatment of their income paid to workers in those companies, and this would essentially mean that if Peter's clients were caught by the legislation they would be required to recognise a deemed payment of salary each time a payment was made to a worker, whether it was expenses of home-to-work travel or dividends. To ensure that promoters and owners of MSCs cannot simply walk away from their PAYE and NIC obligations and liquidate the MSC, there are also provisions to ensure that any tax debts due in respect of PAYE and NIC can be collected from directors and others personally under what are termed the 'transfer of debt provisions'.

The definition of managed service company relies to a large extent on the involvement of a managed service company provider (MSCP: see note 22). Where a company provides the services of individuals who are largely remunerated by dividends, it is the involvement of an MSCP that can cause the MSC legislation to trigger, resulting in potentially significant additional tax liabilities, and possible personal liability for the directors, of both the MSC and the MSCP.

The definition of MSCP is therefore crucial. However, the definition provides a specific exclusion for persons who merely provide legal or accountancy services in a professional capacity. Peter would therefore be keen to ensure that his firm does not meet the definition of MSCP, and the advice he provides to his clients is seen as specific tailored advice suitable for each individual client, rather than a 'packaged solution'. Subjecting his clients to a basic advice structure in which there is no differential for salary, dividends and the variations between the individual's personal circumstances, businesses and the way they work might be viewed as standard packaged solutions, and Peter should be aware that this increases risk. However, if Peter has a range of other clients to whom he provides a wide range of services, then it is unlikely that he would be regarded as an MSCP. The description of an MSCP in the legislation is brief: a person who carries on a business of promoting or facilitating the use of companies to provide the services of individuals.

In any event, the MSCP must be 'involved with' the company, which is defined as follows:

A scheme provider is involved with an MSC if the provider or an associate of the provider:

- benefits financially on an ongoing basis from the provision of services of the individual, or

- influences or controls the provision of services, the way in which payments are made to the individual or his associate, or the company's finances or activities, or

- gives or promotes an undertaking to make good any tax loss.

This level of control or influence is likely to go beyond the advice and services provided by the average professional firm, even where it might be regarded that the level of support goes beyond the normal level of 'accountancy services' provided to these businesses. It is important to recognise that the test of involvement only applies when it has already been established that there is an MSCP present. Peter's practice will generally be an accountancy practice, rather than 'a business of promoting or facilitating the use of companies to provide the services of individuals'. If Peter also has a number of self-employed clients whom he has helped to choose and set up a business, he is prima facie unlikely to have a business within the definition of MSCP unless he clearly fails the 'involvement' test.

During the debates on the 2007 Finance Bill the Minister (HC Finance Bill Public Bill Committee (15 May 2007 pm) col 175) made it clear that even where there was concern that firms of accountants might fall foul of the definition of MSC provider, the concept of influence would go much further than the mere providing of advice, which permits the client to make a choice between appropriate courses of action. It would only be when the client is offered a standard solution or product which he accepts that the involvement would extend to influence. He then went further to state quite categorically that even where the specific exclusion for accountants does not apply, the purpose of the legislation is not to include within the definition of MSC provider accountants, tax advisers, lawyers and company secretaries who provide advice or other professional services to companies in general. Those persons are not in the business of promoting or facilitating the use of companies to provide the services of individuals, nor are they regarded as involved with the company in the way in which the legislation envisages. (HC Finance Bill Public Bill Committee (15 May pm) cols 175 and 176).

Therefore Peter can be reassured that he will not be regarded as an MSCP, and thus his clients will not be regarded as managed service companies by reason of the services he has provided to them.

Explanatory Notes

Determining employment status

1. Employed or self-employed status is determined by the relationship between the parties. This relationship may comprise a great many factors, making differentiation between employment and self-employment difficult, and in some cases uncertain. The differentiation is not based on any statutory definition of employment, but on case law.

    Much of this case law is not primarily related to tax, but concerns employees' rights and employers' obligations. An employee may expect entitlement to sick pay, holiday pay, pensions, insurance, redundancy pay, notice periods, and benefits offered by the employer. Many employment status cases come to light after work has ceased, when the worker claims unfair dismissal, termination pay, or seeks unemployment benefit available only to employees for whom NI contributions have been paid. Much case law derives from a period before contracting by temporary, flexible workers was as widespread as it is today, and its emphasis was towards determining employment rights, vicarious liability, or tax treatment of individuals throughout commerce and industry generally.

    The employer has much more onerous HR obligations to employees than to the self-employed, for instance in providing pensions access, training, increased insurance and health and safety obligations, the time off and benefits mentioned above, and perhaps cars. An employer must operate PAYE and NIC, cope with student loans, and statutory sick pay and maternity pay, wages attachments, benefits in kind and P11Ds, and faces penalties for delay or non-compliance with this multitude of complex obligations.

Why seek self-employed status

2. Employers can protect themselves from the consequences of recategorisation by treating workers as employees, at the cost of additional administration, employer obligations and tax, NIC, and payroll-related cost. As the costs and duties of care tend to be higher for employment, the relevant authorities are unlikely to object to cautious categorisation, although the worker may do so.

    For project or relatively short-term working, it is attractive to employers to take on contractors or agency staff. Typically, the employer will expect to pay a monthly or weekly invoice, perhaps at a higher rate than for employees, but avoiding the administrative and some legal obligations. Contractor companies often find it easier to opt out of the Working Time Regulations conditions.

    The reasons why an employer might wish to avoid an employment relationship are:

    *   reduction in HR and PAYE administration;

    *   reduction in cost of pension and benefits;

    *   reduction in exposure to claims for redundancy and employment rights;

    *   short-term work/project work;

    *   NIC and PAYE savings.

    If the independent contractor has the same costs as the employer, they will tend to be passed on in the contract price, with no saving. Independent contractors can often reduce costs. Reasons for a potential employee wishing to avoid employment are:

    *   avoiding high NI contribution costs;

    *   obtaining relief for expenses on a self-employed basis;

    *   managing their own pension and financial affairs;

    *   reducing tax costs;

- freedom to move from one interesting project to another at short notice.

If the independent contractor can save on costs, part of the saving may be passed to the potential employer.

National insurance costs

3. National insurance has been in existence since the early 20th century, and has long been an additional cost to the employer, although its rates have tended to increase. The difference in cost of national insurance between earnings of employment as opposed to profits from self-employment in 2009/10 for earnings at the upper earnings limit is £1,020 for the individual and £4,884.48 for the employer. The only significant difference in benefit entitlement is that, on reaching state pension age, the self-employed person does not qualify for the S2P addition in respect of that period of work (and, less importantly, jobseeker's allowance in the short-term).

    National insurance contributions are due on the earnings of employed individuals where the thresholds are exceeded, while no national insurance contributions are due on dividends. In personal service companies that are potentially affected by IR35 legislation, it is necessary to demonstrate that the engagement would, in the absence of the corporate or partnership wrapper, be treated as one of self-employment for profits to be available for distribution as dividends. In recent years this has led to payment of low salaries (ie, enough to qualify for NI benefits), while drawing the remaining profits as dividends, thus reducing national insurance contributions to levels below those of sole traders or partnerships.

Tax costs – rates and bands

4. Husband and wife are taxed independently, presenting the opportunity of using the personal allowances and basic rate bands of both spouses. Although salary can be paid to a non-active spouse, it is tax-deductible only if expended wholly and exclusively for the purposes of the trade, and attracts NI contributions if paid at a level above the minimum NIC thresholds. Dividends are generally taxable as the income of the owner of the shares, so shares are often held by both spouses to enable them each to receive dividends, with the intention of using two sets of rates and bands. The resulting tax saving proved to be an incentive for the formation of contractor companies in which both spouses hold shares and receive dividends, while only one of them delivers the substantive services to clients. The Arctic Systems case (*Jones v Garnett* [2007] UKHL 35) was heard by the House of Lords in June 2007, and confirmed that dividends paid on ordinary shares to a spouse out of profits of one main earner can be taxed on the recipient of the dividends. HMRC have stated that legislation will be introduced to reverse the position, although framing such anti-avoidance legislation is difficult and may take some time. Where profits do not derive principally from the work of any particular individual, dividends will continue to be taxed as income of the owner of the shares to which they relate.

HMRC reaction

5. HMRC have reacted in a number of ways as set out below.

    From 6 April 2000, the provision of services through intermediaries legislation (IR35) has, broadly, deemed 95% of the income of an affected company to be earnings of employment liable to PAYE and NIC deductions.

    From 6 April 2007 all income earned through managed service companies must be treated as earnings of the individuals from whom it derives. The deemed payment is calculated net of PAYE and NI contributions (although NIC need not be paid until periods commencing 6 August 2007).

    HMRC also have argued that the settlements legislation (ITTOIA 2005 s 624) applies to some dividends paid to spouses, and that therefore the dividend should be taxed entirely on the spouse earning the income – see Example 27, explanatory note 1. The House of Lords held this not to be the case, but legislation is expected to be introduced to achieve the same effect at some point in the future.

Reclassification

6.   If an individual who has been treated as self-employed is reclassified as an employee, the tax and NI contributions that become payable are the liability of the employer. The employer will also be liable to interest and may be liable to a penalty if the misclassification was careless or deliberate. Settlements often cover many years, and can be for amounts large enough to be crippling to a business. Correct classification between employment and self-employment is therefore of crucial importance to the financial management of all businesses, although the position of contractors and CIS workers tends to be emphasised currently.

Where an individual was treated as self-employed, they should have paid tax under self-assessment. It has been longstanding practice to offset this tax when negotiating a PAYE settlement. Following remarks made by the Special Commissioner in the *Demibourne* case ((2005) SpC 486), in which offset of tax paid under self-assessment was requested, HMRC revised this practice because it became concerned that the employee might now seek to reclaim the tax originally paid.

After extensive consultation, HMRC issued amending Regulations in 2008 (SI 2008/782) which introduced a new power for HMRC to make a direction transferring the liability for the under-deducted PAYE to the employee in cases where self-assessment tax has been paid on the earnings. (Regs 72E to 72G inserted in SI 2003/2682) This removes the anomaly created by the *Demibourne* decision.

Application of PAYE

7.   PAYE applies to earnings from offices or employments. While there may be difficulties in determining employment status, there is rarely difficulty in determining whether an individual is an office-holder or not. Earnings deriving from the holding of an office such as director or company secretary – for instance attending board meetings – are subject to PAYE.

A director's earnings in another capacity – such as working on the company's normal business – are not earnings from an office, and therefore may (rarely) potentially arise from work carried out on self-employed status.

If the earner is an employee and PAYE applies, the income belongs to that earner only, and only his or her allowances and basic rate band can be applied in reduction of the tax. If income arises from self-employment, NI contributions will be lower than those of employment, and additional expenses may potentially be claimed against earnings. However, those earnings will continue to be those of one individual, and there is no possibility of using additional allowances or rate bands by paying dividends. Any salary paid to a spouse must reflect the value of work done and is subject to NI contributions. If income is generated through a limited company to which IR35 does not apply, PAYE and NIC contributions can be reduced by paying low salaries. Furthermore, NI contributions can be avoided in respect of the remaining profits by paying dividends. If the shares are held by more than one individual, a further income tax saving can be made by using the basic rate bands and allowances of more than one individual.

Special cases

8.   There are a number of cases with special tax or NIC treatment, among which are:

   • agency workers

      Individuals supplying services through agencies are treated as employees for both PAYE and NIC, provided that the worker is subject to the right of supervision, direction or control as to the manner in which the services are provided. This does not apply to companies supplying services through agencies, provided the individuals are clearly officers or employees of the company concerned (ITEPA 2003 s 44) and there is no suggestion that the earnings are personal to the individual but have been paid to the company as his nominee, which should mean that PAYE and NIC are applied before the net amount is paid to the company (see *Westek Ltd v CRC* (2007) SpC 629).

- divers and diving supervisors

  Divers and diving supervisors undertaking seabed diving operations in UK are taxed as if carrying out a trade (ITTOIA 2005 s 15), although the deeming rule does not apply for NIC, so they will often have to be on payroll, with an NT PAYE code but paying NIC under Class 1.

- lecturers, teachers and instructors

  Those teaching in an educational establishment other than on an occasional basis are usually deemed to be employees of the establishment for NIC purposes, although self-employed in general law and tax terms (SI 1978/1689 reg 2 Sch 2 para 4).

- managed service companies

  The managed service companies legislation introduced in FA 2007 is covered below.

Employment status

9.   HMRC points out that employment status is a matter of fact and law, not a matter of choice, or something to be agreed between the two parties.

There is no comprehensive statutory definition of employment status, and the criteria for determining it arise largely from case law. Employment status is determined by demonstrating that a contract (written, oral or implicit) exists, and that it is a contract of service (in old-fashioned terms, a master-servant relationship), not a contract for services. This involves the consideration of a number of criteria, and their interaction with each other. As a result each case has to be considered individually on its own merits, and the results are not always predictable.

Irreducible minimum

10.   In the opinion of Stephenson LJ:

'There must, in my judgment, be an irreducible minimum of obligation on each side to create a contract of service.' (*Nethermere (St Neots) Ltd v Gardiner* [1984] ICR 615)

This referred to three criteria given in the *Ready Mixed Concrete (South East) Ltd v Minister of Pension and National Insurance* case in 1968.

'(1) The servant agrees that, in consideration of a wage or other remuneration, he will provide his own work and skill in the performance of some service for his master.

(2) He agrees, expressly or impliedly, that in the performance of that service he will be subject to the other's control in a sufficient degree to make that other master.

(3) The other provisions of the contract are consistent with its being a contract of service.'

The minimum requirements are:

- that the employee provide his/her own work/skill;

- mutuality of obligation;

- a sufficient degree of control; and

- that the other provisions of the contract are consistent with employment.

HMRC tends to place greater emphasis on control than does case law, and places a different emphasis on mutuality of obligation.

Form of contract

11. Where the contract terms can be separately ascertained, usually because they are in writing, HMRC will compare the contract terms to the actual relationship between the parties as demonstrated by their actions. If the contract terms as evidenced by performance of the contract differ from those in the form of the contract, then the terms actually operated will be the ones to be used in determining employment status by HMRC. The decision in *Narich Pty Ltd v Commissioner of Pay-roll Tax for New South Wales* [1984] ICR 286, a Privy Council case, is used by HMRC as authority to assert that behaviour that is not in accordance with the terms of a contract must mean that the contract has been changed, so they must concentrate on actual behaviours rather than the written terms.

However, the actual finding in *Narich* was that, where an express contractual term is in direct conflict with the effect of the contract as a whole, then no effect can be given to that term and it is treated as failing in its purpose, which is not the same point. The finding related to a term in a contract that labelled workers as self-employed while the rest of the contract gave the company so much close control over the work of the personal service of individual workers that they were clearly employees, which is significantly different from asserting that behaviour has, or custom and practice have, changed a written contract.

HMRC's approach was implicitly undermined by the comments of Lord Justice Peter Gibson in *Express & Echo Publications Ltd v Tanton* [1999] ICR 693, who referred to the 'difficulty in approaching the identification of the terms of the agreement by concentrating on what actually occurred rather than looking at the obligations by which the parties were bound.' This reluctance to substitute custom and practice for clear written contracts also helped decide *Staffordshire Sentinel Newspapers Ltd v Potter* (2004) UKEAT/0022/04/DM, which turned, like *Tanton*, on whether a substitution clause meant that a contract was incompatible with a contract of service. The employment judge noted that it is wrong to concentrate on what actually happened rather than looking at the mutual obligations of the parties, unless the contract was sham. Where there is no clear express term in writing, then it may be necessary to look at the overall factual matrix in order to discern the term, but where the term is clear from the contractual document and no sham, the factual matrix is unnecessary. Case law has therefore held that written terms cannot be ignored unless they do not reflect the intention of the parties.

Services performed personally/substitution

12. In *Tanton*, Lord Justice Peter Gibson stated 'it is, in my judgment, established on the authorities that where, as here, a person who works for another is not required to perform his services personally, then as a matter of law the relationship between the worker and the person for whom he works is not that of employee and employer'.

If there is an unfettered right of substitution, then that makes clear that the services need not be performed personally, and if they need not be performed personally, then the contract cannot be a contract of employment, and ITEPA 2003 s 49 (IR35) is excluded. The right of substitution is clearly implied in many contracts, but substitution clauses feature noticeably in 'IR35-friendly' contracts, and sometimes in contracts where it appears unlikely that such a clause would or could be invoked.

HMRC, despite the principles expressed in *Tanton* and *Staffordshire Sentinel*, is likely to argue that a substitution clause is ineffective unless it is invoked – in effect, arguing that if it is not used, it must be a sham. A number of cases have held that any right of substitution is inconsistent with a contract of employment and the case of *Real-Time Civil Engineering Ltd v Callaghan* UKEAT/0516/05/ZT held that the right of substitution could be disregarded only if it did not reflect the intention of the parties. In the case of *Lime-IT v Justin* [2003] STC (SCD) 15, an IT support consultant working through her personal service company was held to be outside IR35 on the grounds that she had negotiated into her company's contract a non-standard condition to the effect that the company had the right to send a substitute of equivalent expertise if it needed to do so. The client had the right to refuse a substitute on any reasonable grounds, but substitution never happened in fact. The Special Commissioner referred to the substitution right, which was never used but was not a sham, as a 'strong indicator of self-employment', quoting *Tanton* in support.

The requirement to perform work personally is a key component of a contract of service, and any real right not to deliver the work personally (ie, to use an agent, subcontractor or employee) is fundamentally incompatible with a contract of service.

Mutuality of obligation

13. This refers to the mutual commitment whereby the employer must offer work under the contractual arrangements, and the employees must accept the work contracted for. Typically, in an employment situation, there is an obligation on the employee to present himself at the appointed hours, and an obligation on the employer to provide work during those hours, on a continuing basis.

In the 1983 employment case of *O'Kelly v Trusthouse Forte plc*, a casual waiter was held not to be an employee because the hotel chain was not obliged to offer him work, and if it did, he was not obliged to accept it. Framework agreements for a series of periods of casual work will not necessarily constitute a contract of service.

Mutuality of obligation is not limited to full-time employment. Arrangements to offer and perform work on any particular day each week may be expected to demonstrate mutuality of obligation, and it should not be overlooked that the minimum mutual obligations of an employment contract set out in the *Ready Mixed Concrete* judgment can just as easily exist in a short-term casual worker contract as in a permanent contract of employment.

Control

14. HMRC tends to regard the right to control as the most significant criterion for determining employment status, giving it much greater weight than the courts currently do. The control test provides no clear-cut criterion for distinguishing employment from self-employment, because in a relationship where one party is paying the other, there is always an element of control. The worker may well have to exercise skill that only he or she possesses, and it is obviously hard to control such skill. There will be many instances where the worker cannot be effectively controlled on a day-to-day basis because the employer has insufficient skill to do so, and because exercise of the employee's skill requires him/her to make the decisions as to what to do. In this case the right to transfer an employee between tasks would indicate control. A help-line operator, even though exercising skill that the employer may lack, will usually be classed as an employee, because the timing, place and nature of the work are effectively controlled by the employer.

At one extreme a standard employment contract with terms requiring the workers to present themselves at the appointed time, to report to the manager, and work to instruction clearly gives a very strong indication of employment.

Elements of control

- right to move workers between jobs: if the work provider can assign the worker to different work without renegotiating the contract, this points to employment rather than self-employment;

- setting particular times: if the work provider can set the specific times at which the work should be performed, this points to employment rather than self-employment;

- specifying where the work is to be done: if the work provider can require the work to be done in a particular place, and direct the worker to move from one place to another, this will be a pointer towards employment rather than self-employment;

- how the work is done: if the work provider can specify how the work is to be done, this is a very strong pointer to employment. However, its absence is not conclusive evidence of self-employment.

Other contract conditions consistent with employment/self-employment

15.   All factors that make the contract appear to be one of employment or otherwise must be taken into consideration. They are to be evaluated to determine the intentions of the parties, or to clarify other criteria, and cannot be used in the manner of a checklist. There is no exhaustive list, and none of the points are likely to be conclusive in isolation.

The following comments of Mr Justice Mummery in the High Court were cited with approval by Lord Justice Nolan in the *Hall v Lorimer* case:

> 'In order to decide whether a person carries on business on his own account it is necessary to consider many different aspects of that person's work activity. This is not a mechanical exercise of running through items on a check list to see whether they are present in, or absent from, a given situation. The object of the exercise is to paint a picture from the accumulation of detail. The overall effect can only be appreciated by standing back from the detailed picture which has been painted, by viewing it from a distance and by making an informed, considered, qualitative appreciation of the whole. It is a matter of evaluation of the overall effect of the detail, which is not necessarily the same as the sum total of the individual details. Not all details are of equal weight or importance in any given situation. The details may also vary in importance from one situation to another.'

In 'painting this picture' any relevant factors may be considered, but a list of the most frequently considered points is given at Example 13.7, and in HMRC's employment status manual. The points selected for consideration below are amongst the most significant.

- Financial risk/reward: employees generally have certainty of being paid for the time they are required to work and may even be paid at a premium rate if they are required to work extra hours to finish a job on time. The self-employed may be able to negotiate fixed rates which may lead to losses, but conversely can allow them to profit through efficiency in work methods or management. Self-employed workers risk not being paid if work is unsatisfactory, or being asked to re-do work that is not up to standard without further payment. They also have to invest in their business to enable it to trade.

- However, employees benefiting from share option schemes would never be considered as self-employed for that reason, nor does investment by an individual as a shareholder of a company affect his employment status with that company.

- Provision of equipment or investment in substantial stock is characteristic of self-employment, to the extent that it may determine self-employment. It can be regarded as related to financial risk, in that there may be no return on investment. An owner-driver of a truck will be regarded as self-employed, even if working closely with one customer; conversely, provision of hand tools will be disregarded.

- 'Part and parcel of the organisation': if the individual is integral to the organisation, this is a very strong pointer to employment. Examples would be working in a managerial or supervisory capacity, or occupying a function central to the existence of the company, such as a nurse in a hospital. Contrast the nurse with a plumber who is called in to fix a leaking pipe in the hospital – the nurse is integral to the functioning of the hospital, while the plumber is ancillary.

- Length of engagement: there is no set length of engagement that determines employment status, and a casual worker can be taken on for one shift as an employee, while, for example, some radio presenters can supply their services to the same broadcasters for years on end without becoming employees. However, the longer the engagement is, the more it is likely to produce control, mutuality of obligations and to lead to the worker becoming an integral part of the host organisation.

- Holiday pay, overtime, employee benefits: in non-tax disputes, these are more likely to be the point at issue rather than the evidence. Provision of employee terms of remuneration is indicative of mutuality of obligations.

HMRC's general guide to self-employed status

16. HMRC's leaflets ES/FS1, ES/FS2 and CIS349, and the employment status section of the website, give details of the Department's interpretation of case law and of its procedures. Officers are required to determine the correct status, not any particular status. HMRC provides an employee status indicator tool on the website, which presents questions that revolve around the following guidance points, which are quoted from the website:

'As a general guide as to whether a worker is an employee or self-employed; if the answer is "Yes" to all of the following questions, then the worker is probably an employee:

- Do they have to do the work themselves?

- Can someone tell them at any time what to do, where to carry out the work or when and how to do it?

- Can they work a set amount of hours?

- Can someone move them from task to task?

- Are they paid by the hour, week, or month?

- Can they get overtime pay or bonus payment?

If the answer is "Yes" to all of the following questions, it will usually mean that the worker is self-employed:

- Can they hire someone to do the work or engage helpers at their own expense?

- Do they risk their own money?

- Do they provide the main items of equipment they need to do their job, not just the small tools that many employees provide for themselves?

- Do they agree to do a job for a fixed price regardless of how long the job may take?

- Can they decide what work to do, how and when to do the work and where to provide the services?

- Do they regularly work for a number of different people?

- Do they have to correct unsatisfactory work in their own time and at their own expense?'

All these points can be seen to be derived from the principles discussed above.

HMRC's employment status tool

17. HMRC provides an Employment Status Indicator (ESI) based on its interpretation of employment status criteria. This tool can be found at http://www.hmrc.gov.uk/calcs/esi.htm. The tool relies on the accuracy of the information input by the user, and the result is not legally binding, although it is understood that HMRC will be bound by the result if the information has been entered accurately and the output pages are printed and retained by the engager. If the circumstances of the engagement change, it is necessary to review the employment status, whether using this tool or any other method. Input is largely by answering 'Yes'/'No'/'Not applicable' to a restricted range of preset questions in a decision tree, which limits the possibility of accurately conveying the substance of the engagement.

HMRC states that this tool may not be used for determining the status of:

- Directors and company office-holders.

- Individuals providing their services through a limited company (IR35).

- Agency workers.

These exceptions cover a substantial fraction of the cases for which guidance would be sought. The tool may be useful for determining employment status under CIS, and general employment status issues.

It is necessary to document use of the tool by taking copies, although enquiries are given a number, and can be displayed for seven days. Clearly, demonstrating that employment status has been carefully and accurately considered, using HMRC's tools and criteria, will be helpful in supporting the decision reached and avoiding penalties for misclassification of workers.

The tool categorises workers by assigning a score of high, medium or low to the following criteria:

- Substitution.

- Control.

- Financial risk.

The questions asked depend on the data entered, and on answers to previous questions, but the absence of the criterion of mutuality of obligations should be noted. For example, if an attempt is made to key in the details of the casual waiter in *O'Kelly v Trust House Forte*, the questions do not allow the casual nature of the engagement to be entered, nor any data concerning mutuality of obligations. It therefore determines the part-time waiter to be an employee, whereas in the case he was held by the court to be self-employed. It is fair to say that many practitioners would also currently advise that casual waiters should be treated as employees, unless quite exceptional circumstances are present.

Since the results of the tool are not legally binding, it is open to the user to disagree with the result given. Because of the limitations of data that can be entered to be taken into consideration, and because mutuality of obligations is not considered, it is likely that its results will not always be accepted. In that case, it is advisable to record the reasons in a sufficiently robust form to be used to support in any dispute with HMRC, and even to seek the agreement of the local HMRC status officer (once located) to the decision taken.

Managed service companies

Background

18. Numerous individuals work as contractors through limited companies known as managed service companies (MSCs). This vehicle is often chosen because large businesses refuse to engage any temporary worker who is self-employed, because of the risk of misclassification and attendant PAYE and NIC arrears. To service these MSCs, a number of companies exist with the principal aim of dealing with all company and tax administration on behalf of MSCs supplying services. Typically, these companies, known as a managed service company providers (MSCPs), will supply company secretarial and payroll services, and organise invoicing and expense claims (on the basis of instructions from their clients), prepare VAT returns, and perhaps undertake CIS compliance if appropriate. All administrative obligations will be met by the MSCP. The individual providing services will expect merely to advise the amount to be invoiced by the MSC in terms of time worked and expenses, and to receive a monthly or weekly statement of salary, dividends and expenses. The individuals providing services may or may not control the MSC that they are working for – some operate through one-man MSCs in which they or their spouses own the shares, while others are shareholders in composite MSCs, whose members are generally otherwise unconnected, apart from being in a similar trade or industry. The MSCP may receive a weekly or monthly fee, or be remunerated by a percentage of the individual's earnings.

The structure of these companies varies, and is individual to each company. Composite companies will group a small number of unrelated contractors into a company in which they hold different classes of share, allowing remuneration to be channelled to them by dividend on the basis of income that they have earned. Where managed personal service companies are used, each contractor has his own company, but all effective control and administration is provided by the MSCP, which will usually be a director through a nominee company. Both these types of provider are likely to advertise tax-efficient remuneration.

The 'IR35' legislation of ITEPA 2003 ss 48–61 applied to these companies up to 5 April 2007. Since the remuneration or dividend that the individuals receive is based directly on their level of earnings, whether channelled to them by issue of multiple classes of share, individual managed companies, or by some other means, it would appear that ITEPA s 53 would be effective in bringing this remuneration within the deemed employment payment arrangements (IR35). However, because employment status has to be determined on a case-by-case basis, and because of the large volume of MSC companies, HMRC had difficulty in policing its application. For the IR35 legislation, ITEPA s 59 sets out the liability for tax on the deemed payment, making tax recoverable from any intermediary in a chain of intermediaries, not from managing companies or directors who are not directly in the chain. In the case of MSCs, duration of contracts may be short, amounts payable may be relatively small, the workers may have returned to a foreign home, and other intermediaries may have no assets by the time HMRC seeks to recover tax, making the IR35 provisions difficult to apply. Compliance with IR35 was notoriously poor: official figures released in 2009 in response to a FOIA request by the Professional Contractors Group showed an average annual Exchequer yield of just £1.5m, which is believed to be lower than the amount spent by HMRC on policing the rules.

A further type of service company exists, the umbrella company. These already tax all remuneration (excluding travel and subsistence payments) through payroll. The MSC legislation does NOT apply to umbrella companies that charge all their remuneration through payroll.

The legislation

19.   To combat the perceived loss of tax and NIC caused by the use of MSCs, FA 2007 s 25 and Sch 3 introduced legislation to prevent the loss of tax. The MSC legislation does not affect companies or partnerships managed by their owners, and such businesses can continue to operate under previous legislation, and may be affected by the IR35 intermediaries legislation instead. From 6 April 2007, the legislation required MSCs to apply PAYE to all income earned by individuals operating through managed service companies.

Deemed employment payment

20.   Almost any payment or benefit that the individual receives through the company is deemed to be earnings from an employment subject to NIC and PAYE at the time of receipt. The amount so deemed includes any payment or benefit made to the worker or his associates by any person which can reasonably be taken to be in respect of the services provided, and typically would be a dividend, which in the absence of the MSC rules would have been non-employment income (ITEPA 2003 s 61E).

In computing the amount of the deemed payment, there is no 5% deduction for expenses as in IR35, and no deduction for the MSCP's fees. The deemed employment payment may only be reduced by the expenses that would have been deductible had the individual been employed directly by the client. This includes expenses incurred wholly, exclusively and necessarily in the performance of the duties, travel expenses, professional subscriptions, employees' liability and indemnity insurance, and any fixed allowances.

However, as the individual is deemed by the legislation to be an employee of the end client, not of the MSC or their own company, travel and accommodation expenses incurred in attending the client's premises will not normally be deductible in computing the deemed payment, as that would have been a permanent workplace. Travel expenses that an employee of the client could have deducted, for attendance at a temporary workplace, may still be excluded by the MSC worker.

The remainder of the deemed payment (if any) is treated as an amount including employer's national insurance contributions, and thus the deemed employment payment can be arrived at.

If tax has been withheld at source from the income, as may be the case with CIS deductions, the 'deemed employment payment' is the amount gross of CIS deductions.

ITEPA 2003 s 61G explains how the deemed employment payment is treated for income tax. In particular it brings the deemed payment within the scope of PAYE provisions, and excludes any deduction from the deemed payment in respect of mileage allowance relief or other expenses – relief having already been given in the computation of the deemed payment.

Definition of a managed service company

21.   A managed service company is one meeting all of the following conditions:

   (a)   its business consists wholly or mainly of providing (directly or indirectly) the services of an individual to other persons; and

   (b)   the greater part of the consideration for providing the services is paid to the individual; and

   (c)   the way in which payments are made results in the individuals receiving net pay greater than they would have received if it were taxed as employment income; and

   (d)   a person who carries on a business of promoting or facilitating the use of these companies (an MSC provider or MSCP) is involved with the company.

Criteria (a), (b) and (c) may be met by ordinary service companies, who remain able to operate as before. This legislation is targeted at MSCPs, who are able to generate companies on an industrial scale that makes them difficult to police. If service companies are provided through an MSCP, employment status and IR35 become irrelevant, and all remuneration or dividends must be taxed as employment income.

Definition of an MSC provider

22.   An MSCP is involved with an MSC if the MSCP or an associate of the MSCP:

   •   benefits financially on an ongoing basis from the provision of services of the individual, or

   •   influences or controls the provision of services, the way in which payments are made to the individual or his associate, or the company's finances or activities, or

   •   gives or promotes an undertaking to make good any tax loss.

Businesses that do no more than 'merely' provide professional legal or accountancy services, and employment agencies, are not considered to be involved with the company as a result of providing their normal professional services. This will not exclude firms of accountants or employment agencies who also act as MSCPs. Furthermore, such companies that are not MSCPs , but are associated with companies that are MSCPs, may be caught by the legislation – for instance by the transfer of tax liabilities provisions in ITEPA 2003 s 688A. HMRC could consider an accountancy firm that recommended a particular MSC company to its clients as being associated with it, because an 'associate' for these purposes includes any person who 'acts in concert' for the purposes of securing that an individual's services are provided by a company, even if there is no ownership or control connection. Provision of comprehensive accountancy and administrative services to a company set up on the initiative of its director, and controlled by him, would not be considered to constitute association.

Distributions

23.   ITEPA 2003 s 61H provides a mechanism for prevention of double taxation if distributions are made. If a 'deemed employment payment' arises, and a distribution is made in the same year or subsequent years, the MSC may claim relief. This is given by reducing the distribution by the amount of the

deemed employment payment (thus retaining the NIC charge and the appropriate tax year). This claim must be made by the recipient of the distribution within five years of 31 January following the tax year in which the distribution is made.

Debt transfer provisions

24. The debt transfer provisions in ITEPA 2003 s 688A are perhaps the most controversial aspect of this legislation. These provisions allow HMRC to collect PAYE and NIC due under the MSC provisions from third parties if the MSC and its directors fail to pay the liabilities.

    Essentially, the section is enabling legislation allowing the detail to be prescribed by secondary legislation, amending the PAYE Regulations (the principal Regulations). These amending Regulations are SI 2007 No 2069 (for PAYE purposes). Equivalent NIC changes were made to SI 2001/1004 and are in Sch 4 Part IIIA. Section 688A(1) allows amendment of the principal Regulations to authorise recovery from specified persons of any amount that an officer of HMRC considers should have been deducted by an MSC in respect of PAYE.

    The persons specified for this purpose are given by s 688A(2). They include directors, office holders and associates of the MSC ('associates' bearing the wide meaning of those acting in concert as described above), MSC providers and a person who has encouraged or been actively involved in the provision by the MSC of the services of the individual. Finally, the provisions are extended to directors, office holders and associates of the last two categories. The debt transfer provisions commenced on 5 August 2007 for the first two categories of third party – directors, office holders and MSC providers, and from 5 January 2008 for the remainder. The debt transfer provisions apply only to PAYE debts arising from the commencement dates, not prior liabilities.

    Subsection (3) provides an exclusion from these provisions for persons merely providing legal or accountancy advice (not services) and for employment agencies concerned solely with placing the services of the workers. This limited exclusion is narrower than that applying to the definition of an MSC provider, but it was considered that the requirement for the third party to have either encouraged or been actively involved in the provision of services through MSC's would sufficiently limit the application of these provisions. For example, it is unlikely that in most situations the client (end user of the services) would be a specified person; however this might arise where a client actively promotes a scheme by transferring existing staff to MSC arrangements.

Calculation of profits for MSCs

25. A deduction is provided in both income tax (for partnerships) by ITTOIA 2005 s 164A and corporation tax (FA 2007 Sch 3) for the amount of the deemed employment payment together with the employer's national insurance contributions paid by the MSC in respect of the deemed payment. In a similar way to the matching rules in the existing intermediaries legislation, the deduction is given in the period in which the deemed payment is treated as made. The deduction is restricted to an amount which would reduce the profits to nil.

Question

Ellis Containers Ltd, which makes up its accounts annually to 31 July, has a wholly owned foreign subsidiary – Ellis Containers (Utopia) Ltd. Ellis Containers Ltd has not made a general 31.3.82 rebasing election.

In the year ended 31 July 2009 Ellis Containers Ltd made disposals of assets as follows:

(a)   A freehold factory which it had purchased when it was first built on 1 May 1981 at a cost of £50,000 including land of £8,000. The factory was used as such until 31 October 1987 and thereafter entirely as offices. On 30 December 2008 it was sold for £255,000 including £55,000 for the land. An initial allowance of 50% had been claimed when the building was first acquired. The market value of the factory (including land) on 31 March 1982 was £95,000.

(b)   On 31 December 2008 the company sold a building that had cost £85,000 on 6 June 1967, including £10,000 for the land. The sale proceeds were £370,000, including £75,000 for the land. The market value at 31 March 1982 was £137,000. The building had been used for industrial purposes until September 1996, then as offices until the date of sale.

(c)   On 2 April 2009 two acres of land were sold for £18,900, being part of a holding of ten acres purchased in November 1987 for £37,250. The market value of the unsold land at 2 April 2009 was £56,700. No question of dealing in land arises, and the land has never been used for the trade.

(d)   The company's freehold interest in a storage depot was sold on 1 October 2008 for £395,000. The depot was acquired in February 1988 for £170,000 and capital expenditure incurred subsequently consisted of £12,750 in June 1989 for temporary partitioning and £19,840 in August 1991 for the replacement of the partitioning by permanent dividing walls. The expenses of the sale consisted of £2,930 valuer's fees.

(e)   Three of the company's machines were sold in April 2009 to different businesses for a total consideration of £4,800. The machines had already been replaced three months previously as part of the company's plan to modernise its fixed plant and machinery. The three machines that were sold had all been acquired in May 2002.

Details of their cost and the proceeds of sale are as follows (£):

	Cost	Proceeds
Cutting machine	1,600	2,650
Folding machine	1,500	1,200
Binding machine	710	950

The company also sold two items of movable machinery, details being as follows:

1st machine bought December 1997 for £7,000, sold March 2009 for £4,500.

2nd machine bought June 1998 for £5,500, sold April 2009 for £4,000.

No balancing charges arose on any of the sales because the pool residue of expenditure covered the proceeds.

(f)   On 1 January 2000 the company was granted a 21-year lease of premises which it used as a showroom and for which it paid a premium of £82,500. On 30 December 2008 the company contracted to sell the lease for £94,000, completion taking place in January 2009.

(g)   In December 2008 the company's sales office building was damaged by fire. On 30 April 2009 the company received £400,000 in compensation from its insurance company. The company intends to use this sum to restore the building to its original condition. The building was purchased new in June

1994 at a cost of £450,000 including land. The insurance company estimated that after the fire the site and the damaged building were worth £320,000.

(h) In June 2009 the company's wholly owned foreign subsidiary, Ellis Containers (Utopia) Ltd, was nationalised by the Government of Utopia and no compensation was received. Requests are continuing to be made to the Utopian authorities for compensation, but it is not expected that they will be successful. The shares in the subsidiary company were acquired in 1976 for £5,000 and were considered to be worth £100,000 in March 1982. An unsecured loan of £80,000 was made to the subsidiary in 1985 and is still outstanding. In the accounts for the year the investment and the loan have each been written down to nil.

On 31 December 2008 a newly built factory was brought into use, having been constructed at a cost of £800,000 since 1 April 2008 on land already owned. The new factory qualified as an industrial building, but was not in an enterprise zone.

The company's trading profits for the year ended 31 July 2009, as adjusted for taxation purposes but before dealing with any balancing adjustments on the sale of the old building, or allowances on the new factory, amounted to £551,820 and it had neither received nor paid any dividends.

1. Calculate the capital gains arising before any claims for relief are made.

   For item (a), the freehold factory, state the position if the sale had concluded as a result of a binding unconditional contract entered into in writing on 15 February 2007, which was completed without any variation in terms.

2. Compute the amount upon which corporation tax is payable for the year ended 31 July 2009 after all available reliefs are claimed.

The following retail price indices should be used in answering this example:

Mar 1982	79.44	
Nov 1987	103.4	
Feb 1988	103.7	
Oct 1990	130.3	
Aug 1991	134.1	
June 1994	144.7	
Jan 2000	166.6	
May 2001	174.2	
Oct 2008	217.7	
Dec 2008	212.9	(rise from Mar 1982: 168.0%)
Apr 2009	211.5	(rise from Mar 1982: 166.2%)

Answer

Ellis Containers Ltd – year ended 31 July 2009

1. Capital gains arising before any claims for relief are made

(a) Disposal of freehold factory

	Using cost £	Using 31.3.82 value £
Sale proceeds December 2008	255,000	255,000
Cost 1981	50,000	
31 March 1982 market value		95,000
Unindexed gain	205,000	160,000
Indexation allowance		
£95,000 × 168.0%	159,600	159,600
	45,400	400

Chargeable gain is therefore £400

If the disposal had taken place as a result of a contract dated 15 February 2007

For disposals on or after 21 March 2007, FA 2007 s 35 withdrew balancing adjustments for industrial and agricultural buildings, as the first step in phasing out IBAs and ABAs over four years. See Example 23 for further details. No calculation of the balancing charge is therefore required, and there is no adjustment to profit for a balancing charge or allowance. The buyer will be able to claim allowances based on the seller's cost/residue of qualifying expenditure, without recalculation.

If, however, the disposal had taken place as a result of an unconditional contract which was entered into in writing before 21 March 2007 and completed without any significant variation in terms before 1 April 2011, then the disposal is taxed under the old regime, which applied when the contract was agreed. Therefore the sale for more than cost would require the allowances given to be clawed back, producing a balancing charge equal to the allowances given. For capital gains tax purposes, the disposal is treated as occurring at the date the contract became unconditional, so the capital gain on the disposal would have been taxed in the year ended 31 July 2007.

(b) Disposal of office building

Chargeable gain:

	Using cost £	Using 31.3.82 value £
Sale proceeds December 2008	370,000	370,000
Cost June 1967	(85,000)	
31 March 1982 value		(137,000)
Unindexed gain	285,000	233,000
Indexation allowance		
137,000 @ 168.0%	(230,160)	(230,160)
	54,840	2,840

Chargeable gain is therefore £2,840.

(c)   **Disposal of land**

	£	£	£
Sale proceeds for 2 acres April 2009 (more than 20% of (£56,700 + £18,900) – see explanatory note 3)		18,900	
Cost of 10 acres in November 1987 = £37,250			
Cost of part disposed of =			

$$37,250 \times \frac{18,900}{(18,900 + 56,700)} \qquad 9,313$$

Indexation allowance

$$\frac{211.5 - 103.4}{103.4} = 104.5\% \qquad\qquad 9,587^* \quad 18,900$$

Chargeable gain   Nil

* restricted to amount to reduce gain to nil. Indexation allowance cannot be used to create a loss.

(d)   **Sale of freehold storage depot**

	£	£	£
Sale proceeds October 2008		395,000	
Less: Sale expenses – valuation fee		2,930	
		392,070	
Less: Cost February 1988	170,000		
Permanent dividing walls August 1991	19,840	189,840	
Unindexed gain		202,230	
Less: Indexation allowance:			
On cost February 1988			

$$\frac{217.7 - 103.7}{103.7} = 109.9\% \times 170,000 \qquad 186,830$$

On permanent dividing walls August 1991

$$\frac{217.7 - 134.1}{134.1} = 62.3\% \times 19,840 \qquad 12,360 \quad 199,190 \quad 3,040$$

(e)   **Sale of machines**

	£	£	£
Dealt with as part of capital allowances computation			
Proceeds deducted from pool (limited to cost)			
Cutting machine	1,600		
Folding machine	1,200		
Binding machine	710		
1st movable machine	4,500		
2nd movable machine	4,000	12,010	
Chargeable gains/allowable losses:			
Cutting machine proceeds April 2009		2,650	
Less: Cost May 2001		1,600	
Unindexed gain		1,050	

$$\textit{Less}: \text{Indexation allowance} \quad \frac{211.5 - 174.2}{174.2} = 21.4\% \times 1,600 \qquad 342 \qquad 708$$

Folding machine – Difference between cost of £1,500 and
proceeds of £1,200 covered by capital allowances, therefore no
allowable loss

Binding machine proceeds April 2009		950	
Less: Cost May 2001		710	
Unindexed gain		240	
Less: Indexation allowance 21.4% × 710		152	88
			796

Both movable machines are sold for less than their cost and also for less than £6,000 each. Since the proceeds must be regarded as £6,000 to calculate an allowable loss, and since indexation allowance cannot be taken into account, there is no allowable loss on either machine.

(f)   **Sale of leasehold interest in showroom**

	£	£	£
Proceeds December 2008			
– contract date is the relevant disposal date			94,000
Cost January 2000		82,500	
Less: Part of purchase price allowed as rent in computing			
trading profits (TCGA 1992 s 39)			
Premium paid	82,500		
Less (21 – 1) × 2% = 40%	33,000		
Assessable as rent on recipient	49,500		

$$\frac{49,500}{21} = £2,357 \qquad\qquad 21,213$$

per annum for January 2000 to December 2008
inclusive   61,287

Depreciated cost under TCGA 1992 Sch 8:

	£	£	£

$$61,287 \times \frac{13 \text{ yrs when disposed of}}{21 \text{ years when acquired}}$$

Substitute TCGA 1992 Sch 8 percentages:

$$61,287 \times \frac{56.167}{74.635}$$

		46,122
Unindexed gain		47,878
Indexation allowance		

$$\frac{212.9 - 166.6}{166.6} = 27.8\% \times 46,122$$

		12,822
Chargeable gain		35,056

(g)   Sales office compensation (treated as part disposal)

	£	£
Compensation from insurance company April 2009	400,000	

Cost June 1994 £450,000

Less: ×

$$\frac{£400,000 \text{ proceeds}}{£400,000 \text{ proceeds} + £320,000 \text{ value remaining}}$$

	£	£
	250,000	
Unindexed gain	150,000	
Less: Indexation allowance		

$$\frac{211.5 - 144.7}{144.7} = 46.2\% \times 250,000$$

	115,500	34,500

(h)   Ellis Containers (Utopia) Ltd

No disposal has yet been made.

2.   Amount on which corporation tax is payable after claiming reliefs

Claims for relief may be made as follows:

Re (a), (b), (e) and (f) (see explanatory note 2)

Since the whole proceeds in each case have been reinvested in the new factory, ((a) £255,000, (b) £370,000, (e) £2,650 and £950 and (f) £94,000 = £722,600) the gains may be rolled over and treated as reducing the base cost of the factory, which will therefore have a capital gains tax base cost of:

Construction expenditure		800,000
Less: Gain on previous factory	400	
Gain on office building	2,840	
Gain on cutting machine	708	
Gain on binding machine	88	
Gain on leasehold showroom	35,056	39,092
		£760,908

Since the cutting and binding machines had been replaced, the small gains of £708 and £88 could have been held over until the replacement machinery is disposed of or no longer in use, or until ten years from its acquisition if sooner. It is, however, preferable to roll over the gains against the cost of the new factory, rather than deferring it for a maximum of ten years.

Re: (g)

Compensation received need not be treated as a disposal if it is used to restore the asset. Instead the compensation can be deducted from the restoration cost, or indeed from the cost of the original acquisition to the extent that the compensation slightly exceeds the restoration costs (see explanatory note 6) (TCGA 1992 s 23).

Hence the calculated gain of £34,500 will not be chargeable at this time if the insurance compensation is used to reinstate the building and a claim for relief is made.

Re: (h) Ellis Containers (Utopia) Ltd

A claim may be made for the shares to be regarded as worthless and consequently treated as sold and immediately reacquired for that nil value. Thus a constructive loss can be claimed at that point and if any proceeds are ever received, a gain will arise to that extent in future (TCGA 1992 s 24(2)). The allowable loss would be £5,000, being smaller than 31 March 1982 value of £100,000.

There is no relief for the unsecured loan (see explanatory note 5).

Computation of profits chargeable to corporation tax	£	£
Trading profit (assumed to be stated *after* the allowance for rent of £2,357 in item (f))		551,820
Industrial buildings allowance on new factory		
Cost £800,000		
Writing down allowance 4% = £32,000		
1.8.08 – 31.3.09 8/12 × 75% × £32,000	16,000	
1.4.09 – 31.7.09 4/12 × 50% × £32,000	5,333	(21,333)
		530,487
Chargeable gains after claims for relief		
Sale of land (c)	Nil	
Sale of storage depot (b)	2,840	
Shares in Ellis Containers (Utopia) Ltd (h)	(5,000)	Nil
Corporation tax payable on		530,487

Explanatory Notes

Lease premiums

1.   References in these notes are to TCGA 1992 unless otherwise stated. Since the acquisition of the leasehold interest in the showroom at part (f) of the example was on the grant of a lease, so that the

grantor would have a tax charge on part of the premium (by way of additional rent) as illustrated, the payer can deduct, in calculating his trading profit, over the period of the lease that part of the premium assessed on the recipient as rent. The interaction of the rent deduction permitted by TCGA 1992 s 39 with the application of the lease depreciation fraction to the cost per TCGA 1992 Sch 8 is not clear in the legislation. HMRC takes the view that the rent deduction is made *before* the depreciation factor is applied to the cost (Capital Gains Manual at CG 71201), as illustrated in the example. This is, in fact, a more beneficial treatment for the taxpayer, since the rent reduction in allowable expenditure is then 'depreciated'.

If the premium paid had been for the *assignment* of a leasehold interest, the vendor would not normally be taxable where the payer is subject to income tax on any part of his proceeds and accordingly no part of the payment would be allowed in calculating the payer's trading profit (CTA 2009 s 63 or the equivalent rules in ITTOIA 2005). Instead, the assignee can claim the same amount of the original premium that the assignor was entitled to deduct, if the lease was originally granted for a period of less than 50 years. See Example 99 for detailed notes on lease premiums.

Rollover relief on replacement of business assets

2. Rollover relief is available in respect of the gains on the old factory, the office building, the storage depot, the cutting and binding machines and the showroom, since all six and the replacement asset –the new factory – are within the classes set out in s 155 and the replacement is acquired within the time limit of 12 months before and three years after the disposals.

The cost of the replacement factory (£800,000) is not, however, sufficient to enable all the gains to be rolled over, so it is necessary to decide how to maximise the available relief. The position is as follows:

	Sale proceeds £	Gain £
Factory	255,000	400
Office building	370,000	2,840
Storage depot	395,000	3,040
Cutting machine	2,650	708
Binding machine	950	88
Showroom	94,000	35,056
	1,117,600	

The maximum deferral of gains is achieved by excluding the office building from the claim. The gain on the office building would still be eligible for rollover/holdover relief if £370,000 was invested in qualifying assets within three years from December 2008 (a balance of (800,000 – (1,117,600 – 370,000) =) £52,400 of the expenditure on the new factory being available towards this amount). If Ellis Containers had wanted to defer the gain, it could have claimed to postpone payment of the tax if it had declared on its tax return that it intended to incur qualifying replacement expenditure within the three years. In fact, after taking into account the loss on the Ellis Containers (Utopia) Ltd shares, none of the gain of £2,840 is chargeable to tax, and if the provisional claim was made the company would have £5,000 unrelieved capital losses to carry forward, so a provisional claim may not be appropriate.

Part disposals of land

3. Where part only of a holding of land is disposed of (other than between spouses/civil partners, or intra-group) and the amount or value of the consideration is not more than 20% of the market value of the land immediately before the disposal and the proceeds do not exceed £20,000, the transferor may claim that this does not constitute a disposal, but that the consideration received be deducted from allowable expenditure in computing a gain on any subsequent disposal of the land. This relief does not, however, apply where in the chargeable period in which the transfer is made, the transferor

made other disposals of land, the total consideration for all disposals of land in that year exceeding £20,000 (s 242). In TCGA 1992 land, unless the context otherwise requires, 'includes messuages, tenements and hereditaments, houses and buildings of any tenure' (s 288). Section 242 expressly excludes leasehold interests with 50 years or less to run. The time limit for the claim for companies is two years from the end of the accounting period of disposal (one year from 31 January following the tax year of disposal for individuals).

On a subsequent disposal of the land the indexation allowance is calculated in the normal way and is then reduced by an indexation amount calculated on the earlier disposal proceeds from the date they were received, thus ensuring that the reduction in the base cost of the land as a result of that earlier disposal only affects the calculation of the indexation allowance from that date and not over the whole period of ownership. For non-corporate taxpayers indexation allowance is not given for periods after April 1998.

In part (c) of the example the disposal proceeds of £18,900 are more than 20% of the value before the disposal (20% of £75,600 = £15,120). Even if they had not been, the company has made other substantial disposals of property in the year thus denying relief under this de minimis provision.

Where part disposals of land are concerned, it may be costly to get a valuation of the whole estate in order to apply the part disposal formula. HMRC will allow the part sold to be treated as a separate asset, using any reasonable means of apportioning part of the total acquisition cost to the part sold. This cannot be done where earlier part disposals have followed the statutory method, unless the alternative method would have given broadly the same result for those disposals (HMRC Statement of Practice D1).

Capital allowances – temporary partitioning

4. The cost of the temporary partitioning in the storage depot is not allowable in calculating the chargeable gain since it is not reflected in the state or nature of the asset at the time of disposal (s 38(1)).

   The cost of the partitioning should, however, have qualified as plant for capital allowances if there was a business requirement for the partitions to be moved (*Jarrold v John Good & Sons* (1963)).

Loss of money lent

5. For companies, the treatment of the loss of money lent is dealt with under the rules for 'loan relationships', profits and losses on disposals being taken out of the capital gains regime and brought into the calculation of a company's income profits. Where a company has guaranteed a debt, however, a payment under the guarantee is outside the loan relationships rules. The company guarantor can, if appropriate, claim relief under the provisions of TCGA 1992 s 253 outlined below.

   The loan relationships rules enable companies to claim relief for the loss of money lent, except for loans between connected persons (see Example 63 explanatory note 7). Connected persons include companies under common control or where one controls the other, as is the case for Ellis Containers Ltd and its subsidiary, Ellis Containers (Utopia) Ltd. Relief is not therefore available in respect of the unsecured loan to the subsidiary.

   For capital gains tax purposes, relief is not normally available in respect of the loss of money lent unless the debt is a 'debt on a security' which means loan stock or similar security, whether secured or unsecured (ss 251 and 132). (This only applies, however, to the original creditor and not to an assignee, for whom an allowable loss or chargeable gain may arise, except that an allowable loss cannot arise if the creditor and the assignee are connected persons – s 251(4).)

   Furthermore, most securities fall within the definition of 'qualifying corporate bonds', which are exempt from capital gains tax (see Example 80 explanatory note 8), so that even though the debt is a 'debt on a security' the loss is not usually allowable under the general rules.

There are provisions in s 253 to enable relief to be claimed for a loss where a loan is made or a guarantee is given and the recipient of the loan is a UK resident who uses the money lent wholly for the purpose of a trade carried on by him, providing the debt is not a 'debt on a security' (s 253). Even if the loan was a debt on a security, loss relief could previously be claimed if the debt was a qualifying corporate bond, where the bond was held on, or issued on or after, 15 March 1989. The relief in this case was limited to the underlying principal of the loan or the amount subscribed for the bond, whichever was lower (ss 254 and 255). Relief under ss 254 and 255 is abolished for loans made on or after 17 March 1998 (FA 1998 s 141).

Where the relief is available, the loss is deemed to arise at the time of the claim that the loan has become irrecoverable, or at the time of the guarantee payment, provided that the debt or the rights acquired by subrogation under the guarantee payment are not assigned (s 253). If they are assigned, then providing the loan does not constitute a qualifying corporate bond, the assignee may claim relief for a loss under s 251 unless he and the debtor are connected persons. For the definition of connected persons for this purpose see Example 73 part (e). Relief under s 253, and under s 254 for pre 17 March 1998 loans, may be given as if the loss had arisen at a time not more than two years before the beginning of the tax year of claim (or for a claim by a company guarantor, not earlier than the first day of the earliest accounting period ending not more than two years before the time of the claim) where the stated conditions are satisfied (ss 253(3A) and 254(8A)). If allowed losses prove in whole or part to be recoverable, a capital gain arises on the amount recovered (or recovered from co-guarantor).

Relief is not available if the loss arises because of an act or omission by the lender, nor is it available where the claimant and borrower are husband and wife or companies in the same group.

By Extra Statutory Concession D38, where someone acquired unquoted stock before 14 March 1989 in respect of shares or securities on a takeover, the stock then becoming a qualifying corporate bond because of FA 1989 s 139, and the stock later becomes of negligible value or gives rise to a loss, the loss may be treated as an allowable loss under s 254.

Assets damaged, lost or destroyed

6. Where an asset is damaged but not lost or destroyed, compensation that is used to restore the asset need not be treated as a disposal. Instead it is treated as reducing the restoration cost in deciding how much of that cost is allowable expenditure on a later disposal.

   No indexation allowance would be calculated at the time of restoration, so that in part (g) of the example the £400,000 compensation received would be balanced by restoration expenditure of the same amount, leaving the original cost intact for the purposes of a later disposal. If the restoration costs exceed the compensation the excess would represent additional allowable expenditure for a later disposal, indexed from the date it was incurred for companies.

   If the compensation exceeds the restoration cost by a small amount ('small' regarded by HMRC as 5% of the compensation), then for assets other than wasting assets the excess may be deducted from the cost of the asset instead of being treated as a part disposal, thus eliminating any current gain but increasing the gain on a subsequent disposal. In those circumstances the available indexation allowance on a later disposal is first of all calculated on the full amount of allowable expenditure, but is then reduced by an indexation amount calculated on the small excess compensation from the date the compensation is received. This ensures that the benefit of indexation on that small amount is not lost for the period from the time the original expenditure is incurred to the date the compensation is received (ss 23 and 57). If the compensation was received before 31 March 1982 the excess over restoration cost would escape tax because it would not affect the 31 March 1982 value. If it was received after 31 March 1982 but before 6 April 1988, it is deducted in arriving at the 31 March 1982 value (but with the same indexation allowance provisions applying to ensure that indexation allowance is not lost for the period up to the receipt of the compensation) (Sch 3 para 4(2)).

If the compensation exceeds the restoration cost by more than 5%, or by any amount for wasting assets, a claim may be made for the part that is used to restore the asset not to be treated as a part disposal but as reducing the allowable expenditure, so that the restoration expenditure does not then count as part of the allowable cost (s 23(3)).

7. If an asset is lost or destroyed, rather than being merely damaged as in part (g) of the example, and any insurance proceeds or compensation received are used to replace the asset within one year of receipt, a claim may be made for the old asset to be deemed to have been disposed of for such consideration as leaves an unindexed gain equivalent to the available indexation allowance, so that the net result is no loss/no gain (s 23). If a building is lost or destroyed, and a replacement is built or acquired on other land, the building may be treated as separate from the land for the purposes of this claim (s 23(6)). If the compensation received exceeds the deemed proceeds for the destroyed asset, the excess is treated as reducing the cost of the replacement (s 23(5)). Where such a reduction occurred between 31 March 1982 and 5 April 1988 and it relates wholly or partly to an asset acquired before 31 March 1982, it is reduced by half in calculating a gain on a disposal on or after 6 April 1988, under the deferred charges provisions of Sch 4 (see Example 82 explanatory note 10).

Assets of negligible value

8. The 'entire loss, destruction, dissipation or extinction' of an asset is treated as a disposal of it, whether or not any compensation is received (s 24). Where this does not apply, but the asset has become of negligible value, a claim may be made to be treated as if the asset had been disposed of and immediately reacquired for that negligible value (s 24(2)), as is shown for the shares in Ellis Containers (Utopia) Ltd in part (h) of the example. The date of the deemed disposal is either the date of the claim or, if the claim so requires, an earlier date falling within the two years before the tax year or company accounting period in which the claim is made. The asset must have been of negligible value on that earlier date (whether or not it was of negligible value before then).

Interaction of capital allowances and capital gains

9. For capital gains purposes, where assets have qualified for capital allowances, the allowances are ignored in computing a gain but are taken into account in computing a loss (the allowances being deducted from 31 March 1982 value when making computations based on that value). This means that capital losses will not arise, since the difference between cost and disposal proceeds is covered by the capital allowances. As far as plant and machinery is concerned, if the item is sold for more than cost, any capital allowances given will be withdrawn by taking into account sale proceeds equal to the original cost, as shown in part (e) of the example. But even if capital allowances are not withdrawn, as in the case of the office building in part (b) of the example, the capital allowances are not taken into account in computing a gain. A similar situation can arise with agricultural buildings – see Example 22 explanatory note 7.

Fixed and movable plant and machinery

10. Gains on plant and machinery are calculated using different rules according to whether the items are fixed or movable. Gains on fixed items are chargeable, subject to a claim for rollover/holdover relief if there is qualifying replacement expenditure. It was held in the case of *Williams v Evans* (1982) that 'fixed' applies to both plant and machinery, so for example, mobile cranes and fork lift trucks would not qualify. Movable items are 'tangible movable property' and are subject to the chattels rules of s 262. These rules provide that a gain is not a chargeable gain if the gross sale proceeds are £6,000 or less. If the proceeds exceed £6,000 the gain is calculated in the usual way (except that it cannot exceed 5/3rds of the excess of the sale proceeds over £6,000 – see Example 77 part (b) for an illustration) and it cannot be deferred.

Claims

11. Capital gains reliefs are not given automatically, and a claim must be made within the normal time limit under TMA 1970 s 43(1), ie within six years from the end of the chargeable period for

companies (five years from 31 January following the tax year for individuals). Ellis Containers must accordingly make claims by 31 July 2015 for the reliefs in relation to replacement of business assets and the compensation used for restoration. (This time period will reduce to four years with effect from 1 April 2010.) In relation to the negligible value claim, in order to establish the loss as a loss of the year to 31 July 2009, the claim must be made not later than 31 July 2011 as indicated in explanatory note 8.

If brought forward losses are to be set against gains, a claim must be made under s 16(2A). Individuals will normally claim relief in their tax returns, with an overall time limit for the claim of five years from 31 January following the end of the tax year. The time limit for companies is six years after the end of the accounting period (four years from 1 April 2010). For both capital gains tax and corporation tax, losses arising after the introduction of self-assessment (ie from 1996/97 for individuals and for accounting periods ending after 30 June 1999 for companies) will be regarded as set off before earlier losses (FA 1995 s 113(2)). This may be particularly relevant in relation to pre 1996/97 losses on transactions with connected persons, because if there was a gain on a later transaction with that person, that gain, together with other gains of the same tax year, would be eligible to be relieved by losses arising in and after 1996/97 before the earlier loss on the disposal to the connected person could be used against it.

See Example 77 explanatory notes 12 to 14 for comments on revisions to earlier returns following the Court of Appeal's decision in *Mansworth v Jelley* and HMRC's responses to it.

Where a claim has been made under FA 1991 s 72 to treat an *income* loss as a capital loss, thereby reducing capital gains (see Example 29 explanatory note 1(e)), and a later claim, such as rollover relief, reduces the gains against which the loss was set, the deemed capital loss that thereby becomes unrelieved is carried forward to set against later gains, but cannot be relieved in any tax year after that in which the trade ceases (s 72(6)). Where such unrelieved losses occur, therefore, they must be separately identified in the amount of capital losses carried forward.

Question

Convey commenced to practise on 1 May 1977.

In 1981 he took Sing into partnership, the balance sheet immediately after the admission being:

Capital accounts:		£	Fixed assets:		£
Convey	10,000		Premises – at cost		7,500
Sing	4,000	14,000			
Current liabilities:			Current assets:		
Creditors	2,000		Work in progress	4,500	
Bank overdraft	4,000	6,000	Debtors	8,000	12,500
		20,000			20,000

It was agreed that the premises, which had been acquired by Convey some time earlier, be vested in both partners, that the profit sharing ratio be two-thirds to Convey and one-third to Sing, and that they should contribute capital as agreed from time to time.

No payments or adjustments were made for goodwill or increase in value of premises on the admission of Sing, although it was acknowledged at that time that should Convey have sought a payment from Sing, the premises were worth £25,000 and the goodwill £10,000.

In April 1993 it was decided to introduce goodwill into the accounts and a value of £75,000 was agreed. The book value of the premises was not disturbed. The value of goodwill on 31 March 1982 is agreed at £30,000, the value of the premises on that day being £20,000.

From 30 April 1994 the profit sharing ratio was altered to give equal shares to Convey and Sing. Although no accounting adjustments were made the partners acknowledged that the premises were currently worth £97,500, and the goodwill £99,000.

In anticipation of the retirement of Convey, a longstanding employee, Dance, was admitted to the partnership from 1 May 2005 as an equal partner. It was agreed that at that stage no payment or accounting adjustments should be made for goodwill and premises.

Convey retired from the business on 30 April 2009, which was his 68th birthday.

Sing and Dance remained as equal partners.

It was agreed that the terms of Convey's retirement should reflect an appropriate amount for his share in the premises and goodwill, the values of which assets were acknowledged as being £420,000 each, the accounts however still showing the premises as having cost £7,500, with £75,000 included for goodwill on the basis of the 1993 valuation, the values in the accounts not having been disturbed.

The profits of the firm have generally increased over time and the relevant tax adjusted profits have been:

		£
Year ended 30 April	1997 (after capital allowances of £20,000)	150,000
	1998 (after capital allowances of £22,000)	168,000
	2003 (after capital allowances of £18,000)	140,000
	2004 (after capital allowances of £25,000)	171,000
	2005 (after capital allowances of £33,000)	130,000
	2006 (after capital allowances of £20,000)	202,000
	2007 (after capital allowances of £30,000)	255,000
	2008 (after capital allowances of £20,000)	280,000
	2009 (after capital allowances of £50,000)	450,000

The retail prices index for the relevant months was March 1982 79.44, April 1993 140.6, April 1994 144.2, April 1998 162.6.

The partners have made general 31 March 1982 rebasing elections in respect of partnership chargeable assets.

Show the taxation implications arising from the above assuming that Convey, on his retirement, in order to reflect the full value of the premises and goodwill, received in addition to the balance on his capital account:

(a)   £280,000 cash, or

(b)   an annuity of £46,000 per annum (having an estimated capital value of £280,000) in consideration of his past services in the partnership, or

(c)   a reduced annuity of £34,500 per annum plus a lump sum of £70,000.

Answer

Capital gains liabilities

    (i)   1981 Admission of Sing   No chargeable gains.

    (ii)   1993 Revaluation of goodwill   See explanatory notes 2 and 4.

(iii)   1994/95 Change in profit sharing ratio on 30 April 1994

Convey disposes of a one-sixth share to Sing.

The property has not been revalued and is therefore at a no loss/no gain value (Sing's cost becomes one-half of the 31.3.82 market value).

The share of goodwill is deemed to be disposed of at the revaluation figure from 1993, because two-thirds of that will have been credited to Convey's capital account. Before the change Convey's share of the 31.3.82 market value is £20,000 and Sing's £10,000. The gain on the disposal by Convey is as follows:

	£
Proceeds of one-sixth share: 75,000/6	12,500
MV 31.3.82: 30,000/6	(5,000)
Indexation: Mar 82–Apr 94 ($\dfrac{144.2-79.44}{79.44}$) = 81.5%	(4,075)
Chargeable gain	3,425

This would have been covered by retirement relief of £3,425 in 1994/95.

Convey's base cost of goodwill is reduced to £15,000 and Sing's base cost of £10,000 is increased by £12,500 incurred in April 1994.

(iv)   2005/06 – Admission of Dance on 1 May 2005

On the admission of Dance on 1 May 2005 Convey and Sing each dispose of a one-sixth share of goodwill and premises to him. The disposal of the premises takes place on a no gain/no loss basis, since there has been no earlier revaluation and no payment by Dance to the partners. Because of the earlier revaluation of goodwill, each of Convey and Sing has deemed disposal proceeds of £12,500, being amounts in their capital accounts not now represented by their share in goodwill.

Their capital gains indexed base costs of their current shares of the assets are as follows:

	Goodwill – Convey £	Goodwill – Sing £	Premises – each £
31.3.82 MV	15,000	10,000	10,000
Indexation to April 1998 ($\frac{162.6-79.44}{79.44}$) = 104.7%	15,705	10,470	10,470
April 1994		12,500	
Indexation to April 1998 ($\frac{162.6-144.2}{144.2}$) = 12.8%		1,600	
	30,705	34,570	20,470
One third of a half share:	10,235	11,523	6,823
Their deemed disposal proceeds are	12,500	12,500	6,823
Capital gains	2,265	977	–

The gains shown would be reduced by business asset taper relief.

After the transaction, the partners' capital gains base costs (excluding indexation for Convey and Sing) are as follows:

			Goodwill £		Premises £
Convey	(March 1982)	(15,000 – 5,000)	10,000	(10,000 – 3,333)	6,667
Sing	(March 1982)	(10,000 – 3,333)	6,667	(10,000 – 3,333)	6,667
	(April 1994)	(12,500 – 4,167)	8,333		
Dance	(May 2005)	(12,500 + 12,500)	25,000	(6,823 + 6,823)	13,646

On disposals after 5 April 2008, no indexation allowance would be available to the partners, but as far as disposals by Dance are concerned, the indexation allowance within his base cost for the premises will need to be identified in the event of a disposal at a loss (see explanatory note 6).

(v)   2009/10 – Retirement of Convey on 30 April 2009

(a)   **Cash settlement**

	Goodwill £	Premises £
(Cash being split pro rata to the agreed values since balance sheet values are not disturbed)		
Base cost for capital gains tax (see (iv))	10,000	6,667
Disposal proceeds	140,000	140,000
Gains	130,000	133,333
Total gains on goodwill and premises		263,333
Less: entrepreneur's relief 4/9 (see explanatory note 9)		(117,037)
Chargeable gain before annual exemption		146,296

The capital gains tax base costs of goodwill and premises for Sing and Dance will each be increased by £70,000 (ie £70,000 on each of two assets for each of two partners, total £280,000), being the amount paid to Convey to acquire his share.

(b) Annuity

	Goodwill £	Premises £
Base cost for capital gains tax plus indexation allowance as in (a)	10,000	6,667
Deemed disposal proceeds (see explanatory notes 4 and 6)	10,000	6,667
No gain no loss	–	–

The capital gains tax base costs of goodwill and premises for each of Sing and Dance will be increased by half (ie their share) of £10,000 and £6,667 respectively.

The annuity itself is not chargeable to capital gains tax (see explanatory note 10) but it will be assessed to income tax in the hands of Convey, and allowed as a charge against income to Sing and Dance, on which they will obtain relief at their marginal rate of tax (see under 'Income tax implications of retirement of Convey' note (b) below).

(c) Annuity plus lump sum

	Goodwill £	Premises £
Base cost for capital gains tax as in (a)	10,000	6,667
Disposal proceeds (split pro rata)	35,000	35,000
Gains	25,000	28,333
Less: entrepreneur's relief (4/9)	(11,111)	(12,592)
Chargeable gains	13,889	15,741

The capital gains tax base costs of premises and goodwill for each of Sing and Dance will be increased by half (ie their share) of £35,000 in each case.

Income tax implications of retirement of Convey

(a) The retirement of Convey on 30 April 2009 will not affect the calculation of the taxable profits of Sing and Dance. The amount assessable on Convey is his share of the profits (net of capital allowances) for the year ended 30 April 2009 less overlap relief for the period 1 May 1996 to 5 April 1997 (calculated on profits *before* capital allowances), ie:

1/3 × (500,000 – CAs 50,000 = 450,000)	150,000
Less: 340/365 × (1/2 × (150,000 + 20,000))	79,178
	£70,822

(b) The receipt of the annuity of £46,000 per annum would be taxable as pension income in the hands of Convey from 2009/10 onwards. The payment of £46,000 per annum is a charge on income for Sing and Dance, and is paid net of basic rate tax, so it is disallowed in computing trading profits. The gross amount paid in the *tax year* (not the accounting period) must be shown in the annual partnership statement, divided between the partners in the way profits are shared in the tax year. Each partner will show his share in his own personal tax return, and relief at the higher rate, if appropriate, would be given in calculating the tax payable (see explanatory note 13).

(c) The annuity of £34,500 would be treated in the same way as under (b) above.

Explanatory Notes

Partnership capital gains

1.   The rules relating to partnership capital gains are contained in TCGA 1992 ss 59 and 286(4), supplemented by a Revenue Statement of Practice originally issued on 17 January 1975 (D12). The statement has been updated, most recently in August 2003. The latest version makes clear that the statement generally applies to the gains of limited liability partnerships (see explanatory note 15).

The position is very complex and there are areas where the approach to be taken is not clear. This is particularly so in relation to the integration of the 31 March 1982 indexation provisions with the 1975 statement. It is considered that the approach taken in this example reflects the views expressed in the practice statements.

Statement of Practice D12 has been supplemented by the issue of Revenue & Customs Brief 03/08 which deals with the application of capital gains tax to the contribution of an asset to a partnership by one partner, which is intended as a capital contribution. While SP D12 had been applied in these situations, that approach is now considered to be erroneous, and now such transactions are treated as a disposal of a fractional share of the asset in return for proceeds equal to the credit on the capital account or, if the partner is connected with the remaining partners, market value.

2.   Any charge to capital gains tax arises in the hands of each individual partner, not the partnership, each partner being deemed to own a proportionate part of the partnership's chargeable assets, being his share under the partnership agreement. The amount of the partner's capital/current account is irrelevant and it is helpful in understanding the capital gains tax aspects of partnerships to remember that a partner's capital/current account arises in one of three ways:

(i)   Cash (or other assets) introduced

(ii)   Profits are retained

(iii)   Assets are revalued, the capital account being credited with the partner's share of the surplus (or debited with his share of the deficit).

If capital is withdrawn, it will comprise a mixture of those three items.

Clearly there is no capital gains tax on withdrawals up to the amount introduced, nor on the withdrawal of retained profits. If, however, amounts are realised (as distinct from the capital account becoming overdrawn) in excess of these two items, they must reflect an upward revaluation of assets or, by implication, a payment for goodwill.

In order for capital gains tax to arise there must be a disposal, and a mere revaluation with a credit to the partners' capital accounts in the profit sharing ratio does not constitute a disposal. A subsequent withdrawal of the capital account on retirement, however, would do so, the liability on revaluation then crystallising. It will also crystallise on the admission of a new partner or a change in profit sharing ratio, since the capital/current account of the partner whose share is being reduced then includes an amount over and above the value of his new share in the chargeable asset concerned – tantamount to his having made a disposal, his capital account containing the proceeds.

3.   In relation to partnership assets a partner is not connected with his fellow partners if the transaction is a bona fide commercial arrangement. This means that unless the partners are otherwise connected, eg father and son (and even then if the same transaction could be expected to have been made were they not so connected), HMRC will accept whatever valuation is placed upon a transaction by the partners and will not substitute market value. In the same way no charge to inheritance tax will arise. Furthermore it renders the holdover relief for business gifts in TCGA 1992 s 165 unnecessary in these situations.

4.   Therefore, on the admission of a partner or a change in profit sharing ratio, no charge to capital gains tax will arise unless there is or has been a revaluation of assets with a corresponding adjustment

in the capital/current accounts, or payment is made for assets. The reason is that on the admission of a partner, any cash he pays into the partnership will not constitute a disposal for capital gains tax purposes on the part of the existing partners if it is credited to the incoming partner's capital account; and unless he pays the existing partners for a share in the goodwill (or other chargeable assets) it will be treated as having been disposed of by the existing partners to the incoming partner for a consideration of such amount that neither chargeable gain nor allowable loss arises for capital gains purposes, the future ownership of each chargeable asset then being in the future capital profit sharing ratio.

Bringing goodwill into the accounts

5.   On the introduction of goodwill into the accounts in 1993 the accounting entries will have been:

	Goodwill *(Asset Account)*	*Capital Accounts* *Convey (2/3rds)*	*Sing (1/3rd)*
Valuation	£75,000	£50,000	£25,000

Upon the profit sharing ratio being altered in 1994 this is tantamount to saying that Convey has disposed of (2/3rds − 1/2 =) 1/6th of the goodwill to Sing. But his capital account still contains the credit of £50,000, so this is equivalent to his having realised £12,500 of chargeable gains – that is £50,000 credited to capital account less £37,500 which is the value of his half share of the goodwill after the change in profit sharing ratio.

The same applies on the introduction of Dance, this time both Convey and Sing making disposals. The calculations are as follows:

	Convey *£*	*Sing* *£*	*Dance* *£*
Amount originally credited to capital account in 1993	50,000	25,000	–
At 30 April 1994			
Disposal on change in profit sharing ratio	(12,500)		
Deemed cost of acquisition for Sing		12,500	
	37,500	37,500	
At 1 May 2005			
Deemed cost of acquisition for Dance			25,000
Disposal by Convey and Sing (since these amounts remain in their capital accounts)	(12,500)	(12,500)	
New share of goodwill in accounts is deemed to be	25,000	25,000	25,000

Effect of rebasing to 31 March 1982 values

6.   Following the rebasing provisions of FA 1988, as applied to partners by SP1/89, for disposals on and after 6 April 1988 partners are able to take advantage of using 31 March 1982 value in computing gains. This effectively means that on 6 April 1988 they are deemed to hold their then shares of partnership assets acquired before 31 March 1982 at either original cost or 31 March 1982 value, whichever shows the lower gain or loss on a disposal, or, as with Convey and Sing, where a general rebasing election has been made, at 31 March 1982 value in any event. Where any no gain no loss disposals (see explanatory note 4) take place on or after 6 April 1988 they will be deemed to be for such consideration as gives a nil result after taking any available indexation allowance into account.

If no gain no loss changes in partnership sharing ratios occurred between 6 April 1985 and 5 April 1988 inclusive, the no gain no loss provisions operated *before* taking indexation allowance into account, so that allowable losses would have been created on such changes. In these circumstances, indexation allowance on disposals on and after 6 April 1988, although computed on 31 March 1982 value if appropriate, is calculated from the date when the indexation allowance was given on the no gain no loss disposal.

For disposals on or after 30 November 1993, indexation allowance cannot be used to create or increase a loss, but can be used to reduce a profit (to nil if appropriate). Accordingly the no gain no loss provisions still apply after taking any available indexation allowance into account, but the base value carried forward must be divided into cost and indexation allowance and in so far as a disposal results in a loss, indexation allowance will be reduced by the amount of loss. Therefore a loss can only arise based upon cost (including indexation allowance for any pre 30 November 1993 transactions) or market value on 31 March 1982 as appropriate.

The modernisation of capital gains tax which took place for disposals on or after 6 April 2008 abolished the cost option on all assets owned since before March 1982, and all such assets are now treated as held at 31 March 1982 market value, whether an election was made or not. This will affect any subsequent disposal of goodwill by Convey and Sing.

7.   Indexation allowance for individuals is no longer available for disposals after 5 April 2008, however, the provisions described above affect the earlier disposals in the Example, and thus affect the cost of assets transferred between the partners. No indexation allowance can apply in respect of any disposals after 5 April 2008, whatever the result.

Retirement relief

8.   Retirement relief is not available for disposals after 5 April 2003. Covey would have enjoyed small amounts of relief on his disposal in 1994, because he was already over 50 at those times, but the full disposal of his interest will not qualify.

Entrepreneur's relief

9.   Relief for entrepreneurs replaces business asset taper relief on the disposal in 2009, taper relief having been abolished for disposals on or after 6 April 2008. The relief is available in respect of the disposal of a partners' share in his business, and thus will apply to Convey's sale. The relief provides a reduction of 4/9 in the chargeable gain, leaving 5/9 in charge. This, when taxed at the standard CGT rate of 18% results in a net 10% tax charge, replicating the benefit of 75% business asset taper relief for 40% taxpayers. The maximum amount of gain which can attract relief is £1 million in the disposer's lifetime.

Annuity to retiring partner

10.   Where an annuity is paid on the retirement of a partner by reason of age or ill health, then capital gains tax is not chargeable on the capitalised value provided the payment is in reasonable recognition of past service and is not a lump sum equivalent or a purchased life annuity.

A reasonable amount is regarded as being the appropriate fraction of the retiring partner's average taxable profits *before* capital allowances or charges of the best three of the last seven tax years in which the partner was required to devote substantially the whole of his time to acting as a partner. The appropriate fraction depends on the complete years of service to the partnership (or a predecessor firm prior to merger) as follows:

Complete years	Fraction
1–5	1/60 per year
6	8/60
7	16/60
8	24/60
9	32/60
10	2/3*

Convey's best three out of the last seven shares of profit in this example are as follows (his 2008/09 share being 1/3 × (450,000 + 50,000) = 166,667 less overlap relief 79,178 = £87,489):

2003/04	½ × £196,000	98,000
2007/08	⅓ × £285,000	95,000
2008/09	⅓ × £300,000	100,000
		£291,000

Average profits 1/3 × £291,000 = £97,000

Maximum annuity which can be disregarded in computing capital gains (SP D12)

* 2/3 × £97,000 = £64,667.

Lump sums and purchased annuities

11. Where a lump sum is paid (or an annuity is *purchased* in addition to the provision of an annuity from the partnership) the whole of the capitalised value of the *annuity from the partnership* plus the lump sum is treated as a payment for chargeable assets (but the capitalised value of the annuity from the partnership does not increase the capital gains tax base cost of those partners paying the annuity – they are after all getting relief for income tax at their marginal rates on such payments). If, however, the sum of the annuity from the partnership plus 1/9th of the lump sum or purchased annuity amounts to less than the 'reasonable amount' defined in note 9, the capitalised value of the annuity from the partnership is not chargeable to capital gains tax, but the lump sum or cost of the purchased annuity remains so (SP 1/79). Note that for income tax purposes a purchased annuity is treated as savings income (ITA 2007 s 18(3)(b)) but a partnership annuity is not.

12. The 'reasonable amount' per note 9 is £64,667. This is compared with:

Scheme (b)	Annuity	£46,000

Scheme (c)	Annuity	34,500
	1/9th × £70,000	7,778
		£42,278

Since in each case the amount is less than £64,667 the capitalised value of the annuity is not chargeable to capital gains tax, but the lump sum in (c) represents part of the disposal proceeds and is brought into the capital gains tax computation as indicated at (v)(c).

Tax position of partners paying the annuity

13. Partnership annuities are charges on income as far as the paying partners are concerned and they are not deductible from trading profits. They are allocated to partners in profit sharing ratios, and the amount deductible from income is the amount paid in the tax year. Purchased annuities must be paid subject to PAYE, but PAYE does not apply to annuities paid by the partnership.

14. If the partners pay a 'reasonable annuity' and continue to do so, there is no gain for the retiring partner, and symmetrical income tax treatment for those paying and receiving. If, instead, the other partners purchase an annuity on the date of retirement, then there will be a gain for the retiring partner by reference to the purchase price and the cost will be added to the other partners' base costs. There is a disadvantage if the partners commence to pay an annuity and then replace it at a later date by buying an annuity. It is likely that the right to receive the annuity is a chargeable asset, and the disposal of it in consideration for the amount paid for the purchased life annuity would give rise to a capital gains tax charge (with minimal taper relief); but the other partners would not at that time acquire any asset, so the cost to them would obtain no tax relief at all.

Limited liability partnerships (LLPs)

15.   LLPs can be formed under the Limited Liability Partnerships Act 2000. For the detailed provisions see Example 27 part (b). As indicated in that example, if an LLP goes into formal liquidation it will be treated as a company from that time, and the partners' shares in the LLP will then be chargeable assets in their own right.

The 2003 version of SP D12 makes it clear that a LLP will be treated for CGT purposes as a 'normal' partnership (that is the partners will be assessed on their shares of the underlying assets and the LLP will be 'transparent') as long as the LLP is within TCGA 1992 s 59A(1) (carrying on a trade or business and not in liquidation).

Goodwill

16.   It is common for partners gradually to increase their share of partnership goodwill over a number of years. It would be open for HMRC to argue that 'shares of goodwill' are 'fungible assets' subject to the share identification rules in TCGA 1992 s 104(3). The 2003 version of SP D12 states that HMRC will not take this view, but will regard a share of partnership goodwill as a single asset that is successively enhanced. This makes the computations much easier.

Question

(A)   Fred Stone owns the following properties in the UK which he lets.

Shop 1	A butcher's shop, the annual rental of which is £13,200 under a 7-year lease expiring on 29 September 2009 and the lease was renewed on that date at £18,800 per annum for 7 years.
Shop 2	A shop selling textiles, the annual rental of which is £12,000 under a 7-year lease expiring on 25 March 2011. The quarter's rent due on 25 March 2009 was not paid until 30 April 2010.
Shop 3	A shop selling light fittings. This was let to a relative of Mr Stone at an annual rental of £2,400 when a commercial rent would have been £10,000. Mr Stone's relative is responsible for all outgoings, with the exception of insurance amounting to £2,500.
Shop 4	This shop had been let at an annual rental of £14,000 until 23 June 2009 when the tenant, who had been selling clothing, informed Mr Stone that he could not afford to pay the rent and vacated the premises forthwith. Mr Stone agreed through his agent to re-let the premises from 25 March 2010 to a new tenant who would be selling pottery imported from Scandinavia. The new rental was £16,000 per annum for 10 years and Mr Stone also received a premium of £6,000 from the incoming tenant on 25 March 2010.

Mr Stone had borrowed money to buy Shops 1, 2 and 4 and the interest payable for 2009/10 was £8,200.

House 1	A furnished house let on weekly tenancies. The house had been purchased in November 2002 with the aid of a bank loan of £62,500. Interest had been paid for 2008/09 amounting to £5,000. The property was let throughout 2009/10. The all-inclusive weekly rental was £160.
House 2	A furnished house also let on weekly tenancies. During 2009/10 the property was let for 43 weeks. The all-inclusive weekly rental was £120.

The houses are not holiday accommodation and are regularly let to one tenant for lengthy periods. House 2 had been empty and available for letting during the weeks when it was not let. Council tax had been paid by the tenants, apart from the period when House 2 was not let, when the tax was paid by Fred Stone. Wear and tear of furniture is claimed at 10% of the gross rents, less water supply charges.

On 31 December 2009, Fred received £8,000 from Super Alpha REIT plc, as a property income distribution.

With the exception of the houses the rents are due in advance on the normal English quarter days: 25 March, 24 June, 29 September and 25 December. Fred makes up his rental accounts to 5 April annually. Details of expenditure for the year ended 5 April 2010, as adjusted for amounts in arrears and advance, were as follows:

Insurance	
Buildings	3,122
Contents	216
Ground rent	610
Repairs and decorating (see notes)	7,145
Accountancy	370
Newspaper advertising	134
Gardeners' wages	380
Water supply charges (house 1 £230, house 2 £310)	540
Council tax	60
	£12,577

Mr Stone employs agents to collect the rents, except that of Shop 3. He pays them 10% of the amount collected (not applicable to the premium). Total rent collected in 2008/09 was £49,216.

Notes on repairs

1. £3,854 was spent on putting Shop 4 into proper condition after the previous tenant had vacated it.

2. £1,050 was spent on dry-rot remedial treatment to House 1. The dry-rot was present in the house when Mr Stone purchased it in November 2003.

3. £1,428 was spent on re-tiling the roof of House 2.

4. All the expenditure on the houses in respect of repairs and decorating relates to the property and not the furniture.

In 2007/08 Mr Stone gave £20,000 to his son Donald as part payment for the son's flat, Donald borrowing a further £80,000. The net interest in 2009/10 was £3,200. To help with expenses, Donald let a furnished room in the flat to a friend and received rent of £60 a week throughout the year. He did not provide any other services. Donald paid for the buildings and contents insurance on the flat amounting to £150, and spent £250 on repairs during 2009/10. He also paid a service charge of £300, water supply charges of £110 and council tax of £400 (his friend making a contribution of £100 to the council tax).

(a)   Calculate Fred Stone's net rental income for tax purposes for 2009/10.

(b)   (i)   State Donald's position in 2009/10 in relation to his rents and expenses.

     (ii)   Indicate what the position would be if Donald took up a job where he was required to live on the premises, and he let the whole flat for an annual rent of £5,500 from 6 April 2010.

(B)   Mrs Morley is a married woman aged 47, whose husband is the director and owner of a prosperous engineering company with profits averaging £300,000 per year. She has a pensionable salary of £30,000 per annum. Her only other source of income is rent from two houses that she purchased on 1 January 1995. One is in London and has been let furnished at a commercial rent continuously since purchase. The other is a furnished holiday house in Suffolk used partly by the family and partly for holiday letting on commercial terms. The house in Suffolk cost £100,000 and there has been no major improvement since, but on 31 October 2008 loft insulation was installed in both houses, at a cost of £1,200 each. Both properties were purchased with the assistance of bank loans, the interest paid in the year ended 5 April 2009 being £3,739 on the loan for the London house and £4,630 on the loan for the Suffolk house.

The Morleys are considering buying a house in Ruritania, which will principally be let as holiday accommodation, but used by the family in the skiing season. The Ruritanian lawyer has advised that this should be purchased through a company formed for the purpose, and they ask your advice as they are concerned about possible benefit in kind charges.

The Suffolk house has been occupied as follows:

		Year ended 2008	5 April 2009
Number of weeks –	let	7	20
	occupied by family	20	20
	empty, available for letting	25	12
		52	52

The income and expenditure for each property for the year ended 5 April 2009, adjusted for accruals and prepayments, was as follows:

		London £	*Suffolk* £
Income –	rent receivable	16,735	7,000
Expenditure –	rates		1,300
	water supply charges	730	520
	insurance	485	364
	cleaning on change of occupants	–	996
	replacement of furniture	390	777
	repairs and decorations	940	1,810
	advertising for lettings	–	263

An allowance of 10% of rent (less rates and water) has been agreed for each property to cover depreciation of furniture.

(a) Calculate Mrs Morley's property income for 2008/09.

(b) State the position relating to pension contributions on the income from the Suffolk house.

(c) Mrs Morley is contemplating the possible sale of the Suffolk house in the summer of 2009, and expects the sale proceeds to be around £485,000 after selling expenses.

   Calculate the amount upon which capital gains tax would be payable if the property was sold at the estimated price on 1 June 2009, that the average period of holiday lettings and availability for letting was 3/5ths, and that Mrs Morley had no other capital transactions in 2009/10 and did not have any brought forward capital losses. Advise Mrs Morley about the implications of sale during 2009/10.

(d) Suggest any tax planning issues that may be relevant in relation to the Suffolk house in 2009/10.

(e) Prepare notes for a response to the request for advice on the foreign letting property.

Answer

(A) Fred Stone

(a) Fred Stone's UK property income assessment 2009/10

Rental income

		£
Shop 1		
6.4.09 – 28.9.09 (176 days) @ £13,200 pa		6,365
29.9.09 – 5.4.10 (189 days) @ £18,800 pa		9,735
Shop 2		12,000
Shop 3		2,400
Shop 4		
6.4.09 – 23.6.09 (79 days) @ £14,000 pa		3,030
25.3.10 – 5.4.10 (12 days) @ £16,000 pa		526
Premium *		4,920
House 1 (160 × 52)		8,320
House 2 (120 × 43)		5,160
		52,456

Expenditure

Interest re Shops 1, 2, 4 and House 1 (8,200 + 5,000)		13,200	
Other expenditure as listed	12,577		
Less: Shop 3 excess of insurance paid over rent received	100	12,477	
Agent's commission – 10% of rent collected £49,216		4,922	
Wear and tear of furniture **		1,294	(31,893)
Fred Stone's property business			20,563
Super Alpha REIT property business income (see note 19)			10,000
Total property income			30,563

*	The part of the premium to be taken as additional rent is:		
	Premium		6,000
	Less 2% × (10 – 1) = 18%		1,080
			£4,920

		House 1	House 2
**	The wear and tear allowance is calculated as follows:		
	Total rent	8,320	5,160
	Less: water supply charges	230	310
		£8,090	£4,850
	10% thereof	£809	£485

(b) Donald

(i) Donald's position in 2008/09

Donald is receiving rent of 52 × £60 = £3,120 and has incurred expenses of (150 + 250 + 300 + 110 + 300 =) £1,110 plus £3,200 interest = £4,310, part of which relates to his own occupation.

Under the 'rent-a-room' relief provisions, he is exempt from tax on the rents, since they do not exceed £4,250. He will not, of course, obtain any additional relief for the expenses.

(ii)

If Donald let the whole property, then he would be taxed on the rental income of £5,500 less allowable expenses, including interest.

Rent-a-room relief cannot be claimed unless the property is the claimant's main residence at some time in the letting period, so the relief would not be available from 6 April 2010. (Had it been, Donald could have elected to pay tax on the excess of the rent over the exempt £4,250, ie on £1,250, if this was more beneficial than the normal UK property income treatment – see explanatory note 14.)

(B) Mrs Morley

(a) Computation of Mrs Morley's UK property income for 2008/09

	London House			*Suffolk House*	
Rent receivable		16,735			7,000
Less: Rates	–		(32/52)	800	
Water supply charges	730		(32/52)	320	
Insurance	485		(32/52)	224	
Cleaning on change of occupants	–			996	
Repairs and decorations	940		(32/52)	1,114	
Advertising for lettings	–			263	
Loft insulation	1,200*	See expl. 28			
10% wear and tear allowance					
On (16,735 – 730)	1,601				
On (7,000 – 1,120)				588	
Interest paid	3,739	8,695	(32/52 × £4,630)	2,850	7,155
		8,040			(155)
Total assessable income					7,885

(b) Personal pension contributions

The income from furnished holiday lettings in the UK is treated as trading income (ITA 2007 s 127) until the end of 2009/10. After that the special treatment of furnished holiday lettings will be abolished in relation to all taxes.

The limit on contributions into pension schemes is 100% of earnings (or £3,600 if lower). In computing earnings the loss on the Suffolk house would be set against other UK property income first and would only reduce the total earnings available if the loss exceeded the profit on the London property.

(c) Amount potentially liable to capital gains tax if Suffolk house is sold on 1 June 2009

	£
Expected sale proceeds after expenses of selling	485,000
Cost on 1 January 1995	100,000
Gain	385,000

of which ⅖ = £154,000 relates to the private use proportion
and ⅗ = £231,000 relates to the holiday letting.

The gain of £154,000 relating to the private proportion would be a chargeable gain, since the property is not Mr and Mrs Morley's main residence.

The gain of £231,000 relating to the holiday letting would be reduced by entrepreneur's relief of 4/9, providing the lettings proportion of 3/5ths applies to the period to the date of disposal (see explanatory note 25), and assuming that Mrs Morley has therefore ceased trading and is selling the asset used in the trade following the cessation, leaving a chargeable gain of £128,333. All of the qualifying conditions for furnished holiday letting treatment would need to be met for at least twelve months leading up to the disposal, so that the necessary condition applying to entrepreneur's relief can be met; this must be confirmed before Mrs Morley commences marketing the property. If a replacement holiday property were acquired within three years after the disposal, the gain could be rolled over and treated as reducing the capital gains tax cost of the holiday let proportion of that property, but in view of the abolition of favourable treatment for furnished holiday lettings there is little time to re-invest and as a subsequent sale would not attract entrepreneur's relief Mrs Morley would be better to re-invest in alternative business property qualifying for roll over relief if she wishes to shelter the gain in this way.

If rollover relief was not available or was not claimed, the amount chargeable to capital gains tax would therefore be £154,000 + £128,333 = £282,333 less Mrs Morley's annual capital gains tax exemption for 2009/10.

(d) **Advice regarding tax planning in relation to the Suffolk home**

The abolition of the favourable treatment of furnished holiday letting activities from 6 April 2010 presents the possibility of tax planning in advance of the change. Mrs Morley might consider the following areas:

1. Capital gains tax

   The planned sale during the summer of 2009 presents Mrs Morley with the ideal opportunity to capitalise on entrepreneur's relief while it remains applicable to the sale. After 5 April 2010 no relief will be available and the gain would be fully chargeable, increasing the amount taxable by £102,667. Before making a final decision on this point, the adviser will need to consider the use of the property in the twelve months leading up to the eventual sale or the cessation of the trade, to ensure that the furnished holiday letting conditions have been met throughout that period.

   If Mrs Morley decided to retain the holiday letting activity it might be worth considering transferring the activity to a limited company to secure the relief. However, there would be a number of complications in that course of action, including the need to raise finance in the limited company to repay the private borrowings, and the potential impact of stamp duty land tax. She would also be liable to tax on a benefit-in-kind in relation to the private occupation of the house, unless she paid market rent for any time the family spent there. The benefit could be assessed in relation to the period the house was available to the family, rather than the period they actually spent there. In summary, in Mrs Morley's case and with the possible disposal in any event, transfer to a limited company would not be a viable alternative.

   The impact of the change in relation to roll over relief has been dealt with in part (c) above.

2. Capital allowances

   After 2009/10 no capital allowances will be due on furniture and equipment in the house. Mrs Morley has the potential availability of £50,000 in AIA during 2009/10 and might consider replacing any equipment or carpets and furniture as appropriate before the end of the year, were she to decide to retain the property. It is not clear what will happen to the tax written down value of capital assets on the cessation of the furnished holiday letting regime, but the expenditure would enable her to set any resulting losses against her income for 2009/10. Should she decide to retain the property she should be advised that a balancing charge may arise at the end of the tax year.

3.   Treatment of losses

Mrs Morley may set any losses arising on the letting activity against other income for the last time in 2009/10. In consequence, if she intends to retain the property she might consider carrying out any repair or redecoration that would be due in the next few years during 2009/10 to secure the deduction from profits and increasing any loss (together with capital allowance claims). She can then set the resulting loss against other income in 2009/10, and also in 2008/09 if she desires. The extended loss provisions in FA 2009 Sch 6 also apply for 2008/09 and 2009/10 losses, but as the relief is given only against profits of the same trade, relief against other income may be preferable.

(e)   **Notes for response on Ruritanian holiday property**

-    We are unable to advise on foreign tax matters. It is essential that these are dealt with by a competent professional trained in the tax law of the jurisdiction concerned. We can obtain a specialist opinion at additional cost if requested.

-    The tax treatment of the property will be determined by the Double Tax Treaty (if any) – see Example 36. However, it is likely that the income will be taxable in both countries, with the result that tax will be paid at the higher of the two rates. If Ruritanian tax is higher than UK tax, then no refund will be available in the UK; if Ruritanian tax is lower than UK tax, then there will be additional UK tax to pay.

-    If Ruritania is in the European Economic Area (EEA), the purchase of the property as a furnished holiday letting activity in private hands (as opposed to through a limited company) would attract favourable tax treatment during 2009/10 only. Budget 2009 announced that the favourable treatment of furnished holiday lettings should be available to properties outside the UK in the EEA, and that retrospective claims would be possible. However, as the intended purchase is during 2009/10, the special tax treatment would be available for that year only. To secure FHL treatment Mrs Morley would need to meet the FHL conditions by the anniversary of purchase, even where this is after 5 April 2010. This would allow losses for 2009/10 to be set against other income, and would also permit capital allowance claims for furniture and equipment in the property (although see part (d) above regarding written down value as at 5 April 2010). See also explanatory note 1.

-    Finance Act 2008 exempts individuals owning a property through a company from benefits in kind charges, however long they have owned the company, subject to conditions. The conditions are:

    –   that the property is owned by a company owned by individuals;

    –   the company's only activities are incidental to its ownership of the property;

    –   the property is the company's only or main asset;

    –   the property must not be funded, directly or indirectly, by a connected company.

    The property must therefore not be funded by Mr Morley's company. The matter of what activities are planned for the holiday property, and to what extent they are merely incidental to ownership, must be resolved. It is however probable that it will be possible to escape the benefits in kind charge. Note that the transfer of the Suffolk home to a limited company described in part (d) above is unlikely to qualify for exemption if the company carries on a businesses of holiday letting.

    However, for the purpose of determining control of the company, spouses are associates of each other (see Example 56, explanatory notes 3 and 4), which would make the two companies associated companies. A company operating a furnished accommodation business will certainly not be considered dormant, so the small company thresholds will be halved. As a result, in the 2009 financial year, the marginal small companies' rate of 29.5% will apply on profits above £150,000. This will be 7.5% above the small companies rate, and will result in an additional £11,250 approximately of corporation tax falling due for Mr Morley's company.

Explanatory Notes

Taxation of rental income

1. The same rules broadly apply to the calculation of rental income for individuals and companies, although there are some differences. HMRC's Property Income Manual deals with the income tax treatment.

    The rules that apply to both individuals and companies are dealt with in notes 2 to 12 below. Rules that apply only for income tax are dealt with in notes 13 and 14 and rules that apply only for companies in notes 15 and 16.

UK property business rules for rental income

2. All UK rental income is treated as relating to a single 'UK property business'. This applies whether the income is from sizeable businesses or from letting a single property, and no matter whether the property is let furnished or unfurnished. The net income from UK furnished holiday lettings is, however, calculated as a separate amount and then added to other property income. The holiday lettings income broadly qualifies as trading income for the purpose of various reliefs – part (B) of the Example and explanatory notes 20 onwards deal with this. Special rules also apply under the 'rent-a-room' scheme for individuals letting rooms in their own home – see note 14.

    Those who run hotels or guest houses, or individuals who provide meals to lodgers or tenants in their own homes, are usually regarded as trading (although the 'rent-a-room' scheme may apply). HMRC considers that where let property is not the taxpayer's home, the income will rarely constitute trading income, even if managing the properties takes up virtually all of the owner's time, although where additional services are provided over and above those normally provided for let property the income from those additional services may be treated as trading income.

Calculation of rental profits

3. Under ITTOIA 2005 s 272, the profits of a UK property business are computed broadly in the same way as business profits, although the income is still unearned income rather than earned income except for furnished holiday lettings – see explanatory note 20 onwards.

    The main rule in relation to allowable expenses is that they must be 'wholly and exclusively' for the purposes of the business. This will include the expenses of travelling to and from the let properties, unless in the case of an individual the trip is partly for private purposes. Provision may be made for bad and doubtful debts. Interest payable is included in allowable expenses for individuals (subject to the wholly and exclusively rule). See note 15 for the treatment of interest for companies. Legal and professional costs of *renewing* a short lease (ie with a term of 50 years or less) are allowable, but not the costs of the first letting, unless it is for less than a year. A change of tenant will not usually affect this treatment (see Revenue's Tax Bulletin December 1996). Capital allowances may be claimed where appropriate (except for fixtures, furniture or plant for use in a dwelling house (CAA 2001 s 35(2)), for which a wear and tear allowance may be available – see note 6). The allowances for vehicles are restricted to the business proportion as for traders (see Example 20 explanatory note 16), although this restriction does not affect companies.

    Expenditure incurred in the seven years before the business started is treated as incurred on the first day of the business (ITTOIA 2005 s 57 (individuals) and CTA 2009 s 61 (companies)), except for *interest* paid by a company, which is dealt with under the loan relationships rules (see note 15).

If property is let for less than a commercial rent for personal reasons (for example, to a relative or friend), expenses relating to the property are restricted by the 'wholly and exclusively' rule, and are not allowed to the extent that they exceed the rent received, nor can the excess expenses be carried forward to a later year. In part (a) of the example, therefore, Fred cannot deduct the excess insurance premium on Shop 3 from his other rental income.

4. Rent and expenses are calculated on the 'earnings basis', ie with adjustments for amounts in arrear and in advance. For income tax purposes, HMRC will, however, accept figures based on receipts and payments for 'small' cases, ie where the gross rental income does not exceed £15,000, providing the cash basis is used consistently and does not produce a result substantially different from the earnings basis.

    The basis period is the tax year for individuals and the accounting period for companies. If individuals do not make up their UK property business accounts for the tax year, the results must be apportioned on a time basis, eg if accounts are drawn up to 30 June, the 2008/09 income would be 86/365ths of the result to 30 June 2009 and 279/365ths of the result to 30 June 2010. (In practice HMRC will accept accounts drawn up to 31 March, providing this is done consistently and does not give materially different results from the strict tax year basis.)

Repair expenditure

5. As far as repair expenditure is concerned, under commercial accounting principles, expenditure to rectify dilapidations that occurred in a previous ownership is allowable so long as the property was in a usable state when acquired (*Odeon Associated Theatres Ltd v Jones* – see Example 15 explanatory note 5). Hence Fred Stone in part (a) of the example has been allowed to deduct the cost of rectifying the dry-rot in House 1.

    Repair expenditure must be distinguished from capital expenditure on improvements, additions and extensions, which is not allowable (although such expenditure would qualify for capital allowances if the let property is an industrial or agricultural building, and see also explanatory notes 6 and 7).

Capital allowances and wear and tear allowance

6. Capital allowances are available on plant and machinery used for the maintenance, repair or management of let premises, but not on items for use in dwelling houses (CAA 2001 s 35). Under CAA 2001 s 15, qualifying expenditure is dealt with in the same way as for trades (see Example 20). It is possible that capital allowances claims may be available in respect of the fittings in the shops, although no details are given of the costs or written down value in the question. Specialist help might be appropriate in identifying the value of equipment for the purposes of capital allowances claims, particularly as some plant may now be treated as integral features.

    By concession B47, the disallowed expenditure on furniture etc in a dwelling house that is furnished to the extent that it can be occupied without additional expenditure by the tenant qualifies for a wear and tear allowance of 10% of rents. An adjustment is made to the 10% calculation to exclude from the rent any additions, if material, for payments that would normally be borne by a tenant, such as water supply charges, as shown in the example. Council tax is usually paid directly by the tenants, but where a property is multi-occupied, the landlord pays it instead (see note 10). In that event, any addition to rent to cover the tenant's share of the council tax should be excluded when making the 10% calculation. In the past some officers allowed a deduction for very short life items, such as crockery and linen, in addition to the 10% deduction. The concession now specifically states that such items are included within the 10% figure.

    In addition to the wear and tear allowance, a deduction may be claimed for the cost of replacing fixtures that are an integral part of buildings, such as baths, toilets, central heating (but excluding any 'improvement element' where the replacements are significantly better than the original items). No deduction is allowed for items a tenant would normally provide for himself in unfurnished accommodation, eg cooker, washing machine, dishwasher.

As an alternative to the 10% allowance, a renewals basis may be claimed, so that no deduction is allowed when assets are acquired but when they are replaced a deduction is given for the full replacement cost.

7.   Where maintenance and repairs of property are made unnecessary because of improvements, additions and alterations, no allowance will normally be given. However if assets are replaced with broadly the same asset a full deduction can be claimed for the replacement and only additional amounts will be capital, eg a replacement kitchen with extra storage (only the extra storage will be disallowed). However if the asset is substantially upgraded then the whole will be disallowed. HMRC will accept that replacing single glazed windows by double glazed equivalents counts as allowable repair expenditure (both for UK property and trading businesses). Generally, if the replacement is part of the 'entirety' and is like-for-like or the nearest modern equivalent the expenditure is allowed as revenue expenditure (see Tax Bulletin June 2002).

8.   Capital allowances are deducted as a business expense and are thus taken into account in arriving at the UK property business profit or loss.

Premiums on leases (ITTOIA 2005 Part 3 Chapter 4)

9.   The premium arising on the grant of a short lease (ie for 50 years or less) by a landlord, as distinct from the assignment of such a lease from one tenant to another, is partly assessable as income, whilst the remainder forms part of a capital gains computation.

That part assessable as income is treated as additional rent and is therefore available to cover expenses (as in Shop 4 in this example) (s 277(3)).

The formula given in the legislation is devised so that the longer the term of the lease, the more of the premium falls into the capital gains computation and the less is regarded as additional rent.

The premium is reduced by 2% for each complete twelve-month period of the lease except the first, in ascertaining that part to be left in as rent (s 277(4)).

Thus:

Lease for	5 yrs	10 yrs	25 yrs	40 yrs	50 yrs
Premium £ or %	100	100	100	100	100
Reduce by 2% for each year except the first (and take this part into a capital gains computation as a part disposal)	8	18	48	78	98
Include as additional rent	92	82	52	22	2

The formula for including the discounted part in a capital gains computation is dealt with in Example 100, which also deals with other aspects of the tax treatment of premiums.

Council tax and business rates

10.   Council tax on let domestic property is usually paid by the tenants, but the landlord will pay when property is in multiple occupation and for periods when, as in this example, property is empty between lettings, although various periods are exempt, such as the first six months for unfurnished property.

For property that is not domestic property, such as business premises, business rates are payable, and the payments are deductible as an expense in the normal way, subject to the rules for void periods for company landlords.

UK property let by a non-resident

11.   Where property is let by a non-resident, the rental income is computed in the same way as for a resident *individual* (ITA 2007 ss 971–972, SI 1995/2902). This applies whether the non-resident

landlord is an individual, or trustees, or a company, except that it does not apply to the rental income of a UK branch of a non-resident company. 'Non-residents' for the purpose of s 971 are those whose 'usual place of abode' is outside the UK, rather than the definition used for other purposes (as to which see Example 12 part A(i)). HMRC regards an individual as having a usual place of abode outside the UK if he is away for more than six months. Companies will not be so treated if they are UK resident for tax purposes. References to non-residents in the remainder of this note should be read accordingly.

Basic rate tax on net property income is normally deducted at source, either by a UK agent handling the let property, or by the tenant where there is no agent, and paid over to HMRC 30 days after the end of each calendar quarter, with a final settling up by the non-resident landlord. Where the tenant pays VAT on the rent, tax need only be deducted from the net of VAT amount. A tenant paying rent of £100 a week or less does not have to deduct tax unless told to do so by HMRC. Neither tenants nor agents have to deduct tax at source if the non-resident registers with the Non-Resident Landlords Scheme, whereby he agrees with HMRC's Centre for Non-Residents to complete any tax returns he receives and to include any tax due on the property income in his payments under self-assessment (ITA 2007 s 972). Non-resident landlords are required to make half-yearly payments on account unless covered by the de minimis thresholds (see Example 41). HMRC have stated that the Centre for Non-Residents will not normally issue self-assessment returns to non-resident individual landlords who have no net tax liability, although returns may still be sent occasionally to ensure that the tax position remains the same. HMRC have produced guidance on its website (see Centre for Non-Residents) covering the detailed provisions.

Overseas property lettings

12. Income from property let abroad is calculated broadly in the same way as for a UK property business (except that the rules for furnished holiday lettings do not apply, nor the income tax rules in ITTOIA 2005 ss 92–94 relating to board and lodging and travelling expenses in connection with foreign trades). In order to calculate the amount of double tax relief available, profits and losses are calculated separately for each property and then aggregated and taxed as the profits of an 'overseas property business' (ITTOIA 2005 s 268 and s 269(2) (individuals), CTA 2009 s 206 (companies)). Losses are carried forward to set against later overseas lettings profits (ICTA 1988 s 379B (individuals), ICTA 1988 s 392B (companies)).

Provisions applicable to individuals

Relief for losses

13. If losses arise, they are carried forward to set against future property income. See Example 18 part (b) for details of the relief available to individuals for excess capital allowances included in a UK property business loss.

Rent-a-room relief

14. Under the 'rent-a-room' relief provisions of ITTOIA 2005 Part 7 Chapter 1, an owner or tenant who lets furnished rooms in his home is exempt from tax on gross rent of up to £4,250 a year. This applies whether the rent would have been charged as UK property income or trading income where the services provided are such that the income would be treated as being from a trade.

The rent taken into account for the relief is the payment for the accommodation plus payments for related goods and services, such as meals, cleaning, laundry etc.

The property must have been the claimant's only or main residence at some time during the letting period in each relevant tax year. The relief cannot be claimed if part of the property is let unfurnished in the same year.

If during the basis period someone else receives rent for letting a room in the property while it is the claimant's only or main residence the available exemption is halved to £2,125. This would apply, for example, to a couple who were jointly receiving rent from tenants, or to other joint owners.

If the taxpayer has any unrelieved losses from letting the property in earlier years in which the rent-a-room relief did not apply, they may be set against any profit on other rented properties in the current year, any unrelieved amount being carried forward to set against later rental profits on other properties. If capital allowances have been claimed, no allowances are due for an exempt year, and any balancing charges arising are added to rents to see if the total is below the exempt limit. The taxpayer may elect for the exemption not to apply to a particular year, which could be to his advantage if he had losses for which he could otherwise claim relief. Such an election only affects the year for which it is claimed and must be made within one year after the 31 January following the relevant tax year. It can be withdrawn within the same period.

Where gross rents exceed £4,250, the taxpayer may either be charged on rents less expenses in the normal way, or alternatively he may elect to be charged on the excess of gross rents over £4,250. If he elects for the alternative basis, no capital allowances are available, but any balancing charge relating to earlier allowances remains assessable. An election for the alternative basis must be made within one year after the 31 January following the relevant tax year, and remains in force until withdrawn, the same time limit applying to the withdrawal.

For the effect of letting part of the home on the capital gains tax exemption see Example 81.

Provisions applicable to companies

Treatment of interest paid and losses

15.   Interest paid by a company in relation to rented property is dealt with under the 'loan relationships' rules (as to which see Examples 63 and 64). If the interest relates to a furnished holiday letting it is deducted from the letting income. See Example 49 explanatory note 6 for the treatment of interest incurred before the commencement of a trade.

16.   If a loss arises, it may be set against the total profits of the same accounting period, or surrendered by way of group relief (see Example 64 explanatory note 5), any unrelieved balance being carried forward to set against future *total* profits.

Finance Act 2006 Part 4 introduced a new regime for real estate investment trusts (REITs). These are companies which are exempt from corporation tax. Distributions from the company are taxed as property income (Schedule A in respect of corporate shareholders).

UK real estate investment trusts

Overview

17.   The REIT regime provides that profits from a company's or group's ring fenced property rental business shall be exempt from corporation tax, provided that at least 90% of those profits are passed through to shareholders as property income distributions (PIDs) within twelve months of the company's year end. These profits are liable to income tax or corporation tax in the hands of the recipients as income from a separate property business.

REIT company – key points

18.   The REIT legislation is found in FA 2006 ss 103–145 as amended by FA 2007 s 51 and Sch 17, and a number of regulations. Exemption is obtained by making an application to HMRC, stating that a number of properties have been moved into the exempt property business ring fence, and that a number of conditions have been fulfilled.

   •   There is an entry charge of 2% of the market value divided by the company's tax rate for properties entering the ring fence (FA 2006 s 102).

Provided that conditions are complied with, the tax exemptions available to the REIT company are:

- exemption from corporation tax on the rental income;

- exemption from capital gains tax on disposal of ring fence properties.

The main conditions to be complied with by the company are:

- it must be quoted on a recognised stock exchange;

- it must not be a close company;

- it must be UK resident and not dual resident;

- it must have one class only of ordinary shares, but may have fixed interest preference shares;

- there is an interest cover restriction, charging excessive interest to tax;

- interest paid on loans must be fixed interest, and not participate in profit;

- there must be a minimum of three properties (individual units count as separate properties);

- no property may represent more than 40% of the portfolio (IFRS valuation/fair value);

- no property may be owner occupied;

- 75% of total profits must arise from the tax-exempt property rental business;

- 75% of the company's assets at the beginning of the period must relate to the tax-exempt property rental business;

- the maximum individual shareholding in the company is limited to less than 10%;

- 90% of profits from the property rental business must be paid as dividends within twelve months of the company's tax period end.

Failure to meet these conditions may cause a tax charge to arise, or for the company to cease qualifying for REIT exemptions.

Distributions

19. Rental income property distributions are not dividends, but are treated as profits of a separate UK property business. There is no tax credit on these distributions; instead tax must be withheld at the basic rate (20%). The distributions are treated as profits of a *separate* property business, and as such, losses from other property businesses may not be offset against them. The offshore landlords' regime does not apply to these distributions. Fred Stone's receipt of £8,000 therefore represents £10,000, less tax at 20%.

There are therefore no tax exemptions for recipients of distributions, the purpose of the scheme being to facilitate holdings in property portfolios. However, because profits have not been subject to corporation tax, the distributions should be higher than they otherwise would have been.

REIT shares may be held in ISAs, PEPs, child trust funds or self-invested personal pensions (SIPPs), where tax relief may be available.

Furnished holiday lettings (ITTOIA 2005 Part 3 Chapter 6)

20. All UK property income of individuals and companies, both from furnished and unfurnished lettings, is treated as being from a single business (ITTOIA 2005 s 264). For full details see part (A) of the Example.

To the extent that rental income relates to qualifying furnished holiday lettings in the UK, or elsewhere in the European Economic Area (EEA) the income and expenses are kept separate and are treated as if the net income arose from a trade, that income being treated as earnings for pension purposes (ITTOIA 2005 s 328). Capital allowances and loss reliefs may be claimed where appropriate (ITTOIA 2005 s 327). For both individuals and companies, any overall profit or loss is included within the result of a UK property business.

As noted above, all beneficial treatment of furnished holiday lettings whether in the UK or elsewhere in the EEA will cease on 5 April 2010. From that date former furnished holiday letting activities will fall within normal property income. It is not presently clear how the treatment of assets on which capital allowances have been claimed will be resolved.

As a result of the announcement, owners of qualifying properties could make a claim to amend their 2007 tax return by an extended deadline of 31 July 2009. The 2008 returns remain open for amendment until 31 January 2010. HMRC have not given any advice about claims made otherwise than by amendment of a tax return.

Capital allowance claims are possible in respect of expenditure incurred on or after the latest of the following three dates:

- the property was first used as a qualifying FHL;

- the date on which the country in which the property is situated joined the EEA; and

- 1 January 1994.

Where the expenditure was incurred on or after these three dates, it will qualify for capital allowances from the date of purchase. For expenditure incurred before the latest of these three dates it will be treated as brought into use for the purposes of a qualifying activity on the latest of the three dates, at its market value at that time.

See Example 37 for pension rules applicable from 6 April 2006. See explanatory notes 25 to 27 for the capital gains position.

Qualifying conditions

21. To qualify for furnished holiday lettings treatment, the property must be available for letting as holiday accommodation on a commercial basis for a total of 140 days or more in the tax year and must be so let for at least 70 of those days. (The 70-day test may be satisfied by averaging periods of occupation of any or all of the holiday accommodation let furnished by the same person (ITTOIA 2005 s 326).) If the accommodation is in the same occupation for a continuous period of more than 31 days then the aggregate of all such long-term occupancy must not exceed 155 days in the tax year (ITTOIA 2005 s 325).

If the property was not let as furnished holiday lettings in the previous tax year then the above tests apply for the period of 12 months from the date of first letting as qualifying furnished holiday accommodation (ITTOIA 2005 s 324).

Where part only of the let accommodation is holiday accommodation, apportionments are made on a just and reasonable basis.

Relief for losses on holiday lettings may be denied on the grounds that the lettings are not on a commercial basis, particularly where property is bought as a holiday home for the family. This was the decision in *Brown v Richardson* (June 1997 SpC 129), where it was held that lettings were made 'with a view to generating revenue to offset costs rather than with a view to the realisation of profits'. See also *Walls v Livesey* (1995 SpC 4) for comments on the different commerciality tests for the holiday lettings provisions (ITTOIA 2005 s 323) and for loss relief (ICTA 1988 s 381(4)). The Revenue gave their views on the implications of these cases in their Tax Bulletin of October 1997.

As far as inheritance tax is concerned, business property relief may not be available, because the lettings would probably be regarded as investments (IHTA 1984 s 105(3)). The HMRC's Capital Taxes Manual indicates, however, that business property relief will probably be available where holiday lettings are very short-term and either the owner or someone acting for him is substantially involved with the holidaymakers in terms of their activities on and from the premises.

Rent-a-room relief

22. The 'rent-a-room' relief provisions outlined in explanatory note 14 above could be claimed if appropriate in respect of furnished holiday accommodation instead of the above rules if the accommodation consisted of furnished rooms in the taxpayer's only or main residence, but not where, as in this example, the holiday home is not the main home.

Capital allowances and wear and tear allowance

23. Although the furnished holiday accommodation provisions enable capital allowances to be claimed, no guidance is given as to how to switch from the 10% wear and tear or renewals basis normally used for let property, nor as to how to deal with property that is within the provisions in one tax year and not the next, such as the Suffolk house in this example, where it did not qualify in 2007/08 because it was let for only 49 days. In practice, it is considered that capital allowances will probably not be claimed and the wear and tear or renewals treatment will continue.

Council tax and business rates

24. Council tax is payable on domestic property. Self-contained holiday accommodation is, however, liable to business rates if it is available for letting for 140 days or more a year (no matter for how long it is actually let), hence the rates payable on the Suffolk house.

   As far as the London house is concerned, if it is let long-term the tenant will pay the council tax. If it is no-one's only or main residence Mrs Morley will pay the council tax, which would be an allowable expense of the letting.

   Any rates and other charges normally borne by a tenant, such as water supply charges, are deducted from rent before calculating the 10% wear and tear allowance.

Capital gains tax

25. The property and other chargeable assets used in the furnished holiday lettings are eligible for capital gains rollover relief if they are replaced (see Example 82) (TCGA 1992 s 241(3)).

   Where a sole trader either sells his business as a going concern, or ceases trading and sells the assets used in the business, entrepreneur's relief is available on the sale – known as a material disposal. The business must have been carried on for at least 12 months. It is therefore necessary that the furnished holiday letting conditions are met for the tax year 2008/09 and the period leading up to the date of sale to ensure that the relief is available.

26. As far as Mrs Morley is concerned, rollover relief could be claimed in respect of the lettings proportion of the gain providing the full business proportion of the proceeds of sale was reinvested in the business proportion of the new property. Gains could continue to be rolled over on a succession of such sales, were it not for the abolition of the relief at the end of 2009/10. Mrs Morley would be best advised to seriously consider the possible sale of the business as it represents a one-off opportunity to save capital gains tax on the disposal of £18,480 (£102,667 at 18%).

27. The gain of £154,000 that would arise on the private proportion of the Suffolk house if it were sold as contemplated is fully chargeable because the house is not the main residence. If it had been, then that part of the gain would have been exempt. Where the only or main residence has been let as residential accommodation, there is an exemption equal to £40,000 or an amount equal to the owner occupier exempt gain whichever is less. The Revenue took the view that this exemption was only available if the lettings had some degree of permanence and a series of short lets would not qualify. They lost a case on the point, however (*Owen v Elliott* (CA 1990) – see Example 81 explanatory note 7), so it would appear that had the Suffolk house been the capital gains tax exempt residence at some time, the residential lettings exemption would be available (TCGA 1992 s 223).

Landlord's energy saving allowance

28. The provisions of the landlord's energy saving allowance (LESA) are contained in ITTOIA 2005 ss 312–314, as amended by FA 2007 ss 17–18 and a number of regulations. These allow landlords carrying on a property business involving a dwelling-house to deduct expenditure on certain energy-saving items incurred before 6 April 2015. These items are:

   - cavity wall insulation;

   - loft insulation;

   - floor insulation;

   - hot water system insulation;

   - draught proofing.

   There is a limit of £1,500 per dwelling, with each flat in a block of flats counting as a separate dwelling. However, no deduction is allowed if the energy-saving item is installed in a dwelling-house in the course of construction, neither in respect of rent-a-room receipts, nor in respect of commercial letting of furnished holiday accommodation.

   For this reason the expenditure incurred on the London house is deductible, while the same expenditure incurred on the holiday letting property is not.

Question

A.

In 2009/10 Henry Non-Dom is a 25-year-old UK resident foreign domiciliary. He has been UK resident since the age of 21 (arriving in the UK on 17 March 2006). He made a remittance basis claim in 2008/09 and made the necessary claim (under what was then ITTOIA 2005 s 831) for his relevant foreign income to be taxed on the remittance basis in prior years (any foreign employment income and foreign chargeable gains automatically being subject to the remittance basis in 2007/08 and prior years).

Taking each scenario in turn explain whether ITA 2007 s 809D, s 809E or s 828C applies (see explanatory notes 4 to 10).

SCENARIO A

Henry has gross foreign interest income in the year of £1,800, no foreign chargeable gains and makes no remittances. He has UK self-employment income of £35,000 and £10 of UK gross bank interest which is taxed at source. He has no other UK income and made no disposals of UK situs chargeable assets in the tax year.

SCENARIO B

Henry has gross foreign interest income in the year of £23,000, aggregate foreign chargeable gains of £250,000 and makes no remittances. He has £82 of UK gross bank interest which is taxed at source. He has no other UK income and made no disposals of UK situs chargeable assets in the tax year.

SCENARIO C

Henry has foreign income in the year of £501,175. This breaks down as:

● £1,175 of gross bank interest; and

● an offshore income gain of £500,000 (total proceeds £1.5 million) that was realised on 17 March 2010.

He has just the one offshore account. He remits £500,000 on 20 December 2009. At that time the account contained £750,285 of foreign income which breaks down as follows:

	Gross £
Current year	875
2008/09	485,750
2007/08	263,660

No foreign chargeable gains accrued to him in 2009/10.

SCENARIO D

Henry has foreign income and foreign chargeable gains in 2009/10 of £365,000. This breaks down as £150,000 of gross interest (received on 31 December 2009) and a foreign chargeable gain of £215,000 (the disposal taking place on 24 June 2009 with proceeds of £650,000 being received and no foreign tax credit). He has just the one offshore account. He remits £363,300 on 17 January 2010. At that time the account contained £1,385,000 which breaks down as follows:

	Gross £
Current year	800,000
2008/09	350,000
2007/08	235,000

No foreign chargeable gains accrued to him in 2009/10. He has UK self-employment income of £315,000 and £2,750 of UK gross bank interest which is taxed at source. He has no other UK income and made no disposals of UK situs chargeable assets in the tax year.

SCENARIO E

In the year to 6 April 2009 Henry did not make any disposals of chargeable assets and received the following income:

- £25,000 of gross UK employment income;

- £10 of UK grossed up dividend income;

- £8,500 of gross taxed foreign employment income (taxed at 15%);

- £75 of gross foreign taxed bank interest (taxed at 15%).

Henry's income is entirely taxed at source with his PAYE code having correctly deducted the necessary income tax from his UK employment income. He did not remit any unremitted foreign income or gains relating to prior tax years and will not be making a remittance basis claim (ITA 2007 s 809B). Accordingly, if it were not for the foreign income that arose in the tax year he would not have to file a UK tax return.

B.

Nicolas Non-Dom is 25 years old. He first came to the UK in 1992/93. His residency pattern between then and 2008/09 is as follows:

Tax Year	UK resident at any time in the tax year
1992/93 – 2003/04	Yes
2004/05 – 2005/06	No
2006/07	Yes
2007/08	No
2008/09	No

He returned to the UK on 15 October 2009.

Assuming Nicolas's aggregate foreign income and gains and his remittances do not qualify him for automatic access to the remittance basis in 2009/10 would a claim to access the remittance basis mean that he has to pay the remittance basis charge in that year?

C.

Lauren and Ellie Non-Dom are UK resident foreign domiciliaries. They are twins who have been UK resident since 29 August 2000 when they started their UK private schooling. Lauren is the elder and was born at 11:51 pm on 5 April 1992. Ellie was born at 00:05 on 6 April 1992.

Both Lauren and Ellie have significant offshore wealth as the result of interest in possession trusts established by their paternal grandparents. They will take an absolute interest at the age of 21 and during their minority are entitled to the income (which is around £300,000 pa). The trust whilst an offshore settlement provides the twins with the same beneficial entitlement to the income as a trust established under the law of England and Wales. The trustees ensure that no trust property is UK situs so all the trust income is foreign situs. The income arising from the trusts has been invested in personal portfolios (held for them, whilst they are minors, on bare trust by their mother) with instructions that investment in UK situs assets is prohibited.

The twins' parents (both of whom are not UK resident) settle all the twins' UK expenses and provide them with a generous monthly allowance.

For 2009/10 the twins' foreign income and foreign chargeable gains are identical and as follows:

		Gross £	Foreign tax credit £
Trust	Interest income	160,000	Nil
Trust	Property income	150,000	37,500
Personal	Interest income	55,000	Nil
Personal	Dividend income	45,000	6,750
Personal	Offshore income gains	95,000	Nil
Personal	Capital gains	50,000	5,000

Neither Lauren nor Ellie will make any taxable remittances to the UK in 2009/10. Both have a UK current account with BZS Bank plc and receive interest income each year. The income from their BZS account is the only source of UK income that arose to the twins in the 2009/10 tax year. Both received gross interest of £75 from which £15 was deducted at source.

The twins did not dispose of any UK situs chargeable assets in 2009/10.

Explain whether either twin can automatically access the remittance basis of taxation, if not whether making the remittance basis claim will mean the remittance basis charge is due and whether based on the foreign income and gains arising in 2009/10 the remittance or arising basis will be the cheaper alternative.

D.

In 2009/10 Jake Non-Dom is a 36-year-old UK resident foreign domiciliary. Jake's taxable UK income in 2009/10 equates to £165,345. His foreign income and foreign chargeable gains are such that he will not qualify for the automatic remittance basis in 2009/10 and will be making the claim and paying the £30,000 remittance basis charge. A nomination of foreign income or gains needs to be made. Jake has the following BCDE Jersey plc bank accounts:

- Account A – an account containing the proceeds from the sale of various foreign chargeable assets disposed of prior to 6 April 2008. Interest arising on this account is paid into account C.

- Account B – an account containing £75,000 of income that derives originally from successful source-ceasing exercises. The £75,000 is part of a larger sum that was remitted to the UK on 17 March 2008. Jake had kept some of the funds in the UK and transferred the surplus offshore on 25 August 2008. Interest arising on this account is paid into account C.

- Account C – an income account receiving gross interest income earned with respect to a number of the other accounts. A total of £950 of interest was paid into this account in 2009/10. The figure of £950 breaks down as £85 of interest earned on the funds within account C and £865 with respect to interest earned on other accounts with the bank.

- Account D – an account into which £1,000 of clean capital was transferred in January 2010. Interest is paid each December so the account balance at 5 April 2010 was still £1,000. Interest of £4 was received in December 2010.

- Account E – an account receiving gross Swiss bond interest of £270,000 in 2009/10. Interest arising on this account is paid into account C.

- Account F – an account into which his Swiss director's fees for April 2009 to February 2010 are paid. The account received £82,500 of net income with tax of £27,500 having being deducted at source. Interest arising on this account is paid into account C.

- Account G – an account into which his March 2010 net Swiss director's fees of £7,500 was paid (with tax of £2,500 having been deducted at source). No interest income arose in 2009/10.

- Account H – an account that in March 2010 was established with a £1,000 transfer from account E. The intention both when the transfer was made and at the end of 2009/10 is that the funds remain in the account indefinitely. Immediately before the transfer to this new account the transferor account contained £650,000 of which £160,000 related to 2007/08, £220,000 to 2008/09 and £270,000 to 2009/10. No interest income arose in 2009/10.

Explain, taking each account in turn, whether funds within the account could be nominated for the purposes of a long-term UK resident foreign domiciliary making a valid remittance basis claim.

E.

Chloe Non-Dom is 22 in 2009/10. She has been UK resident since the age of 13. She has significant offshore wealth and made a remittance basis claim in 2008/09. In that tax year she did not realise any chargeable gains. However, the fact that she made a remittance basis claim meant that in order to be able to access some relief for foreign capital losses she had to make an election under TCGA 1992 s 16ZA. After considering the options carefully it was thought that in the long term Chloe would be better off making the election and this was made on her 2008/09 tax return.

In addition to her offshore assets Chloe has inherited UK wealth from one of her maternal grandmothers and has a UK share portfolio worth £1,500,000 which is managed by LMNO Investment Management.

For 2009/10 Chloe's foreign income and foreign chargeable gains are as follows:

	Gross £	Foreign tax credit £
Gross bond interest	15,000	Nil
Gross interest income – Jersey accounts	35,000	Nil
Gross interest income – Guernsey account	7	Nil
Property income	175,000	17,500
Offshore income gains	217,000	Nil
	442,007	17,500
Capital gains	250,000	Nil

Chloe realised in 2008/09 that under the new regime:

- her personal situation meant that she would never qualify for the automatic remittance basis;

- being a remittance basis user would always be more favourable for her than being taxed on the default arising basis; and

- she had been UK resident in seven of the nine tax years immediately preceding 2008/09 so will have to make a nomination and pay the £30,000 for that year and all future years.

Chloe, therefore, realised that she would need to make a nomination of relevant year foreign income or gains for each tax year that she continues to be UK resident from 2008/09 onwards. She had not used her Guernsey bank account in years. It contained a balance sufficient to ensure that some interest would be earned each tax year and she decided that the small amount of interest earned and the fact that she has never needed recourse to the funds made it ideal for nomination purposes. Her reasons being that it would earn at least £1 of interest each tax year and she was happy to put a freeze on all payments from the account to avoid inadvertent remittances of nominated funds. (See explanatory note 16 for why avoiding inadvertent remittances of nominated funds is advisable.)

Chloe made no remittances in the 2009/10 apart from a possible £10,000 remittance from her Jersey account containing bank interest. She thinks the remittance is exempt as it was a payment for services and she made the payment to an offshore bank account. The £10,000 was to settle her UK lawyers' fees with respect to the purchase of a UK property.

Her UK income in 2009/10 consists of gross bond interest of £55,000 and taxed bank interest of £80 gross. She realised UK chargeable gains of £150,000 and UK chargeable losses of £200,000.

Calculate her tax liability for 2009/10.

Answer

A. Henry Non-Dom

SCENARIO A: In this scenario Henry automatically qualifies for the remittance basis under ITA 2007 s 809D (see explanatory note 6). In 2009/10 Henry meets all the necessary conditions set down in ITA 2007 s 809D(1) being:

- UK resident in the tax year;

- not domiciled in the UK in the tax year;

- his unremitted foreign income and gains are less than £2,000*[1]; and

- he does not come within the ITA 2007 s 828B conditions*[2].

  *[1]   In Henry's case he has not remitted any foreign income and gains in the tax year but still qualifies under s 809D as the total of his foreign income and gains for 2009/10 is less than £2,000.

  *[2]   Without going through all the ITA 2007 s 828B conditions Henry obviously does not qualify for the s 828C exemption as he has no UK employment income (see explanatory note 4 for full details of the s 828B conditions).

Should Henry not wish to be taxed on the remittance basis he can opt out by giving notice on his 2009/10 tax return that he does not wish ITA 2007 s 809D to apply to him for 2009/10.

SCENARIO B: In this scenario Henry automatically qualifies for the remittance basis under ITA 2007 s 809E (see explanatory note 7). In 2009/10 Henry meets all the necessary conditions set down in ITA 2007 s 809E(1):

- he is UK resident in the tax year;

- not domiciled in the UK in the tax year;

- has no UK income and gains in 2009/10 other than taxed investment income not exceeding £100*[1];

- no remittance basis foreign income or gains are remitted to the UK in 2009/10; and

- Henry has been UK resident for less than six of the nine tax years immediately preceding 2009/10*[2].

  *[1]   Henry's only UK income is £82 of gross bank interest.

  *[2]   Henry arrived in the UK in 2005/06 (on 17 March 2006) and has been UK resident since then. The nine-year look back period extends to 2000/01. Accordingly, residence in the nine-year look back period is as follows:

Tax year	UK resident at any time in the tax year	Tax years	Tax years in which UK resident
2000/01	No	1	0
2001/02	No	2	0
2002/03	No	3	0
2003/04	No	4	0
2004/05	No	5	0
2005/06	No	6	1
2006/07	Yes	7	2
2007/08	Yes	8	3
2008/09	Yes	9	4

Henry is UK resident for only four of the nine tax year preceding 2009/10. Accordingly, the condition at s 809E(1)(e)(i) is met.

Should Henry not wish to be taxed on the remittance basis he can opt out by giving notice on his 2009/10 tax return that he does not wish ITA 2007 s 809E to apply to him for 2009/10.

SCENARIO C: In this scenario Henry does not qualify for the automatic remittance basis. He cannot qualify under ITA 2007 s 809E as he has made a £500,000 remittance in the tax year.

The £500,000 is remitted on 20 December 2009 (that is before the disposal of the units in the non-distributor fund). At the time of the remittance only £875 of foreign income and gains has arisen in 2009/10 and so the £500,000 remittance is matched as follows:

1.   £875 of current year foreign income;

2.   £485,750 of foreign income arising in 2008/09;

3.   £13,375 of foreign income arising in 2007/08.

Henry does not qualify under s 809D as the £500,000 remittance is matched to just £875 of foreign income arising in 2009/10 (the remaining £499,125 being matched to prior years). That is remittances made by Henry in 2009/10 are matched to just £875 out of a total of £501,175 of foreign income and gains for the tax year. This means that the amount of Henry's unremitted foreign income and gains for 2009/10 is not less than £2,000 so ITA 2007 s 809D(1)(c) is breached.

If Henry wants to access the remittance basis he will have to make a claim. Note that if he does not make the claim and is taxed on the default arising basis he will be taxed on the entire £501,175 of foreign income arising in the tax year and the element of the £500,000 remittance that was matched to tax years prior to 2009/10 (that is he will also be taxed on a remittance of £499,125 of foreign income).

SCENARIO D: In this scenario Henry automatically qualifies for the remittance basis under ITA 2007 s 809D. He is UK resident in the tax year and foreign domiciled but has no UK employment income so cannot qualify for the ITA 2007 s 828C exemption (with there being no need to consider the other s 828B conditions).

The £363,300 is remitted on 17 October 2009 from an account that immediately before the remittance contains £800,000 of current year (2009/10) receipts. Matching the remittance in line with s 809Q one deems the remittance to represent:

1.   £150,000 of relevant foreign income; and

2.   £213,300 of foreign chargeable gains.

Accordingly, in 2009/10 Henry remitted £363,300 out of a total of £365,000 of foreign income and gains for that year so his unremitted foreign income and gains for 2009/10 is less than £2,000. This means that he meets all the necessary s 809D qualifying conditions in the tax year.

Should Henry not wish to be taxed on the remittance basis he can opt out by giving notice on his 2009/10 tax return that he does not wish ITA 2007 s 809D to apply to him for 2009/10.

SCENARIO E: On the basis that Henry will not make a remittance basis claim in this scenario Henry meets the conditions at s 828B such that the s 828C exemption will be available (see explanatory note 4).

Condition	
UK resident and foreign domiciled	Met
No s 809B remittance basis claim in the tax year	Met
In receipt of UK employment income	Met, £25,000 gross UK employment income

No foreign chargeable gains	Met
All foreign income subject to foreign taxes	Met, 15% tax on all foreign income
The only foreign income that can arise in the tax year is foreign employment income and interest income (as defined in ITTOIA 2005 Part 4 Chapter 2) and the income arising must not exceed specified limits being (1) £10,000 or less of foreign employment income and (2) no more than £100 of interest.	Met, only foreign income is £8,500 gross of employment income and £75 of taxed bank interest
When considering their total worldwide income, if it were all subject to UK tax, the individual would not pay tax on any of this income at a rate in excess of the basic rate of tax.	Met, worldwide income of £33,585. Accordingly no income would be taxed at a rate higher than the 20% basic rate
The individual does not submit a self-assessment tax return for the tax year, and other than the foreign income, has no reason to have to submit a return.	Met

For 2009/10 Henry's UK tax paid was correct and he does not have to complete a tax return or pay any additional tax on his foreign income. As ITA 2007 s 828C is a complete exemption from tax on foreign income arising in the year it is more favourable than the remittance basis so an individual meeting the other qualifications would not be well advised to put him or herself outside the exemption by making a remittance basis claim.

An individual could not qualify for both ITA 2007 s 809E and ITA 2007 s 828C, as to qualify for s 809E there can be no UK employment income whilst in contrast the qualifying conditions for s 828C to apply cannot be met where the individual does not receive UK employment income. It is possible (though in Henry's case it has not happened as he has not remitted any of his £8,575 of foreign income) to come within the qualifying conditions for both s 828C and s 809D. As s 828C is more favourable than the automatic remittance basis this provision has priority (s 828D(1A)).

B.   **Nicolas Non-Dom**

As stated in explanatory note 10, when considering whether the remittance basis charge is in point for 2009/10 the nine year look back period runs from 2000/01 to 2008/09. From the information provided in the case of Nicolas Non-Dom the facts are as follows:

Tax year	UK resident at any time in the tax year	Tax years	Tax years in which UK resident
2000/01	Yes	1	1
2001/02	Yes	2	2
2002/03	Yes	3	3
2003/04	Yes	4	4
2004/05	No	5	4
2005/06	No	6	4
2006/07	Yes	7	5
2007/08	No	8	5
2008/09	No	9	5

Nicolas has been UK resident in only five of the nine tax years immediately preceding 2009/10 and would not, therefore, have to pay the RBC in order to access the remittance basis in that tax year. Note that if his pattern of UK residence had been different and he had been UK resident in seven of the preceding nine tax years he would have had to pay the full £30,000 regardless of the fact that he became UK resident mid-way through 2009/10.

C.   **The Twins**

In the case of Lauren and Ellie Non-Dom the 14 minute interval between their birth times means that in 2009/10 their tax affairs are different:

●   Lauren being born on 5 April 1992 is 18 in the tax year;

●   Ellie being born on 6 April 1992 is under 18 throughout the tax year.

Ellie automatically qualifies for the remittance basis under ITA 2007 s 809E (see explanatory note 8). In 2009/10 Ellie meets all the necessary conditions set down in ITA 2007 s 809E(1):

●   she is UK resident in 2009/10;

●   she is not domiciled in the UK in 2009/10;

●   she has no UK income and gains in 2009/10 other than taxed investment income not exceeding £100*¹;

●   no remittance basis foreign income or gains are remitted to the UK in 2009/10; and

●   as she is under 18 throughout the tax year the fact that Ellie has been UK resident for more than six of the nine tax years immediately preceding 2009/10 does not disqualify her from meeting the s 809E conditions.

       *¹   Ellie's only UK income is £75 of gross bank interest with tax deducted at source.

Ellie can automatically access the remittance basis and does not have to pay the £30,000 remittance basis charge meaning that since she made no remittances she has to pay no UK tax on her foreign income and gains. Being taxed on the remittance basis will clearly result in a far better tax position for 2009/10 for Ellie than opting out and being taxed on the arising basis.

Lauren does not qualify under ITA 2007 s 809E as she is over 18 at the end of the tax year and has been UK resident for more than six of the nine tax years immediately preceding 2009/10. As she has made no remittances and has foreign income well in excess of £2,000 she does not qualify under s 809D. She has no UK employment income so cannot qualify for the ITA 2007 s 828C exemption (with there being no need to consider the other s 828B conditions).

Accordingly, it is necessary to establish whether the arising basis of the remittance basis is more cost effective for Lauren in 2009/10. We know that accessing the remittance basis will cost her £30,000. In addition since she has to make a claim she will not be entitled to her personal allowance or capital gains tax (CGT) annual exemption though given she has no UK capital gains and minimal UK income this is not such an issue in her case.

We know that Lauren made no remittances in 2009/10 so this means that if she claims the remittance basis her additional UK tax liability with respect to her foreign income and gains will be £30,000. Aggregating her trust and personal foreign income and chargeable gains she has:

	Gross	*Foreign tax credit*
	£	*£*
Interest income	215,000	Nil
Property income	150,000	37,500
Dividend income	45,000	6,750
Offshore income gains	95,000	Nil
Capital gains	50,000	5,000

If she were taxed on the arising basis it is clear that even taking into account foreign tax credits and the fact that she will be entitled to a tax credit equal to one-ninth of the gross foreign dividend income that she receives (ITTOIA 2005 s 397A) her tax liability with respect to her foreign income and gains will be well in excess of £30,000. Even if she had only received the gross foreign interest income of £215,000 she would be better of making the remittance basis claim. This is because in 2009/10 an individual taxed on £215,000 of income on the arising basis would have a tax liability of

£75,930 ((£6,475 × 0%) + (£37,400 × 20%) + (£171,125 × 40%)) which is significantly in excess of £30,000. Accordingly, based on the foreign income and gains arising in 2009/10 the remittance will be the cheaper alternative even though Lauren has to pay the £30,000 remittance basis charge.

D.   Jake Non-Dom

See explanatory notes 12 to 20.

ACCOUNT A: this account has not received any foreign income or gains for 2009/10. Accordingly, Jake cannot make a valid nomination for 2009/10 with respect to any foreign income or chargeable gains within this account.

ACCOUNT B: this account has not received any foreign income or gains for 2009/10. Accordingly, Jake cannot make a valid nomination for 2009/10 with respect to any foreign income or chargeable gains within this account.

ACCOUNT C: this account received £950 of interest income in the tax year. All or part of this £950 could be nominated and that would be a valid nomination for 2009/10. Even nominating the entire £950 would not be sufficient to generate a relevant tax increase of £30,000 but that is immaterial. Provided at least £1 of actual foreign income or chargeable gains is nominated for 2009/10 a valid nomination has been made. Any shortfall in the tax increase will be made up by the deemed nomination provisions at ITA 2007 s 809H(4) (see explanatory note 13). To ensure a full description is given for the purposes of the nomination one may wish to just nominate the whole or part of the £85 of interest earned with respect to funds deposited within account C rather than a higher amount and having to provide details of more than one account.

ACCOUNT D: the deposit made in 2009/10 relates to clean capital. This account has not received any foreign income or gains for 2009/10 with the first income receipt being in 2010/11. Accordingly, Jake cannot make a valid nomination for 2009/10 with respect to any foreign income or chargeable gains within this account.

ACCOUNT E: this account received £270,000 of gross bond interest income in the tax year (no foreign tax credits). Disregarding any foreign income, Jake is a higher rate taxpayer (his UK income for the tax year being £165,345). The nomination will be invalid if it gives rise to a tax increase in excess of £30,000(see explanatory note 14). The maximum amount of bond interest that can be nominated for there to be a valid nomination is £75,000 with the minimum being £1. Note that whilst the bond interest is within account D that account is not the source of the income. When providing details of the source of income on Jake's tax return, details of the Swiss bond interest will need to be provided (see explanatory note 11).

ACCOUNT F: this account received £110,000 of gross income in the tax year (£27,500 tax credit). All or part of this £110,000 could be nominated and that would be a valid nomination for 2009/10. This is because the £27,500 tax credit means that the relevant tax increase if the entire £110,000 is nominated will only be £16,500 ((£110,000 × 40%) – £27,500) so there is no possibility of the nomination resulting in a relevant tax increase in excess of £30,000. There will be an insufficient nomination and the shortfall in the tax increase will be made up by the deemed nomination provisions at ITA 2007 s 809H(4) (see explanatory note 13). When providing details of the source of income on Jake's tax return, details of the Swiss director's fees will need to be provided including information with respect to the £27,500 tax credit (see explanatory note 11).

ACCOUNT G: this account received £10,000 of gross income in the tax year (£2,500 tax credit). All or part of this £10,000 could be nominated and that would be a valid nomination for 2009/10. There will be an insufficient nomination and the shortfall in the tax increase will be made up by the deemed nomination provisions at ITA 2007 s 809H(4) (see explanatory note 13). When providing details of the source of income on Jake's tax return, details of the Swiss director's fees will need to be provided including information with respect to the £2,500 tax credit (see explanatory note 11).

ACCOUNT H: This account was established though an offshore transfer from account E. No remittances were made from account H in 2009/10 and at the end of 2009/10 there is no intention for remittances to be made from the account. Accordingly, the offshore transfer provisions at ITA 2007 s 809Q (4). This means that the funds transferred are deemed to be 'the appropriate proportion of each kind of income and gain in the fund immediately before the transfer'. The appropriate proportion is logically defined as the proportion the funds which are transferred equate to when considering the value in the mixed fund immediately before the transfer.

The composition of the accounts is as follows:

	In Account E prior to the transfer £	Transferred to Account H £	Transferred in Account E £
2009/10 foreign interest	270,000	415	269,585
2008/09 foreign interest	220,000	339	219,661
2007/08 foreign interest	160,000	246	159,754
	650,000	1,000	649,000

Accordingly, account H is deemed to contain £415 of Swiss bond interest relating to 2009/10. All or part of this £415 could be nominated and that would be a valid nomination for 2009/10. When providing details of the source of income on Jake's tax return, details of the Swiss bond interest will need to be provided.

E.   **Chloe Non-Dom**

Chloe's UK income in itself is sufficient to mean that she is a higher rate taxpayer. We are told that her maximum potential remittances in the tax year amount to £10,000. It is clear that the remittance basis claim is favourable given that if she is taxed on the arising basis she will have to pay tax at 40% on foreign income of £442,000 with foreign tax credits equating to only £17,500 and on foreign chargeable gains and also at 18% on foreign chargeable gains of £250,000 (though the UK capital losses would reduce the figure on which tax is chargeable).

The £10,000 paid offshore from her foreign interest income for UK services is a remittance. This is because foreign income has been directly used to pay for a service provided in the UK to and for the benefit of Chloe and the service exemption (ITA 2007 s 809W) is not in point. For the service exemption to be available as well as the payment being made overseas (which was the case here) the UK service must be wholly or mainly in connection with foreign property (which was not the case here as the service was wholly with respect to UK property).

As a remittance basis user in 2009/10 she will be taxed as follows (note she has the benefit of neither the personal allowance nor the CGT annual election):

	Income £	Tax credit £
UK bond interest	55,000	Nil
UK taxed bank interest	80	16
Remittance of foreign bank interest	10,000	Nil
	65,080	16

Tax thereon: 37,400 @ 20%	7,480
£27,680 @ 40%	11,072
Remittance basis charge (tax on the £7 of Guernsey bank interest plus tax on the deemed nominated income so the increase equates to £30,000)	30,000

CGT on UK gains of £150,000 @ 18%	27,000
(as the TCGA 1992 s 16ZA(2) loss election has been made and	
2009/10 is a year for which Chloe will be taxed on the	
remittance basis the £200,000 of UK losses are set against the	
£250,000 of unremitted foreign capital gains*)	
Less tax credits	(16)
	75,536

* See explanatory note 29.

Explanatory Notes

What is the remittance basis?

1. The default basis of taxation for income tax and capital gains tax (CGT) is known as the arising basis. Where the arising basis applies for a tax year individuals are taxed on the taxable income deemed to arise and the chargeable gains deemed to accrue to them in the tax year. Whatever their domicile status all UK residents are subject to tax on UK source income and chargeable gains realised on the disposal (or deemed disposal) of UK situs assets on the arising basis.

    The remittance basis is an alternative basis of UK taxation which can only be accessed by individuals who meet specified qualifying criteria (see explanatory note 2). It can apply to foreign income and potentially to foreign chargeable gains of such eligible individuals. Where it does apply such funds are only taxable when remitted to the UK. There are specific rules which govern the remittance basis of taxation and there are some specific items of foreign income and/or gains that the remittance basis cannot apply to. In particular gains under a policy of life assurance, life annuity or on a capital redemption policy are always taxable on the arising basis.

    Finance Act 2008 significantly altered the rules with respect to the remittance basis of taxation. The package of reforms was highly complex and controversial. Finance Act 2009 made changes to the Finance Act 2008 provisions to:

    - ease the compliance burden (particularly for low income taxpayers);

    - make technical corrections where it was agreed that the legislation was found not to be operating as intended;

    - put through anti-avoidance amendments to prevent perceived potential abuse of the remittance basis regime.

    The main remittance basis regime legislation can be found in Income Tax Act 2007 (ITA 2007), Part 14, Chapter 1A. Specific provisions with respect to income tax are contained in Income Tax (Trading and Other Income) Act 2005 (ITTOIA 2005), employment income in Income Tax (Earnings and Pensions) Act 2003 (ITEPA 2003) and capital gains tax (CGT) in Taxation of Chargeable Gains Act 1992 (TCGA 1992). Finance Act 2008 (FA 2008) Sch 7 should also be referred to as it contains the commencement provisions and important transitional provisions.

    This is a highly complex area of UK taxation. These notes address the issues of eligibility for and access to the remittance basis. They also provide a very brief overview with respect to remittances.

Who is potentially eligible to access the remittance basis?

2. Eligibility to access the remittance basis with respect to both foreign income and foreign chargeable gains is only open to foreign domiciliaries who are resident or ordinarily resident in the UK.

Individuals who are UK resident and UK domiciled but not ordinarily resident in the UK can access the remittance basis but only with respect to their foreign income. Such individuals are taxable on foreign gains on the arising basis. References below to remittance basis users include such individuals (though only insofar as foreign income is in point).

Foreign employment income – the benefits of not being ordinarily resident in the UK

3.   Where the individual is a remittance basis user and ordinarily resident in the UK the remittance basis is available only where the foreign employment is with an overseas employer and the duties are wholly performed abroad (with the exception of incidental UK duties). In contrast, for a remittance basis user who is not ordinarily resident in the UK, one contract can cover UK and foreign duties with the foreign duties part being taxed on the remittance basis (the salary will need to be paid initially into an offshore account). The specific rules with respect to the remittance basis and employment income are complex and outside the scope of this work. It is suggested that readers consult Tolley's Expatriate Tax Planning 2009/10.

Exemption from UK tax on foreign income for basic rate UK resident foreign domiciled taxpayers with UK employment income, small amounts of taxed foreign employment income and/or taxed foreign interest income

4.   The general rule is that a claim has to be made to benefit from provisions within double tax agreements. This rule when coupled with the changes with respect to accessing the remittance basis (see explanatory note 5) would have meant that a significant number of tax returns would have had to be submitted where there was little or no tax due. This would have placed a significant administrative burden on both taxpayers and HMRC. The exemption at ITA 2007 s 828C addresses the problem partially. Where the ITA 2007 s 828B qualifying conditions are met the legislation exempts from UK tax the individual's foreign income. Those meeting the ITA 2007 s 828B qualifying conditions would not have had to submit a tax return if it were not for the foreign income so the exemption from paying UK tax on this income removes the need for qualifying individuals to have to file UK tax returns.

To qualify for the exemption an individual must in the relevant tax year be a UK resident foreign domiciliary who does not make a remittance basis claim (ITA 2007 s 828A) and meets the conditions set down in ITA 2007 s828B which can be summarised as follows:

- in the year the individual has income from an employment, the duties of which are performed wholly or partly in the UK;

- no foreign income arises to the individual in the year other than (1) £10,000 or less of foreign employment income subject to a foreign tax, and/or (2) no more than £100 of foreign interest income subject to a foreign tax;

- no foreign chargeable gains whatsoever arise;

- when considering their total worldwide income, if it were all subject to UK tax, the individual would not pay tax on any of this income at a rate in excess of the basic rate of tax; and

- the individual does not make a return under TMA 1970 s 8 for the tax year.

Where the conditions are met this exemption will give a more favourable result than applying the remittance basis to the foreign income for the tax year. This is because the exemption means that no UK tax will arise on the foreign income regardless of whether it remains offshore or is remitted to the UK.

Accessing the remittance basis

5.   One of the fundamental principles underpinning the new remittance basis regime is that, with limited exceptions, those who access the remittance basis should suffer a financial penalty.

The general rule for 2008/09 and subsequent tax years is that individuals who are eligible to access the remittance basis will by default be taxed on the arising basis and will only be able to access the remittance basis if they make a formal claim (the standard means for doing this being to complete the relevant boxes on the 'Residence, remittance basis etc' supplementary pages of their UK self-assessment tax return). The deadline for making the remittance basis claim is the standard claims deadline (TMA 1970 s 43).

Making a remittance basis claim comes with a cost attached. The basic cost is set down at ITA 2007 s 809G and entails the loss of:

- the income tax personal allowance (and where applicable the age allowance);

- the blind person's allowance (if applicable);

- the capital gains annual exempt amount; and

- the married couples'/civil partners' allowance (only claimable where one of the individuals was 65 before 6 April 2000 and operating as a tax reduction relief rather than being a tax-free allowance).

There is also an impact on the individual's capital loss relief entitlement (TCGA 1992 s 16ZA) as explained in explanatory note 29.

In addition to the basic cost of accessing the remittance basis, the £30,000 remittance basis charge (RBC) is due where the individual is aged 18 or over in the tax year and meets the definition of a long-term UK resident (ITA 2007 s 809H). An individual will be a long-term resident if he or she has been UK resident for at least seven of the nine tax years immediately preceding the tax year in question.

There are two statutory exceptions (ITA 2007 s 809D and s 809E – see explanatory notes 6 to 7) to the rule that the remittance basis must be claimed.

For individuals who meet either of the two sets of specified conditions the position is reversed in that the remittance basis is the default basis of taxation. Individuals qualifying automatically for the remittance basis will only be able to access the arising basis if they make a specific claim to opt out of being taxed on the remittance basis (the standard TMA 1970 s 43 claims deadline also applying in this case). Whichever default basis of taxation the individual qualifies for they have a free choice as to whether to make a claim so the other basis will apply. Claims made in previous years in no way fetter an individual's choice in later years. Furthermore, the choices made have no impact on their actual domicile status.

Individuals will be entitled automatically to claim the remittance basis where they meet either the qualifying conditions set down at ITA 2007 s 809D (see explanatory note 7) or ITA 2007 s 809E (see explanatory note 8).

Automatic entitlement to the remittance basis

6. The determination as to whether the individual qualifies for the remittance basis without having to make a claim is made on a year-by-year basis. An individual might meet the conditions such that the remittance basis can be accessed without the need to make a claim in one year and not in another. Having to make a claim for the remittance basis in a tax year does not mean that the individual cannot qualify for automatic access to the remittance basis of taxation in future tax years.

Where an individual automatically qualifies for the remittance basis their entitlement to personal allowances and the CGT annual exemption is unaffected. No remittance basis claim is required on a self-assessment tax return. If a return has to be submitted the necessary questions must be completed to establish that the return is prepared on the remittance basis and that entitlement is automatic.

Unremitted foreign income and foreign chargeable gains under £2,000

7.   ITA 2007 s 809D provides that the remittance basis is automatic for a tax year during which an individual:

- is UK resident;

- is either not domiciled in the UK or is not ordinarily resident in the UK; and

- has aggregate unremitted foreign income and foreign chargeable gains equating to less than £2,000.

The 'less than £2,000' test is with respect to the total foreign income and foreign chargeable gains for the tax year that are not remitted in that tax year. Accordingly, it is not necessary for the individual's total foreign income and gains for the tax year to be less than £2,000. For example, the total foreign income and gains figure could be £500,000 for the tax year and the individual would qualify if £498,001 of those foreign income and gains were remitted to the UK in that year.

Note than there is no split year treatment with respect to the £2,000. This means that if an individual arrives mid-way through the tax year foreign income and gains that arose or accrued in the part of the tax year before UK residence began are taken into account for the purposes of the test.

Individuals who qualify for the automatic remittance basis as they have aggregate unremitted foreign income and foreign chargeable gains for the tax year of less than £2,000 will not have to pay the RBC regardless of how long they have been resident in the UK.

Child or short-term UK resident making no remittances and with minimal UK income arising in the tax year

8.   ITA 2007 s 809E provides that the remittance basis is automatic for a tax year during which an individual:

- is UK resident;

- is either not domiciled in the UK or is not ordinarily resident in the UK;

- meets at least one of the following two qualifying conditions:

    – under 18 throughout the tax year;

    – has been UK resident in not more than six of the nine tax years immediately preceding the year in question;

- either has no UK income or chargeable gains whatsoever or only has £100 or less of investment income that has had actual tax (as opposed to the deemed dividend tax credit) deducted at source, for example bank interest paid net; and

- does not remit any property representing or derived from remittance basis foreign income or foreign chargeable gains.

Claiming the remittance basis (where the individual does not qualify automatically)

9.   As explained above, where the individual is entitled to access the remittance basis but does not qualify for automatic access there is an access cost. This is as follows:

- the loss of personal allowances and the CGT annual exemption (ITA 2007 s 809G);

- the loss of standard capital loss relief on all foreign capital losses (TCGA 1992 s 16ZA); and

- the £30,000 RBC (see explanatory note 10) where the individual is aged 18 or over in the tax year and has been UK resident in at least seven of the nine tax years immediately preceding the year in which the remittance claim is made.

The loss of the personal allowance and CGT annual exemption if a remittance claim is made will mean that amounts previously covered by the personal allowance or CGT annual exemption, such as modest UK income or gains and/or small remittances of foreign income or gains, will be subject to tax.

There is one exception to the general rule that a remittance basis claim results in the loss of allowances in the relevant tax year. The exception arises because certain double tax agreements (DTAs) the UK has entered into have specific provisions which, if the individual meets the conditions, establish that the individual has a right to the same allowances and reliefs as British subjects not resident in the UK. The precise treaty provision needs to be consulted, but very broadly for the treaty provision to apply in this situation the individual must be dual resident with the treaty tiebreaker provisions awarding residence to the other territory.

The countries with whom the text of the DTA with the UK is such that this can happen are: Austria, Belgium, Fiji, France (though not when the new agreement comes into force), Germany, Ireland, Kenya, Luxembourg, Mauritius, Namibia, Netherlands (though when the new agreement comes into force the qualifying conditions are further restricted), Portugal, Swaziland, Sweden, Switzerland and Zambia.

Long-term UK residents: the RBC

10.   As explained above the price an individual has to pay to access the remittance basis is increased if he or she is aged 18 or over in the tax year and is a long-term UK resident. This is because ITA 2007 s 809H imposes the £30,000 RBC on adult long-term UK residents. A long-term UK resident is defined as an individual who has been UK resident in at least seven of the nine tax years immediately preceding the year in which the remittance claim is made (ITA 2007 s 809C(1)(b) and s 809H(1)(c)). For 2009/10 the look back period, when determining if the individual has been UK resident in at least seven of the preceding nine tax years, covers the tax years 2000/2001 to 2008/09 (inclusive).

When considering the seven out of the nine tax years immediately preceding test, all years when the individual is resident in the UK under UK tax law are counted. Accordingly, a year is counted for the purposes of this test if the individual is dual resident. This is the case even if under the terms of a relevant treaty tiebreaker clause the individual is regarded as resident in the other territory (the tiebreaker clause only having effect for the purposes of the treaty provisions).

A child under the age of 18 throughout the tax year does not have to pay the RBC (ITA 2007 s 809C(1)(a) and s 809H(1)(b)). However, one should bear in mind that years of UK residence during the individual's minority are counted when determining if an individual has been resident for seven of the preceding nine tax years.

Long-term UK residents: making the remittance basis claim

11.   In addition to making the basic remittance basis claim an adult long-term UK resident foreign domiciliary (or UK domiciliary who is not ordinarily resident in the UK) must:

●   make an actual nomination of at least £1 of foreign income or foreign chargeable gains that have arisen in the relevant tax year (ITA 2007 s 809C(2)); and

●   avoid making an excessive actual nomination such that the nominated foreign income or chargeable gains gives rise to a relevant tax increase exceeding £30,000.

The nomination is made on the tax return on the supplementary pages for 'Residence, remittance basis etc.' The nomination of foreign income or chargeable gains arising in the tax year is made using box 31 (for foreign income) and/or 32 (for foreign gains). Additional information about the nominated income and/or gains needs to be provided in box 35 'any other information'. The HMRC tax return preparation guidance for the 'Residence, remittance basis etc.' supplementary pages states that:

'Box 35 Any other information

> You must provide details if you have completed boxes 31 or 32 and 33. This information is required to validate your nomination and to confirm any UK Gift Aid donations, double taxation relief claims and so forth.
>
> You should identify the precise income and gains you have nominated at boxes 31 and/or 32, including the country of origin and the type and source of the income (for example, the bank account or employment to which it relates), show the computation of the gain (if applicable) and the exchange rates used.
>
> If you have deducted any expenses or losses from the income or gains in arriving at the final taxable amount then full details of the amounts and nature of those expenses or losses must also be given.'

The choice the individual makes with respect to the foreign income or gains to nominate has no impact on his or her nomination choice in future years.

The £30,000 RBC is collected through the self-assessment system and where the RBC is derived from an actual or a deemed income nomination (see explanatory note 13) the resulting income tax feeds into the payments on account calculation. Such issues need to be considered if consideration is being given to the making of a claim to reduce payments on account.

Long-term UK residents: the nomination process

12. A complicated nomination process has been put in place to try to establish that the RBC is either income tax or CGT, and so should be given credit in the same way as any other income tax or CGT paid, rather than it being seen as a stand-alone tax charge.

    As set down in explanatory note 11, it is a statutory requirement that in order to make a valid remittance basis claim a long-term resident makes a nomination of at least £1 of actual foreign income or gains arising or accruing in the tax year for which the claim is being made.

    The provisions state that nominated foreign income and gains are treated as being taxed on the arising basis (ITA 2007 s 809H(2)) and the tax increase due as a result of the nomination is calculated. Credit is given, in the standard manner, for any foreign tax suffered. As the nominated foreign income and gains are treated as being taxed on the arising basis, one calculates tax on foreign dividend income using the dividend tax rates (and where applicable the ITTOIA 2005 s 397A tax credit should be taken into account).

    A valid nomination will always result in a relevant tax increase of £30,000 and, therefore, a RBC of £30,000. The legislation achieves this result by artificially increasing an insufficient actual nomination (see explanatory note 13) and rejecting an excessive nomination (see explanatory note 14).

The additional top-up deemed nomination provisions

13. As discussed, where a long-term UK resident foreign domiciliary wants to make a remittance basis claim and makes an actual nomination that results in a tax increase of less than £30,000 specific deeming provisions are triggered. For the purposes of carrying out the RBC calculation these provisions deem an additional top-up 'notional' nomination of foreign income, sufficient to result in the necessary £30,000 tax increase, to have been made (ITA 2007 s 809C(4)(a)). Note that it is irrelevant whether the individual does or does not have foreign income that could have been so nominated (ITA 2007 s 809C(4)(b)).

    The deeming provisions apply for the purposes of the RBC tax calculation meaning that the income tax calculated on the deemed foreign income feeds through to the payments on account. However, the deeming provisions are specifically disapplied when considering whether nominated foreign income or gains have been remitted (ITA 2007 s 809H(6)). Accordingly for the purposes of the ITA 2007 ss 809I and 809J legislation (see explanatory note 17) one only considers actual nominated income or chargeable gains.

Excessive nominations

14. The legislation specifies that the nomination must be such that the resulting tax increase does not exceed £30,000 (ITA 2007 s 809C(4)). This means that a remittance basis claim made will not be valid if there is an excessive nomination. If an invalid claim is not repaired within the claims deadline then the taxpayer will not have been entitled to the remittance basis for that tax year. Accordingly, great care should be taken to avoid making an excessive nomination.

Little chance of credit in the UK for the £30,000

15. The individual is unlikely to ever receive credit for the £30,000 as to do so it is necessary for them to have first remitted ALL foreign income and gains subject to tax on the remittance basis since 6 April 2008 (ITA 2007 s 809I). This is unlikely to be achievable because even the deduction of £1 in bank fees from funds representing post-5 April 2008 foreign income or gains would mean that the individual would not be able to remit ALL such foreign income and gains.

Will credit for the £30,000 RBC be given in other territories?

16. Where an individual's tax affairs are such that they would wish to claim credit for the RBC against foreign tax they will not want to make an insufficient nomination. Making an actual nomination such that the increase in the tax liability can be traced to actual foreign income or gains would appear to be the only prospect for being successful in making a claim for credit for the RBC in a foreign territory. The position is uncertain. However, it may be an academic question as the individual may be better off being taxed on the arising basis, or where the remittance basis claim is made, the level of UK tax paid may be higher than in the foreign territory, meaning that individual will have excess foreign tax credits.

Why one should avoid remitting nominated income or gains

17. The legislation has deeming provisions (ITA 2007 s 809I) which mean that, if the individual does remit actual nominated income or gains before having remitted ALL foreign income and gains subject to tax on the remittance basis since 6 April 2008, special matching provisions (ITA 2007 s 809J) are triggered which for tax purposes change reality. As set down in explanatory note 14 in practical terms it is very unlikely that an individual will be able to remit ALL foreign income and gains subject to tax on the remittance basis since 6 April 2008. It is, therefore, likely that if nominated income or gains are remitted these penal rules will be triggered.

The provisions are highly complex. One quantifies the actual foreign income and gains remitted in the tax year and one then determines the actual foreign income and gains received in that tax year and previous tax years back to 2008/09. For tax purposes the individual is taxed on the same amount of remittance basis foreign income and gains that have been remitted but this amount is matched to foreign income and gains in the order set down in the legislation (ITA 2007 s 809J(2)).

Generally the legislative matching order will mean that, where the individual has more than one category of foreign income or gains, the taxpayer will pay more UK tax on the income or gains remitted than would otherwise have been the case.

Example

Lucy is a long-term UK resident foreign domiciliary who is a higher rate taxpayer. She made the remittance basis claim and paid the RBC in 2008/09 and 2009/10. Lucy has two Jersey bank accounts:

– a Jersey income account containing foreign bank interest of £100,000 relating to 2008/09 and 2009/10 (with no tax credit); and
– a Jersey capital proceeds account containing the proceeds (£300,000) from the sale in 2008/09 of a foreign chargeable asset which on sale realised a gain of £100,000 (the £200,000 to acquire the asset having come from clean capital).

In 2009/10 Lucy remits £50,000 from the Jersey capital proceeds account. Under normal circumstances this remittance would be taxable at 18%. However, if with respect to another transaction Lucy has remitted nominated income or gains (with respect to either 2008/09 or 2009/10) and so triggered the ITA 2007 ss 809I and J provisions what has actually happened is ignored. Should these provisions apply Lucy will be taxed as if £50,000 of the foreign bank interest were remitted (so the tax rate is 40% rather than the fixed CGT rate of 18%).

It should be noted that these provisions have no bearing where clean income is remitted. The rules only work to re-characterise the actual remitted foreign income and gains.

Considerations when making the nomination

18. Great care needs to be taken when making the nomination to ensure that a valid nomination is made. As set down in explanatory note 11 to make a valid nomination it is necessary to ensure that:

- at least £1 of foreign income and/or gains arising in the relevant tax year is nominated; and

- that the actual nomination made does not result in an additional tax liability in excess of £30,000.

In addition when making the nomination one will want to avoid triggering the penal matching provisions at ITA 2007 ss 809I and 809J (see explanatory note 17). This means that one will want to ensure that the actual foreign income or gains nominated have not been and will not be remitted to the UK.

To ensure actual nominated income or gains are not remitted it is recommended that steps are taken to ring-fence the funds. If specific measures are not taken there will be a danger of an inadvertent remittance. Commentators have suggested that, where the individual does not need to obtain credit for the £30,000 in a foreign territory, a token nomination is made on the basis that this will reduce the level of the funds that have to be ring-fenced. Ring-fencing actual nominated income or gains in a special account should both avoid an inadvertent remittance and enable the individual to demonstrate that actual nominated income/gains have not been remitted should HMRC enquire.

Nominating foreign income as opposed to foreign gains

19. For the reasons explained above, one will want to avoid remitting the actual nominated income and/or gains. Since the funds cannot be brought into the UK, in cases where one will nominate more than a token amount of income or gains it would be sensible to nominate the category of income and/or gains that would be least tax efficient to remit. This will depend on the individual's circumstances but where the individual has such income this will be any type of foreign income with no notional UK tax credit (so not dividend income), relief or foreign tax credit attached.

Where foreign income is nominated or deemed to have been nominated there is an impact on the payments on account situation going forward (and with respect to the current tax year if a reduction claim was made). In contrast, if foreign gains are nominated the payments on account are unaffected with the £30,000 being part of the balancing payment due by 31 January following the tax year. Accordingly, it would be advantageous to nominate foreign chargeable gains where an individual:

- is certain he or she can ring-fence proceeds from a gain/gains sufficient to increase their tax liability by £30,000 and will never remit these proceeds;

- is happy to provide details with respect to the capital disposal to HMRC; and

- is confident that their tax liabilities will not be increased overall through not being able to remit the proceeds as there will be no need to remit from funds which would give rise to a liability in excess of 18%.

As with so much in connection with the remittance basis regime there is no 'one size fits all' answer and individual circumstances need to be considered carefully.

The downside to making a token nomination

20. As discussed (see explanatory note 16) individuals who want to be able to claim credit for the £30,000 RBC against their tax liabilities in other territories will not want to make an insufficient nomination.

   In theory there is one other category of taxpayer who will want to make a full actual nomination. That is a taxpayer who may be in a position to remit all remittance basis foreign income and gains arising since 6 April 2008 and would then be in a position to remit the nominated foreign income and gains and claim credit for the RBC paid. Where there is an 'insufficient nomination' the tax credit can only be claimed for the RBC pertaining to the actual nominated income or gain. It is thought unlikely that an individual who would opt to pay the £30,000 RBC would ever be in a position where they are able to remit ALL remittance basis foreign income and gains arising since 6 April 2008. This is because such individuals commonly use offshore funds to finance their offshore expenditure. One may want to make a full nomination where there is a genuine possibility that an individual will not use their foreign income and foreign chargeable gains offshore.

The meaning of 'remitted to the UK'

21. The remittance basis regime changed fundamentally with effect from 6 April 2008. The enactment of one extended definition of 'remitted to the UK' was one of the most significant changes.

   From 6 April 2008 there can be a taxable remittance of foreign income even if the source of that income does not exist in the tax year of remittance.

   The main legislative provision defining what constitutes a remittance is ITA 2007 s 809L. In very simple terms it can be said that there will be a taxable remittance where any property representing or derived from foreign income or foreign chargeable gains is brought to, received or used:

   • in the UK by or for the benefit of a relevant person (defined in explanatory note 23); or

   • to provide a service in the UK to or for the benefit or a relevant person (this will be the case regardless of whether the service is paid for offshore or the payment is made in the UK).

   It is important to appreciate how wide this definition is and that it encompasses far more than just cash remittances. Potentially it covers:

   • any form of property brought to, received or used in the UK for the benefit of a relevant person;

   • payment (whether to the service provider's UK or offshore account) for any services provided in the UK to or for the benefit of a relevant person;

   • any use of property representing or derived from foreign income or foreign chargeable gains in connection with a loan or debt which provides, whether directly or indirectly, any UK person with a UK benefit (either in connection with property enjoyed or a service provided to them or for their benefit).

   In addition where remittance basis foreign income or gains are first remitted to the UK after 5 April 2008 there is a tax charge on taxable remittances made in the tax year regardless of whether in that tax year the individual is subject to tax on the arising or remittance basis.

   There are important transitional provisions and ongoing exemptions which when in point mean that there will be no tax liability even though an ITA 2007 s 809L remittance of foreign income and/or foreign chargeable gains has been made. Brief details are provided in explanatory notes 25 and 26.

Tracing

22. Where there is a remittance one has to trace to the source of the original funds and where at any point one finds unremitted foreign income and/or gains there will be a tax charge (unless one of the transitional provisions or ongoing exemptions apply). This is best explained by an example. Toby

remits £70,000 from his Jersey bank account. This represents the proceeds of sale of a painting. A £20,000 foreign chargeable gain arose on the sale. The £50,000 used to acquire the painting was derived from the sale of foreign securities where a gain of £10,000 was realised. The original funds (£40,000) to acquire the securities came from Toby's Jersey interest income account. In total, therefore, Toby will be taxed on foreign chargeable gains of £30,000 and foreign bank interest of £40,000.

The 'relevant person' concept

23. As outlined above for foreign income and foreign chargeable gains arising or accruing after 5 April 2008 there is a deemed remittance by the individual to whom the foreign income arose or the foreign gains accrued where any relevant person in connection with the individual remits property representing or derived from foreign income or relevant foreign gains or receives a UK benefit derived from foreign income or foreign chargeable gains.

    The individual will be taxed on the remittance in exactly the same way whether it is effected or enjoyed by the individual themselves or any other relevant person in connection with the individual. The provisions apply regardless of whether the actions by or with respect to any relevant person result in a UK benefit being incurred on that relevant person or on any other relevant person. Relevant person is defined (s 809M) as:

    (a)   the individual;

    (b)   the individual's husband or wife*;

    (c)   the individual's civil partner*;

    (d)   a child under 18 or grandchild under 18 of someone within category (a) to (c);

    (e)   a close company in which a person falling within any other category is a participator;

    (f)   with effect from 22 April 2009 a company which is a 51% subsidiary of a company meeting the category (e) conditions;

    (g)   a foreign company, that would be a close company if UK resident, in which a person falling within any other category is a participator;

    (h)   the trustees of a settlement where a person falling within any other category is a beneficiary; or

    (j)   a body connected with such a settlement if the body falls within one of the following categories:

          (i) any close company whose participators include the trustees of the settlement;

          (ii) any non-resident company which, if it were UK resident, would be a close company whose participators include the trustees of the settlement;

          (iii) any body corporate controlled by a company within (i) or (ii); or

          (iv) if the settlement is the principal settlement in relation to one or more sub-funds settlements, a person in the capacity as trustee of such a sub-fund settlement.

    *   for the purposes of this legislation individuals living together as husband and wife/civil partners are treated as legal spouses/partners.

    The meaning of relevant person is widely drawn and great care must be taken.

Anti-alienation provisions

24. Specific provisions cover gifts to other individuals (ITA 2007 s 809L(4) and s 809N) and transactions with third parties (ITA 2007 s 809L(5) and s 809O) where the property transferred represents or is derived from foreign income or foreign chargeable gains. There will be a taxable remittance where such transactions result directly or indirectly in any relevant person receiving a UK benefit.

The provisions are wide ranging. However, there are no restrictions on offshore gifts from foreign income and gains to non-relevant persons provided a relevant person does not receive any benefit. Furthermore, important transitional provisions (FA 2008 Sch 7 para 86(4) narrow the definition of relevant person (such that only the individual is considered) where the foreign income or foreign chargeable gains arose prior to 6 April 2008. Funds representing or derived from pre- 6 April 2008 foreign income and/or foreign chargeable gains can be gifted to any person and remitted by that person to the UK without there being a taxable remittance provided the individual to whom the foreign income or gains arose or accrued does not receive any benefit.

Transitional provisions

25. The main transitional provisions are with respect to:

   • the definition of relevant person when considering remittances representing or derived from pre-6 April 2008 foreign income and/or gains (broadly where the remittance represents or derives from pre-6 April 2008 foreign income and/or gains the relevant person definition only includes the individual to whom the foreign income or gains arose or accrued) – FA 2008 Sch 7 para 86(4);

   • property (including money) consisting of or deriving from an individual's relevant foreign income brought to, received or used in the UK before 6 April 2008 for the benefit of a relevant person in connection with the individual to whom the relevant foreign income originally arose (FA 2008 Sch 7 para 86(2));

   • property (excluding money) consisting of or deriving from an individual's relevant foreign income acquired before 12 March 2008 by a relevant person in connection with the individual to whom the relevant foreign income originally arose (FA 2008 Sch 7 para 86(3));

   • relevant foreign income is used to pay the interest with respect to a qualifying pre-12 March 2008 offshore mortgage used to acquire an interest in UK residential property or with respect to a qualifying re-mortgaging transaction (FA 2008 Sch 7 para 90).

Ongoing exemptions

26. The legislation contains seven ongoing exemptions from the remittance definition. These are:

   (1) money paid to the Commissioners – ITA 2007 s 809V;

   (2) consideration for certain UK services (the so called 'services exemption') – ITA 2007 s 809W;

   (3) the public access rule – ITA 2007 s 809X(3), s 809Z and s 809Z1;

   (4) the personal use rule (applicable only to clothing, footwear and jewellery) – ITA 2007 s 809X(4)and s 809Z2;

   (5) the repair rule – ITA 2007 s 809X(5)(a) and s 809Z3;

   (6) the temporary importation rule (across all tax years the property should not have been in the UK for more than 275 countable days) – ITA 2007 s 809X(5)(b) and s809Z4; and

   (7) the less than £1,000 de minimis provision – ITA 2007 s 809X(5)(c) and s 809Z5.

The exemptions with respect to money paid to the Commissioners and consideration for UK services will generally involve the payment of money. The other exemptions relate to the importation of goods (defined as not including money).

For the 'money paid to the Commissioners' exemption to be met, a total of £30,000 can be transferred from funds representing or derived from foreign income and/or foreign gains, to settle the tax liability for a tax year for which the RBC is payable.

For the services exemption to be in point the UK services must be wholly or mainly (over 50%) in connection with foreign property. In addition the qualifying invoice must be settled outside the UK by one or more payments to an offshore bank account held by or on behalf of the service provider.

All the exemptions apply to remittances regardless of whether the funds represent or derive from foreign income or foreign chargeable gains. Each ongoing exemption does, however, have its own specific qualifying conditions. Great care must be taken as it would be very easy to confuse the conditions and make inadvertent remittances.

Where the conditions are met, the provisions with respect to the services exemption mean there will never be a tax liability with respect to foreign income and/or gains used in this way. However, the exemption with respect to money paid to the Commissioners will be lost should HMRC refund the payment(s) made.

The 'less than £1,000 de minimis provision' is a complete exemption, provided that the goods remitted are not converted to money or money's worth while in the UK. Should this happen, there will be a deemed remittance of the original foreign income and/or foreign chargeable gains used to acquire the property.

The public access rule, personal use rule, repair rule and temporary importation rule are described by the legislation as 'relevant rules' and interact such that there is no charge, provided that one of the relevant rules applies. In effect these provisions mean that the tax charge that would have arisen if the exemption was not in point is deferred and will become payable should the asset be within the UK at a time that none of these relevant rules apply.

Statutory rules with respect to the remittance of foreign chargeable gains

27. From 6 April 2008 the gain is deemed to be remitted first where proceeds from the sale of chargeable foreign assets are remitted to the UK (TCGA 1992 s 12). Prior to 6 April 2008 the non statutory practice was that, where funds representing or derived from the proceeds of foreign chargeable assets sold at a gain were remitted, gains were deemed to be remitted in proportion to the quantum of the sales proceeds remitted.

Statutory matching rules with respect to remittances from mixed funds

28. It is important to remember that a mixed fund is not just a bank or building society account – it can be any asset. For example, a painting would be a mixed fund if it were acquired using a mixture of clean capital, foreign employment income and foreign dividend income.

Statutory rules apply to mixed funds containing foreign income and foreign gains arising or accruing after 5 April 2008. There are different rules for matching with respect to remittances to the UK (ITA 2007 s 809Q) and offshore transfers (ITA 2007 s 809R(4)). There is also a general anti-avoidance rule (ITA 2007 s 809S).

Where a fund contains pre- and post-5 April 2008 funds, two sets of matching rules apply (the post-5 April 2008 statutory rules having priority until these funds are deemed to have been remitted).

Complicated rules with respect to foreign capital losses

29. UK resident foreign domiciliaries will be entitled to full relief for foreign capital losses, provided (from 2008/09 onwards) a claim to access the remittance basis is not made. In addition there is the potential to claim a measure of relief for foreign capital losses even if one makes a remittance basis claim (TCGA 1992 ss 16ZA(2)).

The default position if a remittance claim is made is that all foreign capital loss relief is forfeited (TCGA 1992 s 16ZA(3)) whilst the individual remains foreign domiciled. However, to preserve some entitlement to foreign capital loss relief the individual can opt into an alternative loss relief regime by making an irrevocable election. The deadline for making the election is the standard claims period set down at TMA 1970 s 43. Where a valid election is made the new regime applies from the start of the first tax year after 5 April 2008 for which the remittance basis claim is made.

The alternative loss relief regime has specific provisions applying to both UK and foreign capital loss entitlement (TCGA 1992 ss16ZB and 16ZC). Where the election is made the capital loss relief available is complex and varies depending on whether the individual is taxed on the arising or remittance basis in the year and whether remittances representing or derived from foreign chargeable gains are made. Broadly where an election has been made and the remittance basis claimed in a year then ALL capital losses are set off in the following order (TCGA 1992 s 16ZC):

- first against remitted foreign chargeable gains which accrued to the individual in the tax year;

- next against unremitted foreign chargeable gains which accrued to the individual in the tax year; and

- lastly against UK chargeable gains which accrued to the individual in the tax year.

Where the election is made and in a future tax year the arising basis of taxation applies neither the annual exemption nor capital losses can be set off against foreign gains remitted to the UK which arose in an earlier year when the remittance basis applied.

The decision as to whether or not to make the election must be considered very carefully as the individual may be better off forfeiting entitlement to foreign capital losses and keeping the standard entitlement to UK capital losses. A fuller explanation is given in the answer to Example 73(g)(ii).

Question

Calculate the taxable income and chargeable gains that would arise in the following circumstances assuming that in no case is a general 31 March 1982 rebasing election made.

The retail prices index is shown on page (xix). Assume the index to be 210.0 for October 2009 and 211.0 for December 2009, giving index increases from March 1982 of 164.4% to October 2009 and 165.6% to December 2009.

(a) An individual acquired a freehold for £188,000 on 16 May 1992. On 24 June 2009 he grants a lease of the whole premises for 21 years for a premium of £120,000 and a rent of £20,000 per annum, payable quarterly in advance on usual quarter days. The value of the reversion was £256,000.

(b) A lease is granted for 60 years for a premium of £230,000, the value of the reversion being £80,000. The other circumstances are as in (a).

(c) An individual was granted a 40 year lease on 25 December 2002 at a market rental of £20,000 per annum payable quarterly in advance on the usual quarter days and paying a market premium of £50,000. The property is used as a second home. On 25 December 2009 he assigns the unexpired portion of the lease for a premium of £70,000.

(d) The individual in (c) above, instead of assigning the lease, grants a sub-lease at the same rent for 20 years from 25 December 2009 for a market premium of £49,000.

(e) On 1 July 2004 Eric Forbes granted a lease to Jeremy Poulton on payment of a premium of £7,500. The lease was for a period of 17 years and it is considered, having regard to the terms of the lease, that a premium of £120,000 could have been demanded. On 15 January 2009 Jeremy sold the lease to Peter Long for £100,000 and Peter in turn sold the lease on 18 June 2009 to John Field for £150,000.

Compute the amount, if any, chargeable to income tax for 2008/09 and 2009/10 on the assumption that none of the persons involved is a dealer in land.

(f) Rufford Ltd makes up accounts annually to 31 March. On 6 April 1964 it acquired a lease of business premises due to expire on 6 April 2011. It paid £13,860 for the assignment of the lease and incurred £300 of allowable legal and similar fees. On 6 October 2009 it assigned the lease (at arm's length) for £35,000 incurring allowable fees of £1,300. The value of the lease at 6 April 1965 was £12,500, and at 31 March 1982 was £30,000.

(g) Newco Ltd prepares accounts to 31 March. It has a wholly owned subsidiary from which on 2 December 2009 it acquired freehold property at the then market value of £500,000. The cost to the subsidiary in July 2000 was £360,000.

On 31 December 2008 Newco Ltd granted a 21-year lease over three quarters of the property to Antiques Ltd. Newco Ltd received a premium of £220,000, and the rent was £1,000 per month payable in advance on the 1st of each month.

There are three-yearly rent reviews at which point the tenant has an option to terminate the lease, the rent to be determined in the absence of agreement by arbitration. The residual value of the whole property at 31 December 2009 following the grant of the lease was £352,000.

(h) Newport, a trader who has been in business for many years, making up accounts annually to 31 December, was granted a 21 year lease of business premises on 1 July 2009 at a premium of £90,000 and a rent of £20,000 per annum payable quarterly in advance. Show the deductions to be made in respect of the lease in Newport's accounts to 31 December 2009 and indicate the tax treatment if Newport were to assign the lease in five years' time.

Answer

(a)   **Grant of short lease out of freehold**

	£
Premium – 24 June 2009	120,000
Less: Discount (21 – 1 = 20 × 2%) = 40%	48,000
Additional rent	72,000
Normal rent: 24 June 2009 to 5 April 2010 (286 days)	15,671
2009/10 UK property income subject to expenses	87,671
Capital proceeds (total premium 120,000 – 72,000 taxed as additional rent)	48,000

Less: Cost May 1992

$$£188,000 \times \frac{48,000 \text{ proceeds}}{\text{full premium} + \text{reversion}} \qquad 24,000$$

$$120,000 \qquad\qquad 256,000$$

	£
2009/10 Capital gain	24,000

(b)   **Grant of long lease at a premium**

No UK property income liability on the premium since this is a long lease, but a liability on rent as (a):

	£
2009/10 UK property income – rent (286 days)	£15,671

	£
Capital gain – premium 24 June 2009	230,000

Less: Cost May 1992

$$£188,000 \times \frac{230,000 \text{ (cash received)}}{310,000 \text{ (cash and reversion)}} \qquad 139,484$$

2009/10 Capital gain	90,516

(c)   **Assignment of short lease**

Since the lease was acquired at full market value there will be no income tax liability on the premium when the assignment takes place (see note 3).

	£
The capital gain is:	
Premium 25 December 2009	70,000

Less: Cost December 2001

$$£50,000 \times \frac{33 \text{ years unexpired on disposal}}{40 \text{ years unexpired on acquisition}}$$

Substituting relevant percentages:

$$£50,000 \times \frac{(33 \text{ years } =) \ 90.280}{(40 \text{ years } =) \ 95.457}$$ 47,288

2009/10 Capital gain, 22,712

(d) **Grant of sub-lease out of short lease**

	£	£
Premium received 25 December 2009		49,000
Less: Discount (20 − 1 = 19 × 2%) = 38%		18,620
c/f		30,380

		£	£
b/f			30,380
Less: Fraction applicable to sub-lease of premium paid on acquisition –			
Premium paid		50,000	
Less: (40 − 1 = 39 × 2%) = 78%		39,000	
Additional rent		11,000	
20 (years of sub-lease)/40 (years of head lease) × 11,000			5,500
Additional rent			24,880
Normal rent: 25 December 2009		5,000	
25 March 2010	5,000		
Less in advance (79 days out of 91)	4,341	659	5,659

2009/10 UK property income subject to expenses
(including rent payable £5,659) 30,539

Capital gain
Proceeds (full premium) 49,000

Less: Cost December 2001

$$£50,000 \times \frac{\begin{pmatrix} 33 \text{ years unexpired when} \\ \text{sub-lease granted less 13 years} \\ \text{unexpired when sub-lease ends} \end{pmatrix}}{\begin{pmatrix} 40 \text{ years unexpired when lease} \\ \text{acquired} \end{pmatrix}}$$

Substituting relevant percentages:

$$£50,000 \times \frac{(33 \text{ years}) = 90.280 - (13 \text{ years}) = 56.167}{(40 \text{ years}) = 95.457}$$

$$= £50,000 \times \frac{34.113}{95.457}$$ 17,868

31,132

Less: Part of premium assessable as UK property income 24,880

2009/10 Capital gain 6,252

Note that where there is a capital gain the rent deduction cannot convert it to a loss; it can only reduce the gain to nil, so that if the gain had been say £24,000, the result would have been no gain no loss. If the capital gains calculation had resulted in a loss, then that would be the allowable loss for capital gains purposes and the taxable UK property income could not be used to increase the allowable loss.

(e) **Grant of lease at an undervalue**

Amount forgone by Eric Forbes on the grant of the lease to Jeremy Poulton on 1 July 2004 was (120,000 – 7,500 =) £112,500.

Assignment by Jeremy Poulton to Peter Long 15.1.09

Excess of premium received over premium paid (100,000 – 7,500)	92,500
Less: 2 × (17 – 1) = 32%	29,600
Chargeable on Jeremy as UK property income for 2008/09	£62,900

Leaving (112,500 – 92,500 =) £20,000 to be dealt with on subsequent assignments.

Assignment by Peter Long to John Field 18.6.09

Excess of premium received over premium paid (150,000 – 100,000 =) £50,000 but restricted to balance of amount forgone	20,000
Less: 32% as above	6,400
Chargeable on Peter as UK property income 2009/10	£13,600

Unlike other amounts charged to income tax, the amounts charged under these provisions are not excluded from the proceeds in the capital gains computation (TCGA 1992 Sch 8 para 6(2)), so Jeremy will have a capital gains liability by reference to proceeds of £100,000 and Peter by reference to proceeds of £150,000 (see note 3).

(f) **Rufford Ltd – assignment of lease acquired before 6 April 1965**

(i) The gain using cost/6.4.65 value is as follows:

	£
Sale proceeds 6 October 2009	35,000
Less selling expenses	1,300
	33,700

Cost 6 April 1964 (including £300 expenses) £14,160
Allow fraction equivalent to unexpired term of lease at time of disposal, ie:

$$\frac{1\tfrac{1}{2} \text{ years unexpired at disposal}}{46 \text{ years unexpired at acquisition}}$$

Substitute TCGA 1992 Sch 8 percentages
1½ years is a percentage midway between 1 and 2 years)

$$£14,160 \times \frac{8.806}{98.490} = \qquad 1,266$$

	32,434
Less: Indexation allowance on 31 March 1982 value (see (ii) below)	5,495

	£
Overall gain	26,939

$$\text{Proportion after 6 April 1965} = \frac{43\frac{1}{2}}{44\frac{1}{2}} \times 26{,}939$$

	£
Gain	26,334

If election made to use 6 April 1965 value

	£
Sale proceeds less selling expenses as above	33,700

Market value at 6 April 1965

$$£12{,}500 \times \frac{1\frac{1}{2} \text{ (years of lease unexpired at disposal)}}{45 \text{ (years of lease unexpired at 6.4.1965)}}$$

		£
Thus	$£12{,}500 \times \dfrac{8.806}{98.059} =$	1,123

	£
Unindexed gain	32,577
Less: Indexation allowance (see (ii) below)	5,106
Gain	27,471
The gain is the lower of £26,334 and £27,471, ie	26,334

(ii)   The gain using 31.3.82 value is:

	£
Sale proceeds 6 October 2009 less selling expenses as before	33,700

31 March 1982 market value

$$£30{,}000 \times \frac{1\frac{1}{2} \text{ (years unexpired at disposal)}}{28 \text{ (years unexpired at 31.3.82)}}$$

		£
Thus	$£30{,}000 \times \dfrac{8.806}{85.053} =$	3,106

	£
Unindexed gain	30,594
Indexation allowance on depreciated 31 March 1982 value (being higher than depreciated cost £1,266) £3,106 × 164.4%*	(5,106)
Gain	25,488

Therefore the chargeable gain is £25,488 which is included in the company's total profits for the year ended 31 March 2010 and charged at the rate of corporation tax applicable to the company's profits.

(g) **Newco Ltd – intra-group transfer and subsequent lease**

Schedule A liability on grant of lease:

	£	£
Amount received 31 December 2009		220,000
Less: Discount ((21 – 1) × 2%) of £220,000		88,000
Portion taxable as additional rent is		132,000
Rent: 1.1.10 to 31.3.10 3 months @ £1,000		3,000
Property income (subject to expenses) yr ended 31.3.10		135,000
Chargeable gain portion		88,000
Less: Allowable expenditure		
Cost to subsidiary July 2000	360,000	

$$\text{Indexation allowance} \quad \frac{211.0^* - 170.5}{170.5} = 23.8\% \qquad 85,680$$

	£	£
Deemed acquisition cost to Newco Ltd December 2008	445,680	

Cost of part disposed of December 2009
(no further indexation allowance since
disposed of in same month as acquired)

$$3/4 \times 445,680 = 334,260 \times \frac{88,000}{220,000 + 352,000} \qquad\qquad 51,425$$

Chargeable gain year ended 31 March 2010		36,575

    *   Assumed figures

(h) **Newport – premium paid on short lease of business premises**

	£	£
Premium payable 1 July 2009	90,000	
Less: Discount (21 – 1) × 2% = 40%	36,000	
Assessable on landlord as additional rent	54,000	

$$\text{Therefore allowable to Newport} \quad \frac{54,000}{21} = £2,572 \text{ per annum}$$

In year to 31 December 2009:

	£
Deduction re lease premium (6 months) ½ × 2,572	1,286
Rent payable (2 quarters)	10,000
	11,286

If Newport assigned the lease in five years' time, the assignee, providing he was a business tenant, would take over the right to make the annual deductions of £2,572 in respect of the premium (ITTOIA 2005 s 61). Newport would be treated as having made a disposal for capital gains tax, the allowable cost being the premium paid of £90,000, less the total annual deductions allowed to him, less depreciation under TCGA 1992 Sch 8 (see explanatory note 11).

Explanatory Notes

Difference between grant and assignment of lease

1. Example 97 deals with the income tax/corporation tax treatment of let property. This example deals with some additional income aspects and also the capital gains treatment of lease premiums.

2. A *grant* of a new lease by a landlord to a tenant and an *assignment* of an existing lease from one tenant to another must be carefully distinguished for tax purposes. A grant of a new lease for a capital sum is a part disposal of the property for capital gains purposes, but part of the capital sum is charged as income if the lease is for 50 years or less, as detailed below (ITTOIA 2005 s 279). An assignment of an existing lease on the other hand is a disposal of the whole of the assignor's interest in the property and is normally subject only to a capital gains charge.

3. If, however, the premium obtained on the *grant* of a lease for 50 years or less is less than could have been obtained, successive assignors of the lease may be liable to an income tax (or corporation tax) charge on part of the proceeds instead of the proceeds on assignment being wholly a capital gains matter. This situation will prevail until the whole of the premium originally forgone has been charged on subsequent assignments (ITTOIA 2005 s 283). The charge is calculated in the same way as additional rent would have been calculated for the grantor of the lease, using the original lease term, as illustrated in part (e) of the example. Despite the income tax or corporation tax charge, there is no deduction from the proceeds in a capital gains computation on the premium (TCGA 1992 Sch 8 para 6(2)). The charge under ITTOIA 2005 s 283 is treated as part of the profits of a UK property business.

Income tax treatment on grant of short lease followed by sub-lease

4. A premium received on the *grant* of a lease not exceeding 50 years is partly taxable as additional rent. That part so taxable is the premium less 2% for each complete year of the lease except the first (ITTOIA 2005 s 279).

5. If the lessee then sublets at a premium, he may deduct from the amount of his additional rent calculated as in note 4 above the appropriate proportion of the base premium that is taxable, being the proportion that the sub-lease bears to the head lease (ITTOIA 2005 s 288). If he sublets at a rent rather than at a premium, he may deduct the appropriate proportion of the premium he paid from the rent on a day to day basis (ITTOIA 2005 s 292).

    In part (d) of the example, half of the £11,000 'additional rent' on which the head landlord was taxed relates to the 20 year sub-lease, ie £5,500, and this would have been deducted at £275 per annum from the rent payable by the sub-tenant if he had not paid a premium.

    Similar provisions apply where a premium is paid by a business tenant – see explanatory note 11.

6. For both individuals and companies, rental income and expenses are calculated according to commercial accounting principles, with adjustments for amounts in arrear and in advance. Full details are in Example 97.

Grant of short lease out of freehold/long lease

7. Where a short lease (ie not exceeding 50 years) is granted out of a freehold or long lease, that part of the premium not taxed as additional rent is a part disposal for capital gains purposes.

    The value of the reversion (ie the right to receive the rent and possession of the premises at the end of the lease) must be taken into account in calculating the gain arising.

    The denominator in that calculation includes the full premium received, not just the deemed capital portion (TCGA 1992 Sch 8 para 5).

The normal rules for part disposals apply to the capital gains computation (TCGA 1992 s 42). Note that for companies the indexation allowance is calculated on the cost of the part disposed of (or on the same proportion of the 31.3.82 value if appropriate), not on the total cost.

Grant of sub-lease out of short lease

8. Where a short lease is granted out of another short lease, then for capital gains purposes the gain or loss is calculated on the *full premium* according to the wasting asset rules, taking as the cost figure that part of the original expenditure that will waste away during the sub-lease. The part that has wasted away is worked out on a curved line basis, the percentages appropriate to the years concerned being in TCGA 1992 Sch 8 (see page (xvi)). The available indexation allowance is calculated on the depreciated amount. Where the original short lease was acquired before 31 March 1982, then unless a general rebasing election has been made, the gain or loss is calculated using pre March 1982 and post March 1982 rules, with the allowable expenditure being the depreciated 31.3.82 value or depreciated cost/6 April 1965 value, and indexation allowance being on the higher of the depreciated 31 March 1982 value and depreciated cost/6 April 1965 value as the case may be. When the gain has been calculated, the part of the premium chargeable as UK property income is then deducted from the capital gain, but not so as to create a loss, nor can it be added to a loss (TCGA 1992 Sch 8 paras 4 and 5).

Assignment of short lease

9. In calculating the capital gain arising on an *assignment* of a short lease, the cost has to be depreciated on the same curved line basis as in note 8 above, and the same provisions apply in relation to the indexation allowance and assets acquired before 31 March 1982.

Intra-group transfer; term of lease

10. (a) The cost to be used on the acquisition by Newco (part (g)) from its subsidiary is the cost to the subsidiary plus indexation allowance (TCGA 1992 s 171). See Example 83 explanatory note 2 for the special rules which apply where the asset was originally acquired before 31 March 1982 and for the effect of the provisions preventing the use of indexation allowance to create or increase a loss on and after 30 November 1993.

    (b) The term of the lease for the purpose of calculating the exclusion from Schedule A and inclusion as a chargeable gain is considered to be 21 years, even though the tenant has an option to terminate the lease at each three-yearly rent review.

    If the term had been artificially extended in the lease, whilst encouraging the tenant to terminate it earlier because of harsh rent review provisions, the term for calculating the exclusion from Schedule A and inclusion as a chargeable gain would have been taken as the period for which the lease was likely to run (CTA 2009s 244).

Income tax treatment of lease premium paid by business tenant

11. Where a business tenant pays a premium on the grant of a short lease, that part of the premium that is assessable on the landlord as additional rent is allowable to the payer as rent payable, but spread over the period of the lease rather than as a single deduction. The appropriate fraction may accordingly be deducted in arriving at trading profits as shown in part (h) of the example (ITTOIA 2005 s 61).

If the business tenant then assigns the lease, the part of the premium that has been allowed as an expense against income must be excluded from the allowable cost in the capital gains computation, as shown in Example 95 part (f). A new business tenant would then take over the right to make the annual deductions for the balance of the premium.

Surrenders and variations

12.   Where a tenant surrenders a lease in exchange for a new longer lease on broadly the same terms but at a different rent, the surrender is not normally treated as a disposal and acquisition for capital gains purposes (Extra Statutory Concession D39).

13.   Where a leaseholder acquires a superior interest in the land, such as a freehold reversion, HMRC, by Extra Statutory Concession D42, allow indexation allowance on the original cost of the lease, reduced as appropriate under Sch 8, by reference to the date of the original acquisition, even though strictly indexation should run from the date the superior interest is acquired. Indexation on the consideration for the superior interest runs from the date of its acquisition.

Reverse premiums

14.   Where an inducement is provided by a landlord to a tenant to encourage the taking of a lease of land or buildings it is known as a reverse premium. It is provided by CTA 2009 Sch 2 para 24 and ITTOIA 2005 ss 101 and 311 that the receipt of a reverse premium is taxable in the hands of the recipient. If the taxpayer receives the amount in the course of a trade or profession then the amount is taxed in that trade. Under Accounting Standards, the amount will normally be spread over the period of the lease (or to the date of the first rent review if shorter) and taxed over that period. There are anti-avoidance rules to prevent exploitation of this principle by granting a lease on uncommercial terms between connected persons. In such cases the reverse premium is taxable in full in the period in which the lease is granted. Where the tenant is not in business, the premium received is taxed as UK property income, again spread over the lease. No charge arises if the property is the tenant's only or main residence or if the same amount is a deduction as a contribution towards expenditure for capital allowances.

Rent factoring

15.   Some companies have entered into rent factoring schemes, which are in substance equivalent to bank loans. It has, however, been argued that the amounts received are chargeable to corporation tax only as capital gains, which may be offset by losses or reliefs. The Revenue considered that the sums were already taxable as UK property income, but the position was put beyond doubt for transactions entered into on or after 21 March 2000 (ICTA 1988 ss 43A to 43G). Lump sums received for giving up the right to future rental income are charged as UK property income. There are exceptions so that the provisions do not affect genuine investment in property and capital allowances based finance leasing.

Question

(a) Peter and Lucy Hobday, who are UK resident and domiciled, jointly own a villa in southern France, which they spend some weeks at during the summer. They purchased the villa in 2008. They also let the villa on an occasional basis to friends, but the lettings are not advertised publicly. The total rent they received during the year 2009/10 for casual lettings was £4,200, which was for a total of four weeks. In 2009/10 the couple spent a total of seven weeks at the property, and the 'season' lasted for 18 weeks.

The interest on the loan to purchase the property amounts to £8,000 for the year, and the couple pay a service charge for the upkeep of the property of £2,400 per annum. Each visit to the property costs £400 in travelling expenses, and the couple visit the property twice a year to 'open' and 'close' it at each end of the season, attending to cleaning and other tasks while there for two days on each occasion. These visits do not coincide with their own holidays there.

Explain the treatment of the income on the property for UK tax purposes. Advise the couple of any other tax implications that they should consider with regard to their holiday home.

(b) Kate and Richard Simpson are UK resident, but Kate is not UK domiciled. They own a substantial villa in Italy which Kate inherited from her grandparents five years ago, and transferred a half share to Richard. It is the couple's intention to retire to Italy in around six years' time when family commitments permit. The couple spend increasing amounts of time in Italy – around 12 weeks per annum now, and this is likely to increase steadily towards retirement. It is not their intention to let the Italian property. However, Kate and Richard's home in England will probably be let for several years after retirement, until their daughter is ready to occupy it as her family home – at which point ownership will be transferred to her.

Advise the couple of the tax issues associated with their foreign property.

(c) Janek has been working in the UK for four years, running a successful building company. He purchased a house in Poland in the first year he was working in the UK. This is presently rented to his cousin at a rent of £200 per month (which is less than the market rent). Janek's cousin bears all of the expenses related to the house, and carries out any minor repairs that are needed. The rent is banked in Poland in Janek's name. Janek is now considering moving back to Poland, as the economy there is booming. However, he is seeking advice regarding his house. It has increased substantially in value and he is considering selling it and trading up. He would most likely do this before returning to Poland, so that the new property would be ready for him on his return. He estimates that the increase in value of the property is around £60,000 over the period he has owned it. Advise him of the best strategy.

The rate of tax on income in Poland is 19%, as is the rate of tax on capital gains, although gains on property owned for more than five years are exempt from tax. Assume that Janek has no allowances available to set against Polish tax liabilities.

Answer

(a)   Peter and Lucy Hobday – foreign rental income 2009/10

	£	£
Rent received		4,200
Less: allowable expenses		
Loan interest (18 – 7)/52 × £8,000	1,692	
Service charges 11/52 × £2,400	508	
Wear and tear allowance	420	
		2,620
Net Profit		1,580

Notes

(i)   The profit of £1,580 will be taxed on the couple as property income. However, any tax suffered in France will need to be taken into account in determining the UK tax liability on the income, which can be split equally between the couple. Double tax relief will be available to reduce the UK tax burden if this is higher than the tax charge in France, which will normally have been levied on a different income figure as the basis of assessment and allowable expenses varies from that in the UK.

(ii)   The couple should each enter their share of the net income on the Foreign pages of the tax return SA106, on page F4, which requires a summary of the rent and allowable expenses for all foreign properties, and a further analysis by country to claim double tax relief.

(iii)   Had the couple realised a loss on this property, the loss would be carried forward only against profits arising on this property or the profits on any other overseas property they might acquire and let in the future. Losses on overseas lettings cannot be set off against UK property income. Explanatory note 8 provides further information about losses.

(iv)   It is not clear what the capital gains tax position is with regard to the property. If it is regarded as the couple's home for part of the year they are still potentially in time to make an election under TCGA 1992 s 222(5) nominating whether their UK home or their French villa should be regarded as their main residence. If the couple elect within two years of the date of purchase of the French property, they can vary that election at any time in the future. Both the election and any variation of it can be backdated by up to two years. For a detailed example on Private Residence relief see Example 81.

(v)   The couple should also seek advice about the impact of French VAT (TVA) on their letting income, which amounts to charges for holiday accommodation, as this is frequently subject to standard rate VAT. There is a risk that they could exceed the VAT limit in France if their letting income in any year was substantial – and given the length of the season this is possible. VAT registration limits in the rest of the EU are significantly lower than in the UK. They should seek specialist advice on this point as a matter of urgency.

(vi)   The extension of favourable furnished holiday letting treatment to properties in the EEA is not available to Peter and Lucy as they do not let the property on a commercial basis. If this had been the case, the couple would have had until 31 July 2009 to amend their 2007 tax returns and 31 January 2010 to amend the 2008 returns. It is likely that the main benefit would have been the offset of losses against other income, although capital allowance claims could also have been made in respect of furniture and equipment in the house purchased since acquisition (capital allowance claims not having been made in earlier years).

(b)   **Kate and Richard Simpson's Italian villa**

As Kate and Richard do not plan to let their villa in Italy, their tax issues are limited to capital gains tax. However, the situation is complex.

There is no indication that Kate and Richard have made any election under TCGA s 222(5) to nominate which of their homes is to be regarded as their principal private residence. This means that on disposal HMRC will decide on the facts which is to be regarded as their main residence, qualifying for exemption. It is likely, given the facts to date that this would be the home in the UK as although the couple spend increasing amounts of time in Italy they still spend the majority of the year in the UK.

As the election has not been made within two years of acquiring the second home, the couple are out of time to elect, unless they purchase another residence, which would re-start the two-year period allowed. As the Italy home has always been a residence for the couple it is unlikely that their occupation of the Italian home was not of such significance to regard it as their second home in the early part of ownership. It would be wise to assemble the exact facts regarding the period spent in Italy since the property was acquired to ensure that full facts can be provided to HMRC to establish which properties can be treated as their principle private residence for CGT relief when a disposal occurs.

If the UK home is currently regarded as their main residence, then this cannot alter until either another residence is purchased, or the couple actually cease to occupy their home in the UK as their main residence. This would be a question of fact. The couple would notify HMRC of their departure to Italy in any event, and would probably transfer the main residence qualification to the Italian home at that time.

There are other considerations to be taken into account. The letting of the UK home after departure may give rise to a chargeable gain on the property, but this would be subject to letting relief, which would be a maximum of £40,000 each. The last three years of ownership would be exempt from capital gains tax in any event under TCGA s 223 (2). This would probably permit at least three years letting without incurring any capital gains tax, as the let gain due for exemption under letting relief is capped at the amount of the exempt gain. The most appropriate advice regarding the UK home is for the couple to review their ownership of it regularly once they leave the UK.

Once the couple leave the UK for good on retirement, they are likely to become non-UK resident almost immediately, assuming that they do not visit the UK for long periods of time. As non-residents, any gains on either the UK home or the Italian villa would not be taxable in the UK, but the couple should be warned about the temporary non-residence rules, which could adversely affect them in the future. If after a period of time they transferred their UK home to their daughter, then it may be no longer exempt under the scenario outlined above, particularly if they have had difficulties securing an appropriate tenant so that the house had remained empty and therefore did not qualify for letting relief. If, however, before five complete years of non-residence have elapsed they return to the UK – perhaps for health or family reasons – the gain on the property would be assessed on them on their return. Kate and Richard should be aware of this fact and that other capital gains tax planning steps are appropriate to ensure that this problem does not arise.

Finally, there is the possibility that Kate as a non-domiciled individual could shelter any gains on the Italian property by failing to remit them to the UK. However, there are problems with this approach. First, transferring the property into joint names on acquisition means that Richard would accrue half of the gain on the Italian property when sold. Although he could gift his share back to Kate, this may trigger an IHT problem if he dies within seven years, as he is limited to an inter-spouse exemption of £55,000 as Kate is not UK domiciled. Also, the provisions of the Finance Act 2008 limit the remittance basis to those with income or gains of less than £2,000 in any tax year, or those willing to forgo UK personal allowances and for longer term UK residents, to make a payment of £30,000 in respect of unremitted income and gains. This is unlikely to be beneficial should Richard and Kate ever sell the Italian property while still UK resident, so this avenue is pursued no further.

(c)   **Janek's Polish home**

Janek is not UK domiciled. If he sells the house in Poland while he is still resident in the UK for tax purposes he can claim to be taxed on a remittance basis on the gain. As he has never occupied the house, no relief for principal private residence will be available to him, so he will be taxed in full on any gain remitted to the UK, assuming he claims the remittance basis.

A claim for the remittance basis may not, however, be appropriate to Janek, as Polish capital gains tax on real estate is charged at a rate of 19%, although after five years ownership the gain is exempt from tax. As UK capital gains tax is only charged at 18%, Janek is likely to have no tax liability on the gain in the UK, even if it is liable for tax in full; so far he has owned the property for no more than four years. The gain exceeds £2,000 he would suffer loss of his UK personal allowances and capital gains tax exemption if he claimed the remittance basis. The £30,000 charge on unremitted income and gains will not apply to Janek as he has not been UK resident for a sufficient period.

If, alternatively, Janek waits until his return to Poland to sell and repurchase a home, he could not be liable to UK tax as he would by then be non-resident. This would also present to him the opportunity to retain ownership of the Polish property for five years, and thus escape Polish tax on the gain. Janek should, however, be warned that as a UK resident for four years, the temporary non-resident rules would apply to him, and should he return to the UK unexpectedly he may trigger the gain back into charge on arrival. If by then there is no Polish tax charge, UK tax could be chargeable in full at 18% on the gain.

Therefore the advice to Janek regarding the sale of his property is that it is likely to be tax neutral in the UK, and should he wish to sell and repurchase before leaving the UK, no additional UK tax will apply over and above the Polish tax due on the disposal. However, he should seek more specific advice about the incidence of capital gains tax in Poland on the sale of the property.

However, Janek should also be aware that any rent charged in Poland may need to be declared in the UK for income tax purposes following the changes made by Finance Act 2008. Janek should assemble the details of the expenses he bears in relation to the Polish property, and be prepared to account for UK tax on the rentals – particularly as the gross rentals exceed £2,000 per annum and the expenses in relation to the property would seem very small. As it is likely that his net rental income on a UK tax basis exceeds £2,000 Janek would be better off paying tax in the UK on an arising basis, and making a claim for double taxation relief for the tax suffered on the income in Poland. The basic rate of income tax in Poland is also 19%, so additional UK tax would be due if Janek were taxed on an arising basis on his Polish rental income.

Explanatory Notes

Foreign let property

1.   Income from foreign lettings is taxed as property income, on the same basis as UK letting income. The basis of computation of the profit or loss follows the same rules as UK property income, which for individuals is given by ITTOIA 2005 s 272. In particular, expenses incurred wholly and exclusively for the purpose of the overseas letting trade are allowed against the income, splitting any costs which relate to private use of the property or periods when it is not available for letting to provide a deduction for the costs incurred in relation to the period when the property is actually let or available for letting. The allowable costs relate to the period during which the property is open for letting (18 weeks of the year) less the period during which it was not available through owner occupation (seven weeks).

2.   The net income for each property is calculated separately so that the provisions of the various double taxation arrangements apply, and then the net profits are aggregated and taxed as the profits of an 'overseas property business' under ITTOIA ss 268 and 269(2) for individuals.

3. Although the definition of furnished holiday lettings in ITTOIA 2005 ss 323 to 326 are not UK specific, the favourable treatment extended by various parts of the tax code to furnished holiday letting as a 'deemed trade' were not thought to apply to foreign holiday lettings, even if all of the necessary conditions were met. However, in Budget 2009 it was announced that HMRC now consider that the favourable treatment should apply to properties within the European Union. Instead, the relief has been slightly extended to apply to properties in the European Economic Area rather than only the EU. The relief will be withdrawn completely from the end of 2009/10 for all furnished holiday lettings whether in the UK or elsewhere in the EEA.

For more details on the conditions for furnished holiday letting treatment see Example 97.

4. The basis periods for property income are tax years, irrespective of the basis for which the accounts are drawn up, which may be done to meet foreign tax provisions. The rules which determine the profit for foreign tax purposes are irrelevant to the UK tax computation, and the profits must be calculated as if the letting were a normal UK letting, subject to note 5.

5. There are minor differences in allowable expenditure in relation to overseas property lettings. Primarily, this excludes from relief the travelling and related expenses with regard to foreign trades provided in relation to an actual trade carried on by ITTOIA 2005 ss 92–94. These sections permit travel to the place where the trade is carried on to be tax deductible even where the 'wholly and exclusively' rule would not apply; s 92 provides relief for travel and accommodation, plus family expenses in relation to foreign trades. However, where the expenses would qualify in any event as 'wholly and exclusively', s 92 would not apply, and the travelling expenses would be deductible in any event. As regards Peter and Lucy's travel to their villa in France at the beginning and end of the season, this expenditure has a dual purpose, as although the trip does not relate to their own holidays specifically, the season to which the travel relates comprises both let periods and owner occupation. The travel is therefore dual purpose expenditure, and not allowable under the normal rules. The exclusion of ss 92–94 from the list of allowable deductions in ITTOIA 2005 s 272 therefore excludes the travelling expenses.

6. The new style tax return introduced in 2008 includes a change in the layout of the details reported in relation to income from foreign property. Taxpayers are required to prepare multiple copies of boxes 14 to 22 on page 4 to report the income of more than one let property overseas in the year if the properties are in different countries and foreign tax has been suffered. There is no longer any necessity to provide the address of each let property abroad.

7. Where the owner of the property is UK resident but not UK domiciled, the letting income arising is taxed only to the extent remitted to the UK, subject to the changes made by Finance Act 2008. Where the unremitted foreign income and gains of the year do not exceed £2,000 the remittance basis is automatic. Otherwise to access the remittance basis the taxpayer must claim and thus will lose the benefit of UK personal allowances and capital gains tax exemption. For those resident in the UK for seven out of the previous nine years a payment of £30,000 per annum is required as a tax on nominated unremitted foreign income and gains before the remittance basis is available. Foreign letting income taxed on the remittance basis is dealt with by ITTOIA 2005 s 357, which brings the income within the charge to tax on a remittance basis.

8. The treatment of losses on foreign property lettings is given by ITA 2007 s 118. Losses on an overseas property business are treated in the same way as losses on a UK property business, and carried forward against future profits of the same business. For this purpose, a foreign property business (comprising all overseas lettings wherever situated) are separate from a UK property business, and thus any losses on overseas lettings cannot be offset against profits on a UK property business.

Capital gains tax on foreign property

9. The capital gains tax rules apply to foreign property in exactly the same way as to UK property for UK resident and domiciled individuals. It is possible to elect for a foreign home to be the main residence under TCGA 1992 s 222 and thus to qualify for relief from capital gains tax on it, even

where the owners are UK resident for the tax years in question. This would relieve a foreign property from UK tax; it would not, however, affect the treatment of the disposal of that property for foreign tax purposes, and as the incidence of capital gains tax can be higher than the UK flat rate of 18%, there may be no benefit in electing for a foreign home to be the main residence, as double tax relief could prevent UK tax from being due on disposal in any event. (For a detailed study of capital gains in relation to the main residence see Example 81, and in particular Explanatory notes 1 to 3.)

10.   The UK capital gains tax elections available should be reviewed carefully in light of any potential foreign tax charges, for which specific professional advice should be sought.

11.   Where the foreign property is owned by a UK resident but non-domiciled individual any gains of the property would be taxed on an arising basis, unless an election is made for remittance basis. In the case of both Kate and Richard and Janek in this Example, the foreign gains are unlikely to be remitted to the UK given the facts. However, if the disposers are still UK resident at the date of disposal of the foreign property, consideration will have to be given to the availability of an election and costs arising from loss of allowances and loss of use of double tax relief by using the remittance basis after the changes made by Finance Act 2008 s 25 and Sch 7. See explanatory note 7 above for more details.

12.   Each situation should be reviewed on the specific facts and the plans of the client so that appropriate advice can be given about the interplay between the foreign tax likely to arise on the property and the incidence of capital gains tax on the disposal of any UK property to ensure that all aspects have been considered.

INDEX

References are to page numbers.

O